SHIPS OF THE
ROYAL NAVY

THE COMPLETE RECORD
OF ALL FIGHTING SHIPS OF THE ROYAL NAVY

J. J. Colledge

REVISED BY LT-CDR BEN WARLOW

GREENHILL BOOKS · LONDON
STACKPOLE BOOKS · PENNSYLVANIA

Greenhill Books

This edition of
Ships of the Royal Navy:
The Complete Record of all the Fighting Ships of the Royal Navy
First published 2003 by
Greenhill Books, Lionel Leventhal Limited,
Park House, 1 Russell Gardens, London NW11 9NN
and
Stackpole Books, 5067 Ritter Road,
Mechanicsburg, PA 17055, USA

British Library Cataloguing in Publication Data
Colledge, J. J. (James Joseph)
Ships of the Royal Navy: the complete record of all fighting ships
of the Royal Navy from the 15th century to the present – Rev. ed.
1. Great Britain. Royal Navy – History
2. Warships – Great Britain – History
3. Great Britain – History, Naval
I. Title   II. Warlow, Ben
623.8′25′0941

ISBN 1-85367-566-0

Library of Congress Cataloging-in-Publication Data available

Publishing History
Ships of the Royal Navy was originally published in two volumes in 1968.
The volumes were revised and updated in 1987 (Greenhill Books). This is the
first volume fully revised and updated from the 1987 edition.

Edited, designed and typeset by Roger Chesneau
Printed and bound in Great Britain

Contents

Preface

Foreword to the 1987 Edition

Introduction
Scope of the Book
Tonnages
Dimensions
Armament
Building Materials
Building Yards
Early Ship Types
Establishment of Guns
Classes Mentioned in the Text
A Note on Rebuilds
Acknowledgements
References

Abbreviations

SHIPS OF THE ROYAL NAVY: A HISTORICAL INDEX

Preface

This is an updated version of the 1987 edition of Volume 1 of Mr Colledge's excellent work. It has been revised to include ships added to the Fleet since that date, and also the fate of those vessels extant in 1987 but subsequently discarded. Volume 1 contains details of principal warships, whilst Volume 2 covers trawlers, drifters, tugs and requisitioned ships; my own work *Shore Establishments of the Royal Navy* covers static ships and establishments and also nominal depot ships. These three volumes taken together should answer such questions as 'What was HMS ———?'.

For ease of reference, and for the sake of continuity, I have followed the system of presentation used by Mr Colledge, although, in the present volume, the opportunity has been taken to update some of the earlier entries, and some amendment has been made to the order in which the ships are listed. As before, details of the larger classes of warships are listed at the end of this Introduction, in order to avoid unnecessary repetition within the individual entries; similarly, building dates refer, generally, to launch dates. I have continued to designate Canadian ships 'RCN' rather than introduce the term 'CFS'. It must again be emphasised that this summary can provide only a 'snapshot' and a basic guide: statistics such as displacement, armament, and even dimensions, may vary throughout a particular ship's career.

I have been assisted in this revision by Captain Chris Page and the staff of the Naval Historical Branch, and by many others. My thanks go also to Steve Bush, Clive Brookes and Ross Gillett, while to the References listed on page 17 may be added *The Ships of Canada's Naval Forces 1910–1993* by Ken Macpherson and John Burgess.

The main credit for this work must go to Mr Colledge, who provided the basis and the inspiration: many generations will remain indebted to him for his efforts. I therefore hope that revised volume will continue to be helpful to researchers in the naval field. There are bound to be errors and omissions, and I would be grateful to be made aware of any that are noticed.

Ben Warlow
Burnham-on-Crouch, 2003

Foreword to the 1987 Edition

When they appeared nearly twenty years ago, Mr James Colledge's historical indices, the two volmcs of Ships *of the Royal Navy,* immediately became a standard work of reference, indispensable to researchers and enthusiasts alike. Amateurs and professionals appreciated the almost unique combination of simplicity and completeness which, in effect, eliminated a basic level of research.

The one disadvantage of the first edition of *Ships of the Royal Navy* was that it soon became a collector's item, to be found by the fortunate and/or in specialist second hand booksellers, at several times its original publication price. The appearance of this long overdue edition will be welcomed by those who were disappointed the first time around—the feelings of owners of the first edition may, in some cases, be mixed, for it is now superseded.

Since the original text of Volume 1—'Major ships'—went to press in 1968 there have been many changes in the List of the Navy. Nearly 100 ships' names have been resurrected (and *Ships of the Royal Navy* has been at the collective elbow of the Ships' Names Committee as an invaluable source) and some have lived out the full span of their new careers during the two decades. While these additions would justify a revised edition, they are, in practice, almost a minor aspect.

It was inevitable, in collating data on 13,000 ships, that there would be a number of errors and omissions, as well as blanks which the author could not fill. In the years which have passed, Mr Colledge has steadily worked to correct the errors, supplement the data and eliminate the lacunae. In this he has been assisted by members of the World Ship Society, who have already seen, in a special column in their magazine, *Warship Supplement.* the first published form of the amendments. A further significant contribution has also been made by Mr David Lyons, another indefatigably helpful researcher, well known to users of the National Maritime Museum's documentary collection of naval records.

But the work as a whole remains that of J. J. Colledge, who has now improved on excellence. The Navy Historical Library's two battered, broken and annotated copies of the original will now go into honourable retirement to join other 'first editions'—I suspect that many others will be similarly retired.

David Brown
Naval Historical Library, 1987

Introduction

SCOPE OF THE BOOK

This 'ABC' of the ships of the Royal Navy is the result of many years' research in the Admiralty Library and elsewhere, and it is hoped that most of the ships which have served at any time in the British or Commonwealth navies are included. Ships noted as 'Indian' include those of the Hon. East India Company, which developed into the Bombay Marine and later into the Royal Indian Marine. The term 'Australian' is used in the text to cover ships of the various State navies of Australia before the formation of the Royal Australian Navy. Names of ships captured from the French or Spanish are printed in an English form with their English counterparts where convenient, the definite article being omitted except in the few cases when it is known to have been used in the Royal Navy, and 'UNITÉ' for example will have to be read as 'Unite' and 'IMMORTALITÉ' as 'Immortalite'. Mercantile names are printed in italics.

For the sake of brevity, details of the engines of steamships have had to be omitted, as also have most of the changes in armament. For modern ships, [in general] only a tonnage is given, since other details are readily available in current reference books.

Trawlers, tugs etc and auxiliaries are not listed other than as a continuation of a ship name [but see Preface].

TONNAGE

Up to the year 1873, the tonnage is the builder's measurement (bm), a capacity measurement arrived at from, perhaps, the 15th century, by calculating the number of tuns (casks) of wine that the ship could carry. After 1873 displacement tonnage is used, changed in 1926 to standard displacement.

DIMENSIONS

Length and beam are given, the former being that of the gun deck for sailing vessels, which closely approximated to the length between perpendiculars used for the steamships.

ARMAMENT

Until the latter half of the 19th century, guns in the main were smooth-bore muzzle-loaders firing round iron shot, the 'size' of the gun listed being actually the weight of the shot. After this, rifled guns were introduced which later brought about the change in the shape of the projectile fired. Breech loaders were used for a short time in the 1850s, being permanently introduced in the 1880s. Carronades (abbreviated to 'carr.' in the text) took their name from Carron in Scotland, where they were first manufactured in 1777; these were short-barrelled, short-range weapons which had a devastating effect in close action. During the Napoleonic wars, ships of the line and frigates mounted up to twelve of these, 24- or 32-pounders, which were not included in the gun rating of the ship, e.g., a 32-gun frigate mounting 44 weapons. Some of the smaller vessels were often armed almost entirely with carronades. In the text, sailing ship armament is given (when known) only when it differed from the establishment tables.

BUILDING MATERIALS

Shortage of oak during the Napoleonic wars resulted in trials with various softwoods, some 50 frigates and sloops being thus built; they were useless after a few years, as were five frigates so built in 1757. Teak was used for all ships built at Bombay, and pencil cedar for the sloops and schooners built in Bermuda; these were all very durable vessels.

Iron shipbuilding, with a few exceptions, started with the floating batteries of 1855, and iron used in conjunction with surplus timber resulted in composite construction for most of the corvettes and sloops from 1867 to 1889. Steel was used from 1877.

BUILDING YARDS

The first Royal dockyard was founded in 1520 at Woolwich (arguably at Portsmouth), though naval ships had been built there before this. Enlarged in 1701, it was closed in October 1869.

Henry VIII also founded the dockyard at Deptford, which eventually became more important than its near neighbour until the close of the French wars, when it was little used; it was practically derelict by 1818 and closed in 1833 with WORCESTER still on stocks. It reopened in 1843 and finally closed in March 1869.

Portsmouth Dockyard was founded in 1540, though the harbour had been used as a base since 1512, when it superseded Southampton Water. It had a period of decline during the reign of Elizabeth I, when Chatham yard was started.

The dockyard at Chatham dates from 1588 and the Medway then became the main fleet base, the chief enemy threat at that time coming from the Spanish Netherlands. Chatham remained pre-eminent until the advent of the 'Dreadnought' type battleship, whose draught rendered the entrance to the yard rather hazardous. It was enlarged in 1662, and again in 1864–83, and closed in 1984.

A Royal dockyard was started at Harwich in 1650 which lasted until 1714. The site was reopened in 1742 as a private yard under various owners until about 1827.

The next to be founded was at Sheerness in 1667. This, however. was little used after 1674 and was closed in 1686. Reopened two years later and enlarged 1815–26, it finally closed in March 1960.

Plymouth Dockyard was opened in 1691, though the area had long been a naval base. Known as Devonport Dockyard from 1824, it was enlarged in 1844. Milford Dockyard started on the site of Jacobs' private yard in 1794 and moved to Pembroke Dock in 1814. It was closed in 1926.

The remaining two Royal yards at home, Haulbowline (transferred to the Irish government in 1921) and Rosyth, were not building yards.

It will be noticed that most of the private yards were located originally in three main areas adjacent to the royal dockyards—the Thames/Medway group, the Solent/Isle of Wight group and those near Plymouth. There were others on the west and east coasts, and one of these, Yarmouth, needs some comment. Although the east-coast port has been known as Great Yarmouth since the 15th century, this name rarely occurs as such in Admiralty lists. A close study of local records in the Isle of Wight has failed to find any trace of naval building at the Wight Yarmouth, so it seems that all Yarmouth-built vessels must have originated at the east-coast port.

Little need be said about the steamship builders; most of their names would be familiar to the reader. It might be pointed out. however, that only one firm who contracted for the sailing navy still existed in recent times—that of J .S. White of Cowes, who moved there in 1804 and built for the Royal Navy until 1966.

EARLY SHIP TYPES

Many of those in early lists of the Navy are not easily described, since few details of them exist. As far as can be ascertained the *ballinger* (or *balinger*), for instance, seems to have been a moderate-sized oared vessel and the *barge* a larger ship of the same type but fitted with sails. The 16th-century *brigantine* seems to have been an alternative name for the galley. The *busse* was a stoutly built fishing type vessel with three square-rigged masts, though by the 18th century it had two masts only. The *cog* was a merchant type, probably with one square-rigged mast, while the Elizabethan *frigate* remains an enigma. The English *galleasse* was a low, flush-decked vessel fitted with a ram and sometimes with oars, while the *galley* was a very similar craft with three masts and lateen sails; some of these oared galleys were often used as tugs for getting large ships out of harbours. The *hoy* was a coastal store carrier with one square rigged mast, a jib and gaff sails. The *pinnace* in Tudor times was probably a small fast sailing vessel equipped with oars, while the row barge was similar but fitted with a ram. The Stuart *yacht*, of Dutch origin, was cutter rigged with a square topsail.

ESTABLISHMENT OF GUNS

	42pdr	32pdr	24pdr	18pdr	12pdr	9pdr	6pdr	4pdr	3pdr
In 1677:									
1st Rate 100	26	–	–	28	–	–	44	–	–
2nd Rate 90	–	26	–	26	–	–	36	–	2
3rd Rate 70	–	26	–	–	26	–	14	–	4
Ships built after 1716:									
1st Rate 100	28	28	–	–	28	–	16	–	–
2nd Rate 90	26	–	–	26	–	26	12	–	–
2nd Rate 80	26	–	–	–	26	–	30	–	–
3rd Rate 70	–	26	–	–	26	–	18	–	–
3rd Rate 60	–	24	–	–	–	26	10	–	–
4th Rate 50	–	–	–	26	–	22	6	–	–
5th Rate 40	–	–	–	–	20	–	20	–	–
5th Rate 30	–	–	–	–	–	8	20	2	–
6th Rate 20	–	–	–	–	–	–	20	–	–
Ships built after 1740:									
1st Rate 100	28	–	28	–	28	–	16	–	–
2nd Rate 90	–	26	–	26	26	–	12	–	–
3rd Rate 80	–	26	–	26	–	24	4	–	–
3rd Rate 64	–	26	–	26	–	12	–	–	–
4th Rate 58	–	–	24	–	24	–	10	–	–
4th Rate 50	–	–	22	–	22	–	6	–	–
5th Rate 44	–	–	–	20	–	20	4	–	–
6th Rate 20	–	–	–	–	–	20	–	–	–
Ships built after 1757:									
1st Rate 100	28	–	28	–	28	–	16	–	–
2nd Rate 90	–	28	–	30	30	2	–	–	–
3rd Rate 80	–	26	–	–	26	–	28	–	–
Large 74	–	28	30	–	–	16	–	–	–
Small 74	–	28	–	28	–	18	–	–	–
3rd Rate 70	–	28	–	28	–	14	–	–	–
3rd Rate 64	–	–	26	–	26	–	12	–	–
4th Rate 60	–	–	26	–	26	–	8	–	–
4th Rate 50	–	–	–	22	22	–	6	–	–
5th Rate 44	–	–	–	20	–	22	2	–	–
5th Rate 36	–	–	–	–	26	–	10	–	–
5th Rate 32	–	–	–	–	26	–	6	–	–
6th Rate 28	–	–	–	–	–	24	–	–	4
6th Rate 24	–	–	–	–	–	22	–	–	2
6th Rate 20	–	–	–	–	–	20	–	–	–
Sloop 14	–	–	–	–	–	–	14	–	–
Sloop 12	–	–	–	–	–	–	–	12	–
Sloop 10	–	–	–	–	–	–	–	10	–
Sloop 8	–	–	–	–	–	–	–	–	8

	42pdr	32pdr	24pdr	18pdr	12pdr	9pdr	6pdr	4pdr	3pdr
After 1792:									
1st Rate 110	–	30	30	32	18	–	–	–	–
1st Rate 100	28	–	28	–	44	–	–	–	–
	–	30	28	30	12	–	–	–	–
	30	28	–	–	42	–	–	–	–
2nd Rate 98	–	28	–	28	42	–	–	–	–
	–	28	–	60	10	–	–	–	–
2nd Rate 90	–	26	–	26	38	–	–	–	–
3rd Rate 80	–	30	32	–	–	–	18	–	–
Large 74	–	28	30	–	–	16	–	–	–
Common 74	–	28	–	28	–	18	–	–	–
5th Rate 40	–	–	–	28	–	12	–	–	–
5th Rate 38	–	–	–	28	2	8	–	–	–
5th Rate 36	–	–	–	26	2	8	–	–	–
Large 32	–	–	–	26	–	6	–	–	–
Common 32	–	–	–	–	26	–	6	–	–
Sloop 18	–	–	–	–	–	–	18	–	–
Sloop 16	–	–	–	–	–	–	16	–	–

Other ships as in 1757.

CLASSES MENTIONED IN THE TEXT

'A' class submarines: 1,120 tons, 281·7 (oa) × 22·25ft, 1—-in, 1—20mm, 10—TT. 46 ordered 1943–44.

'Acacia' class sloops: 1,200 tons, 250 × 33ft, 2—12pdr, 2—3pdr. 36 ordered 1915.

'Adelaide' class frigates (RAN): 4,100 tons, 445 (last two ships: 453) × 45ft, SSM Harpoon, SAM GDC Pomona, 1—3in, 6—TT, helo. 6 launched 1978–92.

'Albacore' class wood screw gunboats: Av. 232bm, 106 × 22ft, 1—68pdr, 1—32pdr, 2—20pdr. 98 ordered 1855.

'Algerine' class minesweepers: Av. 860 tons, 212·7 (pp), 225 (oa) × 35·2ft, 1—4in, 8—20mm. 115 laid down 1941–44 (inc. 12 RCN and 9 Lend-Lease).

'Anchusa' class sloops: 1,290 tons, 250 × 35ft, 2—4in, 2—12pdr. 33 ordered 1917.

'Ant' class iron screw gunboats: 254 tons, 85 × 26ft, 1—10in. 20 laid down 1870–73.

'Anzac' class frigates (RAN/RNZN): 3,600 tons full load, 387·1 (oa) × 48·6ft SSM Harpoon, SAM Raytheon Sea Sparrow, 1—5in, 6—TT, helo. 10 launched 1994–2003.

'Arabis' class sloops: 1,250 tons, 250 × 33.5ft, 2—4in or 4·7in, 2—3pdr. 36 ordered 1915.

'Ascot' class paddle minesweepers: 810 or (8 vessels) 820 tons, 235 × 29ft, 2—12pdr. 32 ordered 1915 or 1917.

'Astute' class nuclear submarines: 6,500/7,200 tons, 318 (oa) × 35·1ft, Tomahawk, SubHarpoon, 6—TT. First boat laid down 31.01.2001.

'Aubretia' class sloops: As 'Arabis' class but mercantile profile. 6 ordered 1916.

'Bangor' class minesweepers: *Diesel-engined:* 590 tons, 162 (oa) × 28ft, 1—3in. 14 laid down 1939–41 (inc. 10 RCN). *Triple-expansion-engined (TE):* 672 tons, 180 (oa) × 28·5ft, 1—3in. 73 laid down 1940–41 (inc. 36 RCN and 7 RIN). *Turbine-engined:* 656 tons, 174 (oa) × 28·5ft, 1—3in. 26 laid down 1939–41 (inc. 6 RIN).

'Bathurst' class minesweepers: 650 tons, 186·2(oa) × 28ft, 1—4in (1—3in in some), 1—20mm. 63 laid down 1940–42 (inc. 43 RAN and 7 RIN).

'Bay' class frigates: 1,580 tons, 307 (oa) × 38·5ft, 4—4in, 4—40mm, 4—20mm. 26 laid down 1944 as 'Loch' class and altered on stocks, 19 completing as frigates, 4 as survey vessels and 2 as despatch vessels, with 1 cancelled.

'Bay' class coastal minesweepers: 390 tons, 152 (oa) × 28ft, 1—40mm. 20 built for RCN 1952–57.

'Britomart' class wood screw gunboats: Av. 268bm, 330 tons, 120 × 22ft, 2—68pdr. 20 laid down 1859–61.

'C' class destroyers: 1,710 tons, 362·7 (oa) × 35·8ft, 4—4·5in, 4—40mm, 4 or 8—TT. 32 ordered 1942, plus 8 (only 2 named) ordered 1943 but redesignated 'Weapon' class.

'Castle' class corvettes: 1,010 tons, 252 (oa) × 36·7ft, 1—4in, 10—20mm, Squid. 96 ordered 1943–44, inc. 12 RCN. Later re-rated as frigates.

'Captain' class frigates: *Diesel-electric-engined (DE):* 1,085 tons, 289·4(oa) × 35·2ft, 3—3in, 2—40mm, 10—20mm. 34 ordered 1942–43 under Lend-Lease; 32 handed over. *Turbo-electric-engined (TE):* 1,300 tons, 306 (oa) × 36·9ft, 3—3in, 2—40mm, 8—20mm. 46 handed over 1943 under Lend-Lease.

'Catherine' class minesweepers: 890 tons, 215 × 32ft, 1—3in, 6—20mm, 22 handed over under Lend-Lease 1943-44 and 12 retained by the USN.

'Cheerful' class wood screw gunboats: 212bm, 100 × 22ft, 2—32pdr. 20 ordered 1855.

'Cherokee' class brig-sloops: Av. 236bm, 90 × 25ft, 8—18pdr carr., 2—6pdr. 115 laid down 1807–30.

'Clown' class wood screw gunboats: 233bm, 110 × 22ft, 1—68 pdr, 1—32 pdr. 12 ordered 1855.

'Colony' class frigates: 1,318 tons, 304 (oa) × 37·6ft, 3—3in, 4—40mm, 4—20mm, 21 transferred under Lend-Lease 1943–44.

'Cruizer' class brig-sloops: Av. 348bm, 100·5 × 30.5ft, 16—32pdr carr., 2—6pdr. 110 laid down 1797–1826.

'Dapper' class wood screw gunboats: 232bm, 284 tons, 106 × 22ft, 1—68pdr, 2—24pdr. 20 ordered 1854.

'Daring' class (Type 45) destroyers: 7,350 tons, 462·9 (oa) × 65·2ft, 1—4·5in, Phalanx, Harpoon, PAAMS-Sylver-Aster Missile, helo. Up to 12 to replace Type 42 destroyers. Announced 14.7.2000.

'Flower' class corvettes: Av. 925 tons, 190 (pp), 205 (oa) × 33.2ft, 1—4in. 222 laid down 1939–41, inc. 70 RCN and 4 seized French vessels. *Modified 'Flower' class:* Av. 980 tons, 193 (pp) 208·5 (oa) × 33ft, 1—4in, 6—40mm. 57 laid down 1942–44, inc. 36 RCN, 7 under Lend-Lease and 8 transferred to USN.

'Ford' class seaward defence boats: 120 tons, 117·3(oa) × 20ft, 1—40mm. 20 for RN 1952–57, others for South African, Indian, Kenyan, Nigerian and Ghanaian Navies.

'Fly' class river gunboats: 98 tons, 120 × 20ft, 1—4in, 1—12pdr, 1—3pdr. 16 laid down 1916.

'Halifax' class frigates (RCN): 4,770 tons full load, 441·9(oa) × 53·8ft, Harpoon, Sea Sparrow, 1—57mm, Phalanx, 4—TT, 2 helo. 12 launched 1988–95.

'Ham' class inshore minesweepers: 120 tons, 106·4(oa) × 21·2ft, 1—40mm or 20mm. 93 built for RN and others for foreign navies 1952 onwards.

'Hunt' class minesweepers: *Early:* 750 tons, 220 × 28ft, 2—12pdr. 20 ordered 1916. *Later:* 800 tons, 220 × 28.5ft, 1—4in, 1—12pdr (most originally had 1—6pdr only). 119 ordered 1917–18.

'Hunt' class destroyers *Type I:* 907 tons, 264·2 (pp), 280 (oa) × 29ft, 4—4in, 2—20mm (designed for 6—4in, 2—TT; ATHERSTONE completed thus). 20 laid down 1939. *Type II:* 1,050 tons, 264·2 (pp), 280 (oa) × 31·5ft, 6—4in, 2—20mm. 36 laid down 1939–40 (inc. BLENCATHRA, BROCKLESBY, LIDDESDALE: 1,000 tons, 4—4in). *Type III:* 1,087 tons, 264·2 (pp), 280 (oa) × 31·5ft, 4—4in, 2—20mm, 2—TT. 28 laid down 1940–41. *Type IV:* BRECON, BRISSENDEN (see entries for these vessels). All 'Hunt' class destroyers were rated as frigates from 1947.

'Leander' class frigates: 2,650 tons, 372 (oa) × 41/43ft, 2—4·5in, 2—40mm/Seacat, helo. 25 laid down 1959–67 (3 groups, defined by machinery fit: Y100 and Y136 – beam 41ft; Y160 – beam 43ft).

'Ley' class inshore minehunters 123 tons, 106·4 (oa) × 21·2ft, 1—40mm. 10 built for RN 1953–54.

'Loch' class frigates: 1,435 tons, 286 (pp), 307 (oa) × 38·5ft, 1—4in, 4—2pdr, 6—20mm, Squid. 110 ordered. 2 completed as depot ships, 54 cancelled. 26 re-armed as 'Bay' class (4 comp. as survey ships, 2 comp. as despatch vessels, 1 cancelled).

'M' class destroyers: Av. 1,050 tons, 265 × 26·5ft (Thornycroft design: 265 × 27.5ft; Yarrow design: 260 × 26ft), 3—4in, 4—TT. 110 laid down 1913–16.

'Norfolk' class (Type 23) frigates: 3,500 tons 436·2(oa) × 52·8, 1—5in, Harpoon, Seawolf, 4—TT, helo. 16 ships launched 1987–2000.

'Oberon' class diesel/electric submarines: 1,610 tons, 295·2 (oa) × 26·5ft, 8—TT. 13 RN, 6 RAN, 3 RCN, launched 1959–75.

'Philomel' class wood screw gunvessels: 428bm, 570 tons, 145 × 25.5ft, 1—68pdr, 2—24pdr, 2—20pdr. 27 laid down 1859—61.

'Porpoise' class diesel/electric submarines: 1,605 tons, 295·2 (oa) × 26·5ft, 8—TT. 8 launched 1957—59.

'R' class destroyers: Av. 1,065 tons, 265 × 26.5ft, 3—4in, 4—TT. 44 laid down 1915—16. Modified 'R' class: Av. 1,085 tons. 11 laid down 1916.

'Resolution' class ballistic missile submarines: 7,500/8,400 tons, 425 (oa) × 33ft, 16 Polaris ICBM, 6—TT. 4 launched 1966—68.

'River' class frigates: Av. 1,375 tons, 283 (pp), 301·5(oa) × 36ft, 2—4in, 10—20mm. 167 ordered 1941—42, inc. 78 RCN, 22 RAN, 2 tx USN.

'S' class destroyers: Av. 1,075 tons, 265 × 26.5ft (Thornycroft design: 1,087 tons, 267 × 27ft; Yarrow design: 930 tons, 260 × 26ft), 3—4in, 6—TT (reduced to 4—TT). 69 laid down 1917—18.

'S' class submarines: 1931 boats: 640 tons, 202·5 (oa) × 23·75ft. 1934 boats: 670 tons, 208·8 (oa) × 23·5ft. Others: 715 tons, 217 (oa) × 23·75ft. All: 1—3in or 1—4in, 6 or 7—TT. 66 laid down 1931—44. *Note:* All war programme boats were ordered with 'P' numbers and received names in 1.1943. This number is given in the individual entries only if the boat had been launched without a name.

'Sandown' class minehunters: 484 tons (full load), 172·9 (oa) × 34·4ft, 1—30mm. 12 launched 1988—2001.

'Swiftsure' class nuclear submarines: 4,600/4,900 tons, 272 (oa) × 32.2ft, Tomahawk, SubHarpoon, 5—TT. 6 launched 1973—79.

'T' class submarines: 1,090 tons, 265 (pp) 273—275 (oa) (TRITON 277 oa) × 26·5ft, 1—4in, 10— or 11—TT. 58 laid down 1937—44. See note after 'S' class.

'Ton' class coastal minesweepers: 360 tons, 153 (oa) × 28·8ft, 1—40mm. Launched 1953—58. 116 built for RN and other navies. Similar class in RCN ('Bay'). Design used by other navies.

'Trafalgar' class nuclear submarines: 4,740/5,208 tons, 280·1 (oa) × 32·1ft, Tomahawk, SubHarpoon, 5—TT. 7 launched 1981—1991.

'24' class minesweeping sloops: 1,320 tons, 267·5 × 35ft, 2—4in (not in all). 24 ordered 1917.

Type 42 destroyers: *Batch 1:* 3,500 tons, 412 (oa) × 47ft, 1—4·5in, Sea Dart, Phalanx, 4—TT, helo (6 ships). *Batch 2:* 3,800 tons, 412 (oa) × 47ft, 1—4·5in, Sea Dart, Phalanx, 4—TT, helo (4 ships). *Batch 3:* 4,500 tons (4,650 tons after strengthening), 462·8(oa) × 49·2ft, 1—4·5in, Sea Dart, Phalanx, 6—TT, helo (4 ships). 14 in all launched 1971—83.

'U' class submarines: 540 tons, 191·4—196·9 (oa) × 16·1ft, 1—3in, 4—TT. 49 laid down 1937—42 See note after 'S' class.

'Upholder' class diesel/electric submarines: 2,160/2,455 tons, 230·6 (oa) × 25ft, 6—TT. 4 launched 1989—92.

'V' class submarines: 545 tons, 204·4 (oa) × 16·1ft, 1—3in, 4—TT. 34 ordered 1942—43. See note after 'S' class.

'V/W' class destroyers: Av. 1,300 tons, 300(pp) 312(oa) × 29.5ft, 4—4in, 4—TT (6—TT by 1922; 'W' class all built with 6—TT). 51 laid down 1916—17. *Modified 'W' class destroyers:* Av. 1,325 tons, 4—4.7in, 6—TT. 56 ordered 1918.

'Vanguard' class ballistic missile submarines: 15,900 tons dived, 491·8 (oa) × 42ft, 16 Trident ICBM, 4—TT. 4 launched 1992—1998

A NOTE ON REBUILDS

From researches made by Mr Hepper and Mr Lyon, it seems that many of the ships given in Admiralt lists as 'rebuilds' in the early 18th century should count as new ships, though using frames and timbers of ships of the same names of an earlier date. Examples are:

ANTELOPE (1702) BU Woolwich 2.1738. New ship launched Woolwich DY 1741.

BEDFORD (1698) BU 11.1736. New ship launched at Portsmouth DY 1741.

BOYNE (1692) BU 11.1733. New ship launched Deptford 28.5.1739.

CANTERBURY (1693) BU 4.1741. New ship launched Plymouth DY 2.2.1744.

CORNWALL (1692) BU 3.1722. New ship launched Deptford DY 17.10.1726.

CUMBERLAND (1710) BU 10. 1732. New ship launched Woolwich DY 11.7.1739.
DARTMOUTH (1798) BU 9.1736. New ship launched Woolwich DY 22.4.1741.
ELIZABETH (1706) BU 1732. New ship launched Chatham DY 29.11.1737.
FALKLAND (1690) BU 3.1742. New ship launched Bursledon 17.3.1744.
GREENWICH (1666) BU 7.1724. New ship launched Chatham DY 15.2.1730.
HUMBER (1693) BU 11. 1723. New ship launched Portsmouth DY 4.1 .1726.
KINGSTON (1697) BU 11. 1736. New ship launched Plymouth DY 8.10.1740.
LANCASTER (1694) BU 5. 1719. New ship launched Portsmouth DY 1.9.1722.
LION (1709) BU 11. 1735. New ship launched Deptford DY 25.4.1738.
MONMOUTH (1666) BU 7.1739. New ship launched Deptford DY 10.9.1742.
NAMUR (1697) BU 7.1723. New ship launched Deptford DY 13.9.1729.
NASSAU (1706) BU 6.1736. New ship launched Chatham DY 25.9.1740.
NEPTUNE (1683) BU 9.1724. New ship launched Woolwich DY 15.10.1730.
NEWARK (1695) BU 5.1741. New ship launched Chatham DY 27.8.1747.
NORFOLK (1693) BU 2.1717. New ship launched Plymouth DY 21.9.1728.
NOTTINGHAM (1703) BU 4.1739. New ship launched Sheerness DY 17.8.1745.
OXFORD (1694) BU 7.1723. New ship launched Portsmouth DY 10.7.1727.
PEARL (1700) BU 1722. New ship launched Deptford DY 1726.
PRINCE FREDERICK (EXPEDITION, 1679) BU 6.1736. New ship launched Deptford DY 18.3.1740.
PRINCESS MARY (MARY, 1704) BU 1. 1736. New ship launched 3.10.1742.
RAMILLIES (KATHERINE, 1664) BU 8.1741. New ship launched Portsmouth DY 8.2.1749.
RANELAGH (1697) BU 9.1723. New ship launched as PRINCESS CAROLINE 15.3.1740.
ROYAL OAK (1674) BU 5.1737. New ship launched Plymouth DY 29.8.1741.
RUPERT (1666) BU 11.1736. New ship launched Sheerness DY 27.10.1740.
RUSSELL (1692) BU 9.1726. New ship launched Deptford DY 8.9.1735.
ST ALBANS (1706) BU 9.1734. New ship launched Plymouth DY 30.8.1737.
ST GEORGE (1701) BU 11.1726. New ship launched Portsmouth DY 3.4.1740.
SALISBURY (1698) BU as PRESTON 2.1739. New ship launched 18.9.1742.
SEVERN (1695) BU 6.1734. New ship launched Plymouth DY 28.3.1739.
SUFFOLK (1680) BU 1. 1736. New ship launched Woolwich DY 5.3.1739.
SWIFTSURE (1673) BU as REVENGE 6.1740. New ship launched Deptford DY 25.5.1742.
TRIUMPH (1698) BU as PRINCE BU 12.1730. New ship launched Chatham DY 8.8.1750.
WARSPITE (1666) BU as EDINBURGH BU 1741. New ship launched Chatham DY 31.5.1744.
WINDSOR (1695) BU 10.1742. New ship launched Woolwich DY 26.2.1745.
WOOLWICH (1675) BU 8.1736. New ship launched Deptford DY 6.2.1741.

ACKNOWLEDGEMENTS

Grateful thanks are due to the staff of the Admiralty Library; to Mr H. Langley, Captain C. Page and Mr D. Brown of the Naval Historical Branch, Ministry of Defence; to the following members of the World Ship Society: M. Crowdy (founder), J. Meirat (for assistance with French ships), P. Silverstone and F. Dittmar (American Navy), G. Osborn; G. Ransome; R. Coleman; I. Buxton; D. Hepper; and H. T. Lenton; and to Mr D. Lyon of the National Maritime Museum.

REFERENCES

Admiralty Progress Books and Navy Lists, Admiralty Library. World Ship Society records.
British Warship Names (Manning and Walker)
Repertoire des Navires de Guerre Français (Musée de la Marine, Paris)
The Naval Service of Canada (Tucker)
Royal Australian Navy (Gill)
The Naval History of Great Britain (James)

Abbreviations

AA	anti-aircraft	poss.	possible, possibly
ABS	armed boarding steamer	pp	between perpendiculars
ABV	armed boarding vessel	purch.	purchased
acq.	acquired	QF	quick-firing (guns)
AMC	armed merchant cruiser	RAN	Royal Australian Navy
AO	Admiralty Order	RCeyN	Royal Ceylonese Navy
aux.	auxiliary	RCMP	Royal Canadian Mounted Police
av.	average	RCN	Royal Canadian Navy
BU	breaking-up, broken up	recd	recommissioned
c.	circa	RDanN	Royal Danish Navy
Co.	Company	ref.	referred (to as)
cd	commissioned (in the Royal Navy)	repurch.	repurchased
comp.	completed (as, by), completion	req.	requisitioned
conv.	converted (to), conversion (to)	ret.	returned (to)
CTL	constructive total loss	RIM	Royal Indian Marine
DE	diesel-electric	RIN	Royal Indian Navy
DY	Dockyard	RN	Royal Navy
Eng.	Engineering	RNorN	Royal Norwegian Navy
FV	Fishing vessel	RNR	Royal Naval Reserve
GM	guided missile	RNVR	Royal Naval Volunteer Reserve
Govt	Government	RNXS	Royal Naval Auxiliary Service
GWS	guided weapons system(s)	RNZN	Royal New Zealand Navy
helo	helicopter(s)	RPN	Royal Pakistani Navy
HO	handed over (to)	SAN	South African Navy
I.	Island, Isle	SB	Shipbuilding, Shipbuilders
ICBM	inter-continental ballistic missile	S. Bkg	Ship Breaking (or Shipbreaking)
inc.	including	sbkrs	ship breakers
incomp.	incomplete	spec.	speculative, (as a) speculation
Is	Islands, Isles	SR	Ship Repair(er)s
LD	laid down	SY	Shipyard
LU	laid up, lay up	TE	triple-expansion; turbo-electric
MCDV	maritime coast defence vessel	TRV	torpedo recovery vessel
Mod	Modified	TS	training ship
MOT	Ministry of Trade	TT	torpedo tube(s)
MTB	motor torpedo boat	TUFT	taken up from trade
MWT	Ministry of War Transport	tx	transfer(red) (to)
nr	nr	USCG	United States Coast Guard
NY	Navy Yard	USN	United States Navy
NZ	New Zealand	wl	waterline (length)
oa	overall (length)	WW2	World War Two
orig.	original(ly)	YC	yard craft
PO	paid off	=	renamed

A

'A' class submarines 165 tons (first four), 180 tons (others), 100 × 11·5ft (first four), 94 × 12ft (others), 2—TT.

A.1 Vickers 9.7.1902 (ordered as H.6). Sunk 8.1911 target.

A.2 Vickers 16.4.1903. Wrecked 1.1920 while on sale list; wreck sold 22.10.1925 J. H. Pounds, Portsmouth.

A.3 Vickers 9.3.1903. Sunk 17.5.1912 target.

A.4 Vickers 9.6.1903. Sold 16.1.1920 J. H. Lee, Bembridge.

A.5 Vickers 3.3.1904. BU 1920.

A.6 Vickers 3.3.1904. Sold 16.1.1920 J. H. Lee, Bembridge

A.7 Vickers 23.1.1905. Lost 16.1.1914 Whitesand Bay diving into mud.

A.8 Vickers 23.1.1905. Sold 8.10.1920 Philip, Dartmouth.

A.9 Vickers 8.2.1905. BU 1920.

A.10 Vickers 8.2.1905. Sold 1.4.1919 Ardrossan DD Co.

A.11 Vickers 8.3.1905. BU 5.1920 Portsmouth.

A.12 Vickers 8.3.1905. Sold 16.1.1920 J. H. Lee, Bembridge.

A.13 Vickers 18.4.1905. BU 1920.

ABBOTSHAM Inshore minesweeper, 'Ham' class. Blackmore, Bideford, 16.12.1955. Sold 16.6.1967 Pounds, Portsmouth.

ABDIEL (ex-ITHURIEL) Destroyer-minelayer 1,687 tons, 325 × 32ft, 3—4in, 70 mines. Cammell Laird 12.10.1915 (renamed 1915). Sold 7.1936 Rees, Llanelly.

ABDIEL Minelayer, 2,650 tons, 418 (oa) × 39ft, 6—4in, 160 mines. White 23.4.1940. Mined 9.9.1943 Taranto, sank 10.9.1943.

ABDIEL Minelayer, 1,200 tons, 265 (oa) × 38·5ft. Thornycroft 27.1.1967. Sold Vanity Fair Investments Corp.; resold Cantabra Metalurgiea SA; towed from Portsmouth 6.9.1988 to Santander for BU.

ABEILLE Cutter 14. French, captured 2.5.1796 by DRYAD off The Lizard. Listed until 1799.

ABELARD Submarine, 1945 'A' class. Portsmouth DY, cancelled 1945.

ABELIA Corvette, 'Flower' class. Harland & Wolff 28.11.1940. Sold 1947 = *Kraft*; = *Arne Skontorp* 1954. BU Norway 12.1966.

ABERCROMBIE 3rd Rate 74, 1,871 tons. French D'HAUTPOUL, captured 17.4.1809 by squadron in West Indies. Sold 30.4.1817 Mr Freake.

ABERCROMBIE (ex-GENERAL ABERCROMBIE, ex-M.1, ex-ADMIRAL FARRAGUT, ex-FARRAGUT) Monitor, 6,150 tons, 320 × 90ft, 2—14in, 2—6in. Harland & Wolff 15.4.1915 (renamed 20.6.1915). Sold 7.1927 Ward, Inverkeithing.

ABERCROMBIE Monitor, 7,850 tons, 365 × 90ft, 2—15in, 8—4in. Vickers Armstrong, Tyne, 31.3.1942, Arr. 24.12.1954 Ward, Barrow, for BU.

ABERDARE Minesweeper, Later 'Hunt' class. Ailsa, Troon, 29.4.1918. Sold 13.3.1947.

ABERDEEN Sloop, 990 tons, 250 × 36ft, 4—4in. Devonport DY 22.1.1936. Sold 16.12.1948; arr. 18.1.1949 Ward, Hayle, for BU.

ABERFORD Seaward defence boat, 'Ford' class. Yarrow 22.9.1952. Kenyan NYATI 1966; sold 1971.

ABERFOYLE Tender, 210 tons, 100 × 19ft. Purch. 4.11.1920. For disposal 1947. *See DOLPHIN 1938.*

ABERGAVENNY 4th Rate 54, 1,182bm, 160 × 41ft. East Indiaman, purch. 1795. Sold 1807.

ABIGAIL Fireship, 4,143bm. Purch. 1666. Expended 25.7.1666.

ABIGAIL Cutter 3. Captured 12.12.1812 from Danes by HAMADRYAD. Sold 1814.

ABINGDON Minesweeper, Later 'Hunt' class. Ailsa 11.6.1918. Bombed 5.4.1942 Italian aircraft Malta, beached; BU 1950 *in situ.*

ABOUKIR 3rd Rate 74, 1,870bm, 186 × 48ft. French AQUILON, captured 1.8.1798 Battle of the Nile. BU 3.1802 Plymouth.

ABOUKIR 3rd Rate 74, 1,703bm, 172·5 × 47ft. Brindley, Frindsbury, 18.11.1807. Harbour service 6.1824. Sold 16.8.1838 J. Lachlan.

ABOUKIR 2nd Rate 90, 3,080bm, 204 × 60ft. Devonport DY 4.4.1848; undocked 1.1.1858 as screw ship, 3,091bm. Sold 23.11.1877 in Jamaica.

ABOUKIR Armoured cruiser, 12,000 tons, 440 × 69·5ft, 2—9·2in, 12—6in. Fairfield 16.5.1900. Sunk 22.9.1914 by U.9 North Sea.

ABRAHAM Flyboat 4, 202bm. Purch. 1665. Sold 1666.

ABRAMS OFFERING Fireship, 63bm. Purch. 1694. Expended 12.9.1694 Dunkirk.

ABUNDANCE Storeship 24, 673bm, 140 × 32·5ft. Adams, Buckler's Hard, 30.9.1799, purch. 1799. Sold 22.5.1823.

ABUNDANCE *See also ALFRED 1855.*

ABYSSINIA Turret ship (Indian), 2,900 tons, 225 × 42ft, 4—10in MLR. Dudgeon, Poplar, 19.2.1870. Sold 1.1903.

ACACIA Sloop, 'Acacia' class. Swan Hunter 15.4.1915. Sold 9.1922 Dornom Bros.

ACANTHUS Corvette, 'Flower' class. Ailsa 26.5.1941. Lent Norwegian Navy 10.1941–1946. Sold 1946 = *Colin Frye.*

ACASTA 5th rate 40, 1,142bm, 154 × 41ft. Wells, Rotherhithe, 14.3.1797. BU 1.1.1821.

ACASTA Wood screw frigate, 3,202bm, 280 × 50ft. Deptford DY, LD 16.4.1861, cancelled 12.12.1863.

ACASTA Destroyer, 996 tons, 260 × 27ft, 3—4in, 2—TT. John Brown 10.9.1912. Sold 9.5.1921 Ward, Hayle.

ACASTA Destroyer, 1,350 tons, 323 (oa) × 32·5ft, 4—4·7in, 8—TT. John Brown 8.8.1929. Sunk 8.6.1940 by German battlecruisers west of Narvik.

ACASTA Submarine, 1945 'A' class'. Portsmouth DY, cancelled 1945.

ACE Submarine, 1945 'A' class. Devonport DY 14.3.1945, not comp. Arr. 6.1950 Smith & Houston, Port Glasgow, for BU.

ACERTIF Brig-sloop 18. Danish, captured 8.1808 by DAPHNE in Baltic. Sold 1809.

ACHATES 13-gun ship, 100bm, 6—9pdr, 2—4pdr, 5 small. Deptford 11.10.1573. Hulked 1590. Sold 1605.

ACHATES Brig-sloop 10, 'Cherokee' class, 238bm. Brent, Rotherhithe, 1.2.1808. Wrecked 7.2.1810 Guadeloupe.

ACHATES (ex-LE MILAN) Brig-sloop, 16,327bm, 95·5 × 28·5ft. French, captured 3.10.1809. Sold 11.6.1818 Mr Ledger.

ACHATES Destroyer, 982 tons, 260 × 27ft, 3—4in, 2—TT. John Brown 14.11.1912. Sold 9.5.1921 Ward, Rainham.

ACHATES Destroyer, 1,350 tons, 323 (oa) × 32·5ft, 4—4·7in, 8—TT. John Brown 4.10.1929. Sunk 31.12.1942 by ADMIRAL HIPPER in Barents Sea.

ACHATES Submarine, 1945 'A' class. Devonport DY 20.9.1945, not comp. Sunk 6.1950 target off Gibraltar.

ACHERON Bomb vessel 8, 388bm, 108 × 29ft. Purch. 10.1803. Captured 3.2.1805 by French in Mediterranean, burnt.

ACHERON Wood paddle sloop, 722bm, 150 × 33ft, 2—9pdr. Sheerness DY 23.8.1838. Sold 24.9.1855 Sydney.

ACHERON Wood screw sloop, 675bm, 162 × 30ft. Deptford DY, LD 14.10.1861, cancelled 12.12.1863.

ACHERON Torpedo boat (Australian), 16 tons, 78 × 10ft, 1—TT. Built 1879. Sold 12.1902.

ACHERON Destroyer, 773 tons, 245 × 26ft, 2—4in, 2—12pdr, 2—TT. Thornycroft 27.6.1911. Sold 9.5.1921 Ward; resold 20.6.1923 J. J. King for BU.

ACHERON Destroyer, 1,350 tons, 323 (oa) × 32ft, 4—4·7in, 8—TT. Thornycroft 18.3.1930. Sunk 17.12.1940 mine in English Channel.

ACHERON Submarine, 1945 'A' class. Chatham DY 25.3.1947. BU Newport 2.1972.

ACHERON *See also NORTHUMBERLAND 1866.*

ACHILLE Sloop 8. French, captured 1744. Captured 14.11.1745 by Spanish off Jamaica.

ACHILLE 3rd Rate 78, 1,801bm, 178 × 48ft. French, captured 1.6.1794 'Battle of 1st of June'. BU 2.1796 Plymouth.

ACHILLE 3rd Rate 74, 1,981bm, 184 × 50·5ft. Cleveley, Gravesend, 16.4.1798. Sold 11.1865 Castle & Beech.

ACHILLE Storeship 14, 420bm, 97 × 31ft. Purch. 1780. Sold 8.1.1784.

ACHILLES Schooner 8. Purch. 1747. Captured 1748 by Spanish.

ACHILLES 4th Rate 60, 1,234bm, 154 × 42·5ft. Barnard, Harwich, 16.7.1757. Hulked 1780. Sold 1.6.1784.

ACHILLES Iron screw ship, 9,820 tons, 380 × 58ft, 20—100pdr (rearmed 14—9in, 2—7in MLR). Chatham DY 23.12.1863. Base ship = HIBERNIA 1902; = EGMONT 3.1904; = EGREMONT 6.1916; = PEMBROKE 6.1919. Sold 26.1.1923 Granton S. Bkg Co.

ACHILLES Armoured cruiser, 13,550 tons, 480 × 73·5ft, 6—9·2in, 4—7·5in, 24—3pdr. Armstrong 17.6.1905. Sold 9.5.1921 Ward; BU Swansea and Briton Ferry 1923.

ACHILLES Cruiser, 7,030 tons, 554·5 (oa) × 55ft, 8—6in, 8—4in. Cammell Laird 1.9.1932. RIN DELHI 5.7.1948, discarded 5.1978.

ACHILLES Frigate, 'Leander' class, Y160, 2,650 tons, 372 (oa) × 43ft, 2—4·5in, Seacat, helo. Yarrow 21.11.1968. Sold Chile 1.12.1990 = MINISTRO ZENTENO.

ACONITE Corvette, 'Flower' class. Ailsa, Troon, 31.3.1941. Free French ACONIT 7.1941–30.4.1947. Sold 7.1947 = *Terje II.*

ACORN 22-gun ship. Hired 1649–54.

ACORN Sloop 18, 430bm, 110 × 30ft. Croker, Bideford, 30.10.1807. BU 5.1819.

ACORN Sloop 18, 455bm, 112 × 30·5ft. Chatham DY 16.11.1826. Wrecked 14.4.1828 off Halifax, NS.

ACORN Sloop 18, 480bm, 114 × 31ft. Portsmouth DY, cancelled 6.1831.

ACORN Brig 12, 485bm, 105 × 33·5ft, 12—32pdr. Devonport DY 15.11.1838. Coal hulk 1861. Sold 15.2.1869 Yokohama.

ACORN Composite screw sloop, 970 tons, 167 × 32ft, 8—5in. Milford Haven SB Co. 6.9.1884. Sold 15.12.1899 Harris, Bristol; BU 1904.

ACORN Destroyer, 760 tons, 246 × 25ft, 2—4in 2—12pdr, 2—TT. John Brown 1.7.1916. Sold 29.11.1921 Marple & Gillott, Saltash.

ACTAEON 6th Rate 28 (fir-built), 595bm, 118 × 34ft. Chatham DY 30.9.1757. Sold 9.9.1766, unserviceable.

ACTAEON 6th Rate 28, 594bm, 120·5 × 33·5ft. Woolwich DY 18.4.1775. Grounded 29.6.1776 Charlestown, burnt.

ACTAEON 5th Rate 44, 887bm, 140 × 38ft. Randall, Rotherhithe, 29.1.1778. Harbour service 7.1795. Sold 30.4.1802.

ACTAEON 6th Rate 26, 620bm, 121·5 × 34·5ft. Portsmouth DY 31.1.1831. Survey ship 1856; lent Cork Harbour Board 2.1870 as hulk. Sold 2.1889 J. Read, Portsmouth.

ACTAEON Sloop, 1,350 tons, 299·5 (oa) × 38·5ft, 6—4in, 4—40mm. Thornycroft 25.7.1945. Tx West Germany = HIPPER 9.12.1958. Hulk 31.7.1964. Sold 25.10.1967 Eisen & Metall, Hamburg, for BU.

ACTAEON *See also VERNON 1832, ARIADNE 1859, DIDO 1869.*

ACTEON Brig-sloop 16, 335bm. French, captured 3.10.1805 by EGYPTIENNE off Rochefort. BU 10.1816.

ACTIF Gun-brig 10, 165bm, 10—4pdr. French, captured 16.3.1794 by IPHIGENIA in West Indies. Foundered 26.11.1794 off Bermuda.

ACTIVE 6th Rate 28, 594bm, 118·5 × 34ft. Stanton, Deptford, 11.1.1758. Captured 1.9.1778 by French off San Domingo.

ACTIVE Brig-sloop 14, 109bm, 76 × 20ft. Purch. 1776. Captured 1780 by Americans off New York.

ACTIVE Cutter 12. In service 1779. Captured 18.8.1779 by French cutter LE MUTIN in English Channel.

ACTIVE 5th Rate 32, 697bm, 126 × 36ft. Raymond, Northam, 30.8.1780. Wrecked 7.1796 St Lawrence R.

ACTIVE Brig-sloop 14. In service 1782.

ACTIVE 5th Rate 38, 1,058bm, 150 × 41ft. Chatham DY 14.12.1799. Harbour service 2.1826 = ARGO 15.11.1833. BU 10.1860 Plymouth.

ACTIVE 5th Rate 36, 1,627bm, 160 × 49ft, Chatham DY 19.7.1845 (ordered Pembroke). = TYNE (TS) 30.7.1867; = DURHAM 18.11.1867. Sold 12.5.1908; BU Bo'ness.

ACTIVE Iron screw corvette, 3,080 tons, 270 × 42ft, 18—64pdr. Blackwall 13.3.1869. Sold 10.7.1906.

ACTIVE Scout cruiser, 3,360 tons, 385 × 41·5ft, 10—4in. Pembroke Dock 14.3.1911. Sold 21.4.1920.

ACTIVE Destroyer, 1,350 tons, 323 (oa) × 32ft, 4—4·7in, 8—TT. Hawthorn Leslie 9.7.1929. Sold 20.5.1947; BU Troon.

ACTIVE Frigate, Type 21, 2,750 tons, 384 (oa) × 40·5ft, 1—4·5in, Exocet, Seacat, 6—TT, helo. Vosper-Thornycroft 23.11.1972. Tx Pakistani Navy 23.9.1994 = SHAH JAHAN.

ACTIVITY (ex-*Empire Activity*, ex-*Telemachus*) Escort carrier, 11,800 tons, 475 × 66·5ft, 2—4in, 15 aircraft. Caledon 30.5.1942, conv. Sold 4.1946 = *Breconshire*.

ACUTE (Gunboat No 6) Gunvessel 12, 159bm, 75 × 22ft. Randall, Rotherhithe, 4.1797. Sold 10.1802.

ACUTE Gun-brig 12, 178bm, 80 × 22·5ft. Rowe, Newcastle, 21.7.1804. Harbour service 5.1813; later coastguard service until 1831.

ACUTE (ex-ALERT) Minesweeper, 'Algerine' class. Harland & Wolff 14.4.1942 (renamed 12.1941). Destroyed 1964 target.

ACUTE Patrol boat (RAN), 146 tons, 107.5 (oa) × 20ft, 1—40mm. Evans Deakin 26.8.1967; HO Indonesia 6.5.1983 = SILEA.

ADAM & EVE Storeship 20. Dutch, captured 1652. Sold 1657.

ADAM & EVE Hoy 6, 72bm. Dutch, captured 1665. Sunk 1673 as foundation Sheerness.

ADAMANT 4th Rate 50, 1,060bm, 146·5 × 41ft. Baker, Liverpool, 24.1.1780. Harbour service 7.1809. BU 6.1814.

ADAMANT Depot ship, 935 tons, 190 × 32·5ft. Cammell Laird 12.7.1911. Sold 21.9.1932 Rees, Llanelly.

ADAMANT Depot ship, 12,700 tons, 620 × 70·5ft, 8—4·5in. Harland & Wolff 30.11.1940. Arr. Inverkeithing 11.9.1970 for BU.

ADAMANT Submarine tender, 101 (oa) × 25·6ft. Fairey Allday Marine, Cowes, 8.10.1992.

ADAMANT II *See LILY 1915.*

ADDA *See FIDGET 1905.*

ADDER Galley 8. Purch. 1782. Sold 5.1787.

ADDER (Gunboat No 17) Gunvessel 12, 159bm, 75 × 22ft. Barnard, Deptford, 22.4.1797. BU 2.1805.

ADDER Gun-brig 12, 180bm, 85 × 22ft. Ayles, Topsham, 9.11.1805. Captured 9.12.1806 by French while aground on coast of France.

ADDER Gun-brig 12, 182bm, 85 × 22ft. Davy,

Topsham, 28.6.1813. Coastguard 1.1826. Wrecked 1832 nr Newhaven.

ADDER *See SEAGULL 1814.*

ADDER (ex-*Crocodile*) Wood paddle packet, 240bm, 117 × 21ft. GPO vessel, tx 5.1837. Sold 13.5.1870 Wilson Mackay.

ADDER (ex-*Burgoyne*) Tender, 125 tons, 95 × 17.5ft. War Dept vessel, tx 7.1905. = ATTENTIVE II 7.1919. Sold 31.1.1923 Carriden S. Bkg.Co.

ADELAIDE (ex-*Delia Josephine*) Tender, 95bm, 67 × 19ft. Slaver, purch. 1827. Sold 1833 Rio de Janeiro.

ADELAIDE 140bm. Slaver, purch. 5.1848. Wrecked 9.10.1850 Banana I., West Africa.

ADELAIDE *See FIDGET 1905.*

ADELAIDE Light cruiser (RAN), 5,440 tons, 430 × 50ft, 9—6in, 3—4in. Cockatoo DY 27.7.1918. Sold 1.1949 Port Kembla for BU.

ADELAIDE Frigate (RAN), 'Adelaide' class. Todd, Seattle, 21.6.1978.

ADEPT Submarine, 1945 'A' class. Chatham DY, cancelled 23.10.1945, not LD.

ADMIRABLE Submarine, 1945 'A' class. Vickers Armstrong, Tyne, cancelled 1945.

ADMIRAL DEVRIES 3rd Rate 68, 1,360bm, 157 × 44.5ft. Dutch, captured 11.10.1797 Battle of Camperdown. Harbour service 1800. Sold 2.1806 in Jamaica.

ADMIRAL FARRAGUT *See ABERCROMBIE 1915.*

ADMIRALTY Yacht, 115bm, 69 × 20ft. Woolwich DY 21.5.1814. = PLYMOUTH 7.1830; = YC.1 (harbour service) 1866. Sold 10.5.1870 Lethbridge & Drew.

ADMIRALTY Yacht, 136bm, 69 × 21.5ft. Portsmouth DY 28.2.1831 = FANNY (q.v.).

ADONIS Schooner 10, 111bm, 68 × 20ft. Bermuda 1806. Sold 1.9.1814.

ADROIT Patrol boat (RAN), 146 tons, 107.5 (oa) × 20ft, 1—40mm. Evans Deakin 3.2.1968. Expended 8.8.1994 target west of Rottnest I.

ADUR Frigate, 'River' class. Vickers, Montreal, 22.8.1942. Tx RCN = NADUR 1942; tx USN = ASHEVILLE 11.1942.

ADVANCE Patrol boat (RAN), 146 tons, 107.5 (oa) × 20ft, 1—40mm. Walker 16.8.1967. PO 6.2.1988 for RANR use; tx Australian National Maritime Museum 1988.

ADVANTAGE 18-gun ship, 144/182bm, 6—9pdr, 8—6pdr, 4—2pdr. Built 1590. Burnt 1613.

ADVANTAGE 26-gun ship. Dutch, captured 1652. Sold 1655.

ADVANTAGIA Galley, 100bm. Woolwich 1601. Sold 1629.

ADVENTURE Galley 26, 343bm, 4—18pdr, 11—9pdr, 11 small. Built 1594 Deptford. BU 1645.

ADVENTURE 32-gun ship, 438bm, 116 × 28ft. Woolwich DY 1646; rebuilt Chatham 1691 as 4th Rate 44, 117 × 29ft. Captured 1.3.1709 by French off Martinique.

ADVENTURE 5th Rate 40, 530bm, 118 × 32ft. Sheerness DY 16.6.1709. Rebuilt Portsmouth 1726 as 598bm. BU 6.1741 Deptford.

ADVENTURE 4th Rate, 683bm, 124 × 36ft. Blaydes, Hull, 1.10.1741. 32-gun 5th Rate 1758. Sold 20.3.1770.

ADVENTURE Cutter 12, 61bm, 48 × 18ft. Purch. 2.1763. Sold 5.4.1768.

ADVENTURE (ex-RAYLEIGH, ex-*Marquis of Rockingham*) Discovery vessel, 336bm, 99 × 28ft, 10—4pdr. Purch. 11.1771 (renamed 25.12.1771). Fireship 1780. Sold 7.5.1783.

ADVENTURE 5th Rate 44, 896bm, 140.5 × 38.5ft. Perry, Blackwall, 19.7.1784. Troopship 7.1789; harbour service 6.1801. BU 9.1816 Sheerness.

ADVENTURE Torpedo ram, 2,640 tons. Chatham DY, ordered 6.3.1885, cancelled 12.8.1885.

ADVENTURE River gunboat, 85 tons, 75 × 12ft. Yarrow 1891. Re-erected Lake Nyasa 1893; tx BCA Govt 1896. Sold 1921.

ADVENTURE Scout cruiser, 2,670 tons, 374 × 38ft, 10—12pdr. Armstrong 8.9.1904. Sold 3.3.1920 Ward, Morecambe.

ADVENTURE Minelayer, 6,740 tons, 500 × 59ft, 4—4.7in, 280 mines. Devonport DY 18.6.1924. Repair ship 3.1944. Sold 10.7.1947; BU Ward, Briton Ferry.

ADVENTURE *See also AID 1809, RESOLUTE 1855.*

ADVENTURE GALLEY In service 1696–99.

ADVENTURE PRIZE Hoy, 25bm, 38 × 12.5ft. French, captured 1693. Made pitch boat 1695. Sold 1698.

ADVERSARY Submarine, 1945 'A' class. Vickers Armstrong, Tyne, cancelled 1945.

ADVICE Pinnace 9, 50bm, 4—6pdr, 2—4pdr, 3 small. Woolwich DY 1586. Sold 1617.

ADVICE 48-gun ship, 516bm, 118.5 × 31ft. Pett, Woodbridge, 1650. Rebuilt Woolwich 1698 as 550bm. Captured 27.6.1711 by French.

ADVICE 4th Rate 50, 714bm, 131 × 35.5ft. Deptford DY 8.7.1712. = MILFORD 23.5.1744. Sold 11.5.1749.

ADVICE 4th Rate 50, 983bm, 140 × 40ft. Rowcliffe, Southampton, 26.2.1745. BU 10.1756 Portsmouth.

ADVICE Cutter 10, 95bm, 56 × 21ft, 10—3pdr. Purch. 1779. Wrecked 1.6.1793 Bay of Honduras.

ADVICE Cutter 4, 47bm, 45·5 × 16ft, 4—3pdr. Itchen Ferry 1796. Last listed 8.1799.

ADVICE Advice boat, 180bm. Randall, Rotherhithe, 30.12.1800. Sold 1805.

ADVICE (ex-*Vixen*) Wood paddle packet, 197bm, 108 × 20ft. GPO vessel, tx 4.1837. Sold 12.5.1870 J. J. Stark.

ADVICE PRIZE 6th Rate 18, 200bm, 82 × 24·5ft. French, captured 19.6.1704. Sold 10.4.1712.

ADVICE PRIZE Sloop. French, captured 1693. Sold 1695.

ADVISER Pink 8. In service 1654. Captured 1655 by privateer.

AE.1, AE.2 *See under 'E' class submarines.*

AENEAS Submarine, 1945 'A' class. Cammell Laird 9.10.1945. BU Dunston 12.1974.

AEOLUS 5th Rate 32, 704bm, 125·5 × 36ft. West, Deptford, 29.11.1758. Harbour service 5.1796. = GUERNSEY 1800. BU 5.1801.

AEOLUS 5th Rate 32, 910bm, 144 × 37·5ft. Barnard, Deptford, 28.2.1801. BU 10.1817 Deptford.

AEOLUS 5th Rate 46, 1,078bm, 152 × 40ft. Deptford DY 17.6.1825. Harbour service 1855. BU 3.1886 Castle, Thames.

AEOLUS 2nd class cruiser, 3,600 tons, 300 × 44ft, 2—6in, 6—4·7in, 8—6pdr. Devonport DY 13.11.1891. Sold 26.5.1914 Ward, Preston.

AETNA Fireship 8, 283bm, 91 × 26ft. Freame, Hull, 19.3.1691. Captured 18.4.1697 by French.

AETNA (ex-*Mermaid*) Fireship 8, 183bm, 82 × 23ft. Purch. 14.9.1739. Sold 23.10.1746.

AETNA Bomb vessel 8, 300bm, 92 × 27·5ft. Randall, Rotherhithe, 20.6.1776. BU 5.1784.

AETNA (ex-*Success*) Bomb vessel 8, 369bm. Purch. 10.1803. Sold 11.1.1816.

AETNA Bomb vessel 6, 375bm, 106 × 28·5ft. Chatham DY 14.4.1824. Survey vessel 1826. Sold 20.2.1846 Bristol Seamen's Friendly Society.

AETNA Wood screw floating battery, 1,469bm, 172·5 × 44ft, 14—68pdr. Scott Russell, Millwall, LD 9.10.1854, caught fire and launched herself 3.5.1855; BU on river bank.

AETNA Wood screw floating battery, 1,588bm, 186 × 44ft, 16—68pdr. Chatham DY 5.4.1856. Harbour service 1866. Burnt out Sheerness 1873; BU 1874.

AETNA *See also ETNA.*

AFFLECK (ex-OSWALD) Frigate, TE 'Captain' class. Bethlehem, Hingham, 30.6.1943 USN, on Lend-Lease. Badly damaged 7.12.1944; nominally ret. USN 1.9.1945. Sold 4.10.1947 Portuguese owners as hulk.

AFFRAY Submarine, 1945 'A' class. Cammell Laird 20.4.1945. Foundered 17.4.1951 English Channel.

AFRICA 46-gun ship. In service 1694–96.

AFRICA 3rd Rate 64, 1,354bm, 158 × 44·5ft. Perry, Blackwall, 1.8.1761. Sold 15.7.1774.

AFRICA 3rd Rate 64, 1,415bm, 160 × 46ft. Barnard, Deptford, 11.4.1781. Harbour service 9.1798. BU 5.1814 Portsmouth.

AFRICA Cutter. Hired 1803–04.

AFRICA Wood screw sloop, 669bm, 160 × 30ft. Devonport DY 29.3.1862. Sold 13.8.1862 Emperor of China = CHINA.

AFRICA Battleship, 16,350 tons, 439 × 78ft, 4—12in, 4—9·2in, 10—6in, 12—12pdr. Chatham DY 20.5.1905. Sold 30.6.1920 Ellis, Newcastle.

AFRICA Aircraft carrier, 36,800 tons, 720 × 112ft, 16—4·5in, 58—40mm, 100 aircraft. Fairfield, ordered 8.1943, cancelled 10.1945.

AFRICA *See also EURYALUS 1803, GOOD HOPE 1900.*

AFRICAINE 5th Rate 38, 1,085bm, 154 × 40ft. French, captured 19.2.1801 by PHOEBE in Mediterranean. BU 9.1816.

AFRICAINE 5th Rate 46, 1,173bm, 159 × 41ft. Chatham DY 20.12.1827. Sold 9.5.1867 Trinity House as hulk. BU 1903.

AFRIDI Destroyer, 872 tons, 250 × 25ft, 3—12pdr, 2—TT. Armstrong 8.5.1907. Sold 9.12.1919 F. Wilkinson.

AFRIDI Destroyer, 1,870 tons, 377 (oa) × 36·5ft, 8—4·7in, 4—TT. Vickers Armstrong, Tyne, 8.6.1937. Sunk 3.5.1940 air attack off Namsos, Norway.

AFRIKANDER *See TICKLER 1879, GRIPER 1879.*

AGAMEMNON 3rd Rate 64, 1,384bm, 160 × 45ft. Adams, Buckler's Hard, 10.4.1781. Wrecked 16.6.1809 R. Plate.

AGAMEMNON Screw 2nd Rate 91, 3,102bm, 230 × 55·5ft, 36—8in, 54—32pdr. Woolwich DY 22.5.1852. Sold 2.5.1870 W. H. Moore.

AGAMEMNON Battleship, 8,510 tons, 280 × 66ft, 4—12·5in MLR, 2—6in. Chatham DY 17.9.1879. BU 1.1903 Germany.

AGAMEMNON Battleship, 16,500 tons, 435 × 79·5ft, 4—12in, 10—9·2in, 24—12pdr. Fairfield 23.6.1906. Target ship 9.1920. Sold 24.1.1927 Cashmore, Newport.

AGASSIZ Corvette (RCN), 'Flower' class. Burrard DD Co. 15.8.1940. Sold 1946 Irving & Brunswick Motors, Moncton.

AGATE Submarine, 1945 'A' class. Cammell Laird, cancelled 1945.

AGGRESSOR Gun-brig 14, 179bm, 85 × 22ft. Perry, Blackwall, 1.4.1801. Sold 23.11.1815.

AGGRESSOR Submarine, 1945 'A' class. Cammell Laird, cancelled 1945.

AGILE Submarine, 1945 'A' class. Cammell Laird, cancelled 1945.

AGINCOURT (ex-*Earl Talbot*) 3rd Rate 64, 1,440bm, 161 × 46ft. Perry, Blackwall, 23.7.1796, East Indiaman, purch. on stocks. Prison ship = BRISTOL 6.1.1812. Sold 15.12.1814.

AGINCOURT 3rd Rate 74, 1,747bm, 176 × 48·5ft. Plymouth DY 19.3.1817. Harbour service 3.1848; = VIGO 4.1865. Sold 10.1884 Castle, Thames.

AGINCOURT (ex-CAPTAIN) Iron screw ship, 6,621bm, 10,600 tons, 400 × 59·5ft, 17–9in MLR. Laird 27.3.1865 (renamed 1861). Harbour service = BOSCAWEN III 3.1904, = GANGES II 21.6.1906; = C.109 (coal hulk) 9.1908. Arr. 21.10.1960 Ward, Grays, for BU.

AGINCOURT Battleship, 27,500 tons. Portsmouth DY, ordered 1914, cancelled 26.8.1914.

AGINCOURT (ex-SULTAN OSMAN I, ex-RIO DE JANEIRO) Battleship, 27,500 tons, 632 × 89ft, 14–12in, 20–6in. Armstrong 22.1.1913, ex-Turkish, ex-Brazilian, seized 8.1914. Sold 19.12.1922 Rosyth S. Bkg. Co.

AGINCOURT Destroyer, 2,400 tons, 379 (oa) × 40ft, 5–4·5in, 8–TT. Hawthorn Leslie 29.1.1945. BU 10.1974 Sunderland.

AID 18-gun ship, 300bm, 8–9pdr, 2–6pdr, 4–4pdr, 4 small. Deptford 6.10.1562. Rebuilt 1580. BU 1599.

AID Transport 10, 314bm, 105·5 × 26ft, 10–12pdr carr. Brindley, Lynn, 4.4.1809. Survey ship 3.1817; = ADVENTURE 24.5.1821. Sold 19.3.1853

AIGLE 5th Rate 38, 1,003bm, 147·5 × 39ft. French, captured 14.9.1782 off Delaware R. Wrecked 18.7.1798 off Cape Farina, Spain.

AIGLE 5th Rate 36, 990bm, 150 × 39ft. Adams, Buckler's Hard, 23.9.1801. Coal hulk 1853. Sunk in shallow water during torpedo experiments Sheerness; sold 24.11.1870 for BU.

AIMABLE 5th Rate 32, 782bm, 133·5 × 36·5ft. French, captured 19.4.1782. BU 5.1814.

AIMWELL Gunvessel 12, 148bm, 75 × 21ft. Perry, Blackwall, 12.5.1794. BU 11.1811 Sheerness.

AINTHORPE Coastal minesweeper. Thornycroft, ordered 9.9.1950, cancelled 1953.

AIRE Frigate, 'River' class. Fleming & Ferguson 22.4.1943. = TAMAR 3.1946; = AIRE 12.1946. Wrecked 20.12.1946 Bombay Reef.

AIREDALE Destroyer, 'Hunt' class Type III. John Brown 12.8.1941. Sunk 15.6.1942 by German aircraft north of Sollum.

AISNE Destroyer, 2,380 tons, 379 (oa) × 40ft, 5–4·5in, 8–TT. Vickers Armstrong, Tyne, 12.5.1945. Arr. Inverkeithing 26.6.1970 for BU.

AITAPE Patrol boat (RAN), 146 tons, 107.5 (oa) ×

20ft, 1–40mm. Walker 6.7.1967. Tx Papua New Guinea 9.1975. Hulked for spares 1989.

AJAX 3rd Rate 74, 1,615bm, 168 × 48·5ft, Portsmouth DY 23.12.1767. Sold 10.2.1785.

AJAX 3rd Rate 74, 1,953bm, 183 × 49·5ft, Randall, Rotherhithe, 3.3.1798. Burnt 11.2.1807 accident off Tenedos.

AJAX 3rd Rate 74, 1,761bm, 176 × 48·5ft, Perry, Blackwall, 2.5.1809; undocked 1846 as screw ship. BU 1864.

AJAX Battleship, 8,660 tons, 280 × 66ft, 4–12·5in MLR, 2–6in. Pembroke Dock 10.3.1880. Sold 3.1904 Castle, R. Thames.

AJAX Battleship, 23,000 tons, 555 × 89ft, 10–13·5in, 12–4in. Scotts 21.3.1912. Sold 11.1926 Alloa S. Bkg Co., Rosyth and Charlestown, for BU.

AJAX Cruiser, 6,985 tons, 554·5 (oa) × 55·8ft, 8–6in, 8–4in. Vickers Armstrong, Barrow, 1.3.1934. Arr. 13.11.1949 Cashmore, Newport, for BU.

AJAX (ex-FOWEY) Frigate, 'Leander' class, Y100, 2,650 tons, 372 (oa) × 41ft, 2–4·5in, Limbo, helo, (later Ikara, Limbo, helo). Cammell Laird 16.8.1962. Arr. Millom, Cumbria, 3.8.1988 for BU.

AJAX *See also VANGUARD 1835.*

AJDAHA Wood paddle frigate (Indian), 1,440bm. Fletcher, Limehouse, 1846. Sold 4.1863.

AKBAR 3rd Rate 74. LD 4.4.1807 Prince of Wales I., Malabar; cancelled 12.10.1809.

AKBAR Wood paddle frigate (Indian), 1,143bm. Napier, Glasgow, 1841. Sold 2.1859.

AKBAR Minesweeper, 'Catherine' class. General Engineering, Alameda, 12.12.1942 for RN; retained USN.

AKBAR *See also CORNWALLIS 1801, HERO 1816, TEMERAIRE 1876.*

AKERS Fireship, 85bm. Purch. 4.1794. Sold 16.12.1801.

ALAART Sloop 16, 306bm, 94·5 × 27·5ft, 16–24pdr carr. Danish, captured 1807. Retaken 10.8.1809 by Danes off coast of Denmark. *Was to have been renamed CASSANDRA.*

ALACRITY Brig-sloop 18, 'Cruizer' class. Rowe, Newcastle, 13.11.1806. Captured 26.5.1811 by French ABEILLE off Corsica.

ALACRITY Brig-sloop 10, 'Cherokee' class. Deptford DY 29.12.1818. Sold 28.8.1835.

ALACRITY Wood screw sloop, 675bm, 180·5 × 28·5ft. Mare, Blackwall, 20.3.1856. Sold 7.10.1864 Castle, R. Thames.

ALACRITY (ex-*Ethel*) 85bm, 1–12pdr. Purch. 4.11.1872. Sold 1882 Sydney.

ALACRITY Despatch vessel, 1,700 tons, 250 × 32·5ft, 4–5in, 4–6pdr. Palmer 28.2.1885. Sold 9.1913 in Hong Kong.

ALACRITY (ex-*Margarita*, ex-*Seramis*, ex-*Mlada*) Steam yacht/despatch vessel, 1,830grt. Req., conv. to ABV, cd 8.8.1919 as yacht for CinC Far East. PO 7.1922, sold 1923; removed Lloyd's Register 10.7.1939.

ALACRITY Sloop, 1,350 tons, 283 × 38ft, 6—4in. Denny 1.9.1944. Arr. 15.9.1956 Arnott Young, Dalmuir, for BU.

ALACRITY Frigate, Type 21, 2,750 tons, 384 (oa) × 40·5ft, 1—4·5in, Exocet, Seacat, helo, 6—TT. Yarrow 18.9.1974. Tx Pakistani Navy 1.3.1994 = BADR.

ALACRITY *See also SURPRISE 1885.*

ALADDIN Submarine, 1945 'A' class. Cammell Laird, cancelled 1945.

ALAMEIN Destroyer, 2,400 tons, 379 (oa) × 40ft, 5—4·5in, 8—40mm, 10—TT. Hawthorn Leslie 28.5.1945. Arr. 1.12.1964 Hughes Bolckow, Blyth, for BU.

ALARIC 5th Rate 36, 1,020bm. *Name chosen 1811 for IRIS but not used.*

ALARIC Submarine, 1945 'A' class. Cammell Laird 20.2.1946. BU Inverkeithing 7.1971.

ALARM 5th Rate 32, 683bm, 125 × 35·5ft. Barnard, Harwich, 19.9.1758. BU 9.1812 Portsmouth.

ALARM Cutter 4, 81bm, 53 × 19·5ft. Purch. 2.1763. Sold 23.10.1780.

ALARM Galley. Purch. 6.1777 North America. Lost 1.8.1778 Rhode I.

ALARM 6th Rate 24, 635bm, 122 × 34ft. Dutch, captured 28.8.1799 off Texel. = HELDER 4.1800, = HELDIN 24.4.1800. Sold 3.1802.

ALARM 6th Rate 28, 652bm, 125 × 34·5ft. Pembroke Dock, LD 1.1832, cancelled 10.1832.

ALARM 6th Rate 28, 910bm, 131 × 40·5ft. Sheerness DY 22.4.1845. Coal hulk 1860. Sold 7.7.1904.

ALARM Torpedo gunboat, 810 tons, 230 × 27ft, 2—4·7in, 4—3pdr. Sheerness DY 13.9.1892. Sold 9.4.1907 Thames S. Bkg Co.

ALARM Destroyer, 780 tons, 246 × 25ft, 2—4in, 2—12pdr, 2—TT. John Brown 29.8.1910. Sold 9.5.1921 Ward, Hayle.

ALARM Minesweeper, 'Algerine' class. Harland & Wolff 5.2.1942. Badly damaged mine 1.1943, sold 12.1943 Bône for BU.

ALAUNIA II *See MARSHAL NEY 1915.*

ALBACORE (ex-ROYAL LOUIS) Sloop 16, 320bm, 97 × 27ft, 16—6pdr. American privateer, captured 1781 by NYMPHE and AMPHION. Sold 29.4.1784.

ALBACORE Sloop 16, 361bm, 105 × 28ft. Randall, Rotherhithe, 4.1793. Sold 1802.

ALBACORE Sloop 18, 370bm, 106·5 × 28ft. Hillhouse, Bristol, 10.5.1804. Sold 14.12.1815.

ALBACORE Schooner, 37bm, 44 × 15ft. Bermuda 1828. Sold 1832.

ALBACORE Wood screw gunboat, 'Albacore' class. White 3.4.1856. Tankvessel 1874, hulk 1882. BU 6.1885 Bermuda.

ALBACORE Composite screw gunboat, 560 tons, 135 × 26ft, 2—5in, 2—4in. Laird 13.1.1883. Sold 18.5.1906.

ALBACORE Destroyer, 440 tons, 215 × 21ft, 3—12pdr, 2—TT. Palmer 19.9.1906, purch. 3.1909. Sold 1.8.1919 T. R. Sales.

ALBACORE Minesweeper, 'Algerine' class. Harland & Wolff 2.4.1912. Arr. 9.9.1963 Smith & Houston, Port Glasgow, for BU.

ALBAN Schooner 10, 111bm. Bermuda 1806. Wrecked 18.12.1812 off Aldeburgh. *In Danish hands 25.5.1810–11.5.1811.*

ALBAN (ex-WILLIAM BAYARD) Schooner 14, 253bm, 94·5 × 24·5ft. American, captured 12.3.1813 by WARSPITE. BU 18.2.1822.

ALBAN Wood paddle vessel, 294bm, 110 × 25ft, 4—18pdr, 2—18pdr carr. Deptford DY 27.12.1826; brig-sloop, rebuilt as 405bm. BU 5.1860.

ALBAN Wood screw gunvessel, 'Philomel' class. Deptford DY, LD 1.10.1860, cancelled 12.12.1863.

ALBANAISE Brig-sloop 14, 238bm. French, captured 3.6.1800 by PHOENIX off Cape Feno. HO Spanish 23.11.1800 Malaga by mutineers, ret. French Navy.

ALBANY Sloop 14, 270bm, 91 × 26ft. Darby, Gosport, 23.3.1745. Captured 7.7.1746 by French off North America.

ALBANY (ex-*Rittenhouse*) American, purch. 1776. BU 1780.

ALBANY *See also TAVISTOCK 1744.*

ALBATROSS Brig-sloop 16, 366bm, 96 × 30ft. Ross, Rochester, 30.12.1795. Sold 1807 East Indies.

ALBATROSS Survey schooner, 64bm. Purch. 1826. Sold 30.8.1833 Mr Ledger.

ALBATROSS Brig 16, 484bm, 105 × 33ft, 16—32pdr. Portsmouth DY 28.3.1842. BU 19.5.1860.

ALBATROSS Wood screw sloop, 695bm, 185 × 28·5ft, 2—68pdr, 2—32pdr. Chatham DY, LD 1862, cancelled 12.12.1863.

ALBATROSS Composite screw sloop, 940 tons, 160 × 31ft, 2—7in, 2—64pdr. Chatham DY 27.8.1873. BU 2.1889 Chatham.

ALBATROSS Destroyer, 430 tons, 228 × 21ft, 1—12pdr, 5—6pdr, 2—TT. Thornycroft, Chiswick, 19.7.1898. Sold 7.6.1920 J. W. Houston.

ALBATROSS Seaplane carrier (RAN), 4,800 tons, 443·75 (oa) × 61ft, 4—4·7in, 9 aircraft. Cockatoo DY 21.2.1928. Tx RN 1938; repair ship 1942. Sold 19.8.1946 = *Pride of Torquay.*

ALBEMARLE Ship. In service 1664.

ALBEMARLE Fireship 6, 164bm. Purch. 1667. Expended 1667.

ALBEMARLE 2nd Rate 90, 1,376bm, 162 × 44·5ft. Betts, Harwich, 1680. = UNION 29.12.1709; rebuilt 1726 as 1,578bm. BU 11.1749 Chatham.

ALBEMARLE (ex-MENAGERE) 6th Rate 28, 543bm, 125 × 32ft. French, captured 18.12.1779. Sold 1.6.1784.

ALBEMARLE Battleship, 14,000 tons, 405 × 75·5ft, 4—12in, 12—6in. Chatham DY 5.3.1901. Sold 19.11.1919 Cohen, Swansea.

ALBERNI Corvette (RCN), 'Flower' class. Yarrow, Esquimalt, 22.8.1940. Sunk 21.8.1944 by U.480 English Channel.

ALBERT Iron paddle troopship, 459bm, 134 × 37ft, 3 guns. Laird 9.1840. Wrecked 13.7.1843; salved, tx 1.3.1845 Govt of The Gambia.

ALBERT Gunvessel (Australian), 350 tons, 115 × 25ft, 1—9in, 1—6in, 2—9pdr. Armstrong Mitchell 1883. Sold c. 1896.

ALBERTA Wood paddle yacht, 370bm, 391 tons, 160 × 22·5ft. Pembroke Dock 3.10.1863. BU 1912 Portsmouth.

ALBION 3rd Rate 74, 1,662bm, 168 × 46ft. Deptford DY 16.5.1763. Floating battery 1794. Wrecked 26.4.1797 The Swin.

ALBION Armed ship 22, 393bm, 103 × 30ft. Hired 1793–9.1794, purch. 1798. Sold 1803 Sheerness.

ALBION 2nd Rate 90, 3,111bm, 204 × 60ft, 8—8in, 4—68pdr, 78—32pdr. Plymouth DY 3.1842; undocked 21.5.1861 as screw ship 3,117bm. BU 1884.

ALBION 3rd Rate 74, 1,743bm, 175 × 48·5ft. Perry, Blackwall, 17.6.1802. Harbour service 7.1931. BU 6.1836 Deptford.

ALBION Aircraft carrier, 22,000 tons, 650 × 90ft, 32 × 40mm, 50 aircraft. Swan Hunter 6.5.1947. Commando carrier 8.1962. Sold 9.7.1973; resold 11.1973, BU Faslane.

ALBION Battleship, 12,950 tons, 390 × 74ft, 4—12in, 12—6in. Thames Iron Works, Blackwall, 21.6.1898. Sold 11.12.1919 Ward, Morecambe.

ALBION Landing platform dock, 19,560 tons, 577·4 (oa) × 98·1ft, Goalkeeper, 4—20mm, 3 helo, 305 troops. BAe Systems, Barrow, 9.3.2001.

ALBRIGHTON Destroyer, 'Hunt' class Type III. John Brown 11.10.1941. Sold 11.1957 West German Navy = RAULE 9.4.1959.

ALBUERA Destroyer, 2,380 tons, 355 × 40ft, 5—4·5in, 8—40mm, 10—TT. Vickers Armstrong, Tyne, 28.8.1945, not comp. Target. BU 11.1950 Ward, Inverkeithing.

ALBURY Minesweeper, Later 'Hunt' class. Ailsa 21.11.1918. Sold 13.3.1947 Dohmen & Habets, Liége.

ALCASTON Coastal minesweeper, 'Ton' class. Thornycroft 5.1.1953. Tx RAN 30.5.1961 = SNIPE. BU 1985.

ALCESTE 5th Rate 32, 932bm, 145 × 39ft. French, captured 29.8.1793 Toulon, tx Sardinians; recaptured by French 1794; captured again 18.6.1799 by squadron in Mediterranean. Sold 5.1802.

ALCESTE (ex-MINERVE) 5th Rate 38, 1,101bm, 152·5 × 40ft. French, captured 25.9.1806 by squadron off Rochefort. Wrecked 18.2.1817 China Sea.

ALCESTIS Submarine, 1945 'A' class. Cammell Laird, cancelled 1945.

ALCIDE 3rd Rate 64, 1,375bm, 159 × 45ft. French, captured 6.6.1755. Sold 27.5.1772.

ALCIDE 3rd Rate 74, 1,625bm, 168 × 47ft. Deptford DY 30.7.1779. BU 4.1817.

ALCIDE Submarine, 1945 'A' class. Vickers Armstrong, Barrow, 12.4.1945. Sold 18.6.1974 Draper & Sons; BU Hull.

ALCMENE 5th Rate 32, 731bm, 131 × 35·5ft. French, captured 21.10.1779 West Indies. Sold 17.8.1784.

ALCMENE 5th Rate 32, 803bm, 135 × 36·5ft. Graham, Harwich, 8.11.1794. Wrecked 29.4.1809 off Nantes.

ALCMENE *See also JEWEL 1809.*

ALDBOROUGH Ketch 10, 100bm. Johnson, Aldeburgh, 6.5.1691. Accidentally blown up 17.8.1696.

ALDBOROUGH 6th Rate 20, 288bm, 94 × 27ft. Johnson, Blackwall, 6.3.1706. Rebuilt 1727 as 374bm. BU 3.1743 Deptford.

ALDBOROUGH 6th Rate 24, 506bm, 112 × 32ft. Okill, Liverpool, 16.3.1743. Sold 28.11.1749 Deptford.

ALDBOROUGH 6th Rate 20, 440bm, 108 × 30·5ft. Perry, Blackwall, 15.5.1756. BU 9.1777.

ALDBOROUGH *See also LEAMINGTON 1918.*

ALDENHAM Destroyer, 'Hunt' class Type III. Cammell Laird 27.8.1941. Sunk 14.12.1944 mine Adriatic.

ALDERNEY Bomb vessel 8, 263bm, 90·5 × 26ft. Woolwich DY 29.3.1735. Hulked 2.1741 Jamaica.

ALDERNEY (ex-SQUIRREL) 6th Rate 24, 504bm, 112 × 32ft. Reed, Hull, 18.3.1743 (renamed 11.2.1742). Sold 26.6.1749.

ALDERNEY Sloop 12, 235bm, 88·5 × 25ft. Snook, Saltash, 5.2.1757. Sold 1.5.1783.

ALDERNEY Submarine, 1945 'A' class. Vickers Armstrong, Barrow, 25.6.1945. BU 8.1972 Cairnryan.

ALDERNEY Offshore patrol vessel, 925 tons, 195·3 (oa) × 34·2ft, Hall Russell 27.2.1979. PO 31.10.2001; sold Bangladeshi Navy 31.10.2002 = KAPATAK HAYA.

ALDINGTON (ex-PITTINGTON) Coastal mine-sweeper. Camper & Nicholson 15.9.1955. Sold Ghanaian Navy 1964 = EJURA. BU 1979.

ALECTO Fireship 12, 432bm, 109 × 30ft. King, Dover, 26.5.1781. Sold 1802.

ALECTO Wood paddle sloop, 796bm, 164 × 32·5ft. Chatham DY 7.9.1839. BU 11.1865 Castle, R. Thames.

ALECTO Composite paddle vessel, 620 tons, 2 guns. Westwood Bailey, Poplar, 18.4.1882. Sold 12.10.1899 in Sierra Leone.

ALECTO Depot ship, 935 tons, 190 × 32·5ft. Laird 29.8.1911. Sold 7.7.1949; BU Llanelly.

ALERT Cutter 8. In service 1753–54.

ALERT Cutter 10, 133bm, 69 × 26ft. Ladd, Dover, 24.6.1777. Sloop 10.1777. Captured 17.7.1778 by French in English Channel.

ALERT Cutter 10, 202bm, 78 × 25ft. Dover 1778. Captured 10.1780 by French in Bay of Biscay.

ALERT Brig-sloop 14, 205bm, 78·5 × 25ft. King, Dover, 1.10.1779. Sold 2.10.1792 Deptford.

ALERT Schooner 4, 88bm. Purch. 1790. BU 1799.

ALERT Sloop 16, 365bm, 105 × 28ft. Randall, Rotherhithe, 8.10.1793. Captured 5.1794 by French UNITE off coast of Ireland.

ALERT Brig-sloop 8 (Indian), 85bm. Bombay DY 1795.

ALERT (ex-*Oxford*) 393bm, 105 × 29ft, 16—18pdr carr. Collier, purch. 5.1804. Captured 13.8.1812 by American ESSEX off North America.

ALERT Brig-sloop, 'Cruizer' class, 388bm. Pitcher, Northfleet, 14.7.1813. Sold 11.1832 Cristall, Rotherhithe.

ALERT Packet brig 8, 358bm, 95 × 30ft, 8—18pdr. Bottomley, Rotherhithe, 24.9.1835. BU 5.1851.

ALERT Brig 8. Ex-slaver, captured 1848 by BONETTA. Sold 1850.

ALERT Wood screw sloop, 751bm, 160 × 32ft, 17—32pdr. Pembroke Dock 20.5.1856. Survey ship 8.1878. HO 1884 American research society.

ALERT Sloop, 960 tons, 180 × 32ft, 6—4in, 4—3pdr. Sheerness DY 28.12.1894. Lent Basra civil authorities 1906; sold 12.1.1926 Basra as pilot vessel. BU 10.1949.

ALERT *See also ACUTE 1942, DUNDRUM BAY 1945.*

ALERTE Brig-sloop 14, 248bm, 80 × 24ft. French, captured 8.1793 Toulon. Recaptured 18.12.1793; burnt Toulon.

ALEXANDER Fireship 12, 150bm. Captured 1688. Accidentally burnt 11.6.1689.

ALEXANDER 3rd Rate 74, 1,621bm, 169 × 47ft. Deptford DY 8.10.1778. Hulk 1805. BU 11.1819. *In French hands 11.1794–6.1795.*

ALEXANDER Storeship. In service 1788–90.

ALEXANDER Schooner 6, 125bm. Purch. 1796. Sold 1802.

ALEXANDER Discovery vessel. In service 1818–19.

ALEXANDER Transport (New Zealand Govt). Purch. 11.1864. Wrecked 8.8.1865 nr Taranaki, New Zealand.

ALEXANDER (ex-ALEXANDR NEVSKI) Ice-breaker, 6,000 tons. Russian, seized 1917. Ret. Soviet Govt. 1919.

ALEXANDRA (ex-SUPERB) Battleship, 9,490 tons, 325 × 64ft, 2—11in MLR, 10—10in MLR, 6—64pdr. Chatham DY 7.4.1875 (renamed 4.3.187)4. Sold 6.10.1908 Garnham.

ALEXANDRA Screw yacht, 2,050 tons, 275 × 40ft, 2—7pdr. Inglis 30.5.1907. Sold 5.1925 = *Prince Olaf.*

ALEXANDRE 2nd Rate 80, 2,231bm. French, captured 6.2.1806 by Fleet off San Domingo. Harbour service 1811. Sold 16.5.1822.

ALEXANDRIA (ex-REGENEREE) 5th Rate 38, 902bm, 144·5 × 38ft. French, captured 2.9.1801 by Fleet at Alexandria. BU 4.1804.

ALEXANDRIA Tender. In service 1802–03.

ALEXANDRIA 5th Rate 32 (fir-built), 662bm, 127 × 34ft. Portsmouth DY 18.2.1806. BU 7.1818.

ALEXANDRIA Frigate (RCN), 'River' class. Montreal, ordered 1943, cancelled 12.1943.

ALFRED Brig. Hired 1793.

ALFRED 3rd Rate 74, 1,638bm, 169 × 47ft. Chatham DY 22.10.1778. BU 5.1814.

ALFRED Iron screw storeship, 617bm, 170 × 27·5ft, purch. 6.1.1855; = ABUNDANCE 2.1855. Sold 1856.

ALFRED *See also ASIA 1811.*

ALFREDA Ship 20, 440bm. American, captured 9.3.1778. Sold 1782.

ALFRISTON Coastal minesweeper, 'Ton' class. Thornycroft 29.4.1953. = WARSASH 5.1954; = ALFRISTON 1958; = KILMOREY 1961–75. Towed Bruges 28.12.1988 for BU.

ALGERINE Cutter 10, 197bm. King, Upnor, 3.3.1810. Wrecked 20.5.1813 West Indies.

ALGERINE Brig-sloop 10, 'Cherokee' class. Deptford DY 10.6.1823. Foundered 9.1.1826 Mediterranean.

ALGERINE Brig-sloop 10, 'Cherokee' class. Chatham DY 1.8.1829. Sold 30.4.1844 J. Ledger.

ALGERINE Wood screw gunvessel, 299bm, 126 × 23ft, 1—10in MLR. Pitcher, Northfleet, 24.2.1857. Sold 2.4.1872 in Hong Kong = *Algerine* (mercantile); BU 1894.

ALGERINE Composite screw gunvessel, 835 tons, 157 × 29·5ft, 2—5in, 2—64pdr. Harland & Wolff 6.11.1880. Sold 10.5.1892.

ALGERINE Sloop 1,050 tons, 185 × 33ft, 6—4in, 4—3pdr. Devonport DY 6.6.1895. Sold 11.4.1919 as salvage vessel.

ALGERINE Minesweeper, 'Algerine' class. Harland & Wolff 22.1.1941. Sunk 15.11.1942 by Italian submarine ASCIANGHI off Bougie.

ALGERINE *See also TIGRESS 1808.*

ALGIERS 5th Rate 32, 344bm. Captured 1671. Wrecked 1673.

ALGIERS 1st Rate 110, 3,099bm. Pembroke Dock, ordered 1833, cancelled 1848.

ALGIERS Screw 2nd Rate 90, 3,340bm, 219 × 60ft. Devonport DY 26.1.1854. Sold 26.2.1870 Cooper Scott.

ALGIERS *See also ANSON 1860, TRIUMPH 1870.*

ALGOMA Corvette (RCN), 'Flower' class. Port Arthur SY 17.12.1940. Sold 1946 Venezuelan Navy = CONSTITUCION; BU 1962.

ALGONQUIN Escort (RCN), 3,551 tons, 426 (oa) × 50ft, 1—5in, Sea Sparrow, 6—TT, helo, Limbo. Davie SB 23.4.1971.

ALGONQUIN *See also VALENTINE 1943.*

ALICE Minesweeper, 'Catherine' class. General Engineering, Alameda, 12.12.1942 for RN; retained USN.

ALICE & FRANCIS Fireship 6, 266bm. Purch. 1672. Expended 28.5.1672.

ALISMA Corvette, 'Flower' class. Harland & Wolff 17.12.1940. Sold 1947 = *Laconia*.

ALKMAAR 4th Rate 54, 1,041bm, 142·5 × 41ft. Dutch, captured 11.10.1797 Battle of Camperdown. Sold 30.11.1815.

ALLEGIANCE (ex-KING GEORGE) Sloop 14. American, captured 1779. Captured 6.8.1782 by French.

ALLEPIN Fireship 6, 233bm. Purch. 1666. Foundered 1667.

ALLIANCE (ex-ALLIANTE) Storeship 20, 697bm, 130·5 × 35ft. Dutch, captured 22.8.1795 off coast of Norway. Sold 5.1802.

ALLIANCE Submarine, 1945 'A' class. Vickers Armstrong, Barrow, 28.7.1945. Museum boat, Gosport, from 6.1981.

ALLIGATOR 6th Rate 28, 599bm, 121 × 34ft. Jacobs, Sandgate, 18.4.1787. Sold 21.7.1814.

ALLIGATOR Sloop 14, 300bm, 96·5 × 26·5ft. Fisher, Liverpool, 11.11.1780. Captured 26.6.1782 by French LA FEE.

ALLIGATOR 6th Rate 28, 500bm, 114 × 32ft. Cochin 29.3.1821. Harbour service 1846. Sold 30.10.1865 in Hong Kong.

ALLIGATOR Wood screw corvette, 1,857bm, 225 × 43ft. Woolwich DY, LD 1.11.1860, cancelled 12.12.1863.

ALLINGTON CASTLE (ex-ALINGTON CASTLE, ex-AMARYLLIS) Corvette, 'Castle' class. Fleming & Ferguson 29.2.1944 (renamed 6.1944). Arr. 20.12.1958 Young, Sunderland, for BU.

ALNWICK CASTLE Corvette, 'Castle' class. G. Brown 23.5.1944. Arr. 12.1951 King, Gateshead, for BU.

ALONZO Sloop 16, 384bm, 102 × 30ft, 14—24pdr carr., 2—18pdr. Purch. 1.1801. Harbour service 1817. Scuttled 2.1842 outside Leith harbour.

ALPHEA Schooner 10, 112bm, 68 × 20ft, 8—18pdr carr., 2—6pdr. Bermuda 1806. Sunk 10.9.1813 action with French privateer RENARD.

ALPHEUS 5th Rate 36 (pine-built), 949bm, 143·5 × 38·5ft. Wallis, R. Thames, 6.4.1814. Sold 10.9.1817 Mr Bailey.

ALRESFORD Minesweeper, Later 'Hunt' class. Ailsa 17.1919. Sold 13.3.1947 Dohmen & Habets, Liége.

ALTHAM Inshore minesweeper, 'Ham' class. Camper & Nicholson 2.12.1952. Tx Malaysian Navy = SRI JOHORE 1.4.1959. BU 1967.

ALTON *See ARBROATH 1918.*

ALTON CASTLE Corvette, 'Castle' class. Fleming & Ferguson, cancelled 12.1943.

ALVERTON Coastal minesweeper, 'Ton' class. Camper & Nicholson 18.11.1952. = THAMES 8.6.1954; = ALVERTON 2.1962. Sold Eire 11.1970 = BANBA; resold 6.10.1983 Andover Shipping Co., BU Spain.

ALVINGTON Frigate (RCN), 'River' class. Vickers, Montreal, 15.4.1944. = ROYAL MOUNT 6.1944. BU 11.1947.

ALYSSUM Sloop, 'Arabis' class. Earle 5.11.1915. Sunk 18.3.1917 mine off south-west Ireland.

ALYSSUM Corvette, 'Flower' class. G. Brown 3.3.1941. Lent Free French = ALYSSE 8.1941. Sunk 8.2.1942 by U.654 western Atlantic.

AMARANTHE (ex-AMARANTE) Brig-sloop 14, 290bm, 86 × 28ft. French, captured 31.12.1796 by DIAMOND off Alderney. Wrecked 25.10.1799 off Florida.

AMARANTHE (ex-VENUS) 6th Rate 28, 498bm, 112·5 × 31·5ft. Dutch, captured 28.8.1799 off Texel. BU 3.1804 Deptford.

AMARANTHE Brig-sloop 18, 'Cruizer' class, 386bm. Dudman, Deptford, 20.11.1804. Sold 12.10.1815.

AMARANTHUS Corvette, 'Flower' class. Fleming & Ferguson 17.10.1940. Sold 1946.

AMARYLLIS Sloop, 'Arabis' class. Earle 9.12.1915. Sold 30.1.1923 Fryer, Sunderland.

AMARYLLIS *See also ALLINGTON CASTLE 1944.*

AMAZON (ex-PANTHERE) 6th Rate 26, 471bm, 115 × 31ft. French, captured 1745. Sold 10.1763.

AMAZON 5th Rate 32, 687bm, 126 × 35ft. Wells, Rotherhithe, 24.5.1773. BU 6.1794 Plymouth.

AMAZON 5th Rate 36, 934bm, 143 × 38ft. Wells, Rotherhithe, 4.7.1795. Wrecked 14.1.1797 Île de Bas.

AMAZON 5th Rate 38, 1,038bm, 150 × 39·5ft. Woolwich DY 18.5.1799. BU 5.1817 Plymouth.

AMAZON 5th Rate 46, 1,078bm, 151 × 40·5ft. Deptford DY 15.8.1821. 6th Rate, 24 guns, 12.1844. Sold 9.1863 Lethbridge.

AMAZON Wood screw sloop, 1,040bm, 187 × 36ft, 2—6in, 2—64pdr. Pembroke Dock 23.5.1865. Sunk 10.7.1866 collision English Channel.

AMAZON Destroyer, 970 tons, 280 × 26·5ft, 2—4in, 2—TT. Thornycroft 29.7.1908. Sold 22.10.1919 Ward, Preston.

AMAZON Destroyer, 1,330 tons, 323 × 31·5ft, 4—4·7in, 1—3in, 6—TT. Thornycroft 27.1.1926. Arr. 6.10.1948 Troon for BU.

AMAZON Frigate, Type 21, 2,750 tons, 384 (oa) × 40·5ft, 1—4·5in, Seacat, helo, 6—TT. Vosper-Thornycroft 26.4.1971. Tx Pakistani Navy 30.9.1993 = BABUR.

AMBERLEY CASTLE Corvette, 'Castle' class. Austin, Sunderland, 27.11.1943. Weather ship *Weather Adviser* 9.1960; = *Admiral Fitzroy* 1977. BU Troon 1982.

AMBERWITCH Troopship (Indian), 1,010 tons, 175·5 × 27ft. Laird 1862. Sold c. 1890.

AMBLESIDE *See BEAUFORT 1919.*

AMBOYNA (ex-HAERLEM) Brig-sloop 10, 180bm. Dutch, captured 1796. BU 1802.

AMBROSE AMC, 6,600 tons, 388 × 47·5ft. Hired, cd 10.12.1914, purch. 20.10.1915, conv. to depot ship. = COCHRANE 1.6.1938. Sold 8.1946 for BU; arr. 13.11.1946 Ward, Inverkeithing.

AMBUSCADE (ex-EMBUSCADE) 5th Rate 40, 740bm, 132·5 × 36ft. French, captured 21.4.1746. Sold 9.2.1762.

AMBUSCADE 5th Rate 32, 684bm, 126·5 × 35ft. Adams, Deptford, 17.9.1773. Captured 14.12.1798 by French BAYONNAISE, = EMBUSCADE; recaptured 28.5.1803. BU 6.1810 Deptford.

AMBUSCADE (ex-EMBUSCADE) 5th Rate 40, 906bm, 143 × 37·5ft. French, captured 12.10.1798 off Donegal. = SEINE 16.1.1804. BU 8.1813.

AMBUSCADE (ex-POMONE) 5th Rate 38, 1,085bm, 152·5 × 40ft. French, captured 29.11.1811 by ACTIVE and ALCESTE. BU 11.1812 Woolwich.

AMBUSCADE 5th Rate 36, 1,284bm, 159 × 42ft. Woolwich DY, LD 15.4.1830, = AMPHION 31.3.1831, launched 1846 as screw frigate (q.v.).

AMBUSCADE Destroyer, 935 tons, 266 × 27ft, 3—4in, 2—TT. John Brown 25.1.1913. Sold 6.9.1921 Petersen & Albeck.

AMBUSCADE Destroyer, 1,170 tons, 322 (oa) × 31·1ft, 4—4·7in, 6—TT. Yarrow 15.1.1926. Sold 23.11.1946; BU Troon,

AMBUSCADE Frigate, Type 21, 2,750 tons, 384 (oa) × 40·5ft, 1—4·5in, Seacat, helo, 6—TT. Yarrow 18.1.1973. Tx Pakistani Navy 28.7.1993 = TARIQ.

AMBUSH Gunboat 2. Purch. 1815 West Indies. Sold 1815.

AMBUSH Submarine, 1945 'A' class, Vickers Armstrong, Barrow, 24.9.1945. Arr. Inverkeithing 5.7.1971 for BU.

AMBUSH Nuclear submarine, 'Astute' class, BAe Systems, Barrow. To be LD 2002.

AMEER (ex-ALAZON BAY) Escort carrier. LD 1942; retained USN = LISCOMBE BAY.

AMEER (ex-BAFFINS) Escort carrier, 11,420 tons, 468·5 × 69·5ft, 2—4in, 16—40mm, 24 aircraft. Seattle, Tacoma, 18.10.1942; USN, on Lend Lease. Ret. USN 17.1.1946; sold mercantile = *Robin Kirk*.

AMELIA (ex-PROSERPINE) 5th Rate 38, 1,059bm, 151·5 × 39·5ft. French, captured 13.6.1796 by DRYAD off Cape Clear. BU 12.1816.

AMELIA Wood screw gunboat, 'Albacore' class. White 19.5.1856. BU 10.1865 Pembroke Dock.

AMELIA (ex-HAWK) Gunboat, 16 tons, 146 × 23ft, 1—40pdr. Coastguard gunboat (renamed 1888). = COLLEEN 1905, = COLLEEN OLD 1916, = EMERALD 1918, = CUCKOO 1918. Sold 10.8.1922 Cove & Distinn.

AMELIA Minesweeper, 'Catherine' class. General Engineering, Alameda, 9.1.1943 for RN; retained USN.

AMELIA *See also ARGUS 1851.*

AMERICA Armed merchantman. In service 1650–54.

AMERICA 5th Rate 44, 862bm, 139 × 37·5ft. Portsmouth, New England, 4.5.1749. = BOSTON 13.4.1756. Sold 13.9.1757.

AMERICA 4th Rate 60, 1,248bm, 154 × 43ft. Wells Stanton, R. Thames, 21.5.1757. BU 7.1771.

AMERICA 3rd Rate 64, 1,370bm, 158 × 45ft. Deptford DY 5.8.1777. Stranded 1800, salved, prison ship; lent Transport Board 1804. BU 1807.

AMERICA (ex-AMERIQUE) 3rd Rate 74, 1,884bm, 182·5 × 48·5ft. French, captured 1.6.1794 'Battle of the 1st of June'; = IMPETUEUX 1795. BU 12.1813.

AMERICA 3rd Rate 74, 1,758bm, 176 × 48·5ft. Perry, Blackwall, 21.4.1810. 4th Rate 3.1827; target 3.1864. BU 10.1867.

AMERSHAM *See COLLINSON 1919.*

AMERTON Coastal minesweeper, 'Ton' class. Camper & Nicholson 2.1953. = MERSEY 1954; = AMERTON 10.1959. BU Bo'ness 8.1971.

AMETHYST (ex-PERLE) 5th Rate 36, 1,029bm, 150 × 39ft. French, captured 29.8.1793 Toulon. Wrecked 29.12.1795 nr Alderney.

AMETHYST 5th Rate 36, 1,046bm, 150 × 39ft. Deptford DY 22.4.1799. Wrecked 16.2.1811 Plymouth Sound; wreck BU 4.1811.

AMETHYST 6th Rate 26, 923bm, 131 × 41ft. Plymouth DY 7.12.1844. Sold 16.10.1869 for use as cable vessel.

AMETHYST Wood screw corvette, 1,970 tons, 220 × 37ft, 14–64pdr. Devonport DY 10.4.1871. Sold 11.1887 G. Pethwick.

AMETHYST 3rd class cruiser, 3,000 tons, 360 × 40ft, 12–4in, 8–3pdr. Armstrong 5.11.1903. Sold 1.10.1920 Towers, Milford Haven.

AMETHYST Sloop, 1,350 tons, 283 × 38·5ft, 6–4in, 12–20mm. Stephen 7.5.1943. Arr. 19.1.1957 Demmelweek & Redding, Plymouth, for BU.

AMETHYST *See also WAVENEY.*

AMFITRITE 5th Rate 38, 1,036bm, 150 × 40ft. Spanish, captured 25.11.1804 by DONEGAL off Cadiz. = BLANCHE 3.12.1805. Wrecked 4.3.1807 off Ushant.

AMFITRITE *See also AMPHITRITE.*

AMHERST Corvette (RCN), 'Flower' class. St John DY 4.12.1940. Tx Venezuelan Navy 1946 = FEDERACION.

AMITIE Schooner 14. French, captured 1804. Expended 3.10.1804 fireship Boulogne.

AMITY 36-gun ship, 375bm. Purch. 1650. Sold 1667.

AMITY Fireship 6, 252bm. Purch. 1673. Sunk 1673 foundation Sheerness.

AMITY Fireship 10, 100bm, 67·5 × 19ft. Purch. 4.1794. Sold c. 1800.

AMITY Minesweeper, 'Catherine' class. General Engineering, Alameda, 10.2.1943 for RN; retained USN = DEFENSE.

AMOKURA *See SPARROW 1889.*

AMPHION 5th Rate 32, 680bm, 126 × 35ft. Chatham DY 21.12.1780. Blown up 22.9.1796 Hamoaze.

AMPHION 5th Rate 32, 914bm, 144 × 37·5ft. Betts, Mistleythorn, 19.3.1798. Sunk 11.1820 breakwater Woolwich; wreck sold 9.1823 Joiliffe & Banks.

AMPHION (ex-AMBUSCADE) Wood screw frigate, 1,474bm, 177 × 43·5ft. Woolwich DY 14.1.1846 (renamed 31.3.1831). Sold 12.10.1863 Williams. *See AMBUSCADE.*

AMPHION 2nd class cruiser, 4,300 tons, 300 × 46ft, 10–6in. Pembroke Dock 13.10.1883. Sold 15.5.1906 King, Garston.

AMPHION Scout cruiser, 3,440 tons, 385 × 41·5ft,

10–4in. Pembroke Dock 4.12.1911. Sunk 6.8.1914 mine North Sea.

AMPHION Cruiser, 6,908 tons, 562·25 (oa) × 56·8ft, 8–6in, 8–4in. Portsmouth DY 26.7.1934. = PERTH (RAN) 6.1939. Sunk 1.3.1942 torpedoes Sunda Strait action.

AMPHION (ex-ANCHORITE) Submarine, 1945 'A' class. Vickers Armstrong, Barrow, 31.8.1944. Arr. Inverkeithing 6.7.1971 for BU.

AMPHION *See also ANCHORITE 1945.*

AMPHITRITE 6th Rate 24, 513bm, 114 × 32ft. Deptford DY 28.5.1778. Wrecked 30.1.1794 Mediterranean.

AMPHITRITE Ship, 328bm. Hired 1793–94.

AMPHITRITE 5th Rate 40, 1,183bm, 151 × 41·5ft. Dutch, captured 30.8.1799 off Texel. = IMPERIEUSE 1801. BU 4.1805.

AMPHITRITE 5th Rate, 1,064bm, 150 × 49ft. Bombay DY 14.4.1816. Lent 14.7.1862 contractors Plymouth. BU 1.1875 Devonport.

AMPHITRITE 1st class cruiser, 11,000 tons, 435 × 69ft, 16–6in, 14–12pdr. Vickers Maxim, Barrow 5.1.1898. Minelayer 1917 (4–6in, 1–12pdr, 354 mines). Sold 12.4.1920 Ward, Milford Haven.

AMPHITRITE *See also POMONA 1778.*

AMSTERDAM (ex-PROSERPINE) 5th Rate 32, 849bm, 140·5 × 37·5ft. Dutch, captured 4.5.1804 Surinam. Sold 9.1815.

ANACONDA Brig-sloop 18, 387bm, 102·5 × 29ft, 18–9pdr. American privateer, captured 11.7.1814 Chesapeake Bay. Sold 5.7.1815 in Jamaica.

ANACONDA Special Service Vessel (RAN), 316 tons. 5.1945. Tx Army 12.1945.

ANACREON Brig-sloop 16, 151bm, 76 × 21·5ft. French, captured 7.1799. Sold 1802.

ANACREON Sloop 16. In service 8.1804–6.1805.

ANACREON Sloop 16, 427bm, 110 × 29·5ft. LD Sutton, Ringmore, 7.1809, frames tx Plymouth DY 8.1810, launched 1.5.1813. Foundered 28.2.1814 English Channel.

ANACREON Schooner. Built 1815. Tx Customs 1816.

ANCHORITE (ex-AMPHION) Submarine, 1945 'A' class. Vickers Armstrong, Barrow, 22.1.1946. Arr. Troon 24.8.1970 for BU.

ANCHORITE *See also AMPHION 1944.*

ANCHUSA Sloop, 'Anchusa' class. Armstrong 21.4.1917. Sunk 16.7.1918 by U.54 off north coast of Ireland.

ANCHUSA Corvette, 'Flower' class. Harland & Wolff 15.1.1941. Sold 1946 = *Silverlord.*

ANDREW Carrack. Captured 24.8.1417. Foundered 15.8.1420.

ANDREW Submarine, 1945 'A' class. Vickers Armstrong, Barrow, 6.4.1946. Arr. Davies & Cann, Plymouth, 4.5.1977 for BU.

ANDREW *See also ST ANDREW 1622.*

ANDROMACHE 5th Rate 32, 683bm, 126 × 35ft. Barnard, Deptford, 17.11.1781. BU 9.1811.

ANDROMACHE 6th Rate 28, 709bm, 130 × 35ft. Pembroke Dock 27.8.1832. Powder hulk 1854. BU comp. 3.1875 Devonport.

ANDROMACHE 2nd class cruiser, 3,400 tons, 300 × 44ft, 2—6in, 6—4·7in. Chatham DY 14.8.1890. Minelayer 9.1909. Arr. 8.1920 Castle, Plymouth, for BU.

ANDROMACHE Submarine, 1945 'A' class. Vickers Armstrong, Barrow, cancelled 1945.

ANDROMACHE *See also PRINCESS CHARLOTTE 1799.*

ANDROMEDA 6th Rate 28, 609bm, 121 × 36ft. Fabian, East Cowes, 18.11.1777. Lost 10.1780 hurricane off Martinique.

ANDROMEDA 5th Rate 32, 721bm, 129 × 35·5ft. Sutton, Liverpool, 21.4.1784. Harbour service 1808. BU 1811.

ANDROMEDA (ex-HANNIBAL) 6th Rate 24, 812bm, 130 × 37·5ft, 22—32pdr carr., 2—12pdr. American, captured 31.1.1812. Sold 18.4.1816.

ANDROMEDA 5th Rate 46, 1,215bm, 159 × 42ft. Bombay DY 6.1.1829. Sold 24.12.1863 Barnett & Wake.

ANDROMEDA 1st class cruiser, 11,000 tons, 435 × 69ft, 16—6in, 14—12pdr. Pembroke Dock 30.4.1897. = POWERFUL II (TS) 23.9.1913, = IMPREGNABLE II 11.1919, = DEFIANCE 20.1.1931. Arr. 14.8.1956 Burgt, Belgium, for BU.

ANDROMEDA Sloop, 'Anchusa' class. Swan Hunter. Launched 6.1917 as ANDROMEDE (French Navy).

ANDROMEDA Frigate, 'Leander' class, Y160, 2,650 tons, 372 (oa) × 43ft, 2—4·5in, Seacat, helo (later Exocet, Seawolf). Portsmouth DY 4.5.1967. Cd 22.8.1995 Indian Navy = KRISHNA.

ANDROMEDA *See also NIMROD 1828.*

ANEMONE Sloop, 'Acacia' class. Swan Hunter 30.6.1915. Sold 6.9.1922 Marple & Gillott.

ANEMONE Corvette, 'Flower' class. Blyth 22.4.1940. Sold 1949 = *Pelikan*.

ANGEL Bomb vessel 6, 132bm, 60 × 21ft. Purch. 1694. Sold 1697.

ANGELICA Schooner 4 (Canadian lakes). Detroit 1771. Wrecked 12.1783.

ANGLER Wood screw gunboat, 'Cheerful' class. Devonport DY 8.3.1856. BU 1.1869 Haslar.

ANGLER Destroyer, 335 tons, 210 × 19·5ft, 1—12pdr, 5—6pdr, 2—TT. Thornycroft, Chiswick, 2.2.1897. Sold 20.5.1920 Ward, Milford Haven.

ANGLESEA 4th Rate 44, 620bm, 125 × 33ft. Plymouth DY 1694. Rebuilt Chatham 1725 as 5th rate, 601bm. Sunk 1742 breakwater Sheerness. *First ship built at Plymouth DY.*

ANGLESEA 5th Rate 44, 711bm, 126 × 36ft. Blaydes, Hull, 3.11.1742. Captured 28.3.1745 by French APOLLON.

ANGLESEA 5th Rate 44, 714bm, 126 × 36·5ft. Gorrill & Parks, Liverpool, 3.12.1746. Storeship 1759. Sunk 8.1764 breakwater Mount's Cove.

ANGLESEY Patrol boat, 925 tons, 195·3 (oa) × 34·2ft. Hall Russell 18.10.1978. PO due 31.7.2003; tx Bangladeshi Navy (?).

ANGUILLA (ex-HALLOWELL) Frigate, 'Colony' class. Walsh Kaiser, Providence, 14.7.1943. Ret. USN 5.1946.

ANN & CHRISTOPHER Fireship 6, 266bm. Purch. 1672. Sold 1686.

ANN & JUDITH Fireship 6, 264bm. Purch. 1672. Lost in action 1672.

ANNA Storeship 8, 400bm. Hired 1739, purch. 1741. Scuttled 28.8.1741 off Juan Fernandez I., unserviceable.

ANNA Schooner tender 12, 106bm, 73 × 19ft, 12—12pdr carr. Purch. 1805. BU 1809.

ANNA TERESA Gunvessel. Ex-barge, purch. 6.1797.

ANNAN Frigate, 'River' class. Vickers, Montreal, 12.9.1942. Tx USN 11.1942 = NATCHEZ.

ANNAN Frigate, 'River' class. Hall Russell 29.12.1943. Lent RCN 13.6.1944—21.6.1945; sold 27.11.1945 RDanN = NIELS EBBESEN. BU 1963 Odense.

ANNAPOLIS (ex-MACKENZIE) Destroyer, 1,060 tons, 309 × 30·5ft, 3—4in, 1—3in, 6—TT. USN; cd RCN 2.10.1940. TS 1944. BU 1945 Boston Iron & Metal Co.

ANNAPOLIS Frigate/escort (RCN), 2,400 tons, 371 (oa) × 42ft, 2—3in, Limbo, helo, 6—TT. Halifax SY 27.4.1963. PO 1998, moored Vancouver as memorial 1999.

ANNE Ballinger, 120bm. Southampton 1416. Sold 26.6.1424.

ANNE Yacht, 100bm. Woolwich DY 1661. Sold 1686.

ANNE 3rd Rate 70, 1,051bm, 151 × 40ft, 26—32pdr, 26—12pdr, 14—6pdr, 4—3pdr. Chatham DY 1678. Burnt 6.7.1690 Battle of Beachy Head.

ANNE Fireship. Purch. 1702.

ANNE Armed ship 14, 345bm, 104 × 28·5ft. Purch. 1798. Sold 1802.

ANNE Brig 10, 120bm. Hired 1804—09.

ANNE (ex-*Aenne Rickmers*) Seaplane carrier, 4,083grt, 367 × 48ft, 1—12pdr, 2 aircraft. German mercantile, seized 1914 (renamed 5.8.1915). Fleet collier 29.1.1918. Sold 1919.

ANNE *See also BRIDGEWATER 1654.*

ANNE GALLANT Ship, 140/160bm. Built 1512. Wrecked 1518.

ANNE GALLANT Galley 50, 300/450bm. Last listed 1559.

ANNE GALLEY Fireship 8, 302bm, 98 × 26·5ft. Purch. 22.6.1739. Expended 11.2.1744 Toulon.

ANNE ROYAL *See ARK ROYAL 1587.*

ANSON 4th Rate 60, 1,197bm, 150 × 43ft. Ewer, Bursledon, 10.10.1747. Sold 25.6.1773.

ANSON Cutter 6, 95bm, 51 × 22ft. Purch. 2.1763. Sold 15.7.1774.

ANSON 3rd Rate 64, 1,369bm, 159·5 × 45ft. Plymouth DY 4.9.1781. 44-gun ship 1794. Wrecked 29.12.1807 Mount's Bay.

ANSON 3rd Rate 74, 1,742bm, 175·5 × 48·5ft. Steemson, Paul, nr Hull, 11.5.1812. Harbour service 1.1931; convict ship Tasmania 1844. BU 1851 Hobart.

ANSON Screw ship 91, 3,336bm, 245 × 55·5ft. Woolwich DY 15.9.1860. = ALGIERS 11.1.1883. BU 4.1904 Castle.

ANSON Battleship, 10,600 tons, 330 × 68·5ft, 4–13·5in, 6–6in, 12–6pdr. Pembroke Dock 17.2.1886. Sold 13.7.1909 Clarkson; BU Upnor.

ANSON Battlecruiser, sister to HOOD (q.v.). Armstrong, ordered 4.1916, cancelled 10.1918.

ANSON (ex-JELLICOE) Battleship, 35,000 tons, 745 (oa) × 103ft, 10–14in, 16–5·25in. Swan Hunter 24.2.1940 (renamed 2.1940). Arr. 17.12.1957 Faslane for BU.

ANSON *See also DUKE of YORK 1940.*

ANSWER Galleon 21, 200bm, 5–9pdr, 8–6pdr, 2–4pdr, 6 small. Built 1590. Rebuilt Chatham DY 5.1604. Sold 1629.

ANSWER Submarine, 1945 'A' class. Vickers Armstrong, Barrow, cancelled 1945.

ANT Schooner 8, 86bm, 61 × 19ft. French, captured 6.1797. Sold 23.3.1815.

ANT Cutter tender 4, 107bm, 71 × 21ft. Woolwich DY 1815. Dockyard service 1817, later Royal Victoria Yard Craft No 1. Sold 12.11.1869 Mr Hapgood.

ANT Wood screw gunboat, 'Cheerful' class. Devonport DY 22.3.1856. BU 2.1869 Haslar.

ANT Gunboat (New Zealand). Ex-merchantman, purch. 1862. Sold 1864.

ANT Iron screw gunboat, 'Ant' class. Laird 14.8.1873. Boom defence vessel 1917; target 1921. BU 6.1926 Granton S. Bkg Co.

ANT Tender, 545grt, 164·5 × 33ft. Murdoch & Murray 23.7.1913, purch. 5.1913. Sold 12.6.1924 G. Nichol = *Rangitoto*.

ANTAEUS Submarine, 1945 'A' class. Vickers Armstrong, Barrow, cancelled 1945.

ANTAGONIST Submarine, 1945 'A' class. Vickers Armstrong, Barrow, cancelled 1945.

ANTARES Minesweeper, 'Algerine' class. Redfern, Canada, 15.8.1942, on Lend-Lease. Ret. USN 1.1947.

ANTELOPE Galleon 38/44, 384bm, 4–9pdr, 13–6pdr, 8–4pdr, 13 small. Built 1546. Rebuilt 1577; rebuilt 1618 as 512bm. Burnt 1649 by Parliamentarians.

ANTELOPE 50-gun ship, 828bm, Woolwich DY 1651. Wrecked 30.9.1652 off Jutland.

ANTELOPE 4th Rate 54, 684bm, 131·5 × 34·5ft. Taylor, Rotherhithe, 3.1703. Rebuilt Woolwich DY 1741 as 858bm, 134 × 38·5ft. Sold 30.10.1783.

ANTELOPE Sloop 14. Lost 30.7.1784 hurricane off Jamaica.

ANTELOPE Brig 14 (Indian), 199bm. Bombay DY 1793. Sold after 1830.

ANTELOPE 4th Rate 50, 1,107bm, 150 × 41ft. Sheerness DY 10.11.1802. Troopship 1818; harbour service 1.1824. BU 7.1845.

ANTELOPE (ex-*Firefly*) Schooner 14, 172bm, Ex-Spanish prize, purch. 1808. BU 1814.

ANTELOPE Iron paddle sloop, 650bm, 1,010 tons, 170 × 28ft, 3 guns. Mare, Blackwall, 25.7.1846. Sold 20.9.1883 in Malta.

ANTELOPE Torpedo gunboat, 810 tons, 230 × 27ft, 2–4·7in, 4–3pdr, 5–TT. Devonport DY 12.7.1893. Harbour service 1910. Sold 27.5.1919 T. R. Sales.

ANTELOPE Destroyer, 1,350 tons, 323 (oa) × 32·25ft, 4–4·7in, 8–TT. Hawthorn Leslie 27.7.1929. Sold 1.1946; BU Hughes Bolckow, Blyth.

ANTELOPE Frigate, Type 21, 2,750 tons, 384 (oa) × 40·5ft, 1–4·5in, helo, 6–TT. Vosper-Thornycroft 16.3.1972. Lost 24.5.1982 Falklands operations.

ANTELOPE *See also PRESTON 1653.*

ANTHONY Ship. Built 1417.

ANTHONY Ship. In service 1588–99.

ANTHONY Destroyer, 1,350 tons, 323 (oa) × 32·25ft, 4–4·7in, 8–TT. Scotts 24.4.1929. Sold 18.8.1947; BU 5.1948 Troon.

ANTHONY BONAVENTURE 36-gun ship, 450bm. In service 1649. Captured 30.11.1652 by Dutch.

ANTICOSTI (ex-*Jean Tide*) Minesweeper aux. (RCN), 1,076 tons, 191 (oa) × 43ft. Allied Shipping, Vancouver, 1973. Offshore supply vessel, purch. 1988, cd 7.5.1989. Deleted 2000.

ANTIGONISH Frigate (RCN), 'River' class. Yarrow, Esquimalt, 10.2.1944. Sold 10.1946.

ANTIGUA Brig-sloop 14, 157bm, 71·5 × 23·5ft. Privateer, purch. 4.6.1757. Sold 13.8.1763 West Indies.

ANTIGUA Sloop 14. From 8.1779. Sold 12.1.1782.

ANTIGUA (ex-EGYPTIENNE) Prison ship, 856bm, 145 × 37ft. French privateer, captured 25.3.1804. BU 1816.

ANTIGUA Frigate, 'Colony' class. Walsh Kaiser 26.7.1943. Ret. USN 5.1946.

ANTRIM Armoured cruiser, 10,850 tons, 450 × 68·5ft, 4—7·5in, 6—6in, 2—12pdr. John Brown 8.10.1903. Sold 19.12.1922 Hughes Bolckow; arr. Blyth 3.1923 for BU.

ANTRIM GM destroyer, 5,600 tons, 520·5 (oa) × 54ft, 4—4·5in (later 2—4·5in, Exocet, Seacat), 2—20mm, Sea Slug, helo. Fairfield 19.10.1967. Tx Chile 25.6.1984 = ALMIRANTE COCHRANE.

ANZAC Destroyer leader, 1,666 tons, 325 × 32ft, 4—4in, 4—TT. Denny 11.1.1917. Tx RAN 21.3.1919. Sold 8.8.1935 Abrahams & Wilson, Redfern, NSW, to dismantle; hull scuttled 7.5.1936.

ANZAC Submarine, 1945 'A' class. Vickers Armstrong. Barrow, cancelled 1945.

ANZAC Destroyer (RAN), 2,325 tons, 379 (oa) × 41ft, 4—4·5in, 12—40mm, 8—TT. Williamstown DY 20.8.1948. Sold 24.11.1975; BU Hong Kong.

ANZAC Frigate (RAN), 'Anzac' class. Transfield, Williamstown, 16.9.1994.

ANZIO *See LST.3003.*

APELLES Brig-sloop 14, 251bm, 92 × 25·5ft. Woolwich DY 10.8.1808. Sold 15.2.1816.

APHIS River gunboat, 645 tons, 230 × 36ft, 2—6in, 1—3in. Ailsa 15.9.1915. Sold 1947 in Singapore.

APHRODITE Submarine, 1945 'A' class. Vickers Armstrong, Barrow, cancelled 1945.

APOLLO Storeship 20, 744bm, 127·5 × 36·5ft, 16—9pdr, 4—6pdr. French, captured 3.5.1747. Wrecked 12.4.1749 off Madras.

APOLLO 5th Rate 38, 984bm, 146 × 39ft. Perry, Blackwall, 18.3.1794. Wrecked 7.1.1799 Haak Sand, Holland.

APOLLO 5th Rate 36, 956bm, 145 × 38·5ft. Dudman, Deptford, 16.8.1799. Wrecked 2.4.1804 coast of Portugal.

APOLLO 5th Rate 38, 1,086bm, 154·5 × 40ft. Parsons, Bursledon, 27.6.1805. Harbour service; troopship 4.1846. BU 9.1856.

APOLLO 2nd class cruiser, 3,400 tons, 300 × 44ft, 2—6in, 6—4·7in, 8—6pdr. Chatham DY 10.2.1891. Minelayer 8.1909. Arr. 8.1920 Castle, Plymouth, for BU.

APOLLO Cruiser, 7,105 tons, 562·25 (oa) × 56·8ft, 8—6in, 8—4in. Devonport DY 9.10.1934. Tx RAN 14.10.1938 = HOBART. Left Sydney 3.3.1962 for BU Japan.

APOLLO Minelayer, 2,650 tons, 418 (oa) × 39ft, 4—4in, 8—40mm, 100 mines. Hawthorn Leslie 5.4.1943. Arr. 11.1962 Hughes Bolckow, Blyth, for BU.

APOLLO Frigate, 'Leander' class, Y160, 2,650 tons, 372 (oa) × 43ft, 2—4·5in, Seacat, helo. Yarrow 15.10.1970. Sold Pakistani Navy 13.7.1988, HO 14.10.1988 = ZULFIQUAR.

APOLLO *See also GLORY 1763.*

APPLEBY CASTLE Corvette, 'Castle' class. Austin, Sunderland, cancelled 12.1943.

APPLEDORE Minesweeper, Later 'Hunt' class. Ailsa 15.8.1919. Sold 16.10.1920 = *Kamlawti.*

APPLETON Coastal minesweeper, 'Ton' class. Goole SB 4.9.1952. Sold 24.9.1972; BU 11.1972 Neath.

APPROACH Submarine, 1945 'A' class. Vickers Armstrong, Barrow, cancelled 1945.

AQUARIUS (ex-*Hampstead*) Water tanker (RFA), 3,660 tons, 268 × 38ft. Purch. 1902; comp. as depot ship 6.1907. Sold 14.5.1920 mercantile.

AQUILON 6th Rate 28, 599bm, 118·5 × 34ft. Inwood, Rotherhithe, 24.5.1758. Sold 29.11.1776.

AQUILON 5th Rate 32, 724bm, 129 × 36ft. Young & Woolcombe, R. Thames, 23.11.1786. BU 9.1815.

ARAB (ex-JEAN BART) Sloop 16, 424bm, 107 × 30ft. French, captured 29.3.1795 by CERBERUS and SANTA MARGARITA in English Channel. Wrecked 10.6.1796 The Penmarcks.

ARAB (ex-ARABE) Schooner 8, 86bm, 61 × 19ft. French, captured 6.1797. = ANT 1798. Sold 23.3.1815.

ARAB (ex-LE BRAVE) 6th Rate 22, 505bm, 110 × 33ft. French, captured 24.4.1798 by PHOENIX off Cape Clear. Sold 20.9.1810.

ARAB Brig-sloop 18, 'Cruizer' class, 390bm. Pelham, Frindsbury, 22.8.1812. Wrecked 18.12.1823 off Belmullet, Ireland.

ARAB Brig-sloop 16, 481bm, 105 × 33·5ft, 4—32pdr, 12—32pdr carr. Chatham DY 31.3.1847. Coastguard watchvessel No 18 24.5.1863. BU comp. 11.6.1879 Chatham.

ARAB Composite screw sloop, 720 tons, 150 × 28ft, 1—7in ML, 2—64pdr. Napier, Glasgow, 13.10.1874. Rated gunvessel 1876. Sold 1889.

ARAB Destroyer, 470 tons, 218 × 20ft, 1—12pdr, 5—6pdr, 2—TT. Thomson 9.2.1901. Sold 23.7.1919 Fryer, Sunderland.

ARABIS Sloop, 'Arabis' class. Henderson 6.11.1915. Sunk 10.2.1916 by German torpedo boats off Dogger Bank.

ARABIS Corvette, 'Flower' class. Harland & Wolff 14.2.1940. Lent USN = SAUCY 30.4.1942; ret. RN 1945 = SNAPDRAGON. Sold 1946 = *Katina.*

ARABIS Corvette, Modified 'Flower' class. G. Brown 28.10.1943. Arr. 8.1951 Ward, Grays, for BU.

ARACHNE Brig-sloop 18, 'Cruizer' class, 386bm. Hills, Sandwich, 18.2.1809. Sold 1.1837 Ledger.

ARACHNE Sloop 18, 602bm, 115 × 35·5ft, 18– 32pdr. Devonport DY 30.3.1847. BU comp. 12.2.1866 Marshall, Plymouth.

ARARAT Minesweeper (RAN), 'Bathurst' class. Evans Deakin 20.2.1943. Sold 6.1.1961; BU Japan.

ARAXES 5th Rate 36 (red pine-built), 1,070bm, 150·5 × 40ft. Pitcher, Northfleet, 13.9.1813. Sold 10.9.1817 Mr Manlove.

ARBITER (ex-ST SIMON) Escort carrier, 11,420 tons, 468·5 × 69·5ft, 2–4in, 16–40mm, 24 aircraft. Seattle Tacoma 9.9.1943; USN, on Lend-Lease. Ret. USN 3.3.1946, sold = *Caracero*.

ARBROATH (ex-ALTON) Minesweeper, Later 'Hunt' class. Ailsa, cancelled 1918.

ARBUTUS Sloop, 'Anchusa' class, Armstrong 8.9.1917. Sunk 16.12.1917 by UB.5 St George's Channel.

ARBUTUS Corvette, 'Flower' class. G. Brown 5.6.1940. Sunk 9.2.1942 by U.136 Atlantic.

ARBUTUS Corvette, Modified 'Flower' class. G. Brown 26.1.1944. BU 6.1951 Clayton & Davie, Dunston.

ARCADIAN Submarine, 1945 'A' class. Vickers Armstrong, Barrow, cancelled 1945.

ARC-EN-CIEL 4th Rate 50, 1,077bm, 146 × 41ft. French, captured 1756. Sold 6.9.1759.

ARCHER Gun-brig 12, 179bm, 80 × 22·5ft. Perry, Blackwall, 2.4.1801. Sold 14.12.1815.

ARCHER Wood screw sloop, 973bm, 186 × 34ft, 2–68pdr, 12–32pdr. Deptford DY 27.3.1849. Arr. 15.3.1866 Castle, Charlton, for BU.

ARCHER Torpedo cruiser, 1,770 tons, 225 × 36ft, 6–6in, 5–TT. Thomson 23.12.1885. Sold 4.4.1905 Forrester, Swansea.

ARCHER Destroyer, 775 tons, 240 × 25·5ft, 2–4in, 2–12pdr, 2–TT. Yarrow 21.10.1911. Sold 9.5.1921 Ward, Rainham.

ARCHER Escort carrier, 9,000 tons, 469 × 66ft, 3– 4in, 15 aircraft. Sun SB, Chester, 14.12.1939; tx RN on Lend-Lease 17.11.1941. Tx MWT 1945 = *Empire Lagan*; ret. USN 8.1.1946. Sold = *Anna Salen*.

ARCHER Patrol boat (RAN), 146 tons, 107·5 (oa) × 20ft, 1–40mm. Walker 2.12.1967. Sold 10.1974 to Indonesia = SILIMAN.

ARCHER Patrol boat, 49 tons, 68·2 (oa) × 19ft. Watercraft 25.6.1985.

ARCTURUS Minesweeper, 'Algerine' class. Redfern, Toronto, 31.8.1942 on Lend-Lease. Ret. USN 1946. Sold Greek Navy = PYRPOLITIS.

ARD PATRICK Minesweeping sloop, '24' class.

Swan Hunter 6.6.1918. Sold 12.8.1920 Moise Mazza; resold 1.12.1921 Stanlee, Dover.

ARDENT 3rd Rate 64, 1,376bm, 160 × 45ft. Blaydes, Hull, 13.8.1764. Captured 17.8.1779 by French off Plymouth; recaptured 4.1782, = TIGER. Sold 6.1784.

ARDENT 3rd Rate 64, 1,387bm, 160·5 × 45ft. Stares & Parsons, Bursledon, 21.12.1782. Caught fire, blew up 4.1794 off Corsica.

ARDENT (ex-*Princess Royal*) 3rd Rate 64, 1,422bm, 161 × 46ft. Indiaman. Pitcher, Northfleet, 9.4.1796. Harbour service 1812. BU 3.1824 Bermuda.

ARDENT Wood paddle sloop, 801bm, 165 × 33ft, 5–2pdr. Chatham DY 12.2.1841. Arr. 2.3.1865 Castle, Charlton, for BU.

ARDENT Destroyer, 280 tons, 202 × 19ft, 1– 12pdr, 5–6pdr, 2–TT. Thornycroft, Chiswick, 16.10.1894. Sold 10.10.1911.

ARDENT Destroyer, 981 tons, 260 × 27ft, 3–4in, 2–TT. Denny 8.9.1913. Sunk 1.6.1916 Battle of Jutland.

ARDENT Destroyer, 1,350 tons, 323 (oa) × 32·25ft, 4–4·7in, 8–TT. Scotts 26.6.1929. Sunk 8.6.1940 by German battlecruisers off Narvik.

ARDENT Submarine, 1945 'A' class. Vickers Armstrong, Barrow, cancelled 1945.

ARDENT Frigate, Type 21, 2,750 tons, 1–4·5in, Seacat, helo, 6–TT. Yarrow 9.5.1975. Lost 21.5.1982 Falklands operations.

ARDENT Patrol boat (RAN), 146 tons, 107·5 (oa) × 20ft, 1–40mm. Walker 27.4.1968. RANR 6.1982– 7.1984. PO 7.1.1994 navigation training vessel; museum ship 1999.

ARDENT *See also RATTLER 1843.*

ARDROSSAN Minesweeper, 'Bangor' (turbine) class. Blyth 22.7.1941. Sold 1.1.1948; arr. 19.8.1948 Thornaby-on-Tees for BU.

ARETHUSA (ex-ARETHUSE) 5th Rate 32, 700bm, 132 × 34·5ft. French, captured 18.5.1759. Wrecked 19.3.1779 off Ushant.

ARETHUSA 5th Rate 38, 948bm, 141 × 39ft. Hillhouse, Bristol, 10.4.1781. BU 5.1814 Sheerness.

ARETHUSA 5th Rate 46, 1,085bm, 151 × 40·5ft. Pembroke Dock 29.7.1817. Harbour service 6.1836; = BACCHUS 12.3.1844. BU 8.1883 Castle, R. Thames.

ARETHUSA 4th Rate 50, 2,132bm, 3,832 tons, 180 × 53ft, 10–8in, 40–32pdr. Pembroke Dock 20.6.1849, undocked 9.8.1861 as screw frigate. TS 1874. BU 1934 Castle, Thames.

ARETHUSA 2nd class cruiser, 4,300 tons, 300 × 46ft, 10–6in. Napier 23.12.1882. Sold 4.4.1905 Garnham.

ARETHUSA Light cruiser, 3,500 tons, 410 × 39ft, 2—6in, 6—4in. Chatham DY 25.10.1913. Damaged mine, wrecked 11.2.1916 off Harwich.

ARETHUSA Cruiser, 5,220 tons, 506 (oa) × 51ft, 6—6in, 4—4in. Chatham DY 6.3.1934. Arr. 9.5.1950 Cashmore, Newport, for BU.

ARETHUSA Frigate, 'Leander' class, Y100, 2,650 tons, 372 (oa) × 41ft, 2—4·5in, Limbo, helo (later Ikara, Limbo, helo). White 5.11.1963. Expended 1.6.1991 target under tow from Portsmouth.

ARETHUSE 5th Rate 38, 1,064bm, 152 × 39·5ft. French, captured 29.8.1793 Toulon. = UNDAUNTED 1795. Wrecked 27.8.1796 Morant Keys, West Indies.

ARGO 6th Rate 28, 601bm, 118 × 34ft. Bird, Rotherhithe, 20.7.1758. BU comp. 8.11.1776 Portsmouth.

ARGO Schooner 10. Purch. 6.1780. Sold 4.1783.

ARGO 5th Rate 44, 892bm, 141 × 38ft. Baker, Howden Dock, 7.6.1781. Sold 11.1.1816.

ARGO *See also ACTIVE 1799, ESPIEGLE 1880.*

ARGON *See ARGUS 1904.*

ARGONAUT (ex-JASON) 3rd Rate 64, 1,452bm, 166 × 45ft. French, captured 19.4.1782 West Indies. Harbour service 1797. BU 2.1831 Chatham.

ARGONAUT 1st class cruiser, 11,000 tons, 435 × 69ft, 16—6in, 14—12pdr. Fairfield 24.1.1898. Sold 18.5.1920 Ward, Milford Haven; arr. 4.9.1921 for BU.

ARGONAUT Cruiser, 5,450 tons, 512 (oa) × 50·5ft, 10—5·25in. Cammell Laird 6.9.1941. Sold 16.11.1955; BU Cashmore, Newport.

ARGONAUT Frigate, 'Leander' class, Y136, 2,650 tons, 372 (oa) × 41ft, 2—4·5in, Seacat, helo (later Exocet, Seawolf). Hawthorn Leslie 8.2.1966. Towed from Portsmouth 25.1.1995 for BU Spain.

ARGOSY Submarine, 1945 'A' class. Vickers Armstrong, Barrow, cancelled 1945.

ARGUS Sloop 10, 326bm, 103 × 27ft. French privateer, captured 1799. BU 4.1911.

ARGUS 5th Rate 36. Sheerness DY, ordered 1812, cancelled 1812.

ARGUS Brig-sloop 18, 'Cruizer' class, 387bm. Hill, Sandwich, 11.9.1813. Sold 11.7.1827 Mr Freake; sale cancelled; resold 26.3.1828 Ledger.

ARGUS Sloop 18, 480bm, 114 × 31ft. Portsmouth DY, LD 3.1831, cancelled 6.1831.

ARGUS Wood paddle sloop, 981bm, 190 × 33ft. Portsmouth DY 15.12.1849. BU 10.1881.

ARGUS Coastguard vessel, 318bm, 357 tons, 136 × 22ft, 2—32pdr. Green, Blackwall, 1851. = AMELIA 16.4.1872, = FANNY 4.1889. Hulked 1899; BDV 1902. Sold 1907 for BU.

ARGUS Coastguard vessel, 380 tons, 130 × 23ft,

2—6pdr. Bow McLachlan 6.12.1904. = ARGON 1918. Sold 2.1920.

ARGUS (ex-*Conte Rosso*) Aircraft carrier, 14,450 tons, 535 × 68ft, 4—4in, 20 aircraft. Beardmore 2.12.1917, purch. (renamed 8.1916). Harbour service 12.1944. Sold 5.12.1946; BU Ward, Inverkeithing.

ARGUS (ex-*Contender Bezant*) Aviation TS, 18,280 tons (full load), 574·5 (oa) × 99.7ft, 4—30mm, 6 helo. CNR Breda, Venice, 1981; ro-ro container ship (11,445 tons), TUFT 1982, purch. 1984 (renamed 25.3.1987). Primary casualty receiving ship 1990–91.

ARGUS *See also IMOGENE 1864.*

ARGYLL Armoured cruiser, 10,850 tons, 450 × 68·5ft, 4—7·5in, 6—6in, 2—12pdr. Scotts 3.3.1904. Wrecked 28.10.1915 Bell Rock.

ARGYLL Frigate, 'Norfolk' class. Yarrow, Glasgow, 8.4.1989.

ARGYLL *See also BONAVENTURE 1711.*

ARIADNE 6th Rate 20, 430bm, 108 × 30ft. Chatham DY 27.12.1776. Rebuilt Northam 1792 as 6th Rate 24. Sold 7.8.1814.

ARIADNE Advice boat, 187bm. Purch. 5.1805. = DOVE 21.5.05, FLIGHT 1806. Foundered 9.1806.

ARIADNE 6th Rate 20, 511bm, 121·5 × 31ft. Pembroke Dock 10.2.1816. Coal hulk 1837. Sold 23.7.1841.

ARIADNE Wood paddle sloop (Indian), 432bm, 139 × 26ft. Laird 12.1839. Foundered 23.6.1842 off Chusan.

ARIADNE Wood screw frigate, 3,214bm, 4,583 tons, 280 × 51ft, 24—10in, 2—68pdr. Deptford DY 4.6.1859. Harbour service 1884, = ACTAEON 6.6.1905. Sold 11.12.1922.

ARIADNE 1st class cruiser, 11,000 tons, 435 × 69ft, 16—6in, 14—12pdr. Thomson 22.4.1898. Minelayer 3.1917, 4—6in, 1—4in, 400 mines. Sunk 26.7.1917 by UC 65 off Beachy Head.

ARIADNE Minelayer, 2,650 tons, 418 (oa) × 40ft, 4—4in, 4—40mm, 160 mines. Stephen 16.2.1943. BU Dalmuir and Troon 6.1965.

ARIADNE Frigate, 'Leander' class, Y160, 2,650 tons, 372 (oa) × 43ft, 2—4·5in, Seacat, helo. Yarrow 10.9.1971. Tx Chile = GENERAL BAQUEDANO, sailed 15.6.1992.

ARIEL 6th Rate 20, 429bm, 108 × 30ft. Perry, Blackwall, 7.7.1777. Captured 10.9.1779 by French AMAZONE, lent Americans until 1781. Lost 1793.

ARIEL Sloop 16, 314bm, 98 × 27·5ft. Baker, Liverpool, 18.10.1781. Sold 8.1802.

ARIEL Sloop 18, 367bm, 106 × 28ft. Palmer, Yarmouth, 19.4.1806. Sold 12.7.1816 Deptford.

ARIEL Brig 14 (Indian), 160bm. Bombay DY 1809. Foundered 12.3.1820.

ARIEL Brig-sloop 10, 'Cherokee' class. Deptford DY 28.7.1820. Comp. 9.1827 as packet brig. Wrecked 8.12.1828 Sable I.

ARIEL (ex-*Arrow*) Wood paddle packet, 149bm, 108 × 17·5ft. GPO vessel, tx 1.2.1837. Sold 17.5.1850 T. Marston.

ARIEL Wood screw sloop, 486bm, 139 × 28ft, 9—32pdr. Pembroke Dock 11.7.1854. Sold 23.5.1865 Shaw & Thompson.

ARIEL 2nd class gunboat, 436 tons, 125 × 22ft, 2—64pdr MLR, 2—20pdr. Chatham DY 11.2.1873. Coastguard 26.11.1877. Sold 8.1889.

ARIEL Destroyer, 310 tons, 210 × 19·5ft, 1—12pdr, 5—6pdr, 2—TT. Thornycroft, Chiswick, 5.3.1897. Wrecked 19.4.1907 Ricasoli breakwater, Malta, testing harbour defences.

ARIEL Destroyer, ,763 tons, 250 × 26·5ft, 2—4in, 2—12pdr, 2—TT. Thornycroft, Woolston, 26.9.1911. Sunk 2.8.1918 mine in North Sea.

ARIES Minesweeper, 'Algerine' class, Toronto 19.9.1942, on Lend-Lease. Ret. USN 1946; sold Greek Navy = ARMATOLOS.

ARK ROYAL (ex-ARK RALEIGH) Galleon 55, 694bm, 4—60pdr, 4—30pdr, 12—18pdr, 12—9pdr, 6—6pdr, 17 small. Deptford 1587. = ANNE ROYAL; rebuilt Woolwich 1608. Wrecked 4.1636 Tilbury Hope; BU.

ARK ROYAL Seaplane carrier, 7,080 tons, 352·5 × 51ft, 4—12pdr, 4 aircraft. Mercantile, Blyth SB 5.9.1914, purch. 5.1914. Depot ship 1923; = PEGASUS 21.12.1934; catapult ship 4.1941; accommodation ship 1944. Sold 18.10.1946 = *Anita I*; BU 1950.

ARK ROYAL Aircraft carrier, 22,000 tons, 685 × 94ft, 16—4·5in, 72 aircraft. Cammell Laird 13.4.1937. Sunk 14.11.1941 by U.81 off Gibraltar.

ARK ROYAL (ex-IRRESISTIBLE) Aircraft carrier, 36,800 tons, 720 × 113ft, 16—4·5in, 58—40mm, 100 aircraft. Cammell Laird 3.5.1950. BU Cairnryan 9.1980.

ARK ROYAL Aircraft carrier, 20,600 tons, 685·8 (oa) × 90ft, 3 × 6—20mm Phalanx, 16 aircraft, 6 helo. Swan Hunter 2.6.1981. *Originally rated anti-submarine cruiser, ref. INDOMITABLE; named ARK ROYAL 1.12.1978.*

ARLINGHAM Inshore minesweeper, 'Ham' class. Camper & Nicholson 1.4.1953. TRV 4.1967. Sold 1977.

ARMADA 3rd Rate 74, 1,749bm, 176 × 48·5ft. Blackburn, Turnchapel, 22.3.1810. Sold 27.5.1863 Marshall, Plymouth.

ARMADA Destroyer, 2,325 tons, 379 (oa) ×

40·25ft, 4—4·5in, 1—4in, 8—TT. Hawthorn Leslie 9.12.1943. Arr. 18.12.1965 Ward, Inverkeithing, for BU.

ARMERIA Corvette, 'Flower' class. Harland & Wolff 16.1.1941. Sold 1947 = *Deppie*.

ARMIDALE Minesweeper (RAN), 'Bathurst' class. Mort's Dock, Sydney, 23.1.1942. Sunk 21.12.1942 Japanese aircraft off Timor.

ARMIDE 5th Rate 38, 1,104bm, 152 × 40ft. French, captured by squadron off Rochefort 26.9.1806. BU 11.1815.

ARMS OF HOLLAND 34-gun ship. Dutch, captured 1652. Blown up 1656 accident West Indies.

ARMS OF HORN Hulk, 516bm. Dutch 4th Rate, captured 1673. Sunk 1694 foundation Sheerness.

ARMS OF ROTTERDAM 3rd Rate 60, 987bm. Dutch, captured 1673. Hulked 1675. BU 1703.

ARMS OF TERVER 4th Rate 52, 523bm. Dutch, captured 1673. Given away 1674.

ARNO (ex-LIZ) Destroyer, 600 tons, 230 × 22ft, 4—14pdr, 3—TT. Ansaldo, Genoa, 1915; Portuguese, purch. 3.1915. Sunk 23.8.1918 collision destroyer HOPE off Dardanelles.

ARNPRIOR (ex-RISING CASTLE) Corvette, 'Castle' class. Harland & Wolff 8.2.1944. Sold 5.9.1946 to Uruguay = MONTEVIDEO.

ARNPRIOR *See also COURIER 1943.*

ARO (ex-*Albertville*) Depot ship, 3,794grt, 352 × 44ft. Purch. 10.1914. Transport 14.8.1918. Sold 1.1920 W. R. Davis.

ARRAS Sloop, 644 tons, 246 × 31ft, 2—5·5in. French, seized 7.1940 Portsmouth. Free French accommodation ship 5.1941; oil hulk 1943; ret. French Navy 1946.

ARRERNTE *See ARUNTA 1996.*

ARROGANT 3rd Rate 60, 928bm. French, captured 10.3.1705. Foundered 5.1.1709 passage Port Mahon.

ARROGANT 3rd Rate 74, 1,644bm, 168 × 47·5ft. Barnard, Harwich, 22.1.1761. Sheer hulk c. 1801. BU 1810 Bombay.

ARROGANT (ex-*Adasier*) Store hulk 1,439bm. Purch. 7.8.1810. Sold 1842.

ARROGANT Wood screw frigate, 1,872bm, 200 × 46ft, 12—8in, 2—68pdr, 32—32pdr. Portsmouth DY 5.4.1848. Sold 3.1867 Castle & Beech.

ARROGANT 2nd class cruiser, 5,750 tons, 320 × 57·5ft, 4—6in. 6—4·7in (1902: 10—6in, 9—12pdr). Devonport DY 26.5.1896. Depot ship 6.1911. Sold 11.10.1923 Hughes Bolckow, Blyth.

ARROGANT Aircraft carrier, 18,300 tons, 650 × 90ft, 32—40mm, 50 aircraft. Swan Hunter, cancelled 1945.

ARROGANTE Gunvessel 14, 258bm, 92 × 26ft.

French, captured 19.4.1798 by JASON off Brest. = INSOLENT 31.8.1798. Sold 11.6.1818 J. Cristall.

ARROMANCHES (ex-*LCT(8).4086*) Tank landing craft. Tx Army 1958; tx Singapore 1970 = TANGLIN.

ARROW Sloop 20, 386bm, 128·5 × 30ft, 28–32pdr carr. Hobbs, Redbridge, 1796, purch. Captured 4.2.1805 by two French frigates off Gibraltar.

ARROW Cutter 14, 152bm, 91 × 19ft. Deptford DY 7.9.1805. Breakwater from 5.1814. BU 5.1828.

ARROW Cutter 10, 157bm, 64 × 25ft. Portsmouth DY 14.3.1823. BU 1.1852.

ARROW Wood screw despatch vessel, 477bm, 160 × 25·5ft, 2–98pdr. Mare, Blackwall, 26.6.1854. Sold 19.5.1862 Marshall, Plymouth.

ARROW Iron screw gunboat, 'Ant' class. Rennie, Greenwich, 22.4.1871. Sold 1.3.1922 W. H. Webber.

ARROW Destroyer, 1,350 tons, 323·25 (oa) × 32·25ft, 4–4·7in, 8–TT. Vickers Armstrong, Barrow, 22.8.1929. Damaged beyond repair 4.8.1943 Algiers harbour by explosion of ammunition ship *Fort la Montée*; stripped 1944, BU 5.1949.

ARROW Patrol boat (RAN), 146 tons, 107.5 (oa) × 20ft. Walker 17.2.1968. Wrecked 25.12.1974 Darwin.

ARROW Frigate, Type 21, 2,750 tons, 384 (oa) × 40·5ft, 1–4·5in, Exocet, Seacat, helo, 6–TT. Yarrow 5.2.1974. Tx Pakistani Navy 1.3.1994 = KAIBUR.

ARROWHEAD Corvette, 'Flower' class. Marine Industries, Canada, 8.8.1940. Lent RCN until 6.1945. Sold 5.1947 = *Southern Larkspur*.

ARTEMIS Submarine, 1945 'A' class. Scotts 26.8.1946. Sold 12.12.1971 Pounds, Portsmouth, for BU.

ARTFUL Submarine, 1945 'A' class. Scotts 22.5.1947. Sold 16.6.1972; BU Cairnryan.

ARTFUL Nuclear submarine, 'Astute' class. BAe Systems, Barrow. Comp. due 2009.

ARTIFEX (ex-AURANIA) Heavy repair ship, 19,000 tons, 520 × 65ft, 20–20mm. Ex-AMC, conv. comp. 7.1944 (renamed 11.1942). Sold 28.12.1960 Italian sbkrs.

ARTIGO (ex-FERRONIERE) Ship, 140bm. French, captured 1543. Sold 1547.

ARTOIS 5th Rate 40, 1,152bm, 158·5 × 40·5ft. French, captured 1.7.1780. Sold 2.2.1786.

ARTOIS 5th Rate 38, 984bm, 146 × 39ft. Wells, Rotherhithe, 3.1.1794. Wrecked 31.7.1797 nr Rochelle.

ARUN Destroyer, 550 tons, 225 × 23·5ft, 1–12pdr, 5–6pdr, 2–TT (1907: 4–12pdr, 2–TT). Laird 29.4.1903. Sold 30.6.1920 Ward, Hayle.

ARUN Minesweeper, 890 tons (full load), 156·3 (oa) × 34.5ft, 1–40mm. Richards, Lowestoft, 20.8.1985. Tx Brazilian Navy 18.9.1998 = HERCULES, = JOSE BONIFACIO, = BABITONGA.

ARUNDEL 5th Rate 32, 378bm, 109 × 28ft. Ellis, Shoreham, 13.9.1695. Sold per AO 11.6.1713.

ARUNDEL 6th Rate 24, 509bm, 112 × 32·5ft. Chitty & Vernon, Chichester, 23.11.1746. Sold 9.7.1765.

ARUNDEL *See also MEDWAY 1755, WARSPITE 1758.*

ARUNTA Destroyer (RAN), 1,927 tons, 377·5 (oa) × 36·5ft, 6–4·7in, 2–4in, 4–TT. Cockatoo DY 30.11.1940. Foundered 13.2.1969 passage Taiwan for BU.

ARUNTA (ex-ARRERNTE) Frigate (RAN), 'Anzac' class. Transfield, Williamstown, 28.6.1996 (renamed 1993).

ARVE PRINCEN *See HEIR APPARENT 1807.*

ARVIDA Corvette (RCN), 'Flower' class. Morton, Quebec, 21.9.1940. Sold c. 1946 = *La Ceiba*.

ASBESTOS Corvette (RCN), Modified 'Flower' class. Morton, Quebec, 22.11.1943. BU 3.1949.

ASCENSION (ex-HARGOOD) Frigate, 'Colony' class. Walsh Kaiser 6.8.1943. Ret. USN 31.5.1946.

ASCOT Paddle minesweeper, 'Ascot' class. Ailsa 26.1.1916. Sunk 10.11.1918 by UB.67 off Farne Is.

ASGARD Submarine, 1945 'A' class. Scotts, cancelled 1945.

ASHANTI Destroyer, 1,870 tons, 377 (oa) × 36·5ft. 8–4·7in, 4–TT. Denny 5.11.1937. Sold 12.4.1949; BU Troon.

ASHANTI Frigate, Type 81, 2,300 tons, 360 (oa) × 42·5ft, 2–4·5in, 2–40mm, Limbo, helo, 6–TT. Yarrow 9.3.1959. Expended 14.9.1988 target.

ASHBURTON Minesweeper, Later 'Hunt' class. Ailsa, cancelled 1919.

ASHELDHAM Inshore minesweeper, 'Ham' class. Philip 30.9.1952. Tx Malaysia = SRI PERLIS 1.4.1959. BU 1967.

ASHTON (ex-CHERITON) Coastal minesweeper, 'Ton' class. White, Southampton, 5.9.1956. Sold 24.6.1977 for BU Middlesbrough.

ASIA Hulk, 420bm. Purch. 11.12.1694. Foundered 7.4.1701 Bay of Bulls, Newfoundland.

ASIA 3rd Rate 64, 1,364bm, 158 × 44·5ft. Portsmouth DY 3.3.1764. BU 8.1804.

ASIA 3rd Rate 74, 1,763bm, 176 × 48ft. Brindley, Frindsbury, 2.12.1811. = ALFRED 1819; reduced to 50 guns 8.1828. BU 5.1865 Portsmouth.

ASIA 2nd Rate 84, 2,289bm, 197 × 52ft. Bombay DY 19.1.1824. Guardship 1858. Sold 7.4.1908 Merveille, Dunkirk.

ASP (Gunboat No 5) Gunvessel 12, 160bm, 75 × 22ft. Randall, Rotherhithe, 10.4.1797. Sold 1803.

ASP (ex-SERPENT) Sloop 16, 333bm, 99 × 28·5ft. French, captured 17.7.1808 by ACASTA. Sold 16.3.1814.

ASP Cutter. Purch. 1826. Sold 2.1829.

ASP (ex-*Fury*) Wood paddle packet, 112bm, 90 × 16ft. GPO vessel, tx 1837. BU 7.1881 Chatham.

ASPERITY Submarine, 1945 'A' class. Vickers Armstrong, Tyne, cancelled 1945.

ASPHODEL Sloop, 'Arabis' class. Henderson 21.12.1915. Sold 16.6.1920 RDanN = FYLLA.

ASPHODEL Corvette, 'Flower' class. G. Brown 25.5.1940. Sunk 9.3.1944 by U.575 off north-west Spain.

ASSAIL Patrol boat (RAN), 146 tons, 107·5 (oa) × 20ft, 1—40mm. Evans Deakin 18.11.1967. Tx Indonesia 18.10.1985 = SIGUROT.

ASSAM Minesweeper (RIN), 'Bathurst' class. Garden Reach, Calcutta, cancelled 3.1945.

ASSAM *See also BUGLOSS 1943.*

ASSAULT (Gunboat No 4) Gunvessel, 159bm, 75 × 22ft. Randall, Rotherhithe, 10.4.1797. Dockyard lighter 1817. Sold 6.6.1827.

ASSAYE Paddle frigate (Indian), 1,800bm. Bombay DY 15.3.1854. Sold 1863 as sailing vessel; wrecked 1865 off coast of Ireland.

ASSAYE Torpedo gunboat (RIM), 735 tons, 230 × 27ft. 2—4·7in, 4—3pdr, 5—TT. Armstrong 11.2.1890. Sold 5.1904.

ASSIDUOUS (ex-*Jackal*) Schooner, 94bm. Pirate vessel, captured 1823. Sold 5.5.1825.

ASSINIBOINE Frigate (RCN), 2,260 tons, 366 (oa) × 42ft, 4—3in, 2—40mm, Limbo. Marine Industries, Sorel, 12.2.1954. Static TS 1989–94. Sold 1.1995 Crown Assets.

ASSINIBOINE *See also KEMPENFELT 1931.*

ASSISTANCE 50-gun ship, 521bm, 121 × 31ft. Deptford 1650. Rebuilt 1699 as 607bm; rebuilt Limehouse 1712 as 710bm; rebuilt Woolwich 1725 as 750bm. Sunk 14.2.1746 breakwater Sheerness.

ASSISTANCE 4th Rate 50, 1,063bm, 144 × 41·5ft. Ledger, R. Medway, 22.12.1747. Sold 11.8.1773.

ASSISTANCE Transport, 94bm, 59 × 19ft. Plymouth 1771. Sold 1802.

ASSISTANCE 4th Rate 50, 1,045bm, 146 × 41ft. Baker, Liverpool, 12.3.1781. Wrecked 29.3.1802 nr Dunkirk.

ASSISTANCE (ex-*Babod*) Discovery vessel, 420bm, 117 × 28·5ft. Purch. 3.1850. Abandoned 1854 Arctic.

ASSISTANCE Screw storeship, 1,793bm, 283 × 36ft. Purch. 16.1.1855. Laird 5.4.1855. Wrecked 7.6.1860 off Hong Kong; wreck sold 30.7.1860.

ASSISTANCE Iron screw storeship, 2,515 tons, 250 × 38ft, 2 guns. Green, Blackwall, 26.9.1874. Sold 1897.

ASSISTANCE Repair ship, 9,600 tons, 436 × 53ft, 10—3pdr. Raylton Dixon 22.12.1900, purch. 19.9.1900. HO Ward part payment *Majestic* (CALEDONIA, q.v.), arr. 11.3.1937 Pembroke Dock for BU.

ASSISTANCE Repair ship, 7,100 tons, 416 × 57ft, 1—5in, 10—40mm. Maryland DD, Baltimore, 20.6.1944 on Lend-Lease. Ret. USN 15.8.1946.

ASSISTANCE Transport 4, 110bm, 63 × 20ft, 4—3pdr. Purch. 4.1791. Sold 12.10.1802.

ASSOCIATION 2nd Rate 90, 1,459bm, 165 × 45·5ft. Portsmouth DY 1697. Wrecked 22.10.1707 off Scilly Is.

ASSURANCE 42-gun ship, 456bm, 106·5 × 29ft. Deptford 1646. Sold 1698.

ASSURANCE (ex-ASSURE) 3rd Rate 70, 1,102bm, 146 × 42ft. French, captured 12.10.1702. BU 4.1712 Chatham.

ASSURANCE 5th Rate 44, 823bm, 133 × 38ft. Heather, Bursledon, 26.9.1747. Wrecked 24.4.1753 The Needles.

ASSURANCE 5th Rate 44, 898bm, 140 171 × 38ft. Randall, Rotherhithe, 20.4.1780. Troopship 7.1790; harbour service 3.1799. BU 3.1815.

ASSURANCE Wood screw gunvessel, 681bm, 181·5 × 28·5ft. Green, Blackwall, 13.3.1856. Sold 8.3.1870 Marshall, Plymouth.

ASSURANCE Submarine, 1945 'A' class. Scotts, cancelled 1945.

ASSURANCE *See also HOPE 1559.*

ASTARTE Submarine, 1945 'A' class. Scotts, cancelled 1945.

ASTER Sloop, 'Acacia' class. Earle 1.5.1915. Sunk 4.7.1917 mine off Malta.

ASTER Corvette, 'Flower' class. Harland & Wolff 12.2.1941. Sold 29.5.1946; BU McLellan, Bo'ness.

ASTRAEA Storeship, c. 500bm. Spanish, captured 25.3.1739. Burnt 17.1.1743 accident Piscatagua.

ASTRAEA 5th Rate 32, 703bm, 126 × 36ft. Fabian, East Cowes, 24.7.1791. Wrecked 23.3.1808 off Anegada, West Indies.

ASTRAEA 5th Rate 36, 956bm, 145 × 38·5ft. Guillaume, Northam, 5.1810. Harbour service 8.1823. BU 4.1851.

ASTRAEA 2nd class cruiser, 4,360 tons, 320 × 49ft, 2—6in, 8—4·7in, 8—6pdr. Devonport DY 17.3.1893. Sold 1.7.1920 Castle; resold, BU Germany.

ASTREA Wood screw frigate, 2,478bm, 240 × 48ft. Devonport DY, LD 21.10.1861, cancelled 12.12.1863.

ASTREE 5th Rate 38, 1,085bm, 152·5 × 40ft. French, captured 6.12.1810 at reduction of Mauritius. = POMONE 26.10.1811. BU 6.1816.

ASTUTE Submarine, 1945 'A' class. Vickers Armstrong, Barrow, 31.1.1945. Sold Clayton & Davie 2.9.1970; BU Dunston.

ASTUTE Nuclear submarine, 'Astute' class. BAe Systems, Barrow, LD 31.1.2001.

ATALANTA Sloop 14, 300bm, 96·5× 26·5ft. Sheerness DY 12.8.1775. On sale list 13.3.1797; = HELENA 1801. Sold 8.1802.

ATALANTA (ex-SIRO) Schooner 12, 225bm. American, captured 13.1.1814. Recaptured by Americans 1814.

ATALANTA Tender. Deptford DY 1816. Tx Customs Service 1817.

ATALANTA Wood paddle sloop (Indian), 620bm, 6 guns. Built on R. Thames 1836. BU c. 1850.

ATALANTA Brig 16, 549bm, 110 × 35ft, 16−32pdr. Pembroke Dock 9.10.1847. BU comp. Devonport 12.12.1868.

ATALANTA *See also JUNO 1844.*

ATALANTE Brig-sloop 16, 310bm, 98 × 27·5ft. French, captured 10.1.1797 by PHOEBE off Scilly Is. Wrecked 1.2.1807 off Île de Rhe.

ATALANTE Sloop 18, 416bm, 100 × 30ft. Bermuda 8.1808. Wrecked 10.11.1813 off Halifax.

ATALANTE Screw storeship, 295bm. Purch. 7.1860. = MANILLA 19.7.1861; exchanged 28.2.1870 for barque *Ingeberg* (= MANILLA).

ATHABASKAN Destroyer (RCN), 1,927 tons, 377·5 (oa) × 37·5ft, 6−4·7in, 2−4in. Vickers Armstrong, Tyne, 18.11.1941. Sunk 29.4.1944 action with German TBs off French Channel coast.

ATHABASKAN Destroyer (RCN), 1,927 tons, 377·5 (oa) × 37.5ft, 8−4in, 4−40mm, 4−TT. Halifax SY 14.5.1946. BU 7.1969 Italy.

ATHABASKAN Escort (RCN), 3,551 tons, 426 (oa) × 50ft, 1−5in, Sea Sparrow, Limbo, helo, 6−TT. Davie 27.11.1970.

ATHABASKAN *See also IROQUOIS 1941.*

ATHELENEY Minesweeper, Later 'Hunt' class. Clyde SB Co, cancelled 1918.

ATHELING (ex-GLACIER) Escort carrier, 11,420 tons, 468·5 × 69·5ft, 2−4in, 16−40mm, 24 aircraft. Seattle, Tacoma, 7.9.1942. USN, tx RN on Lend-Lease 28.10.1943. Ret. USN 13.12.1946; sold = *Roma*.

ATHELING (ex-MISSION BAY) Escort carrier, 11,420 tons, 468·5 × 69·5ft, 2−4in, 16−40mm, 24 aircraft. Kaiser, Vancouver, 26.5.1943. Retained USN = MISSION BAY.

ATHELING (ex-ANGUILLA BAY) Escort carrier, 11,420 tons, 468·5 × 69·5ft, 2−4in, 16−40mm, 24 aircraft. Kaiser, Vancouver, 12.8.1943. Retained USN = CORREGIDOR.

ATHENIENNE Gun-brig 14, 202bm. French, captured 8.6.1796 by ALBACORE off Barbados. Sold 1802.

ATHENIENNE 3rd Rate 64, 1,404bm, 164 × 44·5ft. French, ex-Maltese, captured 4.9.1800 Malta. Wrecked 20.10.1806 off Sicily.

ATHERSTONE Paddle minesweeper, 'Ascot' class. Ailsa 4.4.1916. Sold 12.8.1927 = *Queen of Kent*. Req. WW2 = QUEEN OF KENT.

ATHERSTONE Destroyer, 'Hunt' class Type I. Cammell Laird 12.12.1939. Sold 23.11.1957; BU Smith & Houston, Port Glasgow.

ATHERSTONE Minesweeper, 615 tons. Vosper-Thornycroft 1.3.1986.

ATHOLL 6th Rate 28, 503bm, 114 × 32ft, 20−32pdr carr., 6−18pdr carr., 2−9pdr. Woolwich DY 23.11.1820. Troopship 7.1832. BU 4.1863 Devonport.

ATHOLL Corvette (RCN), Modified 'Flower' class. Morton, 5.5.1943. BU 10.1952 Steel Co. of Canada.

ATLANTIS Submarine, 1945 'A' class. Vickers Armstrong, Barrow, cancelled 1945.

ATLAS 2nd Rate 90, 1,950bm, 178 × 50ft. Chatham DY 13.2.1782. 3rd Rate 1802; harbour service 1814. BU 5.1821.

ATLAS Screw 2nd Rate 91, 3,318bm, 5,260 tons, 245 × 55·5ft, 34−8in, 1−68pdr, 56−32pdr. Chatham DY 21.7.1860, not comp. Lent 11.1884 Metropolitan Asylum Board. BU 1904.

ATTACK Gunvessel 12, 147bm, 75 × 21ft. Brindley, Frindsbury, 1794. Sold 9.1802.

ATTACK Gun-brig, 181bm, 80 × 22·5ft. Adams, Chapel, 9.8.1804. Captured 16.8.1812 by Danes in Kattegat.

ATTACK Destroyer, 785 tons, 240 × 25·5ft, 2−4in, 2−12pdr, 2−TT. Yarrow 21.12.1911. Sunk 30.12.1917 by UC.34 off Alexandria.

ATTACK Patrol boat (RAN), 146 tons, 107·5 (oa) × 20ft, 1−40mm. Evans Deakin 8.4.1967. Sold to Indonesia 20.2.1985 = SIKUDA.

ATTACKER Escort carrier, 11,420 tons, 468·5 × 69·5ft, 2−4in, 8−40mm, 18 aircraft. Western Pipe & Steel Co. 27.9.1941. Tx RN on Lend-Lease 4.1942; ret. USN 5.1.1946. Sold 1952 = *Castel Forte*.

ATTACKER Training boat, 32 tons, 65·6 (oa) × 17ft, 1−20mm. Fairey Marine, Cowes, 1983. Sold to Lebanon 11.1991 = TRABLOUS 17.7.1992.

ATTACKER *See also LST.3010 1944..*

ATTENTIVE Gun-brig 12, 178bm, 80 × 23ft. Bools & Co., Bridport, 18.9.1804. BU 8.1812 Deptford.

ATTENTIVE (ex-MAGNET) Prison ship, 359bm, 96 × 28·5ft. American brig, captured 1812. BU 1.1817 Portsmouth.

ATTENTIVE Scout cruiser, 2,670 tons, 374 × 38ft, 10—12pdr. Armstrong 24.11.1904. Sold 12.4.1920 Ward, Preston.

ATTENTIVE II *See ADDER 1905.*

AUBRIETIA (Q.13) Sloop, 'Aubrietia' class. Blyth SB 17.6.1916. Sold 25.10.1922 R. H. Partridge.

AUBRIETIA Corvette, 'Flower' class. G. Brown 5.9.1940. Sold 29.7.1946 = *Arnfinn Bergen.*

AUCKLAND Wood paddle frigate (Indian), 946bm, 6—8in MLR. Bombay DY 9.1.1840. Harbour service 1863. Sold c. 1874.

AUCKLAND (ex-HERON) Sloop 1,200 tons, 276 × 37ft, 8—4in. Denny 30.6.1938 (enamed 1937). Sunk 24.6.1941 Italian aircraft off Tobruk.

AUDACIEUX Sloop 14, 408bm, 114·5 × 28·5ft, French, captured 1797. Last listed 1801.

AUDACIOUS 3rd Rate 74, 1,624bm, 168 × 47ft. Randall, Rotherhithe, 23.7.1785. BU 8.1815.

AUDACIOUS Battleship, 6,010 tons, 280 × 54ft, 10—9in MLR, 4—64pdr MLR. Napier 27.2.1869. Depot ship 1902 = FISGARD 4.1904; TS 1.1.1906 = IMPERIEUSE; repair ship 1914. Sold 12.3.1927 Ward; BU Inverkeithing.

AUDACIOUS Battleship, 23,000 tons, 555 × 89ft, 10—13·5in, 12—4in. Cammell Laird 14.9.1912. Sunk 27.10.1914 mine off Tory I.

AUDACIOUS *See also JAMES WATT 1847, EAGLE 1946.*

AUDACITY (ex-*Empire Audacity*, ex-*Hannover*) Escort carrier, 11,000 tons, 435 × 56ft, 1—4in, 6—20mm, 6 aircraft. German, captured 2.1940; comp. as carrier 9.1941. Sunk 21.12.1941 by U.751 Atlantic.

AUGUSTA 4th Rate 60, 1,068bm, 144 × 41·5ft. Deptford DY 1.7.1736. BU comp. 6.7.1765 Portsmouth.

AUGUSTA 3rd Rate 64, 1,381bm, 159 × 44·5ft, Stanton & Wells, Rotherhithe, 24.10.1763. Burnt by American gunfire 23.10.1777 Mud I., USA.

AUGUSTA Yacht, 184bm, 80·5 × 23ft. Deptford DY 1771. = PRINCESS AUGUSTA 23.7.1773. Sold 13.8.1818.

AUGUSTA Gunboat. Ex-barge, purch. 9.1795. In service 1801.

AUGUSTA 3rd Rate 74. Portsmouth DY, LD 1806, cancelled 1809.

AUGUSTA (ex-*Policy*) Schooner. Purch. 1.1819. Sold 24.4.1823.

AUGUSTA Schooner 2 (Indian), 114bm. Bombay DY 1853. In service 1866.

AUGUSTA Minesweeper, 'Catherine' class. General

Engineering, Alameda, 19.4.1943 for RN; retained USN = DEVASTATOR.

AUGUSTA *See also CHARLOTTE 1677.*

AUGUSTE 4th Rate 60, 932bm, 141·5 × 39ft. French, captured 1705. Wrecked 10.11.1716 Anholt.

AUGUSTINE Storeship 26, 360bm. Dutch, captured 1653. Sunk 1655 foundation Harwich.

AUGUSTUS Gunvessel 1. In commission 1798. Wrecked 7.7.1801 Plymouth Sound.

AURICULA Sloop, 'Anchusa' class. Armstrong 4.10.1917. Sold 1.2.1923 J. Hornby.

AURICULA Corvette, 'Flower' class. G. Brown 14.11.1940. Mined 5.5.1942 Courier Bay, Madagascar; foundered next day.

AURICULA Trials vessel, 981 tons, 170·5 (oa) × 36ft. Ferguson 22.11.1979. Sold, towed from Portsmouth 14.6.1995 commercial use = *Lowland Searcher.*

AURIGA Submarine, 1945 'A' class. Vickers Armstrong, Barrow, 29.3.1945. Sold 14.11.1974 Cashmore; BU Newport.

AUROCHS Submarine, 1945 'A' class, Vickers Armstrong, Barrow, 28.7.1945. Arr. 7.2.1967 Troon for BU.

AURORA (ex-ABENAKISE) 5th Rate 36, 946bm, 144 × 38·5ft. French, captured by UNICORN 23.1.1757. BU 4.1763.

AURORA 5th Rate 32, 679bm, 125 × 35ft. Chatham DY 13.1.1766. Burnt out 1770 passage Cape to East Indies.

AURORA 6th Rate 28, 596bm, 121 × 35ft. Perry, Blackwall, 7.6.1777. Sold 3.11.1814.

AURORA Sloop 14 (Indian), 247bm. Bombay DY 1809. Captured by French 9.1810 off Mauritius.

AURORA (ex-CLORINDE) 5th Rate 38, 1,083bm, 152 × 40·5ft. French, captured 26.2.1814 by DRYAD and EUROTUS in Atlantic. BU 5.1851.

AURORA Wood screw frigate, 2,558bm, 227 × 50ft, 1—110pdr, 8—8in, 4—70pdr, 8—40pdr, 18—32pdr. Pembroke Dock 22.6.1861. BU 12.1881.

AURORA Armoured cruiser, 5,600 tons, 300 × 56ft, 2—9·2in, 10—6in. Pembroke Dock 28.10.1887. Sold 2.10.1907 Payton, Milford Haven.

AURORA Light cruiser, 3,500 tons, 410 × 39ft, 2—6in, 6—4in. Devonport DY 30.9.1913. Cd RCN 1.11.1920. Sold 8.1927 A. A. Lasseque, Sorel.

AURORA Cruiser, 5,270 tons, 506 (oa) × 51ft, 6—6in, 8—4in. Portsmouth DY 20.8.1936. Sold 19.5.1948 Chinese Navy = CHUNG KING; = Communist TCHOUNG KING 1949. Sunk Hulu-toa 18/19.3.1950; salved 1951 = HSUANG HO; = PEI CHING. Hulk = KUANG CHOU (1955). Believed BU 1960.

AURORA Frigate, 'Leander' class, Y100, 2,650 tons, 372 (oa) × 41ft, 2—4·5in, Limbo, helo (later Ikara, Limbo, helo). John Brown 28.11.1962. Arrived Millom, Cumbria, 6.9.1990, for BU.

AURORE 5th Rate 32, 860bm. French, captured 29.8.1793 Toulon. Prison ship 1799–c. 1803.

AUSONIA AMC, 19,000 tons, 520 × 65ft, 8—6in, 2—3in. Hired 9.1939. Conv. heavy repair ship 5.1944. BU 9.1965 Spain.

AUSTERE Submarine, 1945 'A' class. Vickers Armstrong, Tyne, cancelled 1945.

AUSTRALIA Armoured cruiser, 5,600 tons, 300 × 56ft, 2—9·2in, 10—6in. Fairfield 25.11.1886. Sold 4.4.1905 King, Troon.

AUSTRALIA Battlecruiser (RAN), 18,800 tons, 555 × 80ft, 8—12in, 14—4in. John Brown 25.10.1911. Sunk 12.4.1924 target off Sydney.

AUSTRALIA Cruiser (RAN), 9,870 tons, 630 (oa) × 68.5ft, 8—8in, 4—4in. John Brown 17.3.1927. Sold 25.1.1955; BU 7.1955 Ward, Barrow.

AUTUMN Sloop 16, 335bm. Purch. 1801. = STROMBOLO (bomb vessel) 15.2.1811. Sold 9.2.1815.

AVELEY Inshore minehunter, 'Ley' class. White, Cowes, 16.2.1953. Sold 21.5.1983 Sea Cadets, Woolwich = TS *Woolwich*. Arr. Pounds, Portsmouth, 21.11.1986 for BU.

AVENGER (ex-VENGEUR) Sloop 16, 330bm. French, captured 17.3.1794 Martinique. Sold 9.9.1802.

AVENGER (ex-*Elizabeth*) Sloop, 208bm. Purch. 8.1803. Foundered 5.12.1803 off Heligoland.

AVENGER (ex-*Thames*) Sloop 18, 390bm. Ex-collier, purch. 5.1804. Wrecked 8.10.1812 off St John's, Newfoundland.

AVENGER Paddle frigate, 1,444bm, 210 × 39ft. Devonport DY 5.8.1845. Wrecked 20.12.1847 off north coast of Africa.

AVENGER AMC, 15,000 tons. Req. 1915–17.

AVENGER (ex-*Rio Hudson*) Escort carrier, 8,200 tons, 468·5 × 66ft, 2—4in, 40—40mm, 15 aircraft. Sun SB Co., Chester, on Lend-Lease 27.11.1940. Sunk 15.11.1942 by U.155 west of Gibraltar.

AVENGER Frigate Type 21, 2,750 tons, 384 (oa) × 40·5ft, 1—4·5in, Exocet, Seacat, helo, 6—TT. Yarrow 20.11.1975. Tx Pakistani Navy 23.9.1994 = TIPPU SULTAN.

AVENGER *See LST.3011 1945, LUCIFER 1778.*

AVERNUS Torpedo boat (Australian), 16 tons, 1—TT. Built 1879. Sold 12.1902.

AVON Brig-sloop 18, 'Cruizer' class. Symons, Falmouth, 31.1.1805. Sunk 27.8.1814 action with American WASP in English Channel.

AVON (ex-*Thetis*) Wood paddle packet, 360bm, 144 × 23ft, 3 guns. GPO vessel, tx 1837. Sold 9.1.1863 Marshall, Plymouth.

AVON Paddle gunboat (New Zealand) 40bm, 60ft, 1—12pdr. Purch. 1862. Sold 12.1863 as coal hulk; = *Clyde*.

AVON Composite screw gunvessel, 467bm, 603 tons, 155 × 25ft, 1—7in, 1—64pdr, 2—20pdr. Portsmouth DY 2.10.1867. Sold 26.4.1890 for BU Charlton.

AVON Destroyer, 355 tons, 210 × 21·5ft, 1—12pdr, 5—6pdr, 2—TT. Vickers 10.10.1896. Sold 1.7.1920 Castle, Plymouth.

AVON Frigate, 'River' class. Hill 19.6.1943. HO Portuguese Navy 5.1949 = NUNO TRISTAO. BU 12.1.1970.

AVON VALE Destroyer, 'Hunt' class Type II. John Brown 23.10.1940. Tx Greek Navy 3.1944–5.1944 = AEGEAN. Arr. 15.5.1958 Young, Sunderland, for BU.

AWAKE Submarine, 1945 'A' class. Vickers Armstrong, Tyne, cancelled 1945.

AWARE Patrol boat (RAN), 146 tons, 107·5 (oa) × 20ft, 1—40mm. Evans Deakin 7.10.1967. RANVR Adelaide 11.1992. PO 17.7.1993; deleted 1993.

AWE Frigate, 'River' class. Fleming & Ferguson 28.12.1943. HO Portuguese Navy 5.1949 = DIOGO GOMES. BU 20.4.1969.

AXFORD Seaward defence boat, 'Ford' class. Simons 3.1953. Tx Nigeria 9.9.1966 = KADUNA; deleted 1975.

AYDON CASTLE Corvette, 'Castle' class. Kingston SY, cancelled 12.1943.

AYLMER (ex-HARMON) Frigate, TE 'Captain' class. Bethlehem, Hingham, 10.7.1943; USN, on Lend-Lease. Ret. USN 5.11.1945.

AZALEA Sloop, 'Acacia' class. Barclay Curle 10.9.1915. Sold 1.2.1923 J. Hornby & Sons.

AZALEA Corvette, 'Flower' class. Cook, Welton & Gemmell 8.7.1940. Sold 5.4.1946 = *Norte*.

AZOV Schooner gunboat, 94bm, 64 × 18·5ft, 2 guns. German, Malta, 14.7.1855. Harbour service 1859. Sold 9.6.1899 in Malta.

AZOV *See also MUTINE 1880.*

AZTEC Submarine, 1945 'A' class. Vickers Armstrong, Tyne, cancelled 1945.

B

'B' class submarines 280 tons, 135 × 13·5ft, 2—
TT (1—12pdr gun added to five boats in 1917 when
conv. to surface patrol vessels).

B.1 (ordered as A.14) Vickers 25.10.1904. Sold
25.8.1921 A. J. Anderson; resold 2.5.1922
J. Smith, Poole.

B.2 Vickers 31.10.1905. Sunk 4.10.1912 collision
with *Amerika* Strait of Dover.

B.3 Vickers 31.10.1905. Sold 20.12.1919 J. Jackson.

B.4 Vickers 14.11.1905. Sold 1.4.1919 Ardrossan DD
Co.

B.5 Vickers 14.11.1905. Sold 25.8.1921 A. J. Anderson; resold 1.3.1922 J. Smith, Poole.

B.6 Vickers 30.11.1905, comp. 8.1917 as surface
patrol boat S.6. Sold 1919 Francotosti, Malta.

B.7 Vickers 30.11.1905, comp. 8.1917 as surface
patrol boat S.7. Sold 31.10.1919 in Malta.

B.8 Vickers 23.1.1906, comp. 8.1917 as surface
patrol boat S.8. Sold 1919.

B.9 Vickers 24.1.1906, comp. 8.1917 as surface
patrol boat S.9. Sold 1919 Francotosti, Malta.

B.10 Vickers 23.3.1906. Sunk 9.8.1916 air attack
while under repair at Venice.

B.11 Vickers 21.2.1906, comp. 8.1917 as surface
patrol boat S.11. Sold 1919 Francotosti, Malta.

BABET 6th Rate 20, 511bm, 119 × 31ft. French,
captured 23.4.1794 off Île de Bas. Foundered 1801
West Indies.

BACCHANTE 6th Rate 20, 642bm, 131 × 33ft.
French, captured 25.6.1803 by ENDYMION in
Atlantic. Sold 27.2.1809.

BACCHANTE 5th Rate 38, 1,077bm, 154 × 39·5ft.
Deptford DY 16.3.1811. Harbour service 2.1837.
BU comp. 20.2.1858 Deptford.

BACCHANTE Wood screw frigate, 2,064bm, 188
× 50·5ft, 28—8in, 22—32pdr. Portsmouth DY,
ordered 1849, cancelled 1851.

BACCHANTE Wood screw frigate, 2,667bm, 235 ×
50ft, 30—8in, 1—68pdr, 20—32pdr. Portsmouth
DY 30.7.1859. BU 1869 Portsmouth.

BACCHANTE Iron screw corvette, 2,679bm, 4,130
tons, 280 × 45·5ft, 14—7in, 2—64pdr. Portsmouth
DY 19.10.1876. Sold 1897 Cohen.

BACCHANTE 1st class cruiser, 12,000 tons, 454 ×
69·5ft, 2—9·2in, 12—6in, 13—12pdr. John Brown
21.2.1901. Sold 1.7.1920 S. Castle, Plymouth.

BACCHANTE Frigate, 'Leander' class, Y160, 2,650
tons, 372 (oa) × 43ft, 2—4·5in, Seacat, helo.
Vickers Armstrong, Tyne, 29.2.1968. Tx RNZN
1.10.1982 = WELLINGTON. PO 5.5.2000. Project
to sink as artificial reef Houghton Bay, New
Zealand, 7.2002.

BACCHUS Cutter 10, 111bm, 68 × 20ft. Bermuda
1806. Captured 1808 by French in West Indies.

BACCHUS Sloop 12, 141bm. Dutch, captured 1807.
BU 1812.

BACCHUS Brig-sloop 18, 'Cruizer' class, 384bm.
Chatham DY 17.4.1813. Towed Harwich 13.8.1829
for use as breakwater.

BACCHUS *See also ARETHUSA 1817.*

BADDECK Corvette (RCN), 'Flower' class. Davie
SB 20.11.1940. Sold 1946 = *Efthalia*.

BADGER Sloop 14, 274bm, 91·5 × 26·5ft, Janvrin,
Bursledon, 5.8.1745. Lost 1762.

BADGER (ex-*Pitt*) Brig 14, 138bm. Purch. 6.1776.
Condemned 1777.

BADGER Brig. Purch. 1777. Sold 1784 in Jamaica.

BADGER Gunvessel 3, 59bm, 61 × 14·5ft, 2—32pdr
carr., 1—24pdr. Dutch hoy, purch. 4.1794. Sold
1802.

BADGER Brig-sloop 10, 'Cherokee' class, 240bm.
Brindley, Frindsbury, 23.7.1808. Mooring vessel
1835. Beached at Cape 22.3.1860, BU 1864.

BADGER (ex-RANGER) Wood screw gunboat,
216bm, 100 × 22ft, 1—68pdr, 1—32pdr, 2—24pdr
howitzers. Pitcher, Northfleet, 23.9.1854
(renamed before launch). BU 6.1864 Portsmouth.

BADGER Iron screw gunboat, 'Ant' class. Chatham
DY 13.3.1872. Sold 6.10.1908 Loveridge,
Hartlepool.

BADGER Destroyer, 799 tons, 240 × 26ft, 2—4in,
2—12pdr, 2—TT. Denny 11.7.1911. Sold 9.5.1921
Ward, Hayle.

BADMINTON Minesweeper, Later 'Hunt' class.
Ardrossan DD 18.3.1918. Sold 19.5.1928 Ward,
Inverkeithing.

BADMINTON *See also ILSTON 1954.*

BADSWORTH Destroyer, 'Hunt' class Type II.

Cammell Laird 17.3.1941. On loan RNorN 16.11.1944 = ARENDAL. Sold 1945 RNorN.

BAGSHOT Minesweeper, Later 'Hunt' class. Ardrossan DD 23.5.1918. = MEDWAY II (depot ship) 1.4.1945; = BAGSHOT 28.2.1946. Sold 1947 Greek sbkrs; sunk 1.9.1951 mine off Corfu while under tow.

BAHAMA 3rd Rate 74, 1,772bm, 175·5 × 48ft. Spanish, captured 21.10.1805 Battle of Trafalgar. Prison ship 1809. BU 12.1814 Chatham.

BAHAMAS (ex-HOTHAM) Frigate, 'Colony' class. Walsh Kaiser 17.8.1943 on Lend-Lease (renamed 1943). Ret. USN 11.6.1946.

BALA Minesweeper, Later 'Hunt' class. Clyde SB Co, cancelled 1918.

BALEINE 6th Rate 20, 702bm, 150 × 32ft. French, captured 10.1760 Pondicherry. Sold 23.6.1767.

BALFOUR (ex-McANN) Frigate, TE 'Captain' class. Bethlehem, Hingham, 10.7.1943 on Lend-Lease. Ret. USN 10.1945.

BALIKPAPAN Landing craft (RAN), 310 tons, 146 (oa) × 37ft. Walker 8.1971. Ordered for Army; tx RAN 22.9.1974.

BALLAHOU Gunvessel. In service 1800.

BALLAHOU Schooner 4, 78bm, 56 × 18ft. Bermuda 1804. Captured 29.4.1814 by American privateer PERRY off coast of North America.

BALLARAT Minesweeper, 'Bathurst' class. Melbourne Harbour Trust, Williamstown, 10.12.1940. Sold 10.7.1947 Hong Kong Shipping Co. = *Carmencita*.

BALLARAT Frigate (RAN), 'Anzac' class. Tenix Defence Systems, Williamstown, 25.5.2002.

BALLINDERRY Frigate, 'River' class. Blyth SB 7.12.1942. HO 7.7.1961 Ward, Barrow, for BU.

BALM Corvette, 'Flower' class. Alex Hall, ordered 30.7.1942, cancelled 12.11.1942.

BALMAIN Frigate (RAN), 'River' class. Sydney, ordered 12.1942, cancelled 12.6.1944.

BALSAM (ex-CHELMER) Corvette, 'Flower' class. G. Brown 30.5.1942 (renamed 5.1941). Arr. 20.4.1947 Cashmore, Newport, for BU.

BALTIC (ex-APITH) Cutter 14. Russian, captured 24.6.1808 by SALSETTE off Norgen Is. Sold 1810.

BALTIMORE 5th Rate 28. Deptford 1695. *Fate unknown.*

BALTIMORE Sloop 14, 251bm, 89 × 25ft. West, Deptford, 30.12.1742. Conv. bomb vessel 1758. Sold 12.1762.

BALUCHI See *PC.55, Torpedo Boat No 1 (RIM) 1888.*

BALUCHISTAN (ex-GREENOCK) Minesweeper (RIN), turbine 'Bangor' class. Blyth SB 11.5.1942 (renamed 1941). Tx RPN 1948. Sold 22.1.1959.

BAMBOROUGH CASTLE Corvette, 'Castle' class. J. Lewis 11.1.1944. Arr. 22.5.1959 Rees, Llanelly, for BU.

BANBURY Paddle minesweeper, 820 tons, 250 × 29ft, 1–3in, 1–12pdr. Ailsa 19.12.1917. Sold 14.9.1923 Hayes, Pembroke Dock.

BANCHORY Minesweeper, Later 'Hunt' class. Ayrshire Co., Irvine, 5.1918. Sold 18.5.1922 B. Zammitt, Malta.

BANDICOOT (ex-*Grenville VII*) Aux. minesweeper (RAN), 242 tons, 95·8 (oa) × 28ft. Tug, Singapore 1982. Purch. 11.8.1990.

BANDOLIER Patrol boat (RAN), 146 tons, 107·5 (oa) × 20ft, 1–40mm. Walker 2.10.1968. Sold 16.11.1973 to Indonesia = SIBARU.

BANFF Corvette (RCN), 'Flower' class. Burrard 18.7.1940; = WETASKIWIN 1941. Sold 1946 Venezuelan Navy = VICTORIA. Sold 1962.

BANFF Minesweeper, turbine 'Bangor' class. Ailsa, LD 20.7.1940. = HYTHE 6.1941, launched 4.9.1941.

BANFF (ex-SARANAC) Cutter, 1,546 tons, 1–5in, 2–3in. Coast Guard cutter, tx on Lend-Lease 30.4.1941. Ret. USCG 27.2.1946 = SEBEC.

BANGOR Minesweeper, diesel 'Bangor' class. Harland & Wolff, Govan, 23.5.1940. Lent RNorN 1946 = GLOMMA; deleted 1.12.1961.

BANGOR Minehunter, 'Sandown' class, Vosper-Thornycroft 16.4.1999.

BANKS Fishery protection/general-purpose vessel (RAN), 207 tons, 101 (oa) × 22ft. Walker 15.12.1959. Deleted 1995.

BANN 6th Rate 20, 466bm, 116 × 30ft. King, Upnor, 8.6.1814. Sold 8.1.1829 H. Cropman,

BANN Iron paddle gunboat, 267bm, 140 × 20ft, 2–8in. Scott Russell 5.7.1856. Sold 18.2.1873 Moss Isaacs for BU.

BANN Frigate, 'River' class. Hill 29.12.1942. Tx RIN 3.12.1945 = TIR. TS 1948 (1–4in, 1–40mm). BU 1979.

BANSHEE Paddle packet, 670bm, 189 × 27ft. Rotherhithe 13.10.1847. BU 1864.

BANSHEE Destroyer, 330 tons, 210 × 19·5ft, 1–12pdr, 5–6pdr, 2–TT. Laird 17.11.1894. Sold 10.4.1912 Ward, Briton Ferry.

BANTERER (ex-BANTER) 6th Rate 22, 532bm, 118·5 × 31·5ft, Temple, South Shields, 24.2.1807 (renamed 1805). Wrecked 4.12.1808 St Lawrence R.

BANTERER Sloop 16, 250bm, 92 × 25·5ft. Woolwich DY 2.6.1810. Sold 6.3.1817 Gordon & Co.

BANTERER Wood screw gunboat, 'Albacore' class. Pitcher, Northfleet, 29.9.1855. Sold 30.12.1872 in Hong Kong.

BANTERER Composite gunboat, 465 tons, 125 ×

23·5ft, 2—64pdr MLR, 2—20pdr BL. Barrow SB 2.11.1880. Sold 14.5.1907 Harris, Bristol.

BANTERER *See also PLUCKY 1870.*

BANTRY *See SWINDON 1918.*

BANTUM Fireship 6, 276bm. Purch. 1672. Lost 1672.

BARBADOES Fireship 8, 223bm. Purch. 1666. Sunk 1667 blockship R. Medway.

BARBADOES Sloop 14, 130bm, 80 × 21·5ft. Purch. 25.11.1757. Sold 15.3.1763.

BARBADOES Brig-sloop 14. Purch. West Indies 1778. Foundered 4.10.1780 hurricane West Indies.

BARBADOES (ex-RHODES) Sloop 14, 270bm. American, captured 15.2.1782 West Indies. Sold 2.12.1784.

BARBADOES (ex-LE BRAVE) 6th Rate 28, 755bm, 140 × 36·5ft, 10—24pdr carr., 24—9pdr, 2—6pdr. French privateer, captured 5.1803, presented 1804 by inhabitants of Barbados. Wrecked 28.9.1812 Sable I.

BARBADOES (ex-HERALD) Brig-sloop 16, 308bm, 102 × 26ft. American, captured 1813. Powder hulk Jamaica until 1817.

BARBADOES 6th Rate 24, 460bm, 115·5 × 30ft. Davy, Topsham. Launched 8.3.1814 as HIND.

BARBADOS (ex-HALSTED) Frigate, 'Colony' class. Walsh Kaiser 27.8.1943 on Lend-Lease (renamed 1943). Ret. USN 13.4.1946.

BARBARA Schooner 14. Purch. 1796. In service 1801.

BARBARA Schooner 10, 112bm, 68 × 20ft. Bermuda 1806. Sold 9.2.1815. *In French hands as privateer PERATY 17.9.1807–17.7.1808.*

BARBETTE (ex-VAILLANTE) 6th Rate 22, 604bm. French privateer, captured 25.6.1805. BU 5.1811.

BARBETTE Patrol boat (RAN), 146 tons, 107·5 (oa) × 20ft, 1—40mm. Walker 10.4.1968. Sold 22.2.1985 to Indonesia = SIADA.

BARBUDA Sloop 16. In service 1780. Lost 2.1782 on surrender of Demerara.

BARCOO Frigate (RAN), 'River' class. Cockatoo DY 26.8.1943. Sold 27.1.1972 for BU Taiwan.

BARFLEUR 2nd Rate 90, 1,476bm, 163 × 46·5ft. Deptford DY 10.8.1697. Rebuilt Deptford 1716 as 1,565bm, 80 guns; hulked 1764. BU 7.1783.

BARFLEUR 2nd Rate 98, 1,947bm, 178 × 50·5ft. Chatham DY 30.7.1768. BU 9.1819 Chatham.

BARFLEUR Battleship, 10,500 tons, 360 × 70ft, 4—10in, 10—4·7in, 2—9pdr. Chatham DY 10.8.1892. Sold 12.7.1910 C. Ewen, Glasgow; resold, BU Hughes Bolckow.

BARFLEUR Destroyer, 2,325 tons, 379 (oa) ×

40·25ft, 4—4·5in, 8—TT. Swan Hunter 1.11.1943. Arr. 29.9.1966 Dalmuir for BU.

BARFLEUR *See also BRITANNIA 1762.*

BARHAM 3rd Rate 74, 1,761bm, 176 × 48·5ft. Perry, Wells & Green, Blackwall, 8.7.1811. Reduced to 50 guns 12.1826. BU 9.1840.

BARHAM Wood screw frigate, 3,027bm, 250 × 52ft, 30—8in, 1—68pdr, 20—32pdr. Portsmouth DY, ordered 1860, cancelled.

BARHAM 3rd class cruiser, 1,830 tons, 280 × 35ft, 6—4·7in, 4—3pdr. Portsmouth DY 11.9.1889. Sold 19.2.1914 Ward, Preston.

BARHAM Battleship, 27,500 tons, 643·7 (oa) × 90·5ft (later 104ft), 8—15in, 14—6in, 2—3in. John Brown 31.12.1914. Sunk 25.11.1941 by U.331 in Mediterranean.

BARK OF BULLEN Ship, 80bm. Captured from French 7.1522. Listed until 1525.

BARK OF MURLESSE Ship, 60bm. Captured from French 7.1522. Listed until 1530.

BARLE Frigate, 'River' class. Vickers, Montreal, 26.9.1942 on Lend-Lease. Ret. USN 27.2.1946.

BARNARD CASTLE *See EMPIRE SHELTER 1944.*

BARNSTAPLE Minesweeper, Later 'Hunt' class. Ardrossan DD 20.3.1919. Sold 1.12.1921 = *Lady Cynthia*; BU 1957.

BARNWELL CASTLE Corvette, 'Castle' class. Kingston SB, Canada, cancelled 12.1943.

BARRACOUTA Sloop 14, 197bm, 75 × 26ft. Cutter, purch. 6.1782. Sold 19.1.1792.

BARRACOUTA Schooner 4, 781bm, 56 × 18ft. Bermuda 1804. Wrecked 2.10.1805 coast of Cuba.

BARRACOUTA Brig-sloop, 'Cruizer' class, 385bm. Bailey, Ipswich, 6.7.1807. Sold 23.3.1815.

BARRACOUTA Brig-sloop 10, 'Cherokee' class, 235bm. Woolwich DY 13.5.1820. Cd as packet brig 5.1829; sold 21.1.1836.

BARRACOUTA Wood paddle sloop, 1,053bm, 6 guns. Pembroke Dock 31.3.1851. BU 12.1881 Chatham.

BARRACOUTA 3rd class cruiser, 1,580 tons, 220 × 35ft, 6—4·7in, 4—3pdr. Sheerness DY 16.5.1889. Sold 4.4.1905 McLellan; resold, BU Bo'ness.

BARRICADE Patrol boat (RAN), 146 tons, 107·5 (oa) × 20ft, 1—40mm. Evans Deakin 29.6.1968. Sold 22.4.1983 to Indonesia.

BARRIE Corvette (RCN), 'Flower' class. Collingwood SY 23.11.1940. Sold 1946 Argentine Navy = GASESTADO; = CAPITAN CANEPA (survey ship) 1956. BU 1972.

BARRINGTON Destroyer leader, 1,750 tons, 318 × 32ft. Cammell Laird, ordered 4.1918, cancelled 26.11.1918.

BARROSA 5th Rate 36, 947bm, 145 × 38·5ft. Deptford DY 21.10.1812. Harbour service 1823. Sold 27.5.1841.

BARROSA Wood screw corvette, 1,700bm, 225 × 41ft, 16—8in, 1—7in, 4—40pdr. Woolwich DY 10.3.1860. BU 1.1877 Chatham.

BARROSA 3rd class cruiser, 1,580 tons, 220 × 35ft, 6—4·7in, 4—3pdr. Portsmouth DY 16.4.1889. Sold 11.7.1905.

BARROSA Destroyer, 2,380 tons, 379 (oa) × 40·25ft, 5—4·5in, 10—TT. John Brown 17.1.1945. Sold 2.8.1978; BU 12.1978 Blyth.

BARWON Frigate (RAN), 'River' class. Cockatoo DY 3.8.1944. Sold 1.1962 Sleigh Bros for BU Japan; left Sydney 17.8.1962.

BASILISK Bomb vessel 4, 163bm, 72 × 23ft. Reading, Wapping, 4.5.1695. BU 1729.

BASILISK Bomb vessel 4, 270bm, 92 × 26ft. Snelgrove, Limehouse, 30.8.1740. Sold 14.8.1750.

BASILISK Bomb vessel 8, 312bm, 92 × 28ft. Wells, Deptford, 10.2.1759. Captured 29.10.1762 by French privateer AUDACIEUX.

BASILISK Gun-brig 12, 186bm, 80 × 23ft. Randall, Rotherhithe, 2.4.1801. Sold 14.12.1815.

BASILISK Cutter 6, 161bm, 67·5 × 24ft, 6—6pdr. Chatham DY 7.5.1822. Sold 1.1846.

BASILISK Wood paddle sloop, 1,031bm, 185 × 34ft. Woolwich DY 22.8.1848. BU 1882 Chatham.

BASILISK Sloop, 1,170 tons, 195 × 28ft, 8—5in. Sheerness DY 6.4.1889. Coal hulk = C.7. Sold 1905 = *Maggie Grech*.

BASILISK Destroyer, 976 tons, 265 × 28ft, 1—4in, 3—12pdr, 2—TT. White 9.2.1910. Sold 1.11.1921 Fryer, Sunderland.

BASILISK Destroyer, 1,360 tons, 323 (oa) × 32·25ft, 4—4·7in, 8—TT. John Brown 6.8.1930. Sunk 1.6.1940 air attack off Dunkirk.

BASILISK *See also GRASSHOPPER 1777.*

BASING 22-gun ship, 255bm. Shish, Walberswick, 1654. = GUERNSEY 1660; fireship 1688. BU 1693.

BASING 6th Rate 18, 121bm. Purch. 1693. Captured 5.2.1694 by French.

BASS Survey/general-purpose vessel (RAN), 207 tons, 101 (oa) × 22ft. Walker 28.3.1960. Sold 2.1994.

BASSINGHAM Inshore minesweeper, 'Ham' class. Vosper, Portsmouth, 24.6.1952. Sold 1966 Pounds, Portsmouth.

BASTION (ex-LCT.4040) Tank landing craft, 657 tons, 225 × 39ft, 4—20mm. Renamed 1956. Sold 15.9.1966 Zambia.

BAT Destroyer, 360 tons, 215 × 21ft, 1—12pdr, 5—6pdr, 2—TT. Palmer, Jarrow, 7.10.1896. Sold 30.8.1919 Hayes, Porthcawl.

BATAAN (ex-KURNAI) Destroyer (RAN), 1,927 tons, 377 (oa) × 36·5ft, 6—4·7in, 2—4in, 4—TT. Cockatoo DY 15.1.1944 (renamed 1944). Sold 1958 T. Carr & Co., Sydney; resold 1962 for BU Japan.

BATAVIA 4th Rate 56, 1,048bm. Dutch, captured 30.8.1799 off Texel. Floating battery 7.1801; harbour service 9.1817. BU 3.1823.

BATH (ex-HOPEWELL) Destroyer, 1,060 tons, 309 × 30·5ft, 3—4in, 1—3in, 6—TT. USN; cd RN 10.1940. Lent RNorN 1.1.1941. Sunk 19.8.1941 by U.201 south-west of Ireland.

BATHGATE Minesweeper, Later 'Hunt' class. Clyde SB Co, cancelled 1918.

BATHURST Brig 10, 170bm. Port Jackson, purch. 7.1821. Survey vessel 1822; Coastguard service 2.1824. Sold 11.4.1858 Castle for BU.

BATHURST Minesweeper, 'Bathurst' class. Cockatoo DY 1.8.1940. Lent RAN. Sold 21.6.1948 Sydney for BU.

BATMAN Iron screw gunboat (Australian), 388 tons, 1—6in, 2—3pdr. Simons, Renfrew, 1883. Listed 1895.

BATTLE Minesweeper, Later 'Hunt' class. Dundee SB Co, cancelled 10.1919; launched incomp. Sold 3.1922 Ward, Inverkeithing.

BATTLEAXE Landing ship dock, 4,270 tons, 454 × 72ft, 1—3in, 20 light. Newport News 21.5.1943 on Lend-Lease. = EASTWAY 8.1943. Ret. USN 5.1947.

BATTLEAXE Destroyer, 1,980 tons, 365 (oa) × 38ft, 6—4in, 6—40mm, 10—TT. Yarrow 12.6.1945. Arr. 20.10.1964 Hughes Bolckow, Blyth, for BU.

BATTLEAXE Frigate, 3,556 tons, 430 (oa) × 48.5ft, Exocet, Seawolf, helo, 6—TT. Yarrow 18.5.1977. Tx Brazilian Navy 30.4.1997 = RADEMAKER.

BATTLEFORD Corvette (RCN), 'Flower' class. Collingwood SY 15.4.1941. Sold 1946 Venezuelan Navy = LIBERTAD.

BATTLER (ex-*Mormacmail* [ii]) Escort carrier, 11,420 tons, 468·5 × 69·5ft, 2—4in, 8—40mm, 18 aircraft. Ingalls 4.4.1942 on Lend-Lease. Ret. USN 12.2.1946.

BATTLER *See also LST.3015 1945.*

BAYFIELD Minesweeper, TE 'Bangor' class. North Vancouver Ship Repair 26.5.1941. Sold 1.1.1948; BU King, Gateshead.

BAYNTUN Frigate, DE 'Captain' class. Boston NY 27.6.1942 on Lend-Lease. Ret. USN 22.8.1945.

BAYONET Patrol boat (RAN), 146 tons, 107.5 (oa) × 20ft, 1—40mm. Walker 6.11.1968. RANR 3.1982; PO 26.6.1988; attached HMAS CERBERUS. Sunk 19.5.1999 Bass Strait.

BAZELY Frigate, DE 'Captain' class. Boston NY

27.6.1942. Tx RN 18.2.1943 on Lend-Lease. Ret.
USN 8.1945.

BEACHAMPTON Coastal minesweeper, 'Ton'
class. Goole SB 29.6.1953. Patrol boat 1971. PO
1.1985; sold 3.1985 Acorn Shipping, BU.

BEACHY HEAD Repair ship, 8,580 tons, 425 ×
57ft, 16–20mm. Burrard, Vancouver, 27.9.1944.
Lent Dutch Navy 1946–49 = VULKAAN. Tx RCN
1954 = CAPE SCOTT. Sold 1977.

BEACON (ex-*Duff*) Fireship, 150bm. Purch.
6.1804. Sold 3.11.1808.

BEACON Mortar vessel, 117bm, 65 × 21ft, 1–13in
mortar. Wigram, Blackwall, 21.4.1855. = MV.16
19.10.1855. Dockyard lighter 5.1862.

BEACON Wood screw gunboat, 'Albacore' class.
Laird 11.2.1856. BU 8.1864.

BEACON Composite screw gunvessel, 465bm, 603
tons, 155 × 25ft, 1–7in MLR, 1–64pdr MLR 2–
20pdr. Chatham DY 17.8.1867. Sold 12.1888.

BEACON *See also METEOR 1823.*

BEACON HILL Frigate (RCN), 'River' class.
Yarrow, Esquimalt, 6.11.1943. Sold 1968.

BEAGLE Brig-sloop (fir-built), 'Cruizer' class,
383bm. Perry, Wells & Green, Blackwall,
8.8.1804. Sold 21.7.1814.

BEAGLE Brig-sloop 10, 'Cherokee' class. Woolwich
DY 11.5.1820. Survey ship 1825; Customs watch-
vessel 1846; = WV.7 in 5.1863. Sold 13.5.1870
Murray & Trainer.

BEAGLE Wood screw gunvessel, 477bm, 160 ×
25·5ft, 2–68pdr ML. Mare, Blackwall, 20.7.1854.
Sold 1863 in Hong Kong = Japanese KANKO
1865. BU 1889.

BEAGLE Schooner 1, 120bm, 80 × 18ft, 1–12pdr.
Cuthbert, Sydney, 5.12.1872. Sold 1883 Sydney.

BEAGLE Sloop, 1,170 tons, 195 × 28ft, 8–5in.
Portsmouth DY 28.2.1889. Sold 11.7.1905.

BEAGLE Destroyer, 950 tons, 269 × 27ft, 1–4in,
3–12pdr, 2–TT. John Brown 16.10.1909. Sold
1.11.1921 Fryer, Sunderland.

BEAGLE Destroyer, 1,360 tons, 323 × 32·25ft, 4–
4·7in, 8–TT. John Brown 26.9.1930. Sold
15.1.1946; arr. 6.1946 Rosyth for BU.

BEAGLE Survey ship, 1,050 tons, 189·6 (oa) ×
37·5ft. Brooke Marine 7.9.1967. PO 7.2.2002; sold
3.2002 yacht company Poole for conv.

BEAR 40-gun ship, 398bm. Prize, rebuilt 1580.
Last listed 1665.

BEAR 36-gun ship. Captured 1664. Sold 1665.

BEATRICE Survey schooner (Australian). Purch.
1868. Sold 1880.

BEATTY *See HOWE 1940.*

BEAUFORT (ex-AMBLESIDE) Survey ship, 800
tons, 1–3pdr. Minesweeper, Ailsa 21.2.1919, conv.

(renamed 1918). Sold 30.6.1938 Cashmore; resold
27.7.1939 Rees, Llanelly.

BEAUFORT Destroyer, 'Hunt' class Type II.
Cammell Laird 15.4.1941. Lent RNorN 1952
= HAUGESUND 30.9.1954. Sold 1956 to
Norway; BU 1965.

BEAUHARNOIS Corvette (RCN), Modified
'Flower' class. Morton 11.5.1944. Sold 1946
= *Colon.*

BEAULIEU 5th Rate 40, 1,020bm, 147·5 × 39·5ft,
28–18pdr, 12–9pdr. Adams, Buckler's Hard,
4.5.1791, spec., purch. 6.1790. BU 8.1806.

BEAULIEU Minesweeper, TE 'Bangor' class. Hong
Kong & Whampoa, LD 22.7.1941. = LANTAU
9.1941. Captured on stocks by Japanese, launched
2.1943 = Minesweeper No 101.

BEAULY FIRTH (ex-EMPIRE SARAWAK) Repair
ship, 8,650 tons, 439 × 62ft, 12–20mm.
Readhead, South Shields, 24.8.1944 (renamed
1944). Sold 1948 = *Stanfirth.*

BEAUMARIS Minesweeper, turbine 'Bangor' class.
Ailsa 31.10.1940. Sold 1.1.1948; BU Ward, Milford
Haven.

BEAUMARIS *See also BOLTON 1918.*

BEAUMONT Sloop 16. American, captured 5.1780
Charlestown. Sold 4.1793.

BEAVER Ketch 6. Royalist. Captured by Parliamentarians 1656. BU 1658.

BEAVER (ex-TRUDAINE) Sloop 18, 338bm, 93 ×
28·5ft, 18–6pdr. French privateer, captured
4.1757. Sold 22.1.1761.

BEAVER Sloop 14, 285bm, 96·5 × 26ft. Inwood,
Rotherhithe, 3.2.1761. Sold 17.7.1783.

BEAVER Sloop 14, 269bm, 94 × 25·5ft. Graham,
Harwich, 29.9.1795. Sold 21.12.1808.

BEAVER Brig-sloop 10, 'Cherokee' class, 236bm.
Bailey, Ipswich, 16.2.1809. Sold 24.6.1829
J. Cristall.

BEAVER (ex-*Salamander*) Wood paddle packet,
114bm, 102 × 16ft. GPO vessel, tx 1837. Dockyard
lighter 1845.

BEAVER Wood screw gunboat, 'Albacore' class.
Wigram, Northam, 28.11.1855. BU 1864 Portsmouth.

BEAVER (ex-*Victor*) Tender, 125 tons, 95 × 17·5ft.
War Dept vessel, tx 1905. Sold 7.7.1911 Laidler,
Sunderland.

BEAVER Destroyer, 810 tons, 240 × 26ft, 2–4in.
2–12pdr, 2–TT. Denny 6.10.1911. Sold 9.5.1921
Ward, Hayle; resold 6.1923 J. J. King for BU.

BEAVER Frigate, 4,100 tons, 480·5 (oa) × 48·4ft,
Exocet, Seawolf, helo, 6–TT. Yarrow 8.5.1982. PO
5.2.1999, towed 26.2.2001 Aliaga for BU.

BEAVER PRIZE (ex-OLIVER CROMWELL) Sloop

18, 263bm, 88 × 27ft. American privateer, captured 18.5.1778 by BEAVER. Wrecked 11.10.1780 St Lucia. *Named CONVERT until 1778.*

BECCLES Minesweeper, Later 'Hunt' class. Dundee SB Co, cancelled 1918.

BECKFORD Seaward defence boat, 'Ford' class. Simons 3.1953. = DEE 1965. Sold 1.1983 Pounds, Portsmouth.

BECKWITH Schooner (Canadian lakes). Kingston, Ontario, 8.7.1816. Sold c. 1837.

BEDALE Destroyer, 'Hunt' class Type II. Hawthorn Leslie 23.7.1941. Lent Polish Navy 4.1942 = SLAZAK; = BEDALE 11.1946. Tx Indian Navy 27.4.1953 = GODAVERI; later TS. Ran aground 1976, salvaged; deleted 1979.

BEDFORD 3rd Rate 70, 1,073bm, 151 × 40ft. Woolwich DY 12.9.1698. Rebuilt Portsmouth 1741 as 1,230bm, 64 guns; hulked 11.1767. Sold 1787.

BEDFORD 3rd Rate 74, 1,606bm, 168·5 × 47ft. Woolwich DY 27.10.1775. Prison ship 1801. BU 10.1817.

BEDFORD Armoured cruiser, 9,800 tons, 440 × 66ft, 14—6in, 9—12pdr. Fairfield 31.8.1901. Wrecked 21.8.1910 Quelport I., China Sea. Wreck sold 10.1910.

BEDFORD GALLEY 5th Rate 34, 372bm, 103 × 29ft. Built New England 1697, purch. 1697. Rebuilt Portsmouth 1709 as 410bm; fireship 1716. Sunk 3.5.1725 foundation Sheerness.

BEDHAM Inshore minesweeper, 'Ham' class. Bolson, Poole, 29.7.1953. Tx Malaysian Navy 1959 = LANKA SUKA. BU 1967.

BEDOUIN Destroyer, 1,870 tons, 377 (oa) × 36·5ft, 8—4·7in, 4—TT. Denny 21.12.1937. Sunk 15.6.1942 Italian airborne torpedo Mediterranean.

BEE Wood screw/paddle vessel, 42bm, 60 × 12·5ft. Chatham DY 28.2.1842. BU 1874.

BEE River gunboat, 645 tons, 230 × 36ft, 2—6in, 1—3in. Ailsa 8.12.1915. Sold 22.3.1939 in Shanghai for BU.

BEE River gunboat, 585 tons. White, Cowes, ordered 1939, cancelled 3.1940.

BEESTON CASTLE Corvette, 'Castle' class. Kingston SB, cancelled 12.1943.

BEGONIA Sloop, 'Acacia' class. Barclay Curle 26.8.1915. Sunk 2.10.1918 collision U.151 off Casablanca while serving as decoy ship Q.10.

BEGONIA Corvette, 'Flower' class. Cook, Welton & Gemmell 18.9.1940. Lent USN = IMPULSE 16.3.1942—1945. Sold 22.7.1946 = *Beganlock*.

BEGUM (ex-*Balinas*) Escort carrier, 11,400 tons, 468·5 × 69·5ft. Seattle, Tacoma, 11.11.1942; tx RN

2.8.1943 on Lend-Lease. Ret. USN 4.1.1946; sold = *Raki.*

BEGUM (ex-NATOMA BAY) Escort carrier, 7,800 tons. Kaiser, Vancouver, 20.7.1943. Retained USN = NATOMA BAY.

BELEM Schooner 4, 88bm. Spanish, captured 27.6.1806 Montevideo. Recaptured by Spanish 12.8.1806 Buenos Aires.

BELETTE 6th Rate 24, 580bm, 120 × 32ft. French, captured 29.8.1793 Toulon. Burnt 20.10.1796 Ajaccio, unserviceable.

BELETTE (ex-BELLIQUEUSE) Sloop 18, 346bm, 104·5× 27·5ft. French, captured 2.1798. Sold 14.9.1801.

BELETTE Brig-sloop 18, 'Cruizer' class, 384bm. King, Dover, 21.3.1806. Wrecked 24.11.1812 Kattegat.

BELETTE Brig-sloop 18, 'Cruizer' class, 386bm Larking, Lynn, 18.6.1814. Sold 26.3.1828 Adam Gordon.

BELFAST Cruiser, 10,000 tons, 613·5 (oa) × 63·3ft (later 66·3ft), 12—6in, 12—4in. Harland & Wolff 17.3.1938. Museum ship 21.10.1971 R. Thames.

BELFORT Sloop, 644 tons, 246 × 31ft, 1—3in. French, seized 3.7.1940 Plymouth. Free French depot ship 9.1940—1944; ret. French Navy 1946.

BELISARIUS 6th Rate 24, 514bm, 164 × 27·5ft. American, captured 7.8.1781 by MEDEA. Sold 2.12.1783.

BELLE ISLE (ex-*Berlin*) 3rd Rate 64, 1,494bm, 168·5 × 45ft. French East Indiaman, captured 1761. Harbour service 12.1784. Sold 3.2.1819.

BELLE ISLE *See also Belleisle.*

BELLE POULE 5th Rate 36, 902bm, 140 × 38ft. French, captured 17.7.1780 by NONSUCH off mouth of R. Loire. Sold 14.9.1801.

BELLE POULE 5th Rate 38, 1,077bm, 151·5 × 40ft. French, captured 13.3.1806 by squadron in south Atlantic. Troopship 1814; prison ship 1815. Sold 11.6.1818.

BELLECHASSE Minesweeper (RCN), TE 'Bangor' class. Burrard, Vancouver, 20.10.1941. Sold 1946.

BELLEISLE (ex-FORMIDABLE) 3rd Rate 74, 1,889bm, 184 × 49ft. French, captured 23.6.1795 Belle Isle. BU 8.1814.

BELLEISLE 3rd Rate 74, 1,709bm, 174 × 48ft. Pembroke Dock 26.4.1819. Reduced to 20-gun troopship 1841; harbour service 5.1854. BU comp. 12.10.1872 Chatham.

BELLEISLE (ex-PEIKI SHEREEF) Coast defence ship, 4,870 tons, 245 × 52ft, 4—12in MLR, 6—6pdr. Samuda, Poplar, 12.2.1876; Turkish, purch. 1878. Wrecked target 4.9.1903; wreck sold 12.4.1904 for BU in Germany.

BELLEISLE Destroyer, 2,380 tons, 379 (oa) ×
40·5ft, 5—4·5in, 10—TT. Fairfield 7.2.1946, not
comp. Arr. 4.1946 Arnott Young for BU Troon.

BELLEISLE *See also Belle Isle.*

BELLEROPHON 3rd Rate 74, 1,643bm, 168 ×
47ft. Graves, Frindsbury, 6.10.1786. Prison ship
10.1815; = CAPTIVITY 5.10.1824. Sold 21.1.1836.

BELLEROPHON Battleship, 4,270bm, 7,551 tons,
300 × 56ft, 10—9in MLR, 5—7in MLR. Chatham
DY 26.5.1865. = INDUS III (TS) 3.1904. Sold
12.12.1922 McLellan, Bo'ness.

BELLEROPHON Battleship, 18,600 tons, 490 ×
82·5ft, 10—12in, 16—4in. Portsmouth DY
27.7.1907. Sold 8.11.1921 Slough Trading Co.;
towed Germany 14.9.1922 for BU.

BELLEROPHON *See also WATERLOO 1818,
TIGER ordered 3.1942, TIGER 1945.*

BELLEVILLE Corvette (RCN), Modified 'Flower'
class. Kingston SB 17.6.1944. Sold 1948 Dominican Navy = JUAN BAUTISTA CAMBIASO.

BELLIQUEUX 3rd Rate 64, 1,372bm, 158 × 45ft.
French, captured 2.11.1758 by ANTELOPE in
Bristol Channel. BU 9.1772.

BELLIQUEUX 3rd Rate 64, 1,379bm, 160 ×
48·5ft. Perry, Blackwall, 5.6.1780. Prison ship
2.1814. BU 3.1816 Chatham.

BELLONA (ex-BELLONE) 6th Rate 30, 541bm,
112 × 33·5ft, 24—9pdr, 6—4pdr. French privateer,
captured 2.2.1747 by NOTTINGHAM in English
Channel. Sold 2.2.1749.

BELLONA 3rd Rate 74, 1,615bm, 168 × 47ft.
Chatham DY 19.2.1760. BU 9.1814 Chatham.

BELLONA Gunvessel 3, 86bm, 62 × 18ft. Purch.
3.1794. Mud boat 1799. BU 8.1805 Woolwich.

BELLONA (ex-BELLONE) 6th Rate 28, 648bm,
132 × 34ft. French, captured 9.7.1806 by
POWERFUL off Ceylon; = BLANCHE 1809. BU
1814.

BELLONA 3rd class cruiser, 1,830 tons, 280 ×
35ft, 6—4·7in, 4—3pdr. Hawthorn 29.8.1890.
Sold 10.7.1906.

BELLONA Scout cruiser, 3,350 tons, 385 × 41ft,
6—4in. Pembroke Dock 20.3.1909. Sold 9.5.1921
Ward, Lelant.

BELLONA Cruiser, 5,770 tons, 512 (oa) × 50·5ft,
8—5·25in, Fairfield 29.9.1942. Lent RNZN 1948–
56. Arr. 5.2.1959 Ward, Briton Ferry, for BU.

BELLONA *See also INDUS 1812.*

BELLWORT Corvette, 'Flower' class. G. Brown
11.8.1941. Tx Irish Govt 1947 = CLIONA. BU
Haulbowline 1.1971.

BELMONT (ex-SATTERLEE) Destroyer, 1,190
tons, 311 × 31ft, 3—4in, 1—3in. 6—TT. USN, cd RN
8.10.1940. Sunk 31.1.1942 by U.82 off Halifax, NS.

BELTON Coastal minesweeper, 'Ton' class. Doig,
Grimsby, 3.10.1955. Sold 28.10.1974; BU Spain.

BELVIDERA 5th Rate 36, 946bm, 145 × 38·5ft.
Deptford DY 23.12.1809. Harbour service
10.1846. Sold 10.7.1906 J. B. Garnham.

BELVIDERA Wood screw frigate, 3,027bm, 250 ×
52ft. Chatham DY, LD 30.4.1860, cancelled
16.12.1864.

BELVOIR Minesweeper, Early 'Hunt' class. Ailsa
8.3.1917. Sold 7.1922 Stanlee, Dover.

BELVOIR Destroyer, 'Hunt' class Type III.
Cammell Laird 18.11.1941. Arr. 21.10.1957
McLellan, Bo'ness, for BU.

BELZEBUB Bomb vessel 8, 334bm, 102·5 × 27·5ft.
Taylor, Bideford, 30.7.1813. BU comp. 23.9.1820.

BELZEBUB Bomb vessel 8, 372bm, 105 × 29ft,
10—24pdr carr., 2—6pdr, 1—13in mortar, 1—10in
mortar. Plymouth DY, ordered 1821, cancelled
1832.

BELZEBUB *See also FIREBRAND 1842.*

BEN LOMOND *See LST.3013 1945.*

BEN NEVIS *See LST.3012 1945.*

BENALLA Minesweeper (RAN), 'Bathurst' class.
Williamstown DY 19.12.1942. Sold 20.2.1958 for
BU Japan.

BENALLA Survey vessel (RAN), 320 tons (full
load), 118·9 (oa) × 45·3ft. Elgo Engineering, Port
Adelaide, 4.9.1989.

BENARES Sloop 14 (Indian), 230bm. Bombay DY
1807. Sold 1836.

BENBOW 3rd Rate 72, 1,773bm, 176·5 × 49ft.
Brent, Rotherhithe, 3.2.1813. Harbour service
2.1848; coal hulk 8.1859. Sold 23.11.1892; BU
1895 Castle, Woolwich.

BENBOW Battleship, 10,600 tons, 330 × 68·5ft,
2—16·25in, 10—6in, 15 small. Thames Iron Works,
Blackwall, 15.6.1885. Sold 13.7.1909 Ward,
Morecambe.

BENBOW Battleship, 25,000 tons, 580 × 89·5ft,
10—13·5in, 12—6in. Beardmore 12.11.1913. Sold
3.1931 Metal Industries, Rosyth.

BEND OR Minesweeping sloop, '24' class. Barclay
Curle 24.9.1918. Sold 12.8.1920 Moise Mazza,
Malta; resold 8.1922 C. A. Beard.

BENDIGO Minesweeper, 'Bathurst' class. Cockatoo
DY 1.3.1941. Sold 5.5.1947 = *Cheung Hing.*

BENDIGO Patrol vessel (RAN), 211 tons. North
Queensland Engineering Co., Cairns, 9.4.1983.

BENGAL *Name chosen 1812 for ex-Danish FIJEN
74, not used.*

BENGAL Minesweeper (RIN), 'Bathurst' class.
Cockatoo DY 28.5.1942. Sold 1960.

BENJAMIN Fireship 6, 130bm. Purch. 1673. Captured 1673 by Dutch.

BENJAMIN & ANN Gunvessel 3, 72bm, 59·5 × 16·5ft. Purch. 1794. *Fate unknown.*

BENTINCK Iron paddle vessel (Indian). Rennie 28.7.1832. For sale 1855.

BENTINCK Frigate, DE 'Captain' class. Mare Island 22.8.1942 for RN; retained USN = BRENNAN.

BENTINCK Frigate, TE 'Captain' class. Bethlehem, Hingham, 3.2.1943 on Lend-Lease. Ret. USN 5.1.1946.

BENTLEY Frigate, TE 'Captain' class. Bethlehem, Hingham, 17.7.1943 on Lend-Lease. Ret. USN 5.11.1945.

BERBERIS Sloop, 'Arabis' class. Henderson 3.2.1916. Sold 30.1.1923 Stuart General Trading Co.

BERBICE Schooner, 121bm. Purch. 1780, condemned 12.9.1788.

BERBICE Schooner 8, 120bm, 73 × 20·5ft, 2–12pdr carr., 6–3pdr. Prize, purch. 1793. Wrecked 11.1796 Dominica.

BERBICE Schooner 4, 78bm. Purch. 1804. Foundered 1806 nr Demerara.

BERE CASTLE Corvette, 'Castle' class. G. Brown, cancelled 12.1943.

BERENICE Paddle sloop (Indian), 630bm, 170 × 29ft, 1–68pdr, 2–32pdr. Napier, Glasgow, 1836. Burnt 31.10.1866 accident Persian Gulf.

BERESFORD *See PRINCE REGENT 1812.*

BERGAMOT Sloop, 'Anchusa' class. Armstrong 5.5.1917. Sunk 13.8.1917 by U.84 in Atlantic.

BERGAMOT Corvette, 'Flower' class. Harland & Wolff 15.2.1941. Sold 5.1946 = *Syros.*

BERGERE Sloop 18, 442bm. French, captured 17.4.1806 by SIRIUS in Mediterranean. BU 10.1811.

BERKELEY Destroyer, 'Hunt' class Type I. Cammell Laird 29.1.1940. Sunk 19.8.1942 by ALBRIGHTON after bomb damage off Dieppe.

BERKELEY Minehunter, 615 tons, 197 (oa) × 32·8ft. Vosper-Thornycroft 4.6.1985. Tx Greek Navy 28.2.2001 = KALLISTO.

BERKELEY CASTLE 48-gun ship. Captured 25.10.1695 by French.

BERKELEY CASTLE Corvette, 'Castle' class. Barclay Curle 19.8.1943. Arr. 29.2.1956 Grays for BU.

BERMAGUI (ex-*Nadgee II*) Aux. minesweeper (RAN), 150 tons. 1973. Hired for trials (renamed 14.3.1994–2000).

BERMUDA Brig-sloop 14, 170bm, 80 × 24ft, 14–12pdr. carr. Purch. 1795 Bermuda while building. Foundered 9.1796 Gulf of Florida.

BERMUDA Sloop 18, 399bm, 100 × 30ft. Bermuda 1805. Wrecked 22.4.1808 Bahamas.

BERMUDA Brig-sloop 10, 'Cherokee' class, 237bm. Pelham, Frindsbury, 20.12.1808. Wrecked 24.11.1816 Gulf of Mexico.

BERMUDA Yacht, 43bm. Pilot boat, presented 1813. BU 9.1841 Bermuda.

BERMUDA Schooner. Purch. 1819. Foundered 3.1821 between Halifax and Bermuda.

BERMUDA Schooner 3, 180bm, 80 × 23ft. Outerbridge & Hollis, Bermuda, 3.1848. Wrecked 24.2.1855 Turks Is.

BERMUDA Cruiser, 8,000 tons, 555·5 (oa) × 62ft, 12–6in, 8–4in. John Brown 11.9.1941. Arr. 26.8.1965 Ward, Briton Ferry, for BU.

BERRY Frigate, DE 'Captain' class. Boston NY 23.11.1942 on Lend-Lease. Ret. USN 15.2.1946.

BERRY HEAD Repair ship, 8,580 tons, 441 (oa) × 57ft, 16–40mm. Burrard, Vancouver, 21.10.1944. Sold Dido Steel Corp; arr. Aliaga, Turkey, 19.3.1990 for BU.

BERWICK 3rd Rate 70, 1,041bm, 151 × 40ft. Chatham DY 1679. Rebuilt 1700 as 1,090bm; hulked 10.1715. BU 1742.

BERWICK 3rd Rate 70, 1,147bm, 151 × 42ft. Deptford DY 23.7.1723. Hulked 5.1743. BU 6.1783.

BERWICK 3rd Rate 70, 1,280bm, 154 × 44ft. Deptford 1743. BU 9.1760 Chatham.

BERWICK 3rd Rate 74, 1,623bm, 168·5 × 47ft. Portsmouth DY 18.4.1775. Captured 7.3.1795 by three French frigates in Mediterranean; recaptured 21.10.1805 Battle of Trafalgar, wrecked off San Lucar.

BERWICK Storeship 22, 512bm, 110 × 33ft. Purch. 11.1781 = SIRIUS (6th Rate) 10.1786. Wrecked 15.3.1790 Norfolk I.

BERWICK 3rd Rate 74, 1,761bm, 176 × 48ft. Perry, Blackwall, 11.9.1809. BU 3.1821.

BERWICK 1st class cruiser, 9,800 tons, 440 × 66ft, 14–6in, 9–12pdr. Beardmore 20.9.1902. Sold 1.7.1920; towed Hamburg 28.8.1922 for BU.

BERWICK Cruiser, 9,750 tons, 630 (oa) × 68·5ft, 8–8in, 8–4in. Fairfield 30.3.1926. Sold 15.6.1948; arr. 12.7.1948 Hughes Bolckow, Blyth, for BU.

BERWICK Frigate, 2,144 tons, 360 × 41ft, 2–4·5in, 1–40mm. Harland & Wolff 15.12.1959. Sunk 8.1986 target North Atlantic.

BERWICK *See also SAN JUAN 1805.*

BESCHERMER 4th Rate 56, 1,052bm. Dutch, captured 30.8.1799 off Texel. Floating battery 7.1801. Lent East India Dock Co. 4.11.1806–8.1838. Sold 9.1838 J. Cristall.

BETANO Landing craft (RAN), 310 tons, 146 (oa) × 33ft. Walker 5.12.1972.

BETONY Corvette, Modified 'Flower' class. Alex

Hall 22.4.1943. Lent RIN 24.8.1945 = SIND; tx RN = BETONY 17.5.1946. Sold 1947 Siamese Navy = PRASAE. Wrecked 1.1951.

BETTY 5th Rate 36, 372bm, 103 × 28·5ft. Purch. 1695. Sold 1702. *In French hands 14.8.1695–1696.*

BEVERLEY (ex-BRANCH) Destroyer, 1,190 tons, 311 × 31ft, 1–4in, 1–3in, 4–20mm. USN, cd RN 8.10.1940. Sunk 11.4.1943 by U.188 south of Greenland after collision SS *Cairnronaon* 9.4.1943.

BEVINGTON Coastal minesweeper, 'Ton' class. White, Southampton, 1.7.1953. Sold 1967 Argentine Navy = TIERRA DEL FUEGO; deleted 1996–97.

BEZAN Yacht 4, 35bm. Presented by Dutch 1661. BU 1687.

BHAMO Paddle gunboat (RIM), 255 tons, 163 × 30ft, 2–MG. Kidderpore DY 1896. Sold c. 1922.

BICESTER Minesweeper, Early 'Hunt' class. Ailsa 8.6.1917. Sold 18.1.1923 Alloa; arr. Charlestown 22.3.1923 for BU.

BICESTER Destroyer, 'Hunt' class Type II. Hawthorn Leslie 5.9.1941. Arr. 22.8.1956 Ward, Grays, for BU.

BICESTER Minehunter, 615 tons, 197 (oa) × 32·8ft. Vosper-Thornycroft 4.6.1985. Tx Greek Navy 31.7.2000 = EUROPE.

BICKERTON (ex-EISELE) Frigate, TE 'Captain' class. Bethlehem, Hingham, 26.7.1943; USN, on Lend-Lease. Sunk 2.8.1944 by VIGILANT after torpedo damage by U.354 in Barents Sea.

BICKINGTON Coastal minesweeper, 'Ton' class. White, Southampton, 3.1953. = CURZON 1954–60. Sold Vickers Dismantling; towed 23.8.1988 Portsmouth to Bilbao for BU.

BIDDEFORD 6th Rate 24, 256bm, 93 × 25ft. Barrett, Harwich, 25.10.1695. Wrecked 12.11.1699 Point Baque.

BIDDEFORD 6th Rate 20, 282bm, 94 × 26·5ft. Deptford DY 14.3.1711. Rebuilt Chatham 1727 as 371bm. Foundered 18.3.1736 off Flamborough Head.

BIDEFORD 6th Rate 24, 433bm, 106 × 31ft. Barnard, Ipswich, 15.4.1740. BU comp. 19.8.1754 Portsmouth.

BIDEFORD 6th Rate 20, 403bm, 105 × 29·5ft. Deptford DY 2.3.1756. Wrecked 30.12.1761 Flamborough Head.

BIDEFORD Minesweeper, Later 'Hunt' class. Ardrossan DD, cancelled 1918.

BIDEFORD Sloop, 1,105 tons, 250 × 34ft, 2–4in. Devonport DY 1.4.1931. Sold 14.7.1949; BU Howells, Milford Haven.

BIENFAISANT 3rd Rate 64, 1,360bm, 159 × 44ft. French, captured 25.7.1758 Louisburg. BU 11.1814.

BIGBURY BAY (ex-LOCH CARLOWAY) Frigate, 'Bay' class. Hall Russell 16.11.1944 (renamed 1944). Sold 11.5.1959 Portuguese Navy = PACHECO PEREIRA. Sold 6.7.1970.

BIHAR Minesweeper (RIN), TE 'Bangor' class. Garden Reach, Calcutta, 7.7.1942. Sold c. 1949.

BILDESTON Coastal minesweeper, 'Ton' class. Doig, Grimsby, 9.6.1952. Sold Vickers Demolition; arr. Bilbao 22.8.1988 for BU.

BILSTHORPE Coastal minesweeper. Thornycroft, ordered 9.9.1950, cancelled.

BIRD Survey sloop. Purch. 4.1764. BU 3.1775 Deptford.

BIRDHAM Inshore minesweeper, 'Ham' class. Taylor 19.9.1955. Sold 1980 Sutton & Smith.

BIRKENHEAD (ex-VULCAN) Iron paddle frigate, 1,400bm, 210 × 37·5ft. Laird 30.12.1845 (renamed 1843). Troopship 1848. Wrecked 26.2.1852 Algoa Bay, South Africa.

BIRKENHEAD (ex-ANTINANARKOS CONDOUROTIS) Light cruiser, 5,235 tons, 430 × 50ft, 10–5·5in, 1–3in. Cammell Laird, ex-Greek, 18.1.1915, purch. 1914. Sold 26.10.1921 Cashmore, Newport.

BIRMINGHAM 2nd class cruiser, 5,440 tons, 430 × 50ft, 9–6 in, 1–3in. Armstrong 7.5.1913. Sold 2.1931 Ward; arr. 12.3.1931 Pembroke Dock for BU.

BIRMINGHAM Cruiser, 9,100 tons, 591·5 (oa) × 61·6ft, 12–6in, 8–4in. Devonport DY 1.9.1936. Arr. 7.9.1960 Ward, Inverkeithing, for BU.

BIRMINGHAM Destroyer, Type 42 Batch 1, 3,150 tons. Cammell Laird 30.7.1973. PO 10.12.1999, towed 20.10.2000 Portsmouth to Spain for BU.

BISHAM Inshore minesweeper, 'Ham' class. Bolson, Poole, 6.3.1954. Burnt accident 29.9.1956 Haslar; wreck sold 8.8.1957.

BITER (Gunboat No 10) Gunvessel 12, 169bm, 75 × 22ft, Wells, Rotherhithe, 13.4.1797. Sold 5.1802.

BITER Gun-brig 12, 177bm, 80 × 22·5ft. Wallis, Blackwall, 27.7.1804. Wrecked 10.11.1805 nr Calais.

BITER Wood screw gunvessel, 301bm, 130 × 22ft. Chatham DY, ordered 26.3.1846, cancelled 22.5.1849.

BITER Wood screw gunboat, 'Dapper' class. Pitcher, Northfleet, 5.5.1855. Coal hulk 24.1.1865; later = T.16. Sold 3.1904 Castle, Woolwich.

BITER (ex-*Sir William Reid*) Tender, 110 tons, 80 × 17ft. War Dept vessel, tx 1905. Sold 5.1923 Dover S. Bkg. Co.

BITER (ex-*Rio Paraw*) Escort carrier, 8,200 tons,

468·5 × 66ft, 3–4 in, 15–20mm, 15 aircraft. Sun SB Co., Chester, 18.12.1940, conv. Tx RN on Lend-Lease 1.4.1942. Tx French Navy 9.4.1945 = DIXMUDE.

BITER Patrol boat, 49 tons, 68·2 (oa) × 19ft. Watercraft 17.10.1985.

BITTERN Sloop 18, 422bm, 110 × 30ft. Adams, Buckler's Hard, 7.4.1796. Sold 30.8.1833 Tibbett & Spence.

BITTERN Brig 12, 484bm, 105 × 34ft. Portsmouth DY 18.4.1840. Sold 20.2.1860 in Hong Kong.

BITTERN Wood screw sloop, 669bm, 160 × 30ft. Devonport DY, LD 17.12.1861, cancelled 16.12.1864.

BITTERN Wood screw gunvessel, 663bm, 805 tons, 170 × 29ft, 1–7in ML, 2–40pdr. Pembroke Dock 20.9.1869. Sold 11.1887 for BU.

BITTERN Destroyer, 360 tons, 210·5 × 21·5ft, 1–12pdr, 5–6pdr, 2–TT. NC&A (Vickers) 1.2.1897. Sunk 4.4.1918 collision SS *Kenilworth* in English Channel.

BITTERN Sloop, 1,190 tons, 266 × 37ft, 6–4in. White, Cowes, 14.7.1937. Sunk 30.4.1940 air attack off Namsos.

BITTERN *See also ENCHANTRESS 1934.*

BITTERSWEET Corvette, 'Flower' class. Marine Industries, Canada, 12.9.1940. Lent RCN until 22.6.1945. Arr. 25.8.1949 Charlestown for BU.

BLACK 8-gun ship. Captured 1653. Sold 1654.

BLACK Sloop, 1,250 tons, 383 × 37·5ft, 6–4in. Yarrow 7.7.1939. Arr. 13.9.1956 Troon for BU.

BLACK BULL (ex-WAPEN VAN EDAW) 36-gun ship, 480bm. Dutch, captured 1665. Recaptured 1666.

BLACK DOG Galliot, 69bm. Dutch, captured 1665. Sunk 1673 foundation Sheerness.

BLACK EAGLE *See FIREBRAND 1831.*

BLACK POSTHORSE Galliot 100bm. Dutch, captured 1665. Given away 1670.

BLACK PRINCE 10-gun ship. Purch. 3.1650. Royalist. Burnt 4.11.1650 by Parliamentarians.

BLACK PRINCE 3rd Rate 74, 1,751bm, 176 × 48·5ft. Woolwich DY 30.3.1816. Prison ship 1848. BU comp. 10.2.1855 Portsmouth.

BLACK PRINCE (ex-INVINCIBLE) Armoured frigate, 6,109bm, 9,210 tons, 380 × 58·5ft, 10–110pdr, 4–70pdr, 26–68pdr (later 4–8in, 22–7in). Napier 27.2.1861 (renamed 1859). TS 1899; = EMERALD 3.1904; = IMPREGNABLE III 6.1910. Sold 21.2.1923.

BLACK PRINCE Armoured cruiser, 13,550 tons, 480 × 73ft, 6–9·2 in, 10–6in, 22–3pdr. Thames Iron Works, Blackwall, 8.11.1904. Sunk 31.5.1916 Battle of Jutland.

BLACK PRINCE Cruiser, 5,770 tons, 512 (oa) × 50·5ft, 8–5·25in, 24 small. Harland & Wolff 27.9.1942. Lent RNZN 1948. BU 8.1962 Japan.

BLACK SNAKE Special Service Vessel (RAN), 80 tons. Savage, Williamstown, 12.1944. Tx North Borneo 11.1945.

BLACK SPREAD-EAGLE (ex-GROENINGEN) 44-gun ship, 367bm. Dutch, captured 1665. Lost in action 1666.

BLACKBURN (ex-BURNHAM) Minesweeper, Later 'Hunt' class. Bow McLachlan 8.1918 (re-named 1918). Sold 17.10.1922 Fryer, Sunderland.

BLACKBURN Aircraft transport, 990 tons, 160 × 30ft, 1–12pdr. Blyth DD 25.3.1944. RNVR drill-ship 1950. Sold 16.7.1968 Pounds, Portsmouth.

BLACKFLY River gunboat, 'Fly' class. Yarrow in sections 1916, launched 22.3.1917 Abadan. Sunk 26.5.1923 collision with bridge at Baghdad while on loan Air Ministry.

BLACKMORE Destroyer, 'Hunt' class Type II. Stephen 2.12.1941. Lent RDanN 1952, = ESBERN SNARE. BU 1966 Sweden.

BLACKMORE KETCH 12-gun ship, 90bm, Chatham DY 1656. Sold 1667.

BLACKMORE LADY 18-gun ship, 180bm. Royalist. Captured 1648 by Parliamentarians. Sold 1650 Lisbon.

BLACKMOREVALE Minesweeper, Early 'Hunt' class. Ardrossan DD 23.3.1917. Sunk 1.5.1918 mine off Montrose.

BLACKPOOL Minesweeper, diesel 'Bangor' class. Harland & Wolff, Govan, 4.7.1940. Sold 1946.

BLACKPOOL Frigate, 2,144 tons, 360 × 41ft, 2–4·5 in, 2–40mm. Thornycroft 14.2.1957. Lent RNZN 7.6.1966. Sold 11.5.1978 for BU.

BLACKWALL 4th Rate 48, 678bm, 131·5 × 34ft. Johnson, Blackwall, 1696. Captured 20.10.1705 by French PROTEE; recaptured 15.3.1808, BU.

BLACKWATER Destroyer, 550 tons, 225 × 23ft, 1–12pdr, 5–6pdr (1907: 4–12pdr), 2–TT. Laird 25.7.1903. Sunk 6.4.1909 collision SS *Hero* off Dungeness.

BLACKWATER Minesweeper, 890 tons (full load), 156·3 (oa) × 34·5ft, 1–40mm. Richards, Great Yarmouth, 29.8.1984. Tx Brazilian Navy 10.7.1998 = VITAL DE OLIVEIRA, later = BENEVENTE.

BLACKWOOD Frigate, DE 'Captain' class. Mare Island 1942 for RN; retained USN = AUSTIN.

BLACKWOOD Frigate, DE 'Captain' class. Boston NY 23.11.1942 on Lend-Lease. Sunk 15.6.1944 by U.764 in English Channel.

BLACKWOOD Frigate, 1,180 tons, 300 × 33ft, 3–40mm. Thornycroft 4.10.1955. BU Troon 11.1976.

BLADE (ex-Z.5) Submarine tender, 263 tons, 195 × 19·5ft, 2—3in. Dutch torpedo boat, cd RN 1.3.1942 (renamed 5.1943). Arr. 10.1945 Troon for BU.

BLAIRMORE Minesweeper (RCN), TE 'Bangor, class. Port Arthur SY 14.5.1942. Sold Marine Industries 3.4.1946; repurch. 7.1951 (Korean crisis). Sold 29.3.1958 Turkish Navy = BEKOZ. BU 1970.

BLAKE 3rd Rate 74, 1,701bm, 172 × 48ft, Deptford DY 23.8.1808. Prison ship 1.1814. Sold 17.10.1816.

BLAKE Screw 2nd Rate 91, 3,716bm, 252 × 57ft. Pembroke Dock, ordered 1860, cancelled 1863.

BLAKE 1st class cruiser, 9,000 tons, 375 × 65ft, 2—9·2in, 10—6in, 16—3pdr. Chatham DY 23.11.1889. Depot ship 8.1908. Sold 9.6.1922 Rees, Llanelly.

BLAKE (ex-TIGER, ex-BLAKE) Cruiser, 9,550 tons, 555·5 (oa) × 64ft, 4—6 in, 6—3in. Fairfield 20.12.1945 (renamed 2.1945); suspended 1946–54, comp. 18.3.1961. Sold 25.8.1982; BU Cairnryan.

BLAKE *See also BOMBAY 1808, TIGER ordered 3.1942.*

BLAKENEY *See BURSLEM 1918.*

BLANCHE 5th Rate 36. French, captured 21.12.1779. Foundered 11.10.1780 hurricane West Indies.

BLANCHE 5th Rate 32, 722bm, 129 × 39·5ft. Calhoun, Bursledon, 10.7.1786. Wrecked 28.9.1799 Texel.

BLANCHE 5th Rate 36, 951bm, 145 × 38ft. Dudman, Deptford, 2.10.1800. Captured 19.7.1805, burnt by French in West Indies.

BLANCHE 5th Rate 46, 1,074bm, 150 × 40·5ft. Chatham DY 26.5.1819. Harbour service 1852. BU 10.1865 Cowes.

BLANCHE Wood screw sloop, 1,268bm, 1,760 tons, 212 × 36ft, 2—7in, 4—64pdr. Chatham DY 17.8.1867. Sold 9.1886 Castle for BU.

BLANCHE 3rd class cruiser, 1,580 tons, 220 × 35ft, 6—4·7in, 4—3pdr. Pembroke Dock 6.9.1885. Sold 11.7.1905 Ward, Preston.

BLANCHE Scout cruiser, 3,360 tons, 385 × 41·5ft, 10—4in. Pembroke Dock 25.11.1909. Sold 27.7.1921 Fryer, Sunderland.

BLANCHE Destroyer, 1,360 tons, 323 (oa) × 32·25ft, 4—4.7 in, 8—TT. Hawthorn Leslie 29.5.1930. Sunk 13.11.1939 mine Thames estuary.

BLANCHE *See also AMFITRITE 1804, BELLONA 1806.*

BLANDFORD 6th Rate 20, 276bm, 94 × 26ft. Woolwich DY 29.10.1711. Foundered 28.3.1719 Bay of Biscay.

BLANDFORD 6th Rate 20, 375bm, 106 × 28·5ft. Deptford 1719. Sold 28.10.1742.

BLANDFORD 6th Rate 24, 455bm, 109 × 31ft.

West, Deptford, 2.10.1741. Sold 12.1763. *Seized by French 13.8.1755 off Brest in retaliation for seizure by British of French ships in Canada in time of peace; later released.*

BLANKNEY Destroyer, 'Hunt' class Type II. John Brown 19.12.1940. Arr. 3.1939 Hughes Bolckow, Blyth, for BU.

BLAST Bomb vessel 4. Johnson, Blackwall, 1695. Pitch boat 1720. BU 1724.

BLAST Bomb vessel 8, 271bm, 91 × 26·5ft. West, Deptford, 28.8.1740. Captured 19.10.1745 by Spanish in West Indies.

BLAST Bomb vessel 8, 303bm, 91·5 × 28ft. Bird, Northam, 27.2.1759. BU 10.1771 Woolwich.

BLAST *See also DRUID 1776.*

BLAXTON Coastal minesweeper, 'Ton' class. Thornycroft 21.6.1955. Tx Eire 1.1.1970 = FOLA. Sold Andover Shipping Co.; arr. Spain 23.3.1988 for BU.

BLAZE Fireship 8, 260bm. Snelgrove, Rotherhithe, 5.3.1691. Expended 22.5.1692 Cherbourg.

BLAZE Fireship 8, 253bm. Purch. 1694. Captured 5.5.1697 by French off Scilly Is.

BLAZE (ex-*America*) Fireship 8, 181bm, 80 × 23·5ft. Purch. 7.9.1739. BU 4.1742 Woolwich.

BLAZE Fireship 10. Purch. 1745. In service 1750.

BLAZE Fireship 10. Purch. 22.7.1756. Sold 28.2.1759 Bombay.

BLAZE Minesweeper, 'Catherine' class. General Engineering, Alameda, 7.5.1943 for RN; retained USN = GLADIATOR.

BLAZER (Gunboat No 12) Gunvessel 12, 159bm, 75 × 22ft. Dudman, Deptford, 14.4.1797. Sold 1.1803.

BLAZER Gun-brig 12, 180bm, 80 × 23ft. Pitcher, Northfleet, 3.5.1804. Sold 15.12.1814.

BLAZER Wood paddle sloop, 527bm, 145 × 28·5ft. Chatham DY 5.1834. Survey ship 1.1843. BU 1853 Portsmouth.

BLAZER Mortar vessel, 117bm, 66 × 20ft, 1—13in mortar. Mare, Blackwall, 5.5.1855. = MV.3 19.10.1855. Tx Thames Conservancy Board 10.1867.

BLAZER Wood screw gunboat, 'Albacore' class. Laird 13.2.1856. = YC.29 (dredger) 6.1868. Sold 4.5.1877 Gibraltar.

BLAZER Iron screw gunboat, 'Ant' class. Portsmouth DY 7.12.1870. Tender 1904; gunboat 8.1914. Sold 19.8.1919 W. Loveridge.

BLAZER Patrol boat, 49 tons, 68·2 (oa) × 19ft. Watercraft 1986, comp. Vosper-Thornycroft 3.1998.

BLEAN Destroyer, 'Hunt' class Type III. Hawthorn Leslie 15.1.1942. Sunk 11.12.1942 by U.443 west of Oran.

BLEASDALE Destroyer, 'Hunt' class Type III. Vickers Armstrong, Tyne, 23.7.1941. Arr. 14.9.1956 Hughes Bolckow, Blyth, for BU.

BLENCATHRA Destroyer, 'Hunt' class, 1,000 tons, 4—4in, Cammell Laird 6.8.1940. Arr. 2.1.1957 Ward, Barrow, for BU.

BLENHEIM 2nd Rate 90, 1,827bm, 176 × 49ft. Woolwich DY 5.7.1761. 3rd Rate 1800. Wrecked 1807 Rodriguez I., Indian Ocean.

BLENHEIM 3rd Rate 74, 1,747bm, 176 × 48.5ft. Deptford DY 31.5.1813. Harbour service 1831; converted to screw 3.1847, 1,822bm, 181 × 48.5ft. BU 1865.

BLENHEIM 1st class cruiser, 9,000 tons, 375 × 65ft, 2—9.2 in, 10—6 in, 16—3pdr. Thames Iron Works, Blackwall, 5.7.1890. Depot ship 1907. Sold 13.7.1926 Ward, Pembroke Dock.

BLENHEIM (ex-*Achilles*) Depot ship, 13,893 tons, 507 × 63ft, 4—4 in, 16 small. Purch. 1940. Arr. 16.3.1948 Ward, Barrow, for BU.

BLENHEIM *Name chosen for ex-Danish CHRISTIAN VII, not used. See also DUCHESS 1679.*

BLESSING Fireship 4, 173bm. Purch. 1666. Lost in action 1666.

BLESSING Fireship 4, 109bm. Purch. 1673. Ex-pended 1673.

BLESSING 'Machine' (fireship), 18bm. Purch. 1694. Sold 1696.

BLICKLING Minesweeper, Later 'Hunt' class. Dundee SB Co, cancelled 1918.

BLIGH (ex-LIDDLE) Frigate, TE 'Captain' class. Bethlehem, Hingham, 31.7.1943; USN, on Lend-Lease. Ret. USN 11.1945.

BLOEMFONTEIN (ex-ROSAMUND) Mine-sweeper (SAN), 'Algerine' class. Renamed 1947. TS 1961. Sold 16.3.1966 The Cape.

BLONDE 5th Rate 32, 704bm, 132 × 34.5ft. French, captured 28.2.1760 by AEOLUS in Irish Sea. Wrecked 21.1.1782 Nantucket Shoal.

BLONDE 5th Rate 32, 678bm, 126 × 35ft. Betts, Mistleythorn, 1783. *Fate unknown. May have been cancelled or renamed.*

BLONDE 5th Rate 32, 682bm, 126.5 × 35ft. Cal-houn, Bursledon, 22.1.1787. Troopship 6.1798. Sold 6.1805.

BLONDE 6th Rate 28, 580bm. French, captured 27.11.1793 by LATONA and PHAETON off Ushant. Sold 1794.

BLONDE 5th Rate 46, 1,103bm, 155 × 40.5ft, 16—32pdr carr., 28—18pdr, 2—9pdr. Deptford DY 12.1.1819. Harbour service 11.1850; = CALYPSO 9.3.1870. Sold 28.2.1895.

BLONDE Wood screw frigate 36, 2,478bm, 240 × 48ft, Woolwich DY, LD 10.9.1860, cancelled 12.12.1863.

BLONDE 3rd class cruiser, 1,580 tons, 220 × 35ft, 6—4.7 in, 4—3pdr. Pembroke Dock 22.10.1889. Sold 11.7.1905; BU Bo'ness.

BLONDE Scout cruiser, 3,350 tons, 385 × 41.5ft, 10—4in. Pembroke Dock 22.7.1910. Sold 6.5.1920 T. C. Pas; BU Holland.

BLONDE *See also HEBE 1782, ISTER 1813, SHAH 1873.*

BLOODHOUND Gun-brig 12, 186bm, 80 × 23ft. Randall, Rotherhithe, 2.4.1801. Sold 18.9.1816.

BLOODHOUND Iron paddle vessel, 378bm, 147 × 23ft. Napier 9.1.1845. BU 1866.

BLOODHOUND Iron screw gunboat, 'Ant' class. Armstrong Mitchell, 22.4.1871. Tender 1905; BDV 1917. Sold 28.6.1921 F. Bevis.

BLOODHOUND Motor torpedo boat, 35 tons, 68 × 19ft, 1—TT. Vosper, Portsmouth, 1937. Wrecked 1.1943 Bincleaves.

BLOODHOUND *See also LONDON.*

BLOOM Tender 14. Purch. 1795. Captured 24.2.1797 by French off Holyhead.

BLOSSOM Sloop 18, 427bm, 108.5 × 30ft. Guill-aume, Northam, 10.12.1806. Survey ship 1825; hulk 1.1833. BU 8.1848.

BLOSSOM (ex-CAREFUL) Wood screw gunboat, 'Cheerful' class. Laird 21.4.1856 (renamed 1855). BU 11.1864 Haslar.

BLOXHAM (ex-BRIXHAM) Minesweeper, Later 'Hunt' class. Ayrshire Co. 11.9.1919 (renamed 1918). Sold incomp. 23.10.1923 Lithgow, Port Glasgow.

BLUEBELL Sloop, 'Acacia' class. Scott 24.7.1915. Sold 26.5.1930 Cashmore, Newport.

BLUEBELL Corvette, 'Flower' class. Fleming & Ferguson 24.4.1940. Sunk 17.2.1945 by U.711 in Barents Sea.

BLUETHROAT Minelayer (RCN), 785 tons. G. T. Davie 15.9.1955.

BLYTH Minesweeper, 'TE 'Bangor' class. Blyth SB 2.9.1940. Sold 25.5.1948 = *Radbourne*. BU 11.1952.

BLYTH Minehunter, 'Sandown' class, Vosper-Thornycroft 4.7.2000.

BOADICEA 5th Rate 38, 1,052bm, 148.5 × 40.5ft. Adams, Buckler's Hard, 12.4.1797. Harbour service 1854. BU 5.1838.

BOADICEA Wood screw frigate 51, 3,353bm, 270 × 52.5ft. Chatham DY, ordered 1861, cancelled 1863.

BOADICEA Iron screw corvette, 4,140 tons, 280 × 45ft, 14—7in MLR, 2—64pdr. Portsmouth DY 16.10.1875. Sold 6.1.1905 Ward, Preston.

BOADICEA Scout cruiser, 3,300 tons, 385 × 41ft, 6—4in. Pembroke Dock 14.5.1908. Harbour service 1.1921. Sold 13.7.1926 Alloa, Rosyth. *Was to have been renamed POMONE 1921.*

BOADICEA Destroyer, 1,360 tons, 323 (oa) × 32·25ft, 4—4·7in, 8—TT. Hawthorn Leslie 23.9.1930. Sunk 13.6.1944 air attack off Portland.

BODENHAM Inshore minesweeper, 'Ham' class. Brooke, Lowestoft, 21.8.1952. HO Saudi Arabia 4.3.1968; deleted 1984.

BODIAM CASTLE Corvette, 'Castle' class. Collingwood SY, cancelled 12.1943.

BOGAM Frigate (RAN), 'River' class. Newcastle, NSW, cancelled 12.6.1944.

BOLD Gunvessel 14, 179bm, 80 × 23ft, 2—32pdr carr., 10—18pdr carr., 2—8in howitzers. Perry & Wells, Blackwall, 16.4.1801. BU 4.1811.

BOLD Gun-brig 12, 182bm, 84·5 × 22ft. Tyson & Blake, Bursledon, 26.6.1812. Wrecked 27.9.1813 Prince Edward I.

BOLD *See also MANLY 1804.*

BOLEBROKE Destroyer, 'Hunt' class Type III. Swan Hunter 5.11.1941. Lent Greek Navy 5.1942–12.11.1959 = PINDOS. BU Greece 1960.

BOLTON Yacht 6, 42bm, 53 × 14·5ft. Portsmouth DY 19.7.1709. BU 1817 Portsmouth.

BOLTON Gun-brig 12. In service 1775. Captured 5.4.1776 by Americans.

BOLTON (ex-BEAUMARIS) Minesweeper, Later 'Hunt' class. Renamed 1918, cancelled 1918.

BOLTON CASTLE Corvette, 'Castle' class. Collingwood SY, cancelled 12.1943.

BOMBARD Patrol boat (RAN), 146 tons, 107·5 (oa) × 20ft, 1—40mm. Walker 6.7.1968. Sold 12.9.1983 Indonesia = SIRIBUA.

BOMBAY 24-gun ship (Indian), 363bm, 90 × 30ft. Bombay DY 1739. Burnt 29.7.1789 accident Bombay.

BOMBAY Storeship. In service 1790.

BOMBAY 5th Rate 38 (Indian), 672bm, 130 × 35ft, 14—24pdr carr., 24—18pdr, 2—9pdr. Bombay DY 1793, purch. 1805. = CEYLON 1.7.1808. Sold 4.7.1857.

BOMBAY 3rd Rate 74, 1,701bm, 174 × 48ft. Deptford DY 28.3.1808. = BLAKE 28.4.1819; harbour service 1828. BU 12.1855 Portsmouth,

BOMBAY 2nd Rate 84, 2,279bm, 196 × 52ft. Bombay DY 17.2.1828. Comp. 5.1861 as screw ship 81, 782bm. Burnt 14.12.1864 accident off Montevideo.

BOMBAY Minesweeper (RIN), 'Bathurst' class. Mort's Dock, Sydney, 6.12.1941. Sold 1960.

BOMBAY CASTLE 3rd Rate 74, 1,628bm, 168 × 47ft. Perry, Blackwall, 14.6.1782. Wrecked 21.12.1796 off R. Tagus. *Was to have been renamed BOMBAY 1.1780.*

BONAVENTURE Warship. Built 1489. Gone by 1509.

BONAVENTURE (EDWARD BONAVENTURE) Ship, 160bm. Built 1551. Wrecked 11.1556 nr Aberdeen.

BONAVENTURE (ELIZABETH BONAVENTURE) 47-gun ship, 300/550bm, 2—60pdr, 2—34pdr, 11—18pdr, 14—9pdr, 18 small. Purch. 1567. In service 1599.

BONAVENTURE 32-gun ship, 410/500bm. Deptford 1621. Lost in action 1653.

BONAVENTURE 4th Rate 50, 703bm, 130 × 35ft. Chatham DY 1711. = ARGYLL 2.1.1715; rebuilt 1722 as 763bm. Sunk 23.11.1748 breakwater Harwich.

BONAVENTURE 2nd class cruiser, 4,360 tons, 320 × 49·5ft, 2—6 in, 8—4·7 in, 8—6pdr. Devonport DY 2.12.1892. Depot ship 1910. Sold 12.4.1920 Forth S. Bkg Co.; arr. Bo'ness 10.1920 for BU.

BONAVENTURE Cruiser, 5,450 tons, 512 (oa) × 50·5ft, 10—5·25in. Scotts 19.4.1939. Sunk 31.3.1941 by Italian submarine AMBRA off Crete.

BONAVENTURE Depot ship, 9,166 tons, 457 × 63ft, 2—4 in, 12—20mm. Greenock DY Co. 27.10.1942, conv. Scotts. Sold 1948.

BONAVENTURE *See also PRESIDENT 1650, POWERFUL 1945.*

BONAVOLIA (ex-ELLYNOR) Galley, 180bm. Presented by France 10.1562 (renamed 1584). Sold 1600.

BONETTA Sloop 4, 57bm. Woolwich 1673. Sold 1687.

BONETTA Sloop 4, 66bm. Deptford 1699. Sold 10.4.1712.

BONETTA Sloop. In service 1718. Sold 28.8.1719.

BONETTA Sloop 3, 66bm. 56 × 17ft. Deptford DY 18.4.1721. Sold 12.1731.

BONETTA Sloop 14, 201bm, 81 × 24ft. Woolwich DY 24.8.1732. Foundered 20.10.1744 off Jamaica.

BONETTA Sloop 10, 227bm. 86·5 × 24·5ft. Bird, Rotherhithe, 4.2.1756. BU 1.11.1776.

BONETTA Sloop 14, 307bm, 97 × 27ft. Perry, Blackwall, 29.4.1779. BU 10.1797. *In French hands 19.10.1781–4.1.1782.*

BONETTA (ex-*Roebuck*) Sloop 18, 272bm. Purch. 11.1781. = SWAN 2.3.1782. Capsized 4.8.1782 off Waterford.

BONETTA Brig-sloop 18, 384bm, 103 × 27ft. French, captured 1797. Wrecked 25.10.1801 coast of Cuba.

BONETTA Sloop 18, 208bm, 86 × 24ft. Purch. 1803. Sold 20.9.1810.

BONETTA Brigantine 3, 319bm, 91 × 29·5ft, 3—32pdr. Sheerness DY 5.4.1836. BU comp. 23.4.1861 Deptford.

BONETTA Iron screw gunboat, 'Ant' class. Rennie 20.5.1871. Sold 12.1.1909 = *Disperser* (salvage vessel). Lost 4.1940.

BONETTA Destroyer, 440 tons, 215 × 21ft, 3—12pdr, 2—TT. Palmer 14.1.1907, spec., accepted 3.1909. Sold 7.6.1920 Ward, Hayle; BU Briton Ferry.

BONITA Dockyard cutter, 78bm, purch. 8.1864, sold 11.87.

BONITO Iron screw gunboat (Australian), 120 tons, 1—64pdr MLR. Built 1884.

BONNE CITOYENNE 6th Rate 20, 511bm, 120 × 31ft, 18—32pdr carr., 2—9pdr. French, captured 10.3.1796 by PHAETON off Cape Finisterre. Sold 3.2.1819 J. Crista

BOOMERANG *See WHITING 1889.*

BOOTLE (ex-BUCKIE) Minesweeper, Later 'Hunt' class. Bow McLachlan 11.6.1918 (renamed 1918). Sold 21.2.1923 Alloa S. Bkg Co.; arr. Charlestown 18.4.1923 for BU.

BOOTLE Minesweeper, turbine 'Bangor' class. Ailsa 23.10.1941. Sold 1.1.1948; arr. 6.1949 Charlestown for BU.

BORAGE Corvette, 'Flower' class. G. Brown 22.11.1941. Tx Ireland = MACHA 1947. BU Haulbowline 1.1971.

BORDER Destroyer, 'Hunt' class Type III. Swan Hunter 3.2.1942. Lent Greek Navy 5.1942 = ADRIAS; mined, CTL 22.10.1943 Mediterranean. BU 11.1945 King, Gateshead.

BORDER CITIES Minesweeper (RCN), 'Algerine' class. Port Arthur 3.5.1943. Sold 1947.

BOREAS 6th Rate 28 (fir-built), 587bm, 118 × 34ft. Woolwich DY 29.7.1757. Sold 29.6.1770, useless.

BOREAS 6th Rate 28, 626bm, 125 × 34ft. Blaydes & Hodgson, Hull, 23.8.1774. Slop ship 1797. Sold 5.1802.

BOREAS 6th Rate 22, 533bm, 119 × 31·5ft. Stone, Yarmouth, 19.4.1806. Wrecked 7.12.1807 Guernsey.

BOREAS Destroyer, 1,360 tons, 323 (oa) × 32·25ft, 4—4·7in, 8—TT. Palmer, Hebburn, 11.6.1930. Lent 4.1944—9.1951 Greek Navy = SALAMIS. Sold 23.11.1951; arr. Rosyth 15.4.1952 for BU.

BOREAS *Name chosen for ex-Danish HARFRUEN, not used.*

BOREHAM Inshore minesweeper, 'Ham' class. Brooke 21.10.1952. Tx Malaysia = JERONG 5.3.1966. BU 1970.

BORER Gunvessel 14, 148bm, 75 × 21ft, 2—32pdr carr., 12—18pdr carr. Randall, Rotherhithe, 17.5.1794. Sold 1810 Heligoland.

BORER Gun-brig 12, 184bm, 85 × 22ft. Tyson & Blake, Bursledon, 27.7.1812. Brig-sloop 14 in 1813. Sold 12.10.1815.

BOSCAWEN Cutter 4, 48bm, 43 × 17ft. Purch. 2.1763. Sold 4.5.1773.

BOSCAWEN 2nd Rate 80, 2,048bm, 187·5 × 51ft. Woolwich DY, LD 1811, cancelled.

BOSCAWEN 3rd Rate 70, 2,212bm, 180 × 54ft. Woolwich DY 3.4.1844. = WELLESLEY No 2 (TS) 21.3.1874. Damaged by fire 3.1914 R. Tyne, BU Blyth. *18 years on slip.*

BOSCAWEN *For training ships with this name, see TRAFALGAR 1841, MINOTAUR 1863, AGINCOURT 1865.*

BOSSINGTON (ex-EMBLETON) Coastal minesweeper, 'Ton' class. Thornycroft 2.12.1955 (renamed 1955). Sold 11.1988, towed 25.2.1989 Portsmouth to Bruges for BU.

BOSTON 5th Rate 32. Built America 1692, pre-sented by citizens of Boston 1694. Captured 4.1.1695 by French in Atlantic.

BOSTON 6th Rate 24, 561bm, 119 × 33ft. Hallowell, Boston, 3.5.1748. BU 2.1752.

BOSTON 5th Rate 32, 676bm, 127·5 × 34·5ft. Inwood, Rotherhithe, 11.5.1762. BU 5.1811.

BOSTON Schooner 6 (Canadian lakes). Navy Island 1764. Burnt 1768.

BOSTON Minesweeper, turbine 'Bangor' class. Ailsa 30.12.1940. Sold 1.1.1948; BU Charlestown.

BOSTON *See also AMERICA 1749.*

BOTHA (ex-ALMIRANTE WILLIAMS) Destroyer leader, 1,742 tons, 320 × 32·5ft, 6—4in, 3—TT. White, Cowes, 2.12.1914; Chilean, purch. 8.1914. Resold 5.1920 Chile = ALMIRANTE WILLIAMS.

BOTTISHAM Inshore minesweeper, 'Ham' class. Ailsa 16.2.1953. Tx Air Ministry 11.1.1966 = No 5001. Sold 11.1973 Gomba Marina.

BOUCLIER Destroyer, 610 tons, 245·5 × 26ft, 2—3·9in. 2—TT. French torpedo boat, seized 3.7.1940 Plymouth. Dutch crew 9.1940; Free French crew 2.1941; TS 1941; ret. French Navy 1946.

BOULOGNE (ex-*Boullogne*) 5th Rate 32, 657bm, 133·5 × 33·5ft. French East Indiaman, captured 3.1762 by VENUS. Storeship 1776. Hulked as part of wharf 7.1784 Halifax, NS.

BOULSTON Coastal minesweeper, 'Ton' class. Richards, Lowestoft, 5.10.1952. = WARSASH 1961. Sold 28.10.1974 H. K. Vickers; BU Hayle.

BOUNCER (Gunboat No 8) Gunvessel 12, 160bm, 75 × 22ft. Wells, Rotherhithe, 4.1797. Sold 4.1802.

BOUNCER Gun-brig 12, 177bm, 80 × 22·5ft. Rowe,

Newcastle, 11.8.1804. Stranded 2.1805 nr Dieppe, captured by French = L'ECUREUIL until 1814.

BOUNCER Wood screw gunboat, 'Albacore' class. Mare, Blackwall, 23.2.1856. Sold 1.2.1871 in Hong Kong.

BOUNCER Steel screw gunboat, 265 tons, 87·5 × 26ft, 1–10 in MLR. Pembroke Dock 15.3.1881. Sold 4.4.1905.

BOUNCER (ex-*Sir Richard Fletcher*) Tender, 100 tons, 77 × 15·5ft. War Dept vessel, tx 1905. Sold 14.5.1920. F. Bevis.

BOUNTIFUL Storeship 46, 778bm, 143·5 × 34·5ft. Purch. 5.2.1782. Sold 1784 Bombay.

BOUNTY (ex-*Bethia*) Armed ship 4, 215bm, 85 × 24·5ft, 4–4pdr. Purch. 23.5.1787. Taken by mutineers 28.4.1789 Otaheite; burnt 1791.

BOURBONNAISE (ex-CAROLINE) 5th Rate 38, 1,078bm, 151·5 × 40ft. French, captured by squadron 16.9.1809 Île Bourbon, Réunion. BU 4.1817.

BOURDELAIS 6th Rate 24, 625bm. French privateer, captured 11.10.1799 off coast of Ireland. BU 8.1804.

BOWEN Minesweeper (RAN), 'Bathurst' class. Walker, Maryborough, 28.7.1942. Sold 18.5.1956 for BU.

BOWES CASTLE Corvette, 'Castle' class. Kingston SY, cancelled 12.1943.

BOWMANVILLE (ex-NUNNEY CASTLE) Corvette (RCN), 'Castle' class. Pickersgill 26.1.1944 (renamed 1943). Sold 5.9.1946 = *Yuan Pei*.

BOWMANVILLE See also COQUETTE 1943.

BOXER (Gunboat No 9) Gunvessel 12, 161bm, 75·5 × 22ft, Wells, Rotherhithe, 11.4.1797. Sold 7.1809.

BOXER Gun-brig 12, 182bm, 84·5 × 22ft. Hobbs, Redbridge, 25.7.1812. Captured 5.9.1813 by American ENTERPRISE off Portland, Maine.

BOXER (ex-*Ivanhoe*) Paddle packet, 159bm, 101 × 19ft. GPO vessel, tx 1.4.1837. Sold c. 27.5.1841 for BU.

BOXER Wood screw gunvessel, 301bm, 130 × 22ft. Chatham DY, LD 5.1846, cancelled 6.1847.

BOXER Wood screw gunboat, 'Dapper' class. Pitcher, Northfleet, 7.4.1855. BU 10.1865 Malta.

BOXER Composite screw gunvessel, 465bm, 605 tons, 155 × 25ft, 1–7in ML, 1–64pdr ML, 2–20pdr. Deptford DY 25.1.1868. Sold 6.1887 for BU.

BOXER Destroyer, 280 tons, 201·5 × 19ft, 1–12pdr, 5–6pdr, 2–TT. Thornycroft, Chiswick, 28.11.1894. Sunk 8.2.1918 collision SS *St Patrick* in English Channel.

BOXER Tank landing ship, 3,620 tons, 390 × 49ft, 8–20mm. Harland & Wolff 12.12.1942. Fighter-

direction ship 1944; radar training vessel 1947. Sold 1.12.1958 Ward, Barrow.

BOXER Frigate, 4,100 tons, 480·5 (oa) × 48·4ft, Exocet, Seawolf, helo, 6–TT. Yarrow 17.6.1981. PO 4.8.1999; allocated target 2003.

BOYNE 2nd Rate 80, 1,160bm, 157 × 41·5ft. Deptford DY 21.5.1692. Rebuilt Blackwall 1708, 1,301bm; rebuilt Deptford 1739, 1,390bm; prison ship 1750. BU comp. 3.1763 Portsmouth.

BOYNE 3rd Rate 70, 1,426bm, 162 × 44·5ft. Plymouth DY 31.5.1766. BU 5.1783.

BOYNE 2nd Rate 98, 2,010bm, 182 × 50ft. Woolwich DY 27.6.1790. Burnt 1.5.1795 accident Spithead.

BOYNE 2nd Rate 98, 2,155bm, 186 × 52ft. Portsmouth DY 3.7.1810. = EXCELLENT (gunnery ship) 1.12.1834; = QUEEN CHARLOTTE 22.11.1859. BU comp. 25.6.1861 Portsmouth.

BOYNE Destroyer, 545 tons, 222 × 23·5ft, 1–12pdr, 5–6pdr (1907: 4–12pdr), 2–TT. Hawthorn 12.9.1904. Sold 30.8.1919 Hayes, Porthcawl.

BRAAK Brig-sloop 14, 255bm. Dutch, seized 2.1795 by FORTUNE at Falmouth. Capsized 23.5.1798 Delaware R.

BRAAK (ex-MINERVA) 6th Rate 24, 613bm, 116·5 × 34·5ft. Dutch, captured 28.8.1799 off Texel. Sold 1802.

BRAAVE 5th Rate 40, 883bm. Dutch, captured 17.8.1796 Saldanha Bay. Harbour service 1811. Sold 20.7.1825.

BRADFIELD Minesweeper, Later 'Hunt' class. Ayrshire Co. 14.5.1919. Sold 10.1920 = *Champavati*.

BRADFORD 24-gun ship, 294bm. Chatham DY 1658. = SUCCESS 1660. Wrecked 1680.

BRADFORD (ex-McLANAHAN) Destroyer, 1,190 tons, 311 × 31ft, 3–4in, 1–3in, 6–TT. USN, cd RN 8.10.1940. Arr. 8.1946 Troon for BU.

BRAID Frigate, 'River' class. Simons 30.11.1943. Tx French Navy 21.1.1944 = L'AVENTURE.

BRAITHWAITE (ex-STRAUB) Frigate, TE 'Captain' class. Bethlehem, Hingham, 31.7.1943 on Lend-Lease. Ret. USN 17.12.1945.

BRAKEL 4th Rate 54, 1,010bm. Dutch, seized 4.3.1796 Plymouth. Troopship 6.1799. Sold 29.9.1814.

BRAMBER CASTLE Corvette, 'Castle' class. Collingwood SY, cancelled 12.1943.

BRAMBLE 14-gun ship, 125bm. Ostend privateer, captured 1656. Fireship 1665. Expended against Dutch 6.1667 R. Medway.

BRAMBLE Schooner 10, 150bm, 79 × 22ft. Bermuda 1808. Sold 14.12.1815.

BRAMBLE Cutter 10, 161bm, 71 × 23·5ft. Plymouth DY 8.4.1822. Survey vessel 4.1842; lent Colonial Dept 31.5.1853 as diving-bell vessel Sydney. Sold 23.12.1876 as lightship.

BRAMBLE Wood screw gunboat, 'Britomart' class. Haslar, LD 1861, cancelled 12.12.1863.

BRAMBLE 1st class gunboat, 715 tons, 165 × 29ft, 6—4in. Harland & Wolff 11.12.1886. = COCKATRICE 6.1896. Sold 3.4.1906 Chatham.

BRAMBLE 1st class gunboat, 710 tons, 180 × 33ft, 2—4in, 4—12pdr. Potter, Liverpool, 26.11.1898. Sold 26.1.1920 Bombay,

BRAMBLE Minesweeper, 875 tons, 230 × 33.5ft, 2—4in. Devonport DY 12.7.1938. Sunk 31.12.1942 by German destroyers in Barents Sea.

BRAMBLE Minesweeper, 'Algerine' class. Lobnitz 26.1.1945. Arr. 8.1961 King, Gateshead, for BU.

BRAMHAM Destroyer, 'Hunt' class Type II. Stephen 29.1.1942. Lent Greek Navy 3.1943–12.11.1959 = THEMISTOKLIS (THERMISTOCLES). BU 1960 Greece.

BRAMPTON Corvette (RCN), Modified 'Flower' class. Morton, cancelled 12.1943.

BRANDON Corvette (RCN), 'Flower' class. Davie SB 29.4.1941. Sold 1946.

BRANDON MCDV (RCN), 'Kingston' class, 962 tons, 181·4 (oa) × 37·1ft, 1—40mm, Halifax SY 3.9.1998.

BRANLEBAS Destroyer, 610 tons, 245·5 × 26ft, 2—3·9in, 2—TT. French torpedo boat, seized 3.7.1940 Portsmouth. Free French crew 10.1940. Foundered 14.12.1940 gale English Channel.

BRANTFORD Corvette (RCN), 'Flower' class. Midland SY 6.9.1941. Sold 1945 = *Olympic Arrow*.

BRANTINGHAM Inshore minesweeper, 'Ham' class. Ailsa 4.12.1953. Tx Malaysia = TEMASEK 1959. BU 1966.

BRAVE Ship. Hired 1588.

BRAVE Xebec, 154bm, 76 × 22·5ft. Captured 1747. Sold 1748.

BRAVE (ex-FORMIDABLE) 3rd Rate 80, 2,249bm, 194·5 × 51·5ft, 32—32pdr, 18—32pdr carr., 30—18pdr, 4—12pdr. French, captured 4.11.1805 in action off coast of Spain. Prison ship 1.1808; powder hulk 10.1814. Sold 4.1816 for BU Plymouth.

BRAVE 3rd Rate 74, 1,890bm. French, captured 6.2.1806 San Domingo. Foundered 12.4.1806 passage Jamaica to Britain.

BRAVE Wood screw gunboat, 'Albacore' class. Laird 11.2.1856. BU 3.1869 Portsmouth.

BRAVE Minesweeper, 'Algerine' class. Blyth DD 4.2.1943. RNVR drillship SATELLITE 9.1951. Arr. 25.11.1958 Clayton & Davie for BU.

BRAVE Frigate, 4,100 tons, 480·5 (oa) × 48·4ft, Exocet, Seawolf, helo, 6—TT. Yarrow 19.11.1983. PO 22.3.1999; allocated target 2003.

BRAVE *Name originally chosen for aircraft carrier WARRIOR 1944 (q.v.).*

BRAVO Floating battery 16, 360bm, 96 × 31ft, 16—18pdr. Woolwich DY 31.5.1794. Deleted 1803.

BRAYFORD Seaward defence boat, 'Ford' class. Inglis 19.2.1954. Tx SAN 30.8.1954 = GELDERLAND. Expended 21.12.1988 target.

BRAZEN Cutter 14, 123bm, 58 × 22ft. Purch. 6.1781. Sold 10.1799.

BRAZEN Sloop 18, 420bm, 110 × 29ft. Portsmouth DY, ordered 6.11.1794, cancelled 1799.

BRAZEN Sloop 18, 363bm, 105 × 28ft. French privateer L'INVINCIBLE GENERAL BUONAPARTE, captured 4.1799 by BOADICEA. Wrecked 26.1.1800 nr Brighton.

BRAZEN 6th Rate 26, 422bm, 110 × 29·5ft. Portsmouth DY 26.5.1808. Floating chapel 1827. BU 7.1848.

BRAZEN Wood screw gunboat, 'Albacore' class. Laird 8.3.1856. BU 8.1864.

BRAZEN Destroyer, 390 tons, 218 × 20ft, 7—12pdr, 5—6pdr, 2—TT. Thomson 3.7.1896. Sold 4.11.1919 J. H. Lee.

BRAZEN Destroyer, 1,360 tons, 323 (oa) × 32·25ft, 4—4·7in, 8—TT. Palmer 25.7.1930. Sunk 20.7.1940 air attack off Dover.

BRAZEN Frigate, 3,556 tons, 430 (oa) × 48·5ft, Exocet, Seawolf, helo, 6—TT. Yarrow 4.3.1980. Tx Brazilian Navy 31.8.1996 = BOSISIO.

BREAM Schooner 4, 80bm, 56 × 18ft, 4—12pdr carr. Bermuda 5.1807. Sold c. 1816.

BREARLEY Inshore minehunter, 'Ley' class. White, Cowes, 16.6.1953. Sold 13.5.1971 Pounds, yacht.

BRECON Destroyer, 1,175 tons, 296 (oa) × 33·3ft, 6—4in, 3—TT. Thornycroft 27.6.1942. Arr. 17.9.1962 Shipbreaking Industries, Faslane, for BU.

BRECON Minehunter, 615 tons. Vosper-Thornycroft 21.6.1978.

BRECONSHIRE Store carrier, 8,952 tons, 482 × 56ft. Taikoo DY 1939, purch. Sunk 27.3.1942 air attack Malta. Wreck BU 1954 Italy.

BREDAH 3rd Rate 70, 1,055bm, 151·5 × 40ft, 26—32pdr, 26—12pdr,4—3pdr, 14 light. Betts, Harwich, 1679. Blown up 12.10.1690 accident Cork.

BREDAH 3rd Rate 70, 1,094bm, 151 × 40·5ft. Woolwich DY 23.4.1692. BU comp. 7.10.1730 Portsmouth.

BREDAH *See also NANTWICH 1654, PRINCE OF ORANGE 1734.*

BRENCHLEY Inshore minehunter, 'Ley' class. Saunders-Roe, Anglesey, 19.7.1954. Sold 11.1.1966.

BRERETON Coastal minesweeper, 'Ton' class. Richards, Lowestoft, 14.5.1953. = ST DAVID 1954; = BRERETON 11.1961. Towed Bruges 28.11.1992 for BU.

BREVDRAGEREN Brig-sloop 12, 182bm, 83 × 23ft, 10–18pdr carr., 2–6pdr. Danish, captured 7.9.1807 Battle of Copenhagen. Prison ship 7.1818; Army depot 1820. Sold 13.10.1825 J. Cristall. *Was to have been renamed COCKATRICE 1812.*

BRIAR (ex-PETER) 16-gun ship, 252bm. Royalist, captured 1651. Fireship 1666; given away 1667.

BRIDGEWATER 58-gun ship, 743bm. Deptford DY 1654. = ANNE 1660. Blown up 2.12.1673 Sheerness.

BRIDGEWATER 5th Rate 32, 411bm, 110·5 × 29ft. Sheerness DY 1698. Fireship 1.1727; rebuilt 1729 as 6th Rate. BU 4.1738.

BRIDGEWATER 6th Rate 24, 436bm, 106 × 30·5ft. Pearson, Lynn, 11.12.1740. Wrecked 18.9.1743 off Newfoundland.

BRIDGEWATER 6th Rate 24, 500bm, 112 × 30ft. Rowcliffe, Southampton, 13.10.1744. Run ashore 28.4.1758 Cuddalore, burnt to avoid capture by French.

BRIDGEWATER Sloop, 1,045 tons, 250 × 34ft, 2–4in. Hawthorn Leslie 14.9.1928. Sold 25.5.1947 Howells, Gelleswick Bay, for BU.

BRIDGNORTH CASTLE Corvette, 'Castle' class. Collingwood SY, cancelled 12.1943.

BRIDLINGTON Minesweeper, diesel 'Bangor' class. Denny 29.2.1940. Tx Air Ministry 1946. BU 2.1960 Plymouth.

BRIDLINGTON *See also GOOLE 1919.*

BRIDPORT Minesweeper, diesel 'Bangor' class. Denny 29.2.1940. Tx Air Ministry 1946. BU 5.1959 Plymouth.

BRIDPORT Minehunter, 'Sandown' class. Vosper-Thornycroft 30.7.1992. PO 31.3.2003.

BRIGADIER *See WORTHING 1928.*

BRIGANDINE Ship, 406bm. Dover 1545. Captured 10.1562 by French.

BRIGANTINE Ship, 90bm. Built 1583. Listed 1588.

BRIGHAM Inshore minesweeper, 'Ham' class. Berthon Boat Co. 17.1.1953. Sold 10.12.1968 Pounds, yacht.

BRIGHTON Tender 14. Purch. 1795. Captured 24.2.1797 by French off Holyhead.

BRIGHTON (ex-COWELL) Destroyer, 1,060 tons, 309 × 30·5ft, 3–4in, 1–3in, 6–TT. USN, cd RN 23.9.1940. Target ship 11.1942; lent 16.7.1944–

28.2.1949 Soviet Navy = ZHARKI. Sold 5.4.1949; BU McLellan, Bo'ness.

BRIGHTON Frigate, 'Rothesay' class, 2,380 tons, 370 (oa) × 41ft, 2–4·5in, 1–40mm (later Seacat, helo). Yarrow 30.10.1959. Sold Dean Marine; arr. R. Medway 16.9.1985 for BU.

BRILLIANT Sloop. In service 1729.

BRILLIANT 5th Rate 36, 718bm, 128·5 × 36ft. Plymouth DY 27.10.1757. Sold 1.11.1776.

BRILLIANT 6th Rate 28, 600bm, 120·5 × 34ft. Adams, Buckler's Hard, 13.7.1779. BU 11.1811 Portsmouth.

BRILLIANT 5th Rate 36, 954bm, 146 × 38·5ft. Lungley, Deptford, 28.12.1814. Reduced to 22 guns 1843; RNR TS 18.1959, = BRITON 8.11.1889. Sold 12.5.1908 Forth S. Bkg Co., Bo'ness.

BRILLIANT 2nd class cruiser, 3,600 tons, 300 × 44ft, 2–6in, 6–4·7in, 8–6pdr. Sheerness DY 24.6.1891. Sunk 23.4.1918 blockship Ostend.

BRILLIANT Destroyer, 1,360 tons, 323 (oa) × 32·25ft, 4–4·7in, 8–TT. Swan Hunter 9.10.1930. Sold 18.8.1947; BU Troon.

BRILLIANT Frigate, 3,556 tons, 430 (oa) × 48·5ft, Exocet, Seawolf, helo, 6–TT. Yarrow 15.12.1978. Tx Brazilian Navy 31.8.1996 = DODSWORTH.

BRILLIANT *See also ORONTES 1813.*

BRILLIANT-PRIZE Sloop 6, 60bm. Captured 1696. Sold 1698.

BRINKLEY Inshore minehunter, 'Ley' class. Saunders-Roe 14.9.1954. Sold 10.1.1966.

BRINTON Coastal minesweeper, 'Ton' class. Cook, Welton & Gemmell 8.8.1952. Sold Pounds, Portsmouth, 12.1997.

BRISBANE Light cruiser (RAN), 5,400 tons, 430 × 50ft, 8–6in, 1–3in. Cockatoo DY 30.9.1915. Sold 16.6.1936; BU Ward, Briton Ferry.

BRISBANE GM destroyer (RAN), Modified 'Charles F. Adams' class, 3,370 tons, 440·8 (oa) × 47·1ft, 2–5in, Harpoon SSM, GDC Pomona SAM, 6–TT. Defoe, Bay City, 5.5.1966. PO 19.10.2001.

BRISEIS Brig-sloop 10, 'Cherokee' class, 239bm. King, Upnor, 19.5.1808. Wrecked 5.11.1816 off Cuba.

BRISEIS Brig-sloop 6, 'Cherokee' class, 230bm. Deptford DY 3.7.1829. Comp. as packet brig. Wrecked 1.1838 passage Falmouth to Halifax.

BRISK Sloop 16, 340bm, 101 × 28ft. Jacobs, Sandgate, 6.5.1784. Sold 5.1805.

BRISK Sloop 18, 371bm, 106 × 28ft. Dartmouth 4.1805. Sold 15.2.1816.

BRISK Brig-sloop 10, 'Cherokee' class, 237bm. Chatham DY 10.2.1819. Sold 7.11.1843 J. Levy, Rochester.

BRISK Wood screw sloop, 1,087bm, 190·5 × 35ft, 2—68pdr, 12—32pdr. Woolwich DY 2.6.1851. Sold 31.1.1870 mercantile.

BRISK Torpedo cruiser, 1,770 tons, 225 × 36ft, 6—6in, 8—3pdr, 1—TT. Thomson 8.4.1886. Sold 15.5.1906 Ward, Preston.

BRISK Destroyer, 780 tons, 246 × 25ft, 2—4in, 2—12pdr, 2—TT. John Brown 20.9.1910. Sold 11.1921 J. Distin, Devonport.

BRISSENDEN Destroyer, 1,175 tons, 296 (oa) × 33·3ft, 6—4in, 3—TT. Thornycroft 15.9.1942. Arr. 3.3.1965 Arnott Young, Dalmuir, for BU.

BRISTOL 48-gun ship, 532bm, 24—18pdr, 6—9pdr, 8—6pdr, 10 small. Portsmouth DY 1653. Rebuilt Deptford 1693 as 670bm. Captured 12.4.1709 by French; recaptured, sunk 25.4.1709 English Channel.

BRISTOL 4th Rate 54, 703bm, 130 × 35ft. Plymouth DY 8.5.1711. Rebuilt Woolwich 1746 as 1,021bm, 50 guns. BU 10.1768 Plymouth.

BRISTOL 4th Rate 30, 1,049bm, 146 × 41ft. Sheerness DY 25.10.1775. Prison ship 1794. BU 6.1810.

BRISTOL Wood screw frigate, 3,027bm, 4,020 tons, 250 × 52ft. Woolwich DY 12.2.1861. Sold 7.1883 Castle for BU.

BRISTOL 2nd class cruiser, 4,820 tons, 430 × 47ft, 2—6in, 10—4in. John Brown 23.2.1910. Sold 9.5.1921 Ward, Hayle.

BRISTOL Destroyer, 6,100 tons, 507 (oa) × 55ft, 1—4·5in, Sea Dart, Ikara, Limbo, helo platform. Swan Hunter 30.6.1969. PO 14.6.1991; harbour TS 22.3.1993.

BRISTOL *See also AGINCOURT 1796.*

BRITANNIA 1st Rate 100, 1,708bm, 167·5 × 48·5ft. Chatham DY 1682. Dismantled 1715. *Frames used for BRITANNIA 1719 (q.v.).*

BRITANNIA 1st Rate 100, 1,894bm, 174·5 × 50ft. Woolwich DY 3.10.1719. Harbour service 1745. BU comp. 9.1749 Chatham.

BRITANNIA 1st Rate 100, 2,116bm, 178 × 52ft. Portsmouth DY 19.10.1762. = PRINCESS ROYAL 6.1.1812; = ST GEORGE 18.1.1812; = BARFLEUR 2.6.1819. BU 2.1825. *11 years on stocks.*

BRITANNIA Storeship 20, 535bm, 115 × 32ft. Purch. 1781. Wrecked 4.1782 Kentish Knock.

BRITANNIA 1st Rate 120, 2,616bm, 205 × 55ft, 2—68pdr, 64—32pdr, 18—32pdr carr., 34—24pdr, 4—18pdr. Plymouth DY 20.10.1820. TS 1.1.1859. BU comp. 20.11.1869 Devonport.

BRITANNIA Battleship, 16,350 tons, 425 × 78ft, 4—12in, 4—9·2in, 10—6in, 14—12pdr. Portsmouth DY 10.12.1904. Sunk 9.11.1918 by UB.50 off Cape Trafalgar.

BRITANNIA Royal yacht, 3,990 tons, 412·2 (oa) ×

55ft, 2—3pdr. John Brown 16.4.1953. PO 11.12.1997, arr. Leith under tow 5.5.1998 for use as exhibition ship.

BRITANNIA *See also PRINCE of WALES 1860.*

BRITOMART Brig-sloop 10, 'Cherokee' class, 238bm. Dudman, Deptford, 28.7.1808. Sold 3.2.1819 G. Bailey.

BRITOMART Brig-sloop 10, 'Cherokee' class, 237bm. Portsmouth DY 24.8.1820. Sold 1843 in Singapore.

BRITOMART Brig 8, 329bm, 93 × 29ft, 8—18pdr. Pembroke Dock 12.6.1847. Coastguard 21.10.1857; = WV.25 in 5.1863. BU comp. 25.7.1874 Chatham.

BRITOMART Wood screw gunboat, 'Britomart' class. Smith, Newcastle, 7.5.1860. Sold 12.1.1892 Castle; resold S. Williams, Dagenham, mooring hulk. BU 6.1946.

BRITOMART 1st class gunboat, 710 tons, 180 × 33ft, 2—4in, 4—12pdr. Potter, Liverpool, 28.3.1899. Sold 6.10.1920 Bombay = *Sakuntala.*

BRITOMART Minesweeper, 875 tons, 230 × 33·5ft, 2—4in. Devonport DY 23.8.1938. Sunk 27.8.1944 in error Allied aircraft off Normandy.

BRITOMART *See also GLOMMEN.*

BRITON 5th Rate 38, 1,080bm, 150 × 40·5ft. Chatham DY 11.4.1812. Convict ship 1841; target 2.1860. BU 9.1860 Portsmouth.

BRITON Wood screw frigate 51, 3,027bm, 250 × 52ft. Portsmouth DY, ordered 1860, cancelled 1863.

BRITON Wood screw corvette, 1,331bm, 1,860 tons, 220 × 36ft, Sheerness DY 6.11.1869. Sold 1887 Bombay.

BRITON *See also BRILLIANT 1814, CALYPSO 1883.*

BRIXHAM Minesweeper, turbine 'Bangor' class. Blyth SB 21.11.1941. Sold 7.7.1948; BU Clayton & Davie.

BRIXHAM *See also BLOXHAM 1919.*

BROADERSCHAP 4th Rate 50, 1,063bm, 140 × 41·5ft. Dutch, captured 28.8.1799 off Texel. Floating battery 1803. BU 10.1805.

BROADLEY Inshore minehunter, 'Ley' class. Blackmore, Bideford, 24.11.1953. Burnt 29.9.1956 accident Haslar; wreck sold 8.8.1957.

BROADSWORD Destroyer, 1,980 tons, 365 (oa) × 38ft, 6—4in, 6—40mm, 10—TT. Yarrow 4.2.1946. Arr. Inverkeithing 10.1968 for BU.

BROADSWORD Frigate, 3,556 tons, 430 (oa) × 48·5ft, Exocet, Seawolf, helo, 6—TT. Yarrow 12.5.1976. Tx Brazilian Navy 30.6.1995 = GREENHALGH.

BROADWATER (ex-MASON) Destroyer, 1,190

tons, 311 × 31ft, 3–4in, 1–3in, 6–TT. USN, cd RN 8.10.1940. Sunk 18.10.1941 by U.101 south of Ireland.

BROADWAY (ex-HUNT) Destroyer, 1,190 tons, 311 × 31ft, 1–4in, 1–3in, 4–20mm, 3–TT. USN, cd RN 8.10.1940. Sold 18.2.1947; arr. 3.1948 Charlestown for BU.

BROCK Schooner 2 (Canadian lakes), 141bm, 69·5 × 22ft. Kingston, Ontario, 4.1817. Sold 1837.

BROCKLESBY Destroyer, 'Hunt' class, 1,000 tons, 4–4in. Cammell Laird 30.9.1940. Arr. Faslane 28.10.1968 for BU.

BROCKLESBY Minehunter, 615 tons. Vosper-Thornycroft 12.1.1982.

BROCKVILLE Minesweeper (RCN), diesel 'Bangor' class. Marine Industries 20.6.1941. RCMP *Macleod* 1950; = BROCKVILLE (RCN) 1951. BU 1961.

BROKE Cutter. Hired 1814.

BROKE (ex-ALMIRANTE GONI) Destroyer leader, 1,704 tons, 331·5 × 32·5ft, 2–4·7in, 2–4in, 4–TT. White 25.5.1914; Chilean, purch. 8.1914. Resold 5.1920 Chile = ALMIRANTE URIBE.

BROKE (ex-ROOKE) Destroyer leader, 1,750 tons, 329·25 (oa) × 32ft, 5–4·7in, 1–3in, 6–TT. Thornycroft 16.9.1920 (renamed 13.4.1921). Damaged 8.11.1942 shore batteries Algiers, foundered under tow 9.11.1942.

BROLGA (ex-*Lumen*) Aux. minesweeper (RAN), 268 tons, 93·2 (oa) × 26·6ft. Lighthouse tender 12.1975, acq. 10.2.1988.

BRONINGTON Coastal minesweeper, 'Ton' class. Cook, Welton & Gemmell 19.3.1953. = HUMBER; = BRONINGTON 1959. Sold 9.1988; towed Manchester 24.1.1989 for use as museum ship (opened 28.10.1992); gifted Historic Warship Collection, towed Birkenhead 11.7.2002.

BROOM *See VERVAIN 1941.*

BROOME Minesweeper, 'Bathurst' class. Evans Deakin 6.10.1941. Sold 8.1946 Turkish Navy = ALANYA; deleted 1975.

BROOMLEY Inshore minehunter, 'Ley' class. Harris, Appledore, 14.4.1953. = WATCHFUL 10.1.1959. Sold 29.1.1968 Electro Marine Eng. Co., London; arr. Rotterdam 21.3.1968 for BU.

BROTHERS Gunvessel 2. Purch. 10.1795. Sold 1.1802.

BROUGH CASTLE Corvette, 'Castle' class. Collingwood SY, cancelled 12.1943.

BRUCE Destroyer leader, 1,800 tons, 320 × 32ft, 5–4·7in, 1–3in, 6–TT. Cammell Laird 26.2.1918. Sunk 22.11.1939 torpedo target off Isle of Wight.

BRUISER (ex-*Robert Stephenson*) Iron screw provision vessel, 580bm, 183 × 25ft. Stockton-on-Tees 8.12.1854, purch. on stocks. Sold 12.1.1857 C. Colman.

BRUISER Tank landing ship, 3,620 tons, 390 × 49ft, 8–20mm. Harland & Wolff 24.10.1942. Sold 1946.

BRUISER *See also LST.3025 1945.*

BRUIZER (Gunboat No 11) Gunvessel 12, 160bm, 75 × 22ft, 2–24pdr, 10–18pdr carr. Wells, Rotherhithe, 11.4.1797. Sold 1.1802.

BRUIZER Gun-brig 12, 180bm, 80 × 23ft, 10–18pdr carr., 2–12pdr. Pitcher, Northfleet, 28.4.1804. Sold 24.2.1815.

BRUIZER Wood screw gunboat, 'Britomart' class. Haslar 23.4.1867. BU 5.1886.

BRUIZER Destroyer, 280 tons, 201·5 × 19ft, 1–12pdr, 5–6pdr, 2–TT. Thornycroft, Chiswick, 27.2.1895. Sold 26.5.1914 Cashmore, Newport.

BRUNE 5th Rate 32, 694bm, 131 × 34·5ft, 26–12pdr, 6–6pdr. French, captured 30.1.1761 by VENUS and JUNO. Sold 2.10.1792.

BRUNE (ex-THETIS) 5th Rate 38, 1,090bm, 154 × 40·5ft. French, captured 10.11.1808 by AMETHYST. Troopship 1810. Sold 16.8.1838 Mr Levy.

BRUNE Iron paddle gunboat, 267bm, 140 × 20ft, 2–8in ML. Scott Russell, Millwall, 30.8.1856. Sold 19.5.1863 in Lagos.

BRUNEI Landing craft (RAN), 310 tons, 146 (oa) × 33ft. Walker 5.10.1971.

BRUNSWICK Schooner (Canadian lakes). Oswego 1765. Condemned 1778.

BRUNSWICK 3rd Rate 74, 1,836bm, 176 × 48·5ft, Deptford DY 30.4.1790. Harbour service 6.1812. BU 8.1826 Sheerness.

BRUNSWICK Screw 3rd Rate 80, 2,492bm. Pembroke Dock 1.6.1855. Sold 3.1867 Marshall. *Ex-3rd Rate, 8 years on stocks.*

BRUTUS Minesweeper, 'Catherine' class. General Engineering, Alemeda, 21.5.1943 for RN; retained USN = IMPECCABLE.

BRYANSFORD Seaward defence boat, 'Ford' class. Inglis 3.1953. Sold 5.1968 Nigeria, = IBADAN II; deleted 1975.

BRYONY Sloop, 'Anchusa' class. Armstrong 27.10.1917. Arr. 3.4.1938 Cashmore, Newport, for BU.

BRYONY Corvette, 'Flower' class. Harland & Wolff 15.3.1941. Sold 1948 Norwegian Govt = POLAR-FRONT II. Listed until 1979.

BUCCANEER Patrol boat (RAN), 146 tons, 107·5 (oa) × 20ft, 1–40mm. Evans Deakin 14.9.1968. Sunk 8.10.1988 gunnery target.

BUCEPHALUS 5th Rate 32, 976bm, 150 × 38ft. Rowe, Newcastle, 3.11.1808. Troopship 5.1814; harbour service 6.1822. BU 9.1834.

BUCEPHALUS Wood screw frigate 51, 3,353bm, 270 × 52·5ft. Portsmouth DY, ordered 1861, cancelled 1863.

BUCHAN NESS Repair ship, 8,580 tons, 425 × 57ft, 16—20mm. West Coast SB, Vancouver, 10.2.1945. Sold 25.9.1959; BU Faslane.

BUCK Dogger 6. Dutch, captured 1672. Sold 1674.

BUCKIE *See BOOTLE 1918.*

BUCKINGHAM 3rd Rate 70, 1,128bm, 151 × 41·5ft. Deptford 13.4.1731. BU 1745.

BUCKINGHAM 3rd Rate 70, 1,436bm, 160 × 45·5ft. Deptford DY 13.4.1751. = GRAMPUS (storeship) 19.4.1777. Lost 11.1778.

BUCKINGHAM *See also REVENGE 1699, EAGLE 1774, ROYAL MOUNT 1944.*

BUCKLESHAM Inshore minesweeper, 'Ham' class. Ardrossan DD 8.8.1952. Sold 1981 Pounds.

BUCTOUCHE Corvette (RCN), 'Flower' class. Davie SB 20.11.1940. Sold 1946 International Iron & Metal Co.

BUDDLEIA *See GIFFARD 1943.*

BUDE Minesweeper, TE 'Bangor' class. Lobnitz 4.9.1940. Sold 1946.

BUFFALO (ex-*Fremantle*) Storeship 12, 468bm, 100 × 31ft. Dudman, Deptford, 3.11.1797, purch. on stocks. Hulked 1814. Sold 30.4.1817.

BUFFALO (ex-*Hindostan*) Storeship 16, 589bm, 120 × 34ft. East Indiaman, purch. 1.11.1813. Timber carrier 1831. Wrecked 28.7.1841 Mercury Bay, New Zealand.

BUFFALO (ex-*Baron von Humboldt*) Iron screw storeship, 440bm, 137 × ?ft. Treasury Dept vessel, tx 5.9.1855 (renamed 26.11.1856). Tx Victualling Dept 1868. Sold 11.1888.

BUFFALO (ex-*Earl de Gray & Ripon*) Iron screw storeship, 335 tons, 150 × 21·5ft. War Dept vessel, tx 1.10.1891. Sold 1903.

BUFFALO Minesweeper, 'Catherine' class. General Engineering, Alameda, 22.6.1943 for RN; retained USN = ARDENT.

BUFFALO *See also CAPTAIN 1743.*

BUGLOSS Corvette, Modified 'Flower' class. Crown 21.6.1943. Tx RIN 19.2.1945 = ASSAM.

BULL 26-gun ship, 343bm. Built 1546. *Rebuilt as ADVENTURE 1594?*

BULL Fireship 4, 121bm. Dutch, captured 1666. Sold 1674.

BULLDOG Gunvessel 4, 58bm, 64 × 14ft. Dutch hoy, purch. 3.1794. Sold 1794.

BULLDOG Sloop 16, 317bm, 98 × 27ft. Ladd, Dover, 10.11.1782. Bomb vessel 1798; powder hulk 1801. BU comp. 12.1829 Portsmouth. *In French hands 27.2—16.9.1801.*

BULLDOG Wood paddle sloop, 1,124bm, 190 × 36ft. Chatham DY 2.10.1845. Stranded 23.10.1865, destroyed while attacking rebel steamer Haiti.

BULLDOG 3rd class gunboat, 'Ant' class. Campbell, Johnston, Woolwich, 17.9.1872. Sold 16.7.1906.

BULLDOG Destroyer, 952 tons, 269 × 28ft, 1—4in, 3—12pdr, 2—TT. John Brown 13.11.1909. Sold 21.9.1920 Ward, Rainham.

BULLDOG Destroyer, 1,360 tons, 323 (oa) × 32·25ft, 4—4·7in, 8—TT. Swan Hunter 6.12.1930. Sold 15.1.1946; arr. 3.1946 Rosyth for BU.

BULLDOG Survey vessel, 1,050 tons, 189·6 (oa) × 37·5ft. Brooke Marine 12.7.1967. PO 26.7.2001; sold 8.2001 for conv. luxury yacht.

BULLEN Frigate, TE 'Captain' class. Bethlehem, Hingham, 17.8.1943 on Lend-Lease. Sunk 6.12.1944 by U.775 off north-west Scotland.

BULLFINCH Wood screw gunboat, 'Albacore' class. Laird 25.2.1856. BU 8.1864.

BULLFINCH Wood screw gunvessel, 664bm, 805 tons, 170 × 29ft, 1—7in ML, 2—40pdr. Sheerness DY 13.2.1868. Sold 6.1885.

BULLFINCH Destroyer, 370 tons, 210 × 20·5ft, 1—12pdr, 5—6pdr, 2—TT. Earle 10.2.1898. Sold 10.6.1919 Young, Sunderland.

BULLFINCH Cable ship, 1,950 tons. In service 1940—80.

BULLFROG Schooner 4 (Canadian Lakes) 96bm. Purch. 17.8.1838. Sold 1841.

BULLFROG Wood screw gunboat, 'Albacore' class. Pitcher, Northfleet, 6.10.1855. BU 6.1875 Sheerness.

BULLFROG Composite screw gunboat, 465 tons, 125 × 23·5ft, 2—64pdr MLR, 2—20pdr. Pembroke Dock 3.2.1881. Harbour service 1905; = EGMONT 3.1923; = ST ANGELO 1.7.1933. Sold 1933.

BULRUSH *See MIMICO 1943.*

BULWARK 3rd Rate 74, 1,620bm, 169 × 47ft. Portsmouth DY, ordered 11.6.1778, cancelled 4.3.1783.

BULWARK (ex-SCIPIO) 3rd Rate 74, 1,940bm, 183 × 49ft. Portsmouth DY 23.4.1807 (renamed 1806). BU 9.1826 Portsmouth.

BULWARK Screw 2nd Rate 81, 3,716bm, 252 × 58ft. Chatham DY, LD 8.1859, suspended 7.3.1861, cancelled 3.1873. BU 1873.

BULWARK Battleship, 15,000 tons, 400 × 75ft, 4—12in 12—6in, 18—12pdr. Devonport DY 18.10.1899. Blown up 26.11.1914 accident R. Medway.

BULWARK Aircraft carrier, 22,000 tons, 650 × 90ft, 32—40mm, 50 aircraft. Harland & Wolff

22.6.1948. Comp. commando carrier 19.1.1960, 16 helo. Arr. Cairnryan 17.4.1984 for BU.

BULWARK Landing platform dock, 19,560 tons, 577·4 (oa) × 98·1ft, Goalkeeper, 4—20mm, 3 helo, 305 troops. BAe Systems, Barrow, 15.11.2001.

BULWARK *See also HOWE 1860.*

BUNA Landing craft (RAN), 310 tons, 146 (oa) × 33ft, Walker, Maryborough, 1972. Tx Papua New Guinea Defence Force 14.11.1974.

BUNBURY Minesweeper (RAN), 'Bathurst' class. Evans Deakin, Brisbane, 16.5.1942. Sold 6.1.1961 for BU Japan.

BUNBURY Patrol boat (RAN), 211 tons. North Queensland Engineering Co. 3.11.1984.

BUNDABERG Minesweeper (RAN), 'Bathurst' class. Evans Deakin 1.12.1941. Left Sydney 20.2.1962 for BU Japan.

BURCHETT Sloop 6. Purch. 6.1708. Captured 6.2.1709 by French.

BURDEKIN Frigate (RAN), 'River' class. Walker, Maryborough, 30.6.1943. Sold 9.1961 for BU Japan.

BURDOCK Corvette, 'Flower' class. Crown 14.12.1940. BU 6.1947 Ward, Hayle.

BURFORD 3rd Rate 70, 1,051bm, 152·5 × 40·5ft. Woolwich DY 1679. Rebuilt Deptford 1699 as 1,113bm. Wrecked 14.2.1719 coast of Italy.

BURFORD 3rd Rate 70, 1,147bm, 151 × 42ft. Deptford DY 19.7.1722. BU 1752.

BURFORD 3rd Rate 70, 1,424bm, 162 × 44·5ft. Chatham DY 1757. Sold 31.3.1785.

BURGES Frigate, DE 'Captain' class. Mare Island 1942 for RN; retained USN = EDGAR G. CHASE.

BURGES Frigate, DE 'Captain' class. Boston NY 26.1.1943 on Lend-Lease. Ret. USN 7.2.1946.

BURGHEAD BAY (ex-LOCH HARPORT) Frigate, 'Bay' class. Hill 3.3.1945 (renamed 1944). Tx Portuguese Navy 11.5.1959 = ALVARES CABRAL. Sold 23.6.1971.

BURLEY Inshore minehunter, 'Ley' class. Dorset Yacht Co., Poole, 6.1.1954. = SQUIRREL 15.12.1959. Sold 29.1.1968 Electro Marine Engineering Co, London; arr. Rotterdam 21.3.1968 for BU.

BURLINGTON 4th Rate 48, 680bm, 131·5 × 34·5ft. Johnson, Blackwall, 1695. BU 8.1733 Sheerness.

BURLINGTON Mine destructor vessel. 1940. = FAIRFAX (q.v.).

BURLINGTON Minesweeper (RCN), TE 'Bangor' class. Dufferin, Toronto, 23.11.1940. Sold 1946 T. Harris.

BURLINGTON *See also PRINCESS CHARLOTTE 1814.*

BURNASTON Coastal minesweeper, 'Ton' class. Fleetlands, Gosport, 18.12.1952. Sold 29.3.1971; BU Newhaven.

BURNET Corvette, Modified 'Flower' class. Ferguson 31.5.1943. Lent RIN 15.5.1945 = GONDWANA; = BURNET 17.5.1946. Sold 15.5.1947 Siamese Navy = BANGPAKONG; deleted 1984.

BURNHAM (ex-AULICK) Destroyer, 1,190 tons, 311 × 31ft, 1—4in, 1—3in, 4—20mm, 3—TT. USN, cd RN 8.10.1940. Target ship 1943. Sold 4.3.1947; arr. 12.1948 Hayes, Pembroke Dock.

BURNHAM *See also BLACKBURN.*

BURNIE Minesweeper, 'Bathurst' class. Mort's Dock, Sydney, 25.10.1940. Sold 1946 Dutch Navy = CERAM; deleted 1958.

BURSLEM (ex-BLAKENEY) Minesweeper, Later 'Hunt' class. Ayrshire Co. 4.1918 (renamed 1918). Sold 19.5.1928 Ward, Inverkeithing.

BURTON *See EXMOOR 1941.*

BURWELL (ex-LAUB) Destroyer, 1,190 tons, 311 × 31ft, 1—4in, 1—3in, 4—20mm, 3—TT. USN, cd RN 8.10.1940. Target ship 1943. Sold 4.3.1947; BU Ward, Milford Haven.

BURY Minesweeper, Later 'Hunt' class. Eltringham 17.5.1919. Sold 20.1.1923 J. Smith.

BUSS Fireship 4, 80bm. Captured 1672. Sold 1694.

BUSTARD (ex-ROYAL GEORGE) Brig-sloop 16, 270bm, 83 × 27ft. Revenue cutter (renamed 1806). Sold 12.10.1815.

BUSTARD Brig-sloop 10, 'Cherokee' class, 327bm. Chatham DY 12.12.1818. Sold 24.6.1829 T. Surflen.

BUSTARD Wood screw gunboat, 'Albacore' class. Pitcher, Northfleet, 20.10.1855. Sold 18.11.1869 in Hong Kong.

BUSTARD Iron screw gunboat, 'Ant' class. Napier 7.1.1871. Reported sold 11.1917 Ward but listed until 1921.

BUSTLER Brig-sloop 16, 209bm, 76 × 25·5ft, 16—6pdr. Purch. 1780. Sold 25.8.1788.

BUSTLER Gun-brig 12, 180bm. 84 × 22ft, 10—18pdr carr., 2—12pdr. Ayles, Topsham, 12.8.1805. Stranded 26.12.1808 nr Cape Gris Nez; captured by French.

BUSY Cutter 10, 190bm, 75 × 26ft, 10—4pdr. Farley, Folkestone, 6.1778, purch. Sold 7.6.1792.

BUSY Brig-sloop 18, 337bm, 96 × 29ft. Graham, Harwich, 20.11.1797. Foundered 1807 Halifax Station.

BUTTERCUP Sloop, 'Arabis' class. Barclay Curle 24.10.1915. Sold 5.2.1920 Hughes & Co. as salvage vessel.

BUTTERCUP Corvette, 'Flower' class. Harland &

Wolff 10.4.1941. Lent RNorN 24.4.1942. Sold 1946.

BUTTERFLY River gunboat, 'Fly' class. Yarrow 1915, re-erected R. Tigris 11.1915. Sold 1.3.1923 locally.

BUTTINGTON Coastal minesweeper, 'Ton' class. Fleetlands, Gosport, 11.6.1953. = VENTURER; = BUTTINGTON; = THAMES 2.1962. Sold 12.5.1970; BU Newhaven.

BUTTRESS (ex-LCT.4099) Tank landing craft, 657 tons, 225 × 39ft, 4–20mm. Fairfield, comp. 12.10.1946. Renamed 1956. Sold 5.1966 French Navy = L.9061.

BUXTON (ex-EDWARDS) Destroyer, 1,190 tons, 311 × 31ft, 1–4in, 1–3in, 4–20mm, 3–TT. USN, cd RN 8.10.1940. Lent RCN 1942; TS (RCN) 10.1943. BU 1945 locally.

BUZZARD Brigantine 3, ex-sloop, 'Cherokee' class, 231bm. Portsmouth DY 23.3.1834. Sold 7.11.1843 Greenwood & Clark.

BUZZARD Wood paddle sloop, 980bm, 185 × 34ft. Pembroke Dock 24.3.1849. BU 1883.

BUZZARD Composite screw sloop, 1,140 tons, 195 × 28ft, 8–5in. Sheerness DY 10.5.1887. Drillship 1904; = PRESIDENT 1.4.1911. Sold 6.9.1921 C. A. Beard; resold Dutch sbkrs.

BUZZARD *See also HAWK 1806.*

BYARD Frigate, DE 'Captain' class. Mare Island 1942 for RN; retained USN = EDWARD C. DALY.

BYARD Frigate, TE 'Captain' class. Bethlehem, Hingham, 6.3.1943 on Lend-Lease. Ret. USN 1.1946.

BYRON Frigate, TE 'Captain' class. Bethlehem, Hingham, 14.8.1943 on Lend-Lease. Ret. USN 11.1945.

C

'C' class submarines 280 tons, 135 × 13·5ft, 2—TT:

C.1 Vickers 10.7.1906. Sold 22.10.1920 Stanlee; resold 14.11.1921 Young, Sunderland.

C.2 Vickers 10.7.1906. Sold 8.10.1920 Maden & McKee.

C.3 Vickers 3.10.1906. Expended 23.4.1918 Zeebrugge.

C.4 Vickers 18.10.1906. Sold 28.2.1922 Hampshire Metal Co.

C.5 Vickers 20.8.1906. Sold 31.10.1919 Malta.

C.6 Vickers 20.8.1906. Sold 20.11.1919 J. A. Walker.

C.7 Vickers 15.2.1907. Sold 20.12.1919 J. Jackson.

C.8 Vickers 15.2.1907. Sold 22.10.1920 Stanlee; resold 14.11.1921 T. Young.

C.9 Vickers 3.4.1907. Sold 7.1922 Stanlee, Dover.

C.10 Vickers 15.4.1907. Sold 7.1922 Stanlee, Dover.

C.11 Vickers 27.5.1907. Sunk 14.7.1909 collision SS *Eddystone* off Cromer.

C.12 Vickers 9.9.1907. Sold 2.2.1920 J. H. Lee.

C.13 Vickers 9.11.1907. Sold 2.2.1920 J. H. Lee.

C.14 Vickers 7.12.1907. Sold 5.12.1921 C. A. Beard, Upnor.

C.15 Vickers 21.1.1908. Sold 28.2.1922 Hampshire Metal Co.

C.16 Vickers 19.3.1908. Sold 12.8.1922 C. A. Beard, Upnor.

C.17 Chatham DY 13.8.1908. Sold 20.11.1919 J. A. Walker.

C.18 Chatham DY 10.10.1908. Sold 26.5.1921 B. Fryer.

C.19 Chatham DY 20.3.1909. Sold 2.2.1920 J. H. Lee.

C.20 Chatham DY 27.11.1909. Sold 26.5.1921 B. Fryer.

C.21 Vickers 26.9.1908. Sold 5.12.1921 C. A. Beard, Upnor.

C.22 Vickers 10.10.1908. Sold 2.2.1920 J. H. Lee.

C.23 Vickers 26.11.1908. Sold 5.12.1921 C. A. Beard, Upnor.

C.24 Vickers 26.11.1908. Sold 26.5.1921 B. Fryer.

C.25 Vickers 10.3.1909. Sold 5.12.1921 C. A. Beard, Upnor.

C.26 Vickers 20.3.1909. Sunk 4.4.1918 Helsingfors Bay to avoid capture; raised 1954, BU.

C.27 Vickers 22.4.1909. Sunk 4.4.1918 Helsingfors Bay to avoid capture; raised 1954, BU.

C.28 Vickers 22.4.1909. Sold 25.8.1921 Fryer, Sunderland.

C.29 Vickers 19.6.1909. Sunk 29.8.1915 mine North Sea.

C.30 Vickers 19.7.1909. Sold 25.8.1921 Fryer, Sunderland.

C.31 Vickers 2.9.1909. Sunk 4.1.1915 off coast of Belgium, cause unknown.

C.32 Vickers 29.9.1909. Stranded 24.10.1917 Gulf of Riga, destroyed.

C.33 Chatham DY 10.5.1910. Sunk 4.8.1915 North Sea, cause unknown.

C.34 Chatham DY 8.6.1910. Sunk 21.7.1917 by U.52 off north coast of Ireland.

C.35 Vickers 2.11.1909. Lost with C.26; raised 1954, BU.

C.36 Vickers 30.11.1909. Sold 25.6.1919 in Hong Kong.

C.37 Vickers 1.1.1910. Sold 26.6.1919 in Hong Kong.

C.38 Vickers 10.2.1910. Sold 25.6.1919 in Hong Kong.

CC.1 (ex-IQUIQUE) Submarine (RCN), 313 tons, 144·5 × 15ft, 5—TT. Seattle 3.6.1913; Chilean, purch. 4.8.1914. Discarded 1925.

CC.2 (ex-ANTOFAGASTA) Submarine (RCN), 310 tons, 157·5 × 15ft, 3—TT. Seattle 31.12.1913; Chilean, purch. 4.8.1914. Discarded 1925.

ÇA IRA 3rd Rate 80, 2,210bm. French, captured off Genoa 14.3.1795. Burnt 11.4.1796 accident San Fiorenzo Bay.

CABOT Brig-sloop 14, 189bm, 74 × 24ft, 14—4pdr. American, captured 26.3.1777 by MILFORD off Nova Scotia, purch. 6.1777. Sold 25.6.1783.

CACHALOT Submarine minelayer, 1,520 tons, 271·5 × 25·5ft, 1—4in, 6—TT, 50 mines. Scotts 2.12.1937. Rammed 8.1941 by Italian torpedo boat PAPA off Cyrenaica, sunk.

CACHALOT Submarine, 1,605 tons, 241 × 26·5ft, 8—TT. Scotts 11.12.1957. Sold 12.11.1979; BU Blyth.

CADDISFLY River gunboat, 'Fly' class. Yarrow 1915. Sold 17.2.1923 Anglo-Persian Oil Co.

CADIZ Fireship, 320bm. Purch. 1688. Expended 19.5.1692 Barfleur.

CADIZ Destroyer, 2,315 tons, 379 (oa) × 40·25ft, 4—4·5in, 8—TT. Fairfield 18.9.1944. Tx Pakistani Navy 1.2.1957 = KAIBAR. Sunk by missile 4.12.1971.

CADMUS Brig-sloop 10, 'Cherokee' class, 237bm. Dudman, Deptford, 26.2.1808. Coastguard watchvessel 2.1835; = WV.24 on 25.5.1863. Sold 12.3.1864 W. Lethbridge.

CADMUS Wood screw corvette, 1,466bm, 200 × 40·5ft. Chatham DY 20.5.1856. BU 9.1879 Devonport.

CADMUS Sloop, 1,070 tons, 185 × 33ft, 6—4in, 4—3pdr. Sheerness DY 29.4.1903. Sold 1.9.1921 in Hong Kong.

CADMUS Minesweeper, 'Algerine' class. Harland & Wolff 27.5.1942. Sold 1.1950 Belgian Navy = GEORGES LECONTE. BU 5.1960 Burcht.

CADMUS *See also DESPATCH 1851.*

CAERLEON Minesweeper, Later 'Hunt' class. Bow McLachlan 12.1918. Sold 4.1922 Stanlee, Dover.

CAESAR 3rd Rate 74, 1,621bm, 169 × 47ft. Plymouth DY, ordered 31.7.1777, cancelled 4.3.1783.

CAESAR 3rd Rate 80, 1,992bm, 181 × 50·5ft. Plymouth DY 16.11.1793. Army depot 2.1814. BU 2.1821.

CAESAR Screw 2nd Rate 90, 2,767bm, 207 × 56ft. Pembroke Dock 7.8.1853. Sold 19.4.1870 C. J. Mare.

CAESAR Battleship, 14,900 tons, 390 × 75ft, 4—12in, 12—6in, 16—12pdr. Portsmouth DY 2.9.1896. Sold 8.11.1921 Slough Trading Co.; left 7.1922 for BU Germany.

CAESAR (ex-RANGER) Destroyer, 'C' class. John Brown 14.2.1944 (renamed 11.1942). Arr. 6.1.1967 Hughes Bolckow, Blyth, for BU.

CAESAR *See also CESAR.*

CAICOS (ex-HANNAM) Frigate, 'Colony' class. Walsh Kaiser 6.9.1943 on Lend-Lease (renamed 1943). Ret. USN 1.1946.

CAIRNS Minesweeper, 'Bathurst' class. Walker, Maryborough, 7.10.1941. Sold 1946 Dutch Navy = AMBON. Tx Indonesian Navy 6.4.1950 = BANTENG. BU Hong Kong 4.1968.

CAIRO Light cruiser, 4,190 tons, 451·4 (oa) × 43·9ft, 5—6in, 2—3in. Cammell Laird 19.11.1918. AA ship 1939. Sunk 12.8.1942 by Italian submarine AXUM off Bizerta.

CAISTOR CASTLE Corvette, 'Castle' class. Lewis 22.5.1944. Arr. 3.1956 Troon for BU.

CALABASH Fireship, 262bm. Captured from Algerines 1680. Sold 1684.

CALCUTTA (ex-*Warley*) 4th Rate 54, 1,176bm, 157 × 41ft, 26—32pdr, 28—18pdr, 2—9pdr. East Indiaman, purch. 1795. Transport (24 guns) 1804. Captured 26.9.1805 by French off Scilly Is. Destroyed 12.4.1809 in action British ships.

CALCUTTA 2nd Rate 84, 2,299bm, 197 × 52·5ft. Bombay DY 14.3.1831. Gunnery ship 1865. Sold 12.5.1908 Castle.

CALCUTTA Light cruiser, 4,190 tons, 451·5 (oa) × 43·9ft, 5—6in, 2—3in. Vickers 9.7.1918. AA ship 1939. Sunk 1.6.1941 air attack off Crete.

CALCUTTA *See also HERCULES 1868, HANDY 1884.*

CALDECOT CASTLE Corvette, 'Castle' class. G. Brown, cancelled 12.1943.

CALDER Frigate, DE 'Captain' class. Mare Island 1942 for RN; retained USN = GILMORE.

CALDER Frigate, DE 'Captain' class. Mare Island 1943 for RN; retained USN = FINNEGAN.

CALDER Frigate, TE 'Captain' class. Bethlehem, Hingham, 27.2.1943 on Lend-Lease. Ret. USN 10.1945.

CALDWELL Sloop 2 (Canadian lakes). Lake Niagara, 1774. Sheer hulk 1790.

CALDWELL (ex-HALE) Destroyer, 1,090 tons, 309 × 30·5ft, 3—4in, 1—3in, 6—TT. USN, cd RN 9.9.1940. Sold 20.3.1945; BU Granton.

CALEDON (ex-HENRI) Sloop 16, c. 220bm. French, captured 1808. Sold 11.1811.

CALEDON Light cruiser, 4,120 tons, 450 (oa) × 43·1ft, 5—6in, 2—3in. Cammell Laird 25.11.1916. AA ship 12.1943. Sold 22.1.1948; arr. 14.2.1948 Dover Industries for BU.

CALEDONIA Brig 3 (Canadian lakes), 1—32pdr carr., 2—24pdr. Amherstburg, Lake Erie, 1807. Captured 9.10.1812 by Americans on Lake Erie; burnt 13.10.1812 by British forces.

CALEDONIA 1st Rate 120, 2,616bm, 205 × 54ft. Plymouth DY 25.6.1808. = DREADNOUGHT (hospital ship) 21.6.1856. BU 1875.

CALEDONIA 2nd Rate 91, 3,715bm, 252 × 57ft; altered 6.1861 to ironclad, 4,125bm, 6,832 tons, 273 × 58ft, 24—7in ML. Woolwich DY 24.10.1862. Sold 30.9.1886; BU Castle, Charlton.

CALEDONIA (ex-*Majestic*) TS 56,621 tons. HO 8.10.1936 by Ward in exchange for obsolete warships, cd 23.4.1937. Burnt 29.9.1939 accident Rosyth; wreck sold 3.1943; raised 12.7.1943, BU Firth of Forth/Inverkeithing.

CALEDONIA *See also IMPREGNABLE 1810.*

CALENDULA Corvette, 'Flower' class. Harland & Wolff 3.1940. Lent USN 12.3.1942—1945 = READY. Sold 22.7.1946 = *Villa Cisneros.*

CALGARY Corvette (RCN), 'Flower' Class. Marine

Industries 23.8.1941. Sold 1946 Victory Transport & Salvage Co.

CALGARY Frigate (RCN), 'Halifax' class. Marine Industries, Sorel, 28.8.1992.

CALLIOPE Brig-sloop 10, 'Cherokee' class, 237bm. Dudman, Deptford, 28.7.1808. BU comp. 13.8.1829 Portsmouth.

CALLIOPE 6th Rate 28, 717bm, 130 × 35·5ft. Sheerness DY 5.10.1837. Floating chapel 1860; factory 1865. BU comp. 1.11.1883 Devonport.

CALLIOPE Screw corvette, 2,770 tons, 235 × 44·5ft, 4–6in, 12–5in. Portsmouth DY 24.7.1884. RNVR drillship 29.10.1907; = HELICON 6.1915; = CALLIOPE 10.1931. Sold 4.10.1951; BU Hughes Bolckow, Blyth.

CALLIOPE Light cruiser, 3,750 tons, 420 × 41·5ft, 2–6in, 8–4in. Chatham DY 17.1.1914. Sold 28.8.1931 Ward, Inverkeithing.

CALLIOPE *See also FALMOUTH 1932*

CALPE (ex-SAN JOSEF) Sloop 14, 209bm, 75·5 × 26·5ft. Spanish, captured 27.10.1800 Malaga. Sold 1802.

CALPE Destroyer, 'Hunt' class Type II. Swan Hunter 28.4.1941. Tx RDanN 1952 = ROLF KRAKE. Sold 10.1966 for BU Sweden.

CALSHOT CASTLE Corvette, 'Castle' class. Inglis, cancelled 12.1943.

CALTON Coastal minesweeper, 'Ton' class. Wivenhoe SY 24.10.1953. Sold 17.6.1968 C. H. Rugg; BU Belgium.

CALYPSO Sloop 16, 342bm, 102 × 28ft. Graves, Deptford, 27.9.1783. Run down and sunk 8.1803 by merchantman in Atlantic.

CALYPSO Sloop 18, 'Cruizer' class, 382bm. Dudman, Deptford, 2.2.1805. BU 3.1921.

CALYPSO Brig-sloop 10, 'Cherokee' class, 239bm. Deptford DY, ordered 1824, = HYAENA 1826, cancelled 1828.

CALYPSO (ex-HYAENA) Brig-sloop 10, 'Cherokee' class, 233bm. Chatham DY 19.8.1826 (renamed 1826). Comp. as yacht (2 guns) for Governor of Malta, removed from Navy List. Ret. RN c. 1830 as packet brig. Foundered 1.2.1833 collision iceberg North Atlantic.

CALYPSO Brig-sloop 10, 'Cherokee' class, 235bm. Woolwich DY, LD 1829, = HYAENA 1830, cancelled 1831.

CALYPSO 6th Rate 20, 731bm, 120 × 37·5ft. Chatham DY 5.1845. BU comp. 29.1.1.1866 Castle & Beech, Charlton.

CALYPSO Screw corvette, 2,770 tons, 235 × 44·5ft, 4–6in, 12–5in, Chatham DY 7.6.1883. TS Newfoundland Govt 2.9.1902; = BRITON 15.2.1916. Sold 7.4.1922 store hulk.

CALYPSO Light cruiser, 4,120 tons, 450 (oa) × 43·1ft, 5–6in, 2–3in. Hawthorn Leslie 24.1.1917. Sunk 12.6.1940 by Italin submarine BAGNOLINI south of Crete.

CALYPSO *See also BLONDE 1819.*

CAM Frigate, 'River' class. G. Brown 31.7.1943. Sold 22.6.1945; BU 7.1945 Young, Sunderland.

CAMBERFORD Seaward defence boat, 'Ford' class. Vosper, Portsmouth, 2.1953. Sold 5.7.1967 in Singapore.

CAMBERLEY Minesweeper, Later 'Hunt' class. Bow McLachlan 28.12.1918. Sold 7.1923 C. A. Beard.

CAMBRIA *See DERG 1943.*

CAMBRIAN 5th Rate 40, 1,160bm, 154 × 41·5ft. Parsons, Bursledon, 13.2.1797. Wrecked 3.1.1828 Mediterranean.

CAMBRIAN 5th Rate 36, 1,622bm, 160 × 49ft, Pembroke Dock 5.7.1841. Hulk 1872; floating factory 1880. Sold 12.1.1892 J. Read.

CAMBRIAN 2nd class cruiser, 4,360 tons, 320 × 49·5ft, 2–6in, 8–4·7in. Pembroke Dock 30.1.1893. = HARLECH (base ship) 2.3.1916; = VIVID 9.1921. Sold 21.2.1923 Young, Sunderland.

CAMBRIAN Light cruiser, 3,750 tons, 420 × 41·5ft, 4–6in, 1–4in, 2–3in. Pembroke Dock 3.3.1916. Sold 28.7.1934 Metal Industries, Rosyth.

CAMBRIAN (ex-SPITFIRE) Destroyer, 'C' class. Scotts 10.12.1943 (renamed 1942). Sold Ward; arr. Briton Ferry 3.9.1971 for BU.

CAMBRIDGE 3rd Rate 70, 881bm, 26–34pdr, 26–12pdr, 16–pdr, 2–3pdr. Deptford DY 1666. Wrecked 19.2.1694 off Gibraltar.

CAMBRIDGE 3rd Rate 80, 1,194bm, 156 × 42ft. Deptford DY 21.2.1695. Rebuilt Woolwich 1715 as 1,286bm. BU comp. 12.2.1750 Chatham.

CAMBRIDGE 3rd Rate 80, 1,615bm, 166 × 47ft. Deptford DY 21.10.1755. Harbour service 1793. BU 7.1808 Plymouth.

CAMBRIDGE 3rd Rate 80, 2,139bm, 187 × 52ft. Deptford DY 23.6.1815. Gunnery ship 8.1856. BU comp. 22.3.1869 Devonport.

CAMBRIDGE *See also WINDSOR CASTLE 1858.*

CAMEL Fireship 6, 130bm. Captured 1667. Expended 1667.

CAMEL (ex-*Yorkshire*) Storeship 26, 516bm, 113 × 31ft. Purch. 1776. Sold 27.8.1784.

CAMEL Storeship, 109bm, 64·5 × 20·5ft. Purch. 1798. Sold 22.4.1831.

CAMEL (ex-*Severn*) Storeship 16, 558bm, 115·5 × 34ft. East Indiaman, purch. 1813. Sold 21.4.1831.

CAMEL Mortar vessel, 117bm, 65 × 21ft, 1–13in mortar. Wigram, Blackwall, 21.4.1855. = MV.14 on 19.10.1855; = YC.6 (crane lighter) 1871.

CAMEL Wood screw gunboat, 'Albacore' class. Green, Blackwall, 3.5.1856. BU 6.1864.

CAMEL *See also MEDIATOR 1782.*

CAMELEON Brig-sloop 16 (fir-built), 314bm, 95 × 28ft. Randall, Rotherhithe, 14.10.1795. BU 4.1811.

CAMELEON Brig-sloop 10, 'Cherokee' class, 240bm. Bombay DY 16.1.1816. BU 4.1849.

CAMELEON Wood screw sloop, 952bm, 1,365 tons, 182 × 33ft. Deptford DY 23.2.1860. Sold 1883.

CAMELEON Destroyer, 747 tons, 246 × 26ft, 2—4in, 2—13pdr, 2—TT. Fairfield 2.6.1910. Sold 15.11.1921 Distin, Devonport.

CAMELEON *See also CHAMELEON.*

CAMELLIA Sloop, 'Acacia' class. Bow McLachlan 25.9.1915. Sold 15.1.1923.

CAMELLIA Corvette, 'Flower' class. Harland & Wolff 4.5.1940. Sold 9.8.1946 = *Hetty W.Vinke.*

CAMERON (ex-WELLES) Destroyer, 1,190 tons, 311 × 31ft, 3—4in, 1—3in, 6—TT. USN, cd RN 9.9.1940. Bombed German aircraft 15.12.1940 Portsmouth, capsized in dock; refloated 23.2.1941, used for shock trials; left Portsmouth 11.1944 for BU Falmouth.

CAMILLA 6th Rate 20, 433bm, 108 × 30ft. Chatham DY 20.4.1776. Harbour service 1814. Sold 13.4.1831.

CAMILLA Sloop 16, 549bm, 110 × 35ft, 16—32pdr. Pembroke Dock 8.9.1847. Foundered 3.1861 China Station.

CAMPANIA Aircraft carrier, 18,000 tons, 601 × 65ft, 6—4·7in, 1—3in, 10 aircraft. Passenger liner, purch. 27.11.1914, name retained; conv. comp. 4.1916. Sunk 5.11.1918 collision ROYAL OAK and GLORIOUS in Firth of Forth.

CAMPANIA Escort carrier, 12,450 tons, 510 × 70ft, 2—4in, 16—20mm, 15 aircraft. Harland & Wolff 17.6.1943. Arr. 11.11.1955 Hughes Bolckow, Blyth, for BU.

CAMPANULA Sloop, 'Arabis' class. Barclay Curle 25.12.1915. Sold 6.9.1922 Cove & Distinn.

CAMPANULA Corvette, 'Flower' class. Fleming & Ferguson 23.5.1940. Arr. 21.8.1947 Clayton & Davie, Dunston, for BU.

CAMPASPE Frigate (RAN), 'River' class. Sydney, ordered 12.1942, cancelled 12.6.1944.

CAMPBELL Schooner 4. Purch. 1796 West Indies. Sold 1803.

CAMPBELL Destroyer leader, 1,800 tons, 320 × 32ft, 5—4.7 in, 1—4in, 6—TT. Cammell Laird 21.9.1918. Sold 18.2.1947; arr. 6.1948 Metal Industries, Rosyth, for BU.

CAMPBELTOWN (ex-BUCHANAN) Destroyer, 1,090 tons, 309 × 30·5ft, 3—4in, 1—3in, 6—TT. USN, cd RN 9.9.1940. Lent Polish Navy 3.1941–9.1941. Expended 28.3.1942 St-Nazaire. *Was to have been lent Dutch Navy 1.1941 = MIDDLE-BURG, not taken over.*

CAMPBELTOWN Frigate, 4,200 tons, 480·5 (oa) × 48·4ft, 1—4.5in, Harpoon, Seawolf, helo, 6—TT. Cammell Laird 7.10.1987.

CAMPERDOWN (ex-JUPITER) 3rd Rate 64, 1,559bm, 167·5 × 46·5ft. Dutch, captured 11.10.1797 Battle of Camperdown. Harbour service 1798. Sold 10.9.1817.

CAMPERDOWN Battleship, 10,600 tons, 330 × 68·5ft, 4—13·5in, 6—6in, 12—6pdr. Portsmouth DY 24.11.1885. Hulk 10.1908. Sold 11.7.1911 Cohen, Swansea.

CAMPERDOWN Destroyer, 2,315 tons, 379 (oa) × 40·25ft, 4—4·5in, 8—TT. Fairfield 8.2.1944. Sold 9.9.1970; BU Faslane.

CAMPERDOWN *See also TRAFALGAR 1820.*

CAMPHAAN Brig-sloop 16. Dutch, captured 22.8.1799 Surinam. Sold 4.1802 for BU.

CAMPION Corvette, 'Flower' class. Crown 26.4.1941. Arr. 20.4.1947 Cashmore, Newport, for BU.

CAMROSE Corvette (RCN), 'Flower' class. Marine Industries 16.11.1940. BU 6.1947 Hamilton, Ontario.

CANADA 3rd Rate 74, 1,605bm 170 × 47ft. Woolwich DY 17.9.1765. Prison ship 3.1810. BU 11.1834 Chatham.

CANADA 1st Rate 112, 2,152bm, 191·5 × 51ft, 36—32pdr, 76—24pdr. Kingston, Ontario, LD c. 1814, cancelled 1832, BU on stocks.

CANADA Screw corvette, 2,380 tons, 225 × 44·5ft, 10—6in. Portsmouth DY 26.8.1881. Sold 10.5.1897 Cohen, Blackwall.

CANADA (ex-ALMIRANTE LATORRE) Battleship, 28,000 tons, 625 × 92·5ft, 10—141n, 14—6in. Armstrong 27.11.1913; Chilean, purch. 9.9.1914. Resold 5.1920 Chile = ALMIRANTE LATORRE. BU 1959 Japan.

CANBERRA Cruiser (RAN), 9,850 tons, 630 (oa) × 68·4ft, 8—8in, 8—4in. John Brown 31.5.1927. Sunk 9.8.1942 after torpedo damage Battle of Savo Island.

CANBERRA Frigate (RAN), 'Adelaide' class. Todd, Seattle, 1.12.1978.

CANCEAUX Armed ship 20, 226bm, 80·5 × 24·5ft. Purch. 2.1764 Quebec. Survey ship 1766. Sold 1783 in Quebec.

CANDYTUFT Sloop, 'Anchusa' class. Armstrong 19.5.1917. Sunk 18.11.1917 by U.39 off Bougie.

CANDYTUFT Corvette, 'Flower' class. Grangemouth DY Co. 8.7.1940. Lent USN 4.3.1942–1945 = TENACITY. Sold 9.7.1946.

CANDYTUFT *See also LONGBRANCH.*

CANNING (ex-GOLCONDA) Troopship (RIM), 2,246 tons, 370 × 36ft. Inglis 15.11.1882.

CANNING *See also LAWRENCE 1886.*

CANOPUS (ex-FRANKLIN) 3rd Rate 80, 2,257bm, 194 × 52·5ft, 32—32pdr, 6—32pdr carr., 36—18pdr, 6—9pdr. French, captured 1.8.1798 Battle of the Nile. Harbour service 1863. Sold 10.1887, BU.

CANOPUS Battleship, 12,950 tons, 390 × 74ft, 4—12in, 12—6in, 12—12pdr. Portsmouth DY 13.10.1897. Sold 18.2.1920 Stanlee, Dover.

CANSO (ex-LOTTERY) Schooner 12, 225bm, 93 × 24ft. American, captured 8.2.1813 Chesapeake Bay. Sold 30.5.1816.

CANSO Minesweeper, TE 'Bangor' class. North Vancouver SR Co. 9.6.1941. Sold 1.1.1948; BU Young, Sunderland.

CANTERBURY Storeship 8, 367bm, 96 × 29ft. Purch. 7.9.1692. Foundered 26.11.1703 nr Bristol; raised, sold.

CANTERBURY 4th Rate 60, 903bm, 145 × 38ft. Snelgrove, Deptford, 18.12.1693. Rebuilt Portsmouth 1722 as 963bm; rebuilt Plymouth 1744 as 1,117bm, 58 guns; harbour service 1761. BU 7.1770 Plymouth.

CANTERBURY Light cruiser, 3,750 tons, 420 × 41·5ft, 4—6in, 1—4in, 2—3in. John Brown 21.12.1915. Sold 27.7.1934 Metal Industries, Rosyth.

CANTERBURY Frigate (RNZN), 'Leander' class, Y160, 2,474 tons, 372 (oa) × 43ft, 2—4·5in, Phalanx, helo, 6—TT. Yarrow 6.5.1970. Due replacement 2005.

CANTERBURY CASTLE Corvette, 'Castle' class. Midland SY, cancelled 12.1943.

CAP DE LA MADELEINE Frigate (RCN), 'River' class. Morton, Quebec, 13.5.1944. BU La Spezia 4.1966.

CAPE BRETON Frigate (RCN), 'River' class. Morton, Quebec, 24.11.1942. Sold 13.12.1947; hull sunk 1948 breakwater.

CAPE BRETON *See also FLAMBOROUGH HEAD 1944.*

CAPE SCOTT *See BEACHY HEAD 1944.*

CAPE WRATH Repair ship, 8,775 tons, 439 × 62ft. West Coast SB, Vancouver, 24.8.1945. Sold 1951 = *Marine Fortune.*

CAPEL Frigate, DE 'Captain' class. Philadelphia NY 1942 for RN; retained USN = ANDRES.

CAPEL Frigate, DE 'Captain' class. Boston NY 22.4.1943 on Lend-Lease. Sunk 26.12.1944 by U.486 off Cherbourg.

CAPELIN Schooner 4, 78bm, 56 × 18ft, 4—12pdr carr. Bermuda 1804. In service 1806.

CAPELIN Cutter 8. Wrecked 30.6.1808 off Brest. *May have been same vessel as previous.*

CAPETOWN Light cruiser, 4,190 tons, 451·5 (oa) × 43·9ft, 5—6in, 2—3in. Cammell Laird 28.6.1919; comp. 2.1922 Pembroke Dock. Sold 5.4.1946; arr. 2.6.1946 Ward, Preston, for BU.

CAPILANO Frigate (RCN), 'River' class. Yarrow, Vancouver, 8.4.1944. Sold 17.11.1947 = *Irving Frances M.*; lost 1953.

CAPRICE (ex-SWALLOW) Destroyer, 'C' class. Yarrow 16.9.1943 (renamed 11.1942). Sold 22.6.1979; BU Queenborough.

CAPTAIN 3rd Rate 70, 1,041bm, 149·5 × 40·5ft, 26—34pdr, 26—12pdr, 18 small. Woolwich DY 1678. Rebuilt 1708 as 1,075bm; rebuilt 1722 as 1,131bm; hulked 2.1739. BU 5.1762 Portsmouth.

CAPTAIN 3rd Rate 70, 1,230bm, 151 × 43·5ft, Woolwich DY 14.4.1743. Reduced to 64 guns 1760; = BUFFALO (storeship) 7.2.1777. BU 10.1783.

CAPTAIN 3rd Rate 74, 1,639bm, 170 × 47ft. Batson, Limehouse, 26.11.1787. Harbour service 12.1809. Burnt 22.3.1813 accident Plymouth; BU 7.1813.

CAPTAIN Iron screw turret ship, 4,272bm, 6,950 tons, 320 × 53ft, 4—12in ML, 2—7in ML. Laird 27.3.1869. Capsized 7.9.1870 storm off Cape Finisterre.

CAPTAIN *See also CARNATIC 1783, ROYAL SOVEREIGN 1786, AGINCOURT 1865.*

CAPTIVITY *See MONMOUTH 1772, BELLERO-PHON 1786.*

CARADOC Iron paddle gunboat, 676bm, 193 × 37ft, 2—6pdr. Ditchburn & Mare, Blackwall, 7.1847. Sold 12.5.1870 E. Bates.

CARADOC Light cruiser, 4,120 tons, 450 (oa) × 43·1ft, 5—6in, 2—3in. Scotts 23.12.1916. Base ship 4.1944. Arr. 3.1946 Ward, Briton Ferry, for BU.

CARAQUET Minesweeper, TE 'Bangor' class. North Vancouver SR Co. 2.6.1941. Sold 29.6.1946 Portuguese Navy = ALMIRANTE LACERDA (survey vessel); tx Mozambique 1975; deleted 1984.

CARCASS Bomb vessel 8, 143bm, 66·5 × 23ft. Taylor, Cuckold's Point, 16.4.1695. Sold 8.1713.

CARCASS Bomb vessel 14, 274bm, 92 × 26ft. Taylor, Rotherhithe, 27.9.1740. Sold 2.3.1748.

CARCASS Bomb vessel 8, 309bm, 92 × 28ft. Stanton, Rotherhithe, 27.1.1759. Sold 5.8.1784.

CARDIFF (ex-FORTUNE) 34-gun ship, 300bm. Dutch, captured 1652. Sold 1658 in Jamaica.

CARDIFF Light cruiser, 4,190 tons, 450 (oa) × 43·9ft, 5—6in, 2—3in. Fairfield 12.4.1917. Sold 23.1.1946; BU Troon.

CARDIFF Destroyer, Type 42 Batch 1, 3,150 tons. Vickers, Barrow, 22.2.1974.

CARDIGAN BAY (ex-LOCH LAXFORD) Frigate, 'Bay' class. Robb 28.12.1944 (renamed 1944). Arr. 5.3.1962 Troon for BU.

CARDINGHAM Inshore minesweeper, 'Ham' class. Herd & Mackenzie, Buckie, 24.6.1952. Sold 4.1967 in Hong Kong for BU.

CAREFUL *See BLOSSOM 1856.*

CAREW CASTLE Corvette, 'Castle' class. Midland SY, cancelled 12.1943.

CARHAMPTON Coastal minesweeper, 'Ton' class. Wivenhoe SY 21.7.1955. Sold 22.6.1970 H. K. Vickers for BU.

CARISBROOKE CASTLE Corvette, 'Castle' class. Caledon 31.7.1943. Arr. 14.6.1958 Faslane for BU.

CARLISLE 4th Rate 60, 912bm, 145 × 38ft. Snelgrove, Deptford, 11.2.1693. Wrecked 28.1.1696 The Shipwash.

CARLISLE 4th Rate 48, 709bm. Plymouth DY 1698. Blown up 19.9.1700 accident The Downs.

CARLISLE Light cruiser, 4,190 tons, 451·5 (oa) × 43·9ft, 5—6in, 2—3in. Fairfield 9.7.1918. AA ship 1940 (8—4in, 4—2pdr). Damaged beyond repair 9.10.1943 air attack Mediterranean; base ship Alexandria 3.1944; hulk 1948 Alexandria, BU 1949 *in situ.*

CARLOTTA Brig-sloop 14, 204bm, 90·5 × 23ft. Captured 1810. BU 5.1815.

CARLPLACE Frigate (RCN), 'River' class. Davie, Lauzon, 6.7.1944. Sold 1946 Dominican Navy = PRESIDENTE TRUJILLO.

CARMEN 5th Rate 32, 908bm, 147 × 37·5ft. Spanish, captured 6.4.1800 by LEVIATHAN and EMERALD off Cadiz. Sold 2.1802.

CARNARVON Armoured cruiser, 10,850 tons, 450 × 68ft, 4—7·5in, 6—6in, 2—12pdr, 22—3pdr. Beardmore 7.10.1903. Sold 8.11.1921 Slough Trading Co.; BU Germany.

CARNARVON BAY (ex-LOCH MADDY) Frigate, 'Bay' class. Robb 15.3.1945 (renamed 1944). Arr. 28.8.1959 Spezia for BU.

CARNATIC 3rd Rate 74, 1,720bm, 172 × 48ft. Deptford 21.1.1783. = CAPTAIN 14.7.1815. BU 9.1825.

CARNATIC 3rd Rate 72, 1,790bm, 177 × 49ft. Portsmouth DY 21.10.1823, not cd. Coal hulk 1.1860; powder hulk 1886; lent War Dept 8.1886–10.1891. Sold 19.2.1914; BU Germany.

CARNATIC (ex-NEWHAVEN) Minesweeper (RIN), turbine 'Bangor' class. Hamilton 9.7.1942 (renamed 10.1941).

CARNATION Brig-sloop 18, 'Cruiser' class, 383bm. Taylor, Bideford, 3.10.1807. Captured

3.10.1808 by French PALINURE off Martinique; burnt 2.1809 Martinique to avoid recapture.

CARNATION Brig-sloop, 'Cruizer' class, 385bm. Durkin, Southampton, 29.7.1813. Breakwater 8.1826. Sold 21.1.1836.

CARNATION Wood screw gunboat, 'Albacore' class. Pitcher, Northfleet, 20.10.1855. BU 1863 Sheerness.

CARNATION Sloop, 'Acacia' class. Greenock & Grangemouth 6.9.1915. Sold 14.1.1922 Stanlee, Dover.

CARNATION Corvette, 'Flower' class. Grangemouth DY Co. 3.9.1940. Lent Dutch Navy 1943–18.2.1945 = FRISO. Sold 31.3.1948 = *Southern Laurel.*

CAROLE S Aux. minesweeper (RAN), 112 tonnes. 1971. Leased 12.3.1993—14.3.1994.

CAROLINA Armed ship. In service 1780. Sold 29.4.1784.

CAROLINA *See also PEREGRINE GALLEY.*

CAROLINE Gunvessel 3, 101bm, 64 × 19·5ft. Barge, purch. 4.1794. Sold 3.1802.

CAROLINE 5th Rate 36, 924 bm, 142·5 × 38ft. Randall, Rotherhithe, 17.6.1795. BU 9.1815.

CAROLINE (ex-AFFRONTEUR) Gun-brig 14, 158bm, 12—12pdr carr., 2—6pdr. French, captured 18.5.1803 by DORIS off Ushant. BU 1806.

CAROLINE Schooner. French, captured 1809. Listed until 1814.

CAROLINE Wood screw gunboat, 'Albacore' class. Green, Blackwall, 9.5.1856. BU 2.1862 Portsmouth.

CAROLINE Sailing gunboat (NZ). Purch. 1859. Sold 1863.

CAROLINE Composite screw corvette, 1,420 tons, 200 × 38ft, 14—5in. Sheerness DY 25.11.1882. Harbour service 1897; = GANGES (TS) 4.1908; = POWERFUL III 9.1913; = IMPREGNABLE IV 11.1919. Sold 31.8.1929.

CAROLINE Light cruiser, 3,750 tons, 420 × 41·5ft, 2—6in, 8—4in. Cammell Laird 29.9.1914. RNVR drillship 1.4.1924.

CARRERE 5th Rate 38, 1,013bm, 151 × 39·5ft, 12—32pdr carr., 22—18pdr, 4—9pdr. French, captured 3.8.1801 by POMONE off Elba. Sold 1.9.1814.

CARRICK (ex-*City of Adelaide*) RNVR drillship, 860 tons, 176·5 × 33·5ft. Hospital hulk, purch. 27.3.1923, cd 5.1925. Accommodation ship 10.1940. Given away 1947 club ship.

CARRICK II (ex-*Indefatigable*, ex-PHAETON) TS, 4,300 tons. Renamed 1941. Arr. 20.1.1947 Ward, Preston, for BU.

CARRIER (ex-*Frisk*) Cutter 10, 54bm, 4—12pdr carr., 6—3pdr. Purch. 1805. Wrecked 5.2.1809 coast of France.

CARRON 6th Rate 20, 460bm, 116 × 30ft, 18—32pdr carr., 2—9pdr. Adams, Buckler's Hard, 9.11.1813. Wrecked 6.7.1820 nr Puri, India.

CARRON Wood paddle vessel, 294bm, 110 × 25ft. Deptford DY 9.1.1827, 'Cherokee' class brig-sloop, conv. on stocks. Lent as coal hulk 1846; breakwater 1848. Left Navy List 6.1877; BU 1.1885 Devonport.

CARRON Mortar vessel, 160bm. Wigram, Blackwall, 28.4.1855. = MV.17 on 19.10.1855; hulked 7.1866. BU 11.1884 Devonport.

CARRON (ex-STRENUOUS) Destroyer, 'C' class. Scotts 28.3.1944 (renamed 11.1942). Arr. 4.4.1967 Ward, Inverkeithing, for BU.

CARRON Minehunter, 890 tons (full load), 156.3 (oa) × 34·5ft, 1—40mm. Richards, Great Yarmouth, 23.9.1983. Tx Bangladeshi Navy 3.9.1994 = SHAIKAT.

CARRONADE Destroyer, 1,980 tons, 365 (oa) × 38ft. 6—4in, 6—40mm, 10—TT. Scotts 4.1946, not comp. Arr. 5.4.1946 Troon for BU.

CARSTAIRS (ex-CAWSAND) Minesweeper, Later 'Hunt' class. Bow McLachlan 18.4.1919 (renamed 1918). = DRYAD 4.1.1924; = CARSTAIRS 15.8.1924. Sold 26.4.1935 Ward, Grays.

CARYSFORT 6th Rate 28, 586bm, 118·5 × 34ft. Sheerness DY 23.8.1766. Sold 28.4.1813.

CARYSFORT 6th Rate 26, 911bm, 130 × 40ft. Pembroke Dock 12.8.1836. Sold 22.11.1861 Ritherdon & Thompson.

CARYSFORT Screw corvette, 2,380 tons, 225 × 44·5ft, 2—7in MLR, 12—64pdr. Elder 26.9.1878. Sold 15.12.1899 King, Garston.

CARYSFORT Light cruiser, 3,750 tons, 420 × 41·5ft, 2—6in, 8—4in. Pembroke Dock 14.11.1914. Arr. 10.1931 McLellan, Bo'ness, for BU.

CARYSFORT Destroyer, 'C' class. White 25.7.1944. Sold 23.10.1970 Cashmore; BU Newport.

CASHEL Minesweeper, Later 'Hunt' class. Bow McLachlan, cancelled 1918.

CASSANDRA 5th Rate 36, 897bm. Sheerness, ordered 16.1.1782, cancelled 2.4.1782.

CASSANDRA Cutter 10, 111bm, 68 × 20ft, 8—18pdr carr., 2—6pdr. Bermuda 1806. Foundered 13.5.1807 off Bordeaux.

CASSANDRA Light cruiser, 4,120 tons, 450 (oa) × 43·1ft, 5—6in, 2—3in. Vickers 25.11.1916. Sunk 5.12.1918 mine Baltic.

CASSANDRA (ex-TOURMALINE) Destroyer, 'C' class. Yarrow 29.11.1943 (renamed 11.1942). Arr. 28.4.1967 Ward, Inverkeithing for BU.

CASSIUS Diving-bell vessel. American schooner, purch. 7.9.1847. Last listed 1852.

CASTILIAN Brig-sloop 18, 'Cruiser' class, 387bm. Hill, Sandwich, 29.5.1809. BU 10.1829.

CASTLE Fireship 8, 329bm. Purch. 1672. Sold 1683.

CASTLEMAINE Minesweeper (RAN), 'Bathurst' class. Williamstown DY 7.8.1941. Museum ship 6.1974 Williamstown.

CASTLEREAGH Survey schooner, 93bm. Purch. 3.4.1846. Sold c. 1848.

CASTLETON (ex-AARON WARD) Destroyer, 1,090 tons, 309 × 30·5ft, 1—4in, 1—3in, 4—20mm, 3—TT. USN, cd RN 9.9.1940. Sold 4.3.1947; arr. 9.1948 McLellan, Bo'ness, for BU.

CASTLETON Coastal minesweeper, 'Ton' class. White, Southampton, 26.8.1957. Tx South African Navy 1958 = JOHANNESBURG. Sold S. A. Metal Co. 9.1988; BU 1989.

CASTOR 5th Rate 36. Dutch, captured 23.5.1781 by FLORA. Captured 20.6.1781 by French FRIPONNE off Cadiz.

CASTOR 5th Rate 32, 681bm, 126 × 35ft. Graham, Harwich, 26.5.1785. Sold 22.7.1819. *In French hands 9–29.5.1794.*

CASTOR 5th Rate 26, 1,293bm, 1,808 tons, 159 × 43ft, 36—32pdr. Chatham DY 2.5.1832. TS 1.1860. Sold 25.8.1902 Sheerness.

CASTOR Light cruiser, 3,750 tons, 420 × 41·5ft, 4—6in, 2—3in. Cammell Laird 28.7.1915. Sold 30.7.1936: arr. 8.1936 Rosyth for BU.

CAT Pink 8. In service 1654. Captured 1656 by 'Dunkirkers'.

CAT Fireship 4, 224bm. Captured 1666. Sold 1668.

CATERHAM Minesweeper, Later 'Hunt' class. Bow MacLachlan 6.3.1919. Sold 26.4.1935 Cashmore, Newport.

CATHERINE Fireship, 95bm, 58·5 × 20ft. Purch. 4.1794. Sold 12.1801.

CATHERINE Minesweeper, 'Catherine' class. Associated SB, Seattle, 7.9.1942 on Lend-Lease. Ret. USN 1946. Sold Turkish Navy = ERDEMLI. PO 1963.

CATHERINE *See also KATHERINE.*

CATO 4th Rate 50, 1,062bm, 146·5 × 41ft. Cleveley, Gravesend, 29.5.1792. Foundered 1783 passage East Indies.

CATO Minesweeper, 'Catherine' class. Associated SB, Seattle, 7.9.1942. Tx RN 28.7.1943 on Lend-Lease. Sunk 6.7.1944 by human torpedo off Normandy.

CATON 3rd Rate 64, 1,407bm, 166 × 44ft. French, captured 19.4.1782 Mona Passage. Harbour service 1798. Sold 9.2.1815.

CATTERICK Destroyer, 'Hunt' class Type III. Vickers Armstrong, Barrow, 22.11.1941. Lent

Greek Navy 5.1946 = HASTINGS. Sold 7.1963 Athens for BU.

CATTISTOCK Minesweeper, Early 'Hunt' class. Clyde SB 21.2.1917. Sold 22.2.1923 Alloa S. Bkg Co.; arr. Charlestown 4.1923 for BU.

CATTISTOCK Destroyer, 'Hunt' class Type I. Yarrow 22.2.1940. BU 7.1957 Cashmore, Newport.

CATTISTOCK Minehunter, 615 tons, 197 (oa) × 32·8ft. Vosper-Thornycroft 22.1.1981.

CAUNTON Coastal minesweeper, 'Ton' class. Montrose SY 20.2.1953. Sold 15.4.1970 for BU Newhaven.

CAUVERY Sloop (RIN), 1,350 tons, 283 × 38·5ft, 6—4in, 12—20mm. Yarrow 15.6.1943. = KAVERI 1968. Sold 1979.

CAVALIER Destroyer, 'C' class. White 7.4.1944. Sold 10.1977 for conv. museum ship. At Southampton 1977, Brighton 1983, Hebburn 1987, Chatham 1999 on.

CAVAN (ex-CLOVELLY) Minesweeper, Later 'Hunt' class. Bow McLachlan (renamed 1918), cancelled 1918.

CAVENDISH (ex-SIBYL) Destroyer, 'C' class. John Brown 12.4.1944 (renamed 11.1942). Arr. Blyth 17.8.1967 for BU.

CAVENDISH *See also VINDICTIVE 1918.*

CAWSAND *See CARSTAIRS.*

CAWSAND BAY (ex-LOCH ROAN) Frigate, 'Bay' class. Blyth DD 26.2.1945 (renamed 1944), comp. Hughes Bolckow, Blyth. Arr. 5.9.1959 Genoa for BU.

CAYMAN (ex-HARLAND) Frigate, 'Colony' class. Walsh, Kaiser, 22.8.1943 on Lend-Lease. Ret. USN 22.4.1946.

CAYUGA Destroyer (RCN), 1,927 tons, 377 (oa) × 37·5ft, 8—4in. Halifax SY 28.7.1945. Arr. 14.10.1964 Faslane for BU.

CC.1, CC.2 *See 'C' class submarines.*

CEANOTHUS Sloop, 'Anchusa' class. Armstrong 2.6.1917. Tx RIN 9.1921 = ELPHINSTONE. Wrecked 29.1.1925 Nicobar Is.

CEANOTHUS *See also FOREST HILL.*

CEDARWOOD Survey vessel (RCN), 566 tons. Govt dept vessel, tx 4.10.1948. For disposal 10.1956.

CELANDINE Sloop, 'Arabis' class. Barclay Curle 19.2.1916. Sold 15.1.1923 Unity S. Bkg Co.

CELANDINE Corvette, 'Flower' class. Grangemouth DY Co. 28.12.1940. Arr. 10.1948 Portaferry for BU.

CELEBES (ex-PALLAS) 5th Rate 36. Dutch, captured 26.7.1806 by GREYHOUND in East Indies. Gone by 1809.

CELERITY *See PIQUE 1942.*

CELT Destroyer, 'C' class. Redesigned, 1,980 tons, 365 (oa) × 38ft, 6—4in; = SWORD 9.1943. White, LD 17.9.1945, cancelled 5.10.1945.

CENSEUR 3rd Rate 74, 1,820bm. French, captured 14.3.1795 by the Fleet off Genoa. Recaptured 7.10.1795 by French Fleet off Cape St Vincent.

CENSOR Gun-brig 12, 186bm, 80 × 23ft, 2—32pdr carr., 10—18pdr carr. Randall, Rotherhithe, 2.4.1801. Sold 11.1.1816.

CENTAUR 6th Rate 24, 504bm, 112 × 32ft Blaydes, Hull, 11.6.1746. Sold 30.1.1761.

CENTAUR (ex-CENTAURE) 3rd Rate 74, 1,739bm, 175·5 × 47·5ft, 28—32pdr, 30—18pdr, 16—9pdr. French, captured 18.8.1759 Lagos. Foundered 21.9.1782 off Newfoundland Banks.

CENTAUR 3rd Rate 74, 1,842bm, 176 × 49ft. Woolwich DY 14.3.1797. BU 11.1819 Plymouth.

CENTAUR Wood paddle frigate, 1,269bm, 200 × 37·5ft. Portsmouth DY 6.10.1845. BU 9.1864 Plymouth.

CENTAUR Light cruiser, 3,750 tons, 420 × 42ft, 5—6in, 2—3in. Armstrong 6.1.1916. Sold 2.1934 King, Troon; arr. 6.3.1934 for BU.

CENTAUR Destroyer, 'C' class. White, ordered 2.1942, redesigned as 1,980 tons, = TOMAHAWK 9.1943, launched 15.8.1946 = SCORPION (q.v.).

CENTAUR Aircraft carrier, 22,000 tons, 650 × 90ft, 20—40mm, 50 aircraft. Harland & Wolff 22.4.1947. Sold 19.7.1972; arr. Cairnryan 6.9.1972 for BU.

CENTAUR *See also ROYAL ARTHUR 1891.*

CENTURION 34-gun ship, 531bm. Pett, Ratcliffe, 1650. Wrecked 25.12.1689 off Plymouth.

CENTURION 4th Rate 48, 614bm, 126 × 33ft. Deptford 1691. BU 1728.

CENTURION 4th Rate 60, 1,005bm, 144 × 40ft. Portsmouth DY 6.1.1732. BU 12.1769 Chatham.

CENTURION 4th Rate 50, 1,044bm, 146 × 40·5ft. Barnard, Harwich, 22.5.1774. Harbour service 1809. Sunk 21.2.1824 at moorings Halifax; raised, BU 1825.

CENTURION 3rd Rate 80, 2,580bm, 190 × 57ft. Pembroke Dock 2.5.1844; undocked 12.11.1855 as screw ship, 2,590bm. Sold 19.4.1870 Lethbridge.

CENTURION Battleship, 10,500 tons, 360 × 70ft, 4—10in, 10—4·7in, 8—6pdr. Portsmouth DY 3.8.1892. Sold 12.7.1910 Ward, Morecambe.

CENTURION Battleship, 23,000 tons, 555 × 89ft, 10—13·5in, 12—4in. Devonport DY 18.11.1911. Conv. target ship Chatham 1926; rated escort ship 1940. Sunk 9.6.1944 breakwater Arromanches.

CENTURION Cruiser, c. 9,000 tons. Projected 1945, cancelled 3.1946.

CENTURION *See also CLARENCE 1812.*

CEPHALUS Brig-sloop 18, 'Cruizer' class, 382bm. Custance, Yarmouth, 10.1.1807. BU comp. 17.3.1830.

CERBERUS 6th Rate 28, 593bm, 119 × 34ft. Fenn, Cowes, 5.9.1758. Abandoned, burnt 7.8.1778 Rhode I.

CERBERUS 5th Rate 32, 701bm, 126 × 35·5ft. Randall, Rotherthithe, 15.7.1779. Wrecked 1783 off Bermuda.

CERBERUS 5th Rate 32, 796bm, 135 × 36ft. Adams, Buckler's Hard, 9.1794. Sold 29.9.1814.

CERBERUS Gun-brig 10, 138bm, 79·5 × 20ft, 10– 18pdr carr. French, captured 29.7.1800 by VIPER at Mauritius. Wrecked 19.2.1804 Berry Head, Torbay.

CERBERUS 5th Rate 46, 1,079bm, 152 × 40·5ft, Plymouth DY 30.3.1827. BU comp. 10.1.1866 Marshall, Plymouth.

CERBERUS Turret ship (Australian), 2,107bm, 3,344 tons, 225 × 45ft, 4–10in ML. Palmer, Jarrow, 2.12.1868. Harbour service 1900; = PLATYPUS II (depot ship) 1918. Sold 23.4.1924 Melbourne Salvage Co.; hull sunk 7.1926 breakwater.

CERBERUS *See also PROTECTOR 1884.*

CERES Sloop 18, 361bm, 108·5 × 27·5ft. Woolwich DY 25.3.1777. = RAVEN 4.7.1782. Captured 15.12.1782 by French in West Indies.

CERES 5th Rate 32, 692bm, 129·5 × 35·5ft. Fearon & Webb, Liverpool, 19.9.1781. Slop ship 1804. BU 3.1830.

CERES Light cruiser, 4,190 tons, 450 (oa) × 43·9ft, 5–6in, 2–3in. John Brown 24.3.1917. Sold 5.4.1946; arr. 12.7.1946 Hughes Bolckow, Blyth, for BU.

CERF Gun-brig 12, 172bm, 74 × 22ft. French, captured 30.11.1803 at San Domingo. Sold 27.8.1806.

CERF *See also CYANE.*

CESAR Brig-sloop 16, 320bm. French, captured 15.7.1806 by boats of squadron in Verdun Roads. Wrecked 3.1807 off R. Gironde.

CESAR *See also CAESAR.*

CESSNOCK Minesweeper, 'Bathurst' class. Cockatoo DY 17.10.1941. Sold 23.4.1947 Chinese sbkrs.

CESSNOCK Patrol boat (RAN), 211 tons. North Queensland Engineering Co. 15.1.1983.

CEYLON (ex-BOMBAY) 5th Rate 38, 672bm, 130 × 35ft, 14–24pdr carr., 24–18pdr, 2–9pdr. Renamed 1.7.1808. Troopship 1813. Sold 4.7.1857 in Malta. *Captured three times by French; finally recaptured 6.12.1810 Mauritius.*

CEYLON Cruiser, 8,800 tons, 555·5 (oa) × 62ft, 9–6in, 8–4in. Stephen 30.7.1942. Sold Peruvian Navy 12.1959, = CORONEL BOLOGNESI 2.1960; deleted 1982; BU 1985.

CH.14 (ex-H.14 *See 'H' class submarines.*

CH.15 (ex-H.15) *See 'H' class submarines.*

CHAILEY Inshore minehunter, 'Ley' class. Saunders-Roe, Anglesey, 11.11.1954. Sold 4.6.1969; BU Canvey I.

CHALEUR Schooner 12, 117bm, 67 × 20ft. Purch. 1764 North America. Sold 6.12.1768. *First schooner in RN.*

CHALEUR Coastal minesweeper (RCN), 370 tons, Port Arthur SY 5.1952. Tx French Navy 9.10.1954 = DIEPPOISE; deleted 1987.

CHALEUR Coastal minesweeper (RCN). 390 tons, 140 × 28ft, 1–40mm. Marine Industries, Sorel, 11.5.1957. PO 10.1998; deleted.

CHALLENGER Brig-sloop 16 (pitch pine-built) 285bm, 96 × 25ft. Wallis, Blackwall, 30.7.1806. Captured 12.3.1811 by French frigate off Mauritius.

CHALLENGER Brig-sloop 18, 'Cruizer' class, 387bm. Hobbs & Hillver, Redbridge, 15.5.1813. 10 guns 1816; mooring vessel 1820; store hulk 1820. Sold 3.1824 Trincomalee.

CHALLENGER 6th Rate 28, 603bm, 125·5 × 33ft. Portsmouth DY 14.11.1826. Wrecked 19.5.1835 coast of Chile.

CHALLENGER Corvette 18, 810bm, 134 × 37·5ft. Chatham DY, ordered 1845, cancelled 1848.

CHALLENGER Wood screw corvette, 1,462bm, 2,306 tons, 200 × 40·5ft, 20–8in, 2–69pdr. Woolwich DY 13.2.1858. Survey ship (4 guns) 1872; hulk 1880. Sold 6.1.1921 J. B. Garnham.

CHALLENGER 2nd class cruiser, 5,917 tons, 355 × 56ft, 11–6in, 9–12pdr. Chatham DY 27.5.1902. Sold 31.5.1920 Ward, Preston.

CHALLENGER Survey ship, 1,140 tons, 200 × 36ft. Chatham DY 1.6.1931. Arr. 12.1.1954 Dover Industries for BU.

CHALLENGER Diving vessel, 6,400 tons, 440 (oa) × 59ft. Scotts, Greenock, 19.5.1981. PO 30.11.1990; sold 2.7.1993 Sub Sea Offshore, left Portsmouth 20.1.1994, LU R. Tyne; left 31.8.1998 for Gdynia, refit and resale Italian owners.

CHAMBLY Corvette (RCN), 'Flower' class. Vickers, Montreal, 29.7.1940. Sold 1946 = *Sonjia Vinke*. BU 1952.

CHAMELEON Sloop 14, 307bm, 97 × 27ft. Randall, Rotherhithe, 26.3.1777. Foundered 11.10.1780 hurricane West Indies.

CHAMELEON (ex-*Hawke*) Brig-sloop 16, 267bm, 78 × 29ft. Purch. 1780. Sold 1.5.1783.

CHAMELEON Minesweeper, 'Algerine' class. Harland & Wolff 6.5.1944. Arr. 3.4.1966 Silloth for BU.

CHAMELEON *See also CAMELEON.*

CHAMOIS Destroyer, 360 tons, 215 × 20·5ft, 1—12pdr, 5—6pdr, 2—TT. Palmer 3.11.1896. Foundered 26.9.1904 Gulf of Patras, Greece, after screw had pierced keel.

CHAMOIS Minesweeper, 'Catherine' class. Associated SB, Seattle, 26.10.1942; tx RN on Lend-Lease 22.10.1943 Ret. USN 10.12.1946; BU 9.1950 Southampton.

CHAMPION 6th Rate 24, 519bm, 114·5× 32ft. Barnard, Ipswich, 17.5.1779. Harbour service 1810. Sold 28.8.1816.

CHAMPION Sloop 18, 456bm, 110 × 31ft. Portsmouth DY 31.5.1824. Harbour service 1859. Wrecked target; BU 10.1867 Portsmouth.

CHAMPION Screw corvette, 2,380 tons, 225 × 44·5ft, 2—7in ML, 12—64pdr. Elder 1.7.1878. Harbour service 1904; = CHAMPION (OLD) 1915. Sold 23.6.1919 Hughes Bolckow, Blyth.

CHAMPION Light cruiser, 3,750 tons, 420 × 41·5ft, 2—6in, 8—4in. Hawthorn Leslie 29.5.1915. Sold 28.7.1934 Metal Industries, Rosyth.

CHAMPION *See also CHEQUERS.*

CHAMPLAIN Brig (Canadian lakes), 111bm. Lake Champlain 1819. Sold c. 1832.

CHAMPLAIN *See also TORBAY 1919.*

CHANCE (ex-GALGO) Sloop 18, 395bm, 99 × 27ft. Spanish, captured 15.11.1799 by CRESCENT off Puerto Rico. Foundered 9.10.1800 West Indies.

CHANCE Minesweeper, 'Catherine' class. Associated SB, Seattle, 27.11.1942; tx RN on Lend-Lease 13.11.1943. Ret. USN 1946. Sold 3.1947 Turkish Navy = EDREMIT. Withdrawn 1973.

CHANTICLEER Brig-sloop 10, 'Cherokee' class, 237bm. List, Cowes, 26.7.1808. Survey ship 4.1828; Customs watchvessel 2.1830; = WV.5 on 25.5.1863. BU 6.1871 Sheerness.

CHANTICLEER Wood screw sloop, 950bm, 185 × 33ft. Portsmouth DY 9.2.1861. Sold 23.1.1875 Castle.

CHANTICLEER Sloop, 1,350 tons, 283 × 38·5ft, 6—4in, 12—20mm. Denny 24.9.1942. Damaged beyond repair 18.11.1943 by U.238 west of Portugal, used as base ship; = LUSITANIA 31.12.1943. BU 1945.

CHAPLET Destroyer, 'C' class. Thornycroft 18.7.1944. Arr. 6.11.1965 Hughes Bolckow, Blyth, for BU.

CHARGER Gun-brig 179bm, 80 × 22·5ft, 1—8in mortar, 10—18pdr carr., 2—18pdr. Dudman, Deptford, 17.4.1801. Sold 9.6.1814.

CHARGER Wood screw gunboat, 'Albacore' class. Pitcher, Northfleet, 13.11.1855. Buoy boat 6.1866, later = YC.3. Sold 7.1887 = *Rescue*. BU 1921.

CHARGER Destroyer, 290 tons, 190 × 18·5ft, 1—12pdr, 5—6pdr, 2—TT. Yarrow, Poplar, 15.5.1894. Sold 14.5.1912, Ward; BU Silvertown.

CHARGER (ex-*Rio de la Plata*) Escort carrier, 8,200 tons, 450 × 69·5ft. Sun SB, Chester, 1.3.1941 for RN, conv. on stocks; retained USN = CHARGER.

CHARGER Escort carrier, 11,420 tons, 468·5 × 69·5ft, 2—4in, 16—40mm, 24 aircraft. Seattle, Tacoma. Launched 16.7.1942 = RAVAGER.

CHARGER Patrol boat, 49 tons, 68·2 (oa) × 19ft. Watercraft 1986, comp. Vosper-Thornycroft 6.1988.

CHARGER *See also COURIER 1830, LST.3026 1944.*

CHARITY (ex-CHARITE) Fireship. French, captured 1650. Expended 1652.

CHARITY 36-gun ship, 453bm. Captured 1653. Captured 3.6.1665 by Dutch. *Also known as GREAT CHARITY 1656.*

CHARITY Sloop (Canadian lakes), Lake Niagara 1770. Lost 1777 Lake Niagara.

CHARITY Destroyer, 'C' class, Thornycroft 30.11.1944. Tx Pakistani Navy 16.12.1958 = SHAH JEHAN. Sunk 4.12.1971 off Karachi.

CHARLES Pinnace 16, 70/110bm, 8—6pdr, 2—2pdr, 6 small. Woolwich 1586. Sold 1616.

CHARLES Pinnace 16, 80/140bm. Built 1620. Last listed 1627.

CHARLES 44-gun ship, 607bm. Woolwich 1632. = LIBERTY 1649. Wrecked 1650.

CHARLES 38-gun ship, 500bm. Royalist. Captured 25.4.1649, = GUINET 1649. Sold 1667.

CHARLES Royal yacht 6, 38bm. Woolwich DY 1662. Tx 1668 Ordnance Office.

CHARLES Fireship 6, 209bm. Purch. 1666. Sold 1667.

CHARLES 1st Rate 96, 1,129bm, 163 × 42·5ft, 26—60pdr, 28—18pdr, 26—9pdr, 16—3pdr. Deptford DY 3.3.1668. = ST GEORGE 1687 (q.v.). BU 1774.

CHARLES Royal yacht 8, 120bm. Rotherhithe 1675. Wrecked 1678 Dutch coast.

CHARLES Fireship 6. Purch. 1688. Expended 5.7.1695 St-Malo.

CHARLES & HENRY Fireship 6, 120bm. Purch. 1688. Wrecked 29.11.1689 off Plymouth.

CHARLES GALLEY 5th Rate 32, 546bm, 131 × 28·5ft, 28—9pdr, 4—3pdr. Woolwich DY 1676. Rebuilt 1693 as 548bm; rebuilt Deptford 1710 as 537bm; = TORRINGTON 7.1729, rebuilt as 594bm; hulk 1740. Sold 12.7.1744.

CHARLES V (ex-CAROLUS V) 4th Rate 52, 600bm. Dutch, captured 1665. Burnt 12.6.1667 by Dutch at Chatham.

CHARLES UPHAM (ex-*Mercandian Queen II*, ex-*Continental Queen*) Military Sealift Vessel (RNZN), 7,955 tons, 432·1 (oa) × 69·2ft. Frederikshavn. Purch. late 1994, arr. Auckland 14.3.1995, cd 18.10.1995. Chartered out Contenemar 5.1998 = *Don Carlos*. Sold Contenemar by 10.2001.

CHARLESTOWN (ex-BOSTON) 6th Rate 28, 514bm, 114 × 32ft. American, captured 12.5.1780 Charlestown. Sold 24.4.1783.

CHARLESTOWN (ex-ABBOTT) Destroyer, 1,060 tons, 309 × 30·5ft, 3—4in, 1—3in, 6—TT. USN, cd RN 23.9.1940. Sold 4.3.1947; BU Young, Sunderland.

CHARLOCK Corvette, Modified 'Flower' class. Ferguson 16.11.1943. = MAHRATTA (RIN) 6.2.1946. Stranded 1947.

CHARLOTTE Royal yacht 8, 143bm, Woolwich DY 1677. Rebuilt 155bm = AUGUSTA 28.7.1761. BU 1771.

CHARLOTTE Cutter 4, 70bm, 46·5 × 20ft. Purch. 2.1763. Sold 14.11.1770.

CHARLOTTE Schooner 8, 8—6pdr. Purch. 1798. Captured 1799 by French = VENGEUR; recaptured 22.11.1799, BU.

CHARLOTTE Schooner 6, 6—3pdr. Purch. 1800. Wrecked 28.3.1801 I. of Ash.

CHARLOTTETOWN Corvette (RCN), 'Flower' class. Kingston SY 10.9.1941. Sunk 11.9.1942 by U.517 in Gulf of St Lawrence.

CHARLOTTETOWN Frigate (RCN), 'River' class. G. T. Davie 16.9.1943. Sold 1947; hull sunk as breakwater 1948.

CHARLOTTETOWN Frigate (RCN), 'Halifax' class. Marine Industries, Sorel, 10.7.1994.

CHARON 5th Rate 44, 891bm, 140 × 38ft, Barnard, Harwich, 8.10.1778. Burnt 10.10.1781 Yorktown.

CHARON 5th Rate 44, 889bm, 140 × 38ft. Hillhouse, Bristol, 17.5.1783. Harbour service 1795; troopship 2.1800. BU 12.1805.

CHARON (ex-*Crusader*) Wood paddle packet, 125bm. GPO vessel, tx 1.4.1837. Sold 18.7.1849 Trinity House.

CHARON Wood screw gunboat, 'Albacore' class. Pitcher, Northfleet, 9.2.1856. BU 10.1865 Marshall, Plymouth.

CHARWELL (ex-AURORE) Sloop 16, 346bm, 102 × 29ft. French, captured 18.1.1801 by THAMES. Sold 28.4.1813.

CHARWELL Storeship (Canadian lakes), 439bm, 108 × 30ft. Kingston, Ontario. In service in 1816. = No 98 in 1832.

CHARWELL Destroyer, 545 tons, 225 × 23·5ft, 1—

12pdr, 5—6pdr (1907: 4—12pdr), 2—TT. Palmer 25.7.1903. Sold 23.6.1919 Ward, Rainham.

CHARWELL *See also MOIRA 1812.*

CHARYBDIS Brig-sloop 18, 'Cruizer' class, 385bm. Richards, Hythe, 28.8.1809. Sold 3.2.1819 Pittman.

CHARYBDIS Brig-sloop 10, 'Cherokee' class, 232bm. Portsmouth DY 27.2.1831. Sold Beatson, Rotherhithe, 7.11.1843.

CHARYBDIS Wood screw corvette, 1,506bm, 2,187 tons, 200 × 40·5ft, 20—8in, 1—68pdr. Chatham DY 1.6.1859. Lent Canadian Govt (TS) 10.1880–8.1882. Sold 1884 Halifax.

CHARYBDIS 2nd class cruiser, 4,360 tons, 320 × 49·5ft, 2—6in, 8—4·7in, 8—6pdr. Sheerness DY 15.6.1893. Conv. 3.1918 cargo carrier; ret. RN 12.1919. Sold 27.1.1922 Bermuda; resold 10.1923, BU Holland.

CHARYBDIS Cruiser, 5,450 tons, 512 (oa) × 50.5ft, 8—4·5in, 8—20mm. Cammell Laird 17.9.1940. Sunk 23.10.1943 by German MTBs in English Channel.

CHARYBDIS Frigate, 'Leander' class, Y160, 2,650 tons, 372 (oa) × 43ft, 2—4·5in, Seacat, helo (later Exocet, Seawolf). Harland & Wolff 28.2.1968. Expended 12.6.1993 target.

CHASER Sloop 18, 320bm, 99 × 28ft. Purch. 1.1.1781 East Indies. Captured 25.2.1782 by French in Bay of Bengal; recaptured 3.1783. Sold 26.8.1784.

CHASER (ex-BRETON, ex-*Mormacgulf*) Escort carrier, 11,420 tons. 468·5 × 69·5ft, 2—4in, 8—40mm, 18 aircraft. Ingalls 19.6.1942 on Lend-Lease, conv. on stocks. Ret. USN 12.5.1946, sold = *Aagtekerk*.

CHASER Training boat, 32 tons, 65·6 (oa) × 17ft. Fairey Marine, Southampton, 1983. Sold to Lebanon 11.1991, left Portsmouth 24.8.1992; = BEIRUT 1993.

CHASER *See also LST.3029 1945.*

CHASSEUR Iron screw floating battery, 543bm. Purch. 28.5.1855. Sold 25.5.1901 Ward, Preston.

CHATHAM Galliot, 91bm. Dutch, captured 1666. Given away 1667.

CHATHAM Sloop 4, 50bm. Chatham DY 1673. Wrecked 1677.

CHATHAM 4th Rate, 696bm, 126 × 34·5ft. Chatham DY 20.4.1691. Rebuilt Deptford 1721 as 756bm; breakwater Sheerness 5.1749. Raised 1762, BU.

CHATHAM Yacht 14, 60bm, 58 × 16ft. Chatham DY 18.7.1716. Sold 28.3.1742.

CHATHAM Yacht 6, 74bm, 59 × 18ft, 6—2pdr. Chatham DY 1.10.1741. Rebuilt Chatham 1793 as

93bm; rebuilt Chatham 1842 as 104bm. BU comp. 9.3.1867 Chatham.

CHATHAM 4th Rate 50, 1,052bm, 147 × 40·5ft. Portsmouth DY 25.4.1758. Harbour service 3.1793; powder hulk 12.1805, = TILBURY 29.6.1810. BU 5.1814 Chatham.

CHATHAM Survey brig 4, 133bm, 80 × 22ft, 4–3pdr. King, Dover, 1788, purch. 12.2.1788. Sold 1830 in Jamaica.

CHATHAM Schooner 4, 93bm, purch. 1790 Halifax. Sold 1794 in Canada.

CHATHAM Sloop. Hired 1793.

CHATHAM Transport, 317bm, 109 × 26ft. Brindley, Frindsbury, 22.6.1811. Sunk 9.1825 breakwater.

CHATHAM (ex-ROYAL HOLLANDAIS) 3rd Rate 74, 1,860bm, 178 × 49ft. French, captured on stocks 17.8.1809 Flushing; frames tx Woolwich DY, ship launched 14.2.1812. Sold 10.9.1817 J. Cristall.

CHATHAM Sheer hulk 1,691bm, 146 × 46·5ft. Chatham DY 2.4.1813. BU comp. 5.8.1876 Chatham.

CHATHAM Iron paddle gunboat (Indian), 375bm. Laird 1835. In service 1850.

CHATHAM 2nd class cruiser, 5,400 tons, 430 × 50ft, 8–6in. Chatham DY 9.11.1911. Lent New Zealand 1920. Sold 13.7.1926 Ward, Pembroke Dock.

CHATHAM Frigate, 4,100 tons, 480·5 (oa) × 48·4ft, 1–4·5in, Harpoon, Seawolf, helo, 6–TT. Swan Hunter 20.1.1988.

CHATHAM DOUBLE Sloop 4, 50bm. Chatham DY 1673. Sold 1683. *Built with double hull.*

CHATHAM HULK Sheer hulk, 714bm, 153 × 32ft, Chatham DY 9.10.1694. BU 10.1813 Chatham.

CHATHAM PRIZE 6th Rate 8, 65bm, 53 × 17ft. French, captured 3.1703 by CHATHAM. Sold 8.1.1707.

CHATSGROVE *See PC.74 1918.*

CHAUDIERE Frigate (RCN), 2,370 tons, 366 (oa) × 42ft, 4–3in, 2–40mm, Limbo, 6–TT. Halifax SY 13.11.1957. Scuttled Sechelt Inlet, BC, 5.12.1992 artificial reef.

CHAUDIERE *See also HERO 1936.*

CHAWTON Coastal minesweeper, 'Ton' class. Fleetlands, Gosport, 24.9.1957. Sold 7.1977 Tees Marine Services.

CHEAM Minesweeper, Later 'Hunt' class. Eltringham 2.7.1919. Sold 18.3.1922 Coaster Construction Co.

CHEBOGUE Frigate (RCN), 'River' class. Yarrow, Esquimalt, 16.8.1943. Torpedoed by U-boat, foundered 11.10.1944 off Swansea; raised, BU 2.1948 Milford Haven.

CHEDABUCTO Minesweeper (RCN), TE 'Bangor' class. Burrard 14.4.1941. Collision SS *Lord Kelvin* in St Lawrence R., beached 6.2.1944.

CHEDISTON Coastal minesweeper, 'Ton' class. Montrose SY 6.10.1953. = MONTROSE 06.1954–10.1957; = CHEDISTON 1958; = CURLEW (RAN) 8.1962. PO 23.4.1990; sold 5.1997 Woolwich Marine, Sydney. Tx Hobart 6.1998, preserved. Planned museum ship Montrose 2003.

CHEERFUL Cutter 12, 111bm, 68 × 20ft, 8–18pdr carr., 4–6pdr. Johnson, Dover, 11.1806. Sold 31.7.1816.

CHEERFUL Wood screw gunboat, 'Cheerful' class. Deptford DY 6.10.1855. BU comp. 16.1.1869 Haslar.

CHEERFUL Destroyer, 370 tons, 210 × 21ft, 1–12pdr, 5–6pdr, 2–TT. Hawthorn 14.7.1897. Sunk 30.6.1917 mine off Shetland Is.

CHEERFUL Minesweeper, 'Algerine' class. Harland & Wolff 21.5.1944. BU 9.1963 Lacmots, Queenborough.

CHEERLY Gun-brig 12, 178bm, 80 × 22·5ft, 10–18pdr carr., 2–9pdr. Boole, Bridport, 10.1804. Sold 9.2.1815.

CHELMER Destroyer, 560 tons, 222 × 23·5ft, 1–12pdr, 5–6pdr (1907: 4–12pdr), 2–TT. Thornycroft, Chiswick, 8.12.1904. Sold 30.6.1920 Ward, Hayle.

CHELMER Frigate, 'River' class. G. Brown 27.3.1943. Arr. 8.1957 Charlestown for BU.

CHELMER *See also BALSAM 1942.*

CHELMSFORD Paddle minesweeper, 'Ascot' class. Ailsa 14.6.1916. Sold 25.11.1927 Hughes Bolckow, Blyth.

CHELSEA (ex-CROWNINSHIELD) Destroyer, 1,090 tons, 309 × 30·5ft, 1–4in, 1–3in, 4–20mm, 3–TT. USN, cd RN 9.9.1940. Lent RCN 11.1942–12.1943; lent Soviet Navy 16.7.1944–24.6.1949 = DERZKY. Sold 12.7.1949; BU McLellan, Bo'ness.

CHELSHAM Inshore minesweeper, 'Ham' class. Jones, Buckie, 9.7.1952. Tx RAF 13.12.1965 = No 5000. Ret., sold 1977.

CHELTENHAM Paddle minesweeper, 'Ascot' class. Ardrossan DD Co. 12.4.1916. Sold 7.10.1927 Cashmore, Newport.

CHEPSTOW Paddle minesweeper, 'Ascot' class. Aryshire Co. 29.2.1916. Sold 25.11.1927 Hughes Bolckow, Blyth.

CHEPSTOW CASTLE Corvette, 'Castle' class. Collingwood SY, cancelled 12.1943.

CHEQUERS (ex-CHAMPION) Destroyer, 'C' class. Scotts 30.10.1944 (renamed 1943). Arr. 23.7.1966 Cashmore, Newport, for BU.

CHERITON 20-gun ship, 232bm. Deptford 1656. = SPEEDWELL 1660. Wrecked 29.6.1676 Novaya Zemlya.

CHERITON Coastal minesweeper, 'Ton' class. White. Launched 5.9.1956 = ASHTON (q.v.).

CHEROKEE (ex-*Codrington*) Armed ship 6, 177bm, 76 × 8.5ft. Purch. 9.1774. = DESPATCH; transport 4.1777. Sold 27.2.1783.

CHEROKEE Brig-sloop 10, 'Cherokee' class, 237bm. Perry, Wells & Green, Blackwall, 24.2.1808. Sold 26.3.1828 J. Cristall.

CHEROKEE Wood paddle vessel, 750bm, 170 × 31ft. Canadian brig, Kingston, Ontario, 22.9.1842. Sold 30.10.1851.

CHEROKEE Wood screw gunboat, 'Albacore' class, Green, Blackwall, 30.4.1856. BU 3.1869 Portsmouth.

CHERUB Sloop 18, 424bm, 108·5× 29·5ft. King, Dover, 27.12.1806. Sold 13.1.1820

CHERUB Wood screw gunboat, 'Britomart' class. Haslar 29.3.1865. Sold 5.5.1890 Castle for BU.

CHESAPEAKE 5th Rate 38, 1,135 bm, 151 × 41ft. American, captured 1.6.1813 by SHANNON in Boston Bay. Sold 18.8.1819 J. Holmes.

CHESAPEAKE 5th Rate 36, 1,622bm, 160 × 49ft. Chatham DY, ordered 1834, cancelled 1851.

CHESAPEAKE Wood screw frigate 51, 2,377bm, 212 × 50ft. Chatham DY 27.9.1855. Sold 1867 Castle & Beech.

CHESTER 4th Rate 48, 663bm, 125 × 34·5ft. Woolwich DY 21.3.1691. Captured 10.10.1707 by French.

CHESTER 4th Rate 50, 704bm, 130 × 35ft. Chatham DY 18.10.1708. Harbour service 8.1743. BU 2.1750.

CHESTER 4th Rate 50, 977bm, 140 × 40·5ft. Wells & Bronsdon, Deptford, 18.2.1743. Sold 28.7.1767.

CHESTER (ex-LAMBROS KATSONIS) Light cruiser, 5,185 tons, 430 × 50ft, 10—5·5in, 1—3in. Cammell Laird 8.12.1915; Greek, ordered 1914 . Sold 9.11.1921 Rees, Llanelly.

CHESTER CASTLE Corvette, 'Castle' class. Collingwood SY, cancelled 12.1943.

CHESTERFIELD 5th Rate 44, 719bm, 128 × 36·5ft. Quallet, Rotherhithe, 31.10.1745. Foundered 21.7.1726 off Bahamas.

CHESTERFIELD (ex-WELBORN C. WOOD) Destroyer, 1,190 tons, 311 × 31ft, 1—4in, 1—3in, 4—20mm, 3—TT. USN, cd RN 1940. Sold 4.3.1947; BU Clayton & Davie, Dunston.

CHESTNUT Ketch 8, 81bm. Portsmouth 1656. Wrecked 1665.

CHEVIOT Destroyer, 'C' class. Stephen 2.5.1944. Arr. 22.10.1962 Ward, Inverkeithing, for BU.

CHEVREUIL Minesweeping sloop, 647 tons, 256 × 28ft, 2—3·9in. French, seized 3.7.1940 Plymouth. Free French crew 1940. Ret. French Navy 1944.

CHEVRON Destroyer, 'C' class. Stephen 23.2.1944. Sold Ward 18.10.1969; BU Inverkeithing.

CHICHESTER 2nd Rate 80, 1,210bm, 157·5× 42ft. Chatham DY 6.3.1695. Rebuilt Woolwich 1706. BU comp. 3.9.1749 Plymouth.

CHICHESTER 3rd Rate 70, 1,401bm, 160 × 45ft, Portsmouth DY 4.6.1753. BU 10.1803.

CHICHESTER 5th Rate 44, 901bm, 140 × 38·5ft. Taylor, Itchenor, 10.3.1785. Storeship 1799; lent 3.1810 West India Dock Co. as TS. BU 6.1815.

CHICHESTER (ex-VAR) Storeship 26, 777bm. French, captured 15.2.1809 by BELLE POULE off Valona. Wrecked 2.5.1811 off Madras.

CHICHESTER 4th Rate 52, 1,468bm, 172 × 44ft. Woolwich DY 12.7.1843. LU Chatham 1843; lent 1866 as TS. Sold 5.1889 Castle.

CHICHESTER Frigate, 2,170 tons, 330 × 40ft, 2—4·5in, 2—40mm. Fairfield 21.4.1955. Arr. Queenborough 17.3.1981 for BU.

CHICOUTIMI Corvette (RCN), 'Flower' class. Vickers, Montreal, 16.10.1940. BU 6.1946 Steel Co. of Canada.

CHICOUTIMI *See also UPHOLDER 1986.*

CHIDDINGFOLD Destroyer, 'Hunt' class Type II. Scotts 10.3.1941. Lent Indian Navy 18.6.1954 = GANGA (q.v.). Sold Indian Navy 4.1959. Later TS; PO 1975. Sold 1975.

CHIDDINGFOLD Minehunter, 615 tons. Vosper-Thornycroft 6.10.1983.

CHIEFTAIN Destroyer, 'C' Class, Scotts 26.2.1945. Arr. Young, Sunderland 20.3.1961 for BU.

CHIGNECTO Minesweeper (RCN), TE 'Bangor' class. North Vancouver SR Co. 12.12.1940. Sold c. 1949.

CHIGNECTO Coastal minesweeper (RCN), 390 tons, 140 × 28ft, 1—40mm. Marine Industries 12.6.1952. Tx 7.4.1954 French Navy = LA BAYONNAISE. Reserve, stricken 1976.

CHIGNECTO Coastal minesweeper (RCN), 390 tons, 140 × 28ft, 1—40mm. G. T. Davie 17.11.1956. PO 19.12.1996; sold 5.1999; BU Victoria.

CHILCOMPTON Coastal minesweeper, 'Ton' class. Herd & Mackenzie 23.10.1953. Sold 26.11.1971 Pounds.

CHILDERS Brig-sloop 14, 202bm, 80 × 25ft. Menetone, R. Thames 7.9.1778. BU 1811 Chatham.

CHILDERS Brig-sloop 18, 'Cruizer' class, 384bm. Portsmouth DY 8.7.1812. BU 3.1822.

CHILDERS Brig-sloop 16, 'Cruizer' class, 385bm. Chatham DY 23.8.1827. Sold 19.8.1865 Holloway

Bros.

CHILDERS Destroyer, 'C' class. Denny 27.2.1945. Arr. 22.9.1963 Spezia for BU.

CHILDERS Torpedo boat (Australian), 65 tons, 113 × 12·5ft, 2—Hotchkiss. Thornycroft, Chiswick, 16.8.1883. Sold 5.8.1918, hulked.

CHILDS PLAY 6th Rate 24, 373bm, 103 × 29·5ft. French, captured 1706. Foundered 30.8.1707 off St Kitts.

CHILLINGHAM Inshore minesweeper, 'Ham' class. McLean, Renfrew, 19.12.1952. Sold 3.8.1969 Société Maseline, Channel Is.

CHILLIWACK Corvette (RCN), 'Flower' class. Burrard 14.9.1940. Sold 1946.

CHILTON Coastal minesweeper, 'Ton' class. Cook, Welton & Gemmell 15.7.1957. Tx South African Navy 1958 = EAST LONDON. PO 5.9.2001.

CHIPPEWAY Schooner 2 (Canadian lakes). Maumee, 1812. Captured 10.9.1813 by Americans on Lake Erie. Burnt 12.1813.

CHITTAGONG *See KATHIAWAR 1942.*

CHIVALROUS Destroyer, 'C' class. Denny 22.6.1945. Tx Pakistani Navy 29.6.1954 = TAIMUR; deleted 28.12.1959; BU Karachi 1.1960.

CHOLMONDELY Cutter, 79bm. Purch. 2.1763. Sold 20.8.1771.

CHRIST Ship, 300bm. Purch. 1512. Captured by Turks 1515.

CHRISTCHURCH CASTLE Corvette, 'Castle' class. Midland SY, cancelled 12.1943.

CHRISTIAN VII 3rd Rate 80, 2,131bm. Danish, captured 7.9.1807 Battle of Copenhagen. Harbour service 1814. BU 3.1838 Chatham. *Was to have been renamed BLENHEIM 1812.*

CHRISTOPHER Cog. King's ship 1338.

CHRISTOPHER Hulk. Listed 1410–12.

CHRISTOPHER (ex-PINELLI) Carrack, 600bm. Genoese, captured 24.8.1417. Sold 5.1423.

CHRISTOPHER 53-gun ship, 400bm. Purch. 1545. Sold 1556.

CHRISTOPHER Pinnace, 15bm. Dates from 1577. Burnt 1578.

CHRISTOPHER Destroyer, 938 tons, 267·5 × 27ft, 3—4in, 2—TT. Hawthorn Leslie 29.8.1912. Sold 9.5.1921 Ward; resold 10.1923 King, Garston.

CHRISTOPHER SPAYNE Galley, 600bm. Spanish, captured 29.6.1417. Given away 8.1418.

CHRYSANTHEMUM Sloop, 'Anchusa' class. Armstrong 10.11.1917. RNVR drillship 1939. Sold Inter Action Children's Charity 1987. Resold Carvel Maritime; arr. arrived Rochester 16.5.1995 for BU.

CHRYSANTHEMUM Corvette, 'Flower' class.

Harland & Wolff 11.4.1941. Lent Free French 1942–5.1847 = COMMANDANT DROGOU. Sold 7.8.1947 = *Terje 10.*

CHUB Wood screw gunboat, 'Cheerful' class. Sheerness DY 15.10.1855. BU comp. 29.1.1869 Haslar.

CHUBB Schooner 4, 80bm, 56 × 18ft, 4—12pdr carr. Bermuda 5.1807. Capsized 14.8.1812 Halifax Station.

CHUBB (ex-EAGLE) Schooner (Canadian lakes), 110bm, 10—18pdr carr , 1—6pdr. American, captured 9.1813 Lake Champlain. Sold 1822.

CHURCH 20-gun ship, 194bm. Captured 1653. Sold 1660.

CHURCHILL (ex-HERNDON) Destroyer, 1,190 tons, 311 × 31ft, 1—4in, 1—3in, 4—20mm, 3—TT. USN, cd RN 9.9.1940. Lent 16.7.1944 Soviet Navy = DEIATELNYI. Sunk 16.1.1945 by U.956 in Arctic.

CHURCHILL Nuclear submarine, 4,400/4,900 tons, 285 (oa) × 33ft, SubHarpoon, 6—TT. Vickers Armstrong, Barrow, 20.12.1968. PO 28.2.1991; LU Rosyth.

CICALA River gunboat, 645 tons, 230 × 36ft, 2—12pdr. Barclay Curle 10.12.1915. Sunk 21.12.1941 Japanese aircraft Hong Kong.

CICERO Minesweeping sloop, '24' class. Swan Hunter 26.7.1918. Sold 1.12.1921 Stanlee, Dover.

CICERO (ex-EMPIRE ARQUEBUS) Infantry landing ship, 11,650 tons, 396 × 60ft, 1—4in, 1—12pdr, 12—20mm. Consolidated Steel Corp., Wilmington, 16.11.1943 on Lend-Lease (renamed 1.1945). Tx MWT 9.1945 = *Empire Arquebus.* Ret. USN 1946. Sold 11.1946 = *Al Sudan.*

CIRCASSIAN (ex-*Swan*) Wood paddle tender, 74bm. Purch. 8.1854 Constantinople. Sold 28.7.1856.

CIRCASSIAN *See also ENTERPRISE 1863, ENTERPRISE 1864.*

CIRCE 6th Rate 28, 598bm, 121 × 34ft. Ladd, Dover, 30.9.1785. Wrecked 16.11.1803 nr Yarmouth.

CIRCE 5th Rate 32, 670bm, 127 × 34ft. Plymouth DY 17.11.1804. Sold 20.8.1814.

CIRCE 5th Rate 46, 1,079bm, 152 × 40·5ft. Plymouth DY 22.9.1827. Harbour service 1866, = IMPREGNABLE IV 1916. Sold 7.1922 S. Castle, Plymouth.

CIRCE Torpedo gunboat, 810 tons, 230 × 27ft, 2—4·7in, 4—3pdr, 3—TT. Sheerness DY 14.6.1892. Sold 30.7.1920 H. Auten & Co.

CIRCE Minesweeper, 'Algerine' class. Harland & Wolff 27.6.1942. RNVR drillship 1956. BU 1967 Dalmuir.

CITADEL (ex-LCT.4038) Tank landing craft, 657 tons, 225 × 39ft. Arrol, Alloa, 29.3.1945 (renamed 1956). Sold Pounds 4.6.1970 for BU.

CLACTON Minesweeper, turbine 'Bangor' class. Blyth SB 18.12.1941. Sunk 31.12.1943 mine off Corsica.

CLARA 5th Rate 38, 958bm, 144·5 × 39ft, 12–32pdr carr., 26–12pdr, 2–9pdr. Spanish, captured 5.10.1804 in Atlantic. Harbour service 1811. Sold 21.7.1814 W. R. King, Mark Lane.

CLARBESTON Coastal minesweeper, 'Ton' class. Richards Ironworks 18.2.1954. Sold H. K. Vickers 22.6.1970.

CLARE (ex-ABEL P. UPSHUR) Destroyer, 1,190 tons, 311 × 31ft, 1–4in, 1–3in, 4–20mm, 3–TT. USN, cd RN 9.9.1940. Sold 25.8.1945; arr. 18.2.1947 Troon for BU.

CLARE CASTLE Corvette, 'Castle' class. Collingwood SY, cancelled 12.1943.

CLARENCE 3rd Rate 74, 1,749bm, 176 × 48ft. Blackburn, Turnchapel, 11.4.1812. = CENTURION 1826. BU 10.1828.

CLARENCE (ex-GOLIATH) 2nd Rate 84, 2,288bm, 196·5 × 52ft. Pembroke Dock 25.7.1827 (renamed 1826). TS 1872. Burnt 17.1.1884 accident R. Mersey.

CLARENCE *See also ROYAL WILLIAM 1833.*

CLARKIA Corvette, 'Flower' class. Harland & Wolff 7.3.1940. Sold 30.7.1947; BU Ward, Hayle.

CLAUDIA Cutter 10, 110bm, 68 × 20ft. Wrecked 20.1.1809 coast of Norway.

CLAVERHOUSE *See MACKAY 1918, M.23 1915.*

CLAVERING CASTLE Corvette, 'Castle' class. Collingwood SY, cancelled 12.1943.

CLAYMORE Landing ship dock, 4,270 tons, 454 × 72ft, 1–3in, 16–20mm. Newport News 19.7.1943. = HIGHWAY 8.1943. Ret. USN 4.1946.

CLAYMORE Destroyer, 1,980 tons, 365 (oa) × 38ft, 6–4in, 6–40mm, 10–TT. Scotts, ordered 3.1945, cancelled 10.1945.

CLAYOQUOT (ex-ESPERANZA) Minesweeper (RCN), TE 'Bangor' class. Prince Rupert DD 3.10.1940 (renamed 1940). Sunk 24.12.1944 by U.806 off Halifax.

CLEMATIS Sloop, 'Acacia' class. Greenock & Grangemouth 29.7.1915. Sold 5.2.1931 Young, Sunderland.

CLEMATIS Corvette, 'Flower' class. Hill 22.4.1940. Arr. 9.1949 Gateshead for BU.

CLEOPATRA 5th Rate 32, 689bm, 126·5 × 35ft. Hillhouse, Bristol, 26.11.1779. BU comp. 21.9.1814 Deptford. *In French hands 17–23.2.1805.*

CLEOPATRA 6th Rate 26, 918bm, 130 × 40·5ft, 24–32pdr, 2–12pdr. Pembroke Dock 28.4.1835. BU 2.1862 Castle & Beech.

CLEOPATRA Paddle sloop (Indian). Pitcher, Northfleet, 1839. Foundered 14.4.1847 Indian Ocean.

CLEOPATRA Screw corvette, 2,380 tons, 225 × 44·5ft, 2–7in, 12–64pdr. Elder 1.8.1878. Harbour service 1905; = DEFIANCE III 1.1922. Sold 7.1931 S. Castle, Millbay.

CLEOPATRA Light cruiser, 3,750 tons, 420 × 41·5ft, 2–6in, 8–4in. Devonport DY 14.1.1915. Sold 26.6.1931 Hughes Bolckow, Blyth.

CLEOPATRA Cruiser, 5,450 tons, 512 (oa) × 50·5ft, 10–5·25 in. Hawthorn Leslie 27.3.1940. Arr. 12.12.1958 Cashmore, Newport, for BU.

CLEOPATRA Frigate, 'Leander' class, Y100, 2,650 tons, 372 (oa) × 41ft, 2–4·5in, Limbo, helo (later Exocet, helo, 6–TT). Devonport DY 25.3.1964. Sold Cross Seas Shipping; beached Alang, India, 31.1.1994, BU.

CLEVELAND Royal yacht 8, 107bm. Portsmouth DY 1671. Sold 1716.

CLEVELAND Destroyer, 'Hunt' class Type I. Yarrow 24.4.1940. Stranded 28.6.1957 nr Swansea on passage Rees, Llanelly, for BU; wreck stripped, blown up 14.12.1959.

CLIFTON Minesweeper, Later 'Hunt' class. Bow McLachlan, cancelled 1918.

CLINKER (Gunboat No 14) Gunvessel 12, 159bm, 75 × 22ft, 2–24pdr, 10–18pdr carr. Dudman, Deptford, 28.4.1797. Sold 10.1802.

CLINKER Gun-brig 14, 180bm, 85 × 22ft. Pitcher, Northfleet, 30.6.1804. Foundered 12.1806 off Le Havre.

CLINKER Gun-brig 12, 183bm, 84 × 22·5ft, 10–18pdr carr., 2–6pdr. Davy, Topsham, 15.7.1813. Coastguard 11.1831; = WV.12 in 5.1863. Sold 24.1.1867.

CLINKER Wood screw gunboat, 'Dapper' class. Pitcher, Northfleet, 2.4.1855. Sold 6.6.1871 Castle.

CLINKER *See also WAVE 1856.*

CLINTON (ex-ESPERANCE) 5th Rate 32, 736bm, 134 × 35ft. French, captured 30.9.1780 by PEARL. Sold 5.7.1784.

CLINTON Minesweeper, 'Algerine' class. Redfern, Toronto, 5.10.1942, on Lend-Lease. Ret. USN 1.1947.

CLIO Brig-sloop 18, 'Cruizer' class, 389bm. Betts, Mistleythorn, 10.1.1807. BU 3.1845 Portsmouth.

CLIO Wood screw corvette, 1,472bm, 2,306 tons, 200 × 40ft. Sheerness DY 8.8.1858. TS 1876. Sold 3.10.1919; BU Bangor.

CLIO Sloop, 1,070 tons, 185 × 33ft, 6–4in, 4–3pdr. Sheerness DY 14.3.1903. Sold 12.11.1920 Bombay.

CLITHEROE CASTLE Corvette, 'Castle' class. Collingwood SY, cancelled 12.1943.

CLIVE Sloop 18 (Indian), 387bm. Bombay DY 1826. Sold 7.1862.

CLIVE Troopship (RIM), 3,570 tons, 300 × 45·5ft. Laird 15.11.1882.

CLIVE Sloop (RIN), 2,100 tons, 240 × 38·5ft, 4—3pdr. Beardmore 10.12.1919. Sold c. 1946.

CLONMEL (ex-STRANRAER) Minesweeper, Later 'Hunt' class. Simons 14.5.1918 (renamed 1918). Sold 7.1922 S. D. Harrison.

CLORINDE 5th Rate 38, 1,161bm, 161 × 41ft, 18—32pdr carr., 28—18pdr, 2—12pdr. French, captured 30.11.1803 San Domingo. Sold 6.3.1817 Mr Freake.

CLOVE TREE (ex-NAGELBOOM) 4th Rate 62, 700bm. Dutch, captured 1665. Recaptured 6.1666 by Dutch.

CLOVELLY *See CAVAN 1918.*

CLOVER Corvette, 'Flower' class. Fleming & Ferguson 30.1.1941. Sold 17.5.1947 = *Cloverlock.*

CLOWN Wood screw gunboat, 'Clown' class. Miller, Liverpool, 20.5.1856. Coal lighter 1867; later = YC.1, then = YC.6. Lost 1871.

CLUN CASTLE Corvette, 'Castle' class. Midland SY, cancelled 12.1943.

CLYDE 5th Rate 38 (fir-built), 1,002bm, 146 × 39ft. Chatham DY 26.3.1796. Rebuilt Woolwich, relaunched 28.2.1806. Sold 8.1814.

CLYDE (ex-*Atalanta*) Tender 4. Cutter, purch. 1805. Sold 1826 Milford Haven.

CLYDE 5th Rate 46, 1,081bm, 1,447 tons, 152 × 40ft. Woolwich DY 9.10.1828. RNR drillship 8.1870. Sold 5.7.1904.

CLYDE Wood screw gunboat (Indian), 300bm, 125 × 23ft, 3 guns. Bombay DY 3.5.1859. Survey vessel 1872. Sold c. 1875.

CLYDE Paddle vessel (Newfoundland Govt), 439 tons, 154·5 × 25ft, 1 gun. Inglis 1900. Wrecked 19.12.1951 off Williamsport, Newfoundland.

CLYDE (ex-WILD SWAN) Base ship, 1,130 tons, 170 × 36ft. Renamed 1.5.1904. = COLUMBINE 7.1913. Sold 4.5.1920 Forth S. Bkg Co. *Was to have been renamed ROMULUS.*

CLYDE Submarine, 1,850 tons, 325 × 28ft, 1—4in, 8—TT. Vickers Armstrong, Barrow, 15.3.1934. Sold 30.7.1946 Joubert, Durban, for BU.

CLYDE *See also CRICHTON 1953.*

CLYDEBANK *See ORISSA 1941.*

COATICOOK Frigate (RCN), 'River' class. Davie SB 25.11.1943. Sold 13.12.1947 Wagner, Stein & Greene; wrecked coast British Columbia while under tow, wreck blown up 2.1962.

COBALT Corvette (RCN), 'Flower' class. Port Arthur SY 17.8.1940. Sold 1946 = *Johanna W. Vinke.*

COBHAM Inshore minesweeper, 'Ham' class. Fairlie Yacht Slip 14.5.1953. Sold 5.1966.

COBOURG Corvette (RCN), Modified 'Flower' class. Midland SY 14.7.1943. Sold 1947 = *Camco.*

COBRA Destroyer, 400 tons, 223 × 20·5ft, 1—12pdr, 5—6pdr, 2—TT. Armstrong 28.6.1899, spec., purch. 8.5.1900. Wrecked 19.9.1901 nr Cromer.

COCHIN Schooner, 54bm, 53·5 × 15·5ft. Cochin 23.4.1820. Tankvessel 1840. Sold 4.1850 Trincomalee.

COCHIN Wood screw gunboat, 'Albacore' class. Green, Blackwall, 8.4.1856. BU 3.1863 Sheerness.

COCHRANE Armoured cruiser, 13,550 tons, 480 × 73·5ft, 6—9·2in, 4—7·5in, 24—3pdr. Fairfield 28.5.1905. Stranded 14.11.1918 R. Mersey; wreck BU.

COCHRANE *See also AMBROSE 1914.*

COCKADE Destroyer, 'C' class. Yarrow 1.3.1944. Arr. 7.1964 Cashmore, Newport, for BU.

COCKATRICE Cutter 14, 181bm, 70 × 26ft. King, Dover, 3.7.1781. Sold 9.1802.

COCKATRICE *Name chosen 1812 for BREV-DRAGEREN (q.v.) but not used.*

COCKATRICE Schooner 6, 182bm 80 × 23·5ft. Pembroke Dock 14.5.1832. Sold 9.1858 at Callao.

COCKATRICE Wood screw gunboat, 'Britomart' class. Smith, Newcastle, 26.5.1860. = YC.10 (luggage lighter) 1882. Sold 1885.

COCKATRICE (ex-*Sir W. Harness*) Tender, 110 tons, 80 × 18ft. War Dept vessel, tx 11.1906. Sold 10.1910 in Bermuda.

COCKATRICE Destroyer, 951 tons, 267·5 × 27ft, 3—4in, 2—TT. Hawthorn Leslie 8.11.1912. Sold 9.5.1921 Ward, Hayle.

COCKATRICE Minesweeper, 'Algerine' class. Fleming & Ferguson 27.10.1942. Arr. 29.8.1963 Ward, Inverkeithing for BU.

COCKATRICE *See also NIGER 1880, BRAMBLE 1886.*

COCKBURN (ex-*Braganza*) Schooner. Steam vessel, purch. 5.1822 Rio. Foundered 1.4.1823 nr Simonstown.

COCKBURN Schooner 1 (Canadian lakes), 70bm. Dates from 1827. Sold 1837.

COCKBURN *See also DRURY 1942.*

COCKCHAFER (ex-SPENCER) Schooner tender 5, 104bm, 69·5 × 19ft, 1—12pdr. 4—12pdr carr. American, captured 1812. Sold 1815.

COCKCHAFER Wood screw gunboat, 'Albacore' class. Pitcher, Northfleet, 24.11.1855. Sold 1872 Shanghai.

COCKCHAFER Composite screw gunboat, 465 tons, 125 × 23·5ft, 2—64pdr ML, 2—20pdr. Pembroke Dock 19.2.1881. Sold 6.12.1905.

COCKCHAFER River gunboat, 645 tons, 230 × 36ft, 2—6in, 2—12pdr. Barclay Curle 17.12.1915. Hulk 1947; sold 1949 in Singapore.

CODRINGTON Destroyer leader, 1,540 tons, 343 (oa) × 33·75ft, 5—4·7in, 8—TT. Swan Hunter 7.8.1929. Sunk 27.7.1940 air attack Dover.

COLAC Minesweeper (RAN), 'Bathurst' class. Mort's Dock, Sydney, 13.8.1941. Oil-tank cleaning vessel 1962. Deleted 1982; sunk 4.3.1987 target.

COLCHESTER 24-gun ship, 287bm. Edgar, Yarmouth, 1654. Sunk in action 1666.

COLCHESTER Ketch 8, 72bm. Colchester 1664. Captured 1667 by French in West Indies.

COLCHESTER 4th Rate 48, 696bm, 131·5 × 34ft. Johnson, Blackwall, 1694. Foundered 16.1.1704 Whitesand Bay.

COLCHESTER 4th Rate 54, 682bm, 130·5 × 34·5ft. Deptford DY 1707. Rebuilt Chatham 1721 as 756bm. BU 1742.

COLCHESTER 4th Rate 50,976bm, 140 × 40ft. Barnard, Harwich, 1744. Wrecked 21.9.1744 off Kentish Knock.

COLCHESTER 4th Rate 50, 978bm, 140·5 × 40ft. Carter, Southampton, 20.9.1746. BU 2.1773 Portsmouth.

COLCHESTER CASTLE Corvette, 'Castle' class. Midland SY, cancelled 12.1943.

COLIBRI Sloop 16, 365bm, 99 × 29·5ft. French, captured 16.1.1809 by MELAMPUS in West Indies. Wrecked 22.8.1813 Port Royal, Jamaica.

COLIBRI Brig-sloop (fir-built). Chatham DY, LD 1.1814, frames taken down, tx Halifax, re-laid. Sold on stocks 5.1815 Halifax.

COLLEEN *See ROYALIST 1883, AMELIA 1888.*

COLLINGWOOD 3rd Rate 80, 2,589bm, 190 × 57ft, 4—68pdr, 72—32pdr, 4—18pdr. Pembroke Dock 17.8.1841; undocked 13.7.1861 Sheerness as screw ship. Sold 3.1867 Castle.

COLLINGWOOD Battleship, 9,150 tons, 325 × 68ft, 4—12in, 6—6in. Pembroke Dock 22.11.1882. Sold 11.5.1909 Hughes Bolckow, Dunston.

COLLINGWOOD Battleship, 19,250 tons, 500 × 84ft, 10—12in, 20—4in. Devonport DY 7.11.1908. Sold 12.12.1922 Cashmore; arr. 3.3.1923 Newport for BU.

COLLINGWOOD Corvette (RCN), 'Flower' class. Collingwood SY 27.7.1940. BU 7.1950 Steel Co. of Canada, Hamilton.

COLLINS Submarine (RAN), 'Collins' class, 3,051/3,353 tons, 255·2 (oa) × 25·6ft, 6—TT. Australian Submarine Corp., Adelaide, 28.8.1993.

COLLINSON (ex-AMERSHAM) Survey ship, 800 tons. Ailsa 30.4.1919 (renamed 1919). Sold 25.10.1922 McLellan, Bo'ness.

COLNE Destroyer, 560 tons, 222 × 23·5ft, 1—12pdr, 5—6pdr (1907: 4—12pdr), 2—TT. Thornycroft, Chiswick, 21.2.1905. Sold 4.11.1919 J. H. Lee, Dover.

COLOMBE Sloop 16, 403bm, 108 × 29ft, 14—32pdr carr., 2—6pdr. French, captured 18.6.1803 by DRAGON off Ushant. BU 1811.

COLOMBO Light cruiser, 4,190 tons, 451·5 (oa) × 43·9ft, 5—6in. Fairfield 18.12.1918. AA ship 1943, 6—4in. Sold 22.1.1948; arr. 1.5.1948 Cashmore, Newport, for BU.

COLOSSUS 3rd Rate 74, 1,703bm, 172 × 48ft. Cleveley, Gravesend, 4.4.1787. Wrecked 10.12.1798 Scilly Is.

COLOSSUS 3rd Rate 74, 1,889bm, 180 × 49ft. Deptford DY 23.4.1803. BU 8.2.1826.

COLOSSUS 3rd Rate 80, 2,590bm, 190 × 57ft, 14—8in. 66—32pdr. Pembroke Dock 1.6.1848; undocked 11.6.1864 as screw ship. Sold 3.1867 Castle & Beech.

COLOSSUS Battleship, 9,150 tons, 325 × 68ft, 4—12in, 5—6in. Portsmouth DY 21.3.1882. Sold 6.10.1908 Ward, Briton Ferry.

COLOSSUS Battleship, 20,000 tons, 510 × 86ft, 10—12in 20—4in. Scotts 9.4.1910. Sold 7.1928 Alloa S. Bkg Co., Rosyth; arr. 5.9.1928 for BU.

COLOSSUS Aircraft carrier, 13,190 tons, 693 (oa) × 80ft, 19—40mm, 48 aircraft. Vickers Armstrong, Tyne, 30.9.1943. Sold 6.8.1946 French Navy = ARROMANCHES. BU 1978 Toulon.

COLTSFOOT Corvette, 'Flower' class. Alex Hall 12.5.1941. Sold 1947 = *Alexandra*.

COLUMBIA (ex-CURLEW) Sloop 18, 294bm, 94·5 × 26ft, 16—18pdr carr., 2—6pdr. American privateer, captured 1813 by ACASTA off Cape Sable. Sold 13.1.1820.

COLUMBIA Wood paddle packet (ex-brig-sloop, 'Cherokee' class), 356bm, 130 × 25ft. Woolwich DY 1.7.1829. Survey vessel 1842; coal hulk 1857. Sold 29.10.1859 in Halifax, NS.

COLUMBIA (ex-HARADEN) Destroyer, 1,060 tons, 209 × 30·5ft, 3—4in, 1—3in, 6—TT. USN, cd RCN 24.9.1940. Storeship 9.1944. Sold 7.8.1945 in Canada.

COLUMBIA Frigate (RCN), 2,370 tons, 366 (oa) × 42ft, 4—3in, 2—40mm, 6—TT, Limbo. Burrard DD 1.11.1956. Harbour TS Esquimalt 1973—93. Scuttled 6.1996 Campbell R., BC, as dive site.

COLUMBINE Brig-sloop 18, 'Cruizer' class, 386bm. Adams, Buckler's Hard, 16.7.1806. Wrecked 25.1.1824 Sapienza I.

COLUMBINE Sloop 18, 492bm, 105 × 33·5ft. Portsmouth DY 1.12.1826. 12-gun brig 1849; coal hulk 4.1854. Sold 12.1.1892 Castle.

COLUMBINE Wood screw sloop, 669bm, 913

tons, 160 × 30ft. Deptford DY 2.4.1862. BU 6.1875 Chatham.

COLUMBINE (ex-*Hiarta*) Tender, 270 tons, 125·5 × 25ft. Purch. 2.1897. Sold 10.7.1907.

COLUMBINE Corvette, 'Flower' class. Hill 13.8.1940. Sold 9.8.1946 = *Lief Welding*.

COLUMBINE *See also CYANE 1806, CLYDE 1913*.

COLWYN Minesweeper, Later 'Hunt' class. Bow McLachlan, = CREDITON 1918, cancelled.

COMBATANT 6th Rate 20, 417bm, 109 × 29·5ft. Betts, Mistleythorn, 3.11.1804. Sold 17.10.1816.

COMBATANT Minesweeper, 'Catherine' class. Associated SB, Seattle, 27.11.1942. Tx RN 13.11.1943 on Lend-Lease. Ret. USN 15.12.1946. Sold 1947 Greek Navy.

COMBUSTION Fireship 8, purch. 1782. Sold 26.8.1784 Mr White; withdrawn from sale, sold 29.11.1784 Mr Maxwell.

COMET Bomb vessel 4, 145bm, 66 × 23ft. Blackwall 1695. Captured 10.10.1706 by French.

COMET Bomb vessel 14, 275bm, 92 × 26ft. Taylor, Rotherhithe, 29.3.1742. Sold 11.5.1749.

COMET Galley 8. In service 1756.

COMET Brig-sloop 10 (Indian), 115bm. Bombay DY 1758.

COMET Sloop 10. Purch. 1777. Sold 15.9.1778.

COMET Fireship 14, 424bm, 109 × 30ft. Game, Wivenhoe, 11.11.1783. Expended 7.7.1800 Dunkirk Roads.

COMET Sloop 18, 427bm, 109 × 30ft. Taylor, Bideford, 25.4.1807. Sold 12.10.1815.

COMET Wood paddle vessel, 238bm, 115 × 21ft, 3 guns. Deptford DY 23.5.1822. BU 1868 Portsmouth. *First steam vessel built by RN. Not on Navy List until 1831.*

COMET Sloop 18, 462bm, 113·5 × 31ft. Pembroke Dock 11.8.1828. = COMUS 31.10.1832. BU comp. 10.5.1862 Chatham.

COMET 3rd class gunboat, 'Ant' class. Portsmouth DY 8.12.1870. Sold 12.5.1908; BU Holland.

COMET Paddle vessel (Indian), 144bm, 2 guns. Built 1880, in service 1890.

COMET Destroyer, 747 tons, 246 × 26ft, 2—4in, 2—12pdr, 2—TT. Fairfield 23.6.1910. Sunk 6.8.1918 by Austrian submarine in Mediterranean.

COMET Destroyer, 1,375 tons, 329 (oa) × 33ft, 4—4·7in, 8—TT. Portsmouth DY 30.9.1931. = RESTIGOUCHE (RCN) 15.6.1938. Sold Foundation Maritime; BU 1946 Halifax.

COMET Destroyer, 'C' class. Yarrow 22.6.1944. Arr. 23.10.1962 Troon for BU.

COMET *See also DILIGENCE 1756, THUNDERER 1831*.

COMFREY Corvette, 'Flower' class. Collingwood SY. Tx USN while building; comp. 21.11.1942 as ACTION.

COMMANDANT D'ESTIENNE D'ORVES *See LOTUS 1942*.

COMMANDANT DETROYAT *See CORIANDER 1941*.

COMMANDANT DOMINE Minesweeping sloop, 630 tons, 256 × 28ft, 2—3·9in. French, seized 3.7.1940 Falmouth. Free French 8.1940; ret. French Navy 1944.

COMMANDANT DROGOU *See CHRYSANTHEMUM 1941*.

COMMANDANT DUBOC Minesweeping sloop, 630 tons, 256 × 28ft, 2—3·9in. French, seized 3.7.1940 Plymouth. Free French 7.1940; ret. French Navy 1944.

COMMERCE DE MARSEILLE 1st Rate 120, 2,747bm, 212 × 55ft. French, captured 29.8.1793 Toulon. Sold 1802.

COMMONWEALTH Battleship, 16,350 tons, 425 × 78ft, 4—12in, 4—9·2in, 10—6in, 12—12pdr. Fairfield 13.5.1903. Sold 18.11.1921; BU Germany.

COMOX Coastal minesweeper (RCN), 370 tons, 140 × 28ft, 1—40mm. Victoria Machinery Co. 24.4.1952. Sold 1958 Turkish Navy = TIREBOLU. Sold 1996.

COMUS 6th Rate 22, 522bm, 118 × 31·5ft. Custance, Yarmouth, 28.8.1806. Wrecked 4.11.1816 Newfoundland.

COMUS Screw corvette, 2,380 tons, 225 × 44·5ft, 4—6in, 8—64pdr. Elder 3.4.1878. Sold 17.5.1904.

COMUS Light cruiser, 3,750 tons, 420 × 41·5ft, 2—6in, 8—4in. Swan Hunter 16.12.1914. Sold 28.7.1934 Ward, Barrow.

COMUS Destroyer, 'C' class. Thornycroft 14.3.1945. Arr. 12.11.1958 Cashmore, Newport, for BU.

COMUS *See also COMET 1828*.

CONCEPTION 5th Rate, 375bm, 98 × 29·5ft. Captured 1690. Condemned 1694; wrecked New England

CONCEPTION Hulk at Jamaica. Purch. 1782. Sold 1783.

CONCORD 24-gun ship. Dutch, captured 1649. Hulk 1653; sold 8.1659.

CONCORD Sloop, 172bm, 77 × 22·5ft. French, captured 3.1697. *Fate unknown*.

CONCORD Light cruiser, 3,750 tons, 420 × 42ft, 5—6in, 2—3in. Armstrong 1.4.1916. Arr. 16.9.1935 Metal Industries, Rosyth, for BU.

CONCORD *See also CORSO 1945*.

CONCORDE 5th Rate 36, 889bm, 143 × 38ft. French, captured 15.2 1783 by MAGNIFICENT. Sold 21.1.1811.

CONDAMINE Frigate (RAN), 'River' class. Newcastle DY, NSW, 4.11.1944. BU 12.1961 Japan.

CONDOR Composite screw gunvessel, 780 tons, 157 × 29·5ft, 1—7in, 2—64pdr. Devonport DY 28.12.1876. Sold 8.1889 G. Cohen.

CONDOR Sloop, 980 tons, 180 × 33·5ft, 6—4in, 4—3dpr. Sheerness DY 17.12.1898. Foundered 3.12.1901 off Cape Flattery.

CONFEDERATE (ex-CONFEDERACY) 5th Rate 32, 959bm, 159·5 × 36·5ft. American, captured 14.4.1781 off Delaware R. BU 31.1782.

CONFIANCE 6th Rate 24. French, captured 1797. In service 1801.

CONFIANCE 6th Rate 22, 490bm, 22—18pdr carr., 2—6pdr. French, captured 4.6.1808 by LOIRE at Mudros. Sold 22.12.1810.

CONFIANCE Schooner 2 (Canadian lakes). Captured 5.10.1813 by Americans on Lake Erie.

CONFIANCE Brig-sloop 18, 'Cruizer' class, 392bm. Ross, Rochester, 30.8.1813. Wrecked 21.4.1822 Crookhaven.

CONFIANCE 5th Rate 36, 831bm, 4—32pdr carr., 7—24pdr carr., 26—24pdr. Île aux Noirs, Lake Champlain, 25.8.1814. Captured 11.9.1814 by Americans on Lake Champlain.

CONFIANCE 5th Rate 32 (Canadian lakes). Built Lake Erie 1818. *Fate unknown.*

CONFIANCE Schooner 2 (Canadian lakes), 95bm, 67·5 × 18ft, 2—24pdr. Lake Erie 1824. In service 1831.

CONFIANCE Wood paddle vessel. Woolwich DY 28.3.1827, conv. from brig-sloop, 'Cherokee' class. Tug 1842. BU 6.1873 Devonport.

CONFIANCE *See also MINERVE 1795.*

CONFLAGRATION (ex-*Loyal Oak*) Fireship 8. Purch. 1781. Wrecked 1781 North America.

CONFLAGRATION Fireship 14, 426bm, 108·5 × 291·5ft. Pelham, Shoreham, 8.10.1783. Destroyed 18.11.1793 to avoid capture by French at Toulon.

CONFLICT Gun-brig 12, 180bm, 80 × 23ft. Dudman, Deptford, 17.4.1801. Wrecked 24.10.1804 coast of France.

CONFLICT Gun-brig 12, 182bm, 84 × 22ft, 10—18pdr carr., 2—12pdr. Davy, Topsham, 14.5.1805. Foundered 9.11.1810 Bay of Biscay.

CONFLICT Gun-brig 12, 181bm, 84 × 22ft, 10—18pdr carr., 2—6pdr. Good, Bridport, 26.9.1812. Hulk 1832. Sold 30.12.1840 in Sierra Leone.

CONFLICT Wood screw sloop, 1,038bm, 185 × 34·5ft, Pembroke Dock 5.8.1846. Rebuilt 1848 Blackwall. Sold 1863.

CONFLICT Schooner 1, 120bm, 80 × 19ft, 1—12pdr. Cuthbert, Sydney, 11.2.1873. Sold 1882 Sydney.

CONFLICT Destroyer, 350 tons, 205·5 × 20ft, 1—12pdr, 5—6pdr, 2—TT. White 13.12.1894. Sold 20.5.1920 Ward, Milford Haven.

CONFOUNDER Gun-brig 12, 183bm, 84 × 22ft, 10—18pdr carr., 2—12pdr. Adams, Southampton, 4.1805. Sold 6.6.1814.

CONFOUNDER Wood screw gunboat, 'Albacore' class. Green, Blackwall, 21.5.1856. BU 10.1864.

CONGO Paddle survey schooner, 83bm, 70 × 16ft, 1—12pdr. Deptford DY 11.1.1816. Built for survey of R. Congo. Sold 15.3.1826 Rye. *Never used under steam; engine removed 1816.*

CONISTON Coastal minesweeper, 'Ton' class. Thornycroft 9.7.1952. Sold 28.1.1970; BU Newhaven.

CONN Frigate, TE 'Captain' class. Bethlehem, Hingham, 21.8.1943 on Lend-Lease. Ret. USN 26.11.1945.

CONQUERANT 3rd Rate 74, 1,681bm, 181·5 × 46ft. French, captured 2.8.1798 Battle of the Nile. Harbour service 1799. BU 3.1802.

CONQUERANTE Patrol vessel, 374 tons, 218 × 26ft, 2—3·9in. French, seized 3.7.1940 Falmouth. Foundered 14.4.1941 nr Falmouth.

CONQUEROR Fireship 8, 308bm, 94 × 28ft. French, captured 1745 by LOWESTOFFE in Mediterranean. Sold 2.3.1748.

CONQUEROR 3rd Rate 70, 1,432bm, 160 × 45ft. Barnard, Harwich, 24.5.1758. Wrecked 26.10.1760 off Plymouth.

CONQUEROR 3rd Rate 74, 1,606bm, 169 × 47ft. Plymouth DY 10.10.1773. BU 11.1794.

CONQUEROR 3rd Rate 74, 1,854bm, 176 × 49ft. Graham, Harwich, 23.11.1801. BU 7.1822 Chatham.

CONQUEROR Screw 1st Rate 101, 3,225bm, 240 × 55ft. Devonport DY 2.5.1855. Wrecked 29.12.1861 Rum Cay, West Indies.

CONQUEROR Battleship, 6,200 tons, 270 × 58ft, 2—12in, 4—6in. Chatham DY 8.9.1881. Sold 9.4.1907 Castle.

CONQUEROR Battleship, 22,500 tons, 545 × 88·5ft, 10—13·5in, 14—4in. Beardmore 1.5.1911. Sold 19.12.1922 Upnor S. Bkg Co.

CONQUEROR Battleship, 42,500 tons, 740 × 105ft, 9—16in, 16—5·25in. John Brown, LD 16.8.1939, suspended 10.1939, cancelled 1940.

CONQUEROR Nuclear submarine, 4,400/4,900 tons, 285 (oa) × 33ft, SubHarpoon, 6—TT. Cammell Laird 28.8.1969. LU 1.9.1990 Devonport.

CONQUEROR *See also WATERLOO 1833.*

CONQUEST Gunvessel 12, 147bm, 75 × 21ft, 10—18pdr carr., 2—12pdr. Brindley, Frindsbury, 7.1794. Sold 30.4.1817.

CONQUEST Screw corvette, 2,380 tons, 225 ×

44·5ft, 2—7in, 12—64pdr. Elder 28.10.1878. Sold 16.3.1899 King, Garston.

CONQUEST Light cruiser, 3,750 tons, 420 × 41·5ft, 2—6in, 8—4in. Chatham DY 20.1.1915. Sold 29.8.1930 Metal Industries, Rosyth.

CONQUESTADOR 4th Rate 60, 1,278bm, 156 × 43·5ft. Spanish, captured 12.8.1762 Havana. Harbour service 10.1775. BU 1782 Chatham.

CONQUESTADOR 3rd Rate 74, 1,1773bm, 176·5 × 48·5ft. Guillaume, Northam, 1.8.1810. 4th Rate 1831; powder hulk 1860. Sold 10.5.1897 H. Scawn, Plymouth.

CONRAD *See DANAE 1918.*

CONSORT Destroyer, 'C' class. Stephen 19.10.1944. Arr. 15.3.1961 Swansea for BU Prince of Wales DD Co.

CONSTANCE 6th Rate 22, 535bm, 121·5 × 31ft. French, captured 9.3.1797 by ST FIORENZO and NYMPHE off Brest. Recaptured by French 12.10.1806 off coast of France.

CONSTANCE 5th Rate 36, 1,622bm, 160 × 49ft. Portsmouth DY, LD c. 1833, cancelled 1844.

CONSTANCE Schooner 3 (Indian), 182bm. Bombay DY 1838. Sold 1877 Rangoon Port Authorities.

CONSTANCE 4th Rate 50, 2,132bm, 180 × 53ft, 10—8in, 40—32pdr. Pembroke Dock 12.3.1846; undocked 15.4.1862 as screw frigate, 2,176 bm. Sold 1875 Castle.

CONSTANCE Screw corvette, 2,590 tons, 225 × 44·5ft, 2—7in, 12—64pdr. Chatham DY 9.6.1880. Sold 15.12.1899 King, Garston.

CONSTANCE Light cruiser, 3,750 tons, 420 × 41·5ft, 4—6in, 2—3in Cammell Laird 12.9.1915. Sold 8.6.1936 Arnott Young, Dalmuir.

CONSTANCE Destroyer, 'C' class. Vickers Armstrong, Tyne, 22.9.1944. Arr. 8.3.1956 Ward, Inverkeithing, for BU.

CONSTANT Gun-brig 12, 180bm, 80 × 22·5ft, 10—18pdr carr., 2—6pdr. Dudman, Deptford, 20.4.1801. Sold 15.2.1816.

CONSTANT JOHN Fireship 6, 180bm. Purch. 1666. Sunk 6.1667 blockship R. Medway.

CONSTANT REFORMATION 42-gun ship, 752bm. Deptford 1619. Captured 1648 by Royalists. Lost at sea 30.9.1651.

CONSTANT WARWICK 42-gun ship, 379bm. Privateer, purch. 20 1.1649. Rebuilt 1666. Captured 12 7.1691 by French.

CONSTITUTION Schooner. Purch. 24.8.1835. Not listed 1837.

CONTENT 3rd Rate 70, 1,130bm, French, captured 7.1695 by CARLISLE. Hulk 7.1703. Sold Lisbon.

CONTENT Storeship, 100bm. Hoy, purch. 5.1708. Sold 15.12.1715.

CONTENT Gunvessel 12, 159bm. Lynn 1797. Wrecked 28.8.1799 on Dutch coast. *There is doubt about this vessel: it may have been a hired brig.*

CONTEST (Gunboat No 16) Gunvessel 14, 159bm, 75 × 22ft, 4—24pdr 10—18pdr carr. Barnard, Deptford, 11.4.1797. BU 10.1799.

CONTEST (ex-HELL-HOUND) Gun-brig 5, 2—32pdr carr., 3—24pdr. Dutch, captured 1799. BU 8.1803 Sheerness.

CONTEST Schooner 14, 14—24pdr carr. Purch. 1799. BU 1799.

CONTEST Gun-brig 12, 178bm, 80 × 23ft, 10—18pdr carr., 2—12pdr. Courtney, Chester, 6.1804. Foundered 12.1809 Atlantic.

CONTEST Gun-brig 12, 180bm, 84 × 22ft, 10—18pdr carr., 2—6pdr. Good, Bridport, 24.10.1812. Wrecked 14.4.1828 North America.

CONTEST Brig 12, 459bm, 109 × 32ft. White, Cowes, 11.4.1846. BU comp. 9.9.1868 Portsmouth.

CONTEST Composite screw gunboat, 455 tons, 125 × 23·5ft, 2—64pdr MLR, 2—20pdr. Doxford 29.8.1874. BU 1889 Devonport.

CONTEST Destroyer, 330 tons, 210 × 19·5ft, 1—12pdr, 5—6pdr, 2—TT. Laird 1.12.1894. Sold 11.7.1911 Ward, Preston.

CONTEST Destroyer, 957 tons, 3—4in, 2—TT. Hawthorn Leslie 7.1.1913. Sunk 18.9.1917 by U-boat south-west of Ushant.

CONTEST Destroyer, 'C' class. White 16.12.1944. Arr. 2.2.1960 Ward, Grays, for BU.

CONVERT 20-gun ship. Hired 1652.

CONVERT 30-gun ship, 324bm. French, captured 1652. Sold 1661.

CONVERT (ex-INCONSTANTE) 5th Rate 36, 930bm. French, captured 29.10.1793 by PENELOPE and IPHIGENIA off San Domingo. Wrecked 8.3.1794 Grand Cayman, West Indies.

CONVERT *See also INCONSTANT 1778.*

CONVERTINE 40-gun ship, 500bm. Royalist, captured 1651. Captured 6.1666 by Dutch. *May be same ship as following.*

CONVERTINE *See DESTINY 1616.*

CONVOLVULUS Sloop, 'Anchusa' class. Barclay Curle 19.5.1917. Sold 1922 Stanlee, Dover.

CONVOLVULUS Corvette, 'Flower' class. Hill 21.9.1940. Sold 21.8.1947; BU Cashmore, Newport.

CONVULSION Mortar vessel 5, 77bm, 60 × 17ft. Brent, Rotherhithe, 31.8.1804. Sold 27.8.1806.

CONWAY 6th Rate 20, 451bm, 108 × 30·5ft. Pelham, Frindsbury, 10.3.1814. Sold 13.10.1825 E. Cohen.

CONWAY 6th Rate 26, 652bm, 125·5 × 34·5ft, 26–32pdr, 2–9pdr. Chatham DY 2.2.1832. TS 2.1859, = WINCHESTER 28.8.1861. BU 6.1871 Sheerness.

CONWAY *See also WINCHESTER 1822, NILE 1839.*

COOK Survey ship (RAN), 1,976 tons, 316·7 (oa) × 44ft. Williamstown DY 27.8.1977. PO 31.10.1990; sold 10.1990 Stability Lines for conv. passenger ship = *Marie Kosmo.*

COOK Survey launch, 11 tons, 34·8 (oa) × 9·2ft Halmatic, Southampton. Comp. by 1996.

COOK *See also PEGWELL BAY 1945.*

COOKE (ex-DEMPSEY) Frigate, DE 'Captain' class. Boston NY 22.4.1943 on Lend-Lease. Ret. USN 8.3.1946.

COOTAMUNDRA Minesweeper (RAN), 'Bathurst' class. Poole & Steel, Sydney, 3.12.1942. Sold 1962.

COOTE Sloop 18 (Indian), 420bm. Bombay DY 1827. Stranded 1.12.1846 nr Calicut.

COPPERCLIFF (ex-HEVER CASTLE) Corvette (RCN), 'Castle' class. Blyth DD 24.2.1944 (renamed 1943). Sold 1946.

COPPERCLIFF *See also FELICITY 1944.*

COQUETTE 6th Rate 28. French, captured 2.3.1783. In service 1785.

COQUETTE (ex-*Queen Mab*) 6th Rate 20, 484bm, 113 × 31ft, 18–32pdr carr., 8–12pdr carr., 1–12pdr, 2–6pdr. Temple, South Shields, 24.4.1807, purch. on stocks. Sold 30.4.1817.

COQUETTE Corvette 18, 731bm, 120 × 37·5ft, 18–32pdr. Chatham DY, ordered 1835, cancelled 1851.

COQUETTE Wood screw gunvessel, 677bm, 181 × 28·5ft, 1–110pdr, 1–68pdr, 2–20pdr. Green, Blackwall, 25.10.1855. BU 1868 Cowes.

COQUETTE Composite screw gunboat, 295bm, 430 tons, 125 × 23ft, 2–64pdr, 2–20pdr. Pembroke Dock 5.4.1871. Sold 8.1889.

COQUETTE Destroyer, 355 tons, 210 × 19·5ft, 1–12pdr, 5–6pdr, 2–TT. Thornycroft, Chiswick, 25.11.1897. Sunk 7.3.1916 mine off East Coast of Britain.

COQUETTE (ex-BOWMANVILLE) Minesweeper, 'Algerine' class. Redfern, Toronto, 24.11.1943 (renamed 6.1943). Arr. 26.5.1958 Charlestown for BU.

COQUILLE 5th Rate 36, 916bm. French, captured 12.10.1798 off coast of Donegal. Burnt 14.12.1798 accident Plymouth.

CORAL SNAKE Special Service Vessel (RAN), 80 tons. LD Melbourne, cancelled 8.1945.

CORDELIA Brig-sloop 10, 'Cherokee' class, 239bm. King, Upnor, 26.7.1808. Sold 12.12.1833.

CORDELIA Wood screw sloop, 579bm, 151 × 29ft,

11–32pdr. Pembroke Dock 3.7.1856. Sold 12.5.1870 Marshall, Plymouth.

CORDELIA Screw corvette, 2,380 tons, 225 × 44·5ft, 10–6in, Portsmouth DY 25.10.1881. Sold 5.7.1904.

CORDELIA Light cruiser, 3,750 tons, 420 × 41·5ft, 2–6in, 8–4in. Pembroke Dock 23.2.1914. Sold 31.7.1923 Cashmore, Newport.

COREOPSIS Sloop, 'Anchusa' class. Barclay Curle 15.9.1917. Sold 6.9.1922 Ward, Preston,; arr. Preston 5.5.1924 for BU.

COREOPSIS Corvette, 'Flower' class. Inglis 19.6.1940. Lent Greek Navy 10.11.1943–7.1952 = KREZIS. Arrived 22.7.1952 Young, Sunderland, for BU. .

CORFE CASTLE Corvette, 'Castle' class. Canada, cancelled 12.1943.

CORIANDER (ex-IRIS) Corvette, 'Flower' class. Hall Russell 9.6.1941 (renamed 26.10.1940). Lent Free French/French Navy 1941–5.1947 = COMMANDANT DETROYAT. Arr. Troon 2.1948 for BU.

CORMORANT (ex-MARCHAULT) Fireship 16, 408bm, 101 × 31ft. French, captured 4.1757. Sold 23.12.1762.

CORMORANT Sloop 14, 304bm, 97 × 27ft. Barnard, Ipswich, 21.5.1776. Captured 24.8.1781 by French off Charlestown.

CORMORANT (ex-RATTLESNAKE) Brig-sloop 12, 198bm. 90 × 22ft, 12–4pdr. American, captured 1781 by ASSURANCE. = RATTLESNAKE 8.1783. Sold 10.10.1786.

CORMORANT Sloop 18, 427bm, 108 × 30ft. Randall, Rotherhithe, 2.1.1794. Blown up 24.12.1796 accident Port-au-Prince, Haiti.

CORMORANT (ex-ETNA) 6th Rate 20, 564bm, 119 × 33ft. French, captured 13.11.1796 by MELAMPUS off coast of France. Wrecked 20.5.1800 coast of Egypt.

CORMORANT (ex-*Blenheim*) Sloop 16, 328bm, 110 × 27ft. Purch. 6.1804. Sold 4.12.1817.

CORMORANT Wood paddle sloop, 1,057bm, 170 × 36ft, Sheerness DY 29.3.1842. BU 8.1853.

CORMORANT Wood screw gunvessel, 675bm, 181 × 28ft, 1–110pdr, 1–68pdr, 2–20pdr. Fletcher, Limehouse, 23.2.1856. Sunk 28.6.1859 in action with Peiho forts, China.

CORMORANT Wood screw sloop, 695bm, 186 × 28·5ft, 2–68pdr, 2–32pdr. Wigram, Blackwall, 9.2.1860. Sold 1870 in Hong Kong.

CORMORANT Composite screw sloop, 1,130 tons, 170 × 36ft, 2–7in, 4–64pdr. Chatham DY 12.9.1877. Harbour service 11.1889; = ROOKE 7.1946. BU 1949 Malaga, Spain.

CORMORANT (ex-SUNDERLAND) Patrol boat, 78·7 (oa) × 18ft. James & Stone, Brightlingsea, 1976. RAF vessel, tx 29.8.1985. Sold 1991 Gibraltar.

CORNEL Corvette, 'Flower' class. Collingwood SY, LD 6.1.1942; tx 1942 USN = ALACRITY.

CORNELIA 5th Rate 32, 909bm, 142·5 × 38ft. Temple, South Shields, 26.7.1808. BU 6.1814.

CORNELIAN (ex-CORNELIUS) 12-gun ship, 100bm. Royalist, captured 1655. Last listed 1660.

CORNERBROOK *See URSULA 1991.*

CORNET CASTLE Corvette, 'Castle' class. Collingwood SY, cancelled 12.1943.

CORNFLOWER Sloop. 'Arabis' class. Barclay Curle 30.3.1916. RNVR drillship 1935. Sold 1940 in Hong Kong = *Tai Hing*; repurch. 9.1940 = CORNFLOWER. Sunk 15.12.1941 air attack Hong Kong.

CORNFLOWER *See also LYSANDER 1943.*

CORNWALL 2nd Rate 80, 1,186bm, 156·5 × 41·5ft. Winter, Southampton, 23.4.1692. Rebuilt Rotherhithe 1706 as 1,241bm; rebuilt Deptford 1726 as 1,350bm. BU comp. 16.7.1761 Chatham.

CORNWALL 3rd Rate 74, 1,634bm, 168·5 × 47·5ft. Wells, Deptford, 19.5.1761. Damaged 19.5.1780 in action with French in West Indies, burnt 30.6.1780 St Lucia unserviceable.

CORNWALL *Name chosen for HEIR APPARENT, captured 1807; not used.*

CORNWALL 3rd Rate 74, 1,751bm, 176 × 48ft. Barnard, Deptford, 16.1.1812. Reduced to 50 guns 1831; = WELLESLEY (TS) 18.6.1869. BU comp. 18.1.1875 Sheerness.

CORNWALL Armoured cruiser, 9,800 tons, 440 × 66ft, 14–6in, 9–12pdr. Pembroke Dock 29.10.1902. Sold 7.7.1920 Ward, Briton Ferry.

CORNWALL Cruiser, 9,750 tons, 630 (oa) × 68·5ft, 8–8in, 6–4in. Devonport DY 11.3.1926. Sunk 5.4.1942 Japanese aircraft Indian Ocean.

CORNWALL Frigate, 4,200 tons. Yarrow 14.10.1985.

CORNWALL *See also WELLESLEY 1815.*

CORNWALLIS Galley 5, 1–24pdr, 4–4pdr. Purch. 1777 North America. Sold 1782.

CORNWALLIS Storeship 14, 443bm, 100 × 30ft. Purch. 3.1781. Foundered 9.1782 Atlantic.

CORNWALLIS (ex-*Marquis Cornwallis*) 4th Rate 54, 1,388bm, 166·5 × 43·5ft. East Indiaman, purch. 1801. = AKBAR (troopship) 13.8.1806; harbour service 9.1824. Sold 1862.

CORNWALLIS 3rd Rate 74, 1,809bm, 177 × 48ft. Bombay DY 12.5.1813; undocked 8.2.1855 as screw ship, 60 guns. Conv. to jetty Sheerness 1865; = WILDFIRE (base ship) 1916. BU 1957 Sheerness.

CORNWALLIS Battleship, 14,000 tons, 405 × 75·5ft, 4–12in, 12–6in, 12–12pdr. Thames Iron Works, Blackwall, 13.7.1901. Sunk 9.1.1917 by U.32 south-east of Malta.

CORNWALLIS *See also LYCHNIS 1917.*

COROMANDEL (ex-*Winterton*) 4th Rate 56, 1,340bm, 169 × 42·5ft. Perry, Blackwall, 9.5.1795; East Indiaman, purch. on stocks. Storeship 1800; harbour service 10.1807. Sold 24.7.1813 in Jamaica.

COROMANDEL (ex-*Tartar*) Wood paddle despatch vessel, 303bm, 172 × 24ft. Purch. 8.1.1855. Sold 17.8.1866 in Hong Kong, = Japanese NARUTO. BU 1876.

COROMANDEL Wood screw frigate (Indian), 1,026bm, 4 guns. R. Thames 1856. In service 1870.

COROMANDEL *See also MALABAR 1804.*

CORONATION 2nd Rate 90, 1,346bm, 160·5 × 45ft, 26–34pdr, 26–18pdr, 26–6pdr, 12–3pdr. Portsmouth DY 1685. Wrecked 3.9.1691 Rame Head.

CORSO Destroyer, 'C' class. Thornycroft 14.7.1945. = CONCORD 6.1946. Arr. 22.10.1962 Inverkeithing for BU.

CORUNNA Destroyer, 2,400 tons, 379 (oa) × 40·25ft, 5–4·5in, 10–TT. Swan Hunter 29.5.1945. Sold 8.8.1974; arr. Sunderland 23.11.1974 for BU, tx Blyth 1975.

COSBY (ex-REEVES) Frigate, TE 'Captain' class. Bethlehem, Hingham, 30.10.1943 on Lend-Lease (renamed 1943). Ret. USN 3.1946.

COSSACK (ex-PANDOUR) 6th Rate 22, 546bm, 119 × 32ft. Temple, South Shields, 24.12.1806 (renamed 1806). BU 6.1816.

COSSACK Steam gunvessel, 483bm, 150 × 26ft. Portsmouth DY, LD 1846, cancelled 1849.

COSSACK (ex-WITJAS) Wood screw corvette, 1,296bm, 195 × 39ft, 20–8in. Pitcher, Northfleet, 15.5.1854; Russian, seized 5.4.1854 Sold 19.5.1875 Castle.

COSSACK Torpedo cruiser, 1,630 tons, 225 × 36ft, 6–6in, 8–3pdr, 3–TT. Thomson 3.6.1886. Sold 4.4.1905 G. Graham.

COSSACK Destroyer, 885 tons, 270 × 26ft, 3–12pdr, 2–TT. Cammell Laird 16.2.1907. Sold 12.12.1919 Ward, Preston.

COSSACK Destroyer, 1,870 tons, 377 (oa) × 36·5ft, 8–4·7in, 4–TT. Vickers Armstrong, Tyne, 8.6.1937. Sunk 27.10.1941 west of Gibraltar four days after being torpedoed by U.563.

COSSACK Destroyer, 'C' class. Vickers Armstrong. Tyne, 10.5.1944. Arr. 1.3.1961 Troon for BU.

COTSWOLD Minesweeper, Early 'Hunt' class. Bow

McLachlan 28.11.1916. Sold 18.1.1923 Alloa S. Bkg Co., Charlestown.

COTSWOLD Destroyer, 'Hunt' class Type I. Yarrow 18.7.1940. Breakwater 1955. Arr. 11.9.1957 Ward, Grays, for BU.

COTTESMORE Minesweeper, Early 'Hunt' class. Bow McLachlan 9.2.1917. Sold 18.1.1923 Alloa S. Bkg Co., Charlestown.

COTTESMORE Destroyer, 'Hunt' class Type I. Yarrow 5.9.1940. Sold 17.9.1950 Egyptian Navy = IBRAHIM EL AWAL 1950; = MOHAMMED ALI 1951; = PORT SAID; deleted 1985–86.

COTTESMORE Minehunter, 615 tons. Yarrow 9.2.1982.

COTTON Frigate, TE 'Captain' class. Bethlehem, Hingham, 21.8.1943 on Lend-Lease. Ret. USN 11.1945.

COUCY Depot ship, 644 tons, 246 × 31ft. French patrol vessel, seized 3.7.1940 Plymouth. Ret. French Navy 1944.

COUNTERGUARD (ex-LCT.4043) Tank landing craft, 675 tons, 225 × 39ft. Arrol 1945 (renamed 1956). Sold 1965 Malaysian Navy = SRI LANGKAWI.

COUNTESS OF HOPETOUN Torpedo boat (Australian), 93 tons, 130 × 13·5ft, 3—3pdr, 3—TT. Yarrow, Poplar, 1891. Sold 4.1924 J. Hill, Melbourne.

COURAGEOUS 1st class cruiser (also 'large light cruiser'; officially 'battle cruiser'), 18,600 tons, 735 × 81ft, 4—15in, 18—4in, 2—3in. Armstrong 5.2.1916. Conv. aircraft carrier 5.1928, 22,500 tons, 16—4·7in, 48 aircraft. Sunk 17.9.1939 by U.29 in Atlantic.

COURAGEOUS Nuclear submarine, 4,400/4,900 tons, 285 (oa) × 33ft, 6—TT. Vickers, Barrow, 7.3.1970. PO 10.4.1992, tx Devonport to LU.

COURAGEUX 3rd Rate 74, 1,721bm, 172 × 48ft, 28—32pdr, 28—18pdr, 18—9pdr. French, captured 13.8.1761. Wrecked 18.12.1796 nr Gibraltar.

COURAGEUX (ex-COURAGEUSE) 5th Rate 32, 932bm, 145 × 39ft. French, captured 18.6.1799 by squadron in Mediterranean. In service 1803.

COURAGEUX 3rd Rate 74, 1,772bm, 181 × 47ft. Deptford DY 26.3.1800. Harbour service 2.1814. BU 10.1832.

COURBET Depot ship, 22,200 tons, 541 × 88·5ft. French battleship, seized 3.7.1940 Portsmouth. Free French until 1941. Sunk 9.6.1944 breakwater Arromanches.

COUREUR (ex-COUREUR) Schooner 8, 138bm, 69 × 23ft, 8—4pdr. French, captured 17.6.1778 by ALERT in English Channel. Captured 21.6.1780 by two American privateers off Newfoundland.

COUREUR (ex-COUREUR) Sloop 20, 355bm, 111 × 27·5ft. French privateer, captured 23.2.1798. Sold 14.9.1801.

COUREUSE Schooner 12. French, captured 25.3.1795 by POMONE off coast of France. Sold 13.4.1799.

COURIER (ex-*George IV*) Wood paddle packet, 733bm, 155·5 × 32·5ft. Purch. 20.8.1830. = HERMES 1831; = CHARGER (coal hulk) 1835. BU 6.1854.

COURIER (ex-ARNPRIOR) Minesweeper, 'Algerine' class. Redfern, Toronto, 22.12.1943 (renamed 6.1943). Arr. 25.3.1959 Rees, Llanelly, for BU.

COURIER *See also QUEEN MAB 1807.*

COURSER (Gunboat No 20) Gunvessel 12, 168bm, 76 × 22·5ft. Hill, Limehouse, 25.4.1797. Sold 8.1803 Customs Board.

COURTENAY Minesweeper (RCN), TE 'Bangor' class. Prince Rupert DD 2.8.1941. Sold 3.4.1946 Union SS Co., Vancouver.

COVENTRY (ex-SAN MIGUEL) 28-gun ship, 191bm. Spanish, captured 1658. Captured 1666 by French.

COVENTRY 4th Rate 48, 670bm. Deptford 1695. Captured 24.7.1704 by French off Scilly Is; recaptured. BU 1709.

COVENTRY 6th Rate 28, 599bm, 118·5 × 34ft. Adams, Beaulieu, 20.5.1757. Captured 10.1.1783 by French in Bay of Bengal.

COVENTRY (ex-CORSAIR) Light cruiser, 4,190 tons, 450 (oa) × 43·9ft, 5—6in, 2—3in. Swan Hunter 6.7.1917 (renamed 1916). AA ship 1937. Sunk 14.9.1942 air attack Mediterranean.

COVENTRY Frigate. Vickers Armstrong, Tyne. Launched 17.8.1962 as PENELOPE, 'Leander' class (q.v.).

COVENTRY Destroyer, Type 42, 3,150 tons. Cammell Laird 21.6.1974. Lost 26.5.1982 Falklands operations.

COVENTRY Frigate, 4,100 tons, 480·5 (oa) × 48·4ft, Exocet, Seawolf, helo, 6—TT. Swan Hunter 8.4.1986. PO 17.1.2002; sold 12.2002 to Romania.

COWDRAY Destroyer, 'Hunt' class Type II. Scotts 12.5.1941. Arr. 3.9.1959 King, Gateshead, for BU. *Renamed ADMIRAL HASTINGS 3.1944–8.1944 for loan to Greek Navy; not taken over.*

COWES CASTLE Corvette, 'Castle' class. Collingwood SY, cancelled 12.1943.

COWICHAN Coastal minesweeper (RCN). Davie SB 12.11.1951. Tx 7.4.1954 French Navy = LA MALOUINE. Reserve 1976, stricken 1977.

COWICHAN Minesweeper (RCN), TE 'Bangor' class. North Vancouver SR Co. 9.8.1940. Sold 1946 mercantile, retained name.

COWICHAN Coastal minesweeper (RCN). Yarrow, Esquimalt, 26.2.1957. PO 9.1997; sold 5.1999 for conv. to yacht.

COWLING CASTLE Corvette, 'Castle' class. Midland SY, cancelled 12.1943.

COWPER Wood paddle vessel, 342bm, 178 × 27ft. Purch. 20.10.1860 Hong Kong. Sold 1861 in Hong Kong = *Fei Seen*

COWRA Minesweeper (RAN), 'Bathurst' class. Poole & Steel 27.5.1943. Sold 6.1.1961; left 21.5.1962 for Japan for BU.

COWSLIP Sloop, 'Anchusa' class. Barclay Curle 19.10.1917. Sunk 18.4.1918 by UB.105 off Cape Spartel.

COWSLIP Corvette, 'Flower' class. Harland & Wolff 28.5.1941. Sold 7.1948 mercantile; BU 4.1949 Troon.

CRACCHER Ballinger, 56bm. Built 1416. Last listed 1420.

CRACCHER Destroyer, 'C' class. White 23.6.1945. = CRISPIN 6.1946. Sold 18.3.1958 Pakistani Navy = JAHANGIR; deleted 1982.

CRACHE-FEU Gunvessel 3, 144bm, 79·5 × 20ft. French, captured 9.5.1795 by squadron off coast of France. BU 1797.

CRACKER (Gunboat No 13) Gunvessel 12, 160bm, 75 × 22ft, 2—24pdr, 10—18pdr carr. Dudman, Deptford, 25.4.1797. Sold 12.1802.

CRACKER Gun-brig 12, 180bm, 80 × 23ft, 10—18pdr carr., 2—6pdr. Pitcher, Northfleet, 30.6.1804. Sold 23.11.1815.

CRACKER Cutter tender, 54bm. White, Cowes, 1826, purch. Sold 11.1842.

CRACKER Schooner. Deptford DY, ordered 1846, cancelled 1850.

CRACKER Wood screw gunboat, 'Dapper' class. Pitcher, Northfleet, 2.4.1855. BU 4.1864.

CRACKER Composite screw gunboat, 465bm, 605 tons, 155 × 25ft, 1—7in, 1—64pdr, 2—20pdr. Portsmouth DY 27.11.1867. BU 1889 Portsmouth.

CRADLEY Inshore minehunter, 'Ley' class. Saunders-Roe 24.2.1955. = ISIS 1963. Sold Pounds 4.1982.

CRAFTY Schooner 12, 146bm. French, captured 1804. Captured 9.3.1807 by three privateers off Gibraltar.

CRAIGIE Minesweeper, Later 'Hunt' class. Clyde SB Co. 5.1918. Sold 18.5.1922 B. Zammitt, Malta.

CRANE 24-gun ship, 253bm, 201 tons, 62 × 25ft, 6—9pdr, 7—6pdr, 6—4pdr, 5 small. Built 1590. Sold 1629.

CRANE Galley 1. Purch. 1777 North America. Sold 20.8.1783 New York.

CRANE Schooner 4, 80bm, 56 × 18·5ft, 4—12pdr carr. Custance, Yarmouth, 26.4.1806. Wrecked 26.10.1808 West Hoe.

CRANE Brig-sloop 18, 'Cruizer' class, 385bm. Brindley, Frindsbury, 29.7.1809. Foundered 30.9.1814 West Indies.

CRANE Packet brig 6, 359bm, 96 × 31ft, 6—18pdr. Woolwich DY 28.5.1839. Sold 11.1.1862 Marshall, Plymouth.

CRANE Destroyer, 360 tons, 215 × 21ft, 1—12pdr, 5—6pdr, 2—TT. Palmer 17.1.1896. Sold 10.6.1919 Ward, New Holland.

CRANE Sloop, 1,350 tons, 283 × 38ft, 6—4in, 12—20mm. Denny 10.11.1942. BU 1965 Queenborough.

CRANEFLY River gunboat, 'Fly' class. Yarrow 8.1915, re-erected 12.1915 R. Tigris. Sold locally 1.3.1923.

CRANHAM Inshore minesweeper, 'Ham' class. White, Cowes, 24.11.1953. Sold Pounds 9.6.1966.

CRANSTOUN Frigate, TE 'Captain' class. Bethlehem, Hingham, 28.8.1943 on Lend-Lease. Ret. USN 12.1945.

CRASH (Gunboat No 15) Gunvessel 12, 2—32pdr carr., 2—24pdr carr., 8—18pdr carr. Barnard, Deptford, 5.4.1797. Sold 9.1802. *In Dutch hands 26.8.1798—11.8.1799.*

CRASH *See also SCOURGE 1794.*

CRAUFURD *See GENERAL CRAUFURD 1915.*

CREDITON Minesweeper, Later 'Hunt' class. Bow McLachlan, LD 1918, = COLWYN 1918, cancelled.

CREOLE 5th Rate 36, 944bm. Tanner, Dartmouth, ordered 17.3.1803, cancelled 2.6.1809.

CREOLE 5th Rate 38, 1,070bm. French, captured 1.7.1803 West Indies. Foundered 2.1.1804 off Jamaica.

CREOLE 5th Rate 36, 949bm, 145 × 38·5ft. Plymouth DY 1.5.1813. BU 8.1833 Deptford.

CREOLE 6th Rate 26, 911bm, 131 × 40·5ft, 24—32pdr, 2—12pdr. Plymouth DY 1.10.1845. BU 3.1875 Devonport.

CREOLE Submarine, 893 tons, 241 × 21ft. French, towed Swansea 70 per cent complete 6.1940, seized 3.7.1940. LU Swansea until 1946; ret. French Navy for comp.

CREOLE Destroyer, 'C' class. White 22.11.1945, Sold Pakistani Navy 20.6.1958 = ALAMGIR; deleted 1982.

CRESCENT 14-gun ship, 167bm. Purch. 1643. Captured 1648 by Royalists. Wrecked 1649.

CRESCENT Fireship 6, 234bm, 85 × 25ft. French, captured 1692 by DOVER. Sold 1698.

CRESCENT (ex-ROSTAN) 5th Rate 32, 731bm, 130·5 × 36ft. French privateer, captured 10.1758 by TORBAY. Sold 13.6.1777.

CRESCENT 6th Rate 28, 611bm, 121 × 34ft. Hillhouse, Bristol, 3.1779. Captured 19.6.1781 by French off Cadiz.

CRESCENT 5th Rate 36, 888bm, 137 × 38·5ft. Calhoun & Newland, Bursledon, 28.10.1784. Wrecked 6.12.1808 coast of Jutland.

CRESCENT 5th Rate 38, 1,084bm, 154·5 × 40ft. Woolwich DY 11.12.1810. Harbour service 1.1840. Sold 1854.

CRESCENT Wood paddle tender, 90bm, 80 × 16ft. Purch. 21.7.1854 Constantinople. Sold 7.7.1855.

CRESCENT 1st class cruiser, 7,700 tons, 360 × 61ft, 1—9·2in, 12—6in, 12—6pdr. Portsmouth DY 30.3.1892. Sold 22.9.1921 Cohen; BU Germany.

CRESCENT Destroyer, 1,375 tons, 329 (oa) × 33ft, 4—4·7in, 1—3in, 8—TT. Vickers Armstrong, Barrow, 29.9.1931. Tx RCN = FRASER 17.2.1937. Sunk 25.6.1940 collision CALCUTTA R. Gironde.

CRESCENT Destroyer, 'C' class. John Brown 20.7.1944. Lent RCN 9.1945; sold RCN 1951. BU 5.1971 Taiwan.

CRESCENT *See also GLORY 1899.*

CRESSY 3rd Rate 74, 1,763bm, 176 × 48·5ft. Brindley, Frindsbury, 7.3.1810. BU 12.1832.

CRESSY Screw 3rd Rate 80, 2,539bm, 198 × 55ft, 14—8in, 66—32pdr. Chatham DY 21.7.1853. Sold 1867 Castle & Beech.

CRESSY Armoured cruiser, 12,000 tons, 440 × 69·5ft, 2—9in, 12—6in, 13—12pdr. Fairfield 4.12.1899. Sunk 22.9.1914 by U.9 in North Sea.

CRESSY *See also UNICORN 1824.*

CRETAN (ex-NETTUNO) Brig-sloop 16, 344bm, 95·5 × 29ft, 14—24pdr carr., 2—6pdr. French, ex-Italian, captured 1.6.1808 by UNITE off Zara. Sold 29.9.1814.

CRETAN Destroyer, 'C' class. Scotts 6.8.1945. = CROMWELL 6.1946; sold 7.1946 RNorN = BERGEN. Sold 1.1967 for BU.

CRICCIETH CASTLE Corvette. 'Castle' class. Morton, Canada, cancelled 12.1943.

CRICHTON Coastal minesweeper, 'Ton' class. Doig, Grimsby, 17.5.1953. = CLYDE 5.1954; = ST DAVID 1961; = CRICHTON 1976. Towed 9.4.1987 Cairnryan for BU.

CRICKET Coastal destroyer, 234 tons, 175 × 17·5ft, 2—12pdr, 3—TT. White 23.1.1906. Rated torpedo boat = TB.1 in 1906. Sold 7.10.1920 Fowey Coaling & Ship Co.

CRICKET River gunboat, 645 tons, 230 × 36ft, 2—6in, 1—3in. Barclay Curle 17.12.1915. Minesweeper 1939; gunboat 1940. Damaged mine 6.1941 off Mersa Matruh; BU 1942 Alexandria.

CRISPIN *See CRACCHER 1945.*

CROCODILE 6th Rate 24, 519bm, 114 × 32ft.

Portsmouth DY 25.4.1781. Lost 1784 off Start Point.

CROCODILE 6th Rate 22, 540bm, 119 × 3 11·5ft. Temple, South Shields, 19.4.1806. BU 10.1816.

CROCODILE 6th Rate 28, 500bm, 114 × 32ft, 20—32pdr carr., 6—18pdr, 2—6pdr. Chatham DY 28.10.1825. Harbour service 8.1850. Sold 22.11.1861 Castle.

CROCODILE Iron screw troopship 4, 173bm, 6,211 tons, 360 × 49ft, 3—4pdr. Wigram, Blackwall, 7.1.1867. Sold 11.5.1894, BU.

CROCUS Sloop 14, 256bm, 92 × 25·5ft. Plymouth DY 10.6.1808. Sold 31.8.1815.

CROCUS Wood screw gunboat, 'Albacore' class. Green, Blackwall, 4.6.1856. BU 7.1864.

CROCUS Sloop, 'Arabis' class. Lobnitz 24.12.1915. Sold 7.1930 Bombay.

CROCUS Corvette, 'Flower' class. Inglis 26.6.1940. Sold 22.7.1946 = *Annlock.*

CROFTON Coastal minesweeper, 'Ton' class. Thornycroft 3.1958. = WARSASH 5.1969—1975. BU Cairnryan 9.4.1987.

CROMARTY Minesweeper, turbine 'Bangor' class. Blyth DD 24.2.1941. Sunk 23.10.1943 mine central Mediterranean.

CROMER Wood screw gunboat, 'Britomart' class. Haslar, Portsmouth, 20.8.1867. Sold 24.8.1886 for BU.

CROMER Minesweeper, TE 'Bangor' class. Lobnitz 7.10.1940. Sunk 9.11.1942 mine Mediterranean.

CROMER Minehunter, 'Sandown' class, Vosper-Thornycroft 6.10.1990. PO 10.10.2001. Static harbour TS Dartmouth 7.2002 = HINDOSTAN.

CROMER CASTLE Corvette, 'Castle' class. Midland SY, cancelled 12.1943.

CROMWELL *See CRETAN 1945.*

CROOME Minesweeper, Early 'Hunt' class. Clyde SB Co. 22.5.1917. Sold 7.1922 Stanlee, Dover.

CROOME Destroyer, 'Hunt' class Type II. Stephen 30.1.1941. Arr. 13.8.1957 Ward, Briton Ferry, for BU.

CROSSBOW Destroyer, 1,980 tons, 365 (oa) × 38ft, 6—4in, 10—TT. Thornycroft 20.12.1945. Sold Ward 14.12.1971; BU Briton Ferry.

CROW 36-gun ship. French, captured 1652. Sold 1656.

CROWN 5th Rate 44, 842bm, 134 × 38ft. Taylor, Rotherhithe, 13.7.1747. Storeship 7.1757. Sold 17.7.1770.

CROWN 3rd Rate, 1,405bm, 160·5 × 45ft. Perry, Blackwall, 15.3.1782. Prison ship 5.1798; powder hulk 1802. BU 3.1816.

CROWN Gunvessel, 73bm, 58 × 17ft. Purch. 3.1794. Sold 10.3.1800.

CROWN Wood screw gunboat, 'Britomart' class. Haslar, Portsmouth, LD 1861, cancelled 12.12.1863.

CROWN Destroyer, 'C' class. Scotts 19.12.1945. Sold 7.1946 RNorN = OSLO. BU Grimstad 7.1968.

CROWN *See also TAUNTON 1654.*

CROWN MALAGO Flyboat 6, 197bm. Spanish, captured 1664. Given away 1667.

CROWN PRIZE 6th Rate 26, 223bm. French, captured 1691. Wrecked 9.2.1692 nr Dartmouth.

CROXTON Paddle minesweeper, 'Ascot' class. Ayrshire Co. 7.4.1916. Sold 3.1922 Ward, Inverkeithing.

CROZIER (ex-VERWOOD, ex-VENTNOR) Survey ship, 800 tons, 220 × 28·5ft, 1—3pdr. Simons 1.7.1919 (renamed 1919). Tx SAN 1921, = PROTEA 11.10.1922. Sold 10.1933.

CROZIERS Destroyer, 'C' class. Yarrow 19.9.1944. Sold 10.10.1946 RNorN = TRONDHEIM. BU 12.1961 Belgium.

CRUELLE Cutter 8. French, captured 1.6.1800 by MERMAID off Toulon. Sold 1801.

CRUISER *See KINGFISHER 1879, CRUIZER 1852.*

CRUIZER (ex-DE MERIC) 6th Rate 24, 280bm. French, captured 5.5.1705 by TRYTON. Wrecked 15.12.1708 Azores.

CRUIZER (ex-*Unity*) Sloop 14, 123bm. Purch. 7.6.1709. Sold 1712.

CRUIZER Sloop 8. Captured 1721. Foundered 1724.

CRUIZER Sloop 8, 100bm, 26 × 20ft. Deptford 24.10.1721. BU 7.1732.

CRUIZER Sloop 14, 200bm, 87·5 × 23ft. Deptford DY 6.9.1732. Sold 22.1.1744.

CRUIZER Sloop 8, 141bm, 75·5 × 20·5ft. Deptford DY 31.8.1752. Burnt 2.10.1776 off South Carolina.

CRUIZER Cutter 14, 199bm, 73·5 × 26ft, 14—4pdr. Purch. 5.1780. Lost 1792 on passage to Gibraltar.

CRUIZER Brig-sloop 18, 'Cruizer' class, 384bm. Teague, Ipswich, 20.12.1797. Sold 3.2.1819 Mr Cockshot.

CRUIZER Brig-sloop 18, 'Cruizer' class, 385bm. Chatham DY 19.1.1828. Sold 3.1849 Bombay. *Last of class.*

CRUIZER Wood screw sloop, 752bm, 960 tons, 160 × 32ft, 17—32pdr. Deptford DY 19.6.1852. Listed as CRUISER from 1857; = LARK (sail TS) 5.1893. Sold 1912 in Malta.

CRUSADER Destroyer, 1,045 tons, 280 × 26ft, 2—4in, 2—TT. White 20.3.1909. Sold 30.6.1920 Ward, Preston.

CRUSADER Destroyer, 1,375 tons, 329 (oa) × 33ft, 4—4·7in, 8—TT. Portsmouth DY 30.9.1931. Tx

RCN 15.6.1938 = OTTAWA. Sunk 14.9.1942 by U.91 Gulf of St Lawrence.

CRUSADER Destroyer, 'C' class. John Brown 4.10.1944. Tx RCN 11.1945. Sold 1964 for BU.

CRYSTAL Destroyer, 'C' class. Yarrow 12.2.1945. Sold 10.10.1946 RNorN = STAVANGER. Sold 1.1967 for BU.

CRYSTAL Trials vessel, 3,040 tons, 413·6 (oa) × 56ft. Devonport DY 22.3.1971. Sold Sam Evans & Sons; towed Rotterdam 18.9.1992.

CUBA (ex-POMONA) 5th Rate 32, Spanish, captured 23.8.1806 by ARETHUSA off Havana. Sold 3.4.1817.

CUBA Schooner tender, 67bm. Slaver, captured 6.1857 by ARAB. BU 3.1866 in Jamaica.

CUBITT Frigate, TE 'Captain' class. Bethlehem, Hingham, 11.9.1943 on Lend-Lease. Ret. USN 1946.

CUCKMERE Frigate, 'River' class. Vickers, Montreal, 24.10.1942 on Lend-Lease. Ret. USN 6.11.1946.

CUCKOO Schooner 4, 78bm, 56 × 18·5ft, 4—12pdr carr. Lovewell, Yarmouth, 12.4.1806. Wrecked 4.4.1810 Texel.

CUCKOO (ex-*Cinderella*) Wood paddle packet, 234bm, 120·5 × 20ft. GPO vessel, tx 1837. Sold 1864.

CUCKOO Iron screw gunboat, 'Ant' class. Laird 14.8.1873. = VIVID (base ship) 1912; = VIVID (OLD) 1920; = YC.37 in 1923. Sold 1958.

CUCKOO *See also AMELIA 1888.*

CUFFLEY Inshore minesweeper. Launched 1955 as WINTRINGHAM (q.v.).

CULGOA (ex-MACQUARIE) Frigate (RAN), 'River' class. Williamstown DY 22.9.1945 (renamed 3.1943). Hulk 1966. Sold 27.1.1972; BU Taiwan.

CULGOA *See also MACQUARIE 1945.*

CULLIN SOUND Repair ship, 10,000 tons, 431 × 56ft, 12—20mm. Gray, Hartlepool, 2.11.1944. Sold 1948 = *James Clunies.*

CULLODEN 3rd Rate 74, 1,487bm, 161·5 × 46·5ft. Deptford DY 9.9.1747. Sold 29.6.1770.

CULLODEN Storeship hoy 2, 35bm, 43 × 16ft. Cleveland, Plymouth, 12.1749. Sold 16.12.1765.

CULLODEN 3rd Rate 74, 1,659bm, 170 × 47ft. Deptford 18.5.1776. Wrecked 23.1.1781 Long I.

CULLODEN 3rd Rate 74, 1,683bm, 170 × 48ft. Randall, Rotherhithe, 16.6.1783. BU 2.1813.

CULLODEN *See also PRINCE HENRY 1747.*

CULVER (ex-MENDOTA) Coastguard cutter, 1,546 tons, 1—5in, 2—3in. USN, tx 30.4.1941 on Lend-Lease. Sunk 31.1.1942 by U.105 in North Atlantic.

CULVERIN Destroyer, 1,980 tons, 341·5 × 38ft, 6—4in, 10—TT. Thornycroft 3.1946, not comp. Arr. 3.1946 Ward, Grays for BU.

CUMBERLAND 3rd Rate 80, 1,219bm, 156 × 42ft. Wyatt, Bursledon, 12.11.1695. Captured 10.10.1707 by French. Sold Spanish Navy = PRINCIPE DE ASTURIAS.

CUMBERLAND 3rd Rate 80, 1,308bm, 156 × 44ft. Deptford DY 1710. Rebuilt Woolwich DY 1739 as 66 guns, 1,401bm. Foundered at anchor 2.11.1760 Goa.

CUMBERLAND (ex-*Alex Robert*) Fireship 8, 181bm, 79 × 23ft. Purch. 29.6.1739. BU comp. 31.3.1742 Sheerness.

CUMBERLAND Fireship 8. In service 1745.

CUMBERLAND 3rd Rate 74, 1,647bm, 169 × 46ft. Deptford DY 29.3.1774. BU 1805 Portsmouth.

CUMBERLAND Schooner, 30bm. Purch. 1803 Port Jackson. Sold 1810. *In French hands 1804–09.*

CUMBERLAND 3rd Rate 74, 1 718bm, 174·5 × 48ft. Pitcher, Northfleet, 19.8.1807. Convict ship 3.1830, = FORTITUDE 15.11.1833. On sale list 2.1870. Sold Castle.

CUMBERLAND 3rd Rate 70, 2,214bm, 180 × 54ft, 6—8in, 64—32pdr. Chatham DY 21.10.1842. TS 1870. Burnt 17.2.1889 R. Clyde; wreck BU 1889 Rosneath Bay.

CUMBERLAND Armoured cruiser, 9,800 tons, 440 × 66ft, 14—6in, 9—12pdr. London & Glasgow Co. 16.12.1902. Sold 9.5.1921 Ward, Briton Ferry; arr. 28.3.1923 for BU.

CUMBERLAND Cruiser, 9,750 tons, 630 (oa) × 68·5ft, 8—8in, 6—4in. Vickers Armstrong, Barrow, 16.3.1926. Arr. 3.11.1959 Cashmore, Newport, for BU

CUMBERLAND Frigate, 4,200 tons. Swan Hunter 21.6.1986

CUPAR (ex-ROSSLARE) Minesweeper, Later 'Hunt' class. McMillan, Dumbarton, 27.3.1918 (renamed 1918). Sunk 5.5.1919 mine off R. Tyne.

CUPID Sloop 14, 290bm, 92·5 × 27ft. Purch. 1777. Foundered 28.12.1778 off coast of Newfoundland.

CUPID Cutter 12, 181bm. Purch. 1781. Sold 1782, unsuitable.

CUPID (Mortar Float No 103) Mortar vessel, 102bm, 60 × 20ft. Laird 13.11.1855. = YC.3 in 8.1865. Gone by 1870.

CURACOA 5th Rate 36, 956bm, 145 × 38·5ft. Kidwell, Itchenor, 23.9.1809. Reduced to 24 guns at Chatham 6.1831. BU 3.1849.

CURACOA Wood screw frigate, 1,570bm, 192 × 43ft, 1—10in, 30—32pdr. Pembroke Dock 13.4.1854. BU comp. 17.7.1869.

CURACOA Screw corvette, 2,380 tons, 225 × 44·5ft, 2—7in, 12—6pdr. Elder, Glasgow, 18.4.1878. Sold 17.5.1904 King, Garston.

CURACOA Light cruiser, 4,190 tons, 450 (oa) × 43·9ft, 5—6in, 2—3in. Pembroke Dock 5.5.1917. AA ship 1939. Sunk 2.10.1942 collision SS *Queen Mary* north of Ireland.

CURIEUX Brig-sloop 18, 315bm, 97 × 28·5ft, 10—18pdr carr., 8—6pdr. French, captured 4.2.1804 by boats of CENTAUR at Fort Royal, Martinique. Wrecked 3.11.1809 West Indies.

CURIEUX (ex-BEARNAIS) Brig-sloop 16, 317bm. French, captured 14.12.1809 by MELAMPUS. Sold 5.1814.

CURLEW Brig-sloop 16 (fir-built), 314bm, 95 × 28ft. Randall, Rotherhithe, 16.7.1795. Foundered 31.12.1796 North Sea.

CURLEW (ex-LEANDER) loop 16, 350bm, 98·5 × 29·5ft, 8—24pdr carr., 6—24pdr, 2—6pdr. Purch. 6.1803. Sold 25.6.1810.

CURLEW Brig-sloop 18, 'Cruizer' class, 386bm. Good, Bridport, 27.5.1812. Sold 28.12.1822 Bombay = *Jenica*.

CURLEW Brig-sloop 10, 'Cherokee' class, 233bm. Woolwich DY 25.2.1830. BU 8.1849.

CURLEW Wood screw sloop, 486bm, 139 × 28ft, 9—32pdr. Deptford DY 31.5.1854. Sold 29.8.1865 Marshall, Plymouth.

CURLEW Wood screw gunvesssel, 665bm, 805 tons, 170 × 29ft, 1—7in, 2—40pdr. Deptford DY 20.8.1868. Sold 7.11.1882.

CURLEW Torpedo sloop, 950 tons, 195 × 28ft, 1—6in, 3—5in, 5—TT, Devonport DY 23.10.1885. Sold 10.7.1906.

CURLEW Light cruiser, 4,190 tons, 450 (oa) × 43·9ft, 5—6in, 2—3in. Vickers 5.7.1917. AA ship 1938. Sunk 26.5.1940 air attack Ofotfjord, Norway.

CURLEW *See also CHEDISTON 1953.*

CURRAGH Minesweeper, Later 'Hunt' class. Eltringham, cancelled 1918.

CURZON Frigate, TE 'Captain' class. Bethlehem, Hingham, 18.9.1943 on Lend-Lease. Ret. USN 1946.

CURZON *See also BICKINGTON 1953.*

CUTLASS Destroyer, 1,980 tons, 341·5 × 38ft, 6—4in, 10—TT. Yarrow 20.3.1946, not comp. Cancelled 1.1946; arr. 20.3.1946 Troon for BU.

CUTLASS Patrol boat (fast training boat), 102 tons. Vosper 2.1970. Sold privately Greece; towed away 11.2.1983.

CUTLASS *See also NORTHWAY 1943.*

CUTTER Ketch 2, 46bm. Portsmouth 1673. Wrecked 1673.

CUTTLE Schooner 4, 78bm, 56 × 18ft, 4—12pdr carr. Bermuda 5.1807. Foundered 1814 Halifax Station.

CUXTON Coastal minesweeper, 'Ton' class. Camper & Nicholson 9.11.1953. Towed Bruges 16.4.1992 for BU.

CYANE Sloop 18, 423bm, 110 × 29·5ft. Wilson, Frindsbury, 9.4.1796. Captured 12.5.1805 by French in West Indies; recaptured 5.10.1805 off Tobago = CERF. Sold 12.1.1809.

CYANE (ex-COLUMBINE) 6th Rate 22, 540bm, 118·5 × 31·5ft. Bass, Topsham, 14.10.1806 (renamed 1805). Captured 20.2.1815 by American CONSTITUTION in Atlantic.

CYBELE Mine destructor vessel, 3,980 tons. Scotts 16.11.1943. BU 10.1946 Troon.

CYCLAMEN Sloop, 'Arabis' class. Lobnitz 22.2.1916. Sold 2.7.1932 Metal Industries, Charlestown.

CYCLAMEN Corvette, 'Flower' class. Lewis 20.6.1940. Sold 1947 = *Southern Briar*.

CYCLOPS 6th Rate 28, 603bm, 120 × 34ft. Menetone, Limehouse, 31.7.1779. Troopship 3.1800. Sold 1.9.1814.

CYCLOPS Wood paddle frigate, 1,195bm, 190 × 37·5ft. 2—98pdr, 4—68pdr. Pembroke Dock 10.7.1839. Sold 26.1.1864 Castle.

CYCLOPS Coast defence turret ship, 3,480 tons, 225 × 45ft, 4—10in. Green, Blackwall, 18.7.1871. Sold 7.7.1903.

CYCLOPS (ex-*Indrabarah*) Repair ship, 11,300 tons, 460 × 55ft, 10—3pdr. Laing, Sunderland, 27.10.1905. Arr. 29.6.1947 Cashmore, Newport, for BU.

CYDNUS 5th Rate 38 (red pine-built), 1,080bm, 150 × 40·5ft. Wigram, Wells & Green, Blackwall, 17.4.1813. BU 2.1816 Portsmouth.

CYGNET Pink 3, 30bm, 1—2pdr, 2—1½pdr. Built 1585. Condemned 1603.

CYGNET 10-gun ship, 233bm. Dunkirk privateer (captured?). Purch. 1643. Sold 1654.

CYGNET Sloop 8, 58bm. Chatham DY 1657. Sold 1664.

CYGNET Survey vessel. Purch. 9.1684. Foundered 1687 off Madagascar.

CYGNET Fireship 8, 100bm. Purch. 1688. Captured 20.9.1693 by French.

CYGNET (ex-GUIRLANDE) Sloop 18, 386bm, 111 × 28·5ft, 18—6pdr. French, captured 7.1758. Sold 1768 in South Carolina.

CYGNET Sloop 14, 301bm, 97 × 27ft. Portsmouth DY 24.1.1776. Sold 8.1802.

CYGNET Sloop 16, 365bm, 106 × 28ft. Palmer, Yarmouth, 6.9.1804. Wrecked 7.3.1815 Courantine R., Guiana.

CYGNET Brig-sloop 10, 'Cherokee' class, 237bm. Portsmouth DY 11.5.1819. Sold 6.8.1835.

CYGNET Brig 8, 359bm, 95 × 30·5ft, 8—18pdr. Woolwich DY 6.4.1840. = WV.30 (Coastguard) 5.1863. BU comp. 3.1.1877 Portsmouth.

CYGNET Wood screw gunvessel, 428bm, 145 × 25·5ft, 1—68pdr, 4—24pdr howitzers. Wigram, Northam, 6.6.1860. BU 8.1868 Portsmouth.

CYGNET Composite screw gunboat, 455 tons, 125 × 23·5ft, 2—64pdr MLR, 2—20pdr. Doxford 30.5.1874. BU 1889.

CYGNET Destroyer, 355 tons, 210 × 19·5ft, 1—12pdr, 5—6pdr, 2—TT. Thornycroft, Chiswick, 8.1.1898. Sold 29.4.1920 Ward, Rainham.

CYGNET Destroyer, 1,375 tons, 329 (oa) × 33ft, 4—4·7in, 8—TT. Vickers Armstrong, Barrow, 29.9.1931. Tx RCN = ST LAURENT 17.2.1937. Sold 1947.

CYGNET Sloop, 1,350 tons, 283 × 38·5ft, 6—4in, 12—20mm. Cammell Laird 28.7.1942. Arr. 16.3.1956 Rosyth for BU.

CYGNET Patrol boat, 190 tons, 120 (oa) × 21·7ft, Dunston 6.10.1975. Sold 28.2.1996 private buyer.

CYNTHIA Sloop 18, 410bm, 113 × 29ft. Wells, Deptford, 23.2.1796. BU 10.1809 Chatham.

CYNTHIA Sloop 16. Listed 1810—15.

CYNTHIA Packet brig 6, 232bm, 87 × 25ft. Purch. 1826. Wrecked 6.6.1827 Barbados.

CYNTHIA Wood screw sloop, 669bm, 160 × 30ft. Devonport DY, LD 2.12.1861, cancelled 12.12.1863.

CYNTHIA Destroyer, 355 tons, 210 × 19·5ft, 1—12pdr, 5—6pdr, 2—TT. Thornycroft, Chiswick, 3.9.1898. Sold 29.4.1920 Ward, Rainham.

CYNTHIA Minesweeper, 'Catherine' class. Associated SB, Seattle, 25.1.1943. Tx RN 7.12.1943 on Lend-Lease. Ret. USN 20.1.1947.

CYRENE 6th Rate 20, 457bm, 115·5 × 30ft. Chapman, Bideford, 4.6.1814. Sold 4.1828 Bombay.

CYRUS Transport 10, 461bm, 111 × 30·5ft. Purch. 1771. Lost 22.4.1786 Barbados.

CYRUS 6th Rate 20, 464bm, 116 × 30ft. Courtney, Chester, 26.8.1813. Sold 23.5.1823 Bennet & Son.

CYRUS Mine destructor vessel, 3,980 tons. Scotts 12.10.1943. Wrecked 5.12.1944 Seine Bay.

CZAREVITCH Troopship (RIM), 1,990 tons, 185 × 32ft. Sunderland 1866. Sold c. 1895.

D

'D' class submarines 550 tons, 150 × 22·5ft, 1—12pdr, 3—TT.

D.1 Vickers 16.5.1908. Sunk 23.10.1918 target.

D.2 Vickers 25.5.1910. Sunk 25.11.1914 by German patrol craft off Wester Eems.

D.3 Vickers 17.10.1910. Sunk accidentally 15.3.1918 by French airship in English Channel.

D.4 Vickers 27.5.1911. Sold 17.12.1921 H. Pounds, Portsmouth.

D.5 Vickers 28.8.1911. Sunk 3.11.1914 mine North Sea.

D.6 Vickers 23.10.1911. Sunk 28.6.1918 by UB.73 off north coast of Ireland.

D.7 Chatham DY 14.1.1911. Sold 19.12.1921 H. Pounds.

D.8 Chatham DY 23.9.1911. Sold 19.12.1921. H. Pounds.

D.9 Chatham DY. Launched 9.11.1912. as E.1 (q.v.).

D.10 Chatham DY. Launched 23.11.1912 as E.2 (q.v.).

DACRES (ex-DUFFY) Frigate, DE 'Captain' Class. Boston NY 19.5.1943 on Lend-Lease. Ret. USN 1.1946.

DAEDALUS 5th Rate 32, 703bm, 126 × 38ft. Fisher, Liverpool, 20.5.1780. Lent Trinity House 10.1803—1806 as hulk. BU 7.1811 Sheerness.

DAEDALUS (ex-CORONA) 5th Rate 38, 1,094bm, 153 × 40ft. French, ex-Venetian, captured 13.3.1811 Lissa. Wrecked 2.7.1813 off Ceylon.

DAEDALUS 5th Rate 46, 1,083bm, 1,447 tons, 152 × 40·5ft. Deptford DY, tx Sheerness DY 2.5.1826. Reduced to 20 guns 1843; RNR drillship 1862. Sold 14.9.1911 J. B.Garnham.

DAEDALUS Light cruiser, 4,765 tons, 445 × 46·5ft, 6—6in, 2—3in. Armstrong, ordered 3.1918, cancelled 11.1918.

DAEDALUS See also THUNDERBOLT 1856.

DAFFODIL Sloop, 'Acacia' class. Scotts 17.8.1915. Sold 22.2.1935 Cashmore, Newport.

DAFFODIL Corvette, 'Flower' class. Lewis 3.9.1940, = DIANELLA 26.10.1940. Arr. 24.6.1947 Portaferry for BU.

DAGGER Destroyer, 1,980 tons, 365 (oa)× 38ft, 6—4in, 10—TT. Yarrow, LD 7.3.1945, cancelled 10.1945.

DAGGER See also OCEANWAY 1943.

DAHLIA Sloop, 'Acacia' class. Barclay Curle 21.3.1915. RNVR drillship 1923. Sold 2.7.1932 Metal Industries, Charlestown.

DAHLIA Corvette, 'Flower' class. Lewis 31.10.1940. Arr. 20.10.1948 Howells, Gelleswick Bay, for BU.

DAINTY (ex-REPENTANCE) Discovery ship. Renamed 1589. Captured 1594 by Spanish.

DAINTY Pink 4. In service 1645.

DAINTY Destroyer, 1,375 tons, 329 (oa) × 33ft, 4—4·7in, 1—3in, 8—TT. Fairfield 3.5.1932. Sunk 24.2.1941 air attack off Tobruk.

DAINTY Destroyer, 2,610 tons, 390 (oa) × 43ft, 6—4·5in, 10—TT. White 16.8.1950. Sold 1.1.1971; BU Cairnryan.

DAISY Pink 4, 4—6pdr. In service 1599.

DAISY Wood screw gunboat, 'Cheerful' class. Westbrook, Blackwall, 20.3.1856. BU 1.1869 Haslar.

DAISY Survey vessel, 510 tons, 125 × 22·5ft. Duthie, Torry, 1911, purch. on stocks 14.2.1911. Sold 3.1920 Newfoundland Govt.

DAKINS Frigate, TE 'Captain' class. Bethlehem, Hingham, 18.9.1943 on Lend-Lease. Ret. USN 1946. BU 1.1947 Holland.

DALHOUSIE Troopship (Indian), 1,060bm. Built 1858. In service 1875.

DALHOUSIE Troopship (RIM), 1,960 tons, 239 × 36ft, 6—6pdr. Caird, Greenock, 5.6.1886.

DALRYMPLE See LUCE BAY 1945.

DALSWINTON Coastal minesweeper, 'Ton' class. White, Southampton, 24.9.1953. = MONTROSE 1962. Sold Pounds 11.11.1972.

DAME DE GRACE Gunvessel 4, 87bm. French, captured 18.3.1799 off coast of Syria. Retaken, sunk by French 8.5.1799.

DAMERHAM Inshore minesweeper, 'Ham' class. Brooke Marine 15.6.1953. Sold 27.9.1966 in Singapore.

DAMPIER See HERNE BAY 1945.

DANAE 5th Rate 38, 941bm, 147·5 × 38ft. French, captured 28.3.1759 by SOUTHAMPTON and MELAMPE. BU comp. 14.6.1771 Chatham.

DANAE 5th Rate 32, 689bm, 129·5 × 35ft. French, captured 13.5.1779 when stranded and abandoned nr St-Malo. Sold 10.1797.

DANAE (ex-VAILLANTE) 6th Rate 20, 508bm, 119 × 31ft, 20—32pdr carr., 12—12pdr carr., 2—6pdr. French, captured 7.8.1798 by INDEFATIGABLE in Bay of Biscay. Taken into Brest by mutinous crew 14.3.1800, HO French 17.3.1800.

DANAE Screw corvette, 1,287bm, 1,760 tons, 212 × 36ft, 2—7in, 4—6pdr. Portsmouth DY 21.5.1867. Lent War Dept 1886 as hulk. Sold 15.5.1906.

DANAE Light cruiser, 4,650 tons, 471 (oa) × 46ft, 6—6in, 2—3in. Armstrong 26.1.1918. Lent 4.10.1944–28.9.1946 Polish Navy = CONRAD. Sold 22.1.1948; arr. 27.3.1948 Ward, Barrow, for BU.

DANAE (ex-VIMIERA) Destroyer, 2,610 tons, 390 (oa) × 43ft, 6—4·5in, 6—40mm, 10—TT. Cammell Laird (renamed 3.1945), cancelled 1.1946.

DANAE Frigate, 'Leander' class, Y136, 2,650 tons, 372 (oa) × 41ft, 2—4·5in, Seacat, helo (later Exocet, Seawolf). Devonport DY 21.10.1965. Sold 25.4.1991 Ecuadoran Navy = MORAN VALVERDE.

DANGEREUSE Gunvessel 6. French, captured 18.3.1799 off coast of Syria. Sold 1800.

DANIEL Fireship 6, 160bm. Purch. 1666. Sold 1667.

DANNEMARK 3rd Rate 74, 1,836bm. Danish, captured 7.9.1807 Battle of Copenhagen. Sold 14.12.1815. *Was to have been renamed MARATHON.*

DANUBE Wood paddle vessel, 110bm. Purch. 8.1854 Constantinople. Sold 23.7.1856.

DANUBE Wood screw gunboat, 'Britomart' class. Haslar, Portsmouth, ordered 1861, cancelled 12.12.1863.

DAPHNE (ex-SIRENE) 6th Rate 24, 574bm 118 × 33·5ft, 8—18pdr carr., 22—9pdr, 2—6pdr. Dutch, captured 17.8.1796. = LAUREL (prison ship) 16.2.1798. Sold 7.6.1821 Holmes, Portsea, for BU.

DAPHNE 6th Rate 20, 429bm, 108 × 30ft. Woolwich DY 21.3.1776. Sold 5.1802. *In French hands 19.1.1795–29.12.1797.*

DAPHNE 6th Rate 22, 540bm, 118·5 × 31·5ft. Davy, Topsham, 2.7.1806. Sold 15.2.1816.

DAPHNE 6th Rate 28, 500bm, 114 × 32ft. Plymouth DY, ordered 1820, cancelled 1832.

DAPHNE Corvette 18, 726bm, 120 × 38ft, 18—32pdr. Pembroke Dock, 6.8.1838. Sold 7.10.1864 Castle.

DAPHNE Wood screw sloop, 1,081bm, 1,574 tons, 187 × 36ft. Pembroke Dock 23.10.1866. Sold 7.11.1882.

DAPHNE Sloop, 1,140 tons, 195 × 28ft, 8—5in. Sheerness DY 29.5.1888. Sold 2.1904.

DAPHNE Sloop, 'Acacia' class. Barclay Curle 19.5.1915. Sold 15.1.1923 Unity S. Bkg Co.

DAPPER Gun-brig 12, 185bm, 85 × 22·5ft, 10—18pdr carr., 2—12pdr. Adams, Chapel, 12.1805. Sold 29.9.1814.

DAPPER Wood screw gunboat, 'Dapper' class. Green, Blackwall, 31.3.1855. Training hulk 1885; cooking depot 1897; = YC.37 in 1909. Sold 10.5.1922 Mr Perry.

DARING Gun-brig 12, 178bm, 80 × 23ft, 12—18pdr carr. Bailey, Ipswich, 10.1804. Destroyed 7.2.1813 Sierra Leone to avoid capture by French.

DARING Sloop, 319bm. Sheerness DY, ordered 14.5.1840, cancelled 4.9.1843.

DARING Brig 12, 426bm, 104 × 31·5ft, 10—32pdr, 2—18pdr. Sheerness DY; tx Portsmouth DY 2.4.1844. Sold 7.10.1864 Castle, Charlton.

DARING Composite screw sloop, 840 tons, 160 × 31·5ft, 2—7in, 2—64pdr. Wigram, Blackwall, 4.2.1874. Sold 8.1889 J. Cohen.

DARING Destroyer, 275 tons, 185 × 19ft, 2—12pdr, 3—6pdr, 3—TT. Thornycroft, Chiswick, 25.11.1893. Sold 10.4.1912.

DARING Light cruiser, 4,765 tons, 445 × 46·5ft, 6—6in, 2—3in. Armstrong, ordered 3.1918, cancelled 11.1918.

DARING Destroyer, 1,375 tons, 329 (oa) × 33ft, 4—4·7in 1—3in, 8—TT. Thornycroft 7.4.1932. Sunk 18.2.1940 by U.23 off Duncansby Head.

DARING Destroyer, 2,610 tons, 390 (oa) × 43ft, 6—4·5in, 6—40mm, 10—TT. Swan Hunter 10.8.1949. Sold 26.5.1971; arr. Blyth 15.6.1971 for BU.

DARING Destroyer, 'Daring' class. BAe/Vosper-Thornycoft. Assembled Scotstoun, first steel cut Govan 28.3.2003. In-service date 11.2007.

DARING *See also FLYING FISH 1873, LANCE 1914.*

DARLASTON Coastal minesweeper, 'Ton' class. Cook, Welton & Gemmell 25.9.1953. Tx Malaysian Navy 24.5.1960 = MAHAMIRU. Expended 1980 target.

DARSHAM Inshore minesweeper, 'Ham' class. Jones, Buckie, 19.11.1952. Sold 1.4.1966 Singapore.

DART Sloop 28, 386bm, 129 × 30ft, 28—32pdr carr. Hobbs, Redbridge, 1796. BU 1809 Barbados.

DART Lugger 8. French, ex-British privateer brig, captured 29.6.1803 by APOLLO in Bay of Biscay. Sold 3.1808.

DART Cutter 10, 49bm, 47 × 16ft. Deptford 1810. Foundered 12.1813.

DART Brigantine 3, 319bm, 90 × 29·5ft, 3—32pdr.

Sheerness DY 1847. = WV.26 on 25.5.1863. BU comp. 9.1.1875 Chatham.

DART Wood screw gunvessel, 'Philomel' class. Mare, Blackwall, 10.3.1860. = KANGAROO 1.4.1882. BU 12.1884.

DART (ex-*Cruiser*) Survey ship, 470 tons, 133 × 25ft, 2 guns. Colonial Office yacht, tx 3.1882. Lent NSW Govt 1904 as TS. Sold 9.5.1912 Sydney.

DART Frigate, 'River' class. Blyth DD 10.10.1942. Sold 11.1956; BU Cashmore, Newport.

DART *See also PC.73 1918, GODETIA 1941.*

DARTINGTON Coastal minesweeper, 'Ton' class. Philip 2.10.1956. Sold 12.2.1970 in Hong Kong for BU.

DARTMOOR Minesweeper, Early 'Hunt' class. Dunlop Bremner 30.3.1917. Sold 2.11.1923 Alloa, Charlestown; arr. 22.4.1923 for BU.

DARTMOUTH 22-gun ship, 260bm. Portsmouth 1655. Fireship 1688; 5th Rate 1689. Wrecked 9.10.1690 I. of Mull.

DARTMOUTH Fireship 4, 127bm. Captured 1672. Sold 1674.

DARTMOUTH 4th Rate 48, 614bm, 122 × 34ft. Shish, Rotherhithe, 24.7.1693. Captured 4.2.1695 by French; recaptured 1702 = VIGO. Wrecked 27.11.1703 Dutch coast.

DARTMOUTH 4th Rate 48, 681bm, 131·5 × 34·5ft. Parker, Southampton, 3.3.1698. Rebuilt Woolwich 1741 as 856bm. Sunk 8.10.1747 in action with Spanish GLORIOSO.

DARTMOUTH 4th Rate 50, 853bm, 134 × 38·5ft. Plymouth DY, ordered 10.1.1746, cancelled 20.3.1749.

DARTMOUTH 5th Rate 36, 952bm, 145 × 38·5ft. Tanner; tx Cook , Dartmouth, 28.8.1813. Harbour service 7.1831. BU comp. 2.11.1854 Deptford.

DARTMOUTH Wood screw frigate, 2,478bm, 240 × 48ft. Woolwich DY, LD 6.11.1860, cancelled 16.12.1864.

DARTMOUTH 2nd class cruiser, 5,250 tons, 430 × 48·5ft, 8—6in, 4—3pdr. Vickers 14.12.1910. Sold 13.12.1930 Metal Industries for BU.

DARWIN Destroyer (RAN), 3,370 tons. Projected 1969, cancelled.

DARWIN Frigate (RAN), 'Adelaide' class. Todd, Seattle, 26.3.1982

DASHER Sloop 18, 402bm, 100 × 30ft. Goodrich, Bermuda, 1797. Convict hulk 1832. BU 3.1838.

DASHER Wood paddle packet, 260bm, 357 tons, 120 × 22ft, 1—12pdr. Chatham DY 5.12.1837. Sold 23.3.1985 Castle for BU.

DASHER Destroyer, 290 tons, 190 × 18·5ft, 1—12pdr, 5—6pdr, 2—TT. Yarrow, Poplar, 28.11.1894. Sold 14.5.1912 King & Sons.

DASHER (ex-*Rio de Janeiro*) Escort carrier, 8,200 tons, 468·5 × 66ft, 3—4in, 15—20mm, 15 aircraft. Sun SB Co. 12.4.1941; tx RN 2.7.1942 on Lend-Lease. Lost 27.3.1943 petrol fire and explosion south of The Cumbraes.

DASHER Patrol boat, 49 tons, 68·2 (oa) × 19ft. Watercraft 1986; comp. Vosper-Thornycroft 5.1988.

DATE TREE 5th Rate. Captured 1678 from Algerines. Foundered 1679.

DAUNTLESS Sloop 18, 426bm, 109 × 29·5ft. Blunt, Hull, 11.1804. Captured 26.5.1807 by French at Danzig.

DAUNTLESS Sloop 18, 423bm, 109 × 29·5ft. Deptford DY 20.12.1808. Sold 27.1.1825.

DAUNTLESS Wood screw frigate, 1,453bm, 210 × 40ft, 4—10in, 2—68pdr, 18—32pdr. Portsmouth DY 5.1.1847. Rebuilt 1850 as 219·5ft, 1,575bm. Sold 1.5.1885.

DAUNTLESS Light cruiser, 4,650 tons, 471 (oa) × 46ft, 6—6in, 2—3in. Palmer 10.4.1918. BU 4.1946 Ward, Inverkeithing.

DAUNTLESS Destroyer, 'Daring' class, BAe/ Vosper-Thornycroft. To be assembled Barrow. First steel to be cut 2004. In-service date 2009.

DAUPHIN Corvette (RCN), 'Flower' class. Vickers, Montreal, 24.10.1940. Sold 1947 = *Cortes*.

DAUPHIN ROYAL Schooner. Purch. 1796 West Indies. Listed 1801.

DAVENHAM Inshore minesweeper, 'Ham' class. Weatherhead, Cockenzie, 23.3.1953. Sold 1.4.1966 in Singapore.

DAVID 20-gun ship, 76bm. Scottish Navy, captured 1685. Sold 1685.

DAWLISH *See DERBY 1918.*

DAWSON Corvette (RCN), 'Flower' class. Victoria Machinery Co. 8.2.1941. Foundered 22.3.1946 Hamilton, Ontario.

DE RUYTER 3rd Rate 64, 1,264bm, 151 × 44ft. Dutch, captured 30.8.1799 off Texel. Harbour service 1900. Wrecked 3.8.1804 hurricane Antigua.

DEALE Dogger 3. Dutch, captured 1672. Sold 1674.

DEALE Yacht 4, 28bm. Woolwich DY 1673. Sold 1686.

DEALE CASTLE 6th Rate 24, 240bm, 92 × 24ft. Deptford 1697. Captured 3.7.1706 by French off Dunkirk.

DEALE CASTLE 6th Rate 24, 272bm, 98 × 26·5ft. Burchett, Rotherhithe, 9.9.1706. Rebuilt Sheerness 1727 as 375bm. Sold 14.8.1746.

DEALE CASTLE 6th Rate 24, 506bm, 112 × 32ft. Golightly, Liverpool, 2.12.1746. BU comp. 30.7.1754 Chatham.

DEALE CASTLE 6th Rate 20, 400bm, 107·5 × 29ft. Perry, Blackwall, 20.1.1756. Foundered 11.10.1780 hurricane off Puerto Rico.

DEANE Frigate, TE 'Captain' class. Bethlehem, Hingham, 25.9.1943 on Lend-Lease. Ret. USN 3.1946.

DECADE 5th Rate 36, 915bm, 143·5 × 38ft. French, captured 24.8.1798 by MAGNANIME and NAIAD off Cape Finisterre. Sold 21.2.1811.

DECCAN Minesweeper (RIN), TE 'Bangor' class. Garden Reach 24.4.1944. Sold c. 1949 = *Kennery* (pilot vessel).

DECIBEL (ex-*Bournemouth Belle*) Experimental tender, 131 × 31·5ft. Bolson, Poole, 21.11.1953. Sold 8.1958 mercantile.

DECOUVERTE Schooner 8, 165bm, 81·5 × 21ft, 8—12pdr carr. French, captured 30.11.1803 San Domingo. Sold 1808.

DECOUVERTE (ex-*Eclipse*) Gun-brig 12, 181bm, 80·5 × 22·5ft, 10—12pdr carr., 2—6pdr. Schooner, purch. 1807. Sold 1816.

DECOY Cutter 10, 203bm. List, Fishbourne, 22.3.1810. Captured 22.3.1814 by French off Calais.

DECOY Wood screw gunboat, 'Cheerful' class. Pembroke Dock 21.2.1856. BU comp. 8.2.1869 Haslar.

DECOY Composite screw gunboat, 295bm, 430 tons, 125 × 22·5ft, 2—64pdr ML, 2—20pdr. Pembroke Dock 12.10.1871. Sold 10.1885.

DECOY Destroyer, 275 tons, 185 × 19ft, 1—12pdr, 3—6pdr, 3—TT. Thornycroft, Chiswick, 2.8.1894. Sunk 13.8.1904 collision ARUN off Wolf Rock.

DECOY Destroyer, 1,375 tons, 329 (oa) × 33ft, 4—4·7in, 1—3in, 8—TT. Thornycroft, Woolston, 7.6.1932. Tx RCN = KOOTENAY 12.4.1943. Sold 28.1.1946.

DECOY Destroyer, 2,610 tons, 390 (oa) × 43ft, 6—4·5in, 6—40mm, 10—TT. Vickers Armstrong, Tyne, ordered 1945, cancelled 1.1946.

DECOY (ex-DRAGON) Destroyer, 2,610 tons, 390 (oa) × 43ft, 6—4·5in, 6—40mm, 10—TT. Yarrow 29.3.1949 (renamed 6.1946). Sold 12.1969 Peruvian Navy = FERRE.

DEDAIGNEUSE 5th Rate 36, 987bm, 144 × 37·5ft, 12—24pdr carr., 26—12pdr, 4—6pdr. French, captured 28.1.1801 by three frigates off coast of Portugal. Sold 21.5.1823.

DEE 6th Rate 20, 447bm, 108 × 30·5ft. Bailey, Ipswich, 5.5.1814. Sold 22.7.1819 Pitman.

DEE Brig-sloop 10, 'Cherokee' class, Woolwich DY, LD 9.1824, = AFRICAN (paddle vessel) 5.1825, launched 30.8.1825. BU 12.1862.

DEE Wood paddle vessel, 704bm, 167 × 30·5ft. Woolwich DY 5.4.1832. Troopship 1855; storeship 1868. BU 1871 Sheerness.

DEE Iron screw gunboat, 363 tons, 110 × 34ft, 3—64pdr. Palmer 4.4.1877. Sold 10.7.1902.

DEE Destroyer, 545 tons, 225 × 23·5ft, 1—12pdr, 5—6pdr (1907: 4—12pdr), 2—TT. Palmer 10.9.1903. Sold 23.7.1919 Ward, Briton Ferry.

DEE *See also BECKFORD 1953, DROXFORD 1954.*

DEEPWATER (ex-W. HOLTZAPFEL) Diving tender, 1,200 tons, 250 × 38ft. German, seized 8.1945. Arr. 13.9.1960 Northam for BU.

DEFENCE 10-gun ship, 160bm. Purch. 1588. Listed until 1599.

DEFENCE 3rd Rate 74, 1,603bm, 168·5 × 47ft. Plymouth DY 31.3.1763. Wrecked 24.12.1811 coast of Jutland.

DEFENCE (ex-MARATHON) 3rd Rate 74, 1,754bm, 176 × 48·5ft, Chatham DY 25.4.1815 (renamed 1812). Convict ship 1849. Burnt accident 14.7.1857; wreck BU 1.1858.

DEFENCE Iron screw ship, 3,270bm, 6,270 tons, 280 × 54ft, 6—110pdr, 10—68pdr. Palmer 24.4.1861. = INDUS (TS) 6.1898; hulk 1922. Arr. 16.8.1935 Cattedown, Plymouth, for BU.

DEFENCE Armoured cruiser, 14,600 tons, 490 × 74·5ft, 4—9·2in, 10—7·5in, 14—12pdr. Pembroke Dock 24.4.1907. Sunk 31.5.1916 Battle of Jutland.

DEFENCE Cruiser, 9,550 tons, 555·5 (oa) × 64ft, 4—6in, 6—3in. Scotts 2.9.1944. = LION 8.10.1957. Sold 12.2.1975 Ward; BU Inverkeithing.

DEFENDER (Gunboat No 21) Gunvessel 12, 168bm, 76 × 22·5ft, 2—24pdr, 10—18pdr carr. Hill, Limehouse, 21.5.1797. Last listed 1802.

DEFENDER Gun-brig 14, 179bm, 80 × 22·5ft. Courtney, Chester, 28.7.1804. Wrecked 14.12.1809 off Folkestone.

DEFENDER (ex-BONNE MARSEILLE) Lugger 8, 81bm, 8—12pdr carr. French privateer, captured 12.1809 by ROYALIST. Sold 1.9.1814.

DEFENDER Destroyer, 762 tons, 240 × 25·5ft, 2—4in, 2—12pdr, 2—TT. Denny 30.8.1911. Sold 4.11.1921 Rees, Llanelly.

DEFENDER Destroyer, 1,375 tons, 329 (oa) × 33ft, 4—4·7in, 1—3in, 8—TT. Vickers Armstrong, Barrow, 7.4.1932. Bombed Italian aircraft off Sidi Barani, foundered under tow 11.7.1941.

DEFENDER (ex-DOGSTAR) Destroyer, 2,610 tons, 390 (oa) × 43ft, 6—4·5in, 6—40mm, 10—TT. Stephen 29.7.1950 (renamed 6.1946). Sold White, St. Davids, 10.5.1972, for BU.

DEFENDER Destroyer, 'Daring' class, BAe/Vosper-Thornycroft. To be assembled Barrow. Name announced 2.2002; firm contract 5.2002.

DEFIANCE Pinnace 8. In Fleet against Spanish Armada 1588. *Probably hired.*

DEFIANCE Galleon 46, 500bm, 14—18pdr, 14—

9pdr 6—6pdr, 12 light. Built Deptford 1590. Re-built Woolwich 1614 as 700bm, 34 guns. Sold 1650.

DEFIANCE 10-gun ship. Royalist, captured 2.1652 from Parliamentarians. Foundered 9.1652 off Anegada, West Indies.

DEFIANCE 3rd Rate 66, 890bm. Johnson & Castle, Deptford, 1666. Burnt 6.12.1668 accident Chatham.

DEFIANCE Sloop. In service 1671–78.

DEFIANCE 3rd Rate 64, 898bm, 144 × 38ft. Chatham DY 1675. Rebuilt Woolwich 1695; 4th Rate 1716; hulk 1743. BU 6.1749 Chatham.

DEFIANCE 4th Rate 69, 147·5 × 42·5ft. West, Deptford, 12.10.1744. Sold 10.4.1766.

DEFIANCE Sloop (Indian). Bombay DY 1766.

DEFIANCE 3rd Rate 64, 1,369bm, 159 × 44ft. Woolwich DY 31.8.1772. Wrecked 18.2.1780 off Savannah R.

DEFIANCE 3rd Rate 74, 1,685bm, 169 × 47·5ft. Randall, Rotherhithe, 10.12.1783. Prison ship 12.1813. BU 5.1817.

DEFIANCE Gunvessel 4, 71bm, 70 × 15ft. Purch. 4.1794. Sold 10.1797.

DEFIANCE Screw 2nd Rate 81, 3,475bm, 5,270 tons, 255 × 56ft, 1—110pdr, 34—8in, 4—70pdr, 10—40pdr, 32—32pdr. Pembroke Dock 27.3.1861. Torpedo schoolship 26.11.1884. Sold 26.6.1931 S. Castle, Plymouth.

DEFIANCE *For vessels renamed DEFIANCE as torpedo schoolships, see PERSEUS 1861, SPAR-TAN 1891, CLEOPATRA 1878, INCONSTANT 1868, ANDROMEDA 1897, VULCAN 1889, FORTH 1938.*

DEGO 3rd Rate 64. French (ex-Maltese ZACHARI), captured 20.9.1800. Sold 1802 in Malta.

DELAWARE 6th Rate 28, 563bm, 118 × 33ft, 28—9pdr. American, captured 27.9.1777 by British Army in Delaware R., purch. 4.1778. Sold 14.4.1783.

DELFT 4-gun ship, 288bm. Dutch, captured 1665. Sold 1668.

DELFT (ex-HERCULES) 3rd Rate 64, 1,266bm, 157 × 43ft. Dutch, captured 11.10.1797 Battle of Camperdown. Powder hulk 8.1802. Sunk 9.1822 breakwater Harwich.

DELHI Light cruiser, 4,650 tons, 472·5 (oa) × 46·5ft, 6—6in, 3—3in. Armstrong 23.8.1918. AA ship 1942. Arr. 5.3.1948 Cashmore, Newport, for BU.

DELHI *See also EMPEROR OF INDIA 1913, ACHILLES 1932.*

DELIGHT Discovery vessel, 120bm. Wrecked 1583.

DELIGHT Hoy 4, 84bm. Purch. 1686. Sold 1713 Portsmouth.

DELIGHT 6th Rate 14, 163bm, 78 × 22ft. Woolwich DY 18.10.1709. Sold 8.1.1712.

DELIGHT Sloop 14, 307bm, 97 × 27ft. Graves, Limehouse, 7.11.1778. Foundered 25.1.1781 North America.

DELIGHT (ex-SANS PAREIL) Sloop 18, 336bm. 97·5 × 28·5ft, 18—24pdr carr. French, captured 20.1.1801 by MERCURY off Sardinia. Sold 4.1805.

DELIGHT Brig-sloop 16, 300bm, 97 × 28ft. Thorn, Fremington, 6.1806. Stranded on coast of Calabria, captured 31.1.1808 by French.

DELIGHT (ex-FRIEDLAND) Sloop 18, 340bm. French, captured 26.3.1808 by STANDARD off Cape Blanco. Sold 1.9.1814.

DELIGHT Brig-sloop 10, 'Cherokee' class, 237bm. Portsmouth DY 10.5.1819. Wrecked 23.2.1824 Mauritius.

DELIGHT Brig-sloop 10, 'Cherokee' class, 231bm. Chatham DY 27.11.1829. Sold 30.4.1844.

DELIGHT Wood screw gunboat, 'Albacore' class. Wigram, Blackwall, 15.3.1856. Sold 11.1867 Halifax = *M. A. Starr.*

DELIGHT Destroyer, 1,375 tons, 329 (oa) × 33ft, 4—4·7in, 1—3in, 8—TT. Fairfield 2.6.1932. Sunk 29.7.1940 air attack off Portland.

DELIGHT Destroyer, 2,610 tons, 390 (oa) × 43ft, 6—4·5in, 6—40mm, 10—TT. Vickers Armstrong, Tyne, ordered 1945, cancelled 1.1946.

DELIGHT (ex-DISDAIN) Destroyer, 2,610 tons, 390 (oa) × 43ft, 6—4·5in, 6—40mm, 10—TT. Fairfield 21.12.1950 (renamed 6.1946). Sold Ward 12.9.1970; BU Inverkeithing.

DELORAINE Minesweeper (RAN), 'Bathurst' class. Mort's Dock 26.7.1941. Sold 8.8.1956 for BU.

DELPHINEN Brig-sloop 16, 306bm, 97 × 27·5ft, 14—24dpr carr., 2—6pdr. Danish, captured 7.9.1807 Battle of Copenhagen. Wrecked 4.8.1808 on Dutch coast. *Was to have been renamed MONDOVI.*

DELPHINIUM Sloop, 'Arabis' class. Napier & Miller 23.12.1915. Sold 13.10.1933 Rees, Llanelly.

DELPHINIUM Corvette, 'Flower' class. Robb 6.6.1940. Sold 2.1949; BU Hayes, Pembroke Dock.

DEMERARA Schooner 6, 106bm. Purch. 1804. Captured 14.7.1804 by French privateer GRAND-DECIDE in West Indies.

DEMERARA (ex-COSMOPOLI) Brig-sloop 18, c. 220bm. French privateer, captured 1806, presented 1808 by inhabitants of Demerara. Listed until 1813.

DEMIRHISAR Destroyer, 1,360 tons, 312 × 33ft, 4—4in, 8—TT. Denny 1941. Turkish, cd RN 1.1942 for passage out to Turkey. HO Turkish Navy 3.1942.

DEMON Destroyer, 2,610 tons, 366 × 43ft, 6—4·5in, 6—40mm, 10—TT. Swan Hunter, ordered 3.1945, cancelled 1.1946.

DENBIGH CASTLE Corvette, 'Castle' class. Lewis 5.8.1944. Damaged 13.2.1945 by U.992, grounded Kola Inlet.

DENNIS Discovery vessel. Lost 1578 Arctic.

DENNIS Storeship, 100bm, 57 × 20ft. Plymouth DY 15.12.1743. Sold 30.8.1833.

DEPENDENCE Galley 7, 129bm, 1—24pdr, 6—4pdr. Purch. 12.1776 North America. Sold 1786.

DEPTFORD Sloop 4. Deptford 1652. Last listed 1659.

DEPTFORD Ketch 10, 89bm. Deptford 1665. Wrecked 26.8.1689 coast of Virginia.

DEPTFORD 4th Rate 50, 616bm, 125 × 33·5ft. Woolwich DY 1687. Rebuilt Woolwich DY 1700 as 667bm; rebuilt 1719 as 710bm. Sold per AO dated 3.5.1726.

DEPTFORD 4th Rate 60, 951bm, 146 × 39ft. Deptford DY 22.8.1732; 50 guns 1752. Sold 23.6.1767.

DEPTFORD Storeship 24, 678bm, 124 × 35·5ft, 4—12pdr, 16—9pdr, 4—6pdr. Deptford DY 29.4.1735. BU 5.1756.

DEPTFORD Tender 12, 158bm, 64 × 21ft. Muddle, Gillingham, 8.1781. Sold 17.2.1863.

DEPTFORD Transport, 198bm, 80·5 × 24ft. Batson, Limehouse, 3.1784. Presented 24.8.1816 to Hibernian Marine Society.

DEPTFORD Transport brig 6. Woolcombe, R. Thames, 2.1788, purch. 25.2.1788. Mooring lighter. BU 6.1862 Chatham.

DEPTFORD Sloop, 990 tons, 250 × 36ft, 2—4·7in, 1—3in. Chatham DY 5.2.1935. Sold 8.3.1948; BU Ward, Milford Haven.

DEPTFORD PRIZE Sloop, 147bm, 74 × 21·5ft. Spanish, captured off Ushant 23.5.1740. Sold 20.11.1744.

DEPTFORD TRANSPORT Storeship hoy, 58bm, 53 × 16ft. Deptford DY 3.1702. Sold 6.1713.

DERBY (ex-DAWLISH) Minesweeper, Later 'Hunt' class. Clyde SB 9.8.1918 (renamed 1918). Sold 7.1946 in Gibraltar; BU Spain.

DERBY HAVEN (ex-LOCH ASSYNT) Depot ship, 1,650 tons, 307 (oa) × 38·5ft, 2—4in, 6—20mm. Swan Hunter 14.12.1944 (renamed 1944). Tx Persian Navy 30.7.1949 = BABR. PO 30.10.1969; deleted 1972.

DERG Frigate, 'River' class. Robb 7.1.1943.

= WESSEX (RNVR drillship) 1951; = CAMBRIA. Arr. 9.1960 Cashmore, Newport, for BU.

DERRINGTON Coastal minesweeper, 'Ton' class. Thornycroft 22.12.1953. = KILLIECRANKIE 1955–60. Sold 2.1971; BU Canvey I.

DERVISH Destroyer, 2,610 tons, 366 × 43ft, 6—4·5in, 6—40mm, 10—TT. White, ordered 3.1945, cancelled 1.1946.

DERWENT Brig-sloop 16, 'Cruizer' class, 382bm. Blackburn, Turnchapel, 23.5.1807. Sold 7.3.1817.

DERWENT Destroyer, 555 tons, 222 × 23·5ft, 1—12pdr, 5—6pdr (1907: 4—12pdr), 2—TT. Hawthorn 14.2.1903. Sunk 2.5.1917 mine off Le Havre.

DERWENT Destroyer, 'Hunt' class Type III. Vickers Armstrong, Barrow, 22.8.1941. Sold 11.1946; BU 2.1947 Ward, Penryn.

DERWENT Frigate (RAN), 2,100 tons, 370 (oa) × 41ft, 2—4·5in, Limbo. Williamstown DY 17.4.1961. Sunk by explosives 21.12.1994 off Rottnest I., Western Australia.

DERWENT *See also HUON 1914.*

DESCHAINEUX Submarine (RAN), 'Collins' class, 3,051/3,353 tons, 255·2 (oa) × 25·6ft, 6—TT. Australian Submarine Corp., Adelaide, 12.3.1998.

DESFORD Seaward defence boat, 'Ford' class. Vosper 3.6.1954. Tx Ceylonese Navy 10.5.1955 = KOTIYA. Sunk Trincomalee 22.12.1964; salvaged, sold.

DESIRE Discovery vessel. In service 1583–93.

DESIRE Ketch 6, 63/84bm. Built 1616. Listed until 1628.

DESIRE Destroyer, 2,610 tons, 366 × 46ft, 6—4·5mm, 10—TT. Hawthorn Leslie, ordered 3.1945, cancelled 1.1946.

DESIREE 5th Rate 36, 1,015bm, 149 × 39ft, 10—32pdr carr., 26—18pdr, 4—9pdr. French, captured 8.7.1800 by DART in Dunkirk Roads. Sold 28.8.1832 Rotherhithe for BU.

DESPATCH Brigantine 2, 77bm, 63·5 × 17ft. Deptford 10.5.1691. Sold 10.4.1712.

DESPATCH Sloop 14, 269bm, 91 × 26ft. Stow & Bartlett, Shoreham, 30.12.1745. Sold 6.1763.

DESPATCH Brig 12, 483bm, 105 × 33·5ft, 12—2pdr. Chatham DY 25.11.1851. = WV.24/ CADMUS 25.5.1863. Sold 13.5.1901 Sheerness.

DESPATCH Light cruiser, 4,765 tons, 472·5 (oa) × 46·5ft, 6—6in, 2—4in. Fairfield 24.9.1919. Sold 5.4.1946, BU Troon.

DESPATCH *See also CHEROKEE 1774, ZEPHYR 1779. See also DISPATCH.*

DESPERANTE Schooner 8. In service 1799–1811.

DESPERATE Gun-brig 12, 179bm, 80 × 23ft, 12—18pdr. White, Broadstairs, 2.1.1805. Mortar brig 1811. Sold 15.12.1814.

DESPERATE Wood screw sloop, 1,038bm, 192 × 34ft. Pembroke Dock 23.4.1849. BU 8.1865 Devonport.

DESPERATE Destroyer, 340 tons, 210 × 19·5ft, 1—12pdr, 5—6pdr, 2—TT. Thornycroft 15.2.1896. Sold 20.5.1920 Ward, Milford Haven.

DESPERATE Light cruiser, 4,765 tons, 445 × 46·5ft, 6—6in, 2—4in. Hawthorn Leslie, ordered 3.1918, cancelled 11.1918.

DESPERATE Destroyer, 2,610 tons, 390 (oa) × 43ft, 6—4in, 6—40mm, 10—TT. John Brown, ordered 3.1945, cancelled 1.1946.

DESTINY 34-gun ship, 460/500bm. Woolwich 1616. = CONVERTINE 1620. Captured 1648 by Royalists. Sold 1650 Lisbon.

DESTRUCTION Mortar vessel 5, 77bm, 60 × 17ft, 1—10in mortar, 4—18pdr carr. Perry, Blackwall, 3.9.1804. Sold 27.8.1806.

DETERMINEE 6th Rate 24, 545bm, 124·5 × 31·5ft. French, captured 1799 by REVOLUTIONNAIRE. Wrecked 26.3.1803 Jersey.

DETROIT (ex-*Adams*) Brig 6 (Canadian lakes), 6—6pdr. American, captured 16.7.1813 while stranded nr Detroit. Recaptured 9.10.1813 Lake Erie, burnt.

DETROIT Sloop 20 (Canadian lakes), 305bm. Amherstburgh, Lake Erie, 8.1813. Captured 10.9.1813 by Americans on Lake Erie.

DEUX AMIS Schooner 14, 220bm. French privateer, captured 12.1796 by POLYPHEMUS. Wrecked 23.5.1799 I. of Wight.

DEVASTATION (ex-*Intrepid*) Bomb vessel 8, 446bm, 104 × 31·5ft, 2—24pdr carr., 6—9pdr, 2 mortars. Purch. 10.1804. Sold 30.5.1816.

DEVASTATION Bomb vessel 14, 372bm, 105 × 29ft, Plymouth DY, LD 1820, cancelled 1831.

DEVASTATION Wood paddle sloop, 1,058bm, 180 × 36ft. Woolwich DY 3.7.1841. BU 9.1866 Castle, Charlton.

DEVASTATION Turret ship, 4,406bm, 9,387 tons, 285 × 62ft, 4—12in MLR. Portsmouth DY 12.7.1871. Sold 12.5.1908 Ward, Morecambe.

DEVERON Frigate, 'River' class. Smith's Dock 12.10.1942. Tx RIN = DHANUSH 1945.

DEVIZES CASTLE Corvette, 'Castle' class. Kingston SY, cancelled 12.1943.

DEVONSHIRE 3rd Rate 80, 1,158bm, 154 × 41·5ft. Wyatt, Bursledon, 5.4.1692. Rebuilt 1704 as 1,220bm. Blown up 10.10.1707 in action with French off The Lizard.

DEVONSHIRE 3rd Rate 80, 1,305bm, 156 × 44ft. Woolwich DY 12.12.1710. Hulked 10.1740. Sold 14.10.1760.

DEVONSHIRE 3rd Rate 74, 1,471bm, 161 × 46ft. Woolwich DY 19.7.1745. BU 10.1772 Portsmouth.

DEVONSHIRE Fireship. Purch. 1804. Expended 3.10.1804 Boulogne.

DEVONSHIRE 3rd Rate 74, 1,742bm, 176 × 48·5ft. Barnard, Deptford, 23.9.1812. Harbour service 11.1849. BU comp. 5.6.1869 Sheerness.

DEVONSHIRE Armoured cruiser, 10,850 tons, 450 × 68·5ft, 4—7·5in, 6—6in, 2—12pdr, 22—3pdr. Chatham DY 30.4.1904. Sold 9.5.1921 Ward, Barrow; BU 10.1923.

DEVONSHIRE Cruiser, 9,850 tons, 630 (oa) × 66ft, 8—8in, 8—4in. Devonport DY 22.10.1927. TS 1947. Sold 16.6.1954; arr. 14.12.1954 Cashmore, Newport, for BU.

DEVONSHIRE GM destroyer 5,600 tons, 520·5 (oa) × 54ft, 4—4·5in, 6—TT Sea Slug, helo. Cammell Laird 10.6.1960. Sunk target 17.7.1984 English Channel.

DEXTEROUS Gun-brig 12, 180bm, 80 × 22·5ft, 2—18pdr, 10—18pdr carr. Adams, Eling, 2.2.1805. Sold 17.10.1816.

DEXTROUS Wood screw frigate 51, 3,353bm, 270 × 52·5ft. Pembroke Dock, ordered 1861, cancelled 1863.

DHYFFE CASTLE Corvette, 'Castle' class. Collingwood 12.1943.

DIADEM 3rd Rate 64, 1,376bm, 160 × 44·5ft. Chatham DY 19.12.1782. Troopship 5.1798. BU 9.1832 Plymouth.

DIADEM Sloop 14, 368bm, 102 × 29ft. Purch. 1801. = FALCON 1802. Sold 31.7.1816.

DIADEM Wood screw frigate, 2,483bm, 240 × 48ft, 20—10in, 2—6pdr, 10—32pdr. Pembroke Dock 14.10.1856. Sold 23.1.1875 Castle, Charlton.

DIADEM 1st class cruiser, 11,000 tons, 435 × 69ft, 16—6in, 14—12pdr. Fairfield 21.10.1896. Sold 9.5.1921 Ward, Morecambe.

DIADEM Cruiser, 5,900 tons, 512 (oa) × 50·5ft, 8—5·25in, 12—20mm. Hawthorn Leslie 26.8.1942. Sold 29.2.1956 Pakistani Navy = BABUR 5.7.1957, = JAHANGIR 1982; deleted 1985.

DIAMANTINA Frigate (RAN), 'River' class. Walker, Maryborough, 6.4.1944. Survey ship 6.1959. PO 29.2.1980. Tx 1980 Queensland Maritime Museum, Brisbane.

DIAMANTINA Minehunter (RAN), 'Huon' class, 720 tons, 172·2 (oa) × 32·5ft, 1—30mm. ADI, Newcastle, NSW, 2.12.2000.

DIAMOND 50-gun ship, 547bm, 127·5 × 31·5ft. Deptford 15.3.1652. Captured 20.9.1693 by French.

DIAMOND 5th Rate 50, 536bm, 117 × 32·5ft. Johnson, Blackwall, 12.10.1708. Rebuilt Deptford 1722 as 595bm, 40 guns. Sold 18.12.1744.

DIAMOND 5th Rate 44, 697bm, 125 × 36ft. Carter, Limehouse, 30.10.1741. Sold 5.10.1756.

DIAMOND 5th Rate 32, 710bm, 130 × 35ft. Blaydes & Hodgson, Hull, 28.5.1774. Sold 30.12.1784.

DIAMOND 5th Rate 38, 984bm, 146 × 39ft. Barnard, Deptford, 17.3.1794. BU 6.1812 Sheerness.

DIAMOND 5th Rate 38, 1,067bm, 150 × 40·5ft, Chatham DY 16.1.1816. Burnt 18.2.1827 accident Portsmouth; wreck BU 6.1827.

DIAMOND 6th Rate 28, 1,051bm, 140 × 42ft, 2—8in, 26—32pdr. Sheerness DY 29.8.1848. Lent as TS 4.1866; = JOSEPH STRAKER 13.1.1868. Sold 9.1885 Castle.

DIAMOND Wood screw corvette, 1,405bm, 1,970 tons, 220 × 37ft, 14—64pdr. Sheerness DY 26.9.1874. Sold 8.1889.

DIAMOND 3rd class cruiser, 3,000 tons, 360 × 40ft, 12—4in, 8—3pdr. Laird 6.1.1904. Sold 9.5.1921 Ward, Grays.

DIAMOND Destroyer, 1,375 tons, 329 (oa) × 33ft, 4—4·7in, 1—3in, 8—TT. Vickers Armstrong, Barrow, 8.4.1932. Sunk 27.4.1941 air attack south of Morea.

DIAMOND Destroyer, 2,610 tons, 390 (oa) × 43ft. 6—4·5in, 6—40mm, 10—TT. John Brown 14.6.1950. Sold Medway Secondary Metals; BU 11.1981 Rainham, Kent.

DIAMOND Destroyer, 'Daring' class, BAe/Vosper-Thornycroft. To be assembled Barrow. First steel to be cut 2002. In-service date 2009.

DIAMOND SNAKE Special Service Vessel (RAN), 80 tons. Savage, Williamstown, 17.5.1945. Tx Army 10.1945.

DIANA 5th Rate 32, 668bm, 124·5 × 35ft. Batson, Limehouse, 30.8.1757. Sold 16.5.1793.

DIANA Schooner 6. Purch. 1775 North America. Abandoned and burnt 28.5.1775 Boston.

DIANA 5th Rate 38, 984bm, 146 × 39ft. Randall, Rotherhithe, 3.3.1794. Sold 1815 Dutch Navy.

DIANA Cutter 10, 150bm, 10—6pdr. Purch. 1807. Wrecked 5.1810 Rodriguez I., Indian Ocean.

DIANA 5th Rate 46, 1,083bm, 151·5 × 40·5ft. Chatham DY 8.1.1822. Harbour service 1868. BU comp. 9.2.1874 Chatham.

DIANA Wood paddle vessel (Indian). Kidderpore DY 12.7.1823, purch. 1824. Sold 1826 Burnese Govt. BU 1835 Calcutta.

DIANA Wood paddle vessel (Indian), 133bm, Currie Sulkie 10.1836. Sold 1846.

DIANA 2nd class cruiser, 5,600 tons, 350 × 54ft, 5—6in 6—4·7in, 9—12pdr. Fairfield 5.12.1895. Sold 1.7.1920 S. Castle, Plymouth.

DIANA Destroyer, 1,375 tons, 329 (oa) × 33ft, 4—4·7in, 1—3in, 8—TT. Hawthorn Leslie 16.6.1932. Tx RCN 6.9.1940 = MARGAREE. Lost 22.10.1940 collision *Port Fairy*, North Atlantic.

DIANA Destroyer, 2,610 tons, 390 (oa) × 43ft, 6—4·5in, 6—40mm, 10—TT. Hawthorn Leslie, ordered 3.1945, cancelled 1.1946.

DIANA (ex-DRUID) Destroyer, 2,610 tons, 390 (oa) × 43ft, 6—4·5in, 6—40mm, 10—TT. Yarrow 8.5.1952 (renamed 6.1946). Sold 1.12.1969 Peruvian Navy = PALACIOS; deleted 1993.

DIANELLA *See DAFFODIL 1940.*

DIANTHUS Sloop, 'Anchusa' class. Barclay Curle 1.12.1917. Sold 3.6.1921 mercantile.

DIANTHUS Corvette, 'Flower' class. Robb 9.7.1940. Sold 5.1947 = *Thorslep.*

DICTATOR 3rd Rate 64, 1,388bm, 159·5 × 45ft. Batson, Limehouse, 6.1.1783. Troopship 6.1798; floating battery 5.1803. BU 6.1817.

DIDO 6th Rate 28, 595bm, 120·5 × 34ft. Stewart & Hall, Sandgate, 27.11.1784. Harbour service 1804. Sold 3.4.1817.

DIDO Corvette 18, 734bm, 120 × 38ft, 18—32pdr. Pembroke Dock 13.6.1836. Coal hulk 1860. Sold 3.3.1903.

DIDO Wood screw corvette, 1,857bm 225 × 42ft. Deptford DY, LD 14.1.1861, cancelled 12.12.1863.

DIDO Wood screw corvette, 1,277bm, 1,755 tons, 212 × 36ft, 2—7in, 2—6pdr. Portsmouth DY 23.10.1869. Hulk 1886; = ACTAEON 11.1906. Sold 17.7.1922 J. B. Garnham.

DIDO 2nd class cruiser, 5,600 tons, 350 × 54ft, 5—6in, 6—4·7in, 9—12pdr. London & Glasgow Co. 20.3.1896. Depot ship 1913. Sold 16.12.1926 May & Butcher, Maldon.

DIDO Cruiser, 5,450 tons, 512 (oa) × 50ft, 10—5·25in, Cammell Laird 18.7.1939. Arr. 16.7.1958 Ward, Barrow, for BU.

DIDO (ex-HASTINGS) Frigate, 'Leander' class, Y100, 2,650 tons, 372 (oa) × 41ft, 2—4·5in, Limbo, helo (later Ikara, Limbo, helo). Yarrow 22.12.1961. Tx RNZN 18.7.1983 = SOUTHLAND; deleted 3.1995.

DIDON 5th Rate 38, 1,091bm. French, captured 10.8.1805 by PHOENIX off Cape Finisterre. BU 8.1811.

DIEPPE *See LST.3016 1944.*

DIGBY Minesweeper (RCN), diesel 'Bangor' class. Davie SB 5.6.1942.

DILIGENCE (ex-INTELLIGENCE) Brigantine 2, 78bm, 64 × 17ft. Deptford 23.3.1693 (renamed 1692). Sold 26.11.1708.

DILIGENCE 6th Rate, 152bm. Purch. 23.5.1709. Sold 1712.

DILIGENCE Sloop 10, 236bm, 88·5 × 24·5ft. Wells, Rotherhithe, 29.7.1756. = COMET (fireship) 27.8.1779. Sold 5.12.1780.

DILIGENCE (ex-SPENCER) Brig-sloop 18, 320bm,

95 × 28ft. Parsons, Bursledon, 24.11.1795 (re-named 1795). Wrecked 9.1800 Honda Bank, Cuba.

DILIGENCE (ex-*Union*) Sloop 14, 361bm, 99 × 29ft, 14—24pdr carr., 2—18pdr. Purch. 5.2.1801. Sold 16.4.1812.

DILIGENCE (ex-*Thistle*) Lugger. Purch. 1812. Sold 15.12.1814.

DILIGENCE Transport, 317bm, 567 tons, 104 × 26ft. Bailey, Ipswich, 30.9.1814. Coal hulk 8.1861; = C.72. Sold 5.7.1904 Portsmouth.

DILIGENCE Wood screw sloop, 950bm, 185 × 33ft. Chatham DY, LD 1862, cancelled 12.12.1863.

DILIGENCE (ex-*Tabaristart*) Depot ship, 7,100 tons, 390 × 46ft, 8—4in. Purch. 29.1.1913, comp. 10.1915. BU 11.1926 Hughes Bolckow, Blyth.

DILIGENCE Repair ship, 4,023 tons, 441·5 × 57ft. Bethlehem, Fairfield, 8.7.1944 on Lend-Lease. Ret. USN 1.1946.

DILIGENCE (ex-*Stena Inspector*) Repair ship, 5,814 tons. Purch. 31.10.1983.

DILIGENT Sloop 10, 236bm, 10—3pdr. Purch. 1776 North America. Captured 7.5.1779 by American PROVIDENCE off Newfoundland. Destroyed 15.8.1779 by RN at Penobscot.

DILIGENT Schooner 8. In service 1781–90.

DILIGENT Schooner 8, 89bm. Purch. 1790. Sold 20.11.1794 for BU.

DILIGENT Brig-sloop 16, 317bm. French, captured 28.5.1806 by RENARD in West Indies. = PRUDENTE 10.1806, = WOLF 1807. BU 6.1811.

DILIGENT *See also PORPOISE 1798.*

DILIGENTE 3rd Rate 68, 1,966bm, 176·5 × 50ft, 28—24pdr, 30—12pdr, 10—9pdr. Spanish, captured 16.1.1780 Cape St Vincent. Sold 2.12.1784.

DILIGENTE Storeship 14. French, captured 1800 West Indies. Sold 11.8.1814.

DILIGENTE Lugger 2, 100bm. French, captured 6.1.1813. Sold 15.12.1814.

DILSTON Coastal minesweeper, 'Ton' class. Cook, Welton & Gemmell 15.11.1954. Tx Malaysian Navy = JERAI 1964. BU 1977.

DINGLEY Inshore minehunter, 'Ley' class. White, Cowes, 3.9.1952. Sold Pounds 16.7.1967.

DIOMEDE 5th Rate 44, 891bm, 140 × 38ft. Hillhouse, Bristol, 18.10.1781. Wrecked 2.8.1795 off Trincomalee.

DIOMEDE (ex-FIRM) 4th Rate 50, 1,123bm, 151 × 41ft. Deptford DY 17.1.1798 (renamed 1794). Sold 8.1815.

DIOMEDE Wood screw sloop, 1,268bm. Projected 12.1866, cancelled 30.4.1867

DIOMEDE Light cruiser, 4,765 tons, 472·5 (oa) × 46.5ft, 6—6in, 2—4in. Vickers 29.4.1919. Sold 5.4.1946; BU Arnott Young, Dalmuir.

DIOMEDE Frigate, 'Leander' class, Y160, 2,650 tons, 372 (oa) × 43ft, 2—4·5in, Seacat, helo. Yarrow 15.4.1969. Sold Pakistani Navy, HO 15.7.1988 = SHAMSHER 14.10.1988.

DIPPER (ex-C.30) Mining tender, 120 tons, 60 × 16·5ft. German, seized 1945 (renamed 1948). Sold 1959.

DIRECTOR 3rd Rate 64, 1,388bm, 159 × 44·5ft. Cleveley, Gravesend, 9.3.1784. Harbour service 4.1796. BU 1.1801.

DIRK Destroyer, 1,980 tons, 365 (oa) × 38ft, 6—4in, 10—TT. Scotts. Not LD, cancelled 10.1945.

DISCOVERY Discovery vessel. In service 1600–20.

DISCOVERY 20-gun ship. Purch. 1651. Burnt 25.5.1655 Jamaica.

DISCOVERY Ketch 6, 75bm, 64 × 16ft, Woolwich DY 9.5.1692. BU 1705 Portsmouth.

DISCOVERY Discovery sloop. Lost 1719 Arctic.

DISCOVERY Storeship 6, 154bm, 74·5, × 22·5ft. Purch. 4.1741. Sold 6.5.1750.

DISCOVERY (ex-*Diligence*) Discovery vessel 8, 299bm, 91·5 × 27·5ft. Purch. 1775. Dockyard transport 5.1781. BU Chatham 10.1797.

DISCOVERY Sloop 10, 337bm, 96 × 27ft, 10—4pdr. Randall, Rotherhithe, 1789, purch. 11.1789. Bomb vessel 1799; convict ship 1818. BU 2.1834 Deptford.

DISCOVERY Survey vessel (Indian). In service 1800. Sold 5.1828.

DISCOVERY Wood screw gunvessel, 425bm, 145 × 25ft. Ordered 1861, cancelled 12.12.1863.

DISCOVERY (ex-*Bloodhound*) Wood screw storeship, 1,247 tons, 160 × 29ft. Purch. 5.12.1874. Sold 2.1902 D. Murray.

DISCOVERY Survey vessel, 480 tons. Dundee SB Co. 1901. Sold 1905 Hudson's Bay Co.; repurch. 1929 as TS. HO 2.4.1979 for preservation.

DISCOVERY Inshore minesweeper (RAN), 178 tons, 101·7 (oa) × 29·5ft, 2—12·7mm. Projected 1987, not comp.

DISDAIN Pinnace, 80bm. In service 1585.

DISDAIN *See also NIGER 1945, DELIGHT 1950.*

DISPATCH Sloop 14. Foundered 31.8.1772 hurricane West Indies. *A sloop sold 27.10.1773 may have been this vessel salved.*

DISPATCH Sloop 6. Captured 12.7.1776 by American privateer TYRANNICIDE. *May have been hired.*

DISPATCH Sloop 16, 300bm, 90·5 × 26·5ft. Deptford DY 10.2.1777. Capsized 8.12.1778 St Lawrence R.

DISPATCH Schooner 8. Purch. 16.10.1780 Jamaica; sold 11.1795.

DISPATCH Sloop. French, captured 1790. Sold 7.8.1801.

DISPATCH Brig-sloop 16 (fir-built), 365bm, 96 × 30·5ft. Nicholson, Chatham, 19.12.1795. Sold Russian Navy 3.1796.

DISPATCH Tender 6. In service 1797–1801.

DISPATCH (ex-INDEFATIGABLE) Sloop 14, 238bm, 90·5 × 25ft, 16—18pdr carr., 2—6pdr. French privateer, captured 4.1799 by ETHALION. Sold 1801.

DISPATCH Brig-sloop 18, 'Cruizer' class, 382bm. Symons, Falmouth, 26.5.1804. BU 9.1811.

DISPATCH Brig-sloop 18, 'Cruizer' class, 388bm. King, Upnor, 7.12.1812. Sold 5.1836.

DISPATCH (ex-*Cornwallis*) Brig storeship 6, 172bm, 77 × 23ft. Transport Office vessel, tx c. 1816. Hulk 1820; sheer hulk 1826. Wrecked 12.1846 Bermuda, ordered BU. *Listed until 1865.*

DISPATCH *See also DESPATCH.*

DITTANY (ex-BEACON) Corvette, 'Flower' class. Collingwood SY 31.10.1942 on Lend-Lease. Ret. USN 20.6.1946; sold 1947 = *Olympic Cruiser.*

DITTISHAM Inshore minesweeper, 'Ham' class. Fairlie Yacht Slip 10.1953. For sale 1982. Towed Dartmouth 22.4.1983 for Sea Cadet use. Sent 4.4.1997 Pounds, Portsmouth, for BU.

DIVER (ex-C.28) Mining tender, 120 tons, 60 × 16·5ft. German, seized 1945 (renamed 1948). Dockyard tug 1960. Sold 1971 in Singapore.

DODMAN POINT Repair ship, 8,580 tons, 439 × 62ft. Burrard, Vancouver, 14.4.1945. Arr. 16.4.1963 Spezia for BU.

DOGSTAR *See DEFENDER 1950.*

DOLPHIN (ex-ANGEL) Ketch 4. Royalist, captured 1648. Sold 1650.

DOLPHIN 30-gun ship. Captured 1652. Sold 1657.

DOLPHIN Ketch 4, 50bm. Condemned 1660 Jamaica.

DOLPHIN Fireship 4, 143bm. Purch. 1666. Sunk 6.1667 blockship R. Medway.

DOLPHIN Sloop 2, 80bm. Deptford DY 1673. Lost in action 1673.

DOLPHIN Fireship 8, 267bm, 93·5 × 24·5ft. Chatham DY 29.3.1690. 5th Rate 1692; rebuilt Portsmouth 1711 as 424bm. BU 1730.

DOLPHIN 6th Rate 20, 428bm, 106 × 36·5ft. Deptford DY 4.1.1731. Fireship 10.1746, = FIREBRAND 29.7.1755; = PENGUIN (6th Rate) 1757. Captured 20.3.1760 by French.

DOLPHIN 6th Rate 24, 511bm, 113 × 32ft. Woolwich DY 1.5.1751. Survey ship 1764—70. BU 1.1777.

DOLPHIN 5th Rate 44, 880bm, 140 × 38ft. Chatham DY 10.3.1781. Troopship 4 in 1800. BU 7.1817.

DOLPHIN (ex-DOLFLIN) 6th Rate 24. Dutch, cap-

tured 15.9.1799 by WOLVERINE and ARROW at Vlie I. Listed until 1801.

DOLPHIN Cutter 4, 93bm, 59 × 20ft, 4—12pdr carr. Purch. 4.6.1801. Sold 1802.

DOLPHIN Brigantine 3, 319bm, 91 × 29ft, 3—32pdr. Sheerness DY 14.6.1836. Customs watchvessel 2.1861. Sold 11.5.1894 for BU.

DOLPHIN Composite screw sloop, 925 tons, 157 × 32ft, 2—6in, 2—5in. Raylton Dixon 9.12.1882. Sail TS 1899; hulk 1907; submarine depot ship 1912. Sold 13.3.1925; foundered under tow 19.4.1925, raised, beached. Accommodation schoolship. BU 1977 Bo'ness.

DOLPHIN (ex-ABERFOYLE) Submarine base tender, 210 tons. Renamed 3.1938. For disposal 1947. *Doubt exists as to whether the name was ever painted up on ABERFOYLE, q.v.*

DOLPHIN *See also WEXFORD 1655, HINDOSTAN 1804, PANDORA 1914.*

DOLPHINS PRIZE Sloop 12, 147bm. French privateer, captured 8.1757. Sold 6.11.1760.

DOLWEN (ex-*Hector Gull*) Buoy tender, 602 tons, 140 (oa) × 29.5ft. P. K. Harris 1962. Stern trawler, purch. 1976. Sold 10.1990 Mira Towage, Malta.

DOMETT (ex-EISNER) Frigate, DE 'Captain' class. Boston NY 19.5.1941 on Lend-Lease. Ret. USN 8.3.1946.

DOMINICA Schooner 6, 85bm. Purch. 1805. BU 1.1808.

DOMINICA (ex-TAPE A L'OEIL) Gun-brig 14, 153bm. French privateer, captured 1807. Capsized 8.1809 off Tortola.

DOMINICA (ex-DUC DE WAGRAM) Schooner 10, 203bm, 89·5 × 23ft, 12—12pdr carr., 2—6pdr. French, captured 1809. Captured 5.8.1813 by American privateer off Charlestown; recaptured 22.5.1814. Wrecked 15.8.1815 off Bermuda.

DOMINICA (ex-HARMAN) Frigate, 'Colony' class. Walsh Kaiser 14.9.1943 on Lend-Lease (renamed 1943). Ret. USN 23.4.1946.

DOMINION Battleship, 16,500 tons, 439 × 78ft, 4—12in, 4—9in, 10—6in, 12—12pdr. Vickers 25.8.1903. Sold 9.5.1921 Ward; LU Belfast; arr. Preston 28.10.1924 for BU.

DON Iron screw gunboat, 363 tons, 110 × 34ft, 3—6pdr. Palmer 14.4.1877. Dockyard barge 1911. Sold 1914 in Malta.

DONCASTER Paddle minesweeper, 'Ascot' class. Ayrshire Co. 15.6.1916. Sold 3.1922 Ward, Inverkeithing.

DONEGAL (ex-HOCHE) 3rd Rate 76, 1,901bm, 182 × 49·5ft. French, captured 12.10.1798 by squadron off north-western Ireland. BU 5.1845 Portsmouth.

DONEGAL Screw 1st Rate 101, 3,245bm, 5,481 tons, 240 × 55ft. Devonport DY 23.9.1858. = VERNON (torpedo schoolship) 14.1.1886. Sold 18.5.1925 Pounds, Portsmouth.

DONEGAL Armoured cruiser, 9,800 tons, 440 × 66ft, 14—6in, 10—12pdr. Fairfield 4.9.1902. Sold 1.7.1920 S. Castle, Plymouth; resold Granton S. Bkg Co.

DONOVAN Minesweeping sloop, '24' class. Greenock & Grangemouth 27.4.1918. Sold 15.11.1922 Ferguson Muir.

DONOVAN *See also EMPIRE BATTLEAXE 1943.*

DOOMBA *See WEXFORD 1919*

DOON Destroyer, 545 tons, 222 × 23·5ft, 1—12pdr, 5—6pdr (1907: 4—12pdr), 2—TT. Hawthorn 8.11.1904. Sold 27.5.1919 Ward, Rainham.

DORDRECHT 3rd Rate 64, 1,440bm, 159·5 × 45ft. Dutch, captured 17.8.1796 Saldanha Bay. Harbour service 1800. Sold 21.5.1823 for BU.

DORIS 5th Rate 36, 913bm, 142 × 38ft. Cleveley, Gravesend, 31.8.1795. Wrecked 21.1.1805 Quiberon Bay.

DORIS 5th Rate 32, 885bm, 142 × 37ft. Record, Appledore, ordered 6.1.1806, cancelled 24.6.1806.

DORIS (ex-*Pitt*) 5th Rate 36, 870bm, 137 × 38ft. East Indiaman, purch. 9.1808. Sold 4.1829 Valparaiso. *Launched 24.3.1807 as SALSETTE, = PITT 3.10.1807, = DORIS 3.4.1808.*

DORIS Wood screw frigate, 2,483bm, 3,803 tons, 240 × 48ft, 20—10in, 2—68pdr, 10—32pdr. Pembroke Dock 25.3.1857. Sold 1885.

DORIS 2nd class cruiser, 5,600 tons, 350 × 54ft, 5—6in, 6—4in, 9—12pdr. NC&A Barrow (Vickers) 3.3.1896. Sold 20.2.1919 Bombay.

DORKING Minesweeper, Later 'Hunt' class. Dundee SB Co. 26.9.1918. Arr. 27.5.1928 Charlestown for BU.

DORNOCH Minesweeper, turbine 'Bangor' class. Ailsa 4.2.1942. Sold 1.1.1948; BU Stockholm Ship Co.

DOROTHEA Discovery vessel. Hired 2.1818, purch. 3.1818. Sold 28.2.1819.

DORSET (ex-DUBLIN) Yacht 10, 164bm, 78 × 22ft. Deptford DY 17.7.1753 (renamed 11.7.1753). Sold 23.3.1815.

DORSETSHIRE 3rd Rate 80, 1,176bm, 153·5 × 42ft. Winters, Southampton, 8.12.1694. Rebuilt Portsmouth 1712 as 1,283bm. Sold 1749.

DORSETSHIRE 3rd Rate 70, 1,436bm, 162 × 45ft. Portsmouth DY 13.12.1757. BU 3.1775.

DORSETSHIRE Cruiser, 9,975 tons, 630 (oa) × 68·5ft, 8—8in, 4—4in. Portsmouth DY 29.1.1929. Sunk 5.4.1942 Japanese air attack Indian Ocean.

DOTEREL (ex-*Escape*) Wood paddle packet,

237bm, 119 × 21ft. GPO vessel, tx 1837. Sold 30.11.1850.

DOTEREL Wood screw gunboat, 'Britomart' class. Miller, Liverpool, 5.7.1860. Sold 6.6.1871 Marshall, Plymouth.

DOTEREL Composite screw sloop, 1,130 tons, 170 × 36ft, 2—7in, 4—64pdr. Chatham DY 2.3.1880. Blown up 26.4.1881 accident off Punta Arenas.

DOTEREL Yacht. Req. 1918. = DOTTER 1918—22.

DOTTEREL Brig-sloop 18, 'Cruizer' class, 387bm. Blake & Scott, Bursledon, 6.10.1808. Hulked 4.1827; sold 9.1848 Bermuda.

DOUGLAS Destroyer leader, 1,800 tons, 320 × 32ft, 5—4·7in, 1—3in, 6—TT. Cammell Laird 8.6.1918. Sold 20.3.1945; BU Ward, Inverkeithing.

DOVE (ex-FORTUNE) Ketch 8, 84bm. Royalist, captured 1644 by Parliamentarians. Sunk 1650.

DOVE Dogger 8. Dutch, captured 1672. Wrecked 1674.

DOVE Ketch 4, 19bm. Deptford DY 1672. Sold 1683.

DOVE Schooner 4, 103bm, 4—12pdr carr. Purch. 5.1805. Captured 5.8.1805 by French.

DOVE Packet brig 6. Purch. 1823. Sold 31.1.1829.

DOVE Wood screw gunboat, 'Albacore' class. Pitcher, Northfleet, 24.11.1855. Sold 14.4.1873 Shanghai.

DOVE Paddle gunboat, 20 tons, 60 × 14ft. Yarrow, Poplar, in sections 1893; re-erected 30.5.1893 East Africa. Tx 1895 BCA Govt.

DOVE Destroyer, 370 tons, 210 × 20·5ft, 1—12pdr, 5—6pdr, 2—TT. Earle 21.3.1898. Sold 27.1.1920 Maden & McKee.

DOVE *See also ARIADNE 1805, KANGAROO 1852.*

DOVER Pink. Royalist, captured 1649. Sold 1650.

DOVER 48-gun ship, 554bm, 119 × 32ft. Castle, Shoreham, 1654. Rebuilt Portsmouth 1695; rebuilt 1716 as 604bm. BU 1730.

DOVER Dogger 8. Dutch, captured 1672. Given away 1677.

DOVER 5th Rate 44, 693bm, 124·5 × 36ft. Bronsdon & Wells, Deptford, 7.1.1740. Sold 6.10.1763.

DOVER 5th Rate 44, 905bm, 140 × 38·5ft. Parsons, Burledson, 5.1786. Burnt 6.8.1806 accident Woolwich.

DOVER (ex-BELLONE) Troopship 38, 692bm, 132 × 35ft. French, captured 11.3.1811 Lissa. Harbour service 2.1825. Sold 21.1.1836.

DOVER Iron paddle packet, 224bm, 110·5 × 21ft. Laird 1840. Stationed from 1849 in The Gambia. Sold 1866. *First iron vessel in RN.*

DOVER *See also DUNCAN 1804.*

DOVER CASTLE Corvette, 'Castle' class. Inglis, cancelled 12.1943.

DOVER PRIZE Hulk, captured 1689. Wrecked 1689.

DOVER PRIZE 5th Rate 32, 330bm, 105 × 27ft. Captured 1693. Sold 1698.

DOVEY (ex-LAMBOURNE) Frigate, 'River' class. Fleming & Ferguson 14.10.1943 (renamed 10.1942). Arr. 20.11.1955 Ward, Preston, for BU.

DOVEY Minehunter, 890 tons (full load), 156.3 (oa) × 34·5ft, 1—40mm. Richards, Great Yarmouth, 7.12.1983. Tx Bangladeshi Navy 3.9.1994 = SUROVI.

DOWNHAM Inshore minesweeper, 'Ham' class. White, Cowes, 1.9.1955. TRV 1967. Sold 1982.

DOWNLEY Inshore minesweeper. Launched 1955 as WOLDINGHAM (q.v.).

DRAGON Ship, 100bm. In service 1512–14.

DRAGON 45-gun ship, 140bm. In service 1542–52.

DRAGON (RED DRAGON) Galleon, 900bm. Deptford 1593. Last mentioned 1613.

DRAGON 38-gun ship, 414bm, 120 × 28·5ft. Chatham DY 1647. Rebuilt Deptford 1690 as 479bm; rebuilt Cuckold's Point 1707 as 719bm. Wrecked 15.3.1711 Alderney. *First ship built at Chatham DY.*

DRAGON 4th Rate 60, 1,067bm, 144 × 42ft. Woolwich DY 11.9.1736. Sunk 7.1757 breakwater Sheerness.

DRAGON 3rd Rate 74, 1,614bm, 168 × 47ft. Deptford DY 4.3.1760. Harbour service 1781. Sold 1.6.1784.

DRAGON Cutter 10, 139bm, 61 × 24ft, 10—4pdr. Purch. 5.1782. Sold 7.1785.

DRAGON 3rd Rate 74, 1,815bm, 178 × 49ft. Wells, Rotherhithe, 2.4.1798. Harbour service 9.1824; = FAME (hulk) 15.7.1842. BU 8.1850.

DRAGON Wood paddle frigate, 1,270bm, 200 × 37·5ft. Pembroke Dock 17.6.1845. Sold 7.10.1864 Castle, Charlton.

DRAGON Composite screw sloop, 1,130 tons, 170 × 36ft, 2—7in, 4—64pdr. Devonport DY 30.5.1878. Sold 24.9.1892.

DRAGON Destroyer, 330 tons, 210 × 19·5ft, 1—12pdr, 5—6pdr, 2—TT. Laird 15.12.1894. Sold 9.7.1912 for BU.

DRAGON Light cruiser, 4,650 tons, 471 (oa) × 46ft, 6—6in, 2—3in. Scotts 29.12.1917. Lent 1.1943 Polish Navy. Sunk 8.7.1944 breakwater Normandy beaches.

DRAGON Destroyer, 'Daring' class, BAe/Vosper-Thornycroft. To be assembled Barrow. Firm contract 05.2002.

DRAGON *See also ORMONDE 1711, LOOKOUT 1914, DECOY 1949.*

DRAGON PRIZE Sloop 8, 60bm. French, captured 28.6.1689. Foundered 12.1.1690 off Thanet.

DRAGONFLY Coastal destroyer, 235 tons, 175 × 17·5ft, 2—12pdr, 3—TT. White 11.3.1906. = TB.2 in 1906. Sold 7.10.1920 Ward, Hayle.

DRAGONFLY River gunboat, 'Fly' class. Yarrow; sections sent out 7.1915. Sold 16.2.1923 Basra.

DRAGONFLY River gunboat, 585 tons, 2—4in, 1—3.7in. Thornycroft 8.12.1938. Sunk 14.2.1942 air attack off Singapore.

DRAKE 16-gun ship, 146bm. Deptford 1653. Sold 1691 in Jamaica.

DRAKE 6th Rate 24, 253bm, 93 × 25ft. Fowler, Rotherhithe, 26.9.1694. Wrecked 20.12.1694 coast of Ireland.

DRAKE Yacht 2, 60bm. Plymouth DY 1705. Rebuilt Plymouth 1727 as 68bm. Sold 16.10.1749.

DRAKE Sloop 14, 175bm, 84 × 22ft. Woolwich DY 8.11.1705. *Rebuilt 1729 as following vessel.*

DRAKE Sloop 14, 207bm, 87 × 23ft. Deptford DY 3.4.1729. BU 7.1740 Deptford.

DRAKE Sloop 14 (Indian), 200bm. Bombay DY 1736. Bomb vessel 1748. Sold 1755.

DRAKE Sloop 14, 206bm, 85 × 24ft. West, Wapping, 2.1740. Wrecked 1742 Gibraltar Bay; wreck sold 13.10.1748.

DRAKE Sloop 14, 249bm, 88 × 25ft. Deptford 1743. Sold 1748.

DRAKE (ex-*Marquis of Granby*) Sloop, 462bm, 111 × 30·5ft, 12—6pdr. Purch. 1770. = RESOLUTION (discovery vessel) 25.12.1771. Captured 9.6.1782 by French SPHINX in East Indies.

DRAKE (ex-*Resolution*) Sloop 14, 275bm, 91 × 26ft, 14—4pdr. Purch. 1777. Captured 24.4.1778 by American RANGER off Belfast.

DRAKE Brig-sloop 14, 221bm, 79 × 26ft. Ladd, Dover, 5.1779. Condemned 7.1800 Jamaica.

DRAKE (ex-TIGRE) Brig-sloop 14, 212bm, 80 × 24ft. French privateer, captured 1799. Wrecked 9.1804 Nevis.

DRAKE (ex-*Earl Mornington*) Sloop 16, 253bm, 104 × 24ft. Purch. 1804. BU 8.1808.

DRAKE Brig-sloop 10, 'Cherokee' class, 235bm. Bailey, Ipswich, 3.11.1808. Wrecked 22.6.1822 Newfoundland.

DRAKE Mortar vessel, 109bm, 60 × 21ft. Launched Portsmouth 25.3.1834 as dockyard lighter, conv. Portsmouth 10.1854. = MV.1 on 19.10.1855; = SHEPPEY (dockyard lighter) 7.7.1856. BU 1867.

DRAKE Wood screw gunboat, 'Clown' class. Pembroke Dock 8.3.1856. Sold 9.2.1869 in Hong Kong.

DRAKE (ex-YC.1, ex-HART) Cutter, 80bm, 54 × 19ft. Renamed 11.1870. BU comp. 6.3.1875 Chatham.

DRAKE Armoured cruiser, 14,100 tons, 529 × 71ft, 2—9·2in, 16—6in, 14—12pdr. Pembroke Dock 5.3.1901. Sunk 2.10.1917 by U.79 in Rathlin Sound.

DRAKE *See also SHELDRAKE 1875, MARSHAL NEY 1915.*

DREADFUL Bomb vessel 4, 147bm, 67 × 23·5ft. Graves, Limehouse, 6.5.1695. Burnt 5.7.1695 to avoid capture.

DREADNOUGHT 40-gun ship. In service 1553. *Existence doubtful.*

DREADNOUGHT 41-gun ship, 450bm, 2—60pdr, 4—18pdr, 11—9pdr, 10—6pdr, 12 small. Deptford 10.11.1573. Rebuilt 1592; rebuilt 1614 as 552bm. BU 1648.

DREADNOUGHT 4th Rate 60, 852bm, 142 × 36·5ft. Johnson, Blackwall, 1691. Rebuilt Blackwall 1706 as 910bm; hulk 1740. BU 9.1748 Portsmouth.

DREADNOUGHT 4th Rate 60, 1,093bm, 144 × 42ft. Wells, Deptford, 23.6.1742. Sold 17.8.1784.

DREADNOUGHT 2nd Rate 98, 2,110bm, 185 × 51ft. Portsmouth DY 13.6.1801. Hospital ship 1827. BU comp. 31.3.1857.

DREADNOUGHT (ex-FURY) Battleship, 10,820 tons, 320 × 64ft, 4—12.5in, 6—QF. Pembroke Dock 8.3.1875 (renamed 1.2.1875). Hulk 1903. Sold 14.7.1908 Ward; BU Barrow (and Preston, from 2.1909)

DREADNOUGHT Battleship, 17,900 tons, 490 × 82ft, 10—12in, 27—12pdr. Portsmouth DY 10.2.1906. Sold 9.5.1921 Ward; arr. Inverkeithing 2.1.1923 for BU.

DREADNOUGHT Nuclear submarine, 3,000/ 3,500 tons, 265·8 (oa) × 32·3ft, 6—TT. Vickers Armstrong, Barrow, 21.10.1960. PO, LU Chatham 1982. Tx Rosyth to LU 13.4.1983.

DREADNOUGHT *See also TORRINGTON 1654, CALEDONIA 1808.*

DREADNOUGHT PRIZE Sloop, 109bm, 62 × 21ft. Captured 1748 by DREADNOUGHT. Sold 1748.

DRIVER Sloop 18, 399bm, 105 × 30ft. Goodrich, Bermuda, 1797. Convict ship 1825. BU 7.1834.

DRIVER Wood paddle sloop, 1,058bm, 180 × 36ft. Portsmouth DY 24.12.1840. Wrecked 8.1861 Mariguana I.

DROCHTERLAND (ex-UNIE) 4th Rate (hulk), 871bm, 135 × 38·5ft. Dutch, captured 28.8.1799 off Texel. Receiving ship 1800; BU 3.1815.

DROGHEDA *See TREDAGH 1654.*

DROMEDARY (ex-*Duke of Cumberland*) Storeship 30, 754bm, 22—9pdr, 8—6pdr. Purch. 1777. Registered as 5th Rate 30 from 10.1779. BU 4.1783.

DROMEDARY Iron screw troopship, 657bm, Samuda, Poplar, 16.1.1862. Sold 21.10.1869 J. P. Tate.

DROMEDARY (ex-*Briton*) Iron screw troopship, 1,122 tons. Purch. 4.11.1873. Sold 1885.

DROMEDARY *See also JANUS 1778, HOWE 1805.*

DROXFORD Seaward defence boat, 'Ford' class. Pimblott, Northwich, 28.1.1954. = DEE 1955; = DROXFORD 1965. Target vessel Milford Haven 1989—93.

DRUDGE Trials gunboat, 890 tons, 125 × 35ft, various guns. Launched Elswick 15.6.1887, purch. 28.2.1901. = EXCELLENT 21.11.1916; = DRYAD 26.1.1919; = DRUDGE 1919. Sold 27.3.1920.

DRUDGE *See also READY 1872.*

DRUID Sloop 10, 212bm. 87·5 × 23·5ft. Barnard, Harwich, 24.2.1761. Sunk 8.1773 breakwater Sheerness.

DRUID (ex-*Brilliant*) Sloop 16, 285bm, 97 × 25·5ft. Purch. 2.9.1776. = BLAST (fireship) 16.9.1779. Sold 25.9.1783.

DRUID 5th Rate 32, 718bm, 129 × 35·5ft. Teast & Tombes, Bristol, 16.6.1783. Troopship 4.1798. BU 10.1813.

DRUID 5th Rate 46, 1,170bm, 159 × 41ft. Pembroke Dock 1.7.1825. Sold 4.1863 Marshall, Plymouth.

DRUID Wood screw corvette, 1,322bm, 1,730 tons, 220 × 36ft. Deptford DY 13.3.1869. Sold 10.11.1886 Castle. *Last ship built at Deptford DY.*

DRUID Destroyer, 770 tons, 240 × 25·5ft, 2—4in, 2—12pdr, 2—TT. Denny 4.12.1911. Sold 9.5.1921. Ward, Briton Ferry.

DRUID *See DIANA 1952.*

DRUMHELLER Corvette (RCN), 'Flower' class. Collingwood SY 5.7.1941. Sold 1946.

DRUMMONDVILLE Minesweeper (RCN), TE 'Bangor' class. Vickers, Montreal, 21.5.1941. Sold 9.1958 = *Fort Albany.*

DRURY Frigate, DE 'Captain' class. Philadelphia NY, LD 1.4.1942 for RN; retained USN = ENSTROM.

DRURY (ex-COCKBURN) Frigate, DE 'Captain' class. Philadelphia NY 24.7.1942 on Lend-Lease (renamed 1942). Ret. USN 8.1945.

DRYAD 5th Rate 36, 924bm, 143 × 38·5ft. Barnard, Deptford, 4.6.1795. Harbour service 1832. BU 2.1860 Portsmouth.

DRYAD Wood screw frigate 51, 3,027bm, 250 × 52ft, 30—8in, 1—68pdr, 20—32pdr. Portsmouth DY, LD 2.1.1860, cancelled 16.12.1864.

DRYAD Wood screw sloop, 1,086bm, 1,574 tons, 187 × 36ft, 9—64pdr. Devonport DY 25.9.1866. Sold 9.1885; BU 4.1886.

DRYAD Torpedo gunboat, 1,070 tons, 250 × 30·5ft, 2—4·7in, 4—6pdr 5—TT. Chatham DY 22.11.1893. = HAMADRYAD (harbour service) 1.1918. Sold 24.9.1920 H. Auten.

DRYAD Light cruiser, 4,765 tons, 445 × 46·5ft, 6—6in, 2—4in. Vickers, ordered 3.1918, cancelled 11.1918.

DRYAD *For navigation schoolships with this name see DRUDGE, RATTLER 1886, CARSTAIRS.*

DUBBO Minesweeper (RAN), 'Bathurst' class. Mort's Dock, Sydney, 7.3.1942. Sold 20.2.1958 for BU in Japan.

DUBBO Patrol boat (RAN), 211 tons. Cairns 21.1.1984.

DUBFORD Seaward defence boat, 'Ford' class. White, Cowes, 2.3.1953. Tx Nigerian Navy 1968 = SAPELE; deleted 1983.

DUBLIN Yacht 10, 148bm, 73 × 22ft. Deptford DY 13.8.1709. BU 10.1752 Deptford.

DUBLIN 3rd Rate 74, 1,562bm, 165 × 47ft. Deptford DY 6.5.1757. BU 13.5.1784 Plymouth.

DUBLIN 3rd Rate 74, 1,772bm, 175 × 48·5ft. Brent, Rotherhithe, 13.2.1812. Reduced to 50 guns 12.1826; harbour service 1845. Sold 7.1885 Castle, Charlton.

DUBLIN 2nd class cruiser, 5,400 tons, 430 × 50ft, 8—6in. Beardmore 30.4.1912. Sold 7.1926 King, Troon.

DUBLIN *See also DORSET 1753.*

DUC D'AQUITAINE 3rd Rate 64, 1,358bm, 159·5 × 44·5ft. 24—24pdr, 26—12pdr, 14—9pdr. French East Indiaman, captured 30.5.1757 by EAGLE and MEDWAY. Foundered 1.1.1761 Bay of Bengal 'on an anchor'.

DUC D'ESTISSAC Sloop 18. French privateer, captured 6.6.1781 by CERBERUS. Sold 30.10.1783.

DUC DE CHARTRES Ship-sloop 18, 426bm, 109 × 30·5ft, 18—6pdr. French privateer, captured 1781 by CUMBERLAND in North America. Sold 1.7.1784.

DUC DE LA VAUGINON (ex-DUC DE LA VAUGUYON) Cutter 12, 12—4pdr. French privateer, captured 1779. Lost 12.1779.

DUCHESS OF CUMBERLAND Sloop 16. Purch. 1781. Wrecked 1781 off Newfoundland.

DUCHESS (ex-DUCHESSE) 24-gun ship. French, captured 1652. Sold 1654.

DUCHESS 2nd Rate 90, 1,364bm, 163 × 45ft, 26—34pdr, 26—18pdr, 26—6pdr, 12—3pdr. Deptford 1679. = PRINCESS ANNE 31.12.1701; = WINDSOR CASTLE 17.3.1702, = BLENHEIM 18.12.1706. BU 8.1763.

DUCHESS Destroyer, 1,375 tons, 329 (oa) × 33ft, 4—4·7in, 1—3in, 8—TT. Hawthorn Leslie 19.7.1932. Sunk 12.12.1939 collision BARHAM off western Scotland.

DUCHESS Destroyer, 2,610 tons, 390 (oa) × 43ft, 6—4·5in, 6—40mm, 10—TT. Thornycroft 9.4.1951. Tx RAN 8.5.1964. BU 6.1980 Japan.

DUCKWORTH Frigate, DE 'Captain' class. Mare Island, LD 15.4.1942 for RN; retained USN = BURDEN R. HASTINGS.

DUCKWORTH (ex-GARY) Frigate, TE 'Captain' class. Bethlehem, Hingham, 1.5.1943 on Lend-Lease. Ret. USN 17.12.1945.

DUDDON *See RIBBLE 1943.*

DUDLEY CASTLE Corvette, 'Castle' class. Inglis, cancelled 12.1943.

DUE REPULSE *See REPULSE 1595.*

DUFF Frigate, DE 'Captain' class. Mare Island, LD 15.4.1942. Retained USN, launched as LE HARDY.

DUFF (ex-LAMONS) Frigate, TE 'Captain' class. Bethlehem, Hingham, 22.5.1943. Ret. USN 1.11.1946. BU 1947 Holland.

DUFFERIN Troopship (RIM), 7,457 tons, 437 × 53ft, 8—4in, 8—3pdr. Vickers 14.8.1904. AMC 1914; TS 1927. Hulk for sale 1955.

DUFTON Coastal minesweeper. 'Ton' class. Goole SB 13.11.1954. Sold Pounds 6.1977; BU Sittingbourne.

DUGUAY TROUIN Sloop 18, 252bm, 86 × 26ft, 4—18pdr, 14—6pdr. French privateer, captured 1780 by SURPRISE off The Dodman. Sold 30.10.1783.

DUKE 12-gun shi. In service 1652.

DUKE 2nd Rate 90, 1,346bm, 163 × 45ft, 26—34pdr 26—18pdr, 26—6pdr, 12—3pdr. Woolwich DY 1682. Rebuilt Chatham; = PRINCE GEORGE 31.12.1701 (q.v.). Lost 1758.

DUKE Fireship 8, 199bm, 83 × 24ft. Purch. 22.6.1739. Expended 16.6.1742 St Tropez.

DUKE Fireship 8, 469bm, 107 × 32·5ft. French, captured 1745. Sold 9.2.1748.

DUKE Storeship 10. Foundered 1.1.1761 nr Pondicherry.

DUKE 2nd Rate 90, 1,931bm, 177·5 × 50ft. Plymouth DY 18.10.1777. Harbour service 9.1799. BU 1843.

DUKE *See also VANGUARD 1678.*

DUKE OF EDINBURGH Armoured cruiser, 13,550 tons, 480 × 73·5ft, 6—9·2in, 10—6in, 22—3pdr. Pembroke Dock 14.6.1904. Sold 12.4.1920 Hughes Bolckow, Blyth.

DUKE OF KENT 1st Rate 170 (4-decker), 221 × 65·5ft. Projected 1809, cancelled.

DUKE OF WELLINGTON (ex-WINDSOR CASTLE) Screw 1st Rate 131, 3,771bm, 6,071 tons, 240·5 × 60ft, 16—8in, 1—68pdr, 114—32pdr. Pembroke Dock 14.9.1852 (renamed 1.10.1852). Harbour service 5.1863. Sold 12.4.1904 Castle, Charlton. *See WINDSOR CASTLE 1852.*

DUKE OF YORK Cutter 4, 54bm, 40·5 × 18ft. Purch. 2.1763. Sold 1.7.1766 Sheerness.

DUKE OF YORK (ex-ANSON) Battleship, 35,000 tons, 745 (oa) × 103ft, 10—14in, 16—5·25 in. John Brown 28.2.1940 (renamed 21.12.1938). BU 2.1958 Faslane.

DUKE WILLIAM Cutter, 65bm. Purch. 2.1763. Lost 5.10.1768.

DULLISK COVE (ex-EMPIRE PERAK) Repair ship, 8,402 tons, 425 × 56ft. Short, Sunderland, 4.9.1944 (renamed 1944). Sold 30.7.1947 = *Kafalonia.*

DULVERTON Destroyer, 'Hunt' class Type II. Stephen 1.4.1941. Sunk 13.11.1943 German aircraft off Kos.

DULVERTON Minehunter, 615 tons. Vosper-Thornycroft 3.11.1982.

DUMBARTON CASTLE 6th Rate 24. Scottish, transferred 29.11.1707. Captured 26.4.1708 by French off Waterford.

DUMBARTON CASTLE Corvette, 'Castle' class. Caledon SB 28.9.1943. BU 3.1961 Gateshead.

DUMBARTON CASTLE Patrol vessel, 1,427 tons, Hall Russell 3.6.1981.

DUMBARTON 6th Rate 20, 191bm. Scottish, captured 1685. Condemned 6.6.1691 Virginia.

DUMBLETON Coastal minesweeper, 'Ton' class. Harland & Wolff 8.11.1957. Tx SAN 28.10.1958 = PORT ELIZABETH. Sold S. A. Metal Co. 9.1988; BU Table Bay.

DUNBAR 3rd Rate 64, 1,082bm, Deptford 1656. = HENRY 1660. Burnt accident 1682.

DUNBAR Minesweeper, turbine 'Bangor' class. Blyth DD 5.6.1941. Sold 1.1.1948; BU Pollock & Brown, Southampton.

DUNCAN (ex-*Carron*) 5th Rate 38, 990bm, 130 × 35ft. Indiaman, Bombay DY 1804, purch. 1804. = DOVER 1807. Wrecked 2.5.1811 off Madras.

DUNCAN 3rd Rate 74, 1,761bm, 176 × 48·5ft. Dudman, Deptford, 2.12.1811. Harbour service 1826. BU 10.1863 Chatham.

DUNCAN Screw 1st Rate 101, 3,727bm, 5,724 tons, 252 × 58ft, 38—8in, 1—68pdr, 62—23pdr. Portsmouth DY 13.1.1859. = PEMBROKE (harbour service) 1890; = TENEDOS 11 9.1905. Sold 11.10.1910.

DUNCAN Battleship, 14,000 tons, 432 (oa) × 75·5ft, 4—12in, 12—6in, 12—12pdr. Thames Iron Works, Blackwall, 21.3.1901. Sold 18.2.1920 Stanlee, Dover.

DUNCAN Destroyer leader, 1,400 tons, 329 (oa) × 33ft, 4—4·7in 1—3in, 8—TT. Portsmouth DY 7.7.1932. Sold 9.1945; arr. 11.1945 Ward, Barrow; BU 2.1949.

DUNCAN Frigate, 1,180 tons, 300 × 33ft, 2—40mm. Thornycroft 30.5.1957. Arr. Kingsnorth, R. Medway, 2.1985 for BU.

DUNCAN Destroyer, 'Daring' class. BAe/Vosper-Thornycroft. To be assembled Barrow. Name announced 2.2002. Firm contract 5.2002.

DUNCANSBY HEAD Repair ship, 9,000 tons, 416 × 57ft. Barrard, Vancouver, 17.11.1944. Sold 12.1969; BU in Spain.

DUNDALK Minesweeper, Later 'Hunt' class. Clyde SB Co. 31.1.1919. Mined 16.10.1940, foundered under tow 17.10.1940 off Harwich.

DUNDAS Corvette (RCN), 'Flower' class. Victoria Machinery 25.7.1941. Sold 23.10.1945.

DUNDAS Frigate, 1,180 tons, 300 × 33ft, 3—40mm, 4—TT. White, Cowes, 25.9.1953. BU 4.1983 Troon.

DUNDEE Sloop, 1,060 tons, 250 × 34ft, 2—4in. Chatham DY 20.9.1932. Sunk 15.9.1940 by U.48 in Atlantic.

DUNDRUM BAY (ex-LOCH SCAMADALE) Frigate, 'Bay' class. Blyth DD 10.7.1945. = ALERT 1945. Sold 13.10.1971 Ward; BU Inverkeithing.

DUNEDIN Light cruiser, 4,650 tons, 472·5 (oa) × 46·5ft, 6—6in, 2—3in. Armstrong 19.11.1918. Sunk 24.11.1941 by U.124 north of Pernambuco.

DUNGENESS Repair ship, 8,580 tons, 416 × 57ft. West Coast SB, Vancouver, 15.3.1945. Sold 9.1947 = *Levuka.*

DUNIRA (ex-ALCMENE) 5th Rate 38, 1,080bm, 153 × 40ft. French, captured 20.1.1814 by VENERABLE off Madeira. = IMMORTALITE 1814. Sold 1.1837.

DUNKERTON Coastal minesweeper, 'Ton' class. Goole SB 8.3.1954. Tx SAN = PRETORIA 8.1955. Sold 7.12.1987 as museum ship Hout Bay, = FV *Madiba* 1999.

DUNKIRK Ketch 2, 33bm. French, captured 1656. Sold 1660.

DUNKIRK (ex-WORCESTER) 4th Rate 48, 662bm, 141·5 × 33·5ft. Renamed 1660. Rebuilt Blackwall 1704 as 906bm; rebuilt Portsmouth 1734 as 965bm, 60 guns. BU 3.1749 Woolwich.

DUNKIRK 4th Rate 60, 1,246bm, 153 × 43ft. Woolwich DY 22.7.1754. Harbour service 9.1778. Sold 8.3.1792.

DUNKIRK Destroyer, 2,380 tons, 379 (oa) × 40·5ft, 5—4·5in, 10—TT. Stephen 27.8.1945. Arr. 22.11.1965 Faslane for BU.

DUNKIRK PRIZE (ex-LE HOCQUART) 6th Rate 24, 299bm. French privateer, captured 15.11.1705. Wrecked 25.10.1708 off Cape Francis, West Indies.

DUNMORE Schooner 4 (Canadian lakes). Detroit 1772. In service 1796.

DUNOON Minesweeper, Later 'Hunt' class. Clyde SB 21.3.1919. Sunk 30.4.1940 mine North Sea.

DUNSTER CASTLE Corvette, 'Castle' class. Midland SY, Ontario, cancelled 12.1943.

DUNVEGAN Corvette (RCN), 'Flower' class. Marine Industries 11.12,1940. Sold 1946 Venezuelan Navy = INDEPENDENCIA. BU 1953.

DUNVER (ex-VERDUN OF CANADA) Corvette (RCN), 'River' class. Morton 10.11.1942 (renamed 1942. Sold 13.12.1947; hull sunk 1949 breakwater Comox.

DUNWICH 6th Rate 24, 250bm, 94 × 24.5ft. Collins & Chatfield, Shoreham, 15.10.1695. Sunk 15.10.1714 breakwater Plymouth.

DUQUESNE 3rd Rate 74, 1,901bm. French, captured 25.7.1803 by BELLEROPHON and VANGUARD off San Domingo. Stranded 1804 Morant Key, West Indies; BU 7.1805.

DURBAN Light cruiser, 4,650 tons, 472.5 (oa) × 46.5ft, 6–6in, 2–3in. Scotts 29.5.1919. Sunk 9.6.1944 breakwater Normandy.

DURBAN Coastal minesweeper (SAN), 'Ton' class. Camper & Nicholson 12.6.1957. PO 23.10.1985; tx Durban as museum ship.

DURHAM *See ACTIVE 1845.*

DURSLEY GALLEY 6th Rate 20, 371bm, 105 × 28.5ft. Deptford 13.2.1718. Sold 21.2.1744; became privateer, captured 8.5.1746 by French.

DURWESTON Coastal minesweeper, 'Ton' class. Dorset Yacht Co. 18.8.1955. Tx Indian Navy 17.8.1956 = KAKINADA; deleted 1984.

DUTIFUL *See RELIANCE 1944.*

DWARF Cutter 10, 203bm, 75 × 26ft. Lowes, Sandgate, 24.4.1810. Wrecked 3.3.1824 Kingstown pier.

DWARF Cutter 2, 50bm, 52 × 15ft. White, Cowes, 1826. Dockyard service, then Coastguard. Sold 1862 Hood, Rye.

DWARF (ex-*Mermaid*) Iron screw vessel, 164bm, 130 × 16ft. Purch. 22.6.1843. Sold 9.1853 J. Broughton. *First screw vessel in RN.*

DWARF Wood screw gunboat, 'Cheerful' class. Westbrook, Blackwall, 8.4.1856. BU 1863 Haslar.

DWARF Composite screw gunvessel, 465bm, 584 tons, 155 × 25ft, 1–7in, 1–64pdr, 2–20pdr. Woolwich DY 28.11.1867. BU 4.1886 Devonport.

DWARF 1st class gunboat, 710 tons, 180 × 33ft, 2–4in, 4–12pdr. London & Glasgow Co. 15.11.1898. Sold 13.7.1926 Ward, Pembroke.

DWARF Tender, 172 tons, 83.5 × 19ft. Philip, Dartmouth, 20.8.1936. Sold 8.3.1962, hulked 1963 Gareloch.

E

'E' class submarines 660 tons, 176 × 22·5ft 1—
12pdr, 4—TT (first eight); 662 tons, 180 × 22·5ft,
1—12pdr, 5—TT (others, except minelayers: 3—TT,
20 mines).

E.1 (ex-D.9) Chatham DY 9.11.1912. Destroyed
8.4.1918 Helsingfors to avoid capture.

E.2 (ex-D.10) Chatham DY 23.11.1912. Sold 7.3.1921
B. Zammit, Malta.

E.3 Vickers 29.10.1912. Sunk 18.10.1914 by U.27 in
North Sea.

E.4 Vickers 5.2.1912. Sold 21.2.1922 Upnor S. Bkg
Co.

E.5 Vickers 17.5.1912. Sunk 7.3.1916 North Sea.

E.6 Vickers 12.11.1912. Sunk 26.12.1915 mine in
North Sea.

E.7 Chatham DY 2.10.1913. Destroyed 5.9.1915
Dardanelles by explosive charge from UB.14 after
being caught in submarine net.

E.8 Chatham DY 30.10.1913. Destroyed 8.4.1918
Helsingfors to avoid capture.

E.9 Vickers 29.11.1913. Destroyed 8.4.1918 Helsingfors to avoid capture.

E.10 Vickers 29.11.1913. Sunk 18.1.1915 North Sea,
cause unknown.

E.11 Vickers 23.4.1914. Sold 7.3.1921 B. Zammit,
Malta.

E.12 Chatham DY 5.9.1914. Sold 7.3.1921
B. Zammit, Malta.

E.13 Chatham DY 22.9.1914. Stranded 3.9.1915
coast of Denmark, interned. Sold 14.12.1921
Petersen & Albeck, Denmark; BU Copenhagen.

E.14 Vickers 7.7.1914. Sunk 27.1.1918 mine off Kum
Kale, Dardanelles.

E.15 Vickers 23.4.1914. Stranded 15.4.1915 Kephez
Point, destroyed 18.4.1915 by boats from
MAJESTIC.

E.16 Vickers 23.9.1914. Sunk 22.8.1916 mine North
Sea.

E.17 Vickers 16.1.1915. Wrecked 6.1.1916 off Texel.

E.18 Vickers 4.3.1915. Sunk 1/2.6.1916.

E.19 Vickers 13.5.1915. Destroyed 8.4.1918
Helsingfors to avoid capture.

E.20 Vickers 12.6.1915. Sunk 5.11.1915 by UB.14 in
Sea of Marmora.

E.21 Vickers 24.7.1915. Sold 14.12.1921 Petersen &
Albeck.

E.22 Vickers 27.8.1915. Sunk 25.4.1916 by UB.18 in
North Sea.

E.23 Vickers 28.9.1915. Sold 6.9.1922 Young, Sunderland.

E.24 Vickers 9.12.1915. Minelayer. Sunk 24.3.1916
mine North Sea.

E.25 Beardmore 23.8.1915, LD for Turkish Navy.
Sold 14.12.1921 Petersen & Albeck.

E.26 Beardmore 11.11.1915, LD for Turkish Navy.
Sunk 6.7.1916 North Sea.

E.27 Yarrow 9.6.1917 (ordered 11.1914, cancelled
4.1915, restarted 8.1915). Sold 6.9.1922 Cashmore, Newport

E.28 Yarrow, ordered 11.1914, cancelled
20.4.1915.

E.29 Armstrong 1.6.1915. Sold 21.2.1922 Upnor
S. Bkg.

E.30 Armstrong 29.6.1915. Sunk 22.11.1916 North
Sea.

E.31 Scotts 23.8.1915. Sold 6.9.1922 Young, Sunderland.

E.32 White 16.8.1916. Sold 6.9.1922 Young, Sunderland.

E.33 Thornycroft 18.4.1916. Sold 6.9.1922 Cashmore, Newport.

E.34 Thornycroft 27.1.1917. Minelayer. Sunk
20.7.1918 mine North Sea.

E.35 John Brown 20.5.1916. Sold 6.9.1922 Ellis &
Co.

E.36 John Brown 16.9.1916. Sunk 17.1.1917 North
Sea.

E.37 Fairfield 2.9.1915. Sunk 1.12.1916 North Sea.

E.38 Fairfield 13.6.1916. Sold 6.9.1922 Ellis & Co.

E.39 Palmer 18.5.1916. Sold 13.10.1921 South
Wales Salvage Co.; foundered 9.1922 under tow.

E.40 Palmer 9.11.1916. Sold 14.12.1921 Petersen &
Albeck.

E.41 Cammell Laird 28.7.1915. Minelayer. Sold
6.9.1922 Ellis & Co.

E.42 Cammell Laird 22.10.1915. Sold 6.9.1922
J. Smith.

E.43 Swan Hunter 1916. Sold 3.1.1921 South Wales

Salvage Co.; stranded, lost under tow St Agnes, Cornwall.

E.44 Swan Hunter 21.2.1916. Sold 13.10.1921 South Wales Salvage Co.

E.45 Cammell Laird 25.1.1916. Minelayer. Sold 6.9.1922 Ellis & Co.

E.46 Cammell Laird 4.4.1916. Minelayer. Sold 6.9.1922 Ellis & Co.

E.47 Fairfield 29.5.1916. Sunk 20.8.1917 North Sea.

E.48 Fairfield 2.8.1916. Target 1920. Sold 7.1928 Cashmore, Newport.

E.49 Swan Hunter 18.9.1916. Sunk 12.3.1917 mine off Shetlands.

E.50 John Brown 13.11.1916. Sunk 1.2.1918 mine North Sea.

E.51 Scotts (ex-Yarrow, tx 3.1915) 30.11.1916. Minelayer. Sold 13.10.1921 South Wales Salvage Co.

E.52 Denny (ex-Yarrow, tx 3.1915) 25.1.1917. Sold 3.1.1921 Brixham Marine & Engineering Co.

E.53 Beardmore 1916. Sold 6.9.1922 Beard.

E.54 Beardmore 1916. Sold 14.12.1921 Petersen & Albeck.

E.55 Denny 5.2.1916. Sold 6.9.1922 Ellis & Co.

E.56 Denny 19.6.1916. Sold 9.6.1923 Granton S. Bkg Co.

E.57 Vickers, LD 5.1916, launched 10.5.1917 as L.1 (q.v.).

E.58 Vickers, LD 5.1916, launched 6.7.1917 as L.2 (q.v.).

A.E.1 (RAN) Vickers 22.5.1913. Sunk 14.9.1914 off Bismarck Archipelago, cause unknown.

A.E.2 (RAN) Vickers 18.6.1913. Scuttled 30.4.1915 after damage by shore batteries, Sea of Marmora.

EAGLE Careening hulk, 894bm. Merchantman, purch. 1592. Sold 1683 Chatham.

EAGLE (ex-AIGLE) 12-gun ship, 150bm. French, captured 1650. Sold 1655.

EAGLE Fireship 6, 50bm. Algerian, captured 1670. Expended 2.5.1671 Bugia Bay.

EAGLE Fireship 6 purch. 1672. Foundered 4.1673 passage St Helena.

EAGLE 3rd Rate 70, 1,053bm, 151·5 × 40·5ft. Portsmouth DY 1679. Rebuilt Chatham 1699 as 1,099bm. Wrecked 22.10.1707 Scilly Is.

EAGLE Advice boat 10, 153bm, 76 × 21ft. Fugar, Arundel, 1696. Wrecked 27.11.1703 Sussex coast.

EAGLE Fireship. Sunk 1745 as breakwater.

EAGLE 4th Rate 58, 1,130bm, 147 × 42ft. Barnard, Harwich, 2.12.1745. Sold 9.6.1767.

EAGLE Sloop 14 (Indian). Bombay DY 1754. *Fate unknown.*

EAGLE 3rd Rate 64, 1,372bm, 160 × 44·5ft. Wells, Rotherhithe, 2.5.1774. Harbour service 1790;

= BUCKINGHAM 15.8.1800. BU 10.1812 Chatham.

EAGLE Gunvessel 4, 71bm 68 × 15ft. Dutch hoy, purch. 1.1794. Sold 11.1804.

EAGLE (ex-VENTEUX) Gun-brig 12, 158bm, 74 × 22ft. French, captured 1803. = ECLIPSE 26.8.1803. Sold 7.4.1807.

EAGLE 3rd Rate 74, 1,723bm, 174 × 48·5ft. Pitcher, Northfleet, 27.2.1804. Reduced to 50 guns 4.1830; TS 10.1860; = EAGLET 1918. Lost by fire 1926; wreck sold 4.1.1927 J. Hornby.

EAGLE Brig (Canadian lakes), 110bm. Built 1812. Captured 4.7.1812 by Americans; retaken 9.1813, = CHUBB. Sold 1822.

EAGLE (ex-ALMIRANTE COCHRANE) Aircraft carrier, 22,790 tons, 625 × 94ft, 9—6in, 4—4in, 21 aircraft. Armstrong 8.6.1918; Chilean battleship, conv. on stocks. Sunk 11.8.1942 by U.73 western Mediterranean.

EAGLE Aircraft carrier, 36,800 tons, 720 × 112ft, Vickers Armstrong, Tyne, LD 19.4.1944, cancelled 1945.

EAGLE (ex-AUDACIOUS) Aircraft carrier, 36,800 tons, 720 × 112ft, 16—4·5in, 58—40mm, 100 aircraft. Harland & Wolff 19.3.1946 (renamed 21.1.1946). Arr. Cairnryan 19.10.1978 for BU.

EAGLE *See also SELBY 1654.*

EAGLE SHALLOP Sloop 6. Built 1648. Listed until 1653.

EAGLET Ketch 8, 54bm. Horsleydown 1655. Sold 1674.

EAGLET Ketch 10, 95bm, 63 × 19ft. Shish, Rotherhithe, 7.4.1691. Captured 5.1693 by French off Arran.

EAGLET Paddle vessel. Hired 1855–57.

EAGLET *See also EAGLE 1804, SIR BEVIS 1918.*

EARL Sloop. Presented 2.1701 by Govt of Jamaica. Made storeship. Sold 15.2.1705.

EARL OF CHATHAM Gunvessel 12. Purch. 1792. Removed from Navy List by 1800.

EARL OF DENBIGH Store hulk, 181bm, 73 × 24ft. Purch. North America for use in Antigua 6.4.1788. Lost 1797.

EARL OF DENBIGH *See also PELICAN 1775.*

EARL OF EGMONT Schooner. Purch. 3.1767. Sold 11.8.1773.

EARL OF NORTHAMPTON Survey sloop. Purch. 26.4.1769. Sold 1774 in Jamaica.

EARL OF PETERBOROUGH (ex-M.8) Monitor, 5,900 tons, 320 × 87ft, 2—12in, 2—6in, 2—12pdr. Harland & Wolff 26.8.1915 (renamed 1915). Sold 8.11.1921 Slough Trading Co.; BU Germany.

EARL ROBERTS *See ROBERTS 1915.*

EARNEST Gun-brig 12, 182bm, 80 × 23ft, 10—

18pdr, 2—18pdr carr. Menzies, Leith, 1.1805. Sold 2.5.1816.

EARNEST Wood screw gunboat, 'Albacore' class. Patterson, Bristol, 29.3.1856. Sold 17.1.1885 Castle.

EARNEST Destroyer, 355 tons, 210·5 × 22ft, 1—12pdr, 5—6pdr, 2—TT. Laird 7.11.1896. Sold 1.7.1920 Castle, Plymouth.

EASTBOURNE Minesweeper, TE 'Bangor' class. Lobnitz 2.12.1940. Sold 28.9.1948; BU Clayton & Davie, Dunston.

EASTBOURNE Frigate, 2,150 tons, 360 × 41ft, 2—4·5in, 2—40mm. Vickers Armstrong, Tyne, 29.12.1955. Sold J. A.White; arr. Inverkeithing 7.3.1985 for BU.

EASTON Destroyer, 'Hunt' class Type III. White 11.7.1942. Arr. 1.1953 Charlestown for BU.

EASTVIEW Frigate (RCN), 'River' class. Vickers, Montreal, 17.11.1943. Sold 13.12.1947 for BU; hull sunk 1948 breakwater Comox.

EASTWAY *See BATTLEAXE 1943.*

ECHO 6th Rate 24, 539bm, 118 × 32·5ft, 24—9pdr. French, captured 5.1758 at Louisburg. Sold 5.6.1770.

ECHO (ex-HUSSARD) Sloop 16. French, captured 5.7.1780 by NONSUCH. Wrecked 1791 Plymouth Sound.

ECHO Sloop 16, 342bm, 101·5 × 27·5ft Barton, Liverpool, 8.10.1782. BU 1797.

ECHO Sloop 16, 341bm, 96 × 29ft. King, Dover, 9.1797. Sold 18.5.1809.

ECHO Brig-sloop 18, 'Cruizer' class, 388bm. Pelham, Frindsbury, 1.7.1809. BU 5.1817.

ECHO Wood paddle vessel, 295bm, 112 × 25ft, Woolwich DY 28.5.1827 (LD sloop, 'Cherokee' class). Tug 1830. Sold 6.1885.

ECHO Destroyer, 1,375 tons, 329 (oa) × 33·5ft, 4—4·7in, 8—TT. Denny 16.2.1934. Lent 5.4.1944–4.1956 Greek Navy = NAVARINON. BU 4.1956 Clayton & Davie, Dunston.

ECHO Survey vessel, 120 tons, 100 × 22ft. White, Cowes, 1.5.1957. Sold 1986.

ECHO Survey ship, 3,470 tons, 295·3 (oa) × 55·1ft, Appledore SY, floated out 1.3.2002.

ECHUCA Minesweeper (RAN), 'Bathurst' class. Williamstown DY 17.1.1942. Tx RNZN 5.1952. BU 4.1967 Pacific Steel Co., Auckland.

ECLAIR 6th Rate 22, 444bm. French, captured 9.6.1793 by LEDA in Mediterranean. Powder hulk 4.1797. Sold 27.8.1806.

ECLAIR Gunvessel 3, 107bm, 60 × 20·5ft, 3—18pdr. French, captured 9.5.1795 by squadron off coast of France. Fitted as schooner 4.1796. Hulked 1802.

ECLAIR Schooner 12, 145bm, 12—12pdr carr. French, captured 18.1.1801 by GARLAND at Guadeloupe. = PICKLE 5.1809. Sold 11.6.1818.

ECLAIR Brig-sloop 18, 'Cruizer' class, 387bm. Warren, Brightlingsea, 8.7.1807. BU 3.1831.

ECLAIR *See also INFERNAL 1843.*

ECLIPSE (Gunboat No 22) Gunvessel 12, 169bm, 76 × 23ft, 2—24pdr, 10—18pdr carr. Perry, Blackwall, 29.3.1797. Sold 9.1802.

ECLIPSE Brig-sloop 18, 'Cruizer' class, 384bm, King, Dover, 4.8.1807. Sold 31.8.1817.

ECLIPSE Brig-sloop 10, 'Cherokee' class, 235bm, = WV.21 on 25.5.1863. Sold 10.11.1863 Castle, Charlton.

ECLIPSE Wood screw sloop, 700bm, 185 × 28·5ft, 2—68pdr, 2—32pdr. Scott Russell, Millwall, 18.9.1860. BU 7.1867 Sheerness.

ECLIPSE (ex-SAPPHO) Wood screw sloop, 1,276bm, 1,760 tons, 212 × 36ft, 2—7in, 4—64pdr, Sheerness DY 14.11.1867 (renamed 1867). Lent War Dept as hulk 1888–92. On sale list 1921.

ECLIPSE 2nd class cruiser, 5,600 tons, 350 × 53ft, 5—6in, 6—4·7in (1904: 11—6in). Portsmouth DY 19.7.1894. Sold 8.1921 G. Cohen.

ECLIPSE Destroyer, 1,375 tons, 329 (oa) × 33·5ft, 4—4·7in, 8—TT. Denny 12.4.1934. Sunk 24.10.1943 mine Aegean.

ECLIPSE *See also EAGLE 1803.*

EDDERTON Coastal minesweeper, 'Ton' class. Doig 1.11.1952. = MYRMIDON (survey vessel) 4.1964. Tx Malaysia = PERANTAU 3.1969; deleted 1990.

EDEN 6th Rate 24, 451bm, 108·5 × 31ft. Courtney, Chester, 19.5.1814. BU 5.1833. *Left submerged in Hamoaze 11.1816–3.1817 to test effect of sea water on dry rot.*

EDEN Destroyer, 555 tons, 220 × 23ft, 1—12pdr, 5—6pdr (1907: 3—12pdr) 2—TT. Hawthorn 14.3.1903. Sunk 18.6.1916 collision SS *France* in English Channel.

EDGAR 3rd Rate 70, 1,046bm, 154 × 40ft. Bailey, Bristol, 29.7.1668. Rebuilt Portsmouth 1700 as 1,119bm. Burnt 10.1711 accident Spithead.

EDGAR 4th Rate 60, 1,297bm, 155 × 44ft. Randall, Rotherhithe, 16.11.1758. Sunk 8.1774 breakwater Sheerness.

EDGAR 3rd Rate 74, 1,644bm, 168 × 47ft. Woolwich DY 30.6.1779. Convict hulk 12.1813; = RETRIBUTION 19.8.1814. BU 2.1835 Deptford.

EDGAR 2nd Rate 80, 2,600bm. Chatham DY; launched as screw ship, 3,308bm, 4.5.1859. = HOOD 29.6.1848. *See HOOD 1848.*

EDGAR Screw 2nd rate 91, 3,094bm, 5,157 tons, 230 × 55·5ft, 8—10in, 36—8in, 2—68pdr, 34—

32pdr. Woolwich DY 23.10.1858. Lent Customs Service as hulk 12.2.1870. Sold 12.4.1904 Castle, Charlton.

EDGAR 1st class cruiser, 7,350 tons, 360 × 60ft, 2—9·2in, 10—6in, 12—6pdr. Devonport DY 24.11.1890. Sold 9.5.1921 Ward; arr. 3.4.1923 Morecambe for BU.

EDGAR Aircraft carrier, 13,350 tons, 630 × 80ft, Vickers Armstrong, Tyne, 26.3.1944. = PERSEUS 6.1944, comp. maintenance carrier. Arr. 6.5.1958 Smith & Houston, Port Glasgow, for BU.

EDGAR Cruiser, c. 9,000 tons. Projected 1945, cancelled 3.1946.

EDGELEY Inshore minehunter, 'Ley' class. Dorset Yacht Co., Poole. *Launched as WRENTHAM (q.v.).*

EDINBURGH (ex-ROYAL WILLIAM) 5th Rate 32, 364bm, 99 × 29ft. Scottish, tx 5.8.1707. Sunk 10.8.1709 breakwater Harwich.

EDINBURGH 3rd Rate 74, 1,772bm, 176·5 × 49ft. Brent, Rotherhithe, 26.1.1811; undocked 31.12.1846 as screw ship. Sold 11.1865 Castle & Beech.

EDINBURGH (ex-MAJESTIC) Turret ship, 9,420 tons, 325 × 68ft, 4—12in, 5—6in, 4—6pdr. Pembroke Dock 18.3.1882 (renamed 16.3.1882). Sold 11.10.1910 Ward, Swansea and Briton Ferry.

EDINBURGH Cruiser, 10,000 tons, 613 (oa) × 63·3ft, 12—6in, 12—4in. Swan Hunter 31.3.1939. Torpedoed 30.4.1942, scuttled 2.5.1942 Barents Sea.

EDINBURGH Destroyer, Type 42 Batch 3, 3,550 tons. Cammell Laird 14.4.1982.

EDINBURGH *See also WARSPITE 1666.*

EDLINGHAM Inshore minesweeper, 'Ham' class. Weatherhead, Cockenzie, 21.7.1955. Burnt 29.9.1956 accident Haslar Creek; wreck sold 8.8.1957.

EDMONTON MCDV (RCN), 'Kingston' class, 962 tons, 181·4 (oa) × 37·1ft, 1—40mm. Halifax SY 16.8.1996.

EDMUNDSTON Corvette (RCN), 'Flower' class. Yarrow, Vancouver, 22.2.1941. Sold 1946 = *Ampala.*

EDWARD Ship. In service 1338.

EDWARD Ketch 6. Sunk 1667 as blockship.

EDWARD *See also HENRY GRACE A DIEU 1514.*

EFFINGHAM Cruiser, 9,750 tons, 605 (oa) × 65·1ft, 7—7·5in, 4—3in, 6—12pdr. Portsmouth DY 8.6.1921. Wrecked 18.5.1940 between Harstad and Bodo, Norway; wreck destroyed 21.5.1940.

EGERIA 6th Rate 26, 424bm, 108·5 × 30ft. Boole, Bridport, 31.10.1807. Harbour service 1825. BU 1865.

EGERIA Composite screw sloop, 940 tons, 160 × 31·5ft, 2—7in, 2—64pdr. Pembroke Dock 1.11.1873. Survey ship 10.1886. Sold 10.1911 Vancouver Navy League.

EGERIA Survey vessel, 160 tons, 106·4 (oa) × 22ft. Weatherhead, Cockenzie, 13.9.1958. Lent 10.12.86 Marine Society = *Jonas Hanway.* Ret. RN 1998, sold 7.1998 to Sutton Smit, Great Wakering, for poss. use as diving support vessel.

EGGESFORD Destroyer, 'Hunt' class Type III. White 12.9.1942. Sold 11.1957 West German Navy = BROMMY. BU 1979.

EGLANTINE Sloop, 'Anchusa' class. Barclay Curle 22.6.1917. Sold 1.12.1921 Stanlee, Dover.

EGLANTINE Corvette, 'Flower' class. Harland & Wolff 11.6.1941. Lent RNorN 29.8.1941. Sold 1946.

EGLINTON Paddle minesweeper, 'Ascot' class. Ayrshire Co. 9.9.1916. Sold 7.1922 King, Garston.

EGLINTON Destroyer, 'Hunt' class Type I. Vickers Armstrong, Tyne, 28.12.1939. Arr. 28.5.1956 Hughes Bolckow, Blyth, for BU.

EGMONT Schooner, 100bm, 62 × 20ft. Purch. 3.1765. Lost 12.7.1776.

EGMONT 3rd Rate 74, 1,648bm, 169 × 47ft. Deptford DY 29.8.1768. BU 11.1799 Chatham.

EGMONT Schooner 10, 199bm. Purch. 1770. Captured 7.1779 by American privateer WILD CAT off Newfoundland.

EGMONT 3rd Rate 74, 1,760bm, 178 × 49ft. Pitcher, Northfleet, 7.3.1810. Storeship 12.1862. Sold 2.1.1875 Rio de Janeiro.

EGMONT *For base ships with this name see ACHILLES 1863, FIREFLY 1877, BULLFROG 1881.*

EGREMONT *See ACHILLES 1863.*

EGREMONT CASTLE Corvette, 'Castle' class. Kingston SY, cancelled 12.1943.

EGRET Sloop, 1,200 tons, 276 × 37·5ft, 8—4in. White 31.5.1938. Sunk 27.8.1943 air attack Bay of Biscay.

EHKOLI Patrol boat (RCN), 84 × 20ft, 1—MG. Victoria Boat & Repair Co. 3.9.1941. Survey vessel 1951.

EIDEREN Sloop 18, 336bm. Danish, captured 7.9.1807 Battle of Copenhagen. BU 6.1813. *Was to have been renamed UTILE.*

EKINS Frigate, TE 'Captain' class. Bethlehem, Higham, 2.10.1943 on Lend-Lease. Badly damaged by mine 16.4.1945; nominally ret. USN 6.1945. BU 1947 Dordrecht.

EL CORSO Brig-sloop 14, 234bm, 90·5 × 24·5ft. Spanish, captured 2.12.1796 by SOUTHAMPTON in Mediterranean. Harbour service 3.1803. Sold 1.9.1814.

EL VIVO Sloop 14, 216bm, 81 × 26ft, 14—18pdr. Spanish, captured 30.9.1800 by FISGARD off coast of Spain. Sold 7.9.1801.

ELEANOR Fireship, 193bm, 85·5 × 24ft. Purch. 22.6.1739. Sunk 5.1742 breakwater Sheerness.

ELECTRA Brig-sloop 16, 285bm, 93 × 26ft. Betts, Mistleythorn, 22.1.1806. Stranded 25.3.1808 coast of Sicily; salved, sold 1808 in Malta.

ELECTRA (ex-ESPIEGLE) Brig-sloop 16, 315bm, 94 × 28ft. French, captured 16.8.1808 by SYBILLE in Atlantic. Sold 11.7.1816.

ELECTRA Sloop 18, 462bm, 113·5 × 31ft. Portsmouth DY 28.9.1837. Sold 17.2.1862 W. Foord.

ELECTRA Destroyer, 385 tons, 218 × 20ft, 1—12pdr, 5—6pdr, 2—TT. Thomson 14.7.1896. Sold 29.4.1920 Barking S. Bkg Co.

ELECTRA Destroyer, 1,375 tons, 329 (oa) × 33·5ft, 4—4·7in, 8—TT. Hawthorn Leslie 15.2.1934. Sunk 27.2.1942 by Japanese cruiser JINTSU Battle of Java Sea.

ELEPHANT Storeship, 314bm, 102 × 26·5ft. French vessel, captured; purch. 5.1705. Hulked 6.1709 Port Mahon.

ELEPHANT (ex-*Union*) Storeship 10, 382bm, 103 × 29ft, 10—4pdr. Purch. 17.7.1776. Sold 2.12.1779 Greenock.

ELEPHANT 3rd Rate 74, 1617bm, 168 × 47·5ft. Parsons, Bursledon, 24.8.1786. Reduced to 58-gun 4th Rate 3.1818. BU 11.1830.

ELEPHANT *See also MINOTAUR 1863, HERMES 1953.*

ELF (ex-*Rainbow*) Tender, 180 tons, 115 × 18ft. Purch. 1911. Sold 6.1924 W. G. Keen.

ELFIN Paddle yacht, 98bm (built of Spanish mahogany). Chatham DY 8.2.1849. On sale list 1901.

ELFIN (ex-*Dundas*) Tender, 125 tons, 98 × 17·5ft. War Dept vessel, tx 1905. Sold 29.2.1928 Ward, Pembroke Dock.

ELFIN Tender, 222 tons, 102 × 26ft. White 20.11.1933. = NETTLE 28.8.1941. On sale list 1957.

ELFREDA (ex-OVERSEER) Minesweeper, 'Catherine' class. Associated SB, Seattle, 25.1.1943; on Lend-Lease from 22.12.1943. Ret. USN. Sold 3.1947 Turkish Navy = CESMI. Withdrawn 1974.

ELGIN Armed ship. In service 1814.

ELGIN (ex-TROON) Minesweeper, Later 'Hunt' class. Simons 3.3.1919 (renamed 1918). Sold 20.3.1945, BU King, Gateshead.

ELIAS 32-gun ship, 406bm. Captured 1653. Foundered 1664.

ELIAS Hulk, 350bm. Spanish ship, captured 1656. Sold 1684.

ELIAS 34-gun ship, 301bm. Captured 1666. Sold 1667.

ELING Gunvessel 12, 149bm, 80·5 × 22·5ft, 12—18pdr carr. Purch. 4.1798. BU 5.1814.

ELIZABETH (GREAT ELIZABETH; ex-*Salvator*) 900bm. Purch. 1514. Wrecked 1514.

ELIZABETH 16-gun vessel, 40bm. In service 1577—88.

ELIZABETH 32-gun ship, 474/643bm. Deptford 1647. Burnt 1667 in action with Dutch in Virginia.

ELIZABETH Hoy. Royalist, purch. 1648. Deserted 1649 to Parliamentarians. Sold 1653.

ELIZABETH 3rd Rate 70, 1,073bm, 152 × 41ft, 26—32pdr, 26—12pdr, 18 small. Castle, Deptford, 1679. Rebuilt Portsmouth 1784 as 1,152bm. Captured 12.11.1704 by French.

ELIZABETH 3rd Rate 70, 1,110bm, 150·5 × 41ft. Stacey, Woolwich, 1.8.1706. Rebuilt Chatham 1737 as 1,224bm, 64 guns. BU comp. 10.5.1766 Portsmouth.

ELIZABETH 3rd Rate 74, 1,617bm, 168 × 47ft. Portsmouth DY 17.10.1769. BU 8.1797 Chatham.

ELIZABETH Gunvessel 3, 50bm. Purch. 7.1795. In service 1801.

ELIZABETH Cutter 10, 110bm. Spanish, captured 3.4.1805 by BACCHANTE off Havana. Foundered 1807 West Indies.

ELIZABETH Schooner 12, 141bm, 73 × 21·5ft. French, captured 1806. Capsized 10.1814.

ELIZABETH 3rd Rate 74, 1,724bm, 174 × 48·5ft. Perry, Blackwall, 23.5.1807. BU 8.1820 Chatham.

ELIZABETH & SARAH Fireship 6, 100bm. Purch. 1688. Sunk 1690 foundation Sheerness.

ELIZABETH BONAVENTURE Galleon 47, 600bm, 2—60pdr, 2—32pdr, 11—18pdr, 14—9pdr, 4—6pdr, 14 small. Built 1567. Rebuilt 1581. BU 1611.

ELIZABETH JONAS Galleon 56, 680bm, 3—60pdr, 6—32pdr, 8—18pdr, 9—9pdr, 9—6pdr, 21 small. Woolwich 3.7.1559. Rebuilt 1598 = ELIZABETH. Sold 1618.

ELK Brig-sloop 18 (fir-built), 'Cruizer' class, 382bm. Barnard, Deptford, 22.8.1804. BU 10.1812.

ELK Brig-sloop 18, 'Cruizer' class, 386bm. Hobbs & Hillyer, Redbridge, 28.8.1813. Sold 21.1.1836.

ELK Brig-sloop 16, 482bm, 105 × 33·5ft, 4—32pdr, 12—32pdr carr. Chatham DY 27.9.1847. = WV.13 (Coastguard) 1863; = WV.28 on 25.5.1863. Sold 30.5.1893.

ELK Composite screw gunvessel, 465bm, 603 tons, 155 × 25ft, 1—7in, 1—64pdr, 2—20pdr. Portsmouth DY 10.1.1868. Tug 1890. Sold 1905 as dredger.

ELLINOR (ex-*Eberhard*) Survey ship, 593grt, 180 (oa) × 27ft. Screw yacht, purch. 1901. *Fate unknown.*

ELLINORE *See BONAVOLIA 1584.*

ELPHINSTONE Sloop 18 (Indian), 387bm. Bombay DY 1824. Sold 7.1862.

ELPHINSTONE (ex-*Hindoo*) Troopship (RIM), 950 tons, 206 × 28ft. Swan Hunter 14.11.1887, purch. 1887. On sale list 1919.

ELPHINSTONE *See also CEANOTHUS 1917.*

ELSENHAM Inshore minesweeper, 'Ham' class. Ailsa 25.5.1955. Sold 9.10.1967 Arabian Federation; deleted 1984.

ELTHAM (ex-PORTSMOUTH?) 5th Rate 44, 678bm, 124 × 36ft. Deptford 1736. BU 6.1763 Plymouth.

ELVIN Sloop 18. Danish, captured 1807. Sold 3.11.1814. *Was to have been renamed HARLEQUIN.*

EMBLETON *See BOSSINGTON 1955.*

EMERALD (ex-EMERAUDE) 6th Rate 28, 571bm, 115·5 × 34ft, 24–pdr, 4–4pdr. French, captured 21.9.1757 by SOUTHAMPTON. BU 11.1761 Portsmouth.

EMERALD 5th Rate 32, 681bm, 125 × 35·5ft. Blaydes, Hull, 8.6.1762. BU 1793.

EMERALD 5th Rate 36, 934bm, 143 × 38·5ft. Pitcher, Northfleet, 31.7.1795. BU 1.1836.

EMERALD Tender, 86bm, 58 × 19ft. Purch. 1820. BU 12.1847.

EMERALD Wood screw frigate 51, 2,913bm, 237 × 52·5ft. 30–8in, 1–68pdr, 20–32pdr. Deptford DY 19.7.1856 (conv. from 4th Rate 60, 2,146bm). Sold 2.12.1869 Castle, Charlton.

EMERALD Composite screw corvette, 2,120 tons, 220 × 40ft, 12–6pdr. Pembroke Dock 18.8.1876. Powder hulk 1898. Sold 10.7.1906 Cox, Falmouth.

EMERALD Light cruiser, 7,600 tons, 571·5 (oa) × 54·5ft, 7–6in, 2–4in. Armstrong 19.5.1920, comp. Chatham 14.1.1926. Sold 23.7.1948; BU Troon.

EMERALD *See also BLACK PRINCE 1861, AMELIA 1888.*

EMERSHAM Wood paddle vessel. Purch. 1830. Sold 1833.

EMILIA Brig. Brazilian slaver, captured 1840, purch. 29.12.1840. *Fate unknown.*

EMILIEN *See TRINCOMALE 1801.*

EMILY Schooner 2 (Indian), 90bm. Bombay DY 1855. Sold 7.1862.

EMPEROR Paddle yacht. Purch. 1856, cd 25.2.1857. Sold 7.1858; later to Japan = BANRYU.

EMPEROR (ex-PYBUS) Escort carrier, 11,420 tons, 468·5 × 69·5ft, 2–4in, 16–40mm, 24 aircraft.

Seattle, Tacoma, 7.10.1942, tx RN 6.8.1943 on Lend-Lease. Ret. USN 12.2.1946.

EMPEROR (ex-NASSUK DAY) Escort carrier, 7,800 tons. Oregon SB Co., LD 19.4.1943 for RN; retained USN, launched 6.10.1943 as SOLOMONS.

EMPEROR OF INDIA (ex-DELHI) Battleship, 25,000 tons, 580 × 89·5ft, 10–13·5in, 14–6in. Vickers 27.11.1913 (renamed 10.1913). Target 1931. Sold 6.2.1932 Metal Industries, Rosyth.

EMPEROR OF INDIA Paddle vessel. Req. 1916–20, 1939–46.

EMPIRE *See REVENGE 1859.*

EMPIRE ANVIL (ex-*Cape Argos*) Landing ship, 11,650 tons, 396 × 60ft, 1–4in, 1–12pdr, 12–20mm. Consolidated Steel Corp., Wilmington, 14.10.1943. = ROCKSAND 11.1944. Ret. USN 6.1946.

EMPIRE ARQUEBUS (ex-*Cape St Vincent*) Landing ship, 11,650 tons, 396 × 60ft, 1–4in, 1–12pdr, 12–20mm. Consolidated Steel Corp., Wilmington, 16.11.1943. = CICERO 1.1945; = *Empire Arquebus* (MWT) 9.10.1945. Tx Egypt mercantile 11.1946 = *Al Sudan*. BU 1987–88.

EMPIRE BATTLEAXE (ex-*Cape Berkeley*) Landing ship, 11,650 tons, 396 × 60ft, 1–4in, 1–12pdr, 12–20mm. Consolidated Steel Corp., Wilmington, 12.7.1943. = DONOVAN 1945; = *Empire Battleaxe* (MWT) 1946. Ret. USN 1947.

EMPIRE BROADSWORD (ex-*Cape Marshall*) Landing ship, 11,650 tons, 396 × 60ft, 1–4in, 1–12pdr, 12–20mm. Consolidated Steel Corp., Wilmington, 16.8.1943. Sunk 2.7.1944 mine off Normandy.

EMPIRE COMFORT (ex-YORK CASTLE) Rescue ship, ex-'Castle' class corvette. Ferguson 20.9.1944 (renamed 1944). Sold 7.1955.

EMPIRE CROSSBOW (ex-*Cape Washington*) Landing ship, 11,650 tons, 396 × 60ft, 1–4in, 1–12pdr, 12–20mm. Consolidated Steel Corp., Wilmington, 30.11.1943. = SAINFOIN 11.1944. Ret. USN 9.1946.

EMPIRE CUTLASS (ex-*Cape Compass*) Landing ship, 11,650 tons, 396 × 60ft, 1–4in, 1–12pdr, 12–20mm. Consolidated Steel Corp., Wilmington, 29.7.1943. = SANSOVINO 1945; = *Empire Cutlass* (MWT) 6.1946. Ret. USN 1947.

EMPIRE GAUNTLET (ex-*Cape Comorin*) Landing ship, 11,650 tons, 396 × 60ft, 1–4in, 1–12pdr, 12–20mm. Consolidated Steel Corp., Wilmington, 23.11.1943. = SEFTON 10.1944. Ret. USN 9.1946.

EMPIRE HALBERD (ex-*Cape Gregory*) Landing ship, 11,650 tons, 396 × 60ft, 1–4in, 1–12pdr,

12—20mm. Consolidated Steel Corp., Wilmington, 24.7.1943. = SILVIO 12.1944; = *Empire Halberd* (MWT) 1946. Ret. USN 6.1948.

EMPIRE JAVELIN (ex-*Cape Lobos*) Landing ship, 11,650 tons, 396 × 60ft, 1—4in, 1—12pdr, 12—20mm. Consolidated Steel Corp., Wilmington, 25.10.1943. Sunk 28.12.1944 by U-boat in English Channel.

EMPIRE LANCE (ex-*Cape Pine*) Landing ship, 11,650 tons, 396 × 60ft, 1—4in, 1—12pdr, 12—20mm. Consolidated Steel Corp., Wilmington, 28.8.1943. = SIR HUGO 8.1945; = *Empire Lance* 1945. Ret. USN 1946.

EMPIRE MACE (ex-*Cape St Roque*) Landing ship, 11,650 tons, 396 × 60ft, 1—4in, 1—12pdr, 12—20mm. Consolidated Steel Corp., Wilmington, 8.9.1943. = GALTEE MORE 1.1945; = *Empire Mace* (MWT) 9.10.1945. Tx Egypt mercantile 11.1946 = *Misr*. Listed until 1982.

EMPIRE PEACEMAKER (ex-SCARBOROUGH CASTLE) Rescue ship, ex-'Castle' class corvette. Fleming & Ferguson 8.9.1944 (renamed 1944). Sold 7.1955; BU Belgium.

EMPIRE RAPIER (ex-*Cape Turner*) Landing ship, 11,650 tons, 396 × 60ft, 1—4in, 1—12pdr, 12—20mm. Consolidated Steel Corp., Wilmington, 21.9.1943. = *Empire Rapier* (MWT) 1945. Ret. USN 1946. *Was to have been renamed SIR VISTO.*

EMPIRE REST (ex-RAYLEIGH CASTLE) Rescue ship, ex-'Castle' class corvette. Ferguson 19.6.1944 (renamed 1944). Arr. 5.6.1952 Ward, Briton Ferry, for BU.

EMPIRE SHELTER (ex-BARNARD CASTLE) Rescue ship, ex-'Castle' class corvette. G. Brown 5.10.1944 (renamed 1944). BU 1955 Belgium.

EMPIRE SPEARHEAD (ex-*Cape Girardeau*) Landing ship, 11,650 tons, 396 × 60ft, 1—4in, 1—12pdr, 12—20mm. Consolidated Steel Corp., Wilmington, 7.11.1943. = ORMONDE 1945; = *Empire Spearhead* (MWT) 1945. Ret. USN 8.1947.

EMPRESS Tender, 100 tons. 77 × 15.5ft. War Dept. vessel, tx 1906. = HERON 25.11.1906. Sold 20.9.1923.

EMPRESS Seaplane carrier, 1,960 tons. Req. 1914–19. Paddle vessel 1939–44.

EMPRESS (ex-*Carnegie*) Escort carrier, 11,420 tons, 468.5 × 69.5ft, 2—4in, 16—40mm, 24 aircraft. Seattle, Tacoma, 30.12.1942 on Lend-Lease. Ret. USN 4.2.1946.

EMPRESS MARY Storeship 16, 650bm, 123 × 34ft. Purch. 17.4.1799. Sunk 1804 breakwater Harwich.

EMPRESS OF INDIA (ex-RENOWN) Battleship, 14,150 tons, 380 × 75ft, 4—13.5in, 10—6in, 16—6pdr. Pembroke Dock 7.5.1891 (renamed 1890). Sunk 41.11.1913 target Start Bay.

EMSWORTH Ketch 4, 40bm. Emsworth 1667. Sold 1683.

EMULOUS Brig-sloop 18, 'Cruizer' class, 384bm. Rowe, Newcastle, 6.1806. Wrecked 7.8.1812 Sable I.

EMULOUS (ex-NAUTILUS) Sloop 14, 213bm. American, captured 6.7.1812 by SHANNON. Sold 8.1817.

EMULOUS Brig-sloop 10, 'Cherokee' class, 235bm. Plymouth DY 16.12.1819. Coastguard 1841. Sold 1864 M. Sargent.

ENARD BAY (ex-LOCH BRACADALE) Frigate, 'Bay' class. Smith's Dock 31.10.1944 (renamed 1944). Arr. 15.11.1957 Faslane for BU.

ENCHANTRESS Sloop 14, 176bm, 80 × 23ft, 14—6pdr. Purch. 1804. Harbour service 6.1813. Listed until 8.1818.

ENCHANTRESS Wood screw sloop, 992bm, 185 × 34.5ft. Pembroke Dock, ordered 1847, cancelled 4.4.1851.

ENCHANTRESS Sloop. Slaver, captured 10.8.1860. by BRISK. Wrecked 20.2.1861 Mozambique Channel. *Was to have been cd in RN.*

ENCHANTRESS Wood paddle despatch vessel, 835bm, 1,000 tons, 220 × 28ft, 2—20pdr. Pembroke Dock 2.8.1862. Sold 1889 Read, Portsmouth, for BU.

ENCHANTRESS Screw yacht, 3,470 tons, 320 × 40ft, 4—3pdr. Harland & Wolff 7.11.1903. Sold 24.6.1935; BU 7.1935 Blyth.

ENCHANTRESS (ex-BITTERN) Sloop, 1,190 tons, 282 (oa) × 37ft, 4—4.7in. John Brown 21.12.1934 (renamed 1934). Sold 1946 = *Lady Enchantress*. Arrived Dunston 16.2.1952 for BU.

ENCHANTRESS *See also HELICON 1865.*

ENCOUNTER Discovery vessel. In service 1616.

ENCOUNTER Gun-brig 12, 185bm, 84.5 × 22.5ft, 10—18pdr carr., 2—12pdr. Guillaume, Northam, 16.5.1805. Wrecked 11.7.1812 off San Lucar, Spain.

ENCOUNTER Wood screw corvette, 953bm, 190 × 33ft. Pembroke Dock 24.9.1846. BU 5.1866 Plymouth.

ENCOUNTER Wood screw corvette, 1,970 tons, 220 × 37ft, 14—64pdr. Sheerness DY 1.1.1873. Sold 10.1888.

ENCOUNTER 2nd class cruiser, 5,880 tons, 355 × 56ft, 11—6in, 9—12pdr. Devonport DY 18.6.1902. RAN 12.1919; = PENGUIN (depot ship) 5.1923. Hull scuttled 9.1932 off Sydney.

ENCOUNTER Destroyer, 1,375 tons, 329 (oa) × 33·5ft, 4—4·7in, 8—TT. Hawthorn Leslie 29.3.1934. Sunk 1.3.1942 by Japanese squadron in Java Sea.

ENDEAVOUR 36-gun ship. Purch. 1652. Sold 1656.

ENDEAVOUR Bomb vessel 4, 60bm. Purch. 11.4.1694. Sold 1696.

ENDEAVOUR Firevessel, 18bm, 34 × 12ft. Purch. 1694. Sold 1696.

ENDEAVOUR Storeship hoy, 18bm, 33 × 12ft. Purch. 1694. Sold 20.7.1705.

ENDEAVOUR Cutter, 55bm. Purch. 11.1763. Sold 24.12.1771.

ENDEAVOUR Sloop 14. Purch. 1763. Foundered 11.10.1780 hurricane off Jamaica.

ENDEAVOUR Schooner 10. Purch. 1775. Sold 1782.

ENDEAVOUR Survey ship, 1,280 tons, 200 × 34ft, 1—3pdr. Fairfield 30.3.1912. Depot ship 1940. Sold 30.9.1946.

ENDEAVOUR (ex-*John Biscoe*, ex-PRETEXT) Antarctic support ship (RNZN), 1,058 tons, 172 × 34·5ft. Purch. and renamed 15.8.1956. Sold 1962.

ENDEAVOUR (ex-NAMAKUGON) Antarctic support ship (RNZN), 1,850 tons, 292 (wl) × 48·5ft. Tx 1962. Ret. USN 6.1971; tx Taiwan = *Lung Chuan*.

ENDEAVOUR Research ship (RCN), 1,560 tons, 215 × 38·5ft. Yarrow, Esquimalt, 4.9.1964.

ENDEAVOUR Replenishment ship (RNZN), 12,390 tons, 453 (oa) × 60ft. Hyundai, South Korea, 14.8.1988.

ENDEAVOUR BARK (ex-*Earl of Pembroke*) Discovery ship 6, 366bm, 100 × 29ft, 6—4pdr. Purch. 3.1768. Sold 7.3.1775.

ENDEAVOUR TRANSPORT Storeship, 211bm. Plymouth DY 1708. Sold 30.7.1713.

ENDURANCE (ex-*Anita Dart*) Antarctic support ship, 2,641grt, 298 (oa) × 46ft. Denmark 5.1956, purch. 1967 (renamed 8.1967). PO 21.11.1991; sold mercantile Incom Ship Trading, arr. Karachi 11.1.1993.

ENDURANCE (ex-POLAR CIRCLE) Antarctic patrol ship, 6,500 tons, 298·6 (oa) × 57·4ft.Ulstein Hatlo, Helsinki, 1990. Leased 1991, cd 21.11.1991, purch. 9.10.1992 (renamed 1992).

ENDYMION 5th Rate 44, 893bm, 140 × 38ft, Graves, Limehouse, 28.8.1779. Wrecked 20.8.1790 Turks Is.

ENDYMION 4th Rate 50, 1,277bm 159·5 × 43ft. Randal, Rotherhithe, 29.3.1797. Harbour service 1860. BU comp. 18.8.1868 Devonport.

ENDYMION Wood screw frigate, 2,486bm 240 ×

48ft. Deptford DY 18.11.1865. Sold 1885 as hulk; BU 1905.

ENDYMION 1st class cruiser, 7,350 tons, 360 × 60ft, 2—9·2in, 10—6in, 12—6pdr. Earl 22.7.1891. Sold 16.3.1920 Evans, Cardiff.

ENDYMION *See also HASTINGS 1740.*

ENGADINE Seaplane carrier, 1,676 tons. Req. 1914—19.

ENGADINE Aircraft transport, 10,700 tons, 464 × 63ft, 2—4in, 12—20mm, 40 aircraft. Denny 26.5.1941. Tx MWT 6.7.1945. Sold 1946 = *Clan Buchanan*

ENGADINE Helicopter support ship, 8,000 tons, 424 (oa) × 58ft, 6 helo. Robb 16.9.1966. Towed Devonport 9.2.1990 to Piraeus; resold sbkrs, arr. Alang 7.2.1996 forBU.

ENGAGEANTE 5th Rate 38, 931bm, 139·5 × 38·7ft. French, captured 23.4.1794 by CONCORDE in English Channel. Harbour service 7.1794. BU 5.1811 Plymouth.

ENGLAND 5th Rate 42, 400bm. Mercantile, hired 1692, purch. 19.8.1693. Sunk 1.2.1695 in action with French off Cape Clear.

ENTERPRISE (ex-ENTERPRISE) 6th Rate 24, 320bm. French, captured 5.1705 in Mediterranean. Wrecked 12.10.1707 off Thornton.

ENTERPRISE 5th Rate 44, 531bm, 118 × 32ft. Lock, Plymouth, 24.4.1709. 'Great repair' Chatham 1718 as 700bm. Hulk 9.1745. Sold 3.4.1749.

ENTERPRISE 6th Rate 28, 594bm, 120·5 × 33·5ft. Deptford 1774. Harbour service 1799. BU 8.1807.

ENTERPRISE Tender 10. Captured 14.5.1775 by Americans in Richelieu R.

ENTERPRISE Wood paddle gunvessel (Indian), 470bm, 133 × 27ft. Gordon, Deptford, 1824, purch. In service 1830.

ENTERPRISE Survey sloop, 471bm, 126 × 28·5ft. Wigram, Blackwall, 5.4.1848. Coal hulk 1860. Sold 15.9.1903.

ENTERPRISE Wood screw sloop, 669bm, 160 × 30ft. Deptford DY, LD 1.5.1861, = CIRCASSIAN 22.7.1862, cancelled 12.12.1863.

ENTERPRISE (ex-CIRCASSIAN) Ironclad sloop, 993bm, 1,530 tons, 180 × 36ft, 2—110pdr, 2—100pdr. Deptford DY 9.2.1864 (renamed 22.7.1862). Sold 11.1886. *Ex-wood screw sloop, as preceding vessel.*

ENTERPRISE Light cruiser, 7,600 tons, 571·5 (oa) × 54·5ft, 7—6in, 2—4in. John Brown 23.12.1919. Sold 11.4.1946; BU Cashmore, Newport.

ENTERPRISE Survey vessel, 120 tons, 100 × 22ft. Blackmore, Bideford, 30.9.1958. Sold 1986.

ENTERPRISE Survey ship, 3,470 tons, 295·3 (oa) × 55·1ft. Appledore SY 2.5.2002.

ENTERPRISE *See also NORWICH 1693, LIVER-POOL 1741, RESOURCE 1778.*

ENTREPRENANTE Cutter, 123bm, 67 × 21·5ft. French, captured (1799?). BU 6.1812.

EPERVIER Brig-sloop 16, 254bm, 94 × 25ft. French privateer, captured 12.11.1797 by CERBERUS off coast of Ireland. Sold 7.9.1801. *Spelt 'EPERVOIR' in some lists.*

EPERVIER Brig-sloop 16, 315bm, 95 × 28·5ft, 16–6pdr. French, captured 27.7.1803 by EGYPTIENNE in Atlantic. BU 6.1811 Chatham.

EPERVIER Brig-sloop, 18, 'Cruizer' class, 388bm. Ross, Rochester, 2.12.1812 Captured 29.4.1814 by American PEACOCK off US East Coast.

EPHIRA Brig-sloop 10, 'Cherokee' class, 237bm. King, Upnor, 28.5.1808. Wrecked 26.12.11 nr Cadiz.

EPHRAIM Firevessel, 170bm. Purch. 1695. Expended 1.8.1695 Dunkirk.

EPINAL Patrol vessel, 644 tons, 246 × 31ft, 2–5·5in. French, seized 3.7.1940 Portsmouth. LU until 1943, then accommodation ship. Ret. French Navy 1945.

EPREUVE Sloop 14, 261bm, 92·5 × 25·5ft, 14–6pdr. French, captured 1760 by NIGER. Foundered 3.1764 Atlantic.

EPSOM Paddle minesweeper, 'Ascot' class. G. Brown 4.5.1916. Sold 3.1922 Ward, Inverkeithing.

EREBUS Rocket vessel, 424bm, 109 × 29·5ft. Owen, Topsham, 20.8.1807. 18-gun sloop 1808, fireship 1809; 24-gun 6th Rate 1810. Sold 22.7.1819 Mr Manlove.

EREBUS Bomb vessel 14, 378bm, 106 × 29ft, 10–24pdr carr., 2–6pdr, 2 mortars. Pembroke Dock 7.6.1826. Screw discovery vessel 1844. Abandoned 22.4.1848 in Arctic. *Listed until 6.1854.*

EREBUS Iron screw floating battery, 1,854bm, 1,954 tons, 187 × 49ft, 16–68pdr. Napier 19.4.1856. Sold 5.1884 for BU.

EREBUS Monitor, 8,000 tons, 380 × 88ft, 2–15in, 8–4in, 2–3in. Harland & Wolff, Govan, 19.6.1916. Arr. 29.1.1947. Ward, Inverkeithing, for BU.

EREBUS *See also INVINCIBLE 1869.*

ERICA Corvette, 'Flower' class. Harland & Wolff 18.6.1940. Sunk 9.2.1943 by mine off Benghazi.

ERIDANUS (ex-LIFFEY) 5th Rate 36 (red pine-built), 945bm, 143 × 38·5ft, 14–32pdr carr. , 26–18pdr. Ross, Rochester, 1.5.1813 (renamed 1812). Sold 29.1.1818 Mr Freake.

ERIDGE Paddle minesweeper, 'Ascot' class, Clyde SB 23.2.1916. Sold 3.1922 Ward, Inverkeithing.

ERIDGE Destroyer, 'Hunt' class Type II. Swan Hunter 20.8.1940. Damaged 8.1942, made base ship. Sold 10.1946 Alexandria.

ERIN (ex-RESHADIEH) Battleship, 23,000 tons, 525 × 91·5ft, 10–13·5in. Vickers 3.9.1913; Turkish, purch. 8.1914. Sold 19.12.1920 Cox & Danks, Queenborough; arr. 2.2.1923 for BU.

ERNE 6th Rate 20, 457bm, 115·5 × 30ft, 18–32pdr carr., 2–9pdr. Newman, Dartmouth, 18.12.1813. Wrecked 1.6.1819 Cape Verde Is.

ERNE Wood screw gunboat, 'Albacore' class. Smith, North Shields, 18.2.1856. BU 1874 Chatham.

ERNE Destroyer, 550 tons, 225 × 23·5ft, 1–12pdr, 5–6pdr, 2–TT. Palmer 14.1.1903. Wrecked 6.2.1915 Rattray Head.

ERNE Sloop, 1,250 tons, 283 × 37·5ft, 6–4in. Furness SB 5.8.1940. = WESSEX (drillship) 4.6.1952. Arr. Antwerp 27.10.1965 for BU.

ERRANT Minesweeper, 'Catherine' class. Associated SB, LD 27.10.1942 for RN; retained USN, launched 25.2.1943 as SPEAR.

ERUPTION (ex-*Unity*) Fireship 4, 74bm, 65·5 × 16·5ft. Purch. 5.1804. Sold 17.6.1807 Mr Freake.

ESCAPADE Destroyer, 1,375 tons, 329 (oa) × 33.5ft, 4–4in, 8–TT. Scotts 30.1.1934. Sold 26.11.1946; arr. Newport 23.2.1947 for BU.

ESCORT Sloop 14, 220bm, 86·5 × 24·5ft. French privateer, captured 1757. Sold 6.12.1768.

ESCORT Gun-brig 12, 184bm, 80 × 22·5ft, 10–18pdr carr., 2–6pdr. Perry, Blackwall, 1.4.1801. Tx Customs Service 8.1815.

ESCORT Wood screw gunboat, 'Albacore' class. Patterson, Bristol, 6.5.1856. BU 10.1865 Pembroke Dock.

ESCORT Destroyer, 1,375 tons, 329 (oa) × 33.5ft, 4–4·7in, 8–TT. Scotts 29.3.1934. Torpedoed 8.7.1940 by Italian submarine MARCONI north of Cyprus, foundered 11.7.1940.

ESK 6th Rate 20, 460bm, 115·5 × 30ft, 18–32pdr carr., 1–12pdr. 2–9pdr. Bailey, Ipswich, 11.10.1813. Sold 8.1.1829.

ESK Wood screw corvette, 1,169bm, 192 × 38·5ft, 20–8in, 1–68pdr. Scott Russell, Millwall, 12.6.1854. BU 1870 Portsmouth.

ESK Iron screw gunboat, 363 tons, 110 × 34ft, 3–64pdr. Palmer 28.4.1877. Sold 4.1903 in Hong Kong.

ESK (ex-*Sir Francis Head*) Tender, 110 tons, 80 × 17ft. War Dept vessel, tx 1905 (renamed 26.11.1906). Sold 6.1920 W. P. Jobson.

ESK Destroyer, 1,375 tons, 329 (oa) × 33·5ft, 4–4·7in, 8–TT. Swan Hunter 19.3.1934. Sunk 31.8.1940 mine north-west of Texel.

ESKDALE Destroyer, 'Hunt' class Type III.

Cammell Laird 16.3.1942. Lent RNorN. Sunk 14.4.1943 by E-boat off The Lizard.

ESKIMO Destroyer, 1,870 tons, 377 (oa) × 36·5ft, 8—4·7in, 4—TT. Vickers Armstrong, Tyne, 3.9.1937. Sold 27.6.1949; BU Troon.

ESKIMO Frigate, Type 81, 2,300 tons, 360 (oa) × 42·5ft, 2—4·5in, 2—40mm, helo, Limbo. White 20.3.1961. Arr. Bilbao 19.5.1992 for BU.

ESPERANCE Sloop. Captured 1626. Given away 1632.

ESPERANCE Sloop 16, 345bm. French, captured 8.1.1795 by ARGONAUT off Chesapeake. Sold 7.6.1798.

ESPERANCE Inshore minesweeper (RAN), 178 tons, 101·7 (oa) × 29·5ft, 2—12·7mm. Projected 1987, not comp.

ESPERANZA *See CLAYOQUOT 1940.*

ESPIEGLE Brig-sloop 16. French, captured 30.11.1793 by NYMPHE and CIRCE off Ushant. Sold 2.1802.

ESPIEGLE Brig-sloop 14, 271bm, 92 × 26ft. French, captured 16.3.1794 by IPHIGENIA in West Indies. Sold 1795.

ESPIEGLE (ex-*Wenbury*) Sloop 16, 305bm, 98 × 27ft. Purch. 6.1804. BU 4.1811 Plymouth.

ESPIEGLE Brig-sloop 18, 'Cruizer' class, 387bm. Bailey, Ipswich, 10.8.1812. Sold 11.1832 T. Ward, Ratcliffe.

ESPIEGLE Brig 12, 443bm, 105 × 32ft, 10—32pdr, 2—18pdr. Chatham DY 20.4.1844. Sold 22.11.1861 Castle & Beech.

ESPIEGLE Composite screw sloop, 1,130 tons, 170 × 36ft, 2—7in, 4—64pdr. Devonport DY 3.8.1880. Boom vessel 1899; = ARGO 3.1904. Sold 25.8.1921 W. Thorpe.

ESPIEGLE Sloop, 1,070 tons, 185 × 33ft, 6—4in, 4—3pdr. Sheerness DY 8.12.1900. Sold 7.9.1923 Bombay. *Last RN ship built with figurehead.*

ESPIEGLE Minesweeper, 'Algerine' class. Harland & Wolff 12.8.1942. BU 1967 Dalmuir.

ESPION Cutter 16. French, captured 24.1.1782. Sold 1784.

ESPION (ex-LE ROBERT) Sloop 16, 275bm. French privateer, captured 13.6.1793. Recaptured 22.7.1794 by French. Recaptured 2.3.1795 = SPY. Sold 7.9.1801.

ESPION (ex-ATALANTE) 5th Rate 36, 986bm, 148 × 39ft, 4—18pdr, 2—18pdr carr., 26—12pdr, 6—6pdr. French, captured 7.5.1794 by SWIFTSURE off Cork. Wrecked 16.11.1799 Goodwin Sands.

ESPION *Name chosen for LITTLE BELT captured 1807. Not used.*

ESPOIR Sloop. Origin unknown. Sold 25.3.1784.

ESPOIR Brig-sloop 14, 251bm, 93 × 25ft, 14—6pdr.

French, captured 11.9.1797 by THALIA in Mediterranean. Sold 9.1804.

ESPOIR Brig-sloop 18, 'Cruizer' class, 385bm. King, Dover, 22.9.1804. BU 4.1821.

ESPOIR Brig-sloop 10, 'Cherokee' class, 233bm. Chatham DY 9.5.1826. Sold 1857.

ESPOIR Wood screw gunvessel, 428bm, 145 × 25·5ft, 1—68pdr, 4—24pdr howitzers. Pembroke Dock 7.1.1860. = YC.19 (dredger) 1869. BU 6.1881 Bermuda.

ESPOIR Composite screw gunvessel, 465 tons, 125 × 23·5ft, 2—64pdr, 2—20pdr. Barrow SB (Vickers) 2.11.1880. Tug 1895. On sale list 1903.

ESPOIR Minesweeper, 'Catherine' class. Associated SB, LD 27.10.1942 for RN; retained USN = TRIUMPH.

ESQUIMALT Minesweeper (RCN), diesel 'Bangor' class. Marine Industries 31.8.1941. Sunk 16.4.1945 by U.190 off Halifax.

ESSEX 60-gun ship, 652bm. Deptford 1653. Captured 6.1666 by French in 'Four Days' Battle'.

ESSEX 3rd Rate 70, 1,059bm, 150 × 40ft. Johnson, Blackwall, 1679. Rebuilt Rotherhithe 1700 as 1,090bm; rebuilt Woolwich 1740 as 1,226bm, 64 guns. Wrecked 21.11.1759 in action Quiberon Bay.

ESSEX 3rd Rate 64, 1,380bm, 158 × 45ft. Wells & Stanton, Rotherhithe, 28.8.1760. Harbour service 1.1777. Sold 22.8.1799.

ESSEX 5th Rate 42, 867bm, 139 × 37·5ft. American, captured 28.3.1814 by PHOEBE off Valparaiso. Convict ship 10.1823. Sold 6.7.1837.

ESSEX Armoured cruiser, 9,800 tons, 440 × 66ft, 14—6in, 9—12pdr. Pembroke Dock 29.8.1901. Sold 8.11.1921 Slough Trading Co.; BU Germany.

ESSEX PRIZE Sloop 16, 152bm, 75 × 22·5ft. French, captured 16.7.1694. Sold 1.10.1702 Deptford.

ESSINGTON Frigate, DE 'Captain' class. Mare Island, LD 30.4.1942 for RN; retained USN = HAROLD C. THOMAS.

ESSINGTON Frigate, TE 'Captain' class. Bethlehem, Hingham, 19.6.1943 on Lend-Lease. Ret. USN 10.1945.

ESSINGTON Coastal minesweeper, 'Ton' class. Camper & Nicholson 9.1954. Tx Malaysian Navy = KINABALU 1964. BU 1980.

ESTHER Cutter 6, 101bm, 50 × 24ft. Purch. 1763. Sold 12.6.1779 J. Linney.

ESTHER Survey vessel, 510 tons, 125·5 × 22·5ft. Duthie Torry 22.11.1911 (ex-trawler), purch. 2.1911. Minesweeper 9.1914. Sold 25.10.1919.

ESTRIDGE (ex-*Vogetstruys*) Careening hulk, 811bm. Dutch, captured 1653. Sunk 1679 foundation Sheerness.

ETCHINGHAM Inshore minesweeper, 'Ham' class.
Ailsa 9.12.1957. Sold 1967 in Hong Kong for BU.

ETHALION 5th Rate 38, 992bm, 146 × 36ft.
Graham, Harwich, 14.3.1797. Wrecked 25.12.1799
Penmarks.

ETHALION 5th Rate 36, 996bm, 152·5 × 38ft.
Woolwich DY 29.7.1802. Harbour service 9.1823;
lent 5.1835 Harwich Corporation as breakwater.
Listed until 6.1877.

ETHALION *See also MARS 1944.*

ETNA (ex-*Charlotte*) Fireship 8, 316bm, 98·5 ×
27ft. Purch. 10.11.1756. Sloop 12.1756. Sold
15.2.1763.

ETNA (ex-*Borryan*) Fireship 8, 294bm, 94·5 ×
27ft. Purch. 1.1771. = SCORPION (sloop)
10.8.1771. Sold 27.12.1780 North America.

ETNA (ex-ETNA) 6th Rate 20, 564bm, 119·5 × 33ft.
French, captured 13.11.1796 by MELAMPUS and
CHILDERS off coast of France. = CORMORANT
1797. Wrecked 20.5.1800 coast of Egypt.

ETNA *See also AETNA.*

ETRUSCO Storeship 24, 918bm, 137·5 × 38·5ft.
Purch. 1794. Foundered 15.8.1798 passage from
West Indies.

ETTRICK Destroyer, 550 tons, 225 × 23·5ft, 1–
12pdr, 5–6pdr (1907: 3–12pdr), 2–TT. Palmer
28.2.1903. Sold 27.5.1919 James Dredging Co.

ETTRICK Frigate, 'River' class. Crown, 5.2.1943.
Lent RCN 29.1.1944–30.5.1945. BU 6.1953 Ward,
Grays.

ETTRICK *See also TAMARISK 1941.*

EUGENIE (ex-LA NOUVELLE EUGENIE) Sloop
16, 241bm, 85 × 26ft, 16–6pdr. French privateer,
captured 1.5.1797. Sold 3.1.1803 Blackheath for
BU.

EUGENIE (ex-*Friends*) Sloop 16, 273bm, 90·5 ×
26ft, 14–18pdr carr., 2–9pdr. Purch. 6.1804.
Sold 22.12.1810.

EUPHRATES (ex-GREYHOUND) 5th Rate 36 (red
pine-built), 943bm,143·5 × 38·5ft, 14–32pdr
carr., 26–18pdr. King, Upnor, 8.11.1813 (renamed
7.12.1812). Sold 29.1.1818 W. Thomas.

EUPHRATES Brig 10 (Indian), 255bm. Bombay
DY 30.6.1828.

EUPHRATES 5th Rate 46, 1,215bm, 159 × 42ft.
Portsmouth DY, LD with teak frames in Bombay,
cancelled 7.2.1831.

EUPHRATES Paddle gunboat, 179bm. Laird, re-
erected 9.1834 R. Euphrates. *Fate unknown.*

EUPHRATES Wood screw frigate, 1,556bm, 210 ×
40·5ft. Deptford DY, LD 1847, cancelled 1849.

EUPHRATES Iron screw troopship, 4,173bm,
6,211 tons, 360 × 49ft, 3–4pdr. Laird 24.11.1866.
Sold 23.11.1894 Portsmouth.

EUPHRATES Light cruiser, 7,600 tons, 535 ×
54·5ft, 7–6in. Fairfield, LD 1918, cancelled 9.1919.

EUPHROSYNE Fireship 14, 125bm. Purch. 1796.
Sold 1802.

EUROPA Hulk, 406bm. Dutch ship, captured
5.1673. Burnt 1675 accident Malta.

EUROPA 3rd Rate 64, 1,370bm, 159 × 41ft.
Adams, Lepe, 21.4.1765. = EUROPE 7.1778. BU
7.1814 Plymouth.

EUROPA Gunboat. Cd 1782 Gibraltar.

EUROPA 4th Rate 50, 1,050bm, 146 × 41ft. Woolwich DY 19.4.1783. Troopship 1798. Sold
11.8.1814.

EUROPA Transport. Hired 1854.

EUROPA 1st class cruiser, 11,000 tons, 435 × 69ft,
16–6in, 14–12pdr, 4–3pdr, John Brown
20.3.1897. Sold 15.9.1920 C. F. Bletto, Malta; BU
Genoa.

EUROTAS 5th Rate 38, 1,084bm, 150 × 40ft, 16–
32pdr carr., 28–24pdr, 2–9pdr. Wigram &
Green, Blackwall, 17.4.1813. BU 8.1817.

EUROTAS 5th Rate 46, 1,170bm, 159 × 41ft.
Chatham DY 19.2.1829; undocked 13.2.1856 as
screw frigate, 1,102bm. Sold 1.11.1865 Castle &
Beech.

EURUS (ex-DRAGON) 6th Rate 24, 547bm, 24–
9pdr. French privateer, captured 1758. Wrecked
26.6.1760 St Lawrence R.

EURUS (ex-ZEFIR) 5th Rate 32, 703bm, 127 ×
35ft, 2–24pdr, 20–24pdr carr. Dutch, seized
6.3.1796 R. Forth. Storeship 10.1803. BU 1834.

EURYALUS 5th Rate 36, 946bm, 145 × 38ft.
Adams, Buckler's Hard, 6.6.1803. Prison ship
1826; = AFRICA 1859. Sold 16.8.1860 Mr Recano,
Gibraltar.

EURYALUS Wood screw frigate, 2,371bm, 212 ×
50ft. Chatham DY 5.10.1853. Sold 3.1867 Castle &
Beech.

EURYALUS Iron screw corvette, 4,140 tons, 280 ×
45·5ft, 16–7in. Chatham DY 31.1.1877. Sold
10.3.1897 Cohen, Blackwall.

EURYALUS Armoured cruiser, 12,000 tons, 440 ×
69·5ft, 2–9·2in, 12–6in, 14–12pdr. Vickers
20.5.1901. Minelayer 1918. Sold 1.7.1920 S. Castle;
BU Germany.

EURYALUS Cruiser, 5,450 tons, 512 (oa) × 50·5ft,
10–5·25in, 8–2pdr. Chatham DY 6.6.1939. Arr.
18.7.1959 Hughes Bolckow, Blyth, for BU.

EURYALUS Frigate, 'Leander' class, Y100, 2,650
tons, 372 (oa) × 41ft, 2–4·5in, 2–40mm, Limbo,
helo (later Ikara, Limbo, helo). Scotts 6.6.1963.
Arribved Millom, Cumbria 6.9.1990 for BU.

EURYDICE 6th Rate 24, 521bm, 114·5 × 32ft.
Portsmouth DY 26.3.1781. BU 3.1834.

EURYDICE 6th Rate 24, 908bm, 141 × 39ft, 24–
32pdr, 2–12pdr. Portsmouth DY 16.5.1843. TS
6.1861. Foundered 24.3.1878 off I. of Wight;
raised, BU 9.1878.

EUSTATIA (SAINT EUSTATIUS) 6th Rate 20,
514bm, 104 × 27·5ft. Dutch, captured 1781. Sold
1783 Antigua.

EVENLODE (ex-DANVILLE) Frigate, 'River' class.
Vickers, Montreal, 9.11.1942 on Lend-Lease. Ret.
USN 5.3.1946.

EVERINGHAM Inshore minesweeper, 'Ham'
class. Philip 4.3.1954. Sold 1983.

EXAMPLE *See LOYAL EXAMPLE 1985.*

EXCALIBUR Submarine, 780 tons, 178 × 16ft,
unarmed. Vickers Armstrong, Barrow, 25.2.1955.
Arr. Barrow 24.2.1970 for BU.

EXCELLENT 3rd Rate 74, 1,645bm, 168 × 47ft.
Graham, Harwich 27.11.1787. Reclassified 4th
Rate, 58 guns, 6.1820; gunnery TS 1830. BU
10.1835 Deptford.

EXCELLENT *See also BOYNE 1810, QUEEN
CHARLOTTE 1810, HANDY 1884, DRUDGE 1901.*

EXCHANGE *See JAMES 1649.*

EXE Destroyer, 550 tons, 225 × 23·5ft, 1–12pdr,
5–6pdr (1907: 3–12pdr), 2–TT. Palmer
27.4.1903. Sold 10.2.1920 Ward, Rainham.

EXE Frigate, 'River' class. Fleming & Ferguson
19.3.1942. Arr. 20.5.1956 Ward, Preston, for BU.

EXERTION Gun-brig 12, 180bm, 84 × 22ft, 10–
18pdr carr., 2–12pdr. Preston, Yarmouth,
2.5.1805. Grounded 8.7.1812 R. Elbe, destroyed to
avoid capture by French.

EXETER 3rd Rate 70, 1,030bm, 150 × 40ft.
Johnson, Blackwall, 1680. Damaged explosion
12.9.1691, hulked; BU 1717 Portsmouth.

EXETER 4th Rate 60, 949bm, 148 × 38ft. Portsmouth DY 26.5.1697. Rebuilt Plymouth 1744 as
1,068bm, 58 guns. BU 11.1763 Portsmouth.

EXETER 3rd Rate 64, 1,340bm, 158·5 × 41ft.
Henniker, Chatham, 26.7.1763. Burnt 12.2.1784
Cape unserviceable.

EXETER Cruiser, 8,390 tons. 575 (oa) × 58ft, 6–
8in, 4–4in. Devonport DY 18.7.1929. Sunk
1.3.1942 in action with Japanese squadron off
Java.

EXETER Frigate, 2,170 tons, 330 × 40ft, 2–4·5in,
2–40mm. Fairfield, ordered 1956, cancelled.

EXETER Destroyer, Type 42, 3,150 tons. Swan
Hunter 25.4.1978.

EXMOOR Destroyer, 'Hunt' class Type I. Vickers
Armstrong, Tyne, 25.1.1940. Sunk 25.2.1941 by E-
boat torpedo off Lowestoft.

EXMOOR (ex-BURTON) Destroyer, 'Hunt' class
Type II. Swan Hunter 12.3.1941 (renamed 6.1941).

Tx RDanN 7.1952 = VALDEMAR SEJR. Sold
10.1966 for BU in Sweden.

EXMOUTH Screw 2nd Rate 90, 3,100bm, 4,382
tons, 204 × 60ft. Devonport DY 12.7.1854. Lent
1877 Metropolitan Asylums Board as TS. Sold
4.4.1905 Cohen; BU Penarth.

EXMOUTH Battleship, 14,000 tons, 405 × 75·5ft,
4–12in, 12–6in, 12–12pdr. Laird 31.8.1901. Sold
15.1.1920 Forth S. Bkg Co., Bo'ness; hulk BU 1922
Holland.

EXMOUTH TS, 300 × 53ft. Vickers 20.4.1905.
Req. as depot ship 1939–45. = *Worcester* 1945.

EXMOUTH Destroyer leader, 1,475 tons, 343 (oa)
× 33·75ft, 5–4·7in, 8–TT. Portsmouth DY
7.2.1934. Sunk 21.1.1940 by U.22 off Moray Firth.

EXMOUTH Frigate, 1,180 tons, 300 × 33ft, 2–
40mm. White 16.11.1955. Arr. Swansea 9.2.1979
for BU.

EXPEDITION 20-gun ship. French, captured
1618. Last listed 1652.

EXPEDITION 30-gun ship, 300bm. Bermondsey
1637. Sold 1667.

EXPEDITION 3rd Rate 70, 1,116bm, 152 × 41ft.
Portsmouth 1679. Rebuilt Chatham 1699 as
1.111bm; = PRINCE FREDERICK 2.1.1715; rebuilt
1740 as 1,740bm, 64 guns. Sold 1784.

EXPEDITION 5th Rate 44, 816bm, 133·5 ×
37·5ft. Okill, Liverpool, 11.7.1747. BU 12.1764
Plymouth.

EXPEDITION Cutter 14, 151bm, 67 × 24ft. Ladd,
Dover, 3.8.1778. Listed until 1801.

EXPEDITION 5th Rate 44, 910bm, 140·5 × 38·5ft.
Randall, Rotherhithe, 29.10.1784. Troopship, 26
guns, 4.1798. BU 2.1817.

EXPERIMENT Sloop. Built 1664. Lost 1687.
Double-hulled.

EXPERIMENT Sloop 4. Built 1667. Listed until
1682.

EXPERIMENT 5th Rate 32, 370bm, 105 × 27·5ft.
Chatham DY 17.12.1689. Rebuilt 1727 Plymouth
as 374bm. BU 7.1738 Portsmouth.

EXPERIMENT 6th Rate 24, 445bm, 107 × 31ft.
Bird, Rotherhithe, 18.4.1740. Sold 15.3.1763.

EXPERIMENT Storeship, 342bm, 96 × 28ft.
Purch. 8.1765. Sold 6.12.1768.

EXPERIMENT Gunvessel. Woolwich 1772. *Fate
unknown.*

EXPERIMENT 4th Rate 50, 923bm, 140 × 40ft.
Adams, Deptford, 23.8.1774. Captured 24.9.1778
by French SAGITTAIRE off east coast of North
America.

EXPERIMENT Brig-sloop 14, 200bm, 80 × 23·5ft.
Purch. 1781. Sold 21.3.1785 Antigua.

EXPERIMENT 5th Rate 44, 892bm, 140 × 38ft.

Fabian, East Cowes, 27.11.1784. Storeship 1795; harbour service 1805. Sold 8.9.1836.

EXPERIMENT Lugger 10, 111bm, 73 × 19ft, 10—12pdr carr. Parkins, Plymouth, 5.1793. Captured 2.10 1796 by Spanish in Mediterranean.

EXPERIMENT Fireship, 85bm, 63 × 17·5ft. Purch. 4.1794. Sold 16.12.1801.

EXPERIMENT Gunvessel 2, 1—18pdr, 1—18pdr carr. Woolwich DY 5.1806. Gone by 1809.

EXPERIMENT Wood paddle sloop (Canadian lakes), 100bm, 97 × 14·5ft. Purch. 21.7.1838. Sold 1848.

EXPLOIT Minesweeper, 'Catherine' class. Associated SB, LD 28.11.1942 for RN; retained USN = VIGILANCE.

EXPLOIT *See also LOYAL EXPLOIT 1988.*

EXPLORER *See LOYAL EXPLORER 1986.*

EXPLORER Submarine, 780 tons, 178 × 16ft, unarmed. Vickers Armstrong, Barrow, 5.3.1954. Sold 8.2.1965 Ward, Barrow.

EXPLOSION (ex-*Gloster*) Bomb vessel 12, 323bm, 96·5 × 27·5ft. Purch. 4.1797. Wrecked 10.9.1807 off Heligoland.

EXPLOSION *See also SWAN 1767.*

EXPRESS Advice boat 6, 77bm, 65·5 × 16ft. Portsmouth DY 1695. Sold 8.1.1712.

EXPRESS Schooner 6, 180bm, 88 × 21ft. Randall, Rotherhithe, 30.1.2.1800. Sold 5.1813 Walters, Rotherhithe.

EXPRESS (ex-*Anna Marie*) Advice boat, 92bm, 65 × 18·5ft. American, purch. 1808. *Fate unknown.*

EXPRESS Schooner 12, 92bm, 64·5 × 18ft. Plymouth DY 5.1815. Sold 26.7.1827 in Malta.

EXPRESS Packet brig 6, 362bm, 95 × 30·5ft, 6—18pdr. Colson, Deptford, 8.10.1835. Sold 11.1.1862 Marshall, Plymouth.

EXPRESS Composite screw gunboat, 455 tons, 125 × 23ft, 2—64pdr, 2—20pdr. Doxford 16.7.1874. Sold 8.1889.

EXPRESS Destroyer, 499 tons, 235 × 25·5ft, 1—12pdr, 5—6pdr, 2—TT. Laird 11.12.1897. Sold 17.3.1921 G. Clarkson, Whitby.

EXPRESS Destroyer, 1,375 tons, 329 (oa) × 33.5ft, 4—4·7in, 8—TT. Swan Hunter 29.5.1934. Tx RCN 3.6.1943 = GATINEAU. On sale list 1947; sold 1956 Mainewaring, Vancouver; hulk sunk as breakwater.

EXPRESS *See also LOYAL EXPRESS 1988.*

EXTRAVAGANT Fireship 10, 276bm, 95 × 25·5ft. French, captured 1692. Expended 19.5.1692 Battle of Barfleur.

EYDEREN *Spelling used in some lists for EIDEREN (q.v.).*

EYEBRIGHT Corvette, 'Flower' class. Vickers, Montreal, 22.7.1940. Lent RCN until 17.6.1945. Sold 17.5.1947 = *Albert W. Vinke.*

F

'F' class submarines 353 tons, 150 × 16ft, 3—TT.

F.1 Chatham DY 31.3.1913. BU 1920 Portsmouth DY.

F.2 White 7.7.1917. Sold 7.1922 C. Welton, Portsmouth.

F.3 Thornycroft 9.2.1916. BU 1920 Portsmouth DY.

F.4–8 Projected 1914, cancelled.

FAGONS 22-gun ship, 262bm. Page, Wivenhoe, 1654. = MILFORD 1660. Burnt 7.7.1673 accident Leghorn.

FAIR RHODIAN Schooner. Purch. 1780. Listed 1781.

FAIR ROSAMOND (ex-*Dos Amigos*) Slaver, purch. 22.2.1831. BU 20.11.1845.

FAIRFAX 50-gun ship, 740bm. Deptford 1649. Burnt 1653 accident Chatham.

FAIRFAX 52-gun ship, 745bm. Chatham DY 1653. Wrecked 1682.

FAIRFIELD Minesweeper, Later 'Hunt' class. Clyde SB 30.5.1919. Sold 3.3.1920 South American Tours, Buenos Aires.

FAIRY Sloop 14, 300bm, 97 × 29ft. Sheerness DY 24.10.1778. Rebuilt Sheerness 1790. BU 7.1811 Portsmouth.

FAIRY Brig-sloop, 'Cruizer' class, 386bm. Taylor, Bideford, 11.6.1812. BU 1.1821 Portsmouth.

FAIRY Brig-sloop 10, 'Cherokee' class, 233bm. Chatham DY 25.4.1826. Survey vessel 1830. Wrecked 13.11.1840 Sussex coast.

FAIRY (ex-*Marco Bazzaris*) Paddle vessel. American, purch. 17.6.1834. *Fate unknown.*

FAIRY Iron screw yacht, 312bm, 145 × 21ft. Ditchburn & Mare, Blackwall, 3.1845. Sold 1.1868.

FAIRY Destroyer, 380 tons, 227·5 × 22ft, 1—12pdr, 5—6pdr, 2—TT. Fairfield 29.5.1897. Foundered 31.5.1918 after ramming UC.75 in North Sea.

FAIRY Minesweeper, 'Catherine' class. Associated SB, Seattle, 5.4.1943 on Lend-Lease. Ret. USN 13.12.1946.

FAIRY QUEEN Schooner 8, 55bm. Purch. 1781. Captured 19.11.1781 by Spanish off R. Orinoco.

FAITH Schooner (Canadian lakes). Detroit 1774. Wrecked 12.1783 on lakes.

FAITHFUL Repair ship, 14,250 tons, 416 × 57ft, 1—5in, 10—40mm. Bethlehem, Fairfield, 10.10.1944 for RN; retained USN = DIONYSUS.

FAL Frigate, 'River' class. Smith's Dock 9.11.1942. Tx Burmese Navy 3.1948 = MAYU. Sold 1979.

FALCON Ballinger. Dates from 1343. Sold 1352.

FALCON Ship. In service 1461–85.

FALCON Pinnace, 83bm, '22 iron & 4 brass guns'. In service 1544–78.

FALCON Ship, 180bm. In service 1603.

FALCON 24-gun ship. Purch. 1646. Gone by 1659.

FALCON 6-gun vessel. Royalist, captured 1647. Last listed 1653.

FALCON (GOLDEN FALCON) 10-gun ship. Dutch, captured 1652; fireship 1653. Sold 1658.

FALCON 5th Rate 36, 349bm. Woolwich 1666. 4th Rate, 42 guns, 1668. Captured 1.5.1694 by French in Mediterranean.

FALCON 6th Rate 24, 240bm, 91·5 × 24·5ft. Barrett, Shoreham, 1694. Captured 10.6.1695 by three French ships off Dodman; recaptured 1703, BU.

FALCON 5th Rate 38. Merchantman, conv. 1694. Captured 3.1.1695 by French.

FALCON 4th Rate 32, 412bm, 106 × 30ft. Deptford 1704. Captured 29.12.1709 by French LE SERIEUX in Mediterranean.

FALCON Sloop 14, 272bm, 91·5 × 26ft. Barnard, Harwich, 12.11.1744. Captured 12.8.1745 by French off St-Malo; recaptured 3.1746 = FORTUNE. Sold 20.3.1770.

FALCON Sloop 14, 270bm, 91·5 × 26ft. Alexander, Rotherhithe, 30.11.1745. 8-gun bomb vessel 1758. Wrecked 19.4.1759 West Indies.

FALCON Sloop 14, 302bm, 95 × 27ft. Portsmouth DY 15.6.1771. Sunk 8.1778 as blockship Narragansett Bay; salved, foundered 9.1779.

FALCON Brig-sloop 14, 201bm, 79 × 25ft. Hills, Sandwich, 23.9.1782. Fireship 6.1800; expended 7.7.1800 Dunkirk Roads.

FALCON Sloop 16. Danish, found abandoned 14.4.1807 Danzig. In service 1808.

FALCON Brig-sloop 10, 'Cherokee' class, 237bm. Pembroke Dock 10.6.1820. Sold 1838 = *Waterwitch*. *Fitted with engine 1833, taken out 1834.*

121

FALCON Wood screw sloop, 992bm, 185 × 34ft. Pembroke Dock, ordered 1847, cancelled 4.4.1851.

FALCON Wood screw sloop, 748bm, 160 × 31·5ft, 17—32pdr. Pembroke Dock 10.8.1854. Sold 27.9.1869 Marshall, Plymouth.

FALCON Composite screw gunvessel, 780 tons, 157 × 29·5ft, 1—7in, 2—64pdr. Laird 4.1.1877. Harbour service 1890. Sold 28.6.1920 E. W. Payne & Co.

FALCON Destroyer, 375 tons, 220 × 21·5ft, 1—12pdr, 5—6pdr, 2—TT. Fairfield 29.12.1899. Sunk 1.4.1918 collision trawler JOHN FITZGERALD in North Sea.

FALCON River gunboat, 372 tons, 150 × 29ft, 1—3·7in howitzer, 2—6pdr. Yarrow 18.5.1931. HO Chinese Navy 2.1942 = LUNG HUAN; = YING THE ('British virtue') 1948; = NAN CHIANG 1950. Listed until 1974.

FALCON *See also DIADEM 1801.*

FALCON FLYBOAT 28-gun ship, 200bm. Dutch, captured 1652. So 1658.

FALCON IN THE FETTERLOCK Pinnace, 26bm, '8 iron & brass guns'. In service 1546. Sold 1549.

FALCON OF THE TOWER Ballinger, 80bm. Dates from 1420. Sold 1423.

FALKLAND 4th Rate 48, 637bm, 128·5 × 33ft. Built New England 1690, purch. 2.3.1696. Rebuilt Chatham 1702; rebuilt Bursledon 1744 as 974bm. Tx 10.8.1768 Victualling Dept.

FALKLAND Sloop 18 (Indian), 494bm. Bombay DY 11.1853. Sold 7.1862.

FALKLAND PRIZE (ex-LA SEINE) 5th Rate 36, 732bm, 133·5 × 35ft. French, captured 24.8.1704 by DREADNOUGHT off Azores. Wrecked 19.12.1705 Sandwich Bay; salved, sold 11.3.1706.

FALMOUTH (ex-ROTTERDAM) 30-gun ship. Dutch, captured 7.1652 English Channel. Sold 1658.

FALMOUTH 4th Rate 58, 610bm, 124 × 33·5ft. Snelgrove, Deptford, 25.6.1693. Captured 4.8.1704 by two French privateers in Mediterranean.

FALMOUTH 4th Rate 50, 700bm, 130 × 35ft. Woolwich DY 26.2.1708. Rebuilt 1729 Woolwich as 760bm. BU 1747 Woolwich.

FALMOUTH 4th Rate 50, 1,047bm, 144 × 41ft. Woolwich DY 7.12.1752. Beached and abandoned 16.1.1765 Batavia as unseaworthy after action at Manila.

FALMOUTH Schooner, 160bm, 70 × 23ft. Topsham 1807. Dockyard service 1808; mortar vessel 5.1824; = YC.1 (dockyard lighter) 1846; = YC.46 in 1870; = FALMOUTH 11.1870. Sold 1883.

FALMOUTH 6th Rate 22, 455bm, 116 × 30ft. Chapman, Bideford, 8.1.1814. Sold 27.1.1825 T. Hutchinson.

FALMOUTH Wood screw sloop, 950bm, 185 × 33ft. Deptford DY, ordered 1860, cancelled 1860.

FALMOUTH Wood screw corvette, 1,857bm, 225 × 43ft. Chatham DY, LD 5.1.1861, cancelled 12.12.1863.

FALMOUTH 2nd class cruiser, 5,250 tons, 430 × 48·5ft, 8—6in. Beardmore 20.9.1910. Sunk 19.8.1916 by U.63 in North Sea.

FALMOUTH Sloop, 1,060 tons, 250 × 34ft, 2—4in. Devonport DY 19.4.1932. = CALLIOPE (drillship) 1.1952. Arr. Hughes Bolckow, Blyth, 30.4.1968 for BU.

FALMOUTH Frigate, 'Rothesay' class, 2,380 tons, 370 (oa) × 41ft, 2—4·5in, 1—40mm, Limbo (later also Seacat, helo). Swan Hunter 15.12.1959. Harbour TS 1984–88. Sold Desgua ces Mata; arr. El Ferrol 8.5.1989 for BU.

FAMA 5th Rate 36, 979bm, 145 × 39ft. Spanish, captured 5.10.1804 by MEDEA and LIVELY off Cadiz. Sold 4.1812.

FAMA Brig-sloop 18, 315bm. Danish, captured 8.1808 by boats of EDGAR off Nyborg. Wrecked 23.12.1808 Baltic.

FAME 20-gun ship. Irish Royalist, purch. 1646. Captured by Parliamentarians 1649. Blown up 1658.

FAME (ex-RENOMMEE) 30-gun ship, 208bm. French, captured 8.1655. Expended 6.1665 fireship.

FAME 6th Rate 24, 316bm, 106 × 26ft. French, captured 7.1709. Recaptured by French 21.9.1710 off Port Mahon.

FAME Sloop 14, 272bm, 14—3pdr. Purch. 1744 Antigua. Foundered 7.1745 Atlantic.

FAME 3rd Rate 74, 1,565bm, 166 × 47ft. Bird, Deptford, 1.1.1759. = GUILDFORD (prison ship) 1799. Sold 30.9.1814.

FAME 3rd Rate 74, 1,745bm, 176 × 48ft. Deptford DY 8.10.1805. BU 9.1817 Chatham.

FAME Wood screw sloop, 669bm, 162 × 30ft. Deptford DY, LD 2.12.1861, cancelled 12.12.1863.

FAME Destroyer, 340 tons, 210·5 × 19·5ft, 1—12pdr, 5—TT. Thornycroft, Chiswick, 15.4.1896. Sold 31.9.1921 in Hong Kong.

FAME Destroyer, 1,350 tons, 329 (oa) × 33·25ft, 4—4·7in, 8—TT. Vickers Armstrong, Barrow, 28.6.1934. HO Dominican Navy 2.1949 = GENERALISSIMO; = SANCHEZ 1962; discarded 1968.

FAME *See also DRAGON 1798.*

FANCY Pinnace. In Armada action 1588. *Probably hired.*

FANCY Gun-brig 12, 181bm, 85 × 22ft, 10—18pdr carr., 2—12pdr. Preston, Yarmouth, 7.1.1806. Foundered 24.12.1811 Baltic.

FANCY Wood screw gunboat, 'Dapper' class. Green, Blackwall, 31.3.1955. Harbour service 1876. Sold 11.7.1905 Portsmouth.

FANCY Minesweeper, 'Algerine' class. Blyth SB 5.4.1943, comp. Hughes Bolckow. Sold. 9.8.1951 Belgian Navy = A. F. DUFOUR. Hulk 1959 = NZADI. Sunk 1980 Congo.

FANDANGO Minesweeper, 260 tons, 130 × 26ft, 1—3pdr. Lytham SB 1917; War Dept tug, tx 1919. Sunk by mine 3.7.1919 Dvina R.

FANFAN Ketch 4, 38bm, 58·5 × 12ft, 4 guns. Deane, Harwich, 1666. Sold 1686; dockyard pitchboat 1693.

FANNY Tender, 20bm, 34 × 11·5ft. Deptford DY 5.1827. BU 8.1835.

FANNY Cutter yacht, 136bm, 68·5 × 22ft. Portsmouth DY 28.2.1831. For disposal 1863.

FANNY Coastguard vessel, 153bm. Cd 12.1860. Sunk 31.10.1878 collision SS *Helvetia* off Tuscar.

FANNY (ex-*Otter*) Coastguard vessel, 155 tons. Yacht, purch. 1.1902. Sold 10.4.1912 = *Trefoil*.

FANNY *See also ARGUS 1851.*

FANTOME Brig-sloop 18, 385bm, 94 × 31ft. French privateer, captured 5.1810 by MELAMPUS. Wrecked 24.11.1814 St Lawrence R.

FANTOME Brig-sloop 16, 483bm, 105 × 33·5ft, 4—32pdr, 12—32pdr carr. Chatham DY 39.5.1839. Sold 7.10.1864 Castle.

FANTOME Composite screw sloop, 727bm, 940 tons, 160 × 31·5ft, 2—7in, 2—6pdr. Pembroke Dock 26.3.1873. Sold 2.1889 Read, Portsmouth, for BU.

FANTOME Sloop, 1,070 tons, 185 × 33ft, 6—4in, 4—3pdr. Sheerness DY 23.3.1901. Survey ship 1906. Sold 30.1.1925 Sydney.

FANTOME Minesweeper, 'Algerine' class. Harland & Wolff 22.9.1942. Arr. 22.5.1947 Ward, Milford Haven, for BU.

FAREHAM Minesweeper, Later 'Hunt' class. Dunlop Bremner 7.6.1918. Minesweeper base ship 1944—45 = ST ANGELO II. Sold 24.8.1948; BU Ward, Hayle.

FARNCOMB Submarine (RAN), 'Collins' class, 3,051/3,353 tons, 255·2 (oa) × 25·6ft, 6—TT, Australian Submarine Corp., Adelaide, 15.12.1995.

FARNDALE Destroyer, 'Hunt' class Type II. Swan Hunter 30.9.1940. Arr. 29.11.1962 Hughes Bolckow, Blyth, for BU.

FARNHAM CASTLE Corvette, 'Castle' class. Crown 25.4.1944. Arr. 31.10.1960 Durkin, Gateshead, for BU.

FARRAGUT *See ABERCROMBIE 1915.*

FASTNET Scout cruiser. Launched 16.7.1904 as PATHFINDER (q.v.).

FAULKNOR (ex-ALMIRANTE SIMPSON) Destroyer leader, 1,694 tons, 331 × 32ft, 4—4in, 4—TT. White 26.2.1914; Chilean, purch. 8.1914. Resold Chilean Navy 5.1920 = ALMIRANTE RIVEROS. BU early 1940s.

FAULKNOR (ex-*Po-On*) River gunboat, 126 tons, 1—3pdr. Purch. 10.1925 Hong Kong. Sold 1928.

FAULKNOR Destroyer leader, 1,457 tons, 343 (oa) × 33·75ft, 5—4·7in, 8—TT. Yarrow 12.6.1934. Sold 22.1.1946; BU Ward, Milford Haven.

FAVERSHAM 5th Rate 40, 561bm, 118 × 32ft. Plymouth DY 22.7.1712. BU 12.1730 Portsmouth.

FAVERSHAM 5th Rate 44, 689bm, 124 × 36ft. Perry, Blackwall, 7.1.1741. Sold 13.4.1749.

FAVERSHAM Minesweeper, Later 'Hunt' class. Dunlop Bremner 19.7.1918. Sold 25.11.1927 Alloa S. Bkg Co.; arr. 21.1.1928 Charlestown for BU.

FAVERSHAM *See also FEVERSHAM.*

FAVORITE Survey cutter. Purch. 1805. Sold c. 1813.

FAVORITE Sloop 18, 427bm, 109 × 29·5ft 16—32pdr, 6—18pdr carr., 2—6pdr. Bailey, Ipswich, 13.9.1806. BU 2.1821.

FAVORITE Ironclad screw corvette, 2,094bm, 3,232 tons, 225 × 47ft, 10—8in MLR. Deptford DY 5.7.1864. Sold 30.3.1886.

FAVOURITE Sloop 14, probably 206bm. Sheerness DY 1740. *Fate unknown. Existence doubtful.*

FAVOURITE Sloop 14, 313bm, 96·5 × 27ft. Sparrow, Shoreham, 15.12.1757. Sold 21.10.1784.

FAVOURITE Sloop 16, 423bm, 108 × 30ft, 12—12pdr carr., 16—6pdr. Randall, Rotherhithe, 1.2.1794. Captured 6.1.1806 by French off Cape Verde = FAVORITE; recaptured 27.1.1807 by JASON off coast of Guiana = GOREE. Prison ship 1814. BU 1817 Bermuda.

FAVOURITE Sloop 18, 434bm, 110 × 31ft. Portsmouth DY 21.4.1829. Coal hulk 8.1859. Sold 17.5.1905 Devonport. *Listed as FAVORITE 1836–56; also bore number C 3 and later C.77 as coal hulk.*

FAWKNER Iron screw gunboat (Australian), 387 tons, 1—6in, 1—6pdr. Built 1887. *Fate unknown.*

FAWN (ex-FAUNE) Brig-sloop 16. French, captured 15.8.1805 by GOLIATH in English Channel. In service 1806.

FAWN Sloop 18, 424bm, 180·5 × 30ft, 18—24pdr carr., 6—18pdr carr. Owen, Topsham, 22.4.1807. Sold 20.8.1818.

FAWN (ex-*Caroline*) Brigantine 6, 169bm, 75 × 23ft. Slaver, purch. 27.5.1840 Rio de Janeiro. Tankvessel 1842. Sold 5.1847 Natal Colonial Govt.

FAWN Wood screw sloop, 751bm, 1,045 tons, 160 × 32ft, 17—32pdr. Deptford DY 30.9.1856. Survey ship 6.1876. Sold 1884.

FAWN Destroyer, 380 tons, 215 × 20·5ft, 1—12pdr, 5—6pdr, 2—TT. Palmer 13 4.1897. Sold 2.7.1919 Ward, New Holland.

FAWN Survey ship, 1,050 tons, 189·6 (oa) × 37·5ft, Brooke Marine 29.2.1968. PO 10.1991; sold 1991 West German interests as offshore support vessel West Africa and China Sea = *Red Fulmar*.

FEARLESS Gunvessel 12, 149bm, 75 × 21ft. Cleveley, Gravesend, 6.1794. Wrecked 2.1804 Cawsand Bay.

FEARLESS Gun-brig 12, 180bm, 80·5 × 22·5ft, 2—18pdr carr., 10—19pdr. Graham, Harwich, 18.12.1804. Wrecked 8.12.1812 off Cadiz.

FEARLESS (ex-*Flamer*) Wood paddle survey vessel, 165bm, 112·5 × 18·5ft. GPO vessel, tx 8.1837. BU 1875 Chatham.

FEARLESS Torpedo cruiser, 1,580 tons, 220 × 34ft, 2—5in, 8—3pdr, 3—TT. Barrow SB (Vickers) 20.3.1886. Sold 11.7.1905 Portsmouth.

FEARLESS Scout cruiser, 3,440 tons, 385 × 41·5ft, 10—4in. Pembroke Dock 12.6.1912. Sold 8.11.1921 Slough Trading Co.; BU Germany.

FEARLESS Destroyer, 1,375 tons, 329 (oa) × 33·25ft, 4—4·7in, 8—TT. Cammell Laird 12.5.1934. Sunk 23.7.1941 by Italian aircraft in Mediterranean.

FEARLESS Assault ship, 11,060 tons, 520 (oa) × 80ft, 2—40mm, Seacat, helo. Harland & Wolff 19.12.1963. PO 2.8.2002; for preservation?

FELICIDADE Schooner. Brazilian slaver, captured 27.2.1845 by WASP off Lagos. Foundered 5.4.1845.

FELICITE 5th Rate 36. French, captured 18.6.1809 by LATONA in West Indies. 16 guns by 1814. Sold 1818.

FELICITY Sloop (Canadian lakes). Detroit 1773. Sold 1795.

FELICITY (ex-RCN COPPERCLIFF) Minesweeper, 'Algerine' class. Redfern, Toronto, 19.1.1944 (renamed 6.1943). Sold 1947 = *Fairfree*.

FELIX Schooner 14, 158bm, 80·5 × 22ft, 14—12pdr carr. French privateer captured 26.7.1803 by AMAZON. Wrecked 23.1.1807 nr Santander.

FELIXSTOWE Minesweeper, TE 'Bangor' class. Lobnitz 15.1.1941. Sunk 18.12.1943 mine off Sardinia.

FELLOWSHIP 28-gun ship, 300bm. Royalist, captured 1643. Careening hulk 1651. Sold 1662.

FELMERSHAM Inshore minesweeper, 'Ham' class. Camper & Nicholson 24.9.1953. Tx Malaysian Navy 5.3.1966 = TODAK. BU 1976.

FENCER (ex-CROTON) Escort carrier, 11,420 tons, 468·5 × 69·5ft, 2—4in, 8—40mm, 18 aircraft. Western Pipe & Steel Co. 4.4.1942 on Lend-Lease. Ret. USN 11.12.1946.

FENCER Patrol/training boat, 32 tons, 65·6 (oa) × 17ft. Fairey Marine 1983. Sold 11.1991 to Lebanon; left Portsmouth 24.8.1992 by ship; = SAIDA 1993.

FENELLA Wood screw gunboat, 'Clown' class. Pitcher, Northfleet, 19.5.1856. Dredger 3.1867. BU 11.1878.

FENNEL Corvette, 'Flower' class. Marine Indus-tries, Sorel, 20.8.1940. Lent RCN until 12.6.1945. Sold 9.8.1946 = *Milliam Kihl*.

FENTON Coastal minesweeper, 'Ton' class. Camper & Nicholson 10.3.1955. BU 1968 Newhaven.

FERGUS (ex-FORT FRANCIS) Corvette (RCN), Modified 'Flower' class. Collingwood SY 30.8.1944 (renamed 4.1943). Sold 16.11.1945 = *Camco II*.

FERMOY Minesweeper, Later 'Hunt' class. Dundee SB 3.2.1919. Damaged beyond repair 30.4.1941 air attack Malta, BU.

FERNIE Destroyer, 'Hunt' class Type I. John Brown 9.1.1940. Arr. 7.11.1956 Smith & Houston, Port Glasgow, for BU.

FEROZE Wood paddle frigate (Indian), 1,450bm, 240 × 44ft. Bombay DY 18.5.1848. Yacht 1863.

FERRET Sloop 10, 128bm, 72 × 20ft. Dummer, Blackwall, 1704. Captured 25.2.1706 by French off Dunkirk.

FERRET Sloop 10, 123bm, 65 × 21ft. Deptford DY 2.4.1711. Captured 1.9.1718 by Spanish Cadiz Bay.

FERRET Sloop 6, 67bm, 55 × 17ft. Woolwich DY 6.5.1721. Sold 18.11.1731.

FERRET Sloop 14, 255bm, 88·5 × 25ft. Bird, Rotherhithe, 10.5.1743. Foundered 24.9.1757 hurricane off Louisburg.

FERRET Sloop 14, 300bm, 95·5 × 27ft. Stanton, Rotherhithe, 6.12.1760. Foundered 8.1776 hurricane West Indies.

FERRET Cutter 6, 83bm, 50 × 20ft. Chatham DY 8.10.1763. Sold 18.6.1781.

FERRET Brig-sloop 12, 202bm, 79 × 25ft. Hills, Sandwich, 17.8.1784. Sold 16.12.1801.

FERRET Gunboat 4, 66bm, 64 × 15ft. Hoy, purch. 4.1794. Sold 5.1802.

FERRET Schooner 6 purch. 1799. Captured 1799 by the Spanish.

FERRET Brig-sloop 18, 'Cruizer' class, 387bm. Tanner, Dartmouth, 4.1.1806. Wrecked 7.1.1813 nr Leith.

FERRET Brig-sloop 10, 'Cherokee' class, 237bm. Portsmouth DY 12.10.1821. Sold 1.1837 H. Bailey.

FERRET Brig 8, 358bm, 95 × 30ft, 8—18pdr. Devonport DY 1.6.1840. Wrecked 29.3.1869 off Dover pier.

FERRET Destroyer, 325 tons, 194 × 19ft, 1—12pdr, 3—6pdr, 2—TT. Laird 9.12.1893. Dismantled 1910 Chatham; sunk 1911 target.

FERRET Destroyer, 750 tons, 246 × 25·5ft, 2—4in, 2—12pdr, 2—TT. White 12.4.1911. Sold 9.5.1921 Ward, Milford Haven.

FERRET *See also NOVA SCOTIA 1812.*

FERRETER Gun-brig 12, 184bm, 80 × 23ft. Perry, Blackwall, 4.4.1801. Captured 31.5.1807 by Dutch R. Ems.

FERVENT Gun-brig 12, 179bm, 80 × 23ft, 2—18pdr, 10—18pdr carr. Adams, Buckler's Hard, 15.12.1804. Mooring lighter Portsmouth 8.1816. BU 1879.

FERVENT Wood screw frigate, 1,453bm, 210 × 40ft. Woolwich DY, ordered 1846, cancelled 1849.

FERVENT Wood screw gunboat, 'Albacore' class. Green, Blackwall, 23.1.1856. BU 2.1879 Devonport.

FERVENT Destroyer, 310 tons, 200 × 19ft, 1—12pdr, 5—6pdr, 2—TT. Hanna Donald, Paisley, 28.3.1895. Sold 29.4.1920 Ward, Rainham.

FEVERSHAM 5th Rate 32, 372bm, 107 × 28ft. Ellis, Shoreham, 1.10.1696. Wrecked 7.10.1711 off Cape Breton.

FEVERSHAM *See also FAVERSHAM.*

FIDELITY Decoy ship, 2,450 tons. Cd 24.9.1940. Lost 30.12.1942

FIDGET Wood screw gunboat, 'Cheerful' class. Joyce, Greenhithe, 7.4.1856. BU 1863 Haslar.

FIDGET Iron screw gunboat, 'Ant' class. Chatham DY 13.3.1872. Hulked 1905.

FIDGET (ex-*Miner 18*) Tender, 70 × 15ft. War Dept vessel, tx 1905. = ADELAIDE 1907; = ADDA 1915; = ST ANGELO 12.1933. Sold 6.1937.

FIERCE (ex-*Desperate*) Schooner 16, 82bm, 59 × 19·5ft. Purch. 1806. BU 1813.

FIERCE Minesweeper, 'Algerine' class. Lobnitz 11.9.1945. Arr. 2.8.1959 Dorkin, Gateshead, for BU.

FIFE GM destroyer, 'County' class, 5,440 tons, 520·5 (oa) × 54ft, 4—4·5in (later 2—4·5in, Exocet, Seacat, helo), 2—20mm, Sea Slug. Fairfield 9.7.1964. Sold Chilean Navy 12.8.1987 = BLANCO ENCALADA.

FIFE NESS Repair ship, 8,580 tons, 439 × 62ft. Burrard, Vancouver, 30.4.1945. Tx Air Ministry 1948 = ADASTRAL.

FIGHTER *See LST.3038 1945.*

FIJI Cruiser, 8,000 tons, 555·5 (oa) × 62ft, 12—6in, 8—4in. John Brown 31.5.1939. Sunk 22.5.1941 air attack south-west of Crete.

FILEY *See RUGBY 1918.*

FINCH (ex-GROWLER) Brig 8 (Canadian lakes), 110bm, 1—18pdr, 6—18pdr carr., 1—6pdr. American, captured 9.1813 Lake Champlain. Recaptured 11.9.1814 by Americans.

FINDHORN Frigate, 'River' class. Vickers, Montreal, 5.12.1942 on Lend-Lease. Ret. USN 20.3.1946.

FINISTERRE Destroyer, 2,315 tons, 379 (oa) × 40·25ft, 4—4in, 1—4in, 8—TT. Fairfield 22.6.1944. Arr. 12.6.1967 Dalmuir for BU.

FINWHALE Submarine, 'Porpoise' class, 1,605 tons, 241 × 26·5ft, 8—TT. Cammell Laird 21.7.1959. Harbour TS 1979–87. Towed 28.3.1988 to Spain for BU.

FIREBALL Minesweeper, 'Algerine' class. Lobnitz, ordered 1943, cancelled 10.1944.

FIREBRAND Fireship 8, 268bm, 92·5 × 25·5ft. Haydon, Limehouse, 31.3.1694. Wrecked 22.10.1707 Scilly Is.

FIREBRAND (ex-*Charming Jenny*) Fireship 8, 221bm, 87·5 × 24·5ft. Purch. 14.8.1739. Sold 19.12.1743.

FIREBRAND Fireship 89bm, 60 × 19ft. Purch. 5.1794. BU 6.1800.

FIREBRAND Fireship, 140bm, 80 × 20ft. French prize, purch. 1804. Wrecked 13.10.1804 off Dover.

FIREBRAND Wood paddle vessel, 494bm, 155 × 26·5ft, 1—18pdr. Curling & Co., Limehouse, 11.7.1831. Rebuilt 1834 as 540bm, 168 × 26·5ft. = BLACK EAGLE 1843. BU 3.1876 Portsmouth.

FIREBRAND (ex-BELZEBUB) Wood paddle frigate, 1,190bm, 190 × 37·5ft. Portsmouth DY 6.9.1842 (renamed 5.2.1842). Sold 7.10.1864 Castle, Charlton.

FIREBRAND Composite screw gunboat, 455 tons, 125 × 23·5ft. 2—64pdr, 2—20pdr. Thomson 30.4.1877. Sold 1905 = *Hoi Tin.*

FIREBRAND (ex-*Lord Heathfield*) Tender, 125 tons, 95 × 17·5ft. War Dept vessel, tx 1906 (renamed 26.11.1906). Sold 10.2.1920 Stanlee, Dover.

FIREBRAND *See also DOLPHIN 1731, PORPOISE 1777, TORCH 1894.*

FIREDRAKE Bomb vessel 12, 202bm, 86 × 27ft. Deptford 1688. Captured 12.11.1689 by French.

FIREDRAKE Bomb vessel 12, 279bm, 85 × 24ft. Deptford 6.1693. Foundered 12.10.1703.

FIREDRAKE Bomb vessel 12, 283bm, 91·5 × 26·5ft. Perry, Blackwall, 26.2.1741. Sold 31.3.1763.

FIREDRAKE (ex-*Ann*) Firevessel. Purch. 1794. Sold 17.6.1807 Mr Freake for BU.

FIREDRAKE Destroyer, 767 tons, 225 × 25·5ft, 2—4in, 2—12pdr, 2—TT. Yarrow 9.4.1912. Sold 10.10.1921 J. Smith.

FIREDRAKE Destroyer, 1,350 tons, 329 (oa) × 33·25ft. 4—4·7in, 8—TT. Vickers Armstrong, Barrow, 28.6.1934. Sunk 17.12.1942 by U.211 in Atlantic.

FIREFLY Galley 8. In service 1781.

FIREFLY (ex-*John Gordon*) Storeship 6, 98bm, 6—12pdr carr. Purch. 1803. Gone by 1805.

FIREFLY Cutter 8, 80bm. Captured 1807. Wrecked 1808 West Indies.

FIREFLY Schooner 6. Bermuda 1828. Wrecked 27.2.1835 coast of British Honduras.

FIREFLY Wood paddle survey vessel, 550bm, 155 × 28ft. Woolwich DY 29.9.1832. BU 1866 Malta.

FIREFLY Composite screw gunboat, 455 tons, 125 × 23·5ft. 2—64pdr, 2—20pdr. Thomson 28.6.1877. Boom defence vessel 1904; = EGMONT (base ship) 3.4.1914; = FIREFLY 1.3.1923. Sold 5.1931.

FIREFLY Coastal destroyer, 235 tons, 175 × 17·5ft, 2—12pdr, 3—TT. White 1.9.1906. = TB.3 in 1906. Sold 7.10.1920 Ward, Hayle.

FIREFLY River gunboat, 'Fly' class. Yarrow in sections 7.1915, re-erected 11.1915 R. Tigris. Sunk by insurgents 6.1924 R. Euphrates. *In Turkish hands 1.12.1915—26.2.1917.*

FIREFLY *See also FLYING FISH 1803.*

FIREQUEEN Iron paddle vessel, 313bm, 164 × 20ft. Purch. 24.7.1847. Sold 4.8.1883.

FIREQUEEN (ex-*Candace*) Yacht, 446 tons, 157 × 23·5ft. Purch. 1882. Sold 5.7.1920 = *Firebird.*

FIRM Floating battery 16, 397bm, 96 × 31ft, 16—18pdr. Deptford DY 19.5.1794. Sold 1803.

FIRM Gun-brig 12, 181bm, 80 × 22·5ft, 10—18pdr carr., 2—12pdr. Brindley, Frindsbury, 2.7.1804. Wrecked 28.6.1811 coast of France.

FIRM Mortar vessel, 117bm, 65 × 21ft, 1—13in mortar. Wigram, Blackwall, 1.3.1855. = MV.11 on 19.10.1855. Sold 1858 in Malta.

FIRM Wood screw gunboat, 'Albacore' class. Fletcher, Limehouse, 22.3.1856. Sold 1872 in China.

FIRM Composite screw gunboat, 455 tons, 125 × 23·5ft, 2—64pdr, 2—20pdr. Earle 14.2.1877. Sold 14.5.1907 Cox, Falmouth.

FIRME (ex-FERME) 3rd Rate 70, 1,288bm, 156 × 43·5ft. French, captured 14.10.1702 Vigo. Sold 12.11.1713 = Russian LEFERM.

FIRME 4th Rate 60, 1,297bm, 154·5 × 43·5ft. Perry, Blackwall, 15.1.1759. Harbour service 5.1784. Sold 10.11.1791.

FIRME (ex-FERME) 3rd Rate 74, 1,805bm. Spanish, captured 22.7.1805 Cape Finisterre. Harbour service 1807. Sold 3.11.1814.

FIRME *See also DIOMEDE 1798.*

FISGARD (ex-RESISTANCE) 5th Rate 44, 1,182bm, 160 × 41ft, 8—32pdr carr., 28—18pdr, 10—9pdr. French, captured 9.3.1797 by SAN FIORENZO and NYMPHE off Brest. Sold 11.8.1814.

FISGARD 5th Rate 46, 1,068bm, 150 × 40·5ft, 16—32pdr carr., 28—18pdr, 2—9pdr. Pembroke Dock 8.7.1819, not cd until 1843. BU comp. 8.10.1879 Chatham.

FISGARD *For ships renamed FISGARD as training ships, see AUDACIOUS 1869, INVINC-IBLE 1869, HINDOSTAN 1841, SULTAN 1870, SPARTIATE 1898, HERCULES 1868, TERRIBLE 1895.*

FISHGUARD (ex-TAHOE) Cutter, 1,546 tons, 1—5in, 2—6pdr. Tx RN 30.4.1941 on Lend-Lease. Ret. USN 4.2.1946.

FISKERTON Coastal minesweeper, 'Ton' class. Doig, Grimsby, 12.4.1957. Sold 1971; BU 1976 Dartford.

FITTLETON Coastal minesweeper, 'Ton' class. White, Southampton, 5.2.1954. = CURZON 1961—75. Sold 20.9.77 Sittingbourne for BU.

FITZROY (ex-PINNER, ex-PORTREATH) Survey ship. Lobnitz 15.4.1919, ex-later 'Hunt' class minesweeper (renamed 1919). Minesweeper 1939. Sunk 27.5.1942 mine off Great Yarmouth.

FITZROY Frigate, TE 'Captain' class. Bethlehem, Hingham, 1.9.1943. Ret. USN 1.1946.

FLAMBEAU (ex-*Good Intent*) Fireship. Purch. 1804. Sold 17.6.1807 J. Bailey.

FLAMBOROUGH 6th Rate 24, 252bm. Chatham DY 1697. Captured 10.10.1705 by French JASON off Cape Spartel.

FLAMBOROUGH 6th Rate 24, 261bm, 94 × 25ft. Woolwich DY 29.1.1707. Rebuilt Portsmouth 1727 as 377bm, 20 guns. Sold 10.1.1748.

FLAMBOROUGH 6th Rate 22, 435bm, 108·5 × 30·5ft. Batson, Limehouse, 14.5.1756. Sold 23.9.1772.

FLAMBOROUGH HEAD Repair ship, 8,580 tons, 441 (oa) × 57ft, 16—20mm. Burrard, Vancouver, 7.10.1944. Tx RCN 31.1.1953 = CAPE BRETON. Sunk 20.10.2001 artificial reef nr Nanaimo, Vancouver I.

FLAMBOROUGH PRIZE (ex-GENERAL LALLY) Sloop 14, 115bm, 66 × 20·5ft, 14—4pdr. French privateer, captured 1757 by FLAMBOROUGH. Sold 15.3.1763.

FLAME Fireship 8, 273bm, 92 × 25·5ft Gressingham, Limehouse, 6.3.1691. Foundered 22.8.1697 West Indies.

FLAMER (Gunboat No 24) Gunvessel 12, 168bm, 76 × 22·5ft, 2—24pdr, 10—18pdr carr. Perry, Blackwall, 1.4.1797. Sold 4.1802.

FLAMER Gun-brig 12, 178bm, 80 × 22·5ft, 10–
18pdr carr., 2–12pdr. Brindley, Frindsbury,
8.5.1804. Harbour service 5.1815; Coastguard
1841. Sold 16.9.1858 Castle, Charlton.

FLAMER Wood paddle vessel, 496bm, 155 ×
26·5ft. Fletcher, Limehouse, 11.8.1831. Wrecked
22.11.1850 West Africa.

FLAMER Mortar vessel, 117bm, 65 × 21ft, 1–13in
mortar. Wigram, Blackwall, 1.3.1855. = MV.10 on
19.10.1856. Malta yard craft = YC.5 by 1866. For
disposal 1901.

FLAMER Wood screw gunboat, 'Albacore' class.
Fletcher, Limehouse, 10.4.1856. Harbour service
1868. Blown ashore 1874 typhoon Hong Kong;
wreck sold 1874.

FLAMINGO Composite screw gunvessel, 780 tons,
157 × 29·5ft, 1–7in, 1–64pdr, 2–20pdr. Devonport DY 13.12.1876. Harbour service 1893. Sold
25.5.1923 Plymouth Sanitary Authority. BU 1931.

FLAMINGO Sloop, 1,250 tons, 299·5 (oa) × 37·5ft,
6–4in. Yarrow 18.4.1939. Sold West German
Navy 21.1.1959 = GRAF SPEE; deleted 1964; sold
25.10.1967 Eisen & Metall KG for BU.

FLASH (ex-*James*) Firevessel, 62bm, 54 × 16ft.
Purch. 5.1804. Sold 17.6.1807 W. Bliss.

FLAX Corvette, Modified 'Flower' class. Kingston
SY 15.6.1942. Lent USN from comp. until 1945
= BRISK. Sold 1945 = *Ariana*.

FLECHE Brig-sloop 14, 227bm. French, captured
21.5.1794 by the Fleet at Bastia. Wrecked
12.11.1793 San Fiorenzo Bay.

FLECHE (ex-LA CAROLINE) Sloop 18, French
privateer, captured 31.5.1798. Wrecked 24.5.1810
mouth of R. Elbe.

FLECHE Sloop 16, 280bm, 93 × 26·5ft. French,
captured 5.9.1801 by VICTOR. Wrecked 24.5.1810
mouth of R. Elbe.

FLEETWOOD Ship. Royalist, 150bm. Captured by
Parliamentarians 1655 = WEXFORD.

FLEETWOOD Sloop, 990 tons, 250 × 36ft, 4–4in.
Devonport DY 24.3.1936. Arr. 10.10.1959 Dorkin,
Gateshead, for BU.

FLEETWOOD *See also FORD 1918.*

FLEUR DE LA MER Schooner 8, 117bm, 72·5
× 19·5ft. Purch. 1808. Foundered 8.1.1811
Atlantic.

FLEUR DE LYS (ex-LA DIEPPOISE) Corvette,
'Flower' class. Smith's Dock 21.6.1940. French,
seized 3.7.1940 Middlesbrough. Sunk 14.10.1941
by U.206 west of Gibraltar.

FLEWENDE FISCHE (ex-FLYVENDFISKE) Brig-
sloop 18, 213bm, 77 × 26ft. Danish, captured
7.9.1807 Battle of Copenhagen. Sold 13.6.1811.
Was to have been renamed VENTURE.

FLEWENDE FISCHE *See also FLYING FISH.*

FLIGHT *See ARIADNE 1805.*

FLINDERS (ex-RADLEY) Survey ship, ex-'Hunt'
class minesweeper, 800 tons, 1–3pdr. Lobnitz
27.8.1919 (renamed 1919). Accommodation ship
8.1940. Sold 8.1945; BU Falmouth.

FLINDERS Survey ship (RAN), 720 tons,
Williamstown DY 29.7.1972. Deleted 1998.

FLINT Minesweeper, Later 'Hunt' class. Eltringham, cancelled 1918.

FLINT CASTLE Corvette, 'Castle' class. Robb
1.9.1943. Arr. 10.7.1958 Faslane for BU.

FLINTHAM Inshore minesweeper, 'Ham' class.
Bolson 10.3.1955. Sold 1982.

FLIRT Ship. In service 1592.

FLIRT Brig-sloop 14, 209bm, 78 × 26ft. King,
Dover, 4.3.1782. Sold 1.12.1795.

FLIRT Wood screw gunboat, 'Cheerful' class. Joyce,
Greenhithe, 7.6.1856. BU 4.1864 Haslar.

FLIRT Gunboat (New Zealand). Purch. 1862. Sold
1864.

FLIRT Composite screw gunvessel, 603 tons,
464bm, 155 × 25ft, 1–7in, 1–64pdr, 2–20pdr.
Devonport DY 20.12.1867. Sold 11.1888 Cohen for
BU.

FLIRT Destroyer, 380 tons, 215 × 20·5ft, 1–12pdr,
5–6pdr, 2–TT. Palmer, Jarrow, 15.5.1897. Sunk
27.10.1916 in action with German destroyer in
Strait of Dover.

FLOCKTON Coastal minesweeper, 'Ton' class.
White, Southampton, 3.6.1954. Sold 28.7.1969 for
BU Queenborough.

FLORA Sloop, 313bm. Deptford, ordered by 1755,
cancelled.

FLORA (ex-VESTALE) 5th Rate 32, 698bm, 132 ×
35ft, 26–12pdr, 6–6pdr. French, captured
8.1.1761 by UNICORN. Scuttled 7.8.1778 to avoid
capture Rhode I.; salved by Americans, became
French privateer FLORE 1784; recaptured
7.9.1798 by PHAETON, sold.

FLORA 5th Rate 36, 868bm, 137 × 38ft. Deptford
DY 6.5.1780. Wrecked 19.1.1809 Dutch coast.

FLORA 5th Rate 36, 1,634bm, 160 × 49ft. Devonport DY 11.9.1844. Harbour service 1851. Sold
9.1.1891.

FLORA 2nd class cruiser, 4,360 tons, 320 × 49·5ft,
2–6in, 8–4·7in, 8–6pdr. Pembroke Dock
21.11.1893. TS by 4.1915 = INDUS II. Sold
12.12.1922; BU Dover.

FLORA *See also GRIPER 1879.*

FLORENTIA Wood screw sloop, 998bm, 185 ×
34·5ft. Woolwich DY, ordered 1847, cancelled
22.5.1849.

FLORENTINA 5th Rate 36, 902bm, 146·5 ×

37·5ft. Spanish, captured 7.4.1800 Cadiz. Sold 1802.

FLORIDA Storeship, 299bm, 95 × 28ft. Purch. 8.1764. BU comp. 7.1772 Deptford.

FLORIDA Storeship 14, 202bm, 68 × 19ft. Purch. 1774 West Indies. Sold 18.5.1778 Pensacola.

FLORIDA (ex-FROLIC) 6th Rate 20, 539bm, 119·5 × 32ft, 18—32pdr carr., 2—9pdr. American, captured 20.4.1814 by ORPHEUS. BU 5.1819 Chatham.

FLORISTON Coastal minesweeper, 'Ton' class. Richards Ironworks 26.1.1955. Sold 27.5.1968 Pounds.

FLORIZEL Minesweeper, 'Catherine' class. Associated SB, Seattle, 20.5.1943, on Lend-Lease from 14.4.1944. Ret. USN 12.1946. Sold Greek Navy.

FLORIZEL *See also LAFOREY 1913.*

FLOWER DE LUCE Pinnace, 30 tons. Dates from 1546. Captured by French 1562.

FLY Sloop 6. Built 1648. Last listed 1652.

FLY Dogger 6. Dutch, captured 1672. Wrecked 1673.

FLY Advice boat 6, 73bm, 62 × 16ft. Portsmouth DY 1694. Wrecked 22.8.1695.

FLY Ketch 4, 70bm, 61·5 × 20ft. Portsmouth DY 1696. Sold 10.4.1712.

FLY Sloop 12, 200bm, 87 × 23·5ft. Sheerness DY 15.9.1732. BU 2.1750 Sheerness.

FLY Sloop 8, 140bm, 75 × 20·5ft. Portsmouth DY 9.4.1752. Sold 23.9.1772.

FLY Cutter, 78bm. Purch. 1.1763. Sold 29.10.1771.

FLY Sloop 14, 300bm, 96 × 26·5ft. Sheerness DY 1776. Foundered 1802 off Newfoundland.

FLY Cutter 14. Purchased 1778. Captured 1781 by French.

FLY Sloop 16, 309bm, 89 × 27ft. Deptford DY 1779. In service 1782.

FLY Brig-sloop 14 (Indian), 176bm. Bombay DY 1793. Captured 1803 by French in Persian Gulf.

FLY Sloop 16, 369bm, 106 × 28ft. Parsons, Bursledon, 26.3.1804. Wrecked 5.1805 Gulf of Florida.

FLY Brig-sloop 16, 285bm, 93 × 26ft. Boole, Bridport, 24.10.1805. Wrecked 29.2.1812 Anholt.

FLY Brig-sloop, 'Cruizer' class, 387bm. Bailey, Ipswich, 16.2.1813. Sold 10.5.1828 Bombay.

FLY Sloop 18, 485bm, 114·5 × 32ft. Pembroke Dock 25.8.1831. Coal hulk 1855. BU 1903. *Also bore number C.2, then C.70, while coal hulk.*

FLY Wood screw gunboat, 'Albacore' class. Fletcher, Limehouse, 5.4.1856. BU 1862.

FLY Composite screw gunvessel, 464bm, 603 tons, 155 × 25ft, 1—7in, 1—64pdr, 2—20pdr. Devonport DY 20.12.1867. Sold 11.1887 Castle for BU.

FLY Minesweeper, 'Algerine' class. Lobnitz 1.6.1942. Sold 30.7.1949 Iran = PALANG. PO 12.1966; deleted 1972; sank, BU.

FLYING FISH Cutter 12, 190bm, 75 × 25·5ft, 12—4pdr. Purch. 4.1778. 14-gun sloop 1781. Wrecked 3.12.1782 off Calais.

FLYING FISH Schooner 6, 80bm, 63 × 17ft, 6—3pdr. French, captured 1793 by PROVIDENCE; recaptured 16.6.1795 by two French privateers in West Indies; captured again as privateer POISSON VOLANT 1797 by MAGICIENNE in West Indies. Gone by 1799.

FLYING FISH (ex-POISSON VOLANT) Schooner 12, 110bm. French, captured 30.6.1803 by squadron off San Domingo. = FIREFLY 1807. Foundered 17.11.1807 West Indies.

FLYING FISH Schooner 4, 70bm, 55 × 18ft, 4—12pdr carr. Bermuda 1804. Captured by her own prisoners (?) 1804.

FLYING FISH (ex-*Lady Augusta*) Schooner 1, 78bm, 62 × 17·5ft. Purch. 1817. Sold 31.1.1821 Antigua.

FLYING FISH Brig 12, 445bm, 103 × 32·5ft, 10—32pdr, 2—18pdr. Pembroke Dock 3.4.1844. BU 8.1852 Portsmouth.

FLYING FISH Wood screw despatch vessel, 871bm, 200 × 30·5ft, 2—68pdr, 4—32pdr. Pembroke Dock 20.12.1855. Arr. 8.1866 Castle, Charlton, for BU.

FLYING FISH (ex-DARING) Composite screw sloop, 940 tons, 160 × 31·5ft, 2—7in, 2—64pdr. Chatham DY 8.11.1873 (renamed 14.1.1873). Comp. as survey ship 4.1880. Sold 12.1888.

FLYING FISH Destroyer, 380 tons, 215 × 20·5ft, 1—12pdr, 5—6pdr, 2—TT. Palmer 4.3.1897. Sold 30.8.1919 T. R. Sales.

FLYING FISH (ex-TILLSONBURG) Minesweeper (RCN), 'Algerine' class. Redfern, Toronto, 16.2.1944 (renamed 6.1943). Tx Ceylonese Navy 7.10.1949 = VIJAYA. Sold 24.5.1967 to Ceylon; BU 4.1975.

FLYING FOX Minesweeping sloop, '24' class. Swan Hunter 28.3.1918. RNVR drillship 24.3.1920. Sold 26.1.1973; BU Cardiff.

FLYING GREYHOUND 24-gun ship, 230bm. Captured 1665. Sold 1667.

FOAM Wood screw gunboat, 'Albacore' class. Wigram, Northam, 8.5.1856. Sold 6.1867 for BU.

FOAM Composite screw gunboat, 430 tons, 125 × 23ft, 2—64pdr, 2—20pdr. Pembroke Dock 29.8.1871. Sold 6.1887 for BU.

FOAM Destroyer, 340 tons, 210 × 19·5ft, 1—12pdr, 5—6pdr. 2—TT. Thornycroft, Chiswick, 8.10.1896. Sold 6.5.1914 Chatham; BU Norway.

FOAM Minesweeper, 'Catherine' class. Associated SB, Seattle, 20.5.1943; tx RN 28.4.1944 on Lend-Lease. Ret. USN 13.11.1946.

FOLEY Frigate, DE 'Captain' class. Mare Island, LD 30.4.1942 for RN; retained USN = WILEMAN.

FOLEY (ex-GILLETTE) Frigate, DE 'Captain' class. Boston NY 19.5.1943 on Lend-Lease. Ret. USN 8.1945.

FOLKESTON Cog (Cinque Ports Fleet). Listed in 1299.

FOLKESTON 4th Rate 44, 496bm, 116 × 31·5ft. Deptford DY 14.10.1703. BU 1727.

FOLKESTON 5th Rate 44, 698bm, 124·5 × 36ft. Bird, Rotherhithe, 8.1.1741. Sold 1.8.1749.

FOLKESTONE Cutter 8, 84bm, Folkestone 13.10.1764. Captured 24.6.1778 by French SURVEILLANTE in English Channel.

FOLKESTONE Sloop, 1,045 tons, 250 × 34ft, 2–4in. Swan Hunter 1.7.1930. Sold 22.5.1947 Howells; BU by Ward 11.1947 Milford Haven.

FORCE Gunvessel 12, 149bm, 75 × 21ft. Pitcher, Northfleet, 1794. Sold 11.1802.

FORD (ex-FLEETWOOD) Minesweeper, Later 'Hunt' class. Dunlop Bremner 19.10.1918 (renamed 1918). Sold 10.1928; resold 8.12.1928 = *Forde*.

FORDHAM Inshore minesweeper, 'Ham' class. Jones, Buckie, 7.8.1956. Sold 1981 Pounds.

FORESIGHT 36-gun ship, 306bm. 14–9pdr, 8–6pdr, 3–4pdr, 11 small. Built 1570. BU 1604.

FORESIGHT 50-gun ship, 524bm, 121 × 32ft. Deptford 1650. Wrecked 4.7.1698 West Indies.

FORESIGHT Scout cruiser, 2,850 tons, 360 × 39ft, 10–12pdr, 8–3pdr. Fairfield 8.10.1904. Sold 3.3.1920 Granton S Bkg Co.

FORESIGHT Destroyer, 1,350 tons, 329 (oa) × 33·25ft, 4–4·7in, 8–TT. Cammell Laird 29.6.1934. Bombed 12.8.1942 Italian aircraft central Mediterranean, sank next day.

FOREST HILL (ex-CEANOTHUS) Corvette (RCN), Modified 'Flower' class. Ferguson 27.10.1943 (renamed 9.1943). Sold 17.7.1948.

FOREST HILL *See also PROVIDENCE 1943.*

FORESTER 22-gun ship. Lydney 1657. Blown up 1672.

FORESTER Hoy 7, 125bm, 66·5 × 20·5ft. Portsmouth DY 2.11.1693. Wrecked 26.8.1752.

FORESTER Hoy 4, 112bm, 63·5 × 20ft. Ewer, Bursledon, 1748. Hulk tx 1828 Coastguard.

FORESTER Gunvessel 4, 172bm, 70 × 24ft. Hoy, purch. 4.1794. In service 1800.

FORESTER Brig-sloop 18, 'Cruizer' class, 385bm, King, Dover, 3.8.1806. Harbour service 1816. Sold 8.3.1819.

FORESTER Brig 10. Deptford DY, ordered 1824, cancelled 1830. *Contract poss. transferred Chatham—see next vessel.*

FORESTER Brig-sloop 10, 'Cherokee' class, 229bm. Chatham DY 28.8.1832. Sold 27.11.1843.

FORESTER Wood screw gunboat, 'Albacore' class. Green, Blackwall, 22.1.1856. = YC.7 1868. Lost 1871 typhoon Hong Kong.

FORESTER Composite screw gunboat, 455 tons, 125 × 23·5ft, 2–64pdr, 2–20pdr. Earle 26.2.1877. Coal hulk 1894. Sold 1904.

FORESTER Destroyer, 760 tons, 246 × 25·5ft, 2–4in, 2–12pdr, 2–TT. White 1.6.1911. Sold 4.11.1921 Rees, Llanelly.

FORESTER Destroyer, 1,350 tons, 329 (oa) × 33·25ft. 4–4·7in. 8–TT. White 28.6.1934. Sold 22.1.1946; arr. 6.1947 Rosyth for BU.

FORFAR Minesweeper, Later 'Hunt' class. Dundee SB Co 11.1918. Sold 3.1922 Ward, Inverkeithing.

FORMIDABLE 2nd Rate 80, 2,002bm, 188 × 49·5ft, 30–32pdr, 32–24pdr, 18–9pdr. French, captured 20.11.1759. BU comp. 24.1.1768 Plymouth.

FORMIDABLE 2nd Rate 90, 1,945bm, 178 × 50ft. Chatham DY 20.8.1777. 3rd Rate, 74 guns, 1813. BU 9.1813 Chatham.

FORMIDABLE 2nd Rate 84, 2,289bm, 3,594 tons, 196 × 52·5ft. Chatham DY 19.5.1825 from frames captured on stocks 18.4.1814 Genoa. Lent 16.7.1869 as TS. Sold 10.7.1906.

FORMIDABLE Battleship, 15,000 tons, 400 × 75ft, 4–12in, 12–6in, 18–12pdr. Portsmouth DY 17.11.1898. Sunk 1.1.1915 by U.24 off Portland Bill.

FORMIDABLE Aircraft carrier, 23,000 tons, 673 × 96ft, 16–4·5in, 36 aircraft. Harland & Wolff 17.8.1939. Arr. Faslane 12.5.1953 for BU.

FORRES (ex-FOWEY) Minesweeper, Later 'Hunt' class. Clyde SB Co 22.11.1918 (renamed 1918). Sold 26.4.1935 Ward, Pembroke, for BU.

FORT ERIE (ex-LA TUQUE) rigate (RCN), 'River' class. G. T. Davie 27.5.1944 (renamed 3.1944). Arr. 22.5.1966 Spezia for BU.

FORT FRANCIS Minesweeper (RCN), 'Algerine' class. Port Arthur SY 30.10.1943. Survey ship 1949.

FORT FRANCIS *See also FERGUS 1944.*

FORT WILLIAM Minesweeper (RCN), TE 'Bangor' class. Port Arthur 30.12.1941. Sold 29.11.1957 Turkish Navy = BODRUM. BU 1970.

FORT WILLIAM *See also LA MALBAIE 1941.*

FORT YORK (ex-MINGAN) Minesweeper, TE 'Bangor' class. Dufferin, Toronto, 24.8.1941 (renamed 8.1941). Sold 26.9.1950 Portuguese Navy

= COMANDANTE ALMEIDA CARVALHO. BU 1975.

FORTE 4th Rate 50, 1,500bm, 170 × 43·5ft, 20—32pdr carr., 30—24pdr, 2—12pdr. French, captured 28.2.1799 by SYBILLE in Bay of Bengal. Wrecked 6.1801 off Jeddah.

FORTE 5th Rate 40. Sheerness DY, ordered 9.7.1801, cancelled. *Re-ordered as next ship.*

FORTE 5th Rate 38, 1,155bm, 157·5 × 40·5ft. Woolwich DY 21.5.1814. BU 10.1844.

FORTE Screw frigate 51, 2,364bm, 3,456 tons, 212 × 50ft. Deptford DY 29.5.1858. Receiving ship 1880; coal hulk 1894. Burnt 23.11.1905 accident Sheerness.

FORTE 2nd class cruiser, 4,360 tons, 320 × 49·5ft, 2—6in, 8—4·7in, 8—6pdr. Chatham DY 9.12.1893. Sold 2.4.1914 Tydeman, Holland.

FORTE *See also PEMBROKE 1812, FURIOUS 1896.*

FORTH 4th Rate 50 (pitch pine-built), 1,251bm, 159 × 42ft, 20—32pdr carr., 28—24pdr, 2—9pdr. Wigram & Green, Blackwall, 14.6.1813. BU 10.1819.

FORTH 5th Rate 44, 1,215bm, 159 × 42ft. Pembroke Dock 1.8.1833; undocked 21.1.1856 as screw frigate, 1,228bm. = JUPITER (coal hulk) 12.1869. Sold 4.8.1883 Castle for BU.

FORTH 2nd class cruiser, 4,050 tons, 300 × 46ft, 2—8in, 10—6in, 3—6pdr. Pembroke Dock 23.10.1886. Sold 8.11.1921 Slough Trading Co.; BU Germany. *Was to have been renamed HOWARD 12.1920.*

FORTH Depot ship, 8,900 tons, 574 (oa) × 73ft, 8—4·5in. John Brown 11.8.1938. = DEFIANCE 2.1972—4.1978. Sold 1985; arr. R. Medway 25.7.1985 for BU by Dean Marine, Kingsnorth.

FORTH *See also TIGRIS 1813.*

FORTITUDE 3rd Rate 74, 1,645bm, 168·5 × 47ft. Randall, Rotherhithe, 22.3.1780. Prison ship 10.1795; powder hulk 5.1802. BU 3.1820.

FORTITUUD *See CUMBERLAND 1807.*

FORTUNE Ship, 100bm. In service 1512.

FORTUNE Ship. In service 1522.

FORTUNE (ex-FORTUNEE) Ship, 300bm. French, captured 1627. Last listed 1635.

FORTUNE 10-gun ship, 84bm. Royalist, purch. 1644. Captured 1644 by Parliamentarians, = DOVE. Lost 1650.

FORTUNE Ship 12. Royalist, captured 1644 by Parliamentarians = ROBERT. Captured 1649 by Irish Royalists.

FORTUNE Ship. Captured 1651. Captured 1652 by Dutch.

FORTUNE Fireship 10. Captured 1652. Last listed 1653.

FORTUNE (ex-FORTUNEE) 32-gun ship. French, captured 1653. Sold 1654.

FORTUNE Fireship 6, 392bm. Captured 1666. Expended 1666.

FORTUNE Flyboat 4, 180bm. Dutch, captured 1666. Sunk 1667 blockship R. Thames.

FORTUNE Flyboat 8, 311bm. Dutch, captured 1672. Sold 1674.

FORTUNE Storeship. Purch. 1699. Wrecked 15.12.1700 coast of Cornwall.

FORTUNE Storeship, 192bm. Captured 1700. Still listed 1702.

FORTUNE Storeship 24, 543bm, 126 × 31ft, Deptford DY 31.5.1709. Sold 12.11.1713.

FORTUNE Sloop 18. In service 1756. Fireship 1759. Sold 20.3.1770. *Was FALCON 1744, q.v., recaptured.*

FORTUNE Brig-sloop 10, 120bm, 70 × 24ft. Purch. 1770. In service 1772.

FORTUNE Sloop 14, 300bm, 97 × 27ft. Woolwich DY 28.7.1778. Captured 26.4.1780 by French in West Indies.

FORTUNE Sloop 14, 120bm, 70 × 24ft. American, captured 1779. Lost 1780.

FORTUNE Brig-sloop 14, 280bm, 85 × 29ft, 14—4pdr. Stewart, Sandgate, 8.1780, purch. on stocks. Wrecked 15.6.1797 nr Oporto.

FORTUNE Sloop 18. French, captured 11.8.1798 by SWIFTSURE off Nile. Recaptured by French 1799?

FORTUNE Destroyer, 1,000 tons, 260 × 27ft, 3—4in, 2—TT. Fairfield 17.5.1913. Sunk 31.5.1916 Battle of Jutland.

FORTUNE Destroyer, 1,350 tons, 329 (oa) × 33·25ft, 4—4·7in, 8—TT. John Brown 29.8.1934. Tx RCN 3.6.1943 = SASKATCHEWAN. BU 1946.

FORTUNE (ex-BELLE ISLE) Coastal minesweeper (RCN), 370 tons, 140 × 28ft, 1—40mm. Victoria Machinery Co 14.4.1953. PO 28.2.1966; sold 1966 for offshore oil exploration = *Edgewater Fortune.*

FORTUNE *See also FALCON 1744.*

FORTUNE PRIZE Fireship 8, 262bm, 89 × 26ft. French, captured 1693. Sold 24.5.1698.

FORTUNEE 5th Rate 40, 948bm, 143·5 × 38ft. French, captured 22.12.1779. Convict ship 10.1785. BU 1800?

FORTUNEE 5th Rate 36, 921bm, 14·5 × 38ft. Perry, Blackwall, 17.11.1800. Sold 29.1.1818 Freake for BU.

FORWARD Gun-brig 12, 179bm, 80 × 22·5ft, 10—18pdr carr., 2—12pdr. Todd, Berwick, 4.1.1805. Sold 14.12.1815.

FORWARD Wood screw gunboat, 'Albacore' class.

Pitcher, Northfleet, 8.12.1855. Sold 28.9.1869 Hill & Beedy, Esquimalt.

FORWARD Composite screw gunboat, 455 tons, 125 × 24ft, 2–6pdr, 2–20pdr. Barrow SB Co. 29.1.1877. Coal hulk 1892. Sold 1904.

FORWARD Scout cruiser, 2,850 tons, 360 × 39ft, 10–12pdr, 8–3pdr. Cammell Laird 27.8.1904. Sold 27.7.1921 Fryer.

FOSTER Frigate (RCN), 'River' class. G. T. Davie, Lauzon, ordered 1943, cancelled 12.1943.

FOTHERINGAY CASTLE Corvette, 'Castle' class. Morton, cancelled 12.1943.

FOUDROYANT 2nd Rate 80, 1,978bm, 18·5 × 50·5ft, 30–32pdr, 32–24pdr, 18–9pdr. French, captured 28.2.1758 by MONMOUTH and SWIFT-SURE. BU 9.1787.

FOUDROYANT 2nd Rate 80, 2,062bm, 184 × 51·5ft. Plymouth DY 31.3.1798. Guardship 1820; TS 1862. Sold 12.1.1892 J. Read; resold German sbkrs; resold J. R. Cobb as TS. Wrecked 16.6.1897 nr Blackpool.

FOUDROYANT *See also TRINCOMALEE 1817, NEPTUNE 1909.*

FOUGUEUX 3rd Rate 64, 1,403bm, 160 × 44ft, 26–32pdr, 28–18pdr, 10–12pdr. French, captured 14.10.1747 Cape Finisterre. BU 5.1759.

FOUNTAIN 34-gun ship. Algerian, captured 1664. Lost 1672 in action.

FOWEY 5th Rate 32, 377bm, 108 × 28ft. Burgess & Briggs, Shoreham, 7.5.1696. Captured 1.8.1704 by French off Scilly Is.

FOWEY 5th Rate 32, 414bm, 108 × 29·5ft. Chatham DY 10.3.1705. Captured 14.4.1709 by French off coast of Portugal.

FOWEY 5th Rate 44, 528bm, 118 × 32ft. Portsmouth DY 7.12.1709. = QUEENBOROUGH 5.11.1744. Sold 8.1746.

FOWEY 5th Rate 44, 709bm, 127 × 36ft. Blaydes, Hull, 14.8.1744. Wrecked 26.6.1748 Gulf of Florida.

FOWEY 6th Rate 24, 513bm, 113·5 × 32ft. Janvrin, Lepe, 4.7.1749. Sunk 10.10.1781 in action with French in Chesapeake Bay.

FOWEY Gunvessel 3. Barge, purch. 6.1795. Sold 1800.

FOWEY Sloop, 1,105 tons, 250 × 34ft, 2–4in. Devonport DY 4.11.1930. Sold.10.1946 = *Fowlock.*

FOWEY *See also FORRES 1918, AJAX 1959.*

FOWY *Named in Navy Lists 1813 in error for TOWEY (q.v.)*

FOX 22-gun ship. French, captured 1650. Expended as fireship 1656 Malaga.

FOX (ex-ST ANTHONY) 14-gun ship, 203bm. Ostender, captured 1658. Expended as fireship 1666.

FOX Fireship 8, 263bm, 93·5 × 25ft. Barrett, Shoreham, 1690. Expended 19.5.1692 La Hogue.

FOX Sloop 6, 68bm, 59 × 16ft. Sheerness DY 1699. Wrecked 2.12.1699 west coast of Ireland.

FOX 6th Rate 24, 273bm, 93 × 26ft. Captured 5.1705 by TRYTON. Wrecked 28.8.1706 Holyhead Bay.

FOX 6th Rate 24, 440bm, 107 × 31ft. Buxton, Rotherhithe, 1.5.1740. Foundered 14.11.1745 off Dunbar.

FOX 6th Rate 24, 503bm, 112 × 32ft. Horn & Ewer, Bursledon, 26.4.1746. Foundered 11.9.1751 hurricane off Jamaica.

FOX Ketch 8 (Indian). Bombay DY 1766. Listed 1772.

FOX 6th Rate 28, 585bm, 120 × 34ft. Calhoun, Northam, 2.9.1773. Captured 7.6.1777 by American HANCOCK; recaptured 8.7.1777 by FLORA; captured again 17.9.1778 by French JUNON.

FOX 5th Rate 32, 697bm, 126 × 35·5ft. Parsons, Bursledon, 2.6.1780. BU 4.1816.

FOX Cutter 10, 104bm, purch. 1794. Sunk 24.7.1797 in action with Spanish at Santa Cruz.

FOX Schooner 14, 150bm. Ex-French prize, purch. 1799. Wrecked 28.9.1799 Gulf of Mexico.

FOX 5th Rate 46, 1,080bm, 151 × 40·5ft. Portsmouth DY 17.8.1829; undocked 18.3.1856 as screw frigate; comp. 3.1862 as screw storeship. BU 3.1882 Devonport.

FOX 2nd class cruiser, 4,360 tons, 320 × 49·5ft, 2–6in, 8–4·7in, 8–6pdr. Portsmouth DY 15.6.1893. Sold 14.7.1920 Cardiff Marine Stores.

FOX Survey vessel, 1,050 tons, 189·6 (oa) × 37·5ft. Brooke Marine 6.11.1967. Sold 4.1989 commercial interests.

FOX *See also NIGHTINGALE 1702.*

FOXGLOVE Sloop, 'Acacia' class. Barclay Curle 30.3.1915. Harbour guardship 1941. Sold 7.9.1946; BU Troon.

FOXHOUND Brig-sloop 18. 'Cruizer' class, 384bm. King, Dover, 30.11.1806. Foundered 31.8.1809 Atlantic.

FOXHOUND (ex-BASQUE) Sloop 16, 348bm, 95 × 29ft. French, captured 13.11.1809. Sold 15.2.1816.

FOXHOUND Brig-sloop 10, 'Cherokee' class, 231bm. Plymouth DY, ordered 28.10.1826, cancelled 21.2.1831.

FOXHOUND Wood screw gunvessel, 681bm, 181·5 × 28·5ft, 1–110pdr, 1–68pdr, 2–20pdr. Mare, Blackwall, 16.8.1856. BU 8.1866 Castle.

FOXHOUND Composite screw gunboat, 455 tons, 125 × 23·5ft, 2–64pdr, 2–20pdr. Barrow SB Co 29.1.1877. Coastguard 1886; coal tug 1897 = YC.20. Sold 1920 as hulk *Arabel.* BU 1975.

FOXHOUND Destroyer, 953 tons, 274 × 27ft, 1–4in, 3–12pdr, 2–TT. John Brown 11.12.1909. Sold 1.11.1921 Fryer, Sunderland.

FOXHOUND Destroyer, 1,350 tons, 329 (oa) × 33·25ft, 4–4·7in, 8–TT. John Brown 12.10.1934. Tx RCN 8.2.1944 = QU'APPELLE. Sold 1948 for BU.

FOYLE Destroyer, 550 tons, 225 × 33·5ft, 1–12pdr, 5–6pdr (1907: 4–12pdr), 2–TT. Laird 25.2.1903. Sunk 15.3.1917 mine Strait of Dover.

FRANCHISE 5th Rate 36, 898bm. French, captured 28.5.1803 by squadron in English Channel. BU 1.1815.

FRANCIS 14-gun ship. Royalist, 85bm. Captured 1657 by Parliamentarians. = OLD FRANCIS 1666; fireship 1672. Sold 1674.

FRANCIS 6th Rate 16, 140bm, 16–6pdr. Deane, Harwich, 1666. Wrecked 1.8.1684 West Indies.

FRANCIS Discovery ship. 1578. Wrecked 1586.

FRANCIS Discovery ship. Captured 1595 by Spanish.

FRANCIS Fireship 4, 211bm. French, captured 1666. Sold 1667.

FRANCIS Gunvessel 5, 60bm, 55·5 × 16ft. Purch. 3.1794. Powder barge 1800. BU 5.1804.

FRANCIS Sloop (Canadian lakes). Detroit 1796. *Fate unknown.*

FRANKLIN (ex-*Adele*) TS (RAN), 288 tons, 145 × 22·5ft. Screw yacht, purch. 1912. Sold 1924. Hired as ADELE 9.1939.

FRANKLIN Survey ship, 830 tons, 230 × 33·5ft. Ailsa 22.12.1937. BU 2.1956 Clayton & Davie, Dunston.

FRASER Frigate (RCN), 2,260 tons, 366 (oa) × 42ft, 4–3in, 2–40mm, Limbo. Burrard 19.2.1953. PO 5.10.1994. Lent Canada National Heritage for preservation Bridgewater, NS, by 1998.

FRASER *See also CRESCENT 1937.*

FRASERBURGH Minesweeper, TE 'Bangor' class. Lobnitz 12.5.1941. Sold 1.1.1948; arr. 3.1948 Thornaby-on-Tees for BU.

FREDERICK WILLIAM (ex-ROYAL FREDER-ICK) Screw 1st Rate 110, 3,241bm, 4,725 tons, 204 × 60ft, 6–68pdr, 100–32pdr, 4–18pdr. Portsmouth DY 24.3.1860 (renamed 18.1.1860). = WORCESTER (TS) 19.10.1876. Sold 7.1948. Foundered 30.8.1948 R. Thames; raised, BU 5.1953 Tennant & Horne, Grays.

FREDERICKSTEIN 5th Rate 32, 680bm, 129·5 × 34·5ft. Danish, captured 7.9.1807 Battle of Copenhagen. BU 6.1813. *Was to have been renamed TERESA.*

FREDERICKSWAERN (ex-FREDERICKS-COARN) 5th Rate 36, 776bm, 130 × 37ft. Danish,

captured 16.8.1807 by COMUS in Baltic. Sold 16.12.1814.

FREDERICTON Corvette (RCN), 'Flower' class. Marine Industries 2.9.1941. Sold 16.11.1945 = *Tra Los Montes.*

FREDERICTON Frigate (RCN), 'Halifax' class. Marine Industries, Sorel, 13.3.1993.

FREESIA Corvette, 'Flower' class. Harland & Wolff 10.1940. Sold 22.7.1946 = *Freelock.*

FREMANTLE Minesweeper (RAN), 'Bathurst' class. Evans Deakin 18.8.1942. Sold 6.1.1961, towed from Sydney 20.2.1962 for BU Japan.

FREMANTLE Patrol vessel (RAN), 200 tons. Brooke Marine 15.2.1979.

FRENCH RUBY *See RUBY 1666.*

FRENCH VICTORY (ex-VICTOIRE) 5th Rate 38, 394bm. French, captured 5.4.1666. Captured 1672 by the Dutch.

FRERE Iron steam gunboat (Indian), 610 tons. Bombay DY 1857. *Fate unknown.*

FRETTENHAM Inshore minesweeper, 'Ham' class. White 18.5.1954. Sold 13.12.1954 French Navy = M.771/TULIPE. Arr. Amsterdam 4.8.1989 for BU.

FREYA (ex-FREDA) 5th Rate 38, 1,022bm. Danish, captured 7.9.1807 Battle of Copenhagen. Sold 11.1.1816. *Was to have been renamed HYPPOL-ITUS; listed 1814 as FRELJA.*

FRIENDSHIP Fireship, 180bm, purch. 1673. Sunk in action 1673.

FRIENDSHIP Cutter, 60bm, purch. 3.1763. Sold 29.10.1771.

FRIENDSHIP Firevessel, 56bm, 51 × 17ft. Purch. 4.1794. BU 9.1801.

FRIENDSHIP Gunvessel 2. Barge, purch. 8.1795. Foundered 9.11. 1801 off Channel Is.

FRIENDSHIP Minesweeper, 'Algerine' class. Toronto SY 24.10.1942 on Lend-Lease. Ret. USN 1.1947.

FRIEZLAND Flyboat 8, 227bm. Dutch, captured 1665. Given to Africa Co. 1672.

FRITHAM Inshore minesweeper, 'Ham' class. Brooke Marine 24.9.1953. Sold 1980.

FRITILLARY Corvette, 'Flower' class. Harland & Wolff 22.7.1941. Sold 19.3.1946 = *Andria.*

FROBISHER Cruiser, 9,750 tons, 605 (oa) × 65·1ft, 7–7·5in, 4–3in, 6–12pdr. Devonport DY 20.3.1920. Sold 26.3.1949; arr. 5.1949 Cashmore, Newport, for BU.

FROBISHER *See also PARKER 1916.*

FROG Dogger 6. Dutch, captured 1673. Sold 1674.

FROLIC Brig-sloop 18, 'Cruizer' class, 384bm. Boole, Bridport, 9.12.1806. BU 11.1813.

FROLIC Brig-sloop 10, 'Cherokee' class, 236bm.

Pembroke Dock 10.6.1820. Sold 16.8.1838 Dowson.

FROLIC Sloop 16, 511bm, 105 × 34ft, 16—32pdr carr. Portsmouth DY 23.8.1842. Sold 7.10.1864 Castle.

FROLIC Composite screw gunvessel, 462bm, 610 tons, 155 × 25ft, 1—7in 1—6pdr, 2—20pdr. Chatham DY 19.2.1872. Drillship 1888; = WV.30 (Coastguard watchvessel) 1893; = WV.41 in 1897. Sold 7.4.1908.

FROLIC Minesweeper. 'Catherine' class. Associated SB, Seattle, 20.6.1943 on Lend-Lease. Ret. USN 1947, sold 3.1947 Turkish Navy = CANDARLI. Withdrawn 1986.

FROME Minesweeper, Later 'Hunt' class. Elthringham, cancelled 1918.

FROME Frigate, 'River' class. Blyth SB 1.6.1943. Tx French Navy 3.1944 = L'ESCARMOUCHE. BU 1961.

FRONTENAC Transport (Canadian), 248grt, 190 × 24ft. Quebec 1930.

FRONTENAC Corvette (RCN), Modified 'Flower' class. Kingston 2.6.1943. Sold 2.10.1945.

FUBBS Royal yacht 12, 148bm, 73·5 × 21ft. Greenwich DY 1682. Rebuilt Woolwich 1701 and Deptford 1724 as 157bm. BU 7.1781.

FUERTE 6th Rate 20. Spanish, captured 3.2.1807 Montevideo. BU 1.1812 Portsmouth.

FULMAR Paddle minesweeper. Ailsa, Troon. Cancelled 12.1918.

FULMINANTE Cutter 8. French, captured 29.10.1798 by ESPOIR in Mediterranean. Wrecked 24.3.1801 coast of Egypt.

FUNDY Coastal minesweeper (RCN), 'Ton' class. St John DD Co. 4.1952. Sold 4.1954 French Navy = LA DUNKERQUOISE; deleted 1986.

FUNDY Coastal minesweeper (RCN), 'Ton' class, Davie, Lauzon, 14.6.1956. PO 1996.

FURIEUSE 5th Rate 38, 1,085bm, 158 × 39ft. French, captured 6.7.1809 by BONNE CITOYENNE in Atlantic. BU 10.1816 Deptford.

FURIOUS (Gunboat No 23) Gunvessel 12, 169bm, 76 × 23ft, 2—24pdr, 10—18pdr carr. Perry, Blackwall 31.3.1797. Sold 10.1802.

FURIOUS Gun-brig 12, 179bm, 80 × 23ft, 10—18pdr carr., 2—12pdr. Brindley, Lynn, 21.7.1804. Sold 9.2.1815.

FURIOUS Wood paddle frigate, 1,287bm, 210 × 36ft, 2—110pdr, 4—40pdr, 10—32pdr. Portsmouth DY 26.8.1850. Coal hulk 3.1867. Sold 1884.

FURIOUS 2nd class cruiser, 5,750 tons, 320 × 57·5ft, 4—6in, 6—4·7in, 9—12pdr. Devonport DY 3.12.1896. = FORTE (hulk) 6.1915. Sold 5.1923

Cohen, Swansea.

FURIOUS 1st class cruiser (also known as 'large light cruiser' and 'battle cruiser'), 19,100 tons, 750 × 88ft, 1—18in (designed for 2—18in), 11—5·5in. Armstrong 15.8.1916. Comp. 3.1818 as aircraft carrier, 10—5·5in, 10 aircraft. Rebuilt 1924, 33 aircraft. Sold 1.1948; BU Dalmuir and Troon.

FURNACE Bomb vessel 4, 144bm. Wells, Horsleydown, 18.4.1695. BU 1725.

FURNACE Bomb vessel 14, 273bm, 92 × 26·5ft. Quallet, Rotherhithe, 25.10.1740. Sold 31.3.1763.

FURNACE Fireship 8, 365bm, 100·5 × 29ft. Fisher, Liverpool, 6.12.1779. Sold 10.4.1783.

FURNACE (Gunboat No 25) Gunvessel 12, 170bm, 76 × 22ft. Perry, Blackwall, 10.4.1797. Sold 10.1802.

FURY Sloop 14, 306bm, 97 × 26·5ft. Lime & Mackenzie, Leith, 18.3.1779. BU 4.1787.

FURY Gunboat 1. Cd 1782 Gibraltar.

FURY Sloop 16, 323bm, 100 × 27ft. Portsmouth DY 2.3.1790. Bomb vessel 16 in 1798. BU 6.1811.

FURY Gunvessel 4, 56bm, 58 × 14·5ft. Dutch hoy, purch. 4.1794. Sold 5.1802.

FURY Bomb vessel 8, 326bm, 102 × 27ft, 8—2pdr carr., 2—6pdr, 1 mortar. Bridport, ordered 30.3.1812, cancelled 3.12.1813.

FURY Bomb vessel 8, 377bm, 109 × 28·5ft, 10—24pdr carr., 2—6pdr, 2 mortars. Ross, Rochester, 4.4.1814. Arctic discovery vessel 1824; bilged in ice 1.8.1825 Regent Inlet.

FURY Wood paddle vessel, 166bm, 90 × 20ft. Purch. 31.7.1834 Bermuda. BU 8.1843 Bermuda.

FURY Wood paddle sloop, 1,124bm, 190 × 36ft. Sheerness DY 31.12.1845. Sold 15.7.1864 Castle & Beech.

FURY Turret ship, 5,030bm, 10,460 tons, 320 × 62ft. Pembroke Dock, LD 10.9.1870, redesigned, = DREADNOUGHT (q.v.) 1.2.1875.

FURY Destroyer, 760 tons, 246 × 25ft, 2—4in 2—12pdr, 2—TT. Inglis, Glasgow, 25.4.1911. Sold 4.11.1921 Rees, Llanelly.

FURY Destroyer, 1,350 tons, 329 (oa) × 33·25ft, 4—4·7in, 8—TT. White 10.9.1934. Damaged 21.6.1944 by mine; arr. 18.9.1944 Ward, Briton Ferry, for BU.

FUZE Firevessel, 55bm, 54·5 × 16ft. Purch. 10.1804. Sold 17.6.1807 T. Freake for BU.

FYEN (ex-FIJEN) 3rd Rate 74, 1,681bm. Danish, captured 7.9.1807 Battle of Copenhagen. Prison ship 1809; sold 1.9.1814. *Was to have been renamed BENGAL. Listed 1814 as FIJEN.*

FYLLA 6th Rate 22, 490bm. Danish, captured 7.9.1807 Battle of Copenhagen. Sold 30.6.1814. *Was to have been renamed LIFFEY.*

G

'G' class submarines 700 tons, 185 × 22·5ft, 1—
3in, 5—TT.

G.1 Chatham DY 14.8.1915. Sold 14.2.1920 Fryer,
Sunderland.

G.2 Chatham DY 23.12.1915. Sold 16.1.1920 Fryer,
Sunderland.

G.3 Chatham DY 22.1.1916. Sold 4.11.1921 Young,
Sunderland.

G.4 Chatham DY 23.10.1915. Sold 27.6.1928 Cashmore, Newport.

G.5 Chatham DY 23.11.1915. Sold 25.10.1922 Cashmore, Newport.

G.6 Armstrong 7.12.1915. Sold 4.11.1921 Young,
Sunderland.

G.7 Armstrong 4.3.1916. Sunk 1.11.1918 North Sea.

G.8 Vickers 1.5.1916. Sunk 14.1.1918 North Sea.

G.9 Vickers 15.6.1916. Sunk 16.9.1917 in error by
British destroyer PETARD off coast of Norway.

G.10 Vickers 11.1.1916. Sold 20.1.1923 J. Smith.

G.11 Vickers 22.2.1916. Wrecked 22.11.1918 off
Hawick.

G.12 Vickers 24.3.1916. Sold 14.2.1920 J. G. Potts.

G.13 Vickers 18.7.1916. Sold 20.1.1923 J. Smith.

G.14 Scotts 17.5.1917. Sold 11.3.1921 Stanlee, Dover.

G.15 White, ordered 30.9.1914, cancelled 20.4.1915.

Torpedo boats (ex-Dutch) 180 tons, 162·5 × 17ft,
2—3in, 3—TT.

G.13 Cd RN as submarine tender 10.1940. BU
2.1943 Ward, Preston.

G.15 Cd RN as submarine tender 10.1940. LU
7.1940; BU 2.1943 Ward, Preston.

GABBARD Destroyer, 2,315 tons, 379 (oa) ×
40·25ft, 4—4·5in, 1—4in, 12—40mm, 8—TT. Swan
Hunter 16.3.1945. Tx Pakistani Navy 3.1.1957
= BADR; deleted 1989.

GABRIEL Ship, 180bm. Purch. 1410. Given away
1413.

GABRIEL Ship. Southampton 1416. *Fate
unknown.*

GABRIEL Discovery vessel, 20bm. In service 1575.

GABRIEL (ex-ABDIEL) Destroyer leader, 1,655
tons, 325 × 32ft, 4—4in, 4—TT. Cammell Laird
23.12.1915 (renamed 1915). Sold 9.5.1921 Ward,
Lelant.

GABRIEL Minesweeper, 'Algerine' class. Lobnitz,
ordered 9.6.1943, cancelled 10.1944.

GABRIEL *See also ITHURIEL 1916.*

GABRIEL HARFLEUR (ex-ST GABRIEL)
Ballinger, 40bm, French, captured 1415. Lost
1420.

GABRIEL ROYAL Ship, 700bm. Purch. 1512.
Listed until 1526.

GADDESDON Minesweeper, Later 'Hunt' class.
Eltringham 30.11.1917. Sold 4.11.1922.

GADFLY Wood screw gunboat, 'Cheerful' class.
Laird 21.4.1856. BU 11.1864.

GADFLY Iron screw gunboat, 265 tons, 87·5 ×
26ft, 1—10in MLR. Pembroke Dock 5.5.1879.
= YC.230 (coal lighter) 18.5.1900. Sold 1918 Cape.

GADFLY Coastal destroyer, 215 tons, 166·5 ×
17·5ft, 2—12pdr, 3—TT. Thornycroft, Chiswick,
24.6.1906. = TB.6 in 1906. Sold 22.10.1920
Stanlee, Dover.

GADFLY River gunboat, 'Fly' class. Yarrow 8.1915
in sections, re-erected 12.1915 R. Tigris. Tx War
Dept 1923.

GADWELL Paddle minesweeper. Ailsa, ordered
1918, cancelled 12.1918.

GAEL Destroyer, c. 2,000 tons, 341·5 × 39·5ft, 4—
4·5in, 6—40mm, 10—TT. Yarrow, ordered
24.7.1944, cancelled 12.12.1945.

GAIETE 6th Rate 20, 514bm, 120 × 31ft. French,
captured 20.8.1797 by ARETHUSA in Atlantic.
Sold 21.7.1808.

GAILLARDIA Sloop, 'Anchusa' class. Blyth DD
19.5.1917. Sunk 22.3.1918 mine Northern Barrage.

GAINSBOROUGH 40-gun ship, 550bm, 122 ×
32ft. Taylor, Plymouth, 1653. = SWALLOW (4th
Rate) 1660. Wrecked 9.2.1692 coast of Ireland.

GAINSBOROUGH (ex-GORLESTON) Minesweeper, Later 'Hunt' class. Eltringham 12.2.1918
(renamed 1918). Sold 6.1928 Alloa S. Bkg Co for
BU.

GALA Destroyer, 570 tons, 222 × 23·5ft, 1—12pdr.
5—6pdr, 2—TT. Yarrow, Poplar, 7.1.1905. Sunk
27.4.1908 collision ATTENTIVE off Harwich.

GALATEA 6th Rate 20, 429bm, 108 × 30ft. Deptford DY 21.3.1776. BU 4.1783.

GALATEA 5th Rate 32, 808bm. 135 × 36·5ft. Parsons, Bursledon, 17.5.1797. BU 5.1809.

GALATEA 5th Rate 36, 947bm, 145 × 38·5ft. Deptford DY 31.8.1810. Coal hulk 8.1836. BU 1849 Jamaica.

GALATEA Wood screw frigate, 3,227bm, 280 × 50ft, 24—10in, 2—68pdr. Woolwich DY 14.9.1859. BU 6.1883 Castle.

GALATEA Armoured cruiser, 5,600 tons, 300 × 56ft, 2—9·2in, 10—6in, 10—3pdr. Napier 10.3.1887. Sold 4.4.1905.

GALATEA Light cruiser, 3,500 tons, 410 × 39ft, 2—6in, 6—4in. Beardmore 14.5.1914. Sold 25.10.1921 Multilocular Co.

GALATEA Cruiser, 5,220 tons, 506 (oa) × 51ft, 6—6in, 8—4in. Scotts 9.8.1934. Sunk 14.12.1941 by U.557 off Alexandria.

GALATEA Frigate, 'Leander' class, Y100, 2,650 tons, 372 (oa) × 41ft. 2—4·5in, Limbo, helo (later Ikara, Limbo, helo). Swan Hunter 23.5.1963. Expended 22.6.1988 target.

GALATHEE Sloop 16. Dutch, captured 30.8.1799 off Texel. Sold 15.10.1807 Cristall for BU Rotherhithe.

GALGO Sloop 12, 164bm, 78·5 × 22ft, 12—4pdr. Spanish, captured 4.1742 English Channel. Sold 24.3.1743.

GALGO Sloop, 272bm, Buxton, Rotherhithe, 17.2.1744. = SWALLOW 31.1.1744 Wrecked 24.12.1744 West Indies.

GALGO (ex-*Garland*) Sloop 16 , 354bm, 102 × 28·5ft, 14—24pdr carr., 2—18pdr. Purch. 1801. Rock transport 1809. Sold 9.6.1814.

GALICIA 3rd Rate 70, Spanish, captured 25.3.1741 Cartagena. Burnt 1741 unseaworthy.

GALLANT (Gunboat No 29) Gunvessel, 169bm, 76 × 22ft, 2—24pdr, 10—18pdr carr. Pitcher, Northfleet, 4.1797. Sold 10.1802.

GALLANT Gun-brig 12, 180bm, 80·5 × 22·5ft, 2—18pdr, 10—18pdr carr. Roxby, Wearmouth, 20.9.1804. Sold 14.12.1815.

GALLANT Destroyer, 1,335 tons, 323 (oa) × 33ft, 4—4·7in, 8—TT. Stephen 26.9.1935. Damaged 10.1.1941 mine, 5.4.1942 air attack Malta; sunk 9.1943 blockship Malta.

GALLANT Destroyer, c. 2,000 tons, 341·5 × 39·5ft, 4—4·5in, 6—40mm, 10—TT. Yarrow, ordered 24.7.1944, cancelled 12.12.1945.

GALLARITA Galley, 100bm. Limehouse 1602. Sold 1629.

GALLION (ex-JESU MARIA JOSEF) Galleon, 570bm. Spanish, captured 1656. Sunk 1670 foundation Portsmouth.

GALLIOT Hoy 4, 49bm. Dutch, captured 1664. Sold 1667.

GALT Corvette (RCN), 'Flower' class. Collingwood SY 28.12.1940. Sold 1946.

GALTEEMORE Minesweeping sloop, '24' class. Osbourne Graham, Sunderland, 1919, cancelled 12.18, sold incomp.

GALTEEMORE *See also EMPIRE MACE 1943.*

GAMBIA Cruiser, 8,000 tons, 555·5 (oa) × 62ft, 12—6in, 8—4in. Swan Hunter 30.11.1940. Sold 15.11.1968.Ward; arr. Inverkeithing 6.12.1968 for BU.

GAMSTON *See SOMERLEYTON 1855.*

GANANOQUE Minesweeper (RCN), TE 'Bangor' class. Dufferin, Toronto, 23.4.1941. LU 1946. Sold 2.1959 Marine Industries.

GANGA (ex-CHIDDINGFOLD) Destroyer (Indian Navy). Renamed 18.6.1954. *See CHIDDINGFOLD 1941.*

GANGES 3rd Rate 74, 1,679bm, 170 × 47·5ft. Randall, Rotherhithe, 30.3.1782. Prison ship until 1811; lent 12.1814 Transport Board. BU 3.1816 Plymouth.

GANGES 2nd Rate 84, 2,248bm, 3,594 tons, 196·5 × 52ft. Bombay DY 10.11.1821. TS 5.1865; = TENEDOS III 21.6.1906; = INDUS V 13.8.1910; = IMPREGNABLE III 12.10.1922. Sold 31.8.1929 for BU.

GANGES *For training ships with this name see MINOTAUR 1863, AGINCOURT 1865, CAROLINE 1882.*

GANNET Brig-sloop 16, 289bm, 88·5 × 28ft, 14—18pdr, 2—6pdr. Purch. 1800. Sold 21.7.1814.

GANNET Brig-sloop 18, 'Cruizer' class, 386bm. Larking & Spong, Lynn, 13.11.1814. Sold 16.8.1838 Mr Soames.

GANNET Composite screw sloop, 1,130 tons, 170 × 36ft, 2—7in, 4—6pdr. Sheerness DY 31.8.1878. = PRESIDENT (TS) 16.5.1903; lent 10.1913 = *Mercury* (TS). Arr. Chatham 6.1987 under tow for preservation.

GANNET Iron screw gunboat (Australian), 346 tons, 1—6in. Built 1884. For sale 1895.

GANNET River gunboat, 310 tons, 177 × 29ft, 2—3in. Yarrow 10.11.1927. Presented Chinese Navy 2.1942 = YING SHAN ('British mountain'). Listed until 1975.

GANNET *See also TRENT 1877, NYMPHE 1888.*

GANNET Wood screw sloop, 579bm, 151 × 29ft, 11—32pdr. Pembroke Dock 29.12.1857. BU 2.1877 Devonport.

GANYMEDE (ex-HEBE) 6th Rate 26, 601bm, 127 × 33ft, 22—32pdr carr., 10—18pdr carr., 2—6pdr. French, captured 5.1.1809 by LOIRE in Atlantic. Convict ship 1819. Capsized 1838, BU.

GANYMEDE Wood screw corvette, 1,857bm, 225

× 43ft. Chatham DY, ordered 1860, cancelled 12.12.1863.

GARDENIA Sloop, 'Anchusa' class. Barclay Curle 27.12.1917. Sold 15.1.1923 Richardson, Westgarth.

GARDENIA Corvette, 'Flower' class. Simons 10.4.1940. Sunk 9.11.1942 collision trawler FLUELLEN off Oran.

GARDINER (ex-O'TOOLE) Frigate, DE 'Captain' class. Boston NY 8.7.1943 on Lend-Lease. Ret. USN 2.1946.

GARLAND (GUARDLAND) Galleon 38/48, 530/700bm, 16—18pdr, 14—9pdr, 4—6pdr, 11 small. Built 1590. Sunk 1618 wharf Chatham.

GARLAND Ship 34/40, 420/550bm. Deptford 1620. Captured 30.11.1652 by Dutch.

GARLAND 5th Rate 44, 496bm, 115·5 × 31ft. Woolwich DY 5.1703. Wrecked 1709.

GARLAND Fireship. In service 1716. Sold 27.9.1744. *Was SCARBOROUGH 1696.*

GARLAND 6th Rate 24, 508bm, 113 × 32ft. Sheerness DY 13.8.1748. Hulked 1768. Sold 2.12.1783.

GARLAND (ex-GUIRLANDE) 6th Rate 20, French, captured 18.8.1762. Sold 1783.

GARLAND Schooner tender 6. Purch. 1798. Gone by 1803.

GARLAND (ex-MARS) 6th Rate 22, 530bm, 124·5 × 31·5ft. French privateer, captured 1.4.1800 by AMETHYST. Wrecked 11.1803 West Indies.

GARLAND 6th Rate 22, 525bm, 118·5 × 31·5ft, 22—32pdr carr., 8—18pdr carr., 2—6pdr. Chapman, Bideford, 25.4.1807. Sold 9.5.1817 Mr Hill.

GARLAND Wood paddle packet, 295bm, 140 × 21ft. Fletcher, Limehouse, 26.2.1846. Sold 1855 Jenkins & Churchward, Dover.

GARLAND Wood screw gunboat, 'Cheerful' class. Laird 7.5.1856. BU 6.1864.

GARLAND Destroyer, 984 tons, 260 × 29ft, 3—4in, 2—TT. Cammell Laird 23.4.1913. Sold 6.9.1921 Petersen & Albeck.

GARLAND Destroyer, 1,335 tons, 323 (oa) × 33ft, 4—4·7in, 8—TT. Fairfield 21.10.1935. Lent 1940–46 Polish Navy. Sold 12.1947 Dutch Navy = MARNIX. BU 10.4.1964 Antwerp.

GARLAND *See also GRANTHAM 1654, SIBYL 1779.*

GARLIES (ex-FLEMING) Frigate, DE 'Captain' class. Boston NY 19.5.1943 on Lend-Lease. Ret. USN 8.1945.

GARNET Wood screw gunboat, 'Clown' class. Pitcher, Northfleet, 31.5.1856. BU 5.1864.

GARNET Composite screw corvette, 2,120 tons, 220 × 40ft, 12—64pdr. Chatham DY 30.6.1877. Sold 12.1904.

GARNET Minesweeper, 'Catherine' class. Associated SB, Seattle, 20.6.1943 on Lend-Lease; = JASPER 4.1944. Ret. USN 12.1946.

GARRY Destroyer, 590 tons, 222 × 23·5ft, 1—12pdr, 5—6pdr (1907: 4—12pdr), 2—TT. Yarrow, Poplar, 21.3.1905. Sold 22.10.1920 J. H. Lee.

GARTH Minesweeper, Early 'Hunt' class. Dunlop Bremner 9.5.1917. Sold 21.2.1923 Alicia, Charlestown.

GARTH Destroyer, 'Hunt' class Type I. John Brown 14.2.1940. Arr. 25.8.1958 Ward, Barrow, for BU.

GASCOYNE Frigate (RAN), 'River' class. Mort's Dock, Sydney, 20.2.1943. Survey ship 6.1959. Sold 27.1.1972; left Sydney 6.7.1972 for BU Osaka.

GASCOYNE Minehunter (RAN), 'Huon' class, 720 tons, 172·2 (oa) × 32·5ft, 1—30mm. ADI, Newcastle, NSW, 11.3.2000.

GASPE Schooner, 102bm, 60 × 20ft. Purch. 5.1764 North America. Burnt 9.6.1772 Rhode I.

GASPE Brig 6. In service 1774. Captured 11.1775 by Americans; recaptured 4.1776, sold.

GASPE Coastal minesweeper (RCN), 'Bay' class. Davie SB, Lauzon, 12.11.1951. Tx Turkish Navy 19.5.1958 = TRABZON. Patrol vessel 1991.

GATINEAU Frigate (RCN), 2,370 tons, 366 (oa) × 42ft, 4—3in, 2—40mm, 6—TT, Limbo. Davie SB 3.6.1957. PO 1998.

GATINEAU *See also EXPRESS 1934.*

GATWICK Paddle minesweeper, 'Ascot' class. Dundee SB 18.4.1916. Sold 3.1922 Ward, Inverkeithing.

GAUNTLET Destroyer, c. 2,000 tons, 341·5 × 39·5ft, 4—4·5in, 6—40mm, 10—TT. Thornycroft, ordered 8.1944, cancelled 12.12.1945.

GAVINTON Coastal minesweeper, 'Ton' class. Doig, Grimsby, 27.7.1953. Arr. Bruges 15.10.1991 for BU.

GAVOTTE Minesweeper, 260 tons, 130 × 26ft, 1—3pdr. Goole SB 3.1911; War Dept tug, tx 12.1917. Ret. 1920 War Dept.

GAWLER Minesweeper, 'Bathurst' class. Broken Hill Co., Whyalla, 4.10.1941. Lent RAN 1942–46. Sold 8.1946 Turkish Navy = AYVALIK. Withdrawn 1963.

GAWLER Patrol boat (RAN), 211 tons, North Queensland Co., Cairns, 9.7.1983.

GAYUNDAH Gunvessel (Australian), 360 tons, 115 × 25ft, 1—8in, 1—6in, 1—3pdr. Armstrong 1884. Sold 1921 mercantile.

GAZELLE Minesweeper, 'Catherine' class. Savannah Machinery 10.1.1943 on Lend-Lease. Ret. USN 12.1946.

GEELONG Minesweeper (RAN), 'Bathurst' class.

Melbourne Harbour Trust 22.4.1941. Sunk 18.10.1944 collision SS *York* between New Guinea and Australia.

GEELONG Patrol boat (RAN), 211 tons, North Queensland Co., Cairns, 23.3.1984.

GELYKNEID 3rd Rate 64, 1,305bm, 156 × 44ft. Dutch, captured 11.10.1797 Battle of Camperdown. Prison ship 1799. Sold 1.9.1814.

GENERAL ABERCROMBIE *See ABERCROMBIE 1915.*

GENERAL CRAUFURD (ex-CRAUFURD, ex-M.7) Monitor, 5,900 tons, 320 × 87ft, 2—12in, 2—6in, 2—12pdr. Harland & Wolff 8.7.1915 (re-named 1915). Sold 9.5.1921 Ward, New Holland; arr. 9.1923 for BU.

GENERAL GRANT *See HAVELOCK 1915.*

GENERAL MONK (ex-GENERAL WASHING-TON) Armed ship 20. American privateer, captured 9.1781 by CHATHAM. Recaptured 8.4.1782 by American privateer HYDER ALI.

GENERAL PLATT (ex-PORTO CORSINI) Gunboat, 280 tons, 2—3in. Italian, salved 1941 Massawa. Sold 6.1946 Massawa.

GENERAL WOLFE (ex-SIR JAMES WOLFE, ex-WOLFE, ex-M.9) Monitor, 5,900 tons, 320 × 87ft, 2—12in, 2—6in, 2—12pdr. Palmer 9.9.1915 (re-named 1915). Sold 9.5.1921 Ward, Hayle; arr. 12.1923 for BU.

GENEREUX 3rd Rate 74, 1,962bm, 185·5 × 49ft. French, captured 18.2.1800 by squadron in Mediterranean. Prison ship 1805. BU 2.1816.

GENISTA Sloop, 'Arabis' class. Napier & Miller 22.2.1916. Sunk 23.10.1916 by U.57 Atlantic.

GENISTA Corvette, 'Flower' class. Harland & Wolff 24.7.1941. Tx Air Ministry 1947 = *Weather Recorder*. BU 10.1961 Antwerp.

GENOA (ex-BRILLANT) 3rd Rate 78, 1,883bm, 181 × 47·5ft. French , captured 18.4.1814 on stocks Genoa, launched there. BU 1.1838.

GENTIAN Sloop, 'Arabis' class. Greenock & Grangemouth 23.12.1915. Sunk 16.7.1919 mine Gulf of Finland.

GENTIAN Corvette, 'Flower' class. Harland & Wolff 6.8.1940. BU 8.1947 Chicks, Purfleet.

GENTILLE 5th Rate 40. French, captured 11.4.1795 by HANNIBAL in English Channel. Sold 9.1802 Portsmouth.

GEORGE Ship. Built 1338 R. Hamble.

GEORGE Carrack, 600bm. Genoese, captured 15.8.1416. Sold 10.8.1425.

GEORGE Ballinger, 120bm. Smallhithe 1420. Sold 8.1423.

GEORGE 28-gun ship, 80bm. Purch. 1546. Listed until 1557.

GEORGE Hoy, 50bm listed 1564–85.

GEORGE Hoy, 100bm. Purch. 1588. Listed until 1603.

GEORGE Fireship. Listed 1652.

GEORGE Dogger 8. Dutch, captured 1672. Sold 1674.

GEORGE Fireship 6, 393bm. Purch. 1672. Sunk 1674 foundation Sheerness.

GEORGE Schooner 8 (Canadian lakes). Listed 1755. Captured 14.8.1756 by French at Oswego.

GEORGE Tender. Listed 1774. Wrecked 26.12.1776 nr Piscatagua, North America.

GEORGE Gunvessel 2, 61bm, 55 × 16·5ft. Purch. 3.1794. Sold 10.1798.

GEORGE Sloop 6, 105bm, 6—4pdr. Captured 1796. Captured 3.1.1798 by two Spanish privateers West Indies.

GEORGEHAM Inshore minesweeper, 'Ham' class. Harris, Appledore, 15.2.1957. Sold 27.11.1967.

GEORGETOWN (ex-MADDOX) Destroyer, 1,060 tons, 309 × 30·5ft, 1—4in, 1—3in, 4—20mm, 3—TT. USN, cd RN 23.9.1940. Lent RCN 9.1942–12.1943; lent Soviet Navy 10.8.1944–9.1952 = ZHOSTKY. Arr. 16.9.1952 Ward, Inverkeithing, for BU.

GEORGIANA Schooner 2 (Indian), 90bm. Bombay DY 1855. Listed 1866.

GERALDTON Minesweeper, 'Bathurst' class. Poole & Steel, Sydney, 16.8.1941. Lent RAN until 1946. Sold 8.1946 Turkish Navy = ANTALYA; = AYVALIK 1963; deleted 1975.

GERALDTON Patrol boat (RAN). North Queensland Co. 22.10.1983.

GERANIUM Sloop, 'Arabis' class. Greenock & Grangemouth 8.11.1915. RAN 1920. Dismantled 1932 Sydney; hull sunk 24.4.1935 target off Sydney.

GERANIUM Corvette, 'Flower' class. Simons 23.4.1940. Sold 24.9.1945 RNorN = THETIS; discarded 1963.

GERMAINE Armed ship 20. Purch. 1779. Captured 1781 (by French?).

GERMAINE Brig-sloop 16, 240bm, 88 × 26ft. Purch. 1782. Sold 25.3.1784.

GERMOON PRIZE 6th Rate 10, 103bm. French, captured 1692. Sunk 4.7.1700 while careening at Porto Bello.

GERRANS BAY (ex-LOCH CARRON) Frigate, 'Bay' class. Smith's Dock 14.3.1945 (renamed 1944). = SURPRISE (despatch vessel) 1945. Arr. 29.6.1965 McLellan, Bo'ness, for BU.

GEYSER Wood paddle sloop, 1,054bm, 180 × 36ft. Pembroke Dock 6.4.1841. BU 1866.

GHURKA Destroyer, 880 tons, 255 × 25·5ft. 3—

12pdr (1911: 5—12pdr), 2—TT. Hawthorn Leslie 29.4.1907. Sunk 8.2.1917 mine off Dungeness.

GHURKA *See also Indian TB.7 1888. See also GURKHA.*

GIBRALTAR 6th Rate 20, 280bm, 94 × 26ft. Deptford DY 18.10.1711. Rebuilt Deptford 1727 as 374bm. Sold 16.3.1748.

GIBRALTAR 6th Rate 20, 430bm, 108 × 30·5ft. Portsmouth DY 9.5.1754. BU comp. 18.11.1773 Portsmouth.

GIBRALTAR Brig 14, 85bm, 63 × 21ft. American, captured 1779. Captured 7.1781 by Spanish off Gibraltar = SALVADOR; recaptured 29.7.1800 by ANSON.

GIBRALTAR (ex-FENIX) 2nd Rate 80, 2,185bm, 179 × 53·5ft. Spanish, captured 16.3.1780. Powder hulk 12.1813; lazaretto 9.1824. BU 11.1836 Pembroke Dock.

GIBRALTAR Screw 1st Rate 101, 3,716bm, 5,724 tons, 252 × 58ft. Devonport DY 16.8.1860. 85 guns 1862 (1—110pdr, 36—8in 4—70pdr, 12—40pdr, 32—32pdr). Lent 1872 as TS. = GRAMPIAN 1889. Sold 1899.

GIBRALTAR 1st class cruiser, 7,700 tons, 360 × 60ft, 2—9·2in, 10—6in, 12—6pdr. Napier, Govan, 27.4.1892. Depot ship 1914. Sold 9.1923 Cashmore, Newport.

GIBRALTAR Aircraft carrier, c. 45,000 tons. Vickers Armstrong, Tyne, ordered 15.9.1943, cancelled 10.1945.

GIBRALTAR PRIZE Sloop 14, 117bm, 59 × 18·5ft, 14—4pdr. French privateer, captured 2.1757 by GIBRALTAR. Sold 22.1.1761.

GIER Brig-sloop 14, 324bm, 91 × 29·5ft, 12—12pdr, 2—6pdr. Dutch, captured 12.9.1799 by WOLVERINE off Texel. BU 9.1803.

GIFFARD (ex-BUDDLEIA) Corvette (RCN), Modified 'Flower' class. Alex Hall 19.6.1943 (renamed 9.1943). Sold 1946; BU 10.1952 Hamilton.

GIFFARD *See also TORONTO 1943.*

GIFFORD Seaward defence boat, 'Ford' class. Scarr, Hessle, 30.6.1954. Tx Nigerian Navy 1968 = BONNY; deleted 1983.

GIFT (ex-DON DE DIEU) 40-gun ship, 490bm. French, captured 1652. = GIFT MAJOR 1658. Expended as fireship 1666.

GIFT (GIFT MINOR; ex-BON JESUS) 16-gun ship, 128bm. Spanish, captured 1658. Sold 1667.

GIFT Destroyer, c. 2,000 tons, 341·5 × 39·5ft, 4—4·5in, 6—40mm, 10—TT. Thornycroft, ordered 8.1944, = GLOWWORM 9.1945, cancelled 12.12.1945.

GIFT (ex-GLOWWORM, ex-GUINEVERE) Destroyer, c. 2,000 tons, 341·5 × 39·5ft, 4—4·5in, 6—

40mm, 10—TT. Denny, ordered 8.1944, renamed 9.1945, 10.1945, cancelled 12.12.1945.

GIFT MINOR *See GIFT 1658.*

GILES Ketch 2,48bm. Purch. 1661. Sold 1667.

GILIA Sloop, 'Anchusa' class. Barclay Curle 15.3.1918. Sold 15.1.1923 Unity S. Bkg Co.

GILLIFLOWER Row-barge, 20bm. In service 1546—52.

GILLIFLOWER 32-gun ship. Royalist, purch. 1651. Deserted to Parliamentarians 1651. Sold 1667.

GIPSY Schooner 19. In service 1799—1804.

GIPSY Schooner 10, 121bm, 69 × 20ft, 10—4pdr. Purch. 12.1804 Jamaica. Sold 1808 in Jamaica.

GIPSY Schooner tender, 70bm, 53 × 18ft. Sheerness DY 27.10.1836. Sold 12.8.1892 W. Meehan.

GIPSY Destroyer, 380 tons, 227 × 22ft, 1—12pdr, 5—6pdr, 2—TT. Fairfield 9.3.1897. Sold 17.3.1921 Beard, Teignmouth; hull used as pontoon Dartmouth until 1937 or later.

GIPSY Destroyer, 1,335 tons, 323 (oa) × 33ft, 4—4·7in, 8—TT. Fairfield 7.11.1935. Sunk 21.11.1939 mine off Harwich.

GIRDLE NESS (ex-PENLEE POINT) Repair ship, 8,580 tons, 425 × 57ft, 16—20mm. Burrard, Vancouver, 28.3.1945 (renamed 10.1944). Sold 10.7.1970; BU Faslane.

GIRONDE Sloop 10, 239bm, 92 × 26ft. French privateer, captured by BOADICEA 9.1800. Sold 7.9.1801.

GLACE BAY (ex-LAUZON) Frigate (RCN), 'River' class. G. T. Davie 6.4.1944. Sold 3.1.1946 Chilean Navy = ESMERALDA; =BAQUEDANO 1952. Sold 29.11.1968 for BU.

GLACE BAY MCDV (RCN), 'Kingston' class, 962 tons, 181·4 (oa) × 37·1ft, 1—40mm, Halifax SY 22.1.1996.

GLACE BAY *See also LAUZON 1944.*

GLADIATOR 5th Rate 44, 882bm, 140 × 38ft. Adams, Buckler's Hard, 20.1.1783. BU 8.1817. *Harbour service vessel, never at sea.*

GLADIATOR Wood paddle frigate, 1,190bm, 190 × 37·5ft, 2—110pdr, 4—10in. Woolwich DY 15.10.1844. BU 3.1879.

GLADIATOR 2nd class cruiser, 5,750 tons, 320 × 57ft, 4—6in, 6—4·7in, 9—12pdr. Portsmouth DY 18.12.1896. Sunk 25.4.1908 collision SS *St Paul* off I. of Wight; raised 10.1908, sold 5.8.1909.

GLADIOLUS Sloop, 'Arabis' class. Connell, Scotstoun, 25.10.1915. Sold 9.1920 Portuguese Navy = REPUBLICA; discarded c. 1943.

GLADIOLUS Corvette, 'Flower' class. Smith's Dock 24.1.1940. Sunk 16.10.1941 by U.568 in North Atlantic.

GLADSTONE Minesweeper (RAN), 'Bathurst' class. Walker, Maryborough, 26.11.1942. Sold 16.6.1956 = *Akuna*

GLADSTONE Patrol boat (RAN), 211 tons. North Queensland Co. 28.7.1984.

GLAISDALE Destroyer, 'Hunt' class Type III. Cammell Laird 5.1.1942. Lent RNorN 1.6.1942. Sold 1946 in Norway.

GLAMORGAN GM destroyer, 5,440 tons, 520·5 (oa) × 54ft, 4—4·5in (later 2—4.5, Exocet), 2—20mm, Sea Slug, helo. Vickers Armstrong, Tyne, 9.7.1964. Sold Chile 1986 = ALMIRANTE LATORRE. PO 31.12.1998, deleted.

GLASGOW (ex-ROYAL MARY) 6th Rate 20, 284bm, 92 × 26·5ft. Scottish, tx 1.5.1707. Sold 20.8.1719.

GLASGOW 6th Rate 24, 504bm, 112 × 32ft. Reed, Hull, 22.5.1745. Sold 8.4.1756.

GLASGOW 6th Rate 20, 452bm, 109 × 30·5ft. Blaydes, Hull, 31.8.1757. Burnt 19.6.1779 accident Montego Bay, Jamaica.

GLASGOW 4th Rate 50 (pitch pine-built), 1,260bm, 159 × 42ft. Wigram & Green, Blackwall, 21.2.1814. BU comp. 29.1.1829 Chatham.

GLASGOW Wood screw frigate, 3,027bm, 4,020 tons, 250 × 52ft, 1—110pdr, 26—8in, 4—70pdr. Portsmouth DY 28.3.1861. Sold 12.1884.

GLASGOW 2nd class cruiser, 4,800 tons, 430 × 47ft, 2—6in, 10—4in. Fairfield 30.9.1909. Sold 29.4.1927 Ward, Morecambe.

GLASGOW Cruiser, 9,100 tons, 591·5 (oa) × 61·7ft, 12—6in, 8—4in. Scotts 20.6.1936. Arr. 8.7.1958 Hughes Bolckow, Blyth, for BU.

GLASGOW Destroyer, Type 42 Batch 1, 3,150 tons. Swan Hunter 14.4.1976.

GLASSERTON Inshore minesweeper, 'Ton' class. Doig, Grimsby, 3.12.1953. Static TS R. Thames 1983–87. Sold Pounds; towed 8.12.1987 Spain for BU.

GLASSFORD Seaward defence boat, 'Ford' class. Dunston, Thorne, 28.3.1955. Tx SAN 23.8.1955 = NAUTILUS. Sold 4.1989 for conv. to yacht.

GLATTON 4th Rate 56, 1,256bm, 164 × 42ft, 28—32pdr carr., 28—18pdr. East Indiaman, purch. 1795. Water depot 1814. Sunk 10.1830 breakwater Harwich.

GLATTON Wood screw floating battery, 1,535bm, 172·5 × 45ft, 14—68pdr. Mare, Blackwall, 18.4.1855. BU 1864.

GLATTON Turret ship, 4,910 tons, 245 × 54ft, 2—12in, 3—6pdr. Chatham DY 8.3.1871. Sold 7.7.1903; BU King, Garston.

GLATTON (ex-BJOERGVIN) Coast defence ship, 5,700 tons, 310 (oa) × 74ft, 2—9·2in, 6—6in.

Armstrong 8.8.1914; Norwegian, purch. 31.1.1915. Blown up 16.9.1918 accident Dover harbour; raised, BU 1925.

GLEANER Survey ketch, 154bm. Hired 12.7.1808, purch. 1809. Dockyard lighter 8.1811. Lost 2.4.1814.

GLEANER Wood screw gunboat, 216bm, 100 × 22ft, 1—68pdr, 1—32pdr, 2—24pdr howitzers. Deptford DY 7.10.1854. Sold 4.1868 Montevideo.

GLEANER Torpedo gunboat, 735 tons, 230 × 27ft, 2—4·7in, 4—3pdr, 3—TT. Sheerness DY 9.1.1890. Sold 4.4.1905 G. Cohen.

GLEANER (ex-*General Stothard*) Tender, 160 tons, 90 × 19ft. War Dept vessel, tx 1906, renamed 26.11.1906. Sold 2.11.1921 M. S. Hilton.

GLEANER Survey vessel, 835 tons, 230 × 33·5ft (1939: 2—4in). Gray, Hartlepool, 10.6.1937. Minesweeper 1939. Sold 20.4.1950; BU 5.1950 Ward, Preston.

GLEANER Survey launch, 22 tons. Emsworth Shipyard 11.1983.

GLEANER See also GULNARE 1833.

GLENARM Frigate, 'River' class. Robb 8.3.1943. = STRULE 1.2.1944. Tx French Navy 25.9.1944 = CROIX DE LORRAINE. BU 1961 Brest.

GLENELG Minesweeper (RAN), 'Bathurst' class. Cockatoo DY 25.9.1942. Sold 2.5.1957 in Hong Kong for BU.

GLENELG See also WHYALLA 1941.

GLENMORE (ex-TWEED) 5th Rate 36 (fir-built), 926bm, 142·5 × 38ft. Woolwich DY 24.3.1796 (renamed 1795). Sold 3.11.1814.

GLENTHAM Inshore minesweeper, 'Ham' class. Ardrossan DY Co. 29.4.1957. Sold 1.4.1966 in Singapore.

GLOBE 24-gun ship, 250/330bm. Captured 1644. Sold 1648.

GLOIRE (GLORY) 5th Rate 44, 748bm, 131 × 36ft. French, captured 3.5.1747 Cape Finisterre. Sold 15.3.1763.

GLOIRE 5th Rate 40, 876bm, 141 × 38ft. French, captured 10.4.1795 by ASTREA in English Channel. Sold 24.3.1902.

GLOIRE 5th Rate 36, 1,153bm, 158 × 41ft. French, captured 25.9.1809 by MARS and CENTAUR in English Channel. BU 9.1912 Chatham.

GLOIRE See also PALMA 1814. See also GLORY.

GLOMMEN Brig-sloop 16, 303bm, 94·5 × 27ft, 16—24pdr carr., 2—6pdr. Danish, captured 7.9.1807 Battle of Copenhagen. Wrecked 11.1809 Barbados. *Was named BRITOMART 21.1.1808.*

GLORIEUX 3rd Rate 74. French, captured 12.4.1782 off Dominica. Foundered 16.9.1782 gale off Newfoundland.

GLORIOSA Corvette, 'Flower' class. Harland & Wolff, ordered 8.4.1940, cancelled 23.1.1941.

GLORIOSO 3rd Rate 74. Spanish, captured 8.10.1747 off Lagos. Sold 13.4.1749.

GLORIOUS 1st class cruiser (also 'large light cruiser'; officially 'battle cruiser') 18,600 tons, 735 × 81ft, 4—15in, 18—4in, 2—3in. Harland & Wolff 20.4.1916. Conv. aircraft carrier comp. 1.1930. Sunk 8.6.1940 by German battlecruisers off Narvik.

GLORY 5th Rate 32, 679bm, 125 × 33ft. Blaydes & Hodgson, Hull, 24.10.1763. = APOLLO 30.8.1774. BU 1.1786 Woolwich.

GLORY (ex-GLOIRE) Lugger 8, 114bm, 70 × 19ft. French, captured 1781. BU 3.1783 Plymouth.

GLORY 2nd Rate 90, 1,944bm, 178 × 50ft. Plymouth DY 5.7.1788. Prison ship 1809; powder hulk 1814. BU comp. 30.7.1825 Chatham.

GLORY Battleship, 12,950 tons, 390 × 74ft, 4—12in, 12—6in, 12—12pdr. Laird 11.3.1899. = CRESCENT (depot ship) 1.5.1920. Sold 19.12.1922 Granton S. Bkg Co.

GLORY Aircraft carrier, 13,190 tons, 630 × 80ft, 19—40mm, 48 aircraft. Harland & Wolff 27.11.1943. Arr. 8.1961 Ward, Inverkeithing, for BU.

GLORY *See also GLORY 1747.*

GLORY IV (ex-ASKOLD) Depot ship, 6,500 tons, 440 × 49ft. Russian cruiser, seized, renamed 3.8.1918. Ret. Soviet Navy 1920.

GLOUCESTER 54-gun ship, 755bm. Graves, Limehouse, 1654. Wrecked 6.5.1682 off Yarmouth.

GLOUCESTER 4th Rate 60, 896bm, 145 × 37·5ft. Clements, Bristol, 5.2.1695. Harbour service 1706. BU 10.1731.

GLOUCESTER 4th Rate 60, 923bm, 144 × 38·5ft. Burchett, Rotherhithe, 25.7.1709. Captured 26.10.1709 by French LYS off Cape Clear.

GLOUCESTER 4th Rate 50, 714bm, 130 × 35ft. Deptford 4.10.1711. BU 20.1.1724 Sheerness.

GLOUCESTER 4th Rate 50, 866bm, 134 × 38·5ft. Sheerness DY 22.3.1737. Damaged 7.1742 storm; burnt 16.8.1742 nr Landrones to avoid capture by Spanish.

GLOUCESTER 4th Rate 50, 986bm, 141 × 40ft. Whetstone & Greville, Rotherhithe, 23.3.1745. Harbour service 1758. BU comp. 13.2.1764 Sheerness.

GLOUCESTER Brig 10 (Canadian lakes), 165bm, 10—12pdr. Kinyton, Ontario, 5.1807. Captured 25.4.1813 by Americans at York, Lake Erie; destroyed 29.5.1813 by British at Sackets Harbour.

GLOUCESTER 3rd Rate 74, 1,770bm, 177 × 49ft.

Pitcher, Northfleet, 27.2.1812. 50-gun 4th Rate 1832; harbour service 1861. Sold 3.1884 Castle, Charlton.

GLOUCESTER 2nd class cruiser, 4,800 tons, 430 × 47ft, 2—6in, 10—4in. Beardmore 28.10.1909. Sold 9.5.1921 Ward, Portishead and Briton Ferry.

GLOUCESTER Cruiser, 9,400 tons, 591·5 (oa) × 62·3ft, 12—6in, 8—4in. Devonport DY 19.10.1937. Sunk 22.5.1941 air attack south-west of Crete.

GLOUCESTER (ex-PANTHER) Frigate, 2,170 tons. Portsmouth DY, ordered 1956, cancelled.

GLOUCESTER Destroyer, Type 42 Batch 3. Vosper-Thornycroft 2.11.1982.

GLOWWORM Coastal destroyer, 255 tons, 166·5 × 17·5ft, 2—12pdr, 3—TT. Thornycroft, Chiswick, 20.12.1906. = TB.7 in 1906. Sold 9.5.1921 Ward, Rainham.

GLOWWORM River gunboat, 645 tons, 230 × 36ft, 2—6in, 2—12pdr. Barclay Curle 5.2.1916. Sold 9.1928 L. Gatt, Malta.

GLOWWORM Destroyer, 1,345 tons, 323 (oa) × 33ft, 4—4·7in, 10—TT. Thornycroft 22.7.1935. Sunk 8.4.1940 by German ADMIRAL HIPPER off Norway.

GLOWWORM (ex-GUINEVERE) Destroyer, c. 2,000 tons, 341·5 × 39·5ft, 4—4·5in, 6—40mm, 10—TT. Denny (renamed 9.1945). = GIFT 10.1945, cancelled 1.12.1945.

GLOWWORM (ex-GIFT) Destroyer, c. 2,000 tons, 341·5 × 39·5ft, 4—4·5in, 6—40mm, 10—TT. Thornycroft, renamed 10.1945, cancelled 12.12.1945.

GLOXINIA Corvette, 'Flower' class. Harland & Wolff 2.7.1940. Arr. 15.7.1947 Chicks, Purfleet, for BU.

GLUCKSTADT Brig-sloop 18, 338bm. 102 × 28ft, 16—18pdr carr., 2—6pdr. Danish, captured 7.9.1807 Batle of Copenhagen. Sold 30.6.1814. *Was to have been renamed RAISON.*

GNAT Wood screw gunboat, 'Cheerful' class. Laird 10.5.1856. BU 8.1864.

GNAT Composite screw gunvessel, 464bm, 155 × 25ft, 1—7in, 1—64pdr, 2—20pdr, Pembroke Dock 26.11.1867. Wrecked 15.11.1868 Balabac I., China Sea.

GNAT Coastal destroyer, 255 tons, 166·5 × 17·5ft, 2—12pdr, 3—TT. Thornycroft, Chiswick, 1.12.1906. = TB.8 in 1906. Sold 9.5.1921 Ward, Rainham.

GNAT River gunboat, 645 tons, 230 × 36ft, 2—6in, 2—12pdr. Lobnitz 3.12.1915. Torpedoed 21.10.1941 by Italian submarine off Bardia, beached Alexandria as AA platform; BU 1945.

GOATHLAND Destroyer, 'Hunt' class Type III.

GODAVARI Fairfield 3.2.1942. Damaged by mine 24.7.1944 off Normandy; arr. 8.1945 Troon for BU

GODAVARI Sloop (RIN), 1,300 tons, 299·5 (oa) × 37·5ft, 6—4in. Thornycroft 21.1.1943. = SIND (RPN) 1948. Sold 2.6.1959 for BU in Pakistan.

GODAVARI *See also BEDALE 1941.*

GODERICH Minesweeper (RCN), 'Bangor' class. Dufferin, Toronto, 15.5.1941. LU 1946. Sold 2.1959 Marine Industries.

GODETIA Sloop, 'Arabis' class. Yarrow 8.1.1916. HO Ward 26.2.1937 part payment *Majestic* (CALEDONIA, q.v.); BU Milford Haven.

GODETIA Corvette, 'Flower' class. Smith's Dock 8.5.1940. Sunk 6.9.1940 collision SS *Marsa* off Northern Ireland.

GODETIA (ex-DART) Corvette, 'Flower' class. Crown 24.9.1941 (renamed 1941). Sold 22.5.1947; BU Ward, Grays.

GOELAN (ex-GOELAND) Sloop 14. French, captured 4.1793 by PENELOPE in West Indies. Sold 16.10.1794.

GOELAN (ex-GOELAND) Brig-sloop 16, 334bm, 19·5 × 28ft. French, captured 13.10.1803 by PIQUE and PELICAN off San Domingo. BU 9.1810.

GOLD COAST (ex-HARVEY) Frigate, 'Colony' class. Walsh Kaiser 21.9.1943 on Lend-Lease (renamed 1943). = LABUAN 1943. Ret. USN 5.1946.

GOLDEN FALCON *See FALCON 1652.*

GOLDEN FLEECE (ex-HUMBERSTONE) Minesweeper, 'Algerine' class. Redfern 29.2.1944 (renamed 6.1943). Arr. 8.8.1960 Rees, Llanelly, for BU.

GOLDEN HIND *See PELICAN 1577.*

GOLDEN HORSE 4th Rate 46, 722bm, 126 × 37ft. Algerian, captured 9.4.1681 by ADVENTURE. Sunk 1688 foundation Chatham.

GOLDEN LION *See LION 1557.*

GOLDEN ROSE Fireship 6, 163bm. Algerian, captured 1681. Sold 1687.

GOLDFINCH Brig-sloop 10, 'Cherokee' class, 237bm. Warwick, Eling, 8.8.1808. Sold 8.11.1838 R. Willis.

GOLDFINCH Wood screw gunboat, 'Albacore' class. Wigram, Blackwall, 2.2.1856. BU 6.1869 Pembroke Dock.

GOLDFINCH 1st class gunboat, 805 tons, 165 × 31ft, 6—4in, 2—3pdr. Sheerness DY 18.5.1889. Survey vessel 2.1902. Sold 14.5.1907 for BU.

GOLDFINCH Destroyer, 747 tons, 246 × 25ft, 2—4in, 2—12pdr, 2—TT. Fairfield 12.7.1910. Wrecked 19.2.1915 Orkneys; wreck sold 4.1919.

GOLIATH 3rd Rate 74, 1,604bm, 168 × 47ft. Deptford DY 19.10.1781. 58-gun 4th Rate 1812. BU 6.1815.

GOLIATH 2nd Rate 80, 2,596bm, 190 × 57ft. Chatham DY 25.7.1842; undocked 30.11.1857 as screw ship. Lent 1870 as TS. Burnt 22.12.1875 accident.

GOLIATH Battleship, 12,950 tons, 390 × 74ft, 4—12in, 12—12pdr. Chatham DY 23.3.1898. Sunk 13.5.1915 by Turkish torpedo boat MUAVENET off Cape Helles.

GOLIATH *See also CLARENCE 1827.*

GOMATI *See LAMERTON 1940.*

GONDWANA Minesweeper (RIN), 'Bathurst' class. Garden Reach, Calcutta, cancelled 2.1945.

GONDWANA *See also BURNET 1943.*

GOOD FORTUNE Dogger 6. Dutch, captured 1665. Sunk 7.1667 blockship R. Medway.

GOOD HOPE (ex-AFRICA) Armoured cruiser, 14,100 tons, 500 × 71ft, 2—9·2in, 16—6in, 12—12pdr. Fairfield 21.2.1901 (renamed 2.10.1899). Sunk 1.11.1914 Battle of Coronel.

GOOD HOPE 35-gun ship, 272bm, 101 × 24ft. In service 1664. Captured 5.1665 by French in North Sea.

GOOD HOPE Flyboat 6, 180bm, 76 × 21ft. Dutch, captured 1665. Sold 1667.

GOOD HOPE (ex-LOCH BOISDALE) Frigate (SAN), 'Loch' class. Blyth DD 5.7.1944 (renamed 1944). Expended False Bay 12.6.1978 breakwater.

GOOD INTENT Gunvessel. In service 1792. Captured 1793 by French.

GOOD INTENT Gunvessel. Purch. 8.1795. BU 12.1801.

GOOD WILL Cutter, 49bm. Purch. 1.1763. Listed until 1768

GOODALL (ex-REYBOLD) Frigate, DE 'Captain' class. Boston NY 8.7.1943; USN, on Lend-Lease. Sunk 29.4.1945 by U-boat Kola Inlet.

GOODSON (ex-GEORGE) Frigate, DE 'Captain' class. Boston NY 8.7.1943; USN, on Lend-Lease. Torpedoed 25.6.1944 off Cherbourg, damaged beyond repair; nominally ret. USN 1.1947; BU 10.1948 Whitchurch.

GOODWIN 6th Rate 6, 74bm, 59 × 16ft. French, captured 1691. Sunk 23.2.1695 by French privateer off Dover.

GOODWOOD Paddle minesweeper, 'Ascot' class. Dundee SB 15.6.1916. Sold 7.1922 Stanlee, Dover.

GOOLE (ex-BRIDLINGTON) Minesweeper, Later 'Hunt' class. Ayrshire Co. 12.8.1919 (renamed 1918). Comp. 4.1926 RNVR drillship; = IRWELL 9.1926. Arr. 27.11.1962 Lacmotts, Liverpool, for BU.

GOOSE BAY MCDV (RCN), 'Kingston' class, 962

tons, 181·4 (oa) × 37·1ft, 1—40mm. Halifax SY 4.9.1997.

GORDON (ex-*Miner*) Tender, 125 tons, 95 × 17·5ft. War Dept vessel, tx 1907. Sold 1907.

GORE (ex-HERZOG) Frigate, DE 'Captain' class. Boston NY 8.7.1943 on Lend-Lease. Ret. USN 5.1946.

GOREE Sloop. French, captured 2.1.1759 at Goree. PO 16.8.1763.

GOREE Sloop 16, 217bm, 89 × 24·5ft, 12—12pdr carr., 4—6pdr. French, captured 1800. Sold 21.4.1806 Heather.

GOREE *See also HAYLING 1729, FAVOURITE 1794.*

GOREY CASTLE *See HEDINGHAM CASTLE 1944.*

GORGON 5th Rate 44, 911bm, 140 × 38·5ft. Perry, Blackwall, 27.1.1785. Storeship 7.1793; floating battery 1805. BU 2.1817.

GORGON Wood paddle frigate (ex-5th Rate), 1,111bm, 178 × 37·5ft, 2—10in, 4—32pdr. Pembroke Dock 31.8.1837. Sold Castle 7.10.1864 for BU.

GORGON Turret ship, 3,560 tons, 225 × 45ft, 4—10in, 4—3pdr. Palmer 14.10.1871. Sold 12.5.1903.

GORGON (ex-NIDAROS) Coast defence ship, 5,700 tons, 310 (oa) × 74ft, 2—9·2in, 4—6in. Armstrong 9.6.1914; Norwegian, purch. 9.1.1915. Sold 28.8.1928 Ward, Pembroke Dock.

GORGON Minesweeper, 'Catherine' class. Savannah Machinery 24.1.1943. Ret. USN 12.1946; sold Greek Navy.

GORLESTON (ex-ITASCA) Cutter, 1,546 tons, 256 (oa) × 42ft, 1—5in, 2—3in. Tx 31.5.1941 on Lend-Lease. Ret. USN 4.1946.

GORLESTON *See also GAINSBOROUGH 1918.*

GOSHAWK Brig-sloop 16 (fir-built), 285bm, 96 × 26ft, 14—24pdr carr., 2—6pdr. Wallis, Blackwall, 17.7.1806. Wrecked 21.9.1813 Mediterranean.

GOSHAWK Brig-sloop 18 (fir-built). Frames made Chatham DY 1814, shipped Halifax, NS, for comp. Canadian lakes. Unsuitable; sold 5.1815 Halifax.

GOSHAWK Wood screw gunboat, 'Albacore' class. Wigram, Blackwall, 9.2.1856. BU 3.1869 Devonport.

GOSHAWK Composite screw gunboat, 430 tons, 125 × 23ft, 2—64pdr, 2—20pdr. Pembroke Dock 23.1.1872. Hulk 1902. Sold c. 1906.

GOSHAWK Destroyer, 760 tons, 240 × 25·5ft, 2—4in, 2—12pdr, 2—TT. Beardmore 18.10.1911. Sold 4.11.1921 Rees, Llanelly.

GOSHAWK *See also NERBUDDA 1847.*

GOSPORT 5th Rate 32, 376bm, 108 × 28ft. Collins & Chatfield, Shoreham, 3.9.1696. Captured 28.8.1706 by French.

GOSPORT 5th Rate 44, 530bm, 118 × 32ft, Woolwich DY 8.3.1707. BU 1735.

GOSPORT 5th Rate 44, 691bm, 124 × 36ft. Snelgrove, Limehouse, 20.2.1741. BU comp. 16.6.1768 Chatham.

GOSSAMER Tender, 48bm, 47 × 16ft. Gosport, purch. 7.1821 on stocks. Sold 22.11.1861 J. Levy, Rochester.

GOSSAMER Torpedo gunboat, 735 tons, 230 × 27ft, 2—4·7in, 4—3pdr, 3—TT. Sheerness DY 9.1.1890. Minesweeper 1908. Sold 20.3.1920 Cornish Salvage Co., Ilfracombe.

GOSSAMER Minesweeper, 835 tons, 230 × 33·5ft, 2—4in. Hamilton 5.10.1937. Sunk 24.6.1942 air attack Kola Inlet.

GOSSAMER *See also M.11 1939.*

GOULBURN Minesweeper, 'Bathurst' class. Cockatoo DY 17.11.1940. Sold 16.3.1947; resold = *Benita.*

GOULD (ex-LOVERING) Frigate, DE 'Captain' class. Boston NY 4.6.1943; USN, on Lend-Lease. Sunk 1.3.1944 by U.358 north of Azores.

GOZO Minesweeper, 'Algerine' class. Redfern 27.1.1943 on Lend-Lease. Ret. USN 1946. Sold Greek Navy = POLEMISTIS; sunk target 1975.

GOZO *See also MALTA 1800.*

GRACE Cutter, 101bm. Purch. 1.1763. BU 12.1772.

GRACE Gunvessel, 70bm, 57 × 17ft. Purch. 3.1794. Sold 10.1798.

GRACE DIEU Ship. Dates from 1390. Given away 1400.

GRACE DIEU Ballinger. Ratcliffe 1402. Given away 12.1409.

GRACE DIEU Ship, 400/600bm. Soper, Southampton, 1418. Struck by lightning 7.1.1439, burnt at Bursledon. *Was never at sea. Ribs still visible at low water; salvage contemplated 1967.*

GRACE DIEU 100-gun ship, 600/1,000bm. Chatham 1488. = REGENT 1489. Lost 10.8.1512 in action with French off I. of Wight.

GRACE OF GOD Discovery vessel. Captured 1568 by Spanish.

GRACIEUSE Schooner 14, 119bm, 72 × 21ft. French privateer, captured 21.10.1804 by BLANCHE in West Indies. Listed until 1808.

GRAFTON 3rd Rate 70, 1,096bm, 150 × 40·5ft Woolwich DY 1679. Rebuilt Rotherhithe 1700 as 1,102bm. Captured 1.5.1707 by French off Beachy Head.

GRAFTON Firevessel, 18bm, 24 × 12ft. Purch. 8.1694. Sold 17.2.1696.

GRAFTON 3rd Rate 70, 1,095bm, 151 × 40·5ft. Swallow & Fowler, Limehouse, 9.8.1709. Rebuilt Woolwich 1725 as 1,133bm. BU 1744.

GRAFTON 3rd Rate 70, 1,414bm, 160 × 45ft. Portsmouth DY 29.3.1750. Sold 25.8.1767.

GRAFTON 3rd Rate 74, 1,650bm, 168 × 47ft. Deptford DY 26.9.1771. Harbour service 1.1792. BU 5.1816 Portsmouth.

GRAFTON 1st class cruiser, 7,350 tons, 360 × 60ft, 2—9·2in, 10—6in, 12—6pdr. Thames Iron Works, Blackwall, 30.1.1892. Sold 1.7.1920 S. Castle, Plymouth.

GRAFTON Destroyer, 1,335 tons, 323 (oa) × 33ft, 4—4·7in, 8—TT. Thornycroft 18.9.1935. Sunk 29.5.1940 torpedo off Dunkirk.

GRAFTON Destroyer, c. 2,000 tons, 341·5 × 39·5ft, 4—4·5in, 6—40mm, 10—TT. White, ordered 8.1944, cancelled 12.12.1945.

GRAFTON Frigate, 1,180 tons, 300 × 33ft, 2—40mm. White 11.1.1957. Sold 7.12.1971; BU Inverkeithing.

GRAFTON Frigate, 'Norfolk' class. Yarrow, Glasgow, 5.11.1994.

GRAMONT (ex-COMTESSE DE GRAMMONT) Sloop 18, 325bm, 98 × 27·5ft, 18—6pdr. French privateer, captured 10.1757. Recaptured 12.7.1762 by French at St John's, Newfoundland.

GRAMPIAN *See GIBRALTAR 1860.*

GRAMPUS Sloop 14, 160bm, 70 × 23ft. Woolwich DY 21.10.1731. Foundered 10.1742 English Channel.

GRAMPUS Sloop 14, 249bm (?), 87 × 25ft. Perry, Blackwall, 27.7.1743. Captured 30.9.1744 by French in Bay of Biscay.

GRAMPUS Sloop 14, 271bm, 92 × 26ft. Reed, Hull, 3.11.1746. = STROMBOLO (fireship) 1775. Hulk 1780 New York.

GRAMPUS 4th Rate 50, 1,062bm, 148 × 40·5ft. Fisher, Liverpool, 8.10.1782. BU 8.1794.

GRAMPUS (ex-*Ceres*) 4th Rate 54, 1,165bm, 157 × 41ft. East Indiaman, purch. 1795. Storeship 2.1797. Wrecked 19.1.1799 Barking Shelf, nr Woolwich.

GRAMPUS (ex-TIGER, renamed 4.3.1802) 4th Rate 50, 1,114bm, 151 × 42ft. Portsmouth DY 20.3.1802. Harbour service 7.1820. Sold 1832.

GRAMPUS Minelaying submarine, 1,520 tons, 271·5 × 25·5ft, 1—4in, 6—TT, 50 mines. Chatham DY 25.2.1936. Sunk 24.6.1940 by Italian torpedo boats CIRCE and CLIO off Sicily.

GRAMPUS Submarine, 'Porpoise' class, Cammell Laird 30.5.1957. Harbour TS 1976—79. Expended 1980 target.

GRAMPUS *See also BUCKINGHAM 1751, TREMENDOUS 1784, NAUTILUS 1910.*

GRANA 6th Rate 28, 528bm, 118 × 32ft. Spanish, captured 25.2.1781 by CERBERUS off Cape Finisterre. Sold 9.1806.

GRANBY Minesweeper (RCN), diesel 'Bangor' class. Davie SB 9.6.1941. Diving tender 1959. On sale list 10.1966; sold 1975.

GRANBY *See also VICTORIAVILLE 1944.*

GRAND TURK 6th Rate 22, 366bm, 101 × 29ft, 20—9pdr, 2—3pdr. French, captured 26.5.1745. Sold 1.5.1749.

GRANDMERE Minesweeper (RCN), TE 'Bangor' class. Vickers, Montreal, 21.8.1941. Sold 1947 = *Eldo.*

GRANDMISTRESS Ship, 450bm. Built 1545. Condemned 1552.

GRANICUS 5th Rate 36 (yellow pine-built), 942bm, 144 × 38·5ft, 14—32pdr carr., 26—18pdr. Barton, Limehouse, 25.10.1813. Sold 3.4.1817.

GRANTHAM 30-gun ship, 265bm, 98·5 × 25·5ft. Furzer, Southampton, 1654. = GARLAND 1660; fireship 1688; 5th Rate 36. Sold 13.5.1698

GRANTHAM Slop ship. Purch. 10.1787. BU 6.1792.

GRAPH (ex-U.570) Submarine, 760 tons, 213 × 20ft, 5—TT. German, captured 28.8.1941 by BURWELL and trawler NORTHERN CHIEF in North Atlantic, renamed 21.9.1941. Grounded 20.3.1944 Islay while under tow.

GRAPPLER (Gunboat No 28) Gunvessel 12, 170bm, 76 × 22ft, 2—24pdr, 10—18pdr carr. Pitcher, Northfleet, 4.1797. Wrecked 31.12.1803 Chansey Reef, burnt by French.

GRAPPLER Iron paddle vessel, 559bm, 165 × 26·5ft. Fairbairn, Poplar, 30.12.1845. Sold 2.2.1850 P. Beech for BU.

GRAPPLER Mortar vessel, 161bm, 66 × 21ft. 1—13in mortar. Wigram, Blackwall, 1.5.1855. = MV.18 on 19.10.1855; hulked 7.1866. Sold 24.4.1896.

GRAPPLER Wood screw gunboat, 'Albacore' class. Wigram, Blackwall, 29.3.1856. Sold 6.1.1868 Esquimalt as merchantman.

GRAPPLER Composite screw gunboat, 465 tons, 125 × 23·5ft, 2—64pdr, 2—20pdr. Barrow SB (Vickers) 5.10.1880. BDV 1904. Sold 14.5.1907 King, Garston.

GRASS SNAKE Special Service Vessel (RAN), 80 tons. Williamstown 1944. Tx North Borneo 12.1945

GRASSHOPPER (ex-*London*) Sloop 14, 276bm, 94 × 27ft. Purch. 29.12.1776. = BASILISK (fireship) 27.8.1779. Sold 4.1783 Plymouth.

GRASSHOPPER Hoy. Muddle, Gillingham, 1799. Sold 1812.

GRASSHOPPER Brig-sloop 18, 'Cruiser' class, 383bm. Richards, Hythe, 29.9.1806. Captured 25.12.1811 by French off Texel.

GRASSHOPPER Brig-sloop 18, 'Cruizer' class, 385bm, Portsmouth DY 17.5.1813. Sold 30.5.1832 T. Ward

GRASSHOPPER Wood screw gunboat, 'Albacore' class. Pitcher, Northfleet, 8.12.1855. Sold 5.1871 Newchang.

GRASSHOPPER Torpedo gunboat, 550 tons, 200 × 23ft, 1–4in, 6–3pdr, 4–TT. Sheerness DY 30.8.1887. Sold 11.7.1905.

GRASSHOPPER Coastal destroyer, 255 tons, 166·5 × 17·5ft. 2–12pdr , 3–TT. Thornycroft, Chiswick, 18.3.1906. = TB.9 in 1906. Sunk 26.7.1916 collision North Sea.

GRASSHOPPER Destroyer, 923 tons, 274 × 28ft, 1–4in, 3–12pdr, 2–TT. Fairfield 23.11.1909. Sold 1.11.1921 Fryer, Sunderland.

GRASSHOPPER River gunboat, 585 tons, 197 × 33ft, 2–4in, 1–3·7in howitzer. Thornycroft 19.1.1939. Beached 14.2.1942 after Japanese air attack nr Singapore.

GRAVELINES Destroyer, 2,135 tons, 379 (oa) × 40·25ft, 4–4·5in, 1–4in, 12–40mm, 8–TT. Cammell Laird 30.11.1944. Arr. 22.3.1961 Rosyth for BU.

GRAYFLY River boat, 'Fly' class. Yarrow 8.1915 in sections. Tx War Dept 1923.

GRAYS Minesweeper, Later 'Hunt' class. Eltringham, cancelled 1918.

GREAT BARBARA Ship, 400bm. Purch. 1513. Listed until 1524.

GREAT BARK Ship, 200/400bm. Built 1512. Sold c. 1531.

GREAT ELIZABETH *See ELIZABETH 1514*

GREAT GALLEY Galleasse, 800bm. Greenwich 1515. Rebuilt 1583 = GREAT BARK, 600bm. Last mentioned 1562.

GREAT HARRY *See HENRY GRACE A DIEU 1514.*

GREAT NICHOLAS *See NICHOLAS REEDE 1512.*

GREAT PINNACE 80bm. Listed 1544–45

GREAT ZABRA Pinnace, 50bm. Listed 1522–25.

GREATFORD Seaward defence boat, 'Ford' class. White 29.1.1953. Sold 8.9.1967; BU Singapore.

GRECIAN (ex-DOLPHIN) Cutter 10, 145bm, 69 × 23ft. Revenue cutter, renamed 20.11.1821. Sold 11.7.1827 Mr Freake.

GRECIAN Brig-sloop 16, 484bm, 105 × 33·5ft, 16–32pdr. Pembroke Dock 24.4.1838. BU comp. 1.11.1865 Marshall.

GRECIAN Minesweeper, 'Catherine' class. Savannah Machinery 10.3.1943. on Lend-Lease. Ret. USN 1947. Sold 3.1947 Turkish Navy = EDINCIK. Withdrawn 1974.

GRECIAN Schooner 10, 224bm. American

privateer, captured 2.5.1814 by JASEUR. Sold 18.4.1822 J. Cristall for BU.

GREEN LINNET Gunvessel 6, 82bm. Purch. 1806. In service 1810. Gone by 1813.

GREENFISH Storeship 2, 67bm, 61 × 16ft. Purch. 1693. Sold 6.3.1705.

GREENFLY Coastal destroyer, 255 tons, 166·5 × 17·5ft, 2–12pdr, 3–TT. Thornycroft 15.2.1907. = TB.10 in 1906. Sunk 10.1.1915 mine North Sea.

GREENFLY River gunboat, 'Fly' class. Yarrow 9.1915 in sections. Sold 1.3.1923 Basra.

GREENOCK (ex-PEGASUS) Iron screw frigate, 1,413bm, 210 × 37·5ft, 6–8in, 4–32pdr. Scotts, Greenock, 30.4.1849, renamed 1846. Sold 8.1852 Australian Screw Shipping Co.

GREENOCK *See BALUCHISTAN.*

GREENWICH 4th Rate 54, 659bm, 136 × 34ft. 24–24pdr, 22–6pdr, 8–4pdr. Woolwich DY 1666. Rebuilt Portsmouth 1699; rebuilt Chatham 1730 as 756bm. Wrecked 20.10.1744 Jamaica.

GREENWICH 4th Rate 50, 1,053bm, 144·5 × 41·5ft. Janvrin, Lepe, 19.3.1747. Captured 18.3.1757 by French.

GREENWICH 6th Rate 26, 754bm, 145·5 × 35ft. East Indiaman, purch. 9.1777. Sold 10.4.1783.

GREENWICH Sloop 12. American, captured 9.1778. Wrecked 22.5.1779 coast of Carolina.

GREENWICH Depot ship, 8,600 tons, 309 × 52ft, 4–4in, 2–6pdr. Dobson, Tyne, 5.7.1915; Greek merchantman, conv. on stocks; comp. Swan Hunter. Sold 11.7.1946 = *Hembury.*

GREENWICH *See also RODNEY 1809.*

GREETHAM Inshore minesweeper, 'Ham' class. Herd & Mackenzie 19.4.1954. Sold 1962 Libyan Navy = ZUARA. BU 1973.

GRENADA Bomb vessel 12, 279bm, 87 × 27ft. Fowler, Rotherhithe, 26.6.1693. Blown up 16.7.1694 Havre de Grâce.

GRENADA (GRENADO) Bomb vessel 4, 148bm, 64 × 23·5ft. Castle, Deptford, 1695. BU 5.1718 Woolwich.

GRENADA (ex-HARMONIE) Brig 10, 141bm, 71·5 × 22ft. French privateer, captured 16.11.1803, presented 1804 by inhabitants of Grenada. Sold c. 1809.

GRENADA (ex-JENA) Sloop 16. French privateer, captured 6.1.1807 by CRUIZER in North Sea. In service 1810–1814.

GRENADE Destroyer, 1,335 tons, 323 (oa) × 33ft, 4–4·7in, 8–TT. Stephen 12.11.1935. Sunk 29.5.1940 air attack Dunkirk.

GRENADE Destroyer, 1,980 tons, 365 (oa) × 38ft, 6–4in, 6–40mm, 10–TT. Scotts, ordered 4.1943, cancelled 1.1945, not LD.

GRENADO Bomb vessel 12, 279bm, 91 × 26ft. Barnard, Ipswich, 22.6.1742. Sloop 1750; sold 30.8.1763.

GRENADO *See also GRENADA 1695.*

GRENVILLE (ex-*Sally*) Schooner 12, 69bm, 55 × 17ft. Purch. 7.8.1763 Newfoundland. Survey brig 1764. BU 3.1775.

GRENVILLE Destroyer leader, 1,666 tons, 312 × 32ft, 4—4in, 4—TT. Cammell Laird 17.6.1916. Sold 12.1931 Rees, Llanelly.

GRENVILLE Destroyer leader, 1,485 tons, 330 (oa) × 34·5ft, 5—4·7in, 8—TT. Yarrow 15.8.1935. Sunk 19.1.1940 mine North Sea.

GRENVILLE Destroyer, 1,730 tons, 362.7 (oa) × 35·8ft, 4—4·7in, 8—TT. Swan Hunter 12.10.1942. Frigate 1954, 2,240 tons, 2—4in, 2—Limbo. BU 1983 Rochester.

GRENVILLE Fishery protection (Canadian Govt) 497 tons, 155 × 31ft. Polson, Toronto, 1915.

GRETNA Minesweeper, Later 'Hunt' class. Eltringham 11.4.1918. Sold 3.10.1928 Alloa, Rosyth.

GREY FOX Patrol boat, 54·1ft (oa). Halmatic, Southampton. Cd 1.1993. = SABRE 11.2002.

GREY WOLF Patrol boat, 54·1ft (oa). Halmatic, Southampton. Cd 1.1993. = SCIMITAR 11.2002.

GREYHOND 5th Rate 40, 494bm, 114 × 31·5ft. Hubbard, Ipswich, 1703. Wrecked 26.8.1711 Tynemouth.

GREYHOUND 45-gun ship, 160bm. Deptford 1545. Rebuilt 1558. Wrecked 1563 off Rye.

GREYHOUND Ship. In service 1585.

GREYHOUND 12-gun ship, 126bm. Woolwich 28.1.1636. Blown up 1656 in action with Spanish.

GREYHOUND 20-gun ship, 145bm. Captured from Royalists 1657. Expended 1666 fireship.

GREYHOUND 6th Rate 16, 180bm, 93 × 21·5ft, 16—6pdr. Portsmouth DY 1672. Sold 13.5.1698.

GREYHOUND Bomb vessel 6, 94bm, 6—4pdr. Purch. 1694. Sold 3.5.1698.

GREYHOUND 6th Rate 20, 276bm, 94 × 26ft. Woolwich DY 21.6.1712. Captured 1.9.1718 by Spanish in St Jermyn's Bay.

GREYHOUND 6th Rate 20, 371bm, 105 × 28·5ft. Stacey, Deptford, 13.2.1719. BU comp. 6.1741 Deptford. *In Spanish hands 4.1722–15.4.1722.*

GREYHOUND 6th Rate 24, 450bm, 108 × 31ft. Snelgrove, Limehouse, 19.9.1741. Sold 5.4.1768.

GREYHOUND Cutter 15, 73bm, 52 × 18ft. Purch. 2.1763. Hulk 1776. Sold 23.10.1780 Sheerness.

GREYHOUND 6th Rate 28, 617bm, 124 × 33ft. Adams, Buckler's Hard, 20.7.1773. Wrecked 1781 nr Deal.

GREYHOUND Cutter 20, 148bm, 20—4pdr.

Purch. 6.1780. = VIPER 1781, 12 guns. Listed until 1803.

GREYHOUND 5th Rate 32, 682bm, 126 × 35ft. Betts, Mistleythorn, 11.12.1783. Wrecked 4.10.1808 Philippines.

GREYHOUND Wood screw sloop, 880bm, 1,260 tons, 173 × 33ft. Pembroke Dock 15.6.1859. Harbour service 9.1869. Sold 3.4.1906.

GREYHOUND Destroyer, 400 tons, 210 × 21ft, 1—12pdr, 5—6pdr, 2—TT. Hawthorn 6.10.1900. Sold 10.6.1919 Clarkson, Whitby.

GREYHOUND Destroyer, 1,335 tons, 323 (oa) × 33ft, 4—4·7in, 8—TT. Vickers Armstrong, Barrow, 15.8.1935. Sunk 22.5.1941 air attack south of Morea.

GREYHOUND Destroyer, c. 2,000 tons, 341·5 × 39·5ft, 4—4·5in, 6—40mm, 10—TT. White, ordered 8.1944, cancelled 12.12.1945.

GREYHOUND *See also EUPHRATES 1813.*

GRIFFIN 12-gun ship, 121bm. Royalist (ex-French), captured 1665 by Parliamentarians. Foundered 1664 off Jamaica.

GRIFFIN Fireship 8, 266bm, 95 × 25ft. Rolfe & Castle, Rotherthithe, 17.4.1690. Rebuilt Sheerness 1702. Sold 21.7.1737.

GRIFFIN (ex-GRIFFON) 5th Rate 44. French, captured 8.1712 off Finisterre. Ret. France 1713.

GRIFFIN Cutter 12, 186bm, 73 × 26ft, 12—4pdr. Purch. 3.1778. Sold 10.8.1786 Chatham.

GRIFFIN Destroyer, 1,335 tons, 323 (oa) × 33ft, 4—4·7in, 8—TT. Vickers Armstrong, Barrow, 15.8.1935. Tx RCN 2.3.1943 = OTTAWA. Sold 1946.

GRIFFON 6th Rate 28, 598bm, 118·5 × 34ft. Janvrin, Burlsedon, 18.10.1758. Wrecked 14.10.1761 nr Bermuda.

GRIFFON Brig-sloop 16, 368bm, 92 × 29ft, 14—24pdr carr. 2—6pdr. French, captured 11.5.1808 by BACCHANTE in West Indies. Sold 11.3.1819 Hill & Co.

GRIFFON Brig-sloop 10, 'Cherokee' class. Deptford DY, ordered 23.5.1820, cancelled 20.8.1828, tx Chatham. *See next entry.*

GRIFFON Brig-sloop 10, 'Cherokee' class. Chatham DY 11.9.1832. Harbour service 1854; coal hulk 1857. BU 2.1869 Portsmouth. *Listed as GRIFFIN from 1858.*

GRIFFON Wood screw gunvessel, 425bm, 145 × 25·5ft, 1—68pdr, 2—20pdr, 2—24pdr howitzers. Pitcher, Northfleet, 25.2.1860. Stranded 10.1866 after collision PANDORA off Little Popo, West Africa.

GRIFFON Composite screw gunvessel, 780 tons, 157 × 29·5ft, 2—5in, 2—64pdr. Laird 16.12.1876. Sold 28.9.1891 Board of Trade = *Richmond* (hulk).

GRIFFON Destroyer, 355 tons, 210 × 20ft 1–
12pdr, 5–6pdr, 2–TT. Laird 21.11.1896. Sold
1.7.1920 Castle, Plymouth.

GRILLE Screw yacht, 2,560 tons, 377 × 44ft.
German, seized 8.1945 in northern Germany. Sold
9.1946 G. Arida.

GRILSE Torpedo boat (RCN), 225 tons, 207 ×
18·5ft, 1–12pdr, 1–TT. Yacht, cd 1914. Sold 1919.

GRIMSBY Sloop, 992 tons, 250 × 36ft, 2–4·7in,
1–3in, Devonport DY 19.7.1933. Sunk 25.5.1941
by Italian aircraft off Tobruk.

GRIMSBY Minehunter, 'Sandown' class, Vosper-
Thornycroft 10.8.1998.

GRINDALL (ex-SANDERS) Frigate, DE 'Captain'
class. Boston NY 4.6.1943 on Lend-Lease. Ret.
USN 8.1945.

GRINDER Tender. Origin unknown. Sold
22.8.1832.

GRINDER Wood screw gunboat, 'Dapper' class.
White 7.3.1855. BU 7.1864 Haslar.

GRINDER Steam sloop, 1,073bm. Sheerness DY,
ordered 3.11.1947, launched 1851 as MIRANDA.

GRIPER (Gunboat No 27) Gunvessel, 170bm, 76 ×
22ft, 2–24pdr, 10–18pdr carr. Pitcher, Northfleet, 10.4.1797. Sold 10.1802.

GRIPER Gun-brig 12, 182bm, 85 × 22ft. Brindley,
Lynn, 24.9.1804. Wrecked 18.2.1807 nr Ostend.

GRIPER Gun-brig 12, 182bm, 85 × 22ft. Richards,
Hythe, 14.7.1813. Arctic discovery sloop 1824, 2
guns; Coastguard 1836; target 1856. BU comp.
11.11.1868 Portsmouth.

GRIPER Wood screw gunboat, 'Albacore' class.
Green, Blackwall, 11.12.1855. BU 3.1.1869 Devonport.

GRIPER Iron screw gunboat, 265 tons, 87·5 × 26ft,
1–10in MLR. Pembroke Dock 15.9.1879 (work
suspended 7.1872–2.1878). = YC.373 (harbour
service) 1905; = FLORA (base ship) 19.6.1923;
= AFRIKANDER 1933. Sold c. 1937.

GRISLE (ex-BURRFISH) Submarine (RCN), 1,525
tons. Cd 11.5.1961. Ret. USN 12.1968.

GROU Frigate (RCN), 'River' class. Vickers, Montreal, 7.8.1943. Sold 13.12.1947 for BU.

GROUPER Schooner 4, 78bm, 56 × 18ft. 4–12pdr
carr. Bermuda 1804. Wrecked 21.10.1811 Guadeloupe.

GROVE Destroyer, 'Hunt' class Type III. Swan
Hunter 29.5.1941. Sunk 12.6.1942 by U.77 north
of Sollum.

GROWLER (Gunboat No 26) Gunvessel, 169bm,
76 × 22·5ft. 10–18pdr carr., 12–9pdr. Perry,
Blackwall, 10.4.1797. Captured 20.12.1797 by
French off Dungeness.

GROWLER Gun-brig 12, 178bm, 80 × 22·5ft. 10–

18pdr carr., 2–12pdr. Adams, Buckler's Hard,
10.8.1804. Sold 31.5.1815.

GROWLER Wood paddle sloop, 1,059bm, 180 ×
36ft. Chatham DY 20.7.1841. BU 1.1854

GROWLER Mortar vessel, 117bm, 65 × 21ft, 1–
13in mortar. Wigram, Blackwall, 31.3.1855.
= MV.4 on 19.10.1855; comp. 16.12.1863 as
landing stage Chatham.

GROWLER Wood screw gunboat, 'Albacore' class.
Wigram, Blackwall, 8.5.1856. BU 8.1864 Malta.

GROWLER Composite screw gunvessel, 464bm,
584 tons, 155 × 25ft, 1–7in, 1–64pdr, 2–20pdr.
Laurie, Glasgow 1.12.1868. Sold 11.1887.

GROWLER *See also LINNET 1813.*

GUACHAPIN Brig-sloop 16, 176bm. Captured
1803. Wrecked 29.7.1811 hurricane Antigua;
salved, sold 1811 Jamaica.

GUADELOUPE Sloop. In service 1762.

GUADELOUPE 6th Rate 28, 586bm, 119 × 33·5ft.
Plymouth DY 5.12.1763. Sunk 10.10.1781 to avoid
capture by French in Virginia; salved, cd by
French. *Ordered 9.1757 from Williams, Milford
Haven; transferred 6.1758 Plymouth.*

GUADELOUPE (ex-NISUS) Sloop 16, 337bm, 99
× 28·5ft, 14–24pdr carr., 2–6pdr. French, captured 12.12.1809 Guadeloupe. Sold 3.11.1814.

GUARDIAN 5th Rate 44, 901bm, 140 × 38·5ft.
Batson, Limehouse, 23.3.1784. Beached 8.2.1790
Table Bay after collision iceberg; sold there
8.2.1791.

GUARDIAN Netlayer, 2,860 tons, 310 × 53ft, 2–
4in Chatham DY. 1.9.1932. Arr. 12.1962 Troon for
BU.

GUARDIAN (ex-*Seaforth Champion*) Support
ship. Purch. 12.19.1982. Sold Pounds 1987.

GUARDLAND *See also GARLAND 1590.*

GUELDERLAND 3rd Rate 64, 1,342bm, 157 ×
44·5ft Dutch, captured 30.8.1799 off Texel (crew
having refused action). Harbour service. Sold
Freake 5.3.1817 for BU.

GUELDERLAND 5th Rate 36, 852bm, 135 × 38ft.
Dutch, captured 19.5.1808. by VIRGINIE in
North Sea. = HELDER 15.8.1809. Sunk 6.1817
breakwater.

GUELPH (ex-SEA CLIFF) Corvette (RCN),
Modified 'Flower' class. Collingwood SY
20.12.1943 (renamed 7.1943). Sold 2.10.1945.

GUEPE Sloop 14, 298bm, 101·5 × 26ft. French
privateer, captured 29.8.1800 Vigo Bay. = WASP
1801. Sold 17.5.1811.

GUERNSEY 4th Rate 48, 680bm, 132 × 34·5ft.
Johnson, Blackwall, 1696. Rebuilt Chatham 1740
as 863bm. Hulk 4.1769. Sold 1786.

GUERNSEY Wood screw sloop, 695bm, 185 ×

28·5ft. Pembroke Dock, ordered 1861, cancelled 12.12.1863.

GUERNSEY Destroyer, c. 2,000 tons, 341·5 × 39·5ft, 4—4·5in, 6—40mm, 10—TT. Denny, ordered 8.1944, cancelled 21.12.1945.

GUERNSEY Patrol vessel, 925 tons, 195·3 (oa) × 34·2ft. Hall Russell 17.2.1977. To PO 31.12.2003; sale to Bangladeshi Navy?

GUERNSEY *See also BASING 1654, AEOLUS 1758.*

GUERRIERE (ex-PEUPLE SOUVERAIN) 3rd Rate 74. French, captured 2.7.1798 Battle of Nile. Sheer hulk 1800. BU 8.1810 Gibraltar.

GUERRIERE 5th Rate 38, 1,092bm, 16—32pdr carr, 30—18pdr, 2—9pdr. French, captured 19.7.1806 by BLANCHE off Faeroes. Captured 19.8.1812 by American CONSTITUTION in Western Atlantic, burnt.

GUILDER DE RUYTER (ex-GELDERSCHE RUITER) 4th Rate 50, 684bm. Dutch, captured 1665. Sold 1667.

GUILDFORD *See FAME 1759.*

GUILDFORD CASTLE *See HESPELER 1943.*

GUILLEMOT Patrol vessel, 580 tons, 243 × 26·5ft, 1—4in. Denny 6.7.1939. Sold 6.6.1950; BU Ward, Grays.

GUINEA *See CHARLES 1648.*

GUINEVERE Destroyer, c. 2,000 tons, 341·5 × 39·5ft, 4—4·5in, 6—40mm, 10—TT. Denny, Ordered 8.1944, = GLOWWORM 9.1945, = GIFT 10.1945, cancelled 12.1945.

GULL *See SWANSTON 1954.*

GULNARE Survey tender. In service 1827.

GULNARE Survey vessel, 146bm. Launched 18.5.1828. In service until 1842. *Hired vessel?*

GULNARE Wood paddle gunvessel, 351bm, 120 × 23ft, 3—18pdr. Built Chatham DY 30.9.1833 for GPO, tx 29.6.1837. Rebuilt 1838 as 371bm = GLEANER. BU 8.1849 Deptford.

GULNARE Survey vessel, 270bm. In service 5.1844–1850. *Hired vessel?*

GULNARE Survey vessel (Canadian), 212bm. Quebec 1851. Listed 1862.

GULNARE Survey cutter, 31bm. Purch. 24.5.1855. Sold 17.4.1863 Glasgow.

GULNARE Survey vessel (Canadian), 500 tons, 110 × 20·5ft. Listed 1893–1936.

GULNARE Survey tender. Purch. 1939. Sold 10.1949.

GURKHA (ex-GHURKA) Destroyer, 1,870 tons, 377 (oa) × 36·5ft, 8—4·7in, 4—TT. Fairfield 7.7.1937 (renamed 1936). Sunk 9.4.1940 air attack off Stavanger.

GURKHA (ex-LARNE) Destroyer 1,920 tons, 362·5 (oa)× 37ft, 8—4in, 8—TT. Cammell Laird 8.7.1940 (renamed 13.6.1940). Sunk by U.133 eastern Mediterranean.

GURKHA Frigate, Type 81, 2,300 tons, 360 (oa) × 42·5ft, 2—4·5in, 2—40mm, Limbo, helo. Thornycroft 10.7.1960. Sold Indonesia 4.1984 = WILHEMUS ZAKARIAS YOHANNES; deleted 2000.

GURKHA *See also GHURKA*

GUYSBOROUGH Minesweeper, TE 'Bangor' class. North Vancouver Ship Repair Co. 21.7.1941. Sunk 17.3.1945 by U.878 off Ushant while on loan RCN.

GYMPIE Minesweeper (RAN), 'Bathurst' class, Evans Deakin, Brisbane, 30.1.1942. Sold 6.1.1961 for BU Japan.

H

'(H)' or 'Holland' class submarines All built Vickers. No 1: 75 tons, 63 × 11ft, 1—TT; Nos 2–5: 105 tons, 63·5 × 12ft, 1—TT.

(H).1 Launched 2.10.1901. Sold 7.10.1913; foundered passage from Portsmouth for BU Briton Ferry. Raised 9.1982; museum boat Gosport.

(H).2 Launched 21.2.1902. Sold 7.10.1913 Pollock/ Brown, Southampton.

(H).3 Launched 10.6.1902. Sold 7.10.1913 F. Rijsdijks.

(H).4 Launched 9.5.1902. Foundered 3.9.1912; raised 1914, target.

(H).5 Launched 21.5.1902. Foundered 8.8.1912 off The Nab under tow for BU.

(H).6 Improved 'Holland' type, launched 9.7.1902 as A.1 (q.v.).

'H' class submarines 364 tons, 150 × 16ft, 4—TT (first 20); 440 tons, 164·5 × 16ft. 4—TT (all others). First 10 built Vickers, Montreal; second 10 built Fore River, USA.

H.1 Comp. 5.1915. Sold 7.3.1921 B. Zammit, Malta.

H.2 Comp. 5.1915. Sold 7.3.1921 B. Zammit, Malta.

H.3 Comp. 3.6.1915. Sunk 15.7.1916 mine off Cattaro.

H.4 Comp. 3.6.1915. Sold 30.11.1921 Agius Bros, Malta.

H.5 Comp. 21.6.1915. Sunk 6.3.1918 collision Irish Sea.

H.6 Comp. 10.6.1915. Stranded 18.1.1916 Dutch coast; interned, sold Dutch Navy 1919 as O.8.

H.7 Comp. 20.6.1915. Sold 30.11.1921 Agius Bros, Malta.

H.8 Comp. 15.6.1915. Sold 29.11.1921 J. Kelly, Arbroath.

H.9 Comp. 24.6.1915. Sold 30.11.1921 Agius Bros. Malta.

H.10 Comp. 27.6.1915. Sunk 19.1.1918 North Sea.

H.11 Comp. 1915. Sold 1921 Stanlee, Dover.

H.12 Comp. 1915. Sold 4.1922 Stanlee, Dover.

H.13 Comp. 3.7.1917 for Chilean Navy = GUALCOLDA.

H.14 Comp. 1918. Tx RCN 6.1919 = CH.14. BU 1925.

H.15 Comp. 14.9.1918. Tx RCN 6.1919 = CH.15. BU 1925.

H.16 Comp. 3.7.1917 for Chilean Navy = TEGUALDA.

H.17 Comp. 7.1917 for Chilean Navy = RUCUMILLA.

H.18 Comp. 7.1917 for Chilean Navy = GUALE.

H.19 Comp. 7.1917 for Chilean Navy = QUIDORA.

H.20 Comp. 7.1917 for Chilean Navy = FRESIA.

H.21 Vickers 20.10.1917. Sold 13.7.1926 Cashmore, Newport.

H.22 Vickers 14.11.1917. Sold 19.2.1929; BU Charlestown.

H.23 Vickers 29.1.1918. Sold 4.5.1934 Young, Sunderland.

H.24 Vickers 14.11.1917. Sold 4.5.1934 Young, Sunderland.

H.25 Vickers 27.4.1918. Sold 19.2.1929; BU Charlestown.

H.26 Vickers 15.11.1917. Sold 21.4.1928 Ward, Pembroke Dock.

H.27 Vickers 25.9.1918. Sold 30.8.1935 Cashmore, Newport.

H.28 Vickers 12.3.1918. Sold 18.8.1944; BU Troon.

H.29 Vickers 8.6.1918. Sold 7.10.1927 Ward, Pembroke Dock.

H.30 Vickers 9.5.1918. Sold 30.9.1935 Cashmore, Newport.

H.31 Vickers 16.11.1918. Sunk 24.12.1941 Bay of Biscay.

H.32 Vickers 19.11.1918. Sold 18.10.1944; BU Troon.

H.33 Cammell Laird 24.8.1918. Sold 1944; BU Troon.

H.34 Cammell Laird 5.11.1918 Sold 1945; BU Troon.

H.35 Cammell Laird, cancelled 1919.

H.36 Cammell Laird, cancelled 1919.

H.37 Cammell Laird, cancelled 1919.

H.38 Cammell Laird, cancelled 1919.

H.39 Cammell Laird, cancelled 1919.

H.40 Cammell Laird, cancelled 1919.

H.41 Armstrong 1918. Damaged collision 1919. Sold 12.3.1920 Young, Sunderland.

H.42 Armstong 5.11.1919. Sunk 23.3.1922 collision destroyer VERSATILE off Gibraltar.

H.43 Armstrong 3.2.1919. Sold 1944; BU Troon.

H.44 Armstrong 17.2.1919. Sold 1944; BU Troon.

H.45 Armstrong, cancelled 1919.

H.46 Armstrong, cancelled 1919.

H.47 Beardmore 19.11.1918. Sunk 9.7.1929 collision submarine L.12.

H.48 Beardmore 31.3.1919. Sold 30.8.1935 Rees, Llanelly.

H.49 Beardmore 15.7.1919. Sunk 27.10.1940 by German surface craft off Dutch coast.

H.50 Beardmore 25.10.1919. Sold 1945; BU Troon.

H.51 Pembroke Dock 15.11.1918. Sold 6.6.1924 Keen, Bristol; resold 17.7.1924 Davo S. Bkg Co.

H.52 Pembroke Dock 31.3.1919. Sold 9.11.1927 New Era Productions.

H.53 Pembroke Dock, cancelled 1919.

HADDOCK Schooner 4, 78bm, 56 × 18ft, 4—12pdr carr. Bermuda 1805. Captured 30.1.1809 by French GENIE in English Channel.

HADLEIGH CASTLE Corvette, 'Castle' class. Smith's Dock 21.6.1943. Arr. 1.1959 Dorkin, Gateshead, for BU.

HAERLEM Sloop 10. Captured 1778. Captured 7.1779 by American privateer.

HAERLEM (ex-HAARLEM) 3rd Rate 64, 1,324bm, 157 × 44·5ft. Dutch, captured 11.10.1797 Battle of Camperdown. Harbour service 1.1811. Sold 2.5.1816.

HAIDA Destroyer (RCN), 1,927 tons, 377 (oa) × 37·5ft, 6—4·7in, 2—4in, 4—TT. Vickers Armstrong, Tyne, 25.8.1942. Presented to City of Toronto 21.8.1964 as memorial.

HALBERD Destroyer, 1,980 tons, 365 (oa) × 38ft, 6—4in, 6—40mm, 10—TT. Scotts, ordered 4.1943, cancelled 1.1945, not LD.

HALCYON (ex-ALCION) Brig-sloop 16, 298bm, 91·5 × 28ft, 14—24pdr carr., 2—6pdr. French, captured 8.7.1803 by NARCISSUS off Sardinia. BU 6.1812.

HALCYON Brig-sloop 18, 'Cruizer' class, 384bm. Larking, Lynn, 16.5.1813. Wrecked 19.5.1814 Jamaica.

HALCYON Brig-sloop 10, 'Cherokee' class. Deptford DY, tx Woolwich DY, ordered 2.11.1818, cancelled 21.2.1831.

HALCYON Torpedo gunboat, 1,070 tons, 250 × 30·5ft, 2—4·7in, 4—6pdr, 5—TT. Devonport DY 6.4.1894. Sold 6.11.1919 J. H. Lee; BU Dover.

HALCYON Paddle minesweeper, 'Ascot' class. Dunlop Bremner 29.3.1916. Sold 14.12.1921 Stanlee, Dover.

HALCYON Minesweeper, 815 tons, 230 × 33·5ft, 2—4in. John Brown 20.12.1933. Sold 19.4.1950; BU Ward, Milford Haven.

HALDON Destroyer, 'Hunt' class Type III. Fairfield 27.4.1942. Lent Free French 12.1942 = LA COMBATTANTE. Sunk 23.2.1945 mine North Sea.

HALF MOON 30-gun ship, captured 1653. Sold 1659.

HALF MOON 46-gun ship, 552bm, 114 × 33·5ft. Captured 1681. Sold 1686.

HALF MOON 32-gun ship, 214bm. Algerian, captured 1685. Fireship 1688, 8 guns. Expended 24.5.1692 La Hogue.

HALIFAX Sloop 22. Oswego, Canada, 1756. Captured 14.8.1756 by French at fall of Oswego.

HALIFAX Schooner 10, 83bm. Purch. 1768, wrecked 15.2.1775.

HALIFAX Schooner. Purch. North America 6.1775. Sold 1780.

HALIFAX (ex-RANGER) Sloop 18, 308bm, 18—6pdr. American, captured 12.5.1780 Charleston. Sold 13.10.1781.

HALIFAX Sloop 18, 378bm, 106·5 × 28·5ft, 16—32pdr carr., 2—6pdr. Halifax, NS, 11.10.1806. BU 1.1814.

HALIFAX Corvette (RCN), 'Flower' class. Collingwood SY 4.10.1941. Sold 1946 = *Halifax* (salvage vessel).

HALIFAX Frigate (RCN), 'Halifax' class. St John SB, 30.4.1988.

HALIFAX *See also MARY 1797.*

HALLADALE Frigate, 'River' class. Inglis 28.1.1944. Sold 1.4.1949 Townsend Bros = *Halladale* (ferry).

HALLOWELL Frigate (RCN), 'River' class. Vickers, Montreal, 28.3.1944. Sold 21.12.1945 = *Sharon;* tx Israeli Navy 1952 = MISNAK; tx RCeyN 1959 = GAJABAHU; discarded 1978.

HALLOWELL *See also ANGUILLA 1943.*

HALSHAM Inshore minesweeper, 'Ham' class. Jones, Buckie, 9.1953. Tx Air Ministry 1966 = No 5002. Tx Royal Corps of Transport 1974 = RICHARD GEORGE MASTERS VC. Sold 1981.

HALSTARR (ex-KENAU HASSELAAR) 5th Rate 32, 700bm. Dutch, captured 1.1.1807 by ARETHUSA at Curaçoa. Listed until 1809.

HALSTED (ex-REYNOLDS) Frigate, TE 'Captain' class. Bethlehem, Hingham, 14.10.1943. Damaged 11.6.1944 by torpedoes, hulked. Nominally ret. USN 1946. Sold 1.11.1946 for BU Holland.

HALSTED *See also BARBADOS 1943.*

HAMADRYAD (ex-NINFA) 5th Rate 36, 890bm. Spanish, captured 26.4.1797 by IRRESISTIBLE off Lisbon. Wrecked 24.12.1797 coast of Portugal.

HAMADRYAD (ex-MATILDA) 5th Rate 36, 966bm. Spanish, captured 25.11.1804 by DONEGAL and MEDUSA off Cadiz. Sold 9.8.1815.

HAMADRYAD 5th Rate 46, 1,082bm, 152 ×
40·5ft. Pembroke Dock 25.7.1823. Lent 3.1866 as
seamen's hospital Cardiff. Sold 11.7.1905.

HAMADRYAD *See also DRYAD 1893.*

HAMBLEDON Minesweeper, Early 'Hunt' class.
Fleming & Ferguson 9.3.1917. Sold 7.1922 Stanlee,
Dover.

HAMBLEDON Destroyer, 'Hunt' class Type I.
Swan Hunter 12.12.1939. Arr. 9.1957 Clayton &
Davie, Tyne, for BU.

HAMILTON (ex-KALK) Destroyer (RCN), 1,060
tons, 309 × 30·5ft, 1—4in, 1—3in, 4—20mm, 3—
TT. USN, cd RCN 23.9.1940. Arr. 7.1945
Baltimore for BU.

HAMPSHIRE 46-gun ship, 490bm, 118 × 30ft.
Deptford 1653. Sunk 26.8.1697 in action with
French PELICAN in Hudson's Bay.

HAMPSHIRE 4th Rate 48, 690bm, 132 × 34·5ft.
Taylor, Cuckold's Point, 3.3.1698. BU 1739 Portsmouth.

HAMPSHIRE 4th Rate 50, 854bm, 134 × 38·5ft
Barnard, Ipswich, 13.11.1741. BU comp.
22.12.1766 Sheerness.

HAMPSHIRE Armoured cruiser, 10,850 tons, 450
× 68·5ft, 4—7·5in, 6—6in, 2—12pdr. Armstrong
24.9.1903. Sunk 5.6.1916 mine off Orkneys.

HAMPSHIRE GM destroyer, 5,440 tons, 520·5
(oa) × 54ft, 4—4·5in, 2—20mm, Sea Slug, helo.
John Brown 16.3.1961. Arr. 28.4.1979 Ward,
Briton Ferry, for BU.

HAMPTON COURT 3rd Rate 70, 1,030bm, 150·5
× 40ft, Deptford DY 1678. Rebuilt Blackwall 1701
as 1,073bm. Captured 1.5.1707 by French off
Beachy Head. Tx Spanish Navy 1712.

HAMPTON COURT 3rd Rate 70, 1,136bm, 151 ×
42ft. Taylor, Rotherhithe, 19.8.1709. Rebuilt
Deptford 1744 as 1,283bm, 64 guns. BU comp.
5.6.1774 Plymouth.

HANDMAID Ship, 80/120bm. Deptford 1573.
Hulked 1600.

HANDY Wood screw gunboat, 'Clown' class.
Pitcher, Northfleet, 31.5.1856. Sold 5.1868 Lagos.

HANDY Trials gunboat, 508 tons, 115 × 37ft, various
guns. Armstrong 1883 (launched 30.12.1882),
purch. 1884. = EXCELLENT 5.1891; = CALCUTTA
1.11.1916; = SNAPPER 8.1917. Sold 27.4.1922.

HANDY Destroyer, 295 tons, 194 × 19ft, 1—12pdr,
5—6pdr, 2—TT. Fairfield 9.3.1895. Sold 1916 in
Hong Kong.

HANDY (ex-JURUA) Destroyer, 1,340 tons, 323
(oa) × 33ft, 4—4·7in, 8—TT. Vickers Armstrong,
Barrow, 29.9.1939; Brazilian, purch. 9.1939.
= HARVESTER 27.2.1940. Sunk 11.3.1943 by
U.432 North Atlantic.

HANDY *See also NYMPHE 1812.*

HANNAM *See CAICOS 1943.*

HANNIBAL 4th Rate 50, 1,054bm, 146 × 41ft,
Adams, Buckler's Hard, 26.12.1779. Captured
21.1.1782. by French HEROS off Sumatra.

HANNIBAL Sloop 14, 220bm, 94 × 25ft. Purch.
1782. Foundered 1788.

HANNIBAL 3rd Rate 74, 1,619bm, 168 × 47ft.
Perry, Blackwall, 15.4.1786. Captured 5.7.1801 by
French when aground at Battle of Algeçiras.

HANNIBAL 3rd Rate 74, 1,749bm, 176 × 48·5ft.
Adams, Buckler's Hard, 5.1810. Harbour service
8.1825. BU 12.1833 Pembroke Dock.

HANNIBAL 2nd Rate 90. Woolwich DY, ordered
14.5.1840, cancelled. *Re-ordered Woolwich as
next ship.*

HANNIBAL Screw 2nd Rate 91, 3,136bm, 4,735
tons, 217 × 58ft. 34—8in, 1—68pdr, 56—32pdr.
Deptford DY 31.1.1854. Hulk 1874. Sold 12.4.1904
Castle.

HANNIBAL Battleship, 14,900 tons, 390 × 75ft,
4—12in, 12—6in, 18—12pdr. Pembroke Dock
28.4.1896. Sold 28.1.1920 M. Yates; BU Italy.

HAPPY Sloop 14, 114bm. Woolwich DY 19.4.1711.
Sold 28.8.1735.

HAPPY Sloop 8, 141bm. 76 × 20·5ft. Woolwich
DY 22.7.1754. Wrecked 14.9.1766 off Great Yarmouth.

HAPPY ENTRANCE 30-gun ship, 404/540bm.
Deptford 8.11.1619. Burnt 28.9.1658 R. Medway.

HAPPY ENTRANCE Fireship. 1665. Expended
1666.

HAPPY LADD Gunboat. Purch. 1855. Sold 8.1856
Turkish Navy.

HAPPY RETURN Firevessel, 846bm. Purch. 1695.
Expended 1.8.1695 Dunkirk.

HAPPY RETURN Discovery ship. 1720.

HAPPY RETURN Minesweeper, 'Algerine' class.
Lobnitz, ordered 1943, cancelled 10.1944.

HAPPY RETURN *See also WINSBY 1654.*

HARDEREEN Flyboat 4, 138bm. Dutch, captured
1665. Sold 1674.

HARDI Sloop 18. French privateer, captured
1.4.1797 by HAZARD off The Skelligs, south-
western Ireland. Sold 1800.

HARDI (ex-LE HARDI) 6th Rate 20, 425bm, 112 ×
30ft. French privateer, captured 29.4.1800.
= ROSARIO 1800. Sold 1.1809.

HARDINGE Troopship (RIM), 6,520 tons, 423·5 ×
51ft, 6—4·7in, 6—3pdr. Fairfield 11.8.1900. Sold
c. 1930.

HARDROCK Frigate (RCN), 'River' class. Montreal, cancelled 12.1943.

HARDY (Gunboat No 30) Gunvessel 12, 170bm, 76

× 22ft, 2—24pdr, 10—18pdr carr. Cleveley, Gravesend, 10.4.1797. Sold 5.1802.

HARDY Gun-brig 12, 178bm. 80·5 × 22·5ft, 2—18pdr, 10—18pdr carr. Roxby, Wearmouth, 7.8.1804. Storeship 1818; hospital ship 11.1821. Sold 6.8.1835 Levy, Rochester.

HARDY Mortar vessel, 117bm, 65 × 21ft, 1—13in mortar. Wigram, Blackwall, 14.3.1855. = MV.12 on 19.10.1855. Sold 21.4.1858 in Malta.

HARDY Wood screw gunboat, 'Albacore' class. Hill, Bristol, 1.3.1856. Sold 9.2.1869 in Hong Kong.

HARDY Destroyer, 295 tons, 196 × 19ft, 1—12pdr, 5—6pdr, 2—TT. Doxford 1895. Sold 11.7.1911 Garnham.

HARDY Destroyer, 898 tons, 263 × 27ft, 3—4in, 1—12pdr, 2—TT. Thornycroft 10.10.1912. Sold 9.5.1921 Ward, Briton Ferry.

HARDY Destroyer leader, 1,505, tons, 337 (oa) × 34ft, 5—4·7in, 8—TT. Cammell Laird 7.4.1936. Beached 10.4.1940 after damage Battle of Narvik.

HARDY Destroyer, 1,730 tons, 362·7 (oa) × 35·7ft, 4—4·7in, 2—40mm, 8—TT. John Brown 18.3.1943. Sunk 30.1.1944 by U.278 Barents Sea.

HARDY Frigate, 1,180 tons, 300 × 33ft, 3—40mm, 4—TT. Yarrow 25.11.1953. Sunk 7.1983 target off Gibraltar.

HARE 10-gun vessel, 30bm. Dates from 1545. Rebuilt 1558 as 40bm. Sold 1573.

HARE Ketch. Royalist, captured 1649; deserted to Parliamentarians 1649. Wrecked 1655.

HARE Pink. Listed 1653–57.

HARE Fireship 6, 180bm. Captured 1665. Burnt 1666 accident.

HARE Dogger 6. Dutch, captured 1672. Sold 1674.

HARE Bomb vessel. Listed 1703.

HARE Sloop 10, 55bm, 53·5 × 15·5ft. Captured 8.9.1709 by SPEEDWELL. Sold 1712.

HARE Minesweeper, 'Algerine' class. Harland & Wolff 20.6.1944. Sold Nigerian Navy 1959 = NIGERIA. BU 1962 Faslane.

HAREBELL Sloop, 'Anchusa' class. Barclay Curle 10.5.1918. Arr. 2.1939 Dalmuir for BU.

HAREBELL Corvette, 'Flower' class. Harland & Wolff, ordered 8.4.1940, cancelled 23.1.1941.

HARFRUEN (ex-HANFRU) 5th Rate 36, 1,030bm, Danish, captured 7.9.1807 Battle of Copenhagen. Sold 29.9.1814. *Was to have been renamed BOREAS.*

HARGOOD Frigate, TE 'Captain' class. Bethlehem, Hingham, 18.12.1943 on Lend-Lease. Ret. USN 3.1946.

HARLAND *See CAYMAN 1943.*

HARLECH *See CAMBRIAN 1893.*

HARLEQUIN Sloop 16, 141bm. *See PORTO 1780.*

HARLEQUIN Schooner 14. Purch. 1796. Listed 1802.

HARLEQUIN Brig-sloop 18, 'Cruizer' class, 385bm. Bailey, Ipswich, 15.7.1813. Sold 4.9.1829 in Jamaica.

HARLEQUIN Gunboat. Purch. 1815 West Indies. Listed 1816 as tender Bermuda.

HARLEQUIN Brig-sloop 16, 433bm, 101·5 × 32ft, 14—32pdr, 2—9pdr. Pembroke Dock 18.3.1836. Coal hulk 1860. Sold 8.1889 Marshall, Plymouth.

HARLEQUIN Wood screw sloop, 950bm, 185 × 33ft. Portsmouth DY, LD 13.2.1861, cancelled 16.12.1864.

HARMAN Fireship. Presented 2.1702 by Govt of Jamaica. Sunk 26 2.1705 Port Royal, Jamaica.

HARMAN *See also DOMINICA 1943.*

HARP Pinnace 8, 20bm. Listed 1546–48.

HARP Ketch 10, 75bm. Dublin 1656. Sold 1671.

HARP Ketch 10, 96bm, 62·5 × 19ft. Frame, Scarborough, 24.4.1691. Captured 6.1693 by French.

HARPENDEN Paddle minesweeper, 'Ascot' class, 820 tons. Ailsa 26.2.1918. Arr. 4.1928 Charlestown for BU.

HARPHAM Inshore minesweeper, 'Ham' class. Jones, Buckie, 14.9.1954. Tx Libyan Navy 1962 = BRAK. BU 1973.

HARPY Sloop 18, 367bm, 103 × 28ft. Fisher, Liverpool, 8.5.1777. Fireship, 10 guns, 8.1779. Sold 21.3.1783.

HARPY Brig-sloop 18, 316bm, 95 × 28ft. King, Dover, 2,1796. Sold 10.11.1817 Mr Kilsby.

HARPY Brig-sloop 10, 'Cherokee' class, 232bm. Chatham DY 16.7.1825. Sold 27.5.1841 Greenwood & Clarke.

HARPY Iron paddle gunboat, 344bm, 500 tons, 141 × 22.5ft. Ditchburn & Mare, Blackwall, 4.3.1845. Tx War Dept 26.10.1892 target. Sold c. 1909.

HARPY Destroyer, 972 tons, 275 × 28ft, 1—4in, 3—12pdr, 2—TT. White 27.11.1909. Sold 1.11.1921 Fryer, Sunderland.

HARRIER Brig-sloop 18 (fir-built) 'Cruizer' class, 383bm. Barnard, Deptford, 22.8.1804. Foundered 3.1809 Indian Ocean.

HARRIER Brig-sloop 18, 'Cruizer' class, 386bm. Bailey, Ipswich, 28.7.1813. Sold 8.1.1829 Tibbetts & Co.

HARRIER Sloop 18, 486bm, 114·5 × 32ft. Pembroke Dock 8.11.1831. BU 3.1840 Portsmouth.

HARRIER Wood screw sloop, 747bm, 160 × 32ft, 17—32pdr. Pembroke Dock 13.5.1845. BU comp. 12.1866 Portsmouth.

HARRIER Wood screw sloop, 895bm, 180 ×

33·5ft. Pembroke Dock, ordered 26.3.1846, cancelled 4.4.1851.

HARRIER Schooner 2, 190 tons, 92·5 × 19ft. Purch. 15.3.1881. Sold 4.1888 London Missionary Society, Sydney.

HARRIER Torpedo gunboat, 1,070 tons, 250 × 30·5ft, 2—4·7in 4—6pdr, 5—TT. Devonport DY 20.2.1894. Sold 23.2.1920 Haulbowline.

HARRIER Minesweeper, 815 tons, 230 × 33·5ft, 2—4in. Thornycroft 17.4.1934. Sold 6.6.1950; BU King, Gatehead.

HARRIOT Storeship 20, 407bm, 107 × 30ft. Purch. 7.1781. Sold 17.3.1784 Bombay.

HARROW Minesweeper, Later 'Hunt' class. Eltringham 30.7.1918. Sold 1947 J. Dacoutos, Malta. BU Genoa.

HART Galley, 56, 300bm. Built 1546, rebuilt 1558. Listed until 1568.

HART 12-gun ship, 120bm. Royalist, captured 1643 by Parliamentarians. Captured 1652 by Dutch.

HART (RED HART) Pink 6. Captured 1653. Sold 1654.

HART Pink 8, 55bm. Woolwich DY 1657. Sold 1683.

HART Dogger 8. Captured 1672. Captured 1673 by Dutch.

HART Ketch 10, 96bm, 62·5 × 19ft. Rolfe & Castle, Rotherhithe, 23.3.1691. Captured 5.1692 by two French privateers off St Ives.

HART Cutter. Deptford 1793. Sold 30.10.1817 J. Edgar.

HART (ex-EMPEREUR) Brig-sloop 16, 152bm, 78·5 × 21ft, 16—12pdr carr. French privateer, captured 6.1805 by EAGLE. Sold 1810 in Jamaica.

HART Composite screw gunvessel, 464bm, 584 tons, 155 × 25ft, 1—7in, 1—64pdr, 2—20pdr. Thomson, Glasgow, 20.8.1868. Sold 12.1888.

HART Destroyer, 295 tons, 185 × 19ft, 1—12pdr, 5—6pdr, 2—TT. Fairfield 27.3.1895. Sold 1912 in Hong Kong.

HART Sloop 1,350 tons, 283 × 38ft, 6—4in, 12—20mm. Stephen 7.7.1943. Sold 1958 West German Navy = SCHEER; PO 1967; sold 17.3.1971 Vebeg, Hamburg, for BU.

HART (ex-STIRLING) Patrol boat, 70.2 tons, 78.7 × 18ft. James & Stone, Brightlingsea, 1976. RAF vessel, tx 29.8.1985. Sold 1991 in Gibraltar.

HART *See also RAPID 1883.*

HARTLAND (ex-PONTCHARTRAIN) Cutter, 1,546 tons, 256 (oa) × 42ft, 1—5in, 2—3in. USN, tx RN 30.4.1941 on Lend-Lease. Sunk 8.11.1942 by French TYPHON and shore batteries Oran.

HARTLAND POINT Repair ship, 8,580 tons, 416 × 57ft. Burrard 4.11.1944. Sold 2.7.1774; BU 2.1979 Santander.

HARTLEPOOL *See KATHIAWAR 1942.*

HARVESTER Minesweeping sloop, '24' class. Barclay Curle 2.11.1918. Sold 8.1922 C. A. Beard.

HARVESTER *See also HANDY 1939.*

HARVEY *See GOLD COAST 1943.*

HARWICH Hoy 5, 52bm. Deane, Harwich, 1660. Sold 1680.

HARWICH 3rd Rate 70, 993bm. Deane, Harwich, 12.4.1674. Wrecked 3.9.1691 off Plymouth.

HARWICH 4th Rate 48, 683bm, 132 × 34·5ft. Deptford 1695. Wrecked 5.10.1700 Amoy, China.

HARWICH Storeship, 56bm. Butler, Harwich, 10.8.1709. Sold 18.11.1714 W. Chamberlain.

HARWICH *See also TIGER 1742, KHYBER 1942.*

HASTINGS 5th Rate 32, 384bm, 109 × 28·5ft. Ellis, Shoreham, 5.2.1695. Wrecked 1697 off Waterford.

HASTINGS 5th Rate 32, 381bm, 109 × 28ft. Betts, Woodbridge, 17.5.1698. Capsized 9.2.1707 off Yarmouth.

HASTINGS 5th Rate 44, 533bm, 118 × 32ft. Portsmouth DY 2.10.1707. Hulk 2.1739. Sold 27.9.1744 privateer.

HASTINGS (ex-ENDYMION) 5th Rate 44, 682bm, 124 × 36ft. Okill, Liverpool, 7.3.1741 (renamed 1739). BU comp. 19.9.1763 Sheerness.

HASTINGS 3rd Rate 74, 1,763bm, 177 × 48·5ft. East Indiaman, purch. 22.6.1819 Calcutta; undocked Portsmouth 5.2.1855 as screw ship. Coal hulk 1870. Sold 9.1885.

HASTINGS 5th Rate 32 (Indian), 566bm. Bombay DY 2.5.1821. BU 1855.

HASTINGS Sloop 1,045 tons, 250 × 34ft, 2—4in. Devonport DY 10.4.1930. Sold 2.4.1946; BU Troon.

HASTINGS *See also OTAGO 1958.*

HASTY (Gunboat No 33) Gunvessel 12, 170bm, 76 × 23ft, 2—24pdr, 10—18pdr carr. Wilson, Frindsbury, 6.1797. Sold 12.1802.

HASTY Gun-brig 12, 182bm, 84 × 23ft, 10—18pdr carr., 2—6pdr. Hill, Sandwich, 26.8.1812. Survey vessel 7.1819; mud-engine Mauritius 1.1827. Still in service 1870.

HASTY Wood screw gunboat, 'Albacore' class. Pitcher, Northfleet, 10.1.1856. Sold 11.1865 Castle, Charlton.

HASTY Destroyer, 290 tons, 190 × 18·5ft, 1—12pdr, 5—6pdr, 2—TT. Yarrow, Poplar, 16.6.1894. Sold 9.7.1912 Cox, Falmouth.

HASTY Destroyer, 1,340 tons, 323 (oa) × 33ft, 4—4·7in, 8—TT. Denny 5.5.1936. Sunk 16.6.1942 eastern Mediterrean by HOTSPUR after being torpedoed.

HASTY *See also LINNET 1906.*

HATHERLEIGH Destroyer, 'Hunt' class Type III. Vickers Armstrong, Tyne, 18.12.1941. Lent Greek Navy 7.1942–12.11.1959 = KANARIS. BU 12.12.1959 Greece.

HAUGHTY (Gunboat No 31) Gunvessel 12, 168bm, 76 × 23ft. Cleveley, Gravesend, 4.1797. Sold 5.1802.

HAUGHTY Gun-brig 12, 178bm, 80 × 22·5ft. Dudman, Deptford, 7.5.1804. Sold 11.1.1816.

HAUGHTY Wood screw gunboat, 'Albacore' class. Pitcher 9.2.1856. Sold 23.5.1867 in Hong Kong.

HAUGHTY Destroyer, 295 tons, 196 × 19ft, 1–12pdr, 5–6pdr, 2–TT. Doxford 18.9.1895. Sold 10.4.1912.

HAUGHTY *See also LARK 1913.*

HAVANNAH 5th Rate 36, 949bm, 145 × 38·5ft. Wilson, Liverpool, 26.3.1811. Lent 19.3.1860 TS. Sold 1905 for BU.

HAVANT Minesweeper, Later 'Hunt' class. Eltringham 24.3.1919. Sold 8.1922 Thornycroft for Siamese Navy = CHOW PRAYA. Stricken 24.8.1971.

HAVANT (ex-JAVARY) Destroyer, 1,340 tons, 323 (oa) × 33ft, 4–4·7in, 8–TT. White 17.7.1939; Brazilian, purch. 4.9.1939. Bombed 1.6.1940 off Dunkirk, sunk by SALTASH.

HAVELOCK Paddle gunboat (Indian), 610bm. Bombay DY 1857. *Fate unknown.*

HAVELOCK (ex-M.2, ex-GENERAL GRANT) Monitor, 6,150 tons, 320 × 90ft, 2–14in, 2–6in, 2–12pdr. Harland & Wolff 29.4.1915 (renamed 1.6.1915, 20.6.1915). Sold 9.5.1921 Ward, retained; resold 20.6.1927 Ward, Preston.

HAVELOCK (ex-JUTAHY) Destroyer, 1,340 tons, 323 (oa) × 33ft, 4–4·7in, 8–TT. White 16.10.1939; Brazilian, purch. 4.9.1939. Sold 31.10.1946; BU Ward, Inverkeithing.

HAVERSHAM Inshore minesweeper, 'Ham' class. McLean, Renfrew, 3.6.1954. TRV 1964–79. PO 1980; towed Southampton 28.10.1985 for BU Spain.

HAVICK Sloop 16, 365bm, 102 × 26ft. Dutch, captured 17.8.1796 Saldanha Bay. Wrecked 9.11.1800 St Aubin's Bay, Jersey.

HAVOCK Gun-brig, 12, 184bm, 85 × 22·5ft. Stone, Yarmouth, 25.7.1805. Lightvessel 9.1821; watchvessel 3.1843. BU 7.1859.

HAVOCK Mortar vessel, 120bm, 65 × 21ft, 1–13in mortar. Mare, Blackwall, 14.3.1855. = MV.5 on 19.10.1855; Customs watchvessel = WV.27. BU 7.1874 Chatham.

HAVOCK Wood screw gunboat, 'Albacore' class. Hill, Bristol, 20.3.1856. Sold 31.3.1870 Yokohama.

HAVOCK Destroyer, 275 tons, 180 × 18·5ft, 1–12pdr, 3–6pdr, 3–TT. Yarrow, Poplar, 12.8.1893. Sold 14.5.1912 Chatham. *First destroyer in RN.*

HAVOCK Destroyer, 1,340 tons, 323 (oa) × 33ft, 4–4·7in, 8–TT. Denny 7.7.1936. Wrecked 6.4.1942 nr Kelibia, Tunisia.

HAVOCK *See also LINNET 1913.*

HAWEA Patrol boat (RNZN), 105 tons, 107 (oa) × 20ft, Brooke Marine 9.9.1974. Deleted 1992.

HAWEA *See also LOCH ECK 1944.*

HAWK Sloop 10, 206bm, 85 × 24ft. Greville, Limehouse, 10.3.1741. BU 10.1747 Deptford.

HAWK Sloop 10, 225bm, 89 × 24ft. Batson, Limehouse, 1.4.1756. Sold 13.8.1781. *In French hands 11.1759–4.2.1761.*

HAWK Sloop 10, 225bm, 89 × 24ft. Barnard, Harwich, 1761. *May have been preceding vessel rebuilt.*

HAWK Schooner. In service 1775. Captured 4.4.1776 by Americans.

HAWK Sloop 16, 333bm, 100 × 28ft. Deptford DY 24.7.1793. BU 5.1803.

HAWK Storeship 4, 68bm, 67 × 15ft. Hoy, purch. 4.1794. Lost 1796.

HAWK Galley. In service 1795. Sold 12.2.1796 Mr Dormer.

HAWK (ex-ATALANTE) Sloop 18, 320bm, 91 × 28ft, 18–18pdr, 2–9pdr. French privateer, captured 8.1803 by PLANTAGENET. Foundered 12.1804 English Channel.

HAWK (ex-LUTIN) Brig-sloop 16, 311bm, 91 × 28ft. French, captured 24.3.1806 by AGAMEMNON and CARYSFORT in West Indies. = BUZZARD 8.1.1812. Sold 15.12.1814.

HAWK Screw coastguard vessel, 372bm, 416 tons, 146 × 23ft, 1–40pdr. White, Cowes, 14.4.1869. = AMELIA 1888. *See AMELIA 1888.*

HAWK (ex-OBERON; ex-*Lady Aline*) Coastguard vessel, 520 tons, 157 × 24ft, 2–7pdr. Purch. 1.1888, renamed 5.5.1888. = UNDINE 1904. Sold 3.4.1906 Chatham.

HAWK *See also SOMERLEYTON 1955.*

HAWKE Discovery vessel, 100bm. Bristol 1593. *Fate unknown.*

HAWKE Ketch 8, 60bm. Woolwich DY 1655. Sold 1667.

HAWKE Fireship 8, 259bm, 94·5 × 25ft. Fream, Wapping, 17.4.1690. Sunk 1712 foundation Plymouth.

HAWKE Sloop 8, 103bm, 62 × 20ft. Chatham DY 23.11.1721. Foundered 10.1739.

HAWKE 3rd Rate 74, 1,754bm, 176 × 48·5ft. Woolwich DY 16.3.1820. Comp. 5.1855 as screw ship. BU 1865.

HAWKE 1st class cruiser, 7,350 tons, 360 × 60ft, 2—9·2in, 10—6in, 12—6pdr. Chatham DY 11.3.1891. Sunk 15.10.1914 by U.9 in North Sea.

HAWKE Cruiser, 8,800 tons, 555·5 (oa) × 64ft, 9—6in. Portsmouth DY. Suspended 1.1945, cancelled 1946.

HAWKESBURY Corvette (RCN), Modified 'Flower' class. Morton, Quebec, 16.11.1943. PO 10.7.1945. Sold (1946?); = *Campuchea* 1950. BU 1956 Hong Kong.

HAWKESBURY Frigate (RAN), 'River' class. Mort's Dock 24.7.1943. Sold 9.1961 for BU; left Sydney 12.9.1962 for BU Japan.

HAWKESBURY Minehunter (RAN), 'Huon' class. 720 tons, 172·2 (oa) × 32·5ft, 1—30mm, ADI, Newcastle, NSW, 24.4.1998.

HAWKINS Cruiser, 9,750 tons, 605 (oa) × 65·1ft, 7—7·5in, 4—3in, 6—12pdr. Chatham DY 1.10.1917. Sold 26.8.1947; BU Dalmuir.

HAWTHORN Pinnace, 20bm. Listed 1546–48.

HAYDON Destroyer, 'Hunt' class Type III. Vickers Armstrong, Tyne, 2.4.1942. Arr. 18.5.1958 Clayton & Davie, Dunston, for BU.

HAYLING Storeship hoy 4, 114bm, 61 × 21ft. Purch. 6.7.1705.

HAYLING Storeship hoy 126bm. Portsmouth DY 1729. Sloop, 10—9pdr, in 1759 = GOREE. BU 1763.

HAYLING Transport hoy 4, 132bm, 67 × 21·5ft. Adams, Buckler's Hard, 1.4.1760. Foundered 1782 English Channel.

HAZARD Sloop 14, 114bm, 63 × 21ft. Woolwich 19.4.1711. Wrecked 12.10.1714 off Boston, New England.

HAZARD Sloop 14, 273bm, 93 × 26ft. Buxton, Rotherhithe, 11.12.1744. Sold 7.9.1749. *In hands of 'Young Pretender' 24.11.1745–4.1746.*

HAZARD Sloop 8, 140bm, 77 × 20·5ft, 8—3pdr. Portsmouth DY 3.10.1749. Sold 11.2.1783.

HAZARD Sloop 16, 423bm, 108 × 30ft. Brindley, Frindsbury, 3.3.1794. Sold 30.10.1917 Mr Spratley.

HAZARD Sloop 18, 431bm, 110·5 × 31ft. Portsmouth DY 21.4.1837. BU comp. 12.2.1866 White. Cowes.

HAZARD Torpedo gunboat, 1,070 tons, 250 × 30·5ft, 2—4·7in, 4—6pdr, 5—TT. Pembroke Dock 17.2.1894. Sunk 28.1.1918 collision English Channel.

HAZARD Minesweeper, 835 tons, 230 × 33·5ft, 2—4in. Gray, Hartlepool, 26.2.1937. Sold 22.4.1949; BU Ward, Grays.

HAZARD PRIZE Sloop 8, 101bm, 62 × 20ft, 8—4pdr. French privateer, captured 10.9.1756. Sold 21.6.1759.

HAZARDOUS (ex-HASARD) 4th Rate 54, 875bm, 137 × 38ft. French, captured 11.1703. Wrecked 11.1706 nr Selsey Bill.

HAZLETON Coastal minesweeper, 'Ton' class. Cook, Welton & Gemmell 6.2.1954. Tx SAN 1955 = KAAPSTAAD. Sold S. A. Metal Co. 9.1988; BU 1989 Table Bay.

HEART OF OAK Firevessel 54bm. Purch. 1794. Sold 12.1796

HEARTSEASE 36-gun ship. Captured 1652. Sold 1656.

HEARTSEASE (ex-PANSY) Corvette, 'Flower' class. Harland & Wolff 20.4.1940 (renamed 1940). Lent USN 18.3.1942–1945 = COURAGE. Sold 22.7.1946 = *Roskva.*

HEARTY Gun-brig 12, 183bm, 85 × 22ft, 10—18pdr carr., 2—12pdr. Bailey, Ipswich, 12.4.1805. Sold 11.7.1816.

HEARTY Brig-sloop 10, 'Cherokee' class, 228bm. Chatham DY 22.10.1824. Packet brig 1.1827. Burnt at sea 9.1827.

HEARTY (ex-*Indra*) Survey ship, 1,300 tons, 212 × 30ft, 4—3pdr. Thomson, Dundee, 18.4.1885 (purch. 1885). Sold 6.11.1920 M. S. Hilton as salvage vessel.

HEARTY (ex-JURUENA) Destroyer, 1,340 tons, 323 (oa) × 33ft, 4—4·7in, 8—TT. Thornycroft 1.8.1939; Brazilian, purch. 9.1939. = HESPERUS 27.2.1940. Sold 26.11.1946; BU Grangemouth.

HEATHER Sloop, 'Aubrietia' class. Greenock & Grangemouth 16.6.1916. Sold 16.2.1932 Midland Iron & Hardware Co., Plymouth. *Served as decoy ship Q.16 until 1918.*

HEATHER Corvette, 'Flower' class. Harland & Wolff 17.9.1940. Sold 22.5.1947; BU Ward, Grays.

HEBE 5th Rate 38, 1,063bm, 150 × 40ft. French, captured 9.1782 by RAINBOW off Île de Bas. = BLONDE 24.12.1805. BU 6.1811.

HEBE 5th Rate 32 (fir-built), 658bm, 127 × 34ft. Deptford DY 31.12.1804. Sold 28.4.1813.

HEBE 5th Rate 46, 1,078bm, 152 × 40ft, 16—32pdr carr., 28—18pdr, 2—9pdr. Woolwich DY 14.12.1826. Receiving ship 1839; hulk 1861. BU comp. 31.3.1873 Chatham.

HEBE Torpedo gunboat, 810 tons, 230 × 27ft, 2—4·7in, 4—3pdr, 3—TT. Sheerness DY 15.6.1892. Minesweeper 1909; depot ship 1910. Sold 22.10.1919 Ward, Preston.

HEBE Minesweeper, 835 tons, 230 × 3 3·5ft, 2—4in. Devonport DY 28.10.1936. Sunk 22.11.1943 mine off Bari.

HEBRUS 5th Rate 36 (yellow pine-built), 939bm, 143 × 38ft, 14—32pdr carr., 28—12pdr, 2—9pdr. Barton, Limehouse, 13.9.1813. Sold 3.4.1817 J. Cristall.

HECATE (Gunboat No 32) Gunvessel 12, 168bm, 76 × 22·5ft. Wilson, Frindsbury, 2.5.1797. Sunk 1809 breakwater Harwich.

HECATE Brig-sloop 18, 'Cruizer' class, 385bm. King, Upnor, 30.5.1809. Sold 30.10.1817 Mr Parker. *Resold Chilean Navy?*

HECATE Wood paddle sloop, 817bm, 165 × 33ft, 1—10in 1—110pdr, 4—32pdr. Chatham DY 30.3.1839. Sold 1865 Castle for BU.

HECATE Iron screw turret ship, 3,480 tons, 225 × 45ft, 4—10in MLR. Dudgeon, Poplar, 30.9.1871. Sold 12.5.1903.

HECATE Survey ship, 1,915 tons, 260·1 (oa) × 49·1ft. Yarrow, Scotstoun, 31.3.1965. Tx disposal list 15.3.1991; = *Sangeeta*, left Portsmouth for Pipaviv, India, for BU; beached 29.1.1994.

HECLA (ex-*Scipio*) Bomb vessel 10, 300bm, 93 × 28ft. Purch. 4.1797. BU 7.1813.

HECLA Bomb vessel 10, 375bm, 105 × 29ft, 10—24pdr carr., 2—6pdr, 1—13in mortar, 1—10in mortar. Barkworth & Hawkes, North Barton, 22.7.1815. Arctic discovery vessel 1819—27. Sold 13.4.1831.

HECLA Wood paddle sloop, 817bm, 165 × 33ft, 2—84pdr, 4—32pdr. Chatham DY 14.1.1839. Sold 15.6.1863 Williams & Co.

HECLA (ex-*British Crown*) Depot ship, 6,400 tons, 391·5 × 39ft, 5—64pdr, 1—40pdr. Harland & Wolff 7.3.1878; purch. 1878. Rebuilt 1912 as 5,600 tons, 4—4in. Sold 13.7.1926 Ward, Preston.

HECLA Depot ship, 10,850 tons, 585 × 66ft, 8—4·5in. John Brown 14.3.1940. Sunk 12.11.1942 by U.515 west of Gibraltar.

HECLA Repair ship, 14,250 tons, 415 × 57ft, 1—5in, 10—40mm. Bethlehem, Fairfield, 31.7.1944 for RN; retained USN = XANTHUS.

HECLA Survey ship, 1,915 tons, 260·1 (oa) × 49·1ft. Yarrow, Blythswood, 21.12.1964. PO 31.3.1997; sold 23.3.1997 Rossmarine = *Bligh*.

HECTOR 22-gun ship, 200/266bm. Captured 1643. Sold 1656.

HECTOR 30-gun ship, 150bm. Captured 1653. Sold 1657.

HECTOR (ex-THREE KINGS) 22-gun ship, 111bm. Royalist (?), captured 1657. Sunk 1665 in action with Dutch.

HECTOR 5th Rate 44, 493bm, 116·5 × 31ft. Burchett, Rotherhithe, 20.2.1703. Rebuilt Plymouth 1721 as 607bm. BU 1742.

HECTOR 5th Rate 44, 720bm, 126 × 36·5ft. Blaydes, Hull, 24.10.1743. Sold 9.12.1762.

HECTOR Cutter. Purch. 2.1763. Sold 4.5.1773.

HECTOR 3rd Rate 74, 1,622bm, 169 × 47ft. Adams, Deptford, 27.5.1774. Prison ship c. 1808. BU 2.1816.

HECTOR 3rd Rate 74. French, captured 12.4.1782. Recaptured 5.9.1782 by French.

HECTOR Iron screw ship, 4,089bm, 6,710 tons, 280 × 56·5ft, 2—8in, 16—7in. Napier 26.9.1862. Sold 11.7.1905 for BU.

HEDINGHAM CASTLE (ex-GOREY CASTLE) Corvette, 'Castle' class. Crown, Sunderland, 30.10.1944 (renamed 1943). Arr. 4.1958 Granton for BU.

HEDINGHAM CASTLE *See also ORANGEVILLE 1944.*

HEIR APPARENT (ex-ARVEPRINDS FREDERICK) 3rd Rate 74. Danish, captured 7.9.1807 Battle of Copenhagen. Sold 3.4.1817 Mr Freake for BU. *Listed as ARVE PRINCLON from 1813. Was to have been renamed CORNWALL.*

HELDER *See ALARM 1799, GUELDERLAND 1808.*

HELDERENBERG 5th Rate 30, 242bm. Dutch, captured 1685 from Duke of Monmouth. Sunk 17.11.1688 collision off I. of Wight.

HELDIN 6th Rate 28, 636bm. 122 × 34ft, 24—12pdr, 4—6pdr. Dutch, captured 28.8.1799 off Texel. Sold 1802.

HELENA Sloop 14, 220bm, 76 × 26·5ft, 14—4pdr. Built 1778. Foundered 3.11.1796 off Dutch coast. *In French hands 9.1778–22.6.1779.*

HELENA Sloop 18, 370bm, 106 × 28ft. Preston, Yarmouth, 26.4.1804. Sold 21.7.1814.

HELENA Brig-sloop 10, 'Cherokee' class, 231bm. Plymouth DY, ordered 26.10.1826, cancelled 21.2.1831.

HELENA Brig-sloop 16, 549bm, 110 × 35ft, 16—32pdr. Pembroke Dock 11.7.1843. Coal hulk 1861; police hulk 11.1863; church ship 12.1868; police hulk 1883. Sold 6.1.1921 Garnham for BU.

HELENA *See also ATALANTA 1775.*

HELFORD Frigate, 'River' class. Hall Russell 6.2.1943. Arr. 29.6.1956 Troon for BU.

HELFORD Minehunter, 890 tons (full load), 156·3 (oa) × 34·5ft, 1—40mm. Richards, Great Yarmouth, 16.5.1984. Tx Bangladeshi Navy 3.9.1994 = SHAIBAL.

HELICON Brig-sloop 10, 'Cherokee' class, 238bm. King, Upnor, 5.8.1808. BU 7.1829 Sheerness.

HELICON Wood paddle despatch vessel, 837bm, 1,000 tons, 220 × 28ft. Portsmouth DY 31.1.1865. = ENCHANTRESS 1.4.1888. Sold 11.7.1905 Laidler, Sunderland.

HELICON *See also CALLIOPE 1884.*

HELIOTROPE Sloop, 'Acacia' class. Lobnitz 10.9.1915. Sold 7.1.1935 Metal Industries; BU Charlestown.

HELIOTROPE Corvette, 'Flower' class. Crown

5.6.1940. Lent USN 3.1942–1945 = SURPRISE. Sold 18.7.1946 = *Heliolock*.

HELMSDALE Frigate, 'River' class. Inglis 5.6.1943. Arr. 7.11.1957 Faslane for BU.

HELMSDALE Minehunter, 890 tons (full load), 156·3 (oa) × 34·5ft, 1–40mm, Richards, Lowestoft, 11.1.1985. Tx Brazilian Navy 31.1.1995 = GARNIER SAM PAIO.

HELMSDALE *See also HUNTLEY 1919.*

HELMSLEY CASTLE Corvette, 'Castle' class. Morton, cancelled 12.1943.

HELVERSON (ex-HILVERSUM) 60-gun ship, 597bm. Dutch, captured 1665. Sunk 7.1667 blockship R. Medway.

HEMLOCK Corvette, 'Flower' class. Harland & Wolff, ordered 8.4.1940, cancelled 23.1.1941.

HENRIETTA Pinnace 6, 68bm. Chatham 1626. Sold 1661.

HENRIETTA Yacht 8, 104bm. Woolwich DY 1663. Sunk 11.8.1673 in action with Dutch.

HENRIETTA Yacht 8, 153bm. Woolwich DY 1679. Sold 1721.

HENRIETTA *See also LANGPORT.*

HENRIETTA MARIA 42-gun ship, 594/792bm. Deptford DY 1.1633. = PARAGON 1650. Burnt at sea 13.7.1655.

HENRY Sloop 16. Purch. 1804. Listed 1805; not listed 1806.

HENRY *See also DUNBAR 1656.*

HENRY GALLEY Galley, 80bm. Built 1512. Lost at sea 1513.

HENRY GRACE A DIEU (GREAT HARRY) Galleon 80, 1,500bm. Woolwich (Erith?) 18.6.1514. Rebuilt Portsmouth 1539 as 1,000bm; = EDWARD 1547. Burnt 27.8.1553 accident.

HENRY OF HAMPTON Ship, 120bm. Purch. 1513. Hulked 1521.

HENRY PRIZE 6th Rate 24, 246bm, × 25·5ft. French, captured 1690. Sold 1698.

HENRYVILLE Frigate (RCN), 'River' class. G. T. Davie, Lauzon, cancelled 12.1943.

HEPATICA Corvette, 'Flower' class. Davie SB 6.7.1940. Lent RCN until 27.6.1945. Arr. 1.1.1948 Rees, Llanelly, for BU.

HERALD 6th Rate 20, 422bm, 109 × 30ft, 8–18pdr carr., 16–6pdr. Carver, Littlehampton, 27.12.1806. BU 9.1817.

HERALD Paddle river gunboat, 82 tons, 90 × 18ft, 4–3pdr. Yarrow, Poplar, 1890. Sold 19.2.1903.

HERALD Survey ship, 2,000 tons, 260·1 (oa) × 49·1ft. Robb-Caledon 4.10.1973. PO 31.5.2001; sold Rossmarine by 7.2001 = *Somerville*.

HERALD *See also TERMAGANT, MERRY HAMPTON 1918.*

HERCULES 3rd Rate 74, 1,608bm, 166·5 × 47ft. Deptford DY 15.3.1759. Sold 17.8.1784.

HERCULES 3rd Rate 74, 1,750bm, 176 × 48·5ft. Chatham DY 5.9.1815. Harbour service 1853. Sold 22.8.1865 in Hong Kong.

HERCULES Iron battleship, 5,234bm, 8,700 tons, 325 × 59ft, 8–10in, 2–9in, 4–7in MLR. Chatham DY 10.2.1868. Coastguard/harbour service from 1881; barracks 1905; = CALCUTTA 1909; = FISGARD II 4.1915. Sold 7.1932 Ward, Morecambe; hulk to Preston 1.12.1932.

HERCULES Battleship, 20,000 tons, 510 × 85ft, 10–12in, 12–4in. Palmer 10.5.1910. Sold 8.11.1921 Slough Trading Co; BU 1922 Germany.

HERCULES Aircraft carrier, 14,000 tons, 695 (oa) × 80ft, 28–40mm, 35 aircraft. Vickers Armstrong, Tyne, 22.9.1945; comp. Harland and Wolff. Tx Indian Navy 1.1957 = VIKRANT 4.3.1961. PO 31.1.1997 (museum ship Mumbai 2002?).

HEREWARD Destroyer, 1,340 tons, 323 (oa) × 33ft, 4–4·7in, 8–TT. Vickers Armstrong, Tyne, 10.3.1936. Torpedoed 29.5.1941 Italian aircraft off Crete.

HEREWARD *See also LAVEROCK 1913.*

HERMES (ex-MERCURIUS) Brig-sloop 12, 210bm, 80 × 27ft. Dutch, captured 12.5.1796 by SYLPH off Texel. Foundered 1.1797.

HERMES Armed ship 22, 331bm, 100 × 28ft. Purch. 1798. Sold 6.1802.

HERMES (ex-*Majestic*) Sloop 16, 339bm, 107 × 27ft, 14–24pdr, 2–6pdr. Purch. 7.1803. Sold 24.3.1810.

HERMES 6th Rate 20, 511bm, 120 × 31ft, 18–32pdr carr., 2–9pdr. Portsmouth DY 22.7.1811. Grounded, burnt 15.9.1814 Mobile, Mississippi.

HERMES Wood paddle sloop, 716bm, 150 × 33ft. Portsmouth DY 26.6.1835. Rebuilt Chatham 1842 as 830bm. BU 1864.

HERMES 2nd class cruiser, 5,600 tons, 350 × 54ft, 11–6in, 9–12pdr. Fairfield 7.4.1898. Fitted to carry seaplanes 1913. Sunk 31.10.1914 by U.27 in Strait of Dover.

HERMES Aircraft carrier, 10,950 tons, 548 × 70ft, 10–6in, 4–4in, 20 aircraft. Armstrong 11.9.1919. Sunk 9.4.1942 Japanese aircraft off Ceylon.

HERMES Aircraft carrier, 18,300 tons, 650 × 90ft, 32–40mm, 45 aircraft. Cammell Laird, cancelled 10.1945.

HERMES (ex-ELEPHANT) Aircraft carrier, 22,500 tons, 650 × 90ft, 17–40mm, 20 aircraft. Vickers Armstrong, Barrow, 16.2.1953 (renamed 5.11.1945). Sold India 11.1986 = VIRAAT.

HERMES *See also MINOTAUR 1816, COURIER 1830.*

HERMIONE 5th Rate 32, 716bm, 129 × 35ft. Teast & Tombs, Bristol, 9.9.1782. HO Spanish in West Indies 22.9.1797 by mutinous crew. Recaptured 25.10.1799 = RETALIATION; = RETRIBUTION 31.1.1800. BU 6.1805 Deptford.

HERMIONE 2nd class cruiser, 4,360 tons, 320 × 49·5ft, 2—6in, 8—4in, 8—6pdr. Devonport DY 7.11.1893. Sold 25.10.1921 Multilocular S. Bkg Co.; resold 18.12.1922 = WARSPITE (TS); resold 9.1940 Ward, Grays, for BU.

HERMIONE Cruiser, 5,450 tons, 512 (oa) × 50·5ft, 10—5·25in, Stephen 18.5.1939. Sunk 6.6.1942 by U.205 eastern Mediterranean.

HERMIONE Frigate, 'Leander' class, Y160, 2,650 tons, 372 (oa) × 43ft, 2—4·5in, Seacat, helo (later Exocet, Seawolf). Stephen 26.4.1967, comp. Yarrow. Sold Samsung (HK) 9.1997; arr. Aland 5.1998 for BU.

HERNE BAY (ex-LOCH EIL) Frigate, 'Bay' class. Smith's Dock 15.5.1945 (renamed 1944). = DAMPIER (survey ship) 9.1946. Sold 13.9.1968; BU Belgium

HERO 3rd Rate 74, 1,574bm, 166 × 47ft. Plymouth DY 28.3.1759. Prison ship 1793; = ROCHESTER 15.9.1800. BU 7.1810 Chatham.

HERO 3rd Rate 74, 1,730bm, 176 × 48ft. Perry, Blackwall, 18.8.1803. Wrecked 5.12.1811 off Texel.

HERO 3rd Rate 74, 1,756bm, 176·5 × 48·5ft. Deptford DY 21.9.1816. = WELLINGTON 4.12.1816; = AKBAR (TS) 10.5.1862. Sold 1908 Ward; arr. Morecombe 8.4.1908 for BU.

HERO Screw 2nd Rate 91, 3,148bm, 234·5 × 55·5ft, 1—110pdr, 34—8in, 4—70pdr, 10—40pdr, 30—32pdr (1862). Chatham DY 15.4.1858. Sold 20.6.1871 Castle, Charlton.

HERO Turret ship, 6,200 tons, 270 × 58ft, 2—12in, 4—6in, 7—6pdr. Chatham DY 27.10.1885. Target 11.1907; sunk as such 18.2.1908; raised, BU.

HERO Destroyer, 1,340 tons, 323 (oa) × 33ft, 4—4·7in, 8—TT. Vickers Armstrong, Tyne, 10.3.1936. Tx RCN 15.11.1943 = CHAUDIERE. Sold 1946.

HEROINE 5th Rate 32, 779bm, 131 × 37ft. Adams, Buckler's Hard, 8.1783. Floating battery 1803. Sold 2.1806.

HEROINE Packet brig 8, 359bm, 95 × 30·5ft, 8—18pdr. Woolwich DY 16.8.1841. Harbour service 1865. BU 12.1878 Devonport.

HEROINE Composite screw corvette, 1,420 tons, 200 × 38ft, 8—6in. Devonport DY 3.12.1881. Sold 28.8.1902 King, Bristol, for BU.

HEROINE *See also VENUS 1758.*

HERON (ex-*Jason*) Sloop 16, 340bm. Purch.

6.1804. = VOLCANO (bomb vessel) 1810. Sold 28.8.1816.

HERON (ex-RATTLESNAKE) Brig-sloop 18, 'Cruizer' class, 387bm. King, Upnor, 22.10.1812 (renamed 1812). BU 3.1831.

HERON Brig 16, 482bm, 105 × 33·5ft, 4—32pdr, 12—32pdr carr. Chatham DY 27.9.1847. Foundered 9.5.1859 off West Africa.

HERON Wood screw gunboat, 'Albacore' class. Miller, Liverpool, 5.7.1860. BU 1881 Jamaica.

HERON River gunboat, 85 tons, 100 × 20ft, 2—6pdr. Yarrow 1897. Tx 1.1899 Govt of Nigeria.

HERON *See also EMPRESS 1906, AUCKLAND 1938.*

HERRING Schooner 4, 78bm, 56 × 18ft, 4—12pdr carr. Bermuda 1804. Foundered 1814 North America.

HERRING Wood screw gunboat, 'Albacore' class. Pitcher, Northfleet, 10.1.1856. BU 8.1865 Sheerness.

HESPELER (ex-GUILDFORD CASTLE) Corvette (RCN), 'Castle' class. Robb 13.11.1943 (renamed 1943). Sold 1946 = *Chilcotin.*

HESPELER *See also LYSANDER 1943.*

HESPER Sloop 18, 424bm, 110 × 29·5ft. Tanner, Dartmouth, 3.7.1809. Sold 8.7.1817.

HESPER (ex-*Hesperus*) Iron screw storeship, 808bm. Tx 24.5.1855 from Treasury Dept. Sold 10.1868.

HESPERUS *See HEARTY 1939.*

HESTOR Fireship 6, 101bm. Purch. 1673. Burnt 1673.

HESTOR Cutter. Listed 1763–67.

HEUREUX 6th Rate 22, 598bm, 127·5 × 33ft, 22—12pdr. French privateer, captured 19.10.1799 by STAG in English Channel. Foundered 1806 Atlantic.

HEUREUX (ex-LYNX) Sloop 16, 337bm. French, captured 21.1.1807 by GALATEA off Caracas. Sold 1.9.1814.

HEVER CASTLE *See COPPERCLIFF 1944.*

HEXHAM Transport 6. Purch. 1798. Listed 1801.

HEXHAM Paddle minesweeper, 'Ascot' class, 820 tons. Clyde SB 15.12.1917. Sold 24.9.1923 Hayes, Pembroke Dock.

HEXTON Coastal minesweeper, 'Ton' class. Cook, Welton & Gemmell 1954. Tx Malaysian Navy 10.1963 = LEDANG. BU 1980.

HEYTHROP Minesweeper, Early 'Hunt' class. Fleming & Ferguson 4.6.1917. Sold 7.1922 Stanlee, Dover.

HEYTHROP Destroyer, 'Hunt' class Type II. Swan Hunter 30.10.1940. Sunk 20.3.1942 by ERIDGE after being torpedoed by U.652 north of Sollum.

HIBERNIA 1st Rate 110, 2,530bm, 203 × 54ft. Plymouth DY 17.11.1804. Base flagship Malta 1855. Sold 14.10.1902. *12 years on stocks.*

HIBERNIA Battleship, 16,350 tons, 425 × 78ft, 4—12in, 4—9·2in, 10—6in, 14—12pdr. Devonport DY 17.6.1905. Sold 8.11.1921 Stanlee; resold, BU Germany.

HIBERNIA *See also PRINCE OF WALES 1765, ACHILLES 1863.*

HIBISCUS Sloop, 'Anchusa' class. Greenock & Grangemouth 17.11.1917. Sold 18.1.1923 Metal Industries, Charlestown.

HIBISCUS Corvette, 'Flower' class. Harland & Wolff 6.4.1940. Lent USN 2.5.1942–1945 = SPRY. Sold 1946 = *Madonna.*

HICKLETON Coastal minesweeper, 'Ton' class. Thornycroft 26.1.1955. Sold 1967 Argentine Navy, = NEUQUEN; deleted 1996.

HIGHBURTON Coastal minesweeper, 'Ton' class. Thornycroft 2.6.1954. BU 7.1978 Middlesbrough.

HIGHFLYER Schooner 8, 144bm, 80 × 20ft. American privateer, captured 9.1.1813 by POICTIERS. Recaptured 8.9.1813 by American PRESIDENT off Nantucket.

HIGHFLYER Tender 2, 81bm, 56 × 19ft, 2—6pdr. Woolwich DY 11.6.1822. Sold 7.8.1833 Ledger, Rotherhithe.

HIGHFLYER Wood screw frigate, 1,153bm. 192 × 36·5ft, 1—10in, 20—8in. Mare, Blackwall, 13.8.1851. BU 5.1871 Portsmouth.

HIGHFLYER 2nd class cruiser, 5,600 tons, 350 × 54ft, 11—6in, 9—12pdr. Fairfield 4.6.1898. Sold 10.6.1921 Bombay.

HIGHLANDER Wood screw gunboat, 'Albacore' class. Hill, Bristol, 4.1856. = YC.51 (dredger) 1868. Sold 5.1884.

HIGHLANDER (ex-JAGUARIBE) Destroyer, 1,340 tons, 323 (oa) × 34ft, 4—4·7in, 8—TT. Thornycroft 17.10.1939; Brazilian, purch. 4.9.1939. Sold 27.5.1946; arr. 8.1947 Rosyth for BU.

HIGHWAY (ex-CLAYMORE) Dock landing ship, 4,270 tons, 454 × 72ft, 1—3in, 16—20mm. Newport News 19.7.1943 on Lend-Lease (renamed 8.1943). Ret. USN 4.1946.

HILDERSHAM Inshore minesweeper, 'Ham' class. Vosper, Gosport, 5.2.1954. Tx Indian Navy 1955 = BIMLIPATAN; deleted 1994–95.

HIMALAYA Iron screw troopship, 3,553bm, 4,690 tons, 340 × 46ft. Mare, Blackwall, 24.5.1853, purch. 7.1854. = C.60 (coal hulk) 12.1895. Sold 28.9.1920 E. W. Payne; sunk 1940 air attack Portland.

HIMALAYA AMC, 6,929 tons. Req. 1914–22.

HINCHINBROOK Sloop 10, 271bm, 91·5 × 26ft. Janvrin, Bursledon, 8.3.1744. Captured 10.11.1746 by French.

HINCHINBROOK (ex-TARTAR) Brig 14. American, captured 1777. Slop ship 1782. Sold 21.3.1783.

HINCHINBROOK Sloop 12. 1778. Captured 4.1778 by Americans.

HINCHINBROOK (ex-ASTREE) 6th Rate 28, 557bm, 115 × 33ft. French, captured 1779. Foundered 19.1.1782 off Jamaica.

HIND 28-gun vessel, 80bm. Built 1545. Sold 1555.

HIND 18-gun ship, 140/500bm. Purch. 1643. Listed until 1651. *In Royalist hands 1648–49.*

HIND Ketch 8, 54bm. Page, Wivenhoe, 1655. Wrecked 11.12.1668.

HIND Dogger 6. Dutch, captured 1672. Recaptured 1674 by Dutch.

HIND Ketch 10, 96bm. Snelgrove, Wapping, 2.4.1691. Captured 7.1.1697 by French in North Sea.

HIND 6th Rate 12, 161bm, 78·5 × 22·5ft. French privateer, purch. 8.6.1709. Stranded 16.9.1709 nr Hurst Castle.

HIND 6th Rate 16, 190bm, 78 × 23·5ft. Captured 21.9.1709 by MEDWAY. Bilged on anchor 29.11.1711 Dublin harbour, sank.

HIND 6th Rate 20, 282bm, 94 × 26ft. Woolwich DY 31.10.1711. Wrecked 7.12.1721 Channel Is.

HIND 6th Rate 24, 510bm, 113 × 32·5ft. Chitty & Vernon, Chichester, 29.11.1740. Storeship 7.1783. Sold 8.1.1784.

HIND Sloop 1741. Sold 6.10.1743.

HIND Sloop 14, 273bm, 91·5 × 26ft. Perry, Blackwall, 19.4.1744. Foundered 1.9.1747 North America.

HIND 6th Rate 28, 592bm, 121 × 35ft. Clayton & Wilson, Sandgate, 22.7.1785. BU 7.1811 Deptford.

HIND Tender 10, 161bm, 72 × 24ft, 10—6pdr. Cowes 1790; built as Revenue cutter. Sold 22.2.1844 E. Smith.

HIND (ex-BARBADOES) 6th Rate 20, 460bm, 115·5 × 30ft. Davy, Topsham, 8.3.1814 (renamed 1813). Sold 6.4.1829 Bombay.

HIND Wood screw gunboat, 'Dapper' class. Thomson, Millwall, 3.5.1855. BU 10.1872 Devonport.

HIND Coastguard yawl, 131bm, 70 × 21ft. White, Cowes, 25.3.1880. Wrecked 27.11.1900 Shipwash.

HIND Destroyer, 770 tons, 240 × 25·5ft, 2—4in, 2—12pdr, 2—TT. John Brown 28.7.1911. Sold 9.5.1921 Ward, BU Preston 1924.

HIND Sloop, 1,350 tons, 283 × 38ft, 6—4in. Denny 30.9.1943. Arr. 10.12.1958 Clayton & Davie, Dunston, for BU.

HINDOSTAN (ex-*Born*) 4th Rate 54, 1,249bm, 160 × 42ft. East Indiaman, purch. 1795. Storeship 1802. Burnt 2.4.1804 accident Rosas Bay, San Sebastian.

HINDOSTAN (ex-*Admiral Rainer*) 4th Rate 50, 887bm. 158·5 × 37ft. East Indiaman, purch. 5.1804. Storeship, 20 guns, 1811; = DOLPHIN 2.9.1819; = JUSTITIA (convict ship) 1830. Sold 24.10.1855.

HINDOSTAN 2nd Rate 80, 2,029bm, 3,242 tons, 186 × 51ft. Plymouth DY 2.8.1841. TS 1868; = FISGARD III 12.10.1905; = HINDOSTAN 8.1920. Sold 10.5.1921 Garnham.

HINDOSTAN *See also CROMER 1990.*

HINDUSTAN Battleship, 16,350 tons, 425 × 78ft, 4—12in, 4—9·2in, 10—6in. John Brown 19.12.1903. Sold 9.5.1921 Ward; LU Belfast; arr. Preston 14. 1973 for BU.

HINDUSTAN Sloop (RIN), 1,190 tons, 280 × 35ft, 2—4in. Swan Hunter 12.5.1930. Tx Pakistani Navy 1948 = KARSAZ. BU 1951.

HINKSFORD Seaward defence boat, 'Ford' class. Richards, Lowestoft, 17.3.1955. Tx Nigerian Navy 9.9.1966 = BENIN; deleted 1982.

HIPPOMENES Sloop 18, 407bm, 96 × 30ft. 16—32pdr carr., 2—9pdr. Dutch, captured 20.9.1803 Demerara. Sold 28.4.1813.

HIRA Gunboat (RIN), 331 tons, 170 × 22ft, 2—3in. Iranian, captured 1941 by RIN forces. Ret. Iran 1946.

HIRONDELLE Gun-brig 14, 210bm. French cutter, captured 28.4.1804 by BITTERN in Mediterranean. Wrecked 3.1808 nr Tunis.

HOBART (ex-LA REVANCHE) Sloop 18, c. 400bm. French privateer, captured 21.10.1794 by RESISTANCE off Sunda. Sold 1803.

HOBART GM destroyer (RAN). Modified 'Charles F. Adams' class, 3,370 tons, 440·8 (oa) × 47ft, 2—5in, Harpoon, SAM GDC Pomona, 6—TT. Defoe SB, Bay City, 9.1.1964. PO 12.5.2000; scuttled 7.2000 off Aldinga Beach.

HOBART *See also APOLLO 1934.*

HODGESTON Coastal minesweeper, 'Ton' class. Fleetlands SY 6.4.1954. = NORTHUMBRIA 1954–60; = VENTURER 1961–75. Sold 9.1988; BU 28.12.1988 Bruges.

HOGUE 3rd Rate 74, 1,750bm, 176 × 48·5ft. Deptford DY 3.10.1811. Comp. screw ship 1848, 1,846bm. BU 1865 Devonport.

HOGUE Armoured cruiser, 12,000 tons, 440 × 69·5ft, 2—9·2in, 12—6in. Vickers 13.8.1900. Sunk 22.9.1914 by U.9 North Sea.

HOGUE Destroyer, 2,315 tons, 379 (oa) × 40·25ft, 4—4·5in, 1—4in, 12—40mm, 8—TT. Cammell

Laird 21.4.1944. Sold 7.3.1962 in Singapore for BU.

HOLCOMBE Destroyer, 'Hunt' class Type III. Stephen 14.4.1942. Sunk 12.12.1943 by U.593 off Bougie.

HOLDERNESS Minesweeper, Early 'Hunt' class. Henderson 9.11.1916. Sold 8.1924 for BU by Cashmore, Newport.

HOLDERNESS Destroyer, 'Hunt' class Type I. Swan Hunter 8.2.1940. Arr. 20.11.1956 Ward, Preston, for BU.

HOLDERNESSE Cutter 10. Origin unknown. Captured 1779 by Spanish in English Channel.

HOLIGHOST Ship. Listed 1400–06

HOLIGOST 'King's ship'. Bt 1300 Sandwich.

HOLIGOST (ex-SANTA CLARA) 6-gun vessel. Spanish, captured 1413. Listed until 1452

HOLIGOST SPAYNE Ship. Captured from Spanish 1.8.1419. Sold 15.6.1423.

Holland submarines *See entry at beginning of 'H' section.*

HOLLESLEY BAY (ex-LOCH FANNICH) Frigate, 'Bay' class. Smith's Dock (renamed 1944). Cancelled 1945.

HOLLY Schooner 10, 150bm, 79 × 22ft. Bermuda 1809. Wrecked 29.1.1814 nr San Sebastian.

HOLLYHOCK Sloop, 'Acacia' class. Barclay Curle 1.5.1915. Sold 7.10.1930 Ward, Pembroke Dock.

HOLLYHOCK Corvette, 'Flower' class. Crown 19.8.1940. Sunk 9.4.1942 by Japanese aircraft east of Ceylon.

HOLM SOUND (ex-*Empire Labuan*) Repair ship, 10,000 tons, 431 × 56ft, 12—20mm. Gray, Hartlepool, 5.9.1944. Sold 4.1948 = *Avisbay.*

HOLMES 5th Rate 24, 220bm. Purch. 1671. Fireship 1677. Sold 1682.

HOLMES Frigate, TE 'Captain' class. Bethlehem, Hingham, 19.12.1943 on Lend-Lease. Ret. USN 12.1945.

HOLMES *See also TOBAGO 1943.*

HOLSTEIN 3rd Rate 64, 1,395bm, 161 × 44·5ft, 24—24pdr, 38—24pdr carr., 2—12pdr. Danish, captured 2.4.1801 Battle of Copenhagen. = NASSAU 1805. Sold 3.11.1814.

HONESTY (ex-CAPRICE) Corvette, Modified 'Flower' class. Kingston, Ontario, 28.9.1942. Tx RN 28.5.1943 on Lend-Lease. Ret. USN 5.1.1946. Sold 1946 as whaler.

HONEYSUCKLE Sloop, 'Acacia' class. Lobnitz 29.4.1915. Sold 6.9.1922 Distin for BU.

HONEYSUCKLE Corvette, 'Flower' class. Ferguson 22.4.1940. BU 11.1950 Ward, Grays.

HONG KONG Paddle tender. Purch. 1856. Sold c. 1858.

HOOD (ex-EDGAR) Screw 2nd Rate 91, 3,308bm, 198 × 56ft. Chatham DY 4.5.1859 (renamed 29.6.1848). Harbour service 1872. Sold 1888. *See EDGAR 1848.*

HOOD Battleship, 14,150 tons, 380 × 75ft, 4–13·5in, 10–6in, 10–6pdr. Chatham DY 30.7.1891. Sunk 4.11.1914 blockship Portland harbour.

HOOD Battlecruiser, 41,200 tons, 860·9 (oa) × 105·3ft, 8–15in, 12–5·5in, 4–4in. John Brown 22.8.1918. Sunk 24.5.1941 in action with German BISMARCK and PRINZ EUGEN south of Greenland.

HOPE Galleon 48, 403/500bm, 2–60pdr, 4–34pdr, 9–18pdr , 11–9pdr, 4–6pdr, 18 small. Deptford 1559. Rebuilt 1604, 600bm, 38 guns = ASSURANCE. BU 1645.

HOPE (ex-ESPERANCE) Ship. French privateer, captured 1626. 'Released' 1630.

HOPE Storeship 26. Purch. 1652. Sold 1657.

HOPE (ex-HOOP) 44-gun ship, 480bm. Dutch, captured 1665. Wrecked 1666.

HOPE Hoy storeship 4, 46bm. Dutch, captured 1666. Recaptured 1672 by Dutch.

HOPE 3rd Rate 70, 1,052bm, 152 × 40·5ft. Deptford DY 1678. Captured 16.4.1695 by French off The Lizard.

HOPE Sloop 14. Listed from 1764. Captured 1779 by American privateer.

HOPE Schooner. Purch. 3.1765. Condemned 14.1776 North America.

HOPE Brig-sloop 14, 232bm, 91·5 × 26·5ft. Purch. 1780. Wrecked 1781 off Savannah.

HOPE (ex-*Lady Washington*) Cutter 12, 156bm, 68 × 24·5ft, 12–4pdr. American, purch. 4.1780. Sold 9.6.1785. *In French hands 16.8–21.8.1781.*

HOPE Gunvessel 3, 68bm, 57·5 × 16·5ft, 1–32pdr carr., 2–18pdr. Hoy, purch. 3.1794. Listed until 1798.

HOPE (ex-STAR) Sloop 14, 220bm. Dutch, captured 18.8.1795 Simons Bay. Sold 1807.

HOPE Brig-sloop 10, 'Cherokee' class, 237bm. Bailey, Ipswich, 22.7.1808. Sold 3.2.1819 T. Pittman for BU.

HOPE Tender 10, 49bm, 47 × 16ft. Deptford 1813. = YC.42 (tankvessel) 7.1863. In service 1880.

HOPE Packet brig 3, 'Cherokee' class, 231bm. Plymouth DY 8.12.1824. Harbour service by 1854. BU 10.1882 Pembroke.

HOPE Destroyer, 745 tons, 246 × 25ft, 2–4in, 2–12pdr, 2–TT. Swan Hunter 6.9.1910. Sold 2.1920 in Malta.

HOPE PRIZE Fireship 2, 91bm. Dutch, captured 1672. Sold 1674.

HOPEWELL Pink 20. Purch. 1652. Sold 1657.

HOPEWELL Fireship 6, 242bm. Purch. 1672. Expended 1673.

HOPEWELL Fireship 8, 253bm, 94 × 25ft. Ellis, Shoreham, 15.4.1690. Burnt 3.6.1690 accident The Downs.

HOPEWELL Fireship 8, 157bm. Purch. 11.8.1690. Expended 19.5.1692 La Hogue.

HOPEWELL Firevessel, 18bm. Purch. 7.1694. Sold 17.2.1696.

HORATIO 5th Rate 38, 1,090bm, 154·5 × 39ft. Parsons, Bursledon, 23.4.1807. Comp. 6.1850 screw ship, 1,175bm. Sold 1865 Castle, Charlton.

HORNBY See *MONTSERRAT 1943.*

HORNET Sloop 14, 272bm, 91 × 26·5ft. Chitty & Quallet, Chichester, 3.8.1745. Sold 3.7.1770. *In French hands 12.1746–10.1747.*

HORNET Cutter 16, 98bm, 50 × 20ft. Purch. 1.1763. Sold 13.3.1772.

HORNET Sloop 14, 305bm, 97 × 27ft. Perry, Blackwall, 19.3.1776. Sold 7.1791.

HORNET Sloop 16. 423bm, 108 × 30ft. Stalkart, Rotherhithe, 3.2.1794. Harbour service 1805. Sold 30.10.1817.

HORNET Gunvessel 4, 60bm, 63 × 14ft. Purch. 3.1794. BU 7.1795.

HORNET Schooner 6, 181bm, 81 × 23·5ft. Chatham DY 24.8.1831; comp. brigantine. BU 7.1845 Chatham.

HORNET Schooner. Woolwich, ordered 12.8.1847, tx Deptford. *Became following ship.*

HORNET Wood screw sloop, 753bm, 160 × 32ft, 17–32pdr. Deptford DY 13.4.1854. BU 1868 White, Cowes.

HORNET Composite screw gunvessel, 465bm, 603 tons, 155 × 25ft, 1–7in, 1–64pdr 2–20pdr. Penn, Stockton-on-Tees, 10.3.1868. Sold 1889.

HORNET Destroyer, 260 tons, 180 × 18·5ft, 1–12pdr, 3–6pdr, 3–TT. Yarrow, Poplar, 23.12.1893. Sold 12.10.1909 Thames S. Bkg Co.

HORNET Destroyer, 770 tons, 240 × 25·5ft, 2–4in, 2–12pdr, 2–TT. John Brown 20.12.1911. Sold 9.5.1921 Ward, Rainham.

HORNPIPE Minesweeper, 260 tons, 130 × 26ft, 1–3pdr. Murdoch & Murray 25.7.1917; War Dept tug, tx 10.1917. Sold 1.5.1920 Crichton Thomson.

HORSEMAN Flyboat 18, 191bm. Dutch, captured 1665. Sunk 7.1667 blockship R. Thames.

HORSHAM Minesweeper (RAN), 'Bathurst' class. Williamstown DY 25.3.1942. Sold 8.8.1956 in Hong Kong for BU.

HORSLEYDOWN Sloop 4. Horsleydown 1652. Sold 1654.

HORSLEYDOWN Sloop 4. Listed 1653. Sold 1656.

HOSTE Destroyer leader, 1,666 tons, 325 × 32ft, 4–4in, 4–TT. Cammell Laird 16.8.1916. Sunk 21.12.1916 collision NEGRO in North Sea.

HOSTE (ex-MITCHELL) Frigate DE 'Captain' class. Boston NY 24.9.1943 on Lend-Lease. Ret. USN 22.2.1945.

HOSTE *See also NYASALAND 1943.*

HOSTILE Destroyer, 1,340 tons, 323 (oa) × 33ft, 4–4·7in, 8–TT. Scotts 24.1.1936. Sunk 23.8.1940 mine off Cape Bon.

HOTHAM Frigate, TE 'Captain' class. Bethlehem, Hingham, 22.12.1943 on Lend-Lease. Nominally ret. USN 13.3.1956. BU 9.1956.

HOTHAM *See also BAHAMAS 1943.*

HOTSPUR 5th Rate 36, 952bm, 145 × 38·5ft. Parsons, Warsash, 13.10.1810. BU 1.1821.

HOTSPUR 5th Rate 46, 1,171bm, 159 × 41ft. Pembroke Dock 9.10.1828. Chapel hulk 1859; = MONMOUTH 1868. Sold 1902.

HOTSPUR Armoured ram (turret ship), 4,331 tons, 235 × 50ft, 1–12in, 2–64pdr. Napier, Govan, 19.3.1870. Sold 2.8.1904.

HOTSPUR Destroyer, 1,340 tons, 323 (oa) × 33ft. 4–4·7in, 8–TT. Scotts 23.3.1936. Tx Dominican Republic 23.11.1948 = TRUJILLO; = DUARTE 1962; deleted 1972.

HOTSPUR *See also LANDRAIL 1913.*

HOUGHTON Coastal minesweeper, 'Ton' class. Camper & Nicholson 22.11.1957. Sold 29.1.1971; BU Plymouth.

HOUND 36-gun ship. Captured 1652. Hulk 1656. BU 1660 Jamaica.

HOUND 18-gun ship, 206bm. Captured 1656. Expended 1666 as fireship.

HOUND Sloop 4, 50bm. Chatham DY 1673. Sold 1686.

HOUND Fireship 8, 257bm, 94 × 25ft. Graves, Limehouse, 18.4.1690. Expended 22.5.1692 Cherbourg.

HOUND Sloop 4, 83bm, 61 × 18ft. Deptford DY 1700. Sold 29.7.1714.

HOUND Sloop 14, 200bm, 87·5 × 23ft. Deptford DY 6.9.1732. BU 6.1745 Deptford.

HOUND Sloop 14, 267bm, 92 × 26ft. Stow & Bartlett, Shoreham, 22.5.1745. Sold 27.10.1773.

HOUND Sloop 14, 305bm, 97 × 27ft. Adams Barnard, Deptford, 8.3.1776. BU 11.1784. *Was French LEVRETTE 1780–82.*

HOUND Sloop 16, 321bm, 100 × 26ft. Deptford DY 31.3.1790. Captured 14.7.1794 by French in Atlantic.

HOUND Brig-sloop 16, 314bm, 95 × 28ft. Hill, Sandwich, 24.3.1796. Wrecked 26.9.1800 Shetlands.

HOUND (ex-*Monarch*) Sloop 16, 333bm, 103 × 27ft, 12–24pdr carr., 4–18pdr. Purch. 2.1801. Bomb vessel 1808. BU 11.1812.

HOUND Brig 8. Woolwich DY, ordered 24.5.1839, cancelled 6.1844, tx Deptford.

HOUND Brig 8, 358bm, 91 × 30·5ft, 8–18pdr. Deptford DY 23.5.1846. Breakwater 1872. Sold 11.1887 Castle, Charlton.

HOUND Minesweeper, 'Algerine' class. Lobnitz 29.7.1942. Arr. 1.9.1962 Troon for BU.

HOUND *See also MASTIFF 1856.*

HOUSE DE SWYTE (ex-HUISTE SWIETEN) 3rd Rate 70, 786bm. Dutch, captured 3.6.1665. Sunk 3.1667 blockship R. Thames.

HOVERFLY River gunboat, 'Fly' class. Yarrow 4.1916 in sections. Sold 16.2.1923 Basra Port Authority.

HOVINGHAM Inshore minesweeper, 'Ham' class. Fairlie Yacht Co. 24.5.1956. Sold 27.9.1966.

HOWE (ex-*Kaikusroo*) Storeship 20, 1,048bm, 150 × 30ft. East Indiaman, purch. 1805. = DROMEDARY 6.8.1806; convict ship 8.1819. Sold 8.1864 in Bermuda.

HOWE 1st Rate 120, 2,619bm, 205 × 56ft. Chatham DY 28.3.1815. BU 2.1854 Sheerness.

HOWE Screw 1st Rate 110, 4,245bm, 275 × 61ft. Pembroke Dock 7.3.1860. = BULWARK (harbour service) 3.12.1885; = IMPREGNABLE 27.9.86; = BULWARK 1.12.19. Sold 18.2.1921 Garnham for BU.

HOWE Battleship, 10,300 tons, 325 × 68ft, 4–13·5in, 6–6in, 12–6pdr. Pembroke Dock 28.4.1885. Sold 11.10.1910 Ward, Swansea; to Briton Ferry 1.1912 for BU.

HOWE Battlecruiser, 36,300 tons, 8–15in, 12–5.5in. Cammell Laird, ordered 4.1916, cancelled 10.1918.

HOWE (ex-BEATTY) Battleship, 35,000 tons, 745 (oa) × 103ft, 10–14in, 16–5·25in. Fairfield 9.4.1940 (renamed 2.1940). Arr. 4.6.1958 Ward, Inverkeithing, for BU.

HOWETT *See PAPUA 1943.*

HOWITZER Destroyer, 1,980 tons, 341·5 × 38ft, 6–4in, 6–40mm, 10–TT. Thornycroft, LD 26.2.1945, cancelled 10.1945.

HUBBERSTON Coastal minesweeper, 'Ton' class. Camper & Nicholson 14.9.1954. Towed Zeebrugge 13.5.1992 for BU.

HUGH LINDSAY Wood paddle sloop (Indian), 441bm. Bombay DY 1829. Sold 1859.

HUGH ROSE Wood screw gunboat (Indian), 300bm, 125 × 23ft, 1–68pdr, 2–24pdr. Bombay DY 18.9.1860. Listed until 1876,

HUGHES Destroyer leader, 1,750 tons. 329 × 32ft,

5–4·7in, 1–3in, 6–TT. Cammell Laird, ordered 4.1917, cancelled 1.19.

HULVUL *See NAIAD 1963.*

HUMBER Fireship 8, 254bm. Built 1690. *Fate unknown.*

HUMBER 2nd Rate 80, 1,223bm, 156 × 42ft. Frame, Hull, 30.3.1693. Rebuilt Deptford 1708 as 1,294bm; rebuilt Portsmouth 1726 as 1,353bm. = PRINCESS AMELIA 1727. BU 6.1752 Portsmouth.

HUMBER 5th Rate 44, 829bm, 134 × 38ft. Smith, Bursledon, 5.3.1748. Wrecked 16.9.1762 Hazeboro Sand.

HUMBER Sloop 16. French, captured 1806. Listed 1808.

HUMBER Wood screw gunvessel, 'Philomel' class. Pembroke Dock, LD 8.2.1861, cancelled 12.12.1863.

HUMBER (ex-*Harar*) Iron screw storeship, 1,640 tons, 246 × 29ft. Earle, Hull, 7.10.1876, purch. 28.5.1878. Sold 1907 = *Lucia Victoria.*

HUMBER (ex-JAVARY) River monitor, 1,260 tons, 265 × 49ft, 2–6in, 2–4·7in howitzers. Vickers 17.6.1913; Brazilian, purch. 8.8.1914. Sold 17.9.1920 F. Rijsdijks as crane ship.

HUMBER Minehunter, 890 tons (full load), 156·3 (oa) × 34·5ft, 1–40mm. Richards, Lowestoft, 17.5.1984. Tx Brazilian Navy 31.1.1995 = AMORIM DO VALLE.

HUMBER *See also BRONINGTON 1953.*

HUMBERSTONE (ex-NORHAM CASTLE, ex-TOTNES CASTLE) Corvette (RCN), 'Castle' class. Inglis 12.4.1944 (renamed 1943). Sold 1946 = *Chang Chen.*

HUMBERSTONE *See also GOLDEN FLEECE 1944.*

HUNTER Dogger. Captured 1646. Sold 1649.

HUNTER (ex-CHASSEUR) Fireship 10. French sloop, captured 1652. Burnt 31.7.1653 in action with Dutch.

HUNTER 6-gun vessel, 50bm. Royalist, captured by Parliamentarians 1656. Foundered 1661.

HUNTER 5th Rate 30, 260bm. Dutch, captured 1672. Listed until 1677.

HUNTER Sloop 4, 46bm. Portsmouth DY 1673. Sold 1683.

HUNTER Fireship 8, 277bm, 94 × 25ft. Shish, Rotherhithe, 29.4.1690. 6th Rate 1710, 24 guns. Captured 20.9.1710 by Spanish off Cape St Mary.

HUNTER Fireship 10. Purch. 7.9.1739. = VULCAN 1740. Hulked Jamaica 10.1743.

HUNTER Sloop 10, 238bm, 89 × 24·5ft. Wells & Stanton, Deptford, 28.2.1756. Captured 23.11.1775 by American privateer off Boston; re-

captured by GREYHOUND. Sold 27.12.1780 New York unfit.

HUNTER Cutter 8, 72bm, 50 × 20ft. Purch. 1.1763. Sold 1771.

HUNTER Sloop 16, 336bm, 103 × 26ft, 16–24pdr. Pender, Bermuda, 1796, purch. on stocks. Wrecked 27.12.1797 Hog I., Virginia.

HUNTER Brig-sloop 18, 310bm, 91 × 28·5ft, 2–24pdr, 16–6pdr. Purch. 5.1801. BU 1809.

HUNTER Brig 10 (Canadian lakes), 180bm. Lake Erie 1812. Captured 10.9.1813 by Americans on Lake Erie.

HUNTER Wood screw gunboat, 'Clown' class. Pitcher, Northfleet, 7.6.1856. On sale list 6.1869. Sold 1884.

HUNTER Destroyer, 295 tons, 194 × 19ft, 1–12pdr, 5–6pdr, 2–TT. Fairfield 28.12.1895. Sold 10.4.1912 Ward, Briton Ferry, for BU.

HUNTER Destroyer, 1,340 tons, 323 (oa) × 33ft, 4–4·7in 8–TT. Swan Hunter 25.2.1936. Damaged in action, lost 10.4.1940 collision HOTSPUR at Narvik.

HUNTER Patrol/training boat 32 tons, 65·6 (oa) × 17ft. Fairey Marine 1983. Sold Lebanon 11.1991 = JBEIL 17.7.1992.

HUNTER *See also TRAILER 1942, LST.3042 1945.*

HUNTLEY (ex-HELMSDALE) Minesweeper, Later 'Hunt' class. Eltringham 18.1.1919 (renamed 1918). Sunk 31.1.1941 air attack eastern Mediterranean.

HUNTSVILLE (ex-WOOLVESEY CASTLE) Corvette (RCN), 'Castle' class. Ailsa 24.2.1944 (renamed 1943). Sold 1946 = *Wellington Kent.*

HUNTSVILLE *See also PROMPT 1944.*

HUON (ex-DERWENT) Destroyer (RAN), 700 tons, 1–4in, 3–12pdr, 3–TT. Cockatoo DY 19.1.1914 (renamed 1913). Dismantled 1929; sunk target 9.4.1930 off Jervis Bay.

HUON Minehunter (RAN), 'Huon' class, 720 tons, 172·2 (oa) × 32·5ft, 1–30mm, Intermarine/ADI, Newcastle, NSW, 25.7.1997.

HURON (ex-OHIO) Schooner 2 (Canadian lakes), 2–24pdr. American, captured 12.8.1814. Listed 1817.

HURON Schooner 2 (Canadian lakes), 66bm, 54 × 17·5ft, 2–24pdr. Kingston, Ontario, 1817. *May have been rebuild of previous vessel.*

HURON Destroyer (RCN), 1,927 tons, 377 (oa) × 37·5ft, 6–4·7in, 2–4in, 4–TT. Vickers Armstrong, Tyne, 25.6.1942. Arr. 20.8.1965 Spezia for BU.

HURON Destroyer (RCN), 4,700 tons (full load), 426 (oa) × 50ft, 1–5in, 1–3in, 6–TT, Limbo, 2 helo. Marine Industries 3.4.1971.

HURRICANE (ex-JAPARUA) Destroyer, 1,340 tons, 323 (oa) × 33ft, 4—4·7in, 8—TT. Vickers Armstrong, Barrow, 29.9.1939; Brazilian, purch. 9.1939. Sunk 24.12.1943 by U.275 in North Atlantic.

HURSLEY Destroyer, 'Hunt' class Type II. Swan Hunter 20.7.1941. Lent Greek Navy 12.1943–12.11.1959 = KRITI. BU 1960.

HURST Paddle minesweeper, 'Ascot' class. Dunlop Bremner 6.5.1916. Sold 3.1922 Ward, Inverkeithing.

HURST CASTLE Corvette, 'Castle' class. Caledon SB 23.2.1944. Sunk 1.9.1944 by U.482 north-west of Ireland.

HURWORTH Destroyer, 'Hunt' class Type II. Vickers Armstrong, Tyne, 10.4.1941. Sunk 22.10.1943 mine east of Kalymnos, Dodecanese.

HURWORTH Minehunter, 615 tons, 197 (oa) × 32·8ft, 1—40mm. Vosper-Thornycroft 25.9.1984.

HUSSAR 6th Rate 28 (fir-built), 586bm, 118·5 × 34ft. Chatham DY 23.7.1757. Captured 5.1762 by French when aground coast of Cuba.

HUSSAR 6th Rate 28, 627bm, 114 × 34ft. Inwood, Rotherhithe, 26.8.1763. Wrecked 1780 nr New York.

HUSSAR (ex-PROTECTOR) 6th Rate 26, 586bm. American, captured 5.1780 by ROEBUCK. Sold 14.8.1783.

HUSSAR Galley 1. American, captured 1780. Sold 1786.

HUSSAR 6th Rate 28, 596bm, 120·5 × 34ft. Wilson, Sandgate, 1.9.1784. Wrecked 27.12.1796 off Île de Bas.

HUSSAR (ex-HUSSARD) Sloop 14, 413bm, 105 × 30ft. French privateer, captured 10.1798 by AMERICA. Sold 1800.

HUSSAR 5th Rate 38, 1,043bm, 150·5 × 39·5ft. Woolwich DY 1.10.1799. Wrecked 2.1804 Bay of Biscay.

HUSSAR 5th Rate 38, 1,077bm, 154 × 40ft. Adams, Buckler's Hard, 23.4.1807. Harbour service 9.1833; target 6.1861. Burnt 1861 accident Shoeburyness in use target.

HUSSAR Torpedo gunboat, 1,070 tons, 250 × 30·5ft, 2—4·7in, 4—6pdr, 5—TT. Devonport DY 3.7.1894. Sold 12.1920; resold 13.7.1921 L. Gatt, Malta, for BU.

HUSSAR Minesweeper, 815 tons, 230 × 33·5ft, 2—4in. Thornycroft 27.8.1934. Sunk 27.8.1944 in error by Allied aircraft off Normandy.

HYACINTH (ex-HAYACINTHE) Sloop. French privateer, captured 11.1692. *Fate unknown.*

HYACINTH 6th Rate 20, 424bm, 109 × 30ft, 16—32pdr carr., 8—18pdr carr., 2—6pdr. Preston, Yarmouth, 30.8.1806. BU 12.1820.

HYACINTH Sloop 18, 435bm, 110 × 31ft. Plymouth DY 6.5.1829. Coal hulk 16.1860. BU comp. 27.11.1871 Portsmouth.

HYACINTH Composite screw corvette, 1,420 tons, 200 × 38ft, 8—6in. Devonport DY 20.12.1881. Sold 25.8.1902; BU King, Bristol.

HYACINTH 2nd class cruiser, 5,600 tons, 350 × 54ft, 11—6in, 9—12pdr. London & Glasgow Co. 27.10.1898. Sold 11.10.1923 Cohen, Swansea.

HYACINTH Corvette, 'Flower' class. Harland & Wolff 19.8.1940. Lent Greek Navy 1943 = APOSTOLIS. BU 1962.

HYAENA 6th Rate 24, 522bm, 114·5 × 32ft. Fisher, Liverpool, 2.3.1778. Captured 27.5.1793 by French CONCORDE in West Indies; recaptured 10.1797 as privateer HYENE, = HYAENA. Sold 2.1802.

HYAENA (ex-*Hope*) 6th Rate 28, 519bm, 132 × 31ft. Purch. 6.1804. Storeship 1813. Sold 18.4.1822 Cockshott.

HYAENA Brig-sloop 10, 'Cherokee' class. 233bm. Chatham DY, LD 3.1825; launched 19.8.1826 as CALYPSO (q.v.).

HYAENA (ex-CALYPSO) Brig-sloop 10, 'Cherokee' class, 239bm. Deptford DY, cancelled 21.2.1831 (renamed 1826).

HYAENA Wood screw gunboat, 'Albacore' class. Mare, Blackwall, 3.4.1856. Sold 8.3.1870. W. E. Joliffe as salvage vessel.

HYAENA Iron screw gunboat, 'Ant' class. Laird 30.8.1873. Sold 3.4.1906 Chatham.

HYDERABAD Decoy ship. 1917–20.

HYDERABAD (ex-NETTLE) Corvette, 'Flower' class. A. Hall 23.9.1941 (renamed 23.4.1941). Sold 1.1.1948; BU 10.1948 Portaferry.

HYDRA 6th Rate 24, 454bm, 109·5 × 30·5ft. Adams & Barnard, Deptford, 8.8.1778. Sold 1.5.1783.

HYDRA 5th Rate 38, 1,024bm, 148 × 39ft. Cleveley, Gravesend, 13.3.1797. Troopship 1812. Sold 13.1.1820.

HYDRA Wood paddle sloop, 818bm, 165 × 33ft. Chatham DY 13.6.1838. Sold 13.5.1870 Castle, Charlton.

HYDRA Coast defence ship, 3,480 tons, 225 × 45ft, 4—10in MLR. Elder, Govan, 28.12.1871. Sold 7.7.1903; BU Genoa.

HYDRA Destroyer, 700 tons, 240 × 25·5ft, 2—4in, 2—12pdr, 2—TT. John Brown 19.2.1912. Sold 9.5.1921 Ward, Portishead.

HYDRA Minesweeper, 'Algerine' class. Lobnitz 29.9.1942. Damaged 10.11.1944 mine, not repaired; BU 11.1945 Ward, Grays.

HYDRA Survey ship, 1,915 tons, 260·1 (oa) × 49ft. Blythswood 14.7.1965. HO Indonesia 18.4.1980 = DEWI KEMBAR.

HYDRANGEA Sloop, 'Arabis' class. Connell, Greenock, 2.3.1916. Sold 7.4.1920 in Hong Kong.

HYDRANGEA Corvette, 'Flower' class. Ferguson 4.9.1940. Sold 1947 = *Hydralock.*

HYGEIA *See LEANDER 1780.*

HYPERION 5th Rate 32, 978bm, 144 × 39.5ft, Gibson, Hull, 3.11.1807. BU 6.1833.

HYPERION Wood screw frigate, 3,202bm, 280 × 50ft. Woolwich DY, ordered 3.2.1861, cancelled 12.1863.

HYPERION Destroyer, 1,340 tons, 323 (oa) × 33ft, 4—4.7in, 8—TT. Swan Hunter 8.4.1936. Torpedoed Italian submarine SERPENTE in Mediterranean, sunk 22.12.1940 by ILEX.

HYTHE (ex-BANFF) Minesweeper, turbine 'Bangor' class. Ailsa 4.9.1941 (renamed 6.1941). Sunk 11.10.1943 by U.37 off Bougie.

I

IBIS Sloop, 1,250 tons, 283 × 37·5ft, 6—4in. Fur-ness SB Co 28.11.1940. Sunk 10.11.1942 by Italian aircraft in western Mediterranean.

IBIS *See also SINGLETON 1955.*

ICARUS Brig-sloop 10, 'Cherokee' class, 234bm. Portsmouth DY 18.8.1814. Coastguard 1839. Sold 4.4.1861.

ICARUS Wood screw sloop, 580bm, 15 × 29ft, 11—32pdr. Deptford DY 22.10.1858. Sold 23.1.1875 Castle, Charlton.

ICARUS Sloop, 950 tons, 167 × 32ft. Devonport DY 27.7.1885. Sold 3.1904.

ICARUS Destroyer, 1,370 tons, 323 (oa) × 33ft, 4—4·7in, 10—TT. John Brown 26.11.1936. Sold 29.10.1946; BU Troon.

ICKFORD Seaward defence boat, 'Ford' class. Rowhedge Ironworks 17.6.1954. Sold 4.9.1967 in Singapore.

IGNITION (ex-*Jean*) Fireship 4, 130bm, 69 × 22ft, 4—12pdr carr. Purch. 5.1804. Wrecked 19.2.1807 off Dieppe.

ILDEFONSO *See SAN ILDEFONSO 1805.*

ILEX Destroyer, 1,370 tons, 323 (oa) × 33ft, 4—4·7in, 10—TT. John Brown 28.1.1937. Sold 1948 in Malta for BU Sicily.

ILFRACOMBE Minesweeper, turbine 'Bangor' class. Hamilton 29.1.1941. Sold 1. 1.1948; BU Clayton & Davie, Tyne.

ILFRACOMBE *See also INSTOW 1919.*

ILLUSTRIOUS 3rd Rate 74, 1,616bm, 168 × 47ft. Adams, Buckler's Hard, 7.7.1789. Wrecked 14.3.1795 Avenza.

ILLUSTRIOUS 3rd Rate 74, 1,746bm, 175 × 48·5ft. Randall, Rotherhithe, 3.9.1803. Gunnery ship 4.1854. BU comp. 4.12.1868 Portsmouth.

ILLUSTRIOUS Battleship, 14,900 tons, 390 × 75ft, 4—12in, 12—6in, 18—12pdr. Chatham DY 17.9.1896. Sold 18.6.1920 Ward, Barrow.

ILLUSTRIOUS Aircraft carrier, 23,000 tons, 673 × 96ft, 16—4·5in, 36 aircraft. Vickers Armstrong, Barrow, 5.4.1939. Arr. 3.11.1956 Faslane for BU.

ILLUSTRIOUS Aircraft carrier (originally rated anti-submarine cruiser, 20,600 tons (full load),

677 (oa) × 90ft, 3—30mm Goalkeeper, 16 aircraft, 6 helo. Swan Hunter 1.12.1978.

ILMINGTON Coastal minesweeper, 'Ton' class. Camper & Nicholson 8.3.1954. Sold 1967 Argentine Navy = FORMOSA.

ILSTON Coastal minesweeper, 'Ton' class. Camper & Nicholson. Launched 14.10.1954 as BADMINTON. Sold for BU 14.4.1970 Bruges.

IMAUM (ex-*Liverpool*) 3rd Rate 76, 1,776bm, 177 × 48·5ft. Bombay DY 10.11.1826. East Indiaman, presented 9.3.1836 by Imam of Muscat. Harbour service 7.1842. BU 1863 Jamaica.

IMMORTALITE 5th Rate 42, 1,010bm, 145 × 39ft. French, captured 20.10.1798 by FISGARD off Brest. BU 7.1806.

IMMORTALITE (ex-INFATIGABLE) 5th Rate 38, 1,157bm. French, captured 24.9.1806 by squadron off Rochefort. BU 1.1811.

IMMORTALITE Wood screw frigate, 3,984bm, 251 × 52ft. Pembroke Dock 25.10.1859. Sold 1883.

IMMORTALITE Armoured cruiser, 5,600 tons, 300 × 56ft, 2—9·2in, 10—6in 10—3pdr. Chatham DY 7.6.1887. Sold 1.1.1907 S. Bkg Co, Blackwall.

IMMORTALITE *See also DUNIRA 1814.*

IMOGEN (ex-DIABLE-A-QUATRE) Sloop 18, 399bm, 108 × 29ft. French privateer, captured 26.10.1800 by THAMES in Bay of Biscay. Foundered 1.3.1805 Atlantic.

IMOGEN Brig-sloop 16, 282bm, 93 × 27ft. Bailey, Ipswich, 11.7.1805. Sold 3.4.1817 Mr Ismay.

IMOGEN Destroyer, 1,370 tons, 323 (oa) × 33ft, 4—4·7in 10—TT. Hawthorn Leslie 30.10.1936. Sunk 16.7.1940 collision GLASGOW off Duncansby Head.

IMOGENE (ex-PEARL) 6th Rate 28, 660bm, 125 × 35ft, 20—32pdr, 6—18pdr, 2—9pdr. Pembroke Dock 24.6.1831 (renamed 23.2.1826). Burnt 19.9.1840 accident Plymouth.

IMOGENE Wood screw corvette, 950bm, 185 × 33ft. Portsmouth DY, ordered 1861, cancelled 12.12.1863.

IMOGENE Coastguard vessel, 300 tons, 139 × 21ft, 2—20pdr. White, Cowes, 1864. = ARGUS 22.1.1884. Sold 1903.

IMOGENE (ex-*Jacamar*) Iron screw yacht, 460 tons, 160 × 24ft. Purch. 1882. = IMPEY 1919. Sold 15.5.1919 Ledger Hill.

IMPERIAL Destroyer, 1,370 tons, 323 (oa) × 33ft, 4–4·7in, 10–TT. Hawthorn Leslie 11.12.1936. Bombed 28.5.1941 German aircraft north of Crete, sunk next day by HOTSPUR.

IMPERIEUSE 5th Rate 40, 1,040bm, 148·5 × 39·5ft. French, captured 11.10.1793 by squadron off Spezia. = UNITE 3.9.1803. Harbour service 1832. BU 1.1858 Chatham.

IMPERIEUSE Wood screw frigate, 2,358bm, 212 × 50ft, 10–8in, 1–68pdr, 40–32pdr. Deptford DY 15.9.1852. Sold 3.1867 Castle & Beech.

IMPERIEUSE Armoured cruiser, 8,400 tons, 315 × 62ft, 4–9·2in. 10–6in, 8–6pdr. Portsmouth DY 18.12.1883. = SAPPHIRE II (depot ship) 2.1905; = IMPERIEUSE 6.1909. Sold 24.9.1913 Ward, Morecambe.

IMPERIEUSE *See also AMPHITRITE 1799, IPHIGENIA 1804, AUDACIOUS 1869. The name was also given to a 1944 training establishment comprising the battleships RESOLUTION and REVENGE (ships' names not changed).*

IMPETUEUX 3rd Rate 74, 1,878bm, 182 × 47·5ft. French, captured 1.6.1794 'Battle of 1st of June'. Burnt 24.8.1794 accident Portsmouth.

IMPETUEUX *See also AMERICA 1794.*

IMPEY *See IMOGENE 1882.*

IMPLACABLE (ex-DUGUAY-TROUIN) 3rd Rate 74, 1,882bm, 3,223 tons, 181 × 49·5ft. French, captured 3.11.1805 Sir Richard Strachan's action. TS 7.1855; lent 1.1912 Mr Wheatly Cobb for preservation. Scuttled 2.12.1949 off The Owers.

IMPLACABLE Battleship, 15,000 tons, 400 × 75ft, 4–12in, 12–6in, 18–12pdr. Devonport DY 11.3.1899. Sold 8.11.1921 Slough Trading Co.; BU Germany.

IMPLACABLE Aircraft carrier, 26,000 tons, 673 × 96ft, 16–4·5in, 72 aircraft. Fairfield 10.12.1942. Arr. 3.11.1955 Ward, Inverkeithing, for BU.

IMPREGNABLE 2nd Rate 98, 1,887bm, 178 × 49ft. Deptford DY 15.4.1789. Wrecked 18.10.1799 nr Chichester.

IMPREGNABLE 2nd Rate 98, 2,406bm, 3,880 tons, 197 × 53·5ft. Chatham DY 1.8.1810. TS 1862. = KENT 9.11.1888; = CALEDONIA 22.9.1891. Sold 10.7.1906 Castle.

IMPREGNABLE *For training ships with this name see HOWE 1860, INCONSTANT 1868, BLACK PRINCE 1861, CIRCE 1827, POWERFUL 1895, ANDROMEDA 1897, CAROLINE 1882, GANGES 1821.*

IMPULSIVE Destroyer, 1,370 tons, 323 (oa) ×

33ft, 4–4·7in 10–TT. White 1.3.1937. Sold 22.1.1946; BU Young, Sunderland.

INCENDIARY Fireship 8, 397bm, 110·5 × 29ft. Mestears, R. Thames, 6.11.1778. Wrecked 1780 off I. of Wight.

INCENDIARY Fireship 16, 422bm, 109 × 30ft, 16–18pdr carr. King, Dover, 12.8.1782. Captured 29.1.1801 by French in Mediterrnean.

INCENDIARY (ex-*Diligence*) Fireship 14, 62bm, 53·5 × 17·5ft. Purch. 1804. Sold 4.1812.

INCHARRAN Frigate (RCN), 'River' class. Davie SB 6.6.1944. Sold 1966 Kingston Mariners' Association.

INCONSTANT (ex-PALLAS) 5th Rate 36, 705bm, 128 × 35·5ft. French, captured 19.7.1778 by VICTORY. = CONVERT 1778. BU 1791.

INCONSTANT 5th Rate 36, 890bm, 138 × 38·5ft. Barnard, Deptford, 28.10.1783. BU 11.1817.

INCONSTANT 5th Rate 46, 1,215bm, 159·5 × 42ft. Deptford DY, tx Sheerness DY, ordered 9.6.1825, cancelled 9.3.1832.

INCONSTANT 5th Rate 36, 1,422bm, 160 × 45·5ft. 36–32pdr. Portsmouth DY 10.6.1836. Sold 8.12.1862 Scott, Cork. BU 10.1866 (by Castle?).

INCONSTANT Iron screw frigate, 4,066bm, 5,880 tons, 337 × 50ft, 10–9in, 6–7in MLR. Pembroke Dock 12.11.1868. Harbour service 1898. = IMPREGNABLE II (TS) 6.1906; = DEFIANCE IV 1.1922; = DEFIANCE II 12.1930. Arr. 4.4.1956 Belgium for BU.

INCONSTANT Light cruiser, 3,500 tons, 410 × 39ft, 2–6in, 6–4in. Beardmore 6.7.1914. Sold 9.6.1922 Cashmore, Newport.

INCONSTANT (ex-MUAVENET) Destroyer, 1,360 tons, 323 (oa) × 33·5ft, 4–4·7in, 8–TT. Vickers Armstrong, Barrow, 24.2.1941; Turkish, purch. 9.1939. Ret. Turkish Navy 9.3.1946; sold 1960.

INCREASE 12-gun ship, 100/133bm. Captured 1645. Wrecked 1650.

INCREASE Ship, 505bm. In service 1650–54. *Possibly hired.*

INDEFATIGABLE 3rd Rate 64, 1,400bm, 160 × 44ft. Adams, Buckler's Hard, 7.1784. Reduced to 38 guns 2.1795. BU 8.1816 Sheerness.

INDEFATIGABLE Armed ship. Purch. 1804. Sold 1805.

INDEFATIGABLE 4th Rate 50, 2,084bm, 176 × 53ft, 50–32pdr. Woolwich DY, ordered 29.11.1832, cancelled 9.3.1834.

INDEFATIGABLE 4th Rate 50, 2,044bm, 2,626 tons, 180 × 51·5ft, 28–8in, 22–32pdr. Devonport DY 27.7.1848. On loan from 3.1.1865 as TS. Sold 26.3.1914.

INDEFATIGABLE 2nd class cruiser, 3,600 tons,

300 × 44ft, 2—6in, 6—4·7in, 13—6pdr. London & Glasgow Co 12.3.1891. = MELPOMENE 11.1.1910. Sold 7.10.1913 Ward, Preston.

INDEFATIGABLE Battlecruiser, 19,200 tons, 555 × 80ft, 8—12in, 20—4in. Devonport DY 28.10.1909. Sunk 31.5.1916 Battle of Jutland.

INDEFATIGABLE Aircraft carrier, 26,000 tons, 673 × 96ft, 16—4·5in, 72 aircraft. John Brown 8.12.1942. Arr. 4.11.1956 Dalmuir for BU.

INDEFATIGABLE *See also PHAETON 1883.*

INDEPENDENCIA Coal hulk. Slaver, purch. 1.12.1843. = ATTENTION 1846. Sold 1847?

INDIAN 44-gun ship, 687bm. Captured 1654. Sold 1659.

INDIAN Sloop 18, 400bm. Bermuda 1805. Sold 24.4.1817.

INDIAN (ex-*Relampago*) Survey schooner. Purch. 24.9.1855. On sale list 7.1856. Sold 1859?

INDIGNANT Gun-brig 12, 182bm, 84 × 22ft, 10—18pdr carr., 2—12pdr, 1—13in mortar. Boole & Good, Bridport, 13.5.1805. BU 6.1811.

INDOMITABLE Battlecruiser, 17,250 tons, 560 × 78ft, 8—12in, 16—4in. Fairfield 16.3.1907. Sold 1.12.1921 Stanlee, Dover; arr. 30.8.1922 for BU.

INDOMITABLE Aircraft carrier, 23,000 tons, 673 × 96ft, 16—4·5in, 36 aircraft. Vickers Armstrong, Barrow, 26.3.1940. Arr. 30.9.1955 Faslane for BU.

INDUS Storeship. East Indiaman, purch. 1790. *Fate unknown.*

INDUS 3rd Rate 74, 1,756bm, 177 × 48·5ft. Dudman, Deptford, 19.12.1812. = BELLONA 3.11.1818. Harbour service 1840. BU comp. 27.6.1868 Devonport.

INDUS Iron paddle gunboat (Indian), 303bm. Laird 1838. Listed 1843.

INDUS 2nd Rate 80, 2,098bm, 3,653 tons, 189 × 51ft. Portsmouth DY 16.3.1839. Guardship 1860. Sold 11.11.1898.

INDUS Gunvessel (Indian), 522bm. Bombay DY 1851. *Fate unknown.*

INDUS Sloop (RIN), 1,190 tons, 280 × 35·5ft, 2—4·7in. Hawthorn Leslie 24.8.1934. Sunk 6.4.1942 Japanese aircraft Akyab, Burma.

INDUS *For training ships with this name see DEFENCE 1861, TEMERAIRE 1876, BELLERO-PHON 1865, VALIANT 1863, GANGES 1821, TRIUMPH 1870, FLORA 1893, VICTORIOUS 1895.*

INDUSTRY Sloop. In service 1765.

INDUSTRY Firevessel, 70bm, 59·5 × 17ft. Purch. 4.1794. BU 8.1795.

INDUSTRY Gunvessel. In service 1806–10.

INDUSTRY Transport, 318bm, 104 × 2–6ft, 4—12pdr carr. Warwick, Eling, 13.10.1814. Harbour service 1820. BU 1846.

INDUSTRY Iron screw storeship, 638bm, 1,100 tons. Mare, Blackwall, 1854, purch. 19.4.1854. BDV 1901. Sold 10.10.1911 Ward, Preston.

INDUSTRY (ex-GLASGOW) Storeship, 1,460 tons, 196 × 30ft. Beardmore 7.6.1901 (renamed 1900). Sunk 19.10.1918 enemy action.

INDUSTRY (ex-*Tay & Tyne*) Storeship, 180 × 26ft. Purch. 26.9.1917. Sold 31.10.1924 C. A. Beard.

INFANTA 3rd Rate 74, 1,918bm, 171·5 × 51·5ft Spanish, captured 1762 Havana. Sold 26.4.1775.

INFANTA DON CARLOS Sloop 16. Spanish, captured 12.1804 by DIAMOND. BU 1811.

INFERNAL Bomb vessel 8, 307bm, 91·5 × 28ft, 8—6pdr. 1—13in mortar. West, Northam, 4.7.1757. Sold 26.10.1774.

INFERNAL Fireship 8, 307bm, 97 × 27·5ft. Perry & Hankey, R. Thames, 6.11.1778, purch. on stocks. Sold 21.3.1783.

INFERNAL Bomb vessel 6, 374bm, 105 × 28·5ft. Barkworth & Hawkes, North Barton, 26.7.1815. Sold 13.4.1831 Mr Snook.

INFERNAL Wood paddle sloop, 1,059bm 180 × 36ft. Woolwich DY 31.5.1843. = ECLAIR 8.1844; = ROSAMOND 10.1846. Floating factory 1863. BU 1865.

INFLEXIBLE Sloop 18, 180bm, 18—12pdr. St John's, Lake Champlain, 1.10.1776. *Fate unknown.*

INFLEXIBLE 3rd Rate 64, 1,386bm, 160 × 46ft. Barnard, Harwich, 7.3.1780. Storeship 12.1793; troopship 7.1809. BU 1820 Halifax, NS.

INFLEXIBLE Wood paddle sloop, 1,122bm, 190 × 36ft. Pembroke Dock 12.4.1845. Sold 1864 Castle & Beech.

INFLEXIBLE Battleship, 11,880 tons, 320 × 75ft, 4—16in MLR, 8—4in. Portsmouth DY 27.4.1876. Sold 15.9.1903 Ward, Birkenhead and Preston.

INFLEXIBLE Battlecruiser, 17,250 tons, 560 × 78ft, 8—12in, 16—4in. John Brown 20.6.1907. Sold 1.12.1921 Stanlee, Dover.

INGERSOL Corvette (RCN), Modified 'Flower' class. Collingwood SY, cancelled 12.1943.

INGLEFIELD Destroyer leader, 1,530 tons, 337 (oa) × 34ft, 5—4·7in, 10—TT. Cammell Laird 15.10.1936. Sunk 25.2.1944 German aircraft Anzio.

INGLESHAM Inshore minesweeper, 'Ham' class. White 23.4.1952. Sold 9.8.1966.

INGLIS Frigate, DE 'Captain' class. Boston NY 2.11.1943 on Lend-Lease. Ret. USN 3.1946.

INGONISH Minesweeper, TE 'Bangor' class. North Vancouver Ship Repair Co. 30.7.1941. Lent RCN until 2.7.1945. Sold 1.1.1948; BU Clayton & Davie, Tyne.

INMAN Frigate, DE 'Captain' class. Boston NY 2.11.1943 on Lend-Lease. Ret. USN 3.1946.

INSOLENT Wood screw gunboat, 'Albacore' class. Pitcher, Northfleet, 26.1.1856. Sold 1.5.1869 Chefoo.

INSOLENT Iron screw gunboat, 265 tons, 87·5 × 26ft, 1–10in MLR. Pembroke Dock 15.3.1881. Gatevessel 1.1918. Foundered 1.7.1922 Portsmouth harbour; wreck sold 18.6.1925 Pounds, Portsmouth.

INSOLENT *See also ARROGANTE 1798.*

INSPECTOR Sloop 16, 310bm, 97 × 27ft. Game, Wivenhoe, 29.4.1782. Sold 2.1802.

INSPECTOR Sloop 16, 250bm. Purch. 1803. Sold 25.6.1810.

INSPECTOR Survey cutter, 60bm. In service 1822.

INSTOW (ex-ILFRACOMBE) Minesweeper, Later 'Hunt' class. Eltringham 15.4.1919 (renamed 1918). Sold 15.11.1920 A. S. Miller = *Tilak.*

INTEGRITY Cutter 6 purch. Australia 1805. Listed until 1810.

INTELLIGENCE Brigantine 4, 75bm. Woolwich DY 11.2.1696. Wrecked 3.2.1700 Douglas Bay, I. of Man.

INTELLIGENT Gun-brig 12, 181bm, 84 × 22ft. Boole & Good, Bridport, 26.8.1805. Sold 14.10.1815, refused by buyer; mooring lighter 8.1816.

INTREPID (ex-SERIEUX) 3rd Rate 64, 1,300bm, 152 × 44ft. French, captured 3.5.1747 Cape Finisterre. BU comp. 2.8.1765 Chatham.

INTREPID 3rd Rate 64, 1,374bm, 160 × 44ft. Woolwich DY 4.12.1770. Harbour service 5.1810. Sold 26.3.1828 Beatson.

INTREPID Sloop 16 (Indian). Bombay 1780. Foundered 10.1800.

INTREPID (ex-PERSEVERANCE, ex-*Free Trade*) Wood screw discovery sloop. Purch. 3.1850 (renamed 3.1850). Abandoned 15.6.1854 Arctic.

INTREPID Wood screw gunvessel, 862bm, 201·5 × 30·5ft, 2–68pdr, 4–32pdr. Wigram, Blackwall, 13.11.1855. Sold 7.10.1864 Marshall, Plymouth.

INTREPID 2nd class cruiser, 3,600 tons, 300 × 44ft, 2–6in, 6–4·7in, 8–6pdr. London & Glasgow Co 20.6.1891. Minelayer 9.1910. Sunk 23.4.1918 blockship Zeebrugge.

INTREPID Destroyer, 1,370 tons, 323 (oa) × 33ft, 4–4·7in, 10–TT. White 17.12.1936. Sunk 26.9.1943 German aircraft Leros harbour.

INTREPID Assault ship, 11,060 tons, 520 (oa) × 80ft, 2–40mm, Seacat, helo. John Brown 25.6.1964. LU 1991; cannibalised 2000–01; for disposal 7.2001.

INVENTION Sloop 4, 28bm. Portsmouth 1673. Sold 1683.

INVER Frigate (RCN), 'River' class. Vickers, Montreal, 5.12.1942 on Lend-Lease. Ret. USN 4.3.1946.

INVERELL Minesweeper (RAN), 'Bathurst' class. Mort's Dock 2.5.1942. Tx RNZN 10.4.1952; deleted 1976.

INVERMORISTON Coastal minesweeper, 'Ton' class. Dorset Yacht Co., Poole, 2.6.1954. Sold Cashmore 2.7.1971; BU Newport.

INVERNESS (ex-DUC DE CHARTRES) 6th Rate 22, 354bm, 105 × 28·5ft. 90–9pdr, 2–3pdr. French privateer, captured 18.1.1746 by EDINBURGH off The Lizard. BU 2.1750 Portsmouth.

INVERNESS Minehunter, 'Sandown' class, Vosper-Thornycroft 27.2.1990.

INVESTIGATOR Survey brig 16, 121bm, 76 × 19ft. Deptford DY 23.4.1811. Police ship 3.1837. BU 10.1857.

INVESTIGATOR Survey sloop (Indian), 450bm. Purch. 1823. *Fate unknown.*

INVESTIGATOR Discovery vessel, 480bm. Purch. 2.1848. Abandoned c. 1853 Arctic.

INVESTIGATOR Wood paddle survey vessel, 149bm. Deptford DY 16.11.1861. Sold 1869 Lagos local authorities.

INVESTIGATOR Wood paddle survey vessel (Indian), 856 tons, 180 × 26ft. Bombay DY 1881. Sold c. 1906.

INVESTIGATOR (ex-*Consuelo*) Survey vessel, 900 tons, 185·5 × 29ft, 1–3pdr. Purch. 12.1903. = SEALARK 29.1.1904. Sold 3.9.1919 Melbourne, mercantile.

INVESTIGATOR Survey vessel (RIM), 1,185 tons, 254 × 33ft. Vickers 11.6.1907. Sold 1934.

INVESTIGATOR (ex-*Patrick Stewart*) Survey vessel (RIM), 1,572 tons, 226 × 37·5ft. Purch. 1934. Sold 19.6.1951 for BU Bombay.

INVESTIGATOR *See also XENOPHON 1798, RESEARCH 1888, TRENT 1942.*

INVETERATE Gun-brig 12, 182bm, 84 × 22ft, 10–18pdr carr., 2–12pdr. Boole & Good, Bridport, 30.5.1805. Wrecked 18.2.1807 nr St-Valery-en-Caux.

INVINCIBLE 3rd Rate 74, 1,793bm, 172 × 49ft. French, captured 3.5.1747 Cape Finisterre. Wrecked 19.2.1758 nr St Helens.

INVINCIBLE 3rd Rate 74, 1,631bm, 168·5 × 47·5ft. Wells, Deptford, 9.3.1765. Wrecked 16.3.1801 Harborough Sands, Yarmouth.

INVINCIBLE 3rd Rate 74, 1,674bm, 170 × 48·5ft. Woolwich DY 15.3.1808. Coal hulk 1857. BU 1.1861.

INVINCIBLE Iron screw ship, 3,774bm, 6,010 tons, 280 × 54ft. 10—9in, 4—64pdr. Napier 29.5.1869. = EREBUS (TS) 4.1904; = FISGARD II 1.1906. Foundered 17.9.1914 off Portland.

INVINCIBLE Battlecruiser, 17,250 tons, 550 × 78ft, 8—12in, 16—4in. Armstrong 13.4.1907. Sunk 31.5.1916 Battle of Jutland.

INVINCIBLE Aircraft carrier (originally rated anti-submarine cruiser), 20,600 tons (full load), 677 (oa) × 90ft, 3—30mm Goalkeeper, 16 aircraft, 6 helo. Vickers, Barrow, 3.5.1977.

INVINCIBLE *See also BLACK PRINCE 1861.*

IPHIGENIA 5th Rate 32, 681bm, 126 × 35ft. Betts, Mistleythorn, 27.12.1780. Burnt 20.7.1801 accident Alexandria.

IPHIGENIA (ex-MEDEA) 5th Rate 38, 1,046bm, 147 × 40ft, 14—32pdr carr., 28—18pdr, 2—9pdr. Spanish, captured 5.10.1804 by squadron in Atlantic. = IMPERIEUSE 1805; harbour service 5.1818. Sold 10.9.1838. *Captured while at peace with Spain.*

IPHIGENIA 5th Rate 36, 870bm, 137 × 38ft. Chatham DY 26.4.1808. Lent 7.1833–48 Marine Society. BU 5.1851 Deptford.

IPHIGENIA 2nd class cruiser, 3,600 tons, 300 × 44ft, 2—6in, 6—4·7in, 8—6pdr. London & Glasgow Co. 19.11.1891. Minelayer 1910. Sunk 23.4.1918 blockship Zeebrugge.

IPSWICH 3rd Rate 70, 1,049bm, 150 × 40ft. Barrett, Harwich, 19.4.1694. Large repair Woolwich 1712 as 1,100bm; rebuilt Portsmouth 1730 as 1,142bm; hulked 5.1757 Gibraltar. BU c. 1764.

IPSWICH Minesweeper, 'Bathurst' class. Evans Deakin 11.8.1941. Lent RAN from 6.1942. Sold 1946 Dutch Navy = MOROTAI. Tx Indonesia 28.12.1949 = HANG TUAH. Sunk 28.4.1958 aircraft off Balikapam.

IPSWICH Patrol boat (RAN), 211 tons. North Queensland Co., Cairns, 25.9.1982.

IRAWADDY Iron river gunboat (Indian), 614 tons. Listed 1887–93. Origin and fate unknown.

IRIS (ex-HANCOCK) 6th Rate 28, 762bm, 137 × 34ft, 26—12pdr, 6—6pdr. American, captured 1777 by RAINBOW. Captured 11.9.1781 by French in Chesapeake R. Destroyed 18.12.1793 by RN while hulked Toulon.

IRIS 5th Rate 32, 688bm, 126 × 35·5ft. Barnard, Deptford, 2.5.1783. Lent 10.1803 Trinity House; = SOLEBAY 18.11.1809. BU 10.1833 Devonport.

IRIS 5th Rate 44, 1,020bm. Danish MARIE, captured 7.9.1807 Battle of Copenhagen. Sold 31.7.1816. *Was to have been renamed ALARIC.*

IRIS 6th Rate 26, 906bm, 131 × 40·5ft. Pembroke Dock 14.7.1840. Sold 16.10.1869 as cable vessel.

IRIS Despatch vessel (2nd class cruiser), 3,730 tons, 300 × 46ft, 10—64pdr. Pembroke Dock 12.4.1877. Sold 11.7.1905.

IRIS Sloop, 'Acacia' class. Lobnitz 1.6.1915. Sold 26.1.1920 C. W. Kellock.

IRIS *See also CORIANDER 1941.*

IRON DUKE Battleship, 6,010 tons, 280 × 54ft, 10—9in, 4—64pdr. Pembroke Dock 1.3.1870. Sold 15.6.1906 Galbraith, Glasgow.

IRON DUKE Battleship, 25,000 tons, 580 × 89·5ft, 10—13·5in, 12—6in. Portsmouth DY 12.10.1912. Harbour service 9.1932. Sold 2.1946; arr. 8.1946 Faslane for BU; hulk resold, arr. 30.11.1948 Port Glasgow for BU.

IRON DUKE Frigate, 'Norfolk' class. Yarrow, Glasgow, 2.3.1991.

IROQUOIS Minesweeping sloop, '24' class. Barclay Curle 24.8.1918. Survey ship 1912. HO Ward 28.6.1937 part payment *Majestic* (CALEDONIA, q.v.); BU Briton Ferry.

IROQUOIS (ex-ATHABASKAN) Destroyer (RCN), 1,927 tons, 377 (oa) × 37·5ft, 6—4·7in, 2—4in, 4—TT. Vickers Armstrong, Tyne, 23.9.1941 (renamed 1940). Arr. 9.1966 Bilbao for BU.

IROQUOIS Destroyer (RCN), 4,700 tons (full load), 426 (oa) × 50ft, 1—5in, 1—3in, 6—TT, Limbo, 2 helo. Marine Industries 28.11.1970.

IRRAWADDY Wood paddle vessel (Indian), 170bm. Kidderpore DY 1.1827. *Fate unknown.*

IRRESISTIBLE 3rd Rate 74, 1,643bm, 168 × 47ft. Barnard, Harwich, 6.12.1782. BU 9.1806.

IRRESISTIBLE Screw 2nd Rate 80, 2,589bm. 3,842 tons, 190 × 57ft. Chatham DY 27.10.1859. Harbour service 9.1868. Sold 1894 Bermuda.

IRRESISTIBLE Battleship, 15,000 tons, 400 × 75ft, 4—12in, 12—6in, 18—12pdr. Chatham DY 15.12.1898. Sunk 18.3.1915 torpedo from shore battery, Dardanelles.

IRRESISTIBLE *See also SWIFTSURE 1787, ARK ROYAL 1950.*

IRVINE Minesweeper, Later 'Hunt' class. Fairfield 8.12.1917. Sold 21.2.1923 J. W. Houston, Mont-rose.

IRWELL *See SIR BEVIS 1918, GOOLE 1919.*

ISABELLA Yacht 8, 94bm, 8—3pdr. Greenwich 1683. Rebuilt Deptford 1703 as 105bm. Sold 13.3.1716.

ISABELLA Yacht 6, 52bm. Chatham DY 1680. Sold 1683.

ISABELLA Discovery vessel. 1818.

ISHAM Inshore minesweeper, 'Ham' class. White 13.9.1954. Tx French Navy 22.4.1955 = M.774/ OILETTE. Arr. Amsterdam 4.8.1989 for BU.

ISINGLASS Minesweeping sloop, '24' class. Greenock & Grangemouth 5.3.1919, not comp. Sold 12.8.1920 Moise Mazza, Malta; retained, sold 15.11.1922 Ferguson Muir & Co.

ISIS 4th Rate 50, 976bm, 142 × 40ft. Harwich. *Probably launched as COLCHESTER 1744 (q.v.).*

ISIS (ex-DIAMANT) 4th Rate 50, 1,013bm, 143 × 40·5ft, 24—24pdr, 24—9pdr, 2—6pdr. French, captured 3.5.1747 Cape Finisterre. Sold 1.7.1766 Chatham.

ISIS 4th Rate 50, 1,051bm, 146 × 41ft. Henniker, R. Medway, 19.11.1774. BU 9.1810.

ISIS 4th Rate 50, 1,190bm, 154·5 × 43ft. Woolwich DY, ordered 1813; lengthened 1816 to 1,321bm, 164 × 43ft, '60 guns' (22—24pdr, 10—24pdr carr., 24—12pdr, 2—6pdr), launched 5.10.1819. Coal hulk 3.1861. Sold 12.3.1867 C. Heddle, Sierra Leone.

ISIS 2nd class cruiser, 5,600 tons, 350 × 54ft, 5—6in, 6—4·7in (1904: 11—6in). London & Glasgow Co. 27.6.1896. Sold 26.2.1920 Granton S. Bkg Co.

ISIS Destroyer, 1,370 tons, 323 (oa) × 33ft, 4—4·7in, 10—TT. Yarrow 12.11.1936. Sunk 20.7.1944 off Normandy. *Probably mined.*

ISIS *Name borne in succession by RNVR tenders FDB.76 (renamed 1950–51); MSS.1785 (1951, foundered 1956 off Ostend): PULHAM (31.7.1956, = PULHAM 1963); CRADLEY (1963).*

ISKRA Schooner, 560 tons, 128 × 25ft. 1917. Purch. by Polish Navy 1922; used as submarine depot ship 1941–45. *See PIGMY.*

ISLE OF WIGHT Yacht 4, 31bm. Portsmouth DY 1676. Rebuilt Portsmouth 1701 as 38bm. Sold 1712.

ISLIP 22-gun ship. Bailey, Bristol, 3.1654. Wrecked 1655 off Inverlochy.

ISTER (ex-BLONDE) 5th Rate 36 (red pine-built), 945bm, 143·5 × 38·5ft, 14—32pdr carr., 28—12pdr. Wallis, Blackwall, 14.7.1813 (renamed 1812). Sold 8.3.1819 Beech for BU.

ISTER Wood screw frigate 36, 2,478bm, 240 × 48ft. Devonport DY, LD 8.11.1860, cancelled 12.1864.

ITCHEN Destroyer, 550 tons, 225 × 23·5ft, 1—12pdr, 5—6pdr, (1907: 4—12pdr), 2—TT. Laird 17.3.1903. Sunk 6.7.1917 by U.99 North Sea.

ITCHEN Frigate, 'River' class. Fleming & Ferguson 29.7.1942. Sunk 22.9.1943 U-boat in North Atlantic.

ITCHEN Minehunter, 890 tons (full load), 156·3 (oa) × 34·5ft, 1—40mm. Richards, Lowestoft, 30.10.1984. Tx Brazilian Navy 8.4.1998 = CALHEIRO DA GRACA; = BRACUI.

ITHURIEL (ex-GABRIEL) Destroyer leader 1,655 tons, 325 × 32ft, 4—4in, 4—TT. Cammell Laird 8.3.1916 (renamed 1915). Sold 8.11.1921 Slough Trading Co.; BU Germany.

ITHURIEL (ex-GAYRET) Destroyer, 1,360 tons, 323 (oa) × 33·5ft, 4—4·7in, 8—TT. Vickers Armstrong, Barrow, 24.2.1941; Turkish, purch. 9.1939. Sunk 28.11.1942 Bône harbour; raised, sold 25.8.1945; BU 8.1946 McLellan, Bo'ness.

IVANHOE Destroyer, 1,370 tons, 323 (oa) × 33ft, 4—4·7in, 10—TT. Yarrow 11.2.1937. Mined 1.9.1940 off Texel; sunk by KELVIN.

IVANHOE *See also LAWFORD1913.*

IVESTON Coastal minesweeper, 'Ton' class. Philip, Dartmouth, 1.6.1954. Sold Sea Cadets; towed to Tilbury 13.8.1993.

IVY Sloop, 'Anchusa' class. Blyth SB 31.10.1917. Sold 2.1920 Howard, Ipswich; resold 2.6.1921 Clan Line.

IVY Corvette, 'Flower' class. Harland & Wolff, ordered 8.4.1940, cancelled 23.1.1941.

IVY *See also MARIGOLD 1915.*

J

'J' class submarines 1,210 tons (J.7 [ii] 1,260 tons), 270 × 23·5ft, 1—4in, 6—TT.

J.1 Portsmouth DY 11.1915. RAN 1919. Sold 26.2.1924 Melbourne Salvage Syndicate; hull scuttled 26.5.1926 off Barwon Heads.

J.2 Portsmouth DY 11.1915. RAN 1919 Sold 26.2.1924 Melbourne Salvage Syndicate; hull scuttled 1.6.1926 off Barwon Heads.

J.3 Pembroke Dock, cancelled 20.4.1915.

J.3 (ex-J.7, renamed 4.1915) Pembroke Dock 4.12.1915. RAN 1919. Sold 1.1926 Hill, Melbourne; hull sunk breakwater Swan I., Victoria.

J.4 Pembroke Dock, cancelled 20.4.1915.

J.4 (ex-J.8, renamed 4.1915) Pembroke Dock 2.2.1916. RAN 1919. Sold 26.2.1924 Melbourne Salvage Syndicate; sank at moorings 10.7.1924 Williamstown; raised, scuttled 1972 off Port Phillip.

J.5 Devonport DY 9.9.1915. RAN 1919. Sold 26.2.1924 Melbourne Salvage Syndicate; hull scuttled 4.6.1926.

J.6 Devonport DY 9.9.1915. Sunk 15.10.1918 in error by decoy ship CYMRIC off Blyth.

J.7 (ii) Devonport DY 21.2.1917. RAN 1919. Sold 11.1929 Morris & Watt, Melbourne; hull sunk 1930 breakwater Hampton, Victoria.

J.4922 *See JUTLAND 1945.*

JACK Sloop 14. Purch. 1780. Captured 21.6.1781 by French off Cape Breton.

JACK TAR Sloop 14, 193bm, 14—4pdr. Captured 1794. Sold 20.11.1794.

JACKAL Cutter 10. Purch. 4.1778. Sold 17.5.1785.

JACKAL Cutter 14, 187bm, 73 × 25·5ft. Purch. 1779. HO French at Calais 27.11.1779 by mutineers; became privateer = BOULOGNE; recaptured 1781. Captured 11.4.1782 by American frigate DEANE.

JACKAL Brig 10, 101bm. Purch. In service 1792.

JACKAL Gun-brig 2, 186bm, 80 × 23ft, 2—18pdr, 10—18pdr carr. Perry, Blackwall, 1.4.1801. Captured 30.5.1807 by French after stranding nr Calais.

JACKAL Iron paddle gunvessel, 340bm, 505 tons, 142·5 × 23ft. Napier 28.10.1844. Sold 11.1887.

JACKAL Destroyer, 745 tons, 246 × 25·5ft, 2—4in, 2—12pdr, 2—TT. Hawthorn Leslie 9.9.1911. Sold 28.9.1920. J. Smith.

JACKAL Destroyer, 1,690 tons, 356·5 (oa) × 35·8ft, 6—4·7in, 10—TT. John Brown 25.10.1938. Damaged 11.5.1942 air attack eastern Mediterranean; sunk 12.5.1942 by JERVIS.

JACKAL *See also WOODCOCK 1885.*

JACKDAW Schooner 10, 80bm, 56 × 18ft. Rowe, Newcastle, 19.5.1806. Captured 1807 'by Spanish Rowboat'; recaptured 15.2.1807. Sold 1.11.1816.

JACKDAW Cutter 4, 108bm, 61 × 20·5ft. Chatham DY 4.8.1830. Schooner 3.1833. Wrecked 11.3.1835 West Indies.

JACKDAW Wood screw gunboat, 'Dapper' class. Thompson, Rotherhithe, 18.5.1855. Cooking depot 1886. Sold 11.1888 C. Wort.

JACKDAW River gunboat, 85 tons, 100 × 20ft, 2—6pdr. Yarrow, Poplar, 1898. Tx 12.1898 West African colonial authorities. Sold c. 1912.

JACKTON Coastal minesweeper, 'Ton' class. Phillip, Dartmouth, 28.2.1955. Tx RAN = TEAL 8.1962. Museum ship Hobart 1977.

JAGUAR Destroyer, 1,690 tons, 356·5 (oa) × 35·8ft, 6—4·7in, 10—TT. Denny 22.11.1938. Sunk 26.3.1942 by U.652 north of Sollum.

JAGUAR Frigate, 2,300 tons, 330 × 40ft, 4—4·5in, 2—40mm. Denny 30.7.1957. Sold Bangladeshi Navy 6.7.1978 = ALI HAIDER.

JAHANGIR *See DIADEM 1942.*

JALOUSE Brig-sloop 18, 384bm, 103 × 27·5ft. French, captured 13.8.1797 by VESTAL in North Sea. BU 3.1807.

JALOUSE Sloop 18, 425bm, 109 × 29·5ft. Plymouth DY 13.7.1809. Sold 8.3.1819 G. T. Young.

JAMAICA Sloop 14, 113bm, 65 × 21·5ft. Deptford DY 30.9.1710. Wrecked 9.10.1715 Grand Cayman, West Indies.

JAMAICA Sloop 14. 273bm, 92 × 26ft. Deptford DY 17.7.1744. Foundered 17.1.1770 off Jamaica.

JAMAICA Sloop 16 purch. 1779. Sold 1783.

JAMAICA (ex-PERCENTE) 6th Rate 26, 520bm, 122 × 31ft. French, captured 21.4.1796 by INTREPID in West Indies. Sold 11.8.1814.

171

JAMAICA 4th Rate 52, 1,487bm, 173 × 44ft, 16–42pdr carr., 36–24pdr. Plymouth DY, ordered 1.7.1825, cancelled 5.3.1829.

JAMAICA Cruiser, 8,000 tons, 555·5 (oa) × 62ft, 12–6in, 8–4in. Vickers Armstrong, Barrow, 16.11.1940. Arr. 20.12.1960 Dalmuir for BU.

JAMAICA *See also JUNO 1938.*

JAMES Ballinger. Acq. 3.1417. Given away 6.1422.

JAMES (ex-EXCHANGE) 30-gun ship, 300bm. Royalist, captured 1649 by Parliamentarians at Kinsale. Listed until 1650.

JAMES 48-gun ship, 660/870bm. Deptford 2.1634. = OLD JAMES 1660. Sold 1682.

JAMES Hoy, 72bm. Dutch, captured 1665. Recaptured 1673 by Dutch.

JAMES & ELIZA Gunvessel 4. Purch. 1796. Gone by 1800.

JAMES BAY (ex-CHANTRY) Coastal minesweeper (RCN), 'Bay' class. Yarrow, Esquimalt, 12.3.1953. PO 28.2.1964; sold 1966 for offshore oil exploration.

JAMES GALLEY 4th Rate 30, 486bm, 112 × 28ft, 26–9pdr, 4–3pdr. Deane, Blackwall, 1676. Made 5th Rate 1691. Wrecked 25.11.1694 Longsand Head.

JAMES WATT (ex-AUDACIOUS) Screw 2nd Rate 80, 3,083bm, 230 × 55·5ft, 8–10in, 36–8in, 34–32pdr. Pembroke Dock 23.4.1853 (renamed 18.11.1847 before LD). Sold 1875 Castle.

JAMUNA *See JUMNA.*

JANISSARY Gunvessel 6. In service 1801.

JANUS 5th Rate 44, 884bm, 140 × 38ft. Batson, Limehouse, 14.5.1778. Storeship 1.1788, = DROMEDARY 3.3.1788. Wrecked 10.8.1800 off Trinidad.

JANUS (ex-ARGO) 5th Rate 32, 704bm, 131 × 36ft, 6–24pdr carr., 26–12pdr, 6–6pdr. Dutch, captured 12.5.1796 by PHOENIX in North Sea. Harbour service 1.1798. Sold 21.2.1811.

JANUS Wood paddle sloop, 763bm, 180 × 30·5ft. Chatham DY 6.2.1844. Sold 4.1856 Castle, Charlton.

JANUS Wood screw gunboat, 'Clown' class. Pembroke Dock 8.3.1856. = YC.6 (coal lighter) 12.1869. Sold 1917 in Hong Kong.

JANUS Destroyer, 320 tons, 200 × 20ft, 1–12pdr, 5–6pdr, 2–TT. Palmer 12.3.1895. Sold 1914 in Hong Kong for BU.

JANUS Destroyer, 1,690 tons, 356·5 (oa) × 35·8ft, 6–4·7in, 10–TT. Swan Hunter 10.11.1938. Sunk 23.1.1944 airborne torpedo Anzio.

JASEUR Brig-sloop 12. French, captured 10.7.1807 by BOMBAY off Andaman Is. Gone by 1810.

JASEUR Brig-sloop 18, 'Cruizer' class, 387bm. Bailey, Ipswich, 2.2.1813. Sold 2.1845.

JASEUR Wood screw gunboat, 310bm, 125 × 23ft, 1–68pdr, 2–24pdr howitzers. Green, Blackwall, 7.3.1857. Wrecked 26.2.1859 Baxo Nuevo, West Indies.

JASEUR Wood screw gunvessel, 'Philomel' class, Deptford DY 15.5.1862. Sold 12.1874 Irish Light Commissioner.

JASEUR Torpedo gunboat, 810 tons, 230 × 27ft, 2–4·7in, 3–4pdr, 3–TT. NC&A (Vickers) 24.9.1892. Sold 11.7.1905.

JASEUR Minesweeper, 'Algerine' class. Redfern, Toronto, 19.4.1944. Arr. 26.2.1956 Hughes Bolckow, Blyth, for BU.

JASMINE Corvette, 'Flower' class. Ferguson 14.1.1941. Sold 1948.

JASMINE *See also JESSAMINE 1915.*

JASON Fireship 6, 146bm. Purch. 1673. Sold 5.1674.

JASON 5th Rate 44, 810bm, 131·5 × 37·5ft. French, captured 3.5.1747 Cape Finisterre. Sold 15.3.1763.

JASON 5th Rate 32, 689bm, 130 × 37ft. Batson, Limehouse, 13.6.1763. Sold 10.2.1785.

JASON 3rd Rate 64, 1,452bm, 166 × 45ft. French, captured 19.4.1782 Mona Passage, West Indies. = ARGONAUT 20.1.1783. BU 2.1831 Chatham.

JASON 5th Rate 38, 384bm, 146 × 39ft, Dudman, Deptford, 3.4.1794. Wrecked 13.10.1798 nr Brest.

JASON 5th Rate 36, 1,053bm, 150 × 40ft, Parsons, Bursledon, 27.1.1800. Wrecked 21.7.1801 Bay of St-Malo.

JASON 5th Rate 32 (fir-built), 661bm, 127 × 34ft. Woolwich DY 21.11.1804. BU 7.1815 Plymouth.

JASON Gun-brig 12. French privateer captured 31.12.1813. Renamed?

JASON 5th Rate 46, 1,162bm. Woolwich DY, ordered 18.7.1817, cancelled 7.2.1831.

JASON Wood screw corvette, 1,711bm, 2,431 tons, 225 × 41ft, 16–8in, 1–7in, 4–40pdr. Devonport DY 10.11.1859. BU 7.1877 Devonport.

JASON Torpedo gunboat, 810 tons, 230 × 27ft, 2–4·7in, 4–3pdr, 3–TT. NC&A (Vickers) 14.5.1892. Minesweeper 1909. Sunk 7.4.1917 mine off west coast of Scotland.

JASON Survey ship, 835 tons, 230 × 33·5ft (1939: 2–4in). Ailsa 6.10.1937. Anti-submarine vessel 1939; minesweeper 1942. Sold 3.9.1946 Wheelock Marden = JASLOCK. BU 2.1950.

JASPER Brig-sloop 10, 'Cherokee' class, 237bm. Bailey, Ipswich, 27.5.1808. Wrecked 21.1.1817 off Plymouth.

JASPER Brig-sloop 10, 'Cherokee' class, 237bm. Portsmouth DY 26.7.1820. Wrecked 11.10.1828 off Santa Maura; wreck sold 1.1831.

JASPER (ex-*Aladdin*) Wood paddle packet,

233bm, 112·5 × 21·5ft. GPO vessel, tx 4.1837. Burnt 15.5.1854 after explosion off Beachy Head.

JASPER Wood screw gunboat, 'Dapper' class. White 2.4.1855. Grounded 24.7.1855 in action Taganrog, Sea of Azov.

JASPER Wood screw gunboat, 301bm, 125 × 23ft, 1—68pdr, 2—24pdr howitzers. Green, Blackwall, 16.3.1857. Sold 2.8.1862 Emperor of China = AMOY.

JASPER *See also GARNET 1943.*

JASTRZAB *See P.551 1941.*

JAVA (ex-MARIA RELIGERSBERGEN) 5th Rate 32, 850bm. Dutch, captured 18.10.1806 by CAROLINE in Indian Ocean. Foundered 2.1807 off Rodriguez I., Indian Ocean.

JAVA (ex-RENOMMEE) 5th Rate 38, 1,083bm. French, captured 20.5.1811 by squadron off Madagascar. Captured 29.12.1812 by American CONSTITUTION off San Salvador, burnt next day.

JAVA 4th Rate 52, 1,460bm, 172 × 44ft. Plymouth DY 16.11.1815. BU comp. 22.11.1862 Portsmouth.

JAVELIN (ex-KASHMIR) Destroyer 1,690 tons, 356·5 (oa) × 35·8ft, 6—4·7in, 10—TT. John Brown 21.12.1938 (renamed 1937). Sold 11.6.1949; BU Troon.

JED Destroyer, 550 tons, 222 × 23·5ft, 1—12pdr, 5—6pdr (1907: 4—12pdr), 2—TT. Thornycroft, Chiswick, 16.2.1904. Sold 29.7.1920 J. & W. Purves, Teignmouth; hull became embankment Dartmouth.

JED Frigate, 'River' class. Hill, Bristol, 30.7.1942. Arr. 25.7.1957 Ward, Milford Haven, for BU.

JELLICOE *See ANSON 1940.*

JEMMY Yacht 4, 26bm, 41 × 12·5ft. Pett, Lambeth, 1662. BU 1722.

JENNET 41-gun ship, 180bm. Portsmouth 1539. Rebuilt 1558 as 200bm. Listed until 1578. *First ship built at Portsmouth.*

JENNET PYRWIN (ex-ANDREW BARTON) Ship. Scottish, captured 1511. Last mentioned 1514.

JERAMIAH Hoy 4, 53bm. Captured 1666. Sold 1667.

JERFALCON Ship, 120bm. Listed 1550–57.

JERSEY 4th Rate 48, 558bm. Starline, Woodbridge, 1654. Captured 18.12.1691 by French in West Indies.

JERSEY 6th Rate 24, 262bm, 94·5 × 25·5ft. Deptford 17.1.1694. = MARGATE 21.10.1698. Wrecked 9.12.1707 nr Cartagena.

JERSEY 4th Rate 48, 677bm, 132 × 34ft. Moore & Nye, East Cowes, 24.11.1698. Hulked 8.1731. Sunk 27.5.1763.

JERSEY 4th Rate 60, 1,065bm, 144 × 41·5ft. Ply-

mouth DY 1736. Hospital ship 3.1771. Abandoned 11.1783 on evacuation of New York.

JERSEY 'Gondola' 7 (Canadian lakes) 52bm. New York 1776. Lost off Valcour I. 11.10.1776; salved 12.10.76 by British, listed until 1779.

JERSEY Cutter 4, 71bm. White, Cowes, 22.3.1860. Sold 8.1873 E. A. S. Mignon.

JERSEY Destroyer, 1,690 tons, 356·5 (oa) × 35·8ft, 6—4·7in, 10—TT. White 26.9.1938. Sunk 2.5.1941 mine entrance to Malta harbour.

JERSEY Patrol vessel, 925 tons, 195·3 (oa) × 34·2ft, Hall Russell 18.3.1976. Sold Bangladeshi Navy, tx Rosyth 28.1.1994 = SHAHEED RAHUL AMIN.

JERVIS Destroyer leader, 1,695 tons, 356·5 (oa) × 35·8ft, 6—4·7in, 10—TT. Hawthorn Leslie 9.9.1939. Sold 3.1.1949; BU Arnott Young, Port Bannatyne.

JERVIS BAY Troop carrier (RAN), 1,250 tons, 284·1ft (oa). Hobart. Cd 10.6.1999 (leased for 2 years from International Catamaran Australia). PO 11.5.2001, deleted.

JESSAMINE Sloop, 'Azalea' class. Swan Hunter 9.9.1915. Sold 21.12.1922 T. E. Evans.

JESUS Ballinger. Acq. 1416. Rebuilt Bursledon 1436 = LITTLE JESUS.

JESUS 1,000-ton ship. Winchelsea 1416. Given away 1446.

JESUS & MARY Galley. Purch. 1409. Sold 1417.

JESUS OF LUBECK Galleon 70, 700bm. Purch. 1544. Captured 1568 by Spanish while trading.

JEWEL (ex-TOPAZE) 5th Rate 38, 1,135bm, 157 × 40·5ft. French, captured 22.1.1809 by squadron in West Indies. = ALCMENE 25.5.1809. BU 2.1816.

JEWEL Minesweeper, 'Algerine' class. Harland & Wolff 20.7.1944. Arr. 7.4.1967 Ward, Inverkeithing, for BU.

JHELUM River gunboat (Indian), 499bm. Bombay DY 1851. *Fate unknown.*

JHELUM *See also NARBADA 1942.*

JOHN Cog, 220bm presented 1413. Wrecked 7.10.1414 coast of France.

JOHN Vessel. Captured 1549. *Fate unknown.*

JOHN 28-gun ship, 275/367bm. Purch. 1646. Wrecked 1652.

JOHN Galliot 4, 81bm. Captured 1666. Sold 1667.

JOHN & ALEXANDER Fireship 8, 178bm. Purch. 1678. Sold 1686.

JOHN & MARTHA Firevessel, 18bm. Purch. 1694. Sold 1698.

JOHN & PETER Dogger 6. Purch. 1666. Given away 1668.

JOHN & SARAH Fireship 4, 132bm. Purch. 1666. Sunk 6.1667 blockship R. Medway.

JOHN BALLINGER Listed 1417. Sold 1420.

JOHN BAPTIST 22-gun ship, 400bm. Purch. 1512. Wrecked c. 1534.

JOHN BAPTIST 22-gun ship. Captured 1652. Fireship 1653. Sold 1656.

JOHN EVANGELIST Ship. Purch. 7.1463. Listed until 1484

JOHN OF DUBLIN Fireship. Captured 1689 from French. Lost 13.1.1690.

JOHN OF GREENWICH 50-ton vessel. Captured 1523. Listed until 1530.

JOHNSON (ex-L'OUTAQUISE) 10-gun vessel (Canadian lakes). French, captured 1760. Lost 11.1764 Lakes.

JOLIETTE Frigate (RCN), 'River' class. Morton 12.11.1943. Sold 3.1.1946 Chilean Navy = IQUIQUE. Sold 29.11.1968 for BU.

JOLLY (ex-JOLIE) 6th Rate 10, 113bm, 67 × 19.5ft. French, captured 6.1693 Lagos. Sold 1698.

JOLLY Sloop 6, 168bm. Purch. 13.6.1709. Sold 29.7.1714.

JONQUIERE Frigate (RCN), 'River' class. G. T. Davie 28.10.1943. Sold 8.1967.

JONQUIL Sloop, 'Acacia' class. Connell 12.5.1915. Sold 5.1920 Portuguese Navy = CARVALHO ARAUJO; survey ship 1937; BU 1959.

JONQUIL Corvette, 'Flower' class. Fleming & Ferguson 9.7.1940. Sold 5.1946 = *Lemnos*.

JOSEPH STRAKER *See DIAMOND 1848.*

JOSEPH Fireship 4, 101bm. Purch. 1666. Burnt 1667 accident.

JOSEPH Fireship 8, 278bm, 99 × 26.5ft. Captured 1692. Sold 1698.

JOSIAH Storeship 30, 664bm, 131 × 34ft. Purch. 8.1694. Hulk 9.1696. Sunk 26.8.1715 breakwater Sheerness.

JOYFUL 6th Rate 10, 106bm, 68 × 18ft. Captured 1694. *Fate unknown.*

JUBILANT Destroyer, 1,690 tons. 356.5 (oa) × 35.8ft, 6—4.7in 10—TT, cancelled 1937, not ordered.

JULIA Brig sloop 16, 284bm, 93 × 26.5ft, 14—24pdr carr., 2—6pdr. Bailey, Ipswich, 4.2.1806. Wrecked 2.10.1817 Tristan da Cunha.

JULIA Schooner (Canadian lakes) 77bm, 64 × 17ft. Kingston, Ontario, 1814. *Fate unknown.*

JULIA Wood screw gunboat, 'Albacore' class. Fletcher, Limehouse, 27.11.1855. BU 2.1866 Marshall, Plymouth.

JULIA Coastguard vessel, 15bm. Purch. c. 1868. Sold 10.4.1891.

JULIA (ex-*Maretanza*) Coastguard vessel, 310 tons, 120 × 20.5ft, 2—7pdr. Yacht, purch. 1.4.1901. Sold 6.11.1920 M. S. Hilton.

JULIAN 6th Rate 14, 104bm, 67 × 19ft. French, captured 1690. Bomb vessel 1694. Sold 3.5.1698.

JULIUS 3rd Rate 74, 1,750bm. Chatham DY, ordered 1807, cancelled 1812.

JUMNA Iron paddle vessel (Indian). Thames 1832. *Fate unknown. First iron steam vessel built on R. Thames.*

JUMNA (ex-ZEBRA) Brig-sloop 16, 549bm, 110 × 35ft, 16—32pdr. Bombay DY 7.3.1848 (renamed 1846). Sold 25.6.1862.

JUMNA Iron screw troopship, 4,173bm, 6,211 tons, 360 × 49ft, 3—4pdr. Palmer 24.9.1866. = C.110 (coal hulk) 1893. Sold 7.1922 A. J. Hellyer as hulk *Oceanic.*

JUMNA Sloop (RIN), 1,300 tons, 299.5 (oa) × 37.5ft, 6—4in. Denny 16.11.1940. Survey vessel 1957. Later = JAMUNA. PO 31.12.1980; BU India.

JUNEE Minesweeper (RAN), 'Bathurst' class. Poole & Steel, Sydney, 16.11.1943. Sold 7.1958.

JUNIPER Schooner 10, 150bm, 79 × 22ft. Bermuda 1808. Sold 3.11.1814.

JUNO 5th Rate 32, 667bm, 128 × 34.5ft. Alexander, Rotherhithe, 29.9.1757. Burnt 7.8.1778 to avoid capture Rhode I.

JUNO 5th Rate 32, 689bm, 126.5 × 35ft. Batson, Limehouse, 30.9.1780. BU 7.1811.

JUNO 6th Rate 26, 923bm, 131 × 41ft, 2—8in, 24—32pdr. Pembroke Dock 1.7.1844. = MARINER (police ship) 10.1.1878; = ATALANTA (TS) 22.1.1878. Foundered 12.2.1880 Atlantic.

JUNO Wood screw corvette, 1,462bm, 2,216 tons, 200 × 40.5ft, 8—64pdr. Deptford DY 28.11.1867. Sold 12.1887.

JUNO 2nd class cruiser, 5,600 tons, 350 × 54ft, 5—6in, 6—4.7in (1904: 11—6in). NC&A (Vickers) 16.11.1895. Sold 24.9.1920 Earle; resold Petersen & Albeck.

JUNO (ex-JAMAICA) Destroyer, 1,690 tons, 356.5 (oa) × 35.8ft, 6—4.7in. 10—TT. Fairfield 8.12.1938 (renamed 9.1938). Sunk 21.5.1941 German and Italian aircraft off Crete.

JUNO Frigate, 'Leander' class, Y136, 2,650 tons, 372 (oa) × 43ft, 2—4.5in, Seacat, helo (later Exocet, Seawolf). Thornycroft 24.11.1965. Arr. Vigo, Spain, 17.2.1995 for BU.

JUNON 5th Rate 36, 1,100bm. French, captured 10.2.1809 by squadron in West Indies. Retaken 13.12.1809 by French.

JUNON (ex-BELLONE) 5th Rate 38. French, captured 6.12.1810 Mauritius. BU 2.1817 Deptford.

JUPITER 4th Rate 50, 1,044bm, 146 × 41ft. Randall, Rotherhithe, 13.5.1778. Wrecked 10.12.1808 Vigo Bay.

JUPITER 4th Rate 50, 1,173bm, 150 × 42ft. Plymouth DY 22.11.1813. Troopship 11.1837; coal hulk 4.1846. BU comp. 28.1.1870 Devonport.

JUPITER Battleship, 14,900 tons, 390 × 75ft, 4—12in 12—6in, 18—12pdr. Thomson 18.11.1895. Sold 15.1.1920 Hughes Bolckow; BU Dewenthaugh.

JUPITER Destroyer, 1,690 tons, 356·5 (oa) × 35·8ft, 6—4·7in, 10—TT. Yarrow 27.10.1938. Torpedoed 27.2.1942 Japanese destroyer Java Sea.

JUPITER Frigate, 'Leander' class, Y160, 2,650 tons, 372 (oa) × 43ft, 2—4·5in, Seacat, helo (later Exocet, Seawolf). Yarrow 4.9.1967. Sold Samsung (HK) 9.1997 for BU; arr. Alang 5.1998.

JUPITER *See also FORTH 1833.*

JUSTE 2nd Rate 80, 2,144bm, 193·5 × 50ft. French, captured Ushant 1.6.1794. BU 2.1811.

JUSTITIA Prison ship, 260bm. Merchantman, purch. 1777. In service 1795.

JUSTITIA 3rd Rate 74, 1,758bm. Danish, captured 7.9.1807 Battle of Copenhagen. BU 3.1817. *Was to have been renamed ORFORD.*

JUSTITIA *See also ZEALAND 1796, HINDOSTAN 1804.*

JUTLAND Destroyer, 2,380 tons, 379 (oa) × 40·5ft, 5—4·5in. 8—40mm, 10—TT. Hawthorn Leslie 2.11.1945, not comp. = J.4922 (contract number) 12.1945; hull used for trials 1947. Arr. 11.9.1957 Rosyth for BU.

JUTLAND (ex-MALPLAQUET) Destroyer, 2,380 tons, 379 (oa) × 40·5ft, 5—4·5in, 8—40mm, 10—TT. Stephen 20.2.1946 (renamed 12.1945). Arr. 14.5.1965 Hughes Bolckow, Blyth, for BU.

K

'K' class submarines 1,880 tons, 334 × 26·5ft, 2—4in, 1—3in, 10—TT.

K.1 Portsmouth DY 14.11.1916. Sunk 17.11.1917 by BLONDE after collision K.4 off coast of Denmark.

K.2 Portsmouth DY 14.10.1916. Sold 13.7.1926 Cashmore, Newport.

K.3 Vickers 20.5.1916. Sold 26.10.1921 Barking S. Bkg Co.

K.4 Vickers 15.7.1916. Sunk 31.1.1918 collision K.6 off May I.

K.5 Portsmouth DY 16.12.1916. Sunk 20.1.1921 Bay of Biscay.

K.6 Devonport DY 31.5.1916. Sold 13.7.1926 Cashmore, Newport.

K.7 Devonport DY 31.5.1916. Sold 9.9.1921 Fryer, Sunderland.

K.8 Vickers 10.10.1916. Sold 11.10.1923 McLellan, Bo'ness.

K.9 Vickers 8.11.1916. Sold 23.7.1926 Alloa, Charlestown.

K.10 Vickers 27.12.1916. Sold 4.11.1921 C. A. Beard; foundered under tow 10.1.1922.

K.11 Armstrong 16.8.1916. Sold 4.11.1921 C. A. Beard.

K.12 Armstrong 23.2.1917. Sold 23.7.1926 Alloa, Charlestown.

K.13 Fairfield 11.11.1916. Foundered on trials 29.1.1917; salved 3.1917 = K.22. Sold 16.12.1926 Young, Sunderland.

K.14 Fairfield 8.2.1917. Sold 1926 Granton S. Bkg Co.

K.15 Scotts 30.10.1917. Sold 8.1924 Upnor S. Bkg Co.

K.16 Beardmore 5.11.1917. Sold 22.8.1924 J. Hornby; resold 9.1924 Alloa S. Bkg Co., Charlestown.

K.17 Vickers 10.4.1917. Sunk 31.1.1918 collision FEARLESS off May I.

K.18 Vickers. Launched 9.7.1917 as M.1 (q.v.).

K.19 Vickers. Launched 19.10.1918 as M.2 (q.v.).

K.20 Armstrong. Launched 19.10.1920 as M.3 (q.v.).

K.21 Armstrong. hull sold incomp. 30.11.1921 Armstrong.

K.22 See K.13.

Modified 'K' class submarines 2,140 tons, 351·5 × 28ft, 3—4in, 10—TT (all ordered 10.6.1918).

K.23 Armstrong, cancelled 26.11.1918.

K.24 Armstrong, cancelled 26.11.1918.

K.25 Armstrong, cancelled 26.11.1918.

K.26 Vickers 26.8.1919, comp. Chatham 15.9.1923. Sold 3.1931 Mamo Bros, Malta.

K.27 Vickers, cancelled 26.11.1918.

K.28 Vickers, cancelled 26.11.1918.

KAHREN *See Indian TB.2 1888.*

KAHU (ex-MANAWANUI) TS (RNZN), 91·5 tons, 88 (oa) × 20ft. Whangerai, cd 28.5.1979.

KALE Destroyer, 545 tons, 22 × 23·5ft, 1—12pdr, 5—6pdr (1907: 4—12pdr), 2—TT. Hawthorn 8.11.1904. Sunk 27.3.1918 mine North Sea.

KALE Frigate, 'River' class. Inglis 24.6.1942. Sold 11.1956; BU Cashmore, Newport.

KALGOORLIE Minesweeper, 'Bathurst' class. Broken Hill 7.8.1941. Lent RAN 4.1942. Sold 8.1946 Dutch Navy = TERNATE; deleted 1.1956.

KAMLOOPS Corvette (RCN), 'Flower' class. Victoria Machinery 7.8.1940. Sold 1946 J. Earl McQueen, Amherstburg.

KAMSACK Corvette (RCN), 'Flower' class. Port Arthur SY 5.5.1941. Sold 1946.

KANDAHAR Destroyer, 1,690 tons, 356·5 (oa) × 35·7ft, 6—4.7in, 10—TT. Denny 21.3.1939. Mined 19.12.1941 off Tripoli, sunk next day by JAGUAR.

KANGAROO Brig-sloop 16 (fir-built), 314bm, 95 × 28ft. Wells, Rotherhithe, 30.9.1795. Sold 2.1802.

KANGAROO Sloop 18, 370bm, 106 × 28ft. Brind-ley, Lynn, 12.9.1805. Sold 14.12.1815.

KANGAROO Survey brig purch. 1818. Wrecked 18.12.1828 West Indies.

KANGAROO (ex-*Las Damas Argentinas*) Schooner tender 3, 84bm, 2—12pdr, 1—2in howitzer. Purch. 1829 Jamaica. Sold 1.1834.

KANGAROO (ex-DOVE) Brig 12, 483bm, 105 × 33·5ft, 4—32pdr, 8—32pdr carr. Chatham DY 31.8.1852 (renamed 1850). = WV.20 (Coastguard) 25.5.1863. Sold 10.5.1897 M. Hayhurst.

KANGAROO Destroyer, 380 tons, 215 × 21ft, 1—12pdr, 5—6pdr, 2—TT. Palmer 8.9.1900. Told

23.3.1920 M. Yates; resold Ward; BU Milford Haven 6.1920.

KANGAROO BDV (RAN). 1940–67.

KANGAROO *See also DART 1860.*

KANIERE *See LOCH ACHRAY 1948.*

KANIMBLA (ex-SAGINAW/LST.1188) Landing ship (RAN), 4,975 tons, 552·3 (oa) × 69·5ft, Phalanx, helo. National Steel Shipbuilding, San Diego, 23.1.1971. USN, acq. 25.8.1994.

KAPUNDA Minesweeper (RAN), 'Bathurst' class. Poole & Steel, Sydney, 23.6.1942. Sold 6.1.1961 for BU Japan.

KAPUSKASING Minesweeper (RCN), 'Algerine' class. Port Arthur SY 22.7.1943. Survey vessel 1959. Sunk 3.10.1978 target.

KARRAKATTA (ex-WIZARD) Torpedo gunboat, 735 tons, 230 × 27ft, 2–4·7in, 4–3pdr, 3–TT. Armstrong 27.8.1889 (renamed 2.4.1890). Sold 11.1.1905 Portsmouth.

KASHMIR Destroyer, 1,690 tons, 356·5 × 35·7ft, 6–4·7in, 10–TT. Thornycroft 4.4.1939. Sunk 23.5.1941 air attack off Crete.

KASHMIR *See also JAVELIN 1938.*

KATHERINE Ship, 200bm. Purch. 1402. BU 1406.

KATHERINE Ship, 210bm. Purch. 2.1415. Sold 1425.

KATHERINE (ex-CATHERINE) 36-gun ship. French, captured 1653. Sold 1658.

KATHERINE Yacht 8, 94bm. Deptford 1661. Captured 1673 by Dutch.

KATHERINE 2nd Rate 82, 1,003bm, 153 × 40ft. Woolwich DY 26.10.1664. Rebuilt 1702; = RAMILLIES 18.12.1706. Rebuilt Portsmouth 1749 as 1,689bm. Wrecked 15.2.1760 Bolt Head. *Also known as ROYAL KATHERINE from 1696.*

KATHERINE Fireship 6, 180bm. Purch. 1672. Expended 1673.

KATHERINE Fireship 6, 264bm. Purch. 1672. Expended 1672.

KATHERINE Yacht 8, 131bm, 8–3pdr. Chatham DY 1674. Rebuilt Deptford 1720 as 166bm, = CATHERINE. Sold 14.9.1801.

KATHERINE Storeship 6, 292bm, 97 × 25ft. Purch. 5.10.1692. Sold 22.5.1701.

KATHERINE *See also CATHERINE.*

KATHERINE BARK Vessel. In service 1222.

KATHERINE BARK Ship, 100bm. Built 1518. Listed until 1525.

KATHERINE BRETON Ballinger. Captured from French 9.1417. Sold 3.1423.

KATHERINE FORTILEZA 700-ton ship. Purch. 1512 from Genoese. Damaged 1521 storm; not listed thereafter.

KATHERINE GALLEY Galley, 80bm. Listed 1512–27.

KATHIAWAR (ex-HARTLEPOOL) Minesweeper (RIN), turbine 'Bangor' class. Blyth 14.7.1942 (renamed 1942). Tx RPN 1948 = CHITTAGONG. Sold 1956.

KATOOMBA (ex-PANDORA) 2nd class cruiser, 2,575 tons, 265 × 41ft, 8–4·7in, 8–3pdr. Armstrong 27.8.1889 (renamed 4.1890). Sold 10.7.1906; BU Morecambe.

KATOOMBA Minesweeper (RAN), 'Bathurst' class. Poole & Steel 16.4.1941. Sold 2.5.1957 for BU Hong Kong.

KEATS (ex-TISDALE) Frigate, DE 'Captain' class. Boston NY 17.7.1943 on Lend-Lease. Ret. USN 2.1946.

KEDLESTON Coastal minesweeper, 'Ton' class. Pickersgill 21.12.1953. = NORTHUMBRIA 1.1955; = KEDLESTON 1955. Towed Bruges 20.4.1992 for BU.

KEITH Destroyer leader, 1,400 tons, 323 (oa) × 32.25ft, 4–4·7in, 8–TT. Vickers Armstrong, Barrow, 10.7.1930. Sunk 1.6.1940 air attack Dunkirk.

KELLETT (ex-UPPINGHAM) Survey ship, 1–3pdr. Simons 31.5.1919 (renamed 1919). Minesweeper 1939, 2–2pdr. Sold 20.3.1945; BU Young, Sunderland.

KELLINGTON Coastal minesweeper, 'Ton' class. Pickersgill 12.10.1954. HO Sea Cadets, Stockton-on-Tees 23.8.1993, purch. 9.2.1999.

KELLY Destroyer leader, 1,695 tons, 356·5 (oa) × 35·7ft, 6–4·7in. 10–TT. Hawthorn Leslie 25.10.1938. Sunk 23.5.1941 air attack off Crete.

KELOWNA Minesweeper (RCN), TE 'Bangor' class. Prince Rupert DD 28.5.1941. Sold 1946 mercantile.

KELVIN Destroyer, 1,690 tons, 356·5 (oa) × 35·7ft, 6–4·7in, 10–TT. Fairfield 19.1.1939. Sold 6.4.1949, BU Troon.

KEMERTON Coastal minesweeper, 'Ton' class' Harland & Wolff 27.11.1953. = KILMORY 1955, = KEMERTON 1961. Sold 25.10.1971; BU 1975 Poole.

KEMPENFELT Destroyer leader, 1,607 tons, 325 × 32ft, 4–4in, 4–TT. Cammell Laird 1.5.1915. Sold 9.5.1921 Ward, Morecambe.

KEMPENFELT Destroyer leader, 1,390 tons, 329 (oa) × 33ft, 4–4·7in, 9–TT. White 29.10.1931. Tx RCN 8.1939 = ASSINIBOINE 18.10.1939. Wrecked 10.11.1945 Prince Edward I; wreck sold 17.7.1952.

KEMPENFELT (ex-VALENTINE) Destroyer leader, 1,730 tons, 362·8 (oa) × 35·7ft, 4–4·7in,

4—40mm, 8—TT. John Brown 8.5.1943. Tx Yugoslav Navy 10.1956 = KOTOR. Withdrawn 1971.

KEMPENFELT *See also VALENTINE 1943.*

KEMPTHORNE (ex-TRUMPETER) Frigate, DE 'Captain' class. Boston NY 17.7.1943 on Lend-Lease. Ret. USN 8.1945.

KEMPTON Paddle minesweeper, 'Ascot' class. Ferguson 3.6.1916. Sunk 24.6.1917 mine off Dover.

KENDAL Minesweeper, Later 'Hunt' class. Fairfield 9.2.1918. Sold 3.10.1928 Alloa, Charlestown.

KENILWORTH CASTLE Corvette. 'Castle' class. Smith's Dock 17.8.1943. Arr. 20.6.1959 Rees, Llanelly, for BU.

KENNET Destroyer, 550 tons, 222 × 23·5ft, 1—12pdr, 5—6pdr, (1907: 4—12pdr), 2—TT. Thornycroft, Chiswick, 4.12.1903. Sold 11.12.1919 J. H. Lee.

KENNINGTON (ex-MERMAID) 6th Rate 24, 429bm, 106 × 30·5ft. Deptford DY 30.6.1736 (renamed 1735). BU 9.1749 Plymouth.

KENNINGTON 6th Rate 20, 437bm, 107·5 × 30·5ft. Adams, Buckler's Hard 1.5.1756. BU comp. 31.1.1774 Sheerness.

KENOGAMI Corvette (RCN), 'Flower' class. Port Arthur SY 5.9.1940. Sold 1946; BU 1950 Steel Co. of Canada, Hamilton

KENORA Minesweeper (RCN), TE 'Bangor' class. Port Arthur 20.12.1941. LU 1946; sold 29.11.1957 Turkish Navy = BANDIRMA; deleted 1980.

KENT 3rd Rate 70, 1,040bm, 151 × 40ft, 26—32pdr, 26—12pdr, 14—4pdr, 4—3pdr. Johnson, Blackwall, 1679. Rebuilt Rotherhithe 1699 as 1,064bm; rebuilt 1724 as 1,130bm. BU 1744.

KENT 3rd Rate 70, 1,309bm, 155 × 44·5ft. Deptford 1746. Hulked 1760 East Indies.

KENT 3rd Rate 74, 1,617bm, 168 × 47ft. Deptford DY 23.3.1762. Sold. 5.8.1784.

KENT 3rd Rate 74, 1,694m, 183 × 50ft. Perry, Blackwall, 17.1.1798. Sheer hulk 1856. BU 1881.

KENT Gunvessel 16 purch. 1798. Sold 1801.

KENT Screw 2nd Rate 91, 3,716bm, 252 × 57·5ft. Portsmouth DY, LD 13.3.1860, cancelled 12.12.1863.

KENT Armoured cruiser, 9,800 tons, 440 × 66ft, 14—6in, 10—12pdr. Portsmouth DY 6.3.1901. Sold 6.1920 in Hong Kong.

KENT Cruiser, 9,850 tons, 630 (oa) × 68·5ft, 8—8in, 4—4in. Chatham DY 16.3.1926. Sold 22.1.1948. BU Troon.

KENT GM destroyer 5,440 tons, 520·5 (oa) × 54ft, 4—4·5in, Sea Slug, helo. Harland & Wolff 27.9.1961. Sold 9.1997 for BU India; left under tow 14.11.1997.

KENT Frigate, 'Norfolk' class, Yarrow, Glasgow, 27.5.1998.

KENT *See also KENTISH 1652, IMPREGNABLE 1810.*

KENTISH Armed merchantman. Purch. 1646. Listed until 1647.

KENTISH 46-gun ship, 601bm. Deptford 1652. = KENT 1660. Wrecked 10.1672 nr Cromer.

KENTVILLE Minesweeper (RCN), TE 'Bangor' class. Port Arthur SY 17.4.1942. LU 1964; sold 29.11.1957 Turkish Navy = BARTIN; deleted 1980.

KENYA Cruiser, 8,000 tons, 555·5 (oa) × 62ft, 12—6in, 8—4in. Stephen 18.8.1939. Arr. 29.10.1962 Faslane for BU.

KEPPEL Brig 14, 75bm, 14—4pdr. American, captured 1778. Sold 5.8.1783 New York.

KEPPEL Destroyer leader, 1,750 tons, 329·25 (oa) × 32ft, 5—4·7in, 1—3in, 6—TT. Thornycroft 23.4.1920. Sold 7.1945; BU Ward, Barrow.

KEPPEL Frigate, 1,180 tons, 300 × 33ft 3—40mm, 4—TT. Yarrow 31.8.1954. Arr. Sittingbourne 29.4.1979 for BU.

KERTCH Schooner gunboat 2, 94bm. German, Malta, 14.7.1855. Yard craft 10.1860 = YC.4. In service 1875.

KESTREL Brigantine, 200bm. Yacht, purch. 5.12.1846. BU 11.1852.

KESTREL Wood screw gunboat, 'Clown' class. Miller, Liverpool, 20.5.1856. Sunk in action 6.1859 Peiho; raised, sold 16.3.1866 Glover & Co., Yokohama; resold Japanese Navy.

KESTREL Composite screw gunvessel, 610 tons, 155 × 25ft, 1—7in, 1—64pdr, 2—20pdr. Chatham DY 29.2.1872. Sold 11.1888.

KESTREL Destroyer, 380 tons, 218 × 20ft, 1—12pdr, 5—6pdr, 2—TT. John Brown 25.3.1898. Sold 17.3.1921 Ward, Rainham.

KEW Minesweeper, late 'Hunt' class. Eltringham, cancelled 1918.

KHARTOUM Destroyer, 1,690 tons, 356·5 (oa) × 35·7ft, 6—4.7in, 10—TT. Swan Hunter 6.2.1939. Beached 23.6.1940 Perim harbour after accidental explosion.

KHEDIVE (ex-*Cordova*) Escort carrier, 11,420 tons, 2—4in, 16—40mm, 24 aircraft. Seattle, Tacoma, 30.1.1943. Tx RN 25.8.1943 on Lend-Lease. Ret. USN 26.1.1946.

KHEDIVE Escort carrier, 7,800 tons. Oregon SB Co., LD 20.7.1943 for RN; retained USN, launched 28.11.1943 as NEHENTA BAY.

KHYBER (ex-HARWICH) Minesweeper (RIN), turbine 'Bangor' class. Hamilton 17.2.1942 (renamed 10.1941). BU 1949.

KIAMA Minesweeper (RAN), 'Bathurst' class.

Evans Deakin 3.7.1943. Tx RNZN 5.1952. BU 1976.

KIAWO River gunboat. River steamer, purch. 1926, cd 25.1.1927. Sold 1930.

'Kil' class patrol gunboats 895 tons, 170 × 30ft, 1–4in.

KILBEGGAN G. Brown 23.9.1918. Sold 14.2.1920 Robinson, Brown & Joplin = *Luckner.*

KILBERRY G. Brown 2.7.1918. Sold 14.2.1920 Robinson, Brown & Joplin = *Bolam.*

KILBIRNIE G. Brown 16.5.1919. Sold 14.2.1920 Robinson, Brown & Joplin.

KILBRIDE Hall Russell 5.1918. Sold 14.2.1920 Robinson, Brown & Joplin = *Scotsgap.*

KILBURN Hall Russell 28.5.1918. Sold 14.2.1920 Robinson, Brown & Joplin, = *Tarset.*

KILCAVAN Hall Russell 1918. Sold 14.2.1920 Robinson, Brown & Joplin.

KILCHATTAN Cook, Welton & Gemmell 13.4.1918. Sold 14.2.1920 Robinson, Brown & Joplin = *Benton.*

KILCHREEST Smith's Dock 8.6.1918. Sold 14.2.1920 Robinson, Brown & Joplin = *Harrogate.*

KILCHRENAN Smith's Dock 15.1.1918. Sold 14.2.1920 Robinson, Brown & Joplin = *Bombardier.*

KILCHVAN Cook, Welton & Gemmell 13.7.1918. Sold 14.2.1920 Robinson, Brown & Joplin = *Belsay.*

KILCLARE Smith's Dock 14.1.1918. Sold 14.2.1920 Robinson, Brown & Joplin.

KILCLIEF Cook, Welton & Gemmell 8.10.1918. Sold 14.2.1920 Robinson, Brown & Joplin = *Tynehome.*

KILCLOGHER Cook, Welton & Gemmell 24.10.1918. Sold 14.2.1920 Robinson, Brown & Joplin = *Northerner.*

KILCOCK Smith's Dock 27.4.1918. Sold 14.2.1920 Robinson, Brown & Joplin = *Spinner.*

KILDALKEY Cochrane 13.3.1918. Sold 14.2.1920 Robinson, Brown & Joplin, name unchanged.

KILDANGAN Cochrane 15.3.1918. Sold 14.2.1920 Robinson, Brown & Joplin = *Bebside.*

KILDARE Cochrane 10.4.1918. Sold 14.2.1920 Robinson, Brown & Joplin = *Milford Haven.*

KILDARY Smith's Dock 1.11.1917. Sold 14.2.1920 Robinson, Brown & Joplin = *Sorcerer.*

KILDAVIN Smith's Dock 13.2.1918. Sold 14.2.1920 Robinson, Brown & Joplin = *Leaside.*

KILDIMO Smith's Dock 27.4.1918. Sold 14.2.1920 Robinson, Brown & Joplin = *Southerner.*

KILDONAN Cochrane 11.4.1918. Sold 21.11.1919 Thornycroft = *Watkin.*

KILDOROUGH Smith's Dock 16.11.1917. Sold 14.2.1920 Robinson, Brown & Joplin = *Wearmouth.*

KILDORRY Smith's Dock 14.2.1918. Sold 14.2.1920 Robinson, Brown & Joplin = *Dempster.*

KILDRESS Cochrane 13.4.1918. Sold 21.11.1919 Thornycroft = *Glynarthan.*

KILDWICK Cochrane 27.4.1918. Sold 21.11.1919 Thornycroft = *Pengham.*

KILDWICK Cochrane 27.4.1918. Sold 14.2.1920 Robinson, Brown & Joplin = *Empleton;* hired 1940 as INDIRA.

KILFENORA Smith's Dock 14.12.1917. Sold 14.2.1920 Robinson, Brown & Joplin, name unchanged.

KILFINNY Cochrane 10.5.1918. Sold 14.2.1920 Robinson, Brown & Joplin = *Kenrhos.*

KILFREE Cochrane 11.5.1918. Sold 21.11.1919 Thornycroft = *Porthminster.*

KILFULLERT Smith's Dock 15.3.1918. Sold 14.2.1920 Robinson, Brown & Joplin = *Wearhome.*

KILGARVAN Smith's Dock 27.5.1918. Sold 14.2.1920 Robinson, Brown & Joplin = *Heather King.*

KILGOBNET Smith's Dock 14.12.1917. Sold 14.2.1920 Robinson, Brown & Joplin = *Maxton.*

KILHAM Smith's Dock 10.6.1918. Sold 14.2.1920 Robinson, Brown & Joplin = *Easterner.*

KILKEEL Smith's Dock 27.3.1918. Sold 14.2.1920 Robinson, Brown & Joplin = *Falconer.*

KILLENA Smith's Dock 9.7.1918. Sold 14.2.1920 Robinson, Brown & Joplin = *Edwin Douglas.*

KILLERIG Smith's Dock 9.7.1918. Sold 11.1920 as salvage vessel, name unchanged.

KILLINEY Smith's Dock 29.7.1918. Sold 14.2.1920 Robinson, Brown & Joplin = *Thropton.*

KILLOUR Smith's Dock 9.8.1918. Sold 1920 = *Narworth.*

KILLOWEN Smith's Dock 6.9.1918. Sold 14.2.1920 Robinson, Brown & Joplin = *Curler.*

KILLYBEGS Smith's Dock 7.9.1918. Sold 14.2.1920 Robinson, Brown & Joplin = *Alwinton.*

KILLYGORDON Smith's Dock 10.10.1918. Sold 14.2.1920 Robinson, Brown & Joplin = *Homeford.*

KILMACRENNAN Smith's Dock 5.11.1918. Sold 14.2.1920 Robinson, Brown & Joplin = *Seghill.*

KILMAINE Smith's Dock 5.11.1918. Sold 14.2.1920 Robinson, Brown & Joplin = *Crofter.*

KILMALCOLM Smith's Dock 8.10.1918. Sold 14.2.1920 Robinson, Brown & Joplin. = *Nigretia.*

KILMALLOCK Smith's Dock 4.12.1918. Sold 14.2.1920 L. Gueret = *Mallock.*

KILMANAHAN Smith's Dock 17.12.1918. Sold 14.2.1920 L. Gueret = *Manahan.*

KILMARNOCK Smith's Dock 31.3.1919. Sold 14.2.1920 L. Gueret, name unchanged.

KILMARTIN Smith's Dock 31.3.1919. Sold 14.2.1920 L. Gueret, = *Mandrake*.

KILMEAD Smith's Dock 1.5.1919. Sold 14.2.1920 L. Gueret = *Mead*. Hired 1940 as MEAD.

KILMELFORD Smith's Dock 14.5.1919. Sold 14.2.1920 L. Gueret = *Melford*.

KILMERSDON Smith's Dock 30.5.1919. Sold 14.2.1920 L. Gueret = *Mersdon*.

KILMINGTON Smith's Dock 30.5.1919. Sold 14.2.1920 L. Gueret = *Mington*.

KILMORE Smith's Dock 17.7.1919. Sold 14.2.1920 L. Gueret = *Newtonia*.

KILMUCKRIDGE Smith's Dock 28.7.1919. Sold 14.2.1920 L. Gueret = *Newton Bay*.

KILMUN Smith's Dock 11.10.1919. Comp. as cable vessel (RFA); sold 16.9.1946.

The following 31 vessels were cancelled in 1918:
KILBRACHAN, KILGLASS (G. Brown, 2); KIL-GOWAN, KILKEE, KILKENNY, KILKENZIE, KILKERRIN, KILKHAMPTON, KILLADOON, KILLALOO, KILLANE, KILLARNEY, KILLARY, KILLEGAN. KILLEGAR (Cochrane, 13); KIL-COLGAN, KILCONNAN, KILCONNELL, KIL-COOLE, KILCORNIE, KILCOT, KILCREGGAN. KILCULLEN, KILCURRIG, KILDALE (Cook, Welton & Gemmell, 10); KILBARCHAN, KILBY, KILBANE, KILBRITTAIN, KILCAR (Hall Russell, 5); KILDPART (Smith's Dock, 1).

'Kil' class patrol sloops 795 tons, 176·5 × 33ft, 1—3in, 3—40mm. All built by Pullman Standard Car Co., Chicago, and supplied to RN under Lend-Lease.

KILBIRNIE Launched 2.5.1943. Ret. USN 12.1946. Sold = *Haugesund*.

KILBRIDE Launched 15.5.1943. Ret. USN 12.1946.

KILCHATTAN Launched 27.5.1943. Ret. USN 12.1946. Sold = *Stravanger*.

KILCHRENAN Launched 13.6.1943. Ret. USN 12.1946.

KILDARY Launched 26.6.1943. Ret. USN 12.1946. Sold = *Rio Vouga*.

KILDWICK Launched 10.7.1943. Ret. USN 12.1946.

KILHAM Launched 2.8.1943. Ret. USN 1946. Sold = *Sognefjord*

KILHAMPTON Launched 3.9.1943. Ret. USN 1946. Sold = *Georgios F.*

KILKENZIE Launched 19.8.1943. Ret. USN 12.1946. Sold, name unchanged.

KILMALCOLM Launched 17.9.1943. Ret. USN 12.1946. Sold = *Rio Agueda*.

KILMARNOCK Launched 1.10.1943. Ret. USN 12.1946. Sold = *Arion*.

KILMARTIN Launched 13.10.1943. Ret. USN 12.1946. Sold = *Marigoula*.

KILMELFORD Launched 23.10.1943. Ret. USN 12.1946.

KILMINGTON Launched 2.11.1943. Ret. USN 12.1946. Sold = *Athinai*.

KILMORE Launched 9.11.1943. Ret. USN 12.1946. Sold = *Despina*.

KILDARTON Coastal minesweeper, 'Ton' class. Harland & Wolff 23.5.1955. Sold 28.7.1969 for BU.

KILLIECRANKIE RNVR tender. *See DERRITON 1953.*

KILMOREY RNVR tenders. *See ALFRISTON 1953, KEMERTON 1953.*

KIMBERLEY Destroyer, 1,690 tons, 356·5 (oa) × 35·7ft, 6—4·7in, 10—TT. Thornycroft 1.6.1939. Sold 30.3.1949; BU Troon.

KINCARDINE (ex-TAMWORTH CASTLE) Corvette (RCN), 'Castle' class. Smith's Dock 26.1.1944 (renamed 1943). Sold 5.9.1946 = *Saada*.

KINCARDINE *See also MARINER 1944.*

KING ALFRED Armoured cruiser, 14,100 tons, 500 × 71ft, 2—9·2in, 16—6in, 12—12pdr. Vickers 28.10.1901. Sold 30.1.1920 F. Rijsdijk; BU Holland.

KING DAVID Storeship. Captured 1653. Sold 1654.

KING EDWARD VII Battleship, 16,350 tons, 425 × 78ft, 4—12in, 4—9·2in, 10—6in, 14—12pdr. Devonport DY 23.7.1903. Sunk 6.1.1916 mine off Cape Wrath.

KING GEORGE Coastguard cutter 60bm. Listed 1863. = FLORA 26.5.1883. Wrecked 12.11.1901 nr Kingstown.

KING GEORGE V (ex-ROYAL GEORGE) Battleship, 23,000 tons, 555 × 89ft, 10—13·5in, 16—4in. Portsmouth DY 9.10.1911 (renamed 1910). Sold 12.1926 Alloa S. Bkg Co.; arr. Rosyth 1.1927 for BU.

KING GEORGE V Battleship, 35,000 tons, 745 (oa) × 103ft, 10—14in, 16—5·25in. Vickers Armstrong, Tyne, 21.2.1939. Arr. 20.1.1958 Dalmuir, then 25.5.1959 Troon.

KING GEORGE V *See also MONARCH 1911.*

KING OF PRUSSIA Cutter. Purch. 3.1763. Lost 6.2.1765 off Ramsgate.

KINGCUP Corvette, 'Flower' class. Harland & Wolff 31.10.1940. Sold 31.7.1946 = *Rubis*.

KINGFISH Brig. Listed 3.1807—7.1814.

KINGFISHER Ship, 269bm. In service 1664-67.

KINGFISHER 46-gun ship, 664bm, 136 × 34ft, 22—18pdr, 20—6pdr, 4—4pdr. Pett, Woodbridge, 1675. Rebuilt Woolwich 1699 as 661bm; hulked 1706. BU 1728 Sheerness.

KINGFISHER Ketch 4, 61bm. Purch. 1684. Captured 3.1690 by French.

KINGFISHER Sloop 14, 275bm, 92 × 26·5ft. Darby, Gosport, 12.12.1745. Bomb vessel 8 from 9.1758 to 3.1760. Sold 3.5.1763.

KINGFISHER Sloop 14, 302bm, 97 × 26·5ft. Chatham DY 13.7.1770. Burnt 7.8.1778 to avoid capture Rhode I.

KINGFISHER Brig-sloop 18, 369bm, 95 × 30·5ft, 18–6pdr. Rochester 1782, purch. on stocks. Wrecked 3.12.1798 Lisbon Bar.

KINGFISHER Sloop 18, 370bm, 106 × 28ft, 16–32pdr carr., 2–6pdr. King, Dover, 10.3.1804. BU 10.1816 Portsmouth.

KINGFISHER Brig-sloop 10, 'Cherokee' class, 237bm. Woolwich DY 11.3.1823. Sold 16.8.1838 Mr Knowland.

KINGFISHER Brig 12, 446bm, 103 × 32·5ft, 10–32pdr, 2–18pdr. Pembroke Dock 8.4.1845. LU 1852; harbour service 1875. Sold 26.4.1890 W. Taylor.

KINGFISHER Composite screw sloop, 1,130 tons, 170 × 36ft, 2–7in, 4–64pdr. Sheerness DY 16.12.1879. = LARK (TS) 10.11.92; = CRUIZER 18.5.1893. Sold 1919.

KINGFISHER River gunboat. Yarrow, ordered 1912, cancelled.

KINGFISHER Patrol vessel, 510 tons, 234 × 26·5ft, 1–4in. Fairfield 14.2.1935. Sold 21.4.1947; BU Stockton Ship & Salvage Co.

KINGFISHER Patrol boat, 190 tons, 120 (oa) × 21·7ft. Dunston 20.9.1974. Sold 28.2.1996 private individual.

KINGFISHER *See also MARTIN 1850.*

KINGHAM Inshore minesweeper, 'Ham' class. White 26.1.1955. Tx French Navy 1955 = PAQUERETTE. Arr. 4.8.1989 Amsterdam for BU.

KINGSALE (ex-*Royalist*) Ketch 10, 91bm. Irish, captured 1656 by Parliamentarians. Sold 1663.

KINGSALE 5th Rate 32, 533bm, 117·5 × 32ft. Studleigh & Stacey, Kinsale, 22.5.1700. Rebuilt Portsmouth 1724 as 607bm. BU 1741.

KINGSALE *See also KINSALE.*

KINGSFORD Seaward defence boat, 'Ford' class. Rowhedge Ironworks 24.3.1955. Sold 7.4.1971; BU Cairnryan 1972.

KINGSMILL Gunvessel 1, 150bm. Listed 1797–1801.

KINGSMILL Frigate, DE 'Captain' class. Boston NY 13.8.1943 on Lend-Lease. Ret. USN 7.1945.

KINGSTON 4th Rate 60, 924bm, 145 × 40ft, 24–24pdr, 26–9pdr, 10–6pdr. Frame, Hull, 13.3.1697. Rebuilt Portsmouth 1719; rebuilt Plymouth 1740 as 1,068bm. Sold 14.1.1762.

KINGSTON (ex-*Caries*) Schooner, 109bm. Slaver, captured 4.1858 by FORWARD. Sunk 1861 as bathing place Kingston, Jamaica. BU 3.1867.

KINGSTON Destroyer, 1,690 tons, 356·5 (oa) × 35·7ft, 6–4·7in, 10–TT. White 9.1.1939. Wrecked 11.4.1942 air attack Malta while in dock; hull used as blockship.

KINGSTON MCDV (RCN), 'Kingston' class, 962 tons, 181·4 (oa) × 37·1ft, 1–40mm. Halifax SY 12.8.1995.

KINGSTON *See also PRINCE REGENT 1814, PORTLAND 1822.*

KINGUSSIE Minesweeper, Later 'Hunt' class. Eltringham, cancelled 1918.

KINNAIRDS HEAD *See MULL OF GALLOWAY 1944.*

KINROSS Minesweeper, Later 'Hunt' class, Fairfield 4.7.1918. Sunk 16.6.1919 mine in Aegean.

KINSALE 5th Rate 44, 701bm, 125 × 36ft. Bird, Rotherhithe, 27.11.1741. Ordered hulked Antigua 7.1758, ordered sold 12.1762.

KINSHA (ex-*Pioneer*) River gunboat, 616 tons, 180 × 30ft, 6 MG. Purch. 11.1900. Sold 30.4.1921 in Shanghai.

KIPLING Destroyer, 1,690 tons, 356·5 (oa) × 35·7ft, 6–4·7in, 10–TT. Yarrow 19.1.1939. Sunk 11.5.1942 air attack eastern Mediterranean.

KIRKLAND LAKE (ex-ST JEROME) Frigate (RCN), 'River' class. Morton 27.4.1944 (renamed 3.1944). Sold 22.9.1947 for BU.

KIRKLISTON Coastal minesweeper, 'Ton' class. Harland & Wolff 18.2.1954. = KILMORY 5.1954–60. BU 20.10.1991 Bruges.

KISTNA Sloop (RIN), 1,350 tons, 299·5 (oa) × 38·5ft, 6–4in. Yarrow 22.4.1943. = KRISHNA. PO 31.12.1981; BU India.

KITCHEN Yacht 8, 101bm, 59 × 19·5ft. Castle, Rotherhithe, 1670. Bomb vessel 7.1692. Sold 25.11.1698.

KITCHENER (ex-VANCOUVER) Corvette (RCN), 'Flower' class. G. T. Davie 18.11.1941 (renamed 11.1941). Sold 1946; BU 4.1949 Hamilton.

KITCHENER *See VANCOUVER 1941.*

KITE Cutter 6, 82bm, 56 × 18·5ft. Deptford DY 7.9.1764. Sold 29.10.1771.

KITE Cutter 12, 218bm, 77·5 × 27·1ft, 12–4pdr. Purch. 4.1778. Rated sloop 4.1779–1783. For BU 12.1793.

KITE Brig-sloop 16 (fir-built), 365bm, 96 × 30·5ft. Barnard, Deptford, 7.1795. Sold 9.1805.

KITE Sloop 16 (fir-built), 284bm, 93 × 26ft. Warren, Brightlingsea, 13.7.1805. Sold 14.12.1815.

KITE (ex-*Aetna*) Wood paddle gunvessel, 300bm,

125 × 23ft. GPO vessel, tx 7.1837. Sold 1864 T. Sar-gent.

KITE Iron screw gunboat, 'Ant' class. Napier 8.2.1871. Sold 18.5.1920 Hughes Bolckow, became dredger.

KITE Sloop, 1,350 tons, 283 × 38·5ft, 6—4in. Cammell Laird 13.10.1942. Sunk 21.8.1944 by U.344 Greenland Sea.

KITTIWAKE Patrol vessel, 530 tons, 234 × 26·5ft, 1—4in. Thornycroft 30.11.1936. Sold 1946 = *Tuch Shing*.

KNARESBOROUGH CASTLE Corvette, 'Castle' class. Blyth SB 29.9.1943. Arr. 16.3.1956 Smith & Houston, Port Glasgow, for BU.

KNOLE Minesweeper, Later 'Hunt' class. Eltringham, cancelled 1918.

KOKANEE Frigate (RCN), 'River' class. Yarrow, Esquimalt, 27.11.1943. Sold 12.1945; = *Bengal* (pilot vessel) 1948.

KONKAN (ex-TILBURY) Minesweeper (RIN), TE 'Bangor' class. Lobnitz 18.2.1942 (renamed 10.1941). Sold 1973.

KOOTENAY Escort (RCN), 2,370 tons, 366 (oa) × 42ft, 4—3in, 2—40mm, 6—TT, Limbo. Burrard 15.6.1954. Towed 6.11.2000 for use as artificial reef Puerto Vallarta, Mexico.

KOOTENAY *See also DECOY 1932.*

KORAAGA (ex-*Grozdana 'A'*) Aux. minesweeper (RAN), 264 tons. 1975; fishing vessel, purch. 16.2.1989. Deleted 2000.

KRAIT Special Service Vessel (RAN). Japanese *Kofuku Maru*, captured 11.12.1941. Tx North Borneo 2.1945. Museum ship 1964 Sydney.

KRAKOWIAK *See SILVERTON 1940.*

KRISHNA Survey brig (Indian). Listed 1841–60.

KRISHNA *See also KISTNA 1943.*

KRONPRINCEN (ex-KRON-PRINDS FREDER-ICK) 3rd Rate 74. Danish, captured 7.9.1807 Battle of Copenhagen. Comp. 12.1809 prison ship. Sold 1.11.1814.

KRONPRINCESSEN (ex-KRONPRINDESSE MARIE) 3rd Rate 74. Danish, captured 7.9.1807 Battle of Copenhagen. Sold 15.12.1814.

KUITAN Patrol boat (RCN), 84 × 20ft, 1 MG. Armstrong, Victoria, 25.9.1941. For disposal 1946.

KUJAWIAK *See OAKLEY 1940.*

KUKRI *See TRENT 1942.*

KUMAON (ex-MIDDLESBROUGH) Minesweeper (RIN), turbine 'Bangor' class. Hamilton 2.5.1942 (renamed 10.1941). BU 1949.

KURNAI *See BATAAN 1944.*

L

'L' class submarines L.1–8: 890 tons, 222 × 23·5ft, 1—4in, 4—TT. L.9–36: 890 tons, 228 × 23·5ft, 1—4in, 6—TT (L.9, L.15, L.17, L.19, L.20, L.26, L.27, L.33: 1—4in, 4—TT; L.14, L.24, L.25: 4—TT, 14 mines). L.50–74, 960 tons, 230·5 × 23·5ft, 2—4in, 6—TT.

L.1 (ex-E.57) Vickers 10.5.1917. Sold 3.1930 Cashmore, Newport; wrecked St Just, BU *in situ*.

L.2 (ex-E.58) Vickers 6.7.1917. Arr. 5.1930 Ward, Grays, for BU.

L.3 Vickers 1.9.1917. Arr. 29.10.1930 Charlestown for BU.

L.4 Vickers 17.11.1917. Arr. 24.2.1934 Ward, Grays, for BU.

L.5 Swan Hunter 26.1.1918. Arr. 20.11.1930 Charlestown for BU.

L.6 Beardmore 14.1.1918. Arr. 1.1935 Cashmore, Newport, for BU.

L.7 Cammell Laird 24.4.1917. Arr. 26.2.1930 Hughes Bolckow, Blyth, for BU.

L.8 Cammell Laird 7.7.1917. Sold 7.10.1930 Cashmore.

L.9 Denny 29.1.1918. Foundered 18.8.1923 Hong Kong; raised 6.9.1923, sold 30.6.1967 in Hong Kong.

L.10 Vickers 24.1.1918. Torpedoed 30.10.1918 by German destroyer S.33 off Texel.

L.11 Vickers 26.2.1918. Sold 16.2.1932 Young, Sunderland.

L.12 Vickers 16.3.1918. Sold 16.2.1932 Cashmore, Newport.

L.14 Vickers 10.6.1918. Sold 5.1934 Cashmore, Newport.

L.15 Fairfield 16.1.1918. Sold 2.1932 Cashmore, Newport.

L.16 Fairfield 9.4.1918. Sold 2.1934 Brechin, Granton.

L.17 Vickers 13.5.1918. Sold 2.1934 Ward, Pembroke Dock.

L.18 Vickers 21.11.1918. Sold 10.1936 Ward, Pembroke Dock.

L.19 Vickers 4.2.1919. Arr. 12.4.1937 Ward, Pembroke Dock, for BU.

L.20 Vickers 23.9.1918. Sold 7.1.1935 Cashmore, Newport.

L.21 Vickers 11.10.1919. Sold 2.1939 Arnott Young; stranded 21.2.1939 under tow; arr. 4.1939 Dalmuir for BU.

L.22 Vickers 25.10.1919. Sold 30.8.1935 Cashmore. Newport.

L.23 Vickers 1.7.1919, comp. 26.8.1924 Chatham. Foundered 5.1946 off Nova Scotia under tow sbkrs.

L.24 Vickers 19.2.1919. Sunk 10.1.1924 collision RESOLUTION off Portland.

L.25 Vickers 13.2.1919. Arr. 10.1935 Cashmore, Newport, for BU.

L.26 Vickers 29.5.1919, comp. 11.10.1926 Devonport. Sold 1945 in Canada for BU.

L.27 Vickers 14.6.1919. BU 1944 Canada.

L.28 Vickers, cancelled 1919.

L.29 Vickers, cancelled 1919.

L.30 Vickers, cancelled 1919.

L.31 Vickers, cancelled 1919.

L.32 Vickers 23.8.1919, not comp. Hull sold 1.3.1920 Leith Salvage Co. = LS.2 (salvage vessel/ Camel). BU Bo'ness 12.1938.

L.33 Swan Hunter 29.5.1919. Sold 2.1932 Ward, Lelant.

L.34 Pembroke Dock, cancelled 1919.

L.35 Pembroke Dock, cancelled 1919.

L.36 Fairfield, cancelled 1919.

L.37–49 Not ordered.

L.50 Cammell Laird, LD 5.1917, cancelled 1.4.1919.

L.51 Cammell Laird, cancelled 1919.

L.52 Armstrong 18.12.1918. Arr. 9.1935 Rees, Llanelly, for BU.

L.53 Armstrong 12.8.1919, comp. 10.1924 Chatham. Arr. 23.1.1939 Ward, Briton Ferry, for BU.

L.54 Denny 20.8.1919, comp. 9.1924 Devonport. Arr. 2.2.1939 Ward, Briton Ferry, for BU.

L.55 Fairfield 21.9.1918. Sunk 9.6.1919 Soviet torpedo boat in Baltic; salved 1928, cd Soviet Navy.

L.56 Fairfield 29.5.1919. Arr. 16.4.1938 Ward, Pembroke Dock, for BU.

L.57 Fairfield, LD 1.1918, cancelled 1.4.1919.

L.58 Fairfield, LD 22.4.1918, cancelled 1.4.1919.

L.59 Beardmore, cancelled 1919

L.60 Cammell Laird, cancelled 1919.

L.61 Cammell Laird, cancelled 1919.

L.62 Fairfield, LD 10.10.18, cancelled 30.11.18.

L.63 Scotts, cancelled 1919.

L.64 Scotts, cancelled 1919.

L.65 Swan Hunter, LD 9.1918, cancelled 29.6.1919.

L.66 Swan Hunter, cancelled 1919.

L.67 Armstrong, LD 11.1917; cancelled 1.4.1919, frames used for Yugoslav HRABRI (comp. 1927).

L.68 Armstrong, LD 12.1917; cancelled 1.4.1919, frames used for Yugoslav NEBOJSA (comp. 1927).

L.69 Beardmore 6.12.1918, comp. 3.1923 Rosyth. Sold 2.1939 Arnott Young, Dalmuir, for BU.

L.70 Beardmore, cancelled. Hull sold 1.3.1920 Leith Salvage Co., renamed LS.3 (salvage vessel/Camel).

L.71 Scotts 17.5.1919. Sold 25.3.1938 Ward, Milford Haven, for BU.

L.72 Scotts, LD 12.1917, cancelled 1.4.1919.

L.73 Denny, cancelled 1919.

L.74 Denny, cancelled 1919.

L'ABONDANCE Storeship 24, 524bm, 182·5 × 29·5ft, 24—9pdr, 4—4pdr. French, captured 1781. Sold 29.4.1784.

L'AGLAIA Sloop 18. French privateer, captured 18.4.1782 by AEOLUS. Sold 5.6.1783.

L'EGYPTIENNE 5th Rate 40, 1,430bm, 170 × 44ft, 28—24pdr, 16—24pdr carr., 4—9pdr. French, captured 2.9.1801 Alexandria. Sold 30.4.1817 for BU.

L'ETOILE Training schooner, 227 tons. French, seized 3.7.1940 Falmouth. HO 9.1940 Free French; LU 1943. Ret. French Navy 1945.

L'HERCULE 3rd Rate 74, 1,876bm, 181 × 48·5ft. French, captured 21.4.1798 by MARS off Bec du Raz. BU 12.1810 Portsmouth.

L'IMPASSIBLE Stationary AA ship, 2,419 tons, 328 × 39ft, 2—40mm. French target ship, seized 3.7.1940 Falmouth. Ret. French Navy 1947.

L'INCOMPRISE Destroyer, 610 tons, 245·5 × 26ft, 2—3·9in, 2—TT. French torpedo boat, seized 3.7.1940 Portsmouth. Cd RN 6.7.1940. Ret. French Navy 1946.

LA CAPRICIEUSE Submarine escort, 630 tons, 256 × 28ft, 2—3·9in. French sloop, seized 3.7.1940 Portsmouth. Ret. French Navy 1945.

LA CHIEFTAIN 5th Rate 36, 945bm, 145 × 38ft, 12—32pdr carr., 26—12pdr, 4—9pdr. French, captured 19.8.1801 by SYBILLE in Seychelles. Sold 1.9.1814.

LA COMBATTANTE *See HALDON 1942.*

LA CORDELIERE Destroyer, 610 tons, 245 × 26ft, 2—3·9in, 2—TT. French, seized 3.7.1940 Portsmouth; cd RN 6.7.1940. Ret. French Navy 1945.

LA FLORE Destroyer, 610 tons, 245 × 26ft, 2—3·9in, 2—TT. French torpedo boat, seized 3.7.1940 Portsmouth. Ret. French Navy 1945.

LA HULLOISE Frigate (RCN), 'River' class. Vickers, Montreal, 29.10.1943. BU La Spezia 4.1966.

LA LOIRE 5th Rate 40, 1,100bm, 153·5 × 40ft, 28—18pdr, 12—9pdr. French, captured 18.10.1798 by ANSON off Ireland. BU 4.1818.

LA MALBAI (ex-FORT WILLIAM) Corvette (RCN), 'Flower' class. Kingston SY 25.10.1941 (renamed 11.1941). Sold 1946.

LA MALOUINE Corvette, 'Flower' class. French, seized 3.7.1940 Middlesbrough. Smith's Dock 21.3.1940. Arr. 22.5.1947 Howells, Gellyswick Bay, Milford Haven, for BU.

LA MELPOMENE Destroyer, 610 tons, 245 × 26ft, 2-3·9in, 2—TT. French torpedo boat, seized 3.7.1940 Portsmouth. Free French 9.1940–10.1942, then RN crew; ret. French Navy 1946.

LA MOQUEUSE Minesweeping sloop 630 tons, 256 × 28ft, 2—3·9in. French, seized 3.7.1940 Falmouth. Free French from 8.1940; ret. French Navy 1945.

LABUAN Landing craft (RAN), 310 tons, 146 (oa) × 33ft. Walker 29.12.1971.

LABUAN *See also GOLD COAST 1943, LST.3501 1944.*

LABURNUM Sloop, 'Acacia' class. Connell 10.6.1915. Drillship 1935. Lost 2.1942 Singapore.

LABURNUM (ex-WAKATAKA) Drillship, 1,890 tons. Japanese minelayer, seized 17.10.1947, renamed 1949.

LACEDAEMONIAN (ex-LACEDMONIENNE) Brig 12, 195bm. French privateer, captured 5.1796 by PIQUE and CHARON in West Indies. Recaptured 5.1797 by French in West Indies.

LACEDAEMONIAN 5th Rate 38, 1,073bm, 150·5 × 40ft. Portsmouth DY 21.12.1812. BU 11.1822.

LACHINE Minesweeper (RCN), diesel 'Bangor' class. Davie SB 14.6.1941. To be tx RCMP 1950 = *Starnes*, cancelled. Conv. tug = *Jacks Bay* 1952.

LACHLAN Frigate (RAN), 'River' class. Mort's Dock, Sydney, 25.3.1944. Tx RNZN 1948 survey ship. Accommodation ship 12.1974–9.1993. Tx Philippines 1994 for BU.

LACHUTE Corvette (RCN), Modified 'Flower' class. Morton, Quebec, 9.6.1944. Sold 1947 Dominican Navy = CRISTOBAL COLON; discarded 1977, wrecked hurricane 31.8.1979.

LADAS Sloop, '24' class. Osbourne Graham, Sunderland, 21.9.1918. Sold 1920; repurch. 1920 mooring vessel. Sold 8.6.1936 Metal Industries, Rosyth.

LADAVA Patrol boat (RAN), 146 tons, 107·5 (oa) × 20ft, 1—40mm. Walker 11.5.1968. Tx Papua New Guinea 9.1975. Damaged by grounding 10.1983; sold 1988.

LADY CANNING Paddle sloop (Indian), 527bm. Bombay DY 24.3.1857. Hulked 1870 Calcutta.

LADY FALKLAND Paddle vessel (Indian). Laird 1854. Foundered under tow 6.5.1854.

LADY LOCH Iron gunboat (Australian), 336 tons, 183 × 24·5ft, 1—6in. Campbell, Melbourne, 1886. Listed until 1901.

LADY NELSON Survey brig 6, purch. 1800. Destroyed 1825 by natives of Babber I., Timor.

LADY PREVOST Schooner 12 (Canadian lakes), 230bm. Amherstburg, Lake Erie, 13.7.1812. Captured 10.9.1813 by Americans.

LADYBIRD River gunboat, 645 tons, 230 × 36ft, 2—6in 2—12pdr. Lobnitz 12.4.1916. Sunk 12.5.1941 Italian aircraft off Tobruk.

LADYBIRD (ex-*Wusueh*) Base ship, 3,400 tons, 295 × 46ft. Purch. 8.1950. Sold 5.1953 China Navigation Co. (original owners).

LADYBIRD Tender, 475 tons, C. D. Holmes, Beverley, 27.1.1970.

LAE Patrol boat (RAN), 146 tons, 107·5 (oa) × 20ft, 1—40mm. Walker 5.10.1967. Tx Papua New Guinea 9.1975. Sold 1988.

LAE *See also LST.3035 1944.*

LAERTES (ex-SARPEDON) Destroyer, 982 tons, 260 × 27ft, 3—4in, 4—TT. Swan Hunter 6.6.1913 (renamed 30.9.1913). Sold 1.12.1921 Stanlee, Dover; arr. 8.3.1922 after stranding nr Newhaven.

LAERTES Minesweeper, 'Algerine' class. Redfern, Toronto, 25.3.1944. Arr. 21.4.1959 Ward, Barrow, for BU.

LAFOREY (ex-FLORIZEL) Destroyer, 995 tons, 260 × 27·5ft, 3—4in. 4—TT. Fairfield 22.8.1913 (renamed 30.9.1913). Sunk 23.3.1917 British mine English Channel.

LAFOREY Destroyer leader, 1,935 tons, 362·5 (oa) × 37ft, 6—4·7in, 8—TT. Yarrow 15.2.1941. Sunk 30.3.1944 by U.223 north of Sicily.

LAGAN Frigate, 'River' class. Inglis 28.7.1942. Damaged 20.9.1943 by torpedo in Atlantic, not repaired; sold 21.5.1946, BU Troon.

LAGOS Destroyer, 2,315 tons, 379 (oa) × 40·25ft, 4—4·5in, 1—4in, 12—40mm, 8—TT. Cammell Laird 4.8.1944. Arr. 6.1967 McLellan, Bo'ness, for BU.

LAL (ex-SIMORGH) Gunboat (RIN), 331 tons, 170 × 22ft, 2—3in. Iranian, captured 1941 by RIN. Ret. Iran 1946.

LALESTON Coastal minesweeper, 'Ton' class. Harland & Wolff 18.5.1954. BU 4.1985.

LAMBOURN *See DOVEY 1943.*

LAMERTON Destroyer, 'Hunt' class Type II. Swan Hunter 14.12.1940. Lent Indian Navy 27.4.1953 = GOMATI. PO 5.1972; BU 6.1973.

LAMPORT *See LANGPORT 1654.*

LANARK Paddle minesweeper, 'Ascot' class, 820 tons. Fleming & Ferguson 18.12.1917. Sold 5.1923 Stanlee, Dover.

LANARK Frigate (RCN), 'River' class. Vickers, Montreal, 10.12.1943. Arr. 22.5.1966 Spezia for BU.

LANCASTER 2nd Rate 80, 1,198bm, 156 × 42ft. Wyatt, Bursledon, 3.4.1694. Rebuilt Portsmouth 1722 as 1,366bm. BU 1743

LANCASTER 3rd Rate 66, 1,478bm, 161 × 46ft. Woolwich DY 1749. BU comp. 10.8.1773 Portsmouth.

LANCASTER (ex-*Pigot*) 3rd Rate 64, 430bm, 173 × 43ft, 26—24pdr, 26—18pdr, 12—9pdr. Randall, Rotherhithe, 29.1.1797; East Indiaman, purch. on stocks. Lent West India Dock Co. 11.3.1815. Sold 30.5.1832 Cristall for BU.

LANCASTER 4th Rate 58, 1,476bm, 173 × 44ft, 26—42pdr carr., 32—24pdr. Plymouth DY 23.8.1823. Sold 17.2.1864 Marshall, Plymouth.

LANCASTER Armoured cruiser, 9,800 tons, 440 × 66ft, 14—6in, 10—12pdr. Armstrong 22.3.1902. Sold 3.3.1920 Ward, Birkenhead and Preston

LANCASTER (ex-PHILIP) Destroyer, 1,090 tons, 309 × 30·5ft, 3—4in, 1—3in, 6—TT. USN, cd RN 23.10.1940. Air target 3.1945. Arr. 30.5.1947 Hughes Bolckow, Blyth, for BU.

LANCASTER Frigate, 'Norfolk' class. Yarrow, Glasgow 24.5.1990.

LANCASTER CASTLE Corvette, 'Castle' class. Fleming & Ferguson 14.4.1944. Arr. 6.9.1960 King, Gateshead, for BU.

LANCE (ex-DARING) Destroyer 997 tons, 260 × 27ft, 3—4in, 4—TT. Thornycroft 25.2.1914 (renamed 30.9.1913). Sold 5.11.1921 Granton S. Bkg Co.

LANCE Destroyer, 1,920 tons, 362·5 (oa) × 37ft, 8—4in, 8—TT. Yarrow 28.11.1940. Sunk 9.4.1942 air attack Malta; raised, towed Chatham, found beyond repair; arr. Ward, Grays, 6.1944 for BU.

LANDGUARD (ex-SHOSHONE) Cutter 1,546 tons, 1—5in, 2—3in. USN, tx RN 20.5.1941 on Lend-Lease. LU 1946; sold 6.10.1949 Madrigal Co., Manila.

LANDRAIL Schooner 4, 80bm, 56 × 18ft, 4—12pdr carr. Sutton, Ringmore, 18.6.1806. Sold c. 1816.

LANDRAIL (ex-*Gipsy King*) Wood paddle tug, 36bm. Purch. 24.5.1855 Constantinople. Sold 21.7.1856 Constantinople.

LANDRAIL Wood screw gunvessel, 'Philomel' class. Deptford DY 28.3.1860. Sold 9.1869 = *Walrus*.

LANDRAIL Torpedo gunvessel, 950 tons, 195 × 28ft, 1—6in, 3—5in, 3—TT. Devonport DY 19.1.1886. Sunk 4.10.1906 target Lyme Bay.

LANDRAIL (ex-HOTSPUR) Destroyer, 983 tons, 260 × 27ft, 3—4in, 4—TT. Yarrow 7.2.1914 (renamed 30.9.1913). Sold 1.12.1921 Stanlee, Dover.

LANGPORT (LAMPORT) 62-gun ship, 794bm. Built Horsleydown, R. Thames, 1654. = HENRI-ETTA 1660. Wrecked 25.12.1689 nr Plymouth.

LANTAU *See BEAULIEU 1941.*

LANTON Coastal minesweeper, 'Ton' class. Harland & Wolff 30.7.1954. Sold 14.4.1970; BU Bruges.

LAPWING Cutter 10, 82bm, 48 × 21ft. White, Broadstairs, 21.1.1764. Lost 31.10.1765.

LAPWING 6th Rate 28, 598bm, 120·5 × 34ft. King, Dover, 21.9.1785. Harbour service 1813. BU 5.1828.

LAPWING Packet brig 6, 'Cherokee' Cass, 228bm. Chatham DY 20.2.1825. Breakwater 6.1845. Sold 22.11.1861 Marshall, Plymouth.

LAPWING Wood screw gunvessel, 675bm, 181·5 × 28·5ft, 1—110pdr, 1—68pdr, 2—20pdr. White, Cowes, 26.1.1856. Sold 1864 Marshall, Plymouth.

LAPWING Wood screw gunvessel, 663bm, 774 tons, 170 × 29ft, 1—7in, 2—40pdr, 1—20pdr. Devonport DY 8.11.1867. Sold 15.4.1885 Castle, Charlton.

LAPWING Composite screw gunvessel, 805 tons, 165 × 31ft, 6—4in, 2—3pdr. Devonport DY 12.4.1889. Sold 10. 11. 19 10 Bombay.

LAPWING Destroyer, 745 tons, 240 × 25·5ft, 2—4in, 2—12pdr, 2—TT. Cammell Laird 29.7.1911. Sold 26.10.1921 Barking S. Bkg Co.

LAPWING Sloop, 1,350 tons, 283 × 38·5ft, 6—4in, 12—20mm. Scotts 16.7.1943. Sunk 20.3.1945 by U-boat off Kola Inlet.

LARGO BAY (ex-LOCH FIONN) Frigate, 'Bay' class. Pickersgill 3.10.1944 (renamed 1944). Arr. 11.7.1958 Ward, Inverkeithing, for BU.

LARK Sloop 16, 430bm, 108 × 29·5ft. Pitcher, Northfleet, 15.2.1794. Foundered 8.8.1809 West Indies.

LARK Survey cutter 2, 109bm, 61 × 21·5ft. Chatham DY 23.6.1830. BU 6.1860 Devonport.

LARK Wood screw gunboat, 'Dapper' class. Deptford DY 15.3.1855. Sold 18.7.1878 Marshall, Plymouth.

LARK (ex-*Falcon*) Survey schooner, 86bm, 75 × 16·5ft. Purch. 27.9.1877 West Indies, = SPARROWHAWK 4.12.1877. Sold 4.9.1889 in Bermuda.

LARK Survey schooner, 166bm, 1—12pdr. Westacott, Barnstaple, 4.12.1880. Sold 12.1887 Sydney.

LARK (ex-HAUGHTY) Destroyer 968 tons, 260 × 27ft, 3—4in, 4—TT. Yarrow 26.5.1913 (renamed 30.9.1913). Sold 20.1.1923, Hayes, Porthcawl.

LARK Sloop, 1,350 tons, 299·5 (oa) × 38·5ft, 6—4in, 12—20mm. Scotts 28.8.1943. Torpedoed 17.2.1945 by U.968 off Kola Inlet, beached Murmansk; salved by Soviets, cd., = NEPTUN. BU 1956.

LARK *See also CRUIZER 1852, KINGFISHER 1879.*

LARKE Pinnace, 50bm. In service 1588.

LARKE 8-gun ship, 86bm. Royalist, captured 1656 by Parliamentarians. Sold 1663.

LARKE 6th Rate 18, 203bm, 76 × 22·5ft. Deane, Blackwall, 1675. Sold 3.5.1698.

LARKE 4th Rate 42, 492bm, 115 × 31·5ft. Wells, Rotherhithe, 2.1703. Rebuilt Woolwich 1726 as 598bm. Hulked 9.1742 Kingston, Jamaica; wrecked there 20.10.1744 hurricane.

LARKE 5th Rate 44, 710bm, 126 × 36ft. Golightly, Liverpool, 30.6.1744. Sold 4.8.1757 Woolwich.

LARKE 5th Rate 32, 680bm, 127 × 34·5ft. Bird, Rotherhithe, 10.5.1762. Burnt 7.8.1778 Rhode I. to avoid capture.

LARKE Cutter 16, 198bm, 74·5 × 26ft, 2—12pdr carr., 16—4pdr. Purch. 1779. Sloop from 1781. Sold 16.1.1784.

LARKSPUR Sloop, 'Acacia' class. Napier & Miller 11.5.1915. Sold 3.1922 Ward, Inverkeithing.

LARKSPUR Corvette, 'Flower' class. Fleming & Ferguson 5.9.1940. Lent USN 11.3.1942 = FURY. Sold 22.7.1946 = *Larkslock*.

LARNE 6th Rate 20, 459bm, 115·5 × 30ft, 18—32pdr carr., 2—9pdr. Bottomley, Lynn, 8.3.1814. Sold 26.3.1828 Castle, Charlton.

LARNE Destroyer, 730 tons, 240 × 25ft, 2—4in, 2—12pdr, 2—TT. Thornycroft, Woolston, 23.8.1910. Sold 9.5.1921 Ward, Lelant.

LARNE Minesweeper, 'Algerine' class. Simons, LD 30.1.1942; contract tx Lobnitz, LD again 25.1.1943, launched 2.9.1943. Sold 1947 Italian Navy = ERITREA. =*Alabarda* 1951; orphanage ship. BU La Spezia 5.1981.

LARNE *See also LIGHTNING 1829, GURKHA 1940.*

LASALLE Frigate (RCN), 'River' class. Davie SB 12.11.1943. Sold 13.12.1947; hull sunk 1948 breakwater.

LASHAM Inshore minesweeper, 'Ham' class. Weatherhead, Cockenzie, 31.5.1954. Sold Scotroy 1981.

LASSOO (ex-MAGIC) Destroyer, 1,010 tons, 260 ×

27ft, 3–4in, 4–TT. Beardmore 24.8.1915 (renamed 15.2.1915). Sunk 13.8.1916 mine North Sea.

LATONA 5th Rate 38, 944bm, 141·5 × 39ft. Graves, Limehouse, 13.3.1781. Harbour service 1813. Sold 2.5.1816.

LATONA 5th Rate 46, 1,071bm, 150 × 40ft. Chatham DY 16.6.1821. Sale list 12.1869. BU comp. 20.3.1875 Chatham.

LATONA 2nd class cruiser, 3,400 tons, 300 × 43ft, 2–6in, 6–4·7in, 8–6pdr. NC&A (Vickers) 22.5.1890. Minelayer 5.1907, 4–4·7in. Sold 22.12.1920 in Malta.

LATONA Minelayer, 2,650 tons, 418 (oa) × 40ft, 6–4·7in, 160 mines. Thornycroft 20.8.1940. Sunk 25.10.1941. Italian aircraft off Libya.

LATROBE Minesweeper (RAN), 'Bathurst' class. Mort's Dock 19.6.1942. Sold 18.3.1956 in Hong Kong for BU.

LAUDERDALE Destroyer, 'Hunt' class Type II. Thornycroft 5.8.1941. Lent Greek Navy 4.5.1946–12.11.1959 = AIGAION. BU 1960 Greece.

LAUNCESTON 5th Rate 42, 528bm, 118 × 32ft. Portsmouth DY 17.10.1711. = PRINCESS LOUISA 1728, rebuilt as 603bm. Wrecked 29.12.1736 Dutch coast.

LAUNCESTON 5th Rate 44, 701bm, 125 × 36ft. Buxton, Rotherhithe, 29.12.1741. Sold 25.3.1784.

LAUNCESTON Minesweeper, 'Bathurst' class. Evans Deakin 30.6.1941. Lent RAN until 1946. Sold 1946 Turkish Navy = AYANCIK; = HAMIT NACI; withdrawn 1965.

LAUNCESTON Patrol boat (RAN), 211 tons. North Queensland Co. 23.1.1982.

LAUNCESTON CASTLE Corvette, 'Castle' class. Blyth SB 27.11.1943. Arr. 3.8.1959 J. A. White, St Davids, for BU.

LAURA Schooner 10, 112bm, 68 × 20ft, 8–18pdr carr., 2–9pdr. Bermuda 1806. Captured 8.9.1812 by French privateer DILIGENT off North America.

LAUREL 50-gun ship, 489bm. Portsmouth 1651. Wrecked 1657.

LAUREL (ex-BECKFORD) Sloop 12, 104bm, 66 × 19ft, 12–4pdr. Privateer, purch. 7.1759. Sold 31.3.1763.

LAUREL Cutter 10, 58bm, 46 × 17ft. Purch. 11.1763. Sold 24.9.1771.

LAUREL 6th Rate 28, 602bm, 120 × 34ft. Raymond, Northam, 27.10.1779. Foundered 10.10.1780 hurricane West Indies.

LAUREL 6th Rate 28, 600bm. Jacobs, Sandgate, cancelled 10.1783. *Builder failed.*

LAUREL (ex-JEAN BART) 6th Rate 22, 424bm,

107 × 30ft. French, captured 15.4.1795 by squadron off Rochefort. Sold 1797 in Jamaica.

LAUREL 6th Rate 22, 526bm, 118·5 × 31·5ft. Boole & Good, Bridport, 2.6.1806. Captured 12.9.1808 by French CANONNIERE off Mauritius; recaptured 12.4.1810 as ESPERANCE, = LAURESTINUS. Wrecked 22.10.1813 West Indies.

LAUREL (ex-FIDELLE) 5th Rate 36, 1,104bm. French, captured 17.8.1809 on stocks Flushing. Wrecked 31.1.1812.

LAUREL 5th Rate 38, 1,088bm, 154·5 × 40ft. Parsons, Warsash, 31.5.1813. Harbour service 1864. BU 11.1885 Castle.

LAUREL (ex-REDGAUNTLET) Destroyer, 965 tons, 260 × 27ft, 3–4in, 4–TT. White 6.5.1913 (renamed 30.9.1913). Sold 1.11.1921 Fryer, Sunderland.

LAUREL *See also DAPHNE 1796.*

LAURESTINUS *See LAUREL 1806.*

LAUZON (ex-GLACE BAY) Frigate (RCN), 'River' class. G. T. Davie 10.6.1944. Sold 12.2.1964. *See GLACE BAY 1944.*

LAVENDER Sloop, 'Acacia' class. McMillan 12.6.1915. Sunk 5.5.1917 by UC.75 in English Channel.

LAVENDER Corvette, 'Flower' class. Alex Hall 27.11.1940. Sold 9.8.1946.

LAVEROCK (ex-HEREWARD) Destroyer, 994 tons, 260 × 27ft, 3–4in, 4–TT. Yarrow 19.11.1913 (renamed 30.9.1913). Sold 9.5.1921 Ward, Grays.

LAVINIA 5th Rate 48, 1,172bm, 158 × 41·5ft. Jacobs, Milford Haven, 6.3.1806. Harbour service 7.1836. Sunk 19.2.1870 collision SS *Cimbria* Plymouth harbour; wreck sold 31.3.1870 A. Dockerill.

LAVINIA *See also SEAHORSE 1830.*

LAWFORD (ex-IVANHOE) Destroyer, 1,003 tons, 260 × 27ft, 3–4in, 4–TT. Fairfield 30.10.1913 (renamed 30.9.1913). Sold 24.8.1922 Hayes, Porthcawl.

LAWFORD Frigate, DE, 'Captain' class. Boston NY 13.8.194 on Lend-Lease. Sunk 8.6.1944 air attack off Normandy.

LAWRENCE Fireship 6, 154bm. Purch. 1672. Expended 1673.

LAWRENCE Iron paddle despatch vessel (Indian), 1,154 tons, 212 × 32ft, 4–4in. Laird 15.6.1886. = OLD LAWRENCE 1918; = CANNING 1919. Listed until 1922.

LAWRENCE Sloop (Indian), 1,225 tons, 230 × 34ft, 4–12pdr. Beardmore 30.7.1919. For disposal 1946.

LAWSON Frigate, DE 'Captain' class. Boston NY 13.8.1943 on Lend-Lease. Ret. USN 3.1946.

LE HAVRE Frigate (RCN), 'River' class. Victoria, BC, cancelled 12.1943.

LE ROBECQUE (ex-LE ROBECQ) Sloop 18, 388bm, 111 × 28ft, 18—6pdr. French, captured 1782. Sold 5.6.1783.

LE TRIOMPHANT *See TRIOMPHANT 1940.*

LEAMINGTON (ex-ALDBOROUGH) Minesweeper, Later 'Hunt' class. Ailsa 26.8.1918 (renamed 1919). Sold 19.5.1928 Ward, Pembroke Dock.

LEAMINGTON (ex-TWIGGS) Destroyer, 1,090 tons, 309 × 30·5ft, 3—4in, 1—3in, 6—TT. USN, cd RN 23.10.1940. Lent RCN 12.1942—12.1943; lent Soviet Navy 16.7.1944—16.11.1950 = ZHGUCHI. Sold 26.7.1951; arr. Cashmore, Newport, 3.12.1951, for BU.

LEANDER 4th Rate 52, 1,044bm, 146 × 40·5ft. Chatham DY 1.7.1780. Captured 17.8.1798 by French GENEREUX; recaptured 3.3.1799 by Russians at Corfu, ret. RN. = HYGEIA (medical depot) 1813. Sold 14.4.1817.

LEANDER 4th Rate 58 (pitch pine-built), 1,572bm, 174 × 45ft, 26—12pdr carr., 32—24pdr. Wigram & Green, Blackwall, 10.11.1813. BU 3.1830.

LEANDER 4th Rate 50, 1,987bm, 181·5 × 51ft, 10—8in, 40—32pdr. Portsmouth DY 8.3.1848; undocked 16.2.1861 as screw ship, 2,760bm. Sold 1867 Castle & Beech.

LEANDER Steel despatch vessel (2nd class cruiser), 4,300 tons, 300 × 46ft, 10—6in. Napier 28.10.1882. Depot ship 1904. Sold 1.7.1920 Castle, Plymouth.

LEANDER Cruiser, 7,270 tons, 554·5 (oa) × 55·1ft, 8—6in, 8—4in. Devonport DY 24.9.1931. Sold 15.12.1949; BU Hughes Bolckow.

LEANDER (ex-WEYMOUTH) Frigate, 'Leander' class, Y100, 2,650 tons, 372 (oa) × 41ft, 2—4·5in, Limbo, helo (later Ikara, Limbo, helo). Harland & Wolff 28.6.1961. Expended 14.9.1989 target.

LEASIDE (ex-WALMER CASTLE) Corvette (RCN), 'Castle' class. Smith's Dock 10.3.1944 (renamed 1943). Sold 1946 = *Coquitlam*; = *Glacier Queen* 1958; hulked as floating hotel 1970.

LEASIDE *See also SERENE 1943.*

LEDA 5th Rate 36, 881bm, 137·5 × 38ft. Randall, Rotherhithe, 12.9.1783. Foundered 11.2.1796 off Madeira.

LEDA 5th Rate 38, 1,071bm, 150 × 40·5ft. Chatham DY 18.11.1800. Wrecked 31.1.1808 nr Milford Haven.

LEDA 5th Rate 36, 947bm, 145 × 38·5ft. Woolwich DY 9.11.1809. Sold 30.4.1817 Cockshott for BU.

LEDA 5th Rate 46, 1,171bm, 159 × 41ft. Pembroke Dock 15.4.1828. Police hulk 5.1864. Sold 15.5.1906 Harris, Bristol.

LEDA Torpedo gunboat, 810 tons, 230 × 27ft, 2—4·7in, 4—3pdr, 3—TT. Sheerness DY 13.9.1892. Minesweeper 1909. Sold 14.7.1920 Cardiff Marine Stores; BU Germany.

LEDA Minesweeper, 815 tons, 230 × 33·5ft, 2—4in. Devonport DY 8.6.1937. Sunk 20.9.1942 by U.435 Greenland Sea.

LEDBURY Destroyer, 'Hunt' class Type II. Thornycroft 27.9.1941. Arr. 5.1958 Charlestown for BU Rosyth.

LEDBURY Minehunter, 615 tons. Vosper-Thornycroft 5.12.1979.

LEDSHAM Inshore minesweeper, 'Ham' class. Bolson, Poole, 30.6.1954. Sold 12.4.1971; BU Newhaven.

LEE Sloop 8. On Canadian lakes 1776.

LEE (ex-*Adder*) Galley 8. Purch. 6.1780. Sold 1784.

LEE 6th Rate 20, 463bm, 115·5 × 30ft, 18—32pdr carr; 2—9pdr. Brindley, Frindsbury, 24.1.1814. BU 5.1822.

LEE Wood screw gunboat, 301bm, 125 × 23ft, 1—10in, 2—24pdr howitzers. Pitcher, Northfleet, 28.2.1857. Sunk 25.6.1859 in action with Peiho forts, China.

LEE Wood screw gunvessel, 'Philomel' class. Wigram, Blackwall, 25.1.1860. BU 3.1875 Sheerness.

LEE Destroyer, 365 tons, 210 × 20ft, 1—12pdr, 5—6pdr, 2—TT. Doxford 21.1.1899. Wrecked 5.10.1909 nr Blacksod Bay.

LEEDS (ex-CONNOR) Destroyer, 1,020 tons, 309 × 30·5ft, 2—4in, 4—20mm. USN, cd RN 13.10.1940. Sold 4.3.1947; BU Ward, Grays.

LEEDS CASTLE Corvette, 'Castle' class. Pickersgill 12.10.1943. Arr. 5.5.1958 Ward, Grays, for BU.

LEEDS CASTLE Patrol vessel, 1,427 tons. Hall Russell 22.10.1980.

LEEUWIN Survey vessel (RAN), 2,170 tons, 233·6 (oa) × 49·9ft. North Queensland Engineering and agents, Cairns, 19.7.1997.

LEGERE 6th Rate 24, 453bm, 116 × 30ft, 6—18pdr carr., 18—pdr. French, captured 22.6.1796 by APOLLO and DORIS off Scilly Is. Wrecked 2.2.1801 nr Cartagena.

LEGERE Gunvessel 6. French, captured 22.8.1798 by ALCMENE off Alexandria. In service 1801.

LEGION (ex-VIOLA) Destroyer, 1,072 tons, 260 × 27ft, 3—4in, 4—TT. Denny 3.2.1914 (renamed 30.9.1913). Sold 9.5.1921 Ward, New Holland.

LEGION Destroyer, 1,920 tons, 362·5 (oa) × 37ft, 8—4in, 8—TT. Hawthorn Leslie 26.12.1939. Sunk 26.3.1942. air attack Malta.

LEICESTER 6th Rate 24, 257bm. Purch. 1667. Sunk 7.1667 blockship R. Thames.

LEIGHTON Armed ship 22. Purch. 1798. Listed 1801. Gone by 1804.

LEITH Armed ship 20. In service 1782.

LEITH Sloop, 990 tons, 250 × 34ft, 2—4·7in, 1—3in. Devonport DY 9.9.1933. Sold 25.11.1946 = *Byron*; to Danish Navy = GALATHEA 1949. BU 1955.

LENNOX (ex-PORTIA) Destroyer, 996 tons, 260 × 27ft, Beardmore 17.3.1914 (renamed 30.9.1913). Sold 26.10.1921 Barking S. Bkg Co.

LENNOX Minesweeper, 'Algerine' class. Simons, cancelled 3.1919, contract tx Lobnitz, launched 15.10.1943. Arr. 1.6.1961 Clayton & Davie, Dunston, for BU.

LENOX 3rd Rate 70, 1,013bm, 15·5 × 40ft. Deptford 1978. Rebuilt Deptford 1701 as 1,089bm, rebuilt Chatham 1723 as 1,128bm. Sunk 4.1756 breakwater Sheerness.

LENOX 3rd Rate 74, 1,579bm, 165·5 × 47ft. Chatham DY 25.2.1758. Sunk 1784 breakwater; raised, BU 5.1789 Plymouth.

LEOCADIA 5th Rate 36, 952bm, 26—12pdr, 10—6pdr. Spanish, captured 1.5.1781 by CANADA. Sold 23.9.1794.

LEOCADIA Brig-sloop 16, 215bm, 85·5 × 24·5ft, 14—12pdr carr., 2—6pdr. Spanish, captured 5.6.1805 by HELENA in Atlantic. Sold 21.7.1814.

LEOCADIA *This name seems also to have been borne for a short time by CLARA 1804 (q.v.).*

LEONIDAS 5th Rate 36, 1,067bm, 150 × 40ft. Pelham, Frindsbury, 4.9.1807. Powder hulk 1872. Sold 23.11.1894 Castle, Charlton.

LEONIDAS (ex-ROB ROY) Destroyer, 987 tons, 260 × 27ft, 3—4in, 4—TT. Palmer 30.10.1913 (renamed 30.9.1913). Sold 9.5.1921 Ward, Hayle; BU 10.1922.

LEOPARD 34-gun ship, 516bm, Woolwich 1635. Captured 4.3.1653 by Dutch.

LEOPARD 54-gun ship, 645bm. Deptford 1659. Hulk 1686. Sunk 7.6.1699 breakwater Sheerness.

LEOPARD Fireship 6, 226bm. Purch. 1672. Expended 1673.

LEOPARD 4th Rate 54, 683bm, 131 × 34·5ft. Swallow, Rotherhithe, 15.3.1703. Rebuilt Woolwich 1721 as 762bm. BU 1739.

LEOPARD 4th Rate 50, 872bm, 134 × 39ft. Perry, Blackwall, 30.10.1741. BU comp. 7.1761.

LEOPARD 4th Rate 50, 1,044bm, 146·5 × 41ft. Portsmouth DY, LD 1.1776; frames to Sheerness DY 9.5.1785, launched 24.4.1790. Troopship 1812. Wrecked 28.6.1814 Anticosti, St Lawrence R.

LEOPARD Gunvessel 4, 65bm, 66·5 × 14·5ft.

Dutch hoy, purch. 4.1794. Dockyard craft 1796. Sold 1808.

LEOPARD Wood paddle frigate, 1,406bm, 218 × 37·5ft, 5—110pdr, 1—68pdr, 4—40pdr, 8—32pdr. Deptford DY 5.11.1850. Sold 8.4.1867 Marshall, Plymouth.

LEOPARD Destroyer, 385 tons, 210 × 20ft, 1—12pdr, 5—6pdr , 2—TT. Vickers 20 3.1897. Sold 6.1919 J. Jackson.

LEOPARD Destroyer, 2,126 tons, 393 × 37·5ft, 5—5.1in, 6—TT. French, seized 3.7.1940 Portsmouth. Free French 9.1940. Sunk 27.5.1943 off Tobruk.

LEOPARD Frigate, 2,300 tons, 330 × 40ft, 4—4·5in, 2—40mm. Portsmouth DY 23.5.1955. BU 10.77 Dartford.

LEOPARD'S WHELP *See THOMAS 1649.*

LETHBRIDGE Corvette (RCN), 'Flower' class. Vickers, Montreal, 21.11.1940. Sold 1952 = *Nicolaas Vinke*.

LETTERSTON Coastal minesweeper, 'Ton' class. Harland & Wolff 26.10.1954. Sold 9.6.1971 Belgian interests.

LEVANT 6th Rate 28, 595bm, 118·5 × 34ft. Adams, Buckler's Hard, 6.7.1758. BU comp. 27.9.1780.

LEVANT (ex-VENUS) Vessel captured 7.9.1807. *Name chosen, not used.*

LEVANT 6th Rate 20, 464bm, 116 × 30ft, 2—32pdr carr. Courtney, Chester, 8.12.1813. BU 10.1820.

LEVEN 6th Rate 20, 457bm, 116 × 30ft, 18—32pdr carr., 2—9pdr. Bailey, Ipswich, 23.12.1813 Survey ship 1820; harbour service 1827. BU 7.1848.

LEVEN Wood screw gunboat, 300bm, 126 × 23ft, 1—10in, 2—24pdr howitzers. Pitcher, Northfleet, 7.3.1857. Sold 21.7.1873 in Shanghai.

LEVEN Destroyer, 370 tons, 218 × 20ft, 1—12pdr, 5—6pdr, 2—TT. Fairfield 28.6.1898. Sold 14.9.1920 Hayes, Porthcawl.

LEVERET Brig-sloop 18, 'Cruizer' class, 384bm. King, Dover, 14.1.1806. Wrecked 10.11.1807 Galloper Rock.

LEVERET Brig-sloop 10, 'Cherokee' class, 237bm. Perry, Wells & Green, Blackwall, 27.2.1808. Sold 18.4.1822 Pittman.

LEVERET Brig-sloop 10, 'Cherokee' class, 232bm. Portsmouth DY 19.2.1825. Sold 7.11.1843.

LEVERET Wood screw gunboat, 'Albacore' class. Pitcher, Northfleet, 8.3.1856. BU 10.1867 Portsmouth.

LEVERTON Coastal minesweeper, 'Ton' class. Harland & Wolff 2.3.1955. Sold Pounds 13.8.1971, BU 1977.

LEVIATHAN 3rd Rate 74, 1,707bm, 172 × 48ft. Chatham DY 9.10.1790. Convict ship 10.1816; target 10. 1846. Sold 7.8.1848 Mr Burns.

LEVIATHAN Armoured cruiser, 14,100 tons, 500 × 71ft, 2—9·2in, 16—6in, 12—12pdr. John Brown 3.7.1901. Sold 3.3.1920 Hughes Bolckow, Blyth.

LEVIATHAN Aircraft carrier, 15,700 tons, 694·5 × 80ft. Swan Hunter (ex-Vickers Armstrong, Tyne) 7.6.1945, not comp. Arr. Faslane 27.5.1968 for BU.

LEVIATHAN *See also NORTHUMBERLAND 1750.*

LEVIS Corvette (RCN), 'Flower' class. G. T. Davie 4.9.1940. Sunk 19.9.1941 by U-boat south of Greenland.

LEVIS Frigate (RCN), 'River' class. G. T.Davie 26.11.1943. Sold 13.12.1947 for BU; hull sunk 1948 breakwater.

LEWES Paddle minesweeper, 'Ascot' class. Fleming & Ferguson 12.3.1918. Sold 3.1922 Ward, Inverkeithing.

LEWES (ex-CONWAY) Destroyer, 1,020 tons, 309 × 30·5ft, 2—4in, 5—20mm. USN, cd RN 23.10.1940. Air target 1943. Scuttled 25.5.1946 off coast of Australia.

LEWISTON Coastal minesweeper, 'Ton' class. Herd & McKenzie 3.11.1959. BU 12.1985.

LEYDEN 3rd Rate 64, 1,307bm, 156 × 44ft, 26—24pdr, 26—18pdr, 2—9pdr. Dutch, captured 30.8.1799 off Texel. Floating battery 1805, 56—24pdr, 10—24pdr carr. Sold 9.2.1815.

LIBERTY Gunvessel 4. Purch. 5.1798. Gone by 1800.

LIBERTY Cutter 14, 187bm, 74·5 × 25·5ft, 14—4pdr. Purch. 1779. Sold 2.1816 Barbados.

LIBERTY Training brig 428bm, 447 tons, 101 × 32·5ft. Pembroke Dock 11.6.1850. Sold 11.7.1905.

LIBERTY (ex-ROSALIND) Destroyer, 975 tons, 260 × 27ft, 3—4in, 4—TT. White 15.9.1913 (renamed 30.9.1913). Sold 5.11.1921 Granton S. Bkg Co.

LIBERTY Minesweeper, 'Algerine' class. Harland & Wolff 22.8.1944. Sold 29.11.1949 Belgian Navy = ADRIEN DE GERLACE. Hulk 1959; sold 1970 for BU Bruges.

LIBERTY *See also CHARLES 1632.*

LICHFIELD (ex-PATRICK) Fireship 20, 233bm. Royalist, captured 1658 by Parliamentarians. = HAPPY ENTRANCE 1665. *Fate unknown.*

LICHFIELD 4th Rate 48, 682bm, 130·5 × 34·5ft. Portsmouth 1694. Rebuilt 1730 Plymouth as 754bm. BU 1744.

LICHFIELD 4th Rate 50, 979bm, 140 × 40ft. Barnard, Harwich, 26.6.1746. Wrecked 28.11.1758 north coast of Africa.

LICHFIELD PRIZE 5th Rate 36, 397bm, 100 × 30·5ft. French, captured 29.7.1703. Sold 24.16.1706 R. Prince.

LICORNE 5th Rate 32, 679bm, 127 × 34·5ft. French, captured 18.6.1778 by AMERICA in English Channel. Sold 2 11.1783.

LICORNE *See also UNICORN 1776.*

LIDDESDALE Destroyer, 'Hunt' class, 1,000 tons, 4—4in. Vickers Armstrong, Tyne 19.8.1940. Sold 1.10.1948; BU King, Gateshead.

LIFFEY 4th Rate 50 (pitch pine-built), 1,240bm, 159 × 42ft, 20—32pdr carr., 28—24pdr, 2—9pdr. Wigram, Blackwall, 25.9.1813. BU 7.1827.

LIFFEY Wood screw frigate, 2,126bm, 3,915 tons, 235 × 50ft. Devonport DY 6.5.1856. Store hulk 1877. Sold 4.1903; hulked Coquimbo.

LIFFEY Destroyer, 550 tons, 222 × 23ft, 1—12pdr, 5—6pdr (1907: 4—12pdr), 2—TT. Laird 24.9.1904. Sold 23.6.1919 Ward, Grays.

LIFFEY *See also ERIDANUS 1813.*

LIGAERA (ex-DILIGENTIA) 6th Rate 22. Spanish, captured 12.1804 by DIANA and PIQUE in West Indies. Sold 1.9.1814.

LIGHTFOOT Destroyer leader, 1,607 tons, 325 × 32ft, 4—4in, 4—TT. White 28.5.1915. Sold 9.5.1921 Ward, New Holland.

LIGHTFOOT Minesweeper, 'Algerine' class. Redfern, Toronto, 14.11.1942 on Lend-Lease. Ret. USN 1946. Sold 1947 Greek Navy = NAVMACHOS; sunk target 1974.

LIGHTNING Fireship 8, 270bm, 91 × 25ft. Taylor, Cuckold's Point, 20.3.1691. Captured 24.11.1705 by French.

LIGHTNING Bomb vessel 8, 275bm, 91 × 26·5ft. 8—14pdr, 2 mortars. Bird, Rotherhithe, 24.10.1740. Capsized 16.6.1746 off Leghorn.

LIGHTNING Fireship 16, 422bm, 109 × 29·5ft. Ayles, Topsham, 14.10.1806. Sold 28.8.1816.

LIGHTNING Wood paddle gunvessel, 296bm, 126 × 23ft, 3 guns. Deptford DY 19.9.1823. BU 1872 Devonport.

LIGHTNING Sloop 18, 463bm, 113·5 × 31ft. Pembroke Dock 2.6.1829. = LARNE 12.9.1832. BU 3.1866 Castle, Charlton,

LIGHTNING Destroyer, 320 tons, 200 × 20ft, 1—12pdr, 5—6pdr, 2—TT. Palmer 10.4.1895. Sunk 30.6.1915 mine North Sea.

LIGHTNING Destroyer, 1,920 tons, 362·5 (oa) × 37ft, 6—4·7in, 8—TT. Hawthorn Leslie 22.4.1940. Sunk 12.3.1943 Italian MTB north of Algeria.

LIGHTNING *See also VIPER 1746, SYLPH 1776, T.B.1 1877.*

LILAC Sloop, 'Acacia' class, Greenock & Grangemouth 29.4.1915. Sold 15.12.1922 Batson Syndicate.

LILY 10-gun ship, 110bm. Purch. 1642. Wrecked 9.1653.

LILY Ketch 6, 64bm, 6—4pdr. Deptford 1657. Sold 1667.

LILY Sloop 6. Deptford 1672. Lost 1673.

LILY (ex-*Swallow*) Brig-sloop 18, 331bm, 108·5 × 30ft. Purch. 1804 Sold 11.1811.

LILY Brig 16, 432bm, 101 × 32·5ft, 14—32pdr, 2—18pdr. Pembroke Dock 28.9.1837. Coal hulk 1860 = C.29; = C.15. Sold 7.4.1908 Castle, Charlton.

LILY Wood screw gunvessel, 702bm, 185 × 28·5ft. 2—68pdr, 2—32pdr. Scott Russell, Millwall, 27.2.1861. BU 10.1867 Sheerness.

LILY Composite screw sloop, 720 tons, 150 × 28·5ft, 1—7in, 2—64pdr. Napier 27.10.1874. Wrecked 16.9.1889 coast of Labrador.

LILY Sloop, 'Acacia' class. Barclay Curle 16.6.1915. = VULCAN II (depot ship) 15.10.1923, = ADAMANT II 1930. Sold 25.6.1930 Cashmore, Newport.

LILY *See also SPENCER 1795.*

LIMBOURNE Destroyer, 'Hunt' class Type III. Stephen 12.5.1942. Damaged by torpedo from German TB, scuttled 23.10.1943 off French Channel coast.

LINARIA (ex-CLASH) Corvette, Modified 'Flower' class. Midland SY 18.11.1942 on Lend-Lease. Ret. USN 27.7.1946, = *Porto Offuro* 1948.

LINCOLN 4th Rate 48, 676bm, 130·5 × 34·5ft. Woolwich 19.2.1695. Foundered 29.1.1703.

LINCOLN (ex-YARNALL) Destroyer, 1,090 tons, 309 × 30·5ft, 1—4in, 1—3in, 20mm, 3—TT. USN, cd RN 10.1940. Lent RNorN 9.1941; lent Soviet Navy = RUZNI 26.8.1944—19.8.1952; sold 9.1952; BU Charlestown.

LINCOLN Frigate, 2,170 tons, 330 × 40ft, 2—4·5in, 2—40mm. Fairfield 6.4.1959. BU White, Inverkeithing 4.1983.

LINDISFARNE Patrol vessel, 925 tons, 195·3 (oa) × 34·2ft, 1—40mm. Hall Russell 1.6.1977. To PO 31.12.2003; for sale to Bangladesh?

LINDSEY Corvette (RCN), Modified 'Flower' class. Midland SY 4.6.1943. Sold 1964 = *North Shore.*

LINDSEY *See also PASLEY 1943.*

LING Corvette, 'Flower' class. Harland & Wolff, ordered 8.4.1940, cancelled 23.1.1941.

LINGANBAR Frigate (RCN), 'River' class. G. T. Davie, cancelled 12.1943.

LINGFIELD Paddle minesweeper, 'Ascot' class. Fleming & Ferguson 29.4.1916. Sold 5.1923 Stanlee, Dover.

LINNET (ex-SPEEDWELL) Gun-brig 14, 198bm, 86 × 22ft, 12—18pdr carr., 2—6pdr. Revenue vessel, renamed 1806. Captured 25.2.1813 by French GLOIRE off Madeira.

LINNET (ex-GROWLER) Brig 16 (Canadian lakes), 350bm, 16—12pdr. Lake Champlain 1813 (renamed 1813). Captured 11.9.1814 by Americans on Lake Champlain.

LINNET Survey cutter, 80bm, 56 × 19ft. Deptford DY 3.1.1817. Sold 7.8.1833 Ledger, Rotherhithe, for BU.

LINNET Packet brig 8, 361bm, 95 × 30·5ft, 8—18pdr. White, Cowes, 27.7.1835. Coastguard 9.1857; = WV.36 on 25.5.1863. Sold 30.10.1866 Marshall, Plymouth.

LINNET Wood screw gunboat, 'Britomart' class. Briggs, Sunderland, 7.6.1860. BU 7.1872 Chatham.

LINNET Composite screw gunvessel, 756 tons, 165 × 29ft, 2—7in, 3—20pdr. Thames Iron Works, Blackwall, 30.1.1880. Sold 27.4.1904 = *Linnet* (salvage vessel).

LINNET (ex-*Napier of Magdala*) Tender, 144 tons, 80 × 18ft. War Dept vessel, tx 11.1906. = HASTY 26.12.1913. Sold 20.2.1932 Reynolds, Torpoint.

LINNET (ex-HAVOCK) Destroyer, 970 tons. 260 × 27ft, 3—4in, 4—TT. Yarrow 16.8.1913 (renamed 30.9.1913). Sold 4.11.1921 Rees, Llanelly

LINNET Minelayer, 498 tons, 145 × 27ft, 1—20mm, 12 mines. Ardrossan DD 24.2.11.1938. Arr. 11.5.1964 Clayton & Davie, Dunston, for BU.

LION 36-gun ship, 120bm. Scottish, captured 1511. Sold 1513.

LION 50-gun ship, 160bm. Built 1536. Listed until 1559.

LION Ship. Scottish, captured 1549. Lost off Harwich.

LION (GOLDEN LION) 40-gun ship, 600bm. Built 1557. Rebuilt 1582 as 500bm, 4—3pdr, 8—18pdr, 14—9pdr, 9—6pdr, 25 small; rebuilt Deptford 1609 as 600bm = RED LION; rebuilt Chatham 1640 as 751bm, 130 × 35·5ft = LION; rebuilt 1658. Sold 16.12.1698.

LION (YOUNG LION) Ketch 6, 44bm, Dutch, captured 1665. Sold 1667; repurch. 1668. Sunk 1673 foundation Sheerness.

LION 5th Rate, c. 300bm, 92·5 × 25·5ft. Algerian, captured 1683. Sold 1683.

LION Hoy 4, 99bm, 54 × 20ft, 4—4pdr. Purch. 2.1702. Captured 12.1707 by French; recaptured 1709; rebuilt Deptford 4.1709 as 108bm. Listed until 1737.

LION 3rd Rate 60, 906bm, 144 × 38ft. Chatham DY 20.1.1709. Rebuilt Deptford 1738 as 1,068bm. Sold 14.3.1765.

LION Transport, 151bm, 72 × 22·5ft. Adams, Buckler's Hard, 3.7.1753. Hulked 1775. Sold 1786.

LION Cutter, 61bm. Purch. 2.1763. Sold 24.9.1771.

LION Discovery vessel. In service 1774–85

LION 3rd Rate 64, 1,378bm, 159 × 45ft. Portsmouth DY 3.9.1777. Sheer hulk 9.1816. Sold 30.11.1837 Chatham for BU.

LION Schooner. Purch. c. 1781. Sold 9.6.1785.

LION Gunvessel 4, 74bm, 67 × 15ft. Dutch hoy, purch. 3.1794. Sold 20.11.1795 Channel Is.

LION Schooner, 88bm. In service 1823. Sold 15.5.1826.

LION 2nd Rate 80, 2,580bm, 190 × 57ft, 12–8in, 68–32pdr. Pembroke Dock 29.7.1847; undocked Devonport 17.5.1859 as screw ship, 2,611bm, 3,482 tons. TS 1871. Sold 11.7.1905 Portsmouth.

LION Battlecruiser, 26,350 tons, 660 × 88·5ft, 8–13·5in, 16–4in. Devonport DY 6.8.1910. Sold 31.1.24 Hughes Bolckow; BU Jarrow and Blyth.

LION Battleship, 42,500 tons, 740 × 105ft, 9–16in, 16–5·25in. Vickers Armstrong, Tyne, LD 4.7.1939, suspended 10.1939, cancelled 1940.

LION *See also DEFENCE 1944.*

LION'S WHELP Vessel, type unknown. Lost at sea 17.5.1591.

LION'S WHELP Ketch 11, 90bm. Purch. 1601. Given away 1625.

LION'S WHELP *Name carried by ten 14-gun sloops, built 1627 and numbered 1 to 10. No 1 sold 1651; No 2 sold 1650; No 3 lost 2.1648; No 4 lost 14.8.1636 off Jersey; No 5 wrecked 8.6.1637 Dutch coast; No 6 wrecked 11.1628 off Ushant; No 7 blown up 1630 in action with French; No 8 hulked 1645; No 9 wrecked 4.1640; No 10 sold 19.10.1654.*

LIONESS (ex-*Lioness*) Storeship 26. East Indiaman, purch. 9.1777. Sold 25.6.1783.

LIONESS (ex-PETROLIA) Minesweeper, 'Algerine' class. Redfern, Toronto, 15.3.1944 (renamed 1943). Arr. 15.11.1956 Rosyth for BU.

LISBURNE Sloop 14. In service 1781. Sold 1.5.1783.

LISMORE Minesweeper, 'Bathurst' class. Mort's Dock, Sydney, 10.8.1940. Lent RAN until 1946. Sold 7.1946 Dutch Navy = BATJAN; deleted 1958.

LISTON Coastal minesweeper, 'Ton' class. Harland & Wolff 23.5.1955. *Launched as KILDARTON.*

LISTOWEL Corvette (RCN), Modified 'Flower' class. Kingston SY, cancelled 12.1943.

LITHGOW Minesweeper (RAN), 'Bathurst' class. Mort's Dock 21.12.1940. Sold 8.8.1956 for BU Hong Kong.

LITTLE BELT (ex-LILLE BELT) 6th Rate 20, 460bm, 18–32pdr carr., 2–9pdr. Danish, captured 7.9.1807 Battle of Copenhagen. Captured 16.5.1811 by American PRESIDENT. Ret. by

Americans, sold 1811 Deptford. *Was to have been renamed ESPION by Americans.*

LITTLE BELT Sloop 2 (Canadian lakes). Lake Erie 1812. Captured 10.9.1813 Lake Erie by Americans.

LITTLE CHARITY 28-gun ship. Captured 1653. Sold 1656.

LITTLE LONDON Smack, 16bm. Chatham DY 1672. Sold 1697.

LITTLE UNICORN *See UNICORN 1665.*

LITTLE VICTORY 5th Rate 28, 175bm. Chatham DY 1665. Expended 8.5.1671 fireship.

LITTLEHAM Inshore minesweeper, 'Ham' class. Brooke Marine, Lowestoft, 4.4.1954. Tx Indian Navy 15.6.1955 = BASSEIN; deleted 1994 or 1995.

LIVELY 5th Rate 30, 309bm, French, captured 25.7.1689. Recaptured 4.10.1689 by French.

LIVELY 6th Rate 12, 125bm. Purch. 7.7.1709. Sold 20.10.1712.

LIVELY 6th Rate 20, 279bm, 95 × 26ft. Plymouth DY 28.5.1713. BU 10.1738 Portsmouth.

LIVELY 6th Rate 24, 439bm, 107 × 31ft. Quallett, Rotherhithe, 16.6.1740. Sold 17.7.1750.

LIVELY 6th Rate 20, 438bm, 108 × 30·5ft. Janvrin, Beaulieu, 10.8.1756. Captured 10.7.1778 by French IPHIGENIE; recaptured 29.7.1781 by PERSEVERANCE. Sold 11.3.1784.

LIVELY Sloop 12, 206bm, 73·5 × 23·5ft, 12–18pdr carr. Purch. 1779. HO 9.12.1782 Spanish at Havana by her American prisoners.

LIVELY 5th Rate 32, 806bm, 135 × 36ft. Nowlan, Northam, 23.10.1794. Wrecked 12.4.1798 Rota Point, nr Cadiz.

LIVELY Storeship 16, 111bm, 64 × 20ft. Parsons, Bursledon, 1797, purch. on stocks. Listed 1802.

LIVELY 5th Rate 38, 1,076bm, 154 × 40ft. Woolwich DY 23.7.1804. Wrecked 26.8.1810 Malta.

LIVELY Cutter. Hired 12.8.1805, purch. 27.8.1805. *Fate unknown.*

LIVELY 5th Rate 38, 1,080bm, 150 × 40·5ft. Chatham DY 14.7.1813. Harbour service 1831. Sold 28.4.1862 Marshall.

LIVELY Wood screw gunboat, 'Albacore' class. Smith, Newcastle, 23.2.1856. Wrecked 23.12.1863 Dutch coast; salved = *Helgolanderin* (mail steamer).

LIVELY Wood paddle despatch vessel, 835bm, 985 tons, 220 × 28ft, 2–20pdr. Sheerness DY 10.12.1870. Wrecked 7.6.1883 nr Stornoway; wreck sold 7.1910.

LIVELY Destroyer, 400 tons, 218 × 20ft, 1–12pdr, 5–6pdr, 2–TT. Laird 14.7.1900. Sold 1.7.1920 S. Castle, Plymouth.

LIVELY Destroyer, 1,920 tons, 362·5 (oa) × 37ft, 8—4in, 8—TT. Cammell Laird 28.1.1941. Sunk 11.5.1942 aircraft off Sollum.

LIVELY *See also SCAMANDER 1813.*

LIVERPOOL (ex-ENTERPRISE) 5th Rate 44, 681bm, 125 × 36ft. Okill, Liverpool, 18.7.1741 (renamed 20.2.1741). Sold 14.9.1756 Woolwich; became privateer. *See LOOE 1759.*

LIVERPOOL 6th Rate 28, 590bm, 118·5 × 34ft. Gorill & Pownell, Liverpool, 10.2.1758. Wrecked 11.2.1778 Long I.

LIVERPOOL 4th Rate 50 (pitch pine-built), 1,240bm, 159 × 40ft, 20—32pdr carr., 28—24pdr, 2—9pdr. Wigram & Green, Blackwall, 21.2.1814. Sold 16.4.1822 Bombay.

LIVERPOOL 4th Rate 58, 1,487bm, 172 × 44ft, 26—42pdr carr., 32—24pdr. Plymouth DY, ordered 9.6.1825, cancelled 5.3.1829.

LIVERPOOL Wood screw frigate, 2,656bm. 235 × 50ft, 1—110pdr, 8—8in, 4—70pdr, 18—32pdr, 8—40pdr. Devonport DY 30.10.1860. Sold 26.6.1875 Castle, Charlton.

LIVERPOOL 2nd class cruiser, 4,800 tons, 430 × 47ft, 2—6in, 10—4in. Vickers 30.10.1909. Sold 1921 Stanlee; resold 8.11.1921 Slough Trading Co.; BU Germany.

LIVERPOOL Cruiser, 9,400 tons, 591·5 (oa) × 62·3ft, 12—6in, 8—4in. Fairfield 24.3.1937. Arr. 2.7.1958 McLellan, Bo'ness, for BU.

LIVERPOOL Destroyer, Type 42 Batch 2. Cammell Laird 25.9.1980.

LIZARD Ship, 120bm. Listed 1512–22.

LIZARD Fireship 16, 165bm. Royalist, captured 1652 by Parliamentarians. Expended 1666.

LIZARD Sloop 4, 40bm. Deptford 1673. Captured 1674 by Dutch.

LIZARD 6th Rate 24, 250bm, 94·5 × 24·5ft. Chatham DY 1694. Wrecked 31.5.1696 off Toulon.

LIZARD 6th Rate 24, 264bm, 95 × 25ft. Sheerness DY 1697. Sold 29.7.1714 S. Eyre.

LIZARD Sloop 14, 272bm, 92 × 26ft. Ewer, Bursledon, 22.12.1744. Wrecked 27.2.1748 Scilly Is.

LIZARD 6th Rate 28, 595bm, 119 × 34ft. Bird, Rotherhithe, 7.4.1757. Harbour service 1795. Sold 22.9.1828.

LIZARD Schooner 18. In service 1782. Sold 1786 East Indies.

LIZARD Wood paddle vessel, 300bm. Woolwich DY 7.1.1840. Sunk 24.7.1843 collision French paddle sloop VELOCE.

LIZARD Iron paddle gunvessel, 340bm, 142 × 22·5ft, 3 guns. Napier, Glasgow, 28.11.1844. BU 4.1869 Chatham.

LIZARD Composite screw gunvessel, 715 tons, 165

× 29ft, 6—4in. Harland & Wolff 27.11.1886. Sold 1905 Sydney for BU.

LIZARD Destroyer, 745 tons, 240 × 25·5ft, 2—4in, 2—12pdr, 2—TT. Cammell Laird 10.10.1911. Sold 4.11.1921 Rees, Llanelly.

LLANDAFF Frigate, 2,170 tons, 339·8 (oa) × 40ft, 2—4·5in, 2—40mm, Squid. Hawthorn Leslie 30.11.1955. Sold Bangladeshi Navy 10.12.76 = UMAR FAROOQ; deleted 1998.

LLANDUDNO Minesweeper, turbine 'Bangor' class. Hamilton 8.11.1940. Sold 8.5.1947 = *Borvik*.

LLEWELLYN Wood paddle packet, 650bm, 190 × 26·5ft. Miller & Ravenhill, Blackwall, 22.1.1848. Sold 1850 City of Dublin S. P. Co.

LLEWELLYN (ex-PICTON) Destroyer, 996 tons, 260 × 27ft, 3—4in, 4—TT. Beardmore 30.10.1913 (renamed 30.9.1913). Sold 10.3.1922 J. Smith.

LOBELIA Sloop, 'Arabis' class. Simons 7.3.1916. Sold 3.1920 Newfoundland Govt.; hulked 1924.

LOBELIA Corvette, 'Flower' class. Alex Hall 1.5.2.1941. Lent Free French 2.1941–4.1947; sold 3.5.1947 = *Thorgeir*.

'Loch' class frigates *See Introduction for details.*

LOCH ACHANALT Robb 23.3.1944. Tx RNZN 13.9.1948 = PUKAKI. BU 1.1966 Hong Kong.

LOCH ACHILTY *See ST BRIDES BAY 1945.*

LOCH ACHRAY Smith's Dock 7.7.1944. Tx RNZN 28.9.1948 = KANIERE. Sold 1966 for BU Hong Kong.

LOCH AFFRIC Ailsa, cancelled 1945.

LOCH ALVIE Barclay Curle 14.4.1944. Sold in Singapore 18.1.1965 for BU.

LOCH ARD Harland & Wolff, Govan, 2.8.1944. Comp. 21.5.1945 as TRANSVAAL (SAN).

LOCH ARKAIG Caledon 7.6.1945. Arr. 28.1.1960 King, Gateshead, for BU.

LOCH ARKLET *See START BAY 1945.*

LOCH ARNISH *See TREMADOC BAY 1945.*

LOCH ASSYNT Swan Hunter 14.12.1944. Comp. 2.8.1945 as DERBY HAVEN. Sold 7.1949 Persian Navy = BABR.

LOCH AWE Harland & Wolff, cancelled 1945.

LOCH BADCALL Pickersgill, cancelled 1945.

LOCH BOISDALE Blyth 5.7.1944. Comp. 1.12.1944 as GOOD HOPE (SAN) (q.v.).

LOCH BRACADALE *See ENARD BAY 1944.*

LOCH CARLOWAY *See BIGBURY BAY 1944.*

LOCH CAROY Pickersgill, cancelled 1945.

LOCH CARRON *See GERRANS BAY 1945.*

LOCH CLUNIE Ailsa, cancelled 1945.

LOCH COULSIDE *See PADSTOW BAY 1945.*

LOCH CRAGGIE Harland & Wolff 23.5.1944. Sold 8.7.1963 Dantos Leal; arr. 25.10.1963 Lisbon for BU.

LOCH CREE Swan Hunter 19.6.1944. Comp. 8.3.1945 as NATAL (SAN) (q.v.).

LOCH CRERAN Smith's Dock, cancelled 1945.

LOCH DOINE Smith's Dock, cancelled 1945.

LOCH DUNVEGAN Hill 25.3.1944. Arr. 25.8.1960 Ward, Briton Ferry, for BU.

LOCH EARN Hill, cancelled 1945.

LOCH ECK Smith's Dock 25.4.1944. Tx RNZN 1.10.1948 = HAWEA; sold 9.1965 for BU Hong Kong.

LOCH EIL Smith's Dock. Launched 15.5.1945 as HERNE BAY (q.v.).

LOCH ENOCK Harland & Wolff, cancelled 1945.

LOCH ERICHT Ailsa, cancelled 1945.

LOCH ERISORT Barclay Curle, cancelled 1945.

LOCH EYE Harland & Wolff, cancelled 1945.

LOCH EYNORT Harland & Wolff, cancelled 1945.

LOCH FADA John Brown 14.12.1943. Sold 21.5.1970; BU Faslane.

LOCH FANNICH Smith's Dock, = HOLLESLEY BAY, cancelled 1945.

LOCH FIONN *See LARGO BAY 1944.*

LOCH FRISA *See WIDEMOUTH BAY 1944.*

LOCH FYNE Burntisland 24.5.1944. Sold Cashmore 7.7.1970; BU Newport.

LOCH GARASDALE *See WIGTOWN BAY 1945.*

LOCH GARVE Hall Russell, cancelled 1945.

LOCH GLASHAN Smith's Dock, cancelled 1945.

LOCH GLASS *See LUCE BAY 1945.*

LOCH GLENDHU Burntisland 18.10.1944. Arr. 14.11.1957 Clayton & Davie, Dunston, for BU.

LOCH GOIL Harland & Wolff, cancelled 1945.

LOCH GORM Harland & Wolff 8.6.1944. Sold 9.1961 = *Orion.*

LOCH GRIAM Swan Hunter, cancelled 1945.

LOCH HARPORT *See BURGHEAD BAY 1945.*

LOCH HARRAY Smith's Dock, cancelled 1945.

LOCH HEILEN *See MORECAMBE BAY 1944.*

LOCH HOURNE Harland & Wolff, cancelled 1945.

LOCH INCHARD Harland & Wolff, cancelled 1945.

LOCH INSH Robb 10.5.1944. Tx Malaysian Navy 2.10.1964 = HANG TUAH; sold for BU 1977.

LOCH KATRINE Robb 21.8.1944. Tx RNZN 1949 = ROTOITI; left 28.11.1966 for Hong Kong for BU.

LOCH KEN Smith's Dock, cancelled 1945.

LOCH KILBIRNIE *See MOUNTS BAY 1945.*

LOCH KILLIN Burntisland 29.11.1943. Arr. 24.8.1960 Cashmore, Newport, for BU.

LOCH KILLISPORT Harland & Wolff 6.7.1944. Sold 20.2.1970; BU Blyth.

LOCH KIRBISTER Swan Hunter, cancelled 1945.

LOCH KIRKAIG Harland & Wolff, cancelled 1945.

LOCH KISHORN Robb, cancelled 1945.

LOCH KNOCKIE Pickersgill, cancelled 1945.

LOCH LARO Harland & Wolff, Cancelled 1945.

LOCH LAXFORD *See CARDIGAN BAY 1944.*

LOCH LINFERN Smith's Dock, cancelled 1945.

LOCH LINNHE Pickersgill, cancelled 1945.

LOCH LOMOND Caledon 19.6.1944. Sold 6.9.1968; BU Faslane.

LOCH LUBNAIG *See WHITESAND BAY 1944.*

LOCH LURGAIN Harland & Wolff, cancelled 1945.

LOCH LYDOCH *See ST AUSTELL BAY 1944.*

LOCH LYON Swan Hunter, cancelled 1945.

LOCH MABERRY Hall Russell, cancelled 1945.

LOCH MADDY *See CARNARVON BAY 1945.*

LOCH MINNICK Smith's Dock, cancelled 1945.

LOCH MOCHRUM *See PEGWELL BAY 1945.*

LOCH MORE Caledon 3.10.1944. Arr. 27.8.1963 Ward, Inverkeithing, for BU.

LOCH MORLICH Swan Hunter 25.1.1944. Tx RNZN 11.4.1949 = TUTIRA. Sold 15.12.1961.

LOCH MUICK (ii) *See THURSO BAY 1945.*

LOCH NELL Robb, cancelled 1945.

LOCH ODAIRN Robb, cancelled 1945.

LOCH OSSAIN Smith's Dock, cancelled 1945.

LOCH QUOICH Blyth 2.9.1944. Arr. 13.11.1957 Clayton & Davie, Dunston, for BU.

LOCH ROAN *See CAWSAND BAY 1945.*

LOCH RONALD Harland & Wolff, cancelled 1945.

LOCH RUTHVEN Hill 3.6.1944. BU 1966 Davies & Cann, Plymouth.

LOCH RYAN Pickersgill, cancelled 1945.

LOCH SCAMADALE *See DUNDRUM BAY 1945.*

LOCH SCAVAIG Hill 9.9.1944. Arr. 5.9.1959 Genoa for BU.

LOCH SCRIDAIN Pickersgill, cancelled 1945.

LOCH SEAFORTH (ex-LOCH MUICK [i]) *See PORLOCK BAY 1945.*

LOCH SHEALLAG Harland & Wolff, cancelled 1945.

LOCH SHIEL Harland & Wolff, cancelled 1945.

LOCH SHIN Swan Hunter 23.2.1944. Tx RNZN 13.9.1948 = TAUPO; sold 15.12.1961.

LOCH SKAIG Smith's Dock, cancelled 1945.

LOCH SKERROW Hill, cancelled 1945.

LOCH STEMSTER Harland & Wolff, cancelled 1945.

LOCH STENNESS Smith's Dock, cancelled 1945.

LOCH STRIVEN Harland & Wolff, cancelled 1945.

LOCH SUNART Harland & Wolff, cancelled 1945.

LOCH SWANNAY *See VERYAN BAY 1944.*

LOCH SWIN Harland & Wolff, cancelled 1945.

LOCH TANNA Blyth, cancelled 1945.

LOCH TARBERT Ailsa 19.10.1944. Arr. 18.9.1959 Genoa for BU.

LOCH TILT Pickersgill, cancelled 1945.

LOCH TORRIDON Swan Hunter 13.1.1945. Comp. 19.10.1945 as WOODBRIDGE HAVEN (depot ship). BU 8.1965 Hughes Bolckow, Blyth.

LOCH TRALAIG Caledon 12.2.1945. Arr. 24.8.1963 McLellan, Bo'ness, for BU.

LOCH TUMMEL Harland & Wolff, cancelled 1945.

LOCH URIGILL Blyth, cancelled 1945.

LOCH VANAVIE Harland & Wolff, cancelled 1945.

LOCH VENNACHAR Blyth, cancelled 1945.

LOCH VEYATIE Ailsa 14.4.1944. Arr. 12.8.1965 Arnott Young, Dalmuir, for BU.

LOCH WATTEN Blyth, cancelled 1945.

LOCHINVAR (ex-MALICE) Destroyer, 1,010 tons, 260 × 27ft, 3—4in, 4—TT. Beardmore 9.10.1915 (renamed 15.2.1915). Sold 25.11.1921 Hayes, Porthcawl, for BU.

LOCHY Frigate, 'River' class. Hall Russell 30.10.1943. Arr. 29.6.1956 Troon for BU.

LOCKEPORT Minesweeper, TE 'Bangor' class. North Vancouver SY 22.8.1941. Lent RCN 5.1942–2.7.1945. Sold 1.1.1948; BU Gateshead.

LOCUST Gun-brig 12, 179bm, 80 × 22·5ft, 2—32pdr carr., 10—10pdr carr. Randall, Rotherhithe, 2.4.1801. Sold 11.8.1814.

LOCUST Paddle gunvessel, 248bm, 420 tons, 120 × 23ft. Woolwich 8.4.1840. Tug 1869. Sold 1895 Sheerness.

LOCUST Destroyer, 385 tons, 210 × 22ft, 1—12pdr, 5—6pdr, 2—TT. Laird 8.12.1896. Sold 10.6.1919 J. Jackson.

LOCUST River gunboat, 585 tons, 2—4in, 1—3.7in howitzer. Yarrow 28.9.1939. RNVR drillship 1951. Sold Cashmore 24.5.1968; BU Newport,

LOFOTEN *See LST.3027 1945.*

LONDON 40-gun ship. Indiaman, purch. 1636. Listed 1653.

LONDON 64-gun ship, 1,104bm. Chatham DY 7.1656. Blown up 7.3.1655 accident The Nore.

LONDON (ex-LOYAL LONDON) 96-gun ship, 1,134bm. Deptford DY 10.6.1666. Partly destroyed by fire 13.6.1667; rebuilt Deptford 1670 as 1,348bm, 161 × 45ft (renamed 1670); rebuilt Chatham 1706 as 1,685bm; rebuilt Chatham 1721 as 1,711bm. BU comp. 10.1747 Chatham.

LONDON Brigantine 16 (Canadian lakes). Oswego, Lake Ontario, 1756. Lost to French 14.8.1756 on the Lakes.

LONDON (ex-*Holden*) Busse 6, 80bm, 64 × 16·5ft. Purch. 10.11.1756. Wrecked 29.4.1758 Senegal R.

LONDON Busse 6. Purch. 1759. Listed until 1764.

LONDON 2nd Rate 90, 1,894bm, 177 × 49·5ft. Chatham DY 24.5.1766. BU 4.1811.

LONDON 2nd Rate 92, 2,598bm, 4,375 tons, 206 × 54·5ft, 10—8in, 82—32pdr. Chatham DY 28.9.1840; undocked Devonport 13.5.1858 as screw ship, 2,687bm, 72 guns. Harbour storeship 4.1874. Sold 1884 in Zanzibar for BU.

LONDON Battleship, 15,000 tons, 400 × 75ft, 4—12in, 12—6in, 18—12 pdr. Portsmouth DY 21.9.1899. Minelayer 5.1918, 3—6in, 1—4in, 240 mines. Sold 4.6.1920 Stanlee; resold, BU Germany.

LONDON Cruiser, 9,850 tons, 632·8 (oa) × 66ft, 8—8in, 8—4in. Portsmouth DY 14.9.1927. Sold 3.1.1950; BU Ward, Barrow.

LONDON GM destroyer 5,440 tons, 520·5 (oa) × 54ft, 4—4·5in, 2—20mm, Sea Slug, Seacat, helo. Swan Hunter 7.12.1961. Tx Pakistani Navy 24.3.1982 = BABUR.

LONDON (ex-BLOODHOUND) Frigate, 4,100 tons, 480·5 (oa) × 48·4ft, Exocet, Seawolf, 6—TT, helo. Yarrow 27.10.1984. PO 11.6.1999; sold to Romania 12.2002.

LONDON *See also ROYAL ADELAIDE 1828.*

LONDONDERRY Sloop, 990 tons, 250 × 36ft, 2—4·7in, 1—3in. Devonport DY 16.1.1935. Sold 8.3.1948; BU Rees, Llanelly.

LONDONDERRY Frigate, 'Rothesay' class, 2,380 tons, 370 (oa) × 41ft, 2—4·5in, 1—40mm, Limbo (later Seacat, helo). White 20.5.1958. Harbour TS 1984—88. Expended 25.6.1989 target.

LONGBOW Destroyer, 1,980 tons, 365 (oa) × 38ft, 6—4in, 6—40mm, 10—TT. Thornycroft, LD 11.4.1945, cancelled 10.1945.

LONGBRANCH (ex-CANDYTUFT) Corvette (RCN), Modified 'Flower' class. Inglis 28.8.1943 (renamed 9.1943). Sold 1946 = *Kent County*.

LONGFORD (ex-MINEHEA) Minesweeper, Later 'Hunt' class. Harkess 15.3.1919 (renamed 1918). Sold 18.1.1923 Col J. Lithgow.

LONGUEUIL Frigate (RCN), 'River' class. Vickers, Montreal, 30.10.1943. Sold 13.1.1946; BU 1948.

LONSDALE Torpedo boat (Australian), 12 tons, 1—TT. Thornycroft 1884. BU 1913.

LOOE 5th Rate 32, 385bm, 110 × 28ft. Plymouth 1696. Wrecked 30.4.1697 off Baltimore, Ireland.

LOOE 5th Rate 32, 390bm, 108 × 29ft. Portsmouth 1697. Wrecked 12.12.1705 Scatchwell Bay, I. of Wight.

LOOE 5th Rate 42, 553bm, 120 × 32·5ft. Johnson, Blackwall, 7.4.1707. Harbour service 1735. Sunk 1737 breakwater.

LOOE 5th Rate 44, 685bm, 124·5 × 36ft. Snelgrove, Limehouse, 29.12.1741. Foundered 5.2.1744 off Cape Florida.

LOOE 5th Rate 44, 716bm, 126 × 36·5ft. Gorill & Parks, Liverpool, 17.8.1745. Sunk 12.1759 breakwater Harwich.

LOOE (ex-LIVERPOOL) 5th Rate 30, 681bm, 124 × 36ft, 20—12pdr, 10—9pdr. Privateer, purch. 9.1759. Sold 6.10.1763.

LOOE Minesweeper, TE 'Bangor' class. Hong Kong & Whampoa, LD 22.7.1941; = LYEMUN 9.1941, captured on stocks 12.1941 by Japanese.

LOOKOUT (ex-DRAGON) Destroyer, 1,002 tons, 260 × 27ft, 3—4in, 4—TT. Thornycroft 27.4.1914 (renamed 30.9.1913). Sold 24.8.1922 Hayes, Porthcawl.

LOOKOUT Destroyer, 1,920 tons, 362·5 (oa) × 37ft, 6—4·7in, 8—TT. Scotts 4.11.1940. Sold 6.1.1948; BU Cashmore, Newport.

LOOSESTRIFE Corvette, 'Flower class. Hall Russell 25.8.1941. Sold 4.10.1946 = *Kallsevni*.

LORD CLIVE (ex-CLIVE, ex-M.6) Monitor, 5,920 tons, 320 × 88ft, 2—12in, 2—6in. Harland & Wolff 10.6.1915 (renamed 8.3.1915, 1915). Sold 10.10.1927 McLellan, Bo'ness.

LORD CLYDE Ironclad battleship, 4,067bm, 7,842 tons, 280 × 59ft, 24—7in MLR. Pembroke Dock 13.10.1864. Sold Castle 11.1885 for BU.

LORD HOWE Cutter, 82bm, 53 × 20ft. Purch. 2.1763. Sold 20.8.1771.

LORD MELVILLE *See MELVILLE 1813.*

LORD NELSON Storeship. Purch. 1800. Sold c. 1807.

LORD NELSON Battleship, 16,500 tons, 435 × 79·5ft, 4—12in 10—9·2in, 15—12pdr. Palmer 4.9.1906. Sold 4.6.1920 Stanlee; resold 8.11.1921 Slough Trading Co.; BU Germany.

LORD RAGLAN *See RAGLAN 1915.*

LORD ROBERTS *See ROBERTS 1915.*

LORD WARDEN Ironclad battleship, 4,080bm, 7,842 tons, 280 × 59ft, 16—8in, 4—7in MLR. Chatham DY 27.5.1865. Sold Castle 2.1889 for BU. *Largest wooden ship built for RN.*

LORING Frigate, DE 'Captain' class. Boston NY 30.8.1943 on Lend-Lease. Nominally ret. USN 1.1947; left Preston 27.3.1947 for Greece for BU.

LOSSIE Frigate, 'River' class. Vickers, Montreal, 29.4.1943 on Lend-Lease. Ret. USN 26.1.1946.

LOTUS Corvette, 'Flower' class. Hill 17.1.1942. Lent Free French 4.1942–5.1947 = COMMANDANT D'ESTIENNE D'ORVES. Sold 23.10.1947 for BU.

LOTUS *See PHLOX 1942.*

LOUIS (ex-TALISMAN) Destroyer, 965 tons, 260 ×

27ft, 3—4in, 4—TT. Fairfield 30.12.1913 (renamed 30.9.1913). Wrecked 31.10.1915 Suvla Bay, destroyed Turkish gunfire.

LOUIS Frigate, DE 'Captain' class. Boston NY 13.8.1943 on Lend-Lease. Ret. 3.1946 USN.

LOUISA Gunvessel 3, 95bm, 66 × 18ft. Hoy, purch. 3.1794. Sold 10.1798.

LOUISA Tender. In service 1814. Sold 22.6.1816.

LOUISA Cutter. Purch. 1835 Canton. Foundered 8.1841 East Indies Station.

LOUISA Wood screw gunboat, 'Albacore' class. Fletcher, Limehouse, 12.1855. Sold 27.8.1867 Lethbridge for BU.

LOUISBURG Corvette (RCN), 'Flower' class. Morton 27.5.1941. Torpedoed 16.2.1943 Italian aircraft off Oran.

LOUISBURG Fireship 8. French, captured 1746. Recaptured 4.1.1747 by French privateer English Channel.

LOUISBURG Corvette (RCN), Modified 'Flower' class. Morton 13.7.1943. Sold 1947 Dominican Navy = JUAN ALEJANDRO ACOSTA; deleted 1978; wrecked 31.8.1979 hurricane.

LOVE & FRIENDSHIP Gunvessel 3. Purch. 1796. Listed 1800.

LOWESTOFFE 5th Rate 28, 357bm, 104·5 × 28ft. Chatham DY 1697. Rebuilt Portsmouth 1723 as 6th Rate 20, 378bm. Sold 12.7.1744.

LOWESTOFFE 6th Rate 24, 512bm, 112 × 32·5ft. Buxton, Deptford, 8.7.1742. Sold 2.2.1748.

LOWESTOFFE 6th Rate 28, 594bm, 119 × 34ft. Graves, Limehouse, 17.5.1756. Sunk 16.5.1760 action with French in St Lawrence R.

LOWESTOFFE 5th Rate 32, 717bm, 130·5 × 35·5ft. West, Deptford, 5.6.1761. Wrecked 11.8.1801 West Indies.

LOWESTOFFE PRIZE Brig-sloop 8. Captured 1777 West Indies. Condemned 9.1779 Jamaica.

LOWESTOFT 5th Rate 38, 870bm, 137 × 38ft. Woolwich DY, ordered 9.7.1801, cancelled 26.7.1805.

LOWESTOFT 2nd class cruiser, 5,440 tons, 430 × 50ft, 9—6in. Chatham DY 23.4.1913. Sold 8.1.1931 Ward, Milford Haven.

LOWESTOFT Sloop, 992 tons, 250 × 34ft, 2—4·7in, 1—3in. Devonport DY 11.4.1934. Sold 4.10.1946 = *Miraflores*.

LOWESTOFT Frigate, 2,150 tons, 370 (oa) × 41ft, 2—4·5in, 1—40mm, 4—GWS. Stephen 23.6.1960. Sunk 8.6.1986 target off Bahamas.

LOYAL (ex-ORLANDO) Destroyer, 995 tons, 260 × 27ft, 3—4in, 4—TT. Denny 10.11.1913 (renamed 30.9.1913). Sold 25.11.1921 Hayes, Porthcawl.

LOYAL Destroyer, 1,920 tons, 362·5 (oa) × 37ft,

6—4·7in, 8—TT. Scotts 8.10.1941. Sold 5.8.1948;
BU Ward, Milford Haven.

LOYAL EXAMPLE Patrol boat, 49 tons, 68·2 (oa)
× 19ft. Watercraft; comp. 13.8.1985 for RNXS
= EXAMPLE.

LOYAL EXPLOIT Patrol boat, 49 tons, 68·2 (oa) ×
19ft. Watercraft; comp. Vosper-Thornycroft
8.1988 for RNXS = EXPLOIT.

LOYAL EXPLORER Patrol boat, 49 tons, 68·2 (oa)
× 19ft. Watercraft; comp. 1.1986 for RNXS,
= EXPLORER.

LOYAL EXPRESS Patrol boat, 49 tons, 68·2 (oa)
× 19ft. Watercraft; comp. Vosper-Thornycroft
26.5.1988 for RNXS = EXPRESS.

LOYAL LONDON *See LONDON 1666.*

LOYALIST (Ex-*Restoration*) Sloop 14, 320bm, 99
× 28ft. Purch. 1780. Captured 30.7.1781 by French
LE GLORIEUX off Cape Henry.

LOYALTY 34-gun ship, 440bm. In service 1650–
53.

LOYALTY Store hulk 400bm. Purch. 11.11.1694
Cadiz. Foundered 7.4.1701 Bay of Bulls.

LOYALTY *See also RATTLER 1942.*

LST (1) Tank landing ships (Mark 1). *Original
classification for three ships launched 1942. See
BOXER, BRUISER, THRUSTER.*

LST (2) Tank landing ships, 1,625 tons. 115 ships
launched 9.1942–7.1943 in USA for Lend-Lease.
Fourteen lost, rest ret. USN 1945–47.

LST (3 Tank landing ships, 2,256 tons, 330 × 54ft,
10—20mm (3001 series) or 4—40mm, 6—20mm
(3501 series).

LST.3001 Vickers Armstrong, Tyne, 15.1.1945. Tx
War Dept 31.10.1946 = *Frederick Clover*. Sold
1966 Govt of Philippines.

LST.3002 Vickers Armstrong, Tyne, 29.3.1945. Tx
Greek Navy 1946 = ALIAKMON. Sold 25.4.1971.

LST.3003 Vickers Armstrong, Tyne, 8.6.1945.
= ANZIO 1947. Sold 8.2.1970; BU Spain.

LST.3004 Vickers Armstrong, Tyne, 30.7.1945,
cancelled incomp.; sold 18.6.1946 = *Rio Teja.*

LST.3005 Vickers Armstrong, Tyne, 1945. BU
incomp. 1945.

LST.3006 Harland & Wolff 3.9.1944. = TROMSO
1947; Tx MOT = *Empire Gannet* 21.9.1956. Sold
1968 in Singapore.

LST.3007 Harland & Wolff 16.9.1944. Lent Greek
Navy 4.1947–2.1962 = AXIOS. Sold 24.7.1962;
BU Genoa.

LST.3008 Harland & Wolff 31.10.1944. Tx RAN
1946. Sold 4.6.1950 R. R. Coots, Sydney.

LST.3009 Harland & Wolff 30.12.1944. Tx War
Dept 1946 = *Reginald Kerr.*

LST.3010 Harland & Wolff 30.9.1944.

= ATTACKER 1947. Tx MOT 1954 = *Empire
Cymric.* Arr. Faslane 1.10.1963 for BU.

LST.3011 Harland & Wolff 12.2.1945. = AVENGER
1947. Tx RIN 1.3.1949, = MAGAR 1951.

LST.3012 Harland & Wolff 12.3.1945. = BEN
NEVIS 1947. Arr. Faslane 12.3.1965 for BU.

LST.3013 Harland & Wolff 24.4.1945. = BEN
LOMOND 1947. Arr. 21.3.1960 Ward, Grays, for
BU.

LST.3014 Barclay Curle 11.11.1944. Tx RAN
7.1946. Sold 4.6.1950 R. R. Coots, Sydney.

LST.3015 Barclay Curle 16.3.1945. = BATTLER
1947. Tx MOT = *Empire Puffin* 1956. BU 7.1966
Spezia.

LST.3016 Hawthorn Leslie 15.12.1944. = DIEPPE
1947. Harbour service 11.1964. Sold 25.2.1980;
BU Santander.

LST.3017 Hawthorn Leslie 28.11.1944. Tx RAN
= TARAKAN 7.12.1948. Sold 12.3.1954 E. A. Marr,
Sydney.

LST.3018 Hawthorn Leslie 12.6.1945, cancelled
1946. Sold = *Rio Minho.*

LST.3019 Swan Hunter 4.9.1944. = VAAGSO 1947.
BU 12.1959 Faslane.

LST.3020 Swan Hunter 31.10.1944. Lent Greek Navy
1947–2.1962 = ALFIOS. Arr. 8.1963 Spezia for BU.

LST.3021 Lithgow 23.10.1944. Tx War Dept
= *Charles McLeod* 1946. BU 7.1968 Spezia.

LST.3022 Lithgow 26.1.1945. RAN 1946. Sold
4.6.1950 R. R. Coots, Sydney.

LST.3023 Lithgow 13.6.1945, cancelled. = *Rio
Tinto.*

LST.3024 Smith's Dock 5.10.1944. Tx War Dept
= *Maxwell Brander* 946. BU 1969 Hong Kong.

LST.3025 Smith's Dock 14.1.1945. = BRUISER
1947. Sold 15.10.1954 in Singapore.

LST.3026 Blyth 30.10.1944. = CHARGER 1947;
= *Empire Nordic* (MOT) 1956. BU 10.1968 Bilbao.

LST.3027 Blyth 26.1.1945. = LOFOTEN 1947.
Helicopter support ship 6.1964. Towed Rosyth
26.10.1993 to Bruges for BU.

LST.3028 Stephen 16.11.1944. Tx War Dept
= *Snowden Smith* 1946. Arr. 14.1.1961 Spezia for
BU; mercantile = *Elbano Primo* 1964

LST.3029 Stephen 12.1.1945. = CHASER 1947.
Sold 1.2.1962; arr. 28.31962 Spezia for BU.

LST.3030 Hall Russell 12.6.1945, cancelled.
= *Clupea.*

LST.3031 Connell 14.12.1944. = SULTAN 1.1959.
Sold 8.12.1970; BU Valencia

LST.3032 Connell 27.4.1945, cancelled. = *Rio
Mondego.*

LST.3033 Pickersgill 11.2.1945. Tx MOT = *Empire
Shearwater* 1956. Sold 16.11.1962; BU Ghent.

LST.3034 Pickersgill 25.8.1945, cancelled. BU 2.1950 Charlestown.

LST.3035 Denny 24.10.1944. Tx RAN 18.7.1946, = LAE 7.12.1948. Sold 14.11.1955, stranded 3.11.1956 Queensland coast on passage Japan for BU.

LST.3036 Ailsa 20.11.1944. = PUNCHER 1947. Sold 12.8.1960; arr. 4.6.1961 Ghent for BU.

LST.3037 Fairfield 30.1.1945. Tx War Dept = *Evan Gibb* 1946. Sold 1963 Italian sbkrs; BU Spezia.

LST.3038 Fairfield 14.3.1945. = FIGHTER 1947. Tx MOT = *Empire Grebe* 10.1956. Sold 1968 in Singapore.

LST.3039 Fairfield 27.6.1945, cancelled. = *Rio Duoro*.

LST.3040 Fairfield; tx Harland & Wolff 22.9.1945, cancelled. BU 17.1.1949 Ward, Hayle.

LST.3041 Harland & Wolff, Govan, 31.10.1944. = *Empire Doric* (MOT) 1954. Arr. 13.1.1960 Port Glasgow for BU.

LST.3042 Harland & Wolff, Govan, 31.1.1945. = HUNTER 1947; = *Empire Curlew* (MOT) 1956. Arr. 26.9.1962 Spezia for BU.

LST.3043 Scotts 27.4.1945. = MESSINA 1947. Sold 9.1980; BU Vigo.

LST.3044 Vickers Armstrong, Barrow, 29.7.1945. = NARVIK 1947. Sold 1.12.1971; BU Antwerp.

LST.3045 Vickers Armstrong, Barrow, 24.10.1945, cancelled. BU 11.1945 Barrow.

LST.3501 Vickers, Montreal, 24.8.1944. Tx RAN 1946, = LABUAN 1949. Sold 14.11.1955; BU 1956 Japan.

LST.3502 Vickers, Montreal, 31.8.1944. Lent Greek Navy 5.1947–2.1962 = STRYMON. Sold 3.7.1962; BU Spezia.

LST.3503 Vickers, Montreal, 12.10.1944. Lent Greek Navy 1947 = ACHELOOS. Sold 26.4.1971 Greek interests.

LST.3504 Vickers, Montreal, 3.11.1944. = PURSUER 1947, = *Empire Tern* (MOT) 1956. BU 1969.

LST.3505 Vickers, Montreal, 23.11.1944. = RAVAGER 1947. Sold 19.6.1961.

LST.3506 Vickers, Montreal, 2.12.1944. Lent Greek Navy 1947 = PINIOS. Sold 28.2.1972; BU Piraeus.

LST.3507 Davie SB 21.10.1944. tX mot = *Empire Gaelic* 1954. Sold 12.8.1960 = *Rjev*.

LST.3508 Davie SB 30.10.1944. = SEARCHER 1947. Arr. 20.6.1949 Milford Haven for BU.

LST.3509 Davie SB 27.11.1944. Tx War Dept = *Humphrey Gale* 1947. Arr. 10.1.1961 Genoa for BU.

LST.3510 Davie SB 28.11.1944. = SLINGER 1947.

Tx MOT = *Empire Kittiwake* 1956. Sold 1968 in Singapore.

LST.3511 Davie SB 29.11.1944. = REGGIO 1947. Arr. 12.8.1960 Ward, Grays, for BU.

LST.3512 Davie SB 25.4.1945. Tx MOT = *Empire Celtic* 1956. Arr. 7.9.1962 Spezia for BU.

LST.3513 Davie SB 26.4.1945. = SALERNO 1947. Sold 8.6.1961 for BU Italy.

LST.3514 Yarrow, Esquimalt, 7.10.1944. = SMITER 1947. Sold 3.1949; wrecked 25.4.1949 under tow off Portugal.

LST.3515 Yarrow, Esquimalt, 16.12.1944. = STALKER 1947. Sold Pounds, Portsmouth; arr. Portsmouth 10.12.2002.

LST.3516 Yarrow, Esquimalt, 15.2.1945. = STRIKER 1947. Sold 8.2.1970; BU Valencia.

LST.3517 Yarrow, Esquimalt, 28.4.1945. = ST NAZAIRE 1947. Tx MOT = *Empire Skua* 1956. Arr. 31.1.1968 Spezia for BU.

LST.3518 Vickers, Montreal, 6.4.1945. = SUVLA 1947. Arr. 8.9.1960 Ward, Grays, for BU.

LST.3519 Vickers, Montreal, 26.4.1945. Tx MOT = *Empire Baltic* 1956. Arr. 10.7.1962 Spezia for BU.

LST.3520 Vickers, Montreal, 2.5.1945. = THRUSTER 1947. Tx MOT = *Empire Petrel* 1956. Sold 1968 in Singapore.

LST.3521 Vickers, Montreal, 27.7.1945. Scuttled incomp. 2.1946 with cargo of gas shells off Halifax, NS.

LST.3522 Davie SB 9.6.1945. = TRACKER 1947. Sold 8.12.1970; BU Spain.

LST.3523 Davie SB 9.7.1945. = TROUNCER 1947, Tx MOT = *Empire Gull* 1956. BU 3.1980 Santander.

LST.3524 Davie SB 25.7.1945. = TRUMPETER 1947. Tx MOT = *Empire Fulmar* 1956. Sold 1968 in Singapore.

LST.3525 Davie SB 29.8.1945. = WALCHEREN 1947. Tx MOT = *Empire Guillemot* 10.1956. For sale 1968.

LST.3526 United SY, Montreal, 11.8.1945, cancelled incomp. 8.1945. Comp. barge = *Mil.462*.

LST.3527 United SY; cancelled 8.1945.

LST.3528 United SY; cancelled 8.1945.

LST.3529 United SY; cancelled 8.1945.

LST.3530 Sorel; cancelled 8.1945.

LST.3531 Sorel; cancelled 8.1945.

LST.3532 Marine Industries, Sorel, 19.5.1945. = ZEEBRUGGE 1947. Sold 16.12.1974; BU Gijon, Spain.

LST.3533 Sorel 1945, cancelled 1945.

LST.3534 Yarrow, Esquimalt, 23.6.1945. Tx MOT = *Empire Cedric* 1956. Arr. 16.9.1960 Ghent for BU.

LST.3535 Yarrow, Esquimalt, 1945, cancelled. BU 1945.

LST.3536 Vickers, Montreal, 1945, cancelled. BU 1945.

LST.3537 Vickers, Montreal, 11.8.1945, cancelled incomp. 8.1945. Comp. barge= *Mil.463.*

LST.3538–3574 Various Canadian builders. All cancelled.

LUCE BAY (ex-LOCH GLASS) Frigate, 'Bay' class. Pickersgill 12.4.1945 (renamed 1944). = DALRYMPLE (survey ship) 4.1947, comp. 10.2.1949 Devonport. Sold 4.1966 Portuguese Navy = ALFONSO DE ALBUQUERQUE; deleted 1983, accommodation ship Lisbon; expended 7.1994 target.

LUCIA (ex-*Spreewald*) Depot ship, 5,805 tons, 367·5 (oa) × 45ft, 2—3pdr. German mercantile, captured 9.1914 by BERWICK; conv. 1916. Sold 4.9.1946 = *Sinai.*

LUCIFER Fireship 8, 339bm, 98 × 28·5ft. Randall, Rotherhithe, 9.10.1778, purch. on stocks. = AVENGER (sloop) 13.12.1779. Sold 12.6.1783 New York.

LUCIFER Fireship. Fitted out 11.1783, not comp. Sold 8.1.1784.

LUCIFER (ex-*Spring*) Bomb vessel 8, 397bm. Purch. 1803. Sold 11.2.1811.

LUCIFER (ex-*Comet*) Wood paddle gunvessel, 387bm, 155 × 22·5ft, 2 guns. GPO vessel, tx 1837. = WV.41 (Coastguard watchvessel) 1875. Sold 1893.

LUCIFER (ex-ROCKET) Destroyer, 987 tons, 260 × 27ft, 3—4in, 4—TT. Palmer 29.12.1913 (renamed 30.9.1913). Sold 1.12.1921 Stanlee, Dover.

LUCIFER *See also TRUMPETER 1942.*

LUDHAM Inshore minesweeper, 'Ham' class. Fairlie Yacht Co. 16.6.1954. Sold Allen, Glasgow, 13.3.1967.

LUDLOW 5th Rate 32, 382bm, 108 × 28·5ft. Mundy, Woodbridge, 12.9.1698. Captured 16.1.1703 by French ADROIT off Goree.

LUDLOW Paddle minesweeper, 'Ascot' class. Goole SB 1.5.1916. Sunk 29.12.1916 mine The Shipwash.

LUDLOW (ex-STOCKTON) Destroyer, 1,020 tons, 309 × 30·5ft, 2—4in, 4—20mm. USN, cd RN 2.10.1940. Beached 5.6.1945 RAF target; sold 5.7.1945.

LUDLOW CASTLE 5th Rate 42, 531bm, 118 × 32ft. Sheerness DY 10.4.1707. Rebuilt Woolwich 1723 as 595bm. Hulked 25.1.1743 Antigua; sold 1749.

LUDLOW CASTLE 5th Rate 44, 725bm, 127 × 36·5ft. Taylor, Rotherhithe, 31.7.1744. Reduced to

6th Rate 24 in 1762. BU comp. 15.6.1771 Portsmouth.

LULLINGTON Coastal minesweeper, 'Ton' class. Harland & Wolff 31.8.1955. Tx Malaysian Navy = TAHAN 4.1966. BU 1982.

LULWORTH (ex-CHELAN) Cutter, 1,546 tons. Tx 2.5.1941 on Lend-Lease. Ret. USN 12.2.1946.

LUNENBURG Corvette (RCN), 'Flower' class. G. T. Davie 10.7.1941. BU 6.1946 Steel Co. of Canada, Hamilton.

LUPIN Sloop, 'Arabis' class. Simons 31.5.1916. Sold 22.3.1946 Pounds, Portsmouth; foundered 1946, raised, BU Portchester.

LURCHER (ex-COMTESSE D'AYEN) Cutter 6, 82bm, 54 × 19·5ft, 6—3pdr. French, captured 1761. Sold 1763 West Indies.

LURCHER Cutter 6, 83bm, 50 × 20ft. Deptford DY 26.9.1763. Sold 1771.

LURCHER Cutter 8. Deptford 1774. Sold 15.12.1778 West Indies.

LURCHER Destroyer, 765 tons, 225 × 25·5ft, 2—4in, 2—12pdr, 2—TT. Yarrow 1.6.1912. Sold 9.6.1922 Cashmore, Newport.

LURCHER *See also PIGMY 1781.*

LUSITANIA *See CHANTICLEER 1942.*

LUTIN Brig-sloop 16. French, captured 25.7.1793 by PLUTO off Newfoundland. Sold 26.1.1796.

LUTINE 5th Rate 36, 932bm, 144 × 39ft, 26—12pdr, 10—6pdr. French, HO 29.8.1793 by Royalists at Toulon, taken away 18.12.1793. Wrecked 9.10.1799 off Vlieland, Holland.

LUTINE Sloop 18, 332bm. French, captured 1799. Prison ship 1801. Sold 1802.

LYCHNIS Sloop, 'Anchusa' class. Hamilton 21.8.1917. Tx RIM = CORNWALLIS 9.1921. BU 1946.

LYDD (ex-LYDNEY) Minesweeper, Later 'Hunt' class. Fairfield 4.12.1918 (renamed 1918). Sold 13.3.1947 Dohmen & Habets, Liége.

LYDIARD (ex-WAVERLEY) Destroyer, 1,003 tons, 260 × 27ft, 3—4in, 4—TT. Fairfield 26.2.1914 (renamed 30.9.1913). Sold 5.11.1921 Granton S. Bkg Co.

LYDNEY *See LYDD 1918.*

LYEMUN *See LOOE 1941.*

LYME 52-gun ship, 764bm, 145 × 35ft. Portsmouth 1654. = MONTAGU 1660, 3rd Rate 836bm. Rebuilt Chatham 1675; rebuilt Woolwich 1698 as 905bm; rebuilt Portsmouth 1716 as 920bm. BU 9.1749.

LYME Pink 4, 118bm. Captured 7.1685 from Duke of Monmouth. Sold 1685.

LYME Dogger, 53bm. Captured 7.1685 with above vessel. Sold 1687.

LYME 5th Rate 32, 38415m, 109 × 29ft. Flint, Plymouth, 1695. Reduced 1720 to 6th Rate, 376bm, 20—6pdr. BU 1.1738 Deptford.

LYME 6th Rate 24, 446bm, 106·5 × 31ft. Taylor, Rotherhithe, 17.5.1740. Foundered 15.9.1747 Atlantic.

LYME 6th Rate 28, 587bm, 118 × 34ft. Deptford DY 10.12.1748. Wrecked 18.10.1760 Baltic.

LYME REGIS (ex-SUNDERLAND) Minesweeper, turbine 'Bangor' class. Stephen 19.3.1942 (renamed 4.1942). Sold 24.8.1948; BU Dorkin, Sunderland.

LYME REGIS *See also RAJPUTANA 1941.*

LYNN 5th Rate 32, 380bm, 108 × 28·5ft. Ellis, Shoreham, 1696. Sold 16.4.1713 F. Sheldon.

LYNN 5th Rate 42, 553bm, 117 × 32·5ft. Sheerness DY 8.4.1715. BU 10.1732 Plymouth.

LYNN 5th Rate 44, 688bm, 124 × 36ft. West, Deptford 7.3.1741. Sold 3.5.1763.

LYNX Sloop 10, 261bm, 88 × 23·5ft. Stanton, Rotherhithe, 11.3.1761. Sold 14.2.1777.

LYNX Sloop 24bm, 95 × 28ft. Randall, Rotherhithe, 10.3.1777, purch. on stocks. Hospital ship 7.1780. Sold 1.5.1783.

LYNX Sloop 16, 425bm, 108 × 30ft. Cleveley, Gravesend, 14.2.1794. Sold 24.4.1813.

LYNX Brigantine 3, 'Cherokee' class, 231bm. Portsmouth DY 2.9.1833. BU 12.1845.

LYNX Wood screw gunvessel, 477bm, 160 × 25·5ft, 2—68pdr. Mare, Blackwall, 22.7.1854. Sold 19.5.1862 Marshall, Plymouth.

LYNX Composite screw gunvessel, 464bm, 584 tons, 155 × 25ft, 1—7in, 1—64pdr, 2—20pdr. Harland & Wolff 25.4.1868. Sold 12.1888.

LYNX Destroyer, 325 tons, 194 × 19ft, 1—12pdr, 3—6pdr, 3—TT. Laird 24.1.1894. Sold 10.4.1912 Ward, Preston.

LYNX Destroyer, 935 tons, 260 × 27ft, 3—4in, 4—TT. London & Glasgow Co. 20.3.1913. Sunk 9.8.1915 mine Moray Firth.

LYNX Frigate, 2,300 tons, 330 × 40ft, 4—4·5in, 2—40mm. John Brown 12.1.1955. HO Bangladesh 12.3.1982 = ABU BAKR.

LYNX *See also PANDORA 1812.*

LYRA Brig-sloop 10, 'Cherokee' class, 240bm. Dudman, Deptford, 22.8.1808. Sold 11.7.1818 Pittman for BU.

LYRA Brig-sloop 10, 'Cherokee' class, 235bm. Plymouth DY 1.6.1821. Sold 3.6.1845 Hull Dock Co.

LYRA Wood screw sloop, 488bm, 139 × 28ft, 9—32pdr. Deptford 26.3.1857. BU 1876 Portsmouth.

LYRA Destroyer, 730 tons, 240 × 25ft, 2—4in, 2—12pdr, 2—TT. Thornycroft, Woolston, 4.10.1910. Sold 9.5.1921 Ward, Milford Haven.

LYS 6th Rate 24, 366bm, 106 × 29ft. French privateer captured 12.1745 by HAMPTON COURT. Sold 13.4.1749.

LYSANDER Brig 4. Listed 1842–44.

LYSANDER (ex-ULYSSES) Destroyer, 976 tons, 260 × 27ft, 3—4in, 4—TT. Swan Hunter 18.8.1913 (renamed 30.9.1913). Sold 9.6.1922 Cashmore, Newport.

LYSANDER (ex-HESPELER) Minesweeper, 'Algerine' class. Port Arthur SY 1.1.1943 (renamed 6.1943). = CORNFLOWER 3.1950–1951. Arr. 23.11.1957 Hughes Bolckow, Blyth, for BU.

M

M. 1–14 *Original designation of fourteen monitors built in 1915 and given, respectively, the following names before completion: ABERCROMBIE, HAVELOCK, RAGLAN, ROBERTS, SIR JOHN MOORE, LORD CLIVE, GENERAL CRAUFURD, EARL OF PETERBOROUGH, GENERAL WOLFE, PRINCE RUPERT, PRINCE EUGENE, SIR THOMAS PICTON, MARSHAL NEY, MARSHAL SOULT.*

'M' class coastal monitors 540 tons (M.29–33: 535 tons), 170 × 31ft, 1—9·2in, 1—3in (M.23—25: 1—7in, 2—3in; M.26: 1—7·5in, 1—3in, 1—12pdr; M.27: 1—4·7in, 2—3in; M29—33: 2—6in, 1—6pdr).

M.15 Gray 28.4.1915. Sunk 11.11.1917 by UC.38 off Gaza.

M.16 Gray 7.5.1915. Sold 29.1.1920 = *Tiga.*

M.17 Gray 12.5.1915. Sold 12.5.1920 = *Toedjoe.*

M.18 Gray 15.5.1915. Sold 29.1.1920 = *Anam.*

M.19 Raylton Dixon 4.5.1915. Sold 12.5.1920 = *Delapan.*

M.20 Raylton Dixon 11.5.1915. Sold 29.1.1920 = *Lima.*

M.21 Raylton Dixon 27.5.1915. Sunk 20.10.1918 mine off Ostend.

M.22 Raylton Dixon 10.6.1915. Minelayer 1919. = MEDEA 1.12.1925. Sold 12.1938 Cashmore; stranded 22.1.1939 under tow nr Padstow.

M.23 Raylton Dixon 18.6.1915. RNVR drillship = CLAVERHOUSE 16.12.1922. Arr. 21.4.1959 Charlestown for BU.

M.24 Raylton Dixon 9.8.1915. Sold 29.1.1920 = *Satoe.* Sunk 29.9.1936 target West Indies.

M.25 Raylton Dixon 24.7.1915. Unable to cross bar Dvina R, blown up 16.9.1919 to avoid capture.

M.26 Raylton Dixon 24.8.1915. Sold 29.1.1920 = *Doewa.*

M.27 Raylton Dixon 8.9.1915. Blown up 16.9.1919 with M.25.

M.28 Raylton Dixon 28.6.1915. Sunk 20.1.1918 gunfire German GOEBEN off Imbros.

M.29 Harland & Wolff 22.5.1915. Minelayer 1919. = MEDUSA 1.12.1925; depor ship = TALBOT 1.9.1941; = MEDWAY II 1943; = MEDUSA

21.9.1944. Sold 9.9.1946; BU 1947 Dover Industries.

M.30 Harland & Wolff 23.6.1915. Sunk 13.5.1916 shore batteries Gulf of Smyrna.

M.31 Harland & Wolff 24.6.1915. Minelayer 1919. = MELPOMENE 1.12.1925; = MENELAUS 23.12.1940. BU 1.1948 Rees, Llanelly.

M.32 Harland & Wolff; tx Workman Clark 22.3.1915. Sold 29.1.1920 = *Ampat.*

M.33 Harland & Wolff; tx Workman Clark 22.5.1915. = MINERVA 1. 12.25; hulked 1940 = C.23. To Hartlepool for restoration 24.7.1987; on display Portsmouth 1999.

'M' class submarines 1,600 tons, 296 (oa) (M.3, M.4: 305 oa) × 24·5ft, 1—12in, 1—3in, 4—TT.

M.1 (ex-K.18) Vickers 9.7.1917 (renamed 1917). Sunk 12.11.1925 off Start Point (rammed SS *Vidar?).*

M.2 (ex-K.19) Vickers 19.10.1918 (renamed 1917). Fitted to carry seaplane 4.1928 Chatham (12in gun removed). Sunk 26.1.1932 off Portland.

M.3 (ex-K.20) Armstrong 19.10.1918 (renamed 1917). Minelayer 1927 (guns removed). Sold 2.1932 Cashmore; arr. Newport 13.4.1932 for BU.

M.4 (ex-K.21) Armstrong, LD 1917 (renamed 1917). Hull sold 30.11.1921 to builder.

'M' class controlled minelayers 300 tons, 110 × 26·5ft, 1—20mm, 10 mines.

M.I Philip, Dartmouth 6.7.1939. = MINER I 1942; = MINSTREL 7.9.1962. Sold 1967.

M.II Philip, Dartmouth, 18.8.1939. = MINER II 1942; = GOSSAMER 1949. Sunk 18.3.1970 target off Portland.

M.III Philip, Dartmouth, 16.11.1939. = MINER III 1942. Sold 2.1977; BU Sittingbourne.

M.IV Philip, Dartmouth, 6.8.1940. = MINER IV 1942. BU 5.1964.

M.V Philip, Dartmouth, 2.11.1940. = MINER V 1942; cable layer = BRITANNIC 1960. RAF target 6.6.1979.

M.VI Philip, Dartmouth, 7.2.1942. = MINER VI 1942. Sold mercantile 16.8.1988 Malta.

M.VII (i) Singapore, ordered 3.10.1940. Destroyed on stocks 2.1942 on fall of Singapore.

M.VII (ii) Philip, Dartmouth. Launched 29.1.1944 = MINER VII. = ETV.VII 1959; trials vessel = STEADY. Sold Pounds 3.1880 for BU.

M.VIII Philip, Dartmouth. Launched 24.3.1943 = MINER VIII. Tender = MINDFUL 7.9.1962. Sold 22.2.1965 D. Arnold = *Rawdhan.*

MACDUFF *See MUNLOCHY 1918.*

MACEDONIAN 5th Rate 38, 1,082bm, 154 × 39·5ft. Woolwich DY 16. 1810. Captured 25.10.1812 by American UNITED STATES in Atlantic.

MACHINE Fireship 12, 390bm, 109 × 28ft. French, captured 15.9.1692. Sunk 9.7.1696 foundation Sheerness.

MACKAY (ex-CLAVERHOUSE) Destroyer leader, 1,800 tons, 320 × 32ft, 5–4·7in, 1–3in, 6–TT. Cammell Laird 21.12.1918 (renamed 1917). Sold 18.2.1947; arr. 6.1949 Charlestown for BU.

MACKENZIE Escort (RCN), 2,380 tons, 366 (oa) × 42ft, 4–3in, 6-TT, Limbo. Vickers, Montreal, 25.5.1961. Scuttled 16.5.1995 artificial reef off Vancouver I.

MACKEREL Dogger captured 1646. Last mentioned 1647.

MACKEREL Schooner 4, 78bm, 56 × 18ft, 4–12pdr carr. Bermuda 1804. Sold 14.12.1815.

MACKEREL Wood screw gunboat, 'Albacore' class. Pitcher, Northfleet, 8.3.1856. BU 7.1862.

MACQUARIE (ex-CULGOA) Frigate (RAN), 'River' class. Mort's Dock, Sydney, 3.3.1945 (renamed 3.1943). Sold 5.7.1962 for BU Japan.

MADAGASCAR (ex-NEREIDE) 5th Rate 38, 1,114bm, 154·5 × 40·5ft. French, captured 26.5.1811 Tamatave. BU 5.1819

MADAGASCAR 5th Rate 46, 1,167bm, 159·5 × 41ft. Bombay DY 15.11.1822. Harbour storeship 10.1853. Sold 5.5.1863 Rio de Janeiro.

MADAGASCAR Wood paddle vessel (Indian). Burnt 9.1841 accident Formosa Channel.

MADANG Patrol boat (RAN), 146 tons, 107·5 (oa) × 20ft, 1–40mm. Evans Deakin 10.8.1968. Tx Papua New Guinea 9.1975. PO 1989.

MADDISTON Coastal minesweeper, 'Ton' class. Harland & Wolff 27.1.1956. Sold 20.10.1974; BU Sunderland

MADRAS (ex-*Lascelles*) 4th Rate 56, 1,426bm, 175 × 43ft. East Indiaman; Wells, Rotherhithe, 4.7.1795. Storeship 1803. Sold 1807 Malta, partly BU.

MADRAS Minesweeper (RIN), 'Bathurst' class. Cockatoo DY 17.2.1942. Sold 1960.

MADRAS *See also MEEANEE 1848.*

MAEANDER 5th Rate 38 (red pine-built), 1,067bm, 150 × 40ft. Pitcher, Northfleet, 13.8.1813. BU 2.1817.

MAEANDER 5th Rate 44, 1,221bm, 159 × 42ft. Chatham DY 5.5.1840. Coal hulk 11.1859. Ordered for BU 10.1865; wrecked 7.1870 gale Ascension I.

MAENAD Destroyer, 'M' class, 1,025 tons. Denny 10.8.1915. Sold 22.9.1921 G. Cohen; BU Germany.

MAENAD Minesweeper, 'Algerine' class. Redfern, Toronto, 8.6.1944. Arr. 18.12.1957 Ward, Grays, for BU.

MAESTERLAND Firevessel 10, 100bm. Dutch, purch. 4.1694. Sold 17.2.1696.

MAGDALA Iron turret ship (Indian), 2,107bm, 3,340 tons, 225 × 45ft, 4–10in MLR. Thames Iron Works, Blackwall, 2.3.1870. Tx RN 31.10.1892; tx RIM 19.2.1903. Sold 1904.

MAGDALEN (MAWDELYN) Ship, 120bm. Listed 1522–25.

MAGDALEN Store hulk, 290bm. French, captured 1698. Sold 24.8.1699 Portsmouth.

MAGDALEN Schooner. Purch. 6.1769 Canada. Sold 23.9.1777 Quebec.

MAGDALEN Schooner, 90bm. Purch. 1780 North America. *Fate unknown.*

MAGIC (ex-MARIGOLD) Destroyer, 'M' class. White 10.9.1915 (renamed 1915). Sold 22.9.1921 G. Cohen; BU Germany.

MAGIC Minesweeper, 'Catherine' class. Savannah Machinery 25.5.1943 on Lend-Lease. Sunk 6.7.1944 human torpedo off Normandy.

MAGIC *See also LASSOO 1915.*

MAGICIAN Ferry service vessel, 1,050 tons, 206 × 38·5ft. Ailsa 27.9.1939. Lent War Dept 1939; tx RN 1944 = MAGICIAN II. Sold 31.12.1951; BU Faslane.

MAGICIENNE 5th Rate 32, 968bm, 144 × 39ft. French, captured 2.9.1781 by CHATHAM in North America. Burnt 27.8.1810 Mauritius to avoid capture by French after grounding.

MAGICIENNE 5th Rate 36, 949bm, 145 × 38·5ft. List, Fishbourne, 8.8.1812. Comp. 11.1831 as 6th Rate 24. BU 3.1845 Portsmouth.

MAGICIENNE Wood paddle frigate, 1,258bm, 210 × 36ft. Pembroke Dock 2.3.1849. BU 9.1866 Marshall, Plymouth.

MAGICIENNE 2nd class cruiser, 2,950 tons, 265 × 42ft, 6–6in, 9–6pdr. Fairfield 12.5.1888. Sold 11.7.1905.

MAGICIENNE Minesweeper, 'Algerine' class. Redfern 24.6.1944. Arr. 20.3.1956 Cashmore, Newport, for BU.

MAGICIENNE *See also OPAL 1875.*

MAGNANIME 3rd Rate 74, 1,823bm, 174 × 49·5ft. French, captured 31.1.1748 by NOTTINGHAM and PORTLAND. BU 4.1775.

MAGNANIME 3rd Rate 64, 1,370bm, 159·5 × 45ft.

Deptford DY 14.10.1780. Reduced to 5th Rate 2.1795, 6—42pdr carr, 26—24pdr, 12—12pdr. BU 7.1813 Sheerness.

MAGNET Brig-sloop 18, 'Cruizer' class, 382bm. Guillaume, Northam, 19.10.1807. Lost 11.1.1809 in ice in Baltic.

MAGNET (ex-ST JOSEPH) Brig-sloop 16. 285bm, 90 × 28ft, French privateer, captured 12.2.1809 by UNDAUNTED in English Channel. Foundered 9.1812 Atlantic.

MAGNET Packet brig 3, 'Cherokee' class, 237bm. Woolwich DY 13.3.1823. Sold 1847.

MAGNET Gunboat (Canadian lakes). Listed 1830–46.

MAGNET Mortar vessel, 155bm, 70 × 23·5ft, 1—13in mortar. Wigram, Northam, 2.5.1855. = MV.15 on 19.10.1855. Dockyard craft 2.1857. BU 6.1867.

MAGNET Wood screw gunboat, 'Albacore' class. Briggs, Sunderland, 29.1.1856. BU 1874 Chatham.

MAGNET *See also SIR SYDNEY SMITH 1812.*

MAGNIFICENT 3rd Rate 74, 1,612bm, 1969 × 47ft. Deptford DY 20.9.1766. Wrecked 25.3.1804 nr Brest.

MAGNIFICENT 3rd Rate 74, 1,732bm, 174 × 48·5ft. Perry, Wells & Green, Blackwall, 30.8.1806. Hospital ship 12.1825. Sold 1843 in Jamaica.

MAGNIFICENT Battleship, 14,900 tons, 390 × 75ft, 4—12in, 12—6in, 18—12pdr. Chatham DY 19.12.1894. Storeship 1.1918. Sold 9.5.1921 Ward, Inverkeithing.

MAGNIFICENT Aircraft carrier, 15,700 tons, 630 × 80ft, 19—40mm, 40 aircraft. Harland & Wolff 16.11.1944. Lent RCN 4.1948–1957. Arr. 12.7.1965 Faslane for BU.

MAGNOLIA Sloop, 'Acacia' class. Scotts 26.6.1915. Sold 2.7.1932 Metal Industries; arr. 27.7.1932 Charlestown for BU.

MAGOG Frigate (RCN), 'River' class. Vickers, Montreal, 22.9.1943. Sold 1947 Marine Industries for BU.

MAGPIE Schooner 4, 76bm, 56 × 18ft. Rowe, Newcastle, 17.5.1806. Captured 19.2.1807 by French at Perros.

MAGPIE Schooner 5, 70bm, 54 × 18ft. McLean, Jamaica, 6.1826. Wrecked 27.8.1826 squall off Cuba.

MAGPIE Cutter 4, 108bm, 61 × 20·5ft. Sheerness DY 30.9.1830. Dockyard tank vessel = YC.6 1845. Still in service 1880; sold 1908?

MAGPIE Wood screw gunboat, 'Dapper' class. Deptford DY 15.3.1855. Wrecked 8.4.1864 Galway Bay.

MAGPIE Wood screw gunvessel, 665bm, 774 tons, 170 × 29ft, 1—7in, 2—40pdr, 1—20pdr. Portsmouth DY 12.11.1868. Survey vessel 1878. Sold 9.1885.

MAGPIE Composite screw gunboat, 805 tons, 165 × 31ft, 6—4in. Pembroke Dock 15.3.1889. BDV 1902; gunboat 1915; depot ship 10.1915. Sold 29.12.1921 Duguid & Stewart.

MAGPIE Sloop, 1,350 tons, 283 × 38·5ft, 6—4in, 12—20mm. Thornycroft 24.3.1943. Arr. 12.7.1959 Hughes Bolckow, Blyth, for BU.

MAGPIE (ex-*Hondo*) Target vessel, 273 tons. Goole 1961–62. Trawler, purch. 6.1982. Tx Hooktone Organisation 1996.

MAHONE Minesweeper (RCN), TE 'Bangor' class. North Vancouver 14.11.1940. Sold 29.3.1958 Turkish Navy = BEYLERBEYI; listed until 1979.

MAHONESA 5th Rate 36, 921bm. Spanish, captured 13.10.1796 by TERPISCHORE off Malaga. BU 7.1798.

MAHRATTA (ex-MARKSMAN) Destroyer, 1,920 tons, 362·5 (oa) × 37ft, 6—4·7in, 8—TT. Scotts 28.7.1942 (renamed 7.1942). Sunk 25.2.1944 by U.956 Barents Sea.

MAHRATTA *See also Indian TB.4 1889, CHARLOCK 1943.*

MAIDA (ex-JUPITER) 3rd Rate 74, 1,899bm. French, captured 6.2.1806 San Domingo. Sold 11.8.1814.

MAIDEN CASTLE Corvette, 'Castle' class. Fleming & Ferguson 8.6.1944. Comp. as rescue ship EMPIRE LIFEGUARD. BU 7.1955

MAIDSTONE 40-gun ship, 555bm. Mundy, Woodbridge, 1654. = MARY ROSE 1660. Captured 12.7.1691 by French in Atlantic.

MAIDSTONE 6th Rate 24, 250bm, 94·5 × 24·5ft. Chatham DY 11.1693. Sold 29.7.1714.

MAIDSTONE 4th Rate 50, 979bm, 140·5 × 40·5ft. Wells, Rotherhithe, 12.10.1744. Wrecked 27.6.1747 off St-Malo.

MAIDSTONE 6th Rate 28, 593bm, 118·5 × 34ft. Seward, Rochester, 9.2.1758. BU 7.1794.

MAIDSTONE 5th Rate 32 (fir-built), 796/804bm, 135 × 36ft. Deptford DY 12.12.1795. BU 8.1810 Chatham.

MAIDSTONE 5th Rate 36, 947bm, 145 × 38·5ft. Deptford DY 18.10.1811. Receiving ship 1832; coal hulk 1839. BU comp. 16.6.1865 Cowes.

MAIDSTONE Depot ship, 3,600 tons, 355 (oa) × 45ft. Scotts 29.4.1912. Sold 31.8.1929.

MAIDSTONE Depot ship, 8,900 tons, 497 × 73ft, 8—4·5in. John Brown 21.10.1937. Arr. Ward, Inverkeithing, 24.5.1978 for BU.

MAIDSTONE *See also ROCHESTER 1693.*

MAJESTIC 3rd Rate 74, 1,623bm, 170·5 × 47ft. Adams & Barnard, Deptford, 11.2.1785. Reduced to 4th Rate 58, 28—42pdr carr., 28—32pdr, 2—12pdr, in 1813. BU 4.1816 after stranding.

MAJESTIC Screw 2nd Rate 80, 2,589bm, 190 × 57ft, 12—8in, 68—32pdr. Chatham DY 1.12.1853. BU 1868 Marshall, Plymouth. *Twelve years on stocks.*

MAJESTIC Battleship, 14,900 tons, 390 × 75ft, 4—12in 12—6in, 18—12pdr. Portsmouth DY 31.1.1895. Sunk 27.5.1915 by U.21 off Cape Helles.

MAJESTIC Aircraft carrier, 16,000 tons, 630 × 80ft, 25—40mm, 24 aircraft. Vickers Armstrong, Barrow, 28.2.1945. Comp. 10.1955 = MELBOURNE (RAN) 28.10.1955. Left Sydney 27.4.1985 under tow Shanghai for BU.

MAJESTIC *See also EDINBURGH 1882.*

MALABAR (ex-*Royal Charlotte*) 4th Rate 54, 1,252bm, 161 × 42ft. Pitcher, Northfleet; East Indiaman, purch. 1795. Foundered 10.10.1796 passage from West Indies.

MALABAR (ex-*Cuvera*) 4th Rate 56, 935bm. Purch. 5.1804. Storeship 20 in 1805, = COROMANDEL 7.3.1815. Convict ship 10.1827. BU comp. 12.1853 Bermuda.

MALABAR Sloop 20 (Indian). In service 1810.

MALABAR 3rd Rate 74, 1,715bm, 174·5 × 48ft. Bombay DY 28.12.1818. Coal hulk 10.1848; = MYRTLE 30.10.1883. Sold 11.7.1905 Portsmouth.

MALABAR Iron screw troopship, 4,713bm, 6,211 tons, 360 × 49ft, 3—4pdr. Napier 8.12.1866. Base ship 1897; = TERROR 1.5.1901. Sale list 1914. Sold 1.1918 R. Tucker, Bermuda.

MALACCA (ex-PENANG) 5th Rate 36, 990bm, 150 × 39ft. Prince of Wales I., Penang, 1809 (renamed 1808). BU 3.1816.

MALACCA Wood screw sloop, 1,034bm, 192 × 34·5ft, 1—10in, 16—32pdr. Moulmein, Burma, 9.4.1853; 6th Rate 26, engined Chatham 1854. Re-engined 1862 as screw corvette. Sold 6.1869 E. Bates; resold Japanese Navy = TSUKUBA; BU 1906.

MALAGA MERCHANT Fireship 4, 206bm. Purch. 1666. Sold 1967.

MALAYA Battleship, 27,500 tons, 639·8 (oa) × 90·5ft (later 104ft), 8—15in, 12—6in, 2—3in. Armstrong 18.3.1915. Sold 20.2.1948; arr. 12.4.1948 Faslane for BU.

MALCOLM Destroyer leader, 1,804 tons, 320 × 32ft, 5—4·7in, 1—3in, 6—TT. Cammell Laird 29.5.1919. Sold 25.7.1945; BU Ward, Barrow.

MALCOLM Frigate, 1,180 tons, 300 × 33ft, 3—40mm, 4—TT. Yarrow 18.10.1955. Sold Ward 13.8.1973; BU Inverkeithing.

MALCOLM *See also VALKYRIE 1917.*

MALHAM Inshore minesweeper, 'Ham' class. Fairlie Yacht Co. 29.8.1958. Sold 10.1959 Ghanaian Navy = YOGADA. BU 1977.

MALICE *See LOCHINVAR 1915.*

MALLAIG Minesweeper, Later 'Hunt' class. Fleming & Ferguson 10.10.1918. Sold 25.11.1927 Hughes Bolckow, Blyth.

MALLARD Gun-brig 12, 178bm, 80 × 22·5ft, 2—18pdr, 10—18pdr carr. Barnard, Deptford, 11.4.1801. Captured 25 12.1804 by French when aground nr Calais.

MALLARD Composite screw gunboat, 455 tons, 125 × 23ft, 2—64pdr, 2—20pdr. Earle, Hull, 4.8.1875. Sold 8.1889.

MALLARD Destroyer, 310 tons, 210·5 × 19·5ft, 1—12pdr, 5—6pdr, 2—TT. Thornycroft 19.11.1896. Sold 10.2.1920 S. Alloa S. Bkg Co.

MALLARD Patrol vessel, 510 tons, 234 × 26·5ft, 1—4in. Stephen 26.3.1936. Sold 21.4.1947; BU Dorkin, Gateshead.

MALLING CASTLE Corvette, 'Castle' class. Morton, cancelled 12.1943.

MALLOW Sloop, 'Acacia' class. Barclay Curle 13.7.1915. RAN 7.1919; dismantled 7.1932. Hull sunk 1.8.1935 target off Sydney.

MALLOW Corvette, 'Flower' class. Harland & Wolff 31.10.1940. Lent Yugoslav Navy 11.1.1944 = NADA; = PARTIZANKA 1946. Sold 28.10.1948 Egyptian Navy = EL SUDAN; deleted 1982.

MALMESBURY CASTLE Corvette, 'Castle' class. Morton, cancelled 12.1943.

MALPEQUE Minesweeper (RCN), TE 'Bangor' class, North Vancouver SY 5.9.1940. Sold 2.1959 Marine Industries.

MALPLAQUET *See JUTLAND 1946.*

MALTA Schooner 10, 162bm, 80·5 × 21·5ft, 10—14pdr. Captured 1800; = GOZO 12.1800. Gone by 1804.

MALTA (ex-GUILLAUME TELL) 2nd Rate 84, 2,265bm, 194·5 × 53ft, French, captured 30.3.1800 by squadron off Malta. Harbour service 1831. BU 8.1840.

MALTA (ex-*Britannia*) Paddle tender purch. 1854. Sold 1856.

MALTA Aircraft carrier, c. 45,000 tons, John Brown, LD 12.1944, cancelled 1945.

MALVERN Minesweeper, Later 'Hunt' class. Fleming & Ferguson 19.12.1919. Sold 26.6.1928 Alloa S. Bkg Co.; BU Charlestown.

MALWA Minesweeper (RIN), TE 'Bangor' class. Garden Reach, Calcutta, 21.6.1944. Tx Pakistani Navy 1948 = PESHAWAR; sold 22.1.1959.

MAMADUKE *See REVENGE 1650.*

MAMBA SSV (RAN). Building Melbourne 1945, cancelled 8.1945.

MAMELUKE Destroyer, 'M' class. John Brown 14.8.1915. Sold 22.9.1921 Cohen; BU Germany.

MAMELUKE Minesweeper, 'Algerine' class. Redfern, Toronto, 19.7.1944. Sold 27.4.1950; BU Thornaby-on-Tees.

MANAWANUI (ex-*Star Perseus*) Diving tender (RNZN), 911 tons, 143 × 31·2ft. Cochrane, Selby, comp. 5.1979. Cd 5.4.1988.

MANCHESTER Cruiser, 9,400 tons, 591·5 (oa) × 62·3ft, 12—6in, 8—4in. Hawthorn Leslie 12.4.1937. Sunk 13.8.1942 Italian MTBs Mediterranean

MANCHESTER Destroyer, Type 42 Batch 3. Vickers, Barrow, 24.11.1980.

MANDARIN Gun-brig 12, 178bm. Scuttled Dutch vessel salved 2.1810 Amboyna. BU 1812.

MANDATE Destroyer, 'M' class. Fairfield 24.7.1915. Sold 22.9.1921 Cohen; BU Germany.

MANDATE Minesweeper, 'Algerine' class. Redfern, Toronto, 9.8.1944. Arr. 12.1957 Rosyth for BU.

MANDRAKE Corvette, Modified 'Flower' class. Morton 22.8.1942. Tx USN 6.4.1943 = HASTE; sold 9.1947 = *Porto Azzura*.

MANILLA Storeship 14, 406bm. Purch. 11.1780. Lost 1782 East Indies.

MANILLA 5th Rate 36, 947bm, 145 × 38·5ft. Woolwich DY 11.9.1809. Wrecked 28.1.1812 Texel.

MANILLA 5th Rate 46, 1,215bm, 159·5 × 42ft. Bombay DY, ordered 5.4.1819, cancelled 21.2.1831.

MANILLA (ex-*Ingeburg*) Storeship, 373bm. Taken over 28.2.1870. Sold 14.8.1872 Yokohama.

MANILLA *See also ATALANTE 1860.*

MANLY (Gunboat No 37, ex-*Experiment*) Gunvessel 12, 157bm, 78 × 21ft, 2—24pdr, 10—18pdr carr. Purch. 4.1797 Leith. Sold 10.1802.

MANLY Gun-brig 12, 178bm, 80 × 22·5ft, 10—18pdr carr., 2—12pdr. Dudman, Deptford, 7.5.1804. Captured 1.1806 by Dutch; recaptured 1.1.1809, = BOLD 13.12.1813. Sold 11.8.1814.

MANLY Gun-brig 12, 180bm, 84 × 22ft. 10—18pdr carr., 2—6pdr. Hill, Sandwich, 13.7.1812. Sold 12.12.1833.

MANLY Mortar vessel, 117bm, 65 × 21ft, 1—13in mortar. Thompson 16.5.1855. = MV.6 on 19.10.1855. Hulked 7.1866.

MANLY Wood screw gunboat, 'Albacore' class. Briggs, Sunderland, 29.1.1856. BU 1.1864 Deptford.

MANLY Destroyer, 883 tons, 260 × 25·5ft, 3—4in, 4—TT. Yarrow 12.10.1914. Sold 26.10.1921 Barking S. Bkg Co.

MANLY Tender, 143 tons, 80 (oa) × 21ft. Dunston 23.7.1981. Sold Pounds 2.1992.

MANNERS Destroyer, 'M' class. Fairfield 15.6.1915. Sold 26.10.1921 Barking S. Bkg Co.

MANNERS Frigate, DE 'Captain' class. Boston NY 17.12.1943 on Lend-Lease. Nominally ret. USN 8.11.1945; sold 1.1947 for BU Greece.

MANOORA (ex-FAIRFAX COUNTY/LST.1193) Landing ship (RAN), 4,975 tons, 552·3 (oa) × 69·5ft. National Steel SB, San Diego, 19.12.1970. USN, acq. 27.9.1994, cd 25.11.1994.

MANSFIELD Destroyer, 'M' class, 1,057 tons. Hawthorn Leslie 3.12.1914. Sold 26.10.1921 Barking S. Bkg Co.

MANSFIELD (ex-EVANS) Destroyer, 1,090 tons, 309 × 30·5ft, 1—4in, 1—3in, 4—20mm, 3—TT. USN, cd RN 23.10.1940. Lent RNorN 12.1940–3.1942; RCN 9.1942–6.1944. Sold 21.10.1944; BU Canada.

MANTIS River gunboat, 645 tons, 230 × 36ft, 2—6in, 1—3in. Sunderland SB Co. 14.9.1915. Sold 20.1.1940 Shanghai.

MANXMAN Seaplane carrier, 2,048 tons. In service 1916–20.

MANXMAN Minelayer, 2,650 tons, 418 (oa) × 40ft, 6—4·7in, 160 mines. Stephen 5.9.1940. Minesweeper support ship 2.1963. Sold Cashmore 1.9.1972; BU Newport.

MAORI Destroyer, 1,035 tons, 280 × 27ft, 2—4in, 2—TT. Denny 24.5.1909. Sunk 7.5.1915 mine North Sea.

MAORI Destroyer, 1,870 tons, 377 (oa) × 36·5ft, 8—4·7in, 4—TT. Fairfield 2.9.1937. Sunk 11/12.12.1942 air attack Malta; salved, scuttled 15.7.1945 off Malta.

MARATHON 2nd class cruiser, 2,950 tons, 265 × 42ft, 6—6in, 9—6pdr. Fairfield 23.8.1888. Sold 11.8.1905 Ward, Preston.

MARATHON *See also DEFENCE 1815.*

MARAZION Minesweeper, Later 'Hunt' class. Fleming & Ferguson 15.4.1919. Sold 3.1933 in Hong Kong.

MARENGO 2nd Rate 80, 1,930bm. French, captured 13.2.1806 by LONDON and AMAZON in Atlantic. Prison ship 9.1809. BU 11.1816.

MARGAREE Escort (RCN), 2,260 tons, 366 (oa) × 42ft, 4—3in, 2—40mm, Limbo. Halifax SY 29.3.1956. Towed from Halifax 13.3.1994 for BU Alang.

MARGAREE *See also DIANA 1932.*

MARGARET Ship. Purch. 1413. Sold 5.1421.

MARGARET Ship. Purch. 7.1461. Listed until 1493.

MARGARET Ship. Captured 1490 from the Scots.

MARGARET 60-ton vessel. Listed 1549.

MARGARET Galliot. In service 1645–74.

MARGARET Galley. Built Pisa, purch. 1671. Given away 1677.

MARGARET Sloop 20. Purch. 6.1744 Jamaica. Sold 9.8.1744.

MARGARET Cutter. Captured 12.6.1775 by Americans.

MARGARET Tender. Dates from 1785. Wrecked 11.1798.

MARGATE Sloop 14, 162bm, 77 × 22·5ft. Deptford 1709. Sold 1712.

MARGATE (ex=GUILLAUME TELL) 6th Rate 24, 438bm, 108 × 31ft, 22–9pdr, 2–4pdr. French privateer, captured 27.10.1746. Sold 7.9.1749.

MARGETT *See JERSEY 1694.*

MARGUERITE Sloop, 'Arabis' class. Dunlop Bremmer 23.11.1915. RAN 1919; dismantled 9.1932; sunk 1.8.1935 target.

MARGUERITE Corvette, 'Flower' class. Hall Russell 8.7.1940. = *Weather Observer* 1947. BU 9.1961.

MARIA 6-gun vessel, 68bm. Built 1626. Condemned 1644.

MARIA Discovery vessel, 70bm. Exploring Hudson Bay 1631.

MARIA Schooner 6 (Canadian lakes). In service 1776.

MARIA Cutter tender 10. In service 1806–12.

MARIA Gun-brig 14, 172bm. Purch. 1807. Captured 29.9.1808 by French LANDES off Guadeloupe.

MARIA Brig 16. In service 1812–15.

MARIA DE LORETO Ship, 800bm. Genoese, seized 1512. Released 1514.

MARIA PRIZE Store hulk, 120bm. Algerian, captured 1684. Sold 27.10.1690 Cadiz.

MARIA SANCTA 50-gun ship, 400bm. Dutch, captured 1665. Burnt by Dutch 13.6.1667 Chatham.

MARIA SANDWICH Carrack, 550bm. Captured 1416. Sold 10.9.1424.

MARIA SPAYNE Ship. Spanish, captured 24.8.1417. Listed 1450.

MARIANA (MARIANA PRIZE; ex-MARIANNE) 6th Rate 18, 202bm, 80·5 × 24ft. French, captured 27.1.1693 Sold 30.8.1698.

MARIANA (MARYANEE) Bomb vessel 4, 82bm. Purch. 4.1694. Sold 13.5.1698.

MARIANA Schooner 10. Spanish, captured 1805 by SWIFT. Listed 1806.

MARIANNE Storeship. Purch. 1788. Listed until 6.1793.

MARIANNE Gun-brig 12. French, captured 18.3.1799. Sold 9.1801.

MARIANNE Receiving ship, 490bm. Slaver, purch. 1858. Ordered for BU Kingston, Jamaica, 2.1864; BU 1867.

MARIE Brig 14, 136bm, 71 × 21·5ft. French, captured 21.11.1797 b JASON. = HALIFAX 16.1800. Listed until 1802.

MARIE (ex-CONSTANCE) Schooner 10, 130bm, 72 × 20ft, 12–12pdr carr., 2–4pdr. French, captured 21.6.1805 by CIRCE. Foundered 16.10.1807 West Indies.

MARIE ANTOINETTE (ex-CONVENTION NATIONALE) Schooner 10, 187bm, 85·5 × 23ft, 10–4pdr. French, captured 9.1793 by squadron off San Domingo. Taken into French West Indian port by mutineers 7.1797.

MARIGOLD 22-gun ship. Portuguese, captured 1650. Sold 1658.

MARIGOLD Hoy 3, 42bm. Portsmouth DY 1653. BU 1712.

MARIGOLD Fireship 4, 332bm. Purch. 1673. Lost 8.1673 in action.

MARIGOLD 4th Rate 44, 495bm. Algerian, captured 1677. Wrecked 1679.

MARIGOLD (ex-IVY) Sloop, 'Acacia' class. Bow McLachlan 27.5.1915 (renamed 1915). Sold 26.1.1920 = *Principe de Piamonte.*

MARIGOLD Corvette, 'Flower' class. Hall Russell 4.9.1940. Sunk 9.12.1942 Italian aircraft off Algiers.

MARIGOLD *See also MAGIC 1915.*

MARINER Gun-brig 12, 180bm, 80 × 23ft, 2–32pdr carr., 10–18pdr carr. Pitcher, Northfleet, 4.4.1801. Sold 29.9.1814.

MARINER Brig 16, 481bm, 105 × 33·5ft 4–32pdr, 12–32pdr carr. Pembroke Dock 19.10.1846. Sold 12.6.1865.

MARINER Composite screw sloop, 970 tons, 167 × 32ft, 8–5in. Devonport DY 23.6.1884. BDV 1903; salvage vessel 1917. Sold 2.1929 Hughes Bolckow, Blyth.

MARINER Minesweeper, 'Algerine' class. Port Arthur SY 9.5.1944. Tx Burmese Navy 18.4.1958 = YAN MYO AUNG; deleted 1982.

MARINER *See also JUNO 1844.*

MARJORAM Sloop, 'Anchusa' class. Greenock & Grangemouth 26.12.1917. To be = PRESIDENT (drillship) 1921 but wrecked 17.1.1921 Flintstone Head on passage Haulbowline to fit out; wreck sold 8.9.1921.

MARJORAM Corvette, 'Flower' class. Harland & Wolff, ordered 8.4.1940, cancelled 23.1.1941.

MARKSMAN Destroyer leader, 1,604 tons, 325 × 32ft, 4–4in, 4–TT. Hawthorn Leslie 28.4.1915. Sold 8.11.1921 Slough Trading Co.; BU Germany.

MARKSMAN Destroyer, 'M' class. Projected 1913, not ordered.

MARKSMAN *See also MAHRATTA 1942.*

MARLBOROUGH (ex-ST MICHAEL) 2nd Rate 96, 1,579bm. Renamed 18.12.1706, rebuilt. Reduced to 68 guns 1752. Foundered 29.11.1762 Atlantic. *See ST MICHAEL 1669.*

MARLBOROUGH 3rd Rate 74, 1,642bm, 169 × 47ft. Deptford 26.8.1767. Wrecked 4.11.1800 nr Belleisle.

MARLBOROUGH 3rd Rate 74, 1,754bm, 175·5 × 48·5ft. Barnard, Deptford, 22.6.1807. BU 7.1835.

MARLBOROUGH Screw 1st Rate 121 (ex-131), 4,000bm, 6,300 tons, 245 × 61ft, 1—110pdr, 16—8in, 6—70pdr, 10—40pdr, 88—32pdr. Portsmouth DY 31.7.1855. TS 1878; = VERNON II 3.1904. Sold 10.1924 A. Butcher; capsized 28.11.1924 off Osea I. under tow sbkrs.

MARLBOROUGH Battleship, 25,000 tons, 580 × 89·5ft, 10—13·5in, 12—6in. Devonport DY 24.11.1912. Sold 27.6.1932 Metal Industries, Rosyth.

MARLBOROUGH Frigate, 'Norfolk' class. Swan Hunter 21.1.1989.

MARLINGFORD Seaward defence boat, 'Ford' class. Yarwood, Northwich, 17.6.1954. Sold Pounds 8.9.1967.

MARLION Pinnace, 40bm. French, captured 1545. Listed until 1549.

MARLION *See also MORSEBY 1915.*

MARLOW Minesweeper, Later 'Hunt' class. Harkess, Middlesbrough, 7.8.1918. Sold 21.4.1928 Alloa S. Bkg Co.; BU Charlestown.

MARMION Destroyer, 'M' class. Swan Hunter 28.5.1915. Sunk 21.10.1917 collision destroyer TIRADE off Lerwick.

MARMION Minesweeper, 'Algerine' class. Harland & Wolff, cancelled 4.1943,

MARMION (ex-ORANGEVILLE) Minesweeper, 'Algerine' class. Port Arthur SY 15.6.1944 (renamed 1943). BU 8.1959 Clayton & Davie, Dunston.

MARNE Destroyer, 'M' class. John Brown 29.5.1915. Sold 29.9.1921 G. Cohen; BU Germany.

MARNE Destroyer, 1,920 tons, 362·5 (oa) × 37ft, 6—4·7in, 8—TT. Vickers Armstrong, Tyne, 30.10.1940. Sold 26.3.1958 Turkish Navy = MARSEAL FEVSI CAKMAK; discarded 1970.

MAROON Tender, 24 tons, 50 × 12ft. Tx 1907 from War Dept. Sold 1907 in Jamaica.

MARQUISE DE SEIGNELAY Sloop 14, 232bm, 97 × 26ft. French privateer, captured 10.12.1780 by PORTLAND and SOLEBAY. Sold 23.3.1786.

MARS 50-gun ship, 396bm. Dutch, captured 1665. Sold 1667.

MARS 3rd Rate 64, 1,374bm, 160 × 45ft, 26—24pdr, 28—12pdr, 10—6pdr. French, captured 10.1746 by NOTTINGHAM off Cape Clear. Wrecked 6.1755 nr Halifax, NS.

MARS 3rd Rate 74, 1,55bm, 165·5 × 46·5ft. Woolwich DY 15.3.1759. Harbour service 1778. Sold 17.8.1784.

MARS 5th Rate 32, 703bm, 130·5 × 35ft. Dutch, captured 3.2.1781 West Indies. Sold 25.3.1784.

MARS 3rd Rate 74, 1,842bm, 176 × 49ft. Deptford DY 25.10.1794. BU 10.1823.

MARS 2nd Rate 80, 2,576bm, 3,482 tons, 190 × 56·5ft, 12—8in, 68—32pdr. Chatham DY 1.7.1848; undocked 23.11.1855 as screw ship; lent 13.5.1869 as TS. Sold 10.6.1929 Ward. *Nine years on stocks.*

MARS Battleship, 14,900 tons, 390 × 75ft, 4—12in, 12—6in, 18—12pdr. Laird 3.3.1896. Sold 9.5.1921 Ward; BU Swansea 11.1921, Briton Ferry 8.1925.

MARS Cruiser, 9,000 tons, Projected 1944, cancelled 3.1946.

MARS (ex-ELTHALION) Aircraft carrier, 13,190 tons. Vickers Armstrong, Barrow 20.5.1944 (renamed 1942). Maintenance carrier = PIONEER 7.1944. Arr. 9.1954 Ward, Inverkeithing, for BU.

MARSHAL NEY (ex-M.13) Monitor, 6,670 tons, 340 × 90ft, 2—15in, 8—4in, 2—12pdr. Palmer 17.6.1915. = VIVID (base ship) 6.1922; = DRAKE 1.1.1934; = ALAUNIA II 1947. Arr. 6.10.1957 Ward, Milford Haven, for BU.

MARSHAL SOULT (ex-M.14) Monitor, 6,400 tons, 355·75 (oa) × 90·25ft, 2—15in, 8—4in, 2—12pdr. Palmer 24.8.1915. Depot ship 1940. Arr. 8.1946 Troon for BU.

MARSOUIN Sloop 16, c. 320bm. French, captured 11.3.1795 by BEAULIEU at Guadeloupe. Listed until 1798.

MARSTON MOOR 54-gun ship, 734bm, 139 × 34·5ft. Johnson, Blackwall, 1654. = YORK 1660. Wrecked 23.11.1703 The Shipwash.

MARTHA & MARY Gunboat. Purch. 5.1797. *Fate unknown.*

MARTIAL Gun-brig 12, 183bm, 84·5 × 22ft, 10—18pdr carr., 2—9pdr. Ross, Rochchester, 17.4.1805. Fishery protection vessel 6.1826; hulked 4.1831. Sold 21.1.1836.

MARTIAL Destroyer, 'M' class. Swan Hunter 1.7.1915. Sold 9.5.1921 Ward, Briton Ferry; arr. 11.1922 for BU.

MARTIN Ship. Captured 1651. Sold 1653.

MARTIN Ship 12, 127bm. Portsmouth 1652. Sold 1667.

MARTIN Ketch 10, 103bm. Parker, Southampton, 24.12.1694. Captured 30.8.1702 by three French privateers off Jersey.

MARTIN Sloop 14, 289bm, 97 × 26ft. Randall, Rotherhithe, 7.2.1761. Sold 1.7.1784.

MARTIN Sloop 16, 329bm, 101 × 27ft. Woolwich DY 8.10.1790. Foundered 10.1800 North Sea.

MARTIN Sloop 18, 367bm, 106 × 28ft. Tanner, Dartmouth, 1.1.1805. Foundered 1806 Atlantic.

MARTIN Sloop 18, 399bm, 100 × 30ft, 16—24pdr carr., 2—9pdr. Bermuda 5.1809. Wrecked 8.12.1817 west coast of Ireland.

MARTIN Sloop 18, 461bm, 108·5 × 29ft. Portsmouth DY 18.5.1821. Foundered 2.1826 off The Cape.

MARTIN Brig 16, 481bm, 105 × 33·5ft, 41—32pdr, 12—pdr carr. Pembroke Dock 19.9.1850. Training brig = KINGFISHER 2.5.1890. Sold 2.10.1907 Collins, Dartmouth.

MARTIN (ex-MAYFLOWER) Training brig 508bm, 6—12pdr. Pembroke Dock 20.1.1890 (renamed 4.1888). Coal hulk = C.23 15.11.1907.

MARTIN Destroyer, 730 tons, 240 × 25ft, 2—4in, 2—12pdr, 2—TT. Thornycroft, Woolston, 15.12.1910. Sold 21.8.1920 Agius Bros, Malta.

MARTIN Destroyer, 1,920 tons, 362·5 (oa) × 37ft, 6—4·7in, 8—TT. Vickers Armstrong, Tyne, 12.12.1940. Sunk 10.11.1942 by U.431 off Algiers.

MARTIN GARCIA Ship. Purch. 7.1470. Listed until 1485.

MARVEL Destroyer, 'M' class. Denny 7.10.1915. Sold 9.5.1921 Ward, Hayle.

MARVEL Minesweeper, 'Algerine' class. Redfern, Toronto, 30.8.1944. Arr. 7.5.1958 Charlestown for BU.

MARY Cinque Ports ship. 1350.

MARY Ship, 120bm. From 1400. Given away 7.1423.

MARY Ship, 120bm. From 1413. Lost 5.1426

MARY Ketch. 1648. Royalist, captured 1649 by Parliamentarians. Not listed thereafter.

MARY Yacht 8, 92bm, 67 × 18·5ft, 8—3pdr. Presented by the Dutch 1660. Wrecked 25.3.1675 Skerries. *First royal yacht in RN.*

MARY Fireship 4, 111bm. Purch. 1666. Sold 1667.

MARY Fireship 4, 108bm. Purch. 1667. Expended 1667.

MARY Ketch 10. Origin unknown. Foundered 19.2.1694 off Gibraltar.

MARY Smack 4, 38bm, 43 × 15ft. Plymouth DY 1702. Rebuilt Plymouth 1728 as 52bm. Lost 3.10.1778 Plymouth Sound.

MARY 3rd Rate 64, 914bm, 145 × 37·5ft. Chatham DY 12.5.1704. Rebuilt as 1,068bm = PRINCESS MARY 26.7.1728. BU 1.1736.

MARY Yacht 8, 155bm. Chatham DY 1677. Rebuilt 1727 as 164bm; rebuilt 1761. BU 4.1816.

MARY Gunvessel 3, 61bm, 54·5 × 16ft. Purch. 3.1794. Sold 10.1798.

MARY Tender 6 purch. 1797. Listed 1805.

MARY Schooner 3 (Canadian lakes). Listed 1812. Captured 1813 by Americans.

MARY Coastguard cutter 30bm. White, Cowes, 1867. Sold 4.4.1905 Chatham.

MARY *See also SPEAKER 1649.*

MARY & JOHN Ship, 180bm. Purch. 1487. Rebuilt 1512. Listed until 1528.

MARY ANN Bomb vessel 4, 82bm. Purch. 4.1694. Sold 13.5.1698.

MARY ANTRIM 14-gun ship. Irish Royalist, captured 1644 by Parliamentarians. = TIGER'S WHELP 1649, lost.

MARY BRETON Ship. Captured from French 1415; recaptured 1421.

MARY FLYBOAT 500-ton ship. Captured 1650. Sold 1657.

MARY FORTUNE 80-ton ship. Portsmouth 1497. Rebuilt 1512 = SWALLOW. Listed until 1527.

MARY GALLEY 5th Rate 32, 462bm, 177 × 29·5ft. Deane, Rotherhithe, 1687. 'Great repair' Deptford 1708 as 536bm; rebuilt Plymouth 1727 as 594bm, 124 × 33·5ft. BU comp. 1.6.1743 Deptford.

MARY GALLEY 5th Rate 44, 716bm, 126 × 36·5ft. Bird, Rotherhithe, 16.6.1744. Sunk 4.1764 breakwater.

MARY GEORGE Ship, 240bm. Purch. 1512. Listed 1526.

MARY GLORIA Ship, 300bm. Purch. 1517. Listed 1522.

MARY GRACE Hoy, 90bm. Captured 1522. Listed until 1525.

MARY GRACE Ship. Purch. 12.1468. Listed until 1480

MARY GRACE Storeship, 100bm. Captured 1560. Listed until 1562.

MARY GUILDFORD Ship, 160bm. Listed 1524–39.

MARY HAMBORO 70-gun ship, 400bm. Purch. 1544 Hamburg. Sold 1555.

MARY HAMPTON Carrack. Genoese, captured 15.8.1416. Foundered 13.7.1420.

MARY IMPERIAL Ship, 100bm. Listed 1513–25.

MARY JAMES Ship, 260bm. Purch. 1512. Listed until 1529.

MARY JAMES Ship, 120bm. Captured 1545. Listed until 1546.

MARY NORWELL Ship, 80bm. Listed 1549.

MARY ODIERNE 70-ton vessel. Captured 1545. *Fate unknown.*

MARY OF ROUEN Ship. Captured 1626. Listed until 1627.

MARY PRIZE 36-gun ship. Captured 1649. Listed 1655.

MARY PRIZE Ship 14, 109bm. Spanish, captured 1654. Captured by Dutch 1666.

MARY PRIZE Fireship 4, 106bm. Dutch merchantman, captured 1666. Lost at sea 1666.

MARY ROSE 60-gun ship, 500bm. Built Portsmouth 1509, rebuilt 1536 as 700bm. Capsized 20.7.1545 in action with French off I. of Wight. Raised 11.10.1982 for preservation.

MARY ROSE Galleon 39, 600bm, 4—34pdr, 11—18pdr, 10—9pdr, 14 smaller. Built 1556; rebuilt 1589 as 495bm. Condemned; used 1618 as part of wharf at Chatham.

MARY ROSE 26-gun ship, 300bm. Deptford 1623. Wrecked 1650 off Flanders coast.

MARY ROSE 32-gun ship. In service 1650–54. *Hired?*

MARY ROSE (ex-MARIA ROSE) Gun-brig 4. French, captured 18.3.1799 off Acre. Sold 1801.

MARY ROSE Destroyer, 'M' class. Swan Hunter 8.10.1915. Sunk 17.10.1917 German cruisers North Sea.

MARY ROSE Tender. Purch. 1918. Sold 4.1922 W. Warren.

MARY ROSE (ex-TORONTO) Minesweeper, 'Algerine' class. Redfern 5.8.1943 (renamed 1943). Arr. 14.11.1957 Dorkin, Gateshead, for BU.

MARY ROSE *See also MAIDSTONE 1654.*

MARY THOMAS Ship, 100bm. Captured 1545. Listed until 1546.

MARY WILLOUGHBY Ship, 140bm. Listed 1535. Captured 1536 by the Scots; recaptured 1547; rebuilt 1551 as 160bm. Sold 1573.

MARYANEE *See MARIANA 1694.*

MARYBOROUGH Minesweeper, 'Bathurst' class. Walker 17.10.1940. Lent RAN 6.1941. Sold 9.5.1947 = *Isobel Queen.*

MARYPORT *See MISTLEY 1918.*

MARYTON Coastal minesweeper, 'Ton' class. Montrose SY 3.4.1958. Sold S. Bkg. (Queenborough) 28.7.1969 for BU.

MASHONA Destroyer, 1,870 tons, 377 (oa) × 36·5ft, 8—4·7in, 4—TT. Swan Hunter 3.9.1937. Sunk 28.5.1941 air attack south-west of Ireland.

MASON Cutter. Listed 1817. Sold 22.4.1817.

MASTIFF (Gunboat No 35, ex-*Herald*) Gunvessel 12, 136bm, 72 × 23ft, 2—32pdr carr., 10—18pdr carr. Purch. 3.1797 Leith. Wrecked 5.1.1800 Yarmouth Roads.

MASTIFF Gun-brig 12, 184bm, 84 × 22·5ft, 10—18pdr carr., 2—6pdr. Taylor, Bideford, 25.9.1813. Survey vessel 8.1825. BU 5.1.1851.

MASTIFF Mortar vessel, 117bm, 65 × 20·5ft, 1—13in mortar. Mare, Blackwall, 5.5.1855. = MV.7 on 19.10.1955; Coastguard watchvessel = WV.37 in 11.1864. BU 9.1875 Chatham.

MASTIFF (ex-HOUND) Wood screw gunboat, 'Albacore' class. Briggs, Sunderland, 22.2.1856 (renamed 1855). BU 10.1863 Deptford.

MASTIFF Iron screw gunboat, 'Ant' class. Armstrong Mitchell 4.4.1871. = SNAPPER 1914. Sold 28.11.1931 sbkrs R. Thames.

MASTIFF Destroyer, 'M' class. Thornycroft 5.9.1914. Sold 9.5.1921 Ward, Briton Ferry.

MATABELE Destroyer, 1,870 tons, 377 (oa) × 36·5ft, 8—4·7in, 4—TT. Scotts 6.10.1937. Sunk 17.1.1942 by U.454 Barents Sea.

MATANE (ex-STORMONT) Frigate (RCN), 'River' class. Vickers, Montreal, 29.5.1943 (renamed 1942). Sold 13.12.1947 for BU; hull sunk 1948 breakwater Oyster Bay.

MATAPAN Destroyer, 2,380 tons, 379 (oa) × 40·5ft, 5—4·5in, 8—40mm, 10—TT. John Brown 30.4.1945. Sold H. K. Vickers 18.5.1979; BU Blyth.

MATAPEDIA Corvette (RCN), 'Flower' class. Morton 14.9.1940. Sold 30.8.1946. BU 12.1950 Steel Co. of Canada, Hamilton, Ontario.

MATCHLESS Destroyer, 'M' class, 1,010 tons. Swan Hunter 5.10.1914. Sold 26.10.1921 Barking S. Bkg Co.

MATCHLESS Destroyer, 1,920 tons, 362·5 (oa) × 37ft, 6—4·7in, 8—TT. Stephen 4.9.1941. Tx Turkish Navy 16.7.1959 = KILICALA PASHA; discarded 1970.

MATHIAS 48-gun ship, 588bm. Dutch, captured 1653. Blown up 12.6.1667 by Dutch at Chatham.

MATILDA (ex-JACOBIN) 6th Rate 28, 573bm, 120 × 33ft. French, captured 30.10.1794 by squadron in West Indies. Hospital ship by 1805. BU 8.1810.

MATILDA (ex-MATHILDE) Schooner 10. French privateer, captured 3.7.1805 by CAMBRIAN. Listed 1805.

MATTHEW Discovery vessel. 1497. *Cabot's vessel.*

MATTHEW Ship, 600bm. Purch. 1539. Listed until 1554.

MAURITIUS Cruiser, 8,000 tons, 555·5 (oa) × 62ft, 12—6in, 6—4in. Swan Hunter 19.7.1939. Arr. 27.3.1965 Ward, Inverkeithing, for BU.

MAVOURNEEN Schooner yacht, 160 tons. Purch. 9.7.1900. Sold 7.1912.

MAWDELYN *See MAGDALEN 1522.*

MAXTON Coastal minesweeper, 'Ton' class. Harland & Wolff 24.5.1956. Towed Francisco Martasa, El Ferrol 17.4.1989 for BU.

MAY FRERE Wood paddle despatch vessel (Indian), 450bm, 168 × 20ft. Bombay DY 1864. *Fate unknown.*

MAYFLOWER (ex-FAME) 20-gun ship. Royalist, captured 1649 by Parliamentarians. Blown up 1658.

MAYFLOWER 20-gun ship. Purch. 1651. Sold 1658.

MAYFLOWER Firevessel, 20bm. Purch. 1694. Sold 17.2.1696.

MAYFLOWER Fireship, 109bm. Hired 27.6.1695, purch. 7.1695. Expended 1.8.1695 Dunkirk.

MAYFLOWER Gunvessel 3, 90bm, 64·5 × 19ft. Purch. 3.1794. Dockyard mudboat 9.1799.

MAYFLOWER Wood screw gunboat, 'Albacore' class. Pitcher, Northfleet, 31.1.1856. BU 8.1867 Sheerness.

MAYFLOWER Corvette, 'Flower' class. Vickers, Montreal, 3.7.1940. BU 1950 Charlestown.

MAYFLOWER *See also MARTIN 1890.*

MAYFLY Torpedo boat, 225 tons, 2—12pdr, 3—TT. Yarrow 29.1.1907. = TB.11 in 1906. Sunk 7.3.1916 mine North Sea.

MAYFLY River gunboat, 'Fly' class. Yarrow 1915 in sections. Lent 1.1918 War Dept. Sold 1.3.1923 Basra.

MAYFORD Seaward defence boat, 'Ford' class. Richards, Lowestoft, 30.9.1954. Sold 28.8.1968 Wessex Power Boats.

MAYO Troopship (RIM), 1,125 tons. Built 1896. Listed 1920.

MAZURKA Minesweeper, 265 tons, 130 × 26ft, 1—2pdr. Murdoch & Murray 13.10.1917 for War Dept; tx. Sold 1.5.1920 Crichton Thompson & Co.

MEADOWSWEET Corvette, 'Flower' class. Hill, Bristol, 28.3.1942. Sold 31.3.1951 = *Gerrit W. Vinke.*

MEAFORD Corvette (RCN), Modified 'Flower' class. Midland SY, cancelled 12.1943.

MECKLENBURGH Cutter. Purch. 1.1763. Sold 1.1768.

MECKLENBURGH Gunvessel. Purch. 1768. Sunk 9.1773 breakwater Sheerness.

MEDA Survey schooner, 150bm. Westacott, Barnstaple, 2.1880, purch. Sold 1887 Western Australia Govt.

MEDA (ex-SDML.3552, ex-SDML.1301) Survey vessel, 72ft (oa). Blackmore, Bideford 8.1.1943; named 1949. Sold 25.5.1966 private individual Gibraltar.

MEDEA (ex-MEDEE) 6th Rate 26. French, captured 4.4.1744 by DREADNOUGHT. Sold 3.1745; privateer = *Boscawen.*

MEDEA 6th Rate 28, 605bm, 120·5 × 33·5ft. Hilhouse, Bristol, 28.4.1778. Sold 1795.

MEDEA 5th Rate 32, 658bm, 127 × 34ft. Woolwich DY, ordered 1800, cancelled.

MEDEA Wood paddle sloop, 835bm, 180 × 32ft, 2—10in, 2—12pdr. Woolwich DY 2.9.1833. Sold 1867.

MEDEA 2nd class cruiser, 2,800 tons, 265 × 41ft, 6—6in, 9—6pdr. Chatham DY 9.6.1888. Sold 2.4.1914.

MEDEA (ex-KRITI) Destroyer, 1,007 tons, 265 × 27ft, 3—4in, 4—TT. John Brown 20.1.1915; Greek, purch. 8.1914. Sold 9.5.1921 Ward, Milford Haven; arr. 10.1922 for BU.

MEDEA *See also M.22 1919, CIRCE 1939.*

MEDEE 5th Rate 36, French, captured 5.8.1800 off Rio by two East Indiamen. Prison ship 1802. Sold 1805.

MEDIATOR Sloop 10, 105bm, 61·5 × 21ft, 10—4pdr. Purch. 4.1745. Captured 29.7.1745 by French privateer off Ostend.

MEDIATOR 5th Rate 44, 879bm, 140 × 37·5ft. Raymond, Northam, 30.3.1782. Storeship = CAMEL 3.3.1788. BU 12.1810.

MEDIATOR (ex-*Ann & Amelia*) 5th Rate 44, 689bm. Indiaman , purch. 6.1804. Fireship 1809. Expended 11.4.1809 Basque Roads.

MEDICINE HAT Minesweeper (RCN), TE 'Bangor' class, Vickers, Montreal, 26.6.1941. Sold 29.11.1957 Turkish Navy = BIGA; BU 1963.

MEDINA 6th Rate 20, 460bm, 116 × 30·5ft. Adams, Buckler's Hard, 13.8.1813. Sold 4.1.1832 Mr Ledger for BU.

MEDINA Wood paddle packet, 889bm, 176 × 33ft. Pembroke Dock 18.3.1840. BU 3.1864.

MEDINA Iron screw gunboat, 363 tons, 110 × 34ft, 3—64pdr. Palmer 3.8.1876. Sold 1904 Bermuda.

MEDINA (ex-REDMILL) Destroyer, 'M' class. White 8.3.1916 (renamed 1915). Sold 9.5.1921 Ward, Milford Haven.

MEDINA *See also PORTSMOUTH 1703.*

MEDITERRANEAN Sloop (xebec) 12, c. 200bm, 92·5 × 21ft, 2—6pdr, 10—3pdr. Captured 1756 Mediterranean. Listed 1757.

MEDORA *See MEDWAY 1916.*

MEDUSA 4th Rate 50, 910bm, 140·5 × 38·5ft. Plymouth DY 23.7.1785. Wrecked 26.11.1798 coast of Portugal.

MEDUSA 5th Rate 32, 920bm, 144 × 37·5ft. Pitcher, Northfleet, 14.4.1801. BU 11.1816.

MEDUSA 5th Rate 46, 1,063bm, 150 × 40·5ft. Woolwich DY, ordered 18.7.1817, re-ordered Pembroke Dock 7.8.1830, cancelled 22.4.1831.

MEDUSA Wood paddle packet, 889bm, 175 × 33ft. Pembroke Dock 31.10.1838. Sold 17.2.1872 Castle, Charlton.

MEDUSA Iron paddle gunboat (Indian), 432bm. Laird 1839. Wrecked 9.12.1853 coast of Bengal.

MEDUSA 2nd class cruiser, 2,800 tons, 265 × 41ft, 6—6in, 9—6pdr. Chatham DY 11.8.1888. Harbour service 1910. Sold 1920 Stanlee; resold 21.10.1921 J. E. Thomas.

MEDUSA (ex-LESVOS) Destroyer, 1,007 tons, 265 × 27ft, 3—4in, 4—TT. John Brown 27.3.1915; Greek, purch. 8.1914. Sunk 25.3.1916 collision destroyer LAVEROCK off Schleswig coast.

MEDUSA (ex-SDML.3516, ex-FDB.76, ex-ML.1387) Survey vessel, 72ft (oa). Newman & Son, Hamworthy, Poole, 20.11.1943. Named 1.1.1961. PO 11.1965; sold 29.5.1968.

MEDUSA *See also M.29 1915.*

MEDWAY 4th Rate 60, 914bm, 145.5 × 38ft. Sheerness DY 20.9.1693. Rebuilt Deptford 1718. Hulk 1740; beached 18.11.1748 as sheer hulk Portsmouth. BU 10.1749 Portsmouth.

MEDWAY 4th Rate 60, 1,080bm, 144 × 41.5ft. Bird, Rotherhithe. *Probably re-ordered as the following ship.*

MEDWAY 4th Rate 60 × 1,204bm, 149.5 × 43ft. Deptford DY 14.2.1755. Receiving ship 6.1787; = ARUNDEL 1802. BU 3.1811.

MEDWAY Storeship (busse) 6, 83bm, 65 × 17ft, 6—4pdr. Purch. 10.11.1756. Dockyard craft 2.1760. Sold 17.4.1764.

MEDWAY 3rd Rate 74, 1,768bm, 176 × 49ft. Pitcher, Northfleet, 19.11.1812. Convict ship 10.1847. Sold 2.11.1865 in Bermuda.

MEDWAY Iron screw gunboat, 363 tons, 110 × 34ft, 3—64pdr. Palmer 3.10.1876. Sold 1904 in Bermuda.

MEDWAY (ex-MEDORA, ex-REDWING) Destroyer, 'M' class. White 19.4.1916 (renamed 1916, 1915). Sold 9.5.1921 Ward, Milford Haven.

MEDWAY Depot ship, 14,650 tons, 545 × 85ft, 6—4in. Vickers Armstrong, Barrow, 19.7.1928. Sunk 30.6.1942 by U.372 off Alexandra.

MEDWAY (ex-MRC.1109, ex-LCT.1109) Depot ship, 200 tons. Renamed 12.1959. Sold 1970 Singapore.

MEDWAY *See also BAGSHOT 1918.*

MEDWAY II *See M.29 1919.*

MEDWAY PRIZE 4th Rate 48, 500bm, 117 × 34ft. French, captured 20.8.1697 by MEDWAY. Hulk 1699. Sunk 1712 foundation Sheerness.

MEDWAY PRIZE 6th Rate 28, 241bm, 92 × 25ft. French, captured 6.9.1704 by MEDWAY. Sold 1713 in Jamaica.

MEDWAY PRIZE (ex-FAVORETTE [?]) 5th Rate 744bm, 128 × 36ft. French, captured 1.1744 East Indies. Sold 13.2.1749.

MEEANEE (ex-MADRAS) 2nd Rate 80, 2,591bm, 190 × 57ft, 12—8in, 68—32pdr. Bombay DY

11.11.1848; undocked 31.10.1857 as screw ship, 60 guns (renamed 19.2.1843). Lent War Dept 5.3.1867 as hospital ship. BU 1906.

MEERMIN (ex-MIERMIN) Brig-sloop 16, 203bm, 74.5 × 26ft, 16—6pdr. Dutch, seized 4.3.1796 Plymouth. Sold 1801.

MEGAERA Fireship 14, 425bm, 109 × 30ft. Teague, Ipswich, 5.1783. Sold 3.4.1817 J. Darkin.

MEGAERA Wood paddle sloop, 717bm, 150 × 32.5ft, 2—9pdr. Sheerness DY 17.8.1837. Wrecked 4.3.1843 coast of Jamaica.

MEGAERA Iron screw frigate, 1,391bm, 207 × 31.5ft. Fairbairn, Millwall, 22.5.1849. Troopship 1855. Beached 16.6.1871 St Paul's I., Indian Ocean, unseaworthy.

MELAMPE 5th Rate 36, 747bm, 134.5 × 35.5ft. French, captured 2.11.1757 by TARTAR. Beached 1764 Antigua.

MELAMPUS 5th Rate 36, 947bm, 141 × 39ft. Hillhouse, Bristol, 8.6.1785. Sold 6.1815 Dutch Navy.

MELAMPUS 5th Rate 46, 1,089bm, 152 × 40.5ft. Pembroke Dock 10.8.1820. Harbour service 1854; lent War Dept 8.8—10.91. Sold 3.4.1906 Harris, Bristol.

MELAMPUS 2nd class cruiser, 3,400 tons, 300 × 43ft, 2—6in, 6—4.7in, 8—6pdr. Vickers 2.8.1890. Sold 14.7.1910 Cohen, Felixstowe.

MELAMPUS (ex-CHIOS) Destroyer, 1,040 tons, 265 × 27ft, 3—4in, 4—TT. Fairfield 16.12.1914; Greek, purch. 8.1914. Sold 22.9.1921 Cohen; BU Germany.

MELBOURNE 2nd class cruiser (RAN), 5,440 tons, 430 × 50ft, 8—6in. Cammell Laird 30.5.1912. Sold 8.12.1928 Alloa S. Bkg Co., Rosyth.

MELBOURNE Frigate (RAN), 'Adelaide' class. Australian Marine Engineering, Williamstown, 5.5.1989.

MELBOURNE *See also MAJESTIC 1945.*

MELBREAK Destroyer, 'Hunt' class Type III. Swan Hunter 5.3.1942. Arr. 22.11.1956 Ward, Grays, for BU.

MELEAGER 5th Rate 32, 682bm, 126 × 35ft, Graves, Frindsbury, 28.2.1785. Wrecked 9.6.1801 Gulf of Mexico.

MELEAGER 5th Rate 36, 875bm, 137 × 38ft. Chatham DY 25.11.1806. Wrecked 30.7.1808 Bare Bush Cay, Jamaica.

MELITA Composite screw sloop, 970 tons, 167 × 32ft, 8—5in. Malta DY 20.3.1888. = BDV 5.1905; = RINGDOVE (salvage vessel) 12.1915. Sold 9.7.1920 Falmouth Docks Board.

MELITA Minesweeper, 'Algerine' class. Redfern,

Toronto, 8.12.1942. = SATELLITE (drillship) 4.1947–1951. Arr. 25.2.1959 Rees, Llanelly, for BU.

MELITA *See also RINGDOVE 1889.*

MELPOMENE 5th Rate 38, 1,014bm, 148 × 39ft. French, captured 10.8.1794 Calvi. Sold 14.12.1815.

MELPOMENE 5th Rate 38, 1,087bm, 153 × 40ft. French, captured 30.4.1815 by RIVOLI off Ischia. Sold 7.6.1821.

MELPOMENE Wood screw frigate, 2,861bm, 237 × 52ft. Pembroke Dock 8.8.1857; ex-4th Rate, 2,147bm. Sold 23.1.1875 Castle, Charlton. *Eight years on stocks.*

MELPOMENE 2nd class cruiser, 2,950 tons, 265 × 42ft, 6–6in, 9–6pdr. Portsmouth DY 20.9.1888. Sold 11.8.1905 Ward, Preston.

MELPOMENE (ex-SAMOS) Destroyer, 1,040 tons, 265 × 26·5ft, 3–4in, 4–TT. Fairfield 1.2.1915; Greek, purch. 8.1914. Sold 9.5.1921 Ward, New Holland.

MELPOMENE *See also INDEFATIGABLE 1891, M.31 1919, LA MELPOMENE 1940.*

MELTON Paddle minesweeper, 'Ascot' class. Hamilton 16.3.1916. Sold 25.11.1927 Hughes Bolckow; resold 2.1928 = *Queen of Thanet.* Hired as minesweeper 1939.

MELTON Tender, 143 tons, 80 (oa) × 21ft. Dunston 6.3.1981.

MELVILLE (ex-NAIADE) Brig-sloop 18, 353bm. French, captured 16.10.1805 by JASON in West Indies. Sold 3.11.1808.

MELVILLE (LORD MELVILLE) Brig 14 (Canadian lakes), 186bm, 73 × 24·5ft. Kingston, Ontario, 20.7.1813. = STAR 22.1.1814. Sold 1837.

MELVILLE 3rd Rate 74, 1,768bm 176·5 × 49ft. Bombay DY 17.2.1817. Hospital ship 3.1857. Sold 1873 in Hong Kong.

MELVILLE Minesweeper (RCN), diesel 'Bangor' class. Davie SB 7.6.1941. Tx RCMP 1950 = *Cygnus.* BU 1961.

MELVILLE Inshore minesweeper (RAN), 178 tons, 101·7 (oa) × 29·5ft, 2–12·7mm. Projected 1987.

MELVILLE Survey vessel (RAN), 2,170tons, 233·6 (oa) × 49·9ft. North Queensland Engineering and Agents, Cairns, 23.6.1998.

MEMNON Paddle sloop (Indian), 1,140bm, 2–64pdr, 4–32pdr. Fletcher, Limehouse, 1841. Wrecked 4.8.1843 nr Cape Guardafui.

MENACE Destroyer, 'M' class. Swan Hunter 9.11.1915. Sold 9.5.1921 Ward, Grays; BU begun 8.2.24.

MENAI 6th Rate 26, 449bm, 108 × 31ft, 18–32pdr carr., 8–12pdr carr., 2–6pdr. Brindley, Frinds-

bury, 5.4.1814. Harbour service 1831; target 1851. BU 4.1853.

MENAI Wood screw corvette, 1,857bm, 225 × 43ft. Chatham DY, LD 5.1.1861, cancelled 16.12.1864. *Frames used for BLANCHE 1865.*

MENAI Tender, 128 tons. Dunston 15.5.1981.

MENDIP Destroyer, 'Hunt' class Type I. Swan Hunter 9.4.1940. Lent Chinese Navy 5.1948 = LIN FU. Sold 15.11.1949 Egyptian Navy = MOHAMED ALI EL KEBIR (1949), = IBRAHIM EL AWAL (1951). Captured by Israeli Navy 31.10.1956 = HAIFA (1.1957); hulk 1970–72; discarded 1972.

MENELAUS 5th Rate 38, 1,077bm, 154 × 40ft. Plymouth DY 17.4.1810. Quarantine hulk 1832; lent Customs 5.1854. Sold 10.5.1897 J. Read, Portsmouth.

MENELAUS *See also M.31 1915.*

MENTOR Armed ship 16. American, captured 1778. Burnt 8.5.1781 to avoid capture by Spanish at Pensacola.

MENTOR (ex-AURORA) Sloop 16. American, captured 1781. Wrecked 16.3.1783 off Bermuda.

MENTOR Destroyer, 'M' class, 1,053 tons. Hawthorn Leslie 21.8.1914. Sold 9.5.1921 Ward, Hayle; arr. 10.1922 for BU.

MENTOR Tender, 143 tons, 80 (oa) × 21ft. Dunston 7.10.1981. Sold Pounds 2.1992.

MEON Frigate, 'River' class. Inglis 4.8.1943. Arr. 14.5.1966 Hughes Bolckow, Blyth, for BU.

MEON Tender, 143 tons, 80 (oa) × 21ft. Dunston 13.5.1982.

MERCURE Sloop 14, 338bm, 103·5 × 27·5ft. French privateer, captured 31.8.1798 by PHAETON. = TROMPEUSE 1799. Foundered 17.5.1800 English Channel.

MERCURIUS Brig-sloop 16, 308bm, 94·5 × 27·5ft, 16–24pdr. Danish, captured 7.9.1807 Battle of Copenhagen. Sold 23.11.1815. *Was to have been renamed TRANSFER.*

MERCURY Galley 6, 80bm, 1–18pdr, 1–6pdr, 4 smaller. Deptford 1592. Sold 1611.

MERCURY Ship, 300bm. R. Thames 16.10.1620. *Fate unknown.*

MERCURY Ship. Purch. 31.8.1622. *Fate unknown.*

MERCURY Advice boat 6, 78bm, 61·5 × 16ft. Portsmouth 3.1694. Captured 19.6.1697 by French privateer off Ushant.

MERCURY Fireship 8, 217bm, 90 × 24ft. Purch. 22.6.1739. Foundered 12.1744.

MERCURY Brigantine, 16–6pdr. Purch. 1744. Captured 1745 by French.

MERCURY 6th Rate 24, 504bm, 113 × 32ft.

Golightly, Liverpool, 13.10.1745. BU comp.
7.8.1753 Woolwich.

MERCURY 6th Rate 20, 433bm, 108 × 30ft.
Barnard, Harwich, 2.3.1756. Wrecked 24.12.1777
off New York.

MERCURY 6th Rate 28, 594bm, 121 × 34ft.
Mestears, R. Thames, 9.12.1779. BU 1.1814
Woolwich.

MERCURY Brig 14 (Indian), 185bm. Bombay DY
1806. Coal hulk by 1865.

MERCURY Tender, 50bm. Rotherhithe 1807. BU
10.1835.

MERCURY 5th Rate 46, 1,084bm, 152 × 40·5ft.
Chatham DY 16.11.1826. Coal hulk 1861. Sold
3.4.1906 Harris, Bristol.

MERCURY Cutter tender, 70bm, 54 × 18ft.
Chatham DY 7.2.1837. = YC.6 (yard craft) 1866,
= PLYMOUTH 8.2.1876. Sold 17.5.1904.

MERCURY Despatch vessel (2nd class cruiser)
3,730 tons, 300 × 46ft, 10—64pdr. Pembroke
Dock 17.4.1878. Depot ship 1906. Sold 9.7.1919
Forth S. Bkg Co., Bo'ness. *Was to have been
renamed COLUMBINE 1912.*

MERCURY (ex-*Illova*) TS 398grt, 139 × 27ft.
Barque, purch. 1887. Sold 1916 coal hulk.

MERCURY *See also GANNET 1878.*

MEREDITH Cutter 10, 83bm, 54·5 × 19·5ft. Purch.
3.1763. Sold 1.7.1784.

MERHONOUR 41-gun ship, 709bm, 4—34pdr,
15—18pdr, 16—9pdr, 4—6pdr, 2 small. Woolwich
1590. Rebuilt Woolwich 1615. Sold 1650.

MERLIN Pinnace 10, 50bm. Built 1579; listed until
1601.

MERLIN Yacht 14, 129bm Chatham DY 1652. Captured 13.10.1665 by Dutch.

MERLIN Yacht 8, 109bm. Shish, Rotherhithe,
1666. Sold 30.8.1698.

MERLIN Sloop 2, 66bm, 59·5 × 16ft. Chatham DY
1699. Sold 1712.

MERLIN Sloop 14, 271bm, 92 × 26ft. Greville &
Whitstone, Limehouse, 1744. Sold 1750.

MERLIN Sloop 10. In service 1753.

MERLIN Sloop 10, 224bm. Quallett, Rotherhithe,
20.3.1756. Captured by French 19.4.1757; recaptured 9.1757 = ZEPHYR; captured again by
French 23.8.1778; recaptured again, burnt 1780.

MERLIN Sloop 10, 304bm, 100 × 26ft, 10—6pdr.
Randall, Rotherhithe, 1.7.1757, purch. on stocks.
Abandoned, burnt 23.10.1777 Delaware R.

MERLIN Sloop 18, 340bm, 101 × 28ft, 18—6pdr,
6—12pdr carr. King, Dover, 1780, purch. on
stocks. Sold 28.8.1795.

MERLIN Sloop 16, 371bm, 106 × 28ft. Dudman,
Deptford, 25.3.1796. BU 1.1803.

MERLIN (ex-*Hercules*) Sloop 16, 395bm, 104 ×
30·5ft, 10—32pdr carr., 4—24pdr carr. Purch.
7.1803. Sold 21.1.1836.

MERLIN Wood paddle packet, 889bm, 175 × 33ft.
Pembroke Dock 18.9.1838. Survey vessel 1854;
gunvessel 1856. Sold 18.5.1863 Williams & Co.

MERLIN Composite screw gunboat, 295bm, 430
tons, 125 × 23ft, 2—64pdr, 2—20pdr. Pembroke
Dock 24.11.1871. Sold 27.2.1891.

MERLIN Sloop, 1,070 tons, 185 × 33ft, 6—4in.
Sheerness DY 30.11.1901. Survey vessel 9.1906.
Sold 3.8.1923 in Hong Kong.

MERMAID Galley, 200bm. Captured 1545. Listed
until 1563.

MERMAID 24-gun ship, 309bm, 105 × 26ft.
Graves, Limehouse, 1651. Rebuilt Woolwich 1689
as 5th Rate 32, 343bm; rebuilt Chatham 1707 as
421bm. BU 6.1734.

MERMAID Fireship 8, 174bm, 78 × 23ft. French,
captured 8.11.1692. Burnt 25.2.1693 accident
Plymouth.

MERMAID 6th Rate 24, 533bm, 115 × 32ft.
Adams, Buckler's Hard, 22.5.1749. Wrecked
6.1.1760 Bahamas.

MERMAID 6th Rate 28, 613bm, 124 × 33·5ft.
Blaydes, Hull, 6.5.1761. Chased ashore 8.7.1778 by
French in Delaware Bay.

MERMAID 5th Rate 32, 693bm, 126 × 35·5ft.
Sheerness DY 29.11.1784 (LD Woolwich, tx
3.1782). BU 11.1815.

MERMAID Gunvessel 1. Purch. 1798 Honduras for
local use. Sold 1800.

MERMAID Survey cutter, 84bm, 56 × 18·5ft.
Purch. 1817 Port Jackson. Grounded 1820; sold
1823.

MERMAID 5th Rate 46, 1,085bm, 152 × 40·5ft.
Chatham DY 30.7.1825. Powder hulk 1850; lent
War Dept 8.5.1863. BU comp. 6.1875 Dublin.

MERMAID Coastguard vessel, 165bm, 88 × 21·5ft.
Purch. 1853. Sold 14.8.1890 Tough & Henderson.

MERMAID Destroyer, 370 tons, 210ft, 1—12pdr,
5—6pdr, 2—TT. Hawthorn 22.2.1898. Sold
23.7.1919 Ward, New Holland.

MERMAID Sloop, 1,350 tons, 299·5 (oa) × 38·5ft,
6—4in. Denny 11.11.1943. Tx West German Navy
5.5.1959 = SCHARNHORST; hulked 1974—89 for
damage control training; towed Zeebrugge
24.4.1990 for BU.

MERMAID (ex-BLACK STAR) Frigate, 2,300 tons.
Ghanaian, purch. 3.1972 from Yarrow. Sold
4.1977 Malaya = HANG TUAH.

MERMAID Survey vessel (RAN), 320 tons (full
load), 118·9 (oa) × 45·3ft. Elgo Engineering, Port
Adelaide, 9.5.1989.

MERMAID *See also RUBY 1708, KENNINGTON 1736, SULLINGTON 1954.*

MEROPE Brig-sloop 10, 252bm, 92 × 25·5ft. Chatham DY 25.6.1808. Sold 23.11.1815.

MERRITTONIA (ex-POINTE CLAIRE) Corvette (RCN), Modified 'Flower' class. Morton 24.6.1944 (renamed 3.1944). Wrecked 30.11.1945 coast of Nova Scotia.

MERRY HAMPTON Minesweeping sloop, '24' class. Blyth SB 19.12.1918. = HERALD (survey vessel) 2.1923. Scuttled 2.1942 Selatar; raised by Japanese, cd 10.1942 = HEIYO; mined 14.11.1944.

MERSEY 6th Rate 26, 451bm, 108·5 × 31ft, 18–32pdr carr., 8–12pdr carr., 2–6pdr. Courtney, Chester, 3.1814. Harbour service 1832. BU 7.1852.

MERSEY Wood screw frigate, 3,733bm, 300 × 52ft, 28–10in, 12–68pdr. Chatham DY 13.8.1858. Sold 23.1.1875 Castle, Charlton.

MERSEY 2nd class cruiser, 4,050 tons, 300 × 46, 2–8in, 10–6in, 3–6pdr. Chatham DY 31.3.1885. Sold 4.4.1905 Isaacs.

MERSEY (ex-MADURA) Gunboat, 1,260 tons, 265 × 49ft, 3–6in, 2–4·7in howitzers. Vickers 1.10.1913; Brazilian river monitor, purch. 8.8.1914. Sold 9.5.1921 Ward, Morecambe; BU 3.1923.

MERSEY Offshore patrol vessel, 1,677 tons, 261·7 (oa) × 44·6ft, 1–20mm, 2–MG. Vosper-Thornycroft. Due in service 11.2003.

MERSEY *Name borne in turn from 1949 by MMS.1075, AMERTON and POLLINGTON as RNVR tenders.*

MERSHAM Inshore minesweeper, 'Ham' class. Harris, Appledore, 5.4.1954. Tx 1955 French Navy = M.773/VIOLETTE; PO 3.1987.

MESSENGER Dogger 6. Dutch, captured 1672. Sold 1673.

MESSENGER Advice boat 6, 73bm. Plymouth 1694. Foundered 30.11.1701 Atlantic.

MESSENGER (ex-*Duke of York*) Wood paddle vessel, 733bm, 156 × 32·5ft. Purch. 20.8.1830. Sold 22.11.1861 Castle.

MESSINA Tender, 143 tons, 80 (oa) × 21ft. Dunston 5.3.1982. For sale 5.1995.

MESSINA *See also LST.3043 1945.*

METEOR (Gunboat No 34, ex-*Lady Cathcart*) Gunvessel 12, 154bm, 74·5 × 22ft, 2–24pdr, 10–18pdr carr. Purch. 3.1797 Leith. Sold 2.1802.

METEOR (ex-*Sarah Ann*) Bomb vessel 8, 364bm, 103 × 29ft, 8–24pdr carr., 1–13in mortar. Purch. 10.1803. Sold 28.5.1811.

METEOR Bomb vessel 8, 378bm, 106 × 29ft, 10–24pdr carr., 2–6pdr, 2 mortars. Pembroke Dock 25.6.1823. = BEACON (survey ship) 1832. Sold 8.1846 Malta.

METEOR Wood paddle vessel, 296bm, 126 × 23ft. Deptford DY 17.2.1824. BU 8.1849 Woolwich.

METEOR River gunboat (Indian), 149bm. Bombay DY 1839. *Fate unknown.*

METEOR Wood floating battery, 1,469bm, 172·5 × 44ft, 14–68pdr. Mare, Blackwall, 17.4.1855. BU 1861.

METEOR Destroyer, 'M' class, 1,070 tons. Thornycroft 24.7.1914. Sold 9.5.1921 Ward, Milford Haven; arr. 10.1922 for BU.

METEOR Destroyer, 1,920 tons, 362.5 (oa) × 37ft, 6–4·7in, 8–TT. Stephen 3.11.1941. HO 29.6.1959 Turkish Navy = PIYALE PASHA; listed until 1979.

METEOR *See also STAR 1805.*

METEORITE *See U.1407.*

MEYNELL Minesweeper, Early 'Hunt' class. Henderson 7.2.1917. Sold 4.11.1922 Lithgow.

MEYNELL Destroyer, 'Hunt' class Type I. Swan Hunter 7.6.1940. Sold 18.10.1954 Ecuadoran Navy, = PRESIDENTE VELASCO IBARRA 8.1955; stricken 5.5.1978.

MICHAEL Ship. Mentioned 1350.

MICHAEL Ship. Captured from Scots 1488. Listed until 1513.

MICHAEL Destroyer, 'M' class. Thornycroft 19.5.1915. Sold 22.9.1921. Cohen; BU Germany.

MICHAEL Minesweeper, 'Algerine' class. Redfern, Toronto, 20.1.1944. Arr. 15.11.1956 McLellan, Bo'ness, for BU.

MICKLEHAM Inshore minesweeper 'Ham' class. Berthon Boat Co. 11.3.1954. Sold 5.8.1966.

MICMAC Destroyer (RCN), 1,927 tons, 377 (oa) × 37·5ft, 6–4·7in, 2–4in 4–TT. Halifax SY 18.9.1943. Sold 1964 Marine Salvage Co.; resold, arr. 10.1964 Faslane for BU.

MIDDLESBROUGH *See KUMAON 1942.*

MIDDLESEX Minesweeper (RCN), 'Algerine' class. Port Arthur SY 27.5.1943. Wrecked 3.12.1946 Bald Island Point, nr Halifax, NS.

MIDDLETON Destroyer, 'Hunt' class Type II. Vickers Armstrong, Tyne, 12.5.1941. Hulked 1955; arr. 4.10.1957 Hughes Bolckow, Blyth, for BU.

MIDDLETON Minehunter, 615 tons. Yarrow 27.4.1983.

MIDGE Cargo vessel. Req. New Zealand 1863. Ret. to owner c. 1864.

MIDGE Wooden paddle gunboat, 209 tons. Limehouse 8.5.1856. BU 10.1864.

MIDGE Composite screw gunvessel, 1–7in, 1–64pdr, 2–20pdr. Elder 21.5.1868. PO 1890; hospital ship Hong Kong 11.1891; sold 1907.

MIDGE Torpedo boat (Queensland Maritime Defence Force), 11 tons, 2 torpedoes. White,

Cowes, 1887. Tx Commonwealth Naval Force; to RAN 1911. Sold 1912.

MIDGE Destroyer, 935 tons, 267·5 × 27ft, 3—4in, 2—TT. London & Glasgow Co. 22.5.1913. Sold 5.11.1921 Granton Sbkg Co.; BU 3.1922.

MIDLAND Corvette (RCN), 'Flower' class. Midland SY 25.6.1941. Sold 1946 Great Lakes Lumber Co.

MIGNONETTE Sloop, 'Arabis' class. Dunlop Bremner 26.1.1916. Sunk 17.3.1917 mine off Galley Head, south-west Ireland.

MIGNONETTE Corvette, 'Flower' class. Hall Russell 28.1.1941. Sold 1946 = *Alexandrouplis*.

MIGNONNE 5th Rate 32, 684bm. French, captured 10.8.1794 by Fleet at Calvi. Burnt 31.7.1797 Puerto Ferrajo useless.

MIGNONNE Sloop 16, 462bm. French, captured 28.6.1803 by GOLIATH at San Domingo. Damaged by grounding 1804; beached Port Royal, Jamaica.

MIGNONNE (ex-PHAETON) Brig-sloop 16, 329bm. French, captured 26.3.1806 by PIQUE in West Indies. = MUSETTE 1806. Sold 1.9.1814.

MILAN (ex-VILLE DE MILAN) 5th Rate 38, 1,097bm, 156 × 40ft. French, captured 23.2.1805 by LEANDER and CAMBRIDGE in Atlantic. BU 12.1815.

MILBROOK Schooner 16, 148bm, 93 × 21·5ft, 16—18pdr carr. Redbridge 1797. Gunvessel 3.1799. Wrecked 25.3.1808 The Burlings.

MILBROOK Destroyer, 'M' class. Thornycroft 12.7.1915. Sold 22.9.1921 Cohen; BU Germany.

MILBROOK Tender, 143 tons, 80 (oa) × 21ft. Dunston 16.12.1981. Sold Pounds 2.1992.

MILDURA (ex-PELORUS) 3rd class cruiser, 2,575 tons, 265 × 41ft, 8—4·7in, 8—3pdr. Armstrong 25.11.1889 (renamed 4.1890). Sold 3.4.1906 Garnham.

MILDURA Minesweeper (RAN), 'Bathurst' class. Mort's Dock, Sydney, 15.5.1941. Sold 9.1965 Brisbane Metal Co.

MILEHAM Inshore minesweeper, 'Ham' class. Blackmore, Bideford, 1.7.1954. Tx French Navy 1955 = M.783/HORTENSIA; deleted 11.1983.

MILFOIL Corvette, 'Flower' class. Morton, Quebec, 5.8.1942. Tx USN 31.3.1943 = INTENSITY.

MILFORD 5th Rate 32, 355bm, 105 × 27·5ft. Woolwich 18.3.1690. Captured 11.1693 by French in North Sea.

MILFORD 5th Rate 32, 385bm, 108 × 28·5ft. Hubbard, Ipswich, 6.3.1695. Captured 7.1.1697 by two French privateers in North Sea.

MILFORD 6th Rate 28, 589bm, 118 × 34ft. Chitty, Milford Haven, 20.9.1759. Sold 17.5.1785.

MILFORD 3rd Rate 78, 1,919bm, 181·5 × 50ft. Jacobs, Milford Haven, 1.4.1809. Harbour service 6.1825. BU 7.1846.

MILFORD Tankvessel. 1816–52.

MILFORD Sloop, 1,060 tons, 250 × 34ft, 2—4in. Devonport DY 11.6.1932. Sold 3.6.1949, BU Ward, Hayle.

MILFORD Tender, 143 tons, 80 (oa) × 21ft. Dunston 22.7.1982. Purch. by Vine Trust for use as Amazon ferry; sailed from Glasgow 3.9.2001 = *Amazon Hope*.

MILFORD *See FAGONS 1654, SCARBOROUGH 1694, ADVICE 1712.*

MILLTOWN Minesweeper (RCN), TE 'Bangor' class. Port Arthur SY 22.1.1942. Sold 2.1959 Marine Industries.

MILNE Destroyer, 'M' class, 1,010 tons. John Brown 5.10.1914. Sold 22.9.1921 Cohen; BU Germany.

MILNE Destroyer, 1,935 tons, 362·5 (oa) × 37ft, 6—4·7in, 8—TT. Scotts 31.12.1941. Tx Turkish Navy 27.4.1959 = ALP ARSLAM; discarded 1970.

MIMICO (ex-BULRUSH) Corvette (RCN), Modified 'Flower' class. Crown, Sunderland, 11.10.1943 (renamed 9.1943). Sold 1950 = *Olympic Victor*.

MIMICO *See also MOON 1943.*

MIMOSA Sloop, 'Acacia' class. Bow McLachlan 16.7.1915. Sold 18.11.1922 South Wales Salvage Co.

MIMOSA Corvette, 'Flower' class. Hill, Bristol, 18.1.1941. Lent Free French 5.1941; sunk 9.6.1942 by U.124 western Atlantic,

MINAS Minesweeper (RCN), TE 'Bangor' class. Burrard 23.1.1941. Arr. 20.8.1959 Seattle for BU.

MINDEN 3rd Rate 74, 1,721bm, 171·5 × 49ft. Bombay DY 19.6.1810. Hospital hulk 4.1842. Sold 4.7.1861 in Hong Kong.

MINDFUL Destroyer, 'M' class. Fairfield 24.8.1915. Sold 22.9.1921 Cohen; BU Germany.

MINDFUL *See also M.VIII 1943.*

MINEHEAD *See LONGFORD 1919.*

MINER I—VIII *See M.I—VIII.*

MINERVA 5th Rate 32, 664bm, 124·5 × 35ft. Quallet, Rotherhithe, 17.1.1759. Captured 28.8.1778 by French CONCORDE; recaptured 4.1.1781 = RECOVERY. Sold 30.12.1784.

MINERVA 5th Rate 38, 941bm, 141 × 39ft. Woolwich DY 3.6.1780. = PALLAS (troopship) 1798. BU 3.1803.

MINERVA Storeship 29, 689bm. Purch. 6.1781. Sold 21.12.1783 Bombay.

MINERVA 5th Rate 32 (fir-built), 661bm, 127 × 34ft. Deptford DY 26.10.1805. BU 2.1815.

MINERVA 5th Rate 46, 1,082bm, 152 × 40·5ft. Portsmouth DY 13.6.1820. Harbour service 1861. Sold 28.2.1895 Portsmouth.

MINERVA 2nd class cruiser, 5,600 tons, 350 × 53ft, 11—6in, 9—12pdr. Chatham DY 23.9.1895. Sold 5.10.1920 Auten.

MINERVA Frigate, 'Leander' class, Y136, 2,650 tons, 372 (oa) × 41ft, 2—4·5in, Seacat, helo (later Exocet, Seawolf). Vickers Armstrong, Tyne, 19.12.1964. Sold Cross Seas Shipping for BU; beached Alang 31.1.1994.

MINERVA *See also M.33 1915.*

MINERVE 5th Rate 38, 1,102bm, 154·5 × 40ft, 4—36pdr carr., 28—18pdr, 12—8pdr. French, captured 24.6.1795 by LOWESTOFT and DIDO in Mediterranean. Stranded 3.7.1803 nr Cherbourg, re captured by French; captured 3.2.1810 as CANONNIERE, = CONFIANCE. Listed until 1814.

MINERVE Prison hulk, 246bm, 90 × 24·5ft. French sloop captured 1803. BU 1811.

MINERVE Submarine, 597 tons, 211 × 20ft, 1—3in, 9—TT. French, seized 3.7.1940 Plymouth. Free French crew from 9.1940. Wrecked 19.9.1945 Portland Bill.

MINGAN *See FORT YORK 1941.*

MINION Ship, 180bm. Built 1523. Rebuilt as 300bm. Given away 1549 to Sir T. Seymour.

MINION Ship, c. 600bm. Purch. 1560. Condemned 1570.

MINION Ketch 6, 22bm. Built 1649. Sold 1669.

MINION Destroyer, 'M' class. Thornycroft 11.9.1915. Sold 8.11.1921 Stough Trading Co; BU Germany.

MINNIKIN Ship. Listed 1594–95.

MINNOW *See X.54 1955.*

MINORCA Storeship 2, 105bm. 63 × 19·5ft, 2—3pdr. Deptford 16.7.1740. Captured by French 6.1756 Minorca.

MINORCA Sloop (xebec) 18, 388bm, 97 × 30·5ft, 18—6pdr. Port Mahon, Minorca, 27.8.1779. Scuttled 21.8.1781 Port Mahon to block passage to harbour.

MINORCA (ex-ALERTE) Brig-sloop 16, 248bm, 85 × 26·5ft. French, captured 18.6.1799 by Fleet in Mediterranean. Sold 5.1802 Port Mahon.

MINORCA Sloop 18. Port Mahon, LD 1799. No trace thereafter. *Possibly HO Spanish Navy 1802 on cession of Minorca.*

MINORCA Brig-sloop 18, 'Cruizer' class, 385bm. Brindley, Lynn, 6.1805. BU 5.1814.

MINORU Minesweeping sloop, '24' class. Swan Hunter 16.6.1919. Sold 25.2.1920 Moise Mazza, Malta.

MINOS Steam vessel (Canadian lakes), 406bm, 153 × 24ft. Chippawa 6.1840. Sold 1852 Mr Weston.

MINOS Destroyer, 'M' class, 883 tons. Yarrow 6.8.1914. Sold 31.8.1920 Ward, Hayle.

MINOTAUR 3rd Rate 74, 1,723bm, 172·5 × 48ft. Woolwich DY 6.11.1793. Wrecked 22.12.1810 Texel.

MINOTAUR 3rd Rate 74, 1,726bm, 171 × 49ft. Chatham DY 15.4.1816. Harbour service 11.1842. = HERMES 27.7.1866. BU 1869 Sheerness.

MINOTAUR (ex-ELEPHANT) Iron screw ship, 6,621bm, 10,690 tons, 400 × 59·5ft, 4—9in, 24—7in, 8—24pdr. Thames Iron Works, Blackwall, 12.12.1863 (renamed 1861). = BOSCAWEN (TS) 3.1904; = GANGES 21.6.1906; = GANGES II 25.4.1913. Sold 30.1.1922; BU Swansea.

MINOTAUR Armoured cruiser, 14,600 tons, 490 × 74·5ft, 4—9·2in, 10—7·5in, 14—12pdr. Devonport DY 6.6.1906. Sold 12.4.1920 Ward, Milford Haven.

MINOTAUR Cruiser, 8,800 tons, 555·5 (oa) × 63ft, 9—6in, 10—4in, 8—40mm. Harland & Wolff 29.7.1943. = ONTARIO (RCN) 7.1944. Sold 6.5.1959; resold, arr. 19.11.1960 Osaka, Japan, for BU.

MINOTAUR Cruiser. Projected 1945, not ordered.

MINOTAUR *See also NEWCASTLE 1936.*

MINSTREL Sloop 18, 423bm, 108·5 × 29·5ft, 16—32pdr carr., 6—18pdr carr. Boole & Goode, Bridport, 23.3.1807. Sold 6.3.1817.

MINSTREL Wood screw gunboat, 'Britomart' class. Portsmouth DY 16.2.1865. Coal hulk 1874. Reportedly sold 1903 but listed until 1906.

MINSTREL Destroyer, 730 tons, 246·5 × 25ft, 2—4in, 2—12pdr, 2—TT. Thornycroft 2.2.1911. Lent Japanese Navy 6.1917–1919 = SENDAN. Sold 1.12.1921 Stanlee, Dover.

MINSTREL Minesweeper, 'Algerine' class. Redfern, Toronto, 5.10.1944. Sold 4.1947 Thai Navy = PHOSAMPTON; sea-going TS 2001.

MINSTREL *See also M.1 1939.*

MINTO Icebreaker (Canadian) 1,100 tons, 225 × 33ft, 4—6pdr. Dundee 1899. Sold 1915 Russian Navy.

MINTO Troopship (RIM), 960 tons, 206 × 31·5ft. 4—3pdr. Laird 1893. Sold 1925.

MINUET Minesweeper, 260 tons, 130 × 26ft, 1—3pdr. War Dept tug, tx on stocks. Day Summers, Southampton, 18.9.1917. Sold 1.5.1920 Crichton Thompson.

MINX (Gunboat No 36, ex-*Tom*) Gunvessel 12, 118bm, 64·5 × 21ft 2—24pdr, 10—18pdr carr. Purch. 4.1797 Leith. Sold 1801.

MINX Gun-brig 12, 180bm, 80 × 23ft, 2—18pdr,

10—18pdr carr. Pitcher, Northfleet, 14.4.1801. Captured 2.9.1809 by Danes off The Scaw.

MINX Schooner 3, 84bm, 60 × 18·5ft. Bermuda 23.12.1829. Sold 6.1833 in Jamaica.

MINX Iron screw gunboat, 303bm, 131 × 22ft. Miller & Ravenhall, Blackwall, 5.9.1846. Tank-vessel 1859. Sold 15.12.1899.

MIRAMICHI Minesweeper (RCN), TE 'Bangor' class. Burrand, Vancouver, 30.5.1941. BU 1949.

MIRAMICHI Coastal minesweeper (RCN), 'Bay' class. St John DD Co. 4.5.1954. Tx French Navy 9.10.1954 = LORIENTAISE; deleted 1986.

MIRAMICHI Coastal minesweeper (RCN), 'Bay' class. Victoria Machinery 22.2.1957. PO 10.1998.

MIRANDA Wood screw corvette, 1,039bm, 185 × 34·5ft, 10—32pdr, 4—20pdr. Sheerness DY 18.3.1851. Sold 2.12.1869 C. Lewis.

MIRANDA Composite screw sloop, 1,130 tons, 170 × 36ft, 2—7in, 4—64pdr. Devonport DY 30.9.1879. Sold 24.9.1892 Reed, Portsmouth, for BU.

MIRANDA Destroyer, 'M' class, 883 tons. Yarrow 27.5.1914. Sold 26.10.1921 Barking S. Bkg Co.

MISCHIEF Destroyer, 'M' class. Fairfield 12.10.1915. Sold 8.11.1921 Slough Trading Co.; BU Germany.

MISTLETOE Schooner 8, 150bm, 79 × 22ft. Bermuda 1809. Sold c. 1826.

MISTLETOE Wood screw gunboat, 'Albacore' class. Briggs, Sunderland, 22.2.1856. BU comp. 28.9.1864 Sheerness.

MISTLETOE Composite screw gunboat, 560 tons, 135 × 26ft, 2—5in, 2—4in. Laird 7.2.1883. BDV 1903. Sold 14.5.1907 S. Bkg Co., London.

MISTLETOE Sloop, 'Anchusa' class. Greenock & Grangemouth 17.11.1917. Sold 25.1.1921 = *Chiapus*.

MISTLEY (ex-MARYPORT) Minesweeper, Later 'Hunt' class. Harkess 19.10.1918 (renamed 1918). Sold 19.5.1928 Ward, Pembroke Dock.

MISTRAL Destroyer, 1,319 tons, 326 × 33ft, 4—5.1in, 6—TT. French, seized 3.7.1940 Portsmouth. Ret. French Navy 1946.

MITCHELL *See HOSTE 1943.*

MOA Coal depot. Ex-brig, purch. 1.1861. Sold 12.1876.

MODBURY Destroyer, 'Hunt' class Type III. Swan Hunter 13.4.1942. Lent 11.1942—23.9.1960 Greek Navy = MIAOULIS. Sold 19.7.1961 for BU Greece.

MODERATE (ex-MODERE) 3rd Rate 64, 887bm, 132·5 × 39·5ft. French, captured 10.1702. Sold 15.12.1713 J. Williamson.

MODESTE 3rd Rate 64, 1,357bm, 158·5 × 44·5ft, 26—24pdr, 28—12pdr, 10—6pdr. French, cap-tured 18.8.1759 Lagos. Harbour service 8.1778. BU 8.1800.

MODESTE 5th Rate 36, 940bm, 143·5 × 38·5ft. French, captured by 17.10.1793 BEDFORD at Genoa. Floating battery 1804. BU 6.1814.

MODESTE (ex-TERPSICHORE) 5th Rate 38, 1,081bm, 152 × 40ft. French, captured 3.2.1814 by MAJESTIC in Atlantic. BU 8.1816.

MODESTE Sloop 18, 562bm, 120 × 33ft. Woolwich DY 31.10.1837. Sold 3.1866 Castle, Charlton.

MODESTE Wood screw corvette, 1,405bm, 1,970 tons, 220 × 37ft, 14—64pdr. Devonport DY 23.5.1873. Sold 8.1.1888. Castle, Charlton.

MODESTE Sloop, 1,350 tons, 283 × 38·5ft, 6—4in. Chatham DY 29.1.1944. Arr. 11.3.1961 White, St Davids, for BU.

MOHAWK Sloop 6 (Canadian lakes). Oswego 1756. Captured 8.1756 by French.

MOHAWK Sloop 18 (Canadian lakes). Oswego 1759. Lost 1764.

MOHAWK Sloop 18, 285bm. Purch. 10.1782. Sold 9.1783

MOHAWK Schooner (Canadian lakes). Kingston, Ontario, 14.5.1795. Condemned 1803.

MOHAWK Sloop. In service 1798. *Fate unknown.*

MOHAWK Gun-brig 10, 148bm. Sold 1814. *Same vessel as VIPER 1810?*

MOHAWK Paddle vessel (Canadian lakes), 174bm, 99 × 19·5ft. Launched 21.2.1843. Sold 13.4.1852 J. F. Parke.

MOHAWK Wood screw gunvessel, 679bm, 181 × 28·5ft. Young & Magnay, Limehouse, 11.1.1856. Sold 20.9.1862 Emperor of China = PEKIN.

MOHAWK Torpedo cruiser, 1,770 tons, 225 × 36ft, 6—6in, 5—TT. Thomson, Glasgow, 6.2.1886. Sold 4.4.1905 Garnham.

MOHAWK Destroyer, 865 tons, 270 × 25ft, 3—12pdr (1911: 5—12pdr), 2—TT. White 15.3.1907. Sold 27.5.1919 Hughes Bolckow, Blyth.

MOHAWK Destroyer, 1,870 tons, 377 (oa) × 36·5ft, 8—4·7in, 4—TT. Thornycroft 5.10.1937. Torpedoed 16.4.1941 by Italian destroyer TARIGO; sunk by HMS JANUS.

MOHAWK Frigate, 2,300 tons, 350 × 42ft, 2—4·5in, 2—40mm. Vickers Armstrong, Barrow, 5.4.1962. Sold 16.9.1982; BU Cairnryan.

MOHAWK *See also ONTARIO 1813.*

MOIRA Schooner 14 (Canadian lakes) Kingston, Ontario, 1812. = CHARWELL (brig, 169bm) 22.1.1814. Powder hulk 1817. Sold 1837.

MONAGHAN (ex-MULLION) Minesweeper, Later 'Hunt' class. Harkess 29.5.1919 (renamed 1918). Sold 15.11.1920 A. S. Miller = *Bao Viagem*.

MONARCA 3rd Rate 68, 1,911bm, 174·5 × 50ft,

28—24pdr, 30—12pdr, 10—9pdr. Spanish, captured 16.1.1780 St Vincent. Sold 13.10.1791.

MONARCH (ex-MONARQUE) 3rd Rate 74, 1,707bm, 175 × 47·5ft. French, captured 14.10.1747 Cape Finisterre. Sold 25.11.1760.

MONARCH 3rd Rate 74, 1,612bm, 168·5 × 47ft Deptford DY 20.7.1765. BU 3.1813.

MONARCH 2nd Rate 84, 2,255bm, 194 × 52ft, 8—8in, 60—32pdr, 16—32pdr carr. Chatham DY 8.12.1832 (ex-Deptford DY, tx 2.1825). Target 1862. BU comp. 3.10.1866 White, Cowes.

MONARCH Iron screw ship, 5,103bm, 8,320 tons, 330 × 57·5ft, 4—12in, 3—7in. Chatham DY 25.5.1868. Guardship 1897; = SIMOOM (depot ship) 3.1904. Sold 4.4.1905 Garnham for BU.

MONARCH Battleship, 22,500 tons, 545 × 88·5ft, 10—13·5in, 16—4in. Armstrong 30.3.1911. Sunk 20.1.1925 target off Scilly Is.

MONCK 60-gun ship, 684bm, 136 × 34·5ft. Portsmouth DY 1659. Rebuilt Rotherhithe 1702 as 4th Rate 50, 808bm. Wrecked 24.11.1720 Yarmouth Roads.

MONCK PRIZE 6th Rate 16, 135bm. Captured 9.9.1709 by MONCK at Cape Morrisco. Sold 6.3.1712.

MONCTON Corvette (RCN), 'Flower' class. St John, New Brunswick, 11.8.1941. Sold 1951.

MONCTON MCDV (RCN), 'Kingston' class, 962 tons, 181·4 (oa) × 37·1ft, 1—40mm. Halifax SY 5.12.1997.

MONDOVI Brig-sloop 16, 211bm, 81·5 × 25ft, 4—12pdr, 12—6pdr. French, captured 13.5.1798 Mediterranean. BU 5.1811.

MONGOOSE Gun-brig 12, 140bm. Dutch, captured 1799. Sold 1803.

MONITOR Destroyer, 'M' class. Projected 1913, cancelled.

MONKEY (ex-*Lark*) Cutter 12, 187bm, 73 × 25·5ft, 12—4pdr. Purch. 9.1780. Sold 23.3.1786.

MONKEY Gun-brig 12, 188bm, 80 × 23ft, 10—18pdr carr., 2—9pdr. Nicholson, Rochester, 11.5.1801. Wrecked 25.12.1810 Belleisle, coast of France.

MONKEY Schooner 3, 70bm, 54 × 18ft. McLean, Jamaica, 6.1826. Wrecked 5.1831 Tampico Bar.

MONKEY (ex-*Courier*) Schooner 6, 68bm, 56 × 18ft. Purch. 25.10.1831. Sold 8.8.1833 in Jamaica.

MONKEY (ex-*Royal Sovereign*) Wood paddle vessel, 212bm, 106·5 × 21ft, 1—6pdr. GPO vessel, tx 3.1837. Tug 1845. Sold 9.1887 Chatham.

MONKSHOOD Corvette, 'Flower' class. Fleming & Ferguson 17.4.1941. Sold 1947 = *W. R. Strang*

MONKTON Coastal minesweeper, 'Ton' class. Herd & McKenzie, Buckie, 30.11.1955. Conv. to

patrol boat 1971—72. Sold in Hong Kong; BU 4.1985 Hing Fat Metals.

MONMOUTH Yacht 8, 103bm. Castle, Rotherhithe, 1666. Sold 25.11.1698.

MONMOUTH 3rd Rate 66, 856bm, 148·5 × 37ft. Chatham DY 3.1667. Rebuilt 1700 Woolwich, 944bm; rebuilt 1742 Deptford, 3rd Rate 64, 1,225bm. BU comp. 28.8.1767 Chatham.

MONMOUTH 3rd Rate 64, 1,370bm, 160 × 45ft. Plymouth DY 18.4.1772. = CAPTIVITY (prison hulk) 20.10.1796. BU 1.1818.

MONMOUTH (ex-*Belmont*) 3rd Rate 64, 1,439bm, 173 × 43·5ft. Randall, Rotherhithe, 23.4.1796; Indiaman, purch. on stocks. Sheer hulk 6.1815. BU 5.1834 Deptford.

MONMOUTH Armoured cruiser, 9,800 tons, 448 × 66ft, 14—6in, 9—12pdr. London & Glasgow Co. 13.11.1901. Sunk 1.11.1914 Battle of Coronel.

MONMOUTH Aircraft carrier, 18,300 tons, 650 × 90ft, 32—40mm, 50 aircraft. Fairfield, cancelled 10.1945.

MONMOUTH Frigate, 'Norfolk' class, Yarrow, Glasgow 23.11.1991.

MONMOUTH *See also HOTSPUR 1828.*

MONMOUTH CASTLE Corvette, 'Castle' class. Lewis, Aberdeen, cancelled 12.1943.

MONNOW Frigate, 'River' class. Hill, Bristol, 4.12.1943. Lent RCN to 11.6.1945. Sold 1946 RDanN = HOLGER DANSKE. BU 1960 Odense.

MONOWAI (ex-*Moana Roa*) Survey ship (RNZN), 2,938 tons. 1960, purch. 1973. Sold Altanamara Shipping 29.9.1998 for conv. to cruise ship; sailed Auckland 6.10.1998.

MONS Destroyer, 'M' class. John Brown 1.5.1915. Sold 8.11.1921 Slough Trading Co.; BU Germany.

MONS Destroyer, 2,380 tons, 355 × 40ft, 5—4in, 8—40mm, 10—TT. Hawthorn Leslie, LD 9.6.1945, cancelled 10.1945.

MONSIEUR 5th Rate 36, 818bm, 139 × 36·5ft, 26—12pdr, 10—6pdr. French privateer, captured 13.3.1780. Sold 5.9.1783 J. Curry.

MONT BLANC 3rd Rate 74, 1,886bm. French, captured 4.11.1805 in Strachan's action. Powder hulk 1811. Sold 8.3.1819 J. Ledger for BU.

MONTAGU 4th Rate 60, 1,218bm, 157 × 42ft. Sheerness DY 15.9.1757. Sunk 8.1774 breakwater Sheerness.

MONTAGU 3rd Rate 74, 1,631bm, 169 × 47ft. Chatham DY 28.8.1779. BU 9.1818.

MONTAGU (ex-MONTAGUE) Battleship, 14,000 tons, 405 × 75·5ft, 4—12in, 12—6in, 12—12pdr. Devonport DY 5.3.1901 (renamed 1901). Wrecked 30.5.1906 Lundy I.

MONTAGU *See also LYME 1654.*

MONTBRETIA Sloop, 'Anchusa' class. Irvine, Glasgow, 3.9.1917. Sold 25.1.1921 = *Chihuahua*.

MONTBRETIA Corvette, 'Flower' class. Fleming & Ferguson 27.5.1941. Lent RNorN 16.9.1941. Sunk 18.11.1942 by U.624 North Atlantic.

MONTEGO BAY Schooner 10 purch. 1796. Listed until 1800.

MONTFORD Seaward defence boat, 'Ford' class. Pimblott 10.10.1957. Sold Nigerian Navy 9.9.1966 = IBADAN; seized by Eastern Region (Biafra) 30.5.1967 = VIGILANCE; sunk Port Harcourt 10.9.1967; salved, BU Lagos.

MONTGOMERY (ex-WICKES) Destroyer, 1,090 tons, 309 × 30·5ft, 1—4in. 1—3in, 4—20mm, 3—TT. USN, cd RN 23.10.1940. Lent RCN 1942–12.1943. Sold 20.3.1945; BU Clayton & Davie, Dunston.

MONTREAL 5th Rate 32, 684bm, 125 × 35·5ft. Sheerness DY 15.9.1761. Captured 4.5.1779 by French BOURGOGNE in Mediterranean. Destroyed 18.12.1793 by Anglo-Spanish forces at Toulon while powder hulk.

MONTREAL Schooner (Canadian lakes). Purch. 18.10.1839. Sold 1848.

MONTREAL Frigate (RCN), 'River' class. Vickers, Montreal, 12.6.1943. BU 1947 Dominion Steel Corp.

MONTREAL Frigate (RCN), 'Halifax' class. St John SB, 28.2.1992.

MONTREAL *See also WOLFE 1813.*

MONTROSE Destroyer leader, 1,800 tons, 320 × 32ft, 5—4·7in, 1—3in, 6—TT. Hawthorn Leslie 10.6.1918. Sold 31.1.1946; BU Hughes Bolckow, Blyth.

MONTROSE Frigate, 'Norfolk' class, Yarrow, Glasgow 31.7.1992.

MONTROSE *Name borne in succession from 1949 by RNVR tenders MMS.1077, CHEDISTON, NURTON, DALSWINTON. See also VALOROUS 1917.*

MONTSERRAT (ex-HORNBY) Frigate, 'Colony' class. Walsh Kaiser, Providence, RI, 28.8.1943 (renamed 9.1943). Ret. USN 6.1946.

MOOLOCK Patrol boat (RCN), 84 × 20ft, 1—MG. Star SY 15.10.1941. Sold 1946.

MOON Pinnace 12, 60bm. Built 1549. Lost 1553 off Gold Coast.

MOON Pinnace 9, 85bm, 4—6pdr, 4—4pdr, 1—1pdr. Deptford 1586. Rebuilt Chatham 1602 as 100bm. Condemned 1626.

MOON Destroyer, 'M' class, 1,007 tons. Yarrow 24.4.1915. Sold 9.5.1921 Ward, Briton Ferry.

MOON Minesweeper, 'Algerine' class. Harland & Wolff, ordered 8.1942, cancelled 4.1943.

MOON (ex-MIMICO) Minesweeper, 'Algerine' class. Redfern 2.9.1943 (renamed 1943). Arr. 13.11.1957 King, Gateshead, for BU.

MOOR (ex-MAURE) 4th Rate 54, 811bm. French, captured 13.12.1710. Sunk 7.3.1716 breakwater Plymouth.

MOORHEN Composite screw gunboat, 455 tons, 125 × 23ft 2—64pdr, 2—20pdr. Napier 13.9.1875. Sold 11.1888.

MOORHEN (ex-COCKATRICE) Paddle vessel, 600 tons, 160 × 25·5ft, 2 guns. Renamed 1896. Sold 1899 Malta.

MOORHEN River gunboat, 180 tons, 160 × 24·5ft, 2—6pdr. Yarrow, Poplar, 13.8.1901. Sold 8.1933 in Hong Kong for BU.

MOORSOM Destroyer, 'M' class. John Brown 21.12.1914. Sold 8.11.1921 Slough Trading Co.; BU Germany.

MOORSOM Frigate, DE 'Captain' class. Boston NY 24.9.1943 on Lend-Lease. Ret. USN 10.1945.

MOOSEJAW Corvette (RCN), 'Flower' class. Collingwood SY 9.4.1941. BU 9.1949 Steel Co. of Canada, Hamilton, Ontario.

MORAY FIRTH (ex-EMPIRE PITCAIRN) Repair ship, 10,100 tons, 431 × 56ft, 12—20mm. Readhead, South Shields, 17.10.1944 (renamed 1944). Sold 1947 = *Linoria*.

MORDAUNT 4th Rate 48, 567bm, 122 × 32·5ft. Deptford 1681, purch. 1683. Stranded 21.11.1691 West Indies.

MORDEN Corvette (RCN), 'Flower' class. Port Arthur SY 5.4.1941. BU 11.1956 Steel Co. of Canada.

MORECAMBE BAY (ex-LOCH HEILEN) Frigate, 'Bay' class. Pickersgill 1.11.1944. Sold 9.5.1961 Portuguese Navy = DOM FRANCISCO DE ALMEDIA; discarded 7.9.1970.

MORESBY (ex-MARLION) Destroyer, 'M' class. White 20.11.1915 (renamed 1914). Sold 9.5.1921 Ward, Grays; BU 1923.

MORESBY Survey ship (RAN), 2,000 tons, 284·5 (oa) × 42ft, 2—40mm. Newcastle DY, NSW, 7.9.1963. PO 13.11.1997. Sold 5.10.1999 Caravelle Investments conv. hospital ship = *Patricia Anne Hotung*.

MORESBY (ex-*Joyce Tide*) Minesweeper aux. (RCN), 1,076 tons, 191 × 43ft, Allied Shipping, Vancouver, 1973 as offshore supply vessel. Purch. 1988, cd. 7.5.1989. Deleted 2000.

MORESBY *See also SILVIO 1918.*

MORGIANA (ex-ACTIF) Brig-sloop 16, 283bm, 96 × 26·5ft, 14—18pdr carr., 2—6pdr. French privateer, captured 30.11.1800 by THAMES in Bay of Biscay. BU 8.1811.

MORGIANA Sloop 18, 400bm, 100 × 30ft. Hill, Bermuda, 12.1811. Sold 27.1.1825 T. Pittman for BU.

MORNE FORTUNEE (ex-MORNE FORTUNE) Schooner 6, 106bm, 65·5 × 21ft, 6–12pdr carr. French privateer, captured 1803, purch. 1804. Wrecked 6.12.1804 West Indies.

MORNE FORTUNEE (ex-REGULUS) Schooner 12, 184bm. French privateer brig, captured 13.12.1804 by PRINCESS CHARLOTTE West Indies. Foundered 9.1.1809 off Martinique.

MORNE FORTUNEE (ex-MORNE FORTUNE) Brig 14. French privateer, captured 8.1808 by BELETTE. BU 10.1813 Antigua.

MORNING STAR Ketch 14, 80bm. Dutch, captured 1672. Given away 1674.

MORNING STAR Cutter, 69bm, 48 × 18·5ft. Purch. 1.1763. Sold 4.5.1773.

MORNING STAR Sloop 16. American privateer, 191bm, captured 14.1.1781. Sold 19.6.1782 Davis, Rotherhithe.

MORNING STAR Sloop 22 (Indian), 350bm. Bombay DY 1799. *Fate unknown.*

MORNING STAR Destroyer, 'M' class. Yarrow 26.6.1915. Sold 1.12.1921 Stanlee, Dover.

MORO (ex-AMERICA) 3rd Rate 74, 1,880bm, 175 × 49·5ft. Spanish, captured 13.8.1762. BU comp. 18.7.1770 Portsmouth.

MORPETH CASTLE Corvette, 'Castle' class. Pickersgill 26.11.1943. Arr. 9.8.1960 Rees, Llanelly, for BU.

MORRIS Destroyer, 'M' class. John Brown 19.11.1914. Sold 8.11.1921 Slough Trading Co.; BU Germany.

MORRIS DANCE Minesweeper, 265 tons, 130 × 26ft, 1–6pdr. War Dept tug, tx 1919. Lytham SB Co. 1918. Sold 1.5.1920 Crichton Thompson.

MORTAR Bomb vessel 12, 260bm, 12–6pdr. Chatham DY 1693. Ran ashore 2.12.1703 Dutch coast.

MORTAR Bomb vessel 14, 280bm, 91 × 26·5ft. Perry, Blackwall, 26.2.1741. Sold 2.3.1748.

MORTAR Bomb vessel 14, 313bm, 92 × 28ft. Wells, Rotherhithe, 14.3.1759. Sold 2.9.1774.

MOSAMBIQUE (ex-MOZAMBIQUE) Schooner 10, 115bm, 67·5 × 20ft, 10–18pdr carr. French privateer, captured 13.3.1804 by EMERALD and DIAMOND. Sold 1810.

MOSELLE Sloop 24, 520bm, 120 × 31ft. French, HO 18.12.1793 by Royalists at Toulon. Recaptured 7.1.1794 by French at Toulon; captured 23.5.1794 by AIMABLE off Hyeres. Sold 9.1802.

MOSELLE Brig-sloop 18, 'Cruizer' class, 385bm. King, Dover, 10.1804. Sold 14.12.1815.

MOSLEM (ex-*Torok*) Iron paddle vessel. Purch. 8.1854 Constantinople. Sold 8.1856.

MOSQUITO Composite screw gunboat, 295bm, 430 tons, 125 × 23ft, 2–64pdr, 2–20pdr. Pembroke Dock 9.12.1871. Sold 12.1888.

MOSQUITO Torpedo boat (Australian), 12 tons, 63 × 7·5ft, 1–TT. Thornycroft, Chiswick, 16.7.1884. Sold c. 1912.

MOSQUITO Paddle river gunboat, 90 tons, 6–3pdr. Yarrow, Poplar, 3.5.1890. Sold 19.12.1902 R. Zambesi.

MOSQUITO Destroyer, 925 tons, 271 × 28ft, 1–4in, 3–12pdr, 2–TT. Fairfield 27.1.1910. Sold 31.8.1920 Ward, Rainham.

MOSQUITO River gunboat, 585 tons, 188 × 33·5ft, 2–4in. Yarrow 14.11.1939. Sunk 1.6.1940 air attack Dunkirk.

MOSQUITO *See also* MUSQUITO.

MOTH Coastal destroyer, 225 tons, 172 × 18ft, 2–12pdr, 3–TT. Yarrow, Poplar, 15.3.1907. = TB.12 in 1906. Sold 10.6.1915 mine North Sea.

MOTH River gunboat, 645 tons, 230 × 36ft, 2–6in, 1–3in. Sunderland SB Co. 9.10.1915. Scuttled 12.12.1941 Hong Kong after bomb damage; salved, cd by Japanese = SUMA; sunk 19.3.1945 mine.

MOTHER SNAKE (ex-*Murchison*, 316/44) Special Service Vessel (RAN), 80 tons. Cd 30.6.1945. Tx North Borneo Govt 11.1945

MOTI (ex-KARKAS) Gunboat (RIN), 331 tons, 170 × 22ft, 2–3in. Iranian, captured 1941 by RIN. Ret. 1946 Iran.

MOUCHERON Brig-sloop 16, 286bm. French, captured 16.2.1801, purch. 1802. Wrecked 9.1807 Dardanelles.

MOUNSEY Destroyer, 'M' class. Yarrow 11.9.1915. Sold 8.11.1921 Slough Trading Co.; BU Germany.

MOUNSEY Frigate, DE 'Captain' class. Boston NY 24.9.1943 on Lend-Lease. Ret. USN 2.1946.

MOUNT EDGCUMBE *See WINCHESTER 1822.*

MOUNTS BAY (ex-LOCH KILBIRNIE) Frigate, 'Bay' class. Pickersgill 8.6.1945. Tx Portuguese Navy 9.5.1961 = VASCO DA GAMA. Sold 21.12.1971.

MOURNE Frigate, 'River' class. Smith's Dock 24.9.1942. Sunk 15.6.1944 by U.767 in English Channel.

MOY Destroyer, 550 tons, 222 × 23·5ft, 1–12pdr, 5–6pdr (1907: 4–12pdr), 2–TT. Laird 10.11.1904. Sold 27.5.1919 T. Oakley.

MOYOLA Frigate, 'River' class. Smith's Dock 27.8.1942. Tx French Navy 15.10.1944 = TONKINOIS. BU Brest 1961.

MULETTE Sloop 18. French, HO 18.12.1793 by Royalists at Toulon. For sale 6.1796.

MULGRAVE 3rd Rate 74, 1,726bm, 176 × 48·5ft. King, Upnor, 1.1.1812. Lazaretto 9.1836; powder hulk 9.1844. BU comp. 12.1854.

MULGRAVE Minesweeper (RCN), TE 'Bangor' class. Port Arthur 2.5.1942. Mined 8.10.1944 English Channel, not repaired; BU 5.1947 Rees, Llanelly.

MULL OF GALLOWAY (ex-KINNAIRDS HEAD) Repair ship, 10,200 tons, 416 × 57ft, 11—40mm. North Vancouver SR Co. 26.10.1944 (renamed 4.1945). BU 1965 Hamburg.

MULL OF KINTYRE Repair ship, 10,200 tons, 416 × 57ft, 11—40mm. North Vancouver SR Co. 5.11.1945. Arr. Hong Kong 25.1.1970 for BU.

MULL OF OA (ex-TREVOSE HEAD) Repair ship, 10,200 tons, 416 × 57ft, 16—20mm. North Vancouver SR Co. 8.11.1945 (renamed 4.1945), cancelled 18.8.1945; comp. = *Turan*.

MULLETT Schooner 5, 78bm, 56 × 18ft. Bermuda 5.1807. Sold 15.12.1814.

MULLETT Wood screw gunvessel, 'Philomel' class. Lungley, Deptford, 13.2.1860. Sold 1872 in Hong Kong.

MULLION See *MONAGHAN 1919*.

MULLION COVE (ex-EMPIRE PENANG) Repair ship, 9,730 tons, 425 × 66ft, 16—20mm. Bartram, Sunderland, 10.7.1944 (renamed 1944). Sold 1948 = *Margaret Clunies*.

MUNLOCHY (ex-MACDUFF) Minesweeper, Later 'Hunt' class. Fleming & Ferguson 12.6.1918 (re-named 1918). Sold 23.11.1922 J. Smith.

MUNSTER Destroyer, 'M' class. Thornycroft 24.11.1915. Sold 15.11.1921 Cashmore, Newport.

MURCHISON Frigate (RAN), 'River' class. Evans Deakin, Brisbane, 31.10.1944. Sold 9.1961 Tolo Mining Co. for BU.

MUROS (ex-ALCIDE) 6th Rate 22, 446bm, 112·5 × 30·5ft, 20—pdr carr., 8—12pdr carr., 2—pdr. French privateer, captured 8.3.1806 by EGYPTIENNE at Muros. Wrecked 24.3.1808 Bay of Honda, Cuba.

MUROS Brig-sloop 14, 252bm, 92 × 25·5ft, 12—24pdr carr., 2—6pdr. Chatham DY 23.10.1809. Sold 18.4.1822 T. Pittman.

MURRAY Destroyer, 'M' class, 1,010 tons. Palmer 6.8.1914. Sold 9.5.1921 Ward, Briton Ferry; BU 1.1923.

MURRAY Frigate, 1,180 tons, 300 × 33ft, 40mm, 4—TT. Stephen 25.2.1955. Sold Arnott Young 14.8.1970; BU Dalmuir.

MURRUMBIDGEE Frigate (RAN), 'River' class. Melbourne Harbour Trust, LD 28.10.1943, cancelled 12.6.1944.

MUSETTE Sloop 22, 312bm, 102 × 27ft. French

privateer, captured 21.12.1796 by HAZARD off Irish coast. Harbour service 1799; floating battery 24 in 1805. Sold 27.8.1806.

MUSETTE See also *MIGNONNE 1806*.

MUSK Corvette, 'Flower' class. Morton, Quebec, 15.7.1942. Tx 1942 USN = MIGHT; sold 10.1946 = *Olympic Explorer*.

MUSKERRY Minesweeper, Early 'Hunt' class. Lobnitz 28.11.1916. Sold 22.1.1923 Rees, Llanelly, for BU.

MUSKET Destroyer, 1,980 tons, 341·5 × 38ft, 6—4in, 6—40mm, 10—TT. White, cancelled 5.10.1945, not LD.

MUSKETEER Destroyer, 'M' class, 900 tons. Yarrow 12.11.1915. Sold 25.11.1921 Hayes, Porthcawl.

MUSKETEER Destroyer, 1,920 tons, 362·5 (oa) × 37ft, 6—4·7in, 8—TT. Fairfield 2.12.1941. Sold 3.12.1955; BU Young, Sunderland.

MUSQUEDOBET (ex-LYNX) Schooner 10, 225bm, 93 × 24ft, 8—18pdr carr., 2—6pdr. American privateer, captured 16.3.1813 Chesapeake Bay. Sold 13.1.1820 Mr Rundle.

MUSQUITO Vessel. In service 1777.

MUSQUITO (ex-VENUS) Schooner 6, 71bm, 55·5 × 17ft. French privateer, captured 1793, purch. 1794. Captured 1799 by Spanish off Cuba.

MUSQUITO Floating battery 4, 309bm, 80 × 32ft, 2—68pdr carr., 2—24pdr. Wells, Rotherhithe, 1795. Wrecked 5.1795 French coast.

MUSQUITO Schooner 12. French, captured 1799. Sold 1802.

MUSQUITO Brig-sloop 18, 'Cruizer' class, 384bm. Preston, Yarmouth, 4.9.1804. Sold 7.5.1822 T. King.

MUSQUITO Brig-sloop, 'Cherokee' class, 231bm. Portsmouth DY 19.2.1825. Sold 7.11.1843 Greenwood & Clark.

MUSQUITO Brig 16, 549bm, 110 × 35ft, 16—32pdr. Pembroke Dock 29.7.1851. Sold 9.7.1862 Prussian Navy.

MUSQUITO See also *MOSQUITO*.

MUSTICO (ex-CATALONIA) Cutter, 59bm, 49·5 × 17ft. Spanish, captured 1800. Harbour service until 1816.

MUTINE (ex-MUTIN) Cutter 14, 215bm, 80 × 26ft, 14—4pdr. French, captured 2.10.1779. = PIGMY 20.1.1798. Wrecked 8.1805 St Aubin's Bay, Jersey.

MUTINE Brig 12. In service 1795.

MUTINE Brig-sloop 16, 349bm, 104·5 × 28ft, 2—36pdr carr., 14—6pdr. French, captured 29.5.1797 Santa Cruz. Sold 1807.

MUTINE Brig-sloop 18, 'Cruizer' class, 386bm.

Ships of the Royal Navy

Chapman, Bideford, 15.8.1806. Sold 3.2.1819
G. Young.

MUTINE Brig 12, 428bm, 112 × 32ft, 10–32pdr,
2–18pdr. Chatham DY 20.4.1844. Wrecked
21.12.1848 nr Venice.

MUTINE Brig-sloop 6, 'Cherokee' class, 231bm.
Plymouth DY 19.5.1825. Sold 27.5.1841
= *Aladdin*.

MUTINE Wood screw sloop, 882bm, 173 × 33ft,
5–40pdr, 12–32pdr. Deptford DY 30.7.1859.
Sold 26.2.1870.

MUTINE Composite screw sloop, 1,136 tons, 170 ×
36, 2–7in, 4–64pdr. Devonport DY 30.7.1880.
BDV 1899; = AZOV 3.1904. Sold 25.8.1921 C. A.
Beard; BU Upnor.

MUTINE Sloop, 980 tons, 180 × 33ft, 6–4in. Laird
1.3.1900. Survey vessel 5.1907; RNVR drillship
9.1925. Sold 16.8.1932. Ward, Briton Ferry.

MUTINE Minesweeper, 'Algerine' class. Harland &
Wolff 10.10.1942. Sold 13.12.1966; BU Barrow.

MV.1–22 *See, respectively, DRAKE, SINBAD 1834;
BLAZER, GROWLER, HAVOCK, MANLY,
MASTIFF, PORPOISE, SURLY, FLAMER, FIRM,
HARDY, RAVEN, CAMEL, MAGNET, BEACON,
CARRON, GRAPPLER, REDBREAST, ROCKET,
PROMPT, PICKLE 1854.*

MYNGS Destroyer, 'M' class, 1,010 tons, Palmer
24.9.1914. Sold 9.5.1921 Ward, Rainham.

MYNGS Destroyer leader, 1,730 tons, 362·8 (oa) ×
35·7ft, 4–4·5in, 2–40mm, 8–TT. Vickers Armstrong, Tyne, 31.5.1943. Sold 5.1955 Egyptian
Navy, = EL QAHER 8.1956; sunk 16.5.1970
Israeli aircraft.

MYOSOTIS Sloop, 'Arabis' class. Bow McLachlan
4.4.1916. Sold 30.1.1923 Fryer, Sunderland.

MYOSOTIS Corvette, 'Flower' class. Lewis
28.1.1941. Sold 2.9.1946 = *Grunningur*.

MYRMIDON 6th Rate 22, 481bm, 114 × 31ft.
Deptford DY 9.6.1781. Harbour service 1798. BU
4.1811.

MYRMIDON 6th Rate 20, 506bm, 120 × 31ft. Milford Haven DY 8.6.1813. BU 1.1823 Portsmouth.

MYRMIDON Iron paddle gunvessel, 374bm, 151 ×
23ft. Ditchburn, Blackwall, 2.1845. Sold 1.12.1858
Fernando Poo.

MYRMIDON Wood screw gunvessel, 697bm, 877
tons, 185 × 28·5ft. Chatham DY 5.6.1867; comp.
10.1967 as survey vessel. Sold 4.1889 in Hong
Kong.

MYRMIDON Destroyer, 370 tons, 215 × 21ft, 1–
12pdr, 5–6pdr, 2–TT. Palmer 26.5.1900. Sunk
26.3.1917 collision SS *Hamborn* English Channel.

MYRMIDON Destroyer, 1,920 tons, 362·5 (oa) ×
37ft, 6–4·7in, 8–TT. Fairfield 2.3.1942. Lent
Polish Navy = ORKAN 11.1942. Sunk 8.10.1943
by U.610 south of Iceland.

MYRMIDON Minesweeper, 'Algerine' class.
Redfern 21.10.1944. Arr. 2.12.1958 Ward, Briton
Ferry, for BU.

MYRMIDON *See also EDDERTON 1952.*

MYRTLE Sloop 18, 429bm, 108·5 × 30ft, 16–
32pdr carr., 8–18pdr carr., 2–6pdr. Chapman,
Bideford, 2.1807. BU 6.1818.

MYRTLE Packet brig 6, 'Cherokee' class, 231bm.
Portsmouth DY 14.9.1825. Wrecked 3.4.1829 off
Nova Scotia.

MYRTLE (ex-*Firefly*) Wood paddle packer, 116bm,
97 × 16ft. GPO vessel, tx 9.1837. Tug 1866. BU
5.1868 Sheerness.

MYRTLE Sloop, 'Acacia' class. Lobnitz 11.10.1915.
Sunk 16.7.1919 mine Gulf of Finland.

MYRTLE *See also MALABAR 1818, MYSTIC 1915*

MYSTIC (ex-MYRTLE) Destroyer, 'M' class. Denny
20.6.1915 (renamed 1915). Sold 8.11.1921 Slough
Trading Co.; BU Germany.

MYSTIC Minesweeper, 'Algerine' class. Redfern
11.11.1944. Arr. 3.5.1958 Rees, Llanelly, for BU.

N

N.1 *See NAUTILUS 1914.*

NAAS Minesweeper, Later 'Hunt' class. Eltringham, cancelled 1919.

NABOB (ex-*Triton*) Storeship 26, 637bm, 136·5 × 33ft. East Indiaman, purch. 9.1777. Hospital ship 1780. Sold 10.4.1783.

NABOB (ex-*Edisto*) Escort carrier, 11,420 tons, 468·5 × 69·5ft, 16—40mm, 24 aircraft. Seattle Tacoma Co. 9.3.1943 on Lend-Lease. Torpedoed 22.8.1944 by U.354 off North Cape, not repaired; left 9.1947 for BU in Holland; resold 1951, retained name *Nabob*.

NADDER Frigate, 'River' class. Smith's Dock 15.9.1943. Tx RIN = SHAMSHER 1944. Tx Pakistani Navy 1947; sold 2.3.1959 for BU.

NADUR *See ADUR 1942.*

NAIAD 6th Rate 26. French, captured 11.6.1783 by SCEPTRE, not cd. Sold 17.8.1784.

NAIAD 5th Rate 38, 1,020bm, 147 × 40ft. Hill, Limehouse, 27.2.1797. Coal depot Callao, Peru, 1.1847. Sold 2.2.1866 Pacific Steam Navigation Co. as coal depot.

NAIAD 2nd class cruiser, 3,400 tons, 300 × 43ft, 2—4·7in 8—6pdr. Vickers 29.11.1890. Minelayer 9.1910. Sold 9.6.1922 King, Troon.

NAIAD Cruiser, 5,450 tons, 512 (oa) × 50·5ft, 10—5·25in. Hawthorn Leslie 3.2.1939. Sunk 11.3.1942 by U.565 south of Crete.

NAIAD Frigate, 'Leander' class, Y100, 2,650tons, 372 (oa) × 41ft, 2—4·5in, 2—40mm, Limbo, helo (later Ikara, Limbo, helo). Yarrow 4.11.1963. Used for hull trials 1989 = HULVUL. Towed from Portsmouth 24.9.1990, expended target.

NAILSEA (ex-NEWQUAY) Minesweeper, Later 'Hunt' class. Inglis, Glasgow, 7.8.1918 (renamed 1918). Sold 25.11.1927 Hughes Bolckow, Blyth.

NAIRANA Seaplane carrier, 3,070 tons, 315 × 45·5ft, 4—12pdr, 7 aircraft. Denny 1916, purch. Sold 1920.

NAIRANA Escort carrier, 14,050 tons, 498 × 68ft, 2—4in, 20—20mm, 15 aircraft. John Brown 20.5.1943, purch. on stocks. Lent Dutch Navy 3.1946—1948. Sold 1948 = *Port Victor*.

NAMUR 2nd Rate 90, 1,442bm, 161 × 46ft. Woolwich DY 28.4.1697. Rebuilt Deptford 1729 as 1,567bm. Wrecked 14.4.1749 East Indies.

NAMUR 2nd Rate 90, 1,814bm, 175 × 49ft. Chatham DY 3.3.1756. 74-gun 3rd Rate 5.1805; harbour service 9.1807. BU 5.1833 Chatham.

NAMUR Destroyer, 2,380 tons, 379 (oa) × 40ft, 5—4·5in, 8—40mm, 10—TT. Cammell Laird 12.6.1945, not comp. Arr. 2.1951 Ward, Barrow for BU.

NANAIMO Corvette (RCN), 'Flower' class. Yarrow, Esquimalt, 28.10.1940. For disposal 10.1945; sold, = *Rene W. Vinke.*

NANAIMO MCDV (RCN), 'Kingston' class, 962 tons, 181·4 (oa) × 37·1ft, 1—40mm. Halifax SY 17.5.1996.

NANCY Schooner (Canadian lakes). Detroit 24.11.1789. Burnt 14.8.1814 by Americans.

NANCY Fireship 72bm, 55·5 × 19ft. Purch. 4.1794. Sold 12.1801.

NANCY Brig 16, ex-cutter. Purch. 1809. Sold 1813.

NANKIN 4th Rate 50, 2,049bm, 2,540 tons, 185 × 51ft, 6—8in, 44—32pdr. Woolwich DY 16.3.1850. Hospital hulk 1866. Sold 28.2.1885; BU 1905.

NANTWICH 28/48-gun ship, 319/511bm. Bailey, Bristol, 13.3.1655. = BREDAH (4th Rate 48) 1660. Wrecked 1666.

NAOMI Frigate (RAN), 'River' class. Sydney, ordered 12.1942, cancelled 12.6.1944.

NAPANEE Corvette (RCN), 'Flower' class. Kingston SY 31.8.1940. BU 6.1946 Steel Co. of Canada, Hamilton, Ontario.

NAPIER Iron river gunboat (Indian), 445bm. Bombay DY 11.9.1844. Listed 1858.

NAPIER Destroyer, 'M' class. John Brown 27.11.1916. Sold 8.11.1921 Slough Trading Co.; BU Germany.

NAPIER Destroyer leader, 1,695 tons, 356·5 (oa) × 35·7ft, 6—4·7in, 10—TT. Fairfield 22.5.1940. Arr. 17.1.1956 Ward, Briton Ferry, for BU.

NAPIER *See also TALISMAN 1915.*

NARBADA Sloop (RIN), 1,300 tons, 283 × 37·5ft, 6—4in. Thornycroft 21.11.1942. Tx Pakistani Navy = JHELUM 1948. BU 7.1959.

NARBADA *See also NERBUDDA.*

NARBROUGH Destroyer, 'M' class. John Brown 2.3.1916. Wrecked 12.1.1918 Pentland Skerries.

NARBROUGH Frigate, TE 'Captain' class. Bethleham, Hingham, 27.11.1943 on Lend-Lease. Ret. USN 2.1946.

NARBROUGH *See also TERMAGANT 1915.*

NARCISSUS 6th Rate 20, 429bm, 108 × 30ft. Plymouth DY 9.5.1781. Wrecked 3.10.1796 Bahamas.

NARCISSUS 5th Rate 32, 894bm, 142 × 38ft. Deptford DY 12.5.1801. Convict ship 12.1823. Sold 1.1837 Levy.

NARCISSUS 6th Rate 28, 601bm, 115 × 35.5ft. Devonport DY, ordered 1846, cancelled 1848.

NARCISSUS 4th Rate 50, 1,996bm. Devonport DY, LD 11.1849, cancelled 23.3.1857.

NARCISSUS Wood screw frigate, 2,665bm, 3,548 tons, 228 × 91ft, 10—8in, 1—64pdr, 40—32pdr. Devonport DY 26.10.1859. Sold 17.2.1883 Castle for BU.

NARCISSUS Armoured cruiser, 5,600 tons, 300 × 56ft 2—9·2in, 10—6in. Earle, Hull, 15.12.1886. Sold 11.9.1906.

NARCISSUS Sloop, 'Acacia' class. Napier & Miller 22.9.1915. Sold 6.9.1922 A. H. Bond.

NARCISSUS Corvette, 'Flower' class. Lewis 29.3.1941. Sold 4.1946 = *Este.*

NARCISSUS *See also NONSUCH 1915.*

NARVIK *See LST.3044 1945.*

NARWHAL Destroyer, 'M' class. Denny 30.12.1915. Collision 1919, broke back; BU 1920 Devonport.

NARWHAL Minelaying submarine, 1,520 tons, 271·5 × 25·5ft, 1—4in, 6—TT, 50 mines. Vickers Armstrong, Barrow, 29.8.1935. Lost 1.8.1940 off Norway, cause unknown.

NARWHAL Submarine, 1,605 tons, 241 × 26·5ft, 8—TT. Vickers Armstrong, Barrow, 25.10.1957. Scuttled 3.8.1983 bottom target off Falmouth

NASEBY 80-gun ship, 1,230bm, 162 × 42ft. Woolwich DY 1655. = ROYAL CHARLES 1660. Captured 12.6.1667 by Dutch at Chatham.

NASSAU Flyboat 4, 180bm. Dutch, captured 1672. Given away 1672.

NASSAU 3rd Rate 80, 1,080bm, 151 × 40ft. Portsmouth DY 1699. Wrecked 30.10.1706 Sussex coast.

NASSAU 3rd Rate 70, 1,104bm, 150·5× 41ft. Portsmouth DY 9.1.1707. Rebuilt Chatham 1740 as 64-gun 3rd Rate, 1,225bm. Sold 4.9.1770.

NASSAU 3rd Rate 64, 1,384bm, 160 × 44·5ft. Hillhouse, Bristol, 28.9.1785. 36-gun troopship 1799. Wrecked 14.10.1799 Dutch coast.

NASSAU Wood screw gunvessel, 695bm, 877 tons,

185 × 28·5ft. Pembroke Dock 20.2.1866: comp. 7.1866 as survey ship. BU 4.1880 Sheerness.

NASSAU *See also HOLSTEIN 1801.*

NASTURTIUM Sloop, 'Arabis' class. McMillan, Dumbarton, 21.12.1915. Sunk 27.4.1916 mine off Malta.

NASTURTIUM (ex-LA PAIMPOLAISE) Corvette, 'Flower' class. Smith's Dock 4.7.1940; French, seized on stocks 3.7.1940. Sold 1946 = *Cania.*

NATAL Armoured cruiser, 13,550 tons, 480 × 73·5ft, 6—9·2in, 4—7·5in, 2—12pdr. 28—3pdr. Vickers Maxim, Barrow, 30.9.1905. Sunk 31.12.1915 internal explosion Cromarty Firth.

NATAL (ex-LOCH CREE) Frigate (SAN), 'Loch' class. Swan Hunter 19.6.1944 (renamed 1944). Survey ship 1957. Sunk 19.9.1972 target off The Cape.

NATHANIELL Fireship 4, 120bm. Purch. 30.8.1689. Sunk 1692 foundation Sheerness.

NAUTILUS Sloop 16, 316bm. 98 × 27ft. Hodgson, Hull, 24.4.1762 (ex-Deptford DY, tx 4.1761). For sale 10.1780.

NAUTILUS Sloop 16, 346bm. 102 × 28ft. Crookenden, Itchenor, 9.1.1784. Wrecked 2.2.1799 Filey Bay.

NAUTILUS Sloop 18, 443bm, 111 × 29·5ft. Jacobs, Milford Haven (Milford Haven DY), 12.4.1804. Wrecked 4.1.1807 Mediterranean.

NAUTILUS Brig-sloop 14 (Indian). Built c. 1794. Captured 18.2.1815 by American PEACOCK in Sunda Strait.

NAUTILUS Brig-sloop 14 (Indian), 185bm. Bombay DY 1806. Wrecked 1834 Red Sea.

NAUTILUS Brig-sloop 18, 'Cruizer' class, 384bm. Betts, Mistleythorn, 5.9.1807. BU 10.1823.

NAUTILUS Brig-sloop 10, 'Cherokee' class, 233bm. Woolwich DY 11.3.1830. TS 1852; hulk 1872. BU comp. 17.10.1878 Devonport.

NAUTILUS Training brig 8, 501 tons, 105 × 33·5ft. Pembroke Dock 20.5.1879. Sold 11.7.1905 Cox, Falmouth.

NAUTILUS Destroyer, 975 tons, 267·5 × 28ft, 1—4in, 3—12pdr, 2—TT. Thames Iron Works, Blackwall, 30.3.1910. = GRAMPUS 16.12.1913. Sold 21.9.1920 Ward, Rainham.

NAUTILUS Submarine, 1,240 tons, 240 × 26ft, 1—12pdr, 6—TT. Vickers 16.12.1914. = N.1 in 1918. Sold 9.6.1922 Cashmore, Newport.

NAVARINO Destroyer, 2,380 tons, 355 × 40ft, 5—4·5in, 8—40mm, 10—TT. Cammell Laird 21.9.1945, not comp. Arr. 4.1946 Ward, Preston for BU.

NAVY Yacht 2, 67bm. Castle, Rotherhithe, 1666. *Fate unknown. Rebuilt as following vessel?*

NAVY Yacht 8, 74bm. Portsmouth 1673. Sold 14.4.1698.

NAVY BOARD (ex-HART) Yacht, 80bm, 56 × 19ft. Cutter, renamed 1822. = HART 1833, then yard craft.

NAVY TRANSPORT Storeship, 107bm. Deptford 1705. Rebuilt 1730. BU 1742.

NAVY TRANSPORT Storeship, 97bm, 64 × 20ft. Purch. 12.1752. Sold 13.10.1791.

NEARCHUS Patrol vessel (RIM), 925 tons, 180 × 29ft, 4–3pdr. Beardmore 15.11.1914. Sold c. 1922.

NEARQUE Sloop 18, 309bm, 94·5 × 20·5ft, 14–24pdr carr., 4–9pdr. French, captured 28.3.1806 by NIOBE in English Channel. Sold 21.7.1814.

NEASHAM Inshore minesweeper, 'Ham' class. White 14.3.1956. Tx RAN 1968 = PORPOISE; for sale 08.1988.

NECKAR 6th Rate 28. French, captured 26.10.1781 by HANNIBAL off The Cape. Foundered 12.1789.

NED ELVIN Brig-sloop 18, 309bm, 98 × 27·5ft, 16–24pdr, 2–6pdr, Danish, captured 7.9.1807 Battle of Copenhagen. Sold 3.11.1814. *Was to have been renamed LEGERE. Also listed as NID ELVIN.*

NEGRESSE Gunvessel 6. French, captured 18.3.1799 by TIGRE off coast of Syria. Sold 1802.

NEGRO Destroyer, 'M' class. Palmer 8.3.1916. Sunk 21.12.1916 collision destroyer HOSTE North Sea.

NEGRO *See also NIGER 1759.*

NELSON 1st Rate 120, 2,617bm, 205 × 44ft. Woolwich DY 4.7.1814; undocked 7.2.1860 as screw ship, 2,736bm, 90 guns; HO NSW Govt 2.1867. Sold 28.4.1898 as store hulk, later coal hulk; BU 9.1928 Launceston.

NELSON Iron armoured frigate, 7,473 tons, 280 × 60ft, 4–10in, 8–9in, 6–20pdr, 3–9pdr. Elder 4.11.1876. TS 1902. Sold 12.7.10; BU Holland.

NELSON Battleship, 33,500 tons, 710 (oa) × 106ft, 9–16in, 12–6in, 6–4·7in. Armstrong, 3.9.1925. Arr. 15.3.1949 Ward, Inverkeithing, for BU.

NEMESIS 6th Rate 28, 598bm, 121 × 33·5ft. Jolly & Smallshaw, Liverpool, 23.1.1780. Sold 9.6.1814. *In French hands 9.12.1795–9.3.1796.*

NEMESIS Iron paddle frigate (Indian), 165 × 29ft, 2–3pdr. Laird 12.1811 For sale 1852.

NEMESIS 5th Rate 46, 1,168bm, 159 × 41ft. Pembroke Dock 19.8.1826. BU comp. 4.7.1866 Marshall, Plymouth.

NEMESIS Destroyer, 740 tons, 246·5 × 25ft, 2–4in, 2–12pdr, 2–TT. Hawthorn Leslie 9.8.1910. Lent Japanese Navy 6.1917–1919 = KANRAN. Sold 26.11.1921 British Legion, Plymouth.

NEMESIS TS. Req. 1940–45.

NENAMOOK Patrol boat (RCN), 84 × 20ft, 1–MG. Victoria Motor Boat & Repairs, Victoria, 10.9.1941. Sold B. C. Packers, Vancouver, 7.1948.

NENE Frigate, 'River' class, Smith's Dock 9.12.1912. Lent RCN 6.4.1944–11.6.1945. Arr. 8.1955 Ward, Briton Ferry, for BU.

NEPAL (ex-NORSEMAN) Destroyer, 1,690 tons, 356·5 (oa) × 35·7ft, 6–4·7in. 10–TT. Thornycroft 4.12.1941 (renamed 1.1942). Arr. 16.1.1956 Ward, Briton Ferry, for BU.

NEPEAN Torpedo boat (Australian), 12 tons, 63 × 7·5ft, 1–TT. Thornycroft, Chiswick 1884. BU 1913.

NEPEAN Destroyer, 'M' class, Thornycroft 22.1.1916. Sold 15.11.1921 Cashmore, Newport; BU 1923.

NEPEAN Frigate (RAN), 'River' class. Sydney, ordered 12.1942, cancelled 12.6.1944.

NEPETA Corvette, 'Flower' class. Morton, Quebec. 28.11.1942. Tx USN 1943 = PERT; sold 10.1946 mercantile.

NEPTUNE 2nd Rate 90, 1,377bm, 164 × 45ft, Deptford DY 17.4.1683. Rebuilt Blackwall 1710 as 1,577bm; rebuilt Woolwich 1730 as 1,573bm; = TORBAY 23.8.1750. Sold 17.8.1784.

NEPTUNE 2nd Rate 90, 1,798bm, 171 × 49ft. Portsmouth DY 17.7.1757. Sheer hulk 1784. BU 10.1816 Portsmouth.

NEPTUNE 2nd Rate 98, 2,111bm, 185 × 51ft, Deptford DY 28.1.1797. BU 10.1818.

NEPTUNE 1st Rate 120, 2,694bm, 206 × 55·5ft, 6–68pdr, 114–32pdr. Portsmouth DY 27.9.1832; undocked 7.3.1859 as screw ship, 72 guns, 2,830bm. Sold 1875 Castle, Charlton.

NEPTUNE Coastguard cutter, 60bm. Built 1863. Sold 4.4.1905 Chatham.

NEPTUNE (ex-INDEPENDENCIA) Battleship, 9,310 tons, 300 × 63ft, 4–12in, 2–9in MLR. Dudgeon, Poplar, 10.9.1874; Brazilian, purch. 3.1878. Sold 15.9.1903 Garnham; BU Germany.

NEPTUNE (ex-FOUDROYANT) Battleship, 19,900 tons, 510 × 85ft, 10–12in, 20–4in. Portsmouth DY 30.9.1909 (renamed 1909). Sold 1.9.1922 Hughes Bolckow, Blyth.

NEPTUNE Cruiser, 7,175 tons. 554·5 (oa) × 55ft, 8–6in, 8–4in. Portsmouth DY 31.1.1933. Sunk 19.12.1941 mine off Tripoli.

NEPTUNE Cruiser, c. 9,000 tons. Projected 1945, cancelled 3.1946, not ordered.

NEPTUNE *See also ROYAL GEORGE 1827.*

NERBUDDA (ex-GOSHAWK) Brig-sloop 12, 445bm, 100 × 32·5ft, 10–32pdr, 2–18pdr. Bombay DY 6.2.1847 (renamed 1845). Foundered 10.7.1856 off The Cape.

NERBUDDA Cutter 2, 49bm. Bombay DY 1835. Sold 7.1862.

NERBUDDA *See also NARBADA.*

NEREIDE 5th Rate 36, 892bm, 140 × 27·5ft. French, captured 20.12.1797 by PHOEBE off Scilly Is. Recaptured 28.8.1810 by French at Mauritius; again captured 6.12.1810 at Mauritius, LU. Sold 1.3.1816.

NEREIDE (ex-VENUS) 5th Rate 38, 1,165bm, 157·5 × 40·5ft. French, captured 18.9.1810 at Réunion by BOADICEA. BU 5.1816.

NEREIDE Wood screw corvette, 1,857bm, 225 × 43ft. Woolwich DY, ordered 1860, cancelled 12.12.1863.

NEREIDE Destroyer, 740 tons, 246·5 × 25ft 2– 12pdr, 2–TT.Hawthorn Leslie 6.9.1910. Sold 1.12.1921 Stanlee, Dover.

NEREIDE Sloop, 1,350 tons, 283 × 38·5ft, 6–4in. Chatham DY 29.1.1944. Arr. 18.5.1958 McLellan, Bo'ness, for BU.

NEREIDE *See also NYMPHE 1812.*

NEREUS 5th Rate 32. Temple, South Shields, 4.3.1809. BU 2.1817.

NEREUS 5th Rate 46, 1,095bm, 152 × 40ft. Pembroke Dock 30.7.1821. Storeship, harbour service 1843. Sold 22.1.1879 J. L. Page, Coquimbo, hulk.

NEREUS Destroyer, 'M' class. Thornycroft 24.2.1916. Sold 15.11.1921 Cashmore, Newport; BU 7.1922.

NERISSA Destroyer, 'M' class, 880 tons. Yarrow 2.1916. Sold 15.11.1921 Cashmore, Newport.

NERISSA Destroyer, 1,690 tons, 356·5 (oa) × 35·7ft, 6–4·7in, 10–TT. John Brown 7.5.1940. Lent Polish Navy 10.1940 = PIORUN; ret. 9.1946 = NOBLE. BU 11.1955 Clayton & Davie, Durston.

NERISSA Minesweeper, 'Algerine' class. Redfern 25.11.1944. Arr. 8.1960 Rees, Llanelly, for BU.

NESBITT Survey launch, 11 tons, 34·8 × 9·2ft. Halmatic, Southampton, comp. 1996.

NESS Destroyer, 555 tons, 222 × 23ft, 1–12pdr, 5– 6pdr (1907: 4–12pdr), 2–TT. White 5.1.1905. Sold 27.5.1919 T. R. Sales.

NESS Frigate, 'River' class. Robb, Leith, 30.7.1942. Sold 9.1956; BU Cashmore, Newport.

NESSUS Destroyer, 'M' class. Swan Hunter 24.8.1915. Sunk 8.9.1918 collision cruiser AMPHITRITE North Sea.

NESSUS Armed river steamer, 150 tons, 1–3pdr. Purch. 1926 Hong Kong. Sold 1929.

NESTOR (ex-FRANKLIN) 6th Rate 28. French privateer, captured 1781 by RAMILLIES and ULYSSES. Sold 1783.

NESTOR Destroyer, 'M' class. Swan Hunter 22.12.1915. Sunk in action 31.5.1916 Battle of Jutland.

NESTOR Destroyer, 1,690 tons, 356·5 (oa) × 35·7ft, 6–4·7in, 10–TT. Fairfield 9.7.1940. Bombed 15.6.1942 Italian aircraft eastern Mediterranean, sank next day.

NETLEY Gun-brig 16, 193bm, 86·5 × 21ft. Schooner, purch. 4.1798. Captured 17.12.1806 by French in West Indies

NETLEY (ex-NIMROD) Schooner 12, 140bm, 76 × 21·5ft, 10–12pdr carr., 2–6pdr. American, captured 1807, purch. 1808. BU 5.1813 Antigua.

NETLEY (ex-DETERMINE) Gun-brig 12, 173bm, 83 × 23.5 f t, 14–18pdr carr., 2–6pdr. French privateer, captured 1807. Wrecked 10.7.1808 West Indies.

NETLEY Cutter 8, 122bm, 64 × 22·5ft, 4–6pdr carr. Plymouth DY 13.3.1823. Foundered 10.1848 Spithead; raised, sold 29.8.1859.

NETLEY Wood screw gunboat, 'Britomart' class. Portsmouth 2.7.1866. Sold 9.1885 Castle for BU.

NETLEY *See also PRINCE REGENT 1812.*

NETTLE (ex-*Pennar*) Tender, 130 tons, 85 × 20ft. War Dept vessel, tx 1905. Sold 1934 = *Topmast I.*

NETTLE Wood screw gunboat, 'Cheerful' class. Pembroke Dock 9.2.1856. BU 1867 Bermuda.

NETTLE *See also THUNDERER 1831, ELFIN 1933, HYDERABAD 1941.*

NETTLHAM Inshore minesweeper, 'Ham' class. White 19.12.1956. Sold Rye Arc 27.11.1967.

NEW ADVENTURE Transport. Purch. 1799. Listed 1800.

NEW GLASGOW Frigate (RCN), 'River' class. Yarrow, Esquimalt, 5.5.1943. Sold 1967.

NEW LISKEARD Minesweeper (RCN). 'Algerine' class. Port Arthur SY 14.1.1944. Survey ship 1959. Sold 1969.

NEW WATERFORD Frigate (RCN), 'River' class. Yarrow, Esquimalt, 3.7.1943. Sold 16.8.1967 for BU.

NEW WESTMINSTER Corvette (RCN), 'Flower' class. Victoria Machinery 14.5.1941. Sold 1947 = *Elisa.*

NEW ZEALAND Battleship, 16,350 tons, 425 × 78ft, 4–12in, 4–9·2in, 10–6in, 14–12pdr. Portsmouth DY 4.2.1904. = ZEALANDIA 1.11.1911. Sold 8.11.1921 Stanlee; BU Germany.

NEW ZEALAND Battlecruiser, 18,800 tons, 555 × 80ft, 8–12in, 10–4in. Fairfield 1.7.1911. Sold 10.12.1922 A. J. Purves; resold, BU Rosyth.

NEW ZEALAND Aircraft carrier, c. 45,000 tons. Cammell Laird, cancelled 2.1946.

NEWARK 2nd Rate 80, 1,217bm, 157 × 42ft. Frame, Hull, 3.6.1695. Rebuilt Chatham 1717 as 1,283bm; rebuilt Chatham 1747 as 1,521bm. BU 6.1787 Chatham.

NEWARK (ex-NEWLYN) Minesweeper, Later 'Hunt' class. Inglis 19.6.1919 (renamed 1918). Sold 6.1928 Ailsa, Charlestown.

NEWARK (ex-RINGGOLD) Destroyer, 1,060 tons, 309 × 30·5ft, 1—4in, 1—3in, 4—20mm, 3—TT. USN, cd RN 5.12.1940. Air target 1.1945. Sold 18.2.1947; BU McLellan, Bo'ness.

NEWASH Schooner 4 (Canadian Lakes), 166bm, 71 × 24·5ft. Chippawa 8.1815. Condemned 3.1832.

NEWBARK Ship, 200bm. Built 1543. Listed until 1565.

NEWBURY 52-gun ship, 766bm. Graves, Lime-house, 4.1654. = REVENGE 1660. Condemned 1678.

NEWBURY Paddle minesweeper, 'Ascot' class. Inglis 3.7.1916. Sold 3.1922 Ward, Inverkeithing; BU 1923.

NEWCASTLE 50-gun ship, 625bm, 131 × 33ft. Pett, Ratcliffe, 1653. Rebuilt Rotherhithe 1692. Wrecked 27.11.1703 nr Chichester.

NEWCASTLE 4th Rate 54, 676bm, 130 × 34ft. Sheerness DY 24.3.1704. Rebuilt Woolwich 1733 as 759bm. BU 1746.

NEWCASTLE 4th Rate 50, 1,052bm, 144 × 41ft. Portsmouth DY 4.12.1750. Foundered 1.1.1761 cyclone off Pondicherry.

NEWCASTLE 4th Rate 60 (pitch pine-built), 1,556bm, 176·5 × 44ft. 26—42pdr carr., 32—24pdr. Wigram & Green, Blackwall, 10.11.1813. Harbour service 6.1824. Sold 6.1850 J. Brown.

NEWCASTLE Wood screw frigate, 3,035bm, 4,020 tons, 250 × 52ft, 30—8in, 1—68pdr, 20—32pdr. Deptford DY 16.10.1860. Powder hulk 1889. Sold 1929.

NEWCASTLE 2nd class cruiser, 4,800 tons, 430 × 47ft, 2—6in, 10—4in. Armstrong 25.11.1909. Sold 9.5.1921 Ward; arr. Lelant 3.5.1923 for BU.

NEWCASTLE (ex-MINOTAUR) Cruiser, 9,100 tons, 591·5 (oa) × 61·7ft, 12—6in. Vickers Arm-strong, Tyne, 23.1.1936 (renamed 1936). Arr. 19.8.1959 Faslane for BU.

NEWCASTLE Destroyer, Type 42 Batch 1. Swan Hunter 24.4.1975.

NEWCASTLE Frigate (RAN), 'Adelaide' class. Australian Marine Engineering, Williamstown, 21.2.1992.

NEWFOUNDLAND Cruiser, 8,800 tons, 555·5 (oa) × 62ft, 9—6in, 8—4in. Swan Hunter 19.12.1941. Sold 2.11.1959 Peruvian Navy = ALMIRANTE GRAU; = CAPITAN QUINONES 1973; hulk 1979.

NEWHAVEN *See CARNATIC 1942.*

NEWMARKET (ex-ROBINSON) Destroyer, 1,060 tons, 309 × 30·5ft, 1—4in, 1—3in, 4—20mm, 3—

TT. USN, cd RN 26.11.1940. Air target 3.1942. Sold 9.1945; BU Rees, Llanelly.

NEWPORT 6th Rate 24, 253bm, 94·5 × 23ft. Portsmouth. Captured 7.4.1694 by French in Bay of Fundy.

NEWPORT Wood screw gunvessel, 425bm, 570 tons, 145 × 15·5ft. Pembroke Dock 20.7.1867; comp. 4.1868 as survey vessel. Sold 3.1881 = *Pandora*.

NEWPORT (ex-SIGOURNEY) Destroyer, 1,060 tons, 309 × 30·5ft, 3—4in, 1—3in, 6—TT. USN, cd RN 26.11.1940. Lent RNorN 3.1941–6.1942. Air target 6.1943. Sold 18.2.1947; BU Brechin, Granton.

NEWPORT *See also ORFORD 1695.*

NEWQUAY *See NAILSEA 1918.*

NEWTON Research vessel/support ship, 3,140 tons, 323.5 (oa) × 53ft. Scott-Lithgow 25.6.1975.

NEZA *See TEST 1942.*

NIAGARA (ex-THATCHER) Destroyer (RCN), 1,060 tons, 309 × 30·5ft, 3—4in, 1—3in, 6—TT. USN, cd RCN 24.9.1940; TS 2.3.1944. BU 12.1947.

NIAGARA *See also ROYAL GEORGE 1809, PRINCE REGENT 1812.*

NICATOR Destroyer, 'M' class. Denny 3.2.1916. Sold 9.5.1921 Ward, Milford Haven.

NICATOR Minesweeper, 'Algerine' class. Redfern, Toronto, LD 5.10.1944, cancelled 8.11.1944.

NICHOLAS Ship. 1398. Given away 1404

NICHOLAS Ship. Purch. 1415. Foundered R. Thames 1419.

NICHOLAS Ballinger, 120bm. Presented 3.1417. Sold 11.9.1422

NICHOLAS Vessel. Captured 1549. Not listed thereafter.

NICHOLAS Fireship. Purch. 1692. Expended 12.7.1694 Dieppe.

NICHOLAS REEDE (GREAT NICHOLAS) Ship, 400bm. Purch. 1512. Listed until 1522.

NICODEMUS 6-gun vessel, 105bm. Privateer, cap-tured 1636. Sold 1657.

NIEMEN 5th Rate 38, 1,093bm, 154·5 × 40ft. French, captured 5.4.1809 by AMETHYST and EMERALD in Bay of Biscay. BU 9.1815.

NIEMEN 6th Rate 28 (fir-built), 502bm, 114 × 31·5ft, 20—32pdr carr., 6—18pdr carr., 2—9pdr. Woolwich DY 23.11.1820. BU comp. 1.1828.

NIEUPORT Gunvessel 14. Purch. 4.1795. Listed until 1810.

NIGELLA Sloop, 'Arabis' class. Hamilton 10.12.1915. Sold 29.11.1922.

NIGELLA Corvette, 'Flower' class. Philip, Dart-mouth, 21.9.1940. Sold 1947 = *Nigelock*.

NIGER 5th Rate 33, 679bm, 125 × 35ft. Sheerness

DY 25.9.1759. Prison ship 1810; = NEGRO 1813. Sold 29.9.1814.

NIGER 5th Rate 38 (red pine-built), 1,066bm, 150 × 40ft. Wigram & Green, Blackwall, 29.5.1813. BU 1820 Halifax, NS.

NIGER Wood screw sloop, 1,013bm 190 × 35ft, 2–68pdr, 12–32pdr. Woolwich DY 18.11.1846. Sold 2.12.1769 Castle.

NIGER Composite paddle vessel, 600 tons, 160 × 25·5ft, 2 guns. Elder 10.3.1880. = COCKATRICE 2.4.1881; = MOORHEN 1896. Sold 1899.

NIGER Torpedo gunboat, 810 tons, 230 × 27ft, 2–4·7in, 4–3pdr, 3–TT. NC&A (Vickers) 17.12.1892. Minesweeper 1909. Sunk 11.11.1914 by U.12 off Deal.

NIGER Minesweeper, 815 tons, 230 × 33·5ft, 2–4in. White 29.1.1936. Sunk 5.7.1942 mine off Iceland.

NIGER Minesweeper, 'Algerine' class. Redfern, Toronto, LD 20.9.1944, cancelled 8.11.1944.

NIGER (ex-DISDAIN) Minesweeper, 'Algerine' class. Lobnitz 1.5.1945 (renamed 11.1944). Arr. 2.2.1966 Silloth for BU by Ardmore Steel Co.

NIGERIA Cruiser, 8,000 tons, 555·5 (oa) × 62ft, 12–6in, 8–4in. Vickers Armstrong, Tyne, 18.7.1939. Tx Indian Navy 29.8.1957 = MYSORE; PO 29.8.1985; BU 1986.

NIGERIA Frigate (Nigerian), 1,750 tons, 341 × 37ft, 2–4in. Wilton-Fijenoord, Holland, 9.1965.

NIGERIA *See also HARE 1944.*

NIGHTINGALE Vessel. Captured 1626. Listed until 1628.

NIGHTINGALE 30-gun ship, 290bm. Horsleydown 1651. Wrecked 16.1.1672 Goodwin Sands.

NIGHTINGALE 6th Rate 24, 251bm, 93 × 24·5ft. Chatham DY 16.12.1702. Captured 26.8.1707 by French; = ROSSIGNOL, recaptured 12.1707 by LUDLOW CASTLE; = FOX. Rebuilt Deptford 1727 as 375bm. BU 1.1737 Deptford.

NIGHTINGALE 6th Rate 24, 253bm, 90 × 2 5·5ft. Johnson, Blackwall, 15.10.1707. Sold 21.6.1716.

NIGHTINGALE 6th Rate 24, 522bm. 114 × 32·5ft. Purch. on stocks 17.6.1746. Bird, Rotherhithe, 6.10.1746. Sunk 8.1773 breakwater Harwich.

NIGHTINGALE Brig-sloop 16, 248bm, 93 × 26·5ft. King, Dover, 29.7.1805. Sold 23.11.1815.

NIGHTINGALE Cutter 6, 122bm. 63·5 × 22ft, 2–6pdr, 4–6pdr carr. Plymouth DY 19.4.1825. Wrecked 17.2.1829 The Shingles.

NIGHTINGALE (ex-*Marchioness of Salisbury*) Packet brig 8, 208bm. Packet, purch. 1829. Sold 24.11.1842 Greenwood & Clark.

NIGHTINGALE Wood screw gunboat, 'Albacore' class. Mare, Blackwall, 22.1922.1855. Sold 16.7.1867 W. Lethbridge.

NIGHTINGALE River gunboat, 85 tons, 100 × 20ft, 2–6pdr. Yarrow 1897. Sold 20.11.1919 in Hong Kong.

NIGHTINGALE Mining tender, 298 tons, 100 × 24·5ft. Portsmouth DY 30.9.1931. Sold 5.7.1957; BU 1958 Pollock Brown, Southampton.

NIJADEN *See NYADEN 1807.*

NILAM (ex-CHAROGH) Gunboat (RIN), 331 tons, 170 × 22ft, 2–3in. Iranian, captured 1941 by RIN. Ret. 1946.

NILE Cutter 12, 166bm, 12–12pdr carr. Purch. 1806. Sold 18.10.1810, rejected by buyer; BU 9.1811.

NILE 2nd Rate 92, 2,598bm, 205 × 54ft,10–8in, 82–32pdr. Plymouth DY 28.6.1839; undocked 30.1.1854 as screw ship, 2,622bm. = CONWAY (TS on loan) 24.7.1876. Stranded 14.4.1953 Menai Strait. Wreck burnt 31.10.1956.

NILE Battleship, 11,940 tons, 345 × 73ft, 4–13·5in, 8–6pdr. Pembroke Dock 27.3.1888. Sold 9.7.1912 Ward, Swansea and Briton Ferry.

NIMBLE Cutter 12, 185bm, 12–4pdr. Purch. 3.1778. Wrecked 11.2.1781 Mounts Bay.

NIMBLE Cutter 12, 168bm, 10–18pdr carr., 2–3pdr. Jacobs, Folkestone, 6.7.1781, purch. on stocks. Grounded, lost 1808 Stangate Creek, Medway; wreck for sale 4.1808.

NIMBLE Cutter 10, 144bm, 65·5 × 23·5ft, 10–12pdr carr., 2–6pdr. Cowes 14.12.1811. Foundered 6.10.1812 North Sea after striking submerged rock.

NIMBLE Cutter 12, 147bm, 68·5 × 23·5ft, 12–12pdr carr. Purch. 1812. Sold 18.4.1816.

NIMBLE Schooner, 570bm. McLean, Jamaica, 1826. Ret. builder 5.1826 unfit for service.

NIMBLE (ex-*Bolivar*) Schooner 5, 168bm, 84 × 22ft. Purch. 1826. Wrecked 4.11.1834 Bahamas Channel.

NIMBLE Wood screw gunvessel, 'Philomel' class. Pembroke Dock 15.9.1860. Harbour service 1879. Sold 10.7.1906 W. R. Jones.

NIMROD (ex-EOLE) Sloop 18, 395bm. French, captured 22.11.1799 by SOLEBAY in West Indies. Sold 21.2.1811.

NIMROD Brig-sloop 18, 'Cruizer' class, 384bm. Bailey, Ipswich, 25.5.1812. Foundered 14.1.1827 Holyhead Bay; wreck sold 1827 Rowland Robert & Co.

NIMROD (ex-ANDROMEDA) Sloop 20, 502bm, 114 × 32ft. Deptford DY 26.8.1828; 6th Rate, renamed 10.5.1827. Coal hulk 2.1853; = C.1; = C.76. Sold 9.7.1907 Hamley & Son.

NIMROD Iron paddle gunboat (Indian), 153bm, 103 × 18ft. Laird 6.1839, re-erected 1840 Basra. Still listed 1859.

NIMROD Wood screw gunvessel, 859bm, 200 × 30·5ft, 2—68pdr, 4—32pdr. Scott Russell 21.4.1856. Sold 2.6.1865 White.

NIMROD Destroyer leader, 1,608 tons, 325 × 32ft. 4—4in, 4—TT. Denny 12.4.1915. Sold 5.11.1926 Alloa, Rosyth.

NIOBE (ex-DIANE) 5th Rate 38, 1,142bm, 156 × 41ft. French, captured 24.8.1800 by squadron off Malta. BU 11.1816.

NIOBE 6th Rate 28, 1,051bm, 140 × 42ft, 2—8in, 26—32pdr. Devonport DY 18.9.1849. Sold 9.7.1862 Prussian Navy.

NIOBE Wood screw sloop, 1,083bm, 187 × 36ft. Deptford DY 31.5.1866. Wrecked 21.5.1874 Miquelon.

NIOBE 1st class cruiser, 11,000 tons, 435 × 69ft, 16—6in, 14—12pdr. NC&A (Vickers) 20.2.1897. Tx RCN 6.9.1910; depot ship 9.1915; BU 1922 Philadelphia.

NIPIGON Minesweeper (RCN), TE 'Bangor' class. Dufferin 1.10.1940. Sold 29.11.1957 Turkish Navy = BAFRA; deleted 1972.

NIPIGON Escort (RCN), 2,400 tons, 371 (oa) × 42ft, 2—3in, 6—TT. Marine Industries 10.12.1961. PO 1.7.1998, deleted.

NISUS 5th Rate 38, 1,074bm, 154 × 39·5ft. Plymouth DY 3.4.1810. BU 9.1822.

NISUS *See also NOBLE 1915.*

NITH Destroyer, 555 tons, 222 × 23ft, 1—12pdr, 5—6pdr (1907: 4—12pdr), 2—TT. White 7.3.1905. Sold 23.6.1919 Ward, Preston.

NITH Frigate, 'River' class. Robb 25.9.1942. Sold 11.1948 Egyptian Navy = DOMIAT; sunk 1.11.1956 by NEWFOUNDLAND.

NITROCRIS Iron paddle gunboat (Indian), 153bm. Laird 1839, re-erected 1840 Basra. *Fate unknown.*

NIZAM Destroyer, 'M' class. Stephen 6.4.1916. Sold 9.5.1921 Ward, Rainham.

NIZAM Destroyer, 1,690 tons, 356·5 (oa) × 35·7ft, 6—4·7in, 10—TT. John Brown 4.7.1940. Arr. 16.11.1955 Ward, Grays, for BU.

NOBLE (ex-NISUS, renamed 1915) Destroyer, 'M' class. Stephen 25.11.1915. Sold 8.11.1921 Slough Trading Co..

NOBLE Destroyer, 1,690 tons, 356·5 (oa) × 35·7ft, 6—4.7in, 10—TT. Denny 17.4.1941. Tx Dutch Navy 11.2.1942 = VAN GALEN; BU 8.2.1957 Hendrick-Ibo-Ambacht.

NOBLE *See also NERISSA 1940.*

NOMAD Destroyer, 'M' class. Stephen 7.2.1916. Sunk 31.5.1916 Battle of Jutland.

NONPAREIL Schooner 14, 210bm, 88 × 24ft. American, captured 1807 Montevideo. Damaged 19.12.1812 storm in Tagus; sold there 1813.

NONPAREIL Destroyer, 'M' class. Stephen 16.5.1916. Sold 9.5.1921 Ward, Briton Ferry.

NONPAREIL Destroyer, 1,690 tons, 356·5 (oa) × 35·7ft, 6—4·7in, 10—TT. Denny 25.6.1941. Tx Dutch Navy 27.5.1942 = TJERK HIDDES; tx Indonesia 1.3.1951 = GADJAH MADA; BU 1961.

NONPAREIL Minesweeper, 'Algerine' class. Redfern, Toronto, LD 23.10.1944, cancelled 8.11.1944.

NONPAREIL *See also PHILIP & MARY 1556.*

NONSUCH 34-gun ship, 400/500bm. Deptford 1646. Wrecked 1664.

NONSUCH Ketch 8, 47bm. Purch. 1654. Sold 1667.

NONSUCH 4th Rate 42, 359bm. Portsmouth 1668. Captured 4.1.1695 by French privateer LE FRANCAIS.

NONSUCH Hoy 5, 95bm. Portsmouth 1686. Sold 5.1.1714.

NONSUCH 4th Rate 48, 677bm, 130·5 × 34ft. Deptford 1696. Rebuilt Portsmouth 1717 as 687bm. Hulk 1740; BU 1745.

NONSUCH 4th Rate 50, 852bm, 133·5 × 39ft. Quallet, Rotherhithe, 29.12.1741. BU 11.1766 Plymouth.

NONSUCH 3rd Rate 64, 1,373bm, 160 × 44·5ft. Plymouth DY 17.12.1774. Floating battery 5.1794. BU 6.1802.

NONSUCH (ex-NARCISSUS) Destroyer, 'M' class. Palmer 7.12.1915 (renamed 1915). Sold 9.5.1921 Ward, Milford Haven; arr. 9.1922 for BU.

NONSUCH Sloop, 1,350 tons, 283 × 38·5ft, 6—4in. Chatham DY, LD 26.2.1945, cancelled 23.10.1945.

NONSUCH *See also PHILIP AND MARY 1556, Z.38 1945.*

NOOTKA Destroyer (RCN), 1,927 tons, 377 (oa) × 37·5ft, 6—4·7in, 2—4in, 4—TT. Halifax SY 26.4.1944. Arr. 6.10.1964 Faslane for BU.

NORANDA Minesweeper (RCN), diesel 'Bangor' class. Davie SB 13.6.1941. Tx RCMP 1947 = *Irvine*. Sold 1962, conv. yacht = *Miriana*. Sank 5.1971 Montego Bay.

NORFOLK 3rd Rate 80, 1,184bm, 156·5 × 41·5ft. Winters, Southampton, 28.3.1693. Rebuilt Plymouth 1728 as 1,393bm. = PRINCESS AMELIA 1.11.1755. Harbour service 4.1777. Tx Customs Service 11.1788.

NORFOLK 3rd Rate 74, 1,556bm, 165·5 × 47ft. Deptford DY 28.12.1757. BU 12.1774 Portsmouth.

NORFOLK Cruiser, 9,925 tons, 635·5 (oa)× 66ft, 8—8in, 8—4in. Fairfield 12.12.1928. Sold

3.1.1950; arr. 19.2.1950 Cashmore, Newport, for BU.

NORFOLK GM destroyer 5,600 tons, 520·5 (oa) × 54ft, 4—4·5in (later 2—4·5in, Exocet), 2—20mm, Sea Slug, Seacat, helo. Swan Hunter 16.11.1967. Sold Chilean Navy (left Britain 2.1982) = PRAT.

NORFOLK Frigate, 'Norfolk' class. Yarrow, Glasgow, 10.7.1987.

NORGE 3rd Rate 74, 1,960bm. Danish, captured 7.9.1807 Battle of Copenhagen. Sold 3.1816. *Was to have been renamed NONSUCH.*

NORHAM CASTLE *See HUMBERSTONE 1944.*

NORMAN Destroyer, 'M' class. Palmer 20.3.1916. Sold 9.5.1921 Ward, Milford Haven.

NORMAN Destroyer, 1,690 tons, 356·5 (oa) × 35·7ft, 6—4·7in 10—TT. Thornycroft 30.10.1940. Arr. 1.4.1958 Cashmore, Newport, for BU.

NORMAN Minehunter (RAN), 'Huon' class, 720 tons, 172·2 (oa) × 32·5ft, 1—30mm. ADI, Newcastle, NSW, 3.5.1999.

NORSEMAN Destroyer, 'M' class. Doxford 15.8.1916. Sold 9.5.1921 Ward, Grays.

NORSEMAN *See also NEPAL 1941.*

NORSYD Corvette (RCN), Modified 'Flower' class. Morton 31.7.1943. On sale list 10.1945; sold = *Balboa*.

NORTH Sloop 18 purch. 1778. Wrecked Halifax 12.12.1779.

NORTH BAY Corvette (RCN), Modified 'Flower' class. Collingwood 27.4.1943. Sold 1946 = *Kent County II*.

NORTH STAR 6th Rate 20, 433bm, 108·5 × 30ft, 16—32pdr carr.,8—18pdr carr., 1—12pdr, 2—6pdr. Tanner, Dartmouth, 21.4.1810. Sold 6.3.1817 Pittman.

NORTH STAR 6th Rate 28, 501bm, 114 × 32ft. Woolwich DY 7.12.1824. BU comp. 15.3.1860 Chatham.

NORTH STAR Wood screw corvette, 1,857bm, 225 × 41ft. Sheerness DY, LD 13.7.1860, cancelled 22.5.1865.

NORTH STAR Destroyer, 'M' class. Palmer 9.11.1916. Sunk 23.4.1918 shore batteries Zeebrugge.

NORTHAMPTON Iron armoured frigate 7,652 tons, 280 × 60ft, 4—10in, 8—9in, 6—20pdr, 3—9pdr. Napier 18.11.1876. TS 6.1894. Sold 4.4.1905 Ward, Morecambe.

NORTHAMPTON *See also SHARPSHOOTER 1888.*

NORTHBROOK Troopship (RIM), 5,820 tons, 360 × 52ft, 6—4·7in, 6—3pdr. John Brown 6.7.1907. Still listed 1924.

NORTHELLA Trawler 1,535 tons, 226 (oa) ×

61·7ft, 1972. TUFT 1982 minesweeper, 1983 target vesel. Navigational TS 1985. PO 29.3.1998, ret. owner.

NORTHESK Destroyer, 'M' class, Palmer 5.7.1916. Sold 9.5.1921 Ward, Rainham.

NORTHOLT Minesweeper, Later 'Hunt' class. Eltringham 21.6.1918. BU 4.1928 Cashmore, Newport.

NORTHREPPS Minesweeper, Later 'Hunt' class. Lobnitz, cancelled 1919.

NORTHUMBERLAND 3rd Rate 70, 1,041bm, 152 × 40·5ft. Bailey, Bristol, 1679. Rebuilt Chatham 1701. Wrecked 27.11.1703 Goodwin Sands.

NORTHUMBERLAND 3rd Rate 70, 1,105bm, 151 × 41ft. Deptford 1705. Rebuilt Woolwich 1721 as 1,133bm. BU 11.1739 Woolwich.

NORTHUMBERLAND 3rd Rate 70, 1,300bm, Woolwich DY 7.10.1743. Captured 8.5.1744 by French CONTENT off Ushant = L'ATLAS.

NORTHUMBERLAND 3rd Rate 70, 1,414bm, 160 × 45ft. Plymouth DY 1.12.1750. Storeship = LEVIATHAN 13.9.1777. Foundered 27.2.1780 passage Jamaica to Britain.

NORTHUMBERLAND 3rd Rate 78, 1,811bm, 179 × 42ft. French, captured 1.6.1794 at 'Battle of 1st of June'. BU 11.1795.

NORTHUMBERLAND 3rd Rate 74, 1,907bm, 182 × 49ft. Barnard, Deptford, 2.2.1798. Hulk 2.1827. BU 7.1850 Deptford.

NORTHUMBERLAND Iron armoured frigate (battleship), 6,621bm, 10,780 tons, 400 × 59·5ft, 4—9in, 22—8in, 2—7in. Mare, Blackwall, 17.4.1866. Depot ship 1898; = ACHERON (TS) 3.1904; hulk C.8 in 1909, C.68 in 1926. Sold 6.1927 Ward; resold as hulk *Stedmound*.

NORTHUMBERLAND Cruiser, 10,000 tons. Devonport DY, ordered 15.5.1929, cancelled 1.1.1930.

NORTHUMBERLAND Frigate (RCN), 'River' class. Victoria, BC, cancelled 12.1943.

NORTHUMBERLAND Frigate, 'Norfolk' class. Swan Hunter 4.4.1992.

NORTHUMBRIA *See HODGESTON 1954, QUAINTON 1957.*

NORTHWAY (ex-CUTLASS) Dock landing ship, 4,270 tons, 454 × 27ft, 1—3in, 16—20mm. Newport News 18.11.1943 on Lend-Lease (renamed 8.1943). Ret. USN 12.1946.

NORWICH 28-gun ship, 265bm. Chatham DY 1655. Wrecked 1682.

NORWICH 4th Rate 48, 616bm, 125·5 × 34ft. Portsmouth DY 1691. Wrecked 6.10.1692 West Indies.

NORWICH 4th Rate 48, 618bm, 125·5 × 34ft.

Deptford DY 1693. Rebuilt Chatham 1718 as 703bm. = ENTERPRISE (5th Rate 44) 23.5.1744. BU 1771 Sheerness.

NORWICH 4th Rate 50, 993bm, 140 × 40·5ft. Perry, Blackwall, 4.7.1745. Sold 24.5.1768.

NORWICH CASTLE Corvette, 'Castle' class. G. Brown, cancelled 12.1943.

NOTTINGHAM 4th Rate 60, 924bm, 146 × 38ft, Deptford 6.1703. Rebuilt Deptford 1719 as 928bm; rebuilt Sheerness 1745 as 1,077bm. Sunk 9.1773 breakwater Sheerness.

NOTTINGHAM Gunvessel 3, 67bm, 57 × 16·5ft. Barge, purch. 3.1794. Sold 18.6.1800.

NOTTINGHAM 2nd class cruiser, 5,440 tons, 430 × 50ft, 9–6in. Pembroke Dock 18.4.1913. Sunk 19.8.1916 by U.52 in North Sea.

NOTTINGHAM Destroyer, Type 42 Batch 2. Vosper-Thornycroft 18.2.1980.

NOTTINGHAM PRIZE 6th Rate 4, 40bm, 46 × 14·5 ×ft. Captured 14.4.1704. Sunk 31.7.1706 breakwater Sheerness.

NOVA SCOTIA (ex-RAPID) Gun-brig 14, 214bm, 84 × 25ft, 12–12pdr carr., 2–6pdr. American privateer, captured 17.10.1812 by MAIDSTONE North America. = FERRET 1813. Sold 13.1.1820.

NOX Minesweeper, 'Algerine' class. Redfern, Toronto, cancelled 8.11.1944, not LD.

NUBIAN (ex-*Procida*) Coal depot, 2,265grt, 326 × 36ft. Purch. 12.1.1901. = C.370 in 1904. Sold 15.7.1912 Simonstown; BU 4.1913 Morecambe.

NUBIAN Destroyer, 985 tons, 280 × 26·5ft, 3–12pdr (1911: 5–12pdr), 2–TT. Thornycroft, Woolston, 20.4.1909. Bow wrecked 27.10.1916 torpedo from German destroyer; stern half joined to bow half of wrecked ZULU Chatham 1917, new ship = ZUBIAN (q.v.).

NUBIAN Destroyer, 1,870 tons, 377 (oa) × 36·5ft, 8–4·7in, 4–TT. Thornycroft 21.12.1937. Sold 11.6.1949; BU Ward, Briton Ferry.

NUBIAN Frigate, Type 81, 2,300 tons, 360 (oa) × 42ft, 2–4·5in, 2–40mm, Limbo, helo. Portsmouth DY 6.9.1960. Expended 27.5.1987 target.

NUESTRA SENORA DEL ROSARIO Galleon 46, 1,000bm. Spanish, captured 1588. BU 1622.

NUGENT Destroyer, 'M' class. Palmer 23.1.1917. Sold 9.5.1921 Ward, Hayle.

NUNNEY CASTLE *See BOWMANVILLE 1944.*

NURTON Coastal minesweeper, 'Ton' class. Harland & Wolff 22.10.1956. = MONTROSE 1958–61; = NURTON 1961–72; = KILLIE-CRANKIE 1972–74. PO 3.12.1993. Sold Pounds 4.1995. *Last 'Ton' class vessel to serve RN.*

NUSA Patrol yacht (RAN), 64 tons. German, captured 13.9.1914 by MELBOURNE off New Ireland. Sold 1921.

NYADEN (NIJADEN) 5th Rate 36, 909bm, 142 × 38ft. Danish, captured 7.9.1807 Battle of Copenhagen. BU 5.1812.

NYASALAND (ex-HOSTE) Frigate, 'Colony' class. Walsh Kaiser 7.9.1943 on Lend-Lease (renamed 1943). Ret. USN 4.1946.

NYMPH Sloop 14, 300bm, 96·5 × 27ft. Chatham DY 27.5.1778. Burnt 28.6.1783 accident Tortola, West Indies.

NYMPHE 5th Rate 36, 937bm, 141 × 38ft. French, captured 10.8.1780 by FLORA off Ushant. Wrecked 18.12.1810 Firth of Forth.

NYMPHE (ex-NEREIDE) 5th Rate 38, 1,087bm, 154 × 40ft. Parsons, Warsash, 12.4.1812 (renamed 1811). Harbour service 3.1836. = HANDY 7.9.1871. BU comp. 3.1875 Chatham.

NYMPHE Wood screw sloop, 1,084bm, 1,574 tons, 187 × 36ft. Deptford DY 24.11.1866. Sold 12.1884.

NYMPHE Composite screw sloop, 1,140 tons, 195 × 28ft, 8–5in. Portsmouth DY 1.5.1888. = WILDFIRE (base ship) 12.1906; = GANNET 1916; = PEMBROKE 7.1917. Sold 10.2.1920; BU Ward, Milford Haven.

NYMPHE Destroyer, 740 tons, 246·5 × 25ft, 2–4in, 2–12pdr, 2–TT. Hawthorn Leslie 31.1.1911. Sold 9.5.1921 Ward, Hayle.

NYMPHE Sloop, 1,350 tons, 283 × 38·5ft, 6–4in. Chatham DY, LD 26.2.1945, cancelled 23.10.1945.

NYMPHEN 5th Rate 36. Danish, captured 7.9.1807 Battle of Copenhagen. Sold 11.1.1816. *Was to have been renamed DETERMINEE.*

O

O.1 *See OBERON 1926.*

OAK Ship. Captured 1652. Lost 31.7.1653 in action with Dutch

OAK Destroyer, 765 tons, 255 × 26ft, 2—4in, 2—12pdr, 2—TT. Yarrow 5.9.1912. Sold 9.5.1921 Ward, Hayle; BU 9.1922.

OAKHAM CASTLE Corvette, 'Castle' class. Inglis 20.7.1944. Tx Air Ministry 8.1957, = *Weather Reporter* 4.1958. Sold H. K.Vickers 2.9.1977; BU 11.1977 Tees Marine, Middlesbrough.

OAKINGTON Coastal minesweeper, 'Ton' class. Harland & Wolff, launched 10.12.1958 as MOSSELBAAI (SAN). Sold S. A. Metal Co. 9.1988; BU 1989 Table Bay.

OAKLEY Minesweeper, Early 'Hunt' class. Lobnitz 10.1.1917. Sold 18.1.1923 Alloa, Charlestown.

OAKLEY Destroyer, 'Hunt' class Type II. Vickers Armstrong, Tyne, 30.10.1940. Tx Polish Navy = KUJAWIAK 6.1941. Mined 16.6.1942 off Malta, foundered in tow.

OAKLEY (ex-TICKHAM) Destroyer, 'Hunt' class Type II. Yarrow 15.1.1942 (renamed 6.1941). Sold 2.10.1958 West German Navy = GNEISENAU. BU 1972.

OAKVILLE Corvette (RCN), 'Flower' class. Port Arthur SB 21.6.1941. Sold 1946 Venezuelan Navy = PATRIA. BU 1962.

OBDURATE Destroyer, 'M' class. Scotts 21.1.1916. Sold 15.11.1921 Cashmore, Newport; arr. 5.1922 for BU.

OBDURATE Destroyer, 1,540 tons, 345 (oa) × 35ft, 4—4in, 8—TT. Denny 19.2.1942. Arr. 30.11.1964 Inverkeithing for BU.

OBEDIENT Destroyer, 'M' class. Scotts 16.11.1916. Sold 2.5.11.1921 Hayes, Porthcawl.

OBEDIENT Destroyer, 1,540 tons, 345 (oa) × 35ft, 4—4in, 8—TT. Denny 30.4.1942. Arr. 19.10.1962 Hughes Bolckow, Blyth, for BU.

OBERON Brig-sloop 16, 283bm, 93 × 26·5ft, 14—24pdr carr., 2—6pdr. Shepherd, Hull, 13.8.1805. BU 5.1816.

OBERON Iron paddle sloop, 649bm, 170 × 28ft. Deptford 2.1.1847. Target 1870. Sunk 1874 mine experiments; raised 1875, sold 16.11.1880 Moss Isaacs.

OBERON Destroyer, 'M' class. Doxford 29.9.1916. Sold 9.5.1921 Ward, Rainham.

OBERON (ex-O.1) Submarine, 1,311 tons, 270 × 28ft, 1—4in, 8—TT. Chatham DY 24.9.1926 renamed 1924). BU 8.1945 Clayton & Davie, Dunston.

OBERON Submarine, 'Oberon' class. Chatham DY 18.7.1959. Sold 1987 Seaforth Group to refit for resale. BU Grimsby 1991.

OBERON *See also HAWK 1888.*

OBERVATEUR Brig-sloop 16, 303bm, 90·5 × 28ft, 14—24pdr carr., 2—6pdr. French, captured 9.6.1806 by TARTAR in West Indies. Sold 1.9.1814.

OBSERVER Brig-sloop 12. Captured (?) 1781. Sold 21.10.1784.

OBSERVER Destroyer, 'M' class. Fairfield 1.5.1916. Sold 30.10.1921 W. & A. T. Burden.

OBSERVER *See also ORIBI 1941.*

OCEAN 2nd Rate 90, 1,833bm, 176 × 49ft. Chatham DY 21.4.1761. Sold 6.1793.

OCEAN 2nd Rate 98, 2,291bm, 197 × 52ft. Woolwich DY 24.10.1805. Depot ship 1841; coal hulk 1853. BU comp. 11.12.1875 Chatham.

OCEAN Ironclad ship, 4,047bm, 6,832 tons, 273 × 57ft, 24—7in. Devonport DY 19.3.1863 (LD 23.8.1968 as 2nd Rate 92). Sold 11.5.1882 Castle, Charlton.

OCEAN Battleship, 12,950 tons, 390 × 74ft, 4—12in, 12—6in, 12—12pdr. Devonport DY 5.7.1898. Sunk 18.3.1915 shore batteries Dardanelles.

OCEAN Aircraft carrier, 13,190 tons, 630 × 80ft, 19—40mm, 48 aircraft. Stephen 8.7.1944. Arr. 6.5.1962 Faslane for BU.

OCEAN Helicopter assault ship, 21,578 tons (full load), 667·3 (oa) × 112·9ft, 8—20mm, Phalanx, 12 helo. Vickers SB, Barrow, and Kvaerner, Govan, 11.10.1995.

OCEANWAY (ex-DAGGER) Dock landing ship, 4,270 tons, 454 × 72ft, 1—3in, 16—20mm. Newport News 29.12.1943 on Lend-Lease (renamed 8.1943). Ret. USN; tx Greek Navy = OKEANOS.

OCELOT Submarine, 'Oberon' class. Chatham DY 5.5.1962. PO 6.9.1991; tx 1992 Chatham Historic DY Trust.

OCKHAM Inshore minesweeper, 'Ham' class. Ailsa SB 12.5.1959. Sold mercantile 1.9.1967.

OCTAVIA 4th Rate 50, 2,132bm, 180 × 53ft, 10–8in, 40–32pdr Pembroke Dock 18.8.1849; undocked 11.4.1861 as screw frigate, 39 guns. BU 8.1876.

OCTAVIA (ex-ORYX) Destroyer, 'M' class. Doxford 21.6.1916 (renamed 1915). Sold 5.11.1921 Granton S. Bkg Co.

OCTAVIA Minesweeper, 'Algerine' class. Redfern 3.12.1942. Sold 27.4.1950; BU Dorkin, Gateshead.

ODIHAM Inshore minesweeper, 'Ham' class. Vosper 21.7.1955. Sold 1980 Sutton & Smith.

ODIN 3rd Rate 74, 1,750bm, 175 × 48ft. Danish, captured 7.9.1807 Battle of Copenhagen. Harbour service 2.1811. Sold 20.7.1825 Cristall for BU.

ODIN Wood paddle frigate, 1,326bm, 208 × 37ft, 5–110pdr, 1–68pdr 4–40pdr, 8–32pdr. Deptford DY 24.7.1846. Sold 1865 Castle & Beech.

ODIN Sloop, 1,070 tons, 185 × 33ft, 6–4in. Sheerness DY 30.11.1901. Sold 12.11.1920 Bombay.

ODIN Submarine, 1,475 tons, 260 × 30ft, 1–4in, 8–TT. Chatham DY 5.5.1928. Sunk 14.6.1940 by Italian destroyer STRALE in Gulf of Taranto.

ODIN Minesweeper, 'Algerine' class. Redfern, Toronto, cancelled 8.11.1944, not LD.

ODIN Submarine, 'Oberon' class, 1,610 tons, 241 × 26·5ft, 8–TT. Cammell Laird 4.11.1960. Arr. Aliaga 10.10.1991 for BU.

ODZANI Frigate, 'River' class. Smith's Dock 19.5.1943. BU 6.1957 Cashmore, Newport.

OFFA Destroyer, 'M' class. Fairfield 7.6.1916. Sold 30.10.1921 W. & A.T. Burden.

OFFA Destroyer, 1,540 tons, 345 (oa) × 35ft, 4–4·7in,1–4in, 4–TT. Fairfield 11.3.1941. Tx Pakistani Navy 3.11.1949 = TARIQ; BU 10.1959 Young, Sunderland.

OFFA See also TRIDENT 1915.

OGRE See TURBULENT 1916.

OISEAU 6th Rate 26. French, captured 23.10.1762 by BRUNE in Mediterranean. *Fate unknown.*

OISEAU 5th Rate 32, 783bm, 146·5 × 34ft, 26–9pdr, 6–6pdr. French, captured 31.1.1779 by APOLLO. Sold 19.6.1783.

OISEAU (ex-CLEOPATRE) 5th Rate 36, 913bm. French, captured 18.1.1793 by NYMPHE off The Start. Prison ship 1810. Sold 18.9.1816.

OJIBWA (ex-ONYX) Submarine (RCN), 'Oberon' class. Chatham DY 29.2.1964 (renamed 2.1964). Out of service 21.5.1998, used for alongside training Halifax.

OKANAGAN Submarine (RCN), 'Oberon' class, 1,610 tons, 241 × 26·5ft, 8–TT. Chatham DY 17.9.1966. PO 1998, cannibalised.

OKEHAMPTON Minesweeper, Later 'Hunt' class. Lobnitz, cancelled 1918.

OLD FRANCIS See FRANCIS 1657.

OLD JAMES See JAMES 1634.

OLD LAWRENCE See LAWRENCE 1886.

OLD PRESIDENT See PRESIDENT 1646, PRESIDENT 1829.

OLD ROEBUCK See ROEBUCK 1688.

OLD SUCCESS See SUCCESS 1650.

OLD TRUELOVE See TRUELOVE 1707.

OLD WARWICK See WARWICK 1643.

OLIVE BRANCH Fireship 6, 204bm. Purch. 1672. Sold 1674.

OLIVE BRANCH Fireship 6, 200bm. Captured 1673. Sunk 1673.

OLIVE BRANCH Fireship. Purch. 1690. Captured 1690 by French.

OLIVE BRANCH Fireship, 72bm, 62·5 × 20ft. Purch. 4.1794. Sold 2.1802.

OLYMPIA Schooner 10, 110bm, 68 × 20ft, 8–18pdr carr., 2–6pdr. Bermuda 1806. Sold 9.2.1815.

OLYMPUS Submarine, 1,475 tons, 260 × 30ft, 1–4in, 8–TT. Beardmore 11.12.1928. Sunk 8.5.1942 mine off Malta.

OLYMPUS Submarine, 'Oberon' class. Vickers Armstrong, Barrow, 14.6.1961. PO 28.7.1989; tx Canada 1989 harbour TS; declared surplus 2002.

OMDURMAN Destroyer, 2,380 tons, 355 × 40ft, 5–4·5in, 8–40mm, 10–TT. Fairfield, LD 8.3.1944, cancelled 10.1945.

ONONDAGA Sloop 22 (Canadian lakes). Oswego 1759. Lost 1764.

ONONDAGA Schooner 6 (Canadian lakes). Raven's Creek 1790. Wrecked 18.12.1793 York.

ONONDAGA Submarine (RCN), 'Oberon' class. Chatham DY 25.9.1965. PO 28.7.2000, tx Canadian War Museum, Ottawa.

ONSLAUGHT Destroyer, 'M' class. Fairfield 4.12.1915. Sold 30.10.1921 W. & A. T. Burden.

ONSLAUGHT Armed river steamer, 102 tons, 1–3pdr. Purch. 1925, cd 26.10.1925. Sold 1928 at Hong Kong.

ONSLAUGHT (ex-PATHFINDER) Destroyer, 1,540 tons, 345 (oa) × 35ft, 4–4·7in, 4–TT. Fairfield 9.10.1941 (renamed 8.1941). Tx Pakistani Navy 24.1.1950 = TUGHRIL; accommodation ship 1987–88.

ONSLAUGHT Submarine, 'Oberon' class. Chatham DY 24.9.1960. Arr. 23.10.1991 Aliaga, Turkey, for BU.

ONSLAUGHT *See also PATHFINDER 1941.*

ONSLOW Destroyer, 'M' class. Fairfield 15.2.1916. Sold 26.10.1921 Barking S. Bkg Co.

ONSLOW (ex-PAKENHAM) Destroyer, 1,550 tons, 345 (oa) × 35ft, 4—4·7in, 4—TT. John Brown 31.3.1941 (renamed 8.1941). Tx Pakistani Navy 30.9.1949 = TIPPU SULTAN; = MUFAFIZ (accommodation ship) 1987–88.

ONSLOW Submarine (RAN), 'Oberon' class, 1,610 tons, 241 × 26·5ft, 8—TT. Scotts, Greenock, 3.12.1968. PO 31.3.1999; tx 1999 Australian National Maritime Museum, Sydney.

ONSLOW *See also PAKENHAM 1941.*

ONTARIO Sloop 12 (Canadian lakes). Oswego 1755. Captured 14.8.1756 by French at Oswego.

ONTARIO Sloop 16 (Canadian lakes). Carlton Island 10.5.1780. Foundered 1.11.1780.

ONTARIO (ex-MOHAWK) Brig-sloop 18, 'Cruizer' class, 384bm. Chapman, Bideford, 26.10.1813 (renamed 1813). Sold 11.1832.

ONTARIO Wood screw corvette, 1,857bm, 225 × 43ft. Woolwich DY, LD 10.9.1860, cancelled 12.12.1863.

ONTARIO *See also MINOTAUR 1943.*

ONYX Brig-sloop 10, 'Cherokee' class, 237bm, Ipswich 8.7.1808. Sold 3.2.1819 T. Pittman for BU.

ONYX Brig-sloop 10, 'Cherokee' class, 236bm. Sheerness DY 24.1.1822. Sold 1.1837 Cristall for BU.

ONYX Iron paddle packet, 292bm, 139 × 21ft. Ditchburn & Mare, Blackwall, 11.1845. Sold 1854 Jenkins & Churchward.

ONYX Wood screw gunboat, 'Cheerful' class. Young & Magnay, Limehouse, 3.4.1856. Dockyard craft 1869. BU 7.1873 Jamaica.

ONYX Torpedo gunboat, 810 tons, 230 × 27ft, 2—4in, 4—3pdr, 3—TT. Laird 7.9.1892. Depot ship 1907. = VULCAN II 6.1919. Sold 1924 King, Garston; resold 9.10.1924 L. Basso, Weymouth.

ONYX Minesweeper, 'Algerine' class. Harland & Wolff 27.10.1942. Arr. 5.4.1967 Ward, Inverkeithing, for BU.

ONYX Submarine, 'Oberon' class, Cammell Laird 16.8.1966. PO 14.12.1990. Tx Warship Preservation Trust 8.1991; tx Birkenhead 11.1991 as museum.

ONYX *See also OJIBWA 1964.*

OPAL (ex-MAGICIENNE) Composite screw corvette, 2,120 tons, 220 × 40ft, 14—64pdr. Doxford 9.3.1875 (renamed 12.2.1875). Sold 11.8.1892.

OPAL Destroyer, 'M' class. Doxford 11.9.1915. Wrecked 21.1.1918 Orkneys; wreck sold 18.8.1932.

OPHELIA Destroyer, 'M' class. Doxford 13.10.1915. Sold 8.11.1921 Slough Trading Co.

OPOSSUM Brig-sloop 10, 'Cherokee' class, 237bm. Muddle, Gillingham, 8.7.1808. Sold 3.2.1819 G. Bailey.

OPOSSUM Brig-sloop 10, 'Cherokee' class, 236bm. Sheerness DY 11.12.1821. Sold 27.5.1841 Levy, Rochester.

OPOSSUM Wood screw gunboat, 'Albacore' class. Wigram, Northam, 28.2.1856. Hospital hulk 1876; mooring vessel 1891; = SIREN 1895. Sold 1896 in Hong Kong.

OPOSSUM Destroyer, 320 tons, 200 × 19ft, 1—12pdr, 5—6pdr, 2—TT. Hawthorn 9.8.1895. Sold 29.7.1920 Ward, Preston.

OPOSSUM Sloop, 1,350 tons, 283 × 38·5ft, 6—4in. Denny 30.11.1944. Arr. 26.4.1960 Demmelweeck & Redding, Plymouth, for BU.

OPOSSUM Submarine, 'Oberon' class, Cammell Laird 23.5.1963. PO 26.8.1993. Tx 10.1996 Pounds, Portsmouth, for BU.

OPPORTUNE Destroyer, 'M' class. Doxford 20.11.1915. Sold 7.12.1923 King, Garston.

OPPORTUNE Destroyer, 1,540 tons, 345 (oa) × 35ft, 4—4in, 8—TT. Thornycroft 24.1.1942. Arr. 25.11.1955 Ward, Milford Haven, for BU.

OPPORTUNE Submarine, 'Oberon' class, 1,610 tons, 241 × 26·5ft. 8—TT. Scotts 14.2.1964. PO Portsmouth 1.6.1993; tx 1996 Pounds, Portsmouth, for BU.

ORACLE Destroyer, 'M' class. Doxford 23.12.1915. Sold 30.10.1921 W. & A. T. Burden.

ORACLE Submarine, 'Oberon' class, Cammell Laird 26.9.1961. PO 8.7.1993. Tx 1997 Pounds, Portsmouth for BU; BU comp. mid-2003.

ORANGE 5th Rate 32, 251bm. Dutch, captured 1665. Lost 1671.

ORANGE Fireship 6, 194bm. Captured 1672. Burnt 1673 accident.

ORANGE TREE 5th Rate 30, 280bm. Algerian, captured 1677. Sold 1687.

ORANGE TREE Fireship 6, 160bm. Purch. 1672. Burnt 1673 accident.

ORANGE TREE Hoy. Captured 1652. Sold 1655.

ORANGEVILLE (ex-HEDINGHAM CASTLE) Corvette (RCN), 'Castle' class. Robb 26.1.1944 (renamed 1943). Sold 5.9.1946 = *Hsi Lin*.

ORANGEVILLE *See also MARMION 1944.*

ORBY Minesweeping sloop, '24' class. Swan Hunter 22.10.1918. Sold 15.11.1922 Ferguson Muir.

ORCADIA Destroyer, 'M' class. Fairfield 26.7.1916. Sold 30.10.1921 W. & A. T. Burden, Poole; BU 1923.

ORCADIA Minesweeper, 'Algerine' class. Port

Arthur SY 8.8.1944. Arr. 3.12.1958 Ward, Briton Ferry, for BU.

ORCHIS Corvette, 'Flower' class. Harland & Wolff 15.10.1940. Damaged 21.8.1944; beached off Coursevilles, Normandy.

ORESTE Brig-sloop 14, 312bm. French, captured 12.1.1810 by SCORPION off Guadeloupe. = WELLINGTON 1.8.1810. BU 9.1812 Portsmouth.

ORESTES (ex-MARS) Brig-sloop 18, 367bm. Dutch, captured 3.12.1781. Foundered 5.11.1799 hurricane Indian Ocean.

ORESTES Sloop 16, 280bm. Purch. 8.1803. Wrecked 12.7.1805 off Dunkirk, burnt.

ORESTES Brig-sloop 16, 284bm, 93 × 26·5ft. Bailey, Ipswich, 23.10.1805. Sold 6.3.1817 Pittman.

ORESTES Sloop 18, 460bm, 110 × 31ft, 16—32pdr carr., 2—9pdr. Portsmouth DY 1.5.1824. Coal hulk 11.1852 (also known as C.28). Sold c. 1905.

ORESTES Wood screw corvette, 1,717bm, 225 × 41ft, 16—8in, 4—40pdr. Sheerness DY 18.8.1860. BU comp. 11.1866 Portsmouth.

ORESTES Destroyer, 'M' class. Doxford 21.3.1916. Sold 30.1.1921 W. & A. T. Burden.

ORESTES Minesweeper, 'Algerine' class. Lobnitz 25.11.1942. Arr. 18.3.1963 West of Scotland S. Bkg Co., Troon.

ORFORD 6th Rate 24, 249bm, 94 × 25ft. Ellis, Shoreham, 29.11.1695. = NEWPORT 3.9.1698. Sold 1714.

ORFORD 3rd Rate 70, 1,051bm, 150·5 × 40·5ft. Deptford 1698. Rebuilt Limehouse 1713 as 1,099bm. Wrecked 14.2.1745 Gulf of Mexico.

ORFORD 3rd Rate 70, 1,414bm, 160 × 45ft. Woolwich DY 1749. Harbour service 3.1777. Sunk 6.1783 breakwater Sheerness.

ORFORD 3rd Rate 74, cancelled 1809.

ORFORD Destroyer, 'M' class. Doxford 19.4.1916. Sold 31.10.1921 W. & A. T. Burden.

ORFORD NESS Repair ship, 8,580 tons, 439 × 62ft, 16—20mm. West Coast SB Co., Canada, 12.4.1945. Sold 1947 = *Rabaul*.

ORFORD PRIZE 5th Rate, 380bm. Captured 7.1703 by ORFORD. Hulked 9.1703.

ORFORD PRIZE 6th Rate 24, 283bm. French, captured 21.10.1708 by ORFORD. Recaptured 27.5.1709 by French off Lundy.

ORIANA Destroyer, 'M' class. Fairfield 23.9.1916. Sold 31.10.1921 W. & A. T. Burden.

ORIBI (ex-OBSERVER) Destroyer, 1,540 tons, 345 (oa) × 35ft, 4—4·7in, 1—4in, 4—TT. Fairfield 14.1.1941 (renamed 11.1940). Tx 18.6.1946 Turkish Navy = GAYRET; BU 1965.

ORIFLAMME 4th Rate 50. French, captured 1.4.1761 by ISIS. *Fate unknown.*

ORILLA Corvette (RCN), 'Flower' class. Collingwood 15.9.1940. BU 1.1951 Steel Co. of Canada, Hamilton.

ORIOLE Destroyer, 'M' class. Palmer 3 1.7.1916. Sold 9.5.1921 Ward, Grays.

ORION 3rd Rate 74, 1,646bm, 170 × 47ft. Adams & Barnard, Deptford, 1.6.1787. BU 7.1814.

ORION Screw 2nd Rate 80, 3,281bm, 238 × 55·5ft, 34—8in, 1—68pdr, 56—32pdr. Chatham DY 6.11.1854. BU 1867 Castle, Charlton.

ORION (ex-BOORDJI ZAFFER) Armoured corvette, 4,870 tons, 245 × 52ft, 4—12in MLR, 6—6pdr. Samuda, Poplar, 23.1.1879; Turkish, purch. 13.2.1878 . = ORONTES (depot ship) 12.1909. Sold 19.6.1913 Malta.

ORION Armoured cruiser, 14,600 tons. Projected 1904, not ordered.

ORION Battleship, 22,500 tons, 545 × 88·5ft, 10—13·5in, 16—4in. Portsmouth DY 20.8.1910. Sold 19.12.1922 Cox & Danks, Queenborough.

ORION Cruiser, 7,215 tons, 554·5 (oa) × 55·7ft, 8—6in, 8—4in. Devonport DY 24.11.1932. Sold 19.7.1949; BU Troon.

ORION Submarine, 558 tons, 219 × 22ft, 1—3in, 9—TT. French, seized 3.7.1940 Falmouth. LU until 5.1943; BU.

ORION Submarine (RAN), 'Oberon' class, Scott-Lithgow 16.9.1974. PO 4.10.1996; gifted to Western Australian Govt; LU = STIRLING, Cockburn Sound, Western Australia. For use as a dive site 2002?

ORISSA (ex-CLYDEBANK1 Minesweeper (RIN), TE 'Bangor' class. Lobnitz 20.11.1941 (renamed 194). BU 1949.

ORKAN *See MYRMIDON 1942.*

ORKNEY Frigate (RCN), 'River' class. Yarrow, Esquimalt, 18.9.1943. Sold 7.10.1947.

ORKNEY Patrol vessel, 925 tons. 195·3 (oa) × 34·2ft, Hall Russell 29.6.1976. PO 27.5.1999. Tx Trinidad and Tobago Defence Force 10.2000; = NELSON 18.12.2000.

ORLANDO 5th Rate 36, 876bm, 137 × 38ft. Chatham DY 20.6.1811. Harbour service 10.1819. Sold 3.1824 Trincomalee.

ORLANDO Wood screw frigate, 3,740bm, 300 × 51ft, 20—10in 12—68pdr. Pembroke Dock 12.6.1858. Sold 15.6.1871 Marshall.

ORLANDO Armoured cruiser, 5,600 tons, 300 × 56ft, 2—9in, 10—6in, 10—3pdr. Palmer 3.8.1886. Sold 11.7.1905 Ward, Morecambe.

ORLANDO *See also LOYAL 1913.*

ORMONDE 4th Rate 54, 704bm, 130 × 35ft. Woolwich DY 18.10.1711. = DRAGON 30.9.1715. BU 1733.

ORMONDE Minesweeping sloop, '24' class. Blyth SB 8.6.1918. Survey vessel 3.1924. Sold 6.8.1937 Ward, Briton Ferry.

ORMONDE *See also EMPIRE SPEARHEAD 1943.*

ORNEN Schooner 12, 143bm, 76 × 21·5ft. Danish, captured 7.9.1807 Battle of Copenhagen. Presented 9.1815 Clyde Marine Society. *Was to have been renamed VICTOIRE.*

ORONOQUE (ex-ORENOQUE) Sloop 18. French privateer (?), captured 1782 Demerara. Recaptured by French 3.2.1785 on loss of Demerara.

ORONTES (ex-BRILLIANT) 5th Rate 36 (red pine-built), 939bm, 143 × 38·5ft, 14—32pdr carr., 26—18pdr. Brindley, Frindsbury, 29.6.1813 (renamed 1812). BU 4.1817.

ORONTES Iron screw troopship, 2,812bm, 4,857 tons, 300 × 44·5ft, 3—4pdr. Laird 22.11.1862. Lengthened 1876 to 5,600 tons. Sold 3.7.1893 for BU R. Thames.

ORONTES *See also SWIFTSURE 1870, ORION 1879.*

OROONOKO Gunvessel 12, 177bm, 80 × 22·5ft, 10—18pdr carr., 2—12pdr. Purch. 1806 West Indies. Sold 1814.

ORPHEUS 5th Rate 32, 708bm, 130 × 35ft. Barnard, Harwich, 7.5.1773. Abandoned and burnt 15.8.1778 Rhode I.

ORPHEUS 5th Rate 32, 688bm, 126·5 × 35ft. Adams & Barnard, Deptford, 3.6.1780. Wrecked 23.1.1807 West Indies.

ORPHEUS 5th Rate 36, 947bm, 145 × 38ft. Deptford DY 12.8.1809. BU 8.1819.

ORPHEUS 5th Rate 46, 1,215bm, 159·5 × 42ft. Chatham DY, ordered 1825, cancelled 7.2.1831.

ORPHEUS Wood screw corvette, 1,706bm, 225 × 41ft, 16—8in, 1—7in, 4—40pdr. Chatham DY 23.6.1860. Wrecked 7.2.1863 Manukau Bar, New Zealand.

ORPHEUS Destroyer, 'M' class. Doxford 17.6.1916. Sold 1.11.1921 Fryer, Sunderland.

ORPHEUS Submarine, 1,475 tons, 260 × 30ft, 1—4in, 8—TT. Beardmore 26.2.1929. Sunk 27.6.1940 by Italian destroyer TURBINE between Malta and Alexandria.

ORPHEUS Submarine, 'Oberon' class. Vickers Armstrong, Barrow, 17.11.1959. PO 23.9.1987; harbour TS. Sold 4.1994 Pounds for BU.

ORQUIJO Sloop 18, 384bm. Spanish, captured 8.2.1805 by PIQUE off Havana. Foundered 10.1805 West Indies.

ORTENZIA Schooner 10. French (ex-Venetian),

captured 16.7.1808 by MINSTREL in Mediterranean. Sold 1812.

ORWELL Wood screw gunboat, 'Britomart' class. Portsmouth DY 27.12.1866. Sold Customs Board 20.12.1890.

ORWELL Destroyer, 360 tons, 218 × 20ft, 1—12pdr, 5—6pdr, 2—TT. Laird 29.9.1898. Sold 1.7.1920 Castle, Plymouth.

ORWELL Destroyer, 1,540 tons, 345 (oa) × 35ft, 4—4in, 8—TT. Thornycroft 2.4.1942. Limited conv. 1942 (2—4in, 4—TT, 2—Squid). Arr. 28.6.1965 Cashmore, Newport, for BU.

ORWELL Minehunter, 890 tons (full load), 156·3 (oa) × 34·5ft, 1—40mm. Richards, Great Yarmouth, 7.2.1985. Tx Guyana Coastguard 22.6.2001 = ESSEQUIBO.

ORYX *See OCTAVIA 1916.*

OSBORNE Wood paddle yacht, 1,856 tons, 250 × 36ft. Pembroke Dock 19.12.1870. Sold 31.7.1908; BU Felixstowe.

OSBORNE *See also VICTORIA AND ALBERT 1843.*

OSHAWA Minesweeper (RCN), 'Algerine' class. Port Arthur 6.10.1943. Survey vessel 1958. For disposal 3.1965.

OSIRIS Destroyer, 'M' class. Palmer 26.9.1916. Sold 9.5.1921 Ward, Rainham.

OSIRIS Submarine, 1,475 tons, 260 × 30ft, 1—4in, 8—TT. Vickers Armstrong, Barrow, 19.5.1928. Sold 9.1946 Durban for BU; BU 1952 Mombasa.

OSIRIS Submarine, 'Oberon' class. Vickers Armstrong, Barrow, 29.11.1962. Sold to Canada for spares 10.1992; towed Garston 9.12.1992 for BU.

OSPREY Sloop 18, 386bm, 102 × 30ft. Pitcher, Northfleet, 7.10.1797. BU 1.1813.

OSPREY Brig 12, 425bm, 101·5 × 32ft, 10—32pdr, 2—18pdr. Portsmouth DY 2.4.1844. Wrecked 11.3.1846 off Hokianga, New Zealand.

OSPREY Wood screw gunvessel, 682bm, 181 × 28·5ft, 1—110pdr, 1—68pdr, 2—20pdr. Fletcher, Limehouse, 22.3.1856. Wrecked 6.1867 coast of South Africa.

OSPREY Composite screw sloop, 1,130 tons, 170 × 36ft, 2—7in, 4—64pdr. Sheerness DY 5.8.1876. Sold 29.4.1890.

OSPREY Destroyer, 380 tons, 227 × 22ft, 1—12pdr, 5—6pdr, 2—TT. Fairfield 17.4.1897. Sold 4.11.1919 J. H. Lee.

OSSINGTON *See REPTON 1957.*

OSSORY 2nd Rate 90, 1,307bm, 161 × 44·5ft. Portsmouth DY 1682. = PRINCE 1705; = PRINCESS 2.1.1716; = PRINCESS ROYAL 1728. BU 1773.

OSSORY Destroyer, 'M' class. John Brown 9.10.1916. Sold 8.11.1921 Slough Trading Co.

OSSORY Minesweeper, 'Algerine' class. Port Arthur SY 3.10.1944. Arr. 4.3.1959 Troon for BU.

OSTEND Gunvessel 1, 40bm. Purch. 4.1795. Listed 9.1809.

OSTRICH Sloop 14, 280bm, 94 × 26·5ft. Purch. 1777. Sold 9.9.1782.

OSTRICH Destroyer, 375 tons, 210 × 21ft, 1–12pdr, 5–6pdr, 2–TT. Fairfield 22.3.1900. Sold 29.4.1920 Barking S. Bkg Co.

OSWALD Submarine, 1,475 tons, 260 × 30ft, 1–4in, 8–TT. Vickers Armstrong, Barrow, 19.6.1928. Rammed 1.8.1940 Italian destroyer VIVALDI south of Calabria.

OSWEGO Sloop 5 (Canadian lakes). Oswego 1755. Captured 14.8.1756 by French at Oswego.

OSWESTRY CASTLE Corvette, 'Castle' class. Crown, Sunderland, cancelled 12.1943.

OTAGO (ex-HASTINGS) Frigate (RNZN), 2,144 tons, 370 (oa) × 41ft, 2–4·5in, Limbo, 4–GWS. Thornycroft 11.12.1958 (renamed 1957). Sold Pacific Steel Co. for BU Auckland; towed Auckland 17–18.8.1987.

OTAMA Submarine (RAN), 'Oberon' class, 1,610 tons. Scott-Lithgow 3.12.1975. PO 15.12.1999. Tx Victoria Community, Hastings, Victoria, 10.2001 for display.

OTTAWA Escort (RCN), 2,260 tons, 366 (oa) × 42ft, 4–3in, 2–40mm, Limbo. Vickers, Montreal, 29.4.1953. Sold Global Shipping, Tampa, 2.1994; left Halifax under tow 4.4.1994 for BU.

OTTAWA Frigate (RCN), 'Halifax' class. Marine Industries, Sorel, 22.11.1995.

OTTAWA *See also CRUSADER 1931, GRIFFIN 1935.*

OTTER Ketch 4, 83bm, 61 × 18ft. Deptford 1700. Captured 28.7.1702 by two French frigates on passage West Indies.

OTTER 6th Rate 14, 167bm, 76 × 22·5ft. Smith, Rotherhithe, 6.3.1709. Sold 8.1.1713.

OTTER Sloop 8, 91bm, 64·5 × 18·5ft. Deptford DY 8.8.1721. Wrecked 13.1.1741 off Aldeburgh.

OTTER Sloop 14, 247bm, 88·5 × 25ft. Buxton, Rotherhithe, 19.8.1742. Sold 16.6.1763.

OTTER Sloop 14, 302bm, 95 × 27ft. Deptford DY 26.10.1767. Wrecked 25.8.1778 coast of Florida.

OTTER Sloop 14. American, captured 1778. Sold 9.10.1783 Plymouth.

OTTER Brig-sloop 14, 202bm, 79 × 25ft, 8–18pdr carr., 14–4pdr. Hills, Sandwich, 17.3.1782. Fireship 1800. Sold 16.12.1801.

OTTER Sloop 18, 365bm, 107 × 28ft, 16–32pdr carr., 2–6pdr. Atkinson, Hull, 2.3.1805. Harbour service 1814. Sold 6.3.1828 J. Holmes.

OTTER (ex-*Wizard*) Wood paddle packet, 237bm,

120 × 21ft. GPO vessel, tx 1837. Gunvessel 1854; tug 1865; coal hulk 1878. Sold 1893.

OTTER Screw gunboat (Australian), 220 tons, 1–64pdr. Ramage & Ferguson 19.7.1884; tug, purch. on stocks. Sold c. 1906. *Hired 9.1939–12.1940.*

OTTER Destroyer, 385 tons, 210 × 20ft, 1–12pdr, 5–6pdr, 2–TT. NC&A (Vickers) 23.11.1896. Sold 25.10.1916 in Hong Kong.

OTTER Submarine, 'Oberon' class, Scotts 17.10.1962. Sold 3.1992 Pounds; plans for re-sale failed; for BU.

OTTRINGHAM Inshore minesweeper, 'Ham' class. Ailsa 22.1.1958. Tx Ghanaian Navy 10.1959 = AFADZATO; BU 1977.

OTUS Submarine, 1,475 tons, 260 × 30ft, 1–4in, 8–TT. Vickers Armstrong, Barrow, 31.8.1928. Sold 5.1946 R. Scott, Durban; hull scuttled 9.1946.

OTUS Submarine, 'Oberon' class, Scotts 17.10.1962. PO 4.1991; sold 1992 Pounds for re-sale; tx Sassnitz 6.2002 museum ship

OTWAY Submarine (RAN), 1,349 tons, 275 × 28ft, 1–4in, 8–TT. Vickers Armstrong, Barrow, 7.10.1926. Tx RN 1931; sold 24.8.1945; BU Ward, Inverkeithing.

OTWAY Submarine (RAN), 'Oberon' class, Scotts 29.11.1966. PO 17.2.1994, harbour TS. Cannibalised 1995; BU 11.1995 Australian Defence Industries, Sydney (casing and fin to Holbrook as exhibit 10.1995).

OUDE Minesweeper (RIN), TE 'Bangor' class. Garden Reach, Calcutta, 3.3.1942. Tx Pakistani Navy 1948= DACCA; sold 22.1.1959.

OUDENARDE Destroyer, 2,380 tons, 255 × 40ft, 5in, 8–40mm, 10–TT. Swan Hunter 11.9.1945, not comp. Target 1947. Arr. 12.1957 Rosyth for BU.

OULSTON Coastal minesweeper, 'Ton' class. Thornycroft 20.7.1954. Tx Irish Navy 11.1970 = GRAINNE; sold 1987; arr. 19.3.1988 San Estaban de Pravias, Spain, for BU.

OUNDLE Minesweeper, Later 'Hunt' class. Lobnitz, cancelled 1919.

OURAGAN Destroyer, 1,319 tons, 326 × 33ft, 4–5·1in, 6–TT. French, seized 3.7.1940 Plymouth. Polish crew 8.1940; Free French 12.1940. LU 1944; ret. French Navy 1946.

OUSE Destroyer, 550 tons, 222 × 23·5ft, 1–12pdr, 5–6pdr (1907: 4–12pdr), 2–TT. Laird 7.1.1905. Sold 22.10.1919 J. H. Lee.

OUTARDE Minesweeper (RCN), TE 'Bangor' class. North Vancouver SR 27.1.1941. Sale list 1946.

OUTRAM Iron river gunboat (Indian), 610bm. Bombay DY 1857. *Fate unknown.*

OUTREMONT Frigate (RCN), 'River' class. Morton 3.7.1943. Arr. 11.4.1966 Spezia for BU.

OVENS Submarine (RAN), 'Oberon' class, 1,610 tons, 241 × 26·5ft, 8—TT. Scotts 4.12.1967. PO 1.12.1995; towed 17.11.1998 Western Australian Maritime Museum, Fremantle.

OVERTON (ex-KARWAR) Coastal minesweeper, 'Ton' class. Camper & Nicholson. Launched 28.1.1956 for Indian Navy, renamed, cd 28.8.1956. Deleted 1984.

OVERYSSEL 3rd Rate 64, 1,226bm, 153·5 × 48ft. Dutch, seized 22.10.1795 by POLYPHEMUS at Queenstown. Hulked 1810 breakwater Harwich. Hulk sold 3.1.1822.

OWEN Survey launch, 11 tons, 34·8 (oa) × 9·2ft. Halmatic, Southampton. Comp. 1996.

OWEN *See also THURSO BAY 1945.*

OWEN GLENDOWER 5th Rate 36, 951bm, 145·5 × 38·5ft. Steemson, Paul (nr Hull), 21.11.1808. Convict ship 10.1842. Sold Gibraltar 1884 F. Danino.

OWEN SOUND Corvette (RCN), Modified 'Flower' class. Collingwood SY 15.6.1943. Sold 2.10.1945 = *Cadia*.

OWL Destroyer, 936 tons, 267·5 × 27ft, 3—4in, 2—TT. London & Glasgow Co. 7.7.1913. Sold 5.11.1921 Granton S. Bkg Co.

OWNERS ADVENTURE Bomb vessel, 115bm. Purch. 1694. Sold 3.5.1698.

OWNERS GOODWILL Firevessel 25bm. Purch. 1694. Sold 1706.

OWNERS LOVE Fireship 10, 500bm. Purch. 1688. Bilged in ice 28.7.1697 Hudson Bay on discovery service.

OXFORD 26-gun ship, 221bm. Deptford 1656. Given to Governor of Jamaica 1668; blown up 1669.

OXFORD 4th Rate 54, 677bm, 127 × 34·5ft. Bailey, Bristol, 1674. Rebuilt Deptford 1702 as 675bm; rebuilt Portsmouth 1727 as 767bm, 50 guns. BU 10.1758 Plymouth.

OXFORD CASTLE Corvette, 'Castle' class. Harland & Wolff 11.12.1943. Arr. 6.9.1960 Ward, Briton Ferry for BU.

OXLEY Submarine (RAN), 1,354 tons, 275 × 28ft, 1—4in, 8—TT. Vickers Armstrong, Barrow, 29.6.1926. Tx RN 1931; sunk in error 10.9.1939 by TRITON off Norway.

OXLEY Submarine (RAN), 'Oberon' class, Scotts 24.9.1965. PO 13.2.1992; arr. 1.6.1992 Cockburn Sound, Western Australia, for BU.

OXLIP Corvette, 'Flower' class. Inglis 28.8.1941. Sold 1946 Irish Naval Service = MAEVE; BU 3.1972 Haulbowline.

P

'P' class patrol boats 613 tons, 230 × 24ft, 1—4in (P.52: 2—4in), 2—TT. Vessels designated 'PC' built as decoy ships, 682 tons, 233 × 25·5ft (except PC.43, 65–68, 70–74: 694 tons, 233 × 27ft), 1—4in, 2—12pdr.

P.11 White, Cowes 14.10.1915. Sold 1.12.1921 Stanlee.

P.12 White, Cowes, 4.12.1915. Sunk 4.11.1918 collision English Channel.

P.13 Hamilton, Glasgow, 7.6.1916. = P.75 on 31.7.1917. Sold 31.7.1923 Dover S. Bkg Industries.

P.14 Connell, Scotstoun, 4.7.1916. Sold 31.7.1923 Cashmore.

P.15 Workman Clark, Belfast, 24.1.1916. Sold 26.11.1921 British Legion, Plymouth.

P.16 Workman Clark, Belfast, 23.3.1916. Sold 26.11.1921 British Legion, Plymouth

P.17 Workman Clark, Belfast, 21.10.1915. Sold 26.11.1921 British Legion, Plymouth

P.18 Inglis, Glasgow, 20.4.1916. Sold 26.11.1921 British Legion, Plymouth.

P.19 Northumberland SB Co., Howden, 21.2.1916. Sold 24.7.1923 British Legion, Richborough.

P.20 Northumberland SB Co., Howden, 3.4.1916. Sold 5.1923 Richardson Westgarth, Saltash.

P.21 Russell, Glasgow, 31.3.1916. Sold 26.11.1921 British Legion, Plymouth.

P.22 Caird, Greenock, 22.2.1916. Sold 12.2.1923 W. G. Keen, Bristol.

P.23 Bartram, Sunderland, 5.3.1916. Sold 24.7.1923 British Legion, Richborough.

P.24 Harland & Wolff, Govan, 24.11.1915. Sold 1.12.1921 Stanlee, Dover.

P.25 Harland & Wolff, Govan, 15.1.1916. Sold 1.12.1921 Stanlee, Dover.

P.26 Tyne Iron SB Co. 22.12.1915. Sunk 10.4.1917 mine off Le Havre.

P.27 Eltringham, South Shields, 21.2.1915. Sold 24.7.1923 British Legion, Richborough.

P.28 Thompson, Sunderland, 6.3.16. Sold 24.7.1923 British Legion, Richborough.

P.29 Gray, West Hartlepool, 6.12.1915. Sold 24.7.1923 British Legion, Richborough.

P.30 Gray, West Hartlepool, 5.2.1916. Sold 24.7.1923 British Legion, Richborough.

P.31 Readhead, South Shields, 5.2.1916. Sold 16.12.1926 Demellweek & Redding, Plymouth.

P.32 Harkess, Middlesbrough, 20.1.1916. Sold 1.12.1921 Stanlee.

P.33 Napier & Miller 8.6.1916. Sold 1.12.1921 Stanlee.

P.34 Barclay Curle 22.3.1916. Sold 1.12.1921 Stanlee.

P.35 Caird, Greenock, 29.1.1917. Sold 15.1.1923 Unity S. Bkg Co., Plymouth.

P.36 Eltringham 25.10.1916. Sold 5.1923 Richardson Westgarth, Saltash.

P.37 Gray, West Hartlepool, 28.10.1916. Sold 18.2.1924 British Legion, Ramsgate.

P.38 Hamilton 10.2.1917. = SPEY 11.2.1925. Sold 5.1938 Ward, Grays.

P.39 Inglis 1.3.1917. Sold 6.9.1922 Marple & Gillet.

P.40 White 1916. BU 1938 Ward, Milford Haven.

P.41 Bartram 23.3.1917. Sold 6.9.1922 Granton S. Bkg Co.

PC.42 Caird, Greenock, 7.6.1917. Sold 1.12.1921 Stanlee.

PC.43 Caird, Greenock, 14.8.1917. Sold 20.1.1923 J. Smith, Poole.

PC.44 Eltringham, South Shields, 25.4.1917. Sold 9.4.1923 E. Suren.

P.45 Gray, West Hartlepool, 24.1.1917. Sold 15.1.1923 Unity S. Bkg Co., Plymouth.

P.46 Harkess, Middlesbrough, 7.2.1917. Sold 28.10.1925 Cashmore, Newport.

P.47 Readhead, South Shields, 9.7.1917. Sold 28.10.1925 Alloa, Charlestown.

P.48 Readhead, South Shields, 5.9.1917. Sold 5.1923 Dover S. Bkg Co.

P.49 Thompson, Sunderland, 19.4.1917. Sold 15.1.1923 Unity S. Bkg Co., Plymouth.

P.50 Tyne Iron SB 25.11.1916. Sold 1.12.1921 Stanlee.

PC.51 Tyne Iron SB 25.11.1916. Sold 18.1.1923 Alloa, arr. 11.1923 Charlestown for BU.

P.52 White, Cowes, 28.9.1916. Sold 51923 Dover S. Bkg Co.

P.53 Barclay Curle 8.2.1917. Sold 18.2.1924 British Legion, Ramsgate.

P.54 Barclay Curle 25.4.1917. Sold 18.2.1924 British Legion, Ramsgate.

PC.55 Barclay Curle 5.5.1917. Tx RIM 2.1922; = BALUCHI 5.1922; sold 1935.

PC.56 Barclay Curle 2.6.1917. Sold 31.7.1923 Dover S. Bkg Co.

P.57 Hamilton, Glasgow, 6.8.1917. Sold 21.5.1920 Egyptian Navy = RAQIB.

P.58 Hamilton, Glasgow, 9.5.1918. Sold 1.12.1921 Stanlee.

P.59 White, Cowes, 2.11.1917. Sold 16.6.1938 Ward; BU Milford Haven.

PC.60 Workman Clark, Belfast, 4.6.1917. Sold 18.2.1924 British Legion, Ramsgate.

PC.61 Workman Clark, Belfast, 19.6.1917. Sold 9.4.1923 E. Suren.

PC.62 Harland & Wolff, Govan, 7.6.1917. Sold 1.12.1921 Stanlee.

PC.63 Connell 2.10.1917. Sold 5.1923 Cashmore, Newport.

P.64 Inglis 30.8.1917. Sold 9.4.1923 Cashmore, Newport.

PC.65 Eltringham, South Shields, 5.9.1917. Sold 18.1.1923 Alloa; arr. 3.1923 Charlestown for BU.

PC.66 Harkess 12.2.1918. Sold 31.7.1923 Hughes Bolckow, Blyth.

PC.67 White 7.5.1917. Sold 1.12.1921 Stanlee.

PC.68 White 29.6.1917. Sold 1.12.1921 Stanlee.

PC.69 Workman Clark, Belfast, 11.3.1918. Tx RIM 5.8.1921; = PATHAN 30.5.1922; sunk 23.6.1940 explosion off Bombay.

PC.70 Workman Clark, Belfast, 12.4.1918. Sold 3.9.1926 Hughes Bolckow, Blyth.

PC.71 White, Cowes, 18.3.1918. Sold 28.10.1925 Alloa; wrecked under tow 25.11.1925 nr South Shields; wreck resold 29.12.1925 North-Eastern Salvage Co.

PC.72 White, Cowes, 8.6.1918. Sold 28.10.1925 Hayes, Porthcawl.

PC.73 White, Cowes, 1.8.1918. = DART 4.1925. Sold Ward 16.6.1938; BU Briton Ferry.

PC.74 White, Cowes, 4.10.1918. Sold 19.7.1948. BU Hayes. *Operated as decoy ship CHATSGROVE 9– 10.1939.*

P.75 (ex-P.13). Renamed 31.7.1917. Sold 31.7.1919 Dover S. Bkg Co.

'U' class submarines *Numbers missing from the following group were given 'U' names 01/ 02.1943 (q.v.):*

P.32 Vickers Armstrong, Barrow, 15.12.1940. Sunk 18.8.1941 mine off Tripoli.

P.33 Vickers Armstrong, Barrow 28.1.1941. Presumed mined off Tripoli; formally PO 20.8.1941.

P.34 Vickers Armstrong, Barrow, 28.4.1941. Sunk 1.4.1942 Italian aircraft Sliema harbour, Malta; raised 7.8.1958, scuttled 22.8.1958 off Malta.

P.38 Vickers Armstrong, Barrow, 9.7.1941. Sunk 25.2.1942 Italian torpedo boats CIRCE and USODIMARE off Tunisia.

P.39 Vickers Armstrong, Barrow, 23.8.1941. Sunk 26.3.1942 air attack Malta; raised and beached 6.1943, BU 1954.

P.48 Vickers Armstrong, Barrow, 15.4.1942. Sunk 25.12.1942 Italian corvette ARDENTE Gulf of Tunis.

P.222 Submarine, 'S' class. Vickers Armstrong, Barrow, 20.9.1941. Sunk 12.12.1942 Italian torpedo boat FORTUNALE off Naples.

P.311 (ex-TUTANKHAMEN, ex-P.311) Submarine, 'T' class. Vickers Armstrong, Barrow, 5.3.1942 (renamed 1.1943). Presumed mined 8.1.1943 off Maddalena.

P.411 Submarine, 1,520 tons, 271·5 × 25·5ft, 1—4in, 6—TT, 50 mines. Scotts, ordered 13.1.1941, cancelled 9.1941.

P.412 Submarine, 1,520 tons, 271·5 × 25·5ft, 1—4in, 6—TT, 50 mines. Scotts, ordered 13.1.1941, cancelled 9.1941.

P.413 Submarine, 1,520 tons, 271·5 × 25·5ft, 1—4in, 6—TT, 50 mines. Scotts, ordered 13.1.1941, cancelled 9.1941.

P.511 (ex-R.3) Submarine, 530 tons, 186 × 18ft, 1— 3in, 4—TT. American, t RN 4.11.1941 on Lend-Lease. Nominally ret. USN 20.12.1944; foundered at moorings 21.11.1947 Karnes Bay; raised, arr. 2.1948 Troon for BU.

P.512 (ex-R.17) Submarine, 530 tons, 186 × 18ft, 1—3in, 4—TT. American, tx RN 9.3.1942 on Lend-Lease. Ret. USN 6.9.1944; BU 11.1945.

P.514 (ex-R.19) Submarine, 530 tons, 186 × 18ft, 1—3in, 4—TT. American, tx RN 9.3.1942 on Lend-Lease. Rammed in error 21.6.1942 minesweeper GEORGIAN North Atlantic.

P.551 (ex-S.25) Submarine, 800 tons, 219 × 20·5ft, 1—4in, 4—TT. American, tx RN 4.11.1941 on Lend-Lease. Lent Polish Navy 11.1941 = JASTRZAB; sunk in error 2.5.1942 by ST ALBANS and SEAGULL off northern Norway.

P.552 (ex-S.1) Submarine, 800 tons, 219 × 20·5ft, 1—4in 4—TT. American, tx RN 20.4.1942 on Lend-Lease. Nominally ret. USN 16.10.1944; BU 6.1946 Durban.

P.553 (ex-S.21) Submarine, 800 tons, 219 × 20·5ft, 1—4in, 4—TT. American, tx RN 14.9.1942 on Lend-Lease. Nominally ret. USN 11.7.1944; sunk 20.3.1945 asdic target.

P.554 (ex-S.22) Submarine, 800 tons, 219 × 20·5ft,

1—4in, 4—TT. American, tx RN 19.6.1942 on Lend-Lease. Ret. USN 11.7.1944; sold 16.11.1945 for BU.

P.555 (ex-S.24) Submarine, 800 tons, 219 × 20·5ft, 1—4in, 4—TT. American, tx RN 10.8.1942 on Lend-Lease. Nominally ret. USN 1945; expended 25.8.1947 tests Portsmouth.

P.556 (ex-S.29) Submarine, 800 tons, 219 × 20·5ft, 1—4in, 4—TT. American, tx RN 5.6.1942 on Lend-Lease. Nominally ret. USN 26.1.1946; sold for BU, stranded Porchester beach 1947; refloated 1965; hulk Pounds 1986.

P.611 (ex-ORUC REIS) Submarine, 683 tons, 193 × 22·5ft, 1—3in, 5—TT. Vickers Armstrong, Barrow, 19.7.1940; Turkish, cd for passage to Turkey. Ret. 1942 Turkish Navy.

P.612 (ex-MURAT REIS) Submarine, 683 tons, 193 × 22·5ft, 1—3in, 5—TT. Vickers Armstrong, Barrow, 20.7.1940; Turkish, cd for passage to Turkey. Ret. 25.5.1942 Turkish Navy.

P.614 (ex-BURAK REIS) Submarine, 683 tons, 193 × 22·5ft, 1—3in 5—TT. Vickers Armstrong, Barrow, 19.10.1940; Turkish, req. 1942. Ret. 12.1945 Turkish Navy.

P.615 (ex-ULUC ALI REIS) Submarine, 683 tons. 193 × 22·5ft, 1—3in, 5—TT. Vickers Armstrong, Barrow, 1.11.1940; Turkish, req. 1942. Sunk 18.4.1943 by U.23 off West Africa.

P.711 *See X.2 1940.*

P.712 (ex-PERLA) Submarine, 620 tons, 197 (oa) × 21ft, 6—TT. Italian, captured 9.7.1942. Tx Greek Navy 1.1943 = MATROZOS.

P.714 Submarine, 629 tons, 197 (oa) × 21ft, 6—TT. Italian BRONZO, captured 12.7.1943. Tx French Navy 1944 = NARVAL.

PACAHUNTA *See POCAHONTAS 1780.*

PACIFIC (ex-PACIFIQUE) Storeship 22, 678bm, 137 × 33ft. French East Indiaman, captured 1777. Sunk 7.1781 breakwater Harwich.

PACIFIC Receiving ship/lightvessel, 110bm. Sloop, purch. 30.12.1844. BU 1868 The Cape.

PACKINGTON Coastal minesweeper, 'Ton' class. Harland & Wolff. Launched 3.7.1958 as WALVISBAII (SAN). PO 5.9.2001.

PACTOLUS 5th Rate 38 (red pine-built), 1,067bm, 150·5 × 40ft. Barnard, Deptford, 14.8.1813. Sold 29.1.1818 Maund.

PACTOLUS 3rd class cruiser, 2,135 tons, 300 × 36·5ft, 8—4in, 8—3pdr. Armstrong 21.12.1896. Depot ship 9.1912. Sold 25.10.1921 Multilocular S. Bkg Co., Stranraer.

PADSTOW *See PANGBOURNE 1918, ROHILKAND 1942.*

PADSTOW BAY (ex-LOCH COULSIDE) Frigate,

'Bay' class. Robb 23.8.1945 (renamed 1944). Arr. 11.8.1959 Spezia for BU.

PAGHAM Inshore minesweeper, 'Ham' class. Jones, Buckie, 4.10.1955. Sold 1983.

PAKENHAM Gunvessel 1. Purch. 1797. In service 1800. Sold (1802?).

PAKENHAM (ex-ONSLOW) Destroyer, 1,550 tons, 345 (oa) × 35ft, 4—4·7in, 4—TT. Hawthorn Leslie 28.1.1941 (renamed 8.1941). Badly damaged 16.4.1943 gunfire Italian torpedo boats CASSIOPEA and CIGNO, sunk by RN forces off Sicily.

PAKENHAM *See also ONSLOW 1941.*

PALADIN Destroyer, 'M' class. Scotts 27.3.1916. Sold 9.5.1921 Ward , Rainham.

PALADIN Destroyer, 1,540 tons, 345 (oa) × 35ft, 4—4·7in, 4—TT. John Brown 11.6.1941. Frigate 1956, 1,800 tons, 2—4in, 2—Squid. Arr. 25.10.1962 Clayton & Davie, Dunston, for BU.

PALINURUS Survey brig (Indian), 192bm. Bombay DY 1823. Listed 1862.

PALINURUS Survey vessel (RIM), 444 tons, 140 × 24ft. Cammell Laird 2.3.1907. Listed 1930.

PALLAS 5th Rate 36, 728bm, 128·5 × 36ft. Wells, Deptford, 30.8.1757. Run ashore 24.3.1783 St George's I. unserviceable.

PALLAS 5th Rate 32, 776bm, 135 × 36ft. Woolwich DY 19.12.1793. Wrecked 4.4.1798 nr Plymouth.

PALLAS 5th Rate 32 (fir-built), 667bm. Plymouth DY 17.11.1804. Wrecked 18.12.1810 Firth of Forth.

PALLAS 5th Rate 36, 951bm, 145·5 × 38·5ft. Portsmouth DY 13.4.1816 (ex-Guillaume, Northam, tx 10.12.1811). Coal hulk 9.1836. Sold 11.1.1862 Marshall, Plymouth.

PALLAS Armoured corvette, 2,372bm, 3,661 tons, 225 × 50ft, 6—7in. Woolwich DY 14.3.1865. Sold 20.4.1886.

PALLAS 2nd class cruiser, 2,575 tons, 265 × 41ft, 8—3pdr. Portsmouth DY 30.6.1890. Sold 7.1906 Bermuda.

PALLAS *See also MINERVA 1780, SHANNON 1803.*

PALLISER Frigate, 1,180 tons, 300 × 33ft, 3—40mm, 4—TT. Stephen 10.5.1956. Arr. Neath 16.3.1983 for BU by Deans Marine.

PALM TREE Hoy, 62bm captured 1665. Sold 1667.

PALMA (ex-IPHIGENIE) 5th Rate 38, 1,066bm, 154 × 40ft. French, captured 16.1.1814 by VENERABLE and CYANE off Maderia. = GLOIRE 12.1814. Sold 10.9.1817.

PALUMA Gunboat (Australian), 360 tons, 115 × 26ft, 1—8in, 1—6in, 1—3pdr. Armstrong Mitchell 5.1884. Tx 1931 Victoria Govt = *Rip*. BU 1957.

PALUMA Survey vessel (RAN), 320 tons (full load), 118·9 (oa) × 45·3ft. Elgo Engineering, Port Adelaide, 6.2.1989.

PANDORA 6th Rate 24, 520bm, 114·5 × 32ft. Adams & Barnard, Deptford, 17.5.1779. Wrecked 28.8.1791 Great Barrier Reef.

PANDORA (ex-PANDOUR) Gun-brig 14, 231bm, 78 × 27ft, 14—4pdr. French, captured 31.8.1795 by CAROLINE in North Sea. Foundered 6.1797 North Sea.

PANDORA Brig-sloop 18, 'Cruizer' class, 383bm. Preston, Yarmouth, 11.10.1806. Wrecked 13.2.1811 Kattegat.

PANDORA Brig-sloop 18, 'Cruizer' class, Woolwich DY, ordered 6.9.1812, = LYNX 24.9.1812, cancelled 9.6.1818.

PANDORA Brig-sloop 18, 'Cruizer' class, 383bm. Deptford DY 12.8.1813. Ship-sloop 1825. On sale list 4.1827; sold 13.4.1831.

PANDORA Packet brig 3, 319bm, 90 × 29ft, 3—32pdr. Woolwich DY 4.7.1833. Coastguard watchvessel 10.1857. Sold 11.1.1862 Marshall, Plymouth.

PANDORA Wood screw gunvessel, 'Philomel' class. Pembroke Dock 7.2.1861. Sold 13.1.1875.

PANDORA 3rd class cruiser, 2,200 tons, 305 × 36·5ft. Portsmouth DY 17.1.1900. Sold 7.10.1913 Ward, Morecambe.

PANDORA (ex-*Sett*) Depot ship, 4,580 tons, 330 × 43ft. Purch. 9.11.1914. = DOLPHIN 3.10.24. Sunk 23.12.1939 mine while under tow Blyth for conv. blockship.

PANDORA (ex-PYTHON) Submarine, 1,475 tons, 260 × 30ft, 1—4in, 8—TT. Vickers Armstrong, Barrow, 22.8.1929 (renamed 1928). Sunk 1.4.1942 Italian aircraft Malta; raised 9.1943, beached; BU 1957.

PANDORA *See also KATOOMBA 1889.*

PANDOUR (ex-EUGENIE) Sloop 16, 248bm, 86 × 24ft, 16—6pdr. French, captured 16.3.1798. = WOLF 1800. BU 3.1802.

PANDOUR (ex-HECTOR) 5th Rate 44, 894bm, 134 × 39ft. Dutch, captured 28.8.1799 Texel. Tx Customs Service 5.1805 store hulk.

PANDOUR *See also COSSACK 1806.*

PANGBOURNE (ex-PADSTOW) Minesweeper, Later 'Hunt' class. Lobnitz 26.3.1918 (renamed 1918). Sold 13.3.1947.

PANSY Sloop, 'Arab' class. Hamilton 1.2.1916. Sold 12.1.1920 as hulk Calcutta Port Commissioners.

PANSY *See also PAUNCEY 1544, HEARTSEASE 1940.*

PANTALOON Brig 10, 340bm, 92 × 29·5ft. Purch. 5.12.1831. BU 8.1852.

PANTALOON Wood screw sloop, 574bm, 151 ×

29ft, 11—32pdr. Devonport DY 26.9.1860. Sold 18.9.1867 Marshall, Plymouth.

PANTHER 4th Rate 54, 683bm, 131·5 × 34·5ft. Popely, Deptford 3.1703. Rebuilt Woolwich 1716, 716bm. Hulked 1.1743. Sold 26.4.1768.

PANTHER 4th Rate 50, 968bm, 140 × 40ft. Plymouth DY 24.6.1746. BU 7.1756 Plymouth.

PANTHER 4th Rate 60, 1,285bm, 154 × 48·5ft. Martin & Henniker, Chatham, 22.6.1758. Hospital ship 1791; prison hulk 1807. BU 11.1813.

PANTHER Sloop 14 (Indian), 181bm. Built 1778. Survey vessel 1802.

PANTHER Destroyer, 385 tons, 210·5 × 21·5ft, 1—12pdr, 5—6pdr, 2—TT. Laird 21.1.1897. Sold 7.6.1920 J. Kelly.

PANTHER Destroyer, 1,540 tons, 345 (oa) × 35ft, 4—4·7in, 4—TT. Fairfield 28.5.1941. Sunk 9.10.1943 air attack Scarpanto Strait.

PANTHER Frigate, 2,300 tons. John Brown, launched 15.3.1957 as BRAHMAPUTRA (Indian Navy). Deleted 1965.

PANTHER *See also GLOUCESTER 1856.*

PAPILLON Gun-brig 10, 145bm, 64 × 22·5ft. French, captured 4.9.1803 by VANGUARD in West Indies. Foundered 1806 Atlantic.

PAPILLON Sloop 16, 345bm, 96 × 29ft, 14—24pdr carr., 2—6pdr. French, captured 19.12.1809 by ROSAMOND in West Indies. Sold 12.10.1815.

PAPUA (ex-HOWETT, ex-PF.84) Frigate, 'Colony' class. Walsh Kaiser, Providence, 10.10.1943 (renamed 1943). Ret. USN 13.5.1946; sold Egypt 1950 mercantile; BU 1956.

PARADOX 14-gun ship, 120bm. Royalist, captured 1649 by Parliamentarians. Sold 1667.

PARAGON Destroyer, 917 tons, 265 × 26·5ft, 3—4in, 4—TT. Thornycroft 21.2.1913. Sunk 18.3.1917 German destroyer torpedo Strait of Dover.

PARAGON *See also HENRIETTA MARIA 1633.*

PARAMOUR Pink 6, 89bm, 64 × 18ft. Deptford 4.1694. Sold 22.8.1706.

PARAPET (ex-LCT.4039) Tank landing craft, 657 tons, 225 × 39ft. Arrol, Alloa, 1945 (renamed 1956). Sold 1966 La Société Maseline, Sark.

PARIS Battleship, 22,189 tons, 541 × 92·5ft. 12—12in, 22—5·5in, French, seized 3.7.1940 Plymouth. Guardship (Polish crew) 8.1940; depot ship, comp. 7.1941. Ret. French Navy 1945.

PARKER (ex-FROBISHER) Destroyer leader, 1,666 tons, 315 × 32ft, 4—4in, 4—TT. Cammell Laird 19.4.1916 (renamed 1915). Sold 5.11.1921 Cashmore, Newport.

PARKES Minesweeper (RAN), 'Bathurst' class. Evans Deakin, Brisbane, 30.10.1943. Sold 2.5.1957 Hong Kong Rolling Mills for BU.

PARRAMATTA Destroyer (RAN), 700 tons, 246 (oa) × 24ft, 1—4in, 3—12pdr, 3—TT. Fairfield 9.2.1910. Dismantled 10.1929 Sydney; hull later sold G. Rhodes, Cowan, NSW, for BU; foundered 8.12.1934 Hawkesby River.

PARRAMATTA Sloop (RAN), 1,060 tons, 266 (oa) × 36ft, 3—4in. Cockatoo DY 18.6.1939. Sunk 28.11.1941 by U.559 off Bardia.

PARRAMATTA Frigate (RAN), 2,100 tons, 370 (oa) × 41ft, 2—4·5in, Limbo, 4—GWS. Cockatoo DY 31.1.1959. Sold 8.1991, left Fremantle 7.5.1992 under tow for BU Pakistan.

PARRAMATTA Frigate (RAN), 'Anzac' class. Tenix Defence Systems, Williamstown, 17.6.2000.

PARRET Frigate, 'River' class. Vickers, Montreal, 29.4.1943 on Lend-Lease. Ret. USN 5.2.1946.

PARROT Ketch 6, 60bm. Chatham DY 1657. Captured 1657 by French.

PARRSBORO Minesweeper, TE 'Bangor' class. Dufferin 12.7.1941. Sold 1.1.1948; BU Hayes, Pembroke Dock.

PARRY SOUND Corvette (RCN), Modified 'Flower' class. Midland SB 13.11.1943. Sold 1950 = *Olympic Champion*.

PARTHIAN Brig sloop 10, 'Cherokee' class. Barnard, Deptford, 13.2.1808. Wrecked 15.5.1828 coast of Egypt.

PARTHIAN Wood screw gunvessel, 486bm, 150 × 26ft. Deptford DY, ordered 26.3.1846, cancelled 6.1849.

PARTHIAN Wood gunboat, 'Albacore' class. Wigram, 8.5.1856. BU comp. 14.9.1864.

PARTHIAN Destroyer, 'M' class. Scotts 3.7.1916. Sold 8.11.1921 Slough Trading Co.; BU Germany.

PARTHIAN Submarine, 1,475 tons, 260 × 30ft, 1—4in, 8—TT. Chatham DY 22.6.1929. Presumed mined 11.8.1943 southern Adriatic.

PARTRIDGE Sloop 18, 423bm, 109 × 29·5ft. Avery, Dartmouth, 15.7.1809. BU 9.1816.

PARTRIDGE Brig-sloop 10, 'Cherokee' class, 235bm. Plymouth DY 22.3.1822. Stranded 28.11.1824 off Texel.

PARTRIDGE Brig-sloop 10, 'Cherokee' class, 231bm. Pembroke Dock 12.10.1829. = WV.32 (Coastguard watchvessel) 25.5.1863. Sold 2.2.1864 Ransome, Southampton.

PARTRIDGE Wood screw gunboat, 'Albacore' class. Wigram, Northam, 29.3.1856. Sold 8.9.1864 Habgood for BU.

PARTRIDGE Composite screw gunboat, 755 tons, 165 × 30ft, 6—4in. Devonport DY 10.5.1888. Sold 1909 Simonstown for Ward, Preston; arr. Preston 6.5.1913.

PARTRIDGE Destroyer, 'M' class. Swan Hunter

4.3.1916. Sunk in action 12.12.1917 German destroyers North Sea.

PARTRIDGE Destroyer, 1,540 tons, 345 (oa) × 35ft, 4—4·7in, 4—TT. Fairfield 5.8.1941. Sunk 18.12.1942 by U.565 west of Oran.

PARTRIDGE Sloop, 1,350 tons, 283 × 38·5ft, 6—4in. Thornycroft, ordered 9.10.1944; cancelled 10.1945.

PASLEY Destroyer, 'M' class. Swan Hunter 15.4.1916. Sold 9.5.1921 Ward, Hayle; arr. 9.1922 for BU.

PASLEY (ex-LINDSAY) Frigate, DE 'Captain' class. Boston NY 30.8.1943 on Lend-Lease (renamed 1943). Ret. USN 8.1945.

PASLEY *See also ST HELENA 1943.*

PAT BARTON Survey launch, 11 tons, 34·8 (oa) × 9·2ft. Halmatic, Southampton, comp. 1996.

PATHAN *See Indian TB.3 1888, PC.69 1918.*

PATHFINDER (ex-FASTNET) Scout cruiser, 2,940 tons, 370 × 39ft, 10—12pdr, 8—3pdr. Cammell Laird 16.7.1904 (renamed 1903). Sunk 5.9.1914 by U.21 North Sea.

PATHFINDER (ex-ONSLAUGHT) Destroyer, 1,540 tons, 345 (oa) × 35ft, 4—4·7in, 4—TT. Hawthorn Leslie 10.4.1941 (renamed 8.1941). Damaged 11.2.1945 Japanese aircraft Ramree I., East Indies. Target trials vessel 1947. Arr. 11.1948 Howells, Milford Haven, for BU.

PATHFINDER Survey vessel (Nigerian), 544grt, 145 × 27ft. White, Cowes, 23.10.1953.

PATHFINDER *See also ONSLAUGHT 1941.*

PATRICIAN Destroyer, 'M' class, 1,004 tons. Thornycroft 5.6.1916. Tx RCN 9.1920; sold 1929; BU Esquimalt.

PATRICK *See LICHFIELD 1658.*

PATRIOT Gunvessel 10. Dutch, captured 1808. Sold 1813.

PATRIOT Destroyer, 'M' class, 1,004 tons. Thornycroft 20.4.1916. Tx RCN 9.1920. Sold 1929 Ward, Briton Ferry.

PATROL Scout cruiser, 2,940 tons, 370 × 39ft, 10—12pdr, 8—3pdr. Cammell Laird 13.10.1904. Sold 21.4.1920 Machinehandel, Holland.

PATROLLER (ex-*Keeweenaw*) Escort carrier, 11,420 tons, 468·5 × 36·5ft, 2—4in, 16—40mm, 24 aircraft. Seattle Tacoma Co. 6.5.1943 on Lend-Lease. Ret. USN 11.12.1946.

PATTON *See SARAWAK 1943.*

PAUL Carrack. Genoese, captured 25.7.1417. Sold 10.9.1424

PAUL (ex-PAULUS) 26-gun ship, 290bm. Captured 1652. Expended as fireship 12.6.1667 against Dutch in R. Thames.

PAULINA Brig-sloop 16, 287bm, 93 × 26·5ft, 14—

24pdr carr., 2–6pdr. Guillaume, Northam, 7.12.1805. Sold 30.5.1816.

PAUNCEY (PANSY) Galleon 97, 450bm. Built 1544. Last listed 1557.

PAUNCEY *See also PANSY 1544.*

PAZ Schooner 12, 10–12pdr. Spanish, captured 3.2.1807 Montevideo. Sold 1814.

'PC' class patrol boats *See under 'P' class patrol boats.*

PEACE Flyboat 8, 225bm. Captured 1672. Sold 1674.

PEACE Fireship 8, 145bm. Purch. 1678. Sold 1687.

PEACOCK Ship. Captured 1651. Sold 1658.

PEACOCK Brig-sloop 18, 'Cruizer' class, 386bm. Bailey, Ipswich, 9.12.1806. Captured 24.2.1831 by American HORNET; sunk.

PEACOCK (ex-WASP) Sloop 18, 434bm. American, captured 18.10.1812 by POICTIERS in Atlantic. Foundered 29.8.1814 off south coast of USA.

PEACOCK Wood screw gunboat, 'Albacore' class. Pitcher, Northfleet, 12.4.1856. BU 3.1869 Portsmouth.

PEACOCK Composite screw gunboat, 755 tons, 165 × 30ft, 6–4in. Pembroke Dock 22.6.1888. Sold 15.5.1906 Ellis, Chepstow.

PEACOCK Sloop 1,350 tons, 283 × 38·5ft, 6–4in. Thornycroft 11.12.1943. Arr. 7.5.1958 Rosyth for BU.

PEACOCK Patrol vessel, 662 tons, 205·3 (oa) × 32·8ft, 1–76mm. Hall Russell 1.12.1982. Sold 1.8.1997 Philippine Navy = EMILIO JACINTO.

PEARD *See SEYCHELLES 1943.*

PEARL Ship. Dates from 1625. Captured 14.5.1635 by French.

PEARL 22-gun ship, 285bm, 103·5 × 25ft. Pett, Ratcliffe, 1651. Sunk 6.8.1697 foundation Sheerness.

PEARL Sloop 4. Listed 1658. Condemned 1660 Jamaica.

PEARL Fireship 6, 162bm. Purch. 1673. Lost in action 1673.

PEARL 4th Rate 42, 559bm, 117 × 33ft. Burchett, Rotherhithe, 5.8.1708. Rebuilt Deptford 1726 as 595bm. Sold 28.6.1744.

PEARL 5th Rate 44, 712bm, 126 × 36ft. Okill, Liverpool, 29.6.1744. Sold 21.6.1759.

PEARL 5th Rate 32, 683bm, 125 × 35·5ft. Chatham DY 27.3.1762. = PROTHEE (receiving ship) 19.3.1825. Sold 4.1.1832 Ledger for BU.

PEARL Sloop 20, 558bm, 119 × 33·5ft. Sainty, Wivenhoe, 17.3.1828 (to builder's design: cancelled 11.7.1825, resumed 23.2.1826). BU 6.1851.

PEARL Wood screw corvette, 1,469bm, 2,187 tons,

200 × 40·5ft, 20–8in, 1–68pdr. Woolwich DY 13.9.1855. Sold Castle 8.1884 for BU.

PEARL 2nd class cruiser, 2,575 tons, 265 × 41ft, 8–4·7in, 8–3pdr. Pembroke Dock 28.7.1890. Sold 7.1906 Simonstown; BU Cohen, Felixstowe.

PEARL *See also IMOGENE 1831.*

PEARL PRIZE 6th Rate 12, 195bm. French, captured 1693. Wrecked 17.5.1694 off Goree.

PEARLEN *See PERLEN 1807.*

PEDRO Schooner 14. Purch. 1796. Listed until 1803.

PEGASE 3rd Rate 74, 1,778bm, 178 × 48ft. French, captured 21.4.1782 by FOUDROYANT in Bay of Biscay. Prison ship 1794. BU 12.1815.

PEGASUS Ship. Built 1585. Rebuilt 1598. Lost 1599.

PEGASUS Sloop 14, 300bm, 96·5 × 27ft. Chatham DY 27.12.1776. Foundered 10.1777 off Newfoundland.

PEGASUS 6th Rate 28, 594bm, 120·5 × 34ft. Deptford DY 1.6.1779. Sold 28.8.1816.

PEGASUS 5th Rate 46, 1,063bm, 150 × 40ft, ordered 23.7.1817 Deptford DY, tx Sheerness 17.2.1825, re-laid 3.1828, cancelled 10.1.1831.

PEGASUS Wood screw sloop, 695bm, 185 × 28·5ft. Woolwich DY, LD 1.1862, cancelled 12.1863.

PEGASUS Composite screw sloop, 1,130 tons, 170 × 36ft, 2–7in, 7–64pdr. Devonport DY 13.6.1878. Sold E. Cohen 11.8.1892 for BU.

PEGASUS 3rd class cruiser, 2,135 tons, 300 × 36·5ft, 8–4in, 8–3pdr. Palmer 4.3.1897. Sunk 20.9.1914 by German KONIGSBERG at Zanzibar.

PEGASUS (ex-*Stockholm*) Seaplane carrier 3,070 tons, 330 × 43ft, 4–12pdr, 9 aircraft. John Brown 9.6.1917, purch. 27.2.1917. Sold 22.8.1931 Ward, Morecambe.

PEGASUS *See also GREENOCK 1849, ARK ROYAL 1914.*

PEGGY Sloop 8, 141bm, 74·5 × 21ft. Deptford DY 26.7.1749. Listed 1769.

PEGGY Fireship. Purch. 1804. Expended 2.10.1804 off Boulogne.

PEGWELL BAY (ex-LOCH MOCHRUM) Frigate, 'Bay' class. Pickersgill 1.9.1945 (renamed 1944). = COOK (survey ship) 15.12.1947. Sold 2.4.1968.

PELARGONIUM Sloop, 'Anchusa' class. Hamilton 18.3.1918. Sold 20.5.1921 Clan Line = *Oaxaca*.

PELICAN 18-gun ship, 100bm. Privateer, with Drake 1577. = GOLDEN HIND 9.1578. Mentioned 1662. *Doubtful if ever in RN.*

PELICAN Ship. Captured 1626. Sold 1629.

PELICAN 10-gun ship. Royalist, 100/130bm. In service 1646–48.

PELICAN 38-gun ship, 500bm. Wapping 1650.
Burnt 2.1656 accident Portsmouth.
PELICAN (ex-*St George*) Sloop 16, 234bm, 87 ×
24·5ft. Purch. 28.4.1757. Sold 3.5.1763.
PELICAN Schooner 10, 150bm, 70 × 21·5ft. French
privateer, captured 1775. Harbour service 1776
Antigua. = EARL OF DENBIGH 1777. Foundered
2.6.1787.
PELICAN 6th Rate 24, 520bm, 114·5 × 22ft.
Adams & Barnard, Deptford, 24.4.1777. Found-
ered 2.8.1781 off Jamaica.
PELICAN (ex-FREDERIC) Brig-sloop 16, 202bm,
85·5 × 23·5ft. French privateer, captured 8.1781
by EMERALD. Sold 1.5.1783 Deptford.
PELICAN Brig-sloop 18 (fir-built), 365bm, 96 ×
30ft. Perry, Blackwall, 17.6.1795. Sold 1806 in
Jamaica.
PELICAN (ex-VOLTIGEUR) Brig-sloop 16,
328bm, 95·5 × 28·5ft, 16—32pdr carr., 2—6pdr.
French, captured 26.3.1806 by PIQUE in West
Indies. Sold 16.4.1812 Deptford.
PELICAN Brig-sloop 18, 'Cruizer' class, 385bm.
Davy, Topsham, 8.1812. Customs watchvessel
1847; = WV.29 on 25.5.1863. Sold 7.6.1865
Fryman, Rye.
PELICAN Wood screw sloop, 952bm, 185 × 33ft,
5—40pdr, 12—32pdr. Pembroke Dock 19.7.1860.
Sold 2.1867 Arthur & Co. = *Hawk*; resold Portu-
guese Navy = INFANTA DOM HENRIQUE.
PELICAN Composite screw sloop, 1,130 tons, 170 ×
36ft, 2—7in, 4—64pdr. Devonport DY 26.4.1877.
Sold 22.1.1901 Hudson Bay Co. as supply ship.
Hulk scuttled 1953.
PELICAN (ex-*Sir J. Jones*) Tender, 100 tons, 77 ×
15ft. War Dept vessel, tx 11.1906. = PETULANT
14.10.1916. Sold 23.5.1927 B. Zammit, Malta.
PELICAN Destroyer, 'M' class. Beardmore
18.3.1916. Sold 9.5.1921 Ward, Briton Ferry, Arr.
Briton Ferry 6.1.1923, Preston 5.1924, for BU.
PELICAN Sloop, 1,200 tons, 276 × 37·5ft, 8—4in.
Thornycroft 12.9.1938. Arr. 29.11.1958 Ward,
Preston, for BU.
PELICAN Survey vessel. Cancelled 1967.
PELICAN PRIZE 34-gun ship. Captured 1653.
Sold 1655.
PELICAN PRIZE Fireship 8, 200bm. French, cap-
tured 7.7.1690 off Dublin. Sunk 26.8.1692
foundation Sheerness.
PELLEW Destroyer, 'M' class. Beardmore
18.5.1916. Sold 9.5.1921 Ward, Briton Ferry; BU
1923.
PELLEW Destroyer, 1,710 tons. Cammell Laird,
ordered 4.1942, cancelled, tx White,
= CARYSFORT, launched 25.7.1944. (q.v.)

PELLEW Frigate, 1,180 tons, 300 × 33ft, 3—
40mm, 4—TT. Swan Hunter 29.9.1954. Sold
H. K.Vickers 26.4.1971; BU Fleetwood.
PELORUS Brig-sloop 18, 'Cruizer' class, 385bm.
Kidwell, Itchenor, 25.6.1808. Sold 10.1841 in
Singapore.
PELORUS Wood screw corvette, 1,462bm, 200 ×
40ft, 20—8in, 1—68pdr. Devonport DY 5.2.1857.
BU 1869 Devonport.
PELORUS 3rd class cruiser, 2,135 tons, 300 ×
36·5ft, 8—4in, 8—3pdr. Sheerness DY 15.12.1896.
Sold 6.5.1920 Ward, Grays.
PELORUS Minesweeper, 'Algerine' class. Lobnitz
18.6.1943. Tx SAN 1947
= PIETERMARITZBURG; accommodation ship
1968—91; scuttled 19.11.1994 False Bay.
PELORUS *See also MILDURA 1889.*
PELTER Gunvessel 14, 149bm, 75 × 21ft. Perry,
Blackwall, 12.5.1794. Sold 10.1802.
PELTER Gun-brig 12, 177bm, 80 × 22·5ft, 10—
18pdr carr., 2—12pdr. Dudman, Deptford,
25.7.1804. Foundered 12.1809 Atlantic.
PELTER Gun-brig 12, 184bm, 84 × 22·5ft, 10—
18pdr carr., 2—6pdr. Tucker, Bideford, 27.8.1813.
Coastguard 1827. Sold 8.8.1862.
PELTER Wood screw gunboat, 218bm, 100 × 22ft,
1—68pdr, 1—32pdr, 2—24pdr howitzers. Pitcher,
Northfleet, 26.8.1854. BU comp. 1.2.1864 Tolpult.
PEMBROKE 28-gun ship, 269bm. Woolwich 1655.
Sunk 1667 collision FAIRFAX off Portland.
PEMBROKE 5th Rate 32, 356bm, 105·5 × 27ft.
Deptford 3.3.1690. Captured 12.2.1694 by French
off The Lizard. Wrecked 1694.
PEMBROKE 4th Rate 60, 908bm, 145 × 37·5ft.
Snelgrove, Deptford, 22.11.1694. Captured
29.12.1709 by French in Mediterranean. Recap-
tured 22.3.1711, foundered.
PEMBROKE 4th Rate 54, 703bm, 130 × 35ft
Plymouth DY 18.5.1710. BU 8.1726 Plymouth.
PEMBROKE 4th Rate 60, 956bm, 144 × 39ft.
Woolwich DY 27.11.1733. Foundered 1745 R.
Medway, raised. Wrecked 13.4.1749 Fort St
David, East Indies.
PEMBROKE 4th Rate 60, 1,222bm, 156 × 42ft.
Plymouth DY 2.6.1757. Hulk 7.1776. BU 8.1793
Halifax, NS.
PEMBROKE 3rd Rate 74, 1,758bm, 176 × 48·5ft.
Wigram, Wells & Green, Blackwall, 17.6.1812;
undocked 3.2.1855 as screw ship; Coastguard
1858; base ship Chatham 4.1873; = FORTE
(receiving hulk) 1890. Sold 1905.
PEMBROKE Minehunter, 'Sandown' class.
Vosper-Thornycroft 15.12.1997.
PEMBROKE *For ships renamed PEMBROKE in*

succession as nominal base ships at Chatham, see TRENT 1877, NYMPHE 1888, ACHILLES 1863, PRINCE RUPERT 1915.

PEMBROKE *See also DUNCAN 1859.*

PEMBROKE CASTLE *See TILLSONBURG 1944.*

PEMBROKE PRIZE Sloop, 196bm, 80 × 23·5ft. Spanish, captured 9.1740. Sold 13.3.1744.

PENANG *See MALACCA 1809.*

PENARTH Minesweeper, Later 'Hunt' class. Lobnitz 21.5.1918. Sunk 4.2.1919 mine off East Coast.

PENDENNIS 3rd Rate 70, 1,093bm, 151 × 40ft. Chatham DY 1679. Wrecked 26.10.1689 Kentish Knock.

PENDENNIS 4th Rate 48, 681bm, 130 × 34·5ft. Deptford DY 15.10.1695. Captured 20.10.1705 by French PROTEE.

PENDENNIS CASTLE Corvette, 'Castle' class. Crown, cancelled 12.1943.

PENELOPE 6th Rate 24, 524bm, 114·5 × 32ft. Baker, Liverpool, 25.6.1778. Captured 10.1780 by her Spanish prisoners.

PENELOPE 5th Rate 32, 721bm, 129 × 36ft. Barton, Liverpool, 27.10.1783. BU 11.1797 Chatham.

PENELOPE 5th Rate 36, 1,051bm, 150 × 40ft. Parsons, Bursledon, 26.9.1798. Troopship 1813. Wrecked 1.5.1815 St Lawrence R.

PENELOPE 5th Rate 46, 1,091bm, 150 × 40·5ft. Chatham DY 13.8.1829 (LD Portsmouth, frames tx Chatham, relaid 11.1827). Comp, 6.1843 as paddle frigate, 1,616bm. Sold 15.7.1864 Castle & Beech for BU.

PENELOPE Armoured corvette, 3,096bm, 4,470 tons, 260 × 50ft, 8–8in, 3–40pdr. Pembroke Dock 18.6.1867. Coastguard 1869; guardship 1891 The Cape; prison hulk 1897. Sold 12.7.1912 The Cape; BU 1914 Genoa.

PENELOPE Light cruiser, 3,500 tons, 410 × 39ft, 2–6in, 6–4in. Vickers 25.8.1914. Sold 10.1924 Stanlee, Dover.

PENELOPE Tender. Purch. 1918. Sold 4.1922 W. Warren.

PENELOPE Cruiser, 5,270 tons, 506 (oa) × 51ft, 6–6in, 8–4in. Harland & Wolff 15.10.1935. Sunk 18.2.1944 by U.410 off Anzio.

PENELOPE (ex-COVENTRY, ex-PANTHER) Frigate, 'Leander' class, Y100, 2,650 tons, 372 (oa) × 41ft, 2–4·5in, helo (later Exocet). Vickers Armstrong, Tyne, 17.8.1962. Sold Ecuador, HO 25.4.1991 = PRESIDENTE ELOY ALFARO.

PENETANG (ex-ROUYN) Frigate (RCN), 'River' class. Davie SB 6.7.1944 (renamed 1944). Tx RNorN 1.1956 = DRAUG. Sold 1966.

PENGUIN Sloop 8, 35bm, 44 × 14·5ft. Woolwich DY 1772, not comp. BU 1785.

PENGUIN (ex-KOMEET) Sloop 16, 336bm, 93 × 29·5ft, 2–18pdr carr., 14–9pdr. Dutch, captured 28.8.1795 by UNICORN off coast of Ireland. Sold 27.7.1809.

PENGUIN Brig-sloop 18, 'Cruizer' class, 387bm. Bottomley, Lynn, 29.6.1813. Captured 23.3.1815 by American HORNET off Tristan da Cunha; foundered 24.1.1815. *Fought final action with US.*

PENGUIN Packet brig 6. 360bm, 95 × 30·5ft, 6–12pdr. Pembroke Dock 10.4.1838. Coastguard watchvessel 1857, = WV.31 on 25.5.1863. Sold 5.6.1871 A. Dockerill.

PENGUIN Wood screw gunvessel, 'Philomel' class. Miller, Liverpool, 8.2.1860. Sold 26.2.1870 Lethbridge & Drew for BU.

PENGUIN Composite screw sloop, 1,130 tons, 170 × 36ft, 2–7in, 4–64pdr. Napier 25.3.1876. Survey ship 1.1890; depot ship 1908 Sydney. Tx RAN 18.3.1913; sold 1924 Waugh, Sydney; crane hulk; burnt 13.12.1960.

PENGUIN *See also DOLPHIN 1731, ENCOUNTER 1902, PLATYPUS 1916.*

PENLEE POINT *See GIRDLE NESS 1945.*

PENN Destroyer, 'M' class. John Brown 8.4.1916. Sold 31.10.1921 W. & A. T. Burden.

PENN Destroyer, 1,540 tons, 345 (oa) × 35ft, 4–4·7in, 4–TT. Vickers Armstrong, Tyne 12.2.1941. Sold 31.1.1950; BU Troon.

PENNYWORT Corvette, 'Flower' class. Inglis 18.10.1941. Sold 1947; BU 1.1949 Troon.

PENSTEMON Sloop, 'Arabis' class. Workman Clark 5.2.1916. Sold 20.4.1920 = *Lila.*

PENSTEMON Corvette, 'Flower' class. Philip 18.1.1941. Sold 1946 = *Galaxidi.*

PENSTON Coastal minesweeper, 'Ton' class. Cook, Welton & Gemmell 9.5.1955. Sold 28.1.1970; BU Newhaven.

PENYLAN Destroyer, 'Hunt' class Type III. Vickers Armstrong, Barrow, 17.3.1942. Sunk 3.12.1942 by E-boats in English Channel.

PENZANCE 6th Rate 246bm, 94·5 × 25ft. Ellis, Shoreham, 22.4.1695, ordered sold 23.9.1713.

PENZANCE 5th Rate 44, 823bm, 135 × 37·5ft. Chitty & Vernon, Chichester, 7.11.1747. Sold 13.5.1766.

PENZANCE Sloop, 1,045 tons, 250 × 34ft, 2–4in. Devonport DY 10.4.1930. Sunk 24.8.1940 by U.34 south of Greenland.

PENZANCE Minehunter, 'Sandown' class, Vosper-Thornycroft 11.3.1997.

PEONY Sloop, 'Acacia' class. McMillan, Dumbarton, 27.10.1915. Sold 20.8.1919 = *Ardana.*

PEONY Corvette, 'Flower' class. Harland & Wolff 4.6.1940. Lent Greek Navy 1943–9.1951 = SAKHTOURIS. Arr. 21.4.1952 Clayton & Davie, Dunston, for BU.

PERA Wood screw store vessel, 126bm. Purch. 11.1855 Constantinople. Sold 11.1856 P&O Steam Navigation Co.

PERDRIX 6th Rate 22, 525bm. French, captured 6.1795 by VANGUARD off Antigua. BU 9.1799.

PEREGRINE Destroyer, 'M' class. John Brown 29.5.1916. Sold 15.11.1921 Cashmore, Newport.

PEREGRINE GALLEY 6th Rate 20, 197bm, 86·5 × 23ft. Sheerness DY 1700. Rebuilt 1733, 1749 as 229bm. Lost 1.1762 Atlantic. *Was yacht CAROLINA 1716, ROYAL CAROLINE 5.1733–1749.*

PEREGRINE PRIZE Sloop, 163bm, 76·5 × 22·5ft. Spanish, captured 8.1742. Sold. 12.14.1743.

PERIM (ex-PHILLIMORE) Frigate, 'Colony' class. Walsh Kaiser 5.11.1943 on Lend-Lease (renamed 1943). Ret. USN 22.5.1946. *Was to have been named SIERRA LEONE.*

PERIWINKLE Corvette, 'Flower' class. Harland & Wolff 24.2.1940. Lent USN 15.3.1942–1945 = RESTLESS. Sold 8.7.1946 = *Perilock.*

PERLEN 5th Rate 38, 1,204bm, 156 × 41·5ft. Danish, captured 7.9.1807 Battle of Copenhagen. Lazaretto 3.1813. Sold 7.1846 J. Brown. *Spelt 'PEARLEN' until 1811, 'PERLIN' from 1836. Was to have been renamed THEBAN in 1808.*

PERSEUS 6th Rate 20, 432bm, 108 × 30ft. Randall, Rotherhithe, 20.3.1776. Bomb vessel 1799. BU.9.1805 Sheerness.

PERSEUS 6th Rate 22, 522bm, 118·5 × 31·5ft, 22–32pdr carr., 8–18pdr carr., 2–6pdr. Sutton, Ringmore, 20.11.1812 Harbour service 5.1818. BU 9.1850 Deptford.

PERSEUS Wood screw sloop, 955bm, 1,365 tons, 185 × 33ft, 5–40pdr, 12–32pdr. Pembroke Dock 21.8.1861. Harbour service 1886; = DEFIANCE II 1904. Sold 26.6.1931.

PERSEUS 3rd class cruiser, 2,135 tons, 300 × 36·5ft, 8–4in, 8–3pdr. Earle, Hull, 15.7.1897. Sold 26.3.1914 Poulson.

PERSEUS Submarine, 1,475 tons, 260 × 30ft, 1–4in, 8–TT. Vickers Armstrong, Barrow, 22.5.1929. Sunk 1.12.1941 by Italian submarine ENRICO TOTI off Zante.

PERSEUS *See also EDGAR 1944.*

PERSEVERANCE 5th Rate 36, 882bm, 137 × 38·5ft. Randall, Rotherhithe, 10.4.1781. Sold 21.5.1823 J. Cristall for BU.

PERSEVERANCE (ex-*Sobraon*) Iron screw troopship, 1,967bm, 273 × 68ft. Mare, Blackwall,

13.7.1854; Russian, purch. from builder 5.1854. Wrecked 21.10.1860 Cape Verde Is.

PERSEVERANCE *See also INTREPID 1850.*

PERSIAN Brig-sloop 18, 'Cruizer' class, 390bm. List, Cowes, 2.5.1809. Wrecked 16.6.1813 Silver Keys.

PERSIAN Brig-sloop 16, 484bm, 105 × 33·5ft, 4–32pdr, 12–32pdr carr. Pembroke Dock 7.10.1839. BU 3.1866 Castle.

PERSIAN Minesweeper, 'Algerine' class. Redfern 12.2.1943 on Lend-Lease. Ret. USN 12.1946.

PERSIAN *See also WALLAROO 1890.*

PERSIMMON Minesweeping sloop, '24' class. Osbourne Graham, Sunderland, 4.3.1919. Sold 12.8.1920 Moise Mazza; sale cancelled; sold 13.10.1922 Dundas Simpson.

PERSIMMON Landing ship, 12,864 tons. 1943–46.

PERSISTENT *See PETARD 1941.*

PERT (ex-BONAPARTE) Brig-sloop 16, 260bm, 84·5 × 23ft, 18–12pdr carr. French privateer, captured 12.11.1804 by CYANE in West Indies. Wrecked 16.10.1807 West Indies.

PERT (ex-SERPENT) Brig-sloop 18, 239bm, 97 × 24ft. French, captured 17.7.1808 by ACASTA off La Guira. BU 10.1813.

PERT Wood screw gunboat, 'Cheerful' class. Young & Magnay, Limehouse, 3.4.1856. BU comp. 12.3.1864.

PERT Composite screw gunvessel, 464bm, 155 × 25ft, 1–7in, 1–64pdr, 2–20pdr. Reid, Glasgow, 22.6.1868. Sold 12.1888.

PERTH GM destroyer (RAN), 3,370 tons, 440·8 (oa) × 47ft, 2–5in, SSM Harpoon, SAM GDC Pomona, 6–TT. Defoe SB 26.9.1963. PO 15.10.1999; dive site King Sound, south-western Australia.

PERTH Frigate (RAN), 'Anzac' class, Tenix Defence Systems, Williamstown. Delivery scheduled 2004.

PERTH *See also AMPHION 1934.*

PERUVIAN Brig-sloop 18, 'Cruizer' class, 383bm. Parsons, Warsash, 26.4.1808. BU 2.1830.

PESAQUID Frigate (RCN), 'River' class. Victoria, BC, cancelled 8.1943.

PESHAWAR *See MALWA 1944.*

PET Wood screw gunboat, 'Cheerful' class. Pembroke Dock 9.2.1856. Hulked 1865. Sold 12.4.1904 Castle. *Also known as C.17 from 1900.*

PET (ex-*Sir Francis Chapman*) Tender, 110 tons, 80 × 18ft. War Dept vessel, tx 11.1906. Sold 13.1.1909 in Jamaica.

PETARD Destroyer, 'M' class. Denny 24.3.1916. Sold 9.5.1921 Ward; arr. 10.1923 Grays for BU.

PETARD (ex-PERSISTENT) Destroyer, 1,540 tons, 345 (oa) × 35ft, 4—4·7in, 4—TT. Vickers Armstrong, Tyne, 27.3.1941 (renamed 1941). Frigate 1956, 1,800 tons, 2—4in, 5—40mm, 4—TT, 2—Squid. BU 1967 McLellan, Bo'ness.

PETER Carrack. Genoese, captured 25.7.1417. Sold mercantile 10.1424.

PETER 10-gun vessel, 120bm. Captured 1645. Listed 1647.

PETER 10-gun vessel. Irish Royalist, captured 1649 by Parliamentarians. Listed until 1652.

PETER 32-gun ship. Captured 1652. Sold 1653.

PETER Flyboat 4, 180bm. Dutch, captured 1665. Sold 1668.

PETER POMEGRANATE Ship, 450bm. Built 1510. Rebuilt 1536 as 600bm, 90 guns = PETER. Listed until 1552.

PETERBOROUGH Corvette (RCN), Modified 'Flower' class. Kingston SY 15.1.1944. Sold Dominican Navy 1947 = GERADO JANSEN; BU 1972.

PETERBOROUGH See also EARL OF PETER-BOROUGH 1915.

PETEREL (ex-*Duchess of Manchester*) Survey sloop 4, 138bm, 71 × 21·5ft, 4—3pdr. Purch. 4.1777. Sold 28.5.1788.

PETEREL Schooner 6, 280bm, 95 × 26ft. Woolwich DY, ordered 18.7.1829, cancelled 28.2.1831.

PETEREL Packet brig 6, 359bm, 95 × 30·5ft, 6—12pdr. Pembroke Dock 23.5.1838. Sold 11.1.1862 Marshall, Plymouth.

PETEREL Wood screw sloop, 669bm, 913 tons, 160 × 30ft, 1—40pdr, 6—32pdr, 4—20pdr. Devonport DY 10.11.1860. Coal hulk 12.1885. Sold 1901.

PETEREL Destroyer, 370 tons, 215 × 21ft, 1—12pdr, 5—6pdr, 2—TT. Palmer 30.3.1899. Sold 30.8.1919 T. R. Sales.

PETEREL River gunboat, 310 tons, 177 × 29ft, 2—3in. Yarrow 18.7.1927. Sunk 8.12.1941 by Japanese cruiser IDZIMO at Shanghai.

PETEREL Patrol vessel, 190 tons, 120 (oa) × 21·7ft. Dunston 14.5.1976. Sold 4.1991 Heuvelman Shipping & Trading, Holland, for resale Rotterdam.

PETERELL Sloop 16, 365bm, 105 × 28ft. Wilson, Frindsbury, 4.3.1794. Harbour service 1817. Sold 11.7.1827.

PETERHEAD Minesweeper, TE 'Bangor' class. Blyth 31.10.1940. Sold 10.5.1948; BU 5.1948 Hayes, Pembroke Dock.

PETERMAN Dogger 6. Captured 1672. Sold 1674.

PETERSFIELD Minesweeper, Later 'Hunt' class. Lobnitz 3.3.1919. Wrecked 11.11.1931 Tung Yung I., China.

PETERSHAM Inshore minesweeper, 'Ham' class. McLean, Renfrew, 12.1.1955. Tx French Navy 1955 = M.782/CAPUCINE; deleted 1985.

PETROLIA (ex-SHERBORNE CASTLE) Corvette (RCN), 'Castle' class. Harland & Wolff 24.2.1944 (renamed 1943). Sold 1946 = *Bharatlaxmi*.

PETROLIA See also LIONESS 1944.

PETULANT See PELICAN 1906.

PETUNIA Sloop, 'Arabis' class. Workman Clark 3.4.1916. Sold 15.12.1922 Batson Syndicate.

PETUNIA Corvette, 'Flower' class. Robb, Leith, 19.9.1940. Tx Chinese Navy 1.1946 = FU PO; lost 20.3.1947.

PEVENSEY CASTLE Corvette, 'Castle' class. Harland & Wolff 11.1.1944. Tx Air Ministry 1959; = *Weather Monitor* 12.5.1961; = *Admiral Beaufort* 1977. BU Troon 1982.

PEYTON Destroyer, 'M' class. Denny 2.5.1916. Sold 9.5.1921. Ward, Morecambe.

PEYTON See also TORTOLA 1943.

PHAETON Fireship 8, 263bm, 91·5 × 25·5ft. Castle, Deptford, 19.3.1691. Burnt in action 19.5.1692 La Hogue.

PHAETON (ex-*Poole*) Fireship 10, 214bm, 84 × 24·5ft. Purch. 14.9.1739. Sold 22.7.1743.

PHAETON 5th Rate 38, 944bm, 141 × 39ft. Smallshaw, Liverpool, 12.6.1782. Sold 11.7.1827 Freak, retained; sold 26.3.1828 Cristall for BU.

PHAETON 4th Rate 50, 1,942bm, 185 × 49·5ft, 8—8in, 42—32pdr. Deptford DY 25.11.1848; undocked 12.12.1859 as screw frigate, 2,396bm. BU 1875 Chatham.

PHAETON Despatch vessel (2nd class cruiser), 4,300 tons, 300 × 46ft, 10—6in. Napier 27.2.1883. Sold 1913 as TS, = *Indefatigable* 1.1.1914; = CARRICK II 1941 (q.v.).

PHAETON Light cruiser, 3,500 tons, 410 × 39ft, 2—6in, 6—4in. Vickers. 21.10.1914. Sold 16.1.1923 King, Troon.

PHAETON See also SYDNEY 1934.

PHEASANT (ex-FAISAN) Sloop 14, 291bm. 106 × 25ft 14—6pdr. French, captured 4.1761 by ALBANY. Foundered 8.1761 English Channel.

PHEASANT Cutter 12, 149bm, 66 × 24ft 12—4pdr. Purch. 3.1778. Capsized 20.6.1781 English Channel

PHEASANT Sloop 18, 365bm, 106 × 30ft. Edwards, Shoreham, 17.4.1798. Sold 11.7.1827 Ledger for BU.

PHEASANT Sloop 18, 481bm, 116 × 31ft. Plymouth DY, ordered 30.1.1829, cancelled 1.11.1832.

PHEASANT Wood screw gunboat, 'Albacore' class. Pitcher, Northfleet, 1.5.1856. BU 8.1877 Sheerness.

PHEASANT Composite screw gunboat, 755 tons, 165 × 30ft, 6—4in. Devonport DY 10.4.1888. Sold 15.5.1906 Cox, Falmouth.

PHEASANT Destroyer, 'M' class. Fairfield 23.10.1916. Sunk 1.3.1917 mine off Orkneys.

PHEASANT Sloop, 1,350 tons, 283 × 38·5ft, 6—4in. Yarrow 21.12.1942. Arr. 15.1.1963 Troon for BU.

PHILIP Ship, 130bm. Purch. 3.1414. Sold 10.4.1418.

PHILIP & MARY Galleon 44, 550bm. Built 1556. Rebuilt 1584, 600bm, 2—60pdr, 3—34pdr, 7—18pdr, 8—9pdr, 12—6pdr, 24 smaller = NONPAREIL. Rebuilt 1603 619bm = NONSUCH. Sold c. 1645.

PHILLIMORE *See PERIM 1943.*

PHILOCTETES Depot ship, 13,980 tons, 507 × 63ft, 4—4in. Purch. 8.1940, comp. Belfast 6.1.1942. Sold 22.1.1948. BU Cashmore, Newport, 11.1948.

PHILOMEL Brig-sloop 18, 'Cruizer' class, 384bm. Poole, Bridport, 11.9.1806. Sold 30.4.1817 Manlove.

PHILOMEL Brig-sloop 10, 'Cherokee' class. Portsmouth DY 28.4.1823. Sold 12.12.1833.

PHILOMEL Brig 8, 360bm, 95 × 30ft, 8—18pdr. Devonport DY 28.3.1842. Coastguard watchvessel 1857; = WV.23 on 25.5.1863. Foundered 1869 R. Swale; sold 2.1870 Hayhurst & Clasper for salvage, BU.

PHILOMEL Wood screw gunvessel, 'Philomel' class. White 10.3.1860. Sold 2.6.1865 White, Cowes, for BU.

PHILOMEL Wood screw gunvessel, 64bm, 774 tons, 170 × 29ft. Deptford DY 29.10.1867. Sold 14.4.1886.

PHILOMEL 2nd class cruiser, 2,575 tons, 265 × 41ft, 8—7in, 8—3pdr. Devonport DY 28.8.1890. Base ship Wellington, NZ, 3.1921. Sold 17.1.1947 Strongman & Co.; hulk scuttled 6.8.1949 off east coast of New Zealand.

PHIPPS (ex-TWO LYDIAS [?]) Schooner 14. Dutch, captured 1808. BU 12.1812.

PHLEGETHON Iron paddle gunvessel (Indian), 510bm. Laird 1839. Listed 1853.

PHLOX Corvette, 'Flower' class. Robb, Leith, 16.1.1942. = LOTUS 4.1942. Sold 1947.

PHOEBE 5th Rate 36, 926bm, 143 × 38·5ft. Dudman, Deptford, 29.9.1795. Slop ship 10.1826. Sold 27.5.1841 J. Cristall for BU.

PHOEBE 4th Rate 51, 2,044bm, 180 × 52ft, 10—8in, 1—68pdr, 40—32pdr. Devonport DY 12.4.1854; undocked 10.4.1860 as screw frigate, 2,896bm. BU 1875 Castle.

PHOEBE 2nd class cruiser, 2,575 tons, 265 × 41ft, 8—4·7in, 8—3pdr. Devonport DY 1.7.1890. Sold 10.7.1906 A. Anderson, Copenhagen.

PHOEBE Destroyer, 'M' class. Fairfield 20.11.1916. Sold 15.11.1921 Cashmore, Newport.

PHOEBE Cruiser, 5,450 tons, 512 (oa) × 50·5ft, 8—5·25in. Fairfield 25.3.1939. Arr. 1.4.1956 Hughes Bolckow, Blyth, for BU.

PHOEBE Frigate, 'Leander' class, Y136, 2,650 tons, 372 (oa) × 41ft, 2—4·5in, Seacat, helo (later Exocet, Seawolf). Stephen 8.7.1964. Sold Victoria Paper Stock Co.; towed Portsmouth 13.10.1992 for BU India.

PHOENIX 20-gun ship, 60bm. Purch. 1546. Rebuilt 1558, 70bm. Sold 1573.

PHOENIX 20-gun ship, 246bm. Chatham 27.2.1613. Listed until 1624.

PHOENIX 38-gun ship, 414bm. Woolwich 1647. Wrecked 1664. *In Dutch hands 7.9–26.11.1652.*

PHOENIX Ship, 780bm. Dutch, captured 1665. Sunk 6.1667 blockship R. Thames.

PHOENIX 5th Rate 42, 368bm, Portsmouth DY 1671. Burnt 12.4.1692 nr Malaga to avoid capture by French.

PHOENIX Bomb vessel 8, 86bm, 55 × 19·5ft. Purch. 1692. Sold 3.5.1698.

PHOENIX Fireship 8, 256bm, 91 × 25·5ft. Dalton & Gardner, Rotherhithe, 16.3.1694. Rebuilt Plymouth 1709 as 6th Rate 24, 273bm; rebuilt Woolwich 1727 as 376bm, 106 × 28ft. Hulked 1742. Sold 28.6.1744.

PHOENIX 6th Rate 24, 514bm, 112·5 × 32·5ft. Graves, Limehouse, 27.7.1743. Hospital hulk 1755. Sold 9.12.1762.

PHOENIX 5th Rate 44, 856bm, 141 × 37ft. Batson, Limehouse, 25.6.1759. Foundered 4.10.1780 hurricane off Cuba.

PHOENIX 5th Rate 36, 884bm, 137 × 38·5ft. Parsons, Bursledon, 15.7.1783. Wrecked 20.2.1816 nr Smyrna.

PHOENIX Wood paddle sloop, 802bm. Chatham DY 25.9.1832 (ordered 1.1831 Woolwich). Conv. 1845 screw sloop, 809bm, 174·5× 32ft. Sold 26.1864 Castle.

PHOENIX Composite screw sloop, 1,124 tons, 170 × 36ft, 2—7in, 4—64pdr. Devonport DY 16.9.1879. Wrecked 12.9.1882 Prince Edward I.

PHOENIX Sloop, 1,050 tons, 185 × 32·5ft, 6—4in. Devonport DY 25.4.1895. Capsized 18.9.1906 typhoon Hong Kong; raised, sold 7.1.1907.

PHOENIX Destroyer, 765 tons, 246 × 26ft, 2—4in, 2—12pdr, 2—TT. Vickers 9.10.1911. Sunk 14.5.1918 by Austrian submarine U.XXVII in Adriatic.

PHOENIX Submarine, 1,457 tons, 260 × 30ft, 1–4in, 8–TT. Cammell Laird 3.10.1929. Sunk 17.7.1940 Italian torpedo boat ALBATROS off Sicily.

PHOENIX *See also TAURANGA 1889.*

PHOSPHORUS (ex-Dutch *Haasje*) Fireship 4, 115bm, 4–12pdr carr. Purch. 6.1804. Sold 24.3.1810.

PICKLE Schooner 5, 118bm, 68 × 21ft. Bermuda 1827. BU 1847 Bermuda.

PICKLE (ex-*Eolo*) Brig 168bm. Slaver, captured 1852 by ORESTES. Listed until 1854.

PICKLE Mortar vessel, 155bm, 70 × 23·5ft, 1–13in mortar. Mare, Blackwall, 23.5.1855. = MV.22 on 19.10.1855. BU comp. 20.10.1865 Marshall, Plymouth.

PICKLE Wood screw gunboat, 'Albacore' class. Pitcher, Northfleet, 3.5.1856. BU comp. 12.4.1864.

PICKLE Iron screw gunboat, 'Ant' class. Campbell Johnston, North Woolwich, 15.11.1872. Dockyard lighter 1906.

PICKLE Minesweeper, 'Algerine' class. Harland & Wolff 3.8.1943. Tx Ceylonese Navy 6.4.1959 = PARAKARAMA; BU 23.9.1964 Singapore.

PICKLE *See also STING 1800, ELCAIR 1801.*

PICOTEE Corvette, 'Flower' class. Harland & Wolff 19.7.1940. Sunk 12.8.1941 by U.568 off Iceland.

PICTON Coastal minesweeper, 'Ton' class. Cook, Welton & Gemmell, Selby, 20.10.1955. Sold S. Bkg (Queenborough) 28.7.1969.

PICTON *See also LLEWELLYN 1913, SIR THOMAS PICTON 1915.*

PICTOU (ex-*Bonne Foi*) Brig-sloop 16, 215bm, 83 × 25ft. Captured 20.4.1813. Captured 14.2.1814 by American CONSTITUTION.

PICTOU (ex-*Zebra*) Schooner 14, 283bm. Purch. 1814. Sold, 13.8.1818 Mr Hughes.

PICTOU Corvette (RCN), 'Flower' class. Davie SB, Lauzon, 5.10.1940. Sold 1949 = *Olympic Chaser*.

PIEMONTAISE 5th Rate 38, 1,093bm. French, captured 8.3.1808 by ST FIORENZO off Ceylon. BU 1.1813 Woolwich.

PIEMONTAISE *See also PRESIDENT 1806.*

PIERCER Gunvessel 16, 147bm, 75 × 21ft. King, Dover, 6.1794. Sold 30.5.1802.

PIERCER Gun-brig 12, 178bm, 80 × 22·5ft, 10–18pdr carr., 2–12pdr. Ayles, Topsham, 29.7.1804. Presented 6.1814 to Govt of Hanover as guard-ship.

PIGEON Schooner 4, 85bm. Purch. 1804. Wrecked 11.1805 Texel.

PIGEON (ex-*Fanny*) Schooner. Purch. 1805. Lost 1805. *May have been previous vessel.*

PIGEON Schooner 4, 75bm, 56 × 18·5ft, 4–12pdr carr. Custance, Yarmouth, 26.4.1806. Wrecked 15.1.1809 nr Margate.

PIGEON (ex-*Brothers*) Wood paddle tender. Purch. 15.8.1854 Constantinople; sold 7.1856 Constantinople.

PIGEON Wood screw gunboat, 'Britomart' class. Briggs, Sunderland, 7.6.1860. BU 29.9.1876 Devonport.

PIGEON Composite screw gunboat, 755 tons, 165 × 30ft, 6–4in. Pembroke Dock 5.9.1888. Sold 15.5.1906 V. Grech, name unchanged.

PIGEON Destroyer, 'M' class. Hawthorn Leslie 3.3.1916. Sold 9.5.1921 Ward, New Holland.

PIGEON *See also VARIABLE 1827.*

PIGMY Cutter 12, 181bm, 69·5 × 25·5ft. 12–4pdr. King, Dover, 2.1781. Captured 22.12.1781 by French when ashore nr Dunkirk; recaptured 7.1782 English Channel; = LURCHER 31.5.1783; = PIGMY 7.1783. Wrecked 16.12.1793 The Motherbank.

PIGMY Gun-brig 14, c. 200bm. Purch. 1806. Wrecked 2.3.1807 nr Rochefort.

PIGMY Schooner 10, 197bm, 83 × 23ft, 10–12pdr carr. King, Upnor, 24.2.1810. Cutter 1819. Sold 21.5.1823 Cristall.

PIGMY (ex-*Sybil*) Wood paddle packet, 227bm, 114·5 × 21ft. GPO vessel, tx 4.1837. BU 1879 Portsmouth.

PIGMY Composite screw gunboat, 755 tons, 165 × 30ft, 6–4in. Sheerness DY 27.7.1888. Sold 4.4.1905 Cox, Falmouth.

PIGMY (ex-*Sir Lothian Nicholson*) Tender, 100 tons. War Dept vessel, tx 1905. BU 1938.

PIGMY (ex-ISKRA) Depot ship, 560 tons, 128 × 35ft. Polish, renamed 1940. Cd 30.12.1940–31.3.1941 = PIGMY; = ISKRA 1941; recd 23.11.1942–13.3.1945 = PIGMY. Ret. Polish Govt 4.1948. *See ISKRA 1941.*

PIGMY *See also MUTINE 1779, RANGER 1779, RANGER 1806.*

PIGOT Gallev 8, 8–2pdr. Purch. 7.1778 North America. Captured 28.10.1778 by Americans at Rhode I.

PIKE Schooner 4, 78bm, 56 × 18ft, 4–12pdr carr. Bermuda 1804. Captured 20.4.1807 by French privateer MARAT.

PIKE Cutter 10. In service 1809–11.

PIKE (ex-DART) Schooner 14, 251bm, 93 × 24·5ft. 12–12pdr carr., 2–6dpr. American, captured 1813. Wrecked 5.2.1836 coast of Jamaica.

PIKE (ex-*Spitfire*) Wood paddle packet, 111bm, 89 × 16ft. GPO vessel, tx 1837. BU 7.1868.

PIKE Iron screw gunboat, 'Ant' class. Campbell

Johnston, North Woolwich, 16.10.1872. BDV 1908. Sold 27.3.1920 G. Sharpe.

PILCHARD Schooner 4, 78bm, 56 × 18ft, 4—12pdr carr. Bermuda 1805. Sold 23.2.1813.

PILFORD *See PITCAIRN 1943.*

PILOT (ex-PILOTE) Brig-sloop 14, 218b, 78·5 × 26ft, 14—4pdr. French cutter, captured 2.10.1779 by JUPITER. Sold 5.1799.

PILOT Brig-sloop 18, 'Cruizer' class, 383bm. Guillaume, Northam, 6.8.1807. Sold 26.3.1828 Adam Gordon.

PILOT Brig-sloop 16, 485bm, 105 × 33·5ft, 12—32pdr carr., 4—3pdr. Plymouth DY 9.6.1838. Sold 11.1.1862 Marshall, Plymouth.

PILOT Training brig 8, 501 tons, 105 × 33·5ft. Pembroke Dock 12.11.1879. Sold 2.10.1907 Adrien Merveille, Dunkirk; resold, BU Holland.

PIMPERNEL Corvette, 'Flower' class. Harland & Wolff 16.11.1940. Sold 6.2.1948; BU Portaferry 10.1948.

PINCHER (Gunboat No 39, ex-*Two Sisters*) Gunvessel 12, 160bm, 74 × 22·5ft, 2—24pdr, 10—18pdr carr. Purch. 3.1797 Leith. Sold 4.1802.

PINCHER Gun-brig 12, 180bm, 80·5 × 22·5ft, 10—18pr carr., 2—12pdr. Graham, Harwich, 28.8.1804. Sold 17.5.1816.

PINCHER Schooner 5, 118bm, 69 × 21ft. Bermuda 1827. Capsized 6.3.1838 off The Owers; raised, sold 31.8.1838.

PINCHER Wood screw gunboat, 216bm, 100 × 22ft, 1—68pdr, 1—32pdr, 2—24pdr howitzers. Pitcher, Northfleet, 5.9.1854. BU comp. 17.2.1864.

PINCHER Iron screw gunboat, 265 tons, 85 × 26ft, 1—10in. Pembroke Dock 5.5.1879. Sold 11.7.1905 Portsmouth.

PINCHER Destroyer, 975 tons, 267·5 × 28ft, 1—4in, 3—12pdr, 2—TT. Denny 15.3.1910. Wrecked 24.7.1918 Seven Stones.

PINCHER Minesweeper, 'Algerine' class. Harland & Wolff 19.1.1943. Arr. 7.3.1962 Clayton & Davie, Dunston, for BU.

PINEHAM Inshore minesweeper, 'Ham' class. McLean, Renfrew, 9.5.1955. Tx French Navy 10.11.1955 = M.789/PETUNIA. BU 26.9.1985.

PINK Corvette, 'Flower' class. Robb 16.2.1942. Torpedoed 27.6.1944, not repaired. BU 1947 Rees, Llanelly.

PINNER *See FITZROY 1919.*

PINTAIL Patrol vessel, 580 tons, 224 × 251·5ft, 1—4in. Denny 18.8.1939. Sunk 10.6.1941 mine off R. Humber.

PIONEER Gun-brig 14. Listed 1804–07.

PIONEER Cutter 12, 197bm, 83 × 23ft, 10—12pdr carr., 2—6pdr. King, Upnor, 10.3.1810. Schooner

1813; cutter 1819; Coastguard vessel 4.1824. Sold 4.9.1849 Plymouth.

PIONEER (ex-*Eider*) Wood screw discovery vessel, 342bm. Purch. 2.3.1850. Abandoned 1854 Arctic; name removed from Navy List 25.10.1854.

PIONEER Wood screw gunvessel, 868bm, 200 × 30·5ft, 1—110pdr, 1—60pdr. 2—40pdr. Pembroke Dock 19.1.1856. BU 1865 Marshall, Plymouth.

PIONEER Iron paddle gunboat (Australian), 140 × 20ft, 2—12pdr. Russell, Sydney, 1862. *Fate unknown.*

PIONEER Wood paddle survey vessel, 142bm. Colonial Office vessel, tx 1864. PO 26.6.1873; sold 8.1873 Wm Holt, Fernando Po.

PIONEER Composite paddle vessel, 576 tons, 160 × 25·5ft, 6—20pdr. Blumer, Sunderland, 26.10.1874. BU 1888.

PIONEER 3rd class cruiser, 2,200 tons, 305 × 36·5ft, 8—4in 8—3pdr. Chatham DY 26.6.1899. Tx RAN 28.12.1912, cd 1.3.1913; PO 7.11.1916; sold 1924 Sydney; hull scuttled 18.2.1931 off Sydney.

PIONEER River gunboat, 40 tons, 75 × 12·5ft, 1—3pdr. Yarrow 1892; dismantled, tx Lake Nyasa, re-erected 1893. Tx BCA Govt 1.1894.

PIONEER *See also MARS 1944.*

PIORUN *See NERISSA 1940.*

PIQUE 5th Rate 38, 906bm. French, captured 6.1.1795 by BLANCHE in West Indies. Wrecked in action with French SEINE 29.6.1798 French Channel coast.

PIQUE (ex-PALLAS) 5th Rate 36, 1,028bm, 146·5 × 39·5ft. French, captured 6.2.1800 by squadron off coast of France. Sold 22.7.1819 Freake for BU

PIQUE 5th Rate 46, 1,215bm, 159 × 42ft. Plymouth DY, ordered 9.6.1825, cancelled 16.6.1832.

PIQUE 5th Rate 36, 1,633bm, 160 × 49ft, 36—32pdr. Plymouth DY 21.7.1834. Receiving ship 1872; lent as hospital hulk 30.3.1882. Sold 12.7.1910 Cox, Falmouth.

PIQUE 2nd class cruiser, 3,600 tons, 300 × 43·5ft, 2—6in, 6—4·7in, 8—6pdr. Palmer 13.12.1890. Sold 9.5.1911 F. E. Rudge.

PIQUE Destroyer, 1,710 tons, Cammell Laird, ordered 4.1942, cancelled 11.1942, tx White, = CAVALIER (q.v.).

PIQUE (ex-CELERITY) Minesweeper, 'Catherine' class. Associated SB, Seattle, 26.10.1942 on Lend-Lease (renamed 1942). Ret. USN 1946; tx Turkish Navy 4.1947 = EREGLI; withdrawn 1973.

PIRIE Minesweeper, 'Bathurst' class. Broken Hill 12.1941. Lent RAN 10.1942. Sold 8.1946 Turkish Navy = AMASRA; withdrawn 1971.

PIROUETTE Minesweeper, 290 tons, 130 × 26ft,

1–3pdr. Rennie Forrest, Wivenhoe, 1.11.1917; War Dept tug, tx on stocks 1917. Ret. War Dept 1920.

PITCAIRN (ex-PILFORD) Frigate, 'Colony' class. Walsh, Kaiser, 15.10.1943 on Lend-Lease (renamed 1943). Ret. USN 6.1946.

PITT Cutter, 100bm, 59 × 20·5ft. Purch. 1.1763. Foundered 5.8.1766 Atlantic.

PITT Schooner 12 purch. 1805. = SANDWICH 1807. BU 10.1809 . *Still listed 1.1810.*

PITT 3rd Rate 74, 1,751bm, 176 × 48·5ft. Portsmouth DY 13.4.1816. Coal hulk 1853. BU comp. 17.3.1877 Portsmouth.

PITT Screw 2nd Rate 91, 3,716bm, 252 × 57·5ft. Chatham DY, ordered 5.3.1860, cancelled 12.12.1863.

PITT *See also DORIS 1808, TRAFALGAR 1820.*

PITTINGTON *See ALDINGTON 1955.*

PLACENTIA Sloop 14. Purch. 1779. Wrecked 1782 off Newfoundland.

PLACENTIA Brig-sloop 6, 42bm, 45 × 15ft. Jeffery & Street, Newfoundland, 1790. Wrecked 8.5.1794 Newfoundland.

PLANET River gunboat (Indian), 397bm. Bombay DY 1840. Listed 1863.

PLANTAGENET 3rd Rate 74, 1,777bm, 181 × 47ft. Woolwich DY 22.10.1801. BU 5.1817.

PLASSY Torpedo gunboat (RIM), 735 tons, 230 × 27ft, 2–4·7in, 3–TT. Armstrong 5.7.1890. Sold 17.5.1904.

PLASSY *See also PUNJAUB 1854.*

PLATYPUS Depot ship (RAN), 3,476 tons, 310 × 44ft. John Brown 28.10.1916. = PENGUIN 16.8.1929, = PLATYPUS 3.1941 Sold 20.2.1958 for BU in Japan.

PLATYPUS II *See CERBERUS 1868.*

PLAY PRIZE 5th Rate 30, 367bm, 97·5 × 28ft. French, captured 1689. Sunk 4.8.1697 Harwich 'to secure the graving place'.

PLESSISVILLE Frigate (RCN), 'River' class. G. T. Davie, cancelled 1944.

PLOVER (ex-MORGEN STAR) 26-gun ship. Dutch, captured 1652. Either sunk in action 2.1653 or sold 1657.

PLOVER Sloop 18, 422bm, 110 × 30ft. Betts, Mistleythorn, 23.4.1796. Sold 8.3.1819 Young, Limehouse.

PLOVER Brig-sloop 10, 'Cherokee' class, 237bm. Portsmouth DY 30.6.1821. Sold 27.5.1841 Cristall.

PLOVER (ex-*Bentinck*) Survey cutter, 237bm. Purch. 2.1842. Sold 24.11.1854 San Francisco.

PLOVER Wood screw gunboat, 'Albacore' class. Pitcher, Northfleet 8.9.1855. Sunk 25.6.1859 in action with Pei Ho forts, China.

PLOVER Wood screw gunvessel, 'Philomel' class. Green, Blackwall, 19.1.1860. Sold 12.9.1865 = *Hawk.*

PLOVER Wood screw gunvessel, 663bm, 805 tons, 170 × 29ft, 1–7in, 2–40pdr. Deptford DY 20.2.1867. Sold Castle 8.1885 for BU

PLOVER Composite screw gunboat, 755 tons, 165 × 30ft, 6–4in. Pembroke Dock 18.10.1888. BDV 1904. Sold 47.4.1927 Gibraltar.

PLOVER Destroyer, 'M' class. Hawthorn Leslie 19.4.1916. Sold 9.5.1921 Ward, Hayle.

PLOVER Minelayer, 805 tons, 180 × 37·5ft, 1–12pdr. Denny 8.6.1937. Sold 26.2.1969; BU Inverkeithing.

PLOVER Patrol vessel, 662 tons, 205·3 (oa) × 32·8ft, 1–76mm. Hall Russell 12.4.1983. Sold 1.8.1997 Philippines Navy = APOLINARIO MABINI.

PLUCKY Steam tender, 212bm. Purch. 1856; sold 1858.

PLUCKY Iron screw gunboat, 196bm, 213 tons, 80 × 25ft, 1–9in. Portsmouth DY 13.7.1870. = BANTERER 6.1915. Sold 1928.

PLUCKY Destroyer, 'M' class. Scotts 21.4.1916. Sold 9.5.1921 Ward, Briton Ferry; arr. 5.1924 Preston for BU.

PLUCKY Minesweeper, 'Algerine' class. Harland & Wolff 29.9.1943. Arr. 15.3.1962 Clayton & Davie, Dunston, for BU.

PLUMPER Gunvessel 12, 149bm, 74 × 21ft. Randall, Rotherhithe, 17.5.1794. Sold 1.1802.

PLUMPER Gun-brig 12, 178bm, 81 × 22ft. Dudman, Deptford, 7.9.1804. Captured 16.7.1805 by French off St-Malo.

PLUMPER Gun-brig 12, 177bm, 80 × 22·5ft. Halifax, NS, 29.12.1807. Wrecked 5.12.1812 Bay of Fundy.

PLUMPER Gun-brig 12, 181bm, 84 × 22·5ft. Good, Bridport, 9.10.1813. Sold 12.12.1833.

PLUMPER Wood screw sloop, 490bm, 140 × 27·5ft. Portsmouth DY 5.4.1848. Sold 2.6.1865 White, Cowes.

PLUMPTON Paddle minesweeper, 'Ascot' class. McMillan 20.3.1916. Sunk 19.10.1918 mine off Ostend.

PLUTO (ex-*Roman Emperor*) Fireship 8, 272bm, 92 × 26ft. 14–4pdr. Purch. 21.8.1745; sold 10.9.1747.

PLUTO (ex-*New Concord*) Fireship 8, 270bm, 86 × 27ft. Purch. 31.12.1756; sold 23.12.1762.

PLUTO Fireship 14, 426bm, 109 × 30ft. Stewart, Sandgate, 1.2.1782. Sold 19.7.1817 Warwick.

PLUTO Wood paddle gunvessel, 365bm, 135 × 24ft. Woolwich DY 28.4.1831. BU 3.1861.

PLUTO Minesweeper, 'Algerine' class. Port Arthur SY 21.10.1944. Sold 13.9.1972; BU Dalmuir.

PLUTO *See also TAMAR 1758.*

PLYM Gunvessel. Packet brig, fitted out 10.1795. Sold 9.1802.

PLYM Frigate, 'River' class. Smith's Dock 4.2.1943. Expended 3.10.1952 atomic tests Monte Bello Is.

PLYMOUTH 60-gun ship, 752bm, 140 × 34·5ft. Taylor, Wapping, 1653. Rebuilt Blackwall 1705, 900bm, 64 guns. Foundered 11.8.1705.

PLYMOUTH Sheer hulk, 524bm, 121 × 32ft. Purch. 19.5.1689. BU 1730.

PLYMOUTH 4th Rate 60, 922bm, 144 × 38ft. Plymouth DY 25.5.1708. Rebuilt Chatham 1722, 955bm. BU comp. 3.4.1764 Portsmouth.

PLYMOUTH Yacht 6, 88bm, 64·5 × 18ft, 6—2pdr. Plymouth DY 1755. BU 9.1793 Plymouth.

PLYMOUTH Transport, 64bm, 51·5 × 17ft. Plymouth 1778. Sunk 1815 breakwater.

PLYMOUTH Yacht 8, 96bm, 64 × 18·5ft. Plymouth DY 2.11.1796. BU 7.1830.

PLYMOUTH Transport 8. Built 1786. Sold 14.12.1815.

PLYMOUTH Frigate, 'Rothesay' class, 2,380 tons, 370 (oa) × 41ft, 2—4·5in, 1—40mm, Limbo (later also Seacat, helo). Devonport DY 20.7.1959. PO 30.4.1988; museum ship Plymouth 1988–90; tx Warship Preservation Trust 20.4.1990, Glasgow 1990–92, Birkenhead 1992.

PLYMOUTH *See also ADMIRALTY 1814.*

PLYMOUTH PRIZE 6th Rate 16, 134bm. Captured 19.7.1709. Captured 21.12.1709 by French off Scilly Is.

PLYMOUTH TRANSPORT Storeship, 109bm, 70 × 19ft. Plymouth DY 1704. Rebuilt Shoreham 1742, 160bm. Sold 1806.

POCAHONTAS Sloop 14, 242bm, 91 × 25·5ft. Purch. 2.10.1780 New York. Condemned 26.7.1782. *Also listed as PACAHUNTA.*

POCHARD Paddle minesweeper. Ailsa, Troon, cancelled 1918.

PODARGUS Brig-sloop 14, 254bm, 92 × 25·5ft, 12—24pdr carr., 2—6pdr. Portsmouth DY 26.5.1808. Sold 7.8.1833 Ledger, Rotherhithe, for BU.

POICTIERS 3rd Rate 74, 1,765bm, 176·5 × 48·5ft. King, Upnor, 9.12.1809. BU comp. 23.3.1857 Chatham.

POICTIERS Destroyer, 2,380 tons, 355 × 40ft, 5—4·5in, 8—40mm, 10—TT. Hawthorn Leslie 4.1.1946, not comp. BU 4.1946 Sunderland.

POINTE CLAIRE *See MERRITTONIA 1944.*

POLACCA Sloop 12, 146bm, 67·5 × 22ft. French, captured 1756. BU 1761.

POLAR CIRCLE *See ENDURANCE 1990.*

POLARIS Minesweeper, 'Algerine' class. Port Arthur SY 13.12.1944. Arr. 26.9.1956 Ward, Briton Ferry, for BU.

POLECAT Brig-sloop 14 purch. 1782. Captured 1782 by French in North America.

POLLINGTON Coastal minesweeper, 'Ton' class. Camper & Nicholson 10.10.1957. = MERSEY 10.1959–1975. BU Cairnryan 5.4.1987.

POLLUX Radar TS, 2,461 tons, 200 × 50·5ft. French minelayer, seized 3.7.1940 Portsmouth. Ret. French Navy 1946.

POLPERRO *See PONTYPOOL 1918.*

POLRUAN Minesweeper, turbine 'Bangor' class. Ailsa 18.7.1940. BU 1950 Sunderland.

POLSHAM Inshore minesweeper, 'Ham' class. Morgan Giles 13.10.1958. Sold 2.1967 Port of London Authority = *Maplin.*

POLYANTHUS Sloop, 'Anchusa' class. Lobnitz 24.9.1917. Sold 20.5.1921 Clan Line = *Colima.*

POLYANTHUS Corvette, 'Flower' class. Robb 30.11.1940. Sunk 20.9.1943 by U-boat south of Greenland.

POLYPHEMUS 3rd Rate 64, 1,409bm, 160 × 45ft, Sheerness DY 27.4.1782. Powder hulk 9.1813. BU comp. 15.9.1827 Chatham.

POLYPHEMUS Wood paddle sloop, 801bm, 164 × 33ft, 5—32pdr. Chatham DY 28.9.1840. Wrecked 29.1.1856 coast of Jutland.

POLYPHEMUS Torpedo ram 2,640 tons, 240 × 40ft, 2—pdr, 5—TT. Chatham DY 15.6.1881. Sold 7.7.1903 Cohen.

POLYPHEMUS Aircraft carrier, 18,300 tons, 650 × 90ft. Devonport DY, cancelled 10.1945.

POLYPHEMUS *See also SOUTHAMPTON 1936.*

POMONA (ex-CHEVERT) Sloop 18, 364bm, 108 × 27·5ft, 18—6pdr. French, captured 30.1.1761. Wrecked 8.1776 hurricane West Indies.

POMONA 6th Rate 28, 594bm, 120·5 × 33ft. Raymond, Northam, 22.9.1778. = AMPHITRITE 14.7.1795. BU 8.1811.

POMONE 5th Rate 44, 1,239bm, 159 × 42ft, 18—32pdr carr., 26—24pdr 2—9pdr. French, captured 23.4.1774 by squadron off Île de Bas. BU 12.1802.

POMONE 5th Rate 38, 1,076bm, 150 × 40ft. Brindley, Findsbury, 17.1.1805. Wrecked 14.1.1811 The Needles.

POMONE Wood screw frigate, 3,027bm, 250 × 52ft. Chatham DY, ordered 5.3.1860, cancelled 12.1863.

POMONE 3rd class cruiser, 2,135 tons, 300 × 36·5ft, 8—4in, 8—3pdr. Sheerness DY 25.11.1897. Training hulk 1.1910. Sold 25.10.1922 J. H. Lee, Dover.

POMONE *See also ASTREE 1810.*

POMPEE 3rd Rate 80, 1,901bm, 182 × 49ft. French, captured 29.8.1793 Toulon. BU 1.1817.

PONDICHERRY Transport 10, 697bm, 10–12pdr. Purch. 11.1780. Sold 26.3.1784.

PONIARD Destroyer, 1,980 tons, 341·5 × 38ft, 6–40mm, 10–TT. Scotts, cancelled 1.1945, not LD.

PONTEFRACT Paddle minesweeper, 'Ascot' class. Murdoch & Murray 2.5.1916. Sold 6.9.1922 H. H. Bond.

PONTYPOOL (ex-POLPERRO) Minesweeper, Later 'Hunt' class. Lobnitz 25.6.1918 (renamed 1918). Sold 18.5.1922 B. Zammitt.

POOLE 5th Rate 32, 381bm, 108·5 × 28ft. Nye, Cowes, 1696. Fireship 1719. Sunk 5.1737 foundation Harwich.

POOLE 5th Rate 44, 706bm, 126 × 36ft. Blaydes, Hull, 5.6.1745. BU comp. 12.8.1765 Portsmouth.

POOLE Minesweeper, turbine 'Bangor' class. Stephen 25.6.1941. Sold 1.1.1948; BU Pembroke Dock.

POPHAM Inshore minesweeper, 'Ham' class. Vosper 11.1.1955. Sold 17.2.1976 mercantile.

POPHAM *See also SOMALILAND 1943.*

POPINJAY Galleon. Built 1587. Condemned 1601.

POPPY Sloop, 'Arabis' class. Swan Hunter 9.11.1915. Sold 9.4.1923 Rees, Llanelly.

POPPY Corvette, 'Flower' class. Alex Hall 20.11.1941. Sold 1946 = *Rami*.

PORCUPINE Sloop 16, 314bm, 94·5 × 28ft. Purch. on stocks 19.7.1746. Taylor, Rotherhithe, 20.9.1746. Sold 31.3.1763.

PORCUPINE Sloop 16, 160bm. Purch. 1777 Jamaica. Sold 17.1.1788.

PORCUPINE 6th Rate 24, 520bm, 114·5 × 32ft. Graves, Deptford, 17.12.1777. BU 4.1805.

PORCUPINE 6th Rate 22, 525bm, 118·5 × 31ft. Owen, Topsham, 26.1.1807. Sold 18.4.1816.

PORCUPINE 6th Rate 28, 500bm, 114 × 32ft, 20–32pdr, 6–18pdr carr., 2–6pdr. Plymouth DY, ordered 1.6.1819, cancelled 1.11.1832.

PORCUPINE Wood paddle vessel, 382bm, 141 × 24ft. Deptford DY 17.6.1844. Sold 1883.

PORCUPINE Destroyer, 320 tons, 200 × 20ft, 1–12pdr, 5–6pdr, 2–TT. Palmer 19.9.1895. Sold 29.4.1920 Ward, Rainham.

PORCUPINE Destroyer, 1,540 tons, 345 (oa) × 35ft, 4–4·7in, 4–TT. Vickers Armstrong, Tyne, 10.6.1941. Torpedoed 9.12.1942 by U.602 Mediterranean, not repaired; base ship 1943. Sold 6.5.1946; BU 1947 Plymouth (stern section BU Southampton).

PORCUPINE (ex-BARRACOUTA) Survey ship, 1,050 tons. Brooke Marine, cancelled 1967 (renamed 1967).

PORGEY Schooner 4, 80bm, 56 × 18ft, 4–12pdr carr. Bermuda 5.1807. Foundered 1812 West Indies.

PORLOCK *See PRESTATYN 1918.*

PORLOCK BAY (ex-LOCH SEAFORTH, ex-LOCH MUICK) Frigate, 'Bay' class. Hill 14.6.1945 (renamed 1944). Tx Finnish Navy 19.3.1962 = MATTI KURKI; stripped Helsinki 1.1976 for BU.

PORPOISE (ex-*Annapolis*) Sloop 16, 285bm. Purch. 1777. = FIREBRAND (fireship) 23.7.1778. Burnt, blew up 11.10.1781 off Falmouth.

PORPOISE Storeship 14, 700bm. Purch. 8.1780. Sold 1.1783 Bombay.

PORPOISE Storeship, 324bm, 96 × 28ft. Hill, Deptford, 16.5.1798. = DILIGENT 5.1.1801. Sold 1802.

PORPOISE (ex-INFANTA AMELIA) Storeship 10, 308bm, 93 × 28ft, 10–6pdr. Spanish sloop, captured 6.8.1799 by ARGO off Portugal. Wrecked 17.8.1903 coral reef off coast of New South Wales.

PORPOISE (ex-*Lord Melville*) Storeship 10, 399bm, 100 × 30ft, 8–18pdr carr., 2–6pdr. Purch. 1804. Sold 16.1.1816.

PORPOISE Mortar vessel, 117bm, 65 × 21ft, 1–13in mortar. Thompson 26.5.1855. = MV.8 on 19.10.1855; hulked as bathing place 7.1866. Sold 25.6.1885 Castle.

PORPOISE Wood screw gunboat, 'Albacore' class. Pitcher, Northfleet, 7.6.1856. BU comp. 22.2.1864.

PORPOISE Torpedo cruiser, 1,770 tons, 225 × 36ft, 6–6in, 8–3pdr. Thomson, Glasgow, 7.5.1886. Sold 10.2.1905 Bombay.

PORPOISE Destroyer, 934 tons, 265 (oa) × 26·5ft, 3–4in, 2–TT. Thornycroft 21.7.1913. Sold 23.2.1920 Thornycroft for resale to Brazilian Navy = ALEXANDRINO DEALENCA.

PORPOISE Minelaying submarine, 1,500 tons, 267 × 30ft, 1–4in. 6–TT, 50 mines. Vickers Armstrong, Barrow, 30.8.1932. Sunk 19.1.1945 Japanese aircraft Strait of Malacca.

PORPOISE Submarine, 1,605 tons, 241 × 26·5ft, 8–TT. Vickers Armstrong, Barrow, 25.4.1956. Sunk 1985 aircraft target Mediterranean

PORT ANTONIO Brig 12, 69bm, 59·5 × 21ft. Purch. 1779. LU Jamacia 1784.

PORT ARTHUR Corvette (RCN), 'Flower' class. Port Arthur SY 18.9.1941. BU 1946.

PORT COLBORNE Frigate (RCN), 'River' class. Yarrow, Esquimalt, 21.4.1943. Sold 17.11.1947 for BU.

PORT HOPE Minesweeper (RCN), TE 'Bangor' class. Dufferin, Toronto, 14.12.1941. Sold 2.1959 Marine Industries.

PORT MAHON 6th Rate 20, 282bm, 94 × 26·5ft. Deptford 18.10.1711. BU 5.1740 Plymouth.

PORT MAHON 6th Rate 24, 437bm, 106·5 × 30·5ft. Buxton, Deptford, 26.8.1740. Sold 29.6.1763.

PORT MAHON Brig-sloop 18, 277bm, 91·5 × 25ft, 18—18pdr. Captured 15.11.1798 on stocks Port Mahon, launched 1798. Police hulk 1.1817. Sold 8.1837 Woolwich.

PORT MORANT Armed ship. Spanish, captured 1780. Sold 1784 in Jamaica.

PORT ROYAL Sloop 18. Dates from 1762. Captured 8.5.1781 by Spanish at Pensacola.

PORT ROYAL Schooner 10, origin unknown. Captured 5.1769 by French in West Indies. Recaptured 18.10.1797 = RECOVERY. Sold 1801.

PORT ROYAL (ex-COMTESSE DE MAUREPAS) Sloop 14. French privateer, captured 6.1779 by privateer COUNTESS of SCARBOROUGH. Listed 1783.

PORT WESPAGNE Schooner 14, 190bm. Presented 1806 by inhabitants of Trindad. Sold in 1811.

PORTAGE Minesweeper (RCN), 'Algerine' class. Port Arthur SY 21.11.1942. BU 1959.

PORTCHESTER CASTLE Corvette, 'Castle' class. Swan Hunter 21.6.1943. Arr. 5.1958 Troon for BU.

PORTCULLIS Pinnace, 20bm. Built 1546. Listed until 1563.

PORTCULLIS (ex-LCT.4044) Tank landing craft, 657 tons, 225 × 39ft. Arrol, Alloa, 22.8.1945 (renamed 1956). Sold Pounds 4.6.1970.

PORTIA Brig-sloop 14, 253bm, 92 × 25·5ft 12—24pdr carr., 2—6pdr. Deptford DY 30.10.1810. Sold 6.3.1817.

PORTIA Wood screw gunvessel, 428bm, 145 × 25·5ft. Deptford DY, LD 1861, cancelled 12.12.1863.

PORTIA Destroyer, 'M' class. Scotts 10.8.1916. Sold 9.5.1921 Ward, Milford Haven; arr. 9.1922 for BU.

PORTIA *See also LENNOX 1914.*

PORTISHAM Inshore minesweeper, 'Ham' class. Dorset Yacht Co. 3.11.1955. RNXS 1980. Sold 23.1.1989 Sutton's Boatyard, Great Wakering.

PORTLAND 4th Rate 50, 605bm. Taylor, Wapping, 1652. Burnt 12.4.1692 to avoid capture by French.

PORTLAND 4th Rate 48, 636bm, 125·5 × 34ft. Woolwich DY 28.3.1693. Rebuilt Portsmouth 1723, 772bm. BU 1743.

PORTLAND 4th Rate 50, 1,044bm, 146 × 40·5ft. Sheerness DY 11.4.1770. Storeship 10 in 1800; prison hulk 1.1802. Sold 19.5.1817 D. List.

PORTLAND 4th Rate 50, 976bm, 140 × 40ft. Snelgrove, Limehouse, 11.10.1774. Sold 15.3.1763.

PORTLAND Gunvessel. Barge, purch. 9.1795. Sold 1. 1802.

PORTLAND (ex-KINGSTON) 4th Rate 52, 1,4767bm, 173 × 44·5ft. Plymouth DY 8.5.1822 (renamed 1817). Sold 19.5.1862 Castle, Charlton.

PORTLAND Minesweeper, TE 'Bangor' class. Taikoo DY, Hong Kong, LD 12.7.1941; = TAITAM 9.1941, lost on stocks 12.1941. Comp. 4.1944 as Japanese minesweeper *101*; sunk 10.3.1945 US air attack.

PORTLAND Frigate, 'Norfolk' class. Yarrow, Glasgow 15.5.1999.

PORTLAND BILL Repair ship, 8,580 tons, 425 × 57ft, 16—20mm. Burrard, Vancouver, 18.5.1945. Sold 1.1951 Stag Line = *Zinnia*.

PORTLAND PRIZE (ex-AUGUSTE) 4th Rate 50, 866bm, 134 × 38·5ft, 22—18pdr, 24—9pdr, 4—6pdr. French, captured 9.2.1746 by PORTLAND. Sold 17.5.1749.

PORTO (ex-ARLEQUIN) Sloop 16, 141 bm. French, captured by SURPRISE 6.6.1780. = HARLEQUIN 1782. Sold 6.1782

PORTREATH *See FITZROY 1919.*

PORTSMOUTH 46-gun ship, 422bm. Portsmouth 1649. Captured 7.1689 by French MARQUIS, blown up.

PORTSMOUTH Ketch 14, 90bm. Portsmouth 1665. Captured 1673 by Dutch.

PORTSMOUTH Sloop 6, 43bm. Portsmouth 1667. Captured 1672 by Dutch.

PORTSMOUTH Yacht 8, 133bm, 70 × 20·5ft, 8—3pdr. Woolwich 1674. Rebuilt Woolwich 1679 as bomb vessel, 143bm. Wrecked 27.11.1703 The Nore.

PORTSMOUTH 5th Rate 32, 412bm, 106·5 × 29·5ft. Portsmouth 13.5.1690 Captured 1.10.1696 by French.

PORTSMOUTH Yacht 6, 50bm, 52 × 15ft 6—2pdr. Portsmouth DY 9.1.1702. Rebuilt 8.1772, 66bm, 53 × 17ft = MEDINA. BU 8.1832 Portsmouth.

PORTSMOUTH 5th Rate 42, 532bm, 118·5 × 32ft. Deptford 1.4.1707. Hospital ship 1720. BU 10.1728 Deptford.

PORTSMOUTH Storeship 24, 694bm, 125 × 36ft. Rowcliff, Southampton, 12.6.1741. Lost 3.12.1747 nr The Longsands.

PORTSMOUTH Yacht 6, 83bm, 59·5 × 19ft, 6—2pdr. Portsmouth DY 30.9.1742. Rebuilt Portsmouth 1794 as 102bm. BU comp. 4.9.1869 Portsmouth.

PORTSMOUTH Transport 4, 114bm, 64 × 24ft, 4—3pdr. Purch. 6.1747. Sold 25.8.1767.

PORTSMOUTH (ex-*Beckford*) Busse 6, 79bm, 63 × 16·5ft, 6—4pdr. Purch. 10.11.1756. Lost 2.1758 Senegal.

PORTSMOUTH Transport 4. Bird, Rotherhithe, 5.10.1759. *Fate unknown.*

PORTSMOUTH (ex-WOOLWICH) Storeship, 317bm, 110 × 26ft. Milford Haven 28.9.1811. Coal hulk 3.1828. BU 8.1834.

PORTSMOUTH PRIZE 6th Rate 10, 106bm. French, captured 29.7.1694. Recaptured 28.9.1696 by French.

PORTSMOUTH SHALLOP Sloop 4. French, captured 1655. Captured 7.1655 by Royalists; fate unknown.

PORTWAY (ex-SPEAR) Dock landing ship, 4,270 tons, 454 × 72ft, 1—3in, 16—20mm. Newport News 11.4.1944 on Lend-Lease (renamed 8.1943); retained USN.

POSEIDON Submarine, 1,475 tons, 260 × 30ft, 1—4in, 8—TT. Vickers Armstrong, Barrow, 21.6.1929. Sunk 9.6.1931 collision SS *Yuta* off Wei Hai Wei.

POST Brigantine. Listed 1562—66.

POSTBOY Advice boat 6, 73bm. Plymouth 1694. Captured 1.10.1694 by French off Calais.

POSTBOY Advice boat 4, 77bm, 65·5 × 16ft. Portsmouth 1695. Captured 3.7.1695 by French FACTEUR DE BRISTOL off Plymouth.

POSTBOY Brigantine 4, 76bm. Deptford 1696. Captured 1.6.1702 by French off Beachy Head.

POSTILLION (ex-POSTILLON) 6th Rate 10, 117bm, 65 × 20ft. French, captured 9.1702 by WORCESTER. Wrecked 7.5.1709 nr Ostend.

POSTILLION (ex-DUC D'AIGUILLON) Sloop 18, 365bm, 97 × 29·5ft, 18—6pdr. French privateer, captured 15.4.1757. Sold 3.5.1763.

POSTILLION Schooner 10. Purch. 1776. Sold 1779 Newfoundland.

POSTILLION Minesweeper, 'Algerine' class. Redfern 18.3.1943 on Lend-Lease. Ret. USN 12.1946.

POTENTILLA Corvette, 'Flower' class. Simons, Renfrew, 18.12.1941. Lent RNorN 16.1.1942–13.3.1944. Sold 13.3.1946; BU Dorkin, Gateshead.

POULETTE 6th Rate 28, 480bm. French, handed over by Royalists 18.12.1793 Toulon. Burnt unseaworthy 20.10.1796 Ajaccio.

POULETTE (ex-FOUDROYANT) 6th Rate 20, 513bm, 120 × 31ft. French privateer, captured 2.1799 by PHOENIX. Sold 2.1814.

POULMIC Patrol vessel, 350 tons, 121 × 26·5ft. French, seized 3.7.1940 Plymouth. Free French 8.1940. Lost 6.10.1940 off Plymouth.

POUNCER (Gunboat No 38, ex-*David*) Gunvessel 12, 165bm, 77 × 22ft, 2—24pdr, 10—18pdr carr. Purch. 3.1797 Leith. Sold 9.1802.

POUNDMAKER Frigate (RCN), 'River' class. Vickers, Montreal, 21.4.1944. Sold 1947 Peruvian Navy = TENIENTE FERRE; = FERRE 1963; BU 1966.

POWDERHAM Inshore minesweeper, 'Ham' class. White 27.11.1958. = WATERWITCH (survey vessel) 1964. Sold Perch Sbkrs 1986.

POWERFUL 3rd Rate 74, 1,627bm, 168·5 × 47ft. Perry, Blackwall, 3.4.1783. BU 5.1812 Chatham.

POWERFUL 2nd Rate 84, 2,296bm, 196 × 52·5ft. Chatham DY 21.6.1826.Target 1860; BU comp. 29.8.1864.

POWERFUL 1st class cruiser, 14,200 tons, 500 × 71ft, 2—9·2in, 12—6in, 16—12pdr. Vickers 24.7.1895. = IMPREGNABLE (TS) 11.1919. Sold 31.8.1929 Hughes Bolckow for BU.

POWERFUL Aircraft carrier, 14,000 tons, 630 × 80ft, 30—40mm, 34 aircraft. Harland & Wolff 27.2.1945. Suspended 5.1946—7.1952. Tx RCN 17.1.1956 = BONAVENTURE, 16,000 tons, 8—3in, 7—40mm, 34 aircraft; BU 1971 Taiwan.

POWERFUL II *See* ANDROMEDA 1897.

POWERFULL III *See* CAROLINE 1882.

PREMIER (ex-*Estero*) Escort carrier, 11,420 tons, 468·5 × 69·5ft, 16—40mm, 24 aircraft. Seattle Tacoma 22.3.1943 on Lend-Lease. Ret. USN 12.4.1946.

PRESCOTT Corvette (RCN), 'Flower' class. Kingston SY 7.1.1941. Sold 1946.

PRESIDENT 26-gun ship, 220bm. Purch. 1646. Sold 1656. *Known as OLD PRESIDENT from 1650.*

PRESIDENT 42-gun ship, 462bm, 124 × 30ft. Deptford 1650. = BONAVENTURE 1660. Rebuilt 1666, 597bm, 126 × 33ft. BU 1711.

PRESIDENT (ex-PRESIDENTE) 5th Rate 38, 1,148bm, 157·5 × 40·5ft. French, captured 27.9.1806 Atlantic. = PIEMONTAISE 1815. BU 12.1815.

PRESIDENT 4th Rate 60, 1,533bm, 173 × 44·5ft. American, captured 15.1.1815 by squadron off New York. BU 6.1818.

PRESIDENT 4th Rate 52, 1,537bm, 173·5 × 45ft. Portsmouth DY 20.4.1829. RNR drillship 4.1862. Sold 7.7.1903. *Known as OLD PRESIDENT from 25.3.1903.*

PRESIDENT *For drillships with this name, see* GANNET 1878, BUZZARD 1887, MARJORAM 1917, SAXIFRAGE 1918.

PRESTATYN (ex-PORLOC) Minesweeper, Later 'Hunt' class. Lobnitz 6.11.1918 (renamed 1918). Sold 1.1923 Rees.

PRESTON 40-gun ship, 516bm. Cary, Woodbridge, 1653. = ANTELOPE 1660. Sold 1693.

PRESTON 4th Rate 50, 1,044bm, 143·5 × 41·5ft. Deptford DY 7.2.1757. Sheer hulk 10.1785. BU 1.1815 Woolwich.

PRESTON *See also SALISBURY 1698.*

PRESTONIAN Frigate (RCN), 'River' class. Davie SB 22.6.1944. Tx RNorN 4.1956 as TROLL. Submarine depot ship 1965 = HORTEN. Discarded 1972.

PREVENTION Sloop 4, 46bm. Portsmouth 1672. Sold 1683.

PREVOST Schooner 10. Listed 1807–09.

PREVOYANTE 5th Rate 40, 803bm. French, captured 17.5.1795 with RAISON by THETIS and HUSSAR off Chesapeake Bay. Storeship 1809. Sold 22.7.1819 Beech for BU.

PRIMROSE Ship, 160bm. Listed from 1523. Rebuilt 1538 as 240bm. Listed until 1545.

PRIMROSE Discovery vessel, 240bm. Listed 1551. Sold 1555.

PRIMROSE Ship, 800bm. Purch. 1560. Sold 1578.

PRIMROSE Hoy, 80bm. Built 1590; rebuilt 1612. Condemned 1618.

PRIMROSE 22-gun ship, 287bm. Wapping 1651. Wrecked 1656 Seven Stones.

PRIMROSE Brig-sloop 18, 'Cruizer' class, 384bm. Nickells, Fowey, 5.8.1807. Wrecked 22.1.1809 The Manacles.

PRIMROSE Brig-sloop 18, 'Cruizer' class, 383bm. Portsmouth DY 22.1.1810. BU 8.1831.

PRIMROSE Wood screw gunboat, 'Albacore' class. Pitcher, Northfleet, 3.5.1856. BU comp. 25.5.1864.

PRIMROSE Sloop, 'Acacia' class. Simons 29.6.1915. Sold 9.4.1923 Rees, Llanelly.

PRIMROSE Corvette, 'Flower' class. Simons 8.5.1940. Sold 9.8.1946 = *Norfinn*.

PRIMULA Sloop, 'Arabis' class. Swan Hunter 6.12.1915. Sunk 1.3.1916 by U.35 in Mediterranean.

PRIMULA Corvette, 'Flower' class. Simons 22.6.1940. Sold 22.7.1946 = *Marylock*.

PRINCE 1st Rate 100, 1,395bm, 167 × 45·5ft. Chatham DY 1670. Rebuilt 1692 = ROYAL WILLIAM (q.v.).

PRINCE 2nd Rate 90, 1,871bm, 177·5 × 49ft. Woolwich DY 4.7.1788. Rebuilt Portsmouth 1796, 2,088bm, 194·5 × 49ft (ship halved and lengthened). BU 11.1 1837.

PRINCE Transport, 2,710 tons. Hired 1854. Lost 1854.

PRINCE Destroyer, 'M' class. Stephen 26.7.1916. Sold 9.5.1921 Ward, Hayle.

PRINCE *See also OSSORY 1682, TRIUMPH 1698, RAJAH 1943.*

PRINCE ALBERT Iron screw turret ship,

2,537bm, 3,687 tons, 240 × 48ft, 4—9in MLR. Samuda, Poplar, 23.5.1864. Sold 16.3.1899 Ward, Preston.

PRINCE ALBERT *See also PRINCESS ROYAL 1853.*

PRINCE ARTHUR Brig-sloop 10, 'Cherokee' class, 239bm. Dudman, Deptford, 28.7.1808. Sold 12.1808 Emperor of Morocco.

PRINCE AUGUSTUS FREDERICK Cutter 8, 69bm, 56 × 18ft, 8—4pdr. Listed 1816–21.

PRINCE CONSORT (ex-TRIUMPH) Ironclad frigate 4,045bm, 273 × 58·5ft, 11—7in, 24—68pdr. Pembroke Dock 26.6.1862 (renamed 14.2.1862). Sold 3.1882 Castle for BU.

PRINCE DE NEUCHATEL Schooner 18, 328bm, 110·5 × 25·5ft. French privateer (in US service), captured 28.12.1814 by squadron in Atlantic. Capsized in dock 1815, badly damaged; sold 1815.

PRINCE EDWARD (ex-MARS) 3rd Rate 62, 1,075bm, 144 × 42ft. Dutch, captured 4.2.1781 West Indies. Harbour service 9.1782. Sold 24.3.1802.

PRINCE EDWARD 5th Rate 44, 715bm, 126·5 × 36ft. Bird, Rotherhithe, 2.9.1745. Sold 16.6.1766.

PRINCE EDWARD Brig-sloop 14. Purch. 1780. Captured 1782 by her American prisoners.

PRINCE EUGENE (ex-M.II) Monitor, 5,920 tons, 320 × 88ft, 2—12in, 2—6in. Harland & Wolff, Govan, 14.7.1915 (renamed 1915). Sold 9.5.1921 Ward, Preston; arr. 8.1923 for BU.

PRINCE FREDERICK (ex-REVOLUTIE) 3rd Rate 64, 1,270bm, 157 × 43ft. Dutch, captured 17.8.1796 at The Cape. Hospital ship by 1804. Sold 5.6.1817 G. Bailey.

PRINCE FREDERICK *See also EXPEDITION 1679.*

PRINCE GEORGE (ex-DUKE) 2nd Rate 90, 1,364bm, 163 × 45ft. Rebuilt, renamed 3.12.1701; rebuilt Deptford 1723, 1,586bm. Burnt 13.4.1758 accident at sea. *See DUKE 1682.*

PRINCE GEORGE Cutter, 62bm. Purch. 2.1763. Sold 20.9.1771.

PRINCE GEORGE 2nd Rate 90, 1,955bm, 177·5 × 50·5ft. Chatham DY 31.8.1772. Sheer hulk 1832. BU 1.1839.

PRINCE GEORGE Battleship, 14,900 tons, 390 × 75ft, 4—12in, 12—6in, 16—12pdr. Portsmouth DY 22.8.1895. = VICTORIOUS II (harbour service) 1918. Sold 29.1.1921 Cohen; resold, stranded 30.12.1921 off Kamperduin under tow Germany for BU.

PRINCE HENRY (ex-CULLODEN) 5th Rate 44, 819bm, 133 × 37·5ft. Gorrill, Liverpool, 12.7.1747 (renamed 14.3.1747). BU 1766 Plymouth.

Ships of the Royal Navy

PRINCE HENRY AMC (RCN). 1939.

PRINCE OF ORANGE (ex-BREDAH) 3rd Rate 70, 1,128bm, 151 × 41·5ft. Stacey, Deptford, 5.9.1734 (renamed at launch). 4th Rate 60, reduced, 8.1748; sheer hulk 1772. Sold 5.1810.

PRINCE OF WALES (ex-HIBERNIA) 3rd Rate 74, 1,623bm, 170 × 47ft. Bird & Fisher, Milford Haven, 4.6.1765 (renamed 20.10.1763). BU 8.1783 Plymouth.

PRINCE OF WALES 2nd Rate 90, 2,010bm, 182 × 51ft. Portsmouth DY 28.6.1794. BU 12.1822 Portsmouth. *Ten years on stocks.*

PRINCE OF WALES Transport 38. Purch. 1795. Listed in 1801.

PRINCE OF WALES Sloop 14 (Indian), 248bm. Bombay DY 1805. *Fate unknown.*

PRINCE OF WALES Screw 1st Rate 121, 3,994bm, 6,201 tons, 252 × 60ft, 1—110pdr, 16—8in, 6—70pdr, 10—40pdr, 88—32pdr. Portsmouth DY 25.1.1860. = BRITANNIA (TS) 3.3.1869. Hulk 9.1909. Sold 13.11.1914 Garnham; resold Hughes Bolckow, arr. 7.1916 Blyth for BU. *Twelve years on stocks.*

PRINCE OF WALES Battleship, 15,000 tons, 400 × 75ft, 4—12in, 12—6in, 18—12pdr. Chatham DY 25.3.1902. Sold 12.4.1920 Ward, Milford Haven.

PRINCE OF WALES Battleship, 35,000 tons, 745 (oa) × 103ft, 10—14in, 16—5·25in. Cammell Laird 3.5.1939. Sunk with REPULSE (q.v.) 10.12.1941 Japanese air attack off east coast of Malaya.

PRINCE REGENT Schooner 8 (Canadian lakes), 187bm, 72 × 21ft. Toronto 7.1812. = BERESFORD 1813; = NETLEY 22.1.1814; = NIAGARA (base ship). BU 1843.

PRINCE REGENT 4th Rate 56 (Canadian lakes), 1,294bm, 161 × 43ft, 6—68pdr carr., 22—32pdr carr., 32—24pdr. Kingston, Ontario, 15.4.1814. = KINGSTON 9.12.1814. Sold 1.1832.

PRINCE REGENT Yacht, 282bm, 96 × 25·5ft. Portsmouth DY 30.5.1820. To be presented 1836 to Imam of Muscat.

PRINCE REGENT 1st Rate 120, 2,613bm, 205 × 54·5ft. Chatham DY 12.4.1823; undocked 27.5.1861 as screw ship, 78 guns, 2,672bm. BU 1873. *Eight years on stocks.*

PRINCE ROYAL 64-gun ship, 890bm. Woolwich DY 25.9.1610. Rebuilt Woolwich 1641, 1,187bm. Burnt 13.6.1666 by Dutch, aground on The Galloper. *Named RESOLUTION 1650–1660.*

PRINCE RUPERT (ex-M.10) Monitor, 5,950 tons, 320 × 88ft, 2—12in, 2—6in. Hamilton 20.5.1915 (renamed 1915). = PEMBROKE (base ship) 24.4.1922; = PRINCE RUPERT 1.9.1922. Sold 5.1923 Beardmore.

PRINCE RUPERT Frigate (RCN), 'River' class. Yarrow, Esquimalt, 3.2.1943. Sold 13.12.1947; hull sunk 1948 breakwater Comox.

PRINCE WILLIAM Flyboat 4, 253bm. Captured 1665. Captured 1666 by Dutch.

PRINCE WILLIAM (GUISPUSCOANO) 3rd Rate 64, 1,346bm, 153 × 44ft, 26—24pdr, 28—12pdr, 10—9pdr. Spanish, captured 1780. Sheer hulk 2.1791. BU 9.1817.

PRINCESS (ex-PRINCESSA) 3rd Rate 70, 1,709bm, 165 × 50ft, 28—32pdr, 28—18pdr, 14—9pdr. Spanish, captured 8.4.1740. Hulk 1760. Sold 30.12.1784 Portsmouth.

PRINCESS (ex-*Williamstadt en Boetzlaar*) 6th Rate 28, 677bm. Dutch East Indiaman, captured 14.9.1795 The Cape. Floating battery (26 guns) 1800. Sold 4.1816 Liverpool.

PRINCESS *See also OSSORY 1682.*

PRINCESS ALICE Iron paddle packet, 270bm, 140 × 20·5ft, 1 gun. Purch. 27.1.1844. BU comp. 16.7.1878 Devonport.

PRINCESS AMELIA 3rd Rate 80, 1,579bm, 165 × 47·5ft. Woolwich DY 7.3.1757. Sold 11.6.1818 Snook for BU. *Left Navy List 11.1788 on loan to Customs.*

PRINCESS AMELIA 3rd Rate 74, 1,906bm, 182 × 49ft. Chatham DY, LD 1.1.1799, cancelled 3.1800.

PRINCESS AMELIA *See also HUMBER 1693, NORFOLK 1693.*

PRINCESS ANNE *See DUCHESS 1679.*

PRINCESS AUGUSTA (ex-PRINCE FREDERICK) Yacht 218bm. Danish, launched 20.8.1785 for Prince Royal of Denmark, sent Britain 1816, cd RN 25.7.1816. Sold 13.8.1818 Ledger for BU.

PRINCESS AUGUSTA *See also AUGUSTA 1771.*

PRINCESS CAROLINA (PRINCESS CAROLINE; ex-PRINDSESSE CAROLINA) 3rd Rate 74, 1,637bm. Danish, captured 7.9.1807 Battle of Copenhagen. Sold 9.2.1815. *Was to have been renamed BRAGANZA.*

PRINCESS CAROLINE (ex-PRINCESS CAROLINA) 5th Rate 44, 862bm, 129 × 39ft. Dutch, captured 30.12.1780 by MARLBOROUGH. Receiving ship 8.1791. Sunk 1799 breakwater Harwich.

PRINCESS CAROLINE *See also RANELAGH 1697, ROTTERDAM 1781.*

PRINCESS CHARLOTTE (ex-JUNON) 5th Rate 38, 1,029bm, 149 × 39·5ft, 16—32pdr carr., 26—18pdr, 4—9pdr. French, captured 18.6.1799 by Fleet in Mediterranean. = ANDROMACHE 6.1.1812. BU 6.1828 Deptford.

PRINCESS CHARLOTTE Schooner listed 1805–06.

PRINCESS CHARLOTTE (ex-VITTORIA) 5th Rate 42 (Canadian lakes), 815bm, 121 × 37·5ft, 2—68pdr carr., 14—32pdr carr., 26—24pdr. Kingston, Ontario, 15.4.1814 (renamed 1814). = BURLINGTON 9.12.1814. Sold 1.1833, BU.

PRINCESS CHARLOTTE 1st Rate 104, 2,443bm, 198·5 × 54ft. Portsmouth DY 14.9.1825. Receiving ship 1858. Sold 1875 in Hong Kong.

PRINCESS LOUISA 4th Rate 60, 1,143bm, 148 × 42·5ft. Carter, Limehouse, 1744. BU comp. 14.12.1766 Chatham.

PRINCESS LOUISA *See also LAUNCESTON 1711, SWALLOW 1732.*

PRINCESS MARGARET Minelayer, 5,070 tons, 395·5 (oa) × 54ft, 2—4in, 2—3in, 400 mines. Denny 24.6.1914; hired 26.12.1914, purch. 14.6.1919. Sold 30.5.1929 Galbraith; resold, arr. 2.7.1929 Hughes Bolckow, Blyth, for BU.

PRINCESS MARIA 38-gun ship. Captured 1652. Wrecked 1658 Goodwin Sands.

PRINCESS MARY Yacht built 1688. Sale date unknown. *Lasted until 1827 as mercantile* Betty Cairns.

PRINCESS MARY *See also MARY 1704.*

PRINCESS OF ORANGE (ex-WASHINGTON) 3rd Rate 74 1,565bm, 165 × 45ft. Dutch, captured 30.8.1799 Texel. Powder hulk 1812. Sold Ledger 18.4.1822 for BU.

PRINCESS ROYAL Storeship 24, 541bm, 123 × 32ft. Purch. 21.11.1739. Sold 4.6.1750.

PRINCESS ROYAL 2nd Rate 90. 1,973bm, 177·5 × 50·5ft. Portsmouth DY 18.10.1773. 98 guns 1800, 74 guns 1807. BU 10.1807.

PRINCESS ROYAL (ex-PRINCE ALBERT) Screw 2nd Rate 91, 3,129bm, 217 × 58ft. Portsmouth DY 23.6.1853 (renamed 26.3.1842). Sold 1872 Castle, Charlton.

PRINCESS ROYAL Battlecruiser, 26,350 tons, 660 × 88·5ft, 8—13·5in, 16—4in. Vickers 29.4.1911. Sold 19.12.1922 A. J. Purves; resold, BU Rosyth S. Bkg Co.

PRINCESS ROYAL *See also OSSORY 1682.*

PRINCESS SOPHIA FREDERICA (ex-PRINDSESSE SOPHIE FREDERICA) 3rd Rate 74, 1,763bm. Danish, captured 7.9.1807 Battle of Copenhagen. Prison ship c. 1811. BU 9.1816. *Was to have been renamed CAMBRIDGE.*

PRINCESSA 3rd Rate 70, 1,967bm, 170 × 51ft, 28—24pdr, 30—18pdr, 12—9pdr. Spanish, captured 16.1.1780 Cape St Vincent. Sheer hulk 8.1784. BU 12.1809 Portsmouth.

PRINCESSE 4th Rate 54, 602bm. Lydney 1660. BU 1680.

PRINS ALBERT Landing ship 1941—46.

PRIVET Corvette, 'Flower' class. Morton 10. 12.1942. Tx USN 1942 = PRUDENT.

PROCRIS Brig-sloop 18, 'Cruizer' class, 384bm. Custance, Yarmouth, 27.12.1806. Sold 23.11.1815.

PROCRIS Brig-sloop 10, 'Cherokee' class, 236bm. Chatham DY 21.6.1822. Sold 1.1837.

PROCRIS Wood screw gunboat, 'Albacore' class. Pitcher, Northfleet, 13.3.1856. Harbour service 1869. Sold 31.5.1893 T. Hockling; BU Stonehouse.

PROGRESSO Tankvessel. Slaver, captured, purch. 23.4.1844. BU 3.1869.

PROHIBITION Sloop 4, 68bm. Sheerness DY 1699. Captured 14.8.1702 by French off Land's End.

PROJECT Mortar boat 98bm, 70 × 17·5ft, 1—10in mortar. Woolwich DY 26.3.1806. BU 12.1810.

PROMETHEUS Fireship 18, 432bm, 109·5 × 30ft. Thompson, Southampton, 27.3.1807. Harbour service 5.1819. = VETERAN 2.5.1839. BU 8.1852.

PROMETHEUS Wood paddle sloop, 796bm, 164 × 33ft, 5—32pdr Sheerness DY 21.9.1839. Sold 1863 Castle, Charlton.

PROMETHEUS 3rd class cruiser, 2,135 tons, 300 × 36·5ft, 8—4in, 8—3pdr. Earle, Hull, 20.10.1898. Sold 28.5.1914 Ward; BU at Preston.

PROMPT 5th Rate 32 (fir-built). Frames made Chatham DY, sent Canada early 1814 for re-erection on lakes. Ordered for sale 21.7.1814 Quebec, 'it not being possible to get them to the lakes'.

PROMPT (ex-*Josephine*) Schooner. Slaver, captured 10.1840, purch. 22.1.1842. Sold 1845.

PROMPT Schooner. Slaver captured 1845, purch. 17.7.1845. Sold c. 1847.

PROMPT Mortar vessel, 155bm, 70 × 23·5ft, 1—13in mortar. Mare, Blackwall, 23.5.1855. = MV.21 on 19.10.1855. BU comp. 27.9.1865 Marshall, Plymouth.

PROMPT Wood screw gunboat, 'Albacore' class. Pitcher, Northfleet, 21.5.1856. BU comp. 6.5.1864.

PROMPT (ex-HUNTSVILLE) Minesweeper, 'Algerine' class. Redfern 30.3.1944 (renamed 6.1943). Damaged 8.5.1945 mine, not repaired. Sold 16.1.1947; BU Rainham, Kent.

PROMPT PRIZE (ex-PROMPT) 3rd Rate 70, 1,391bm, 158 × 45ft. French, captured 12.10.1702 Vigo. Ordered 20.5.1703 to be used as part of wharf at Chatham.

PROMPTE 6th Rate 20, 509bm, 119 × 31ft. French, captured 28.5.1793 by PHAETON in Bay of Biscay. BU 7.1813.

PROSELYTE (ex-*Stanislaus*) 5th Rate 32, 687bm, 135 × 33·5ft. Purch. 12.1780. Sold 10.2.1785.

PROSELYTE Floating battery 24, 950bm. French

frigate, HO by Royalists 28.8.1793 Toulon. Sunk 11.4.1794 batteries Bastia.

PROSELYTE (ex-JASON) 5th Rate 32, 748bm, 133 × 36ft. Dutch, captured 8.6.1796 from mutinous crew Greenock. Wrecked 4.9.1801 St Martin, West Indies.

PROSELYTE (ex-*Ramillies*) Armed ship 24, 404bm. Purch. 6.1804. Bomb vessel 4.1808. Wrecked 1.1809 Baltic.

PROSERPINE Sloop (?). Purch. 1756 Port Mahon. Lost to French 1756.

PROSERPINE (ex-*Maryland Islander*) Fireship 12, 253bm, 91 × 25.5ft. Purch. 3.1.1757. Sold 15.2.1763.

PROSERPINE 6th Rate 28, 596bm, 120.5 × 33ft. Barnard, Harwich, 7.7.1777. Wrecked 1.2.1799 nr Cuxhaven.

PROSERPINE (ex-BELLONE) 5th Rate 36, 852bm, 141 × 38ft. French, captured 12.10.1798 by ETHALION off north coast of Ireland. Hulk 1799. Sold Freake 27.8.1806 for BU.

PROSERPINE 5th Rate 32, 922bm, 144.5 × 37.5ft, 10—24pdr carr., 26—18pdr, 4—9pdr. Steemson, Paul, nr Hull, 6.8.1807. Captured 27.2.1809 by two French frigates.

PROSERPINE 5th Rate 46, 1,063bm, 150 × 40ft. Plymouth DY 1.12.1830. Sold 21.1.1864 R. Ridley.

PROSERPINE 3rd class cruiser, 2,135 tons, 300 × 36.5ft, 8—4in, 8—3pdr. Sheerness DY 5.12.1896. Sold 30.11.1919 Alexandria; BU 1923 Genoa.

PROSPERITY Storeship 22, 687bm, 132 × 34.5ft. Purch. 3.1782. Receiving ship 1.1784. BU 10.1796.

PROSPERO (ex-*Albion*) Bomb vessel 8, 400bm, 107 × 30.5ft, 8—24pdr carr., 1—13in mortar, 1—10in mortar. Purch. 10.1803. Wrecked 18.2.1807 off Dieppe.

PROSPERO Brig-sloop 14, 251bm, 92 × 26.5ft. Woolwich DY 9.11.1809. Sold 30.5.1816.

PROSPERO (ex-*Belfast*) Wood paddle packet, 249bm, 129 × 20.5ft. GPO vessel, tx 7.8.1837. BU 10.1866 Marshall, Plymouth.

PROSPEROUS Vessel. In service 1598.

PROSPEROUS Hoy, 68bm. Chatham DY 1665. Burnt 6.1667 by Dutch at Chatham.

PROSPEROUS Fireship 6, 206bm. Purch. 1666. Sold 1667.

PROSPEROUS Pink 120bm. Listed 1676.

PROSPERPINE Wood screw sloop, 1,268bm. Projected 18.12.1866, cancelled 5.1867.

PROTEA *See CROZIER 1919, ROCKROSE 1941.*

PROTECTOR 5th Rate 44 (Indian). Listed 1749. Foundered 1.1.1761 cyclone off Pondicherry.

PROTECTOR Fireship. In service 1758.

PROTECTOR Gun-brig 12, 178bm, 80 × 22.5ft.

Warren, Brightlingsea, 1.2.1805. Survey vessel 4.1817. Sold 30.8.1833 W. Woolcombe for BU.

PROTECTOR Wood screw gunboat, 'Britomart' class. Portsmouth DY, LD 1861, cancelled 12.12.1863.

PROTECTOR Cruiser (Australian), 920 tons, 188 × 30ft, 1—8in, 5—6in. Armstrong 1884. = CERBERUS (harbour service) 1.4. 1921; = PROTECTOR 1924. Sold 10.10.1924 J. Hill, Melbourne; resold 1931 = *Sidney*; lost collision off Gladstone 7.1943 on loan US Army.

PROTECTOR Netlayer 2,900 tons, 310 × 53ft, 2—4in. Yarrow 20.8.1936. Antarctic patrol ship 1955, 3,450 tons. Sold 10.2.1970; BU Inverkeithing.

PROTECTOR Support ship (RAN), 20,270 tons. Cockatoo DY, cancelled 1974

PROTECTOR (ex-*Seaforth Saga*) Patrol vessel, 802 tons, 1991.5 (oa) × 38.7ft. Selby 1975, purch. 2.1983. Sold Pounds 1987; resold Honduras 4.6.1988 mercantile, arr. Ostend 4.6.1988.

PROTECTOR (ex *Blue Nabilla*, ex-*Osprey*) Submarine support ship (RAN), 670 tons, 140.1 (oa) × 31.2ft. Stirling Marine Services 1984. Trials and safety vessel 11.1990. Sold 1998 civilian use.,

PROTEUS (ex-*Talbot*) 6th Rate 26, 675bm, 125 × 34ft, 20—9pdr, 6—4pdr. Indiaman, purch. 2.1777, receiving ship. Sold 1783 Newfoundland unfit.

PROTEUS Submarine, 1,475 tons, 260 × 30ft, 1—4in, 8—TT. Vickers Armstrong, Barrow, 23.7.1929. Sold 26.2.1946; BU Troon.

PROTHEE (ex-PROTEE) 3rd Rate 64, 1,481bm, 164 × 44.5ft. French, captured 24.2.1780. Prison ship 1799. BU 9.1815.

PROTHEE *See also PEARL 1762.*

PROVIDENCE 30-gun ship, 304bm. Bermondsey 1637. Wrecked 1668.

PROVIDENCE Fireship 6, 150bm. Purch. 1665. Sunk in action 1666.

PROVIDENCE Fireship 6, 180bm. Purch. 1672. Lost 1673.

PROVIDENCE Fireship 8, 175bm. Purch. 1678. Sold 1686.

PROVIDENCE Sloop 12. American, captured 14.8.1779 Penobscot. Listed 1780.

PROVIDENCE 5th Rate 32, 514bm, 114 × 32ft. American, captured 12.5.1780 Charlestown. Sold 11.3.1784.

PROVIDENCE Storeship 16, 462bm, 110 × 30.5ft. Purch. 1782. Sold 25.3.1784.

PROVIDENCE Sloop 12, 420bm, 107 × 29ft. Purch. 2.1791. Wrecked 16.5.1797 Formosa.

PROVIDENCE Schooner 14 purch. 1796. Expended 2.10.1804 fireship Boulogne.

PROVIDENCE (ex-QUAIL) Cutter tender, 80bm. ;

Ordered renamed 31.1.1822, renaming cancelled 11.4.1822

PROVIDENCE Coastguard cutter, 40bm. Harvey, Wivenhoe, 1866. Sold 17.3.1870 Liverpool.

PROVIDENCE (ex-FOREST HILL) Minesweeper, 'Algerine' class. Redfern 27.10.1943 (renamed 6.1943). Arr. 17.5.1958 Young, Sunderland,for BU.

PROVIDENCE PRIZE Ketch 29bm. French, captured 19.4.1691. Recaptured 16.1707 by French.

PROVO Schooner listed 1805–07.

PROWSE *See ZANZIBAR 1943.*

PRUDENT 3rd Rate 64, 1,367bm, 159 × 44·5ft. Woolwich DY 28.9.1768. Harbour service 7.1779. Sold 11.3.1814.

PRUDENT *See also DILIGENT 1806.*

PRUDENTE 5th Rate 38, 897bm, 136 × 38ft. French, captured 2.6.1779 by RUBY in West Indies. Sold 3.1.1803.

PSYCHE 5th Rate 36, 848bm, 139 × 36ft. French, captured 14.2.1805 by SAN FIORENZO off coast of India. Sold 1812.

PSYCHE 5th Rate 32 (fir-built). Frames made Chatham DY, sent Canada early 1814 for re-erection on lakes. Ordered for sale 21.7.1814 Quebec 'as not possible to get to the lakes.' *Some of the material may have been used for the following ship.*

PSYCHE 4th Rate 56, 769bm, 130 × 36·5ft. Kingston, Ontario, 25.12.1814, not comp. Sold 1837.

PSYCHE Wood paddle despatch vessel, 835bm, 250 (oa) × 28ft. Pembroke Dock 29.3.1862. Wrecked 15.12.1870 nr Catania; wreck blown up 2.1871.

PSYCHE Coastguard vessel. Purch. 1.1878. Sold 1884 T. Chalmers, Leith.

PSYCHE 3rd class cruiser, 2,135 tons, 300 × 36·5ft. 8–4in, 8–3pdr. Devonport DY 19.7.1898. Tx RAN 1.7.1915. Sold 21.7.1922 Waterside Ship Chandlery, Melbourne,

PSYCHE *See also RINGAROOMA 1889.*

PUCK Schooner gunboat, 1–32pdr. Purch. 1855. Foundered 8.1856 on passage from Balaclava for Turkish Navy.

PUCKERIDGE Destroyer, 'Hunt' class Type II. White 6.3.1941. Sunk 6.9.1943 by U.617 off Gibraltar.

PUFFIN Patrol vessel, 510 tons, 234 × 26·5ft, 1–4in. Stephen 5.5.1936. Sold 16.1.1947; BU Ward, Grays.

PUISSANT 3rd Rate 74, 1,794bm. French, HO 29.8.1793 by Royalists at Toulon. Harbour service 5.1796. Sold 11.7.1816.

PUKAKI Patrol boat (RNZN), 105 tons, 107·5 (oa) × 20ft. Brooke Marine 1.3.1974. Deleted 1992.

PUKAKI *See also LOCH ACHANALT 1944.*

PULHAM Inshore minesweeper, 'Ham' class. Saunders-Roe, Anglesey, 10.1.1956. Sold 10.8.1966, yacht.

PULTUSK (ex-AUSTERLITZ) Sloop 16, 200bm. French privateer, captured 5.4.1807 by CIRCE in West Indies. BU 1810 Antigua.

PUMA Frigate, 2,300 tons, 330 × 40ft, 4–4·5in, 2–40mm. Scotts 30.6.1954. Arr. Blyth 10.12.1976 for BU.

PUMBA Gunboat (Australian), 450 tons, 1–5in. Govt hopper built 1887. Listed 1901.

PUNCHER (ex-*Willapa*) Escort carrier, 11,420 tons, 468·5 × 69·5ft, 2–4in, 16–40mm, 24 aircraft. Seattle Tacoma 8.11.1943 on Lend-Lease. Ret. USN 16.1.1946.

PUNCHER Patrol boat, 49 tons, 68·2 (oa) × 19ft. Watercraft 1986, comp. Vosper-Thornycroft 7.1988.

PUNCHER *See also LST.3036 1944.*

PUNCHESTON Coastal minesweeper, 'Ton' class. Richards, Lowestoft, 20.11.1956. Sold 3.5.1972; BU 1977 Dartford.

PUNJAB Minesweeper (RIN), 'Bathurst' class. Mort's Dock, Sydney, 11.10.1941. Sold c. 1949.

PUNJABI Destroyer, 1,870 tons, 377 (oa) × 36·5ft, 8–4·7in, 4–TT. Scotts 18.12.1937. Sunk 1.5.1942 collision battleship KING GEORGE V North Atlantic.

PUNJAUB (ex-PLASSY) Paddle frigate (Indian), 1,031bm, 10–8in. Bombay DY 21.4.1854. Sold 1863 barque = *Tweed*.

PUNTOONE Sheer hulk, 267bm. For use 1677 Tangier. Condemned Cadiz 12.11.1691.

PURSUER (ex-ST GEORGE, ex-*Mormacland* [ii]) Escort carrier, 11,420 tons, 468·5 × 69·5ft, 2–4in, 8–40mm, 18 aircraft. Ingalls 18.7.1942 on Lend-Lease. Ret. USN 12.2.1946.

PURSUER Patrol boat, 49 tons, 68·2 (oa) × 19ft. Watercraft 1986, comp. Vosper-Thornycroft 2.1988.

PURSUER *See also LST.3504 1944.*

PUTTENHAM Inshore minesweeper, 'Ham' class. Thornycroft, Hampton, 25.6.1956. Sold 1980.

PYL Brig-sloop 16. Dutch, seized 4.3.1796 Plymouth. Fireship 1798. Sold 31.8.1801.

PYLADES (ex-HERCULES) Sloop 18, 399bm, 90·5 × 30·5ft. Dutch privateer, captured 3.12.1781. BU 3.1790.

PYLADES Sloop 16, 367bm, 105 × 28ft. Mestears, Rotherhithe, 4.1794. Wrecked 26.11.1794 Shetlands; salved, sold Leith; repurch. 1796; resold 11.1815.

PYLADES Sloop 18, 433bm, 110 × 30·5ft 16–

32pdr carr., 2—9pdr. Woolwich DY 29.6.1824. BU 5.1845.

PYLADES Wood screw corvette, 1,278bm. 193 × 38·5ft, 20—8in, 1—68pdr. Sheerness DY 23.11.1854. Sold 23.1.1875 Castle, Charlton.

PYLADES Composite screw corvette, 1,420 tons, 200 × 38ft, 14—5in. Sheerness DY 5.11.1884. Sold 3.4.1906 Cohen, Felixstowe.

PYLADES Destroyer, 'M' class. Stephen 28.9.1916. Sold 9.5.1921 Ward, Hayle; arr. 9.1922 for BU.

PYLADES Minesweeper, 'Catherine' class. Savannah Machinery 27.6.1943 on Lend-Lease. Sunk 8.7.1944 torpedo off Normandy.

PYRAMUS 5th Rate 36, 920bm, 141 × 38·5ft. Portsmouth DY 22.1.1810 (originally LD 4.1806 Greensward, Itchenor; frames sent Portsmouth 5.08, relaid 11.08). Receiving ship 1832. BU 11.1879 Halifax, NS.

PYRAMUS 3rd class cruiser, 2,135 tons, 300 × 36·5ft, 8—4in, 8—3pdr. Palmer 15.5.1897. Sold 21.4.1920; BU Holland.

PYRRHUS Minesweeper, 'Algerine' class. Port Arthur SY 19.5.1945. Arr. 8.9.1956 Cashmore, Newport, for BU.

PYTCHLEY Minesweeper, Early 'Hunt' class. Napier & Miller 24.3.1917. Sold 7.1922 Stanlee, Dover.

PYTCHLEY Destroyer, 'Hunt' class Type I. Scotts 13.2.1940. Arr. 1.12.1956 Rees, Llanelly, for BU.

PYTHON *See PANDORA 1929.*

Q

QU'APPELLE Escort (RCN), 2,380 tons, 366 (oa) × 42ft, 4—3in, 6—TT, Limbo. Davie SB 2.5.1960. PO 31.7.1992.

QU'APPELLE *See also FOXHOUND 1934.*

QUADRA Survey ship (RCN), 5,600 tons. Burrard 4.7.1966. Sold 10.1982.

QUADRANT Destroyer, 1,705 tons, 358·25 (oa) × 35·7ft. 4—4·7in, 8—TT. Hawthorn Leslie 28.2.1942. Tx RAN 10.1945; frigate 1954, 2,200 tons, 2—4in, 2—40mm, Squid; sold 7.1.1963.

QUADRILLE Minesweeper, 260 tons, 130 × 26ft, 1—3pdr. Ferguson 21.9.1917; War Dept tug, tx on stocks. Sold 5.1.1920 Crichton Thompson & Co.

QUAIL Schooner 4, 75bm, 56 × 18·5ft, 4—12pdr carr. Custance, Yarmouth, 26.4.1806. Sold 11.1.1816.

QUAIL Cutter tender, 80bm, 56 × 18·5ft. Deptford DY 31.1.1817. BU comp. 10.4.1829. *Was to have been renamed PROVIDENCE 1.1822.*

QUAIL Cutter 4, 108bm, 61 × 20·5ft. Sheerness DY 30.9.1830. Fitted out 2.1859 for Liberian Govt.

QUAIL Wood screw gunboat, 'Albacore' class. Wigram, Blackwall, 2.6.1856. BU 9.1861 Malta.

QUAIL Destroyer, 395 tons, 213·5 × 21·5ft, 1— 12pdr, 5—6pdr, 2—TT. Laird 24.9.1895. Sold 23.7.1919 Ward, New Holland.

QUAIL Destroyer, 1,705 tons, 358·25 (oa) × 35·7ft, 4—4·7in, 8—TT. Hawthorn Leslie 1.6.1942. Mined 15.11.1943 south of Calabria, foundered under tow 18.6.1944 between Bari and Taranto.

QUAINTON Coastal minesweeper, 'Ton' class. Richards, Lowestoft, 10.10.1957. = NORTHUM-BRIA 4.1960—1972. Sold H. K. Vickers 8.1979; BU Blyth.

QUAKER Ketch 10, 79bm. Purch. 1671. Sold 5.1698.

QUALICUM Minesweeper, TE 'Bangor' class. Dufferin 3.9141. Sold 9.2.1949; BU Charlestown.

QUALITY Destroyer, 1,705 tons, 358·25 (oa) × 35·7ft, 4—4·7in, 8—TT. Swan Hunter 6.10.1941. Tx RAN 10.1945; sold 10.4.1958 for BU Japan.

QUANGTUNG Iron paddle vessel (Indian), 523bm, 900 tons, 185 × 25ft, 6—9pdr. Laird 1863. Listed 1891.

QUANTOCK Destroyer, 'Hunt' class Type I. Scotts 22.4.1940. Sold 18.10.1954 Ecuadoran Navy, = PRESIDENTE ALFARO 16.8.1955; sold 1978.

QUATSINO Minesweeper (RCN), TE 'Bangor' class. Prince Rupert DD Co. 9.1.1941. Sold 1949 = *Concord.*

QUEBEC 5th Rate 32, 685bm, 125 × 35·5ft. Barnard, Harwich, 14.7.1760. Blown up 6.10.1779 in action with French SURVEILLANTE off Ushant.

QUEBEC Schooner. Purch. 1775. Wrecked New-foundland 11.9.1775.

QUEBEC 5th Rate 32, 700bm, 126·5 × 35·5ft. Stares & Parsons, Bursledon, 24.5.1781. BU 7.1816.

QUEBEC Corvette (RCN), 'Flower' class. Morton, Quebec, 12.11.1941. = VILLE DE QUEBEC 1942. Sold 1947.

QUEBEC *See also UGANDA 1941.*

QUEEN 2nd Rate 98, 1,876bm, 177·5 × 49·5ft. Woolwich DY 18.9.1769. Reduced to 74 guns 10.1811. BU 4.1821.

QUEEN Ship, 250bm. Built 1225. *Fate unknown.*

QUEEN Paddle sloop (Indian), 766bm. Pitcher, Northfleet, 1839. Listed 1860.

QUEEN (ex-ROYAL FREDERICK) 1st Rate 110, 3,104bm, 204·5 × 60ft,10—8in, 100—32pdr. Portsmouth DY 15.5.1839 (renamed 12.4.1839); undocked 5.4.1859 as screw ship, 3,249bm, 86 guns. BU 1871 Castle, Charlton.

QUEEN Battleship, 15,000 tons, 400 × 75ft, 4—12in, 12—6in, 18—12pdr. Devonport DY 8.3.1902. Sold 4.11.1920 Ward, Preston: arr. 5.8.1921 from Birkenhead for BU.

QUEEN (ex-*St Andrews*) Escort carrier, 11,420 tons, 468·5 × 69·5ft, 2—4in, 16—40mm, 24 aircraft. Seattle Tacoma 2.8.1943 on Lend-Lease. Ret. USN 31.10.1946.

QUEEN *See also ROYAL CHARLES 1673.*

QUEEN CHARLOTTE 1st Rate 100, 2,286bm, 190 × 52·5ft. Chatham DY 15.4.1790. Blown up 17.3.1800 accident off Leghorn.

QUEEN CHARLOTTE 1st Rate 104, 2,289bm, 190 × 53·5ft. Deptford DY 17.5.1810. = EXCELLENT (gunnery TS) 31.12.1859. Sold 12.1.1892 J. Read, Portsmouth.

QUEEN CHARLOTTE Sloop 16 (Canadian lakes), 280bm, 16—12pdr carr. Fort Erie 1812, purch. 1813. Captured 19.9.1813 by Americans on Lake Erie.

QUEEN CHARLOTTE *See also BOYNE 1810.*

QUEEN ELIZABETH Battleship, 27,500 tons, 646·2 (oa) × 90·5ft, 8—15in, 16—6in (later 12—6in), 2—3in. Portsmouth DY 16.10.1913. Sold 19.3.1948; arr. 7.7.1948 Arnott Young, Dalmuir, for BU.

QUEEN MAB (ex-COUREER) Sloop 18, 490bm. Danish, captured 7.9.1807 Battle of Copenhagen. = COURIER c. 1808. Sold c. 1812.

QUEEN MARY Battlecruiser, 26,500 tons, 658 × 89ft, 8—13·5in, 16—4in. Palmer 20.3.1912. Sunk 31.5.1916 Battle of Jutland.

QUEEN OF KENT *See ATHERSTONE 1916.*

QUEENBOROUGH Yacht 4, 27bm. Chatham DY 1671. Rebuilt Sheerness 1718 as 46bm. Sold 11.7.1777.

QUEENBOROUGH 6th Rate 24, 262bm, 96·5 × 25ft. Sheerness DY 22.12.1694. Rebuilt Portsmouth 1709. Sold 20.8.1719.

QUEENBOROUGH 6th Rate 24, 519bm, 113·5 × 32·5ft Sparrow, Rotherhithe, 21.1.1747. Foundered 1.1.1761 cyclone off Pondicherry.

QUEENBOROUGH Destroyer, 1,705 tons, 358·25 (oa) × 35·7ft, 4—4·7in, 8—TT. Swan Hunter 16.1.1942. Tx RAN 10.1945; frigate 1954, 2,200 tons, 2—4in, 2—40mm, Limbo; sold 8.4.1975; BU Hong Kong.

QUEENBOROUGH *See also FOWEY 1709.*

QUENTIN Destroyer, 1,705 tons, 358·25 (oa) × 35·7ft, 4—4·7in. 8—TT. White 5.11.1941. Sunk

2.12.1942 Italian airborne torpedo north of Algiers.

QUESNEL Corvette (RCN), 'Flower' class. Victoria Machinery 12.11.1940. BU 1946.

QUEST Survey vessel (RCN), 2,130 tons, 235 (oa) × 42ft. Burrard 9.7.1968.

QUIBERON Destroyer, 1,705 tons, 358·25 (oa) × 35·7ft, 4—4·7in, 8—TT. White 31.1.1942. Tx RAN 7.1942; frigate 7.1957, 2,200 tons, 2—4in, 2—40mm, Limbo; sold 15.2.1972; BU Japan.

QUICKMATCH Destroyer, 1,705 tons, 358·25 (oa) × 35·7ft, 4—4·7 in, 8—TT. White 11.4.1942. Tx RAN 9.1942; frigate 9.1955, 2—4in, 2—40mm, 2—Limbo; sold 27.1.1972; BU 7.1972 Japan.

QUILLIAM Destroyer, 1,725 tons, 358·25 (oa) × 35·7ft, 4—4·7in, 8—TT. Hawthorn Leslie 29.11.1941. Tx Dutch Navy 11.1945 = BANCKERT; BU 8.2.1957 Burght.

QUINTE Minesweeper (RCN), TE 'Bangor' class. Burrard 8.3.1941. On sale list 8.1947; sold Dominion Steel Corp for BU.

QUINTE Coastal minesweeper (RCN), 'Bay' class, 890 tons. Port Arthur SY 8.8.1953. PO 26.2.1964; declared surplus 1965.

QUITTANCE 25-gun ship, 257bm, 2—18pdr, 6—9pdr, 7—6pdr, 4—4pdr, 6 smaller. Built 1590. Condemned 1618.

QUORN Minesweeper, Early 'Hunt' class. Napier & Miller 4.6.1917. Sold 18.9.1922 J. Smith.

QUORN Destroyer, 'Hunt' class Type I. White 27.3.1940. Sunk 3.8.1944 explosive motor boat off Normandy.

QUORN Minehunter, 615 tons, 197 (oa) × 32·8ft. Vosper-Thornycroft 23.1.1988.

R

'R' class submarines 420 tons, 163 (oa) × 16ft, 6—TT.

R.1 Chatham DY 25.4.1918. Sold 20.1.1923 J. Smith.

R.2 Chatham DY 25.4.1918. Sold 21.2.1923 E. Suren.

R.3 Chatham DY 8.6.1918. sold 21.2.1923 E. Suren.

R.4 Chatham DY 8.6.1918. Sold 26.5.1934 Young, Sunderland.

R.5 Pembroke Dock (ex-Devonport DY), LD 3.1918, cancelled 28.8.1919.

R.6 Pembroke Dock (ex-Devonport DY), LD 3.1918, cancelled 28.8.1919.

R.7 Vickers 14.5.1918. Sold 21.2.1923 E. Suren.

R.8 Armstrong 12.8.1918. Sold 21.2.1923 E. Suren.

R.9 Vickers 28.6.1918. Sold 21.2.1923 E. Suren.

R.10 Armstrong 5.10.1918. Sold 19.2.1929 Cashmore, Newport; arr. 3.1930.

R.11 Cammell Laird 16.3.1918. Sold 21.2.1923 J. Smith.

R.12 Cammell Laird 9.4.1918. Sold 21.2.1923 J. Smith.

RABY CASTLE Corvette, 'Castle' class. Morton, Quebec, cancelled 12.1943.

RACCOON Yacht (RCN). 1940–42.

RACEHORSE (ex-MARQUIS DE VANDREVIL) Bomb vessel 8, 385bm, 96·5 × 30ft. French privateer, captured 1757, purch. 28.4.1757. On Arctic discovery 1773. Captured 12.1776 by American ANDREA DORIA; destroyed 15.11.1777 by RN in Delaware Bay.

RACEHORSE Sloop 16, 183bm, 68 × 20·5ft. Purch. 1777. Captured 14.8.1778 by French = SENEGAL; recaptured 2.11.1780 from French. Blew up 22.11.1780.

RACEHORSE Schooner 10, purch. 1778. Wrecked 1.1779 Beachy Head.

RACEHORSE Sloop 16, 354bm, 102 × 28ft. Fisher, Liverpool, 20.10.1781, purch. on stocks. BU 5.1799.

RACEHORSE Brig-sloop 18, 'Cruizer' class, 385bm, Hamilton & Breed, Hastings, 17.2.1806. Wrecked 14.12.1822 I. of Man.

RACEHORSE Sloop, 18, 438bm, 110 × 31ft. Plymouth DY 24.5.1830. Coal hulk 1860. Sold 1901.

RACEHORSE Wood screw gunvessel, 695bm, 186 × 28·5ft, 1—110pdr, 2—20pdr. Wigram, Blackwall, 19.3.1860. Wrecked 4.11.1864 nr Chefoo, China.

RACEHORSE Destroyer, 400 tons, 210 × 21ft, 1—12pdr, 5—6pdr, 2—TT. Hawthorn 8.11.1900. Sold 23.3.1920 M. Yates; resold Ward, BU 1921 Milford Haven.

RACEHORSE Destroyer, 1,705 tons, 358·25 (oa) × 35·7ft, 4—4·7in, 8—TT. John Brown 1.6.1942. Sold 8.11.1949; arr. 12.1949 Troon for BU.

RACER Cutter 12, 203bm, 75 × 26ft. Baker, Sandgate, 24.4.1810. Stranded 24.5.1810 French coast; captured by French.

RACER Cutter 6, 123bm, 63·5 × 22ft, 2—6pdr, 4—6pdr carr. Pembroke Dock 4.4.1818, ordered sold 4.5.1830 Malta.

RACER (ex-INDEPENDENCE) Schooner 12, 250bm, 93·5 × 25ft, 12—12pdr carr., 2—6pdr. American privateer, captured 9.11.1812. Wrecked 10.10.1814 Gulf of Florida.

RACER Brig-sloop 16, 431bm, 101 × 32·5ft, 14—32pdr carr., 2—12pdr. Portsmouth DY 18.7.1833. Sold 9.1852 Wilson & Co.

RACER Wood screw sloop, 579bm, 151 × 29ft, 11—32pdr. Deptford DY 4.11.1857. BU 1876 Portsmouth.

RACER Composite screw gunvessel, 970 tons, 167 × 32ft, 8—5in. Devonport DY 6.8.1884. Sloop 1885, salvage vessel 1917. Sold 6.11.1928 Hughes Bolckow, Blyth.

RACHEL Fireship 6, 134bm. Purch. 1672. Sunk in action 1673.

RACKHAM Inshore minesweeper, 'Ham' class. Saunders-Roe 27.4.1956. Sold Pounds 16.7.1967.

RACOON Brig-sloop 14. Dates from 1780. Captured 12.9.1782 by two French ships.

RACOON Brig-sloop 16, 317bm, 95 × 28ft. Randall, Rotherhithe, 14.10.1795. BU 4.1806.

RACOON Sloop 18, 426bm, 109 × 29·5ft. Preston, Yarmouth, 30.3.1808. Convict ship 1819. Sold 16.8.1838.

RACOON Wood screw corvette, 1,467bm, 200 × 40·5ft, 20—8in, 2—68pdr. Chatham DY 25.4.1857. BU 1877 Devonport.

RACOON Torpedo cruiser, 1,770 tons, 225 × 36ft,

6—6in, 8—3pdr, 3—TT. Devonport DY 6.5.1887. Sold 4.4.1905 G. Cohen.

RACOON Destroyer, 913 tons, 266 × 28ft, 1—4in, 3—12pdr, 2—TT. Cammell Laird 15.2.1910. Wrecked 9.1.1918 west coast of Ireland.

RADIANT Destroyer, 'R' class, 1,035 tons. Thornycroft 5.11.1916. Sold 21.6.1920 Thornycroft for resale Siam; = PHRA RUANG 9.1920.

RADLEY *See FLINDERS 1919.*

RADNOR Minesweeper, Later 'Hunt' class. Lobnitz, cancelled 1918.

RADSTOCK Destroyer, 'R' class. Swan Hunter 3.6.1916. Sold 29.4.1927 Ward, Grays.

RAGLAN (ex-LORD RAGLAN, ex-M.3, ex-ROBERT E. LEE) Monitor, 6,150 tons, 320 × 90ft, 2—14in, 2—6in, 2—12pdr. Harland & Wolff, Govan, 29.4.1915 (renamed 23.6.1915, 20.6.1915, 1915). Sunk 20.1.1918 by German GOEBEN off Imbros.

RAIDER Destroyer, 'R' class. Swan Hunter 17.7.1916. Sold 29.4.1927 G. Cohen.

RAIDER Destroyer, 1,705 tons, 358·25 (oa) × 35·7ft, 4—4·7in, 8—TT. Cammell Laird 1.4.1942. Tx Indian Navy 9.9.1949 = RANA; BU 1976.

RAIDER Patrol boat, 49 tons, 68·2 (oa) × 19ft, 1—20mm. Kingfisher Boats, Falmouth, comp. 23.1.1998.

RAIKES Transport. Purch. 9.1780. Captured 6.6.1782 by French in East Indies.

RAIL River gunboat. Yarrow, ordered 1912, cancelled 1913.

RAILLEUR Sloop 14. French, captured 11.1.1783 by CYCLOPS North America. *Fate unknown.*

RAILLEUR Sloop 20, 261bm, 89·5 × 26ft. French privateer, captured 17.11.1797 by BOADICEA. Foundered 17.5.1800 English Channel.

RAILLEUR (ex-*Henry*) Sloop 16, 271bm. Purch. 6.1804. Sold 22.12.1810.

RAINBOW Galleon 26, 384bm, 6—34pdr, 12—18pdr, 7—9pdr, 1—6pdr. Deptford 1586. Rebuilt 1602; rebuilt 1617, 548bm, 64 guns. Sunk 1680 breakwater Sheerness.

RAINBOW 5th Rate 32, 346bm, 103·5 × 27·5ft. French, captured 1697. Sold 20.9.1698.

RAINBOW 5th Rate 44, 831bm, 133·5 × 38ft. Carter, Limehouse, 30.5.1747. Troopship 1.1776; harbour service 6.1784. Sold 2.1802.

RAINBOW Brig-sloop 16. French, captured 1806. Sold 1807.

RAINBOW (ex-IRIS) 6th Rate 28, 587bm, 20—32pdr., 6—18pdr carr., 2—6pdr. French, captured 3.1.1809 by AIMABLE in Texel. Sold 23.5.1815.

RAINBOW 6th Rate 28, 503bm, 114 × 32ft, 20—32pdr carr., 6—18pdr carr., 2—9pdr. Chatham DY 2.11.1823. Sold 8.11.1838 Buck.

RAINBOW Wood screw gunboat, 'Albacore' class. Laird 8.3.1856. Survey vessel 1857; TS 1873. Sold 11.1888 Castle, Charlton.

RAINBOW 2nd class cruiser, 3,600 tons, 300 × 43ft, 2—6in, 2—4·7in, 8—6pdr. Palmer 25.3.1891. Tx RCN 4.8.1910; depot ship 7.1917; sold 1920 as freighter.

RAINBOW Submarine, 1,475 tons, 260 × 30ft, 1—4in, 8—TT. Chatham DY 14.5.1930. Sunk 1940 Italian submarine TOTI off Calabria; formally PO 19.10.1940.

RAINBOW (ex-ARGONAUT) Submarine (RCN). American, cd 2.12.1968. PO 31.12.1974 for BU.

RAISON 6th Rate 26, 472bm, 2—18pdr carr., 2—12pdr., 20—9pdr, 6—6pdr. French, captured with PREVOYANTE 17.5.1795 by THETIS and HUSSAR off Chesapeake Bay. Sold 5.1802.

RAISONNABLE 3rd Rate 64, 1,327bm, 159 × 44ft, 26—24pdr, 20—12pdr, 10—6pdr. French, captured 29.5.1758 by DORSETSHIRE and ACHILLES. Lost 3.2.1762 Martinique.

RAISONNABLE 3rd Rate 64, 1,386bm, 160 × 44·5ft. Chatham DY 10.12.1768. Receiving ship 11.1810. BU 3.1815.

RAJAH (ex-PRINCE, ex-*McClure*) Escort carrier, 11,420 tons, 468·5 × 69·5ft, 2—4in, 16—40mm, 24 aircraft. Seattle Tacoma 18.5.1943 (renamed 12.1942). Ret. USN 13.12.1946.

RAJPUT *See Indian TB.6 1889.*

RAJPUTANA (ex-LYME REGIS) Minesweeper (RIN), TE 'Bangor' class. Lobnitz 31.12.1941 (renamed 1941). BU 1961.

RALEIGH 5th Rate 32, 697bm, 131·5 × 34·5ft, 32—12pdr. American, captured 28.9.1778 by EXPERIMENT and UNICORN. Sold 17.7.1783.

RALEIGH Brig-sloop 18, 'Cruizer' class, 383bm. Hurry, Howden Dock, 24.12.1806. Target 8.1839. Sold 27.5.1841.

RALEIGH 4th Rate 50, 1,939bm, 180 × 51ft, 6—8in, 44—32pdr. Chatham DY 8.5.1845. Wrecked 14.4.1857 nr Macao.

RALEIGH Wood screw frigate, 3,027bm, 250 × 52ft. Pembroke Dock, ordered 5.3.1860; cancelled 12.12.1863.

RALEIGH Iron screw frigate, 3,215bm, 5,200 tons, 280 × 48·5ft, 2—9in, 20—64pdr. Chatham DY 1.3.1873. Sold 11.7.1905 Ward, Morecambe.

RALEIGH Cruiser, 9,750 tons, 605 (oa) × 65ft, 7—7·5in, 6—12pdr. Beardmore 28.8.1919. Wrecked 8.8.1922 coast of Labrador; destroyed 1926—27 target.

RAMBLER (ex-*Good Intent*) Cutter 10, 139 bm, 65·5 × 22·5ft. . Purch. 4.1778. Foundered 10.10.1785; raised, refitted; sold 24.5.1787.

RAMBLER Brig-sloop 14, 193bm, 75·5 × 25·5ft, 14—6pdr. Cutter, purch. 12.1796. Sold 18.10.1816.

RAMBLER (ex-RAMBLE) Wood screw gunboat, 'Cheerful' class. Pembroke Dock 21.2.1856 (renamed 1855). BU 1.1869 Haslar.

RAMBLER Composite screw gunvessel, 835 tons, 157 × 29·5ft, 1—7in, 2—64pdr. Elder, Glasgow, 26.1.1880. Survey vessel 1884. Sold 23.1.1907.

RAME HEAD Repair ship, 8,580 tons, 416 × 57ft, 16—20mm. Vancouver Ship Repairs 22.11.1944.

RAMILLIES 3rd Rate 74, 1,619bm, 168·5 × 47ft. Chatham DY 15.4.1763. Damaged hurricane, burnt 16.9.1782 off Newfoundland Banks.

RAMILLIES 3rd Rate 74, 1,670bm, 170·5 × 48·5ft. Randall, Rotherhithe, 12.7.1785. Harbour service 6.1831. BU 2.1850 Deptford.

RAMILLIES Battleship, 14,150 tons, 380 × 75ft, 4—13·5in, 10—6in, 16—6pdr. Thomson 1.3.1892. Sold 7.10.1913 G. Cohen.

RAMILLIES Battleship, 25,750 tons, 620·8 (oa) × 88·5ft (later 102ft), 8—15in, 14—6in. Beardmore 12.9.1916. Harbour service 5.1945. Sold 20.2.1948; BU Cairnryan.

RAMILLIES Nuclear submarine, ordered 26.6.1964, cancelled 15.2.1965

RAMILLIES *See also KATHERINE 1664.*

RAMPART (ex-LCT.4037) Tank landing craft, 657 tons, 225 × 39ft. Arrol, Alloa, 1945 (renamed 1956). Tx War Dept 1965 = *Akyab*. BU 1991.

RAMPISHAM Inshore minesweeper, 'Ham' class. Bolson, Poole 1.5.1957. = SQUIRREL 10.12.1957; = RAMPISHAM 15.12.1959. Sold 10.8.1966 mercantile.

RAMSEY (ex-MEADE) Destroyer, 1,190 tons, 311 × 31ft, 3—4in, 1—3in, 6—TT. USN, cd RN 26.11.1940. Air target 6.1943. Sold 18.2.1947; arr. 7.1947 McLellan, Bo'ness for BU.

RAMSEY Minehunter, 'Sandown' class, Vosper-Thornycroft 25.11.1999.

RAMSEY *See also ROSS 1919.*

RANEE (ex-*Niantic*) Escort carrier, 11,420 tons, 468·5 × 69·5ft, 2—4in, 16—40mm, 24 aircraft. Seattle Tacoma 2.6.1943 on Lend-Lease. Ret. USN 21.11.1946.

RANELAGH 2nd Rate 80, 1,199bm, 158·5 × 42ft. Deptford DY 25.6.1697. = PRINCESS CAROLINE 1728. Rebuilt Woolwich 1731 as 1,353bm. BU comp. 28.4.1764 Chatham.

RANGER (ex-DEUX COURONNES) 6th Rate 24, 639bm, 123 × 34·5ft, 24—9pdr. French privateer, captured 5.5.1747 by GLOUCESTER in English Channel.

RANGER Sloop 8, 142bm, 75 × 20·5ft. Woolwich DY 7.10.1752. Sold 16.1.1783.

RANGER Cutter, 201bm, 80·5 × 26ft. Purch. 1779; = PIGMY 1781; sloop. Sold 21.10.1784.

RANGER Cutter 14, 195bm, 75 × 25·5ft, 14—4pdr. Purch. 2.1787. Captured 28.6.1794 by French off Brest. Recaptured 14.10.1797 = VENTURER. Sold 2.1803 Gibraltar.

RANGER Sloop 16, 361bm, 105 × 28ft. Hill & Mellish, Limehouse, 19.3.1794. Captured 17.7.1805 by French, burnt.

RANGER Brig-sloop, 208bm, 82·5 × 24·5ft. Built R. Thames 1797, purch. *Fate unknown.*

RANGER Cutter 16, 217bm, 80 × 26ft. Avery, Dartmouth, 5.1806, purch. = PIGMY 29.5.1806. Lost 6.1814.

RANGER Sloop 18, 428bm, 109 × 29·5ft. Thorn, Fremington, 5.9.1807. BU 2.1814.

RANGE 6th Rate 28, 502bm, 113·5 × 32ft, 20—32pdr carr., 6—18pdr carr., 2—9pdr. Portsmouth DY 7.12.1820. Sold 11.1832 J. Jackson.

RANGER Packet brig 8, 363bm, 96 × 30·5ft. Bottomley, Rotherhithe, 25.7.1835. Hulk 1860. Sold 1867 Dublin.

RANGER Wood screw gunvessel, 'Philomel' class. Deptford DY 26.11.1859. Sold 3.11.1869 Moss Isaacs.

RANGER Composite screw gunvessel, 835 tons, 157 × 29·5ft, 1—7in, 2—64pdr. Elder 12.2.1880. Sold 24.9.1892 as salvage vessel. Hired 11.1914—1919 as ammunition hulk. BU 1947.

RANGER Destroyer, 320 tons, 200 × 19ft, 1—12pdr, 5—6pdr, 2—TT. Hawthorn 4.10.1895. Sold 20.5.1920 Riddle & Co.

RANGER Patrol boat, 49 tons, 68·2 (oa) × 19ft. Watercraft 1986, comp. Vosper-Thornycroft 9.1988.

RANGER *See also CAESAR 1944.*

RANKIN Submarine (RAN), 'Collins' class, 3,051/3,353 tons, 255·2 (oa) × 25·6ft, 6—TT. Australian Submarine Corp., Adelaide, 7.11.2001.

RANUNCULUS Corvette, 'Flower' class. Simons 25.6.1941. Lent Free French 1941—46 = RENONCULE. Sold 1947 = *Southern Lily.*

RAPID Gun-brig 12, 178bm, 80 × 22·5ft, 2—18pdr, 10—18pdr carr. Davy, Topsham, 20.10.1804. Sunk 18.5.1808 batteries R. Tagus.

RAPID Brig-sloop 14, 261bm, 92 × 25·5ft, 12—24pdr carr., 2—6pdr. Davy, Topsham, 22.10.1808. Sold 10.12.1814.

RAPID Schooner 12, 90bm. French, captured 1808. Wrecked 3.1814 The Saintes, West Indies.

RAPID Brig-sloop 10, 'Cherokee' class, 235bm. Portsmouth DY 17.8.1829. Wrecked 12.4.1838 off Crete.

RAPID Brig 8, 319bm, 90 × 29·5ft. Portsmouth DY

3.6.1840. Sold 1.1856 MacDonald & Co., Singapore.

RAPID Wood screw sloop, 672bm, 913 tons, 160 × 30·5ft, 1—40pdr, 6—32pdr, 4—20pdr. Deptford DY 29.11.1860. BU 9.1881 Malta.

RAPID Composite screw corvette, 1,420 tons, 200 × 38ft, 2—6in, 10—5in. Devonport DY 21.3.1883. Hulk 1906; coal hulk C.7 in 1912; = HART (accommodation ship) 1916. Sold 1948 Gibraltar.

RAPID Destroyer, 'M' class, 1,033 tons. Thornycroft 15.7.1916. Sold 20.4.1927 G. Cohen.

RAPID Destroyer, 1,705 tons, 358—25 (oa) × 35·7ft, 4—4·7in, 8—TT. Cammell Laird 16.7.1942. Frigate 1952, 2,300 tons, 2—4in, 2—40mm, Squid. Sunk 3.9.1981 target Atlantic.

RAPOSO Gun-brig 10, 173bm. Spanish, captured 7.1.1806 by boats of FRANCHISE off Campeche. Destroyed to prevent capture 15.2.1808 nr Cartagena.

RATTLE Gun-brig 14. Listed 1802–05.

RATTLER Sloop 16, 342bm, 102 × 28ft. Wilson, Sandgate, 22.3.1783. Sold 6.9.1792.

RATTLER Sloop 16, 360bm, 105 × 28ft. Raymond, Northam, 21.3.1795. Sold 12.10.1815.

RATTLER (Gunboat No 41, ex-*Hope*) Gunvessel 12, 158bm, 72·5 × 22·5ft, 2—24pdr, 10—18pdr carr. Purch. 3.1797 Leith. Sold 1802.

RATTLER (ex-ARDENT) Wood screw sloop, 888bm, 176·5 × 32·5ft. Sheerness DY 12.4.1843 (renamed 1842). BU comp. 26.11.1856 Fulcher, Woolwich.

RATTLER Wood screw sloop, 950bm, 185 × 13ft, 5—40pdr, 12—32pdr. Deptford DY 18.3.1862. Wrecked 24.9.1868 China Station.

RATTLER Composite screw gunboat, 715 tons, 165 × 29ft, 6—4in. Armstrong Mitchell 4.8.1886. Harbour service 1910. = DRYAD (navigation schoolship) 9.1919. Sold 10.1924.

RATTLER Minesweeper, 'Algerine' class. Harland & Wolff 9.12.1942. = LOYALTY 6.1943. Sunk 22.8.1944 by U.480 in English Channel.

RATTLESNAKE Cutter 10, 185bm, 69·5 × 26ft. Farley, Folkestone, 7.6.1777. Sloop 1779. *A 14-gun sloop wrecked 2.10.1782 off Trinidad may have been this vessel.*

RATTLESNAKE Sloop 14, 198bm, 84 × 22ft. Captured 1779. Lost 1781 (East Indies?).

RATTLESNAKE Sloop 16, 326bm, 100 × 27ft. Chatham DY 7.1.1791. Sold 3.11.1814.

RATTLESNAKE 6th Rate 28, 503bm, 114 × 32ft, 20—32pdr carr., 6—18pdr carr., 2—9pdr. Chatham DY 26.3.1822. Survey ship, 2 guns, 1845. BU comp. 13.1.1860 Chatham.

RATTLESNAKE Wood screw corvette, 1,705bm,

2,431 tons, 225 × 41ft. 16—8in, 1—7in, 4—40pdr. Chatham DY 9.7.1861. BU 3.1882 Devonport.

RATTLESNAKE Torpedo gunboat, 550 tons, 200 × 23ft, 1—4in, 6—3pdr, 4—TT. Laird 11.9.1886. Sold 1910.

RATTLESNAKE Destroyer, 946 tons, 270 × 28ft, 1—4in, 3—12pdr, 2—TT. London & Glasgow Co. 14.3.1910. Sold 9.5.1921 Ward, Milford Haven.

RATTLESNAKE Minesweeper, 'Algerine' class. Lobnitz 23.2.1943. Sold 11.1957; arr. 10.1959 Brunton, Grangemouth, for BU.

RATTLESNAKE *See also CORMORANT 1781, HERON 1812.*

RATTRAY HEAD Repair ship, 8,580 tons, 416 × 57ft. North Vancouver Ship Repairs 8.6.1945, not comp, cancelled 18.8.1945, comp. as *Iran*.

RAVAGER (ex-CHARGER) Escort carrier, 11,420 tons, 468·5 × 69·5ft, 2—4in, 16—40mm, 24 aircraft. Seattle Tacoma 16.7.1942 on Lend-Lease (renamed 1942). Ret. USN 27.2.1946.

RAVAGER *See also LST.3505 1944.*

RAVEN 36-gun ship. Captured 1652. Captured 4.1654 by Dutch.

RAVEN (ex-ST CORNELIUS) 6-gun vessel. French (?), captured 1656. Listed until 1659.

RAVEN Sloop 14, 273bm, 31 × 26ft. Blaydes, Hull, 4.7.1745. Sold 31.3.1763.

RAVEN Sloop 14 (fir-built), 365bm, 96 × 30·5ft. Wallis, Blackwall, 11.1.1796. Wrecked 3.2.1798 nr Cuxhaven.

RAVEN (ex-ARETHUSE) Brig-sloop 18, 390bm, 107·5 × 29·5ft. French, captured 10.10.1799 by CRESCENT off L'Orient. Wrecked 6.7.1804 nr Mazzara, coast of Sicily.

RAVEN Brig-sloop 18, 'Cruizer' class, 384bm. Perry, Blackwall, 25.7.1804. Wrecked 29.1.1805 Cadiz Bay.

RAVEN Brig-sloop 16 (fir-built), 282bm, 96 × 26ft, 14—24pdr carr., 2—6pdr. Warren, Brightlingsea, 12.8.1805. Sold 18.9.1816.

RAVEN Survey cutter 4, 108bm, 61 × 20·5ft. Pembroke Dock 21.10.1829. Quarantine ship 1.1848; Coastguard 1850. Sold 28.10.1859 Aldeburgh.

RAVEN Mortar vessel, 155bm, 70 × 23·5ft, 1—13in mortar. Green, Blackwall, 19.4.1855. = MV.13 on 19.10.1855, ordered sold 11.7.1856 Constantinople.

RAVEN Wood screw gunboat, 'Albacore' class. Laird 8.3.1856. Sold 13.4.1875 Castle, Charlton.

RAVEN Composite screw gunboat, 465 tons, 125 × 23·5ft, 2—64pdr, 2—20pdr. Samuda, Poplar, 18.5.1882. Diving tender 1904. Sold 13.3.1925.

RAVEN Seaplane carrier, 4,678 tons. Ex-German. In service 1915–17.

RAVEN *See also VESUVIUS 1771, CERES 1777.*
RAYLEIGH *See ADVENTURE 1771.*
RAYLEIGH CASTLE *See EMPIRE REST 1944.*
READING Minesweeper, Later 'Hunt' class. Lobnitz, cancelled 1919.
READING (ex-BAILEY) Destroyer, 1,190 tons, 311 × 31ft 3–4in, 1–3in. 6–TT. USN, cd RN 26.11.1940. Air target 10.1942. Sold 24.7.1945; BU Ward, Inverkeithing.
READY (Gunboat No 42, ex-*Minerva*) Gunvessel 12, 152bm, 70 × 22·5ft, 2–24pdr, 10–18pdr carr. Purch. 3.1797 Leith. Sold 12.1802.
READY Wood screw gunboat, 'Clown' class. Briggs, Sunderland, 12.5.1856. BU comp. 25.1.1864.
READY Wood screw gunvessel, 462bm, 610 tons, 155 × 25ft, 1–7in, 1–64pdr, 2–20pdr. Chatham DY 24.9.1872. Tankvessel 1894. = DRUDGE 10.1916. Sold 25.2.1920 Bermuda.
READY Destroyer, 'M' class, 1,033 tons. Thornycroft 26.8.1916. Sold 13.7.1926 King, Garston.
READY Minesweeper, 'Algerine' class. Harland & Wolff 20.3.1943. Sold 4.7.1951 Belgian Navy = JAN VAN HAVERBEKE. BU 7.3.1961 Bruges.
REAPER (ex-*Winjah*) Escort carrier, 11,420 tons, 468·5 × 69·5ft, 2–4in, 16–40mm, 24 aircraft. Seattle Tacoma 22.11.1943 on Lend-Lease. Ret. USN 20.5.1946.
REBUFF Gun-brig 12, 180bm, 84 × 22ft. Richards, Hythe, 30.5.1805. Sold 15.12.1814.
RECOVERY 20-gun ship, 300bm. Captured 1646. Sold 1655.
RECOVERY 26-gun ship. Captured 1652. Sold 1656.
RECOVERY Sloop 14. American, captured 1782. Sold 1785 West Indies.
RECOVERY *See also PORT ROYAL 1769, MINERVA 1759.*
RECRUIT Brig-sloop 18, 'Cruizer' class, 383bm. Hills, Sandwich, 31.8.1806. Sold 7.8.1822 R. Forbes.
RECRUIT Brig-sloop 10, 'Cherokee' class, 235bm. Portsmouth DY 17.8.1829. Foundered 1832 off Bermuda.
RECRUIT Iron brig 12, 462bm, 114·5 × 30·5ft. Ditchburn & Mare, Blackwall, 10.6.1846. Sold 28.8.1849 Mr Mare; conv. to screw ship, resold = *Harbinger*. *Only iron-built sailing vessel in RN.*
RECRUIT (ex-NIX) Iron paddle gunboat, 540bm, 178 (wl) × 26ft, 4–8in, 4–32pdr. Prussian, exchanged 12.1.1855 with SALAMANDER for 5th Rate THETIS. Sold 23.9.1869 E. Bates.
RECRUIT Destroyer, 385 tons, 218 × 20ft, 1–12pdr, 5–6pdr, 2–TT. Thomson 22.8.1896. Sunk 1.5.1915 by U-boat nr Galloper Lightvessel.

RECRUIT Destroyer, 'R' class. Doxford 9.12.1916. Sunk 9.8.1917 by *UB 16* in North Sea.
RECRUIT Minesweeper, 'Algerine' class. Harland & Wolff 26.10.1943. BU 9.1965 Ward, Barrow.
RED DEER Minesweeper (RCN), TE 'Bangor' class. Vickers, Montreal, 12.5.1941. Sold 2.1959 Marine Industries.
RED DRAGON *See DRAGON 1593.*
RED GALLEY *See SUBTLE 1544.*
RED HART *See HART 1653.*
RED LION *See LION 1557.*
REDBREAST Gun-brig 12, 178bm, 80 × 22·5ft. Preston, Yarmouth, 27.4.1805. Tx Customs Service 7.1815 as hulk. Sold 4.6.1850 Liverpool.
REDBREAST Cutter tender 12, 80bm, 56 × 18·5ft. Woolwich DY 18.2.1817. Sold 1850 J. Brown.
REDBREAST Mortar vessel, 155bm, 70 × 23·5ft, 1–13in mortar. Green, Blackwall, 5.5.1855. = MV.19 on 19.10.1855. BU comp. 27.9.1865 Marshall, Plymouth.
REDBREAST Wood screw gunboat, 'Albacore' class. Laird 11.3.1856. BU comp. 24.9.1864.
REDBREAST Composite screw gunboat, 805 tons, 165 × 31ft, 6–4in. Pembroke Dock 25.4.1889. Sold 1910.
REDBRIDGE Schooner 16, 148bm, 80 × 21·5ft. Redbridge 1796, purch. Captured 4.8.1803 by French off Toulon.
REDBRIDGE (ex-OISEAU) Schooner 12, 170bm, 81 × 21·5ft. French, captured 1803, purch. 1805. Wrecked 4.11.1806 West Indies.
REDBRIDGE Schooner 10, 131bm. Purch. 1804. Foundered 1.3.1805 nr Jamaica.
REDBRIDGE (ex-ARISTOTLE) Schooner 10, 172bm, 80·5 × 22ft, 8–12pdr carr., 2–6pdr. American, captured 1807. Sold 1814.
REDCAR Paddle minesweeper, 'Ascot' class. Ayrshire DY Co. 31.7.1916. Sunk 24.6.1917 mine off Dover.
REDGAUNTLET Destroyer, 'R' class. Denny 23.11.1916. Sold 7.1927 King, Garston.
REDGAUNTLET *See also LAUREL 1913.*
REDMILL Frigate, TE 'Captain' class. Bethlehem, Hingham, 2.10.1943 on Lend-Lease. Torpedoed 27.4.1945, not repaired. Sold by USN 2.1947; BU.
REDMILL *See also MEDINA 1916.*
REDOUBT (ex-*Rover*) Floating battery 20, 386bm, 97·5 × 30ft, 20–24pdr carr. Purch. 3.1793. Sold 20.5.1802.
REDOUBT Destroyer, 'R' class. Doxford 28 10.1916. Sold 13.7.1926 J. Smith.
REDOUBT Destroyer, 1,705 tons, 358·25 (oa) × 35·7ft, 4–4·7in, 8–TT. John Brown 2.5.1942. Tx Indian Navy 4.7.1949 = RANJIT; BU 1979.

REDOUBT (ex-LCT.4001) Tank landing craft, 657 tons, 225 × 39ft. Stockton Co., Thornaby-on-Tees, 27.7.1945 (renamed 1956). Sold 1.1956 as ferry *Dimitris*.

REDOUBTABLE 3rd Rate 74, 1,759 bm, 176·5 × 48·5ft. Woolwich DY 26.1.1815. BU 5.1841 Chatham.

REDOUBTABLE *See also REVENGE 1892.*

REDPOLE Brig-sloop 10, 'Cherokee' class, 239bm. Guillaume, Northam, 29.7.1808. Sunk 8.1828 in action with pirate vessel CONGRESS off Cape Frio.

REDPOLE Composite screw gunboat, 805 tons, 165 × 31ft, 6—4in. Pembroke Dock 13.6.1889. Sold 15.5.1906 Cox, Falmouth.

REDPOLE Destroyer, 720 tons, 246 × 25ft, 2—4in, 2—12pdr, 2—TT. White 24.6.1910. Sold 9.5.1921 Ward, Milford Haven.

REDPOLE Sloop, 1,350 tons, 283 × 38·5ft, 6—4in. Yarrow 25.2.1943. Arr. 20.11.1960 St David's for BU.

REDPOLE (ex-*Sea Otter*) Patrol boat, 159 tons. Fairmile 1967. RAF vessel, tx 10.1984. Sold 28.2.1996 private individual.

REDSHANK Paddle minesweeper. Projected 1918, not ordered.

REDSTART Minelayer, 498 tons, 145 × 27ft, 1—20mm, 12 mines. Robb 3.5.1938. Scuttled 19.12.1941 Hong Kong.

REDWING Brig-sloop 18, 'Cruizer' class, 383bm. Warren, Brightlingsea, 30.8.1806. Foundered 6.1827 off West Africa. *Fought last action with Spain, 11.1808.*

REDWING Sloop 18, 481bm, 116 × 31ft. Plymouth DY, ordered 30.1.1829, cancelled 1.11.1832.

REDWING (ex-*Richmond*) Wood paddle packet, 139bm, 144 × 15·5ft. GPO vessel, tx 1.4.1837. Sold 17.1.1849.

REDWING Wood screw gunboat, 'Dapper' class. Pitcher, Northfleet, 9.3.1855. Harbour service 1857. Sold 2.12.1878.

REDWING (ex-ESPOIR) Composite screw gunboat, 461 tons, 125 × 23·5ft, 2—64pdr, 2—20pdr. Pembroke Dock 25.5.1880 (renamed 3.6.1879). Sold 4.4.1905 Chatham.

REDWING (ex-*Sir Charles Pasley*) Tender, 120 tons, 93 × 18ft. War Dept vessel, tx 1905. Sold 26.6.1931. *Was to have been renamed REDSTART 1916.*

REDWING Tender, 225 tons, 102 × 25ft. White 19.10.1933. Sold 16.1.1957 Everard & Sons.

REDWING *See also MEDWAY 1916.*

REEDHAM Inshore minesweeper, 'Ham' class. Saunders-Roe 19.8.1958. Sold Pounds 8.8.1966; became yacht *Marisa*.

REEVES *See COSBY 1943.*

REFUGE *See RESOLUTE 1850.*

REGENT Brig 14, 350bm, 97 × 29ft, 10—12pdr carr., 2—9pdr, 2—6pdr. Purch. 1816. Revenue Service 1831.

REGENT Submarine, 1,475 tons, 260 × 30ft, 1—4in, 8—TT. Vickers Armstrong, Barrow, 11.6.1930. Sunk 16.4.1943 mine Taranto Strait.

REGENT *See also GRACE DIEU 1488.*

REGGIO *See LST.3511 1944.*

REGINA Corvette (RCN), 'Flower' class. Marine Industries 14.10.1941. Sunk 8.8.1944 mine English Channel.

REGINA Frigate (RCN), 'Halifax' class. Marine Industries, Sorel, 25.10.1991.

REGULUS 5th Rate 44, 889bm, 140 × 38ft. Raymond, Northam, 10.2.1785. Troopship 1793. BU 3.1816.

REGULUS Brig-sloop 14. French privateer, captured 13.12.1804 by PRINCESS CHARLOTTE in West Indies. Listed 1806.

REGULUS Submarine, 1,475 tons, 260 × 30ft, 1—4in, 8—TT. Vickers Armstrong, Barrow, 11.6.1930. Lost Taranto Strait, cause unknown; formally PO 6.12.1940.

REGULUS (ex-LONGBRANCH) Minesweeper, 'Algerine' class. Toronto 18.9.1943 (renamed 1943). Sunk 12.1.1945 mine Corfu Channel.

REINDEER Brig-sloop 18, 'Cruizer' class, 385bm. Brent, Rotherhithe, 15.8.1804. Captured 28.6.1814 by American WASP English Channel, burnt.

REINDEER Packet brig 8, 'Cherokee' class, 230bm. Plymouth DY 29.9.1829. Harbour service 5.1841. Sold 1847. *Listed until 1856.*

REINDEER Wood screw sloop, 953bm, 185 × 33ft, 1—110pdr, 5—64pdr. Chatham DY 29.3.1866 (cancelled 5.1865, restarted). BU 12.1876 Chatham.

REINDEER Composite screw sloop, 970 tons, 167 × 32ft, 8—5in. Devonport DY 14.11.1883. BDV 1904; salvage vessel 1917. Sold 12.7.1924 Halifax SY as salvage vessel.

RELENTLESS Destroyer, 'M' class, 900 tons. Yarrow 15.4.1916. Sold 5.11.1926 Cashmore, Newport.

RELENTLESS Destroyer, 1,705 tons, 358·25 (oa) × 35·7ft, 4—4·7in, 8—TT. John Brown 15.7.1942. Frigate 1951, 2,300 tons, 2—4in, 2—40mm, Limbo. Sold Ward 29.4.1971; BU Inverkeithing.

RELIANCE Discovery vessel, 394bm, 90 × 30ft. Purch. 12.1793. Harbour service 1800. Sold 12.10.1815.

RELIANCE Tender 12. In service 1812–15.

RELIANCE (ex-*Knight Companion*) Repair ship, 9,220 tons, 469·5 × 58ft. Purch. 14.11.1912. Sold 17.12.1919.

RELIANCE Repair ship, 14,250 tons, 416 × 57ft, 1—5in, 10—40mm. Bethlehem, Fairfield. Launched 13.9.1944 as DUTIFUL on Lend-Lease; retained USN = LAERTES.

RENARD Sloop 18. French, captured 5.1780 by BRUNE in West Indies. BU 1784.

RENARD Sloop 18, 347bm, 101 × 28ft, 16—18pdr carr., 2—6pdr. French privateer, captured 14.11.1797 by CERBERUS. Sold 1805.

RENARD Schooner 14, 137bm. French, captured 11.1803 by squadron in Mediterranean. Sold 1.1809, BU.

RENARD Wood screw sloop, 682bm, 181·5 × 28·5ft, 1—110pdr, 1—68pdr, 2—20pdr. Mare, Blackwall, 23.4.1856. BU 3.1866 Castle, Charlton.

RENARD Schooner, 120bm, 80 × 17ft, 1—12pdr. Cuthbert, Sydney, 16.1.1873. Sold 1883 Sydney.

RENARD Torpedo gunboat, 810 tons, 230 × 27ft, 2—4·7in, 4—3pdr, 3—TT. Laird 6.12.1892. Sold 4.4.1905 McLellan, Bo'ness.

RENARD Destroyer, 918 tons, 266 × 28ft, 1—4in, 3—12pdr, 2—TT. Cammell Laird 13.11.1909. Sold 31.8.1920 Ward, New Holland.

RENARD *See also REYNARD.*

RENDLESHAM Inshore minesweeper, 'Ham' class. Brooke Marine, Lowestoft, 13.10.1954. Tx French Navy 1955 = M.781/ AUBEPINE. Sold 1974.

RENEGADE Schooner 4, 94bm. Purch. 7.1823; sold 8.1.1826.

RENFREW Corvette (RCN), Modified 'Flower' class. Kingston, Ontario, cancelled 12.1943.

RENIRA Schooner tender, 86bm. Ordered purch. 18.5.1847. Sold 1850.

RENNIE Tender, 40bm. Plymouth 18.3.1813. Became tankvessel. BU 6.1863 Chatham.

RENNINGTON Coastal minesweeper, 'Ton' class. Richards, Lowestoft, 27.11.1958. Sold 1967 Argentine Navy = CHACO.

RENOMMEE 5th Rate 38. French, captured 20.7.1796 by ALFRED in West Indies. BU 9.1810.

RENOWN (ex-RENOMMEE) Fireship 20. French, captured 12.1651 by NONSUCH. Sold 1654.

RENOWN (ex-RENOMMEE) 5th Rate 30, 669bm, 127 × 35ft. French, captured 9.1747 by DOVER. BU 5.1771 Woolwich.

RENOWN 4th Rate 50, 1,050bm, 146 × 40·5ft. Fabian, Northam, 4.12.1774. BU 12.1794. *Named 19.11.1774 but stuck on ways.*

RENOWN (ex-ROYAL OAK) 3rd Rate 74, 1,899bm, 182 × 49·5ft. Dudman, Deptford,

2.5.1798 (renamed 15.2.1796). Harbour service 1.1814. BU 5.1835.

RENOWN Screw 2nd Rate 91, 3,319bm, 244·5 × 55·5ft, 34—8in, 1—68pdr, 56—32pdr. Chatham DY 28.3.1857. Sold 24.3.1870 to North German Confederation Navy.

RENOWN Battleship, 12,350 tons, 380 × 72ft, 4—10in, 10—6in, 14—12pdr. Pembroke Dock 8.5.1895. Sold 2.4.1914 Hughes Bolckow, Blyth.

RENOWN Battlecruiser, 26,500 tons, 794·1 (oa) × 90ft (later 102·8ft), 6—15in, 17—4in, 2—3in. Fairfield 4.3.1916. Sold 19.3.1948; arr. 8.8.1948 Metal Industries, Faslane, for BU.

RENOWN Nuclear submarine, 'Resolution' class. Cammell Laird 25.2.1967. PO 24.2.1996, LU Rosyth.

RENOWN *See also VICTORIA 1887, EMPRESS of INDIA 1891, REVENGE 1915.*

REPTON (ex-WICKLOW) Minesweeper, Later 'Hunt' class. Inglis 29.5.1919 (renamed 1918). Sold 10.1920 Bombay SN Co. = *Rupavati.*

REPTON (ex-OSSINGTON) Coastal minesweeper 'Ton' class. Harland & Wolff 1.5.1957 (renamed 1956). Sold Pounds 8.1982.

REPUBLICAINE Schooner 18. French, captured 14.10.1795 by MERMAID and ZEBRA in West Indies. Sold c. 1802.

REPULSE (DUE REPULSE) Galleon 50, 622bm. Deptford 1595. Rebuilt 1610 as 764bm. Listed until 1645.

REPULSE (ex-BELLONE) 5th Rate 32, 676bm, 122·5 × 35ft. French, captured 21.2.1759 by VESTAL. Foundered 12.1776 off Bermuda.

REPULSE Cutter 10, 136bm, 64·5 × 23ft. Purch. 1779. Listed until 1781.

REPULSE 3rd Rate 64, 1,387bm, 160 × 44·5ft. Fabian, East Cowes, 28.11.1780. Wrecked 10.3.1800 off Ushant.

REPULSE Cutter 12, 12—4pdr. Purch. 3.1780. Wrecked 3.1782 off Yarmouth.

REPULSE Gunvessel 4, 54bm, 63 × 13·5ft. Hoy, purch. 3.1794. BU 4.1795.

REPULSE 3rd Rate 74, 1,727bm, 174 × 48·5ft. Barnard, Deptford, 22.7.1803. BU 9.1820.

REPULSE Screw 2nd Rate 91, 3,087bm, 230 × 55·5ft. Pembroke Dock 27.9.1855. = VICTOR EMMANUEL 7.1855; receiving ship 1873. Sold 1899.

REPULSE Ironclad ship, 3,749bm, 6,190 tons, 252 × 58ft, 12—8in. Woolwich DY 25.4.1868. Sold 2.1889.

REPULSE Battleship, 14,150 tons, 380 × 75ft, 4—13·5in, 10—6in, 16—6pdr. Pembroke Dock 27.2.1892. Sold 11.7.1911 Ward, Morecambe.

REPULSE Battlecruiser, 26,500 tons, 794·5 (oa) ×

90ft (later 102·8ft), 6—15in, 17—4in, 2—3in. John Brown (ex-Palmer) 8.1.1916. Sunk with PRINCE OF WALES (q.v.) 10.12.1941 Japanese air attack off east coast of Malaya.

REPULSE Nuclear submarine, 'Resolution' class. Vickers Armstrong, Barrow, 11.11.1967. PO 28.8.1996; LU 1997 Rosyth.

REQUIN Gun-brig 12, 165bm, 71 × 24ft. French, captured 20.2.1795 by THALIA in English Channel. Wrecked 1.1.1801 nr Quiberon.

REQUIN Brig 16. In service 1802.

RESEARCH Tender. Purch. 12.3.1846. BU 6.1859.

RESEARCH (ex-TRENT) Ironclad screw sloop, 1,253bm, 1,741 tons, 195 × 38·5ft, 4—7in. Pembroke Dock 15.8.1863 (renamed 9.1862). Sold 1884. *See TRENT.*

RESEARCH (ex-INVESTIGATOR) Paddle survey vessel, 520 tons, 155 × 24ft, 1—6pdr. Chatham DY 4.12.1888 (renamed 5.11.1887). Sold 29.7.1920 Ward, New Holland.

RESEARCH Survey vessel, 757 tons, 142 (oa) × 32ft. Philip, Dartmouth, 18.4.1939, not comp. Arr. 20.10.1952 Hocking Bros, Plymouth, for BU.

RESERVE 42-gun ship, 538bm, 118 × 32·5ft. Pett, Woodbridge, 1650. Rebuilt Deptford 1701 as 580bm. Foundered 27.11.1703 off Yarmouth.

RESERVE 4th Rate 54, 675bm, 130 × 34·5ft. Deptford 3.1704. = SUTHERLAND 2.1.1716; hospital ship 5.1741. Condemned 10.3.1744 Port Mahon; ordered BU 15.11.1754.

RESISTANCE 5th Rate 44, 895bm, 140 × 38ft. Graves, Deptford, 11.7.1782. Blown up 24.7.1798 Banca Strait.

RESISTANCE 5th Rate 36, 963bm, 145 × 38·5ft. Parsons, Bursledon, 29.4.1801. Wrecked 31.5.1803 off Cape St Vincent.

RESISTANCE 5th Rate 38, 1,081bm, 154 × 40ft. Ross, Rochester, 10.8.1805. Troopship 1842. BU comp. 17.4.1858 Chatham.

RESISTANCE Armoured frigate, 3,710bm, 6,070 tons, 280 × 51ft, 6—7in, 10—68pdr, 2—32pdr. Westwood & Baillie, Millwall, 11.4.1861. Target 1885. Sold 11.11.1898; foundered 4.3.1899 Holyhead Bay; raised, BU 1900 Garston.

RESISTANCE Battleship, 25,750 tons. Devonport DY, ordered 1914, cancelled 26.8.1914.

RESOLUE Brig-sloop 10. French, captured 16.8.1795 with three others by Fleet in Alassio Bay. Listed until 1802.

RESOLUE 5th Rate 36, 877bm, 140 × 37·5ft. French, captured 13.10.1798 by MELAMPUS off north coast of Ireland. Slop ship 1805. BU 9.1811.

RESOLUTE Gun-brig 12, 181bm, 84 × 22ft, 10—18pdr carr., 2—12pdr. King, Dover, 17.4.1805.

Tender 3.1814; diving bell vessel 6.1816; convict hulk 1844. BU 1852 Bermuda.

RESOLUTE Screw frigate, 1,235bm. Portsmouth DY, ordered 25.4.1847, tx Sheerness 8.1.1949; cancelled 23.3.1850.

RESOLUTE (ex-REFUGE, ex-*Ptarmigan*) Discovery vessel, 424bm, 115 × 28·5ft. Purch. 21.2.1850 (renamed 3.1850). Abandoned 10.9.1855 Arctic; salved by Americans; arr. Britain 12.12.1856, LU Chatham; BU comp. 16.8.1879 Chatham.

RESOLUTE Iron screw storeship, 1,793bm, 283 × 36·5ft. Laird 19.2.1855, purch. on stocks 16.1.1855. = ADVENTURE (troopship) 16.2.1857. BU 1877 Chatham.

RESOLUTE Coastal minesweeper (RCN), 'Bay' class, 390 tons. Kingston SY 20.6.1953. PO 14.2.1964; declared surplus 1965.

RESOLUTION 3rd Rate 70, 885bm, 148 × 37·5ft. Deane, Harwich, 6.12.1667. Rebuilt Chatham 1698. Foundered 27.11.1703 Sussex coast.

RESOLUTION 3rd Rate 70, 1,103bm, 151 × 41ft. Woolwich DY 15.3.1705. Run ashore 21.3.1707 to avoid capture by French at Ventimiglia.

RESOLUTION 3rd Rate 70, 1,118bm, 150 × 41·5ft. Deptford DY 25.3.1708. Wrecked 10.1.1711 nr Barcelona.

RESOLUTION 3rd Rate 74, 1,569bm, 165·5 × 47ft. Bird, Northam, 14.12.1758. Wrecked 20.11.1759 Quiberon.

RESOLUTION 3rd Rate 74, 1,612bm, 168 × 47ft. Deptford DY 12.4.1770. BU 3.1813 Portsmouth.

RESOLUTION Cutter 14, 200bm, 14—4pdr. Purch. 6.1779. Foundered 6.1797 North Sea.

RESOLUTION Battleship, 14,150 tons, 380 × 75ft, 4—13·5in, 10—6in, 16—6pdr. Palmer 28.5.1892. Sold 2.4.1914; BU Holland.

RESOLUTION Battleship, 25,750 tons, 620·2 (oa) × 88·5ft (later 101·5ft), 8—15in, 14—6in, 2—3in. Palmer 14.1.1915. Harbour service 1945. Sold 5.5.1948; BU Metal Industries, Faslane.

RESOLUTION Nuclear submarine, 'Resolution' class. Vickers Armstrong, Barrow, 15.9.1966. PO 22.10.1994; LU Rosyth.

RESOLUTION (ex-TENACIOUS) Survey ship (RNZN), 2,262 tons, 224 (oa) × 43ft. Halter Marine, Moss Point. Cd USN 29.8.1989; LU 1995. Acquired RNZN 9.1996; cd 13.12.1997.

RESOLUTION *See also PRINCE ROYAL 1610, TREDAGH 1654, DRAKE 1770.*

RESOURCE 6th Rate 28, 603bm, 120·5 × 33·5ft. Randall, Rotherhithe, 10.8.1778. Floating battery 22 in 1804. = ENTERPRIZE (harbour service) 17.4.1806. Sold 28.8.1816

RESOURCE Repair ship, 12,300 tons, 500 × 83ft, 4—4in. Vickers Armstrong, Barrow, 27.11.1928. BU 2.1954 Ward, Inverkeithing.

RESTIGOUCHE Frigate (RCN), 2,370 tons, 366 (oa) × 42ft, 4—3in, 2—40mm, 6—TT, Limbo. Vickers, Montreal, 22.11.1954. Towed from Esquimalt 6.11.2000 for use as artificial reef Acapulco, Mexico.

RESTIGOUCHE *See also COMET 1931.*

RESTLESS Survey vessel (Canadian) 203 tons. Listed 1906–36.

RESTLESS Destroyer, 'R' class. John Brown 22.8.1916. HO Ward 23.11.1936 part payment *Majestic* (CALEDONIA, q.v.); BU Briton Ferry.

RESTORATION 3rd Rate 70, 1,018bm, 150·5 × 40ft. Betts, Harwich, 1678. Rebuilt 1702 as 1,045bm. Wrecked 27.11.1703 Goodwin Sands.

RESTORATION 3rd Rate 70, 1,106bm, 151 × 41ft. Deptford DY 1.8.1706. Wrecked 9.11.1711 off Leghorn.

RETALIATION *See HERMIONE 1782.*

RETALICK Frigate, TE 'Captain' class. Bethlehem, Hingham, 9.10.1943 on Lend-Lease. Ret. USN 10.1945.

RETFORD Minesweeper, Later 'Hunt' class. Lobnitz, cancelled 1919.

RETRIBUTION (ex-WATT) Wood paddle frigate 1,641bm, 220 × 40·5ft, 6—8in, 4—32pdr. Chatham DY 2.7.1844 (renamed 26.4.1844). Sold 15.7.1864 Castle & Beech for BU.

RETRIBUTION 2nd class cruiser, 3,600 tons, 300 × 44ft, 2—6in, 6—4·7in. Palmer 6.8.1891. Sold 4.4.1911 F. E. Rudge.

RETRIBUTION *See also EDGAR 1779, HERMIONE 1782.*

RETRIEVER Destroyer, 'R' class, 1,034 tons. Thornycroft 15.1.1917. Sold 26.7.1927 Hughes Bolckow, Blyth.

REUNION 5th Rate 36, 951bm. French, captured 20.10.1793 by CRESCENT off Cherbourg. Wrecked 7.12.1796 The Swin.

REVENGE Galleon 46, 580bm. Launched 10.1577. Captured 31.8.1591 by Spanish squadron off Azores. Foundered 5.9.1591.

REVENGE 42-gun ship, 457bm. Merchantman, purch. 1650 by Royalists. Deserted to Parliamentarians 1652 = MARMADUKE. Sunk 6.1667 blockship R. Medway.

REVENGE 3rd Rate 70, 1,065bm, 150 × 40·5ft. Miller, Deptford, 1699. = BUCKINGHAM 16.6.1711; hulk 2.1727. Sunk 5.1745 foundation.

REVENGE 6th Rate 28 (Indian), c. 420bm. Bombay DY 22.9.1755. Foundered 19.4.1782 Indian Ocean.

REVENGE Brig-sloop 14. In service 1778. Captured 1779 by Americans.

REVENGE Cutter 8 purch. 1796. Listed until 1798.

REVENGE 3rd Rate 74, 1,954bm, 183 × 50ft. Chatham DY 13.4.1805. BU 10.1849.

REVENGE Screw 2nd Rate 91, 3,322bm, 5,260 tons, 245 × 55·5ft, 34—8in, 1—68pdr, 56—32pdr. Pembroke Dock 16.4.1859. Base ship 8.1872; = EMPRESS (TS) 3.1891. Sold 31.12.1923; BU Appledore.

REVENGE Battleship, 14,150 tons, 380 × 75ft, 4—13·5in, 10—6in, 16—6pdr. Palmer 3.11.1892. = REDOUBTABLE ('bombarding ship') 2.8.1915, 4—12in, 6—6in. Sold 6.11.199 Ward; BU Swansea and Briton Ferry.

REVENGE (ex-RENOWN) Battleship, 25,750 tons, 625·8 (oa) × 88·5ft (later 101·5ft), 8—15in, 14—6in, 2—3in. Vickers Armstrong, Barrow, 29.5.1915 (renamed 22.10.1913). Harbour service 1945. Arr. 5.9.1948 Ward, Inverkeithing, for BU.

REVENGE Nuclear submarine, 'Resolution' class. Cammell Laird 15.3.1968. LU 28.5.1995 Rosyth.

REVENGE *See also NEWBURY 1654, SWIFTSURE 1673.*

REVOLUTIONAIRE (ex-REVOLUTIONNAIRE) 5th Rate 38, 1,148bm, 157 × 40·5ft. French, captured 21.10.1794 by ARTOIS off Brest. BU 10.1822.

REYNA 3rd Rate 74, 1,849bm, 173 × 48·5ft. Spanish, captured 13.8.1762 Havana. Sold 13.5.1772.

REYNARD Brig-sloop 10. 'Cherokee' class, 238bm. King, Upnor, 15.12.1808. Sold Pitman 29.1.1818 for BU.

REYNARD Brig-sloop 10, 'Cherokee' class, 237bm. Pembroke Dock 26.10.1821. = RENARD 1828; mooring vessel 1841. BU 8.1857.

REYNARD Wood screw sloop, 516bm, 148 × 27·5ft, 8—32pdr. Deptford DY 21.3.1848. Wrecked 31.5.1851 Pratas Shoal, China Sea.

REYNARD *See also RENARD.*

RHADAMANTHUS Wood paddle sloop, 813bm, 175 × 27·5ft. Plymouth DY 16.4.1832. BU comp. 8.2.1864 Sheerness.

RHIN 5th Rate 38, 1,080bm, 152 × 40ft. French, captured 27.7.1806 by MARS off Rochefort. Quarantine hulk 1838. Sold 26.5.1884 Castle, Charlton.

RHINOCEROS Transport 20, 711bm. Purch. 1781. Sold 1.6.1784.

RHODIAN Brig-sloop 10, 'Cherokee' class, 240bm. Guillaume, Northam, 3.1.1809. Wrecked 21.2.1813; wreck sold 1813 in Jamaica.

RHODODENDRON Sloop, 'Anchusa' class. Irvine 15.10.1917. Sunk 5.5.1918 by U.70 in North Sea.

RHODODENDRON Corvette, 'Flower' class. Harland & Wolff 2.9.1940. Sold 17.5.1947 = *Maj Vinke*.

RHUDDLAN CASTLE Corvette, 'Castle' class. Crown, cancelled 12.1943.

RHYL Minesweeper, TE 'Bangor' class. Lobnitz 21.6.1940. Sold 28.9.1948; BU King, Gateshead.

RHYL Frigate, 2,380 tons, 370 (oa) × 41ft, 2—4·5in, 1—40mm, Limbo (later also Seacat, helo). Portsmouth DY 23.4.1959. Expended 8.1985 target.

RIBBLE Destroyer, 590 tons, 225 × 23·5ft, 1—12pdr (1907: 4—12pdr), 5—6pdr, 2—TT. Yarrow 19.3.1904. Sold 29.7.1920 Ward, Preston.

RIBBLE Frigate, 'River' class. Simons 23.4.1943. Tx Dutch Navy 25.6.1943 = JOHAN MAURITS VAN NASSAU; BU 1959.

RIBBLE (ex-DUDDON) Frigate, 'River' class. Blyth 10.11.1943. Lent RCN 24.7.1944–11.6.1945. Arr. 9.7.1957 Hughes Bolckow, Blyth, for BU.

RIBBLE Minehunter, 890 tons (full load), 156·3 (oa) × 34·5ft, 1—40mm. Richards, Great Yarmouth, 7.5.1985. Tx Brazilian Navy 31.1.1995 = GARNIER SAMPAIO.

RICHARD 3rd Rate 70, 1,108bm. Woolwich 1658. = ROYAL JAMES 1660. Destroyed 13.6.1667 by Dutch at Chatham.

RICHARD Fireship 4, 198bm. Purch. 1666. Expended 1666.

RICHARD & JOHN Fireship 10, 160bm. Purch. 1688. Sunk 1692 foundation Harwich.

RICHMOND Yacht 8, 64bm. Purch. 1672. Sold 1685.

RICHMOND (ex-*Dauphin*) 6th Rate 24. French East Indiaman, captured 1.1745. Sold 28.11.1749.

RICHMOND 5th Rate 32, 664bm, 127 × 34ft. Buxton, Deptford, 12.11.1757. Captured 11.9.1781 by French AIGRETTE off Chesapeake.

RICHMOND Gun-brig 14, 183bm, 84·5 × 22·5ft, 12—18pdr carr., 2—6pdr. Greensward, Itchenor, 2.1.1806. Sold 29.9.1814.

RICHMOND (ex-FAIRFAX) Destroyer, 1,090 tons, 309 × 30·5ft. 3—4in, 1—3in, 6—TT. USN, cd RN 5.12.1940. Lent RCN 8.1943–12.1943; lent Soviet Navy 16.7.1944–24.6.1949 = ZHIVUCHI, Sold 12.7.1949; BU Brunton, Grangemouth.

RICHMOND Frigate, 'Norfolk' class, Swan Hunter 6.4.1993.

RICHMOND *See also WAKEFIELD 1655*.

RIFLE Destroyer, 1,980 tons, 341·5× 38ft, 6—4in. 6—40mm, 10—TT. Denny, LD 30.6.1944, cancelled 27.12.1945.

RIFLEMAN Gun-brig 12, 187bm, 80 × 22·5ft. Perry, Blackwall, 1804, purch. 6.1804. Sold 27.7.1809.

RIFLEMAN Brig-sloop 18, 'Cruizer' class, 387bm. King, Upnor, 12.8.1809. Sold 21.1.1836.

RIFLEMAN Wood screw gunvessel, 486bm, 150 × 26·5ft. Portsmouth DY 10.8.1846. Sold 18.11.1869 in Hong Kong.

RIFLEMAN Wood screw gunvessel, 462bm, 610 tons, 155 × 25ft, 1—7in, 1—64pdr, 2—20pdr. Chatham DY 20.11.1872. Sold 26.4.1890.

RIFLEMAN Destroyer, 720 tons, 246 × 25ft, 2—4in, 2—12pdr, 2—TT. White 22.8.1910. Sold 9.5.1921 Ward, Briton Ferry; BU 1923.

RIFLEMAN Minesweeper, 'Algerine' class. Harland & Wolff 25.11.1943. Sold 13.9.1972; BU Fleetwood.

RIGOROUS Destroyer, 'R' class. John Brown 30.9.1916. Sold 5.11.1926 Cashmore, Newport.

RIMOUSKI Corvette (RCN), 'Flower' class. Davie SB 3.10.1940. BU 12.1950 Steel Co. of Canada.

RINALDO Brig-sloop 10, 'Cherokee' class, 237bm. Dudman, Deptford, 13.7.1808. Packet brig 2.1824. Sold 6.8.1835.

RINALDO Wood screw sloop, 951bm, 1,365 tons, 185 × 33ft, 5—40pdr, 12—32pdr. Portsmouth DY 26.3.1860. Sold 4.1884.

RINALDO Sloop, 980 tons, 180 × 33ft, 6—4in. Laird 29.5.1900. Sold 21.10.1921 W. Thomas, Anglesey.

RINALDO Minesweeper, 'Algerine' class. Harland & Wolff 20.1.1943. Arr. 16.8.1961 Dorkin, Gateshead, for BU.

RINGAROOMA (ex-PSYCHE) 2nd class cruiser, 2,575 tons, 265 × 41ft, 8—4·7in, 8—3pdr. Thomson 10.12.1889 (renamed 2.4.1890). Sold 15.5.1906 Forth S. Bkg Co.; BU Bo'ness.

RINGDOVE Brig-sloop 18, 'Cruizer' class, 385bm. Warpen, Brightlingsea, 16.10.1806. Sold 11.6.1829 Halifax, NS.

RINGDOVE Brig-sloop 16, 429bm, 101 × 32·5ft, 14—32pdr, 2—18pdr. Plymouth DY 6.1833. BU 8.1850.

RINGDOVE Wood screw gunvessel, 674bm, 181 × 28·5ft, 1—110pdr, 1—68pdr, 2—20pdr. White 22.2.1856. Sold 2.6.1865; BU 11.1866 White, Cowes.

RINGDOVE Wood screw gunvessel, 666bm, 774 tons, 170 × 29ft, 1—7in, 2—40pdr. Portsmouth DY 4.9.1867. Sold 17.5.1882.

RINGDOVE Composite screw gunboat, 805 tons, 165 × 31ft, 6—4in. Devonport DY 30.4.1889. = MELITA (salvage vessel) 7.12.1915. Sold 22.1.1920 Ship Salvage Corp.

RINGDOVE Minelayer, 498 tons, 145 × 27ft, 1—20mm, 12 mines. Robb 16.6.1938. Sold 8.9.1950 Pakistan Govt as pilot vessel.

RINGDOVE *See also MELITA 1888.*

RINGWOOD Minesweeper, Later 'Hunt' class. Lobnitz, cancelled 1919.

RIOU Frigate, TE 'Captain' class. Bethlehem, Hingham, 23.10.1943. Ret. USN 28.2.1946.

RIPLEY (ex-SHUBRICK) Destroyer, 1,190 tons, 311 × 31ft, 3—4in, 1—3in, 6—TT. USN, cd RN 26.11.1940. Sold 20.3.1945; BU Young, Sunderland.

RIPLINGHAM Inshore minesweeper, 'Ham' class. Brooke Marine, Lowestoft, 11.1.1955. Tx French Navy 1955 = M.788/MYOSOTIS; deleted 1985.

RIPON Aircraft transport, 990 tons, 160 × 30ft, 1—12pdr, 2—20mm. Pollock, Faversham, 15.3.1945. Sold 25.2.1959 for BU.

RIPON *See also RIPPON.*

RIPPLE Wood screw gunboat, 'Albacore' class. Wigram, Blackwall, 2.6.1856. BU 4.1865 Marshall, Plymouth.

RIPPON 3rd Rate 64, 924bm, 144·5 × 38·5ft. Deptford DY 23.8.1712. Rebuilt Woolwich 1735 as 4th Rate 60, 1,021bm. BU 1751.

RIPPON 4th Rate 60, 1,229bm, 155·5 × 42·5ft, Woolwich DY 20.1.1758. Harbour service 1801. BU 1.1808.

RIPPON 3rd Rate 74, 1,770bm, 176·5 × 48ft. Blake & Scott, Bursledon, 8.8.1812. BU 3.1821.

RIPPON *See also RIPON.*

RIPPON'S PRIZE (ex-CONDE DE CHINCAN) 6th Rate 28, 396bm, 105·5 × 30ft. Spanish, captured 1744. Sold 1747.

RISING CASTLE *See ARNPRIOR 1944.*

RIVAL Destroyer, 'M' class, 900 tons. Yarrow 14.6.1916. Sold 13.7.1926 Cashmore, Newport.

RIVER PLATE Destroyer, 2,380 tons, 355 × 40ft, 5—4·5in, 8—40mm, 10—TT. Swan Hunter, LD 11.4.1945, cancelled 10.1945.

RIVER SNAKE Special Service Vessel (RAN), 80 tons. Miller Bunning 1944. Tx North Borneo Govt 11.1945.

RIVIERE DU LOUP Corvette (RCN), Modified 'Flower' class. Morton, Quebec, 2.7.1943. Sold 1947 Dominican Navy = JUAN B. MAGGIOLO. BU 1972.

RIVOLI 3rd Rate 74, 1,804bm. French, captured 22.2.1812 by VICTORIOUS in Mediterranean. BU 1.1819.

ROB ROY Destroyer, 'R' class. Denny 29.8.1916. Sold 13.7.1926 King, Garston.

ROB ROY *See also LEONIDAS 1913.*

ROBERT (ex-FORTUNE) 12-gun vessel, 133bm. Royalist, captured 1642 by Parliamentrians. Recaptured 1649 by Irish Royalists.

ROBERT Fireship 4, 122bm. Purch. 1666. Sold 1667.

ROBERT Fireship 4, 112bm. Purch. 1672. Sunk 1674 foundation Sheerness.

ROBERT Gunvessel 3, 87bm, 65 × 18·5ft. Purch. 3.1794. Sold 26.12.1799.

ROBERT E. LEE *See RAGLAN 1915.*

ROBERTS (ex-EARL ROBERTS, ex-M.4, ex-STONEWALL JACKSON) Monitor, 6,150 tons, 320 × 91ft, 2—14in, 2—6in, 2—12pdr. Swan Hunter 15.4.1915 (renamed 22.6.1915, 19.6.1915, 31.5.1915). Sold 9.5.1921 Ward, retained; HO Ward 11.9.1936 part payment *Majestic* (CALEDONIA, q.v.); arr. 19.9.1936 at Preston for BU.

ROBERTS Monitor, 7,970 tons, 373 (oa) × 90ft, 2—15in, 8—4in. John Brown 1.2.1941. Harbour service 1956. Sold 6.1965; arr. 3.8.1965 Ward, Inverkeithing, for BU.

ROBIN River gunboat, 85 tons, 108 × 20ft, 2—6pdr. Yarrow 1897 in sections; re-erected Hong Kong. Sold 9.1928 in Hong Kong.

ROBIN River gunboat, 226 tons, 150 × 27ft, 1—3·7in howitzer, 1—6pdr. Yarrow 7.3.1934. Scuttled 25.12.1941 Hong Kong.

ROBUST 3rd Rate 74, 1,624bm, 168·5 × 47ft. Barnard, Harwich, 25.10.1764. Harbour service 1812. BU 1.1817.

ROBUST Screw 2nd Rate 91, 3,716bm, 252 × 58ft. Devonport DY, LD 31.10.1859; suspended 12.3.1861, cancelled 1872.

ROC Aircraft transport 990 tons, 160 × 30ft, 1—12pdr, 2—20mm. Blyth SB 28.3.1945. Sold 1.1959 Greek owners; resold R. Duvall, Quebec.

ROCHESTER 4th Rate 48, 607bm, 125·5 × 32·5ft. Chatham DY 1693. Rebuilt Deptford 1715 as 719bm. = MAIDSTONE (hospital ship) 27.9.1744. BU 10.1748 Woolwich.

ROCHESTER 4th Rate 50, 1,034bm, 146 × 40ft. Deptford DY 3.8.1749. Sold 3.4.1770.

ROCHESTER Sloop, 1,105 tons, 250 × 34ft, 2—4in. Chatham DY 16.7.1931. Sold 6.1.1951; BU Clayton & Davie.

ROCHESTER *See also HERO 1759.*

ROCHESTER PRIZE (ex-GRACIEUSE) 6th Rate 18, 200bm, 88 × 22·5ft. French, captured 18.5.1702 by ROCHESTER. Sold 10.4.1712.

ROCHFORT 2nd Rate 80, 2,082bm, 193 × 49·5ft. Jacobs, Milford Haven, 6.4.1814. BU comp. 20.6.1826 Chatham.

ROCKCLIFFE Minesweeper (RCN), 'Algerine' class. Port Arthur SY 19.1.1943. BU 1960.

ROCKET (ex-*Busy*) Fireship 4, 62bm, 52·5 × 17ft. Purch. 1804. Sold 17.6.1807 G. Bailey for BU.

ROCKET Iron paddle tender, 70bm, 90 × 12·5ft. Fairburn, Limehouse, 7.1842. BU 6.1850 Woolwich.

ROCKET Mortar vessel, 156bm, 70 × 23·5ft, 1–13in mortar. Green, Blackwall, 5.5.1855. = MV.20 on 19.10.1855. BU comp. 27.9.1865 Marshall, Plymouth.

ROCKET Wood screw gunboat, 'Albacore' class. Laird 21.4.1856. BU 10.1864.

ROCKET Composite screw gunvessel, 464bm, 584 tons, 155 × 25ft, 1–7in, 1–64pdr, 2–20pdr. London Engineering Co., Poplar, 8.4.1868. Sold 12.1888.

ROCKET Destroyer, 325 tons, 205·5 × 19·5ft, 1–12pdr, 5–6pdr, 2–TT. Thompson 14.8.1894. Sold 10.4.1912.

ROCKET Destroyer, 'R' class. Denny 2.7.1916. Sold 16.12.1926 Ward, Inverkeithing.

ROCKET Destroyer, 1,705 tons, 358·25 (oa) × 35·7ft, 4–4·7in, 8–TT. Scotts 28.10.1942. Frigate 7.1951, 2–4in, 2–Squid. Arr. 3.1967 Dalmuir for BU.

ROCKET See also LUCIFER 1913.

ROCKHAMPTON Minesweeper (RAN), 'Bathurst' class. Walker, Maryborough, 26.6.1941. Sold 6.1.1961; BU 5.1962 Japan.

ROCKINGHAM (ex-SWASEY) Destroyer, 1,190 tons, 311 × 31ft, 1–4in, 1–3in, 4–20mm, 3–TT. USN, cd RN 26.11.1940. Air target 1.1944. Sunk 27.9.1944 mine off Aberdeen.

ROCKROSE Corvette, 'Flower' class. Hill, Bristol, 26.7.1941. Tx SAN 9.1947 = PROTEA (survey ship). Sold 1962 = *Justin*; BU 1967.

ROCKSAND Minesweeping sloop, '24' class. Swan Hunter 10.7.1918. Sold 15.11.1922 Ferguson Muir.

ROCKSAND See also EMPIRE ANVIL 1943.

ROCKWOOD Destroyer, 'Hunt' class Type III. Vickers Armstrong, Barrow, 13.6.1942. Damaged 11.11.1943 air attack Aegean, not fully repaired (ret. Britain under own power 1944); PO 7.6.1944; sold 2.1946; arr. 8.1946 King, Gateshead, for BU.

RODINGTON Coastal minesweeper, 'Ton' class. Fleetlands SY 24.2.1955. Sold H. K. Vickers 12.5.1972; BU Fleetwood.

RODNEY Cutter 4. In service 1759.

RODNEY Brig-sloop (?) 16. In service 1781. Captured 23.1.1782 by French at Demerara.

RODNEY 3rd Rate 74, 1,754bm, 176·5 × 47·5ft. Barnard, Deptford, 8.12.1809. = GREENWICH 17.3.1827, 50 guns. Sold 8.9.1836.

RODNEY 2nd Rate 92, 2,598bm, 206 × 54·5ft, 10–8in, 82–32pdr. Pembroke Dock 18.6.1833; undocked Chatham 11.1.1860 as screw ship, 2,770bm, 70 guns. BU 2.1884. *Six years on stocks.*

RODNEY Battleship, 10,300 tons, 325 × 68ft, 4–13·5in, 6–6in, 12–6pdr. Chatham DY 8.10.1884. Sold 11.5.1909 Ward, Morecambe.

RODNEY Battlecruiser, 33,600 tons, 810 × 105ft, 8–15in, 16–5·5in. Fairfield, ordered 4.1916, suspended 3.1917, cancelled 10.1918.

RODNEY Battleship, 33,900 tons, 710·25 (oa) × 106·1ft, 9–16in, 12–6in, 8–4in. Cammell Laird 17.12.1925. Arr. 26.3.1948 Ward, Inverkeithing, for BU.

ROE Ketch 8, 57bm. Page, Wivenhoe, 1665. Wrecked 1670.

ROE Dogger 6 captured 1672. Lost in action 1673.

ROE Ketch 10, 93bm. Haydon, Limehouse, 8.4.1691. Wrecked 12.10.1697 York R., North America.

ROEBUCK Flyboat purch. 1.1585 from Dutch. *With Raleigh in North America.*

ROEBUCK 10-gun vessel, 90bm. Woolwich 28.3.1636. Lost 1641 collision.

ROEBUCK 14-gun ship, 110bm. Captured 1646 from Spanish 'Dunkirkers'. Royalist Navy 1648. Captured 11.1649 by Parliamentarians at Kinsale; sold there 1651.

ROEBUCK 34-gun ship. Captured 1653. Hulk 1664. Sold 1668.

ROEBUCK 6th Rate 16, 129bm. Deane, Harwich, 1666. Sold 1683.

ROEBUCK Fireship 6, 70bm. Purch. 1688. = OLD ROEBUCK 1690. Sunk 1696 foundation Portsmouth.

ROEBUCK Fireship 8, 299bm, 96 × 25·5ft. Snelgrove, Wapping, 17.4.1690. Foundered 24.2.1701 off Ascension. *With Dampier 1695 as 5th Rate, 26 guns.*

ROEBUCK 5th Rate 42, 494bm, 115 × 31·5ft. Portsmouth DY 5.4.1704. Dismantled 1725; rebuilt 1733 Woolwich as 598bm, 124 × 33·5ft. Sunk 4.1743 breakwater Sheerness.

ROEBUCK 5th Rate 44, 708bm, 126 × 36ft. Rowcliffe, Southampton, 21.12.1743. Sold 3.7.1764.

ROEBUCK 5th Rate 44, 886bm, 140 × 38ft. Chatham DY 28.4.1774. Hospital ship 7.1790; troopship 1799; guardship 1803; floating battery 1805. BU Sheerness 7.1811.

ROEBUCK Wood screw gunvessel, 865bm, 200 × 30·5ft, 1–110pdr, 1–60pdr, 4–20pdr. Scott Russell, Millwall, 22.3.1856. Sold 1864 Castle, Charlton.

ROEBUCK Destroyer, 400 tons, 210 × 21ft, 1–12pdr, 5–6pdr, 2–TT. Hawthorn 4.1.1901. BU 1919 Portsmouth.

ROEBUCK Destroyer, 1,705 tons, 358·25 (oa) × 35·7ft, 4–4·7in, 8–TT. Scotts 10.12.1942. Frigate 2.1953, 2,300 tons, 2–4in, 2–40mm, Squid. Sold Ward 12.6.1968; BU Inverkeithing. *Was 'launched' by a near-missing bomb and submerged for nine months.*

ROEBUCK Survey ship, 1,477 tons, 210 (oa) ×
42·6ft, Brooke Marine 14.11.1985. Was to PO
1.4.2003, but retained (to PO 2014).

ROGER DE COVERLEY Minesweeper, 265 tons,
130 × 26ft, 1—3pdr. Ferguson 19.7.1917; War Dept
tug, tx on stocks. = COVERLEY 1918. Sold
1.5.1920.

ROHILKHAND (ex-PADSTOW) Minesweeper
(RIN), turbine 'Bangor' class. Hamilton
29.10.1942 (renamed 1942). Sold 1960.

ROLLA Gun-brig 10, 152bm, 80·5 × 21ft. French,
captured 21.2.1806 by squadron at The Cape. Sold
24.3.1810.

ROLLA Brig-sloop 10, 'Cherokee' class, 238bm.
Pitcher, Northfleet 13.2.1808. Sold 18.4.1822
T. Pitman.

ROLLA Brig-sloop 10, 'Cherokee' class, 231bm.
Plymouth DY 10.12.1829. BU comp. 15.9.1868
Portsmouth.

ROMAN (ex-TEULIE) Brig-sloop 18, 333bm.
French, ex-Venetian, captured 1.6.1808 by UNITE
in Adriatic. Sold 1.9.1814.

ROMAN EMPEROR Fireship 8, 272bm, 92 ×
26ft, 8—4pdr. Purch. 16.5.1757. Sold 16.6.1763.

ROMNEY 4th Rate 48, 683bm, 121 × 34·5ft. Johnson, Blackwall, 1694. Wrecked 22.10.1707 Scilly
Is.

ROMNEY 4th Rate 54, 710bm, 130·5 × 35ft.
Deptford DY 2.12.1708. Rebuilt Deptford 1726,
756bm; reduced to 44 guns 6.1745. Sold 21.7.1757.

ROMNEY 4th Rate 50, 1,046bm, 146 × 40·5ft.
Woolwich DY 8.7.1762. Wrecked 19.11.1804 off
Texel.

ROMNEY 4th Rate 58, 1,227bm, 154·5 × 43ft.
Pelham, Frindsbury, 24.2.1815. Troopship 1820;
depot for freed slaves Jamaica 6.1837. Sold
12.1845 in Jamaica.

ROMNEY Minesweeper, TE 'Bangor' class. Lobnitz
3.8.1940. Sold 18.1.1950; BU Granton.

ROMOLA Destroyer, 'R' class. John Brown
14.5.1916. Sold 13.3.1930 King, Troon.

ROMOLA Minesweeper, 'Algerine' class. Port
Arthur SY 19.5.1945. Arr. 19.11.1957 Demmelweek
& Redding, Plymouth.

ROMULUS 5th Rate 44, 885bm, 140 × 38ft.
Adams, Buckler's Hard, 17.12.1777. Captured
19.2.1781 by French EVEILLE off Chesapeake
Bay.

ROMULUS 5th Rate 36, 879bm, 137 × 38·5ft.
Graves, Deptford, 21.9.1785. Troopship 7.1799;
harbour service 1813. BU 11.1816 Bermuda.

ROO Pinnace, 80bm. Built 1545. Captured 1547 by
French.

ROOK Schooner 4, 80bm, 56 × 18ft, 4—12pdr carr.

Sutton, Ringmore, 21.5.1806. Captured 10.1808
by two French privateers in West Indies.

ROOKE *See BROKE 1920.*

RORQUAL Minelaying submarine, 1,520 tons,
271·5ft, 1—4in, 6—TT, 50 mines. Vickers Armstrong, Barrow, 21.7.1936. Arr. 17.3.1946 Cashmore, Newport, for BU.

RORQUAL Submarine, 1,605 tons, 241 × 26·5ft,
8—TT. Vickers Armstrong, Barrow, 5.12.1956.
Arr. Plymouth 5.5.1977 for BU Davies & Cann.

ROSA Schooner 12. Listed 1802–03.

ROSA Tender 4, 155bm, 4—3pdr. Hired 27.3.1804
(later purch.?). Listed 1808–14.

ROSALIND Destroyer, 'R' class, 1,037 tons.
Thornycroft 14.10.1916. Sold 13.7.1926 King,
Garston.

ROSALIND *See also LIBERTY 1913.*

ROSAMOND 6th Rate 20, 429bm, 108·5 × 30ft,
18—24pdr carr., 8—18pdr carr., 2—6pdr. Temple,
South Shields, 27.1.1807. Sold 14.12.1815.

ROSAMUND Minesweeper, 'Algerine' class. Port
Arthur SY 20.12.1944. Tx SAN 9.1947 = BLOEM-
FONTEIN. Sold 3.1966.

ROSAMOND *See also INFERNAL 1843.*

ROSARIO (ex-DEL ROSARIO) Hulk 1,150bm.
Spanish galleon, captured 1588. BU 1622 Chatham.

ROSARIO (ex-NUESTRA SENORA DEL
ROSARIO) Fireship 14, 210bm. Spanish, cap-
tured 24.5.1797 by ROMULUS off Cadiz.
Expended 7.7.1800 Dunkirk Roads.

ROSARIO Brig-sloop 10, 'Cherokee' class, 236bm.
Bailey, Ipswich, 7.12.1808. Sold 11.1832 Levy,
Rochester.

ROSARIO Wood screw sloop, 673bm, 913 tons,
160 × 30ft, 1—40pdr, 6—32pdr, 4—20pdr.
Deptford DY 17.10.1860. Sold Castle 31.1.1884 for
BU.

ROSARIO Sloop, 980 tons, 180 × 33ft, 6—4in.
Sheerness DY 17.12.1898. Depot ship 1910. Sold
11.11.1921 in Hong Kong.

ROSARIO Minesweeper, 'Algerine' class. Harland
& Wolff 3.4.1943. Tx Belgian Navy 15.1.1953 = DE
MOOR; BU 19.5.1970 Bruges.

ROSARIO *See also HARDI 1800.*

ROSE 'King's ship'. 1222.

ROSE Cinque Ports ship. 1300. Captured 9.1338 by
French.

ROSE Ballinger, 30bm acquired 2.1419. Sold
17.2.1425

ROSE Galley, 80bm. Listed 1512–21.

ROSE Pink 6, 55bm. Woolwich 1657. Tx 1661 Irish
Packet Service.

ROSE Fireship 4, 112bm. Algerian, captured 1670.
Expended 1671.

ROSE Dogger 6. Dutch, captured 1672. Lost 1673.

ROSE 5th Rate 28, 230bm, 93·5, × 24ft. Edgar, Yarmouth, 1674. Fireship 1689. Sold 20.9.1698.

ROSE (SALLY ROSE) 6th Rate 16, 180bm, 64 × 23ft. Salee pirate vessel, captured 1684. Sold 1696.

ROSE 6th Rate 20, 151bm. Purch. 6.6.1709. Sold 6.3.1712.

ROSE 6th Rate 20, 273bm, 94 × 26ft. Chatham DY 25.4.1712. Rebuilt Woolwich 1724 as 377bm; hulked 10.1739. Sold 1744.

ROSE 6th Rate 24, 448bm, 106 × 31ft. Bird, Rotherhithe, 14.8.1740. Sold 29.7.1755.

ROSE 6th Rate 24, 449bm, 110 × 30ft. Blaydes, Hull, 8.3.1757. Sunk 9.1779 blockship Savannah.

ROSE 6th Rate 28, 594bm, 121 × 33·5ft. Stewart & Hall, Sandgate, 1.7.1783. Wrecked 28.6.1794 Jamaica.

ROSE Cutter. Listed 1805–06.

ROSE Sloop 18, 367bm, 106 × 28ft. Hamilton, Hastings, 18.5.1805. Sold 30.10.1817 Pitman for BU.

ROSE Sloop 18, 398bm, 104·5 × 30ft. Portsmouth DY 1.6.1821. BU 5.1851.

ROSE Wood screw gunboat, 'Albacore' class. Laird 21.1.1856. BU 8.1868 Devonport.

ROSE Survey cutter, 37bm. Purch. 20.5.1857. Stranded 20.7.1864; wreck sold 9.8.1864.

ROSE Coastguard yawl, 131bm, 70 × 21ft. White, Cowes, 12.4.1880. Sold 10.7.1906 R. Jones, Rhyl.

ROSE Corvette, 'Flower' class. Simons 22.9.1941. Lent RNorN 23.10.1941. Sunk 26.10.1944 collision frigate MANNERS North Atlantic.

ROSEBAY (ex-SPLENDOR) Corvette, 'Flower' class. Kingston SY 11.2.1943 on Lend-Lease. Ret. USN 20.3.1946; sold = *Benmark.*

ROSEBUSH 24-gun ship, 268bm. Captured 1653. Hulk 1664. Sold 1668.

ROSEMARY Sloop, 'Arabis' class. Richardson Duck, Stockton-on-Tees, 22.11.1915. Sold 17.12.1947; BU Ward, Milford Haven.

ROSS (ex-RAMSEY, renamed 1918) Minesweeper, Later 'Hunt' class. Lobnitz 12.6.1919. Sold 13.3.1947.

ROSSLARE *See CUPAR 1918.*

ROSTHERN Corvette (RCN), 'Flower' class. Port Arthur SY 30.11.1940. BU 6.1946 Steel Co. of Canada.

ROTA 5th Rate 38, 1,102bm, 153·5 × 40ft. Danish, captured 7.9.1807 Battle of Copenhagen. Sold 11.1.1816. *Was to have been renamed SENSIBLE.*

ROTHER Destroyer, 540 tons, 222 × 23·5ft, 1–12pdr, 5–6pdr (1907: 4–12pdr), 2–TT. Palmer 5.1.1904. Sold 23.6.1919 Ward, Briton Ferry.

ROTHER Frigate, 'River' class. Smith's Dock 20.11.1941. Arr. 22.4.1955 West of Scotland S. Bkg Co., Troon, for BU.

ROTHERHAM Destroyer, 1,750 tons, 358·25 (oa) × 35·7ft, 4–4·7in, 8–TT. John Brown 21.3.1942. Tx Indian Navy 29.7.1949 = RAJPUT; BU 1976.

ROTHESAY Minesweeper, turbine 'Bangor' class. Hamilton 18.3.1941. BU 4.1950 Ward, Milford Haven.

ROTHESAY Frigate, 'Rothesay' class, 2,380 tons, 370 (oa) × 41ft, 2–4·5in, 1–40mm, Limbo (later also Seacat, helo). Yarrow 9.12.1957. Arr Santander 7.11.1988 for BU.

ROTOITI Patrol boat (RNZN), 105 tons, 120 (oa) × 20ft. Brooke Marine 8.5.1974. Deleted 1992.

ROTOITI *See also LOCH KATRINE 1944.*

ROTTERDAM Hulk, 937bm. Dutch ship, captured 1672. BU 1703.

ROTTERDAM 4th Rate 50, 878bm, 134·5 × 38·5ft. Dutch, captured 5.1.1781 by WARWICK. Sold 17.7.1806 Beatson. *Named PRINCESS CAROLINE 1799–1806.*

ROUYN *See PENETANG 1944.*

ROVER (ex-CUMBERLAND) Sloop 16, 316bm, 76·5 × 22·7ft. American (1777), captured 1779. Captured 13.9.1780 by French; recaptured 2.1781. Wrecked 1781 Sandyhook.

ROVER Sloop 16, 356bm, 104 × 26ft, 16–24pdr. Pender, Bermuda, 1796, purch. on stocks. Wrecked 3.6.1798 Gulf of St Lawrence.

ROVER Brig-sloop 18, 'Cruizer' class, 385bm. Todd, Berwick, 13.2.1808. Sold 26.3.1828 Adam Gordon.

ROVER Sloop 18, 481bm, 115 × 31·5ft. Chatham DY, ordered 30.1.1829. *Redesigned as the following ship.*

ROVER Sloop 18, 590bm, 113 × 35·5ft, 16–32pdr 2–9pdr. Chatham DY 17.7.1832. BU 9.1845.

ROVER Brig 16, 560bm, 110 × 35ft, 16–32pdr. Pembroke Dock 21.6.1853. Sold 9.7.1862 Prussian Navy.

ROVER Iron screw corvette, 3,460 tons, 280 × 43·5ft, 2–7in, 16–64pdr. Thames Iron Works, Blackwall, 12.8.1874. Sold 1893.

ROVER Submarine, 1,475 tons, 260 × 30ft, 1–4in, 8–TT. Vickers Armstrong, Barrow, 11.6.1930. Sold 30.7.1946 Joubert, Durban, for BU.

ROWENA Destroyer, 'R' class. John Brown 1.7.1916. HO Ward 27.1.1937 part payment *Majestic* (CALEDONIA, q.v.); BU Milford Haven.

ROWENA Minesweeper, 'Algerine' class. Lobnitz 5.6.1944. Arr. 23.10.1958 Dorkin, Gateshead, for BU.

ROWLEY Frigate, TE 'Captain' class. Bethlehem,

Hingham, 30.10.1943 on Lend-Lease. Ret. USN 11.1945.

ROXBOROUGH (ex-FOOTE) Destroyer, 1,060 tons, 309 × 30·5ft, 1—4in, 1—3in, 4—20mm, 3—TT. USN, cd RN 23.9.1940; lent Soviet Navy 10.8.1944–7.2.1949 = DOBLESTNI. Sold 5.4.1949; BU Clayton & Davie, Dunston.

ROXBURGH Armoured cruiser, 10,850 tons, 450 × 68·5ft, 4—7·5in, 6—6in. 2—12pdr, 22—3pdr. London & Glasgow Co. 19.1.1904. Sold 1921 Stanlee; resold 8.11.1921 Slough Trading Co.; BU Germany.

ROYAL ADELAIDE (ex-LONDON) 1st Rate 104, 2,446bm, 4,122 tons, 198 × 54ft. Plymouth DY 28.7.1828 (renamed 10.5.1827). Depot ship 7.1860. Sold 4.4.1905 Laidler, Sunderland; BU Dunkirk. *Nine years on stocks.*

ROYAL ADELAIDE Yacht, 50bm, 50 × 15ft. Sheerness DY 12.1833, re-erected Virginia Water 5.1834 for use of Prince of Wales (model of frigate PIQUE). BU 1877.

ROYAL ALBERT Screw 1st Rate 121, 3,726bm, 5,517 tons, 233 × 61ft. Woolwich DY 13.5.1854. Sold 9.1884 Castle. *Ten years on stocks.*

ROYAL ALFRED Ironclad ship, 4,068bm, 6,707 tons, 273 × 57·5ft, 10—9in, 8—7in. Portsmouth DY 15.10.1864. Sold Castle 12.1884 for BU.

ROYAL ANNE *See ANDREW 1670, ROYAL CHARLES 1673, ROYAL GEORGE 1756.*

ROYAL ANNE GALLEY 5th Rate 42, 511bm, 127 × 21ft. Woolwich 18.6.1709. Foundered 10.11.1721 off The Lizard.

ROYAL ARTHUR (ex-CENTAUR, renamed 1890) 1st class cruiser, 7,700 tons, 360 × 61ft, 1—9·2in, 12—6pdr. Portsmouth DY 26.2.1891. Sold 8.1921 G. Cohen; BU Germany.

ROYAL CAROLINE Sloop 10, 232bm, 90 × 24·5ft. Deptford DY 29.1.1749. = ROYAL CHARLOTTE 1761. *Fate unknown.*

ROYAL CAROLINE *See also PEREGRINE GALLEY 1700.*

ROYAL CHARLES 1st Rate 100, 1,443bm, Portsmouth DY 1673. = QUEEN 1693, rebuilt Woolwich as 1,658bm, = ROYAL GEORGE 9.9.1715; rebuilt Woolwich as 1,801bm, 172 × 49·5ft, = ROYAL ANNE 19.1.1756. BU 1767.

ROYAL CHARLES *See also NASEBY 1655.*

ROYAL CHARLOTTE Sloop 10 (Canadian lakes). Built Navy Island 1764. Listed 1770.

ROYAL CHARLOTTE (ex-CHARLOTTE) Transport 14, 520bm, 14—6pdr. French privateer, captured 1780. Sold 10.4.1783 Milford Haven.

ROYAL CHARLOTTE (ex-CHARLOTTE) Yacht 10, 232bm, 90 × 25ft. BU 7.1820.

ROYAL CHARLOTTE Yacht 6, 202bm, 85·5 × 23ft. Woolwich DY 22.11.1824. BU 10.1832.

ROYAL CHARLOTTE *See also ROYAL CAROLINE 1749.*

ROYAL ESCAPE (ex-*Surprise*) Yacht 4, 34bm, 42 × 14·5ft. Purch. 1660. Rebuilt 1714, 1736 as transport, 74bm. BU 9.1791. *Vessel in which the future King Charles II escaped after the Battle of Worcester.*

ROYAL ESCAPE Storeship, 107bm, 63 × 21ft. Carter, R. Thames, 1743. Sold 17.7.1750.

ROYAL ESCAPE Transport, 110bm, 64 × 20ft. Nowlan, Northam, 29.11.1792. Dockyard service after 1816; = YC.4 Sheerness by 1866. BU Sheerness 2.1877.

ROYAL EXCHANGE 32-gun ship. In service 1594–1620.

ROYAL FREDERICK *See QUEEN 1839, FREDERICK WILLIAM 1860.*

ROYAL GEORGE (ex-ROYAL ANNE) 1st Rate 100, 2,047bm, 178 × 51·5ft. Woolwich DY 18.2.1756 (renamed 19.1.1756). Foundered 29.8.1782 Spithead.

ROYAL GEORGE Sloop 20 (Canadian lakes). Listed 1776.

ROYAL GEORGE (ex-UMPIRE) 1st Rate 100, 2,286bm, 190 × 52·5ft. Chatham DY 15.9.1788 (renamed 9.1782). BU 2.1822.

ROYAL GEORGE Sloop 20 (Canadian lakes), 340bm, 97 × 28ft. Kingston, Ontario, 7.1809. = NIAGARA 22.1.1814. Sold 1837.

ROYAL GEORGE Yacht, 330bm, 103 × 26·5ft. Deptford DY 17.7.1817. Harbour service 1843. BU 9.1905.

ROYAL GEORGE (ex-NEPTUNE) 1st Rate 120, 2,616bm, 20·5 × 54·5ft. Chatham DY 22.9.1827 (renamed 12.2.1822); undocked 22.6.1853 as screw ship, 102 guns. Sold 23.1.1875 Castle, Charlton.

ROYAL GEORGE *See also ROYAL CHARLES 1673, ROYAL JAMES 1675, KING GEORGE V 1911.*

ROYAL JAMES 28-gun ship, 321bm. Royalist, 1654. Captured 1654 by Parliamentarians = SORLINGS. Wrecked 17.12.1717.

ROYAL JAMES 1st Rate 100, 1,426bm Portsmouth DY 1671. Sunk 28.5.1672 Battle of Solebay.

ROYAL JAMES 1st Rate 100, 1,486bm, 163 × 45·5ft. Portsmouth DY 1675. = VICTORY 1691; rebuilt Chatham 1695; = ROYAL GEORGE 27.10.1714; = VICTORY 9.9.1715. Burnt 1721 accident; dismantled 4.1721.

ROYAL JAMES *See also RICHARD 1658.*

ROYAL KATHERINE *See KATHERINE 1664.*

ROYAL LOUISE 5th Rate 32. Woolwich DY 1732. *Fate unknown. Renamed?*

ROYAL MOUNT Frigate (RCN), 'River' class. Davie SB 28.4.1944. = BUCKINGHAM 6.1944. Arr. 4.1966 Spezia for BU.

ROYAL MOUNT *See also ALVINGTON 1944.*

ROYAL OAK 2nd Rate 76, 1,021bm. Portsmouth DY 1664. Burnt 13.6.1667 by Dutch at Chatham.

ROYAL OAK 3rd Rate 70, 1,107bm, 157·5 × 40·5ft. Deptford 1674. Rebuilt Chatham 1690 as 1,154bm; rebuilt Woolwich 1713 as 1,108bm; rebuilt Plymouth 1741 as 1,224bm, 64 guns. BU comp. 8.4.1764 Plymouth.

ROYAL OAK 3rd Rate 74, 1,606bm, 168·5 × 47ft. Plymouth DY 13.11.1769. Prison ship 11.1796; = ASSISTANCE 25.10.1805. BU 11.1815.

ROYAL OAK 3rd Rate 74, 1,759bm, 175 × 48ft. Dudman, Deptford, 4.3.1809. Harbour service 12.1825. BU 1850 Bermuda.

ROYAL OAK Ironclad frigate 4,056bm, 273 × 58ft, 11—7in, 24—68pdr. Chatham DY 10.9.1862. Sold 30.9.1885.

ROYAL OAK Battleship, 14,150 tons, 380 × 75ft, 4—13·5in, 10—6in, 16—6pdr. Laird 5.11.1892. Sold 14.1.1914 Ward, Briton Ferry.

ROYAL OAK Battleship, 25,750 tons, 620·8 (oa) × 88·5ft (later 102ft), 8—15in, 4—6in, 2—3in. Devonport DY 17.11.1914. Sunk 14.10.1939 by U.47 in Scapa Flow.

ROYAL OAK *See also RENOWN 1798.*

ROYAL SAVAGE (ex-BRAVE SAVAGE) Sloop. Built 1775 St Jean, Canada. Sunk 10.1775 American batteries Richelieu R.; salved by Americans = YANKEE.

ROYAL SOVEREIGN (ex-SOVEREIGN OF THE SEAS) 100-gun ship, 1,545bm, 168 × 48·5ft. Renamed 1660, rebuilt Chatham. Rebuilt 1685 as 1,683bm. Burnt accident 29.1.1696 Chatham preparing to rebuild again. *See SOVEREIGN 1637.*

ROYAL SOVEREIGN 1st Rate 100, 1,883bm, 175 × 50·5ft. Woolwich DY 7.1701. Rebuilt 1728 Chatham. BU 4.1768 Chatham.

ROYAL SOVEREIGN 1st Rate 100, 2,175bm, 184 × 52ft. Plymouth DY 11.9.1786. = CAPTAIN (harbour service) 17.5.1825. BU 8.1841 Plymouth. *Twelve and a half years on stocks.*

ROYAL SOVEREIGN Yacht, 278bm, 96 × 26ft. Deptford DY 5.1804. BU 11.1849 Pembroke Dock.

ROYAL SOVEREIGN 1st Rate 110. Portsmouth DY, ordered 12.2.1833; = ROYAL FREDERICK 12.4.1839; = FREDERICK WILLIAM (q.v.).

ROYAL SOVEREIGN Screw 1st Rate 121, 3,765bm, 240·5 × 62ft, 1—110pdr, 16—8in, 6—70pdr, 10—40pdr, 88—32pdr. Portsmouth DY 25.4.1857. Conv. 4.1862—8.1864 ironclad turret ship, 5,080 tons, 5—9in. Sold 5.1885.

ROYAL SOVEREIGN Battleship, 14,150 tons, 380 × 75ft, 4—13·5in, 10—6in, 16—6pdr. Portsmouth DY 26.2.1891. Sold 7.10.1913; BU Genoa.

ROYAL SOVEREIGN Battleship, 25,750 tons, 620·8 (oa) × 88·5ft (101·5ft), 8—15in, 14—6in, 2—3in. Portsmouth DY 29.4.1915. Lent Soviet Navy 30.5.1944—9.2.1949 = ARCHANGELSK. Sold 5.4.1949; BU Inverkeithing.

ROYAL TRANSPORT 6th Rate 18, 220 bm, 90 × 23·5ft. Chatham DY 11.12.1695. Presented 14.3.1698 Czar of Muscovy.

ROYAL WILLIAM (ex-PRINCE) 1st Rate 100, 1,568bm, 167·5 × 47ft. Renamed 1692. Rebuilt Portsmouth 1719 as 1,918bm, 84 guns; guardship c. 1790. BU 8.1813. *See PRINCE 1670.*

ROYAL WILLIAM 1st Rate 120, 2,694bm, 205 × 55·5ft. Pembroke Dock 2.4.1833; undocked 9.2.1860 as screw ship 72 guns. = CLARENCE (TS) 1885. Burnt accident 26.7.1899 R. Mersey.

ROYALIST Schooner 14. Purch. 1797. Listed 1801.

ROYALIST Gunvessel 4. Purch. 8.1798. Gone by 1800.

ROYALIST Brig-sloop 18, 'Cruizer' class, 385bm. Hills, Sandwich, 10.1.1807. Sold 3.2.1819 W. Harper.

ROYALIST Brig-sloop 10, 'Cherokee' class, 231bm. Portsmouth DY 12.5.1823. Sold 8.11.1838 Mr Lindon.

ROYALIST (ex-*Mary Gordon*) Brig 6, 249bm, 88 × 25·5ft. Purch. 9.7.1841 China. Lent police as hulk 7.1856. Sold 14.2.1895.

ROYALIST Wood screw sloop, 669bm, 913 tons, 160 × 30ft, 1—40pdr, 6—32pdr, 4—20pdr. Devonport DY 14.12.1861. BU 9.1875 Chatham.

ROYALIST Composite screw corvette, 1,420 tons, 200 × 38ft, 2—6in, 10—5in. Devonport DY 7.3.1883. Harbour service 2.1900; = COLLEEN 1.12.1913. Tx 19.2.1923 Irish Govt.

ROYALIST Light cruiser, 3,500 tons, 410 × 39ft, 2—6in, 6—4in. Beardmore 14.1.1915. Sold 24.8.1922 Cashmore, Newport.

ROYALIST Submarine, 1,475 tons, 260 × 30ft, 1—4in, 8—TT. Beardmore, LD 10.6.1929, cancelled 7.1929.

ROYALIST Cruiser, 5,770 tons, 512 (oa) × 50·5ft, 8—5·25in, 12—20mm. Scotts 30.5.1942. Tx RNZN 1956; sold 11.1967; BU Osaka.

RUBIS Submarine, 669 tons, 216 × 23·5ft, 1—3in, 5—TT, 32 mines. French, tx RN 7.1940 by her captain (Free French). Served RN until 1945.

RUBY 48-gun ship, 556bm, 125·5 × 31·5ft. Deptford 15.3.1652. Rebuilt Deptford 1706 as 675bm. Captured 10.10.1707 by French MARS.

RUBY (FRENCH RUBY; ex-RUBIS) 3rd Rate 66,

968bm, 139·5 × 38ft. French, captured 17.9.1666. Damaged in storm, hulked 1682. BU 1685.

RUBY 4th Rate 54, 707bm, 130·5 × 35ft. Deptford DY 25.3.1708. = MERMAID 23.5.1744. Sold 19.5.1748.

RUBY 4th Rate 50, 989bm, 141·5 × 40·5ft. Ewer, Bursledon, 3.8.1745. BU 5.1765 Plymouth.

RUBY 3rd Rate 64, 1,369bm, 159·5 × 44·5ft. Woolwich DY 26.11.1776. Receiving ship 1813. BU 4.1821 Bermuda.

RUBY Iron paddle tender, 73bm, 91 × 14ft. Acreman, Bristol, 7.1842. Sold 2.11.1846 Mr Barnard.

RUBY Wood screw gunboat, 215bm, 100 × 22ft, 1—68pdr, 1—32pdr, 2—24pdr howitzers. Deptford DY 7.10.1854. BU 10.1868.

RUBY Composite screw corvette, 2,120 tons, 220 × 40ft, 12—64pdr. Earle, Hull, 9.8.1876. = C.10 (coal hulk) 12.1904. Sold 2.1921.

RUBY Destroyer, 720 tons, 246 × 25ft, 2—4in, 2—12pdr, 2—TT. White 4.11.1910. Sold 9.5.1921 Ward, Grays.

RUBY PRIZE 4th Rate 44, 420bm, 108 × 31ft. French, captured 1695. Sold 1698.

RUGBY (ex-FILEY) Minesweeper, Later 'Hunt' class. Dunlop Bremner 6.9.1918 (renamed 1918). Sold 25.11.1927 Hughes Bolckow, Blyth.

RULER (ex-*St Joseph*) Escort carrier, 11,420 tons, 468·5 × 69·5ft 2—4in, 16—40mm, 24 aircraft. Seattle Tacoma 21.8.1943 on Lend-Lease. Ret. USN 29.1.1946.

RUNCORN Minesweeper, Later 'Hunt' class. Lobnitz, cancelled 1918.

RUNNYMEDE Frigate (RCN), 'River' class. Vickers, Montreal, 27.11.1943. BU 1948.

RUPERT 3rd Rate 66, 832bm, 144 × 36·5ft. Deane, Harwich, 26.1.1666. Rebuilt 1703 Plymouth as 930bm; rebuilt Sheerness 1740 as 1,060bm, 60 guns. BU 11.1769.

RUPERT Iron armoured turret ship, 5,440 tons, 250 × 53ft, 22—64pdr. Chatham DY 12.3.1872. Sold 10.7.1907 Bermuda.

RUPERT Submarine, 1,475 tons, 260 × 30ft, 1—4in, 8—TT. Cammell Laird, ordered 28.2.1929, cancelled 7.1929.

RUPERT Frigate, TE 'Captain' class. Bethlehem, Hingham, 31.10.1943 on Lend-Lease. Ret. USN 3.1946.

RUPERT'S PRIZE 6th Rate 18, 180bm. French, captured 22.12.1692 by RUPERT. Sold 10.12.1700.

RUPERT'S PRIZE Sloop 6, 142bm, 71 × 21·5ft. Spanish, captured 5.1741 by RUPERT. Sold 6.10.1743.

RUSHCUTTER Inshore minesweeper (RAN), 178 tons, 101·7 (oa) × 29·5ft, 2—12·7mm, Carrington Slipways 3.5.1986. PO 28.7.2000; deleted 2001.

RUSHEN CASTLE Corvette, 'Castle' class. Swan Hunter 15.7.1943. Tx Air Ministry 26.9.1960 = *Weather Surveyor*. Sold Pounds 7.7.1977 for use as salvage vessel; left under tow 11.5.1982 for BU Germany.

RUSSELL 2nd Rate 80, 1,177bm, 155·5 × 41·5ft. Portsmouth DY 3.6.1692. Rebuilt Deptford 1735 as 1,350bm. Sunk 1762 breakwater Sheerness.

RUSSELL 3rd Rate 74, 1,642bm, 168·5 × 47·5ft. West, Deptford, 10.11.1764. Sold 1811 East Indies.

RUSSELL 3rd Rate 74, 1,751bm, 176·5 × 48ft. Deptford DY 22.5.1822; undocked 2.2.1855 as screw ship. BU 1865. *Eight years on stocks.*

RUSSELL Battleship, 14,000 tons, 405 × 75·5ft, 4—12in, 12—6in, 12—12pdr. Palmer, Jarrow, 19.2.1901. Sunk 27.4.1916 mine off Malta.

RUSSELL Frigate, 1,180 tons, 300 × 33ft, 3—40mm, 4—TT. Swan Hunter 10.12.1954. Sold Pounds; arr. Portsmouth 1.7.1985 for BU.

RUTHERFORD Frigate, TE 'Captain' class. Bethlehem, Hingham, 23.10.1943 on Lend-Lease. Ret. USN 10.1945.

RYE 5th Rate 32, 384bm, 109·5 × 28·5ft. Sheerness DY 1696. Rebuilt 1717 as 6th Rate, 371bm, 24 guns. Breakwater 1727. BU 12.1735.

RYE 6th Rate 24, 371bm. Chatham DY 6.10.1727. BU 12.1735.

RYE 6th Rate 24, 446bm, 106·5 × 31ft. Bird, Rotherhithe, 1.4.1740. Wrecked 29.11.1744 Norfolk coast.

RYE 6th Rate 24, 510bm, 113 × 32·5ft. Carter, Southampton, 11.2.1745. Sold 15.3.1763.

RYE Wood screw gunvessel, 428bm, 145 × 25ft. Pembroke Dock, ordered 5.3.1860, cancelled 12.12.1863.

RYE Minesweeper, turbine 'Bangor' class. Ailsa, Troon, 19.8.1940. Sold 24.8.1948; BU Purfleet.

S

'S' class submarines 265 tons, 148·5 (oa) ×
14·5ft, 2–TT. All three built by Scotts, Greenock;
all ceded Italian Navy 25.10.1915.

S.1 Launched 28.2.1914.

S.2 Launched 14.4.1915.

S.3 Launched 10.6.191, not cd in RN.

S.1 *See SWORDFISH 1916.*

SABINE (ex-REQUIN) Brig-sloop 18, 338bm, 96 ×
28·5ft, 16–24pdr carr., 2–6pdr. French, captured
28.7.1808 by VOLAGE in Mediterranean. Sold
29.1.1818 T. Pitman for BU.

SABINE *See also SABRINA 1876.*

SABLE Destroyer, 'R' class. White 28.6.1916. Sold
8.1927 Hughes Bolckow, Blyth.

SABLE *See also SALMON 1916.*

SABRE Destroyer, 'S' class. Stephen 23.9.1918.
Sold 11.1945; BU Brunton, Grangemouth.

SABRE Patrol boat, 102 tons. Vosper 21.4.1970.
Sold 1986.

SABRE *See also GREY FOX 1993.*

SABRINA 6th Rate 20, 427bm, 108·5 × 30ft, 16–
24pdr carr., 8–18pdr carr., 2–6pdr. Adams,
Chapel, 1.9.1806. Sold 18.4.1816.

SABRINA Schooner. In service 1838.

SABRINA Wood screw sloop, 669bm, 160 × 30ft,
4–64pdr. Pembroke Dock, ordered 1860, cancelled 12.12.1863.

SABRINA Iron screw gunboat, 363 tons, 110 ×
34ft, 3–64pdr. Palmer 3.10.1876. = SABINE
(diving tender) 1916; = VIVID 1920. Sold 7.1922
Fryer, Sunderland.

SABRINA Destroyer, 'M' class, 900 tons. Yarrow
24.7.1916. Sold 5.11.1926 Cashmore, Newport.

SACKVILLE Corvette (RCN), 'Flower' class. St John
DD 15.5.1941. Cable vessel 1956; survey vessel 1966.
PO 12.1982 for conv. museum ship Halifax, NS.

SACRETT Ship, 160bm. Captured 1556. Listed
until 1559.

SAFARI (ex-P.211) Submarine, 'S' class. Cammell
Laird 18.11.1941. HO 7.1.1946 Cashmore; foundered 8.1.1946 on passage Newport.

SAFEGUARD (Gunboat No 43) Gunvessel 12,
172bm, 79 × 22ft, 2–24pdr, 10–18pdr carr.
Purch. 3.1797 Leith. Sold 9.1802.

SAFEGUARD Gun-brig 12, 178bm, 80 × 22·5ft,
10–18pdr carr., 2–12 dr, 1–8in mortar. Davy,
Topsham, 4.8.1804. Captured 29.6.1811 by Danes.

SAFEGUARD Coastguard hulk (brig). In service
1849–62.

SAFEGUARD Coastguard vessel, 875 tons, 160 ×
29ft, 2–3pdr. Day Summers, Southampton,
24.6.1914. Sold 13.2.1920 = *Safeguarder*.

SAFETY (ex-*Eclair*) Schooner 12, 180bm. Guardship West Indies 1808; prison ship 1810; not
listed again until 1841, then receiving hulk
Tortola. BU 1879.

SAGA Submarine, 'S' class. Cammell Laird
14.3.1945. Sold 11.10.1948 Portuguese Navy
= NAUTILLO.

SAGESSE 6th Rate 28, 481bm. French, captured
8.9.1803 by THESEUS in West Indies. Sold
7.6.1821.

SAGUENAY Destroyer (RCN), 1,337 tons, 321·25
(oa) × 32·75ft, 4–4.7in, 8–TT. Thornycroft
11.7.1930. Damaged, TS 8.1943. Sold 17.7.1948 for
BU.

SAGUENAY Escort (RCN), 2,260 tons, 366 (oa) ×
42ft, 4–3in, 2–40mm, Limbo. Halifax SY
30.7.1953. Scuttled 25.6.1994 dive centre
Lunenburg, NS.

SAHIB (ex-P.212) Submarine, 'S' class. Cammell
Laird 19.1.1942. Sunk 24.4.1943 Italian corvette
GABBIANO north of Sicily.

SAINFOIN *See EMPIRE CROSSBOW 1943. See
also SANFOIN.*

ST AGATHE Frigate (RCN), 'River' class. Quebec,
cancelled 12.1943.

ST ALBANS 4th Rate 50, 615bm, 128 × 33·5ft.
Deptford 1687. Wrecked 8.12.1693 nr Kinsale.

ST ALBANS 4th Rate 54, 687bm, 131 × 34·5ft.
Burchett, Rotherhithe, 27.8.1706. Rebuilt Ply-
mouth 1718 as 853bm. Wrecked 20.10.1744 off
Jamaica.

ST ALBANS 4th Rate 60, 1,207bm, 150 × 43·5ft.
West, Deptford, 23.12.1747. Sold 14.3.1765.

ST ALBANS 3rd Rate 64, 1,380bm, 159·5 × 44·5ft.
Perry, Blackwall, 12.9.1764. Floating battery
9.1803. BU 6.1814.

ST ALBANS (ex-THOMAS) Destroyer, 1,060 tons, 309 × 30·5ft, 3—4in, 1—3in, 6—TT. USN, cd RN 23.9.1940. Lent RNorN 4.1941; lent Soviet Navy 16.7.1944—28.2.1949 = DOSTOINI. Sold 5.4.1949; BU Charlestown.

ST ALBANS Frigate, 'Norfolk' class. Yarrow, Glasgow, 6.5.2000.

ST ALBANS PRIZE 6th Rate 18, 262bm. French, captured 9.10.1691. Sold 13.5.1698.

ST ANDREW Galleon 50, 900bm, 8—18pdr, 21—9pdr, 7—6pdr, 14 smaller. Spanish, captured 6.1596 Cadiz. Given away 1604.

ST ANDREW 42-gun ship, 587bm. Deptford 1622. Wrecked 1666. *Known as ANDREW during the Commonwealth.*

ST ANDREW 1st Rate 96, 1,318bm, 159 × 44ft. Woolwich DY 1670. Rebuilt as 1st Rate 100, 1,722bm, 170 × 48ft = ROYAL ANNE 8.7.1703. BU 5.1727. *Listed until 1756.*

ST ANGELO Base ship, 150 tons, 78 × 18ft. Scott, Bowling, 18.3.1935 for use as dockyard tug. Sunk 30.5.1942 mine off Malta.

ST ANGELO *See also BULLFROG 1881, FIDGET 1905.*

ST ANGELO II *See FAREHAM 1918.*

ST ANNE Ship, 350bm. French, captured 1626. Sold 1630.

ST ANNE 3rd Rate 64, 1,407bm, 165 × 44ft, 26—24pdr, 28—18pdr, 10—9pdr. French, captured 25.5.1761 by squadron West Indies. Sold 2.10.1784.

ST AUSTELL BAY (ex-LOCH LYDOCH) Frigate, 'Bay' class. Harland & Wolff 18.1.1944 (renamed 1944). Arr. 4.7.1959 Charlestown for BU.

ST BONIFACE Minesweeper (RCN), 'Algerine' class. Port Arthur 5.11.1942. Sold 1946, name unchanged.

ST BRIDES BAY (ex-LOCH ACHILTY) Frigate, 'Bay' class. Harland & Wolff 16.1.1945 (renamed 1944). Arr. 3.9.1962 Faslane for BU.

ST CATHERINES Frigate (RCN), 'River' class. Yarrow, Esquimalt, 6.12.1942. Weather ship 1950. BU Japan 1968.

ST CHRISTOPHER (ex-*Mohawk*) Sloop 18. French privateer, presented 1807 by inhabitants of St Kitts. Listed until 1810.

ST CLAIR (ex-WILLIAMS) Destroyer, (RCN), 1,060 tons, 309 × 30·5ft, 3—4in, 1—3in, 6—TT. USN, cd RCN 24.9.1940. Depot ship 12.1943. BU 2.1947.

ST CLAUDE Ship, 300bm. Captured 1625. Given away 1632.

ST COLUMBA Wood paddle packet, 720bm, 198·5 × 27ft. Laird 5.7.1847, purch. on stocks. Sold 1850 City of Dublin SP Co.

ST CROIX (ex-McCOOKE) Destroyer (RCN), 1,190 tons, 311 × 31ft, 3—4in, 1—3in, 6—TT. USN, cd RCN 24.9.1940. Sunk 20.9.1943 by U.305 south of Iceland.

ST CROIX Frigate (RCN), 2,370 tons, 366 (oa) × 42ft, 4—3in, 2—40mm, 6—TT, Limbo. Marine Industries 15.11.1956. Sold Jacobson Metals, Chesapeake; towed from Halifax, NS, 9.4.1991 for BU.

ST DAVID 4th Rate 54, 646bm. Lydney 1667. Foundered 11.11.1690 Portsmouth harbour, raised 8.1691, hulked. Sold 20.8.1713.

ST DAVID (ex-*Suffolk Monarch*) Minesweeper, 392 tons, 120·7 (oa) × 29·2ft. Trawler, Woolwich 1972. Cd 25.11.1978 for South Wales RNVR; ret. 11.1983 owner.

ST DAVID *Name borne in succession from 1949 by RNVR tenders MMS.1733, BRERETON, CRICHTON.*

ST DENNIS 38-gun ship, 396bm. Captured 1625. Hulk 1634. Sold 1645.

ST EDOUARD Frigate (RCN), 'River' class. G. T. Davie, cancelled 12.1943.

ST EUSTATIA 6th Rate 26. Dutch, captured 1781 West Indies. Sold 1784 West Indies.

SAINT EUSTATIUS *See EUSTATIA 1781.*

ST FERMIN Brig, 250bm, 80 × 26ft. Spanish, captured 8.1.1780. Recaptured 4.1780 by Spanish off Gibraltar.

ST FIORENZO (ex-MINERVE) 5th Rate 38, 1,032bm, 14—32pdr carr., 26—18pdr, 2—9pdr. French, captured 19.2.1794. Harbour service 1812. BU 9.1837. *Found sunk San Fiorenzo, Corsica, and raised.*

ST FIORENZO Wood screw frigate, 2,066bm, 188 × 50·5ft. Woolwich DY, LD 6.1850, cancelled 4.1856.

ST FLORENTINE (ex-COMPTE DE SAINT-FLORENTIN) 4th Rate 60, 1,109bm, 148 × 41·5ft, 24—24pdr, 26—12pdr, 10—6pdr. French privateer, captured 4.4.1759. Sunk 5.1771 breakwater Sheerness.

ST FRANCIS (ex-BANCROFT) Destroyer (RCN), 1,190 tons, 311 × 31ft, 3—4in, 1—3in, 6—TT. USN, cd RCN 24.9.1940. TS 1944. Sunk 14.7.1945 collision SS *Winding Gulf* off Sagonnet Point, Rhode I., passage Philadelphia for BU.

ST GEORGE 60-gun ship, 594bm. Burrell, Deptford 1622. Hulked 1687. Sunk 20.10.1697 blockship Sheerness.

ST GEORGE Ship. Captured 1626. Listed until 1632.

ST GEORGE (ex-CHARLES) 1st Rate 96, 1,129bm, 163 × 42·5ft. Renamed 1687. Rebuilt Portsmouth 1701 as 1,470bm; rebuilt Portsmouth 1740 as 1,655bm, 166 × 48·5ft. BU 9.1774.

ST GEORGE Discovery ship, 654bm, 132 × 34ft. Purch. 3.12.1701. Sunk 20.2.1716 foundation Chatham.

ST GEORGE 2nd Rate 98, 1,950bm, 177·5 × 50ft. Portsmouth DY 4.10.1785. Wrecked 24.12.1811 coast of Jutland.

ST GEORGE 1st Rate 120, 2,694bm, 205 × 55·5ft. Plymouth DY 27.8.1840; undocked 19.3.1859 as screw ship, 2,864bm. Sold 1883 Castle; BU 11.1883. *Thirteen years on stocks.*

ST GEORGE 1st class cruiser, 7,700 tons, 360 × 61ft, 2—9·2in, 10—6in, 12—6pdr. Earle, Hull, 23.6.1892. Depot ship 1909. Sold 1.7.1920 S. Castle, Plymouth.

ST GEORGE *See also BRITANNIA 1762.*

ST HELENA (ex-PASLEY) Frigate, 'Colony' class. Walsh Kaiser 20.10.1943 on Lend-Lease (renamed 1943). Ret. USN 23.4.1946.

ST JACOB Fireship 4, 175bm. Captured 1666. Sold 1667.

ST JACOB Fireship 4, 276bm. Purch. 1667. Expended 1667.

ST JACOB Dogger 6. Captured 1672. Sold 1674.

ST JAMES Ship. Captured 1625. Listed until 1628.

ST JAMES Destroyer, 2,325 tons, 379 (oa) × 40·25ft, 4—4·5in, 1—4in, 12—40mm, 8—TT. Fairfield 7.6.1945. Arr. 19.3.1961 Cashmore, Newport, for BU.

ST JEAN D'ACRE Screw 1st Rate 101, 3,199bm, 238 × 55·5ft, 28—8in, 1—68pdr, 72—32pdr. Plymouth DY 23.3.1853. Sold 1.1875 Castle, Charlton; BU 10.1875.

ST JOHN Schooner, 115bm. Purch. 5.1764 North America. Condemned 15.2.1777.

ST JOHN Cutter 14, 90bm. Purch. 1780 North America. Listed 1781.

ST JOHN Frigate (RCN), 'River' class. Vickers, Montreal, 25.8.1943. Sold 17.11.1947 Halifax SY; BU 1948.

ST JOHN PRIZE Advice boat 61, 70bm, 59 × 16·5ft. French, captured 9.1695. Recaptured 5.9.1696 by French.

ST JOHNS Frigate (RCN), 'Halifax' class. Marine Industries, Sorel, 12.2.1995.

ST JOSEPH Sloop 8. French, captured 7.1696. Sold 24.8.1699.

ST JOSEPH Hoy, 70bm. Purch. 24.11.1704 Lisbon. Sold 4.1710.

ST KATHERINE Dogger 6. Captured 1672. Lost 1673.

ST KITTS Destroyer, 2,315 tons, 379 (oa) × 40·25ft, 4—4·5in, 1—4in, 14—40mm, 8—TT. Swan Hunter 4.10.1944. Arr. 19.2.1962 Young, Sunderland, for BU.

ST LAMBERT Corvette (RCN), Modified 'Flower' class. Morton 6.11.1943. Sold 1946 = *Chrysi Hondroulis.*

ST LAURENT Escort (RCN), 2,265 tons, 366 (oa) × 42ft, 4—3in, 2—40mm. Vickers, Montreal, 30.11.1951. Sold Dartmouth Salvage Co. 27.9.1979; resold, foundered 12.1.1980 under tow for BU.

ST LAURENT *See also CYGNET 1931.*

ST LAWRENCE Schooner. Purch. Halifax 5.1764. Blown up 26.7.1766 lightning strike off Cape Breton.

ST LAWRENCE Schooner 10, 114bm. Purch. 7.1767. Sold 6.2.1776.

ST LAWRENCE Schooner. Purch. 1775 North America. Sold 1783.

ST LAWRENCE (ex-ATLAS) Schooner 12, 240bm, 12—12pdr carr., 1—9pdr. American privateer, captured 13.6.1813 off North Carolina. Recaptured 26.2.1815 by American privateer CHASSEUR in West Indies.

ST LAWRENCE 1st Rate 112 (Canadian lakes), 2,305bm, 198 × 52·5ft. Kingston, Ontario, 10.9.1814. Sold 1.1832.

ST LAWRENCE *See also SHANNON 1806.*

ST LEWIS (ex-SAINT-LOUIS) 5th Rate 42, 460bm, 113 × 30·5ft. French, captured 1697. Hulk 1701. Wrecked 1707 Jamaica.

ST LOE (ST LOOE) Yacht 4, 47bm. Plymouth DY 1700. Sold 2.8.1716.

ST LUCIA (ex-ENFANT PRODIGUE) Gun-brig 14, 183bm, 85·5 × 23ft, 14—4pdr. French privateer, captured 24.6.1803 by EMERALD in West Indies. Recaptured 1.1807 by French in West Indies.

ST LUCIA Destroyer, 2,380 tons, 355 × 40ft, 5—4·5in, 8—40mm, 10—TT. Stephen, LD 19.1.1945, cancelled 10.1945.

ST MARTIN 6th Rate 18, 177bm, 78·5 × 23ft. French, captured 1691. Sunk 24.4.1695 breakwater Portsmouth.

ST MARY Cog. Cinque Ports vessel. 1299.

ST MARY Ship, 100bm. Purch. 1626. Given away 1628.

ST MARYS (ex-DORAN) Destroyer, 1,060 tons, 309 × 30·5ft, 3—4in, 1—3in, 6—TT. USN, cd RN 23.9.1940. Sold 20.3.1945; arr. 12.1945 Rosyth for BU.

ST MATHEW (ex-SAN MATEO) Galleon 50, c. 900bm, 4—60pdr, 4—34pdr, 16—18pdr, 14—9pdr, 4—6pdr, 6 smaller. Spanish, captured 6.1596 Cadiz. Given away 1604.

ST MICHAEL 2nd Rate 90, 1,080bm, 155 × 41·5ft. Portsmouth DY 1669. = MARLBOROUGH 18.12.1706 (q.v.).

ST NAZAIRE *See LST.3517 1945.*

ST NICHOLAS Fireship 4, 108bm, 7 0·5 × 19ft. Purch. 4.1694. Expended 12.7.1694 Dieppe.

ST PATRICK 4th Rate 48, 621bm. Bailey, Bristol, 5.1666. Captured 5.2.1667 by Dutch.

ST PATRICK (ex-SHAMROCK) Tankvessel 1917–23 (renamed 1.11.1917).

ST PAUL (ex-PAULUS) 4th Rate 48, 291bm. Dutch, captured 1665. Burnt in action 1666.

ST PAUL Fireship 4, 290bm. Dutch, captured 1666. Sold 1667.

ST PAUL 5th Rate 32, 260bm. Algerian, captured 1679. Fireship 1688. Sold 3.5.1698.

ST PETER Dogger 6. Captured 1672. Captured 1674 by Dutch.

ST PHILIPS CASTLE Sloop. Purch. 1780. Sold 10.4.1783.

ST PIERRE Sloop 1796. Wrecked 12.2.1796 off Port Negro.

ST PIERRE (ex-DILIGENTE) Sloop 18, 371bm. French, captured 2.1809 Martinique. Sold 1.9.1814.

ST PIERRE Frigate (RCN), 'River' class. Quebec Co. 1.12.1943. Sold 1947 Peruvian Navy = TENIENTE PALACIOS; = PALACIOS 1953; BU 1966.

ST ROMUALD Frigate (RCN), 'River' class. G. T. Davie, cancelled 12.1943.

ST STEPHEN Frigate (RCN), 'River' class. Yarrow, Esquimalt, 6.2.1944. Tx 1958 Dept of Transport, weather ship. Sold 1969 mercantile.

ST THOMAS (ex-SANDGATE CASTLE) Corvette (RCN), 'Castle' class. Smith's Dock 28.12.1943 (renamed 1943). Sold 1946 = *Camosum*; = *Chilcotin* 1958; = *Yukon Star* 1958. Hulked 1970 floating hotel. BU 1974 Tacoma.

ST THOMAS *See also SEABEAR 1943.*

ST VINCENT Fireship 8, 197bm. French, captured 18.6.1692. Sold 3.5.1698.

ST VINCENT (ex-SAN VICENTE) Sloop 14, 276bm, 83 × 24ft. Spanish, captured 1780 in West Indies. Sold 4.1783 North America.

ST VINCENT 1st Rate 120, 2,601bm, 4,672 tons, 205 × 54ft. Plymouth DY 11.3.1815. Harbour service (flagship and depot ship) from 10.1841; TS 1.1.1862. Sold 17.5.1906 Castle.

ST VINCENT Battleship, 19,250 tons, 500 × 84ft, 10–12in, 20–4in. Portsmouth DY 10.9.1908. Sold 1.12.1921 Stanlee, Dover.

STE THERESE Frigate (RCN), 'River' class. G. T. Davie SB 16.10.1943. Sold 12.1966.

SAINTES Destroyer, 2,325 tons, 379 (oa) × 40–25ft, 4–4·5in, 1–4in, 14–40mm, 8–TT. Hawthorn Leslie 19.7.1944. Sold 26.6.1972; arr. Cairnryan 1.9.1972 for BU.

SAKER Pinnace, 50bm. Listed 1545–65.

SALADIN Destroyer, 'S' class. Stephen 17.2.1919. Sold 29.6.1947; BU Rees, Llanelly.

SALAMANDER 48-gun ship, 300/450bm. Scottish, captured 1544. Listed until 1559.

SALAMANDER Bomb vessel 10, 134bm, 64·5 × 21·5ft. Chatham DY 1687. Rebuilt Woolwich 1703 as 122bm. Sold 20.8.1713.

SALAMANDER Bomb vessel 10, 265bm. 84 × 27·5ft. Woolwich DY 7.7.1730. Sold 13.3.1743.

SALAMANDER (ex-*Pelham*) Fireship 8, 304bm, 96 × 27·5ft, 8–6pdr. Purch. 6.9.1745. Sold 23.6.1748.

SALAMANDER (ex-*Applewhite & Frere*) Fireship 8, 260bm, 89 × 26ft 8–6pdr. Purch. 5.1.1757. Sold 30.12.1761.

SALAMANDER (ex-*United*) Firevessel 78bm, 59·5 × 18ft. Purch. 5.1804. Sold 17.6.1807 J. Cristall for BU.

SALAMANDER Wood paddle sloop, 818bm, 175·5 × 32ft. Sheerness DY 16.5.1832. Sold Castle 12.1883 for BU.

SALAMANDER Torpedo gunboat, 735 tons, 230 × 27ft, 2–4·7in, 4–3pdr, 3–TT. Chatham DY 31.5.1889. Sold 15.5.1906 Ashdown, London.

SALAMANDER Minesweeper, 815 tons, 230 × 33·5ft, 2–4in. White 24.3.1936. Sold 15.12.1946; arr. Blyth 7.5.1947 for BU.

SALAMANDER *See also SHARK 1776.*

SALAMAUA Landing craft (RAN), 310 tons, 146 (oa) × 33ft. Walker 27.7.1972. Tx Papua New Guinea 14.11.1974.

SALAMINE Brig-sloop 18, 240bm, 93·5 × 25ft. French, captured 18.6.1799 by EMERALD in Mediterranean. Sold 1802 Malta.

SALAMIS Wood paddle despatch vessel, 835bm, 929 tons, 220 × 28ft, 2–9pdr. Chatham DY 19.5.1863. BU 1883 Sheerness.

SALCOMBE *See SUTTON 1918.*

SALDANHA (ex-CASTHOR) 5th Rate 40, 1,065bm, 147 × 40ft. Dutch, captured 17.8.1796 Saldanha Bay. Harbour service 2.1798. Sold 1.1806 Plymouth.

SALDANHA 5th Rate 36, 951bm, 145 × 39ft. Temple, South Shields, 8.12.1809. Wrecked 4.12.1811 Lough Swilly.

SALERNO *See LST.3513 1945.*

SALFORD (ex-SHOREHAM) Minesweeper, Later 'Hunt' class. Murdoch & Murray 3.4.1919 (renamed 1918). Sold 10.1920 Bombay SN Co. = *Vegavati*.

SALISBURY 4th Rate 48, 682bm, 134·5 × 34ft. Herring, Buckler's Hard, 18.4.1698. Captured 10.4.1703 by French ADROIT, recaptured

15.3.1708; = PRESTON 2.1.1716; rebuilt 1742 as
853bm. Hulk 9.1748 Trincomalee; BU 11.1749
Trincomalee.

SALISBURY 4th Rate 54, 703bm, 130 × 35ft.
Chatham DY 3.7.1707. Rebuilt Portsmouth 1726
as 756bm; hulked 2.1744. Sold 1.5.1749.

SALISBURY 4th Rate 50, 976bm, 140 × 40ft.
Ewer, East Cowes, 29.1.1745. Condemned
24.4.1761 East Indies.

SALISBURY 4th Rate 50, 1,051bm 146 × 40·5ft.
Chatham DY 2.10.1769. Wrecked 13.5.1796 nr San
Domingo.

SALISBURY 4th Rate 58, 1,199bm, 154·5 × 43ft.
Deptford DY 21.6.1814. Sold 1.1837 Beatson for BU.

SALISBURY (ex-CLAXTON) Destroyer, 1,090
tons, 309 × 30·5ft, 1–4in, 1–3in, 4–20mm, 3–
TT. USN, cd RN 5.12.1940. Lent RCN 9.1942–
1944. Sold 26.6.1944 in Canada.

SALISBURY Frigate, 2,170 tons, 339·8 (oa) × 40ft,
2–4·5in, 2–40mm, Squid. Devonport DY
25.6.1953. Expended 30.9.1985 target.

SALLY Storeship 14, 398bm. Purch. 4.5.1781. Sold
2.12.1783.

SALLY ROSE *See ROSE 1684.*

SALLYPORT (ex-LCT.4064) Tank landing craft,
657 tons, 225 × 39ft. Arrol, Alloa, 1945 (renamed
1956). Sold Malta 4.1966 Greek interests.

SALMON Destroyer, 310 tons, 200 × 19·5ft, 1–
12pdr, 5–6pdr, 2–TT. Earle, Hull, 15.1.1895. Sold
14.5.1912 Cashmore, Newport.

SALMON Destroyer, 'R' class. Harland & Wolff,
Govan, 7.10.1916. = SABLE 2.12.1933. HO Ward
28.1.1937 part payment *Majestic* (CALEDONIA,
q.v.); arr. Hayle 3.1937 for BU.

SALMON Submarine, 670 tons, 193 × 24ft, 1–3in,
6–TT. Cammell Laird 30.4.1934. Sunk 9.7.1940
mine off Norway.

SALORMAN Cutter 10, 121bm. Danish, captured
10.8.1808 by boats of EDGAR off Nyborg.
Wrecked 22.12.1809 Baltic. *Spelt 'SALOMAN' in
James.*

SALSETTE *See DORIS 1808.*

SALTASH Sloop 14, 200bm, 85·5 × 23·5ft. Plymouth DY 7.9.1732. Sold 22.10.1741.

SALTASH Sloop 14, 221bm, 89 × 24ft. Bird,
Rotherhithe, 1741, purch. on stocks. Wrecked
18.4.1742 coast of Portugal.

SALTASH Sloop 14, 248bm, 88 × 25ft. Quallett,
Rotherhithe, 30.12.1742. Foundered 24.6.1746 off
Beachy Head.

SALTASH Sloop 14, 270bm, 91 × 26ft. Allin &
Quallett, Rotherhithe, 19.12.1746. Sold 15.2.1763.

SALTASH Storeship, 106bm. Chichester 9.12.1748.
Wrecked 26.8.1752.

SALTASH Store lighter, 85bm, 55 × 19ft. Purch.
1756. BU 1775.

SALTASH Store lighter, 125bm, 63·5 × 22·5ft.
Topsham 1809. Sold 12.7.1831.

SALTASH Minesweeper, Later 'Hunt' class.
Murdoch & Murray 25.7.1918. Sold 13.3.1947.

SALTBURN Minesweeper, Later 'Hunt' class.
Murdoch & Murray 9.10.1918. Sold 23.10.1946
Gifford, Bude; wrecked 12.1946 under tow off
Hartland Point; salved, BU 1948.

SALVADOR DEL MUNDO 1st Rate 112,
2,398bm, 191 × 54·5ft, 30–32pdr, 32–24pdr,
32–12pdr, 15–9pdr. Spanish, captured 14.2.1797
Battle of Cape St Vincent. BU 2.1815.

SALVATORE V Aux. minesweeper (RAN). Hired
9.1986–2.1992.

SALVIA Sloop, 'Aubrietia' class. Irvine, Glasgow,
16.6.1916. Sunk 20.6.1917 by U.94 west of Ireland
while decoy ship Q.15.

SALVIA Corvette, 'Flower' class. Simons 6.8.1940.
Sunk 24.12.1941 by U.568 west of Alexandria.

SAMARAI Patrol boat (RAN), 100 tons. Evans
Deakin 14.7.1967. Tx Papua New Guinea 9.1975.

SAMARANG Sloop 18. Portsmouth DY, ordered
6.9.1815, cancelled 30.9.1820.

SAMARANG 6th Rate 28, 500bm, 113·5 × 32ft.
Cochin 1.1.1822. Guardship 5.1847. Sold 10.1883
Gibraltar.

SAMARANG *See also SCIPIO 1807.*

SAMPHIRE Corvette, 'Flower' class. Smith's Dock
14.4.1941. Sunk 30.1.1943 by U-boat in
Mediterranean.

SAMPSON 20-gun ship, 300bm. Captured 1643.
Given away 1646 in exchange for 26-gun
PRESIDENT.

SAMPSON 32-gun ship. Captured 1652. Lost
18.2.1653 in action with Dutch.

SAMPSON 32-gun ship. Captured 1652. Sold 1658.

SAMPSON 3rd Rate 64, 1,380bm, 160 × 44·5ft.
Woolwich DY 8.5.1781. Hulk 1802. BU 5.1832
Levy, Rochester.

SAMPSON Wood paddle frigate, 1,299bm, 203 ×
37·5ft. Woolwich DY 1.10.1844. Sold 15.7.1864
Castle & Beech.

SAMSON Fireship 12, 240bm. Purch. 1678.
Expended 14.3.1689.

SAN ANTONIO Sloop 4, 67bm, 55 × 17ft. Pirate
vessel captured 4.1700 from Captain Kidd. Sunk
4.8.1707 foundation Jamaica.

SAN ANTONIO 3rd Rate 64, 1,392bm, 159·5 ×
44·5ft. Spanish, captured 12.8.1762 Havana. Sold
28.3.1775.

SAN ANTONIO (ST ANTOINE) 3rd Rate 74,
1,700bm. French, captured 12.7.1807 off Cadiz.

Prison ship 1809, powder hulk 9.1814. Sold 11.7.1827, sale cancelled; resold 26.3.1828 J. Ledger for BU.

SAN CARLOS Storeship 22, 676bm, 125 × 35·5ft, 8–18pdr carr., 14–6pdr. Spanish privateer frigate, captured 12.12.1779 by SALISBURY in West Indies. Sold 5.8.1784.

SAN DAMASO 3rd Rate 74, 1,812bm, 175 × 48ft. Spanish, captured 17.2.1797 off Trinidad. Prison ship 1800. Sold 30.9.1814.

SAN DOMINGO 3rd Rate 74, 1,820bm. Woolwich DY 3.3.1809. Sold 18.4.1816.

SAN DOMINGO Destroyer, 2,380 tons, 355 × 40ft, 5–4·5in, 8–40mm, 10–TT. Cammell Laird, LD 9.12.1944, cancelled 10.1945.

SAN GENARO 4th Rate 60. Spanish, captured 13.8.1762 Havana. Wrecked 1.1763 The Downs.

SAN GIORGIO Repair hulk, 9,232 tons, 430 × 69ft. Italian cruiser found sunk in shallow water Tobruk, cd 3.1944–1945.

SAN ILDEFONSO 3rd Rate 74, 1,752bm. Spanish, captured 21.10.1805 Battle of Trafalgar. = ILDEFONSO (provision depot) 1813. BU 1816.

SAN JOSEF 1st Rate 114, 2,457bm, 195 × 54ft. Spanish, captured 14.2.1797 Battle of Cape St Vincent. Gunnery TS 1837. BU 5.1849 Devonport.

SAN JUAN (ex-SAN JUAN NEPOMUCENO) 3rd Rate 74, 1,740bm. Spanish, captured 21.10.1805 Battle of Trafalgar. Listed on harbour service until 1816. Sold 8.1.1818 Gibraltar. *Was named BERWICK for a period in 1805.*

SAN LEON Brig-sloop 16. Spanish, captured 28.11.1798 by squadron in Atlantic. Sold 1800.

SAN MIGUEL 3rd Rate 74, 1,925bm, 176 × 49ft, 28–32pdr, 30–18pdr, 16–9pdr. Spanish, captured 10.9.1782 by garrison of Gibraltar while crew ashore. Sold 1.12.1791.

SAN NICOLAS 3rd Rate 80, 1,942bm, 180 × 49·5ft. Spanish, captured 14.2.1797 Battle of Cape St Vincent. Prison ship 1800. Sold 3.11.1814.

SAN RAFAEL 3rd Rate 80, 2,230bm. Spanish, captured 22.7.1805 during Calder's action off Cape Finisterre. Prison ship 1806. Sold 9.1810.

SAN YSIDRO 3rd Rate 72, 1,836bm, 176 × 49ft. Spanish, captured 14.2.1797 Battle of Cape St Vincent. Prison ship 1797. Sold 3.11.1814.

SANDFLY Floating battery 14, 360bm, 80 × 32ft. Wells, Rotherhithe, 1795. BU 1803.

SANDFLY Wood screw gunboat, 'Albacore' class. Pitcher, Northfleet, 1.9.1855. Sold 5.11.1867 W. Lethbridge for BU.

SANDFLY (ex-*Tasmanian Maid*) Paddle gunboat (NZ Govt) 90bm, 2–12pdr. Purch. 6.1863. Sold 1865.

SANDFLY Survey schooner, 120bm, 1–12pdr. Cuthbert, Sydney, 5.12.1872. Sold 1883 Sydney.

SANDFLY Torpedo gunboat, 525 tons, 200 × 23ft, 1–4in, 6–3pdr, 4–TT. Devonport DY 30.9.1887. Sold 1905 Malta.

SANDFLY Coastal destroyer, 235 tons, 175 × 17·5ft, 2–12pdr, 3–TT. White 30.10.1906. = TB.4 in 1906. Sold 7.10.1920 Ward; ran ashore on passage Pebble Ridge, nr Westward Ho!

SANDFLY Destroyer, 750 tons, 246 × 26ft, 2–4in, 2–12pdr, 2–TT. Swan Hunter 26.7.1911. Sold 9.5.1921 Ward, Milford Haven; arr. 10.1922 for BU.

SANDGATE CASTLE *See ST THOMAS 1943.*

SANDHURST (ex-*Manipur*) Repair ship, 11,500 tons, 470 × 58ft, 4–4in, 2–6pdr. Hired 1914 as dummy battlecruiser INDOMITABLE, purch. 1915, conv. comp. 9.1916. Arr. 4.1946 Arnott Young, Dalmuir, for BU.

SANDOWN Paddle minesweeper, 'Ascot' class. Dunlop Bremner 6.7.1916. Sold 3.1922 Ward; BU Inverkeithing 12.1923.

SANDOWN Minehunter, 'Sandown' class, Vosper-Thornycroft 18.4.1988.

SANDPIPER River gunboat, 85 tons, 108 × 20ft, 2–6pdr. Yarrow, Poplar, 2.7.1897. Sold 18.10.1920 in Hong Kong.

SANDPIPER River gunboat, 185 tons, 160 × 30·5ft, 1–3.7in howitzer, 1–6pdr. Thornycroft 6.6.1933. Tx Chinese Navy 2.1942 = YING HAO ('British Hero'). Listed until 1974.

SANDPIPER Patrol boat, 190 tons, 120 (oa) × 21·7ft, Dunston 20.1.1977. Sold C & H Heuvelmann Shipping & Trading, Holland, 4.1991 for resale Rotterdam.

SANDRINGHAM Inshore minesweeper, 'Ham' class. McLean, Gourock, 16.4.1957. Sold Pounds 1986 mercantile.

SANDWICH 2nd Rate 90, 1,346bm, 161·5 × 44·5ft. Betts, Harwich, 1679. Rebuilt Chatham 1712 as 1,573bm. Hulk 1752. BU comp. 24.3.1770 Chatham.

SANDWICH 2nd Rate 98, 1,869bm, 176 × 49ft. Chatham DY 14.4.1759. Floating battery 1780; harbour service 10.1790. BU 1810 Chatham.

SANDWICH (ex-*Majority*) Armed ship 24. Purch. 1780. Captured 24.8.1781 by French off Charlestown.

SANDWICH Cutter 10, 113bm, 66·5 × 20·5ft, 10–12pdr carr. Purch. 1804. Sold 1805 in Jamaica.

SANDWICH 3rd Rate 74, 2,039bm, 192 × 49ft. Milford Haven DY, LD 12.1809, cancelled 22.3.1811.

SANDWICH Sloop, 1,043 tons, 250 × 34ft, 2–4in. Hawthorn Leslie 29.9.1928. Sold 8.1.1946.

SANDWICH *See also PITT 1805.*

SANFOIN Minesweeping sloop, '24' class. Greenock & Grangemouth 10.6.1918. Sold 15.11.1922 Ferguson Muir.

SANGUINE Submarine, 'S' class. Cammell Laird 15.2.1945. Sold Israeli Navy 1958 = RAHOV 3.1959.

SANS PAREIL 3rd Rate 80, 2,245bm, 193·5 × 51·5ft, 2—42pdr carr., 8—32pdr carr., 30—32pdr, 32—24pdr carr., 22—12pdr. French, captured 1.6.1794 'Battle of 1st of June'. Sheer hulk 1810. BU 10.1842 Devonport.

SANS PAREIL Screw 2nd Rate 81, 2,339bm, 200 × 52ft, 1—10in, 30—8in, 50—32pdr. Devonport DY 18.3.1851. Sold 3.1867 Marshall, Plymouth.

SANS PAREIL Battleship, 10,470 tons, 340 × 70ft, 2—16.25in, 1—10in, 2—6in, 9—6pdr. Thames Iron Works, Blackwall, 9.5.1887. Sold 9.4.1907 Ward, Birkenhead & Preston.

SANSOVINO *See EMPIRE CUTLASS 1943.*

SANTA DOROTEA 5th Rate 34, 958bm. Spanish, captured 15.7.1798 by LION in Mediterranean. BU 6.1814 Portsmouth.

SANTA GERTRUYDA 5th Rate 36. Spanish, captured 7.12.1804 by POLYPHEMUS and LIVELY off Cape St Mary. Receiving ship 11.1807. BU 6.1811.

SANTA LEOCADIA Listed 1814. *Probably refers to LEOCADIA, q.v.*

SANTA MARGARITA 5th Rate 38, 993bm, 145·5 × 39ft, 8—18pdr carr., 26—12pdr, 10—6pdr. Spanish, captured 11.11.1779 coast of Portugal. Quarantine ship 1817. Sold 8.9.1836.

SANTA MARIA 4th Rate 50, 400bm. Dutch, captured 1665. Burnt 12.6.1667 by Dutch at Chatham.

SANTA MONICA 5th Rate 32, 956bm, 145 × 38·5ft, 8—18pdr carr., 26—12pdr, 10—6pdr. Spanish, captured 14.9.1779 by PEARL. Wrecked 28.3.1782 off Tortola.

SANTA TERESA 5th Rate 30, 949bm, 144 × 38·5ft. Spanish, captured 6.2.1799 by ARGO off Majorca. Sold 9.1802.

SANTON Coastal minesweeper, 'Ton' class. Fleetlands SY 18.8.1955. Sold 1967 Argentine Navy = CHUBUT; deleted 1996.

SAPPHIRE 36-gun-ship, 442bm. Ratcliffe 1651. Run ashore 31.3.1671 to avoid capture by French.

SAPPHIRE 5th Rate 32, 346bm, 106 × 27ft. Deane, Harwich, 1675. Sunk 11.9.1696 by French in Bay of Bulls, Newfoundland.

SAPPHIRE 4th Rate 42, 534bm, 118 × 32·5ft. Portsmouth DY 9.1708. Hulked 2.1740. Sold 1.5.1745.

SAPPHIRE 5th Rate 44, 686bm, 124 × 36ft.

Carter, Limehouse, 21.2.1741. Reduced to 32 guns 7.1756. Hulked by 1780. Sold 11.3.1784.

SAPPHIRE Sloop 18, 426bm, 108·5 × 30ft. Brindley, Lynn, 11.11.1806. Sold 18.4.1822 Manlove.

SAPPHIRE 6th Rate 28, 604bm, 119 × 34ft. Portsmouth DY 31.1.1827. Sold 5.11.1864 Trincomalee.

SAPPHIRE Wood screw corvette, 1,405bm, 1,970 tons, 220 × 37ft, 14—64pdr. Devonport DY 24.9.1874. Sold 24.9.1892 G. Cohen.

SAPPHIRE 3rd class cruiser, 3,000 tons, 360 × 40ft. 12—4in, 8—3pdr. Palmer 17.3.1904. Sold 9.5.1921 Ward, Grays.

SAPPHIRE II *See IMPERIEUSE 1883.*

SAPPHIRE'S PRIZE Sloop 10, 164bm, 78·5 × 22ft. Spanish, captured 5.1745. Wrecked 15.9.1745.

SAPPHO Brig-sloop 18, 'Cruizer' class, 384bm. Bailey, Ipswich, 15.12.1806. BU 1830 Halifax, NS.

SAPPHO Brig-sloop 16, 428bm, 101 × 32·5ft, 14—32pdr, 2—9pdr. Plymouth DY 3.2.1837. Foundered 1859 Australian station.

SAPPHO Wood screw sloop, 950bm, 185 × 33ft. Deptford DY, LD 1.5.1861, cancelled 12.12.1863.

SAPPHO Composite screw sloop, 727bm, 940 tons, 160 × 31·5ft, 2—7in, 2—64pdr. Wigram, Blackwall, 20.11.1873. Sold 12.1887 Castle. *Originally ordered from Oswald & Co., Sunderland.*

SAPPHO 2nd class cruiser, 3,400 tons, 300 × 43ft, 2—6in, 6—4·7in, 8—6pdr. Samuda, Poplar, 9.5.1891. Sold 18.3.1921 S. Castle, Plymouth.

SAPPHO *See also ECLIPSE 1867.*

SARABANDE Minesweeper, 265 tons, 130 × 26ft, 1—3pdr. Goole SB 16.8.1918; War Dept tug, tx on stocks. Ret. War Dept 1921. BU 10.1926 Ward, Preston.

SARACEN Brig-sloop 18 (fir-built), 'Cruizer' class, 384bm. Perry, Wells & Green, Blackwall, 25.7.1804. BU 5.1812.

SARACEN Brig-sloop 18, 'Cruizer' class, 387bm. Boole, Bridport, 25.7.1812. Sold 18.8.1819 W. Wilkinson.

SARACEN Brig-sloop 10, 'Cherokee' class, 228bm. Plymouth DY 30.1.1831. Survey vessel 2.1854; exchanged 10.9.1862 Singapore part payment for *Young Queen.*

SARACEN (ex-*Young Queen*) Survey brig 75bm. Purch. 10.9.1862, renamed 29.12.1862. Sold 13.3.1870.

SARACEN Destroyer, 980 tons, 272 × 26ft, 2—4in, 2—TT. White 31.3.1908. Sold 22.10.1919 Ward, Preston.

SARACEN (ex-P.247) Submarine, 'S' class.

Cammell Laird 16.2.1942. Sunk 18.8.1943 Italian corvette MINERVA off Corsica.

SARAH Fireship 4, 89bm. Purch. 1666. Sold 1667.

SARAH Fireship 6, 143bm. Purch. 1678. Sold 1686.

SARAWAK (ex-PATTON) Frigate, 'Colony' class. Walsh Kaiser 25.10.1943 on Lend-Lease (renamed 1943). Ret. USN 5.1946.

SARDINE Sloop 16, 300 bm. French, captured 9.3.1796 by EGMONT off Tunis. Sold 1806.

SARDOINE Sloop 14, 255bm, 94·5 × 25ft, 14– 4pdr. French, captured 4.1761 Bay of Biscay. Sold 26.4.1768.

SARDONYX Destroyer, 'S' class. Stephen 27.5.1919. Arr. 23.6.1945 Ward, Preston, for BU.

SARNIA Minesweeper (RCN), TE 'Bangor' class. Dufferin, Toronto, 21.1.1942. Sold 29.3.1958 Turkish Navy = BUYUKDERE; deleted 1972.

SARPEDON Brig-sloop 10, 'Cherokee' class, 241bm. Warwick, Eling, 1.2.1809. Foundered 1.1.1813.

SARPEDON Destroyer, 'R' class'. Hawthorn Leslie 1.6.1916. Sold 13.7.1926 Alloa, Charlestown.

SARPEDON *See also LAERTES 1913.*

SARPEN Brig-sloop 18, 309bm. Danish, captured 7.9.1807 Battle of Copenhagen. BU 8.1811.

SARTINE 5th Rate 32, 802bm, 132·5 × 36ft. French, captured 25.8.1778 by SEAHORSE and COVENTRY. Wrecked 26.11.1780 off Mangalore, East Indies.

SASKATCHEWAN Escort (RCN), 2,380 tons, 366 (oa) × 42ft, 4–3in, 6–TT, Limbo. Victoria 1.2.1961. Dive site 7.1997 off Nanaimo, Vancouver I.

SASKATCHEWAN *See also FORTUNE 1934.*

SASKATOON Corvette (RCN), 'Flower' class. Vickers, Montreal, 7.11.1940. Sold 1947 = *Tra los Montes*; = *Olympic Fighter* 1950; *Otori Maru No 6* 1956; = *Kyo Maru No 20* 1961; last listed 1977–78.

SASKATOON MCDV (RCN), 'Kingston' class, 962 tons, 181·4 (oa) × 37·1ft, 1–40mm. Halifax SY 30.3.1998.

SATELLITE Brig-sloop 16, 289bm, 93 × 26·5ft, 14–24pdr carr., 2–6pdr. Hills, Sandwich, 3.1806. Foundered 31.12.1810 English Channel.

SATELLITE Brig-sloop 18, 'Cruizer' class, 385bm. List, Fishbourne, 9.10.1812. Sold 3.1824 East Indies.

SATELLITE Sloop 18, 456bm, 112 × 31ft, 16–32pdr carr., 2–9pdr. Pembroke Dock 2.10.1826. BU 2.1849.

SATELLITE Paddle gunboat (Indian), 335bm, 2–12pdr. Bombay DY 1840. Listed 1860.

SATELLITE Wood screw corvette, 1,462bm, 2,187 tons, 200 × 40·5ft, 20–8in, 1–68pdr. Devonport DY 26.9.1855. BU 1879 Devonport.

SATELLITE Composite screw corvette, 1,420 tons, 200 × 38ft, 2–6in, 10–5in. Sheerness DY 13.8.1881. RNVR drillship 1904. Sold 21.10.1947 J. G. Potts.

SATELLITE *See also MELITA 1942, BRAVE 1943.*

SATISFACTION 26-gun ship, 290bm. Captured 1646. Wrecked 19.11.1663 Dutch coast.

SATISFACTION Fireship, 84bm, 64·5 × 18ft. Purch. 4.1794. Sold 5.1802.

SATURN 3rd Rate 74, 1,646bm, 168 × 47·5ft. Raymond, Northam, 22.11.1786. 4th Rate 58 in 12.1813. Harbour service 9.1825. BU comp. 1.2.1868 Pembroke Dock.

SATURN Destroyer, 'S' class. Stephen, cancelled 1919.

SATYR Destroyer, 'R' class. Beardmore 27.12.1916. Sold 16.12.1926 Ward, Milford Haven.

SATYR (ex-P.214) Submarine, 'S' class. Scotts 28.9.1942. Lent French Navy 2.1952–8.1961 = SAPHIR. BU 4.1962 Charlestown.

SAUDADOES Sloop 10, 83bm. Portsmouth 1669. Rebuilt Deptford 1673 as 180bm, 6th Rate. Captured 23.2.1696 by French.

SAUDADOES PRIZE 5th Rate 36, 385bm, 103·5 × 29ft. French, captured 9.1692. Sunk 1712 foundation Plymouth.

SAUK (ex-SOMERS) Schooner 2 (Canadian lakes), 87bm, 58·5 × 19ft. American, captured 12.8.1814. Listed until 1831.

SAULT STE MARIE *See THE SOO 1942.*

SAUMAREZ Destroyer leader, 1,673 tons, 315 × 32ft, 4–4in, 4–TT. Cammell Laird 14.10.1916. Sold 8.1.1931 Ward, Briton Ferry.

SAUMAREZ Destroyer leader, 1,750 tons, 362·9 (oa) × 35·7ft, 4–4·7in, 6–40mm, 8–TT. Hawthorn Leslie 20.11.1942. Sold 8.9.1950; BU 10.1950 Charlestown. *Had been mined 22.10.1946 off Corfu.*

SAUNDERS Destroyer leader, 1,750 tons, 329·25 (oa) × 32ft. Thornycroft, cancelled 1.1919.

SAVAGE Sloop 14. Purch. 1748. Wrecked 1748 The Lizard.

SAVAGE Sloop 8, 144bm, 74 × 21ft. Woolwich DY 24.3.1750. Wrecked 16.9.1776 Louisburg, NS.

SAVAGE Sloop 14, 302bm, 97 × 27ft. Barnard, Ipswich, 28.4.1778. Hulked 10.1804. Sold 31.8.1815.

SAVAGE Brig-sloop 16, 284bm 93 × 26ft. Adams, Chapel, 30.7.1805. Sold 3.2.1819 J. Tibbut.

SAVAGE Brig-sloop 10, 'Cherokee' class, 227bm. Plymouth DY 29.12.1830. Dockyard chain lighter 7.1853. BU 1866.

SAVAGE Wood screw gunboat, 'Albacore' class.

Mare, Blackwall, 5.5.1856. = YC.3 (mooring lighter) 1864. BU 9.1888 Malta.

SAVAGE Destroyer, 897 tons, 264 × 28ft, 1—4in, 3—12pdr, 2—TT. Thornycroft 10.3.1910. Sold 9.5.1921 Ward, Portishead.

SAVAGE Destroyer, 1,710 tons, 362·9 (oa) × 35·7ft, 4—4·5in, 2—40mm, 8—TT. Hawthorn Leslie 24.9.1942. Arr. 11.41962 Cashmore, Newport for BU.

SAVANNAH Brig-sloop 14. In service 1779. Sunk 16.9.1779 to block Savannah R.

SAWFLY River gunboat, 'Fly' class. Yarrow 1915. Sold 1.3.1923 Basra.

SAXIFRAGE Sloop, 'Anchusa' class. Lobnitz 29.1.1918. = PRESIDENT (drillship) 9.4.1921. For preservation 1986.

SAXIFRAGE Corvette, 'Flower' class. Hill, Bristol, 24.10.1941. Sold 8.1947 = *Polarfront I*. Listed until 1979.

SAXLINGHAM Inshore minesweeper, 'Ham' class. Berthon Boat Co., Lymington, 17.10.1955. Sold Ross & Cromarty County Council 24.4.1968.

SCAMANDER (ex-LIVELY) 5th Rate 36 (red pine-built), 941bm, 143 × 38·5ft, 14—32pdr carr., 26—18pdr, 2—9pdr. Brindley, Frindsbury, 13.7.1813 (renamed 1812). Sold 22.7.1819 Ledger for BU.

SCARAB River gunboat, 645 tons, 230 × 36ft. 2—6in, 1—3in. Wood Skinner, Newcastle, 7.10.1915. Lent Burmese Govt 5.1946–6.1947. BU 5.1948 Singapore.

SCARAB Tender, 213 tons. Holmes 26.5.1971. Sold 24.9.1996 Echoscan, Leeds.

SCARBOROUGH Ketch 10, 94bm. Frame, Scarborough 2.5.1691. Captured 12.1.1693 by French.

SCARBOROUGH 5th Rate 32, 374bm, 105 × 29ft. Woolwich DY 15.2.1694. Captured 18.7.1694 by French off north coast of Ireland = DUC DE CHAULNES; recaptured 15.2.1696 = MILFORD. Rebuilt 1705 as 421bm. Wrecked 18.6.1720 Cape Corrientes.

SCARBOROUGH 5th Rate 32, 391bm, 108 × 28·5ft. Parker, Southampton, 1696. Captured 21.10.1710 by French on coast of Guinea; recaptured 31.3.1712 = GARLAND. Sold 27.9.1744.

SCARBOROUGH 5th Rate 32, 416bm, 108 × 29·5ft. Sheerness DY 5.1711. Rebuilt Stacey, Deptford, 1720 as 6th Rate 20, 378bm. Sold 25.8.1739.

SCARBOROUGH Hospital ship, 501bm, 117 × 31·5ft. Purch. 21.11.1739. Sold 18.12.1744.

SCARBOROUGH 6th Rate 24, 442bm, 106 × 31ft. Perry, Blackwall, 31.5.1740. Sold 13.4.1749.

SCARBOROUGH 6th Rate 22, 433bm, 107·5 × 30·5ft. Blaydes, Hull, 17.4.1756. Foundered 5.10.1780 hurricane West Indies.

SCARBOROUGH 3rd Rate 74, 1,745bm, 176 × 48·5ft. Graham, Harwich, 29.3.1812. Sold 8.9.1836.

SCARBOROUGH Sloop, 1,045 tons, 250 × 34ft, 2—4in. Swan Hunter 14.3.1930. Sold 3.6.1949; BU Stockton Ship & Salvage Co.

SCARBOROUGH Frigate, 2,150 tons, 360 × 41ft, 2—4·5in, 2—40mm. Vickers Armstrong, Tyne, 4.4.1955. Sold Pakistan 1975, not taken over. Arr. Blyth 31.8.1977 for BU.

SCARBOROUGH CASTLE *See EMPIRE PEACEMAKER 1944.*

SCEPTRE 3rd Rate 64, 1,398bm, 160 × 44·5ft. Randall, Rotherhithe, 8.6.1781. Wrecked 5.12.1799 Table Bay.

SCEPTRE 3rd Rate 74, 1,727bm, 171 × 48ft. Dudman, Deptford, 11.12.1802. BU 2.1821.

SCEPTRE Destroyer, 'R' class. Stephen 18.4.1917. Sold 16.12.1926 Ward, Briton Ferry.

SCEPTRE Submarine, 'S' class. Scotts 9.1.1943. BU 9.1949 Gateshead.

SCEPTRE Nuclear submarine, 'Swiftsure' class. Vickers 20.11.1976.

SCIMITAR Destroyer, 'S' class. John Brown 27.2.1918. Arr. 30.6.1947 Ward, Briton Ferry, for BU.

SCIMITAR Patrol boat, 102 tons. Vosper-Thornycroft 4.12.1969. Sold mercantile 1983.

SCIMITAR *See also GREY WOLF 1993.*

SCIPIO Fireship 8, 171bm, 71·5 × 23ft. Purch. 28.9.1739. Sold 24.2.1746.

SCIPIO 3rd Rate 64, 1,387bm, 160 × 44·5ft. Barnard, Deptford, 22.10.1782. BU 10.1798.

SCIPIO (PSYCHE) Sloop 18, 408bm. Dutch, captured 1.9.1807. = SAMARANG 19.4.1808. Sold 24.3.1814 Bombay.

SCIPIO *See also BULWARK 1807.*

SCIPION 3rd Rate 74, 1,810bm. French, HO 29.8.1793 by Royalists at Toulon. Burnt 20.11.1793 accident off Leghorn.

SCIPION 3rd Rate 74, 1,884bm, 183 × 48·5ft. French, captured 4.11.1805 Strachan's action. BU 1.1819.

SCORCHER Submarine, 'S' class. Cammell Laird 18.12.1944. BU 1962 Charlestown.

SCORPION Sloop 14, 276bm, 91 × 26·5ft. Wyatt & Major, Beaulieu, 8.7.1746. Sank 9.1762 Irish Sea.

SCORPION Sloop 16, 342bm, 102 × 27·5ft. Ashman, Shoreham, 26.3.1785. Sold 6.12.1802.

SCORPION Gunvessel 4, 70bm, 66·5 × 15ft. Purch. 3.1794. Sold 11.1804.

SCORPION Brig-sloop 18, 'Cruizer' class, 384bm. King, Dover, 17.10.1803. Sold 3.2.1819 G. Young.

SCORPION Brig-sloop 10, 'Cherokee' class,

228bm. Plymouth DY 28.7.1832. Survey vessel 1848; lent Thames Police 3.3.1858. BU comp. 17.10.1874 Chatham.

SCORPION (ex-EL TOUSSON) Iron turret ship, 1,857bm, 2,751 tons, 220 × 42·5ft, 4—9in. Laird 4.7.1863; Turkish, purch. 10.1863. Guardship 10.1869 Bermuda. Sold 2.1903 Bermuda; lost 17.6.03 on passage Boston.

SCORPION Destroyer, 916 tons, 264 × 28ft, 1—4in, 3—12pdr, 2—TT. Fairfield 19.2.1910. Sold 26.10.1921 Barking S. Bkg Co.

SCORPION River gunboat, 670 tons, 209 (oa) × 34·5ft, 2—4in, 1—3·7in howitzer. White 20.12.1937. Sunk in action 13.2.1942 Japanese destroyers in Banka Strait.

SCORPION (ex-SENTINEL) Destroyer, 1,710 tons, 362·75 (oa) × 35·7ft, 4—4·7in, 2—40mm, 8—TT. Cammell Laird 26.8.1942 (renamed 1942). Sold 1.10.1945 Dutch Navy = KORTENAER. Arr. Ghent 18.7.1963 for BU.

SCORPION (ex-TOMAHAWK, ex-CENTAUR) Destroyer, 1,980 tons, 365 (oa) × 38ft, 6—4in, 6—40mm, 10—TT. White 15.8.1946 (renamed 9.1943). Sold 4.6.1971; BU Bo'ness.

SCORPION *See also ETNA 1771.*

SCOTSMAN Destroyer, 'S' class. John Brown 30.3.1918. HO Ward 13.7.1937 part payment *Majestic* (CALEDONIA, q.v.); BU Briton Ferry.

SCOTSMAN Submarine, 'S' class. Scotts 18.8.1944. Arr. 19.11.1964 Troon for BU.

SCOTSTOUN Repair ship, 3,300 tons, 132 × 31ft. Stern-wheel river steamer. Yarrow 1916 in sections, re-erected 10.1916 Abadan. Sold 4.1920 Basra.

SCOTT Destroyer leader, 1,800 tons, 320 × 32ft, 5—4·7in, 1—3in, 6—TT. Cammell Laird 18.10.1917. Sunk 15.8.1918 North Sea, probably by UC.17.

SCOTT Survey ship, 830 tons, 230 × 33·5ft, 1—3pdr. Caledon, Dundee, 23.8.1938. Escort 1939–40. Arr. 30.6.1965 Troon for BU.

SCOTT Survey ship, 13,600 tons, 430·1 (oa) × 70·5ft. Appledore Shipbuilders 13.10.1996.

SCOURGE Galley 8. Purch. 1779. Listed until 3.1784.

SCOURGE Brig-sloop 14, 234bm, 80·5 × 27ft, 16—6pdr. Allin, Dover, 26.10.1779, purch. on stocks. Foundered 7.11.1795 off Dutch coast.

SCOURGE Gunvessel 4, 67bm, 66 × 15ft. Dutch hoy, purch. 4.1794. = CRASH 1798. BU 9.1803.

SCOURGE (ex-ROBUSTE) Sloop 22, 372bm, 103 × 29ft. French, captured 15.1.1796 by POMONE in West Indies. Sold 8.1802.

SCOURGE (ex-*Herald*) Sloop 16, 340bm, 107 × 27·5ft, 14—32pdr carr., 2—6pdr. Purch. 6.1803. Sold 18.4.1816.

SCOURGE Wood paddle sloop, 1,128bm, 190 × 36ft. Portsmouth DY 8.11.1844. BU 1865 Castle, Charlton.

SCOURGE Iron screw gunboat, 'Ant' class. Chatham DY 25.3.1871. = C.79 (dockyard craft) 1904. Listed 1930.

SCOURGE Destroyer, 922 tons, 267 × 28ft, 1—4in, 3—12pdr, 2—TT. Hawthorn Leslie 11.2.1910. Sold 9.5.1921 Ward, Briton Ferry.

SCOURGE Destroyer, 1,710 tons, 362·8 (oa) × 35·7ft, 4—4·7in, 2—40mm, 8—TT. Cammell Laird 8.12.1942. Sold 1.2.1946 Dutch Navy = EVERTSEN; to BU 7.1963 Hendrik Ido Ambacht.

SCOUT 'Bark' 10, 132bm, 4—6pdr, 6—2pdr. Deptford 1577. Condemned 1604.

SCOUT Sloop 6. Listed 1648. Captured 1649 by Royalists.

SCOUT Advice boat 6, 38bm. Portsmouth 1694. Sold 7.7.1703.

SCOUT Brig-sloop 14, 276bm, 82 × 29ft, 14—4pdr. Smith, Folkestone, 30.7.1780, purch. on stocks. Captured 24.8.1794 by French CELESTE off Cape Bon.

SCOUT (ex-VENUS) Sloop 18, 406bm, 111 × 29ft. French, captured 22.10.1800 by FISGARD in Atlantic. Wrecked 25.3.1801 The Shingles.

SCOUT (ex-PREMIER CONSUL) Sloop 18, 448bm, 113 × 30ft, 18—24pdr carr., 2—6pdr. French privateer, captured 5.3.1801 by DRYAD off coast of Ireland. Foundered 1802 off Newfoundland.

SCOUT Brig-sloop 18, 'Cruizer' class, 382bm. Atkinson, Hull, 7.8.1804. Sold 11.7.1827 Ledger for BU.

SCOUT Sloop 18, 488bm, 116 × 31ft. Chatham DY 15.6.1832. BU 10.1852.

SCOUT Wood screw corvette, 1,462bm, 2,187 tons, 200 × 40·5ft, 20—8in, 1—68pdr. Woolwich DY 30.12.1856. BU 1877 Chatham.

SCOUT Coastguard cutter, 80bm. Built 1861. Sold 2.1870 B. Ackerley.

SCOUT Torpedo cruiser, 1,580 tons, 220 × 34ft, 4—5in, 8—3pdr, 11—TT. Thomson 30.7.1885. Sold 5.7.1904.

SCOUT Destroyer, 'S' class. John Brown 27.4.1918. Arr. 29.3.1946 Ward, Briton Ferry, for BU.

SCRUBB Survey schooner, 80bm. Purch. 1815. Sold 19.5.1828.

SCRUBB Tender, 30bm. Purch. 1823. Sold 10.1.1832 in Jamaica.

SCYLLA Brig-sloop 18, 'Cruizer' class, 385bm. Davy, Topsham, 29.6.1809. BU 1.1846.

SCYLLA Wood screw corvette, 1,467bm, 2,187 tons, 200 × 40·5ft, 20—8in, 1—68pdr. Sheerness DY 19.6.1856. Sold Castle 7.11.1882 for BU.

SCYLLA 2nd class cruiser, 3,400 tons, 300 × 43ft, 2–6in, 6–4·7in, 8–6pdr. Samuda, Poplar, 17.10.1891. Sold 2.4.1914.

SCYLLA Cruiser, 5,450 tons, 512 (oa) × 50·5ft, 8–4·5in. Scotts 24.7.1940. Mined 23.6.1944, not repaired. Sold 12.4.1950; BU Ward, Barrow.

SCYLLA Frigate, 'Leander' class, Y160, 2,650 tons, 372 (oa) × 43ft, 2–4·5in, Seacat, helo (later Exocet, Seawolf). Devonport DY 8.8.1968. PO 14.12.1993' projected artificial reef 2003 White-sand Bay.

SCYTHE Destroyer, 'S' class. John Brown 25.5.1918. Sold 28.11.1931 Cashmore, Newport.

SCYTHIAN Submarine, 'S' class. Scotts 14.4.1944. Arr. 8.8.1960 Charlestown for BU.

SEA CLIFF Frigate (RCN), 'River' class. Davie SB 8.7.1944. Sold 3.3.1946 Chilean Navy = COVA-DONGA. BU 1968.

SEA CLIFF *See also GUELPH 1943.*

SEA DEVIL Submarine, 'S' class. Scotts 30.1.1945. Arr. Newhaven 2.1966 for BU.

SEA GLADIATOR Aircraft transport, 990 tons, 160 × 30ft. Pollock, Faversham, cancelled, launched 24.9.1949 as *Goldlynx.*

SEA HURRICANE Aircraft transport, 990 tons, 160 × 30ft. Pollock, Faversham, cancelled, launched 18.12.1948 as *Goldhind.*

SEA RIDER Flyboat 8, 350bm. Captured 1665. Sold 1668.

SEA ROBIN Submarine, 'S' class. Cammell Laird, cancelled 1945.

SEA ROVER Submarine, 'S' class. Scotts 8.2.1943. Sold 10.1949; BU Faslane from 6.1950.

SEA SNAKE Special Service Vessel (RAN), 80 tons. Savage 18.1.1945. Tx North Borneo 6.12.1945

SEABEAR Destroyer, 'S' class. John Brown 6.7.1918. Sold 5.2.1931 Ward, Grays.

SEABEAR (ex-ST THOMAS) Minesweeper, 'Algerine' class. Redfern 6.11.1943 (renamed 1943). Arr. 12.12.1958 Ward, Preston, for BU.

SEADOG (ex-P.216) Submarine, 'S' class. Cammell Laird 11.6.1942. Sold 24.12.1947; BU 8.1948 Troon.

SEAFIRE Destroyer, 'S' class. John Brown 10.8.1918. HO Ward 14.9.1936 part payment *Majestic* (CALEDONIA, q.v.); BU Inverkeithing.

SEAFLOWER Brig-sloop 16, 208bm, 72·5 × 26ft, 16–4pdr. Purch. 4.1782. Captured 28.9.1808 by French off Bencoolen.

SEAFLOWER Brig-sloop 16 listed 1809. Sold 1.9.1814.

SEAFLOWER Cutter 4, 116bm, 60 × 21·5ft. Portsmouth DY 20.5.1830. BU comp. 8.10.1866 Castle, Charlton.

SEAFLOWER Training brig 8, 454 tons, 8–6pdr.

Pembroke Dock 25.2.1873. Workshop 1.1904. Sold 7.4.1908 Castle, Charlton.

SEAFORD 6th Rate 24, 294bm, 98·5 × 26ft. Herring, Bursledon, 1695; purch. 27.12.1695. Captured 5.5.1697 by French off Scilly Is.

SEAFORD 6th Rate 24, 248bm, 93 × 24·5ft. Portsmouth DY 1697. Rebuilt Deptford 1724 as 375bm. BU 6.1740 Woolwich.

SEAFORD 6th Rate 24, 432bm, 106 × 30·5ft. Stowe & Bartlett, Shoreham, 6.4.1741. BU comp. 7.8.1754 Woolwich.

SEAFORD 6th Rate 22, 109 × 30·5ft. Deptford DY 3.9.1754. Sold 16.1.1784.

SEAFORD Minesweeper, TE 'Bangor' class. Taikoo DY, Hong Kong, LD 12.7.1941, = WAGLAN 9.1941; lost on stocks 12.1941. Launched 20.3.1943 as Japanese minesweeper *102.* Ret. RN 1947; BU 1948 Uraga.

SEAFORD PRIZE 6th Rate 12, 86bm, 62·5 × 18ft. French, captured 4.1708 by SEAFORD. Sold 13.10.1712.

SEAFORTH Gun-brig 14, 215bm. Purch. 1805. Capsized 2.1806 squall West Indies.

SEAFORTH *The French privateer brig DAME ERNOUF, captured 8.2.1805 by CURIEUX in the West Indies, was also reported as being renamed SEAFORTH in 1806.*

SEAFOX Aircraft transport, 990 tons, 160 × 30ft. Pollock, Faversham, 16.5.1946. Store carrier 10.1953. Sold 12.1958 = *Roubahe Darya.*

SEAGULL Brig-sloop 16 (fir-built), 318bm, 105 × 28ft. Wells, Rotherhithe, 7.1795. Foundered 12.1804.

SEAGULL Brig-sloop 16, 285bm(?), 93 × 26·5ft. King, Dover, 1.7.1806. Captured 19.6.1808 by Danes, burnt.

SEAGULL (ex-SYLPHE) Brig-sloop 16, 343bm, 98·5 × 2 8·5ft, 12–24pdr carr., 4–9pdr. French, captured 11.8.1808 by COMET off Martinique. Sold 21.7.1814.

SEAGULL Cutter. 1814. In service 1825. Revenue Service? = ADDER 16.4.1817.

SEAGULL Schooner 6, 279bm, 95 × 26ft. Chatham DY 21.11.1831. BU 10.1852.

SEAGULL Wood screw gunboat, 'Albacore' class. Pitcher, Northfleet, 4.8.1855. Sold 7.10.1864 Marshall, Plymouth.

SEAGULL Wood screw gunvessel, 663bm, 805 tons, 170 × 29ft, 1–7in, 2–40pdr. Devonport DY 6.3.1868. Sold 11.1887.

SEAGULL Torpedo gunboat, 735 tons, 230 × 27ft, 2–4·7in, 4–3pdr, 3–TT. Chatham DY 31.5.1889. Minesweeper 1909. Sunk 30.9.1918 collision Firth of Clyde.

SEAGULL Minesweeper, 815 tons, 230 × 33·5ft, 2—4in. Devonport DY 28.10.1937. Survey ship 1945. Arr. 5.1956 Demmelweek & Redding, Plymouth, for BU.

SEAGULL (ex-5001) Long-range recovery and support craft, 159 tons, 120·3 (oa) × 23·5ft. Fairmile, Berwick-upon-Tweed, comp. 1970. RAF vessel, tx 1991. Tx RMAS 1.2.1991.

SEAHAM Minesweeper, TE 'Bangor' class. Lobnitz 16.6.1941 Sold 11.8.1947 Rangoon Port Commissioners = *Chinthe.*

SEAHORSE Ship. Captured 1626. Last mentioned 1635.

SEAHORSE Hoy. Captured 1654. Sold 1655.

SEAHORSE Firevessel 10, 70bm 57 × 17ft. Purch. 4.1694 from Dutch. Became water boat. Sunk 12.10.1698 foundation Sheerness.

SEAHORSE 6th Rate 24, 256bm, 94 × 24·5ft. Hayden, Limehouse, 27.9.1694. Wrecked 14.3.1704 coast of Jamaica.

SEAHORSE 6th Rate 14, 161bm, 76 × 22·5ft. Yeames, Limehouse, 4.11.1709. Wrecked 26.12.1711 nr Dartmouth.

SEAHORSE 6th Rate 20, 282bm, 94 × 26ft. Portsmouth DY 13.2.1712. Rebuilt Stacey, Deptford, 1727 as 374bm. Sold 28.7.1748.

SEAHORSE 6th Rate 24, 519bm, 114 × 32ft. Barnard, Harwich, 13.9.1748. Sold 30.12.1784.

SEAHORSE 5th Rate 38, 998bm, 146 × 39·5ft. Stalkart, Rotherhithe, 11.6.1794. BU 7.1819.

SEAHORSE 5th Rate 46, 1,215bm, 159× 42ft. Pembroke Dock 21.7.1830. Screw frigate 7.1847; screw mortar vessel, 1,258bm, 3.1856; = LAVINIA (coal hulk) 5.5.1870. Sold 1902.

SEAHORSE Submarine, 640 tons, 187 × 23·5ft, 1—3in, 6—TT. Chatham DY 15.11.1932. Sunk 7.1.1940 by German minesweeper in Heligoland Bight.

SEAL Destroyer, 385 tons, 218 × 20ft, 1—12pdr, 5—6pdr, 2—TT. Laird 6.3.1897. Sold 17.3.1921 Ward, Rainham.

SEAL Minelaying submarine, 1,520 tons, 271·5 × 25·5ft, 1—4in, 6—TT, 50 mines. Chatham DY 27.9.1938. Captured in sinking condition 2.5.1940 by Germans in Kattegat; scuttled 3.5.1945; later raised, BU.

SEAL (ex-5000) Long-range recovery and support craft, 159 tons, 120·3 (oa) × 23·5ft. Brooke Marine, comp. 8.1967. RAF vessel, tx 1991. Tx RMAS 1.2.1991. Sold 10.2002.

SEALARK Cutter 4, 80bm, 56 × 18ft, 4—12pdr carr. Wheaton, Brixham, 1.8.1806. Wrecked 18.6.1809 East Coast.

SEALARK (ex-FLY) Schooner 10, 178bm, 79 × 22·5ft, 10—12pdr carr. American, captured 29.12.1811. Sold 13.1.1820.

SEALARK Brig-sloop 10, 'Cherokee' class, 231bm. Plymouth DY, LD 11.1830, cancelled 2.1831.

SEALARK Brig 8, 319bm, 90 × 29·5ft. Portsmouth DY 27.7.1843. Training brig 1875, 311bm. Sold 11.11.1898.

SEALARK *See also INVESTIGATOR 1903.*

SEALION Submarine, 670 tons, 193 × 24ft, 1—3in, 6—TT. Cammell Laird 16.3.1934. Scuttled 3.3.1945 asdic target off I. of Arran.

SEALION Submarine, 'Porpoise' class, Cammell Laird 31.12.1959. PO 18.12.1987; sold 9.7.1988 Charity Action for display; resold, arr. Blyth 28.3.1990 for BU.

SEAMEW Coastguard vessel, 330bm, 376 tons, 143 × 22ft, 1—32pdr. Inland Revenue vessel, tx 1857. Sold 3.4.1906 T. Trattles.

SEAMEW River gunboat, 262 tons, 160 × 27ft, 2—3in. Yarrow 16.1.1928. Sold 27.8.1947 Basra.

SEANYMPH Cutter 8. In service 1782.

SEANYMPH (ex-P.223) Submarine, 'S' class. Cammell Laird 29.7.1942. Arr. 6.1948 Troon for BU.

SEARCHER Brigantine built 1562. Sold 1564.

SEARCHER Destroyer, 'S' class. John Brown 11.9.1918. Sold 25.3.1938 Ward, Barrow.

SEARCHER Escort carrier, 11,420 tons, 468·5 × 69·5ft, 2—4in, 16—40mm, 24 aircraft. Seattle Tacoma 20.7.1942 on Lend-Lease. Ret. USN 29.11.1945.

SEARCHER *See also LST.3508 1944.*

SEASCOUT Submarine, 'S' class. Cammell Laird 24.3.1944. Arr. 14.12.1965 Swansea for BU Briton Ferry.

SEAWOLF Destroyer, 'S' class. John Brown 2.11.1918. Sold 23.2.1931 Cashmore, Newport.

SEAWOLF Submarine, 670 tons, 193 × 24ft, 1—3in, 6—TT. Scotts 28.11.1935. Sold 11.1945 Marine Industries, Montreal.

SECURITY Prison ship, 646bm. Purch. 1778. Sold 10.4.1783 Chatham.

SECURITY Storeship, 142bm, 66 × 22·5ft. Plymouth DY 10.3.1785. Probably dockyard service. Listed until 1852.

SECURITY Prison ship, 250bm, 814 × 25ft. Purch. 1794 Halifax, NS (where used). Sold per AO 28.6.1802.

SEDGEFLY River gunboat, 'Fly' class. Yarrow 9.1916. For disposal 1919 Basra.

SEDGEMOOR 4th Rate 50, 633bm, 123 × 34·5ft. Chatham DY 1687. Wrecked 2.1.1689 St Margaret's Bay.

SEFTON Minesweeping sloop, '24' class. Barclay Curle 6.7.1918. Sold 8.1922.

SEFTON Coastal minesweeper, 'Ton' class. White's, Southampton 15.9.1954. Sold C. H. Rugg, London 2.7.1968 for BU Belgium.

SEFTON *See also EMPIRE GAUNTLET 1943.*

SEINE 5th Rate 38, 1,146bm, 156·5 × 40·5ft, 8–32pdr carr., 28–18pdr, 12–9pdr. French, captured 30.6.1798 by JASON and PIQUE in English Channel. Wrecked 5.6.1803 off Texel.

SEINE (ex-CERES) 5th Rate 38, 1,074bm, 152 × 40ft. French, captured 6.1.1814 by NIGER and TAGUS off Cape Verde Is. BU 5.1823.

SEINE *See also AMBUSCADE 1798.*

SELBY 22-gun ship, 305bm. Taylor, Wapping, 1654. = EAGLE 1660; fireship 1674. Sunk 1694 foundation Sheerness.

SELBY Storeship. Purch. 4.1781. Sold 2.12.1783.

SELBY Armed ship 22, 354bm, 100 × 28ft. Purch. 1798. Sold 12.1801.

SELENE Submarine, 'S' class. Cammell Laird 24.4.1944. Arr. 6.6.1961 King, Gateshead, for BU.

SELKIRK Minesweeper, Later 'Hunt' class. Murdoch & Murray 2.12.1918. Sold Dohmen & Habets 17.5.1947; BU Liége.

SELSEY BILL Repair ship, 8,580 tons, 425 × 57ft. Burrard, Vancouver, 11.7.1945, cancelled 30.8.1945, comp. as *Waitemata*.

SEMIRAMIS 5th Rate 36, 944bm, 145 × 38·5ft. Deptford DY 25.7.1808. Reduced to 24 guns 1827. BU 11.1844.

SEMIRAMIS Paddle sloop (Indian). R. Thames 1837. Foundered 13.2.1839; raised, = CHARGER 1841; coal hulk Aden.

SEMIRAMIS Iron paddle frigate (Indian), 1,143bm, 189 × 34ft. Bombay DY 26.2.1842. Hulked 1863.

SENATOR Destroyer, 'S' class. Denny 2.4.1918. HO Ward 7.9.1936 part payment *Majestic* (CALEDONIA, q.v.); BU Jarrow.

SENECA Sloop 18 (Canadian lakes). Oswegatchie 1771. Listed 1788.

SENEGAL Sloop 14, 292bm, 97 × 26ft. Bird, Rotherhithe, 24.12.1760.

SENEGAL *See also RACEHORSE 1777.*

SENESCHAL Submarine, 'S' class. Scotts 23.4.1945. Arr. 23.8.1960 Clayton & Davie, Dunston, for BU.

SENNEN (ex-CHAMPLAIN) Cutter, 1,546 tons, 256 (oa) × 42ft, 1–4in, 1–3in. USCG, cd RN 12.5.1941 on Lend-Lease. Ret. USCG 3.1946.

SENSIBLE 5th Rate 36, 946bm. French, captured 27.6.1798 by SEAHORSE in Mediterranean. Wrecked 2.3.1802 nr Trincomalee.

SENTINEL (ex-*Friendship*) Gun-brig 12, 194bm, 81 × 24ft, 10–18pdr carr., 2–9pdr. Purch. 7.1804. Wrecked 10.10.1812 Rugen I., Baltic.

SENTINEL (ex-INCHKEITH) Scout cruiser, 2,895 tons, 360 × 40ft, 10–12pdr, 8–3pdr. Vickers 19.4.1904 (renamed 1903). Sold 18.1.1923 Young; arr. Sunderland 20.6.1923 after stranding.

SENTINEL Submarine, 'S' class. Scotts 27.7.1945. Sold 28.2.1962 Lynch, Rochester; BU Gillingham.

SENTINEL (ex-*Seaforth Warrior*, ex-*Edda Sun*) Patrol vessel, 1,710 tons (934grt), 203·6 (oa) × 42·6ft. Huumwerft, Husum, 1975. Purch. 2.1983; cd RN 14.1.1984. PO 30.4.1992; sold EDT Transport, Cyprus, 1.1993.

SENTINEL *See also SCORPION 1942.*

SEPOY Wood screw gunvessel, 483bm, 150 × 26ft. Portsmouth DY, ordered 26.3.1846, cancelled 22.5.1849.

SEPOY Wood screw gunboat, 'Albacore' class. Smith, North Shields, 13.2.1856. BU 4.1868.

SEPOY Destroyer, 'S' class. Denny 22.5.1918. Sold 2.7.1932 Cashmore, Newport.

SEPOY Minesweeper, 'Catherine' class. Gulf SB, Madisonville, 17.1.1943 for RN; retained USN = DEXTROUS.

SERAPH Destroyer, 'S' class. Denny 8.7.1918. Sold 4.5.1934 Ward, Pembroke Dock.

SERAPH (ex-P.219) Submarine, 'S' class. Vickers Armstrong, Barrow, 25.10.1941. Arr. 20.12.1965 Ward, Briton Ferry, for BU.

SERAPIS 5th Rate 44, 886bm, 140 × 38ft. Randall, Rotherhithe, 4.3.1779. Captured 23.9.1779 by American privateer BON HOMME RICHARD off Flamborough Head; tx French Navy.

SERAPIS 5th Rate 44, 886bm, 140 × 38ft. Hillhouse, Bristol, 7.11.1782. Storeship 20 in 1.1795; floating battery 7.1801; storeship 1803. Sold 17.7.1826 in Jamaica.

SERAPIS Iron screw troopship, 4,173bm, 6,211 tons, 360 × 49ft, 3–4pdr. Thames SB Co., Blackwall, 2.9.1866. Sold 23.11.1894.

SERAPIS Destroyer, 'S' class. Denny 17.9.1918. Sold 25.1.1934 Rees, Llanelly.

SERAPIS Destroyer, 1,710 tons, 362·8 (oa) × 35·8ft, 4–4·7in, 2–40mm, 8–TT. Scotts 25.3.1943. Tx Dutch Navy 10.1943 = PIET HEIN; arr. Ghent 30.5.1962 for BU.

SERENE Destroyer, 'S' class. Denny 30.11.1918. HO Ward 14.9.1936 part payment *Majestic* (CALEDONIA, q.v.); BU Inverkeithing.

SERENE (ex-LEASIDE) Minesweeper, 'Algerine' class. Redfern 18.10.1943 (renamed 1943). Arr. 8.3.1959 Rees, LLanelly, for BU.

SERINGAPATAM 5th Rate 46, 1,152bm, 157·5 × 40·5ft. Bombay DY 5.9.1819. Receiving ship 7.1847; coal hulk 1852. BU 6.1873 The Cape.

SERPENT 60-ton vessel. Captured 1562. Last mentioned 1563.

SERPENT Bomb vessel 12, 260bm, 86 × 26·5ft, 12—6pdr. Chatham DY 1693. Wrecked 12.2.1694 nr Gibraltar.

SERPENT Bomb vessel 4, 140bm, 70 × 23ft. Chatham DY 1695. Captured 15.10.1703 by French privateer in Atlantic.

SERPENT Bomb vessel 12, 275bm, 93 × 26ft. Snelgrove, Limehouse, 15.3.1742. Wrecked 1.9.1748.

SERPENT Bomb vessel 12. Reported built at Sandgate 1771. *Not traced.*

SERPENT Sloop 16, 322bm, 98 × 27ft. Jacobs, Sandgate, LD 2.1783, cancelled 10.1783. *Builder failed.*

SERPENT Sloop 16, 321bm, 100 × 27ft. Plymouth DY 3.12.1789. Foundered 9.1806 West Indies.

SERPENT Gunvessel 4, 57bm, 65 × 14ft. Dutch hoy, purch. 4.1794. 'Supposed broken up in 1796.'

SERPENT Sloop 18, 423bm, 109 × 29·5ft. Sheerness DY, LD 1810, cancelled 8.9.1810.

SERPENT Brig-sloop 16, 434bm, 101·5 × 32ft, 14—32pdr, 2—18pdr. Fletcher, Limehouse, 14.7.1832. Target 12.1857. BU 7.1861 Portsmouth.

SERPENT Wood screw gunvessel, 695bm, 877 tons, 185 × 28·5ft, 2—68pdr, 2—32pdr. Mare, Blackwall, 23.6.1860. Sold 1875 Castle, Charlton.

SERPENT Torpedo cruiser, 1,770 tons, 225 × 36ft, 6—6in, 8—3pdr, 5—TT. Devonport DY 10.3.1887. Wrecked 10.11.1890 nr Corcubion Bay, northern Spain.

SESAME Destroyer, 'S' class. Denny 30.12.1918. Sold 4.5.1934. Cashmore, Newport.

SESOSTRIS Paddle sloop (Indian), 876bm. R. Thames 1839 or 1840. Transferred 1853 Bengal Govt.

SETTER Destroyer, 'R' class. White 18.8.1916. Sunk 17.5.1917 collision SYLPH off Harwich.

SEVEN SISTERS Gunvessel 4. Hoy, purch. 1794. Sold 18.8.1800.

SEVEN STARS 60-ton vessel. Listed 1549—54.

SEVEN STARS Galley 5, 140bm. Baker, Chatham, 1586. Listed until 1603.

SEVEN STARS 14-gun ship, 144bm. Listed 1615—24.

SEVENOAKS (ex-ZEVENWOLDEN) 4th Rate 52, 684bm. Dutch, captured 1665. Recaptured 1666 by Dutch.

SEVERN 4th Rate 48, 683bm, 131 × 34·5ft. Johnson, Blackwall, 1695. Rebuilt Plymouth 1739 as 853bm. Captured 19.10.1746 by French TERRIBLE; recaptured 14.10.1747, BU.

SEVERN 4th Rate 50, 1,061bm, 144 × 41ft. Barnard, Harwich, 10.7.1747. Sold 2.1.1759.

SEVERN 5th Rate 44, 904bm, 140 × 38·5ft. Hillhouse, Bristol, 29.4.1786. Wrecked 21.12.1804 Channel Is.

SEVERN 4th Rate 50 (pitch pine-built), 1,240bm, 159 × 42ft, 20—32pdr carr., 28—24pdr, 2—9pdr. Wigram & Green, Blackwall, 14.6.1813. Sold 20.7.1825 J. Ledger.

SEVERN 5th Rate 46, 1,215bm, 159 × 42ft. Pembroke Dock, ordered 9.6.1825, cancelled 7.2.1831.

SEVERN 4th Rate 50, 1,986bm, 180 × 50ft. Chatham DY 24.1.1856; undocked 8.2.1860 as screw frigate, 2,767bm. BU 1876.

SEVERN 2nd class cruiser, 4,050 tons, 300 × 46ft, 2—8in, 10—6in. Chatham DY 29.9.1885. Sold 4.4.1905 G. Garnham.

SEVERN (ex-SOLIMOES) River monitor, 1,260 tons, 265 × 49ft, 2—6in, 2—4·7in howitzers. Vickers 19.8.1913; Brazilian, purch. 8.8.1914. Sold 9.5.1921 Ward, Preston; arr. 23.3.1923 for BU.

SEVERN Submarine, 1,850 tons, 325 × 28ft, 1—4in, 8—TT. Vickers Armstrong, Barrow, 16.1.1934. Sold 1946 T. Hassanally, Bombay.

SEVERN Offshore patrol vessel, 1,677 tons, 261·7 (oa) × 44·6ft, 1—20mm, 2—MG. Vosper-Thornycroft 4.12.2002.

SEVERN *See ALSO TAGUS 1813.*

SEYCHELLES (ex-PEARD) Frigate, 'Colony' class. Walsh Kaiser 30.10.1943 on Lend-Lease (renamed 1943). Ret. USN 6.1946.

SEYMOUR Destroyer leader, 1,673 tons, 315 × 32ft, 4—4in, 4—TT. Cammell Laird 31.8.1916. Sold 7.1.1930 Cashmore, Newport.

SEYMOUR Frigate, TE 'Captain' class. Bethlehem, Hingham, 1.11.1943 on Lend-Lease. Nominally ret. USN 1.1946; BU Ward, Barrow.

SHACKLETON *See SHARPSHOOTER 1936.*

SHAH (ex-BLONDE) Armoured frigate, 4,210bm, 6,250 tons, 334 × 52ft, 2—9in, 16—7in, 8—64pdr. Portsmouth DY 9.1873 (renamed 1873). = C.470 (coal hulk) 12.1904. Sold 19.9.1919 W. B. Smith; wrecked 1926 Bermuda.

SHAH (ex-*Jamaica*) Escort carrier, 11,420 tons, 468·5 × 69·5ft, 2—4in, 16—40mm, 24 aircraft. Seattle Tacoma 21.4.1943 on Lend-Lease. Ret. USN 6.12.1945.

SHAKESPEARE Destroyer leader, 1,750 tons, 329 (oa) × 32ft, 5—4·7in, 1—3in, 6—TT. Thornycroft 7.7.1917. HO Ward 2.9.1936 part payment *Majestic* (CALEDONIA, q.v.); BU Jarrow.

SHAKESPEARE (ex-P.221) Submarine, 'S' class. Vickers Armstrong, Barrow, 8.12.1941. Sold 14.7.1946 Ward, Briton Ferry.

SHALFORD Seaward defence boat, 'Ford' class.

Yarrow 21.8.1952. Sold 8.9.1967 Singapore for BU.

SHALIMAR Submarine, 'S' class. Chatham DY 22.4.1943. Arr. 7.1950 Troon for BU.

SHAMROCK Schooner 8, 150bm, 79 × 22ft. Bermuda 15.9.1808. Wrecked 25.2.1811 Cape Santa Maria.

SHAMROCK Gun-brig 12, 180bm, 84 × 22ft. Larking, Lynn, 8.8.1812. Harbour service 11.1831; = WV.18 (Coastguard watchvessel) 25.5.1863. Sold 24.1.1867.

SHAMROCK Wood screw gunboat, 'Albacore' class. Pitcher, Northfleet, 13.3.1856. Sold 4.1867 Marshall, Plymouth.

SHAMROCK Destroyer, 'S' class. Doxford 26.8.1918. HO Ward 23.11.1936 part payment *Majestic* (CALEDONIA, q.v.); BU Milford Haven.

SHANNON 6th Rate 28, 587bm, 118·5 × 33·5ft. Deptford DY 13.8.1757. BU comp. 30.12.1765 Portsmouth.

SHANNON 5th Rate 32 (fir-built), 796bm, 135 × 36·5ft. Deptford DY 9.2.1796. Sold 5.1802.

SHANNON (ex-PALLAS) 5th Rate 36, 881bm. Brindley, Frindsbury, 2.9.1803 (renamed 11.1802). Ran ashore in gale 10.12.1803 nr La Hogue, burnt to avoid capture.

SHANNON 5th Rate 38, 1,066bm, 150 × 40ft. Brindley, Frindsbury, 5.5.1806. Receiving ship 1832; = ST LAWRENCE 11.3.1844. BU comp. 12.11.1859 Chatham.

SHANNON Schooner 10 (Canadian lakes). Listed 1814.

SHANNON Schooner 2 (Indian), 90bm. Listed 1832.

SHANNON Wood screw frigate, 2,667bm, 235 × 50ft, 30—8in, 1—68pdr, 20—32pdr. Portsmouth DY 24.11.1855. Sold 31.5.1871 Castle for BU.

SHANNON Iron screw frigate, 5,390 tons, 260 × 54ft, 2—10in, 7—9in, 6—20pdr. Pembroke Dock 11.12.1875. Sold 15.12.1899 King, Garston.

SHANNON Armoured cruiser, 14,600 tons, 490 × 75·5ft, 4—9·2in, 10—7·5in, 16—12pdr. Chatham DY 20.9.1906. Sold 12.12.1922 McLellan, Bo'ness.

SHARK Sloop 14, 201bm, 80 × 24·5ft. Portsmouth DY 7.9.1732. Sold 2.12.1755.

SHARK Sloop 16, 313bm, 96 × 27ft. Purch. on stocks 11.1775; Randall, Rotherhithe 9.3.1776. = SALAMANDER (fireship) 23.7.1778. Sold 14.8.1783.

SHARK Sloop 16, 304bm, 97 × 27ft. Walton, Hull, 25.11.1779. Receiving ship Jamaica by 1805. Foundered 13.1.1818.

SHARK 6th Rate 28 purch. 1780. Foundered 30.11.1780 storm North America.

SHARK Gunvessel 4, 63bm, 64·5 × 14·5ft. Dutch hoy, purch. 4.1794. HO French 11.12.1795 by mutinous crew at La Hogue.

SHARK Destroyer, 325 tons, 205 × 19·5ft, 1—12pdr, 5—6pdr, 2—TT. Thompson 22.9.1894. Sold 11.7.1911 Ward, Preston.

SHARK Destroyer, 935 tons, 267 × 27ft, 3—4in, 2—TT. Swan Hunter 30.7.1912. Sunk 31.5.1916 Battle of Jutland.

SHARK Destroyer, 'S' class. Swan Hunter 9.14.1918. Sold 5.2.1931 Ward, Inverkeithing.

SHARK Submarine, 670 tons, 193 × 24ft, 1—3in, 6—TT. Chatham DY 31.5.1934. Sunk 6.7.1940 by German minesweepers off Skudesnes, Norway.

SHARK Destroyer, 1,710 tons, 362·8 (oa) × 35·7ft, 4—4·7in, 2—40mm. 8—TT. Scotts 1.6.1943. Lent RNorN 8.3.1944 = SVENNER. Sunk 6.6.1944 by German MTBs off Le Havre.

SHARKE Brigantine 8, 58bm, 58 × 15ft. Deptford 20.4.1691. Sold 25.11.1698 L. Towne.

SHARKE Sloop 14, 66bm. Deptford 1699. Captured 30.3.1703 by French.

SHARKE Sloop 14, 114bm, 65 × 20·5ft. Deptford DY 20.4.1711. Rebuilt Deptford 1722 as 124bm. Sold 3.8.1732.

SHARPSHOOTER Gun-brig 12, 178bm, 80 × 22·5ft. Warren, Brightlingsea, 2.2.1805. Sold 17.5.1816.

SHARPSHOOTER Iron screw gunvessel, 503bm, 150·5 × 27ft. Ditchburn & Mare, Blackwall, 25.7.1846. Sold 2.12.1869.

SHARPSHOOTER Torpedo gunboat, 735 tons, 230 × 27ft, 2—4·7in, 4—3pdr, 3—TT. Devonport DY 30.11.1888. = NORTHAMPTON (harbour service) 1912. Sold 27.3.1922; BU Beard, Upnor.

SHARPSHOOTER Destroyer, 'R' class. Beardmore 27.2.1917. Sold 29.4.1927 Ward, Briton Ferry.

SHARPSHOOTER Minesweeper, 835 tons, 230 × 33·5ft, 2—4in. Devonport DY 10.12.1936. = SHACKLETON (survey vessel) 6.1953. Arr. Troon 20.11.1965 for BU.

SHAVINGTON Coastal minesweeper, 'Ton' class. White, Southampton, 25.4.1955. Arr. Cairnryan 5.4.1987 for BU.

SHAWINIGAN Corvette (RCN), 'Flower' class. G. T. Davie 16.5.1941. Sunk 25.11.1944 by U.1228 in Cabot Strait.

SHAWINIGAN MCDV (RCN), 'Kingston' class, 962 tons, 181·4 (oa) × 37·1ft, 1—40mm, Halifax SY 1.11.1996.

SHEARWATER Brig-sloop 10, 'Cherokee' class, 237bm. Rowe, Newcastle, 21.11.1808. Sold 11.1832 Beaton for BU.

SHEARWATER (ex-*Dolphin*) Wood paddle packet, 343bm, 137 × 23ft. GPO vessel, tx 1837. Sold 2.7.1857 Malta.

SHEARWATER Wood screw sloop, 669bm. 913 tons, 160 × 30ft, 4—64pdr. Pembroke Dock 17.10.1861. BU comp. 5.2.1877 Sheerness

SHEARWATER Sloop, 980 tons, 180 × 33ft, 6—4in. Sheerness DY 10.2.1900. Tx RCN 1915 depot ship. Sold 5.1922 Western Shipping Co., Canada.

SHEARWATER Patrol vessel, 580 tons, 234 × 25·5ft, 1—4in. White 18.4.1939. Sold 21.4.1947; BU Stockton Ship & Salvage Co.

SHEDIAC Corvette (RCN), 'Flower' class. Davie SB 29.4.1941. Sold 1951 = *Jooske W. Vinke*. BU Spain 1965.

SHEEAN Submarine (RAN), 'Collins' class, 3,051/ 3,353 tons, 255·2 (oa) × 25·6ft, 6—TT, Australian Submarine Corp., Adelaide, 3.5.1999.

SHEERNESS Smack 2, 18bm. Chatham 1673. Sunk 24.4.1695 foundation Sheerness.

SHEERNESS 5th Rate 32, 359bm, 106 × 27·5ft. Sheerness DY 1691. Rebuilt Deptford 1731 as 6th Rate 428bm. Sold 5.6.1744.

SHEERNESS 6th Rate 24, 506bm, 112 × 32ft. Buxton, Rotherhithe, 8.10.1743. Sold 26.7.1768.

SHEERNESS Store lighter 109bm. Bennett, Faversham, 1759. BU 1811.

SHEERNESS 5th Rate 44, 906bm, 141 × 38·5ft. Adams, Buckler's Hard, 16.7.1787. Wrecked 7.1.1805 nr Trincomalee.

SHEERNESS Tender 4, 148bm, 4—3pdr. Wilson, Sandgate, 1788, purch. on stocks 6.8.1788. BU 5.1811.

SHEERNESS Tender 10 purch. 1791. Sold 1810?

SHEFFIELD Cruiser, 9,100 tons, 591·5 (oa) × 61·8ft, 12—6in, 8—4in. Vickers Armstrong, Tyne, 23.77.1936. Arr. 9.1967 Faslane for BU.

SHEFFIELD Destroyer, Type 42 Batch 1, 3,150 tons. Vickers 10.6.1971. Lost 10.5.1982 Falklands operations.

SHEFFIELD Frigate, 4,100 tons. 480·5 (oa) × 48·4ft, Exocet, Seawolf, 6—TT, helo. Swan Hunter 26.3.86. Formally PO 14.11.2002; sold Chile = ALMIRANTE WILLIAMS 10.2003.

SHELBURNE (ex-RACER) Schooner 14, 221bm, 94 × 24ft. American privateer, captured 16.3.1813. Sold 10.1817.

SHELDRAKE Brig-sloop 16, 285bm, 93 × 26·5ft. Richards, Hythe, 20.3.1806. Sold Chilean Navy = ALMIRANTE WILLIAMS 10.2003.

SHELDRAKE Brig-sloop 10, 'Cherokee' class, 228bm. Pembroke Dock 19.5.1825. Sold 1855 per order dated 3.1853.

SHELDRAKE Wood screw gunboat, 'Albacore' class. Pitcher, Northfleet, 1.9.1855. Sold 30.6.1865 Montevideo.

SHELDRAKE Composite screw gunboat, 455 tons, 125 × 23·5ft, 2—64pdr, 2—20pdr. Napier, Glasgow, 3. 7.1875. = DRAKE (drillship) 13.3.1888; = WV.29 in 1893; = DRAKE 1906. Sold 3.4.1906 Meyer Isaacs.

SHELDRAKE Torpedo gunboat, 735 tons, 230 × 27ft, 2—4·7in, 4—3pdr, 3—TT. Chatham DY 30.3.1889. Sold 9.7.1907 S. Bkg Co., London.

SHELDRAKE Destroyer, 748 tons, 240 × 25ft, 2—4in, 2—12pdr, 2—TT. Denny 18.1.1911. Sold 9.5.1921 Ward, Grays.

SHELDRAKE Patrol vessel, 530 tons, 234 × 26·5ft, 1—4in. Thornycroft 28.1.1937. Sold 12.8.1946 = *Tuck Loon*.

SHEPPARTON Minesweeper (RAN), 'Bathurst' class. Williamstown DY 15.8.1941. BU 1958 Japan.

SHEPPARTON Survey vessel (RAN), 320 tons (full load), 118·9 (oa) × 45·3ft. Elgo Engineering, Port Adelaide. Cd 24.1.1990.

SHERATON Coastal minesweeper, 'Ton' class. White, Southampton, 20.7.1955. Sold Pounds 12.1997.

SHERBORNE Cutter 10, 86bm, 35 × 19ft. Woolwich DY 3.12.1763. Sold 1.7.1784.

SHERBORNE (ex-TARBERT) Minesweeper, Later 'Hunt' class. Simons 27.6.1918 (renamed 1918). Sold 19.5.1928 Ward, Inverkeithing.

SHERBORNE CASTLE *See PETROLIA 1944.*

SHERBROOKE Corvette (RCN), 'Flower' class. Marine Industries 25.10.1940. BU 5.1947 Steel Co. of Canada.

SHERWOOD (ex-RODGERS) Destroyer, 1,190 tons, 311 × 31ft, 3—4in, 1—3in, 6—TT. USN, cd RN 23.10.1940. Air target 8.1942; beached 10.1943 as rocket target; listed 'destroyed' 1946.

SHETLAND Patrol vessel, 925 tons, 195·3 (oa) × 34·2ft. Hall Russell 22.11.1976. PO 30.6.2002; tx Bangladeshi Navy 31.7.2002.

SHIEL Frigate, 'River' class. Vickers, Montreal, 26.5.1943 on Lend-Lease. Ret. USN 4.3.1946.

SHIFNAL Minesweeper, Later 'Hunt' class. Lobnitz, cancelled 1918.

SHIKARI Destroyer, 'S' class. Doxford 14.7.1919; comp. Chatham 3.1924. Arr. 4.11.1945 Cashmore, Newport, for BU.

SHINCLIFE Paddle minesweeper, 'Ascot' class, 820 tons. Dundee SB 29.1.1918. Sold 3.1922 Ward, Inverkeithing.

SHIPHAM Inshore minesweeper, 'Ham' class. Brooke Marine 14.7.1955. Sold 1986 Pounds.

SHIPPIGAN Minesweeper, TE 'Bangor' class. Dufferin, Toronto, 27.9.1941. Sold 1.1.1948; BU 6.1949 Charlestown.

SHIPTON Frigate (RCN), 'River' class. Quebec, cancelled 12.1943.

SHIRLEY Galley 6 purch. 1745. Condemned 1747.

SHIRLEY Paddle minesweeper, 'Ascot'class, 820 tons. Dunlop Bremner 28.9.1917. Sold 8.4.1919 James Dredging Co.

SHISH Smack/yacht built 1670. *Fate unknown.*

SHOALHAVEN Frigate (RAN), 'River' class. Walker, Maryborough, 14.12.1944. Arr. 8.1962 Japan for BU.

SHOALWATER Inshore minesweeper (RAN), 178 tons, 101·7 (oa) × 29·5ft, 2—12·7mm. Carrington Slipways 20.6.1987.

SHOREHAM 5th Rate 32, 359bm, 103 × 28ft. Ellis, Shoreham, 6.1.1694. Rebuilt Woolwich 1720 as 20-gun 6th Rate, 379bm. Sold 5.6.1744.

SHOREHAM 6th Rate 24, 514bm, 113 × 32·5ft. Reed, Hull, 13.5.1744. Sold 4.4.1758.

SHOREHAM Sloop, 1,105 tons, 250 × 34ft, 2—4in. Chatham DY 22.11.1930. Sold 4.10.1946 = *Jorge Fel Joven.*

SHOREHAM Minehunter, 'Sandown' class. Vosper-Thornycroft 9.4.2001.

SHOREHAM *See also SALFORD 1919.*

SHOREHAM PRIZE Sloop 12, 73bm, 57 × 17ft. French (?), captured 26.8.1709. Sold 11.9.1712.

SHOREHAM PRIZE Sloop. Captured 1746. Lost 1747 Oporto.

SHOULTON Coastal minesweeper, 'Ton' class. Montrose DY 10.9.1954. Sold 2.2.1981; BU Blyth.

SHREWSBURY 2nd Rate 80, 1,257bm, 158 × 42·5ft. Portsmouth DY 6.2.1695. Rebuilt Deptford 1713 as 1,314bm. BU 2.1749 Portsmouth.

SHREWSBURY 3rd Rate 74, 1,594bm, 166 × 47ft. Wells, Deptford, 23.2.1758. Condemned 1783, scuttled off Jamaica.

SHREWSBURY Minesweeper, Later 'Hunt' class. Napier & Miller 12.2.1918. Sold 25.11.1927 Alloa, Charlestown.

SHREWSBURY CASTLE Corvette, 'Castle' class. Swan Hunter 16.8.1943. Lent RNorN = TUNSBERG CASTLE 17.4.1944. Sunk 12.12.1944 mine Kola Inlet.

SHRIKE Paddle minesweeper. Projected 1918, cancelled (not ordered).

SHRIMP *See X.52 1954.*

SHRIVENHAM Inshore minesweeper, 'Ham' class. Bolson, Poole. 28.3.1956. Sold 21.2.1969 Port of London Authority.

SHROPSHIRE Cruiser, 9,830 tons, 633 (oa) × 66ft, 8—8in, 8—4in. Beardmore 5.7.1928. Lent

RAN 1.1943. Arr. 20.1.1955 Arnott Young, Dalmuir, and 9.1955 Troon, for BU.

SIBYL 6th Rate 28, 599bm, 120·5 × 33·5ft. Adams, Buckler's Hard, 2.1.1779. = GARLAND 14.7.1795. Wrecked 16.7.1798 off Madagascar.

SIBYL (ex-P.217) Submarine, 'S' class. Cammell Laird 29.4.1942. Arr. 3.1948 Troon for BU.

SIBYL *See also CAVENDISH 1944.*

SIBYL *See also SYBILLE.*

SICKLE (ex-P.224) Submarine, 'S' class. Cammell Laird 27.8.1942. Sunk (probably mined) 6.1944 off Greece.

SIDLESHAM Inshore minesweeper, 'Ham' class. Harris, Appledore, 25.3.1955. Sold Pounds 16.7.1967; became club ship.

SIDMOUTH Minesweeper, TE 'Bangor' class. Robb 15.3.1941. Sold 18.1.1950; BU Charlestown.

SIDON Wood paddle frigate, 1,329bm, 211 × 37ft, 4—56pdr, 4—3pdr. Deptford DY 26.5.1846. Sold 15.7.1864 Castle & Beech.

SIDON Submarine, 'S' class. Cammell Laird 4.9.1944. Sunk 16.6.1955 accidental torpedo explosion Portland; raised 1955, sunk 6.1957 asdic target off Portland.

SIERRA LEONE *See PERIM 1943.*

SIKH Destroyer, 'S' class. Fairfield 7.5.1918. Sold 26.7.1927 Granton S. Bkg Co.

SIKH Destroyer, 1,870 tons, 377 (oa) × 36·5ft, 8—4in, 4—TT. Stephen 13.12.1937. Sunk 14.9.1942 shore batteries Tobruk.

SIKH *See also Indian TB.5 1889.*

SILENE Sloop, 'Anchusa' class. 13.3.1918. Sold 29.12.1921 Stanlee, Dover.

SILVERTON Destroyer, 'Hunt' class Type II. White 4.12.1940. Lent Polish Navy 5.1941–9.1946 = KRAKOWIAK. Arr. 3.1959 Ward, Grays, for BU.

SILVIO Minesweeping sloop, '24' class. Barclay Curle 20.4.1918. = MORESBY (RAN survey ship) 4.1925. Escort 1940. Sold 3.2.1947; BU Newcastle, NSW.

SILVIO *See also EMPIRE HALBERD 1943.*

SIMCOE Corvette (RCN), Modified 'Flower' class. Morton, Quebec, cancelled 12.1943.

SIMOOM Iron screw frigate, 1,980bm, 2,240 tons, 246 × 41·5ft, 2—6in, 4—56pdr, 14—32pdr. Napier, Govan, 24.5.1849. Troopship 1852. Sold 6.1887 Collings, Dartmouth.

SIMOOM Destroyer, 'R' class. John Brown 30.10.1916. Sunk 23.1.1917 torpedo German S.50 North Sea.

SIMOOM Destroyer, 'S' class. John Brown 26.1.1918. Sold 8.1.1931 Metal Industries, Charlestown.

SIMOOM (ex-P.225) Submarine, 'S' class. Cammell

Laird 12.10.1942. Sunk 19.11.1943 off Dardanelles, cause unknown.

SIMOOM *See also TERRIBLE 1845, MONARCH 1868.*

SINBAD Dockyard lighter, 109bm. Pembroke Dock 27.2.1834. Conv. mortar vessel 10.1854 Deptford; = MV.2 on 19.10.1855; = SINBAD (YC.3) 10.1856. BU comp. 10.11.1866 Woolwich.

SIND Minesweeper (RIN), 'Bathurst' class. Garden Reach, Calcutta, cancelled 3.1945.

SIND *See also GODAVERI 1943, BETONY 1943.*

SINGLETON Coastal minesweeper, 'Ton' class. Montrose SY 23.11.1955. = IBIS (RAN) 9.1962. Sold 1985 Sydney.

SIOUX Gate vessel 1940. = INDIAN 1944–45.

SIOUX *See also VIXEN 1943.*

SIR BEDIVERE Landing ship, 3,270 tons, 412·1 (oa) × 59·8ft (6,700 tons full load, 440·8ft oa, after 1994–98 refit), 4–20mm. Hawthorn Leslie 20.7.1966.

SIR BEVIS Minesweeping sloop, '24' class. Barclay Curle 11.5.1918. = IRWELL (drillship) 9.1923; = EAGLET 1926. BU 1971.

SIR CARADOC (ex-*Grey Master*) Landing ship, 5,980 tons, 407·4 (oa) × 52·5ft. Comp. 1.1973 Norway, chartered 17.3.1983. Sold 28.6.1988 by Nitre Shipping to Rogaland Kystferger, Norway = *Stamveien*.

SIR EDWARD HAWKE Schooner. Built 1768, purch. 1768 North America. Sold 11.8.1773.

SIR EDWARD HUGHES 5th Rate 38, 962bm. East Indiaman, presented 1806. = TORTOISE (storeship 22) 28.11.1807; coal hulk 11.1824; store hulk 8.1841. Ordered for BU 18.10.1859 Ascension I.

SIR FRANCIS DRAKE (ex-*Asia*) 5th Rate 38, 751bm, 132·5 × 35·5ft. Purch. 1805. Sold 13.10.1825.

SIR GALAHAD Landing ship, 3,270 tons. Stephen 19.4.1966. Lost 24.6.1982 Falklands operations.

SIR GALAHAD Landing ship, 8,585 tons, 462 (oa) × 63·9ft, 2–20mm, 2–MG, helo. Swan Hunter 13.12.1986.

SIR GERAINT Landing ship, 3,270 tons, 412·1 (oa) × 59·8ft, 2/4–20mm. Alex Stephen 26.1.1967. LU 16.9.2002.

SIR HUGO Minesweeping sloop. Greenock & Grangemouth 20.9.1918. Sold 25.6.1930 Cashmore, Newport.

SIR HUGO *See also EMPIRE LANCE 1943.*

SIR ISAAC BROCK 6th Rate 28 (Canadian lakes). Building 1813 at York, Toronto. Destroyed on stocks 27.4.1813.

SIR JAMES WOLFE *See GENERAL WOLFE 1915.*

SIR JOHN MOORE (ex-M.5) Monitor, 5,906 tons, 320 × 87ft, 2–12in, 4–6in, 2–12pdr. Scotts 31.5.1915 (renamed 1915). Sold 8.11.1921 Slough Trading Co.; BU Germany.

SIR LAMORAK (ex-*Lakespear Ontario*, ex-*Lady Catherine*, ex-*Lune Bridge*, ex-*Anu*, ex-*Norcliffe*, ex-*Anu*) Landing ship, 5,230 tons, 355·2 (oa) × 66·9ft. Comp. 12.1972 Norway (renamed 1972–81), chartered 11.8.1983–1.1986. Mercantile = *Merchant Trader* 1986, = *Mols Trader* 1987.

SIR LANCELOT Landing ship, 3,270 tons, 412·1 (oa) × 59·8ft, 2/4–20mm. Fairfield 25.6.1963. Sold 1.6.1989 = *Lowland Lancer*; resold Singaporean Navy = PERSEVERANCE 10.1992, cd 5.5.1994.

SIR PERCIVALE Landing ship, 3,270 tons, 412·1 (oa) × 59·8ft, 2/4–20mm. Hawthorn Leslie 4.10.1967.

SIR SYDNEY SMITH (ex-*Governor Simcoe*) Brig 10 (Canadian lakes), 72 × 22ft, 10–18pdr carr. Purch. 1812. = MAGNET 22.1.1814. Burnt 5.8.1814 to avoid capture by Americans.

SIR THOMAS PICTON (ex-PICTON, ex-M.12) Monitor, 5,900 tons, 320 × 87ft, 2–12in, 2–12pdr. Harland & Wolff 30.9.1915 (renamed 8.3.1915). Sold 8.11.1921 Slough Trading Co.; arr. 21.12.1922 Bremen for BU.

SIR TRISTRAM Landing ship, 3,270 tons, 412·1 (oa; 441·2ft after refit) × 59·8ft, 2/4–20mm. Hawthorn Leslie 12.12.1966.

SIR VISTO Minesweeping sloop, '24' class. Osbourne Graham, Sunderland, 24.3.1919. Sold 8.1920 Moise Mazza.

SIR VISTO *See also EMPIRE RAPIER 1943.*

SIRDAR Destroyer, 'S' class. Fairfield 6.7.1918. Sold 4.5.1934 Cashmore, Newport.

SIRDAR Submarine, 'S' class. Scotts 26.3.1943. Arr. 31.5.1965 McLellen, Bo'ness, for BU.

SIREN 6th Rate 24, 504bm, 112·5 × 32ft. Snelgrove, Limehouse, 3.9.1745. Sold 26.1.1764.

SIREN 6th Rate 28, 603bm, 120·5 × 33·5ft. Henniker, Rochester, 2.11.1773. Wrecked 10.11.1777 off Rhode I.

SIREN 5th Rate 32, 886bm, 142 × 37·5ft. Record, Appledore, ordered 16.7.1805, cancelled 24.6.1806.

SIREN (ex-SYREN) Hospital hulk, 298bm, 94 × 27ft. American, captured 1814. Listed until 1815.

SIREN Brig-sloop 16, 549bm, 110 × 35ft, 16–32pdr. Woolwich DY 23.4.1841. BU comp. 14.12.1868 Portsmouth.

SIREN Steam tender, 145bm, 105 × 17ft. Laird 21.10.1855. Sold Atwood & Co. 12.1863. *Built for use by Royalty at Bermuda. Not in Navy Lists.*

Ships of the Royal Navy

SIREN *See also OPOSSUM 1856. See also SIRENE, SYEREN, SYREN.*

SIRENE Sloop 16, 320bm, 92·5 × 26ft. French, captured 8.1794 by INTREPID and CHICHESTER off San Domingo. Wrecked 8.1796 Bay of Honduras.

SIRIUS 5th Rate 36, 1,049bm, 149 × 40ft. Dudman, Deptford, 12.4.1797. Destroyed 24.8.1810 Mauritius to avoid capture by French.

SIRIUS 5th Rate 38, 1,090bm, 155 × 40ft. Tyson & Blake, Bursledon, 11. 9.1813. Target 7.1860. BU comp. 23.9.1862 Portsmouth. *Last ship built at Bursledon.*

SIRIUS Wood screw sloop, 1,268bm, 1,760 tons, 212 × 36ft, 2—7in, 4—64pdr. Portsmouth DY 24.4.1868. Sold 1885 Castle, Charlton.

SIRIUS 2nd class cruiser, 3,600 tons, 300 × 43·5ft, 2—6in, 6—4·7in, 8—6pdr. Armstrong Mitchell 27.10.1890. Sunk 23.4.1918 blockship Ostend.

SIRIUS Cruiser, 5,450 tons, 512 (oa) × 50·5ft, 10 × 5·25in. Portsmouth DY 18.9.1940. Arr. 15.10.1956 Hughes Bolckow, Blyth for BU.

SIRIUS Frigate, 'Leander' class, Y136, 2,650 tons, 372 (oa) × 41ft, 2—4·5in, Seacat, helo (later Exocet, Seawolf). Portsmouth DY 22.9.1964. Towed from Milford Haven 18.9.1998, expended target in Atlantic.

SIRIUS *See also BERWICK 1781.*

SKATE Destroyer, 295 tons, 195 × 20·5ft, 1—12pdr, 5—6pdr, 2—TT. NC&A (Vickers) 13.3.1895. Sold 9.4.1907 Cox, Falmouth.

SKATE Destroyer, 'R' class. John Brown 11.1.1917. Sold 4.3.1947; arr. 20.7.1947 Cashmore, Newport, for BU.

SKEENA Destroyer (RCN), 1,337 tons, 321·25 (oa) × 32·75ft, 4—4·7in, 8—TT. Thornycroft 10.10.1930. Wrecked 25.10.1944 off Iceland; wreck sold 6.1945 locally.

SKEENA Escort (RCN), 2,260 tons, 366 (oa) × 42ft, 4—3in, 2—40mm, Limbo. Burrard 19.8.1952. Left Halifax 3.7.1996 under tow India for BU.

SKILFUL Destroyer, 'R' class. Harland & Wolff, Govan, 3.2.1917. Sold 13.7.1926 King, Garston.

SKIOLD 3rd Rate 74, 1,747bm, 174·5 × 48ft. Danish, captured 7.9.1807 Battle of Copenhagen. Harbour service 1808. Sold 20.7.1825 J. Ledger for BU.

SKIPJACK (ex-CONFIANCE) Schooner 10, 115bm, 71·5 × 19ft. French privateer, captured 23.8.1808 by BELETTE. BU 1812.

SKIPJACK Schooner 5, 118bm, 60·5 × 21ft. Bermuda 1827. Wrecked 6.1841 Cayman Is.

SKIPJACK Wood screw gunboat, 'Albacore' class.

Pitcher, Northfleet, 4.8.1855. Cooking depot 1874. BU comp. 4.2.1879 Devonport.

SKIPJACK Torpedo gunboat, 735 tons, 230 × 27ft, 2—4·7in, 4—3pdr, 3—TT. Chatham DY 30.4.1889. Minesweeper 1909. Sold 23.4.1920 Hammond Lane Foundry Co.

SKIPJACK Minesweeper, 815 tons, 230 × 33·5ft, 2—4in. John Brown 18.1.1934. Sunk 1.6.1940 air attack off Dunkirk.

SKIPJACK (ex-SOLEBAY) Minesweeper, 'Algerine' class. Redfern, Toronto, 7.4.1943 (renamed 10.1942). Arr. 3.1959 Hughes Bolckow, Blyth, for BU.

SKIRMISHER Scout cruiser, 2,895 tons, 360 × 40ft, 10—12pdr, 8—3pdr. Vickers 7.2.1905. Sold 3.3.1920 Ward, Preston.

SKUA *See WALRUS 1945.*

SKYLARK Brig-sloop 16, 283bm, 93 × 26·5ft. Rowe, Newcastle, 2.1806. Burnt 3.5.1812 nr Boulogne to avoid capture by French.

SKYLARK Brig-sloop 10, 'Cherokee' class. Pembroke Dock 6.5.1826. Wrecked 25.4.1845 Kimmeridge Ledge.

SKYLARK Wood gunboat, 'Dapper' class. Pitcher, Northfleet, 3.5.1855. Gunnery tender 1884. Sold 10.7.1906 Garnham.

SKYLARK (ex-*General Elliot*) Tender, 110 tons, 80 × 17ft. War Dept vessel, tx 1906 (renamed 11.1906). Sold 21.10.1930 Ward; BU Grays.

SKYLARK Minelaying tender, 302 tons, 98 × 24·5ft. Portsmouth DY 15.11.1932. = VERNON 9.12.1938; = VESUVIUS 4.1941. Sold 5.7.1957; BU 2.1958 Pollock Brown, Southampton.

SLADEN Paddle river gunboat (Indian), 270 tons, 161 × 30ft, 2—12pdr. Listed 1886–1921.

SLANEY 6th Rate 20, 460bm, 116 × 30ft. Brindle, Frindsbury, 9.12.1813. Receiving ship 1832. BU 1838 Bermuda.

SLANEY Wood screw gunboat, 301bm, 125 × 23ft, 1—10in, 2—24pdr howitzers. Pitcher, Northfleet 17.3.1857. Wrecked 9.5.1870 typhoon nr Hong Kong.

SLANEY Iron screw gunboat, 363 tons, 110 × 34ft, 3—64pdr. Palmer, Jarrow 28.4.1877. Diving tender 1906. Reported sold 30.8.1919 Ward, Grays; arr. Grays 10.10.1919, Rainham 3.1.1923, for BU. *Listed until 1921.*

SLEUTH Submarine, 'S' class. Cammell Laird 6.7.1944. Arr. 15.9.1958 Charlestown for BU.

SLIGO Minesweeper, Later 'Hunt' class. Napier & Miller 23.3.1918. Sold 4.11.1922 Col J. Lithgow.

SLINGER Aircraft catapult vessel, 875grt. Built Renfrew 1917; hopper, purch. Sold 16.10.1919 M. S. Hilton.

SLINGER (ex-*Chatham*) Escort carrier, 11,420
tons, 468·5 × 69·5ft, 2—4in, 16—40mm, 24
aircraft. Seattle Tacoma 19.9.1942 on Lend-Lease.
Ret. USN 27.2.1946.

SLINGER *See also LST.3510 1944.*

SLOTHANY (ex-SLOT VAN HONINGEN) 3rd
Rate 60, 772bm. Dutch , captured 1665. Hulked
1667. Sold 1686.

SLUYS Destroyer, 2,315 tons, 379 (oa) × 40·25ft,
4—4·5in, 8—TT. Cammell Laird 28.2.1945. Tx
Iranian Navy 26.1.1967 = ARTIMEZ. Hulk by 1995.

SMETHWICK Minesweeper, Later 'Hunt' class.
Lobnitz, cancelled 1918.

SMILAX (ex-TACT) Corvette, Modified 'Flower'
class. Collingwood SY 24.12.1942. Ret. USN
20.3.1946.

SMITER (ex-*Vermillion*) Escort carrier, 11,420
tons, 468·5 × 69·5ft, 2—4in, 16—40mm, 24
aircraft. Seattle Tacoma 27.9.1943 on Lend-Lease.
Ret. USN 6.4.1946.

SMITER Patrol boat, 49 tons, 68·2 (oa) × 19ft.
Watercraft. Comp. 2.1986.

SMITER *See also LST.3514 1944.*

SMITHS FALLS Corvette (RCN), Modified
'Flower' class. Kingston SY 19.8.1944. Sold 1950
= *Olympic Lightning*; = *Otori Maru No 16* 1956;
= *Kyo Maru No 23* 1961; last listed 1977–78.

SNAKE Sloop 14. Purch. 6.1777. Captured
13.6.1781 by two American privateers in Atlantic.

SNAKE Sloop 14. Purch. 1777. Slop ship 1782. Sold
2.4.1783. *Previous vessel recaptured?*

SNAKE Sloop 18, 'Cruizer' class (ship-rigged),
386bm. Adams, Bucklers' Hard, 18.12.1797. Sold
18.4.1816.

SNAKE Brig-sloop 16, 434bm, 101·5 × 32ft, 14—
32pdr, 2—18pdr. Fletcher, Limehouse, 3.5.1832.
Wrecked 29.8.1847 Mozambique Channel.

SNAKE Steam tender (Indian), 40bm. Bombay DY
1838. Harbour service hulk 1863.

SNAKE Wood screw gunvessel, 480bm 160 ×
25·5ft, 2—68pdr. Mare, Blackwall, 6.9.1854. Sold
1864 Marshall, Plymouth.

SNAKE Iron screw gunboat, 'Ant' class. Chatham
DY 25.3.1871. Comp. as dockyard cable lighter
23.9.1907 = YC.15.

SNAKEFLY River gunboat, 'Fly' class. Yarrow
1916. Sold 1.3.1923 Basra.

SNAP (ex-PALINUR) Brig-sloop 16, 310bm, 92·5 ×
28·5ft, 16—24pdr carr., 2—6pdr. French, captured
31.10.1808. BU 6.1811.

SNAP Gun-brig 12, 181bm, 84 × 22·5ft, 10—18pdr
carr., 2—6pdr. Russell, Lyme Regis, 25.7.1812.
Survey vessel 1823; powder hulk 1827. Sold
4.1.1832 Levy, Rochester.

SNAP (ex-*Cacique*) Steam transport. Slaver, captured 1847, purch. 4.5.1847. Sold 2.1848.

SNAP Wood screw gunboat, 'Dapper' class. Pitcher,
Northfleet, 3. 2.1855. Sold 1868 in Hong Kong;
resold Japanese Navy = KAKU TEN KAN.

SNAP Iron screw gunboat, 'Ant' class. Campbell
Johnstone, North Woolwich, 11.12.1872. Sold
11.5.1909 Deeker, Hull.

SNAPDRAGON Sloop, 'Arabis' class. Ropner,
Stockton-on-Tees 21.12.1915. Sold 4.5.1934
Cashmore, Newport.

SNAPDRAGON Corvette, 'Flower' class. Simons
3.9.1940. Sunk 19.12.1942 air attack central
Mediterranean.

SNAPDRAGON *See also ARABIS 1940.*

SNAPPER Cutter. Whitstable 1782, purch. 1782.
Sold 29.9.1817 J. Cristall. *Probably Revenue
Service vessel 1790.*

SNAPPER Cutter 4, 78bm, 56 × 18ft, 4—12pdr
carr. Bermuda 1804. Captured 15.7.1811 by
French lugger RAPACE.

SNAPPER Gun-brig 12, 184bm, 84·5 × 22·5ft.
Hobbs & Hillyer, Redbridge, 27.9.1813. Coastguard 5.1824. Sold 1865 Castle per order dated
3.7.1861.

SNAPPER Wood screw gunboat, 218bm, 284 tons,
100 × 22ft, 1—68pdr, 1—32pdr, 2—24pdr howitzers. Pitcher, Northfleet, 4.10.1854. Coal hulk
1865. Sold 1906.

SNAPPER Destroyer, 310 tons, 200 × 19·5ft, 1—
12pdr, 5—6pdr, 2—TT. Earle, Hull 30.1.1895. Sold
14.5.1912 King, Gateshead.

SNAPPER Submarine, 670 tons, 193 × 24ft, 1—
3in, 6—TT. Chatham DY 25.10.1934. Sunk 2.1941
Bay of Biscay, cause unknown.

SNAPPER *See also MASTIFF 1871.*

SNAPPER II *See HANDY 1884.*

SNIPE Gun-brig 12, 185bm, 80·5 × 23ft, 2—32pdr
carr., 10—18pdr carr. Adams, Buckler's Hard,
2.5.1801. Comp. 2.1816 as dockyard mooring
lighter. BU 5.1846.

SNIPE Cutter 6, 122bm, 64 × 22ft, 2—6pdr, 4—
6pdr carr. Pembroke Dock 28.6.1828. BU 11.1860
Devonport.

SNIPE Wood screw gunvessel, 'Philomel' class.
Scott Russell, Millwall, 5.5.1860. BU 5.1868
Sheerness.

SNIPE Coastguard vessel, 20bm. Watkins, Blackwall, 26.11.1874. Foundered 3.2.1914; raised, sold
16.5.1914.

SNIPE River gunboat, 85 tons, 108 × 20ft, 2—
6pdr. Yarrow, Poplar, 1898. Reported sold
20.11.1919 Hong Kong. *Still listed 1921.*

SNIPE Sloop, 1,350 tons, 283 × 38·5ft, 6—4in.

Denny (ex-John Brown) 20.12.1945. Arr. 23.8.1960 Cashmore, Newport, for BU.

SNIPE *See also ALCASTON 1953.*

SNOWBERRY Corvette, 'Flower' class. Davie SB 8.8.1940. Lent RCN until 8.6.1945. BU 8.1947 Thornaby-on-Tees.

SNOWDROP Sloop, 'Acacia' class. McMillan 7.10.1915. Sold 15.1.1923 Unity S. Bkg Co.

SNOWDROP Corvette, 'Flower' class. Smith's Dock 19.7.1940. Sold 17.5.1947; BU 1949 Tyneside.

SNOWFLAKE (ex-ZENOBIA) Corvette, 'Flower' class. Smith's Dock 22.8.1941 (renamed 8.1941). Tx Air Ministry 1947 = *Weather Watcher*. Arr. 5.5.1962 Dublin for BU.

SOBERTON Coastal minesweeper, 'Ton' class. Fleetland SY, Gosport, 20.11.1956. Towed Bruges 15.7.1998 for BU.

SOBO Depot ship, 4,160 tons, 345 × 44ft. Purch. 10.1914. Sold 12.2.1920 W. R. Davies & Co.

SOCIETY Fireship 6, 318bm. Purch. 1673. Expended 1673.

SOCIETY Bomb vessel 8, 102bm. Purch. 4.1694. Sold 3.5.1698.

SOCIETY Hospital ship, origin unknown. Captured 23.8.1697 by French.

SOESDYKE Yacht 8, 116bm. Purch. 24.3.1692. Rebuilt Deptford 1702 as 109bm. Sold 13.7.1713.

SOKOTO Depot ship, 3,870 tons, 345 × 42ft. Purch. 10.1914. Sold 9.8.1919. mercantile.

SOLEBAY 6th Rate 24, 256bm, 92 × 25ft. Snelgrove, Deptford, 9.1694. Wrecked 25.12.1709 Boston Rock, nr Lyme Regis.

SOLEBAY 6th Rate 20, 272bm, 96 × 25ft. Portsmouth DY 21.8.1711. Fireship 1727; hospital ship 6.1742. Sold 23.6.1748.

SOLEBAY 6th Rate 24, 429bm, 106 × 30·5ft. Plymouth 20.7.1742. Sold 15.3.1763. *In French hands 8.1744–4.1746.*

SOLEBAY 6th Rate 28, 619bm, 124 × 33·5ft. Airey, Newcastle, 9.9.1763. Wrecked 25.1.1782 Nevis.

SOLEBAY 5th Rate 32, 683bm, 126·5 × 35ft. Adams & Barnard, Deptford, 26.3.1785. Wrecked 11.7.1809 coast of Africa.

SOLEBAY Destroyer, 2,325 tons, 379 (oa) × 40.25ft, 4–4·5in, 10–40mm, 8–TT. Hawthorn Leslie 22.2.1944. Arr. 11.8.1967 Troon for BU.

SOLEBAY *See also IRIS 1783, SKIPJACK 1943.*

SOLENT Storeship, 125 tons, 100 × 17·5ft. War Dept vessel, tx 1907. Sold 1907 in Hong Kong.

SOLENT Submarine, 'S' class. Cammell Laird 8.6.1944. Arr. 28.8.1961 Troon for BU.

SOLITAIRE 3rd Rate 64, 1,521bm. French, captured 6.12.1782 by RUBY and POLYPHEMUS. Sold 5.1786.

SOLWAY FIRTH (ex-EMPIRE LAGOS) Repair ship, 10,000 tons, 431 × 56ft. Short, Sunderland, 31.10.1944. Sold 1946 = *Kongsborg.*

SOMALI Destroyer, 1,870 tons, 377 (oa) × 36·5ft, 8–4·7in, 4–TT. Swan Hunter 24.8.1937. Torpedoed 20.9.1942 by U.703, foundered 24.9.1942 south of Iceland.

SOMALILAND (ex-POPHAM) Frigate, 'Colony' class. Walsh Kaiser 11.11.1943 (renamed 1943). Ret. USN 31.5.1946.

SOMERLEYTON (ex-GAMSTON) Coastal minesweeper, 'Ton' class. Richards Ironworks, Lowestoft, 17.9.1955. Tx RAN 18.7.1962 = HAWK. Sold 1.1976.

SOMERS Schooner 10. Listed 1807–12.

SOMERSET 3rd Rate 80, 1,354bm, 158 × 44·5ft. Woolwich DY 21.10.1731. BU 10.1746 Chatham.

SOMERSET 3rd Rate 64, 1,436bm, 160 × 42·5ft. Chatham DY 18.7.1748. Wrecked 12.8.1778 nr Cape Cod.

SOMERSET Frigate, 'Norfolk' class. Yarrow, Glasgow 25.6.1994.

SOMERSETT 3rd Rate 80, 1,263bm, 158 × 42·5ft. Chatham DY 1698. Hulked 1715. BU 7.1740 Woolwich.

SOMME Destroyer, 'S' class. Fairfield 10.9.1918. Sold 25.8.1932 Ward, Pembroke Dock.

SOMME Destroyer, 2,380 tons, 379 (oa) × 40.25ft, 5–4·5in, 8–40mm, 10–TT. Cammell Laird, LD 24.2.1945, cancelled 10.1945.

SONNE Galley 8, 50bm. Listed 1546–62.

SONNE Pinnace 5, 40bm, 1–9pdr, 4–2pdr. Chatham 1586. Listed until 1599. *First RN vessel built at Chatham.*

SOPHIA (SPEAKER'S PRIZE) 26-gun ship, 300bm. Captured 1652. Sold 1667.

SOPHIA 12-gun vessel, 145bm. Captured 1685 from Earl of Argyll by KINGFISHER. Fireship 1688; hoy 1690. BU 1713.

SOPHIA Discovery vessel, 150bm. Purch. 11.5.1850. Sold 5.5.1853.

SOPHIE 6th Rate 28, 802bm, 132·5 × 34·5ft. French merchantman, captured 12.9.1782 by WARWICK. Sold 17.8.1784.

SOPHIE (ex-PREMIER CONSUL) Sloop 18, 388bm, 108·5 × 29ft. French privateer, captured 3.1798 by ENDYMION. BU 1809 Deptford.

SOPHIE Firevessel, 56bm. Purch. 6.1804. Sold 17.6.1807 T. Graham.

SOPHIE Brig-sloop 18, 'Cruizer' class, 387bm. Pelham, Frindsbury, 8.9.1809. Sold 15.8.1825 East Indies.

SORCERESS Destroyer, 'R' class. Swan Hunter 29.8.1916. Sold 29.4.1927 Ward, Inverkeithing.

SOREL Corvette (RCN), 'Flower' class. Marine Industries 16.11.1940. Sold 16.10.1945.

SORLINGS 5th Rate 32, 362bm, 102·5 × 28·5ft. Barrett, Shoreham, 19.3.1694. Captured 20.10.1705 by French LE JERSEY off Dogger Bank. Recaptured 2.1711, sold.

SORLINGS 5th Rate 42, 506bm, 116·5 × 40ft. Sheerness DY 18.2.1706. Wrecked 17.12.1717 East Friesland.

SORLINGS (ex-*Elizabeth*) Survey vessel, 64bm, 52 × 17ft. Purch. 1789. Dockyard lighter 1809. For BU 1833.

SORLINGS See also ROYAL JAMES 1654.

SOUDAN Iron steam vessel, 250bm, 113 × 22ft. Laird 7.1840. Wrecked 1844 coast of Nigeria.

SOUTHAMPTON 4th Rate 48, 609bm, 122 × 34ft. Parker & Winter, Southampton 10.6.1693. Rebuilt Deptford 1700 as 636bm; hulked Jamaica 5.1728. BU 1771.

SOUTHAMPTON 5th Rate 32, 671bm, 124·5 × 35ft. Inwood, Rotherhithe, 5.5.1757. Wrecked 27.11.1812 Bahamas.

SOUTHAMPTON 4th Rate 60, 1,476bm, 172·5 × 44·5ft. Deptford DY 7.11.1820. Lent Hull Committee 18.6.1867 as TS. Sold 26.6.1912 Hughes Bolckow, Blyth.

SOUTHAMPTON 2nd class cruiser, 5,400 tons, 430 × 50ft, 8–6in. John Brown 11.5.1912. Sold 13.7.1926 Ward, Pembroke Dock.

SOUTHAMPTON (ex-POLYPHEMUS) Cruiser, 9,100 tons, 591·5 (oa) × 61·8ft, 12–6in, 8–4in. John Brown 10.3.1936 (renamed 1936). Bombed 10.1.1941 east of Malta, scuttled next day.

SOUTHAMPTON Destroyer, Type 42 Batch 2. Vosper-Thornycroft 29.1.1979.

SOUTHDOWN Minesweeper, Early 'Hunt' class. Simons 7.5.1917. Sold 16.12.1926 Granton S. Bkg Co.

SOUTHDOWN Destroyer, 'Hunt' class Type I. White 5.7.1940. Arr. 1.11.1956 Ward, Barrow, for BU.

SOUTHLAND See DIDO 1961.

SOUTHSEA CASTLE 5th Rate 32, 373bm, 106·5 × 28ft. Knowles, Redbridge, 1.8.1696. Wrecked 15.9.1697 Dove Sand.

SOUTHSEA CASTLE 5th Rate 32, 387bm, 108 × 28·5ft. Deptford 1697. Stranded 12.11.1699 I. of Ash, West Indies.

SOUTHSEA CASTLE 5th Rate 42, 546bm, 119·5 × 32·5ft. Swallow, Rotherhithe, 18.11.1708. Sold 1744.

SOUTHSEA CASTLE 5th Rate 44, 712bm, 126 × 36ft. Okill, Liverpool, 18.8.1745. Storeship 1.1760, 22–9pdr, 6–2pdr. Lost 8.1762 Manila.

SOUTHWOLD Destroyer, 'Hunt' class Type II.

White 29.5.1941. Sunk 24. 3.1942 mine off Malta.

SOUTHWOLD See also STOKE 1918.

SOVERANO 3rd Rate 74, 1,875bm, 175 × 49·5ft. Spanish, captured 8.1762. BU comp. 14.8.1770 Portsmouth.

SOVEREIGN (TRINITY SOVEREIGN) 800-ton ship. Built 1488. Rebuilt 1510. Listed until 1521.

SOVEREIGN (SOVEREIGN OF THE SEAS) 100-gun ship, 1,141bm. Woolwich DY 14.10.1637. Rebuilt 1660 = ROYAL SOVEREIGN (q.v.).

SOVEREIGN Nuclear submarine, 'Swiftsure' class. Vickers, Barrow 17.2.1973.

SOVEREIGN OF THE SEAS See SOVEREIGN 1637.

SPANIARD Galleon. Presented 1522 by King of Spain. Not mentioned after 1523.

SPANISH MERCHANT Fireship 8, 250bm. Purch. 1678. Sold 1686.

SPANKER Floating battery 24, c. 500bm, 111·5 × 42·5ft, 24–24pdr carr., 2–10in mortars. Barnard, Deptford, 14.6.1794. Left Navy List 31.8.1810.

SPANKER Wood screw gunboat, 'Albacore' class. Green, Blackwall, 22.3.1856. BU 8.1874 Chatham.

SPANKER Torpedo gunboat, 735 tons, 230 × 27ft, 2–4·7in, 4–3pdr, 3–TT. Devonport DY 27.2.1889. Minesweeper 1909. Sold 20.3.1920 Cornish Salvage Co., Ilfracombe.

SPANKER Minesweeper, 'Algerine' class. Harland & Wolff 20.1.1943. Sold Belgian Navy 25.2.1953 = DE BROUWER; BU Ghent 9.1.1968.

SPARHAM Inshore minesweeper, 'Ham' class. Vosper, Gosport, 14.10.1954. Tx French Navy 30.9.1955 = M.785/HIBISCUS; deleted 1986.

SPARK Submarine, 'S' class. Scotts 28.12.1943. Sold 28.10.1949; BU Faslane 10.1950.

SPARKLER Gun-brig 12, 159bm, 75 × 22ft, 2–24pdr, 10–18pdr carr. Randall, Rotherhithe, 4.1797. Sold 9.1802.

SPARKLER Gun-brig 12, 178bm, 80·5 × 22·5ft, 2–18pdr, 10–18pdr carr. Warren, Brightlingsea, 6.8.1804. Wrecked 14.1.1808 Dutch coast.

SPARROW Pink 16, 60bm. Captured 1653. Sold 1659.

SPARROW (ex-*Rattler*) Cutter 12, 123bm, 66·5 × 22·5ft, 10–12pdr carr., 2–6pdr. Purch. 1796. BU 1805.

SPARROW Brig-sloop 16, 284bm, 96 × 26ft. Preston, Yarmouth, 29.7.1805. Sold 17.10.1816.

SPARROW Cutter 10, 160bm, 70·5 × 24ft. Pembroke Dock 28.6.1828. Survey ketch 1844. BU 8.1860 Devonport.

SPARROW Wood screw gunvessel, 'Philomel' class. Scott Russell, Millwall, 7.7.1860. BU 1868 Marshall, Plymouth.

SPARROW Composite screw gunboat, 805 tons, 165 × 31ft, 6—4in, 2—3pdr. Scotts 26.9.1889. Tx NZ Govt 10.7.1906 = AMOKURA (TS). Sold 2.1922 as coal hulk. BU 1955.

SPARROW Sloop, 1,350 tons, 283 × 38·5ft, 6—4in. Denny (ex-John Brown) 18.2.1946. Arr. 26.5.1958 Charlestown for BU.

SPARROWHAWK Brig-sloop 18, 'Cruizer' class, 385bm. Warren, Brightlingsea, 20.8.1807. Sold 27.5.1841.

SPARROWHAWK Wood screw gunvessel, 676bm, 181 × 28·5ft, 1—7in, 2—40pdr. Young & Magnay, Limehouse, 9.2.1856. Sold 1872 Esquimalt.

SPARROWHAWK Destroyer, 360 tons, 210 × 21ft, 1—12pdr, 5—6pdr, 2—TT. Laird 8.10.1895. Wrecked 17.6.1904 mouth of Yangtse.

SPARROWHAWK Destroyer, 935 tons, 260 × 27ft, 3—4in, 4—TT. Swan Hunter 12.10.1912. Sunk 31.5.1916 collision BROKE and CONTEST Battle of Jutland.

SPARROWHAWK Destroyer, 'S' class. Swan Hunter 14.5.1918. Sold 5.2.1931 Ward, Grays.

SPARROWHAWK *See also LARK 1877.*

SPARTAN 5th Rate 38, 1,084bm, 154 × 40ft. Ross, Rochester, 16.8.1806. BU 4.1822.

SPARTAN 5th Rate 46, 1,215bm, 159 × 42ft. Portsmouth DY, ordered 13.9.1824, cancelled 7.2.1831.

SPARTAN 6th Rate 26, 911bm, 313 × 40·5ft, 2—8in, 24—32pdr. Devonport DY 16.8.1841. Sold 19.5.1862 Castle.

SPARTAN Wood screw sloop, 1,269bm, 1,755 tons, 212 × 36ft, 2—7in, 4—64pdr. Deptford DY 14.11.1868. Sold 7.11.1882 Castle.

SPARTAN 2nd class cruiser, 3,600 tons, 300 × 43·5ft, 2—6in, 6—4·7in, 8—6pdr. Armstrong Mitchell 25.2.1891. Harbour service 1907. = DEFIANCE 8.1921. Sold 26.6.1931.

SPARTAN Cruiser, 5,770 tons, 512 (oa) × 50·5ft, 8—5·25in. Vickers Armstrong, Barrow, 27.8.1942. Sunk 29.1.1944 air attack Anzio.

SPARTAN Nuclear submarine, 'Swiftsure' class. Vickers 7.4.1978.

SPARTIATE 3rd Rate 74, 1,949bm, 182·5 × 50ft. French, captured 1.8.1798 Battle of the Nile. Sheer hulk 8.1842. BU comp. 30.5.1857.

SPARTIATE 1st class cruiser, 11,000 tons, 435 × 69ft, 16—6in, 12—12pdr. Pembroke Dock 27.10.1898. = FISGARD 6.1915. Sold 7.1932 Ward, Pembroke Dock.

SPEAKER 50-ton ship, 727bm, 142 × 35ft. Woolwich 1649. = MARY 1660, 60 guns. Wrecked 27.11.1703 Goodwin Sands.

SPEAKER Gunvessel. Presented by Barbados merchants 10.1756. Listed 1799.

SPEAKER (ex-*Delgada*) Escort carrier, 11,420 tons, 468·5 × 69·5ft, 2—4in, 16—40mm, 24 aircraft. Seattle Tacoma 20.2.1943 on Lend-Lease. Ret. USN 17.7.1946.

SPEAKER'S PRIZE *See SOPHIA 1652.*

SPEAR Destroyer, 'S' class. Fairfield 9.11.1918. Sold 13.7.1926 Alloa, Charlestown.

SPEAR Destroyer, 1,980 tons, 341·5 × 38ft, 6—4in, 6—40mm, 10—TT. Denny, LD 29.9.1944, cancelled 27.12.1945.

SPEAR *See also PORTWAY 1944.*

SPEARFISH Submarine, 670 tons, 193 × 24ft, 1—3in, 6—TT. Cammell Laird 21.4.1936. Sunk 1940 by U.34 off Norway, formally PO 5.8.1940.

SPEARHEAD Submarine, 'S' class. Cammell Laird 2.10.1944. Sold 8.1948 Portugese Navy = NEPTUNO.

SPEARMINT Minesweeping sloop, '24' class. Swan Hunter 23.9.1918. Sold 29.11.1922 Hallamshire Metal Co.

SPEEDWELL Galley. French, captured 1.1560 Firth of Forth. BU 1580.

SPEEDWELL Fireship 8, 120bm. Purch. 1688. Sunk 1692 breakwater Portsmouth.

SPEEDWELL Fireship 8, 259bm, 94 × 25ft, Gressingham, Rotherhithe, 3.4.1690. Rebuilt Limehouse 1702 as 5th Rate 28, 274bm. Wrecked 21.11.1720 Dutch coast.

SPEEDWELL Sloop 14, 271bm, 91·5 × 26·5ft. Buxton, Deptford, 9.11.1744. Sold 13.11.1750.

SPEEDWELL Sloop 8, 142bm, 75·5 × 20·5ft. Chatham DY 21.10.1752. = SPITFIRE (fireship) 27.8.1779. Sold 5.12.1780.

SPEEDWELL Cutter, origin unknown. Captured 4.4.1761 by French ACHILLE at Vigo.

SPEEDWELL Sloop 18. Listed 1775.

SPEEDWELL Cutter 16, 193bm, 75·5 × 26ft, 16—4pdr. Purch. 5.1780. Foundered 18.2.1807 off Dieppe.

SPEEDWELL Schooner 5. Purch. 1815. Sold 1.1834 in Jamaica.

SPEEDWELL Survey cutter, 73bm, 56 × 18ft. Purch. 12.7.1841. Sold 5.1855 Canada.

SPEEDWELL Wood screw gunvessel, 'Philomel' class. Deptford 12.2.1861. BU 7.1876 Chatham.

SPEEDWELL Torpedo gunboat, 735 tons, 230 × 27ft, 2—4·7in, 4—3pdr, 3—TT. Devonport DY 15.3.1889. Minesweeper 1909. Sold 20.3.1920 Cornish Salvage Co., Ilfracombe.

SPEEDWELL Minesweeper, 815 tons, 230 × 33·5ft, 2—4in. Hamilton 21.3.1935. Sold 5.12.1946 = *Topaz.*

SPEEDWELL *See also SWIFTSURE 1573, CHERITON 1656.*

SPEEDWELL PRIZE 6th Rate 20, 155bm, 75·5 × 22ft. Captured 4.10.1708 by SPEEDWELL. Sold 1712.

SPEEDY Brig-sloop 14, 208bm, 78 × 26ft. King, Dover, 29.6.1782. Captured 2.7.1801 by French in Mediterranean. *Also in French hands 6.1794–3.1795.*

SPEEDY Gunvessel (Canadian lakes). Kingston, Ontario, 1798. Foundered 8.10.1804.

SPEEDY (ex-*George Hibbert*) Brig-sloop 16, 379bm, 101·5 × 29·5ft. Purch. 7.1803. Sold 3.1818.

SPEEDY Cutter 6, 123bm, 64 × 22·5ft, 2—6pdr, 4—6pdr carr. Pembroke Dock 28.6.1828. = YC.11 (dockyard mooring lighter) 8.1853. BU 1866.

SPEEDY Wood screw gunboat, 'Britomart' class. Lamport, Workington, 18.7.1860. Sold Castle 8.1889 for BU.

SPEEDY Torpedo gunboat, 810 tons, 230 × 27ft, 2—4·7in, 4—3pdr, 3—TT. Thornycroft, Chiswick, 18.5.1893. Sunk 3.9.1914 mine off Humber estuary.

SPEEDY Destroyer, 'S' class, 1,087 tons. Thornycroft 1.6.1918. Sunk 24.9.1922 collision tug Sea of Marmara.

SPEEDY Minesweeper, 875 tons, 230 × 33·5ft, 2—4in. Hamilton 23.11.1938. Sold 5.11.1946 = *Speedon*.

SPEEDY Jetfoil 117, tons. Seattle 9.7.1979. Sold mercantile 1986

SPENCE Sloop 8, 114bm, 64·5 × 20ft. Deptford DY 13.3.1722. BU 3.1730.

SPENCE Sloop 12, 207bm, 87 × 23ft. Deptford DY 24.6.1730. Sold 10.6.1748.

SPENCER (ex-*Sir Charles Grey*) Brig-sloop 16, 200bm, 92·5 × 22ft, 14—12pdr carr., 2—4pdr. Purch. 1795. = LILY 1800. Captured 15.7.1804 by French privateer DAME AMBERT off North America; recaptured 20.3.05 by RENARD, blew up.

SPENCER 3rd Rate 74, 1,917bm, 181 × 49·5ft. Adams, Buckler's Hard, 10.5.1800. BU 4.1822.

SPENCER *See also DILIGENCE 1795.*

SPENSER Destroyer leader, 1,750 tons, 329·25 (oa) × 32ft, 5—4·7in, 1—3in, 6—TT. Thornycroft 22.9.1917. HO Ward 29.9.1936 part payment *Majestic* (CALEDONIA, q.v.); BU Inverkeithing.

SPEY 6th Rate 20, 463bm, 116 × 30ft, 18—32pdr carr., 2—9pdr. Warwick, Eling, 8.1.1814. Sold 18.4.1822.

SPEY Brig-sloop 10 'Cherokee' class, 231bm. Pembroke Dock 6.10.1827. Packet brig, 4 guns, 1833. Wrecked 28.11.1940 Racoon Key, West Indies.

SPEY Wood screw gunboat, 'Albacore' class. Pitcher, Northfleet, 29.3.1856. BU 12.1863 Deptford.

SPEY Iron screw gunboat, 363 tons, 110 × 34ft, 3—64pdr. Palmer 5.10.1876. Sold 1923.

SPEY Frigate, 'River' class. Smith's Dock 12.1941. Sold 11.1948 Egyptian Navy = RASHEID; deleted 1990.

SPEY Minehunter, 890 tons (full load), 156·3 (oa) × 34·5ft, 1—40mm, Richards, Lowestoft 22.5.1985. Tx Brazilian Navy 10.7.1998 = QALVARO ALBERTO; = BOCAINIA.

SPEY *See also P.38 1917.*

SPHINX 6th Rate 24, 520bm, 114 × 32·5ft. Allen, Rotherhithe, 10.12.1748. Sold 28.8.1770.

SPHINX 6th Rate 20, 431bm, 108 × 30ft. Portsmouth DY 25.10.1775. BU 1811 Portsmouth.

SPHINX Composite paddle vessel, 1,130 tons, 200 × 32ft, 1—6in, 6—4in. Green, Blackwall, 28.11.1882. Sold 27.7.1919 Calcutta.

SPHINX Minesweeper, 875 tons, 230 × 33·5ft, 2—4in. Hamilton 7.2.1939. Foundered 3.2.1940 Moray Firth after damage air attack.

SPHYNX Brig-sloop 10, 'Cherokee' class, 238bm. Bombay DY 25.1.1815. Sold 6.8.1835.

SPHYNX Wood paddle sloop, 1,056bm 180 × 36ft. Woolwich DY 17.2.1846. BU 1881 Devonport.

SPIDER (ex-ARAIGNEE) Schooner 12, 169bm, 69 × 24ft, 12—4pdr. French privateer, captured 9.1782. Sold 1806 Malta.

SPIDER (ex-VIGILANTE) Brig-sloop 14, 280bm, 92 × 25ft, 6—18pdr carr., 12—8pdr. Spanish, captured 4.4.1806 by RENOMMEE in Mediterranean. BU 1815 Antigua.

SPIDER Schooner 6, 183bm, 80 × 23ft. Chatham DY 23.9.1835. Packet 10.1847. Sold 22.11.1861.

SPIDER Wood screw gunboat, 'Albacore' class. Smith, North Shields, 23.2.1856. Sold 12.5.1870 Castle.

SPIDER Torpedo gunboat, 525 tons, 200 × 23ft, 1—4in, 6—3pdr, 4—TT. Devonport DY 17.10.1887. Sold 5.1903 Malta; BU Ward, Preston.

SPIDER Coastal destroyer, 235 tons, 175 × 17·5ft, 2—12pdr, 3—TT. White 15.12.1906. = TB.5 in 1906. Sold 7.10.1920 Ward, Briton Ferry.

SPIKE Flyboat, 321bm. Algerian, captured 1679. Exchanged 1680.

SPIKENARD Corvette, 'Flower' class. Davie SB 10.8.1940. Lent RCN from 12.1940. Sunk 10.2.1942 by U.136 in North Atlantic.

SPINDRIFT Destroyer, 'S' class. Fairfield 30.12.1918. Sold 7.1936 Ward, Inverkeithing.

SPIRAEA Sloop, 'Anchusa' class. Simons 1.11.1917. Sold 6.9.1922 Distin Syndicate.

SPIRAEA Corvette, 'Flower' class. Inglis 31.10.1940. Sold 8.1945 = *Thessaloniki*.

SPIRIT Submarine, 'S' class. Cammell Laird 20.7.1943. Arr. 4.7.1950 Ward, Grays, for BU.

SPITEFUL Gunvessel 12. Dutch hoy, purch. 1794. Listed 1800.

SPITEFUL (Gunboat No 18) Gunvessel 12, 159bm, 75·5 × 22ft, 2—24pdr, 10—18pdr carr. Barnard, Deptford, 24.4.1797. Convict hulk 1818. BU 7.1823.

SPITEFUL Wood paddle sloop, 1,054bm, 180 × 36ft. Pembroke Dock 24.3.1842. Sold Castle 9.1883.

SPITEFUL Destroyer, 365 tons, 215 × 21ft, 1—12pdr, 5—6pdr, 2—TT. Palmer 11.1.1899. Sold 14.9.1920 Hayes, Porthcawl.

SPITEFUL Submarine, 'S' class. Scotts 5.6.1943. Lent French Navy 25.1.1952—11.1958 = SIRENE. Arr. 15.7.1963 Faslane for BU.

SPITFIRE Galley 8. Purch. North America, cd 25.1.1778. Captured 19.4.1779 by French SURVEILLANTE Rhode I.

SPITFIRE Fireship 14, 198bm. Purch. 1780. *Fate unknown.*

SPITFIRE Fireship 16, 424bm, 110 × 29·5ft. Teague, Ipswich, 19.3.1783. Sold 30.7.1825.

SPITFIRE Schooner 4, 61bm, 59·5 × 14ft, 4—3pdr. Purch. 1793. Capsized 2.1794 off San Domingo.

SPITFIRE Schooner, 64bm. French, captured 1798. Gone by 1800.

SPITFIRE Wood paddle vessel, 553bm, 155 × 27·5ft, 2 guns. Woolwich DY 26.3.1834. Wrecked 10.9.1842 nr Jamaica.

SPITFIRE Wood paddle gunvessel, 432bm, 595 tons, 147 × 25ft, 5 guns. Lungley, Deptford, 26.3.1845. Survey vessel 1851, tug 1862. BU 1888 Bermuda.

SPITFIRE Destroyer, 330 tons, 200 × 19ft, 1—12pdr, 5—6pdr, 2—TT. Armstrong 7.6.1895. Sold 10.4.1912 Ward, Preston.

SPITFIRE Destroyer, 935 tons. 260 × 27ft, 3—4in. 4—TT. Swan Hunter 23.12.1912. Sold 9.5.1921 Ward, Hayle.; arr. for BU 10.1922.

SPITFIRE *See also SPEEDWELL 1752, CAMBRIAN 1943.*

SPLENDID Ship listed 1597. *Fate unknown.*

SPLENDID Destroyer, 'S' class. Swan Hunter 10.7.1918. Sold 8.1.1931 Metal Industries, Charlestown.

SPLENDID (ex-P.228) Submarine, 'S' class. Chatham DY 19.1.1942. Scuttled 21.4.1943 after damage by German destroyer HERMES off Corsica.

SPLENDID Nuclear submarine, 'Swiftsure' class. Vickers 5.10.1979.

SPORTIVE Destroyer, 'S' class. Swan Hunter

19.9.1918. HO Ward 25.9.1936 part payment *Majestic* (CALEDONIA, q.v.); arr. 25.9.1936 Inverkeithing for BU.

SPORTSMAN (ex-P.229) Submarine, 'S' class. Chatham DY 17.4.1942. Lent French Navy 1951 = SIBYLLE. Sunk 24.9.1952 off Toulon.

SPRAGGE Fireship 10. Purch. 1673. Lost 1693. *See YOUNG SPRAGGE 1673.*

SPRAGGE Fireship. 1677.

SPRAGGE Destroyer leader, 1,750 tons, 329·25 (oa) × 32ft. Thornycroft, cancelled 1.1919.

SPRAGGE Frigate, TE 'Captain' class. Bethlehem, Hingham, 16.10.1943 on Lend-Lease. Ret. USN 2.1946.

SPRAT *See X.53 1955.*

SPREAD EAGLE Fireship 6, 240bm. Dutch, captured 1666. Lost 6.1 666 in action with Dutch.

SPRIGHTLY Cutter 10. King, Dover 16.8.1777. Capsized 12.1777 off Guernsey.

SPRIGHTLY Cutter 10, 151bm, 66 × 24ft. King, Dover 4.8.1778. Captured 10. 2.1881 by French in Mediterranean, scuttled.

SPRIGHTLY (ex-*Lively*) Cutter 14, 120bm, 64 × 22·5ft, 12—12pdr carr., 2—4pdr. Purch. 1805. BU 5.1815.

SPRIGHTLY Cutter 6. Pembroke Dock 3.6.1818. Tx Revenue Service 1819.

SPRIGHTLY (ex-*Harlequin*) Wood paddle packet, 234bm, 120 × 21ft. GPO vessel, Tx 1837. Sold 1889.

SPRIGHTLY Destroyer, 400 tons, 218 × 20ft, 1—12pdr, 5—6pdr, 2—TT. Laird 25. 9.1900. Sold 1.7.1920 S. Castle, Plymouth.

SPRIGHTLY Submarine, 'S' class. Cammell Laird, cancelled 1945.

SPRINGBOK Destroyer, 'R' class. Harland & Wolff, Govan, 9.3.1917. Sold 16.12.1926 Granton S. Bkg Co.

SPRINGER Submarine, 'S' class. Cammell Laird 14.5.1945. Tx Israeli Navy 9.10.1958= TANIN; Listed for disposal 1972.

SPRINGHILL Frigate (RCN), 'River' class. Yarrow, Esquimalt, 7.9.1943. Sold 17.11.1947 Halifax SY for BU.

SPRITE 30-ton vessel. Captured 1558. Listed 1559.

SPUR Submarine, 'S' class. Cammell Laird 17.11.1944. Sold 11.1948 Portuguese Navy = NARVAL. BU 1.10.1969.

SPURN POINT Repair ship, 8,580 tons, 425 × 57ft. Burrard 8.6.1945. Sold 10.7.1947 = *Lakemba.*

SPY Pinnace 9, 49bm, 4—6pdr, 2—4pdr, 3—2pdr. Limehouse 1586. Listed until 1613.

SPY 200-ton vessel. R. Thames 18.10.1620. *Fate unknown. May have been ship given as purch.*

8.1622 and listed until 1626.

SPY Shallop 6, 40bm. Listed 1644–52.

SPY Sloop 4, 28bm. Deane, Harwich, 1666. Sold 1683.

SPY Fireship 8, 253bm, 91·5ft, Taylor, Cuckold's Point, 3.4.1690. Burnt 12.1.1693 accident Portsmouth.

SPY Brigantine 6, 78bm, 64 × 17ft. Woolwich DY 15.4.1693. BU 2.1706 Sheerness.

SPY Sloop 8, 103bm, 62 × 20ft. Portsmouth DY 9.12.1721. Sold 2.12.1731.

SPY Sloop 14, 201bm, 85·5 × 23·5ft. Chatham DY 25.8.1732. Sold 25.4.1745.

SPY Sloop 10, 222bm, 86 × 24·5ft. Inwood, Rotherhithe, 3.2.1756. Sold 3.9.1773.

SPY Cutter, 58bm. 47·5 × 18ft. Purch. 1.1763. Sold 4.5.1773.

SPY Sloop 14, 306bm, 96·5 × 27ft. Graves, Limehouse, 6.4.1776. Wrecked 16.6.1778 off Newfoundland.

SPY (ex-*Comet*) Sloop 16, 227bm. Purch. 6.1804. Sold 12.1813.

SPY Brigantine 3, 320bm, 90 × 29·5ft, 3–32pdr. Sheerness DY 24.3.1841. Sold 20.1.1862 Montevideo.

SPY Coastguard cutter, 40bm. Listed from 10.1864. Sold 5.7.1904 Portsmouth.

SPY *See also ESPION 1782.*

SQUIB (ex-*Diligent*) Fireship. Purch. 10.1804. Wrecked 10.1805 nr Deal.

SQUIRREL Discovery vessel. With Sir Humphrey Gilbert 1582. Lost 1583.

SQUIRREL Yacht 4, 37bm. Chatham DY 10.12.1694. Sold 8.7.1714.

SQUIRREL 6th Rate 20, 258bm, 93 × 25ft. Portsmouth DY 14.6.1703. Captured 21.9.1703 by two French privateers off Hythe, Kent.

SQUIRREL 6th Rate 20, 260bm, 93·5 × 24·5ft. Portsmouth DY 28.10.1704. Captured 7.7.1706 by French = ECUREUIL; recaptured 15.3.1708, foundered.

SQUIRREL 6th Rate 24,262bm, 94 × 26ft. Stacey, Woolwich, 29.12.1707. Rebuilt Woolwich 1727 as 377bm. Sold 17.10.1749.

SQUIRREL 6th Rate 20, 404bm, 107·5 × 29ft. Woolwich DY 23.10.1755. Sold 16.1.1783.

SQUIRREL 6th Rate 24, 563bm, 119 × 32·5ft. Barton, Liverpool, 9.5.1785. Sold 6.3.1817 J. Cristall for BU.

SQUIRREL Brig-sloop 12, 428bm, 447 tons, 101·5 × 32ft. Pembroke Dock 8.8.1853. BU comp. 11.2.1879 Devonport.

SQUIRREL Coastguard cutter, 40bm. Built 1866. Sold 4.4.1905 Chatham.

SQUIRREL Coastguard vessel, 230 tons, 103 × 21ft, 2–3pdr. Workman Clark 21.12.1904. Cable vessel 1917. Sold 16.11.1921 = *Vedra*.

SQUIRREL Minesweeper, 'Algerine' class. Harland & Wolff 20.4.1944. Scuttled 24.7.1945 off Puket, Siam, after mine damage.

SQUIRREL *Name borne in succession by fishery protection vessels MFV.1151 (1.11.1948– 14.6.1956), MSML.2154 (14.6.1956–9.12.1957), RAMPISHAM (10.12.1957–15.12.1959), BURLEY (19.12.1959–). See also ALDERNEY 1743.*

ST(E) ––– *Treated as SAINT(E)* –––.

STADTHOUSE (STADHUIS VAN HAARLEM) Hulk, 440bm. Dutch ship, captured 1667. Sunk 28.10.1690 Sheerness 'to secure the graving place'.

STAFFORD (ex-STAITHES) Minesweeper, Later 'Hunt' class. Rennoldson 20.9.1918 (renamed 1918). Sold 26.6.1928 Alloa S. Bkg Co.

STAG 5th Rate 32, 707bm, 125 × 36ft. Stanton, Rotherhithe, 4.9.1758. BU 7.1783.

STAG 5th Rate 32, 792bm, 135 × 36ft. Chatham DY 28.6.1794. Wrecked 6.9.1800 Vigo Bay.

STAG 5th Rate 36, 947bm, 145 × 38·5ft. Deptford DY 25.7.1812. BU 9.1821.

STAG 5th Rate 46, 1,218bm, 159·5 × 42ft. Pembroke Dock 2.10.1830. BU comp. 8.8.1866 Marshall, Plymouth.

STAG Coastguard yawl, 120bm, 63 × 21ft. Built 1861. Sold 1891.

STAG Destroyer, 345 tons, 210 × 20ft, 1–12pdr, 5– 6pdr, 2–TT. Thornycroft 18.11.1899. Sold 17.3.1921 Ward, Grays.

STAITHES *See STAFFORD 1918.*

STALKER (ex-HAMLIN) Escort carrier, 11,420 tons, 468·5 × 69·5ft, 2–4in, 8–40mm, 18 aircraft. Western Pipe & Steel Co. 5.3.1942 on Lend-Lease. Ret. USN 29.12.1945.

STALKER *See also LST.3515 1944.*

STALWART Destroyer, 'S' class. Swan Hunter 23.10.1918. Tx RAN 6.1919. Sold 4.6.1937 Sydney.

STALWART Repair ship (RAN), 14,500 tons, 515·5 (oa) × 67·5ft. Cockatoo DY 7.10.1966. Deleted 15.12.1989; sold 5.1990 Marlines (Sea Royal Ferries, Cyprus) = *Her Majesty M.*

STANDARD 3rd Rate 64, 1,370bm, 159·5 × 44·5ft. Deptford DY 8.10.1782. Harbour service 11.1799. BU 17.1816.

STANLEY (ex-McCALLA) Destroyer, 1,190 tons, 311 × 31ft, 1–4in, 1–3in, 4–20mm, 3–TT. USN, cd RN 23.10.1940. Sunk 19.12.1941 by U.574 south-west of Portugal.

STAR Sloop 14. Purch. 1779. Sold c. 1785.

STAR Brig-sloop 18 (fir-built), 365bm, 96 × 30·5ft. Perry, Blackwall, 29.8.1795. Sold 1.1802.

STAR Tender, 41bm, 48 × 14ft. Woolwich DY 1808. Sold 22.9.1828 Levy, Rochester, for BU.

STAR Packet brig 8, 358bm, 95 × 30·5ft, 8—18pdr. Woolwich DY 29.4.1835. Coastguard watchvessel 9.1857; = WV.11 on 25.5.1863. BU c. 1899.

STAR Wood screw sloop, 695bm, 185 × 28·5ft, 2—pdr, 2—32pdr. Mare, Blackwall, 15.12.1860. BU 1877 Plymouth.

STAR Destroyer, 360 tons, 215 × 20·5ft, 1—12pdr, 5—6pdr, 2—TT. Palmer 11.8.1896. Sold 10.6.1919 Ward, New Holland.

STAR *See also MELVILLE 1813. See also STARR.*

STARFISH Destroyer, 310 tons, 195 × 20·5ft, 1—12pdr, 5—6pdr, 2—TT. NC&A (Vickers) 26.1.1895. Sold 14.5.1912 Ward, Preston.

STARFISH Destroyer, 'R' class. Hawthorn Leslie 27.9.1916. Sold 21.4.1928 Alloa S. Bkg Co., Charlestown.

STARFISH Submarine, 640 tons, 187 × 33·5ft, 1—3in, 6—TT. Chatham DY 14.3.1933. Sunk 9.1.1940 German minesweeper M.7 in Heligoland Bight.

STARLING Gun-brig 12, 184bm, 85 × 22ft. Adams, Buckler's Hard, 4.4.1801. Wrecked 18.12.1804 nr Calais.

STARLING Gun-brig 12, 181bm, 84·5 × 22ft. Rowe, Newcastle, 5.1805. Sold 29.9.1814.

STARLING Cutter 10, 151bm. Chatham DY 3.5.1817. BU 8.1828.

STARLING Schooner 4, 108bm, 61 × 20·5ft. Pembroke Dock 31.10.1829. Survey vessel 1834. Sold 2.1844 in China.

STARLING Composite screw gunboat, 465 tons, 125 × 23ft, 2—64pdr, 2—20pdr. Samuda, Poplar, 19.4.1882. Sold 4.4.1905 = *Stella Maris*.

STARLING (ex-*Miner 17*) Tender. War Dept vessel, tx 1905 (renamed 26.11.1906). Sold 14.9.1923 T. Round, Sunderland.

STARLING Sloop, 1,350 tons, 283 × 38·5ft, 6—4in. Fairfield 14,10.1942. Arr. 6.7.1965 Lacinots, Queenborough, for BU.

STARLING Wood screw gunboat, 'Dapper' class. Pitcher, Northfleet, 1.2.1955. Sold 1.12.1871 in Hong Kong.

STARLING Patrol vessel, 662 tons, 205·3 (oa) × 32·8ft, 1—76mm, Hall Russell 7.9.1983. Sold 1.8.1997 Philippines Navy = ARTIMIO RICARTE.

STARR 16-gun ship, 130bm. Purch. 1643. Sold 1652.

STARR Fireship 4, 121bm. Purch. 1667. Expended 1667.

STARR Bomb vessel 8, 117bm. Johnson, Blackwall, 1694, purch. 4.1694. Wrecked 29.5.1712 West Indies.

STARR Sloop 18, 371bm, 106 × 28ft. Tanner, Dart-

mouth, 26.7.1805. = METEOR (bomb vessel) 1812. Sold 16.10.1816.

STARR *See also STAR.*

START BAY (ex-LOCH ARKLET) Frigate, 'Bay' class. Harland & Wolff 15.2.1945 (renamed 1944). BU 7.1958 Cashmore, Newport.

STARWORT Corvette, 'Flower' class. Inglis 12.2.1941. Sold 8.1946 = *Southern Broom*.

STATELY 3rd Rate 64, 1,388bm, 160 × 44·5ft. Raymond, Northam, 27.12.1784. Troopship 8.1.1799. BU 7.1814.

STATESMAN Submarine, 'S' class, Cammell Laird 14.9.1943. Lent French Navy 1952–5.11.1959 = SULTANE. Sold 3.1.1961 Pounds, Portsmouth.

STATICE (ex-VIM) Corvette, Modified 'Flower' class. Collingwood SY 10.4.1943 on Lend-Lease. Ret. USN 21.6.1946.

STATIRA 5th Rate 38, 1,080bm, 154 × 40ft. Guillaume, Northam, 7.7.1807. Wrecked 26.2.1815 coast of Cuba.

STATIRA 5th Rate 46, 1,218bm, 159 × 42·5ft. Plymouth DY, LD 12.1823, cancelled 31.8.1832.

STAUNCH (Gunboat No 44) Gunvessel 12. Rochester 1.5.1797; purch. 1797. Sold 1803 West Indies.

STAUNCH Gun-brig 12, 182bm, 80 × 23ft. Tanner, Dartmouth, 21.8.1804. Wrecked 6.1811 off Madagascar.

STAUNCH Wood screw gunboat, 'Albacore' class. Pitcher, Northfleet, 31.1.1856. Sold 12.1866 in Hong Kong.

STAUNCH Iron screw gunboat, 200bm, 180 tons, 75 × 25ft, 1—9in. Armstrong Mitchell 4.12.1867. Sold 1904.

STAUNCH Destroyer, 748 tons, 240 × 25ft, 2—4in, 2—12pdr, 2—TT. Denny 29.10.1910. Sunk 11.11.1917 by UC.38 off coast of Palestine.

STAVERENS Gun-brig. Origin unknown. Sold 13.6.1811.

STAVOREEN 4th Rate 48, 544bm. Captured 1672. Sold 1682.

STAWELL Frigate (RAN), 'Bathurst' class. Williamstown DY 3.4.1943. Tx RNZN 5.1952. Sold Pacific Scrap, Auckland, 9.1968.

STAYNER Frigate, TE 'Captain' class. Bethlehem, Hingham, 6.11.1943 on Lend-Lease. Ret. USN 11.1945.

STEADFAST Destroyer, 'S' class. Palmer 8.8.1918. Sold 28.7.1934 Metal Industries, Charlestown.

STEADFAST Minesweeper, 'Catherine' class. Gulf SB, Chickasaw, 17.1.1943 on Lend-Lease. Ret. USN 24.12.1946; sold Greek Navy.

STEADY Storeship 14. Purch. 2.1782. Sold 25.3.1784.

STEADY (Gunboat No 19) Gunvessel 12, 168bm, 76 × 22·5ft, 2—24pdr, 10—18pdr carr. Hill, R. Thames, 24.4.1797. Sold c. 1802.

STEADY Gun-brig 12, 180bm, 85 × 22ft. Richards, Hythe, 21.7.1804. Sold 9.2.1815.

STEADY Wood screw gunvessel, 'Philomel' class. Miller, Liverpool, 8.2.1860. Sold 12.5.1870 W. & T. Joliffe.

STEADY *See also M.VII 1944.*

STEDHAM Inshore minesweeper, 'Ham' class. Blackmore, Bideford, 12.1.1955. Tx French Navy 1955 = M.776/JASMINE; deleted 1985.

STELLARTON Corvette (RCN), Modified 'Flower' class. Morton, Quebec, 27.4.1944. Sold 1946 Chilean Navy = CASMA; BU 2.7.1969.

STEPDANCE Minesweeper, 265 tons, 130 × 26ft, 1—6pdr. War Dept tug, tx/cd 4.1919. Sold 1.5.1920 Crichton Thompson.

STERLET Submarine, 670 tons, 193 × 24ft, 1—3in, 6—TT. Chatham DY 22.9.1937. Sunk 18.4.1940 by German trawler in Skaggerak.

STERLING Destroyer, 'S' class. Palmer 8.10.1918. Sold 25.8.1932 Rees, Llanelly.

STERLING *Gun-brig listed in some sources as wrecked 18.12.1804 nr Calais, but believed to be an erroneous reference to STARLING 1801 (q.v.), also given as wrecked 18.12.1804 in same location.*

STETTLER Frigate (RCN), 'River' class. Vickers, Montreal, 10.9.1943. Sold H&M Enterprises, Victoria, BC, 8.1967.

STEVENSTONE Destroyer, 'Hunt' class Type III. White 23.11.1942. Arr. 2.9.1959 Clayton & Davie, Dunston, for BU.

STICKLEBACK *See X.51 1954.*

STING Cutter 10, 126bm, 73 × 20·5ft. Purch. 1800. = PICKLE 1902. Wrecked 27.7.1808 off Cadiz.

STINGAREE Iron gunboat (Australian), 450 tons, 1—5in. Hopper, conv. 1887. Listed 1895.

STIRLING CASTLE 3rd Rate 70, 1,059bm, 151 × 40·5ft. Deptford 1679. Rebuilt Chatham 1699 as 1,087bm. Wrecked 27.11.1703 Goodwin Sands.

STIRLING CASTLE 3rd Rate 70, 1,122bm, 151 × 41ft. Chatham DY 21.9.1705. Rebuilt Woolwich 1723 as 1,138bm; hulked 8.1739. BU comp. 4.12.1771 Sheerness.

STIRLING CASTLE 3rd Rate 70, 1,225bm, 151 × 43·5ft. Chatham DY 24.4.1742. Lost 1762 Havana.

STIRLING CASTLE 3rd Rate 64, 1,374bm, 159 × 44·5ft. Chatham DY 28.6.1775. Wrecked 5.10.1780 West Indies.

STIRLING CASTLE 3rd Rate 74, 1,774bm, 176·5 × 48·5ft. Ross, Rochester, 31.12.1811. Convict ship 4.1839. BU comp. 6.9.1861.

STOAT *See WEAZEL 1906.*

STOCKHAM Frigate, TE 'Captain' class. Bethlehem, Hingham, 31.10.1943 on Lend-Lease. Ret. USN 2.1946.

STOIC Submarine, 'S' class. Cammell Laird 9.4.1943. Sold 7.1950; BU Dalmuir.

STOKE (ex-SOUTHWOLD) Minesweeper, Later 'Hunt' class. Rennoldson 8.7.1918 (renamed 1918). Sunk 7.5.1941 air attack Tobruk.

STONECROP Corvette, 'Flower' class. Smith's Dock 12.5.1941. Sold 17.5.1947 = *Silver King.*

STONEFLY River gunboat, 'Fly' class. Yarrow 9.1915. Sold 1.3.1923 Basra.

STONEHENGE Destroyer, 'S' class. Palmer 19.3.1919. Wrecked 1.11.1920 nr Smyrna: wreck sold 26.3.1921.

STONEHENGE Submarine, 'S' class. Cammell Laird 23.3.1943. Sunk 15.3.1944 Strait of Malacca.

STONETOWN Frigate (RCN), 'River' class. Vickers, Montreal, 28.3.1944. Tx Dept of Transport 1950 as weather ship. Sold 1969 Vancouver.

STONEWALL JACKSON *See ROBERTS 1915.*

STORK 36-gun ship, 397bm. Dutch, captured 1652. Hulk 1653. Sold 1663.

STORK Sloop 10, 233bm, 88·5 × 24·5ft. Stowe, Shoreham, 8.11.1756. Captured 16.8.1758 by Spanish in West Indies.

STORK Sloop 18, 427bm, 108 × 30ft. Deptford DY 29.11.1796 Sold 30.5.1816.

STORK Wood screw gunboat, 'Dapper' class. Pitcher, Northfleet, 7.4.1855. Coal hulk 1874. Sold 4.1884 for BU.

STORK Composite screw gunboat, 465 tons, 125 × 23·5ft, 2—64pdr, 2—20pdr. Samuda, Poplar, 18.5.1882. Survey ship 1887; lent 3.1913 as TS. BU 1950 Shaws of Kent, Lower Rainham; hull used as wharf.

STORK Destroyer, 'R' class. Hawthorn Leslie 15.11.1916. Sold 7.10.1927 Cashmore, Newport.

STORK Survey vessel (sloop) 1,190 tons, 266 × 37ft, 4—3pdr. Denny 21.4.1936. Escort 1939, 4—4·7in. Arr. 6.1958 Troon for BU.

STORM Submarine, 'S' class. Cammell Laird 18.5.1943. BU 11.1949 Troon.

STORMCLOUD Destroyer, 'S' class. Palmer 30.5.1919. Sold 28.7.1934 Metal Industries, Charlestown.

STORMCLOUD Minesweeper, 'Algerine' class. Lobnitz 28.12.1943. Arr. 2.8.1959 King, Gateshead, for BU.

STORMONT Brig-sloop 16, c. 175bm, 80 × 23·5ft. Purch. 1781. Captured 23.1.1782 by French at surrender of Demerara; = STORMON until 1786.

STORMONT Sloop. American privateer, captured 14.2.1782 by PROTHEE. Sold 1.7.1784.

STORMONT Frigate (RCN), 'River' class. Vickers, Montreal, 14.7.1943. Sold 1947, mercantile; = *Christina* (yacht) 1951.

STORMONT *See also MATANE 1943.*

STORMY PETREL Paddle minesweeper. Murdoch & Murray, cancelled 10.1918.

STORNOWAY Minesweeper, TE 'Bangor' class. Robb 10.6.1941. Sold 11.9.1946 mercantile.

STOUR Destroyer, 570 tons, 220 × 24ft, 4—12pdr, 2—TT. Laird 3.6.1905 spec., purch. 12.1909. Sold 30.8.1919 J. Smith.

STRAFFORD 4th Rate 50, 703bm, 130·5 × 35ft. Plymouth DY 16.7.1714. BU 1733.

STRAFFORD 4th Rate 50, 1,067bm, 144 × 41·5ft. Chatham DY 24.7.1735. Sunk 1756 breakwater Sheerness.

STRAHAN Minesweeper (RAN), 'Bathurst' class. Newcastle DY, NSW, 12.7.1943. Sold 6.1.1961 for BU Japan.

STRANRAER *See CLONMEL 1918.*

STRATAGEM Submarine, 'S' class. Cammell Laird 21.6.1943. Sunk 22.11.1944 Japanese patrol craft off Malacca.

STRATFORD Minesweeper (RCN), TE 'Bangor' class. Dufferin 14.2.1942. Disposal list 1946.

STRATHADAM Frigate (RCN), 'River' class. Yarrow, Esquimalt, 20.3.1944. Sold 1947 mercantile Uruguay; tx 1950 Israeli Navy = MISGAV; BU 1959.

STRATHROY Corvette (RCN), Modified 'Flower' class. Midland SY, Ontario, 30.8.1944. Sold 1946 Chilean Navy = CHIPANO; BU 2.7.1969.

STRATTON Coastal minesweeper, 'Ton' class. Dorset Yacht Co. 29.7.1957. Tx 1958 SAN = KIMBERLEY; PO 1999, deleted.

STRENUOUS Gun-brig 12, 180bm, 84 × 22ft, 10—18pdr carr., 2—12pdr. Rowe, Newcastle, 16.5.1805. Sold 1.9.1814.

STRENUOUS Destroyer, 'S' class. Scotts 9.11.1918. Sold 25.8.1932 Metal Industries, Charlestown.

STRENUOUS (ex-VITAL) Minesweeper, 'Catherine' class. Gulf SB, Madisonville, 7.9.1942; tx RN 5.1943 on Lend-Lease. Nominally ret. USN 12.1946; LU Woolston until 4.1956; BU 7.1956 Germany.

STRENUOUS *See also CARRON 1942.*

STRIKER (ex-PRINCE WILLIAM) Escort carrier, 11,420 tons, 468·5 × 69·5ft, 2—4in, 8—40mm, 18 aircraft. Weston Pipe & Steel Co. 7.5.1942 on Lend-Lease. Ret. USN 2.1946.

STRIKER Training boat, 32 tons, 65·6 (oa) × 17ft, Fairey Marine, Southampton 1983. Sold 11.1991 Lebanon, = JOUNIETH 17.7.1992.

STRIKER *See also LST.3516 1945.*

STROMBOLI Bomb vessel (Indian), 68bm. Bombay DY 1793. *Fate unknown.*

STROMBOLI Wood paddle sloop, 967bm, 180 × 34·5ft Portsmouth DY 27.8.1839. Sold 8.1866.

STROMBOLO Fireship 8, 266bm, 91·5 × 2 5·5ft. Johnson, Blackwall, 7.3.1691. Rebuilt 1704. Sold 20.8.1713.

STROMBOLO (ex-*Mollineaux*) Fireship 8, 217bm, 88 × 24ft. Purch. 7.9.1739. Sold 9.2.1743.

STROMBOLO (ex-*Owner's Goodwill*) Fireship 8, 268bm, 93 × 26ft. Purch. 31.12.1756. Sold 26.4.1768.

STROMBOLO (ex-*Leander*) Bomb vessel 8, 371 bm, 100 × 29ft. Purch. 4.1797. BU 7.1809.

STROMBOLO *See also GRAMPUS 1746, AUTUMN 1801.*

STRONGBOW Destroyer, 'M' class, 898 tons. Yarrow 30.9.1916. Sunk 17.10.1917 in action with two German cruisers in North Sea.

STRONGBOW Submarine, 'S' class. Scotts 30.8.1943. BU 4.1946 Ward, Preston.

STRONGHOLD Destroyer, 'S' class. Scotts 6.5.1919. Sunk 4.3.1942 in action with Japanese squadron 300 miles south of Java.

STRULE *See GLENARM 1943.*

STUART Destroyer leader, 1,800 tons, 320 × 32ft, 5—4·7in, 1—3in, 6—TT. Hawthorn Leslie 22.8.1918. RAN 10.1933; fast store carrier 1944. Sold 2.1947 T. Carr & Co.

STUART Frigate (RAN), 2,100 tons, 370 (oa) × 41ft, 2—4·5in, 4—GWS, Limbo. Cockatoo DY 8.4.1961. PO 26.7.1991. Left Fremantle 13.3.1992 tow for BU Pakistan.

STUART Frigate (RAN), 'Anzac' class. Tenix Defence Systems, Williamstown, 17.4.1999.

STUBBINGTON Coastal minesweeper, 'Ton' class. Camper & Nicholson 8.8.1956. Arr. Bilbao 26.9.1989 for BU.

STUBBORN (ex-P.238) Submarine, 'S' class. Cammell Laird 11.11.1942. Sunk 30.4.1946 asdic target off Malta.

STURDY Destroyer, 'S' class. Scotts 25.6.1919. Wrecked 30.10.1940 Tiree.

STURDY Submarine, 'S' class. Cammell Laird 30.9.1943. Sold 7.1957 Malta; arr. 9.5.1958 Clayton & Davie for BU.

STURGEON Destroyer, 310 tons, 195 × 20·5ft, 1—2pdr, 5—6pdr, 2—TT. NC&A (Vickers) 21.7.1894. Sold 14.5.1912 Thames S. Bkg Co.

STURGEON Destroyer, 'R' class. Stephen 11.1.1917. Sold 16.12.1926 Plymouth & Devon S. Bkg Co.

STURGEON Submarine, 640 tons, 187 × 23·5ft,

1–3in, 6–TT. Chatham DY 8.1.1932. Lent Dutch Navy 11.10.1943–14.9.1945 = ZEEHOND. BU 1.1946 Granton.

STYGIAN Submarine, 'S' class. Cammell Laird 30.11.1943. Sold 28.10.1949; BU Metal Industries, Ardgour, 8.1950.

STYX Wood paddle sloop, 1,057bm, 180 × 36ft. Sheerness DY 26.1.1841. BU 4.1866.

STYX Minesweeper, 'Algerine' class. Collingwood SY. Laid down 18.7.1944; cancelled 8.11.1944.

Submarine No 1 etc (Holland submarines) *See entries at start of 'H' section.*

SUBSTITUTE Cutter. Purch. 1782. Sold 14.8.1783.

SUBTLE (RED GALLEY) Galley 31, 200bm. Listed 1544–60.

SUBTLE Schooner 12, 125bm. Purch. 1808. Foundered 30.11.1812 off St Barts, West Indies.

SUBTLE Submarine, 'S' class. Cammell Laird 27.1.1944. BU 7.1959 Charlestown.

SUBTLE *See also VIGILANT 1806.*

SUCCESS (OLD SUCCESS) (ex-JULES) 34-gun ship, 450bm. French, captured 19.10.1650; renamed 1660. Sold 1662.

SUCCESS Fireship 6, 127bm. Purch. 1672. Foundered 1673.

SUCCESS Store hulk, 524bm. Purch. 20.8.1692. Sunk 13.1.1707 breakwater Sheerness.

SUCCESS Sloop 10, 110bm. Purch. 6.1709. Captured 11.4.1710 by French off Lisbon.

SUCCESS Storeship 24, 546bm, 126·5 × 31ft. Deptford DY 10.9.1709. Hulked 2.1730. Sold 6.12.1748.

SUCCESS 6th Rate 20, 275bm, 94·5 × 26ft. Portsmouth DY 30.4.1712. Fireship 1739. Sold 22.7.1743.

SUCCESS Sloop 14 (Indian). Bombay DY 1736. *Fate unknown.*

SUCCESS 6th Rate 24, 436bm, 106 × 30·5ft. Blaydes, Hull, 14.8.1740. BU 1779.

SUCCESS Ketch 14 (Indian). Bombay DY 1754. *Fate unknown.*

SUCCESS 5th Rate 32, 683bm, 126 × 35ft. Sutton, Liverpool, 10.4.1781. Convict ship 1.1814. BU 1820 Halifax, NS.

SUCCESS Gunvessel 3. Barge, purch. 9.1797. Sold 1.1802.

SUCCESS 6th Rate 28, 504bm, 114 × 32ft, 20– 32pdr, 6–18pdr carr., 2–6pdr. Pembroke Dock 30.8.1825. Harbour service 1832. BU 6.1849.

SUCCESS Wood screw sloop, 950bm, 185 × 33ft, 2–110pdr, 5–64pdr. Pembroke Dock, not LD, cancelled 12.1863.

SUCCESS Destroyer, 385 tons, 210 × 21ft, 1– 12pdr, 5–6pdr, 2–TT. Doxford 21.3.1901. Wrecked 27.12.1914 nr Fifeness.

SUCCESS Destroyer, 'S' class. Doxford 29.6.1918. Tx RAN 6.1919. Sold 4.6.1937 Sydney.

SUCCESS Destroyer, 1,710 tons, 362·8 (oa) × 35·7ft, 4–4·7in, 2–40mm, 8–TT. White 3.4.1943. Tx RNorN 8.1943 = STORD; BU Burght 1959.

SUCCESS Supply ship (RAN), 17,930 tons (deep load). Cockatoo DY 3.3.1984.

SUCCESS *See also BRADFORD 1958.*

SUDBURY Corvette (RCN), 'Flower' class. Kingston 31.5.1941. Sold 1949 Badwater Towing Co. as tug, name unchanged.

SUFFISANTE Brig-sloop 14, 236bm, 86 × 29ft. French, captured 31.8.1795 by Fleet off Texel. Wrecked 15.12.1803 off Queenstown.

SUFFISANTE (ex-VIGILANTE) Brig-sloop 16, 358bm. French, captured 30.6.1803 San Domingo (renamed 12.1803). Sold 6.1807.

SUFFOLK 3rd Rate 70, 1,401bm, 151 × 40ft. Johnson, Blackwall, 1680. Rebuilt Blackwall 1699 as 1,075bm; rebuilt Woolwich 1739 as 1,224bm, 64 guns. BU comp. 12.6.1765.

SUFFOLK (SUFFOLK HAGBOAT) Storeship 30, 477bm, 177 × 30·5ft. Purch. 7.1694. Sold 15.12.1713.

SUFFOLK 3rd Rate 74, 1,616bm, 168 × 47ft. Randall, Rotherhithe, 22.2.1765. BU 2.1803.

SUFFOLK Armoured cruiser, 9,800 tons, 440 × 66ft, 14–6in, 10–12pdr. Portsmouth DY 15.1.1903. Sold 1.7.1920 S. Castle, BU Germany 1922.

SUFFOLK Cruiser, 9,800 tons, 630 (oa) × 68·5ft, 8–8in, 8–4in. Portsmouth DY 16.2.1926. Sold 25.3.1948; BU Cashmore, Newport.

SUFFOLK *See also SULTAN 1775.*

SUFFOLK HAGBOAT *See SUFFOLK 1694.*

SUIPPE Sloop, 604 tons, 250 × 28·5ft, 4–3.9in. French, seized 3.7.1940 Falmouth, not cd. Sunk 14.4.1941 air attack Falmouth; raised, BU.

SULHAM Inshore minesweeper, 'Ham' class. Fairlie Yacht Co. 24.3.1955. Tx French Navy 1955 = M.787/JONQUILLE. BU 1985.

SULINA (ex-*Panscova*) Iron paddle vessel. Purch. 19.8.1854 Constantinople. Sold 8.1856.

SULLINGTON Coastal minesweeper, 'Ton' class. Doig, Grimsby, 7.4.1954. = MERMAID (survey vessel) 4.1965. Sold A. K. Vickers 5.9.1970; BU Fleetwood.

SULPHUR Fireship 8. Purch. 7.1778 North America. Sold 4.4.1783.

SULPHUR (ex-*Severn*) Bomb vessel 8, 355bm, 97 × 29ft. Purch. 4.1797. Sold 10.6.1816.

SULPHUR Bomb vessel 10, 375bm, 105·5 × 28ft, 10–24pdr carr. 2–3pdr, 2 mortars. Chatham DY

26.1.1826. Survey vessel 1835; harbour service 1843. BU comp. 20.11.1857. *Last bomb vessel in Navy List.*

SULTAN Schooner, 536bm. Purch. 18.3.1768. Sold 11.8.1773.

SULTAN 3rd Rate 74, 1,614bm, 168·5 × 47ft. Barnard, Harwich, 23.12.1775. Prison ship 2.1797, = SUFFOLK 1805. BU 1.1816.

SULTAN 3rd Rate 74, 1,751bm, 175 × 48·5ft. Dudman, Deptford, 19.9.1807. Receiving ship 1860, then target. BU comp. 28.1.1864.

SULTAN Battleship, 5,234bm, 9,290 tons, 325 × 59ft, 8—10in, 4—9in. Chatham DY 31.5.1870. = FISGARD IV 1.1.1906; = SULTAN (training hulk) 1932. Sold 13.8.1946; arr. 8.10.1946 Dalmuir for BU.

SULTAN HISAR Destroyer, 1,360 tons. Denny 1941, for Turkish Navy. Cd RN 12.1941 for passage Turkey; HO Turkey 1942.

SUMMERSIDE Corvette (RCN), 'Flower' class. Morton 7.5.1941. BU 6.1946 Steel Co. of Canada.

SUMMERSIDE MCDV (RCN), 'Kingston' class, 962 tons, 181·4 (oa) × 37·1ft, 1—40mm. Halifax SY 4.10.1998.

SUNDERLAND 4th Rate 60, 915bm, 145 × 38ft. Winter, Southampton, 17.3.1694. Hulked 1715. Sunk 1737 foundation Sheerness.

SUNDERLAND 4th Rate 60, 951bm, 144 × 39ft. Chatham DY 30.4.1724. Rebuilt Portsmouth 1744 as 1,123bm. Foundered 1.1.1761 cyclone off Pondicherry.

SUNDERLAND *See also LYME REGIS 1942.*

SUNDEW Corvette, 'Flower' class. Lewis 28.5.1941. Lent Free French 1942—6.1947 = ROSELYS. Sold 23.10.1947; arr. 5.1948 Troon for BU.

SUNFISH Destroyer, 315 tons, 200 × 19ft, 1— 12pdr, 5—6pdr, 2—TT. Hawthorn 23.5.1895. Sold 7.6.1920 J. Kelly.

SUNFISH Submarine, 670 tons, 193 × 24ft, 1—3in, 6—TT. Chatham DY 30.9.1936. Lent Soviet Navy 1944 = B.1; sunk in error 27.7.1944 by British aircraft on passage northern Russia.

SUNFLOWER Sloop, 'Acacia' class. Henderson 28.5.1915. Sold 27.1.1921 Rangoon Port Commissioners = *Lanbya.*

SUNFLOWER Corvette, 'Flower' class. Smith's Dock 19.8.1940. BU 8.1947 Ward, Hayle.

SUNN 12-gun ship. Captured 1651. Sold 1654.

SUNN PRIZE 6th Rate 24, 214bm, 81 × 24ft. French, captured 4.8.1692. Sold 1701. *In French hands 17.6.1693—8.10.1696.*

SUNN PRIZE 6th Rate 22, 215bm, 83 × 24ft. French, captured 4.7.1704 by LICHFIELD. Recap-

tured 18.1.1708 by French privateer off The Needles.

SUNSTAR Minesweeping sloop, '24' class. Swan Hunter, cancelled 3.12.1918. Sold incomp. 29.11.1922 Hallamshire Metal Co.

SUPERB (ex-SUPERBE) 3rd Rate 64, 1,029bm, 143·5 × 40ft. French, captured 29.7.1710 by KENT off The Lizard. BU 1732.

SUPERB 4th Rate 60, 1,068bm, 144 × 41·5ft. Woolwich DY 1736 BU 7.1757 Sheerness.

SUPERB 3rd Rate 74 1,612bm, 168 × 47ft. Deptford DY 27.10.1760. Wrecked 5.11.1783 off Tellicherry, India.

SUPERB 3rd Rate 74, 1,919bm, 182 × 49ft. Pitcher, Northfleet, 19.3.1798. BU comp. 17.4.1826.

SUPERB 2nd Rate 80, 2,583bm, 190 × 57ft, 12— 8in, 68—32pdr. Pembroke Dock 6.9.1842. BU comp. 18.2.1869 Portsmouth.

SUPERB (ex-HAMIDIYEH) Battleship, 9,310 tons, 332 × 59ft, 16—10in, 6—4in, 6—6pdr. Thames Iron Works, Blackwall, 16.11.1875; Turkish, purch. 20.2.1878. Sold 15.5.1906 Garnham.

SUPERB Battleship, 18,600 tons, 490 × 82·5ft, 10—12in, 16—4in. Armstrong 7.11.1907. Sold 12.12.1922 Stanlee, Dover.

SUPERB Cruiser, 8,800 tons, 555·5 (oa) × 64ft, 9—6in, 10—4in. Swan Hunter 31.8.1943. Arr. 8.8.1960 Arnott Young, Dalmuir and Troon, for BU.

SUPERB Nuclear submarine, 'Swiftsure' class. Vickers 30.11.1974. Scheduled to PO 2003.

SUPERB *See also ALEXANDRA 1875.*

SUPERBE 6th Rate 22, 619bm, 120 × 35ft. French, captured 10.10.1795 by VANGUARD in West Indies. Prison ship Martinique 1796. Sold 1798.

SUPERIERE Schooner 14, 197bm, 86·5 × 23·5ft, 12—18pdr carr., 2—12pdr. French, captured 30.6.1803 off San Domingo. Sold 16.3.1814 Ledger for BU.

SUPERLATIVA Galley 7, 100bm. Deptford 1601. Sold 1629.

SUPPLY Fireship 6, 230bm. Purch. 1672. Expended 1673.

SUPPLY Fireship 9, 130bm. Purch. 1688. *Fate unknown.*

SUPPLY Armed tender 4, 175bm, 79·5 × 22·5ft. Bird, R. Thames, 1759. Sold 17.7.1792.

SUPPLY (ex-*Prince of Wales*) Storeship 26, 512bm. Purch. 10.1777. Burnt 14.6.1779 accident St Kitts.

SUPPLY Storeship 20, 491bm, 115 × 31ft. Purch. 12.1781. Sold 25.3.1784.

SUPPLY (ex-*New Brunswick*) Storeship 10 (birchbuilt), 388bm, 97·5 × 20·5ft. Purch. 10.1793. BU 1806 New South Wales.

SUPPLY Transport, 222bm, 86 × 24·5ft. Pitcher, Northfleet, 2.7.1798. BU 10.1834.

SUPPLY Iron screw storeship, 638bm, 1,100 tons. Purch. on stocks 4.1854. Ditchburn & Mare, Blackwall, 3.6.1854. BU comp. 8.2.1879 Chatham.

SUPREME Submarine, 'S' class. Cammell Laird 24.2.1944. Sold 7.1950; BU Troon.

SURCOUF Submarine, 2,880 tons, 361 × 29·5ft, 2—8in, 2—37mm, 10—TT. French, seized 3.7.1940 Plymouth. Free French 8.1940; sunk in error 18.2.1942 by SS *Thomson Likes* in Caribbean.

SURF (ex-P.239) Submarine, 'S' class. Cammell Laird 10.12.1942. Sold 28.10.1949; arr. 7.1950 Faslane for BU.

SURFACE Submarine, 'S' class. Cammell Laird, cancelled 1945.

SURGE Submarine, 'S' class. Cammell Laird, cancelled 1945.

SURINAM (ex-HUSSARD) Sloop 18, 414bm, 20—4pdr. French, captured 20.4.1799 Surinam; captured 7.1803 by Dutch at Curaçao; recaptured 1.1.1807, re-added 1808. Listed until 1809.

SURINAM (ex-PYLADES) Sloop 16. Dutch, captured 4.5.1804 Surinam. Listed until 1808.

SURINAM Sloop 18, 'Cruizer' class, 384bm. Ayles, Topsham, 1.1805. Sold 20.7.1825 Ledger for BU.

SURLY Cutter 10, 137bm, 63 × 23·5ft. Johnson, Dover, 15.11.1806. Dockyard lighter 2.1833. Sold 1.1837.

SURLY Mortar vessel, 117bm, 65 × 21ft, 1—13in mortar. Wigram, Blackwall, 31.3.1855. = MV.9 on 19.10.1855. BU 11.1863.

SURLY Wood screw gunboat, 'Albacore' class. Smith, North Shields, 18.3.1856. Sold 1869 T. Begbie.

SURLY Destroyer, 310 tons, 205 × 19ft, 1—11pdr, 5—6pdr, 2—TT. Thomson 10.11.1894. Sold 23.3.1920 Ward, Milford Haven.

SURPRISE (ex-UNITE) 6th Rate 24, 579bm, 24—32pdr carr., 8—18pdr carr., 4—6pdr. French, captured 20.4.1796 by INCONSTANT in Mediterranean. Sold 2.1802 Deptford.

SURPRISE (ex-*Surprise*) Schooner 10. French merchantman, captured 1799 by BRAVE in East Indies. Sold 1800.

SURPRISE 5th Rate 38, 1,072bm, 150·5 × 40ft. Milford Haven DY (ex-Jacobs) 25.7.1812. Convict ship 6.1822, ordered sold 2.10.1837.

SURPRISE (ex-TIGRESS) Schooner 2 (Canadian lakes), 74bm, 57 × 17·5ft, 1—24pdr, 1—24pdr carr. American, captured 3.9.1814 Lake Erie. Listed until 1832.

SURPRISE Wood screw gunvessel, 680bm, 181 × 28·5ft, 1—110pdr, 1—68pdr, 2—2pdr.Wigram, Blackwall, 16.3.1856. BU 11.1866 Marshall, Plymouth.

SURPRISE Despatch vessel, 1,650 tons, 250 × 32·5ft, 4—5in, 4—6pdr. Palmer 17.1.1885. = ALACRITY 1913. Sold 1919.

SURPRISE Destroyer, 'M' class, 910 tons. Yarrow 25.11.1916. Sunk 23.12.1917 mine North Sea.

SURPRISE *See also GERRANS BAY 1945.*

SURPRIZE 6th Rate 24, 508bm, 112·5 × 32ft. Wyatt & Major, Beaulieu, 27.1.1745. BU 7.1770.

SURPRIZE 6th Rate 28, 594bm, 120·5 × 33·5ft. Woolwich DY 13.4.1774. Sold 17.4.1783.

SURPRIZE (ex-BUNKER HILL) Sloop 18. American, captured 1778 St Lucia. Sold 1783 Sheerness.

SURPRIZE Cutter 10, 135bm, 67·5 × 29ft, 10—3pdr. Purch. 2.1780. Sold 30.10.1786.

SURPRIZE Cutter 10, 130bm, 69 × 22·5ft, 10—3pdr. Purch. 10.1786. Sold 2.10.1792 Sheerness.

SURREY Cruiser, 10,000 tons, 590 × 66ft, 8—8in. PortsmouthDY, cancelled 1.1.1930.

SURVEILLANTE 5th Rate 36, 1,094bm. French, captured 30.11.1803 by squadron in West Indies. BU 8.1814.

SURVEYOR Schooner 6. American, captured 12.6.1813 by boats of NARCISSUS. Gone by 1814.

SUSSEX 46-gun ship, 600bm. Portsmouth DY 1652. Blown up 12.1653 accident.

SUSSEX 3rd Rate 80, 1,203bm, 157 × 41·5ft. Chatham DY 11.4.1693. Wrecked 19.2.1694 nr Gibraltar.

SUSSEX Cruiser, 9,830 tons, 633 (oa) × 66ft, 8—8in, 8—4in. Hawthorn Leslie 22.2.1928. Sold 3.1.1950; arr. 23.2.1950 Dalmuir and 7.1950 Troon.

SUSSEX *See also UNION 1756.*

SUSSEXVALE (ex-VALDORIAN) Frigate (RCN), 'River' class. Davie SB 12.7.1944 (renamed 1944). Sold Kennedy & Mitsui, Vancouver, 12.1966 for BU.

SUTHERLAND 4th Rate 50, 874bm, 134 × 38·5ft. Taylor, Rotherhithe, 15.10.1741. Sold 5.6.1770.

SUTHERLAND Frigate, 'Norfolk' class. Yarrow, Glasgow, 9.3.1996.

SUTHERLAND *See also RESERVE 1704.*

SUTLEJ 4th Rate 50, 2,066bm, 180 × 51ft, 28—8in, 22—32pdr. Pembroke Dock 17.4.1855; undocked 26.3.1860 as screw frigate, 3,066bm. BU 1869 Portsmouth.

SUTLEJ Armoured cruiser, 12,000 tons, 440 × 69·5ft, 2—9·2in, 12—6in, 12—12pdr. John Brown 18.11.1899. Sold 9.5.1921 Ward, LU Belfast; arr. 15.8.1924 Preston for BU.

SUTLEJ Sloop (RIN), 1,250 tons, 299·5 (oa) ×

37·5ft, 6–4in. Denny 1.10.1940. Survey ship post-war. PO 31.12.1978; deleted 1982–83; BU India.

SUTTON (ex-SALCOMBE) Minesweeper, Later 'Hunt' class. McMillan, Dumbarton, 8.5.1918 (renamed 1918). Sold Dohmen & Habets 7.1947 for BU.

SUVLA *See LST.3518 1945.*

SVENNER *See SHARK 1943.*

SWAGGERER (ex-BONAPARTE) Brig 16, 300bm. French privateer, captured 1809. BU 1815.

SWALE Destroyer, 550 tons, 222 × 23·5ft, 1–12pdr, 5–6pdr (1907: 4–12pdr), 2–TT. Palmer 20.3.1905. Sold 23.6.1919 Ward, Preston.

SWALE Frigate, 'River' class. Smith's Dock 16.1.1942. Arr. 4.3.1955 Faslane for BU.

SWALLOW 53-gun ship, 240bm. Built 1544. Rebuilt 1558 as 300bm; rebuilt 1580 as 415bm, 40 guns. Sold 1603.

SWALLOW Discovery vessel, 100bm. With Borrough in Arctic 1558. Captured 1568 by Spanish.

SWALLOW Pinnace 8, 2–4pdr, 1–2pdr, 5 smaller. Built 1573. Condemned 1603.

SWALLOW 40-ton vessel. With Sir Humphrey Gilbert in Newfoundland 1583.

SWALLOW 40-gun ship, 478bm. Deptford 1634. Royalist from 1648. Sold 1653 in France.

SWALLOW Ketch 6, 56bm. Deptford 1657. Tx Irish Packet Service 1661.

SWALLOW Sloop 2, 68bm. Deptford 1672. Lost 1673.

SWALLOW Sloop 6, 66bm. Chatham DY 30.9.1699. Captured 19.4.1703 by French privateer off The Maes.

SWALLOW 4th Rate 54, 672bm, 130 × 34·5ft. Deptford 2.1703. Rebuilt Chatham 1719 as 710bm. BU 1728.

SWALLOW 4th Rate 60, 951bm, 144 × 39ft. Plymouth DY 6.10.1732. = PRINCESS LOUISA 16.1.1737. BU 1742.

SWALLOW Sloop 14, 278bm, 92 × 26·5ft. Bird, Rotherhithe, 14.12.1745. Impress service 1762. Sold 20.6.1769.

SWALLOW Discovery vessel. With Carteret in Pacific 1766. BU 1769.

SWALLOW Sloop 14, 302bm, 96 × 27ft. Deptford DY 30.12.1769. Foundered 12.1777 Atlantic.

SWALLOW Ketch 14 (Indian). Bombay DY 1770. Lost 1776.

SWALLOW Packet 14 (Indian), 200bm. Bombay DY 2.4.1777. Sold 1780 Danish Navy captured 1782 by RN = SILLY. Sold 1784 mercantile. *Vessel SILLY not traced.*

SWALLOW Sloop 14, 226bm, 79·5 × 26·5ft. Ladd,

Dover, 2.4.1779. Driven ashore nr Long I. 26.8.1781 by four American privateers.

SWALLOW Sloop 16, 262bm, 78 × 29ft. Fabian, East Cowes 10.1781; cutter, purch. on stocks. Sold 20.8.1795.

SWALLOW Tender. In service 1793–95.

SWALLOW Brig-sloop 18 (fir-built), 365bm, 96 × 30·5ft. Perry, Blackwall, 10.9.1795. Sold 8.1802.

SWALLOW Brig-sloop 18, 'Cruizer' class, 387bm. Tanner, Dartmouth, 24.12.1805. BU 11.1815.

SWALLOW Cutter tender, 46bm, 45 × 16ft. Deptford 1811. Lost 1825.

SWALLOW (ex-*Marquis of Salisbury*) Brig-sloop 10, 236bm. Packet, purch. 7.1824. Sold 8.9.1836.

SWALLOW (ex-*Ferret*) Wood paddle packet, 133bm. GPO vessel, tx 1.4.1837. BU 3.1848.

SWALLOW Wood screw sloop, 486bm, 139 × 28ft, 9–32pdr. Pembroke Dock 12.6.1854. Sold 12.1866

SWALLOW Wood screw gunvessel, 664bm, 805 tons, 170 × 24ft, 1–7in, 2–40pdr. Portsmouth DY 16.11.1868. Sold 18.10.1882 A. Tobin.

SWALLOW Composite screw sloop, 1,130 tons, 195 × 28ft, 8–5in. Sheerness DY 27.10.1885. Sold 1904 McCausland & Sons.

SWALLOW Destroyer, 'S' class. Scotts 1.8.1918. HO Ward 24.9.1936 part payment *Majestic* (CALEDONIA, q.v.); BU Inverkeithing.

SWALLOW Patrol vessel, 662 tons, 205·3 (oa) × 32·8ft, 1–76mm, Hall Russell 30.3.1984. Sold to Irish Navy = CIARA 21.11.1988.

SWALLOW *See also MARY FORTUNE 1497, GAINSBOROUGH 1653, GALGO 1744,e CAPRICE 1943. The name SWALLOW has been borne by 39 British naval vessels, one dockyard craft, two vessels of The Hon. East India Company and at least two revenue cutters.*

SWALLOW KETCH Ketch 6, 54bm. Purch. 1661. Sold 1674.

SWALLOW PRIZE 6th Rate 18, 119bm, 68 × 20·5ft. French, captured 1693. Recaptured 22.2.1696 by French privateer off Weymouth.

SWALLOW PRIZE 5th Rate 32. French, captured 3.1704 by SWALLOW. Wrecked 29.7.1711 off Corsica.

SWAN Sloop 14, 280bm, 91 × 26·5ft. Hinck, Chester, 14.12.1745. Sold 31.3.1763.

SWAN Sloop 14, 302bm, 96·5 × 27ft. Plymouth DY 21.11.1767. Sold 1.9.1814. *Bore name EXPLOSION 10.1779–1783 while in use as fireship.*

SWAN Cutter 10, 90bm, 10–6pdr. Purch. 1788 for Revenue Service, tx RN 1790. Wrecked 26.5.1792 off Shoreham.

SWAN Cutter 10. Purch. 1792 for Revenue Service, tx RN 1795. Captured 1795 by French.

SWAN Cutter 10, 144bm, 65·5 × 23ft, 10—12pdr carr. Cowes 1.11.1811. Lent 5.1844 Church Missionary Society. BU comp. 7.12.1874 Sheerness.

SWAN Wood screw gunboat, 'Albacore' class. Smith, North Shields, 12.4.1856. Coal hulk 1869. Sold 1906.

SWAN Destroyer (RAN), 700 tons, 246 × 24ft, 1—4in, 3—12pdr, 3—TT. Cockatoo DY 11.12.1915. Stripped 9.1929; hulk foundered 2.2.1934 Hawkesbury R.

SWAN Sloop (RAN), 1,060 tons, 250 × 36ft, 3—4in. Cockatoo DY 28.3.1936. TS 1956. Sold 5.6.1964 Hurley & Dewhurst, Sydney.

SWAN Frigate (RAN), 2,100 tons, 370 (oa) × 41ft, 2—4·5in, 6—TT, Williamstown DY 16.12.1967. Scuttled 4.12.1997 as dive site Geographe Bay, Western Australia.

SWAN *See also BONETTA 1781.*

SWANN Ballinger, 120bm. Acq. 3.1417. Sold 1.4.1423.

SWANN 25-ton vessel. With Drake 1572.

SWANN Flyboat, 50bm. With Drake 1577. Lost 1578.

SWANN 'Frigat', 60bm. Listed 1632–33.

SWANN 22-gun ship, 200bm. Captured 1652. Sold 1654.

SWANN Flyboat 6, 162bm. Dutch, captured 1665. Sold 1666.

SWANN Smack, 24bm. Deane, Harwich, 1666. Captured 1673 by Dutch.

SWANN Fireship 2, 71bm. Purch. 1667. Expended 1667.

SWANN 5th Rate 32, 246bm, 85 × 26ft. Dutch, captured 1673. Fireship, 10 guns, 1688–89. Wrecked 15.6.1692 earthquake Jamaica.

SWANN 6th Rate. Algerian, captured 1684. Sold 1684.

SWANN 6th Rate 24, 249bm, 93·5 × 24·5ft. Castle, Deptford, 1694. Foundered 17.8.1707.

SWANN 6th Rate 12, 162bm, 78·5 × 22ft. Dummer, Rotherhithe, 17.9.1709. Sold 8.1.1713.

SWANN PRIZE Spanish 'Dunkirker', captured 1636. Sunk 10.1638 off Guernsey.

SWANSEA Frigate (RCN), 'River' class. Yarrow, Esquimalt, 19.12.1942. Sold Marine Salvage 16.8.1967; BU Savone, Italy.

SWANSTON Coastal minesweeper, 'Ton' class. Doig, Grimsby, 1.7.1954. Tx RAN = GULL 19.7.1962. Sold 1.1976.

SWASHWAY (ex-SWORD) Dock landing ship, 4,270 tons, 454 × 72ft, 1—5in, 12—40mm. Newport News 10.5.1944 for RN (renamed 8.1943); retained USN = RUSHMORE.

SWEEPSTAKE (SWEEPSTAKES) 80-ton ship. Portsmouth 1497. Rebuilt 1511. Listed until 1527.

SWEEPSTAKE Galleon 84, c. 300bm. Built 1535. Listed until 1559.

SWEEPSTAKES 5th Rate 36, 376bm, 109 × 28·5ft. Edgar, Yarmouth, 1666. 4th Rate 42 in 1669; 5th Rate 1691. Sold 13.5.1698.

SWEEPSTAKES 5th Rate 32, 416bm, 108·5ft. Stacey, Woolwich, 20.9.1708. Captured 16.4.1709 by two French privateers off Scilly Is.

SWEEPSTAKES (ex-GLOIRE) 5th Rate 42, 657bm, 122 × 35ft. French, captured 14.5.1709 by CHESTER. Sold 5.6.1716.

SWEETBRIAR Sloop, 'Anchusa' class. Swan Hunter 5.10.1917. Sold 7.10.1927 Cashmore, Newport.

SWEETBRIAR Corvette, 'Flower' class. Smith's Dock 26.6.1941. Sold 29.7.1946 = *Star IX*.

SWIFT 60-ton ship. Listed 1549–54.

SWIFT 6th Rate 20, 288bm, 87·5 × 26·5ft. French, captured 1689. Sunk 24.4.1695 breakwater Portsmouth.

SWIFT Brigantine 6, 80bm, 63 × 17ft. Chatham DY 1695. Foundered 17.8.1696.

SWIFT Advice boat 10, 154bm, 78 × 21·5ft. Moore, Arundel, 1697. Wrecked 24.1.1698 North Carolina.

SWIFT Sloop 4, 65bm. Portsmouth DY 1699. Captured 18.8.1702 by French privateer DUC DE BOURGOGNE off Scilly Is.

SWIFT Sloop 12, 123bm, 73·5 × 20ft. Woolwich 25.10.1704. Sold 20.8.1719.

SWIFT Sloop 12, 93bm, 60·5 × 19ft. Woolwich DY 19.8.1721. Sold 7.7.1741.

SWIFT Sloop 10, 203bm, 85 × 23·5ft. Carter, Limehouse, 30.5.1741. Wreck sold 10.1756.

SWIFT (ex-COMTE DE VALENCE) Cutter 10, 88bm, 54 × 19·5ft. French privateer, captured 1760, purch. 16.1.1761. Recaptured 30.6.1762 off Ushant by French privateer.

SWIFT Cutter 6, 54bm, 50 × 17ft. Purch. 1.1763. Sold 4.5.1773.

SWIFT Sloop 14, 271bm, 91 × 26ft. Graves, Limehouse, 1.3.1763. Lost 3.1770 off coast of Patagonia.

SWIFT Sloop 8. Purch. 3.1773 Antigua. Sold 13.5.1784.

SWIFT Sloop 14, 303bm, 97 × 27ft. Portsmouth DY 9.1.1777. Wrecked, burnt 11.1778 off Cape Henry.

SWIFT (ex-MIDDLETON) Sloop 16. American, captured 1779. Captured 11.8.1782 by French RESOLUE = RAPIDE.

SWIFT Sloop 16, 329bm, 100 × 27ft. Portsmouth DY 5.10.1793. Foundered 4.1797 Chinese waters.

SWIFT Schooner, 47bm, 44·5 × 16ft. Purch. 1794. BU 1803.

SWIFT Gunvessel (Canadian lakes). Kingston, Ontario, 1798. *Fate unknown.*

SWIFT (ex-*Pacific*) Brig-sloop 16, 327bm. Purch. 6.1804. Sold 3.11.1814.

SWIFT Cutter tender, 80bm, 55·5 × 18·5ft. Woolwich DY 15.2.1817. Sold 8.1821.

SWIFT Packet brig 8, 361bm, 95·5 × 30·5ft, 8–18pdr. Colson, Deptford, 21.11.1835. Mooring vessel 1861 The Cape = YC.3. Sold 1866.

SWIFT Composite screw gunvessel, 756 tons, 165 × 29ft, 2–7in, 3–20pdr. Green, Blackwall, 29.11.1879. Sale ordered 4.2.1902 Hong Kong; = *Swift*; = *Hoi Ching.*

SWIFT Torpedo boat, 125 tons, 153 × 17·5ft, 6–3pdr, 3–TT. White, Cowes, 1885, purch. 1885. = TB.81 in 1887. Sold 22.10.1921 J. E. Thomas.

SWIFT Destroyer, 1,825 tons, 345 × 34ft, 4–4in, 2–TT (1917: 2,170 tons, 1–6in, 2–4in), Cammell Laird 7.12.1907. Sold 9.11.1921 Rees, Llanelly.

SWIFT Destroyer, 1,710 tons, 362·8 (oa) × 35·7ft, 4–4·7in, 2–40mm, 8–TT. White 15.6.1943. Sunk 24.6.1944 mine off Normandy.

SWIFT Patrol vessel, 662 tons, 205·3 (oa) × 32·8ft, 1–76mm, Hall Russell 11.9.1984. Sold Irish Navy = ORLA 2.11.1988.

SWIFT CURRENT Minesweeper (RCN), TE 'Bangor' class. Vickers, Montreal, 29.5.1941. Sold Turkish Navy 29.3.1958 = BOZCAADA; in service until 1971.

SWIFTSURE Galleon 41, 360bm, 2–60pdr, 5–18pdr, 12–9pdr, 8–6pdr, 14 smaller. Deptford 1573. Rebuilt 1592 as 416bm. = SPEEDWELL 1607, 40 guns. Lost 11.1624 nr Flushing.

SWIFTSURE 46-gun ship, 746bm. Deptford 1621. Rebuilt Woolwich 1653 as 898bm. Captured 1.6.1666 by Dutch.

SWIFTSURE 3rd Rate 70, 978bm, 149 × 38·5ft. Deane, Harwich, 8.4.1673. Rebuilt Deptford 1696 as 987bm; 3rd Rate 64, 1,104bm = REVENGE 2.1.1716; rebuilt Deptford 1742 as 1,258bm. Sold 24.5.1787.

SWIFTSURE 3rd Rate 70, 426bm, 160 × 45ft. Deptford DY 25.5.1750. Sold 2.6.1773.

SWIFTSURE 3rd Rate 74, 1,612bm, 169 × 47ft. Wells, Deptford, 4.4.1787. Captured 24.6.1801 by French in Mediterranean; recaptured at Trafalgar = IRRESISTIBLE; prison ship. BU 1.1816 Chatham.

SWIFTSURE 3rd Rate 74, 1,724bm, 173 × 48ft. Adams, Buckler's Hard, 23.7.1804. Receiving ship 5.1819. Sold 18.10.1845 Barnard.

SWIFTSURE Iron armoured ship, 3,893bm, 6,910 tons, 280 × 55ft, 10–9in, 4–6pdr. Palmer, Jarrow, 15.6.1870. = ORONTES (harbour service) 3.1904. Sold 4.7.1908 Castle.

SWIFTSURE (ex-CONSTITUCION) Battleship, 11,800 tons, 436 × 71ft, 4–10in, 14–7·5in, 14–14pdr. Armstrong 12.1.03; Chilean, purch. 3.12.1903. Sold 18.6.1920 Stanlee, Dover.

SWIFTSURE Cruiser, 8,800 tons, 555·5 (oa) × 64ft, 9–6in, 10–4in. Vickers Armstrong, Tyne, 4.2.1943. Arr. 17.10.1962 Ward, Inverkeithing, for BU.

SWIFTSURE Nuclear submarine, 'Swiftsure' class. Vickers 7.9.1971. PO 1.5.1992, LU Rosyth.

SWINDON (ex-BANTRY) Minesweeper, Later 'Hunt' class. Ardrossan DD 25.12.1918 (renamed 1918). Sold 1.12.1921 = *Lady Cecilia.*

SWINGER Gunvessel 14, 147bm, 75·5 × 21ft. Hill, Limehouse, 31.5.1794. Sold 10.1802.

SWINGER Gunvessel 6. Purch. 1798 Honduras for local use. Listed 1799.

SWINGER Gun-brig 12, 178bm, 80 × 22·5ft, 2–18pdr, 10–18pdr carr. Davy, Topsham, 9.1804. BU 6.1812.

SWINGER Gun-brig 12, 180bm, 84 × 22ft, 10–18pdr carr., 2–6pdr. Goode, Bridport, 15.5.1813. Mooring lighter 2.1829. BU 3.1877.

SWINGER Wood screw gunboat, 'Dapper' class. Pitcher, Northfleet, 10.5.1855. BU 9.1864.

SWINGER Composite screw gunboat, 295bm, 430 tons, 125 × 22·5ft, 2–64pdr, 2–20pdr. Pembroke Dock 7.2.1872. Hulked 1895. Sold 6.1924 Rodgers & Co.

SWORD (ex-CELT) Destroyer, 1,980 tons. White, cancelled 5.10.1945 (renamed 9.1943).

SWORD *See also* SWASHWAY *1944.*

SWORD DANCE Minesweeper, 265 tons, 130 × 26ft, 1–6pdr. Lytham SB 1918; War Dept tug, tx 1919. Sunk 24.6.1919 mine.

SWORDFISH Destroyer, 330 tons, 200 × 19ft, 1–12pdr, 5–6pdr, 2–TT. Armstrong Mitchell 27.2.1895. Sold 11.10.1910 Cashmore, Newport.

SWORDFISH Steam submarine, 932 tons, 231·5 (oa) × 23ft, 2–12pdr, 6–TT. Scotts 18.3.1916. = S.1 in 4.1916; conv. surface patrol boat = SWORDFISH 7.1917. Sold 7.1922 Pounds, Portsmouth; resold Hayes, Porthcawl, 1923?

SWORDSMAN Destroyer, 'S' class. Scotts 28.12.1918. Tx RAN 6.1919; sold 4.6.1937 Sydney.

SWORDFISH Submarine, 640 tons, 187 × 23·5ft, 1–3in, 6–TT. Chatham DY 7.11.1931. Sunk off I. of Wight. *Probably mined.*

SYBILLE 5th Rate 44, 1,091bm, 154 × 40ft, 28–18pdr, 16–9pdr. French, captured 17.6.1794 by ROMNEY in Mediterranean. Harbour service 7.1831. Sold 7.8.1833.

SYBILLE 5th Rate 36, 1,633bm, 160 × 49ft, 36–

32pdr. Pembroke Dock 15.4.1847. BU 1866 Plymouth.

SYBILLE 2nd class cruiser, 3,400 tons, 300 × 43ft, 2—6in, 6—4·7in, 8—6pdr. Stephenson, Newcastle, 27.12.1890. Wrecked 16.1.1901 Lamberts Bay, South Africa.

SYBILLE Destroyer, 'M' class, 900 tons. Yarrow 5.2.1917. Sold 5.11.1926 Cashmore, Newport.

SYBILLE *See also SIBYL.*

SYCAMORE Destroyer, 'S' class. Stephen, cancelled 1919.

SYDENHAM Paddle gunvessel, 596bm, 170 × 27ft. Purch. 11.1841 Montreal. Sold 7.1846 Malta.

SYDNEY Survey brig 6, 139bm, 72 × 21ft, 6—12pdr carr. Purch. 1813. Sold 27.1.1825 J. Sheldrick.

SYDNEY 2nd class cruiser (RAN), 5,440 tons, 430 × 50ft, 8—6in. London & Glasgow Co. 29.8.1912. BU 4.1929 Cockatoo DY, Sydney.

SYDNEY (ex-PHAETON) Cruiser, 6,830 tons, 562·25 (oa) × 56·8ft, 8—6in, 8—4in. Swan Hunter 22.9.1934 (renamed 9.1935). Torpedoed 19.11.1941 by German AMC KORMORAN in Pacific.

SYDNEY Frigate (RAN), 'Adelaide' class. Todd, Seattle, 26.9.1980.

SYDNEY *See also TERRIBLE 1944.*

SYEREN 3rd Rate 74, 1,491bm. Danish, captured 7.9.1807 Battle of Copenhagen. Harbour service 1809. Sold 1.9.1814, retained; resold 23.11.1815.

SYLPH (ex-*Lovely Lass*) Sloop 14, 274bm, 85 × 27·5ft. Purch. 1776; = LIGHTNING (fireship) 25.8.1779. Sold 1.5.1783.

SYLPH (ex-*Active*) Sloop 18, 224bm, 80·5 × 26ft, 18—4pdr. Cutter, purch. 5.1780. Captured 3.2.1782 by French at loss of Demerara.

SYLPH Sloop 18 (fir-built), 365bm, 96 × 30·5ft. Barnard, Deptford, 3.9.1795. BU 4.1811.

SYLPH Schooner 8 (Indian). Bombay DY 1806. Captured 1808 by pirates.

SYLPH Brig-sloop 18, 400bm, 100 × 30ft. Tynes, Bermuda, 1812. Wrecked 17.1.1815 Long I.

SYLPH Tender, 114bm, 62 × 21ft. Woolwich DY 15.6.1821. Lent Customs Service 15.9.1862 as watchvessel. Sold 7.1888. *Not listed until 1832.*

SYLPH Destroyer, 'R' class. Harland & Wolff, Govan, 15.11.1916. Sold 16.12.1926 Cashmore; stranded 28.1.1927 Aberavon, BU.

SYLVIA Cutter 10, 110bm, 68 × 20ft. Bermuda 1806. Sold 30.5.1816.

SYLVIA Cutter 6, 70bm, 52·5 × 18ft. Portsmouth DY 24.3.1827. Survey vessel 3.1842. Sold 9.1859 Londonderry.

SYLVIA Wood screw sloop, 695bm, 865 tons, 185 × 28·5ft, 2—68pdr, 2—32pdr. Woolwich DY 20.3.1866. Comp. 10.1866 as survey vessel. Sold Cohen 8.1889 for BU.

SYLVIA Destroyer, 350 tons, 210 × 21ft, 1—12pdr, 5—6pdr, 2—TT. Doxford 3.7.1897. Sold 23.7.1919 Ward, New Holland.

SYLVIA Minesweeper, 'Algerine' class. Lobnitz 28.2.1944. Sold 16.9.1958 Malta; arr. 24.10.1958 King, Gateshead, for BU.

SYREN 6th Rate 24, 514bm, 114 × 32ft. Baker, Howden Dock, Tyne, 29.7.1779. Wrecked 1.1781 Sussex coast.

SYREN 5th Rate 32, 679bm, 126 × 35ft. Betts, Mistleythorn, 24.9.1782. Harbour service 1805. BU 9.1822.

SYREN Training tender, 54bm. Purch. 29.6.1878, attached to BRITANNIA. Sold 1912.

SYREN Destroyer, 390 tons, 215 × 21ft, 1—12pdr, 5—6pdr, 2—TT. Palmer 20.12.1900. Sold 14.9.1920 Hayes, Porthcawl.

SYREN *See also SIREN, SIRENE, SYEREN.*

SYRINGA Sloop, 'Anchusa' class. Workman Clark 29.9.1917. Sold 31.3.1920 Egyptian Navy = SOLLUM.

SYRTIS Submarine, 'S' class. Vickers Armstrong, Barrow, 4.2.1943. Sunk 28.3.1944 mine off Bodo, Norway.

T

TABARD Submarine, 'T' class. Scotts (ex-Vickers, Barrow) 21.11.1945. Sold Cashmore 2.1.1974; BU Newport.

TACITURN Submarine, 'T' class. Vickers Armstrong, Barrow, 7.6.1944. Sold Ward 23.7.1971; BU Briton Ferry.

TACTICIAN Destroyer, 'S' class. Beardmore 7.8.1918. Sold 2.1931 Metal Industries, Charlestown.

TACTICIAN Submarine, 'T' class. Vickers Armstrong, Barrow, 29.7.1942. Arr. 6.12.1963 Cashmore, Newport, for BU.

TACTICIAN Nuclear submarine. Ordered 10.9.1984. *Probably refers to sixth 'Trafalgar' class submarine ordered. See TALENT.*

TADOUSSAC Minesweeper (RCN), TE 'Bangor' class. Dufferin, Toronto, 2.8.1941. Sold 18.10.1946 = *Alexandre.*

TAFF Frigate, 'River' class. Hill, Bristol 11.9.1943. Arr. 6.1957 Cashmore, Newport for BU.

TAGUS (ex-SEVERN) 5th Rate 38 (red pine-built), 949bm, 143·5 × 38·5ft. List, Fishbourne, 14.7.1813 (renamed 1812). Sold 19.4.1822 Beatson for BU.

TAIN Minesweeper, Later 'Hunt' class. Simons, cancelled 1919.

TAITAM *See PORTLAND 1941.*

TAKU (ex-HAI LUNG) Destroyer, 305 tons, 193·5 × 20ft, 6—3pdr, 3—TT. Chinese, captured 17.6.1900 China. Sold 25.10.1916 in Hong Kong.

TAKU Submarine, 'T' class. Cammell Laird 20.5.1939. Sold 11.1946; BU Rees, Llanelly.

TALAPUS Patrol boat (RCN), 84 × 20ft. Armstrong Bros, Victoria, 2.7.1941. Sold 1946.

TALAVERA (ex-THUNDERER) 3rd Rate 74, 1,718bm, 174 × 48·5ft. Woolwich DY 15.10.1818 (renamed 23.7.1817). Burnt 27.9.1840 accident Plymouth.

TALAVERA Destroyer, 2,380 tons, 355 × 40ft, 5—4·5in, 8—40mm, 10—TT. John Brown 27.8.1945, not comp. Arr. 1.1946 Troon for BU.

TALAVERA *See also WATERLOO 1818.*

TALBOT Ship. Listed 1585.

TALBOT Ketch 10, 94bm, 62 × 19ft. Taylor, Cuck-old's Point, 6.4.1691. Wrecked 15.10.1694. *In French hands 6.1691–11.1693.*

TALBOT Sloop 18, 484bm, 113·5 × 31ft, 18—32pdr carr., 8—12pdr carr., 1—12pdr, 2—6pdr. Heath, Teignmouth, 22.7.1807. Sold 23.11.1815.

TALBOT 6th Rate 28, 500bm, 114 × 32ft, 20—32pdr, 6—18pdr carr., 2—6pdr. Pembroke Dock 9.10.1824. Powder hulk 2.1855. Sold 5.3.1896 C. P. Ogilvie.

TALBOT 2nd class cruiser, 5,600 tons, 350 × 53ft, 11—6in, 9—12pdr. Devonport DY 25.4.1895. Sold 6.12.1921 Multiocular S. Bkg Co.

TALBOT *See also M.29 1915.*

TALENT Submarine, 'T' class. Vickers Armstrong, Barrow, 17.7.1943. Lent Dutch Navy = ZWAARD-VISCH 6.12.1943. BU 1963.

TALENT Submarine, 'T' class. Vickers Armstrong, Barrow, ordered 1944, tx Scotts, cancelled 1945.

TALENT Nuclear submarine, 'Trafalgar' class. Vickers, Barrow 15.4.1988. *Possibly ordered as TACTICIAN (q.v.).*

TALENT *See also TASMAN 1945.*

TALISMAN (ex-NAPIER) Destroyer, 1,098 tons, 300 × 28·5ft, 5—4in, 4—TT. Hawthorn Leslie 15.7.1915; Turkish (renamed 15.2.1915). Sold 9.5.1921 Ward, Grays.

TALISMAN Submarine, 'T' class. Cammell Laird 29.1.1940. Sunk 9.1942 Sicilian Channel, cause unknown.

TALISMAN *See also LOUIS 1913.*

TALLY—HO! (ex-P.317) Submarine, 'T' class. Vickers Armstrong, Barrow, 23.1.1942. Arr. 10.2.1967 Ward, Briton Ferry, for BU.

TALYBONT Destroyer, 'Hunt' class Type III. White 3.2.1943. Arr. 14.2.1961 Charlestown for BU.

TAMAR Sloop 16, 343bm, 96·5 × 27·5ft. Snook, Saltash, 23.1.1758. = PLUTO (fireship) 23.9.1777. Captured 30.11.1780 by French.

TAMAR Store lighter, 126bm, 65 × 21ft. Cowes 1795, purch. 1795. BU 1798.

TAMAR 5th Rate 38 (fir-built), 999bm, 146 × 39ft. Chatham DY 26.3.1796. BU 1.1810 Chatham.

TAMAR 6th Rate 26, 451bm, 108 × 31ft. Brindley,

Frindsbury, 23.3.1814. Coal hulk 3.1831. Sold 3.1837.

TAMAR Iron screw troopship, 2,812bm, 4,650 tons, 320 (oa) × 45ft, 3—6pdr. Samuda, Poplar, 5.1.1863. Base ship 1897. Scuttled 12.12.1941 Hong Kong.

TAMAR *See also AIRE 1943.*

TAMARISK Sloop, 'Aubrietia' class. Lobnitz 2.6.1916. Sold 17.10.1922 Fryer, Sunderland. *Also operated as Q.11.*

TAMARISK (ex-ETTRICK) Corvette, 'Flower' class. Fleming & Ferguson 28.7.1941 (renamed 1941). Lent Greek Navy 11.1943–1952 = TOMPAZIS. Sold 20.3.1963 Marine Craft Constructors; BU Greece.

TAMWORTH Minesweeper, 'Bathurst' class. Walker, Maryborough, 14.3.1942. Lent RAN until 1946. Sold 1946 Dutch Navy = TIDORE; tx Indonesia = PATI UNUS 28.12.1949; BU 1969.

TAMWORTH CASTLE *See KINCARDINE 1944.*

TANAIS 5th Rate 38 (red pine-built), 1,085bm, 150·5 × 40·5ft. Ross, Rochester, 27.10.1813. Sold Beatson 8.3.1819 for BU.

TANATSIDE Destroyer, 'Hunt' class Type III. Yarrow 30.4.1942. Lent Greek Navy 9.2.1946–1.1964 = ADRIAS. Sold 14.1.1964 Greece for BU.

TANCRED Destroyer, 'R' class. Beardmore 30.6.1917. Sold 17.5.1928 Cashmore, Newport; stranded, BU Port Talbot.

TANG Schooner 4, 78bm, 56 × 18ft, 4—12pdr carr. Bermuda 9.1807. Foundered 1808 Atlantic.

TANGANYIKA Minesweeper, 'Algerine' class. Lobnitz 12.4.1944. Arr. 2.9.1963 Ward, Inverkeithing, for BU.

TANTALUS Submarine, 'T' class. Vickers Armstrong, Barrow, 24.2.1943. BU 11.1950 Ward, Milford Haven.

TANTIVY Submarine, 'T' class. Vickers Armstrong, Barrow, 6.4.1943. Sunk 1951 asdic target Cromarty Firth.

TAPAGEUR Cutter 14, 14—4pdr. French, captured 4.1779. Wrecked 1780 West Indies.

TAPAGEUSE Brig-sloop 14. French, captured 6.4.1806 by boats of PALLAS off Bordeaux. *Fate unknown.*

TAPIR Submarine, 'T' class. Vickers Armstrong, Barrow, 21.8.1944. Lent Dutch Navy 1948–53 = ZEEHOND. Arr. 14.12.1966 Faslane for BU.

TAPTI Survey brig (Indian). Listed 1843–51.

TARA Destroyer, 'S' class. Beardmore 12.10.1918. Sold 17.12.1931 Rees, Llanelly.

TARAKAN Landing craft (RAN), 310 tons, 146 (oa) × 33ft. Walker 16. 3.1972.

TARAKAN *See also LST.3017 1944.*

TARANAKI Frigate (RNZN), 2,144 tons, 370 (oa) × 41ft, 2—4·5in, Limbo. White 19.8.1959. Sold Pacific Steel; towed 8.9.1983 to Auckland for BU.

TARANTELLA Minesweeper, 265 tons, 130 × 26·5ft, 1—12pdr, 1—6pdr. War Dept tug, tx on stocks. Hamilton 22.10.1917. Sold 1921 mercantile.

TARANTULA River gunboat, 645 tons, 230 × 36ft, 2—6in, 1—3in. Wood Skinner, Newcastle, 8.12.1915. Depot ship 1941. Dismantled 1946; hull sunk 1.5.1946 target off Ceylon.

TARBAT NESS Repair ship, 8,580 tons, 424·5 × 57ft. West Coast SB, Vancouver, 29.5.1945, cancelled 18.8.1945; comp. 1.1947 as *Lautoka.*

TARBAT NESS Store carrier 15,500 tons. 1967–81.

TARBERT *See SHERBORNE 1918.*

TARLETON Brig-sloop 14. Dates from 1782. Captured 1782 by French.

TARLETON Fireship 14. French, captured 18.12.1793 at Toulon. Listed until 1798. *French records give this as the 1782 vessel recaptured.*

TARLTON Coastal minesweeper, 'Ton' class. Doig, Grimsby, 10.11.1954. Sold 1967 Argentine Navy = RIO NEGRO; deleted 1996–97.

TARN Submarine, 'T' class. Vickers Armstrong, Barrow, 29.11.1944. Tx Dutch Navy 1945 = TIJGERHAAL; BU 1966.

TARPON Destroyer, 'R' class. John Brown 10.3.1917. Sold 4.8.1927 Cashmore, Newport.

TARPON Submarine, 'T' class. Scotts 17.10.1939. Sunk 14.4.1940 German minesweeper M.6 North Sea.

TARTAN (ex-TARTANE?) Advice boat 6, 49bm. French, captured 1692. Recaptured 17.6.1695 by French.

TARTAN 5th Rate 32, 420bm, 108 × 30ft. Woolwich DY 9.1702. Rebuilt Deptford 1733 as 6th Rate, 429bm. BU comp. 4.1755 Deptford.

TARTAR 6th Rate 28, 587bm, 118 × 34ft. Randall, Rotherhithe, 3.4.1756. Wrecked 4.1797 San Domingo.

TARTAR 5th Rate 32, 885bm, 142 × 37·5ft. Brindley, Frindsbury, 27.6.1801. Wrecked 18.18.1811 Baltic.

TARTAR 5th Rate 36, 949bm, 145 × 38·5ft. Deptford DY 6.4.1814. Receiving ship 3.1830. BU comp. 30.9.1859.

TARTAR (ex-WOJN) Wood screw corvette, 1,296bm, 195 × 39ft, 110pdr, 14—8in, 4—40pdr. Pitcher, Northfleet, 17.5.1854; Russian, seized on stocks. BU 2.1866 Castle, Charlton.

TARTAR Torpedo cruiser, 1,770 tons, 225 × 36ft, 6—6in, 8—3pdr, 3—TT. Thomson 28.10.1886. Sold 3.4.1906 Forrester, Swansea.

TARTAR Destroyer, 870 tons, 260 × 26ft, 3—
12pdr, 2—TT, Thornycroft, Woolston, 25.6.1907.
Sold 9.5.1921 Ward, Hayle.

TARTAR Destroyer, 1,870 tons, 377 (oa) × 36·5ft,
8—4·7in, 4—TT. Swan Hunter 21.10.1937. Sold
6.1.1948; BU Cashmore, Newport.

TARTAR Frigate, Type 81, 2,300 tons, 360 (oa) ×
42·5ft, 2—4·5in, 2—40mm, Limbo, helo. Devonport DY 19.9.1960. Sold Indonesian Navy 1984
= HASANUDDIN; deleted 2000.

TARTAR PRIZE (ex-VICTOIRE) 6th Rate 28, 4—
9pdr, 24—6pdr. French privateer, captured 3.1757
by TARTAR. Wrecked 2.3.1760 Mediterranean.

TARTARUS (ex-*Charles Jackson*) Bomb vessel 8,
344bm, 94·5 × 28·5ft. Purch. 4.1797. Wrecked
20.12.1804 Margate Sands.

TARTARUS Fireship 16, 423bm, 108·5 × 30ft.
Davy, Topsham, 10.1806. Sloop from 3.1808, 22—
24pdr carr., 8—18pdr carr., 2—9pdr. Sold
15.2.1816.

TARTARUS Paddle gunvessel, 523bm, 145 ×
28·5ft, 2—9pdr. Pembroke Dock 23.6.1834. BU
11.1860 Malta.

TARTARUS Wood screw gunvessel, 695bm, 185 ×
28·5ft, 2—68pdr, 2—32pdr. Pembroke Dock, LD
25.10.1860, cancelled 16.12.1864.

TASMAN Submarine, 'T' class. Vickers Armstrong,
Barrow, 13.2.1945. = TALENT 4.1945. Sold
6.1.190; arr. Troon 28.2.1970 for BU.

TASMANIA Destroyer, 'S' class. Beardmore
22.11.1918. Tx RAN 6.1919; sold 4.6.1937
Penguins, Sydney.

TATTOO Destroyer, 'S' class. Beardmore
28.12.1918. Tx RAN 6.1919. Sold 9.1.1937 Penguins, Sydney.

TATTOO Minesweeper, 'Catherine' class. Gulf SB,
Chickasaw, 27.1.1943 on Lend-Lease. Ret. USN
1947; tx Turkey 3.1947 = CARSAMBA;
wWithdrawn 1983.

TAUNTON 48-gun ship, 536bm, 120 × 32ft.
Castle, Rotherhithe, 1954. = CROWNE 1660. Rebuilt Deptford 1704 as 650bm. Wrecked 29.1.1719
off R. Tagus.

TAUPO Patrol vessel (RNZN), 105 tons, 120 (oa) ×
20ft. Brooke Marine 25.7.1975. Deleted 1992.

TAUPO *See also LOCH SHIN 1944.*

TAURANGA (ex-PHOENI) 2nd class cruiser, 2,575
tons. 265 × 41ft, 8—4·7in, 8—3pdr. Thomson
28.10.1889 (renamed 2.4.1890). Sold 10.7.1906
Ward, Preston.

TAURUS Destroyer, 'R' class. Thornycroft
10.3.1917. Sold 18.2.1930 Metal Industries,
Charlestown.

TAURUS (ex-P.339) Submarine, 'T' class. Vickers

Armstrong, Barrow, 27.6.1942. Lent Dutch Navy
1948–2.1953 = DOLFIJN. BU 4.1960 Clayton &
Davie, Dunston.

TAVISTOCK Sloop 14, 269bm, 91 × 26ft. Darby,
Gosport, 22.3.1744. = ALBANY 20.8.1747. Sold
3.5.1763.

TAVISTOCK 4th Rate 50, 1,601bm, 144 × 41ft.
Blaydes, Hull, 26.8.1747. Hulked 1761. BU comp.
24.12.1768 Woolwich.

TAVY Storeship, 171bm, 71·5 × 24ft. Franks
Quarry, Plymouth, 1797. Dockyard luggage lighter
7.1862 = YC.11. BU 1.1869 Devonport.

TAVY Frigate, 'River' class. Hill, Bristol, 3.4.1943.
Arr. 18.7.1953 Cashmore, Newport, for BU.

TAY Sloop 18. 460bm, 116 × 30ft, 18—32pdr carr.,
2—9pdr. Adams, Buckler's Hard, 26.11.1813.
Wrecked 11.11.1816 Gulf of Mexico.

TAY Iron screw gunboat, 363 tons, 110 × 34ft, 3—
64pdr. Palmer, Jarrow, 19.10.1876. Sold
22.10.1920 Stanlee, Dover.

TAY Frigate, 'River' class. Smith's Dock 18.3.1942.
Arr. 28.9.1956 S. Bkg Industries, Rosyth, for BU.

TE KAHA Frigate (RNZN), 'Anzac' class. Transfield, Williamstown 22.7.1995.

TE MANA Frigate (RNZN), 'Anzac' class. Transfield, Williamstown 10.5.1997.

TEAL River gunboat, 180 tons, 160 × 24·5ft.
Yarrow, Poplar, 18.5.1901. Sold 10.1931 Shanghai.

TEAL *See also JACKTON 1955.*

TEAZER Gunvessel 14, 148bm, 75 × 21ft. Dudman,
Deptford, 26.5.1794. Sold 10.1802.

TEAZER Gunvessel 6. Schooner. Purch. 1798
Honduras for local use. *Fate unknown.*

TEAZER Gun-brig 12, 177bm, 80 × 22·5ft, 2—
18pdr, 10—18pdr carr. Dudman, Deptford,
16.7.1804. Sold 3.8.1815.

TEAZER Wood screw tender, 296bm, 130 × 22ft, 2
guns. Chatham DY 25.6.1846. BU 1862 Castle,
Charlton.

TEAZER Composite gunvessel, 464bm, 603 tons,
155 × 25ft, 1—7in, 1—64pdr, 2—20pdr. Laird
28.4.1868. BU 12.1887 Chatham.

TEAZER Destroyer, 320 tons, 200 × 19·5ft, 1—
12pdr, 5—6pdr, 2—TT. White 2.2.1895. Sold
9.7.1912 Cox, Falmouth; resold Cashmore,
Newport.

TEAZER Destroyer, 'R' class. Thornycroft
31.4.1917. Sold 6.2.1931 Cashmore, Newport.

TEAZER Destroyer, 1,710 tons, 362·8 (oa) × 35·7ft,
4—4·7in, 2—40mm, 8—TT. Cammell Laird
7.1.1943. Frigate 2.1952, 2,200 tons, 2—4in, Squid.
Arr. 7.8.1965 Arnott Young, Dalmuir, for BU.

TECUMSETH Schooner 2 (Canadian lakes),
166bm, 70·5 × 24·5ft. Moore, Chippewa, 8.1815.

Condemned 3.1832; foundered c. 1833 Penetanguishene; raised 1953.

TEDWORTH Minesweeper, Early 'Hunt' class. Simons 20.6.1917. Diving tender 8.1923. Sold 5.1946; BU Ward, Hayle.

TEES Wood screw sloop, 950bm, 185 × 33ft. Chatham DY, ordered 5.3.1860, cancelled 12.1863.

TEES Iron screw gunboat, 363 tons, 110 × 34ft. 3–64pdr. Palmer 19.10.1876. Sold 9.7.1907 Harris Bros, Bristol.

TEES 6th Rate 28, 452bm, 108 × 31ft, 18–32pdr carr., 8–12pdr carr., 2–6pdr. Taylor, Bideford, 17.5.1817. Lent 10.1826 as church ship. Sold 28.6.1872 Liverpool.

TEES Frigate, 'River' class. Hall Russell 20.5.1943. Arr. 16.7.1955 Cashmore, Newport, for BU.

TEIGNMOUTH Sloop 16 (Indian), 257bm. Bombay DY 1799. *Fate unknown.*

TEIGNMOUTH *See also TRING 1918.*

TELEGRAPH (ex-VENGEANCE) Schooner 14, 180bm, 83·5 × 22·5ft, 12–12pdr carr., 2–6pdr. American privateer, captured 1813. Wrecked 21.1.1817 Mount Batten, Plymouth.

TELEMACHUS Destroyer, 'R' class. John Brown 21.4.1917. Sold 26.7.1927 Hughes Bolckow, Blyth.

TELEMACHUS Submarine, 'T' class. Vickers Armstrong, Barrow, 19.6.1943. Arr. 28.8.1961 Charlestown for BU.

TEME Frigate, 'River' class. Smith's Dock 11.11.1943. Torpedoed 29.3.1945 by U.246 off Falmouth, not repaired; sold 8.12.1945; BU Rees, Llanelly.

TEMERAIRE 3rd Rate 74, 1,685bm, 169 × 48ft. French, captured 18.8.1759 Lagos. Sold 6.1784.

TEMERAIRE 2nd Rate 98, 2,121bm, 185 × 51ft. Chatham DY 11.9.1798. Prison ship 12.1813; receiving ship 6.1820. Sold 16.8.1838 Beatson, Rotherhithe, for BU.

TEMERAIRE Iron screw ship, 8,540 tons, 285 × 62ft, 4–11in, 4–10in. Chatham DY 9.5.1876. = INDUS II (TS) 4.1904. = AKBAR 1.1915. Sold 26.5.1921 Rijsdijk S. Bkg Co.

TEMERAIRE Battleship, 18,600 tons, 490 × 82·5ft, 10–12in, 16–4in. Devonport DY 24.8.1907. Sold 1.12.1921 Stanlee, Dover.

TEMERAIRE Battleship, 42,500 tons, 740 × 105ft, 9–16in, 16–5·25in. Cammell Laird, LD 1.6.1939, suspended 10.1939, cancelled 1944.

TEMPEST Destroyer, 'R' class. Fairfield 26.1.1917. HO Ward 28.1.1937 part payment *Majestic* (CALEDONIA, q.v.); BU Briton Ferry.

TEMPEST Submarine, 'T' class. Cammell Laird 10.6.1941. Sunk 13.2.1942 by Italian torpedo boat CIRCE in Gulf of Taranto.

TEMPLAR (ex-P.316) Submarine, 'T' class. Vickers Armstrong, Barrow, 26.10.1942. Sunk asdic target 1950; raised 4.12.1958, arr. 17.7.1959 Troon for BU.

TEMPLE 3rd Rate 70, 1,429bm, 160 × 45ft. Blaydes, Hull, 3.11.1758. Foundered 18.12.1762 West Indies.

TENACIOUS Destroyer, 'R' class. Harland & Wolff, Govan, 21.5.1917. Sold 26.6.1928 Ward, Briton Ferry.

TENACIOUS Destroyer, 1,710 tons, 362·8 (oa) × 35·7ft, 4–4·7in, 2–40mm, 8–TT. Cammell Laird 24.3.1943. Frigate 4.1952, 2–4in, Squid. Arr. 29.6.1965 Troon for BU.

TENACITY Patrol boat, 165 tons, Vosper 18.2.1969, purch. 4.4.1972. Sold 9.1983 Marine Turbocraft; for re-sale 1985; for conv. yacht 1993 Portishead; damaged, wreck removed 5.2001.

TENASSERIM Paddle vessel (Indian). Listed 1839–53.

TENASSERIM Iron screw frigate (Indian), 2,570bm, 250 × 35ft. R. Thames 1872. Harbour service 1900–06.

TENBY Minesweeper, turbine 'Bangor' class. Hamilton 10.9.1941. Sold 1.1.1948; BU Clayton & Davie, Dunston.

TENBY Frigate, 2,150 tons, 360 × 41ft, 2–4·5in, 2–40mm. Cammell Laird 4.10.1955. Sold 1975 to Pakistan, not taken over. Arr. Briton Ferry 15.9.1977 for BU.

TENEDOS 5th Rate 38, 1,083bm, 150 × 40·5ft. Chatham DY 11.4.1812. Convict hulk 4.1843. BU comp. 20.3.1875 Bermuda.

TENEDOS Wood screw sloop, 1,275bm, 1,760 tons, 212 × 36ft, 2–7in, 4–64pdr. Devonport DY 13.5.1870. Rated corvette from 1875. Sold 11.1887 Pethwick, Plymouth.

TENEDOS Destroyer, 'S' class. Hawthorn Leslie 21.10.1918. Sunk 5.4.1942 Japanese air attack south of Colombo.

TENEDOS *For training ships with this name, see TRIUMPH 1870, DUNCAN 1859, GANGES 1821.*

TEREDO Submarine, 'T' class. Vickers Armstrong, Barrow, 27.4.1945. Arr. 5.6.1965 Ward, Briton Ferry, for BU.

TERMAGANT 6th Rate 26, 378bm, 110·5 × 28ft, 4–12pdr carr., 22–6pdr. Hillhouse, Bristol, 3.6.1780, purch. on stocks. Reduced to 18-gun sloop 5.1782. Sold 28.8.1795.

TERMAGANT Sloop 18, 427bm, 110 × 30ft, 18–32pdr carr., 8–12pdr carr., 2–6pdr. Dudman, Deptford, 23.4.1796. Sold 3.2.1819 Graham.

TERMAGANT 6th Rate 28, 500bm, 114 × 32ft. Cochin 15.11.1822. = HERALD 15.5.1824, survey ship. Sold 28.4.1862 Castle, Charlton.

TERMAGANT Brigantine 3, ex-'Cherokee' class, 231bm. Portsmouth DY 26.3.1838. Sold 3.1845.

TERMAGANT Wood screw frigate, 1,560bm, 210 × 40ft, 1—110pdr, 16—8in, 6—40pdr. Deptford DY 25.9.1847. Sold 3.1867 Castle & Beech for BU.

TERMAGANT (ex-NARBROUGH) Destroyer, 1,098 tons, 300 × 28·5ft, 5—4in, 4—TT. Hawthorn Leslie 26.8.1915; Turkish (renamed 15.2.1915). Sold 9.5.1921 Ward; arr. Briton Ferry 25.1.1923 for BU.

TERMAGANT Destroyer, 1,710 tons, 362·8 (oa) × 35·7ft, 4—4·7in, 2—40mm, 8—TT. Denny 22.3.1943. Frigate 1953, 2—4in, Squid. Arr. 5.11.1965 Arnott Young, Dalmuir, for BU.

TERN Paddle minesweeper. Murdoch & Murray, cancelled 1918.

TERN River gunboat, 262 tons, 160 × 27ft, 2—3in. Yarrow 29.8.1927. Scuttled 19.12.1941 Hong Kong.

TERNATE Sloop 16 (Indian), 257bm. Bombay DY 1801. Listed 1830.

TERPSICHORE 6th Rate 24, 467bm, 114 × 31ft, 24—6pdr. French, captured 28.2.1760 by squadron off I. of Man. Sold 4.11.1766.

TERPSICHORE 5th Rate 32 683bm 1 126 × 35ft, Betts, Mistleythorn, 17.12.1785. Receiving ship 1818. BU 11.1830.

TERPSICHORE Sloop 18, 602bm, 115 × 35·5ft, 18—32pdr. Wigram, Blackwall, 18.3.1847. Sunk 4.10.1865 torpedo trials Chatham; raised, BU 1.1866 Castle & Beech.

TERPSICHORE 2nd class cruiser, 3,400 tons, 300 × 43ft, 2—6in, 6—4·7in, 8—6pdr. Thompson 30.10.1890. Sold 28.5.1914 Ward, Briton Ferry.

TERPSICHORE Destroyer, 1,710 tons, 362·8 (oa) × 35·7ft, 4—4·7in, 2—40mm, 8—TT. Denny 17.6.1943. Frigate 11.1954. Arr. 17.5.1966 Troon for BU.

TERRA NOVA Escort (RCN), 2,370 tons, 366 (oa) × 42ft, 4—3in, 2—40mm, 6—TT, Limbo. Victoria Machinery 21.6.1955. Extended reserve 1997–2002 Halifax.

TERRAPIN Submarine, 'T' class. Vickers Armstrong, Barrow, 31.8.1943. Damaged by depth charges 19.5.1945 Pacific, not repaired; arr. 6.1946 Troon for BU.

TERRIBLE 6th Rate 26, 253bm, 92·5 × 25ft. Ellis, Shoreham, 15.6.1694. Captured 20.9.1710 by Spanish off Cape St Marys.

TERRIBLE Bomb vessel 14, 263bm, 83 × 27·5ft. Stacey, Deptford, 4.8.1730. Sold 9.2.1748.

TERRIBLE 3rd Rate 74, 1,590bm, 164 × 47·5ft. French, captured 14.10.1747 off Cape Finisterre. BU comp. 16.2.1763 Chatham.

TERRIBLE 3rd Rate 74, 1,644bm, 169 × 47ft. Barnard, Harwich, 4.9.1762. Damaged in action with French off Chesapeake Bay, burnt 11.9.1781 unseaworthy.

TERRIBLE 3rd Rate 74 1,660bm, 170·5 × 47·5ft. Wells, Rotherhithe, 28.3.1785. Receiving ship 5.1823; coal hulk 4.1829. BU 3.1836 Deptford.

TERRIBLE (ex-SIMOOM) Wood paddle frigate, 1,858bm, 3,189 tons, 226 × 42·5ft, 8—68pdr, 8—56pdr, 3—12pdr. Deptford DY 6.2.1845 (renamed 12.1842). Sold 7.7.1879 for BU. *First four-funnelled ship in RN.*

TERRIBLE 1st class cruiser, 14,200 tons, 500 × 71ft, 2—9·2in, 12—6in, 16—12pdr. Thomson 27.5.1895. = FISGARD III (TS) 8.1920. Sold 7.1932 Cashmore.

TERRIBLE Aircraft carrier, 14,000 tons, 630 × 80ft, 30—40mm, 34 aircraft. Devonport DY 30.9.1944. Tx RAN 16.10.1948 = SYDNEY; fast transport 3.1962, 4—40mm; left Sydney 23.12.75 for South Korea for BU.

TERROR Bomb vessel 4, 149bm, 66 × 23·5ft. Davis, Limehouse, 11.1.1696. Captured 17.10.1704 by French at Gibraltar, burnt.

TERROR Bomb vessel 14, 278bm, 92 × 26·5ft. Greville & Whetstone, Limehouse, 13.3.1741. Sold 3.12.1754.

TERROR Bomb vessel 8, 301bm, 91·5 × 27·5ft. Barnard, Harwich, 16.1.1759. Sold 9.8.1774.

TERROR Bomb vessel 8, 307bm, 92 × 28ft. Randall, Rotherhithe, 2.6.1779. Sold 13.8.1812.

TERROR Gunvessel 4, 69bm, 66·5 × 15ft. Dutch hoy, purch. 3.1794. Sold 11.1804.

TERROR Bomb vessel 10, 326bm, 102·5 × 27·5ft. Davy, Topsham, 29.6.1813. Discovery vessel 5.1836. Abandoned 1848 Arctic.

TERROR Iron screw floating battery 1,971bm, 1,844 tons, 186 × 48·5ft, 16—68pdr. Palmer, Jarrow 28.4.1856. Base ship Bermuda 1857. Sold Walker & Co. 1902 Bermuda.

TERROR Monitor, 8,000 tons, 380 × 88ft, 2—15in, 8—4in, 2—3in. Harland & Wolff 18.5.1916. Sunk 24.2.1941 Italian aircraft off Derna.

TERROR *See also MALABAR 1866.*

TEST Destroyer, 570 tons, 220 × 24ft, 4—12pdr, 2—TT. Laird 14.1.1907 spec., purch. 12.1909. Sold 30.8.1919 Loveridge & Co.

TEST Frigate, 'River' class. Hall Russell 30.5.1942. Lent RIN 5.1946–4.1947 = NEZA. Arr. 25.2.1955 Faslane for BU.

TETCOTT Destroyer, 'Hunt' class Type II. White 12.8.1941. Arr. 24.9.1956 Ward, Milford Haven, for BU.

TETRARCH Destroyer, 'R' class. Harland & Wolff,

Govan, 20.4.1917. Sold 28.7.1934 Metal Industries, Rosyth.

TETRARCH Submarine, 'T' class. Vickers Armstrong, Barrow, 14.11.1939. Sunk 2.11.1941 western Mediterranean, cause unknown.

TEVIOT Destroyer, 590 tons, 225 × 23·5ft, 1—12pdr, 5—6pdr (1907: 4—12pdr), 2—TT. Yarrow 7.11.1903. Sold 23.6.1919 Ward, Morecambe.

TEVIOT Frigate, 'River' class. Hall Russell 12.10.1942. Lent SAN 6.1945–7.1946. Sold 29.3.1955; BU Ward, Briton Ferry.

TEXEL (ex-CERBERUS) 3rd Rate 64, 1,317bm. Dutch, captured 30.8.1799 Texel. Sold 11.6.1818 Beatson for BU.

THAIS Sloop 18, 431bm, 109 × 30ft. Tanner, Dartmouth, 19.8.1806. Sold 13.8.1818. *Also served as fireship.*

THAIS Brig-sloop 10, 'Cherokee' class, 231bm. Pembroke Dock 12.10.1829. Foundered 12.1833 off west coast of Ireland.

THAKENHAM Inshore minesweeper, 'Ham' class. Fairlie Yacht Co. 9.9.1957. Sold Pounds 1977.

THALIA 5th Rate 46, 1,082bm, 151·5 × 40·5ft. Chatham DY 1.1830 (ex-Portsmouth, tx 5.1827). Harbour service 12.1855. BU comp. 25.11.1867 White, Cowes.

THALIA Wood screw corvette, 1,459bm, 2,240 tons, 200 × 40·5ft, 8—64pdr. Woolwich DY 14.7.1869. Troopship 10 in 1886; powder hulk 1891; base ship cd 2.1915. Sold 16.9.1920 Rose Street Foundry. *Last ship built at Woolwich DY.*

THALIA *See also UNICORN 1782.*

THAMES 5th Rate 32, 656bm, 127 × 34·5ft. Adams, Buckler's Hard, 10.4.1758. BU 9.1803. *In French hands 24.10.93–7.6.96 as TAMISE.*

THAMES Cutter tender, 65bm, 51·5 × 17·5ft. Rochester 1805. = YC.2 (dockyard craft) 1866. Sold 1872.

THAMES 5th Rate 32 (fir-built), 662bm, 127 × 34ft. Chatham DY 24.10.1805. BU 10.1816.

THAMES Bomb vessel 6 (Indian), 102bm. Bombay DY 1814. *Fate unknown.*

THAMES 5th Rate 46, 1,088bm, 151·5 × 40·5ft. Chatham DY 21.8.1823. Convict ship 1841. Sunk 6.6.1863 at moorings Bermuda; wreck sold J. Murphy.

THAMES 2nd class cruiser, 4,050 tons, 300 × 46ft, 2—8in, 10—6in. Pembroke Dock 3.12.1885. Depot ship 1903. Sold 13.11.1920 = *General Botha* (TS The Cape); = THAMES (accommodation ship) 1942; scuttled 13.5.1947 Simons Bay.

THAMES Submarine, 1,805 tons, 325 × 28ft, 1—4in, 8—TT. Vickers Armstrong, Barrow, 26.2.1932. Sunk 23.7.1940 mine off Norway.

THAMES *Name borne in succession from 1949 by RNVR tenders MMS.1789, ALVERTON, BUTTINGTON.*

THANE (ex-*Sunset*) Escort carrier, 11,420 tons, 468·5 × 69·5ft, 2—4in, 16—40mm, 24 aircraft. Seattle Tacoma 15.7.1943 on Lend-Lease. Torpedoed 15.1.1945 by U.482 off Clyde Lightvessel, not repaired. Nominally ret. USN 5.12.1945; arr. Faslane 12.1945; BU begun 4.1947.

THANET Destroyer, 'S' class. Hawthorn Leslie 5.11.1918. Sunk 27.1.1942 Japanese squadron off Malaya.

THANKERTON Coastal minesweeper, 'Ton' class. Camper & Nicholson 4.9.1956. Tx Malaysian Navy = BRINCHANG 5.1966;. BU 1982.

THATCHAM Inshore minesweeper, 'Ham' class. Jones, Buckie, 25.9.1957. Sold Pounds 1986.

THE PAS Corvette (RCN), 'Flower' class. Collingwood SY 16.8.1941. BU 6.1946.

THE SOO Minesweeper (RCN), 'Algerine' class. Port Arthur 15.8.1942. = SAULT STE MARIE 1944. Sold 11.1959; BU 5.1960.

THEBAN 5th Rate 36, 954bm, 145 × 48·5ft. Parsons, Warsash, 22.12.1809. BU 5.1817.

THEBAN 5th Rate 46, 1,215bm, 159·5 × 42ft. Portsmouth DY, ordered 13.9.1824, cancelled 7.2.1831.

THEBAN Submarine, 'T' class. Vickers Armstrong, Barrow, ordered 18.4.1942, cancelled 18.10.1944.

THEODOCIA *See VENTURER 1807.*

THERMOPYLAE Submarine, 'T' class. Chatham DY 27.6.1945. Sold 26.5.1970; BU Troon.

THESEUS 3rd Rate 74, 1,660bm, 170× 47·5ft. Perry, Blackwall, 25.9.1786. BU 5.1814 Chatham.

THESEUS 1st class cruiser, 7,350 tons, 360 × 60ft, 2—9·2in, 10—6in, 12—6pdr. Thames Iron Works, Blackwall, 8.9.1892. Sold 8.11.1921 Slough Trading Co.; BU Germany.

THESEUS Aircraft carrier, 13,350 tons, 630 × 80ft, 19—40mm, 48 aircraft. Fairfield 6.7.1944. Arr. 29.5.1962 Ward, Inverkeithing, for BU.

THETFORD MINES Frigate (RCN), 'River' class. Morton, Quebec, 30.10.1943. Sold 3.1.1946 mercantile.

THETIS Storeship 22, 720bm. Plymouth DY 1717. *Fate unknown.*

THETIS 5th Rate 44, 720bm, 126·5 × 36ft. Okill, Liverpool, 15.4.1747. Hospital ship 7.1757. Sold 9.6.1767.

THETIS 5th Rate 32, 686bm, 126 × 35ft. Adams, Buckler's Hard, 2.11.1773. Wrecked 12.5.1781 off St Lucia.

THETIS 5th Rate 38. 946bm, 141·5 × 39ft. Rotherhithe 23.9.1782. Sold 9.6.1814.

THETIS 6th Rate 24. Dutch, captured 23.4.1796 Demerara. Scuttled Demerara.

THETIS Schooner 8. Purch. 1796. Listed 1800.

THETIS Gun-brig 10 (Indian), 185bm. Bombay DY 1810. Listed 1836.

THETIS 5th Rate 46, 1,086bm, 151 × 40·5ft, Pembroke Dock 1.2.1817. Wrecked 5.12.1830 Cape Frio, Brazil.

THETIS 5th Rate 36, 1,524bm, 164·5 × 46·5ft, 4—8in, 32—32pdr. Devonport DY 21.8.1846. Tx Prussian Navy 12.1.1855 exchange for two gunboats.

THETIS Wood screw corvette, 1,322bm, 1,860 tons, 220 × 35·5ft, 14—64pdr. Devonport DY 26.10.1871. Sold 11.1887 Pethwick, Plymouth.

THETIS 2nd class cruiser, 3,400 tons, 300 × 43ft, 2—6in, 6—4·7in, 8—6pdr, Thomson 13.12.1890. Minelayer 8.1907. Sunk 23.4.1918 blockship Zeebrugge.

THETIS Submarine, 'T' class. Cammell Laird 29.6.1938. Foundered 1.6.1939 Liverpool Bay; raised, = THUNDERBOLT 4.1940. Sunk 13.3.1943 by Italian corvette CICOGNA north of Sicily.

THISBE 6th Rate 28, 596bm, 120·5 × 33·5ft. King, Dover, 25.11.1783. Sold 9.8.1815.

THISBE 5th Rate 46, 1,083bm, 151·5 × 40·5ft. Pembroke Dock 9.9.1824. Lent 13.8.1863 as church ship Cardiff. Sold 11.8.1892 W. H. Caple.

THISBE Destroyer, 'R' class. Hawthorn Leslie 8.3.1917. HO Ward 31.8.1936 part payment *Majestic* (CALEDONIA, q.v.); BU Pembroke Dock.

THISBE Minesweeper, 'Algerine' class. Redfern, Toronto, 12.4.1943. Arr. 12.1957 Charlestown for BU.

THISTLE Schooner 10, 150bm, 79 × 22ft. Bermuda 27.9,1808. Wrecked 6.3.1811 off New York.

THISTLE Gun-brig 12, 185bm, 84·5 × 22·5ft, 10—18pdr carr., 2—6pdr. Ross, Rochester, 13.7.1812. BU 7.1823.

THISTLE Wood screw gunboat, 'Dapper' class. Pitcher, Northfleet, 3.2.1855. BU comp. Deptford 11.11.1863.

THISTLE Composite screw gunvessel, 465bm, 603 tons, 155 × 25ft, 1—7in, 1—64pdr, 2—20pdr. Deptford DY 25.1.1868. Sold 11.1888 Read, Portsmouth.

THISTLE 1st class gunboat, 710 tons, 180 × 33ft, 2—4in, 4—12pdr. London & Glasgow Co. 22.6.1899. Sold 13.7.1926 Ward, Pembroke Dock.

THISTLE Submarine, 'T' class. Vickers Armstrong, Barrow, 25.10.1938. Sunk 10.4.1940 by U.4 off Skudesnes, Norway.

THOLEN *See THULEN.*

THOMAS Ship. Mentioned 1350.

THOMAS 4-gun vessel, 180bm. Built 1420. Sold 1423.

THOMAS 10-gun vessel. Royalist, captured 1649 by Parliamentarians = LEOPARD'S WHELP. *Fate unknown.*

THOMAS Schooner. Purch. 1796. Listed until 1799.

THOMAS Fireship. Purch. 1808. Expended 1809.

THOMAS & ELIZABETH Fireship 10. Purch. 1688. Expended 24.5.1692 Cape la Hogue.

THOR Submarine, 'T' class. Portsmouth DY 18.4.1944, not comp. BU 7.1946 Rees, Llanelly.

THORLOCK Corvette (RCN), Modified 'Flower' class. Midland SY, Ontario, 15.5.1944. Sold 1946 Chilean Navy = PAPUDO.

THORN Sloop 14, 306bm, 96·5 × 27ft, 14—32pdr carr., 2—6pdr. Betts, Mistleythorn, 17.2.1779. Lent 1799 as TS. Sold 28.8.1816. *In French hands 25.8.1779—20.8.1782.*

THORN Destroyer, 400 tons, 210 × 20·5ft, 1—12pdr, 5—6pdr, 2—TT. Thomson 17.3.1900. BU 1919 Portsmouth DY.

THORN Submarine, 'T' class. Cammell Laird 18.3.1941. Sunk 6.8.1942 by Italian torpedo boat PEGASO in Mediterranean.

THORNBROUGH Frigate, TE 'Captain' class. Bethlehem, Hingham, 13.11.1943 on Lend-Lease. Nominally ret. USN 30.1.1947; BU 1947 Greece.

THORNBURY CASTLE Corvette, 'Castle' class. Ferguson, cancelled 12.1943.

THORNHAM Inshore minesweeper, 'Ham' class. Taylor, Shoreham, 18.3.1957. BU 5.1985 G&T Services, Charlton.

THOROUGH Submarine, 'T' class. Vickers Armstrong, Barrow, 30.10.1943. Arr. 29.6.1961 Clayton & Davie, Dunston, for BU.

THOULEN *See THULEN.*

THRACIAN Brig-sloop 18, 'Cruizer' class, 383bm. Brindley, Frindsbury, 15.7.1809. BU comp. 6.6.1829.

THRACIAN Destroyer, 'S' class. Hawthorn Leslie 5.3.1920, comp. 1.4.1922 Sheerness. Bombed Japanese aircraft Hong Kong, beached 24.12.1941; salved, cd 9.1942 as Japanese patrol boat *101*. Ret. RN 4.9.1945; sold 2.1946 in Hong Kong; BU 1947.

THRASHER (ex-*Adamant*) Gun-brig 12, 154bm, 10—18pdr carr., 2—9pdr. Warren, Brightlingsea, 1804, purch. 6.1804. Sold 3.11.1814.

THRASHER Wood screw gunboat, 'Albacore' class. Green, Blackwall, 22.3.1856. Sold by order dated 9.5.1883.

THRASHER Destroyer, 395 tons, 210 × 21·5ft, 1—12pdr, 5—6pdr, 2—TT. Laird 5.11.1895. Sold 4.11.1919 Fryer.

THRASHER Submarine, 'T' class. Cammell Laird 28.11.1940. Arr. 9.3.1947 Ward, Briton Ferry, for BU.

THREAT Submarine, 'T' class. Vickers Armstrong, Barrow, cancelled 1945, not LD.

THRUSH (ex-PRINCE OF WALES) Brig-sloop 18, 307bm. Revenue brig, renamed 12.9.1806. Powder hulk 10.1809 Port Royal, Jamaica. Wrecked 7.1815; sold.

THRUSH Wood screw gunboat, 'Clown' class. Briggs, Sunderland, 12.5.1856. BU comp. 14.3.1864.

THRUSH 1st class gunboat, 805 tons, 165 × 31ft, 6—4in, 2—3pdr. Scotts, Greenock, 22.6.1889. Coastguard 1906; cable ship 1915; salvage ship 1916. Wrecked 11.4.1917 nr Glenarm, Northern Ireland.

THRUSTER Destroyer, 'R' class. Hawthorn Leslie 10.1.1917. Arr. 16.3.1937 Ward, Grays, for BU.

THRUSTER Tank landing ship, 3,620 tons, 390 × 49ft, 8—20mm. Harland & Wolff 24.9.1942. Tx Dutch Navy 1945 = PELIKAAN.

THRUSTER *See also LST.3520 1945.*

THULE (ex-P.325) Submarine, 'T' class. Devonport DY 22.10.1942. Arr. 14.9.1962 Ward, Inverkeithing, for BU.

THULEN (THOULEN, THOLEN) 5th Rate 36. Dutch, seized 8.6.1796 Plymouth. BU 1811.

THUNDER Bomb vessel 54, 147bm, 65·5 × 23·5ft. Snelgrove, Deptford, 1695. Captured 21.3.1696 by French privateer off Dutch coast.

THUNDER Bomb vessel 6, 254bm, 28 × 27·5ft, 6—9pdr, 1 mortar. Spanish, captured 10.1720. Ordered BU 27.3.1734.

THUNDER Bomb vessel 8, 272bm, 91·5 × 26·5ft. Bird, Rotherhithe, 30.8.1740. Foundered 20.10.1744 hurricane off Jamaica.

THUNDER Bomb vessel 8, 301bm, 91·5 × 28ft. Heneker, R. Medway (Chatham?), 15.3.1759. Sold 2.9.1774.

THUNDER (ex-*Racehorse*) Bomb vessel 8, 314bm, 98 × 27ft. Purch. 7.1771 India. Captured 17.8.1778 by French off Rhode I.

THUNDER Bomb vessel 8, 305bm, 92 × 28ft. Randall, Rotherhithe, 18.5.1779. Foundered 1.1781 English Channel.

THUNDER (ex-DUGUSE ERWARTUNG) Bomb vessel 8, 230bm. Dutch, captured 1797. Sold 22.2.1802.

THUNDER (ex-*Dasher*) Bomb vessel 8, 384bm, 111·5 × 28ft. Purch. 10.1803. Sold 30.6.1814.

THUNDER Bomb vessel, 326bm, 102·5 × 27·5ft. Brindley, Frindsbury, ordered 1812, cancelled.

THUNDER Bomb vessel 12, 372bm, 105 × 29ft,

10—24pdr carr., 2—6pdr, 2 mortars. Deptford DY 4.8.1829. Survey vessel 6.1.1833. BU 5.1851.

THUNDER Wood ironclad floating battery, 1,469bm, 172·5 × 43ft, 14—68pdr. Mare, Blackwall, 17.4.1855. BU 6.1874 Chatham.

THUNDER Minesweeper (RCN), TE 'Bangor' class. Dufferin 19.3.1941. Sold 1947 Marine Industries.

THUNDER Coastal minesweeper (RCN), 'Ton' class, 370 tons. Vickers, Montreal, 17.7.1952. Tx French Navy 1954 = LA PAIMPOLAISE; deleted 1987.

THUNDER Coastal minesweeper (RCN), 'Ton' class, 390 tons. Port Arthur 27.10.1956. PO 9.1997.

THUNDERBOLT 5th Rate 32, 530bm, 119 × 32ft. French, captured 1696. Hulked 1699. BU 1731.

THUNDERBOLT Wood paddle sloop, 1,058bm, 180 × 36ft. Portsmouth DY 13.1.1842. Wrecked 3.2.1847 Cape Recife, South Africa.

THUNDERBOLT Iron screw floating battery, 1,954bm, 186 × 48·5ft, 16—68pdr. Samuda, Poplar, 22.4.1856. Floating pierhead Chatham 13.11.1873; rammed by tug, sunk 3.4.1948; raised, BU 1949 on river bank. *Bore name DAEDALUS 1916—19 as nominal depot ship for Royal Naval Air Service.*

THUNDERBOLT *See also THETIS 1938.*

THUNDERER 3rd Rate 74, 1,609bm, 166·5 × 47ft. Woolwich DY 19.3.1760. Wrecked 5.10.1780 West Indies.

THUNDERER Ketch 14 (Canadian lakes) Built 1776. *Fate unknown.*

THUNDERER 3rd Rate 74, 1,690bm, 171 × 47·5ft. Wells, Rotherhithe, 13.11.1783. BU 3.1814.

THUNDERER 2nd Rate 84, 2279bm, 196 × 52ft. Woolwich DY 25.1831. Target 5.1863; = COMET 21.4.1869; = NETTLE 9.3.1870. Sold 25.11.1901. *Eight and a half years on stocks.*

THUNDERER Turret ship, 4,407bm, 9,390 tons, 285 × 62·5ft, 4—12in. Pembroke Dock 25.3.1872. Sold 13.9.1909 Garnham.

THUNDERER Battleship, 22,500 tons, 545 × 88·5ft, 10—13·5in, 16—4in. Thames Iron Works, Blackwall, 1.2.1911. Sold 12.1926 Hughes Bolckow, Blyth.

THUNDERER Battleship, 42,500 tons, 740 × 105ft, 9—16in, 16—5·25in. Fairfield, LD 1939, suspended 10.1939, cancelled 1944.

THUNDERER *See also TALAVERA 1818.*

THURSO BAY (ex-LOCH MUICK) Frigate, 'Bay' class. Hall Russell 19.10.1945 (renamed 1944). Comp. 23.9.1949 Chatham as survey ship OWEN. Sold 3.7.1970; BU Blyth.

THYME Corvette, 'Flower' class. Smith's Dock 25.7.1941. Tx Air Ministry 1947 = *Weather Explorer;* = *Epos* 1958.

TIARA Submarine, 'T' class. Portsmouth DY 18.4.1944, not comp. BU 6.1947 Dover Industries.

TIBENHAM Inshore minesweeper, 'Ham' class. McGruer 10.3.1955. Tx French Navy 1955 = M.784/GERANIUM; deleted 1987.

TIBER 5th Rate 38, 1,076bm, 150 × 40ft. List, Fishbourne, 10.11.1813. Sold 1.1820 Durkin, Southampton.

TIBER 5th Rate 46, 1,215bm, 159 × 42ft. Portsmouth DY, ordered 9.6.1825, cancelled 7.2.1831.

TICKHAM *See OAKLEY 1942.*

TICKLER Brig-sloop 12, c. 250bm, 94 × 25ft. Purch. 1781. Captured 1783 by French in West Indies.

TICKLER Gunvessel 12, 148bm, 75 × 21ft. Hill, Limehouse, 28.5.1794. Sold 5.1802.

TICKLER Gunvessel 1. Purch. 9.1798 Honduras local use. Listed 1800.

TICKLER Gun-brig 12, 178bm, 80·5 × 22·5ft, 2–18pdr, 10–18pdr carr. Warren, Brightlingsea, 8.8.1804. Captured 4.6.1808 by Danes in Great Belt.

TICKLER (ex-*Lord Duncan*) utter 14, 114bm. Purch. 1808. Sold 28.8.1816.

TICKLER Wood screw gunboat, 'Albacore' class. Pitcher, Northfleet, 8.9.1855. BU comp. Deptford 21.11.1863.

TICKLER Iron screw gunboat, 265 tons, 85 × 26ft, 1–10in. Pembroke Dock 15.9.1879. Dockyard lighter 1902; = AFRIKANDER (base ship) 26.2.1919; = AFRIKANDER II in 1933. BU 1937 Simonstown.

TIGER 22-gun ship, 120/200bm, 6–9pdr, 14–6pdr, 2–2pdr. Built 1546. Rebuilt 1570; floating battery 1600. Condemned 1605.

TIGER Discovery vessel, 260bm. In Arctic 1613.

TIGER 32-gun ship, 457bm, 100 × 29·5ft. Deptford 1647. Rebuilt Deptford 1681 as 448bm; rebuilt Rotherhithe 1701 as 613bm; rebuilt Sheerness 1722 as 712bm. Wrecked 12.1.1743 Tortuga, West Indies.

TIGER 4th Rate 50, 976bm, 140 × 40ft. Barnard, Harwich, 22.12.1743. = HARWICH 28.11.1743. Wrecked 4.10.1760 I. of Pines, Cuba.

TIGER 4th Rate 60, 1,21815m, 151 × 43ft. Wells & Stanton, Rotherhithe, 23.11.1747. Hulk 1760. Sold 12.5.1765 Bombay.

TIGER 3rd Rate 74, 1,886bm, 169 × 51ft. Spanish, captured 13.8.1762 Havana. Sold 10.6.1784.

TIGER Gunvessel 4, 80bm, 68 × 16ft, 3–32pdr carr., 1–24pdr. Dutch hoy, purch. 3.1794. Sold 1798.

TIGER Gun-brig 12, 131bm. In service 1808–12. *Revenue cutter built Bridport 1805, transferred?*

TIGER Wood paddle sloop, 1,221bm, 250 × 36ft, 2–10in, 14–32pdr. Chatham DY 1.12.1849. Rated frigate 1852. Grounded 12.5.1854 action nr Odessa; Russian = TIGR.

TIGER Destroyer, 400 tons, 210 × 21ft, 1–12pdr, 5–6pdr, 2–TT. John Brown 19.5.1900 spec., purch. Sunk 2.4.1908 collision BERWICK off St Catherines, I. of Wight.

TIGER Battlecruiser, 28,500 tons, 600 × 90·5ft, 8–13·5in, 12–6in. John Brown 15.12.1913. Sold 2.1932 Ward, Inverkeithing, BU.

TIGER Cruiser, 8,800 tons, 555·5 (oa) × 64ft, 9–6in, 10–4in. Vickers Armstrong, Tyne, ordered 3.1942, = BELLEROPHON 17.8.1942, LD 8.1944, = BLAKE 12.1944, = BELLEROPHON 2.1945, cancelled 3.1946.

TIGER (ex-BELLEROPHON) Cruiser, 9,550 tons, 555·5 (oa) × 64ft, 4–6in, 6–3in (later 2–6in, helo). John Brown 25.10.1945 (renamed 2.1945). Arr. Castellon, Spain, 28.9.1986 for BU. *Designed armament: 9–6in, 10–4in.*

TIGER *See also ARDENT 1764, GRAMPUS 1802, BLAKE 1942, BLAKE 1945.*

TIGER BAY (ex-ISLAS MALVINAS) Patrol boat, 81 tons. Argentinian, captured in Falklands 6.1982. Sold 1986.

TIGER PRIZE 4th Rate 48, 645bm. Algerian, captured 3.1678 by RUPERT. Sunk 14.2.1696 foundation Sheerness.

TIGER SNAKE SSV (RAN), 78 tons, Savage 6.1944. Tx North Borneo 11.1945.

TIGER'S WHELP *See MARY ANTRIM 1649.*

TIGRE 3rd Rate 80, 1,887bm, 182 × 48·5ft. French, captured 23.6.1795 with two other vessels by Fleet off L'Orient. BU 6.1817.

TIGRESS Gun-brig 12, 168bm, 76 × 22·5ft, 2–24pdr, 10–18pdr carr, Brindley, Lynn, 11.9.1797. Sold 1.1802.

TIGRESS Gun-brig 12, 177bm, 80 × 22·5ft, 2–18pdr, 10–18pdr carr. Dudman, Deptford, 1.6.1804. Captured 2.8.1808 by Danes in Great Belt.

TIGRESS (ex-PIERRE CZAR) Gun-brig 12, 219bm, French, captured 29.6.1808. = ALGERINE 21.4.1814. Sold 29.1.1818.

TIGRESS Destroyer, 750 tons, 246 × 26ft, 2–4in, 2–12pdr, 2–TT. Hawthorn Leslie 20.12.1911. Sold 9.5.1921 Ward, Milford Haven; arr. 9.1922 for BU.

TIGRIS (ex-FORTH) 5th Rate 36, 934bm, 143 × 38·5ft. Pelham, Frindsbury, 26.6.1813 (renamed 1812). Sold 11.6.1818 for BU.

TIGRIS 5th Rate 46, 1,215bm, 159·5 × 42ft. Plymouth DY, LD 6.1822, cancelled 31.8.1832. *Frames made in Bombay.*

TIGRIS Survey brig 10 (Indian), 258bm, 93 × 26ft, Bombay DY 20.4.1829. Sold 7.1862.

TIGRIS Iron paddle gunboat (Indian), 109bm. Laird 1834 in sections, re-erected 5.1834 Basra. Lost 21.5.1835 R. Euphrates.

TIGRIS Paddle vessel (Indian), 192 tons, 132 × 18ft. Bombay DY 1882. Sold 1904 = *Amarapoora.*

TIGRIS Submarine, 'T' class. Chatham DY 31.10.1939. Sunk 10.3.1943 Gulf of Naples, cause unknown.

TILBURY 4th Rate 54, 691bm, 130 × 34·5ft. Chatham DY 1699. BU 1726.

TILBURY 4th Rate 60, 963bm, 144 × 39ft. Chatham DY 2.6.1733. Burnt 21.9.1742 accident off Hispaniola.

TILBURY 4th Rate 58, 1,124bm, 147 × 42ft. Portsmouth DY 20.7.1745. Foundered 24.9.1757 hurricane off Louisburg.

TILBURY Wood screw gunboat, 'Albacore' class. Pitcher, Northfleet, 29.3.1856. BU 12.1865 Marshall, Plymouth.

TILBURY Destroyer, 'S' class. Swan Hunter 13.6.1918. Sold 2.1931 Rees, Llanelly.

TILBURY *See also CHATHAM 1758, KONKAN 1942.*

TILFORD Seaward defence boat, 'Ford' class. Vosper 21.11.1956. Sold Pounds 8.9.1967.

TILLSONBURG (ex-PEMBROKE CASTLE) Corvette (RCN), 'Castle' class. Ferguson 12.2.1944 (renamed 1943). Sold 5.9.1946 = *Ta Ching*, = *Chiu Chin* (1947); tx Chinese Communist Navy = KAO-AN 1952; discarded 1963.

TILLSONBURG *See also FLYING FISH 1944.*

TIMMINS Corvette (RCN), 'Flower' class. Yarrow, Esquimalt, 26.6.1941. Sold 1946 = *Guayaquil.*

TINGIRA (ex-*Sobraon*) Training shp (RAN), 1,800 tons. Purch. 1912. Sold 3.11.1927 W. M. Ford; BU 1940.

TINTAGEL Destroyer, 'S' class. Swan Hunter 9.8.1918. Sold 16.2.1932 S. Castle, Plymouth.

TINTAGEL CASTLE Corvette, 'Castle' class. Ailsa 13.12.1943. Arr. 6.1958 Troon for BU.

TINY Wood screw gunboat, 'Cheerful' class. Young & Magnay, Limehouse, 8.5.1856. BU comp. 28.1.1864.

TIPPERARY (ex-ALMIRANTE RIVEROS) Destroyer leader, 1,737 tons, 320 × 32·5ft, 6—4in, 3—TT. White 5.3.1915; Chilean, purch. 8.1914. Sunk 1.6.1916 Battle of Jutland.

TIPPU SULTAN *See ONSLOW 1941.*

TIPTOE Submarine, 'T' class. Vickers Armstrong, Barrow, 25.2.1944. Sold Pounds 16.4.1971.

TIR *See BANN 1942.*

TIRADE Destroyer, Modified 'R' class. Scotts 21.4.1917. Sold 15.11.1921 Cashmore, Newport.

TIRELESS Submarine, 'T' class. Portsmouth DY 19.3.1943. Sold Cashmore 20.9.1968; BU Newport.

TIRELESS Nuclear submarine, 'Trafalgar' class. Vickers 17.3.1984.

TISDALE Frigate (RCN), 'River' class. Montreal, cancelled 1944.

TISIPHONE 6th Rate 20, 425bm, 109 × 30ft. Ladd, Dover, 9.5.1781. Floating battery, 16 guns, 7.1803. Sold 11.1.1816.

TITANIA Depot ship, 5,270 tons, 335 × 46ft. Clyde SB Co. 4.3.1915, purch. 1915. BU 6.1948 Metal Industries, Faslane.

TIVERTON Minesweeper, Later 'Hunt' class. Simons 24.9.1918. Sold 12.1938 Ward, Grays.

TOBAGO (ex-TRUMBULL) Brig-sloop 14. American, captured 1777 by VENUS. Sold 1783.

TOBAGO Schooner 10, 120bm. Purch. 1805. Captured 18.10.1806 by French privateer GENERAL ERNOUF. Recaptured 24.1.1809 as VENGEUR; sold.

TOBAGO Destroyer, 'S' class, 1,085 tons. Thornycroft 15.7.1918. Damaged 12.11.1920 mine; sold 9.2.1922 Malta.

TOBAGO (ex-HONG KONG, ex-HOLMES) Frigate, 'Colony' class. Walsh Kaiser 27.9.1943 on Lend-Lease (renamed 1943). Ret. USN 13.5.1946.

TOBRUK Destroyer (RAN), 2,325 tons, 379 (oa) × 411ft, 4—4·5in, 12—40mm, 10—TT. Cockatoo DY 20.12.1947. Sold 27.1.1972 for BU Japan.

TOBRUK Landing ship (RAN), 3,300 tons, 417 (oa) × 60ft. Carrington Slip, Newcastle, NSW, 1.3.1980.

TOKEN Submarine, 'T' class. Portsmouth DY 19.3.1943. Sold Pounds 18.2.1970; BU Cairnryan.

TOMAHAWK Destroyer, 'S' class, 930 tons. Yarrow 16.5.1918. Sold 26.6.1928 King, Garston.

TOMAHAWK *See also WATERWAY 1944, SCORPION 1946.*

TONBRIDGE Minesweeper, Later 'Hunt' class. Simons 5.11.1918. Sold 19.5.1928 Ward, Briton Ferry.

TONBRIDGE CASTLE Corvette, 'Castle' class. Austin, Sunderland, cancelled 12.1943. *Was to have been transferred to RCN.*

TONGHAM Inshore minesweeper, 'Ham' class. Miller, St Monance, 30.11.1955. Sold Pounds 1980; resold 1981 Greek interests.

TONNANT 3rd Rate 80, 2,281bm, 194 × 52ft. French, captured 1.8.1798 Battle of the Nile. BU 3.1821.

TOOWOOMBA Minesweeper, 'Bathurst' class. Walker, Maryborough, 26.3.1941. Lent RAN from 10.1941. Sold Dutch Navy 1946 = BOEROE; deleted 5.1984.

TOOWOOMBA Frigate (RAN), 'Anzac' class. Tenix Defence Systems, Williamstown, LD 26.7.2002.

TOPAZE 5th Rate 38, 916bm, 144·5 × 38ft. French, HO 12.1793 by Royalists at Toulon. Sold 1.9.1814.

TOPAZE (ex-ETOILE) 5th Rate 38, 1,060bm, 151·5 × 40ft. French, captured 27.3.1814 by HEBRUS off La Hogue. Receiving ship 2.1823; target 3.1850. BU 12.1851.

TOPAZE Wood screw frigate 51, 2,659bm, 3,915 tons, 235 × 50ft, 30—8in, 1—68pdr, 20—32pdr. Devonport DY 12.5.1858. Sold Castle 14.2.1884.

TOPAZE 3rd class cruiser, 3,000 tons, 360 × 40ft, 12—4in, 8—3pdr. Laird 23.7.1903. Sold 22.9.1921 Cohen; BU Germany.

TORBAY 2nd Rate 80, 1,202bm, 156 × 42ft. Deptford DY 16.12.1693. Rebuilt Woolwich 1719 as 1,296bm. BU comp. 1.1.1749 Portsmouth.

TORBAY Destroyer, 'S' class, 1,087 tons. Thornycroft 6.3.1919. Tx RCN 1.3.1928 = CHAMPLAIN; sold 1937.

TORBAY Submarine, 'T' class. Chatham DY 9.4.1940. Sold 19.12.1945; BU Ward, Briton Ferry.

TORBAY Nuclear submarine, 'Trafalgar' class, Vickers 8.3.1985.

TORBAY *See also NEPTUNE 1683.*

TORCH (ex-*Fortune*) Fireship, 91bm. Purch. 10.1804. Sold 17.6.1807.

TORCH (ex-TORCHE) Sloop 18, 557bm. French, captured 16.8.1805 by GOLIATH and CAMILLA English Channel. BU 6.1811. *One Admiralty source gives vessel BU 1811 as fireship, ex-Fortune, purch.*

TORCH Iron paddle gunvessel, 340bm, 141 × 22·5ft, 1—32pdr. Ditchburn, Blackwall, 25.2.1845. Sold 15.5.1856 Sydney.

TORCH Wood screw gunvessel, 'Philomel' class. Green, Blackwall, 24.12.1859. BU 9.1881 Malta.

TORCH Sloop, 690 tons, 180 × 32·5ft, 6—4in. Sheerness DY 28.12.1894. HO New Zealand Govt 16.8.1917 as TS = FIREBRAND. Sold 7.1920 New Zealand.

TORCH Destroyer, 'S' class, 930 tons. Yarrow 16.3.1918. Sold 7.11.1929 King, Garston.

TORCH TRV, 698 tons (deep load). Hall Russell 7.8.1979. Sold 1999 IMS International.

TOREADOR Destroyer, 'S' class, 1,087 tons. Thornycroft 7.12.1918. Tx RCN 1.3.1928 = VANCOUVER. Sold 1937; arr. Vancouver 24.4.1937 for BU.

TOREADOR TRV, 680 tons. Hall Russell 14.2.1980. Sold 12.1997 Trent Shipping of Leicester as rig supply vessel West Africa; resold 1999 Oil and Industrial Services, St Vincent.

TORMENTOR Gunvessel. Purch. 1794 West Indies. *Fate unknown.*

TORMENTOR Destroyer, 'R' class. Stephen 22.5.1917. Sold 7.11.1929 King for Troon, wrecked in tow 13.12.29 coast of South Wales.

TORMENTOR TRV, 680 tons. Hall Russell 6.11.1979.

TORNADO Destroyer, 'R' class. Stephen 4.8.1917. Sunk 23.12.1917 mine North Sea.

TORNADO TRV, 680 tons. Hall Russell 24.5.1979.

TORONTO Schooner (Canadian lakes). York, Lake Toronto, 8.1799. Wrecked; BU 1781 York.

TORONTO Schooner (Canadian lakes). Listed 1813. Wrecked 2.6.1817 on lakes.

TORONTO (ex-*Sir Charles Adam*) Wood paddle vessel (Canadian lakes). Purch. 7.1838. Sold 1843.

TORONTO (ex-GIFFARD) Frigate (RCN), 'River' class. Davie SB 18.9.1943 (renamed 1943). Tx RNorN 4.1956 = GARM; = VALKYRIEN (depot ship) 1964; BU 1977.

TORONTO Frigate (RCN), 'Halifax' class. St John SB 18.12.1990.

TORONTO *See also MARY ROSE 1943.*

Torpedo boats, 1st class:

No 1 (ex-LIGHTNING) 27 tons, 84·5 × 11ft, 1—TT. Thornycroft 1877. Sold 1910.

Nos 2–12 28 tons, 87 × 11ft, 1—TT. Thornycroft 1878–79. Nos 4 and 6 sold 1906; Nos 7 and 10—12 sold 1904; others sold c. 1905.

No 13 28 tons, 87 × 11ft, 2—TT. Maudslay, Lambeth, 1878. Sold 5.1897.

No 14 33 tons, 88 × 11ft, 2—TT, Yarrow 1877. Sold c. 1905.

No 15 28 tons, 87 × 11ft, 2—TT. Hanna Donald, Paisley, 1879. Sold c. 1905.

No 16 28 tons, 87 × 11ft, 2—TT. Lewien, Poole, 1878. Not to Admiralty requirements, not accepted; sold by builder to Chinese Navy 8.1879.

No 17 33 tons, 86 × 11ft, 2—TT. Yarrow 1877. Sold 1970 in Malta.

No 18 33 tons, 86 × 11ft, 2—TT. Yarrow 1877. Sold 1904 in Gibraltar

No 19 28 tons, 87 × 11ft, 2—TT. White 1878. Sold 1899.

No 20 28 tons, 87 × 11ft, 2—TT. Rennie, Greenwich, 1880. Sold 1905 in Hong Kong.

Nos 21, 22 63 tons, 133 × 12·5ft, 3—TT. Thornycroft 1885. Sold 1907 in Malta.

Nos 23, 24 67 tons, 113 × 12·5ft, 2—3pdr, 3—TT. Yarrow 1885–86. Sold 1906 or 1907.

Nos 25–29 60 tons, 127·5 × 12·5ft, 4–TT. Thorny-croft 1886. Nos 25–27 sold 2.10.1919 Maden & McKee; No 28 stranded 29.7.1898 Kalk Bay, South Africa, and sunk 12.1898 target; No 29 sold 1.7.1919 Cape Town.

Nos 30–33 64 tons, 125 × 13ft, 2–3pdr, 5–TT. Yarrow 1886. No 31 sold 1913; No 33 sold 1.8.1919; others sold c. 1905.

Nos 34–38 64 tons, 125 × 14·5ft, 5–TT. White 1886. No 34 sold 2.10.1919 Maden & McKee; others sold 27.11.1919 in Hong Kong.

Nos 39, 40 40 tons, 100 × 12·5ft, 1–TT. Yarrow 1885 for Chilean Navy, purch. 1888; sold 2.1905 Esquimalt.

Nos 41–60 60 tons, 127·5 × 12·5ft, 2–3pdr, 4–TT. Thornycroft 1886. Nos 41, 45, 49 and 54 all sold 1.8.1919; Nos 42 and 57 sold 2.10.1919 Maden & McKee; Nos 43 and 44 sold 18.12.1919 in Malta; No 47 sold c. 1908; No 48 sold c. 1915; Nos 50 and 55 sold 23.2.1920 R. Longmate; Nos 51 and 59 sold c. 1913; No 53 sold 1913, Nos 52 and 58 sold 19.12.1919 Multilocular S. Bkg Co.; No 60 sold 1.7.1919 The Cape; No 46 wrecked under tow 27.12.1915 Mediterranean, salved, BU 1920; No 56 foundered under tow 17.5.1906 off Dami-etta.

Nos 61–79 75 tons, 125 × 13ft, 2–3pdr, 5–TT. Yarrow 1886. No 61 sold 1909; No 62 sold 1905; Nos 63 and 70 sold 18.12.1919 in Malta; No 64 wrecked 21.3.1915 Aegean; Nos 65 and 78 sold 2.10.1919 Maden & McKee; Nos 66, 68 and 76 sold 30.6.1920 Ward, Hayle; Nos 67 and 74 sold 27.1.1920 Willoughby, Plymouth; No 69 sold c. 1908; No 71 sold 5.7.1923 B. Newton; No 72 sold 19.12.1919 Ward, Rainham; No 73 sold 6.2.1923 L. Basso, Weymouth; No 75 sunk 8.8.1892 collision No 77 off The Maidens; No 77 sold 27.3.1920 Stanlee, Dover; No 79 sold 19.12.1919 Ward, Grays.

Note: All boats up to TB.79 which survived the year 1906 had a '0' added to their numbers to avoid confusion with the coastal TBs, which had been renamed TB.1–36 in that year (e.g., the original TB.25 became TB.025.)

No 80 105 tons, 135 × 14ft, 4–3dr, 5–TT. Yarrow 1887. Sold 22.1.1921 J. E. Thomas.

No 81 (ex-SWIFT) 125 tons, 150 × 17·5ft, 6–3pdr, 3–TT. White 1885. purch. Sold 22.10.1921 J. E. Thomas.

Nos 82–87 85 tons, 130 × 13·5ft, 3–3pdr, 3–TT. Yarrow 1889. Nos 82, 85 and 86 sold 22.10.1921 J. E.Thomas; No 83 sold 12.10.1919 Brand; No 84 sunk 17.4.1906 collision ARDENT; No 87 sold 27.3.1920 Stanlee, Dover.

Nos 88, 89 112 tons, 142 × 14·5ft, 3–3pdr, 3–TT. Yarrow 1894. Both sold 13.10.1919 Brand.

No 90 100 tons, 140 × 14·5ft, 3–3pdr, 3–TT. Yarrow 1895. Capsized 24.4.1919 off Gibraltar.

Nos 91–93 130 tons, 140 × 15·5ft, 3–3pdr, 3–TT. Thornycroft 1894. Nos 91 and 93 sold 13.10.1919 Brand; No 92 sold 1920 Gibraltar.

Nos 94–96 130 tons, 140 × 15·5ft, 3–3pdr, 3–TT. White 1893. Nos 94 and 95 sold with No 91; No 96 sunk 1.11.1915 collision troopship *Tringa* off Gibraltar.

No 97 130 tons, 140 × 15·5ft, 3–3pdr, 3–TT. Laird 16.9.1893. Sold 1920 in Gibraltar.

Nos 98, 99 178 tons, 160 × 17ft, 3–3pdr, 3–TT. Thornycroft 1901. No 98 sold 30.6.1920 Ward, Preston; No 99 sold 29.7.1920 Ward, Hayle.

Nos 100–106 *See Nos 1–7 RIM boats.*

Nos 107, 108 178 tons, 160 × 17ft, 3–3pdr, 3–TT. Thornycroft 1901. No 107 sold 29.7.1920 Ward, Morecambe; No 108 sold 29.7.1920 Willoughby, Plymouth.

Nos 109–113 200 tons, 166 × 17·5ft, 3–3pdr, 3–TT. No 109 Thornycroft 22.7.1902, sold 27.3.1920 Stanlee, Dover; No 110 Thornycroft 5.9.1902, sold with No 109; No 111 Thornycroft 31.10.1902, sold 10.2.1920 Ward, Grays; No 112 Thornycroft 15.1.1903, sold with No 111; No 113 Thornycroft 12.2.1903, sold 19.12.1919 Ward, Grays.

Nos 114–117 205 tons, 165 × 17·5ft, 3–3pdr, 3–TT. No 114 White 8.6.1903, sold 1919 Ward, Grays (moved Rainham 1920); No 115 White 19.11.1903, sold 1919 Ward, Rainham; No 116 White 21.12.1903, sold 22.10.1921 J. E. Thomas, Newport; No 117 White 18.2.1904, sunk 10.6.1917 collision SS *Kamouraska* English Channel (salved?).

Note: Dockyard lighter No 80 'ex-TB.117' was sold 31.3.1921 W. T. Beaumont.

Torpedo boats, 2nd class:

Nos 1–12 (wood-built) 12 tons, 1 spar torpedo. All built White 1883–88. No 2 sold 1900; Nos 1, 3, 4, 7, 8 and 10 sold by 1905; No 5 sold 1909; No 6 sold by 1907, Nos 9 and 11 sold 1912; No 12 sold 1910.

Nos 38–100 (steel-built) 15 tons, 2–TT (except Nos 38–50, 96 and 97: 1–TT). Nos 1–62, 64–73, 76–95, 98–100 all Thornycroft 1878–86; Nos 38–50 all Yarrow 1887–89; No 63 Hereschoff Co., USA; Nos 74, 75, 96, 97 all Yarrow 1883. Nos 55, 58–61, 79, 81, 90, 91 and 97 all sold 1902; No 92 condemned 1900; No 75 sold 1903; Nos 50, 52–54, 56, 57, 84 all sold 1904; Nos 66, 73 and 87 sold 1905; Nos 49, 69, 70, 74, 76–78, 82, 94, 96 all sold 1906; Nos 39–44, 51, 65, 80, 89 and 99 all sold 1907; No 100 sold 1908; No 71 sold 1909;

Nos 45–48 and 95 sold 1912; No 68 tx Newfoundland Govt; No 62 foundered 21.10.1890 under tow by BUZZARD off North America.

Note: A yard craft 'ex-TB.9' was BU at Devonport in 1919.

Indian (RIM) boats, tx RN in 1892:

No 1 (BALUCHI) 96 tons, 134·5 × 14·5ft, 5–TT. Thornycroft 1888. = No 100 in 1901. Sold 1909.

No 2 (KAHREN) 96 tons, 134·5 × 14·5ft. 5–TT. Thornycroft 1888. = No 102 in 1901. Sold 1909.

No 3 (PATHAN) 96 tons, 134·5 × 14·5ft, 5–TT. Thornycroft 1888. = No 103 in 1901. Sold 1909.

No 4 (MAHRATTA) 95 tons, 130 × 14·5ft, 5–TT. White 1889. = No 104 in 1901. Sold 29.7.1920 Willoughby.

No 5 (SIKH) 95 tons, 130 × 14·5ft, 5–TT. White 1889. = No 105 in 1901. Sold 27.1.1920 Willoughby, Plymouth.

No 6 (RAJPUT) 95 tons, 130 × 14·5ft, 5–TT. White 1889. = No 106 in 1901. Sold 11.10.1910 Cashmore, Newport.

No 7 (GHURKA) 92 tons, 130·5 × 14ft, 5–TT. McArthur, Paisley 1888. = No 101 in 1901. Sold 27. 3.1920 Stanlee, Dover.

Tasmanian Govt:

No 1 12 tons, 63 × 7·5ft, 1 spar torpedo. Thornycroft 1884. Deleted 1910.

New Zealand:

Nos 1–4 12 tons, 63 × 7·5ft, 1 spar torpedo. Thornycroft 1884. No 1 sold 1900; No 2 BU 1913.

Ex-coastal destroyers:

Nos 1–12 *CRICKET, DRAGONFLY, FIREFLY, SANDFLY, SPIDER, GADFLY, GLOWWORM, GNAT, GRASSHOPPER, GREENFLY, MAYFLY, MOTH, respectively, renamed 1906 (q.v.).*

No 13 256 tons, 182 × 18ft, 2–12pdr, 3–TT. White 10.7.1907. Sunk 26.1.1916 collision North Sea.

No 14 256 tons, 182 × 18ft, 2–12pdr, 3–TT. White 26.9.1907. Sold 7.10.1920 Philip, Dartmouth, for use as pontoon jetty; still such 1966.

No 15 256 tons, 182 × 18ft, 2–12pdr, 3–TT. White 19.11.1907. Sold 7.10.1920 Ward; arr. Briton Ferry 29.1.1921 for BU.

No 16 256 tons, 182 × 18ft, 2–12pdr, 3–TT. White 23.12.1907. Sold 7.10.1920 Ward; arr. Briton Ferry 29.1.1921 for BU.

No 17 251 tons, 180 × 18ft, 2–12pdr, 3–TT. Denny 21.12.1907. Sold 1919 Gibraltar.

No 18 251 tons, 180 × 18ft, 2–12pdr, 3–TT. Denny 15.2.1908. Sold 1920 Gibraltar.

No 19 280 tons, 178·5 × 20·5ft, 2–12pdr, 3–TT. Thornycroft 7.12.1907. Sold 9.5.1921 Ward, Grays.

No 20 280 tons, 178·5 × 20·5ft, 2–12pdr, 3–TT. Thornycroft 21.1.1908. Sold 9.5.1921 Ward, Grays.

No 21 308 tons, 185 × 18·5ft, 2–12pdr, 3–TT. Hawthorn 20.12.1907. Sold 7.10.1920 Maden & McKee, resold 8.1924 Hayes, Portcawl.

No 22 308 tons, 185 × 18·5ft, 2–12pdr, 3–TT. Hawthorn 1.2.1908. Sold 7.10.1920 Maden & McKee; resold 8.1924 Hayes, Porthcawl.

No 23 253 tons, 177·5 × 18ft, 2–12pdr, 3–TT. Yarrow 5.12.1907. Sold 9.5.1921 Ward, Grays.

No 24 292 tons, 177 × 18ft, 2–12pdr, 3–TT. Palmer 19.3.1908. Wrecked 28.1.1917 Dover breakwater.

No 25 283 tons, 182 × 18ft, 2–12pdr, 3–TT. White 28.7.1908. Sold 9.5.1921 Ward, Grays.

No 26 283 tons, 182 × 18ft, 2–12pdr, 3–TT. White 28.8.1908. Sold 9.5.1921 Ward, Grays; BU Rainham.

No 27 283 tons, 182 × 18ft, 2–12pdr, 3–TT. White 29.9.1908. Sold 9.5.1921 Ward, Rainham.

No 28 283 tons, 182 × 18ft, 2–12pdr, 3–TT. White 29.10.1908. Sold 9.5.1921 Ward, Rainham.

No 29 259 tons, 180 × 18ft, 2–12pdr, 3–TT. Denny 29.8.1908. Sold 28.11.1919 in Malta.

No 30 259 tons, 180 × 18ft, 2–12pdr, 3–TT. Denny 29.9.1908. Sold 28.11.1919 in Malta.

No 31 287 tons, 178·5 × 18·5ft, 2–12pdr, 3–TT. Thornycroft 10.10.1908. Sold 9.5.1921 Ward, Rainham.

No 32 287 tons, 178·5 × 18·5ft, 2–12pdr, 3–TT. Thornycroft 23.11.1908. Sold 9.5.1921 Ward, Rainham.

No 33 306 tons, 185 × 18·5ft, 2–12pdr, 3–TT. Hawthorn 22.2.1909. Sold 24.8.1922 Cashmore, Newport.

No 34 306 tons, 185 × 18·5ft, 2–12pdr, 3–TT. Hawthorn 22.2.1909. Sold 9.5.1921 Ward, Rainham.

No 35 298 tons, 177 × 18ft, 2–12pdr, 3–TT. Palmer 19.4.1909. Sold 24.8.1922 Cashmore, Newport.

No 36 298 tons, 177 × 18ft, 2–12pdr, 3–TT. Palmer 6.5.1909. Sold 9.5.1921 Ward, Rainham.

TORQUAY Frigate, 2,150 tons, 370 (oa) × 41ft, 2–4·5in, 2–40mm, Limbo. Harland & Wolff 1.7.1954. Towed Portsmouth 1.7.1987 for BU Barcelona.

TORRENS Destroyer (RAN), 700 tons, 246 × 24ft, 1–4in, 3–12pdr, 3–TT. Cockatoo DY 28.8.1915. Sunk 24.11.1930 target off Sydney Heads.

TORRENS Frigate (RAN), 2,100 tons, 370 (oa) × 41ft, 2–4·5in, Limbo. Cockatoo DY 28.9.1968. Expended 15.6.1999 target for FARNCOMB west of Perth.

TORRENT Destroyer, 'R' class. Swan Hunter 26.11.1916. Sunk 23.12.1917 mine North Sea.

TORRENT TRV, 680 tons. Clelands 29.3.1971. Sold 5.11.2000 Suffolk Petroleum, Port Harcourt.

TORRID Destroyer, 'R' class. Swan Hunter 10.2.1917. HO Ward 27.1.1937 part payment *Majestic* (CALEDONIA, q.v.); wrecked 16.3.1937 under tow for Hayle, nr Trefusis Point; BU 1940 *in situ.*

TORRID TRV, 680 tons. Clelands 7.9.1971. Sold Dutch interests 1.1992 Moerdijk.

TORRIDE Gunvessel 7. French fireship, captured 25.8.1798 by boats of GOLIATH off R. Nile. Listed 1802.

TORRIDGE Frigate, 'River' class. Blyth 16.8.1943. Tx French Navy 1944 = SURPRISE; tx Morocco = AL MAOUNA 1964; BU 1975.

TORRINGTON 62-gun ship, 732bm. Johnson, Blackwall, 1654. = DREADNOUGHT 1660. Foundered 16.18.1690 off North Foreland.

TORRINGTON 5th Rate 44, 711 bm, 126 × 36ft. Rowcliffe, Southampton, 15.1.1743. Sold 30.8.1763.

TORRINGTON Frigate, TE 'Captain' class. Bethlehem, Hingham, 27.11.1943 on Lend-Lease. Ret. USN 1946.

TORRINGTON *See also CHARLES GALLEY 1676.*

TORTOISE (ex-*Grenville*) Storeship 26. Purch. 1777. Foundered 9.1779 off Newfoundland.

TORTOISE Store lighter, 109bm, 60·5 × 20·5ft. Barnard, Deptford, 17.7.1780. Lost 11.1787.

TORTOISE (ex-*Russian Eagle*) Storeship 16. Purch. 12.1781. Sold 10.1.1785.

TORTOISE Store lighter, 144bm, 69 × 22ft. Sibrell, Plymouth, 27.4.1789. BU 1.1863 Plymouth.

TORTOISE *See also SIR EDWARD HUGHES 1806.*

TORTOLA (ex-PEYTON) Frigate, 'Colony' class. Walsh Kaiser 16.11.1943 on Lend-Lease (renamed 1943). Ret. USN 22.5.1946.

TOTEM Submarine, 'T' class. Devonport DY 28.9.1943. Sold 1964 Israeli Navy, = DAKAR 10.11.1967; lost 25.1.1968 passage Israel.

TOTLAND (ex-CAYUGA) Cutter, 1,546 tons, 256 (oa) × 42ft, 1—5in, 3—3in. Cd RN 12.5.1941 on Lend-Lease. Ret. USN 5.1946.

TOTNES Paddle minesweeper, 'Ascot' class. McMillan 17.5.1916. Sold 3.1922 Ward, Inverkeithing.

TOTNES CASTLE *See HUMBERSTONE 1944.*

TOURMALINE Composite screw corvette, 2,120 tons, 220 × 40ft, 12—64pdr. Raylton Dixon, Middlesbrough, 30.10.1875. Coal hulk 1799, = C.115 in 12.04. Sold 11.1920 as coal hulk.

TOURMALINE Destroyer, 'S' class, 1,087 tons, Thornycroft 12.4.1919. Sold 11.1931 Ward, Grays.

TOURMALINE (ex-USAGE) Minesweeper, 'Catherine' class. Gulf SB, Madisonville, 4.10.1942; to RN 7.6.1943 on Lend-Lease. Ret. USN 1947; tx Turkish Navy = CARDAK; withdrawn 1974.

TOURMALINE *See also CASSANDRA 1943.*

TOURTERELLE 6th Rate 28, 581bm, 126 × 32ft. French, captured 13.3.1795 by LIVELY off Ushant. Sunk 1816 breakwater Bermuda.

TOWER Smack 4. Purch. 1668. Sold 1674.

TOWER Tender 6, 145bm, 4—12pdr. Bridport 1809. Lent Thames Police 1.1817. Sold 27.1.1825 J. Ledger.

TOWER Destroyer, Modified 'R' class. Swan Hunter 5.4.1917. Sold 17.5.1928 Cashmore. Newport.

TOWEY 6th Rate 24, 448bm, 108 × 30·5ft. Adams, Buckler's Hard, 6.5.1814. BU 11.1822.

TOWEY *See also TOWY.*

TOWNSVILLE Minesweeper (RAN), 'Bathurst' class. Evans Deakin, Brisbane, 13.5.1941. Sold 8.8.1956 Delta Shipping Co.; BU 1962 Japan.

TOWNSVILLE Patrol boat (RAN), 211 tons. Cairns 16.5.1981.

TOWY Frigate, 'River' class. Smith's Dock 4.3.1943. Arr. 27.6.1956. Smith & Houston, Port Glasgow, for BU.

TOWY *See also TOWEY.*

TOWZER Gunvessel 1. Purch. 1798 West Indies. Listed 1799.

TRACKER (ex-*Mormacmail*) Escort carrier, 11,420 tons, 468·5 × 69·5ft, 2—4in, 16—40mm, 24 aircraft. Seattle Tacoma 7.3.1942 on Lend-Lease. Ret. USN 29.11.1945.

TRACKER Patrol boat, 49 tons, 68·2 (oa) × 19ft, 1—20mm. Kingfisher Boats, Falmouth, comp. 16.11.1997.

TRACKER *See also LST.3522 1945.*

TRACOUN Sloop 14. Purch. 1782. *Fate unknown.*

TRADEWIND Submarine, 'T' class. Chatham DY 11.12.1942. Arr. 14.12.1955 Charlestown for BU.

TRAFALGAR 1st Rate 106, 2,404bm, 196 × 53·5ft. Chatham DY 26.7.1820. = CAMPERDOWN 22.2.1825. Harbour service 1854; coal hulk 1857. = PITT 29.8.1882. Sold 15.5.1906 Castle. *Seven years on stocks.*

TRAFALGAR 1st Rate 110, 2,694bm, 205·5 × 55·5ft. Woolwich DY 21.6.1841; undocked 21.3.1859 as screw ship, 2,900bm; = BOSCAWEN 1873. Sold 10.7.1906 Castle, Thames. *Eleven and a half years on stocks.*

TRAFALGAR Battleship, 11,940 tons, 345 × 73ft, 4—13·5in, 6—4·7in, 8—6pdr. Portsmouth DY 20.9.1887. Sold 9.5.1911 Garnham.

TRAFALGAR Destroyer, 2,325 tons, 379 (oa) ×
40·25ft, 4—4·5in, 1—4in, 10—40mm, 8—TT. Swan
Hunter 12.1.1944. Sold Arnott Young 8.6.1970;
BU Dalmuir.

TRAFALGAR Nuclear submarine, 'Trafalgar' class.
Vickers 1.7.1981.

TRAIL Corvette (RCN), 'Flower' class. Burrard
16.10.1940. BU 8.1950 Steel Co. of Canada,
Hamilton.

TRAILER (ex-BLOCK ISLAND, ex-*Momac-
penn*) Escort carrier, 11,420 tons, 468·5 × 69·5ft,
2—4in, 8—40mm, 18 aircraft. Ingalls, Pascagoula,
22.5.1942 on Lend-Lease. = HUNTER 11.1942.
Ret. USN 29.12.1945.

TRALEE Minesweeper, Later 'Hunt' class. Simons
17.12.1918. Sold 2.7.1929 Hill, Dover.

TRAMONTANA Bark 21, 150bm, 12—6pdr, 7—
4pdr, 2—2pdr. Deptford 1586. BU 1618.

TRANSCONA Minesweeper (RCN), diesel 'Bangor'
class. Marine Industries 26.4.1941. Tx RCMP
1950 = *French*; BU 1961 La Have, NS.

TRANSFER (ex-TEMERAIRE) Sloop 14. French
cutter, captured 1795 by DIDO in Mediterranean.
BU 1803.

TRANSFER (ex-QUARTRE FRERES) Sloop 12,
181bm, 80 × 23·5ft, 12—6pdr. French privateer,
captured 21.11.1797. Sold 1802 Malta.

TRANSIT Schooner 12, 261bm, 129 × 22·5ft.
Bailey, Ipswich, 3.3.1809; later shortened to
214bm, 112·5 × 22·5ft. Sold 12.10.1815.

TRANSIT Iron screw troopship, 2,587bm, 302·5 ×
41·5ft. Mare, Blackwall, 20.3.1855, purch. on
stocks. Wrecked 10.7.1857 Banka Strait.

TRANSPORTER (TRANSPORT LIGHTER) Ketch
7, 92bm. Sheerness 1677. Rebuilt Deptford 1709
as 100bm; sold 8.1.1713 J. Fox.

TRANSVAAL (ex-LOCH ARD) Frigate (SAN),
'Loch' class. Harland & Wolff, Govan, 2.8.1944
(renamed 1944). PO 14.8.1964; expended
3.8.1978 breakwater False Bay.

TRAVE 5th Rate 38, 1,076bm. French, captured
23.10.1813 by ANDROMACHE in Atlantic. Sold
7.6.1821.

TRAVELLER Wood paddle vessel (Canadian
lakes). Purch. 30.4.1839. Sold 1844 mercantile.

TRAVELLER Wood screw gunboat, 'Albacore'
class. Green, Blackwall, 13.3.1856. BU comp.
28.12.1863 Portsmouth.

TRAVELLER Submarine, 'T' class. Scotts
27.8.1941. Sunk 1942 Gulf of Taranto, cause
unknown; formally PO 12.12.1942.

TREDAGH (DROGHEDA) 50-gun ship, 771bm.
Ratcliffe 1654. = RESOLUTION 1660. Burnt
25.7.1666 in action with Dutch.

TREEKRONEN 3rd Rate 74, 1,746bm, 175·5 ×
48ft. Danish, captured 7.9.1807 Battle of
Copenhagen. Receiving ship 1809. Sold 20.7.1825
Beatson for BU.

TRELAWNEY Storeship 14, 350bm, 106 × 29ft,
10—9pdr, 4—3pdr. Purch. 2.1743. Sold 19.5.1747.

TREMADOC BAY (ex-LOCH ARNISH) Frigate,
'Bay' class. Harland & Wolff 29.3.1945 (renamed
1944). Arr. 18.9.1959 Genoa for BU.

TREMATON CASTLE Corvette, 'Castle' class.
Morton, Quebec, cancelled 12.1943.

TREMENDOUS 3rd Rate 74, 1,656bm, 170·5 ×
48·5ft. Barnard, Deptford, 30.10.1784. Rebuilt
1810 as 1,706bm;, = GRAMPUS 23.5.1845,
reduced to 50 guns. Powder hulk 1856. Sold
10.5.1897 J. Read, Portsmouth.

TRENCHANT Destroyer, Modified 'R' class. White
23.12.1916. Sold 15.11.1928 for BU.

TRENCHANT Submarine, 'T' class. Chatham DY
24.3.1943. Sold 1.7.1963; arr. 23.7.1963 Faslane
for BU.

TRENCHANT Nuclear submarine, 'Trafalgar'
class, Vickers, Barrow, 3.11.1986.

TRENT 6th Rate 28 (fir-built), 587bm, 118·5 ×
34ft. Woolwich DY 31.10.1757. Sold 21.6.1764
unserviceable.

TRENT 5th Rate 36 (fir-built), 926bm, 142·5 ×
38ft. Woolwich DY 24.2.1796. Hospital ship 1803;
receiving ship 1818. BU 2.1823 Haulbowline.

TRENT Wood screw sloop, 950bm, 185 × 33ft.
Pembroke Dock, LD 3.9.1861, = RESEARCH
9.1862, launched 15.8.1863 as ironclad sloop. *See
RESEARCH 1863.*

TRE Iron screw gunboat, 363 tons, 110 × 34ft, 3—
64pdr. Palmer, Jarrow, 23.8.1877. = PEMBROKE
9.1905; = GANNET (diving tender) 6.1917. Sold
21.2.1923 Dover S. Bkg Co.

TRENT Frigate, 'River' class. Hill, Bristol
10.10.1942. Tx RIN 4.1946 = KUKRI; = INVESTI-
GATOR (survey vessel) 1951. BU 1975.

TRENTONIAN Corvette (RCN), Modified 'Flower'
class. Kingston SY 1.9.1943. Sunk 22.2.1945 by
U.1004 off Falmouth.

TREPASSY Brig-sloop 14. Purch. 1779. Captured
28.5.1781 by American ALLIANCE; recaptured.
Sold 29.4.1784.

TREPASSY Brig, 42bm, 45 × 15ft. Lester & Stone,
Newfoundland, 1790. Sold 12.1803 Newfoundland.

TRESCO (ex-MICHAEL) 24-gun ship. Royalist,
captured 1651 by Parliamentarians. Wrecked
1651.

TRESHAM Inshore minesweeper, 'Ham' class.
Morgan Giles, Teignmouth, 11.5.1954. Sold 1966

Reardon Smith Nautical College, Cardiff
= *Margherita II.*

TRESPASSER (ex-P.312) Submarine, 'T' class.
Vickers Armstrong, Barrow, 29.5.1942. Arr.
26.9.1961 Gateshead for BU.

TREVOSE HEAD *See MULL OF OA 1945.*

TRIAD Submarine, 'T' class. Vickers Armstrong,
Barrow, 5.5.1939. Sunk 20.10.1940 off Libya,
cause unknown.

TRIAL Cutter 12. Listed 1781–94.

TRIAL Cutter 12, 123bm, 65 × 21·5ft, 4–12pdr
carr., 8–3pdr. Dunsterville, Plymouth, 9.9.1790.
Sold 1814.

TRIAL Gunvessel 6. Listed 1805–11.

TRIAL Coal hulk. Listed 1843. Sold 3.2.1848.

TRIAL *See also TRYALL.*

TRIBUNE 5th Rate 36, 916bm, 8–32pdr carr.,
26–12pdr, 8–6pdr. French, captured 8.6.1796 by
UNICORN off Ireland. Wrecked 16.11.1797 Thrum
Shoal, Halifax, NS.

TRIBUNE 5th Rate 36, 884bm, 137 × 38·5ft.
Parsons, Bursledon, 5.7.1803. 6th Rate 24 from
1832. Wrecked 28.11.1839 nr Tarragona.

TRIBUNE Wood screw corvette, 1,570bm, 192 ×
43ft, 1–10in, 30–32pdr. Sheerness DY 21.1.1853.
Sold 8.1866 Marshall, Plymouth.

TRIBUNE 2nd class cruiser, 3,400 tons, 300 ×
43ft, 2–6in, 6–4·7in, 8–6pdr. Thomson
24.2.1891. Sold 9.5.1911 Cashmore, Newport.

TRIBUNE Destroyer, 'S' class. White 28.3.1918.
Sold 17.12.1931 Cashmore, Newport.

TRIBUNE Submarine, 'T' class. Scotts 8.12.1938.
BU 11.1947 Ward, Milford Haven.

TRIDENT 3rd Rate 64, 1,366bm 159 × 44·5ft.
Plymouth DY 20.4.1768. Sold 3.7.1816 in Malta.

TRIDENT Iron paddle sloop, 850bm 180 × 31·5ft.
Ditchburn & Mare, Blackwall, 16.12.1845. BU
1.1866 Castle.

TRIDENT (ex-OFFA) Destroyer, 1,098 tons, 300 ×
28·5ft, 5–4in, 4–TT. Hawthorn Leslie 20.11.1915;
Turkish, renamed 15.2.1915. Sold 9.5.1921 Ward,
Grays.

TRIDENT Submarine, 'T' class. Cammell Laird
7.12.1938. Arr. 17.2.1946 Cashmore, Newport, for
BU.

TRIDENT *See also TRYDENT.*

TRILLIUM Corvette, 'Flower' class. Vickers,
Montreal, 26.6.1940. Lent RCN until 27.6.1945.
Sold 17.5.1947 = *Olympic Runner*; = *Otori Maru
No 10* 1956; = *Kyo Maru No 16* 1959; last listed
1972–73.

TRIMMER (ex-ANTIBRITON) Brig-sloop 14,
275bm, 84 × 24·5ft, 14–6pdr. American (?)
cutter, captured 1782 by STAG. Sold 6.1801.

TRINCOMALEE Sloop 16, 315bm. Prize, purch.
1799. Blown up 12.10.1799 in action with the
French privateer IPHIGENIE in Strait of Bab el
Mandib.

TRINCOMALEE (ex-GLOIRE) Sloop 16, 320bm.
French privateer, captured 23.3.1801 by
ALBATROSS in Indian Ocean. Recaptured 1803
by French; captured again 25.9.1818 by
CULLODEN in East Indies, re-added = EMILIEN.
Sold c. 1808.

TRINCOMALEE 5th Rate 46, 1,066bm, 1,447
tons, 150·5 × 40ft. Bombay DY 12.10.1817 26-gun
6th Rate 9.1847; RNR drillship 1.1861. Sold
19.5.1897 J. Read; resold as TS *Foudroyant*.
Towed 24.7.1987 West Hartlepool for preservation (comp. 2002). *Oldest RN ship still afloat.*

TRINCOMALEE Destroyer, 2,380 tons, 355 ×
40ft, 5–4·5in, 8–40mm, 10–TT. John Brown
8.1.1946, not comp. Arr. 2.1946 Troon for BU.

TRINCULO Brig-sloop 18, 'Cruizer' class, 389bm.
Tyson & Blake, Bursledon, 15.7.1809. BU 7.1841.

TRINCULO Wood screw gunboat, 'Britomart'
class. Banks, Plymouth, 15.9.1860. Wrecked
5.9.1870 after collision SS *Moratin* off Gibraltar.

TRING (ex-TEIGNMOUTH) Minesweeper, Later
'Hunt' class. Simons 23.8.1918 (renamed 1918).
Sold 7.10.1927 Alloa; BU Charlestown.

TRINIDAD Schooner 10. Listed 1805–09.

TRINIDAD Destroyer, 'S' class. White 8.4.1918.
Sold 16.2.1932 Ward, Grays.

TRINIDAD Cruiser, 8,000 tons, 555·5 (oa) × 62ft,
12–6in. 8–4in. Devonport 21.3.1940. Bombed
30.4.1942 German aircraft Barents Sea; scuttled
15.5.1942.

TRINITY Ship, 120bm. Purch. 1413. Sold 1418.

TRINITY Ship, 80bm. Captured 1545. Not listed
thereafter.

TRINITY Coastal minesweeper (RCN). 'Bay' class,
370 tons. G. T. Davie 31.7.1953. Tx Turkish Navy
1958 = TERME; patrol vessel 1991.

TRINITY HENRY 64-gun ship, 250bm. Listed
1530. Sold 1566.

TRINITY HENRY Ship, 80bm. Listed 1519–25.

TRINITY ROYAL Ship, 540bm. Built 1398, rebuilt
1416. Abandoned 1429.

TRINITY SOVEREIGN *See SOVEREIGN 1488.*

TRIOMPHANT (LE TRIOMPHANT) Destroyer,
2,569 tons, 411 × 39ft, 5–5.5in, 9–TT. French,
seized 3.7.1940 Plymouth. Free French 8.1940.
Ret. French Navy 1945.

TRISTRAM Destroyer, Modified 'R' class. White
24.2.1917. Sold 9.5.1921 Ward, Briton Ferry; BU
begun 29.8.24.

TRITON 6th Rate 28, 620bm, 124 × 33·5ft. Adams,

Buckler's Hard, 1.10.1771. BU 1.1796. *Buckler's Hard records give launch date as 1773.*

TRITON 5th Rate 32 (fir-built), 856bm, 142 × 36ft. Barnard, Deptford, 5.9.1796. Harbour service 1800. Hulked 1817; BU 1820 Newfoundland.

TRITON Iron paddle sloop, 654bm, 170 × 28ft. Ditchburn & Mare, Blackwall, 24.10.1846. Sold 1872 Moss Isaacs.

TRITON Paddle survey vessel, 410 tons. Samuda, Poplar, 4.3.1882. Harbour service 1914; lent 24.6.1919 Gravesend Sea School. BU 10.1961 Bruges.

TRITON Submarine, 'T' class. Vickers Armstrong, Barrow, 5.10.1937. Sunk 18.12.1940 Italian torpedo boat CLIO southern Adriatic.

TRITON Research vessel/trimaran frigate, 1,200 tons, 323·89 (oa) × 73·8ft, Vosper-Thornycroft 6.5.2000, not cd. *Managed by DERA/Qinetiq.*

TRITON *See also TRYTON.*

TRIUMPH Galleon 68, 741bm. Built 1561. Rebuilt 1596 as 928bm, 4—60pdr, 3—34pdr, 17—18pdr, 8—9pdr, 36 small. Sold 1618.

TRIUMPH 44-gun ship, 898bm. Durell, Deptford, 1623. BU 1687.

TRIUMPH 2nd Rate 90, 1,482bm, 160 × 46ft. Chatham DY 1698. = PRINCE 27.8.1714. Rebuilt Chatham 1750 as 1,677bm, 168·5 × 48ft. BU 1775 Plymouth.

TRIUMPH (ex-TRIUNFO) Sloop 18. Spanish, captured 23.11.1739 Puerto Bello. Foundered 1.1740 West Indies.

TRIUMPH 3rd Rate 74, 1,825bm, 171·5 × 50ft. Woolwich DY 3.3.1764. Harbour service 10.1813. BU 6.1850 Pembroke Dock.

TRIUMPH Screw 2nd Rate 91, 3,715bm, 252 × 57·5ft. Pembroke Dock. = PRINCE CONSORT 14.2.1862, launched 26.6.1862 as armoured frigate, 4,045bm. (q.v.)

TRIUMPH Iron armoured ship, 3,893bm, 6,640 tons, 280 × 55ft, 10—9in, 4—64pdr. Palmer 27.9.1870. = TENEDOS (depot ship; TS) 4.1904; = INDUS IV 1912; = ALGIERS 1.1915. Sold 7.1.1921 Fryer, Sunderland.

TRIUMPH (ex-LIBERTAD) Battleship, 11,985 tons, 436 × 71ft, 4—10in, 14—7·5in, 14—14pdr. Vickers 15.1.1903; Chilean, purch. 3.12.1903. Sunk 25.5.1915 by U.21 off Gallipoli.

TRIUMPH Submarine, 'T' class. Vickers Armstrong, Barrow, 16.2.1938. Sunk 14.1.1942 Aegean, cause unknown.

TRIUMPH Aircraft carrier, 13,350 tons, 630 × 80ft, 19—40mm, 48 aircraft. Hawthorn Leslie 2.10.1944. Repair ship 12.1964, 4—40mm. Left Chatham 9.12.1981 for BU Spain.

TRIUMPH Nuclear submarine, 'Trafalgar' class. Vickers, Barrow, 16.2.1991.

TROIS RIVIERES Minesweeper (RCN). diesel 'Bangor' class. Marine Industries 30.6.1941. Tx RCMP 1950 = *MacBrien.* Sold for BU 1960.

TROJAN Destroyer, 'S' class. White 20.7.1918. HO Ward 24.9.1936 part payment *Majestic* (CALEDONIA, q.v.); BU Inverkeithing.

TROLLOPE Frigate, TE 'Captain' class. Bethlehem, Hingham, 20.11.1943, on Lend-Lease. Damaged by torpedo 6.7.1944, not repaired. Nominally ret. USN 1.1947; arr. 7.1951 Troon for BU.

TROMP (VANTROMP) 4th Rate 60, 1,040bm, 144 × 41ft. Dutch, captured 17.8.1796 The Cape. Harbour service 1799. Sold 9.8.1815.

TROMPEUSE Brig-sloop 16, 342bm. French, captured 12.1.1794 by SPHINX off Cape Clear. Wrecked 15.7.1796 nr Kinsale.

TROMPEUSE (ex-MERCURE) Sloop 18, 338bm. French privateer, captured 5.1797 by MELAMPUS in Bay of Biscay. Foundered 17.5.1800 English Channel.

TROMPEUSE Sloop 18, 380bm, 101 × 30ft. French, captured 4.3.1800. BU 3.1811.

TROMSO *See LST.3006 1944.*

TROON *See ELGIN 1919.*

TROOPER Submarine, 'T' class. Scotts 5.3.1942. Sunk 17.10.1943 Aegean. *Probably mined.*

TROUBRIDGE Destroyer, 1,730 tons, 362·8 (oa) × 35·7ft, 4—4·7in, 2—40mm, 8—TT. John Brown 23.9.1942. Frigate 1957, 2,240 tons, 2—4in, 2—3in, 2—40mm, Limbo. Sold Cashmore 27.2.1970; BU Newport.

TROUNCER (ex-*Perdito*) Escort carrier, 11,420 tons, 468·5 × 69·5ft, 2—4in, 8—40mm, 18 aircraft. Seattle Tacoma 16.6.1943 on Lend-Lease. Ret. USN 3.3.1946.

TROUNCER *See also LST.3523 1945.*

TRUANT Destroyer, 'S' class. White 18.9.1918. Sold 28.11.1931 Rees, Llanelly.

TRUANT Submarine, 'T' class. Vickers Armstrong, Barrow, 5.5.1939. Sold 19.12.1945; wrecked under tow Briton Ferry 12.1946.

TRUCULENT Destroyer, 'M' class, 900 tons. Yarrow 24.3.1917. Sold 29.4.1927 Cashmore, Newport.

TRUCULENT (ex-P.315) Submarine, 'T' class. Vickers Armstrong, Barrow 12.9.1942. Sunk 12.1.1950 collision *Dvina* off The Nore; raised, sold 8.5.1950; BU Ward, Grays.

TRUE BRITON Cutter 10, 190bm. Purch. 3.1778. Captured 9.8.1780 by French. *Perhaps re-captured: a cutter with this name was sold 9.6.1785.*

TRUELOVE (ex-KATHERINE) 14-gun ship, 100bm. Royalist, captured 1647 by Parliamentarians. Fireship 1668. Lost 1673.

TRUELOVE Ship 20, 259bm. Purch. 1650. *Fate unknown.*

TRUELOVE Bomb vessel 4, 65bm. Purch. 4.1694. Sold 24.5.1698.

TRUELOVE (OLD TRUELOVE until 1823) Hoy, 76bm, 66·5 × 17·5ft. Portsmouth DY 11.1707. Rebuilt Portsmouth 1720 as 58bm.

TRUELOVE Minesweeper, 'Algerine' class. Redfern, Toronto, 8.7.1943. Arr. 23.11.1957 Hughes Bolckow, Blyth.

TRUMP Submarine, 'T' class. Vickers Armstrong, Barrow, 25.3.1944. Sold Cashmore 23.7.1971. BU Newport.

TRUMPET Firevessel. Dutch hoy, purch. 4.1694. Sunk 24.4.1695 foundation Portsmouth.

TRUMPETER (ex-LUCIFER, ex-*Bastian*) Escort carrier, 11,420 tons, 468·5 × 69·5ft, 2—4in, 8—40mm, 18 aircraft. Seattle Tacoma 15.12.1942 on Lend-Lease (renamed 1942). Ret. USN 6.4.1946.

TRUMPETER Patrol boat, 49 tons, 68·2 (oa) × 19ft. Watercraft 1986, comp. Vosper-Thornycroft 9.1988.

TRUMPETER *See also LST.3524 1945.*

TRUNCHEON Submarine, 'T' class, Devonport DY 22.2.1944. Tx Israeli Navy 1968 = DOLPHIN; BU 1977.

TRURO Minesweeper, Later 'Hunt' class. Simons 16.4.1919. Sold 19.5.1928 Ward, Milford Haven.

TRURO Minesweeper (RCN), diesel 'Bangor' class. Davie SB 5.6.1942. Tx RCMP 1945 = *Herchmer*; sold mercantile 1947 = *Gulf Mariner*; abandoned Fraser R., BU 1964.

TRUSTY 4th Rate 50, 1,088bm, 150·5 × 40·5ft. Hillhouse, Bristol, 9.10.1782. Troopship 8.1799; prison ship 5.1809. BU 4.1815.

TRUSTY Armoured wood screw floating battery, 1,539bm, 173·5 × 45ft, 14—68pdr. Green, Blackwall, 18.4.1855. BU 1864 Castle.

TRUSTY Destroyer, 'S' class. White 6.11.1918. HO Ward 25.9.1936 part payment *Majestic* (CALEDONIA, q.v.); BU Inverkeithing.

TRUSTY Submarine, 'T' class. Vickers Armstrong, Barrow, 14.3.1941. Sold 1.1947; BU Ward, Milford Haven.

TRYALL Pink. Listed 1645–47.

TRYALL Sloop 14, 113bm, 64·5 × 20·5ft. Deptford DY 30.9.1710. Rebuilt Deptford 1719 as 142bm. BU 10.1731.

TRYALL Hoy. Origin unknown. Sold 13.5.1713 Plymouth to E. Bailing.

TRYALL Sloop 14, 201bm, 84 × 23·5ft. Stacey, Deptford, 6.9.1732. Scuttled 4.10.1741 South Seas, unserviceable.

TRYALL Sloop 14, 272bm, 91·5 × 26ft. Deptford DY 17.7.1744. BU 1.1776.

TRYALL *See also TRIAL.*

TRYDENT (ex-TRIDENT) 4th Rate 58, 762bm, 129·5 × 36·5ft. French, captured 1695. Sunk 3.7.1702 breakwater Harwich.

TRYDENT (ex-TRIDENT) 3rd Rate 64, 1,258bm, 151 × 44ft. French, captured 14.10.1747 Finisterre. Sold 15.3.1763.

TRYDENT *See also TRIDENT.*

TRYPHON Destroyer, 'S' class, 930 tons. Yarrow 22.6.1918. Stranded 4.5.1919; sold 27.9.1920 Agius Bros, Malta

TRYRIGHT Galley. Probably French, captured 1.1560 Fith of Forth. Listed until 1579.

TRYTON (ex-TRITON) 5th Rate 42, 661bm, 128 × 34·5ft. French, captured 10.1702 Vigo. Sold 4.10.1709 Woolwich.

TRYTON Sloop in commission 1741. *No further details known.*

TRYTON 6th Rate 24, 501bm, 113 × 32ft. Heather, Bursledon, 17.8.1745. Burnt East Indies 28.4.1758 to avoid capture by French.

TRYTON *See also TRITON.*

TRYTON PRIZE (ex-ROYAL) 6th Rate 28, 274bm, 75 × 26·5ft. French privateer, captured 3.3.1705 by TRYTON. Sold 26.11.1713.

TSINGTAU Repair ship, 1,970 tons, 279 × 44ft. German, seized 1945. BU 1950 Clayton & Davie, Dunston.

TUBEROSE Sloop, 'Anchusa' class. Swan Hunter 16.11.1917. Sold 15.1.1923 Unity S. Bkg Co.

TUDOR (ex-P.326) Submarine, 'T' class. Devonport DY 23.9.1942. Sold 1.7.1963; arr. Faslane 23.7.1963 for BU.

TUI (ex-CHARLES H. DAVIS) Survey ship (RNZN), 1,380 tons, 208·9 (oa) × 40ft, Christy, Wisconsin 30.6.1962. USNS, purch. 8.1970. Sunk 20.2.1999 dive wreck off Tutukaka.

TULIP 32-gun ship. Captured 1652. Sold 1657.

TULIP Dogger 6. Dutch, captured 1672. Sold 1672.

TULIP Sloop 2, 22bm. Deptford 1672. Lost 1673.

TULIP Sloop, 'Aubrietia' class. Richardson Duck, Stockton-on-Tees, 15.7.1916. torpedoed 30.4.1917 by U.62 in Atlantic, foundered under tow of DAFFODIL. *Operated as decoy ship Q.11.*

TULIP Corvette, 'Flower' class. Smith's Dock 4.9.1940. Sold 5.1947 = *Olympic Conqueror*.

TUMULT Destroyer, 'S' class, 930 tons. Yarrow 17.9.1918. Sold 3.10.1928 Alloa S. Bkg Co., Charlestown.

TUMULT Destroyer, 1,710 tons, 362·8 (oa) × 35·7ft, 4–4·7in, 2–40mm, 8–TT. John Brown 9.11.1942. Frigate 10.1954, 2–4in, Squid. Arr. 25.10.1965 Arnott Young, Dalmuir, for BU.

TUNA Torpedo boat (RCN), 130 tons, 153 × 15ft, 1–3pdr, 2–TT. Purch. 1915 (?). Sold 1920.

TUNA Submarine, 'T' class. Scotts 10.5.1940. Sold 19.12.1945; arr. 24.6.1946 Ward, Briton Ferry, for BU.

TUNSBERG CASTLE *See SHREWSBURY CASTLE 1943.*

TURBULENT Gun-brig 12, 181bm, 84·5 × 22ft. Tanner, Dartmouth, 17.7.1805. Captured 10.6.1808 by Danes in Malmo Bay.

TURBULENT (ex-OGRE) Destroyer, 1,098 tons, 300 × 28·5ft, 5–4in, 4–TT. Hawthorn Leslie 5.1.1916; Turkish (renamed 15.2.1915). Sunk 1.6.1916 Battle of Jutland.

TURBULENT Destroyer, 'S' class. Hawthorn Leslie 29.5.1919. HO Ward 25.8.1936 part payment *Majestic* (CALEDONIA, q.v.); BU Inverkeithing.

TURBULENT Submarine, 'T' class. Vickers Armstrong, Barrow, 12.5.1941. Sunk c. 23.3.1943 Italian MTB off Sardinia.

TURBULENT Nuclear submarine, 'Trafalgar' class. Vickers 1.12.1982.

TURPIN Submarine, 'T' class. Chatham DY 5.8.1944. Sold Israeli Navy 1965 = LEVIATHAN; BU 1975.

TURQUOISE Composite screw corvette, 2,120 tons, 220 × 40ft, 12–64pdr. Earle, Hull, 22.4.1876. Sold 24.9.1892 Pounds, Hartlepool.

TURQUOISE Destroyer, 'S' class, 930 tons. Yarrow 9.11.1918. Sold 1.1932; BU Charlestown.

TUSCAN Brig-sloop 16, 334bm. French, ex-Italian RONCO, captured 2.5.1808 by UNITE in Gulf of Venice. Sold 29.1.1818 T. Pitman for BU.

TUSCAN Destroyer, 'S' class, 930 tons. Yarrow 1.3.1919. Sold 25.8.1932 Metal Industries, Charlestown.

TUSCAN Destroyer, 1,710 tons, 362·8 (oa) × 35·7ft, 4–4·7in, 2–40mm, 8–TT. Swan Hunter 28.5.1942. Frigate 8.1953, 2–4in, Squid. Arr. 26.5.1966 McLellan, Bo'ness, for BU.

TUTANKHAMEN *See P.311 1942.*

TUTBURY CASTLE Corvette, 'Castle' class. Morton, Quebec, cancelled 12.1943.

TUTIRA *See LOCH MORLICH 1944.*

TWEED 5th Rate 32, 661bm, 128·5 × 34ft. Blaydes, Hull, 20.4.1759. Sold 1776.

TWEED Sloop 18, 431bm, 109 × 30ft. Iremonger, Littlehampton, 10.1.1807. Wrecked 5.11.1813 Shoal Bay, Newfoundland.

TWEED 6th Rate 28, 500bm, 113·5 × 32ft, 20–32pdr carr., 6–18pdr carr., 2–9pdr. Portsmouth DY 14.4.1823. Sold 1852 Willson & Co.

TWEED Wood screw frigate, 3,027bm, 250 × 52ft. Pembroke Dock, LD 3.7.1860, cancelled 16.12.1864.

TWEED Iron screw gunboat, 363 tons, 110 × 34ft, 3–64pdr. Palmer 23.8.1877. Sold 21.11.1905 in Hong Kong.

TWEED Frigate, 'River' class. Inglis 24.11.1942. Sunk 7.1.1944 by U.305 south-west of Ireland.

TWEED *See also GLENMORE 1796.*

TWO LIONS 48-gun ship, 552bm, 115·5 × 33·5ft. Captured 1682. Sold 1687.

TYLER Frigate, TE 'Captain' class. Bethlehem, Hingham, 20.11.1943 on Lend-Lease. Ret. USN 11.1945.

TYNE 6th Rate 24, 446bm, 108·5 × 30·5ft, 18–32pdr carr., 8–12pdr carr., 2–6pdr. Davy, Topsham, 20.4.1814. Sold 27.1.1825 T. Pitman for BU.

TYNE 6th Rate 28, 600bm, 125 × 33ft. Woolwich DY 30.11.1826. Storeship 1848. Sold 17.2.1862 Castle & Beech for BU.

TYNE (ex-*Mariotis*) Iron screw storeship, 3,560 tons, 320 × 34ft, 2–24pdr. Armstrong 19.1.1878, purch. 8.3.1878. Foundered 15.11.1920 gale off Sheerness while on Sale List.

TYNE Depot ship, 10,850 tons, 585 × 66ft, 8–4in. Scotts 28.2.1940. Sold H. K. Vickers 25.7.1972; BU Barrow.

TYNE Offshore patrol vessel, 1,677 tons, 261·7 (oa) × 44·6ft, 1–20mm, 2–MG. Vosper-Thornycroft 29.5.2002.

TYNE *See also ACTIVE 1845.*

TYNEDALE Destroyer, 'Hunt' class Type I. Stephen 5.6.1940. Sunk 12.12.1943 by U.593 off Bougie.

TYRANT Destroyer, 'M' class, 900 tons. Yarrow 19.5.1917. Arr.15.1.1939 Cashmore, Newport, for BU.

TYRIAN Brig-sloop 10, 'Cherokee' class, 239bm. Guillaume, Northam, 16.12.1808. Sold 22.7.1819.

TYRIAN Brig-sloop 10, 'Cherokee' class, 233bm. Woolwich DY 16.9.1826. Quarantine hulk 1847; Coastguard depot ship 1866. Sold 11.8.1892.

TYRIAN Wood screw gunboat, 'Britomart' class. Courtenay, Newhaven, 7.9.1861. Tug in Jamaica 1883; sold 1891 in Jamaica.

TYRIAN Destroyer, 'S' class, 930 tons. Yarrow 2.7.1919. Arr. 26.3.1930 Metal Industries, Charlestown, for BU.

TYRIAN Destroyer, 1,710 tons, 362·8 (oa) × 35·7ft, 4–4·7in, 2–40mm, 8–TT. Swan Hunter 27.7.1942. Frigate 5.1953, 2–4in, Squid. Arr. 4.3.1965 Troon for BU.

TYRONE Gunvessel 2. Listed 1798–1800.

U

U-boats (ex-German):

U.190 Surrendered RCN 11.5.1945 Newfoundland, cd 14.5.1945. Sunk 21.10.1947 anti-submarine exercises.

U.889 Surrendered RCN 13.5.1945 Shelburne. Tx USN 12.1.1946.

U.1407 Cd RN 25.9.1945. = METEORITE 6.1947. BU 9.1949 Ward, Barrow.

Note: Of the many U-boats which surrendered, the following were used for trials purposes: U.249, U.712 (listed until 1948), U.776, U.875, U.953 (listed until 1948), U.1023, U.1105, U.1108 (listed until 1948), U.1171 (listed until 1948), U.2326 (tx French Navy 1945), U.2348 (listed until 1948), U.2518 (tx French Navy 1948), U.3017 (arr. 30.10.1949 Cashmore, Newport, for BU).

UFTON *See UPTON 1956.*

UGANDA Cruiser, 8,800 tons, 555·5 (oa) × 62ft, 9—6in, 8—4in. Vickers Armstrong, Tyne, 7.8.1941. Tx RCN = QUEBEC 14.1.1952; arr. 6.2.1961 Osaka, Japan, for BU.

ULEX Submarine, 'V' class. Vickers Armstrong, Barrow, cancelled 2.1944, not LD.

ULLESWATER Destroyer, 'M' class, 923 tons. Yarrow 4.8.1917. Sunk 15.9.1918 U-boat North Sea.

ULLSWATER (ex-P.31) Submarine, 'U' class. Vickers Armstrong, Barrow, 27.11.1940 (renamed 2.1943). = UPROAR 4.1943. Sold 13.2.1946; BU Ward, Inverkeithing.

ULSTER Destroyer, Modified 'R' class. Beardmore 10.10.1917. Sold 21.4.1928 Ward, Pembroke Dock.

ULSTER Destroyer, 1,710 tons, 362·7 (oa) × 35·7ft, 4—4·7in, 2—40mm, 8—TT. Swan Hunter 9.11.1942. Frigate 1953, 2—4in, Limbo. Sold Ward 4.8.1980; BU Inverkeithing

ULTIMATUM (ex-P.34) Submarine, 'U' class. Vickers Armstrong, Barrow, 11.2.1941. Sold 23.12.1949; BU Smith & Houston.

ULTOR (ex-P.53) Submarine, 'U' class. Vickers Armstrong, Barrow, 12.10.1942. Arr. 22.1.1946 Ward, Briton Ferry, for BU.

ULYSSES 5th Rate 44, 887 bm, 140 × 38ft. Fisher, Liverpool, 14.7.1779. Troopship 6.1790. Sold 11.1.1816.

ULYSSES Destroyer, Modified 'R' class. Doxford 24.3.1917. Sunk 29.10.1919 collision SS *Ellerie* Firth of Clyde.

ULYSSES Destroyer, 1,710 tons, 362·7 (oa) × 35·7ft, 4—4·7in, 2—40mm, 8—TT. Cammell Laird 22.4.1943. Frigate 1953—55, 2—4in, Limbo. Sold Davies & Cann 29.10.1979; BU Plymouth.

ULYSSES *See also LYSANDER 1913.*

UMBRA (ex-P.35) Submarine, 'U' class. Vickers Armstrong, Barrow, 15.3.1941. Sold 9.7.1946; BU Hughes Bolckow, Blyth.

UMPIRE Destroyer, Modified 'R' class. Doxford 9.6.1917. Sold 7.1.1930 Metal Industries, Charlestown.

UMPIRE Submarine, 'U' class. Chatham DY 30.12.1940. Accidentally rammed and sunk by trawler 19.7.1941 North Sea.

UMPIRE *See also ROYAL GEORGE 1788.*

UNA (ex-KOMET) Sloop (RAN), 1,438 tons, 210 × 31ft, 3—4in, 2—12pdr. German, captured 11.10.1914 by yacht NUSA off north coast of New Britain. Sold 1921 = *Akuna*.

UNA Submarine, 'U' class. Chatham DY 10.6.1941. Sold 11.4.1949; BU Rees, Llanelly.

UNBEATEN Submarine, 'U' class. Vickers Armstrong, Barrow, 9.7.1940. Bombed in error 11.11.1942 British aircraft Bay of Biscay.

UNBENDING (ex-P.37) Submarine, 'U' class. Vickers Armstrong, Barrow, 12.5.1941. Sold 23.12.1949; BU 1950 Dorkin, Gateshead.

UNBRIDLED Submarine, 'V' class. Vickers Armstrong, Tyne, cancelled 20.11.1943, not LD.

UNBROKEN (ex-P.42) Submarine, 'U' class. Vickers Armstrong, Barrow, 4.11.1941. Lent Soviet Navy 1944—49 = B.2. Arr. 9.5.1950 King, Gateshead, for BU.

UNDAUNTED (ex-BIEN VENUE) 6th Rate 28. French storeship, captured 17.3.1794 by squadron at Martinique. Sold 24.7.1795.

UNDAUNTED Gunvessel. Dutch, captured 13.8.1799 by boats of PYLADES off Dutch coast. Sold 1800.

UNDAUNTED 5th Rate 38, 1,086bm, 155 × 40ft. Woolwich DY (ex-Graham, Harwich) 17.10.1807. Target 1856. BU comp. 12.1860.

UNDAUNTED Wood screw frigate, 3,039bm, 4,020 tons, 250 × 52ft. Chatham DY 1.1.1861. Sold 7.11.1882 Castle.

UNDAUNTED Armoured cruiser, 5,600 tons, 300 × 56ft, 2—9·2in, 10—6in, 10—3pdr. Palmer 25.11.1886. Sold 9.4.1907 Harris, Bristol.

UNDAUNTED Light cruiser, 3,500 tons, 410 × 39ft, 5—6in, 6—4in. Fairfield 28.4.1914. Sold 9.4.1923 Cashmore, Newport.

UNDAUNTED Submarine, 'U' class. Vickers Armstrong, Barrow, 20.8.1940. Sunk 13.5.1941 off Libya, cause unknown.

UNDAUNTED Destroyer, 1,710 tons, 362·7 (oa) × 35·7ft, 4—4·7in, 2—40mm, 8—TT. Cammell Laird 19.7.1943. Frigate 1954, 2—4in, Limbo. Sunk 11.1978 target Atlantic.

UNDAUNTED *See also ARETHUSE 1793.*

UNDINE Iron paddle packet, 284bm. Purch. 13.2.1847. Sold 5.2.1854 Jenkins & Churchward, Dover.

UNDINE Wood screw gunvessel, 428bm, 145 × 25·5ft. Deptford DY, LD 31.12.1861, cancelled 12.12.1863.

UNDINE (ex-*Morna*) Schooner, 280 tons, 114 × 23ft. Purch. 15.3.1881. Sold 4.1888 Millar, Sydney.

UNDINE Destroyer, Modified 'R' class. Fairfield 22.3.1917. Sold 4.1928 Ward; wrecked off Horse Fort, Portsmouth; wreck sold 27.8.1928 Middlesbrough Salvage Co.

UNDINE Submarine, 'U' class. Vickers Armstrong, Barrow, 5.10.1937. Sunk 7.1.1940 German minesweepers off Heligoland.

UNDINE Destroyer, 1,710 tons, 362·7 (oa) × 35·7ft, 4—4·7in, 2—40mm, 8—TT. Thornycroft 1.6.1943. Frigate 1954, 2—4in, Limbo. Arr. 15.11.1965 Cashmore, Newport, for BU.

UNDINE *See also HAWK 1888, WILDFIRE 1888.*

UNGAVA Minesweeper (RCN), TE 'Bangor' class. North Vancouver SR Co. 9.10.1940. Sold c. 1947 T. Harris, Barber, NJ.

UNGAVA Coastal minesweeper (RCN), 'Bay' class. Davie SB 20.5.1953. Sold Turkish Navy 1958 = TEKIRDAG; patrol vessel 1991; BU Aliaga, Turkey, 3.2002.

UNICORN 36-gun ship, c. 240bm. Scottish, captured 1544. Sold 1555.

UNICORN 56-gun ship, 700bm. Woolwich 2.1634. Sold 27.1.1687.

UNICORN (LITTLE UNICORN) (ex-EENHOORN) 18-gun ship, 185bm. Dutch, captured 1665. Expended as fireship 2.6.1666.

UNICORN Fireship 6, 180bm. Purch. 1666. Sunk 6.1667 Chatham blockship.

UNICORN 6th Rate 28, 581bm, 118 × 33·5ft. Plymouth DY 7.12.1748. BU comp. 9.12.1771 Sheerness.

UNICORN 6th Rate 20, 433bm, 108 × 30ft. Randall, Rotherhithe, 23.3.1776. Captured 4.9.1780 by French ANDROMAQUE in West Indies = LICORNE; recaptured 20.4.1781. BU 8.1787 Deptford.

UNICORN 5th Rate 36, 881bm, 137 × 38·5ft. Calhoun, Bursledon, 7.11.1782. = THALIA 15.8.1783. BU 7.1814.

UNICORN 5th Rate 32, 791bm, 135 × 36ft. Chatham DY 12.7.1794. BU 3.1815 Deptford

UNICORN 5th Rate 46, 1,084bm, 151·5 × 40·5ft. Chatham DY 30.3.1824. Powder hulk 1860; RNR drillship 11.1873 Dundee. HO Unicorn Preservation Society 29.9.1968. *Bore name UNICORN II 2.1939, then CRESSY 20.11.1941—14.7.1959.*

UNICORN Aircraft maintenance carrier, 14,750 tons, 564 × 90ft, 8—4·5in, 35 aircraft. Harland & Wolff 20.11.1941. Arr. 15.6.1959 Dalmuir for BU; hulk to Troon 3.1960.

UNICORN Submarine, 'Upholder' class, Cammell Laird 16.4.1992. Tx RCN = WINDSOR 5.7.2001.

UNION 5th Rate. Origin unknown. Burnt 1693 to avoid capture by French. *Hired vessel?*

UNION 2nd Rate 90, 1,781bm, 171 × 48·5ft. Chatham DY 25.9.1756. Hospital ship by 1799; = SUSSEX 6.2.1802. BU 10.1816 Chatham.

UNION Gunvessel 3, 81bm, 59·5 × 18ft. Barge, purch. 3.1794. Listed until 1798.

UNION Cutter. In service 1806. BU 6.1810.

UNION 2nd Rate 98, 2,149bm, 186 × 52ft. Plymouth DY 16.9.1811. BU 3.1833.

UNION Schooner 3, 85bm, 60 × 19ft Purch. 1823. Wrecked 17.5.1828 West Indies.

UNION Submarine, 'U' class. Vickers Armstrong, Barrow, 1.10.1940. Sunk 22.7.1941 by Italian patrol boat in central Mediterranean.

UNION *See also ALBEMARLE 1680.*

UNIQUE Schooner 10, 120bm, 74 × 21ft. French, captured 1803. Recaptured 23.2.1806 by French privateer in West Indies.

UNIQUE (ex-DUQUESNE) Gun-brig 12, 183bm. French privateer, captured 3.9.1807 by BLONDE in West Indies. Burnt 31.5.1809 Guadeloupe by French.

UNIQUE Submarine, 'U' class. Vickers Armstrong, Barrow, 6.6.1940. Sunk 24.10.1942 west of Gibraltar, cause unknown.

UNISON (ex-P.43) Submarine, 'U' class. Vickers Armstrong, Barrow, 5.11.1941. Lent Soviet Navy

1944–49 = B.3. Arr. 19.5.1950 Stockton-on-Tees for BU.

UNITE 5th Rate 38, 893bm, 142·5 × 37·5ft. French, captured 12.4.1796 by REVOLUTIONNAIRE off coast of France. Sold 5.1802.

UNITE *See also IMPERIEUSE 1793.*

UNITED (ex-P.44) Submarine, 'U' class. Vickers Armstrong, Barrow, 18.12.1941. Arr. 12.2.1946 Troon for BU.

UNITY (ex-EENDRACHT) 32-gun ship. Dutch, captured 2.1665. Recaptured 12.6.1667 by Dutch at Chatham.

UNITY Flyboat 4, 172bm. Dutch, captured 1672. Given away 1672.

UNITY Fireship 6, 120bm. Purch. 1688. Rebuilt Portsmouth 1707 as hoy, 130bm, 67 × 21·5ft. Sold 27.10.1773.

UNITY Hoy, 80bm, 60 × 18·5ft. Plymouth DY 1728. Sold 20.12.1788.

UNITY Storevessel, 142bm, 66 × 22·5ft. Hooper, Torpoint, 1788. = YC.13. BU 1878.

UNITY Destroyer, 954 tons, 265 × 26·5ft, 3–4in, 2–TT. Thornycroft 19.9.1913. Sold 25.10.1922 Rees, Llanelly.

UNITY Submarine, 'U' class. Vickers Armstong, Barrow, 16.2.1938. Sunk 29.4.1940 collision SS *Atle Jarl* off R. Tyne.

UNITY II Hoy 4, 79bm, 59 × 18ft. Chatham DY 19.8.1693. Sold 8.1.1713.

UNITY III Hoy 4, 79bm, 59 × 18ft. Chatham DY 1693. Sold 8.1.1713.

UNIVERSAL (ex-P.57) Submarine, 'U' class. Vickers Armstrong, Tyne, 10.11.1942. Sold 2.1946 Cashmore; BU 2.1946 Ward, Milford Haven.

UNRIVALLED (ex-P.45) Submarine, 'U' class. Vickers Armstrong, Barrow, 16.2.1942. Arr. 22.1.1946 Ward, Briton Ferry, for BU.

UNRUFFLED (ex-P.46) Submarine, 'U' class. Vickers Armstrong, Barrow, 19.12.1941. BU 1.1946 West of Scotland S. Bkg. Co., Troon.

UNRULY (ex-P.49) Submarine, 'U' class. Vickers Armstrong, Barrow, 28.7.1942. Arr. 2.1946 Ward, Inverkeithing, for BU.

UNSEEN (ex-P.51) Submarine, 'U' class. Vickers Armstrong, Barrow, 16.4.1942. Arr. 11.5.1949 Ward, Hayle, for BU.

UNSEEN Submarine, 'Upholder' class, Cammell Laird 14.11.1989. Tx RCN = VICTORIA 6.10.2000.

UNSHAKEN (ex-P.54) Submarine, 'U' class. Vickers Armstrong, Barrow, 17.2.1942. BU 3.1946 West of Scotland S. Bkg Co., Troon.

UNSPARING (ex-P.55) Submarine, 'U' class. Vickers Armstrong, Tyne, 28.7.1942. Sold 14.2.1946; BU Inverkeithing.

UNSWERVING Submarine, 'U' class. Vickers Armstrong, Tyne, 19.7.1943. Arr. 10.7.1949 Cashmore, Newport, for BU.

UNTAMED (ex-P.58) Submarine, 'U' class. Vickers Armstrong, Tyne, 8.12.1942. Foundered 30.5.1943; raised 5.7.1943, = VITALITY. Sold 13.2.1946; arr. 3.1946 Troon for BU.

UNTIRING Submarine, 'U' class. Vickers Armstrong, Tyne, 20.1.1943. Lent Greek Navy 7.1945–1952 = XIFIAS. Sunk 25.7.1957 asdic target off Start Point.

UPAS Submarine, 'V' class. Vickers Armstrong, Barrow, LD 10.18.1943, cancelled 2.1944.

UPHOLDER Submarine, 'U' class. Vickers Armstrong, Barrow, 8.7.1940. Sunk 14.4.1942 by Italian torpedo boat PEGASO off Tripoli.

UPHOLDER Submarine, 'Upholder' class. Vickers 2.12.1986. For tx RCN = CHICOUTIMI 2003?

UPPINGHAM *See KELLETT 1919.*

UPRIGHT Submarine, 'U' class. Vickers Armstrong, Barrow, 21.4.1940. Sold 19.12.1945; arr. Troon 3.1946 for BU.

UPROAR *See ULLSWATER 1940.*

UPSHOT Submarine, 'V' class. Vickers Armstrong, Barrow, 24.2.1944. Arr. 22.11.1949 Ward, Preston, for BU.

UPSTART (ex-P.66) Submarine, 'U' class. Vickers Armstrong, Barrow, 24.11.1942. Lent Greek Navy 9.8.1943–1952 = AMFITRITE. Sunk 29.7.1957 asdic target off I. of Wight.

UPTON (ex-UFTON) Coastal minesweeper, 'Ton' class. Thornycroft 15.3.1956. Arr Bruges 22.10.1991 for BU.

UPWARD Submarine, 'V' class. Vickers Armstrong, Tyne, cancelled 20.11.1943, not LD.

URANIA Destroyer, 1,710 tons, 362·7 (oa) × 35·7ft, 4–4·7in, 2–40mm, 8–TT. Vickers Armstrong, Barrow, 19.5.1943. Frigate 1954, 2–4in, Limbo. Sold 16.12.1970; BU Faslane.

URANIE (ex-TARTU) 5th Rate 38, 1,100bm, 154·5 × 40ft, 16–32pdr carr., 28–12pdr, 2–9pdr. French, captured 5.1.1797 by POLYPHEMUS off Ireland. Sold 10.1807. *Original French name spelt 'TARTU' in French lists, 'TORTUE' in James.*

URCHIN Gunvessel, 154bm. Purch. 1797. Foundered 12.10.1800 under tow HECTOR Tetuan Bay.

URCHIN Destroyer, Modified 'R' class. Palmer 7.6.1917. Sold 7.1.1930 Metal Industries, Charlestown.

URCHIN Submarine, 'U' class. Vickers Armstrong, Barrow, 30.9.1940. Lent Polish Navy 11.1941–1946 = SOKOL; = P.97 in 1946. BU 1949.

URCHIN Destroyer, 1,710 tons, 362·7 (oa) × 35·7ft,

4–4·7in, 2–40mm, 8–TT. Vickers Armstrong, Barrow, 8.3.1954. Frigate 1953–54, 2–4in, Limbo. Arr. 6.8.1967 Troon for BU.

URE Destroyer, 550 tons, 222 × 23·5ft, 1–12pdr, 5–6pdr (1907: 4–12pdr), 2–TT. Palmer 25.10.1903. Sold 27.5.1919 T. R. Sales.

UREDD (ex-P.41) Submarine, 'U' class' Vickers Armstrong, Barrow, 24.8.1941. Lent RNorN 12.1941. Sunk c. 24.2.1943 off Bodo, cause unknown.

URGE Submarine, 'U' class. Vickers Armstrong, Barrow, 19.8.1940. Sunk 6.5.1942 by Italian torpedo boat PEGASO in eastern Mediterranean.

URGENT Gun-brig 12, 178bm, 80 × 22·5ft. Bass, Lympstone, 2.11.1804. Sold 31.7.1816.

URGENT (ex-*Colonsay*) Wood paddle packet, 561bm, 170·5 × 26ft. GPO vessel , tx 27.7.1837. Sold 12.1850 H. Hall.

URGENT (ex-*Assaye*) Iron screw troopship, 1,981bm, 2,801 tons, 723 × 38ft, 2–pdr. Mare, Blackwall, 2.4.1855, purch. on stocks. Depot ship 1876. Sold 6.1903 Butler & Co.

URSA Destroyer, Modified 'R' class. Palmer 23.7.1917. Sold 13.7.1926 J. Smith.

URSA Destroyer, 1,710 tons, 362·7 (oa) × 35·7ft. 4–4in, 2–40mm 8–TT. Thornycroft 22.7.1943. Frigate 1954, 2–4in, Limbo. Arr. 25.91967 Cashmore, Newport, for BU.

URSULA Destroyer, Modified 'R' class. Scotts 2.8.1917. Sold 19.11.1929 Cashmore, Newport.

URSULA Submarine, 'U' class. Vickers Armstrong, Barrow, 16.2.1938. Lent Soviet Navy 1944–49 as B.4. Sold 5.1950; BU Brechin, Granton.

URSULA Submarine, 'Upholder' class, Cammell Laird 28.2.1991. Tx RCN = CORNERBROOK 10.3.2003.

URTICA Submarine, 'V' class. Vickers Armstrong, Barrow, 23.3.1944. BU 3.1950 Ward, Milford Haven.

USK Destroyer, 590 tons, 225 × 23·5ft, 1–12pdr, 5–6pdr (1907: 4–12pdr), 2–TT. Yarrow 25.7.1903. Sold 29.7.1920 Ward, Morecambe.

USK Submarine, 'U' class. Vickers Armstrong, Barrow, 7.6.1940. Sunk 3.5.1941 off Cape Bon, Tunisia. *Probably mined.*

USK Frigate, 'River' class. Smith's Dock 3.4.1943. Sold 1948 Egyptian Navy.

USURPER (ex-P.56) Submarine, 'U' class. Vickers Armstrong, Tyne, 24.9.1942. Sunk 10.1943 by German patrol vessel UJ.2208 in Gulf of Genoa.

UTHER Submarine, 'U' class. Vickers Armstrong, Tyne, 6.4.1943. Sold 2.1950; arr. 20.2.1950 Ward, Hayle, for BU.

UTILE 6th Rate 24, 279bm, 89·5 × 26·5ft, 14–24pdr, 2–6pdr. French, captured 9.6.1796 by SOUTHAMPTON in Mediterranean. Sold 7.6.1798.

UTILE Brig-sloop 16. French, captured 1.4.1799 by BOADICEA in English Channel. Foundered 11.1801 Mediterranean.

UTILE (ex-*Volunteer*) Sloop 16, 340bm. Purch. 6.1804. Sold 30.6.1814.

UTMOST Submarine, 'U' class. Vickers Armstrong, Barrow, 20.4.1940. Sunk 24.11.1942 by Italian GROPPO west of Sicily.

UTOPIA Submarine, 'V' class. Vickers Armstrong, Barrow, cancelled 2.1944, not LD.

UTRECHT 3rd Rate 64, 1,331bm. Dutch, captured 30.8.1799 Texel. Hulk by 1810. Sold 23.3.1815.

V

'V' class submarines 364 tons, 147·5 (oa) × 16ft, 2–TT.

V.1 Vickers 23.7.1914. Sold 29.11.1921 J. Kelly. *Believed resold Ward, Rainham.*

V.2 Vickers 17.2.1915. Sold 29.11.1921. J. Kelly. *Believed resold Ward, Rainham.*

V.3 ickers 1.4.1915. Sold 8.10.1920 J. W. Towers.

V.4 Vickers 25.11.1915. Sold 8.10.1920 J. W. Towers.

VAAGSO *See LST.3019 1944.*

VAGABOND Submarine, 'V' class. Vickers Armstrong, Tyne, 19.9.1944. Arr. 26.1.1950 Cashmore, Newport for BU.

VALDORIAN *See SUSSEXVALE 1944.*

VALENTINE Barge, 100bm. Built 1418. Sold 1.3.1424.

VALENTINE Destroyer leader, 'V/W' class. Cammell Laird 24.3.1917. Escort 4.1940. Beached 15.5.1940 mouth of R. Schelde after air attack; BU 1953.

VALENTINE (ex-KEMPENFELT) Destroyer, 1,710 tons, 362·7 (oa) × 35·7ft, 4—4·7in, 2—40mm, 8—TT. John Brown 2.9.1943 (renamed 1942). Tx RCN 28.2.1944 = ALGONQUIN; BU Halifax 1952.

VALENTINE *See also KEMPENFELT 1943.*

VALERIAN Sloop, 'Arabis' class. Rennoldson 21.2.1916. Foundered 22.10.1926 hurricane off Bermuda.

VALEUR 6th Rate 24, 321bm, 101 × 27·5ft, French, captured 5.5.1705 by WORCESTER. Fireship 3.1716, ordered BU Deptford 14.3.1718.

VALEUR 6th Rate 28, 524bm, 115·5 × 32·5ft. French, captured 18.10.1759 by LIVELY. Sold 26.1.1764.

VALHALLA Destroyer leader, 'V/W' class, 1,339 tons. Cammell Laird 22.5.1917. Sold 17.12.1931 Cashmore, Newport.

VALIANT 3rd Rate 74, 1,799 bm, 171·5 × 49·5ft. Chatham DY 10.8.1759. Harbour service 11.1799. BU 4.1826 Sheerness.

VALIANT 3rd Rate 74, 1,718bm, 174 × 48·5ft. Perry, Wells & Green, Blackwall, 24.1.1807. BU 11.1823 Portsmouth.

VALIANT 3rd Rate 76, 1,925bm, 182 × 50ft, 4—

68pdr carr., 26—32pdr, 12—32pdr carr., 28—24pdr, 6—12pdr. Plymouth DY, ordered 9.6.1825, cancelled 11.1832.

VALIANT Iron armoured ship, 4,063bm, 6,710 tons, 280 × 56·5ft, 2—8in, 16—7in. Westwood Baillie, Poplar, 14.10.1863. Harbour service 1888; depot ship 1897; = INDUS IV (depot ship) 1904; = VALIANT (OLD) 1916; = VALIANT III 1919; oil hulk 1924. Arr. 9.12.1956 Zeebrugge for BU.

VALIANT Battleship, 27,500 tons, 639·8 (oa) × 90·5ft, 8—15in, 14—6in. Fairfield 4.11.1914. Sold 19.3.1948; arr. 16.8.1948 Cairnryan for BU. Hulk to Troon 3.1950.

VALIANT Nuclear submarine, 4,400/4,900 tons, 285oa) × 33ft, SubHarpoon, 6—TT. Vickers Armstrong, Barrow, 3.12.1963. PO 6.1994, LU Devonport. *Originally referred to in some sources as INFLEXIBLE.*

VALKYRIE (ex-MALCOLM) Destroyer leader, 'V/W' class, 1,325 tons. Denny 13.3.1917 (renamed 1916). HO Ward 24.8.1936 part payment *Majestic* (CALEDONIA, q.v.); BU Inverkeithing.

VALLEYFIELD Frigate (RCN), 'River' class. Morton 7.7.1943. Sunk 7.5.1944 off Cape Race, probably by U.548.

VALOROUS Sloop 18, 422bm, 109·5 × 29·5ft. Blunt, Hull, 11.1804. Army depot 1810. Sold 7.5.1817.

VALOROUS 6th Rate 20, 514bm, 122 × 31ft. Pembroke Dock 10.2.1816. BU comp. 13.8.1829 Chatham.

VALOROUS Wood paddle frigate, 1,257bm, 2,300 tons, 210 × 26ft. Pembroke Dock 30.4.1851. Sold 27.2.1891 Marshall, Plymouth. *Last paddle frigate built.*

VALOROUS (ex-MONTROSE) Destroyer leader, 'V/W' class, 1,325 tons. Denny 8.5.1917 (renamed 1916). Escort 6.1939. Sold 4.3.1947; BU Stockton Shipping & Salvage, Thornaby.

VAMPIRE Destroyer leader, 'V/W' class, 1,316 tons. White 21.5.1917. RAN 10.1933. Sunk 9.4.1942 Japanese aircraft Bay of Bengal.

VAMPIRE Submarine, 'V' class. Vickers Armstrong, Barrow, 20.7.1943. Arr. 5.3.1950 King, Gateshead, for BU.

VAMPIRE Destroyer (RAN), 2,610 tons, 390 (oa) × 43ft, 6—4·5in, 8—40mm, 5—TT, Limbo. Cockatoo DY 27.10.1956. PO 13.8.1986. Tx 1987 Australian National Maritime Museum.

VANCOUVER Destroyer, 'V/W' class. Beardmore 28.12.1917. = VIMY 1.4.1928. Escort 5.1942. BU 12.1947 Metal Industries, Rosyth.

VANCOUVER (ex-KITCHENER) Corvette (RCN), 'Flower' class. Yarrow, Esquimalt, 26.8.1941 (renamed 11.1941). Sold 1946.

VANCOUVER Survey ship (RCN), 5,600 tons. Burrard 29.6.1965. Sold 10.1982 mercantile.

VANCOUVER Frigate (RCN), 'Halifax' class. St John SB, 8.7.1989.

VANCOUVER *See also TOREADOR 1918, KITCHENER 1941.*

VANDAL (ex-P.64) Submarine, 'U' class. Vickers Armstrong, Barrow, 23.11.1942. Wrecked 24.2.1943 Firth of Clyde.

VANESSA Destroyer, 'V/W' class. Beardmore 16.3.1918. Escort 6.1942. Sold 4.3.1947; arr. 5.9.1948 Charlestown for BU by Metal Industries.

VANGUARD Galleon 31, 450bm, 108 × 32ft, 4—32pdr, 14—18pdr, 11—9pdr, 2—6pdr. Woolwich 1586. Rebuilt Chatham 1615 as 650bm, 40 guns; rebuilt Woolwich 1631 as 731bm, 56 guns. Sunk 12.6.1667 blockship Rochester.

VANGUARD 2nd Rate 90, 1,357bm, 126 × 45ft. Portsmouth DY 1678. Overset 26.11.1703 R. Medway, raised 1704, rebuilt Chatham 1710 as 1,551bm; rebuilt as 1,625bm = DUKE 26.7.1728. BU 8.1769 Plymouth.

VANGUARD 3rd Rate 70, 1,419bm, 160 × 45ft. Ewer, East Cowes, 16.4.1748. Sold 13.4.1774.

VANGUARD Gunvessel 4. Spanish, captured 1780. Sold 1783.

VANGUARD 3rd Rate 74, 1,644bm, 168 × 47ft. Deptford DY 6.3.1787. Prison ship 12.1812; powder hulk 9.1814. BU 9.1821 Portsmouth.

VANGUARD 3rd Rate 78, 2,609bm, 190 × 57ft. Pembroke Dock 25.8.1835. = AJAX 20.10.1867. BU 6.1875 Chatham.

VANGUARD Battleship, 3,774bm, 6,010 tons, 280 × 54ft, 10—9in, 4—6in. Laird 3.1.1870. Sunk 1.9.1875 collision IRON DUKE off coast of Wicklow.

VANGUARD Battleship, 19,250 tons, 490 × 84ft, 10—12in, 20—4in. Vickers 22.2.1909. Sunk 9.7.1917 internal explosion Scapa Flow; raised, BU 1927 Tyne.

VANGUARD Battleship, 42,500 tons, 814·3 (oa) × 108·5ft, 8—15in, 16—5·25in, 71—40mm. John Brown 30.11.1944. Arr. 9.8.1960 Faslane for BU.

VANGUARD Nuclear submarine, 'Vanguard' class, Vickers, Barrow, 4.3.1992.

VANITY Ship. In service 1650—54. *Probably hired.*

VANITY Destroyer, 'V/W' class. Beardmore 3.5.1918. Escort 7.1940. Sold 4.3.1947; BU Brunton, Grangemouth.

VANNEAU Gun-brig 6, 120bm. French, captured 6.6.1793 by COLOSSUS in Bay of Biscay. Wrecked 21.10.1796 nr Porto Ferrajo, Italy.

VANOC Destroyer, 'V/W' class. John Brown 14.6.1917. Escort 11.1943. Sold 26.7.1945; stranded Penrhyn, BU Ward *in situ.*

VANQUISHER Destroyer, 'V/W' class. John Brown 18.8.1917. Escort 4.1943. Sold 4.3.1947; arr. 12.1948 Charlestown for BU.

VANSITTART Destroyer, Modified 'W' class. Beardmore 17.4.1919. Escort 6.1942. Sold 25.2.1946; arr. 5.5.1946 Cashmore, Newport, for BU.

VANTAGE Destroyer, Modified 'W' class. Beardmore, LD 16.9.1918, = VIMY 1918, cancelled 9.1919.

VANTAGE Submarine, 'V' class. Vickers Armstrong, Tyne, cancelled 23.1.1944.

VANTROMP *See TROMP 1796.*

VANTRUMP Flyboat 8, 312bm. Dutch, captured 1665. Sold 1667.

VARANGIAN Submarine, 'U' class. Vickers Armstrong, Tyne, 4.3.1943. Sold 6.1949; BU King, Gateshead.

VARIABLE (ex-*Redbridge*) Sloop/schooner 12, 210bm. Purch. 1808. 'Name removed from Navy List 23.11.1814.'

VARIABLE (ex-*Edward*) Schooner 14, 324bm, 104·5 × 27·5ft, 12—24pdr carr., 2—6pdr. Purch. 1814. BU 2.1817.

VARIABLE Brig-sloop 10, 'Cherokee' class, 231bm. Pembroke Dock 6.10.1827. = PIGEON (packet brig 6) 1829, ordered sold 27.7.1847.

VARIANCE Submarine, 'V' class. Vickers Armstrong, Barrow, 22.5.1944. Tx RNorN 8.1944 = UTSIRA; sold 12.1962; BU 12.1965 Hamburg.

VARNE Submarine, 'U' class. Vickers Armstrong, Barrow, 22.1.1943. Tx RNorN 28.3.1943 = ULA; BU 12.1965 Eckardt, Hamburg.

VARNE Submarine, 'V' class. Vickers Armstrong, Tyne, 24.2.1944. BU 9.1958.

VASHON Destroyer, Modified 'W' class. Beardmore, cancelled 12.1918.

VAUGHAN Sloop 14 Purch. 1781. Sold 17.7.1783.

VAUTOUR Brig-sloop 16, 336bm. French, captured 8.1809 on stocks Flushing; tx Chatham, comp. 15.9.1810. Foundered 8.1813.

VECTIS Destroyer, 'V/W' class. White 4.9.1917.

HO Ward 25.8.1936 part payment *Majestic*
(CALEDONIA, q.v.); BU Inverkeithing.

VEGA Coal hulk, 304bm. Slaver brig, captured
1860 by LYRA, purch. 2.4.1860. Sold 23.2.1863.

VEGA Destroyer, 'V/W' class. Doxford 1.9.1917.
Escort 10.1939. Sold 4.3.1947; arr. 26.3.1948
Clayton & Davie, Dunston, for BU.

VEGREVILLE Minesweeper, TE 'Bangor' class.
Vickers, Montreal, 7.8.1941. BU 5.1947 Ward,
Hayle.

VEHEMENT Destroyer, 'V/W' class. Denny
6.7.1917. Sunk 1.8.1918 mine North Sea.

VEHEMENT Submarine, 'V' class. Vickers Armstrong, Tyne, cancelled 23.1.1944.

VELDT Submarine, 'V' class. Vickers Armstrong,
Barrow, 19.7.1943. Lent Greek Navy 1944–
10.12.1957 = PIPINOS. Arr. 23.2.1958 Clayton &
Davie, Dunston, for BU.

VELOX (ex-PYTHON) Destroyer, 420 tons, 210 ×
21ft, 1–12pdr, 5–6pdr, 2–TT. Hawthorn
11.2.1902 spec., purch. 7.6.1902. Sunk 25.10.1915
mine nr The Nab.

VELOX Destroyer, 'V/W' class. Doxford 17.11.1917.
Escort 4.1942. Sold 18.2.1947; arr. 11.1947
Charlestown for BU.

VENDETTA Destroyer, 'V/W' class. Fairfield
3.9.1917. RAN 10.1933. Scuttled 2.7.1948 off
Sydney Heads.

VENDETTA Destroyer (RAN), 2,610 tons, 390 (oa)
× 43ft, 6–4·5in, 8–40mm, 5–TT, Limbo.
Williamstown DY 3.5.1954. PO 10.10.1979. Towed
Sydney 11.1.1987 for BU China.

VENERABLE 3rd Rate 74, 1,669bm, 170·5 ×
47·5ft. Perry, Blackwall, 19.4.1784. Wrecked
24.11.1804 off Torbay.

VENERABLE 3rd Rate 74, 1,716bm, 174 × 48ft.
Pitcher, Northfleet, 12.4.1808. Harbour service
10.1825. BU 10.1838 Plymouth.

VENERABLE Battleship, 15,000 tons, 400 × 75ft,
4–12in, 12–6in 18–12pdr. Chatham DY
2.11.1899. Sold 4.6.1920 Stanlee; resold, BU
Germany.

VENERABLE Aircraft carrier, 13,190 tons, 630 ×
80ft, 19–40mm, 48 aircraft. Cammell Laird
30.12.1943. Sold Dutch Navy 1.4.1948, = KAREL
DOORMAN 5.1948; tx Argentine Navy 1968 = 25
DE MAYO; sold 7.8.1998; towed to Alang 1999 for
BU.

VENETIA Destroyer, 'V/W' class. Fairfield
29.10.1917. Sunk 19.10.1940 mine Thames
estuary.

VENGEANCE 6th Rate 28, 53315m, 117 × 32·5ft,
24–9pdr, 4–4pdr. French, captured 2.1758 by
HUSSAR. Sunk 10.1766 breakwater Plymouth.

VENGEANCE 3rd Rate 74, 1,627bm, 166 × 46ft.
Randall, Rotherhithe, 25.6.1774. Prison ship
1.1808. BU 1.1816 Portsmouth.

VENGEANCE Tender. Dutch hoy, purch.
21.11.1793. Sold 11.1804.

VENGEANCE 4th Rate 50, 1,370bm, 160 × 41·5ft.
French, captured 20.8.1800 by SEINE in Mona
Passage. Damaged by stranding 1801, BU.

VENGEANCE 2nd Rate 84, 2,284bm, 196·5 × 52ft,
2–68pdr carr., 28–32pdr, 14–32pdr carr., 40–
24pdr. Pembroke Dock 27.7.1824. Receiving ship
1861. Sold 10.5.1897.

VENGEANCE Battleship, 12,950 tons, 390 × 74ft,
4–12in, 12–6in, 12–12pdr. Vickers 25.7.1899.
Sold 1.12.1921 Stanlee, Dover; arr. 9.1.1923 for
BU.

VENGEANCE Aircraft carrier, 13,190 tons, 630 ×
80ft, 19–40mm, 48 aircraft. Swan Hunter
23.2.1944. Tx Brazilian Navy 13.12.1956 = MINAS
GERAIS; de-stored 2001; for preservation (?)
2002; sold 7.2002 private buyer, LU Rio de
Janeiro.

VENGEANCE Nuclear submarine, 'Vanguard'
class. Vickers, Barrow 19.9.1998. *Originally
referred to in some sources as VALIANT.*

VENGEFUL Destroyer, Modified 'W' class. Beardmore, cancelled 12.1918.

VENGEFUL Submarine, 'V' class. Vickers Armstrong, Barrow, 20.7.1944. Lent Greek Navy
1945–57 = DELFIN. Arr. 22.3.1958 King,
Gateshead, for BU.

VENGEUR 3rd Rate 74, 1,765bm, 176·5 × 48ft.
Graham, Harwich, 19.6.1810. Receiving ship
2.1824. BU 8.1843.

VENOM (ex-GENIE) Gun-brig 8, 128bm, 65·5 ×
23ft 4–18pdr carr., 4–6pdr. French, captured
31.5.1796 by squadron in Mediterranean. Listed
until 1799.

VENOM Destroyer, Modified 'V' class. John Brown
21.12.1918. = VENOMOUS 24.4.1919. Escort
8.1942. Sold 4.3.1947; arr. 7.1947 Charlestown for
BU.

VENOM Submarine, 'V' class. Vickers Armstrong,
Tyne, cancelled 23.1.1944.

VENOMOUS *See VENOM 1918.*

VENTNOR *See CROZIER 1919.*

VENTURE Training schooner (RCN), 250 tons,
126·5 × 27·5ft, 2–3pdr. Meteghan, NS, 6.1937.
Sold 1946.

VENTURER (ex-NOUVELLE ENTERPRISE)
Schooner 10, 126bm. 72 × 20·5ft. French privat-
eer, captured 27.12.1807 by NIMROD in West
Indies. = THEODOCIA 1812. Sold 15.12.1814.

VENTURER Submarine, 'V' class. Vickers Armstrong, Barrow, 4.5.1943. Sold 1946 RNorN = UTSTEIN; BU 1964 Sweden.

VENTURER (ex-*Suffolk Harvester*) Minesweeper, 392 tons, 120·7 (oa) × 29·2ft. Woolwich 1972. Trawler, cd 25.11.1978 for Severn RNVR. Ret. 11.1983 owner.

VENTURER *See also RANGER 1787.*

VENTUROUS Destroyer, 'V/W' class. Denny 21.9.1917. HO Ward 25.8.1936 part payment *Majestic* (CALEDONIA, q.v.); BU Inverkeithing.

VENUS 5th Rate 36, 722bm, 128·5 × 36ft. Okill, Liverpool, 11.3.1758. Reduced to 32 guns 3.1792; = HEROINE 1809; harbour service 1817. Sold 22.9.1828.

VENUS 5th Rate 36, 942bm. Danish, captured 7.9.1807 Battle of Copenhagen. Harbour service 1809. Sold 9.8.1815. *Was to have been renamed LEVANT 1809.*

VENUS 5th Rate 46, 1,069bm, 153·5 × 40ft. Deptford DY 10.8.1820. Lent Marine Society 1848–62 as TS. Sold 7.10.1864 Castle, Charlton.

VENUS 2nd class cruiser, 5,600 tons, 350 × 54ft, 5–6in, 6–4·7in (1904: 11–6in). Fairfield 5.9.1895. Sold 22.9.1921 Cohen; BU Germany.

VENUS Destroyer, 1,710 tons, 362·7 (oa) × 35·7ft, 4–4·7in, 4–40mm, 8–TT. Fairfield 23.2.1943. Frigate 1952, 2,240 tons, 2–4in, 2–40mm, 2–Squid. Sold Ward 6.11.1972; BU Briton Ferry.

VERBENA Sloop, 'Arabis' class. Blyth DD 9.11.1915. Sold 13.10.1933 Rees, Llanelly.

VERBENA Corvette, 'Flower' class. Smith's Dock 1.10.1940. Sold 17.5.1947 Wheelock Marden.

VERDUN Destroyer, 'V/W' class. Hawthorn Leslie 21.8.1917. Escort 7.1940. Arr. Ward, Inverkeithing 3.3.1946

VERDUN OF CANADA *See DUNVER 1942.*

VERITY Destroyer, Modified 'W' class. John Brown 19.3.1919. Escort 10.1943. Sold 4.3.1947, arr. 14.9.1947 Cashmore, Newport, for BU.

VERNON Armed ship 14. Listed 1781–82.

VERNON 4th Rate 50, 2,080bm, 2,388 tons, 176 × 52·5ft, 50–32pdr. Woolwich DY 1.5.1832. Torpedo schoolship 1876; = ACTAEON 14.1.1886. Sold 14.9.1923.

VERNON *For the various ships renamed VERNON as torpedo schoolships see DONEGAL 1858, MARLBOROUGH 1855, WARRIOR 1860, SKYLARK 1932.*

VERONICA Sloop, 'Acacia' class. Dunlop Bremner 27.5.1915. Sold 22.2.1935 Cashmore, Newport.

VERONICA Corvette, 'Flower' class. Smith's Dock 17.10.1940. Lent USN 21.3.1942–1945 = TEMPTRESS. Sold 1946 = *Verolock.*

VERSATILE Destroyer, 'V/W' class. Hawthorn

Leslie 31.10.1917. Escort 10.1943. Sold 7.5.1947; BU Brechin, Granton, arr. 10.9.1948.

VERTU *See VIRTUE 1803.*

VERULAM Destroyer, 'V/W' class. Hawthorn Leslie 3.10.1917. Sunk 4.9.1919 mine Gulf of Finland.

VERULAM Destroyer, 1,710 tons, 362·7 (oa) × 35·7ft, 4–4·7in. 2–40mm, 8–TT. Fairfield 22.4.1943. Frigate 1952, 2–4in, 2–40mm, 2–Squid. Sold Cashmore 1.9.1972; BU Newport.

VERVAIN (ex-BROOM) Corvette, 'Flower' class. Harland & Wolff 12.3.1941 (renamed 1.1941). Sunk 20.2.1945 by U.1208 south of Ireland.

VERVE Submarine, 'V' class. Vickers Armstrong, Tyne, cancelled 23.1.1944.

VERWOOD *See CROZIER 1919.*

VERYAN BAY (ex-LOCH SWANNAY) Frigate, 'Bay' class. Hill, Bristol, 11.11.1944 (renamed 1944). Arr. 1.7.1959 Charlestown for BU.

VESPER Destroyer, 'V/W' class. Stephen 15.12.1917. Escort 5.1943. Sold 4.3.1947; arr. Ward, Inverkeithing, 14.3.1949 for BU.

VESTA Schooner 10, 111bm, 63 × 20·5ft, 10–18pdr carr. Bermuda 1806. Sold 11.1.1816.

VESTAL 5th Rate 32, 659bm, 124·5 35ft. Barnard & Turner, Harwich, 17.6.1757. BU 1775.

VESTAL 6th Rate 20, 429bm, 108 × 30ft. Plymouth DY 23.5.1777. Foundered 10.1777 off Newfoundland.

VESTAL 6th Rate 28, 601bm, 120 × 34ft. Batson, Limehouse, 24.12.1779. Troopship 3.1800; lent Trinity House 10.1803. Sold 2.1816 Barbados.

VESTAL Brig 10 (Indian), 159bm. Bombay DY 1809. *Fate unknown.*

VESTAL 6th Rate 26, 913bm, 130 × 40·5ft, 24–32pdr, 2–12pdr. Sheerness DY 6.4.1833. BU comp. 17.2.1862 Castle & Beech.

VESTAL Wood screw sloop, 1,081bm, 1,574 tons, 187 × 36ft, 9–64pdr. Pembroke Dock 16.11.1865. Sold 12.1884 Castle.

VESTAL Sloop, 980 tons, 180 × 33ft, 6–4in, 4–3pdr. Sheerness DY 10.2.1900. Sold 21.10.1921 Thomas, Anglesey.

VESTAL Minesweeper, 'Algerine' class. Harland & Wolff 19.6.1943. Sunk 26.7.1945 Japanese aircraft off Puket, Siam.

VESUVE Gunvessel 3, 160bm, 74 × 22·5ft, 3–18pdr. French, captured 3.7.1795 by MELAMPUS off St-Malo. Sold 12.1802.

VESUVIUS Fireship 8, 248bm, 92 × 25ft. Taylor, Cuckold's Point, 30.3.1691. Expended 19.11.1693 St-Malo.

VESUVIUS Fireship 8, 269bm, 92 × 25·5ft. Barrett, Shoreham, 4.12.1693, purch. on stocks.

Stranded 26.11.1703 Spithead; refloated 12.03, condemned 7.9.1705.

VESUVIUS (ex-*Worcester*) Fireship 16, 200bm, 83 × 24ft. Purch. 12.9.1739. BU 10.1742 Deptford.

VESUVIUS (ex-*King of Portugal*) Fireship 8, 299bm, 91·5 × 28ft 8—4pdr. Purch. 17.11.1756. Sloop 12.1756. Sold 3.5.1763.

VESUVIUS Fireship 8, 8—4pdr. Randall, Rotherhithe, 15.5.1771. = RAVEN (sloop) 10.8.1771. Sold 19.7.1780 New York.

VESUVIUS Bomb vessel 8, 299bm, 91·5 × 27·5ft. Perry, Blackwall, 3.7.1776. Sold 3.8.1812.

VESUVIUS Bomb vessel 8, 298bm (?). Purch. 4.1797. Sold 13.8.1812.

VESUVIUS Bomb vessel 8, 326bm, 102·5 × 27·5ft. Davy, Topsham, 1.5.1813. Sold 22.7.1819.

VESUVIUS Bomb vessel 8, 372bm, 105 × 29ft, 10—24pdr carr., 2—6pdr, 2 mortars, ordered Deptford DY 1823; tx Chatham DY 8.1828, LD 8.1830, cancelled 10.1.1831.

VESUVIUS Wood paddle sloop, 970bm, 180 × 34·5ft, 4 guns. Sheerness DY 11.7.1839. Sold White 6.1865 for BU Cowes.

VESUVIUS Iron screw torpedo vessel, 244 tons, 90 × 22ft, 4—TT. Pembroke Dock 24.3.1874. Sold 14.9.1923 Cashmore; foundered under tow Newport.

VESUVIUS Torpedo-discharge lighter. Purch. 1933. = TL.1 in 1940.

VESUVIUS *See also SKYLARK 1932.*

VETCH Corvette, 'Flower' class. Smith's Dock 27.5.1941. Sold 8.1945 = *Patrai*.

VETERAN 3rd Rate 64, 1,397bm, 160·5 × 45ft. Fabian, East Cowes 14.8.1787. Prison ship 1799. BU 6.1816.

VETERAN Destroyer, Modified 'W' class. John Brown 26.4.1919. Escort 1941. Sunk 26.9.1942 by U.404 in North Atlantic.

VETERAN *See also PROMETHEUS 1807.*

VETO Submarine, 'V' class. Vickers Armstrong, Barrow, cancelled 23.1.1944.

VICEROY Destroyer, 'V/W' class, 1,325 tons. Thornycroft 17.11.1917. Escort 12.1940. Sold 17.5.1947; arr. Brechin, Granton, 10.9.1948 for BU

VICTOIRE Lugger 14. Purch. 1795. Listed until 1800.

VICTOIRE (VICTORIE) Firevessel, 73bm, 63 × 16·5ft, 2—4pdr. French privateer schooner, captured 28.12.1797 by TERMAGANT off Spurn Point. Sold 16.12.1801.

VICTOR Brig-sloop 10. Purch. 1777. Foundered 5.10.1780 hurricane West Indies.

VICTOR Sloop 14. American, captured 1779. Listed until 1782.

VICTOR Sloop 18, 385bm, 101 × 31ft. Brindley, Lynn, 19.3.1798. PO 5.9.1808 sale East Indies.

VICTOR (ex-IENA) Brig-sloop 18, 425bm, 16—32pdr carr., 2—6pdr. French, captured 8.10.1808 by MODESTE in Bay of Bengal. Recaptured 2.11.1809 by French BELLONE same area; again captured 2.12.1810 at Mauritius, sold. *Original French name spelt 'JENA' in British lists. 6pdr armament taken out of previous ship.*

VICTOR Brig-sloop 18, 'Cruizer' class, 382bm. Bombay DY 29.1814. Foundered 8.1842 Atlantic.

VICTOR Wood screw gunvessel, 859bm, 201·5× 30·5ft, 1—110pdr, 1—60pdr, 4—20pdr. Blackwall 24.11.1855. Sold 11.1863 = *Scylla*; tx Confederate Navy = RAPPAHANNOCK.

VICTOR Destroyer, 954 tons, 260 × 26·5ft, 3—4in, 2—TT. Thornycroft 28.11.1913. Sold 20.1.1923. King, Garston.

VICTOR EMANUEL *See REPULSE 1855.*

VICTORIA Wood paddle sloop (Indian), 705bm, 5 guns. Bombay DY 10.1839. Sold c. 1864.

VICTORIA Wood screw sloop (Australian), 580bm, 13—32pdr. Young & Magnay, Limehouse, 7.1855. Survey vessel 1864. Sold 8.1894 W. Marr, Williamstown; BU 8.1895.

VICTORIA Screw 1st Rate 121, 4,127bm, 6,959 tons, 260 × 60ft, 32—8in, 1—68pdr, 88—32pdr. Portsmouth DY 12.11.1859. Sold 5.1893 for BU.

VICTORIA Coastguard yawl, 131bm, 70 × 21ft. Built 1864. Sold 4.4.1905 Chatham.

VICTORIA Screw gunvessel (Australian), 530 tons, 140 × 27ft, 1—10in, 2—13pdr. Armstrong Mitchell 6.1883. Sold 1896 = *Victoria*

VICTORIA (ex-RENOWN) Battleship, 10,470 tons, 340 × 70ft, 2—16·25in, 1—10in, 12—6in, 12—6pdr. Armstrong Mitchell 9.4.1887 (renamed 18.3.1887). Sunk 22.6.1893 collision CAMPERDOWN off Tripoli.

VICTORIA *See also WINDSOR CASTLE 1858, UNSEEN 1989.*

VICTORIA & ALBERT Wood paddle yacht, 1,034bm, 225 (oa) × 33 (oa) ft. Pembroke Dock 26.4.1843. = OSBORNE 22.12.1854. BU 1868 Portsmouth.

VICTORIA & ALBERT (ex-WINDSOR CASTLE) Wood paddle yacht, 2,345bm, 2,470 tons, 329 (oa) × 69 (oa) ft. Pembroke Dock 16.1.1855 (renamed 12.1854). BU 1904 Portsmouth.

VICTORIA & ALBERT Screw yacht, 4,700 tons, 380 × 40ft. Pembroke Dock 9.5.1899. Accommodation ship 1939. Arr. Faslane 6.12.1954 for BU.

VICTORIAVILLE Frigate (RCN), 'River' class. G. T. Davie 23.6.1944. = GRANBY (diving tender) 21.12.1966. PO 31.12.1973; sold for BU 1974.

VICTORIE See *VICTOIRE 1797.*

VICTORIEUSE Brig-sloop 12, 350bm, 103 ×
27·5ft, 2—36pdr carr., 12—12pdr. French, captured 31.8.1795 by Fleet off Texel. BU 7.1805.

VICTORIOUS 3rd Rate 74, 1,683bm, 170·5 × 47ft.
Perry, Blackwall, 27.4.1785. BU 8.1803 Lisbon.

VICTORIOUS 3rd Rate 74, 1,724bm 173 × 47·5ft.
Adams, Buckler's Hard, 20.10.1808. Receiving
ship 5.1826. BU 1.1862 Portsmouth.

VICTORIOUS Battleship, 14,900 tons, 390 × 75ft,
4—12in, 12—6in, 16—12pdr. Chatham DY
19.10.1895. Repair ship 3.1916; = INDUS II 1920.
Sold 19.12.1922 A. J. Purves; resold 4.1923
Stanlee, Dover.

VICTORIOUS Aircraft carrier, 23,000 tons, 673 ×
96ft, 16—4·5in, 36 aircraft. Vickers Armstrong,
Tyne, 14.9.1939. Rebuilt 1958 as 38,530 tons, 12—
3in, 6—40mm, 54 aircraft. Sold S. Bkg. Industries
20.6.1969; BU Faslane.

VICTORIOUS Nuclear submarine, 'Vanguard'
class. Vickers, Barrow 29.9.1993.

VICTORIOUS II See *PRINCE GEORGE 1895.*

VICTORY (ex-*Great Christopher*) 42-gun ship,
565bm. Purch. 1560. Rebuilt 1586, 12—18pdr,
18—9pdr, 6—6pdr, 20 smaller. BU 1608.

VICTORY 42-gun ship, 541bm. Deptford 1620.
Rebuilt Chatham 1666 as 2nd Rate 82, 1,020bm.
BU 1691 Woolwich.

VICTORY 1st Rate 100, 1,921bm, 174·5 × 50·5ft.
Portsmouth DY 23.2.1737. Wrecked 5.10.1744 The
Casquets. *Technically, rebuilt from frames of
ROYAL JAMES 1675 (q.v.), restarted 6.3.1726.*

VICTORY Schooner 8 (Canadian lakes). Navy
Island, Canada, 1764. Burnt (by French?) 1768.

VICTORY 1st Rate 100, 2,142bm, 186 × 52ft.
Chatham DY 7.5.1765. Rebuilt 1801 as 2,164bm;
harbour service 1824. Drydocked 1.1922 Portsmouth.

VICTORY PRIZE Ship. Captured. Listed 1663–67.

VIDAL Survey ship, 1,940 tons, 297 × 40ft, 4—
3pdr. Chatham DY 31.7.1951. BU 6.1976 Bruges.

VIDETTE Destroyer, 'V/W' class. Stephen
28.2.1918. Escort 1.1943; sold 4.3.1947; BU
Brunton, Grangemouth.

VIGILANT Schooner 8 (Canadian lakes). Oswego
Lake, Ontario, 1755. Captured 14.8.1756 by
French at Oswego.

VIGILANT 3rd Rate 64, 1,347bm, 159·5 × 44·5ft.
Adams, Buckler's Hard, 6.10.1774. Prison ship
1799. Foundered 1.1806 Portsmouth harbour;
raised 4.1806, BU 4.1816.

VIGILANT (ex-*Empress of Russia*) Armed ship
20, 14—24pdr, 6—6pdr. Purch. 1777 North America. Burnt 1780 Beaufort, South Carolina, unfit.

VIGILANT Schooner 4, 61bm. Purch. 1803. Sold
1808.

VIGILANT (ex-IMPERIAL) Schooner 8, 102bm.
French, captured 24.5.1806 by CYGNET off
Dominica. = SUBTLE 20.11.1806. Wrecked
26.10.1807 off Bermuda.

VIGILANT Cutter 12, 161bm, 67·5 × 21·5ft. Deptford DY 18.4.1821. Sold 11.1832 W. Clarke.

VIGILANT Wood screw frigate, 1,536bm, 210 ×
40ft. Portsmouth DY, ordered 26.3.1846, cancelled 22.5.1849.

VIGILANT Wood screw gunvessel, 680bm, 181 ×
28·5ft, 1—110pdr, 1—68pdr, 2—20pdr. Mare,
Blackwall, 20.3.1856. Ordered sold 25.2.1869
Bombay.

VIGILANT Wood paddle despatch vessel, 835bm,
1,000 tons, 2—20pdr. Devonport DY 17.2.1871.
Sold 10.1886 in Hong Kong.

VIGILANT Destroyer, 400 tons, 210 × 21ft, 1—
12pdr, 5—6pdr, 2—TT. John Brown 16.8.1900
spec., purch. 31.3.1900. Sold 10.2.1920 South
Alloa S. Bkg Co.

VIGILANT Destroyer, 1,710 tons, 362·7 (oa) ×
35·7ft, 4—4·7in, 2—40mm, 8—TT. Swan Hunter
18.10.1943. Frigate 1952—53, 2—4in, Squid. Arr.
4.6.1965 S. Bkg Industries, Faslane, for BU.

VIGILANT Patrol boat 3.1975. = MEAVY 7.1986.

VIGILANT Nuclear submarine, 'Vanguard' class.
Vickers, Barrow 14.10.1995. *Originally referred
to in some sources as VENERABLE.*

VIGILANTE (ex-VIGILANT) 4th Rate 58,
1,318bm, 154 × 43·5ft, 24—24pdr, 24—12pdr, 10—
6pdr. French, captured 5.1745 by SUPERB off
Cape Breton. Sold 11.12.1759.

VIGILANTE (ex-ALERTE) Cutter 4. French, captured 8.1793. Burnt 18.12.1793 at evacuation of
Toulon.

VIGO 3rd Rate 74, 1,787bm, 177 × 48ft. Ross,
Rochester, 21.2.1810. Receiving ship 1827. BU
8.1865 Marshall, Plymouth.

VIGO Destroyer, Modified 'W' class. John Brown,
cancelled 12.1918.

VIGO Destroyer, 2,315 tons, 379 (oa) × 40—25ft,
4—4·5in, 1—4in, 14—40mm, 8—TT. Fairfield
27.9.1945. Arr. 6.12.1964 Faslane for BU.

VIGO See also *DARTMOUTH 1693, AGINCOURT
1817.*

VIGOROUS Destroyer, Modified 'W' class. John
Brown, LD 1918, = WISTFUL 6.1918, cancelled
12.18.

VIGOROUS Submarine, 'V' class. Vickers Armstrong, Barrow, 15.10.1943. Sold 23.12.1949; BU
Stockton-on-Tees.

VIKING Destroyer, 1,090 tons, 280 × 27·5ft, 2—4in,

2—TT. Palmer 14.9.1909. Sold 12.12.1919 Ward, Briton Ferry. *Only six-funnelled vessel in RN.*

VIKING Training ketch (RNZN). Listed 1937–45.

VIKING Submarine, 'V' class. Vickers Armstrong, Barrow, 5.5.1943. Tx RNorN 1946 = UTVAER; sold Sarisburg, Sweden, 1964.

VILLE DE PARIS 1st Rate 104, 2,347bm, 187 × 53·5ft. French, captured 12.4.1782 by Fleet in West Indies. Foundered 9.9.1782 gale off Newfoundland.

VILLE DE PARIS 1st Rate 110, 2,351bm, 190 × 53ft. Chatham DY 17.7.1795. Harbour service 1825. BU 6.1845 Pembroke Dock.

VILLE DE QUEBEC Frigate (RCN), 'Halifax' class. Marine Industries, Sorel, 16.5.1991.

VILLE DE QUEBEC *See also QUEBEC 1941.*

VIMIERA (ex-PYLADE) Brig-sloop 16, 304bm, 91 × 28ft, 14—24pdr carr., 2—6pdr. French, captured 21.10.1808 by POMPEE. Sold 1.9.1814.

VIMIERA Destroyer, 'V/W' class. Swan Hunter 22.6.1917. Escort 1.1940. Sunk 9.1.1942 mine Thames estuary.

VIMIERA *See also DANAE 1945.*

VIMY *See VANCOUVER 1917, VANTAGE 1918.*

VINCEJO Brig-sloop 16, 277bm. Spanish, captured 19.3.1799 by CORMORANT in Mediterranean. Captured 20.5.1804 by French in Quiberon Bay.

VINDEX (ex-*Viking*) Seaplane carrier, 2,950 tons, 350·5 × 42ft, 4—12pdr, 1—6pdr, 7 aircraft. Hired 15.3.1915, purch. 9.1915. Sold 12.2.1920 Isle of Man Steam Packet Co.

VINDEX Escort carrier, 13,455 tons, 499·5 × 68·5ft, 2—4in, 15 aircraft. Swan Hunter 4.5.1943. Sold 2.10.1947 = *Port Vindex.*

VINDICTIVE Galley 8. Purch. North America 1779. Listed until 1784.

VINDICTIVE (ex-BELLONA) 6th Rate 28, 506bm, 112 × 32ft. Dutch, captured 17.8.1796 Saldanha Bay. Left Navy List 7.1810. BU 1816 Sheerness.

VINDICTIVE 3rd Rate 74, 1,758bm, 176 × 4 8·5ft. Portsmouth DY 23.11.1813. Reduced to 50 guns 10.1832. Storeship 1862 Fernando Poo, then Jellah Coffee; ret. Fernando Poo for sale 1871, foundered. Sold as wreck 24.11.1871.

VINDICTIVE 2nd class cruiser, 5,750 tons, 320 × 54ft, 4—6in, 6—4·7in (1904: 10—6in). Chatham DY 9.12.1897. Sunk 10.5.1918 blockship Ostend; raised 8.1920, BU.

VINDICTIVE (ex-CAVENDISH) Cruiser aircraft carrier, 9,750 tons, 605 (oa) × 65·1ft, 4—7·5in, 4—3in, 4—12pdr, 6 aircraft. Harland & Wolff 17.1.1918 (renamed 1918). Cruiser 1925, 7—7·5in; TS 1937; repair ship 1940. Sold 2.1946; BU Hughes Bolckow, Blyth.

VINEYARD Submarine, 'V' class. Vickers Armstrong, Barrow, 8.5.1944. Lent French Navy 1944–11.1947 = DORIS; arr. 6.1950 Charlestown for BU.

VIOLA Sloop, 'Aubrietia' class. Ropner, Stockton-on-Tees, 14.7.1916. Sold 17.10.1922 Fryer, Sunderland. *Served as decoy ship Q.14.*

VIOLA *See also LEGION 1914.*

VIOLENT Destroyer, 'V/W' class. Swan Hunter 1.9.1917. HO Ward 8.3.1937 part payment *Majestic* (CALEDONIA, q.v.); BU Inverkeithing.

VIOLET Ship, 220bm. In Armada Fleet 1588. *Hired vessel?*

VIOLET 44-gun ship, 400bm. Captured 1652. BU 1672.

VIOLET Lugger, 82bm, 60·5 × 18·5ft, 10—12pdr carr. Customs Service vessel, tx 1806. BU 6.1812.

VIOLET Tender. Purch. on stocks 20.6.1835 Scheveningen. Sold 24.11.1842.

VIOLET Iron paddle packet, 292bm. Ditchburn & Mare, Blackwall, 1.12.1845. Sold 1854 Jenkins & Churchward.

VIOLET Wood screw gunboat, 'Albacore' class. Ditchburn & Mare, Blackwall, 9.1.1856. Sold 7.10.1864 Marshall.

VIOLET Destroyer, 350 tons, 210 × 21ft, 1—12pdr, 2—TT. Doxford 3.5.1897. Sold 7.6.1920 J. Houston, Montrose.

VIOLET Corvette, 'Flower' class. Simons 30.12.1940. Sold 17.5.1947 mercantile.

VIPER Sloop 14, 270bm, 91 × 26ft. Durrell, Poole, 11.6.1746. = LIGHTNING (fireship) 29.7.1755, 8—4pdr. Sold 30.12.1762.

VIPER Sloop 10, 228bm, 88·5 × 24·5ft. West, Deptford, 31.3.1756. Captured 1762 by French.

VIPER Cutter 12. Dates from 1762. Wrecked 11.10.1780 Gulf of St Lawrence.

VIPER Cutter 10, 149bm, 10—3pdr. Purch. North America, cd 17.7.1777. Foundered 15.12.1779 off Newfoundland. *Was to have been sold 2.1780.*

VIPER Galley 8. Purch. 1779; listed until 1785.

VIPER Gunvessel 4, 69bm, 65·5 × 45ft. Dutch hoy, purch. 1794. BU 1801 Portsmouth.

VIPER Cutter 14, 14—4pdr. Purch. 1.1797. Sold 10.1809.

VIPER (ex-*Niger*) Cutter 8, 104bm, 63 × 20·5ft. White, Cowes, 1809; purch. 1809. Sold 11.8.1814.

VIPER Gun-brig 10, 148bm. Purch. 1810. = MOHAWK 1810? Not listed 1811.

VIPER Schooner 6, 183bm, 80 × 23ft. Pembroke Dock 12.5.1831. BU 5.1851.

VIPER Wood screw gunvessel, 477bm, 160 × 25·5ft, 2—68pdr. Green, Blackwall, 22.7.1854. Sold 19.5.1862 Marshall.

VIPER Iron armoured gunvessel, 737bm, 1,230 tons, 160 × 32·5ft, 2–7in, 2–20pdr. Dudgeon, Limehouse, 21.12.1865. Harbour service 1890; tankvessel 1901. Sold 1908 Bermuda.

VIPER Destroyer, 440 tons, 210 × 21ft, 1–12pdr, 5–6pdr, 2–TT. Hawthorn 6.9.1899. Wrecked 3.8.1901 Bushon I., nr Alderney. *First turbine destroyer.*

VIPER *See also GREYHOUND 1780.*

VIPERE Cutter 4. French privateer, captured 1793. Wrecked 12.1793 Hieres Bay.

VIPERE Brig-sloop 16, 290bm, 95·5 × 26·5ft, 2–pdr carr., 16–6pdr. French privateer, captured 23.1.1794 by FLORA in English Channel. Foundered 2.1.1797 off mouth of R. Shannon.

VIRAGO Gun-brig 12, 181bm, 84·5 × 22ft. Tanner, Dartmouth, 23.9.1805. Sold 30.5.1816.

VIRAGO Wood paddle sloop, 1,059bm, 180 × 36ft. Chatham DY 25.7.1842. BU 1876 Chatham.

VIRAGO Destroyer, 395 tons, 210·5 × 21·5ft, 1–12pdr, 5–6pdr, 2–TT. Laird 19.11.1895. Sold 10.10.1919 in Hong Kong; BU China.

VIRAGO Destroyer, 1,710 tons, 362·7 (oa) × 35·7ft, 4–4·7in, 2–40mm. 8–TT. Swan Hunter 4.2.1943. Frigate 1952, 2–4in, 2–40mm, Squid. Arr. 6.1965 Faslane for BU.

VIRGIN Fireship 4, 148bm. Purch. 1666. Expended 1667.

VIRGIN Sloop 12. Origin unknown. Sold 1764. *In French hands as VIERGE 5–9.1760.*

VIRGIN PRIZE 5th Rate 32, 322bm, 95 × 28ft. French, captured 1690. Sold 20.9.1698.

VIRGINIA 6th Rate 28, 802bm (?), 132·5 × 34·5ft, 28–9pdr. American, captured 30.3.1778 when aground Chesapeake Bay. BU 12.1782.

VIRGINIE 5th Rate 38, 1,066bm, 151·5 × 40ft. French, captured 23.4.1796 by INDEFATIGABLE in Atlantic. Receiving ship 1817. Sold 11.7.1827 for BU.

VIRGINIA Schooner 4. Purch. 1796. Gone by 1800.

VIRGINIA (ex-VIRGINIE) Brig-sloop. French transport, captured 14.3.1808. Sold 11.1811.

VIRGINIA Coal hulk, 195bm. Barque, purch. 22.1.1862. BU 3.1866 Bermuda.

VIRILE Submarine, 'V' class. Vickers Armstrong, Barrow, LD 2.11.1943, cancelled 23.1.1944.

VIRTUE (VERTU) (ex-VERTU) 5th Rate 40, 1,073bm. French, captured 30.11.1803 San Domingo. BU 12.1810.

VIRTUE Submarine, 'V' class. Vickers Armstrong, Barrow, 28.11.1943. Arr. 19.5.1946 Cochin, India, for BU.

VIRULENT Destroyer, Modified 'W' class. John Brown, cancelled 12.1918.

VIRULENT Submarine, 'V' class. Vickers Armstrong, Tyne, 23.5.1944. Lent Greek Navy 29.5.1946–3.10.1958 = ARGONAFTIS. Left Malta 11.1958 for Tyne, broke adrift, stranded north coast of Spain; sold 1961 *in situ.*

VISCOUNT Destroyer, 'V/W' class, 1,325 tons. Thornycroft 29.12.1917. Escort 12.1941. Sold 20.3.1945; BU 5.1945 Clayton & Davie, Dunston.

VISIGOTH Submarine, 'V' class. Vickers Armstrong, Barrow, 30.11.1943. Sold 3.1949; arr. 20.2.1950 Ward, Hayle, for BU.

VISITANT Submarine, 'V' class. Vickers Armstrong, Barrow, cancelled 23.1.1944, not LD.

VITALITY *See UNTAMED 1942.*

VITTORIA Destroyer, 'V/W' class. Swan Hunter 29.10.1917. Torpedoed 1.9.1919 Soviet MTB in Baltic.

VITTORIA *See also PRINCESS CHARLOTTE 1814.*

VIVACIOUS Destroyer, 'V/W' class. Yarrow 3.11.1917. Escort 12.1942. Sold 4.3.1947; arr. 10.1948 Charlestown for BU.

VIVID Wood paddle packet, 352bm, 350 tons, 150 × 22ft, 2 guns. Chatham DY 7.2.1848. Sold 1894.

VIVID (ex-*Capercaillie*) Iron screw yacht, 550 tons, 192 × 24ft, 1 gun. Purch. 26.9.1891. Base ship Devonport from 1.1892. Sold 20.11.1912. Wrecked 7.1913 off Colonsay.

VIVID Submarine, 'V' class. Vickers Armstrong, Tyne, 15.9.1943. Arr. 10.1950 Faslane for BU.

VIVID *For nominal base ships with this name, see CUCKOO 1873, SABRINA 1876, CAMBRIAN 1893, MARSHAL NEY 1915.*

VIVIEN Destroyer, 'V/W' class. Yarrow 16.2.1918. Escort 10.1939. Sold 18.2.1947; arr. 11.1947 Charlestown for BU.

VIXEN Gun-brig 14, 186bm, 80·5 × 23ft. Adams, Buckler's Hard, 9.1.1801. Sold 28.3.1815.

VIXEN Wood paddle sloop, 1,054bm, 180 × 36ft, 1–110pdr, 1–10in, 4–32pdr. Pembroke Dock 4.2.1841. Sold 12.11.1862 Castle, Charlton.

VIXEN Armoured composite gunboat, 754bm, 1,230 tons, 160 × 32ft, 2–7in, 2–20pdr. Lungley, Deptford, 18.11.1865, ordered BU 11.10.1895 Bermuda. *First twin-screw and first composite vessel in RN.*

VIXEN Destroyer, 400 tons, 210 × 20ft, 1–12pdr, 5–6pdr, 2–TT. Vickers Maxim 29.3.1.1900. Sold 17.3.1921 Ward, Grays.

VIXEN Destroyer, 1,710 tons, 362·7 (oa) × 35·7ft, 4–4·7in, 2–40mm, 8–TT. White 14.9.1943. Tx RCN 5.3.1944 = SIOUX; frigate 11.1959, 2–4·7in, 4–TT; arr. 28.8.1965 Spezia for BU.

VLIETER (ex-MARS) 5th Rate 40, 1,357bm, 156 ×

45ft. Dutch, captured 30.8.1799 Texel. Floating battery 7.1801; sheer hulk 1809. BU 4.1817.

VOLADOR Brig-sloop 16, 273bm. Spanish (?), captured 1807. Wrecked 23.10.1808 Gulf of Coro, West Indies.

VOLAGE 6th Rate 22, 523bm, 119 × 31·5ft. French privateer, captured 23.1.1798 by MELAMPUS off south-western Ireland. BU 8.1804.

VOLAGE 6th Rate 22, 530bm, 118 × 31·5ft. Chapman, Bideford, 23.3.1807. Sold 29.1.1818.

VOLAGE 6th Rate 28, 516bm, 111 × 32ft. Portsmouth DY 19.2.1825. Survey ship 4.1847; lent War Dept 19.10.1864 as powder hulk. BU comp. 12.12.1874 Chatham.

VOLAGE Iron screw corvette, 2,322bm, 3,080 tons, 270 × 42ft, 6—7in, 6—6·3in. Thames Iron Works, Blackwall, 27.2.1869. Sold 17.5.1904 Cohen, London, for BU. *Ordered as CERBERUS, renamed 2.5.1867.*

VOLAGE Destroyer, Modified 'W' class. John Brown, cancelled 12.1918.

VOLAGE Destroyer, 1,710 tons, 362·7 (oa) × 35·7ft, 4—4·7in, 2—40mm, 8—TT. White 15.12.1943. Frigate 1952, 2—4in, 2—40mm, Squid. Sold Pounds, Portsmouth, 28.10.1972.

VOLANTE Schooner. Origin unknown. Captured 1775 by Americans.

VOLATILE Submarine, 'V' class. Vickers Armstrong, Tyne, 20.6.1944. Lent Greek Navy 5.1946—10.1958 = TRIANA. Arr. 23.12.1958 Clayton & Davie, Dunston, for BU.

VOLATILLIA Galley 7, 100bm. Deptford 1602. Sold 1629.

VOLCANO Fireship 8, 247bm, 89 × 25·5ft, 8—32pdr carr. Purch. 1778, cd 31.7.1778. Sold 7.5.1781.

VOLCANO Bomb vessel 8. Purch. 1780, sold 8.1.1784.

VOLCANO (ex-*Cornwall*) Bomb vessel 8, 368bm, 100 × 29ft. Purch. 3.1797. Sold 22.12.1810.

VOLCANO Bomb vessel 8, 372bm, 105 × 29ft. Plymouth DY, ordered 18.5.1819, cancelled 10.1.1831.

VOLCANO Wood paddle sloop, 720bm, 150·5 × 33ft, 2—9pdr. Portsmouth DY 29.6.1836. Floating factory 1862. BU 11.1894 Portsmouth.

VOLCANO Destroyer, Modified 'W' class. John Brown, cancelled 12.1918.

VOLCANO *See also HERON 1804.*

VOLONTAIRE 5th Rate 38, 1,084bm, 152 × 40ft. French, captured 4.3.1806 The Cape. BU 2.1816.

VOLPE Gunvessel 1. Captured 1808? Lost 1809? *Not traced.*

VOLTIGEUR (ex-AUDACIEUX) Sloop 18, 408bm, 115 × 28·5ft. French privateer, captured 4.1798 by MAGNANIME. Sold 8.1802.

VOLUNTEER (ex-*Harmony*) Gunvessel 12,

135bm, 2—18pdr, 10—18pdr carr. Purch. 6.1804. Sold 6.1812.

VOLUNTEER Destroyer, Modified 'W' class. Denny 17.4.1919. Escort 1943. Sold 4.3.1947; arr. Granton 12.1947 for BU Brechin.

VORACIOUS Submarine, 'V' class. Vickers Armstrong, Tyne, 11.11.1943. Arr. 19.5.1946 Cochin, India, for BU.

VORSECHTERKITE Armed transport 167bm, 77·5 × 24ft. Dutch, captured 1800. Sold 1802.

VORTEX Submarine, 'V' class. Vickers Armstrong, Barrow, 19.8.1944. Lent French Navy 1944–47 = MORSE; lent Danish Navy 1947–16.1.1958 = SAELEN. Arr. 8.1958 Faslane for BU.

VORTIGERN Destroyer, 'V/W' class. White 15.10.1917. Sunk 15.3.1942 German MTB torpedo off Cromer.

VOTARY Destroyer, Modified 'W' class. Denny, LD 18.6.1918, cancelled 12.1918.

VOTARY Submarine, 'V' class. Vickers Armstrong, Tyne, 21.8.1944. Tx RNorN 7.1946 = UTHAUG; sold 1965.

VOX Submarine, 'U' class. Vickers Armstrong, Barrow, 23.1.1943. Lent French Navy 5.1943–7.1946 = CURIE. = P.67 in 7.1946. Arr. 2.5.1949 Ward, Milford Haven, for BU.

VOX Submarine, 'V' class. Vickers Armstrong, Barrow, 28.9.1943. Arr. 19.5.1946 Cochin for BU.

VOYAGER Destroyer, 'V/W' class. Stephen 8.5.1918. Tx RAN 10.1933. Grounded 23.9.1942 south coast of Timor after Japanese air attack, destroyed by crew.

VOYAGER Destroyer (RAN), 2,610 tons, 390 (oa) × 43ft, 6—4·5in, 8—40mm, 5—TT, Limbo. Cockatoo DY 1.3.1952. Sunk 11.2.1964 collision MELBOURNE off Jervis Bay.

VRYHEID (ex-VRIJHEID) 3rd Rate 72, 1,562bm, 167·5 × 46ft. Dutch, captured 11.10.1797 Battle of Camperdown. Prison ship 1799. Sold 6.1811.

VULCAN Fireship 8, 273bm, 91 × 25·5ft. Shish, Rotherhithe, 21.2.1691. Sunk 10.8.1709 breakwater Sheerness.

VULCAN (ex-*Hunter*) Fireship 8, 253bm, 89 × 26ft, 8—6pdr. Purch. 7.9.1739. Hulked 10.1743 Jamaica.

VULCAN (ex-*Mary*) Fireship 8, 225bm, 87 × 24·5ft, 8—6pdr. Purch. 21.8.1745. Sold 9.11.1749.

VULCAN Fireship. American merchantman, 1777. Sunk in action 10.10.1781 Yorktown.

VULCAN Fireship 14, 425bm, 109 × 29·5ft. Edwards, Shoreham, 12.9.1783. Destroyed to avoid capture 18.12.1793 evacuation of Toulon.

VULCAN (ex-*Hector*) Bomb vessel 10, 320bm. Purch. 1796. Sold 5.1802 Madagascar.

VULCAN Iron screw frigate, 1,747bm, 220 × 41ft. Ditchburn & Mare, Blackwall, 27.1.1849. Troopship 1851, 1,764bm. Sold 1.2.1867 as barque *Jorawur*.

VULCAN Depot ship cruiser, 6,620 tons, 350 × 58ft, 8—4·7in, 12—3pdr. Portsmouth DY 13.6.1889. = DEFIANCE III 17.2.1931. Arr. 12.1955 Belgium for BU.

VULCAN II *See ONYX 1892, LILY 1915.*

VULPINE Submarine, 'V' class. Vickers Armstrong, Tyne, 28.12.1943. Lent RDanN 9.1947–1958 = STOREN. Arr. 29.4.1959 Faslane for BU.

VULTURE Ketch 6. Royalist, captured 1648 by Parliamentarians. *Fate unknown.*

VULTURE 10-gun vessel, 88bm. Privateer, captured 1656. Sold 1663.

VULTURE Sloop 4, 68bm. Deptford 1673. Sold 1686.

VULTURE Fireship 8, 270bm, 93 × 25ft. Deptford 18.4.1690. Captured 10. 12.1708 by French in Atlantic.

VULTURE Sloop 14, 267bm, 91·5 × 26ft. Graves, Limehouse, 4.5.1744. Sold 30.1.1761.

VULTURE Sloop 14, 269bm, 91·5 × 26ft. Davis, Northam, 14.1.1763. BU 8.1771.

VULTURE Sloop 14, 304bm, 97 × 27ft. Wells, Deptford, 18.3.1776. Sold 8.1802.

VULTURE (ex-*Warrior*) Sloop 16, 391bm, 105 × 30ft. Purch. 6.1803. Sold 30.9.1814.

VULTURE Wood paddle frigate, 1,191bm, 190 × 37·5ft. Pembroke Dock 21.9.1843. Sold 1866 Castle, Charlton.

VULTURE Wood screw gunvessel, 664bm, 805 tons, 170 × 29ft, 1—7in, 2—40pdr. Sheerness DY 6.11.1869. Sold 9.1885 Castle, Charlton.

VULTURE Destroyer, 380 tons, 218 × 20ft, 1—12pdr, 2—TT. Thomson 22.3.1898. Sold 27.5.1919 Hayes, Porthcawl.

VULTURE *See also PEMBROKE PRIZE 1740.*

W

W.1 Submarine, 340 tons, 171·5 × 15·5ft, 2—TT. Armstrong 19.11.1914. Tx Italian Navy 23.8.1916.

W.2 Submarine, 340 tons, 150 × 17ft, 2—TT. Armstrong 15.2.1915. Tx Italian Navy 23.8.1916.

W.3 Submarine, 340 tons, 150 × 17ft, 2—TT. Armstrong 28.7.1915. Tx Italian Navy 23.8.1916.

W.4 Submarine, 340 tons, 150 × 17ft, 2—TT. Armstrong 11.9.1915. Tx Italian Navy 7.8.1916; lost 4.8.1917.

WAAKZAAMHEID 6th Rate 24, 504bm, 114·5 × 31·5ft. Dutch, captured 24.10.1798 by SIRIUS off Texel. Sold 9.1802.

WAGER 6th Rate 24, 559bm, 123 × 32ft. Purch. 21.11.1739. Wrecked 14.5.1741 south coast of Chile.

WAGER 6th Rate 24, 511bm, 112·5 × 32·5ft. Quallett, Rotherhithe, 2.6.1744. Sold 11.11.1763.

WAGER Destroyer, Modified 'W' class. Denny, LD 2.8.1918, cancelled 12.1918.

WAGER Destroyer, 1,710 tons, 362·7 (oa) × 35·7ft. 4—4·7in, 2—40mm, 8—TT. John Brown 1.11.1943. Tx Yugoslav Navy 10.1956 = PULA; withdrawn 1971.

WAGGA Minesweeper (RAN), 'Bathurst' class. Mort's Dock 25.7.1942. Sold 3.1962.

WAGLAN *See SEAFORD 1941.*

WAGTAIL Schooner 4, 76bm, 56·5 × 18·5ft, 4—12pdr carr. Lovewell, Yarmouth, 12.4.1806. Wrecked 13.2.1807 Azores.

WAIKATO Frigate (RNZN), 'Leander' class, Y160, 2,650 tons, 372 (oa) × 43ft, 2—4·5in, Seacat, helo. Harland & Wolff 18.2.1965. Scuttled 25.10.2000 artificial reef off Tutukaka Harbour.

WAKATAKA *See LABURNUM 1949.*

WAKE Destrover, Modified 'W' class. Denny, LD 14.10.1918, cancelled 12.1918.

WAKEFIELD 26-gun ship, 232bm, 90 × 24·5ft. Portsmouth 1655. = RICHMOND 1660. Fireship 1688–89. Sold 30.8.1698.

WAKEFUL Destroyer, 'V/W' class. John Brown 6.10.1917. Sunk 29.5.1940 by German MTB off Dunkirk.

WAKEFUL (ex-ZEBRA) Destroyer, 1,710 tons, 362·7 (oa) × 35·7ft, 4—4·7in, 2—40mm, 8—TT.

Fairfield 30.6.1943 (renamed 1.1943). Frigate 1953, 2—4in, 2—40mm, Squid. Sold Ward 10.6.1971; BU Inverkeithing.

WAKEFUL (ex-*Dan*, ex-*Hercules*) Tender, 492/65. Tug, orig. Swedish, cd 4.1974. PO 30.10.1987; sold 6.1988 Hellenic Salvage Tugboats = *Aegean Pelago.*

WAKEFUL *See also ZEBRA 1944.*

WALCHERN *See LST.3525 1945.*

WALDEGRAVE Destroyer, Modified 'W' class. Denny, cancelled 12.1918, not LD.

WALDEGRAVE Frigate, TE 'Captain' class. Bethlehem, Hingham, 4.12.1943 on Lend-Lease. Ret. USN 12.1945.

WALDEMAAR 3rd Rate 80. Danish, captured 7.9.1807 Battle of Copenhagen. Prison ship 1812. BU 8.1816. *Was to have been renamed YARMOUTH 1808.*

WALKER Destroyer, 'V/W' class. Denny 29.11.1917. Escort 5.1943. Sold 15.3.1946; BU Troon.

WALKERTON Coastal minesweeper, 'Ton'class. Thornycroft 21.11.1956. TS 1971 Dartmouth. PO 20.6.1986. Arr Middlesbrough 20.12.1990 to BU.

WALLACE (ex-*Lyons*) Iron paddle vessel, 128bm, 112·5 × 20ft. Purch. 7.1855. Sold 1869 Pollock & Brown.

WALLACE Destroyer leader, 1,750 tons, 329·25 (oa) × 32ft, 5—4·7in, 1—3in 6—TT. Thornycroft 26.10.1918. Escort 9.1939. Sold 20.3.1945; BU Clayton & Davie, Dunston.

WALLACEBURG Minesweeper (RCN), 'Algerine' class. Port Arthur SY 17.12.1942. Tx Belgian Navy 31.7.1959 = GEORGES LECOINTE. BU 1969.

WALLAROO (ex-PERSIAN) 2nd class cruiser, 2,575 tons, 265 × 41ft, 8—4·7in, 8—3pdr. Armstrong 5.2.1890 (renamed 2.4.1890). Harbour service 1906; = WALLINGTON 5.3.1919. Sold 27.2.1920 G. Sharpe.

WALLAROO Minesweeper (RAN), 'Bathurst' class. Poole & Steele 18.2.1942. Sunk 11.6.1943 collision SS *Gilbert Costin* off Fremantle.

WALLAROO (ex-*Grenville V*) Aux. minesweeper (RAN), 242 tons, 95·8 × 28ft. Singapore 1982; tug, purch. 11.8.1990.

WALLER Submarine (RAN), 'Collins' class, 3,051/
3,353 tons, 255·2 (oa) × 25·6ft, 6—TT. Australian
Submarine Corp., Adelaide, 14.3.1997.

WALLFLOWER Sloop, 'Arabis' class. Irvine SB
Co. 8.11.1915. Sold 28.8.1931 Ward, Inverkeithing.

WALLFLOWER Corvette, 'Flower' class. Smith's
Dock 14.11.1940. Sold 29.7.1946 = *Asbjorn
Larsen*.

WALLINGTON *See WALLAROO 1890.*

WALMER *See WEM 1919.*

WALMER CASTLE *See LEASIDE 1944.*

WALNEY (ex-SEBAGO) Cutter, 1,546 tons, 250
(oa) × 42ft, 2—5in, 2—6pdr. USN, cd RN
12.5.1941 on Lend-Lease. Sunk 8.11.1942 gunfire
shore batteries and French destroyers Oran.

WALNEY Minehunter, 'Sandown' class. Vosper-
Thornycroft 25.11.1991.

WALPOLE Destroyer, 'V/W' class. Doxford
12.2.1918. Mined 6.1.1945 North Sea, not
repaired. Sold 8.2.1945; BU Ward, Grays.

WALRUS Destroyer, 'V/W' class. Fairfield
27.12.1917. Stranded 12.2.1938 Filey Bay; refloated 29.3.1938, BU 10.1938.

WALRUS Aircraft transport, 990 tons, 160 × 30ft.
Blyth DD Co. 28.5.1945. = SKUA 1953. Sold
28.2.1962; mercantile 12.1962.

WALRUS Submarine, 'Porpoise' class, Scotts
22.9.1959. Sold Seaforth Group 1987 to refit for
resale; BU Grimsby 1991.

WALTON Destroyer, Modified 'W' class. Denny,
cancelled 12.1918, not LD.

WANDERER 6th Rate 20, 431bm, 109·5 × 30ft,
16—32pdr carr., 6—12pdr carr., 2—6pdr. Betts,
Mistleythorn, 29.9.1806. Sold 6.3.1817.

WANDERER Brig-sloop 16, 428bm, 100·5 ×
32·5ft, 14—32pdr, 2—9pdr. Chatham DY
10.7.1835. BU 3.1850 Chatham.

WANDERER Wood screw gunvessel, 675bm, 181
× 28·5ft, 1—110pdr, 1—68pdr, 2—20pdr. Green,
Blackwall, 22.11.1855. Arr. 31.8.1866 Castle,
Charlton, for BU.

WANDERER Composite screw sloop, 925 tons,
157 × 32ft, 2—5in. Raylton Dixon, Middlesbrough
8.2.1883. Training brig 1894. Sold Ward 2.1907
for BU Preston.

WANDERER Paddle ferry 1917. = WARDEN
1918–21.

WANDERER Destroyer, Modified 'W' class.
Fairfield 1.5.1919. Escort 4.1943. Sold 1.1946; BU
Hughes Bolckow, Blyth.

WARBURTON Frigate (RAN), 'River' class. Evans
Deakin, ordered 2.6.1942, cancelled 12.6.1944.

WARKWORTH CASTLE Corvette 'Castle' class.
Fleming & Ferguson, cancelled 12.1943.

WARMINGHAM Inshore minesweeper, 'Ham'
class. Thornycroft, Hampton, 23.4.1954. Sold
Pounds 1983.

WARNING (ex-STEECE) Signal station vessel,
97bm, 70·5 × 18ft. Danish gun-brig, captured
1807. Sold 15.12.1814.

WARRAMUNGA Destroyer (RAN), 1,927 tons,
377·5 (oa) × 36·5ft, 6—4·7in, 2—4in, 4—TT.
Cockatoo DY 7.2.1942. Sold 15.2.1963 for BU
Japan.

WARRAMUNGA (ex-WARUMUNGU) Frigate
(RAN), 'Anzac' class. Tenix Defence Systems,
Williamstown, 23.5.1998.

WARREGO Sloop (RAN), 1,060 tons, 250 × 36ft,
3—4in. Cockatoo DY 10.2.1940. BU 1966 Rozelle
Bay, Sydney.

WARREGO Destroyer (RAN), 700 tons, 246 (oa) ×
24ft, 1—4in, 3—12pdr, 3—TT. Fairfield 4.4.1911 in
sections, re-erected Sydney, launched 4.1911.
Dismantled 9.1929 Cockatoo DY. *Hull sank
22.7.1931 Cockatoo wharf, later blown up.*

WARREN Destroyer, Modified 'W' class. Chatham
DY (ex-Fairfield), cancelled 9.1919.

WARREN HASTINGS Troopship (RIM), 3,910
tons. NC&A (Vickers) 18.4.1893. Wrecked
14.1.1897 Réunion.

WARRINGTON 30-gun ship, 200bm. Purch. or
hired 14.7.1692. Captured 1693 by French.

WARRIOR 3rd Rate 74, 1,642bm 169 × 47·5ft.
Portsmouth DY 18.16.1781. Receiving ship 1818;
convict ship 2.1840. BU comp. 12.1857 Woolwich.

WARRIOR Iron armoured ship, 6,109bm, 9,210
tons, 380 × 58·5ft, 11—110pdr, 26—68pdr.
Thames Iron Works, Blackwall, 29.12.1860. Depot
ship 7.1902; = VERNON III 3.1904; hulk
WARRIOR 1923; = C.77 in 1945. = WARRIOR,
HO for preservation 1979.

WARRIOR Armoured cruiser, 13,550 tons, 480 ×
73·5ft, 6—9in, 4—7.5in, 24—3pdr. Pembroke Dock
25.11.1905. Disabled 31.5.1916 Battle of Jutland,
foundered 1.6.1916.

WARRIOR (ex-BRAVE) Aircraft carrier, 13,350
tons, 630 × 80ft, 19—40mm, 48 aircraft. Harland
& Wolff 20.5.1944 (renamed 1942). Lent RCN
1.1946–2.1948. Tx Argentine Navy 7.1958,
= INDEPENDENCIA 11.1958; deleted 1.1971, BU.

WARRNAMBOOL Minesweeper (RAN), 'Bathurst' class. Mort's Dock, Sydney, 8.5.1941. Sunk
13.9.1947 mine off Cockburn Reef, Queensland.

WARRNAMBOOL Patrol vessel (RAN), 211 tons.
Cairns 25.10.1980.

WARSASH *See BOULSTON 1952, ALFRISTON
1953.*

WARSPIGHT *See WARSPITE 1596.*

WARSPITE (WARSPIGHT) Galleon, 648bm, 2—60pdr. 2—34pdr, 13—18pdr, 10—9pdr, 2—6pdr. Built 1596. Harbour service 1635. Sold 1649.

WARSPITE 3rd Rate 70, 898bm, 142 × 38ft. Johnson & Castle, Blackwall, 8.6.1666. Rebuilt Rotherhithe 1702 as 952bm; = EDINBURGH 2.1.1716; rebuilt Chatham 1721 as 1,119 bm; rebuilt Chatham 1744 as 1,286bm, 64 guns. BU 12.1771 Plymouth.

WARSPITE 3rd Rate 74, 1,580bm, 166 × 47ft. West, Deptford, 8.4.1758. Harbour service 1778. = ARUNDEL 3.1800. BU 11.1801.

WARSPITE 3rd Rate 76, 1,890bm, 180 × 49ft. Chatham DY 16.11.1807. Reduced to 50 guns 1840; lent Marine Society 27.3.1862 as TS. Burnt 3.1.1876 accident Woolwich; wreck sold 2.2.1876 McArthur & Co.

WARSPITE Armoured cruiser, 8,400 tons, 315 × 62ft, 4—9·2in, 6—6in. Chatham DY 29.1.1884. Sold 4.4.1905 Ward, Preston; arr. Mersey 3.10.1905, then Preston, for BU.

WARSPITE Battleship, 27,500 tons, 644·8 (oa) × 90·5ft, 8—15in, 14—6in. Devonport DY 26.11.1913. Sold 12.7.1946; wrecked 23.4.1947 under tow to breakers, wreck resold R. H. Bennett, Bristol.

WARSPITE Nuclear submarine, 4,400/4,900 tons, 285 (oa) × 33ft, SubHarpoon, 6—TT. Vickers Armstrong, Barrow, 25.9.1965. PO by 6.1991 at Devonport, LU *in situ*.

WARSPITE *See also WATERLOO 1833, HERMIONE 1893.*

WARWICK (OLD WARWICK) 22-gun ship, 186bm. Privateer, captured 1643; renamed 1650. BU 1660.

WARWICK 4th Rate 48, 909bm, 130·5 × 34·5ft. Deptford 1696. Rebuilt Rotherhithe 1710 as 721bm. BU 1726.

WARWICK 4th Rate 60, 951bm, 144 × 39ft. Plymouth DY 25.10.1733. Captured 11.3.1756 by French L'ATLANTE. Recaptured 24.1.1761 by MINERVA, BU.

WARWICK 4th Rate 50, 1,073bm, 151 × 40ft. Portsmouth DY 28.2.1767. Receiving ship 9.1783. Sold 24.3.1802.

WARWICK Destroyer, 'V/W' class. Hawthorn Leslie 28.12.1917. Escort 5.1943. Sunk 20.2.1944 by U.413 off north Cornwall.

WARWICK *See also CONSTANT WARWICK 1649.*

WASAGA Minesweeper (RCN), TE 'Bangor' class. Burrard 12.12.1940. Sold 1946 Marine Industries.

WASKESIU Frigate (RCN), 'River' class. Yarrow, Esquimalt 6.12.1942. Sold 1947, = *Hooghly* 1950.

WASP Sloop 8, 140bm, 73·5 × 21ft. Portsmouth DY 4.7.1749. Sold 4.1.1781.

WASP Brig-sloop 16, 207bm, 73·5 × 26ft. Folkestone 1780, purch. 1782. Fireship 4.1798, 8—18pdr. Expended 7.7.1800 Dunkirk Roads.

WASP Gunvessel 4, 63bm 64·5 × 14·5ft. Dutch hoy, purch. 3.1794. Sold 22.11.1801.

WASP Brig-sloop 18, 'Cruizer' class, 387bm. Davy, Topsham, 9.7.1812. BU 9.1847.

WASP Wood screw sloop, 973bm, 186·5 × 34ft, 2—68pdr, 12—32pdr. Deptford DY 28.5.1850. Sold 2.12.1869 Marshall.

WASP Composite screw gunboat, 465 tons, 125 × 23·5ft, 2—64pdr, 2—20pdr. Barrow SB (Vickers) 5.10.1880. Wrecked 9.1884 Tory I.; wreck sold 11.1910 Cornish Salvage Co.

WASP Torpedo boat (Australian), 12 tons, 63 × 8ft, 1—TT. Thornycroft, Chiswick 1884. Sold c. 1906.

WASP Composite screw gunboat, 715 tons, 165 × 29ft, 6—4in. Armstrong Mitchell 13.9.1886. Foundered c. 10.10.1887 after leaving Singapore.

WASP *See also ESPION 1782, GUEPE 1800.*

WASPERTON Coastal minesweeper, 'Ton' class. White, Southampton, 28.2.1956. Sold Pounds 1986.

WASSANAER 3rd Rate 64, 1,270bm, 169 × 42·5ft. Dutch, captured 11.10.1797 Battle of Camperdown. Powder hulk 1804. Sold 13.8.1818 J. Ledger for BU.

WATCHFUL (ex-*Jane*) Gunvessel 12, 169bm, 76 × 23ft, 10—18pdr carr., 2—9pdr. Purch. 6.1804. Tender 3.1811. Sold 3.11.1814.

WATCHFUL Wood screw gunboat, 'Clown' class. Smith, North Shields, 4.6.1856. Sold 1.2.1871 in Hong Kong.

WATCHFUL Composite screw gunboat, 560 tons, 135 × 26ft, 2—5in, 2—4in. Laird 13.2.1883. BDV 1903. Sold 14.5.1907.

WATCHFUL Coastguard vessel, 612 tons, 154 (oa) × 25ft, 2—3pdr. Hall Russell 26.4.1911. Sold 15.5.1920 Newfoundland Govt.

WATCHFUL *Name borne in succession as fishery protection vessels by MFV.1080 (10.1946–11.1955), ML.2840 (11.1955–1.1959), BROOMLEY (10.1.1959–1965).*

WATCHMAN Destroyer, 'V/W' class. John Brown 2.12.1917. Escort 1941. BU 7.1945 Ward, Inverkeithing.

WATERFLY River gunboat, 'Fly' class. Yarrow 1915. Sold 17.2.1923 Anglo Persian Oil Co., Basra.

WATERHEN Destroyer, 'V/W' class. Palmer 26.3.1918. Tx RAN 10.1933. Sank 30.6.1941 off Sollum after air attack previous day.

WATERHEN Sloop, 1,350 tons, 283 × 38·5ft, 6—4in. Denny, cancelled 2.11.1945.

WATERHEN Destroyer (RAN), 2,610 tons, 390 (oa) × 43ft, 6—4·5in, 6—40mm, 10—TT. Williamstown DY, cancelled 1954.

WATERHOUND 32-gun ship. Captured 1652. Sold 1656.

WATERLOO (ex-TALAVERA) 3rd Rate 80, 2,056bm, 192 × 50ft. Portsmouth DY 16.10.1818 (renamed 23.7.1817). = BELLEROPHON 5.10.1824; harbour service 1848. Sold 12.1.92 J. Read.

WATERLOO 1st Rate 120, 2,694bm, 218 × 55ft. Chatham DY 10.6,1833; undocked 12.11.1859 as screw ship. = CONQUEROR 27.2.1862, 2,845bm; = WARSPITE (TS, Marine Society) 11.8.1876. Burnt 20.1.1918 R. Thames.

WATERLOO Destroyer, 2,380 tons, 355 × 40ft, 5—4·5in, 8—40mm, 10—TT. Fairfield, LD 14.6.1945, cancelled 10.1945.

WATERWAY (ex-TOMAHAWK) Dock landing ship, 4,270 tons, 454 × 72ft, 1—3in, 16—20mm. Newport News 24.5.1944 for RN (renamed 8.1943); retained USN = SHADWELL.

WATERWITCH Brig-sloop 10, 319bm, 90·5 × 29·5ft, 8—18pdr carr., 2—6pdr. Yacht, purch. 15.11.1834. Sold 22.11.1861 Castle, Charlton.

WATERWITCH Iron hydraulic gunboat, 777bm, 1,205 tons, 162 × 32ft, 2—7in, 2—20pdr. Thames Iron Works, Blackwall, 28.6.1866. Sold 26.4.1890 Castle, Charlton.

WATERWITCH (ex-*Lancashire Witch*) Iron screw survey vessel, 620 tons, 160 × ?ft. Purch. 17.3.1893. Rammed and sunk 1.9.1912 while at anchor Singapore.

WATERWITCH (ex-*Rechid Pasha*) Despatch vessel, 400 tons, 165 (oa) × 26ft. Turkish, purch. 1915 on completion by Fairfield. Sold 1921 Turkish Govt.

WATERWITCH Minesweeper, 'Algerine' class. Lobnitz 22.4.1943. Sold G. Deckers 9.10.1970.

WATERWITCH *See also POWDERHAM 1958.*

WATSON Destroyer, Modified 'W' class. Devonport DY (ex-Fairfield), cancelled 9.1919.

WATT *See RETRIBUTION 1844.*

WAVE Wood screw gunboat, 'Albacore' class. Wigram, Northam, 25.6.1856. Coal hulk 1869; = CLINKER 30.12.1882. Sold 1890.

WAVE (ex-*Edeline*) Wood screw tender, 308 tons, 134 × ?ft. Purch. 27.11.1882. Sold 1907.

WAVE (ex-*Buyak Ada*) Despatch vessel, 400 tons, 201 × 28ft. Rennie Forrest, Wivenhoe, 7.2.1914; Turkish, purch. 1914. = WAYWARD 8.1919. Foundered under tow 11.11.1922 off coast of Anatolia.

WAVE Destroyer, Modified 'W' class. Fairfield, cancelled 12.1918.

WAVE Minesweeper, 'Algerine' class. Lobnitz 18.8.1944. Arr. 4.4.1962 King, Gateshead, for BU.

WAVE RIDER Aux. minesweeper (RAN). Fishing vessel, leased 4.1989–3.1991.

WAVENEY Destroyer, 550 tons, 220 × 23·5ft, 1—12pdr, 5—6pdr (1907: 4—12pdr), 2—TT. Hawthorn 16.4.1903. Sold 10.2.1920 Ward, Grays.

WAVENEY Frigate, 'River' class. Smith's Dock 30.4.1942. Arr. 12.1957 Troon for BU.

WAVENEY (ex-AMETHYST) Minehunter, 890 tons (full load), 156·3 (oa) × 34·5ft, 1—40mm. Richards, Lowestoft, 8.9.1983. Tx Bangladeshi Navy 3.9.1994 = SHAPLA.

WAVERLEY *See LYDIARD 1914.*

WAYFARER Destroyer, Modified 'W' class, cancelled 12.1918, not ordered.

WAYLAND (ex-ANTONIA) Repair ship, 18,750 tons, 528 × 65ft, 4—4in. Purch. 1940, conversion comp. 17.8.1942 (renamed 1942). Sold 1.1948; arr. Cairnryan 4.1948, Troon 4.1949 for BU.

WAYWARD *See WAVE 1914.*

WEAR Destroyer, 550 tons, 222 × 23·5ft, 1—12pdr, 5—6pdr (1907: 4—12pdr), 2—TT. Palmer 21.1.1905. Sold 4.11.1919 Ward, Grays.

WEAR Frigate, 'River' class. Smith's Dock 1.6.1942. Arr. 29.10.1957 Young, Sunderland, for BU.

WEAZEL Wood screw gunboat, 'Dapper' class. Pitcher, Northfleet, 19.3.1855. Sold 18.11.1869 in Hong Kong.

WEAZEL Iron screw gunboat, 'Ant' class. Laird 4.9.1873. = C.118 (oil fuel lighter) 1904.

WEAZEL (ex-*Sir W. Green*) Tender, 110 tons, 80 × 17ft. War Dept vessel, tx 1906 (renamed 26.11.1906). = STOAT 1.12.1918. Sold 14.9.1923.

WEAZEL Destroyer, Modified 'W' class. Fairfield, cancelled 12.1918.

WEAZLE Sloop 10, 128bm, 72 × 20ft. Dummer, Blackwall 1704. Sold 20.11.1712.

WEAZLE Sloop 8, 102bm, 61·5 × 20ft. Woolwich DY 7.11.1721. Sold 30.11.1732.

WEAZLE Sloop 16, 308bm, 94·5 × 27·5ft. Taylor & Randall, Rotherhithe 22.5.1745, purch. on stocks 22.4.1745. Captured 13.1.1779 by French BOUDEUSE in West Indies.

WEAZLE Brig-sloop 14, 202bm, 79 × 25·5ft. Hills, Sandwich, 18.4.1783. Wrecked 12.1.1799 Barnstaple Bay.

WEAZLE Brig-sloop 16, 214bm, 77 × 26ft, 12—10pdr carr., 4—6pdr. King, Dover, 1799, purch. 3.1799. Wrecked 1.3.1804 off Gibraltar.

WEAZLE Brig-sloop 18, 'Cruizer' class, 388bm. Owen, Topsham, 2.3.1805. Sold 23.11.1815.

WEAZLE Schooner 10, 141bm. Purch. 1808. Listed 1811.

WEAZLE Brig-sloop 10, 'Cherokee' class, 237bm. Chatham DY 26.3.1822. Sold 30.4.1844 W. Beech for BU.

WEDGEPORT Minesweeper, TE 'Bangor' class. Dufferin, Toronto, 2.8.1941. Sold 11.9.1946.

WELCOME Pink 8, 100bm. Listed 1644. Captured 1647 by French.

WELCOME 36-gun ship, 367bm. Captured 1652. Sunk 6.1667 blockship R. Medway.

WELCOME 36-gun ship, 400bm. Captured 1652. Expended 1673 as fireship.

WELCOME Destroyer, Modified 'W' class. Hawthorn Leslie, LD 9.4.1918, cancelled 12.1918.

WELCOME Minesweeper, 'Algerine class. Lobnitz 14.11.1944. Arr. 3.5.1962 Dunston for BU Dorkin.

WELFARE King's ship. Mentioned 1350.

WELFARE Destroyer, Modified 'W' class. Hawthorn Leslie, LD 22.6.1918, cancelled 12.1918.

WELFARE Minesweeper, 'Algerine' class. Redfern 15.7.1943. BU 11.1957 Ward, Grays.

WELLAND Destroyer, 590 tons, 225 × 23.5ft, 1—12pdr, 5—6pdr (1907: 4—12pdr), 2—TT. Yarrow 14.4.1904. Sold 30.6.1920 Ward, Preston.

WELLESLEY 3rd Rate 74, 1,746bm, 176 × 48.5ft. Bombay DY 24.2.1815. Guardship 1854; = CORNWALL (TS) 18.6.1868. Sunk 24.9.1940 air attack R. Thames.

WELLESLEY Destroyer, Modified 'W' class. Hawthorn Leslie, LD 30.8.1918, cancelled 12.18.

WELLESLEY *See also CORNWALL 1812.*

WELLESLEY No 2 *See BOSCAWEN 1844.*

WELLINGTON Sloop, 990 tons, 250 × 36ft, 2—4.7in, 1—3in. Devonport DY 29.5.1934. Sold 6.2.1947 as HQ ship for The Hon. Company of Master Mariners.

WELLINGTON *See also ORESTE 1810, HERO 1816, BACCHANTE 1968.*

WELLS Cutter 10, 84bm, 48 × 21ft. Folkestone 6.1764. Sold 24.11.1780.

WELLS (ex-TILLMAN) Destroyer, 1,090 tons, 309 × 30.5ft, 1—4in, 1—3in, 3—TT. USN, cd RN 5.12.1940. Sold 24.7.1945; BU Troon.

WELSHMAN Minelayer, 2,650 tons, 418 (oa) × 40ft, 6—4.7in, 160mines. Hawthorn Leslie 4.9.1940. Sunk 1.2.1943 by U.617 off Crete.

WEM (ex-WALMER) Minesweeper, Later 'Hunt' class. Simons 12.9.1919 (renamed 1918). Sold 22.4.1921 Cutch Steam Navigation Co.

WEMBDON Minesweeper, Later 'Hunt' class. Simons, cancelled 1919.

WENNINGTON Coastal minesweeper, 'Ton' class. Doig, Grimsby, 6.4.1955. Tx Indian Navy 30.8.1956 = CUDDALORE; deleted 1984.

WENSLEYDALE Destroyer, 'Hunt' class Type III.

Yarrow 20.6.1942. Damaged collision 11.1944, not repaired. Sold 15.2.1946; arr. 2.1947 Hughes Bolckow, Blyth, for BU.

WENTWORTH Frigate (RCN), 'River' class. Yarrow, Esquimalt, 6.3.1943. Sold 17.11.1947 Halifax SY; BU 1948 Dominion Steel Corp.

WEREWOLF Destroyer, Modified 'W' class. White 17.7.1919, not comp, cancelled 9.1919, BU.

WESER (ex-SALAMANDER) Iron paddle gunboat, 590bm, 178 (wl) × 26ft, 4—8in. Prussian, taken 12.1.1855 with RECRUIT in exchange for frigate THETIS. Harbour service 1866. Sold 29.10.1873 Malta.

WESER 5th Rate 44, 1,081bm. French, captured 21.10.1813 by squadron off Ushant. Sold 17.9.1817 for BU.

WESSEX Destroyer, 'V/W' class. Hawthorn Leslie 12.3.1918. Sunk 24.5.1940 air attack off Calais.

WESSEX (ex-ZENITH) Destroyer, 1,710 tons, 362.7 (oa) × 35.7ft, 4—4.7in, 5—40mm, 8—TT. Fairfield 2.9.1943 (renamed 1.1943). Tx SAN = JAN VAN RIEBEECK 29.3.1950; limited conv. frigate 1964–66, 4—4in, 4—40mm, 4—TT, helo; sunk 25.3.1980 target off Cape Town.

WESSEX *See also ERNE 1940, DERG 1943, ZENITH 1944.*

WESTBURY Frigate (RCN), 'River' class. Montreal, cancelled 12.1943.

WESTCOTT Destroyer, 'V/W' class. Denny 14.2.1918. Escort 7.1943. Sold 8.1.1946 for BU West of Scotland S. Bkg Co.

WESTERGATE 34-gun ship, 274bm. Captured 1653. Lost 1664 West Indies.

WESTERNLAND (ex-*Regina*) Repair ship, 16,479grt, 575 × 68ft. Purch. 1.1943. Sold 7.1947; BU Hughes Bolckow, Blyth.

WESTERNPORT Inshore minesweeper (RAN), 178 tons, 101.7 (oa) × 29.5ft, 2—12.7mm, Projected 1987, not comp.

WESTMINSTER Destroyer, 'V/W' class. Scotts 24.2.1918. Escort 12.1939. Sold 4.3.1947; BU 8.1948 Metal Industries.

WESTMOUNT Minesweeper (RCN), TE 'Bangor' class. Dufferin 14.3.1942. Tx Turkish Navy 29.3.1958 = BORNOVA; deleted 1972.

WESTON (ex-WESTON SUPER MARE) Sloop, 1,060 tons, 250 × 34ft, 2—4in. Devonport DY 23.7.1932 (renamed 1932). Sold 22.5.1947; BU Howells, Gelleswick Bay.

WESTPHAL Destroyer. Modified 'W' class. White (ex-Hawthorn Leslie), cancelled 12.1918.

WESTWARD HO! Destroyer, Modified 'W' class. White (ex-Hawthorn Leslie), cancelled 12.1918.

WETASKIWIN *See BANFF 1940.*

WETHERBY Paddle minesweeper, 'Ascot' class, 820 tons. Murdoch & Murray 2.3.1918. Sold 10.6.1924 Alloa S. Bkg Co., Charlestown.

WEWAK Landing craft (RAN), 310 tons, 146 (oa) × 33ft. Walker 18.5.1973.

WEXFORD (ex-FLEETWOOD) 14-gun ship, 150bm. Royalist, captured 1655 by Parliamentarians. = DOLPHIN 1660. Expended 1665 fireship.

WEXFORD Minesweeper, Later 'Hunt' class. Simons 10.10.1919. Sold 1.12.1921 Stanlee; resold mercantile. Served in WW2 as DOOMBA.

WEXHAM Inshore minesweeper, 'Ham' class. Taylor, Shoreham, 3.4.1954. Tx French Navy 1955 = M.772/ARMOISE; deleted 1987.

WEYBOURNE Minesweeper, Later 'Hunt' class. Inglis 21.2.1919. Sold 4.10.1928 Ward, Pembroke Dock.

WEYBURN Corvette (RCN), 'Flower' class. Port Arthur SY 26.7.1941. Sunk 22.2.1943 mine off Gibraltar.

WEYMOUTH (ex-CAVENDISH) 14-gun ship, 230bm. Royalist, captured 1645 by Parliamentarians. Sold 1662.

WEYMOUTH 4th Rate 48, 673bm, 132·5 × 34·5ft. Portsmouth DY 1693. Rebuilt Woolwich 1718 as 715bm. BU comp. 6.1.1732.

WEYMOUTH 4th Rate 60, 1,061bm, 144 × 41·5ft. Plymouth DY 31.3.1736. Wrecked 16.2.1745 Antigua.

WEYMOUTH 4th Rate 60, 1,198bm, 150 × 43ft. Plymouth DY 1752. BU comp. 12.2.1772 Chatham.

WEYMOUTH (ex-*Earl Mansfield*) 4th Rate 56, 1,434bm, 175·5 × 43ft. Wells, Rotherhithe, 30.9.1795; East Indiaman, purch. on stocks. Storeship, 26 guns, 1798. Wrecked 21.1.1900 Lisbon Bar.

WEYMOUTH (ex-*Wellesley*) 5th Rate 36, 826bm, 136 × 37ft. Indiaman, purch. 1804. Storeship, 16 guns, 1811; convict ship 10.1828. Sold 10.3.1865 Bermuda.

WEYMOUTH Wood screw corvette, 1,857bm, 225 × 43ft. Sheerness DY, LD 10.1860, cancelled 12.12.1863.

WEYMOUTH 2nd class cruiser, 5,250 tons, 430 × 48·5ft, 8–6in. Armstrong 18.11.1910. Sold 2.10.1928 Hughes Bolckow, Blyth.

WEYMOUTH *See also LEANDER 1961.*

WHADDON Destroyer, 'Hunt' class Type I. Stephen 16.7.1940. Arr. 5.4.1959 Faslane for BU S. Bkg. Industries.

WHARTON Survey ship, 1,565 tons, ordered Chatham DY 20.6.1949 ,cancelled 19.9.1951.

WHEATLAND Destroyer, 'Hunt' class Type II.

Yarrow 7.6.1941. Hulk 1955. Arr. 20.9.1957 McLellan, Bo'ness, for BU.

WHEELER Destroyer, Modified 'W' class. Scotts, LD 7.1918, cancelled 12.1918.

WHELP Destroyer, Modified 'W' class. Pembroke Dock (ex-Scotts), cancelled 9.1919.

WHELP Destroyer, 1,710 tons, 362·7 (oa) × 35·7ft, 4–4·7in, 6–40mm, 8–TT. Hawthorn Leslie 3.6.1943. Tx SAN = SIMON VAN DER STEL 23.2.1953; limitd conv. frigate 1963, 4–4in, 4–40mm, 4–TT, helo; BU 1976 Durban.

WHELP *See also LIONS WHELP sloops 1627.*

WHIMBREL Sloop, 1,300 tons, 299·5 (oa) × 37·5ft, 6–4in. Yarrow 25.8.1942. Sold 11.1949 Egygtian Navy = El MALEK FAROUK; = TARIQ 1954; for preservation?

WHIMBREL (ex-NSC.1012) Repair craft, 200 tons, 171 × 39ft. LCT, renamed 1954. Sold Pounds 6.1881; resold mercantile.

WHIP Destroyer, Modified 'W' class. Scotts, cancelled 12.1918.

WHIPPET Destroyer, Modified 'W' class. Scotts, cancelled 12.1918.

WHIPPINGHAM Inshore minesweeper, 'Ham' class. Taylor, Chertsey, 28.8.1954. Tx French Navy 1955 = M.786/DAHLIA; deleted 1992.

WHIPSTER Brigantine 4, 64bm. Deptford 1672. Sold 1683.

WHIRLWIND Destroyer, 'V/W' class. Swan Hunter 15.12.1917. Sunk 5.7.1940 by U.34 southwest of Ireland.

WHIRLWIND Destroyer, 1,710 tons, 362·7 (oa) × 35·7ft, 4–4·7in, 5–40mm, 8–TT. Hawthorn Leslie 30.8.1943. Frigate 1953, 2–4in, 2–40mm, Squid. Foundered Cardigan Bay 29.10.1974 target.

WHITAKER Destroyer, Modified 'W' class. Denny, cancelled 12.1918.

WHITAKER Frigate, TE 'Captain' class. Bethlehem, Hingham, 12.12.1943 on Lend-Lease. Damaged 1.11.1944 by U.483 off Malin Head, not repaired. Nominally ret. USN 3.1945; BU 1948 Whitchurch.

WHITBY Storeship 14, 434bm, 108 × 30ft, 14–6pdr. Purch. 12.1780. Sold 27.10.1785.

WHITBY Corvette (RCN), Modified 'Flower' class. Midland SY 18.9.1943. Sold 30.8.1946 = *Bengo*.

WHITBY Frigate, 2,150 tons, 360 × 41ft, 2–4·5in, 2–40mm. Cammell Laird 2.7.1954. Sold 30.10.1978; BU Queenborough.

WHITE BEAR 40-gun ship, 729bm, 3–60pdr, 11–34pdr, 7–18pdr, 10–9pdr, 9 smaller. Built 1563; rebuilt 1599 as 732bm. Sold 1629.

WHITE BEAR Destroyer, Modified 'W' class. Fairfield, cancelled 12.1918.

WHITE ROSE Flyboat 6, 180bm. Captured 1666. Sold 1667.

WHITEHALL Destroyer, Modified 'W' class. Swan Hunter 11.9.1919, comp. Chatham 7.1924. Escort 8.1942. Arr. Ward, Barrow, 25.7.1945 for BU.

WHITEHAVEN Armed ship 14. Origin unknown. Burnt 9.1747 accident off coast of Ireland. *Probably hired.*

WHITEHAVEN Minesweeper, turbine 'Bangor' class. Philip, Dartmouth, 29.5.1941. Arr.8.1948 Ward, Briton Ferry, for BU.

WHITEHEAD Destroyer, Modified 'W' class. Swan Hunter, cancelled 12.1918.

WHITEHEAD Trials vessel, 2,900 tons. Scotts 5.5.1970. Sold INCOM; towed to India, arr 9.1993 for BU.

WHITEHORSE MCDV (RCN), 'Kingston' class, 962 tons, 181·4 (oa) × 37·1ft, 1—40mm, Halifax SY 28.2.1997.

WHITESAND BAY (ex-LOCH LUBNAIG) Frigate, 'Bay' class. Harland & Wolff 16.12.1944 (renamed 1944). Arr. 13.2.1956 S. Bkg Industries, Charlestown, for BU.

WHITING 6-gun vessel, 45bm. Captured 6.1711. Sold 10.4.1712 P. Ford.

WHITING Schooner 4, 78bm, 56 × 18ft, 4—12pdr carr. Bermuda 1805. Captured 22.8.1812 by French privateer LE DILIGENT North America.

WHITING (ex-ARROW) Schooner 12, 225bm, 98 × 24ft, 12—12pdr carr. American, captured 1812. Wrecked 21.9.1816 Padstow harbour.

WHITING Wood screw gunboat, 'Albacore' class. Wigram, Northam, 9.1.1856. BU 12.1881.

WHITING Torpedo gunboat, 735 tons, 230 × 27ft, 2—4·7in, 4—3pdr. Armstrong Mitchell 24.7.1889. = BOOMERANG 2.4.1890. Sold 11.7.1905 Portsmouth.

WHITING Destroyer, 360 tons, 215 × 21ft, 1—12pdr, 5—6pdr, 2—TT. Palmer 26.8.1896. Sold 27.11.1919 in Hong Kong; BU China

WHITLEY Destroyer, 'V/W' class. Doxford 13.4.1918. Escort 10.1938. Beached 19.5.1940 nr Nieuport after air attack.

WHITSHED Destroyer, Modified 'W' class. Swan Hunter 31.1.1919. Sold 18.2.1947, arr. 4.1948 King, Gateshead, for BU.

WHITTON Coastal minesweeper, 'Ton' class. Fleetlands SY. Launched 30.1.1956 as CANNANORE (Indian Navy). PO 1980; deleted 1984.

WHYALLA (ex-GLENELG) Minesweeper, 'Bathurst' class. Broken Hill, Whyalla, 12.5.1941 (renamed 3.1941). Lent RAN from 1.1942. Sold 9.5.1947 as pilot vessel *Rip*.

WHYALLA Patrol boat (RAN), 211 tons. Cairns 22.5.1982.

WICKLOW *See REPTON 1919.*

WIDEMOUTH BAY (ex-LOCH FRISA) Frigate, 'Bay' class. Harland & Wolff 19.10.1944 (renamed 1944). Arr. 23.11.1957 Hughes Bolckow, Blyth, for BU.

WIDGEON Schooner 4, 80bm, 56 × 18ft, 4—12pdr carr. Wheaton, Brixham, 19.6.1806. Wrecked 20.4.1808 Scottish coast.

WIDGEON Wood paddle packet, 164bm, 200 tons, 108 × 18ft. Chatham DY 12.9.1837. Sold 3.1884.

WIDGEON Composite screw gunboat, 805 tons, 165 × 31ft, 6—4in, 2—3pdr. Pembroke Dock 9.8.1889. Sold 15.5.1906 Castle, Charlton.

WIDGEON River gunboat, 195 tons, 2—6pdr. Yarrow 16.4.1904. Sold 10.1931 Shanghai.

WIDGEON Patrol vessel, 530 tons, 234 × 26·5ft, 1—4in. Yarrow 2.2.1938. Sold 21.4.1947; arr. 25.9.1947 King, Gateshead, for BU.

WIDNES (ex-WITHERNSEA) Minesweeper, Later 'Hunt' class. Napier & Miller 28.6.1918 (renamed 1918). Beached 20.5.1941 Suda Bay after air attack; salved by Germans, = 12.V4 (patrol vessel), = UJ.2109; sunk 17.10.1943 RN destroyers in Dodecanese.

WIGMORE CASTLE Corvette, 'Castle' class. Midland SY, cancelled 12.1941.

WIGTOWN BAY (ex-LOCH GARASDALE) Frigate, 'Bay' class. Harland & Wolff 26.4.1945 (renamed 1944). Arr. 4.1959 Faslane for BU.

WILBERFORCE Iron screw survey vessel, 459bm, 138 × 27ft. Laird 10.1840, purch. on stocks. BU 6.1850 West Africa.

WILD 6th Rate 12, 97bm. French, captured 1692. Recaptured 18.6.1694 by French.

WILD BOAR Flyboat 6, 172bm. Captured 1665. Sold 1667.

WILD BOAR Brig-sloop 10, 'Cherokee' class, 238bm. Pelham, Frindsbury, 9.7.1808. Wrecked 15.2.1810 Runnelstone, Scilly Is.

WILD GOOSE Sloop, 1,300 tons, 283 × 37·5ft, 6—4in. Yarrow 14.10.1942. Arr. 27.2.1956 McLellan, Bo'ness, for BU.

WILD SWAN Composite screw sloop, 1,130 tons, 170 × 36ft, 2—7in, 4—64pdr. Napier 28.1.1876. = CLYDE 1.5.1904 (q.v.).

WILD SWAN Destroyer, Modified 'W' class. Swan Hunter 17.5.1919. Damaged air attack, sunk 17.6.1942 collision Spanish trawler Bay of Biscay.

WILDFIRE (ex-*John*) Firevessel, 64bm, 61 × 16·5ft. Purch. 1804. Sold 17.6.1807 Freake for BU.

WILDFIRE (ex-*Watersprite*) Wood paddle packet, 186bm, 116·5 × 18·5ft. GPO vessel, tx 1.1838. Sold W. Walker 12.1888.

WILDFIRE (ex-*Hiawatha*) Screw yacht tender, 453 tons, 162 × 22ft. Purch. 26.1.1888. Base ship Sheerness 4.1889. = UNDINE 1.1907. Sold 9.7.1912 Ward, Preston.

WILDFIRE *See also CORNWALLIS 1813, NYMPHE 1888.*

WILDMAN Fireship 12. Captured 1652. Sold 1658.

WILHELMINA (ex-FURIE) 5th Rate 32, 827bm, 133 × 37·5ft. Dutch, captured 24.10.1798 by SIRIUS off Texel. Sold 1813 in Penang.

WILK Submarine, 965 tons, 246 × 18ft, 1—3.9in, 6—TT, 38 mines. Polish, served RN (Polish crew) 1939–6.1942, LU. Ret. Polish Navy 3.1951.

WILKIESTON Coastal minesweeper, 'Ton' class. Cook, Welton & Gemmell 26.6.1956. Sold White, St Davids, 9.1976 for BU.

WILLIAM Dogger 8. Dutch, captured 1672. Sold 1674.

WILLIAM Ketch 10. Origin unknown. Foundered 19.2.1694 off Gibraltar.

WILLIAM Gunvessel 3, 80bm, 59 × 18ft, 3—12pdr. Purch. 3.1794. Sold 11.1801.

WILLIAM Storeship 22, 374bm, 99·5 × 29ft. Purch. 4.1798. Wrecked 11.11.1807 Gut of Canso.

WILLIAM Storeship 12. Listed 1808. BU 8.1810 Woolwich. *Previous vessel salved?*

WILLIAM & ELIZABETH Firevessel. Purch. 1695. Expended 1.8.1695 Dunkirk.

WILLIAM & MARY Firevessel. Purch. 1694. Expended 12.9.1694 Dunkirk.

WILLIAM & MARY Yacht 10, 172bm, 76·5 × 22·5ft. Chatham DY 9.1694. Sold 14.9.1801 for BU.

WILLIAM & MARY Yacht 8, 199bm, 85 × 23ft. Deptford DY 14.11.1807. BU 4.1849.

WILLIAMSON (ex-IROQUOISE) Sloop 10. French, captured 1760. Lost 1761.

WILLIAMSTOWN Frigate (RAN), 'River' class, cancelled 1944.

WILLOUGHBY Destroyer, Modified 'W' class. Swan Hunter, cancelled 12.1918.

WILLOWHERB (ex-VITALITY) Corvette, Modified 'Flower' class. Midland SY 24.3.1943 on Lend-Lease. Ret. USN 11.6.1946.

WILTON Destroyer, 'Hunt' class Type II. Yarrow 17.10.1941. Arr. 30.11.1959 Faslane for BU.

WILTON Minehunter, 615 tons, Vosper-Thornycroft 18.1.1972. PO 27.7.1994; sold 8.2001, towed to Southampton for conv. for use as yacht club Leigh-on-Sea or on R. Orwell.

WIMMERA Frigate (RAN), 'River' class. Sydney, ordered 12.1942, cancelled 12.6.1944.

WINCHELSEA 6th Rate 24, 441 bm, 106 × 31ft. Carter, Limehouse, 3.5.1740. BU 8.1761 Portsmouth. *In French hands 10–27.10.1758.*

WINCHELSEA Cutter. Purch. 1.1763. Sunk 4.1774 breakwater Sheerness.

WINCHELSEA 5th Rate 32, 679bm, 125 × 35ft. Sheerness DY 31.5.1764. Rebuilt 1782; prison ship 1805. Sold 3.11.1814.

WINCHELSEA Destroyer, 'V/W' class. White 15.12.1917. Escort 4.1942. Sold 20.3.1945; BU Metal Industries, Inverkeithing.

WINCHELSEY 5th Rate 32, 364bm, 103·5 × 38·5ft. Wyatt, Redbridge, 13.8.1694. Captured 6.6.1706 by four French privateers off Hastings.

WINCHELSEY 5th Rate 26, 422bm, 105·5 × 30·5ft. Johnson, Blackwall, 9.9.1706. Foundered 29.8.1707 hurricane Leeward Is.

WINCHELSEY 5th Rate 36, 414bm, 108 × 30ft. Purch. 2.1708. Reduced to 6th Rate 5.1716. BU 12.1735. *In French hands 8.2–2.3.1709.*

WINCHESTER 4th Rate 60, 933bm, 146·5 × 38ft. Wyatt, Bursledon, 11.4.1693. Foundered 24.9.1695 off Cape Florida.

WINCHESTER 4th Rate 48, 673bm, 130 × 34·5ft. Wells, Rotherhithe, 17.3.1698. Rebuilt Plymouth 1717 as 711bm. Hulked 2.1774. BU comp. 5.7.1781 Chatham.

WINCHESTER 4th Rate 50, 987bm, 140·5 × 40·5ft. Bird, Rotherhithe, 5.1744. Sold 20.6.1769.

WINCHESTER Cutter 8, 69bm, 47 × 20ft, 4 carr., 8—3pdr. Purch. 1763. *Fate unknown.*

WINCHESTER 4th Rate 52, 1,487bm, 173 × 44·5ft, 16—42pdr carr., 36—24pdr. Woolwich DY 21.6.1822. = CONWAY (TS) 11.1861; = MOUNT EDGCOMBE 1.9.1876. Sold 8.4.1921.

WINCHESTER Destroyer, 'V/W' class. White 1.2.1918. Escort 5.1940. Sold 5.3.1946; BU Ward, Inverkeithing.

WINCHESTER *See also CONWAY 1832.*

WINDFLOWER Sloop, 'Anchusa' class. Workman Clark 12.4.1918. Sold 7.10.1927 Cashmore, Newport.

WINDFLOWER Corvette, 'Flower' class. Davie SB 4.7.1940. Lent RCN from 10.1940. Sunk 7.12.1941 collision SS *Zypenberg* North Atlantic.

WINDRUSH Frigate, 'River' class. Robb, Leith, 18.6.1943. Tx French Navy 2.1944 = LA DECOUVERTE; expended 1975 target.

WINDSOR 4th Rate 60, 912bm, 146·5 × 38ft. Snelgrove, Deptford, 31.10.1695. Rebuilt Deptford as 951bm; rebuilt Woolwich 1745 as 1,201bm. BU 6.1777.

WINDSOR Destroyer, 'V/W' class. Scotts 21.6.1918. Sold 4.3.1947; arr. 5.1949 Charlestown for BU.

WINDSOR *See also UNICORN 1992.*

WINDSOR CASTLE 2nd Rate 90, 1,462bm. Woolwich DY 1678. Wrecked 28.4.1693 nr Deal.

WINDSOR CASTLE 2nd Rate 98, 1,874bm, 177·5 × 50ft. Deptford DY 3.5.1790. Reduced to 74 guns 6.1814. BU 5.1839 Pembroke Dock.

WINDSOR CASTLE 1st Rate 120, 3,700bm, 241 × 60ft. Pembroke Dock 14.9.1852. = DUKE OF WELLINGTON (screw ship) 1.10.1852 (q.v.).

WINDSOR CASTLE (ex-VICTORIA) 1st Rate 116, 3,101bm, 204 × 60ft. Pembroke Dock 26.8.1858; conv. on stocks to screw ship, '100 guns' (30—8in, 1—110pdr, 4—70pdr, 6—40pdr, 56—32pdr), 1862 (renamed 6.1.1855). = CAMBRIDGE (gunnery ship) 1869. Sold 24.6.1908 Cox, Falmouth. *Fourteen years on stocks.*

WINDSOR CASTLE Armed merchantman. Russian, seized 1918–19.

WINDSOR CASTLE *See also DUCHESS 1679, VICTORIA & ALBERT 1855.*

WINNIPEG Minesweeper (RCN), 'Algerine' class. Port Arthur 19.9.1942. Sold 7.8.1959 Belgian Navy = A. F. DUFOUR. BU 1966.

WINNIPEG Frigate (RCN), 'Halifax' class, Marine Industries, Sorel, 5.12.1993.

WINSBY 50-gun ship, 608bm. Edgar, Yarmouth, 1654. = HAPPY RETURN 1660. Captured 4.11.1691 by French = HEUREUX RETOUR until 1709.

WINTER Destroyer, Modified 'W' class. Swan Hunter, cancelled 12.1918.

WINTRINGHAM Inshore minesweeper, 'Ham' class. White 24.5.1955. Tx RAN 1967 = SEAL; Diving Tender 1001; for sale 8.1988.

WISHART Destroyer, Modified 'W' class, 1,350 tons, 312·25 (oa) × 30·8ft. Thornycroft 18.6.1919. Sold 20.3.1945; BU Ward, Inverkeithing.

WISTARIA Sloop, 'Arabis' class. Irvine, Glasgow, 7.12.1915. Sold 18.1.1931 Ward, Inverkeithing.

WISTFUL *See VIGOROUS 1918.*

WISTON Coastal minesweeper, 'Ton' class. Wivenhoe SY 3.6.1958. Sold H. K. Vickers 9.8.1982 for BU Blyth.

WITCH Destroyer, Modified 'W' class, 1,350 tons, 312·25 (oa) × 30·8ft. Thornycroft 11.11.1919. Sold 12.7.1946; BU Brechin, Granton.

WITHERINGTON Destroyer, Modified 'W' class. White 16.1.1919. Sold 20.3.1947 Metal Industries; wrecked 29.4.1947 under tow to Charlestown.

WITHERNSEA *See WIDNES 1918.*

WIVENHOE Ketch 8, 83bm. Page, Wivenhoe, 1666. Fireship 1673. Sold 1683.

WIVERN (ex-EL MONASSIR) Iron coast defence ship, 1,899bm, 2,751 tons, 224 × 42·5ft, 4—9in. Laird 29.8.1863; Turkish (ex-Confederate), purch. 10.1863. Harbour service 1898. Sold 5.1922 in Hong Kong.

WIVERN Destroyer, Modified 'W' class. White

16.4.1919. Sold 18.2.1947; arr. 10.1948 Metal Industries, Rosyth, for BU Metal Industries.

WIZARD Brig-sloop 16. 283bm, 96·5 × 26ft. Sutton, Ringmore, 11.1805. Sold 17.10.1816.

WIZARD Brig-sloop 10, 'Cherokee' class, 231bm. Pembroke Dock 24.5.1830. Wrecked 8.2.1859 Berehaven.

WIZARD Wood screw gunboat, 'Britomart' class. Smith, Newcastle, 3.8.1860. BU 1879 Malta.

WIZARD Destroyer, 320 tons, 200 × 19·5ft, 1—12pdr, 5—6pdr, 2—TT. White 26.2.1895. Sold 20.5.1920 Ward, Milford Haven.

WIZARD Destroyer, 1,710 tons, 362·7 (oa) × 35·7ft, 4—4·7in, 5—40mm, 8—TT. Vickers Armstrong, Barrow, 29.9.1943. Frigate 1954, 2—4in, 2—40mm, Squid. Arr. 7.3.1967 Ward, Inverkeithing, for BU.

WIZARD *See also KARRAKATTA 1889.*

WOLDINGHAM Inshore minesweeper, 'Ham' class. White 30.11.1955. Sold Pounds 29.9.1966, yacht.

WOLF Sloop 14, 244bm, 87 × 25ft. Stacey, Deptford, 20.11.1731. Wrecked 2.3.1741 coast of Florida.

WOLF Sloop 14, 246bm, 89 × 25ft. West, Deptford, 27.2.1742. Wrecked 31.12.1748 coast of Ireland. *In French hands 14.11.1745–1747.*

WOLF Sloop 10, 141bm, 75·5 × 20·5ft. Chatham DY 24.5.1754. Sold 15.8.1781.

WOLF Armed ship 8. Origin unknown. Wrecked 7.1780 off Newfoundland.

WOLF Gunvessel 4, 68bm, 61·5 × 15·5ft, 3—32pdr, 1—24pdr. Dutch hoy, purch. 3.1794. BU 8.1803.

WOLF Brig-sloop 16 (fir-built), 367bm, 106 × 28ft, 16—32pdr carr., 2—6pdr. Tanner, Dartmouth, 4.6.1804. Wrecked 5.9.1806 Bahamas.

WOLF Brig-sloop 14, 253bm, 92 × 25·5ft. Woolwich DY 16.9.1814. Sold 27.1.1825 T. S. Benson.

WOLF Cutter tender, 81bm, 55 × 19ft, 6—6pdr, 2—3pdr. White, Cowes, 1801. BU 1829 Portsmouth. *Used also by on Revenue Service.*

WOLF Sloop 18, 454bm, 113·5 × 31ft. Portsmouth DY 1.12.1826. Hulk 5.1848; coal hulk 7.1859. BU comp. 5.8.1878 Devonport.

WOLF Wood screw gunboat, 'Albacore' class. Mare, Blackwall, 5.7.1856. BU comp. 8.7.1864.

WOLF Destroyer, 385 tons, 218 × 20ft, 1—12pdr, 5—6pdr, 2—TT. Laird 2.6.1897. Sold 1.7.1921 S. Castle, Plymouth.

WOLF Yacht (RCN). 1940–46.

WOLF *See also PANDOUR 1798, DILIGENT 1806. See also WOOLF.*

WOLFE Sloop 20 (Canadian lakes), 426bm, 102 × 30·5ft. Kingston, Ontario, 5.5.1813. = MONTREAL 22.1.1814. Sold 1.1832.

WOLFE 1st Rate 104 (Canadian lakes), 2,152bm, 191·5 × 50·5ft. Kingston, Ontario, LD 1814, cancelled 1831; hull destroyed on stocks 31.7.1832 by storm.

WOLFE (ex-*Montcalm*) AMC, 16,420grt, 550 × 70ft, 7—6in, 2—12pdr. Cd 21.11.1939, purch. Conv. depot ship 5.1942, 19,557 tons, 4—4in. Arr. 8.11.1952 Faslane for BU.

WOLFE *See also GENERAL WOLFE 1915. See also WOLF, WOOLF.*

WOLFHOUND Destroyer, 'V/W' class. Fairfield 14.3.1918. Escort 4.1940. Sold 18.2.1948; BU Granton.

WOLLONDILLY Frigate (RAN), 'River' class. Sydney, ordered 12.1942, cancelled 12.6.1944.

WOLLONGONG Minesweeper, 'Bathurst' class. Cockatoo DY 5.7.1941. Lent RAN from 10.1941. Sold 1946 Dutch Navy = BANDA; tx Indonesia 6.4.1950 = RADJAWAL; tx Hong Kong 4.1968 for BU.

WOLLONGONG Patrol boat (RAN), 211 tons. Cairns 17.8.1981.

WOLSEY Destroyer, 'V/W' class, 1,325 tons, 312·1 (oa) × 30·75ft, Thornycroft 16.3.1918. Escort 12.1939. Sold 4.3.1947; BU Young, Sunderland.

WOLVERENE Wood screw corvette, 1,703bm, 2,431 tons, 225 × 41ft, 16—8in, 1—7in, 4—40pdr. Woolwich DY 29.8.1863. Tx Australia 1881 TS. Sold 24.8.1923 sheer hulk.

WOLVERINE (ex-*Raider*) Gun-brig 12, 286bm, 98 × 27·5ft, 6—24pdr carr., 2—18pdr, 5—12pdr carr. Purch. 3.1798. Sunk 24.3.1804 in action with French privateer BLONDE western Atlantic.

WOLVERINE Brig-sloop 18, 'Cruizer' class, 387bm. Owen, Topsham, 1.3.1805. Sold 15.2.1816.

WOLVERINE Brig-sloop 16, 428bm, 101 × 32·5ft, 14—32pdr, 2—9pdr. Chatham DY 13.10.1836. Wrecked 11.8.1855 Courtown Bank.

WOLVERINE Destroyer, 914 tons, 266 × 28ft, 1—4in, 3—12pdr, 2—TT. Cammell Laird 15.1.1910. Sunk 12.12.1917 collision sloop ROSEMARY off Donegal.

WOLVERINE Destroyer, Modified 'W' class. White 17.7.1919. Sold 28.1.1946; BU Troon.

WOLVERTON Coastal minesweeper, 'Ton' class. Montrose SY 22.10.1956. Sold 6.1985 at Hong Kong; floating clubhouse/restaurant, burnt out 1991.

WOODBRIDGE HAVEN *See LOCH TORRIDON 1945.*

WOODCOCK Cutter 4, 76bm, 56 × 18·5ft, 4—12pdr carr. Crane, Yarmouth, 11.4.1806. Wrecked 13.2.1807 Azores.

WOODCOCK Wood screw gunboat, 'Clown' class.

Smith, North Shields, 6.6.1856. Sold 1871 in Hong Kong.

WOODCOCK Fishery protection vessel, 750 tons, 148 × 26ft. Purch. 4.1885. = JACKAL 1.5.1886. Sold 10.7.1906.

WOODCOCK River gunboat, 150 tons, 148·5 × 24ft, 2—6pdr. Thornycroft 1897 in sections, relaunched China 8.4.1898. Sold 1927 in Hong Kong.

WOODCOCK Sloop, 1,300 tons, 283 × 37·5ft, 6—4in. Fairfield 26.11.1942. Arr. 28.11.1955 S. Bkg Industries, Rosyth, for BU.

WOODLARK Gun-brig 12, 182bm, 80·5 × 23ft, 10—18pdr carr, 2—18pdr. Menzies, Leith, 1.1805. Wrecked 13.11.1805 nr Calais.

WOODLARK Brig-sloop 16, 'Cherokee' class, 237bm. Rowe, Newcastle, 17.11.1808. Sold 29.1.1818.

WOODLARK Survey tender, 81bm, 55·5 × 18·5ft, 2—6pdr. Deptford DY 31. 7.1821; LD as revenue cutter. Sold 23.9.1863.

WOODLARK Wood screw gunvessel, 663bm, 805 tons, 170 × 29ft, 1—7in, 2—40pdr. Chatham DY 9.3.1871. Sold 9.3.1887 Bombay.

WOODLARK River gunboat, 150 tons, 148·5 × 24ft, 2—6pdr. Thornycroft, Chiswick, 1897 in sections. Sold 7.1928 in Hong Kong.

WOODLARK *See also YAXHAM 1958.*

WOODPECKER Destroyer, Modified 'W' class. Projected 1918, not ordered.

WOODPECKER Sloop, 1,300 tons, 283 × 37·5ft, 6—4in. Denny 29.6.1942. Torpedoed 20.2.1944 by U-boat North Atlantic, foundered 7 days later.

WOODRUFF Corvette, 'Flower' class. Simons 28.2.1941. Sold 1947 = *Southern Lupin.*

WOODSTOCK Corvette (RCN), 'Flower' class. Collingwood SY 10.12.1941. Sold 1.3.1948 = *Olympic Winner*; = Otori *Maru No 20* 1956; = *Akitsu Maru* 1957; BU 1975 Etajima.

WOOLASTON Coastal minesweeper, 'Ton' class. Herd & McKenzie 6.3.1958. Sold Liguria Maritime 14.11.1980; BU Sittingbourne.

WOOLF (ex-LOBO) 16-gun ship, 120bm. Spanish, captured 1656. Sold 1663.

WOOLF Fireship 8, 253bm, 93 × 25ft. Castle, Deptford, 18.4.1690. Expended 23.5.1692 Cherbourg.

WOOLF Sloop 2, 65bm. Portsmouth 1699. Sold 10.4.1712. *In French hands 24.6.1704–1708, 19—21.6.1708.*

WOOLF *See also WOLF, WOLFE.*

WOOLSTON Destroyer, 'V/W' class, 1,325 tons, 312·1 (oa) × 30·75ft. Thornycroft 27.4.1918. Escort 10.1939. Sold 18.2.1947; BU Brunton, Grangemouth.

WOOLVESEY CASTLE *See HUNTSVILLE 1944.*
WOOLWICH Sloop 4, 57bm. Woolwich 1673.
Wrecked 1675.
WOOLWICH 4th Rate 54, 741bm, 138·5 × 35·5ft.
Woolwich DY 1675. Rebuilt Woolwich 1702 as
761bm, 50 guns; rebuilt Deptford 1741 as 866bm.
BU 6.1747 Chatham.
WOOLWICH 5th Rate 44, 825bm, 133·5 × 38ft.
Darley & Janvrin, Beaulieu, 7.3.1749. Sold
30.12.1762.
WOOLWICH Storeship. Woolwich DY 11.2.1755.
Listed 1760. *May have been WOOLWICH
TRANSPORT (q.v.), rebuilt and renamed.*
WOOLWICH 5th Rate 44, 907bm, 140 × 38·5,ft.
Calhoun & Newland, Bursledon, 15.12.1785. Store-
ship by 1794. Wrecked 6.11.1813 West Indies.
WOOLWICH (ex-*Marianne*) Tender 6, 169bm,
6—3pdr. Purch. 30.1.1788. Sold 3.11.1808.
WOOLWICH Store lighter, 114bm, 63·5 × 20·5ft.
Woolwich DY 1815. = PORT ROYAL 1818. *Fate
unknown.*
WOOLWICH Depot ship, 3,380 tons, 320 × 40ft,
2—4in. London & Glasgow Co. 5.9.1912. Sold
13.7.1926 Ward, Hayle.
WOOLWICH Depot ship, 8,750 tons, 575 × 64ft,
4—4in. Fairfield 20.9.1934. Arr. 10.1962 Arnott
Young, Dalmuir, for BU.
WOOLWICH *See also PORTSMOUTH 1811.*
WOOLWICH TRANSPORT Hoy 4, 45bm, 48·5 ×
15ft. Woolwich DY 17.10.1705; rebuilt Woolwich
1726 as 65bm. Sold 25.8.1767.
WORCESTER 48-gun ship, 662bm, 141·5 × 33·5ft.
Woolwich 1651. = DUNKIRK 1660 (q.v.).
WORCESTER 4th Rate 48, 684bm, 132 × 35ft.
Winter, Southampton, 31.5.1698. Rebuilt Dept-
ford 1714 as 719bm. BU 1733.
WORCESTER 4th Rate 60, 1,061bm, 144 × 41·5ft.
Portsmouth DY 20.12.1735. BU comp. 5.9.1765
Plymouth.
WORCESTER 3rd Rate 64, 1,380bm, 159 × 44·5ft.
Portsmouth DY 17.10.1769. Hulk 1.1788. BU
12.1816 Deptford.
WORCESTER 4th Rate 52, 1,468bm, 172 × 44ft,
4—8in, 30—32pdr, 16—32pdr carr., 2—12pdr.
Deptford DY 10.10.1843. Lent 1862 as TS. BU
8.1885 Castle, Charlton. *Twenty-three years on
stocks.*
WORCESTER Destroyer, Modified 'W' class.
White 24.10.1919. Mined 23.12.1943 North Sea,
not repaired. Accommodation ship 5.1944;
= YEOMAN 6.1945. Sold 17.9.1946; BU Ward,
Grays, 2.1947.
WORCESTER *See also FREDERICK WILLIAM
1860.*

WORCESTER PRIZE 6th Rate 14, 140bm, 73 ×
21ft. French, captured 1.1705 by WORCESTER.
Recaptured 6.10.1708 by French off Land's End.
Also in French hands 27.5–14.6.1708.
WORTHING Cross-Channel ferry, 2,294grt. 1928,
req. 9.1939, cd 13.11.1940. = BRIGADIER, hired
as TS 1940; landing ship 1942. Ret. 1946 owners
= *Worthing.*
WORTHING Minesweeper, turbine 'Bangor' class.
Philip 22.8.1941. Sold 7.7.1948; BU Stockton
Shipping & Salvage, Thornaby.
WOTTON Coastal minesweeper, 'Ton' class. Philip
24.4.1956. Tx 2.1986 R. Thames for Sea Cadets.
Towed Portsmouth 19.11.1992 to Belgium for BU.
WRANGLER (Gunboat No 40, ex-*Fortune*) Gun-
vessel 12, 138bm, 72·5 × 30ft, 2—24pdr, 10—
18pdr carr. Purch. 3.1797 Leith. Sold 12.1802.
WRANGLER Gun-brig 12, 177bm, 80 × 22·5ft,
10—18pdr carr., 2—12pdr. Dudman, Deptford,
28.5.1805. Sold 14.12.1815.
WRANGLER Wood screw gunvessel, 477bm, 160
× 25·5ft, 2—68pdr. Green, Blackwall, 19.6.1854.
BU 5.1866 Castle, Charlton.
WRANGLER Composite screw gunboat, 465 tons,
125 × 23·5ft, 2—64pdr, 2—20pdr. Barrow SB
(Vickers) 5.10.1880. Coastguard 1891; BDV 1903.
Sold 2.12.1919; BU Dover.
WRANGLER Destroyer, Modified 'W' class. White,
LD 3.2.1919, cancelled 9.1919.
WRANGLER Destroyer, 1,710 tons, 362·7 (oa) ×
35·7ft, 4—4·7in, 5—40mm, 8—TT. Vickers Arm-
strong, Barrow, 30.12.1943. Conv. frigate 1951–
52, 2—4in, 2—40mm, Squid. Tx SAN
= VRYSTAAT 29.11.1956; sunk 1976 target off
South Africa.
WREN Destroyer, Modified 'W' class. Yarrow
11.11.1919. Sunk 27.7.1940 air attack off Aldeburgh.
WREN Sloop, 1,300 tons, 283 × 37·5ft, 6—4in.
Denny 11.8.1942. Arr. 2.2.1956 S. Bkg Industries,
Rosyth, for BU.
WRENN 12-gun vessel. Captured 1653. Sold
29.9.1657.
WRENN Pink 10, 103bm, 64 × 19ft. Stigant, Redbridge, 21.3.1694. Captured 28.3.1697 by French
off Rye.
WRENTHAM (ex-EDGELEY) Inshore mine-
sweeper 'Ham' class. Dorset Yacht Co. 8.2.1955
(renamed 11.1953). Sold 10.8.1966.
WRESTLER Destroyer, 'V/W' class. Swan Hunter
25.2.1918. Escort 4.1943; mined 6.6.1944, not
repaired. Sold 20.7.1944; BU Cashmore, Newport.
WRYNECK Destroyer, 'V/W' class. Palmer
13.5.1918. Escort 10.1940. Sunk 27.4.1941 air
attack south of Morea.

WRYNECK Sloop, 1,350 tons, 283 × 38·5ft, 6—4in, Denny, cancelled 2.11.1945.

WULASTOCK Frigate (RCN), 'River' class. Victoria, BC, cancelled 12.1943.

WYE 6th Rate 24, 447bm, 108 × 31ft. Hobbs, Redbridge 17.8.1814. Convict ship 1828, ordered BU 10.1852.

WYE (ex-*Hecla*) Iron screw storeship, 700bm. Treasury Dept vessel, tx 24.5.1855 (renamed 6.6.1855). Sold 3.7.1866.

WYE Iron screw storeship, 1,370 tons. Osbourne Graham, Sunderland, 1873, purch. 17.12.1873. Sold 3.4.1906 Adrienne Merveille, Dunkirk, for BU.

WYE Destroyer, Modified 'W' class. Yarrow, LD 1.1918, cancelled 9.1919.

WYE Frigate, 'River' class. Robb, Leith, 16.8.1943. Arr. 22.2.1955 Troon for BU.

X

X.1 Submarine, 2,780 tons, 350 × 30ft, 4—5·2in, 6—TT. Chatham DY 16.6.1923. Arr. 12.1936 Ward, Pembroke Dock, for BU.

X.2 (ex-GALILEO GALILEI) Submarine, 880 tons, 231 (oa) × 22·5ft. 8—TT. Italian, captured 19.6.1940 by trawler MOONSTONE in Red Sea. = P.711 in 8.1942. BU 1946 Port Said.

'X' class 'midget' submarines 27 tons, 2 explosive charges. All built 1943–44. X.3–4 Varley Marine; X.5–10 Vickers Armstrong, Barrow; X.20, 21 Broadbent, Huddersfield; X.22, 23 Markham, Chesterfield; X.24, 25 Marshall, Gainsborough; XT.1–6 Vickers Armstrong, Barrow. The following, ordered 5.1943, were cancelled 12.1943: XT.7–11 Broadbent; XT.2, XT.19 Markham; XT.14–18 Marshall. X.3, X.4 BU 1945; X.5–10 all lost 9.1943 or 10.1943 attacks on German battleship TIRPITZ in Altafjord; X.20, 21 listed until 10.1945; X.22 lost 7.2.1944 collision SYRTIS in Pentland Firth; X.23 listed until 1.1945; X.24 preserved at Gosport; X.25, XT.1, XT.2 listed until 10.1945; XT.3–6 listed until 6.1945.

'X.51' class midget submarines 35 tons, 50 × 6·5ft, 2 explosive charges. All Built Vickers Armstrong, Barrow.

X.51 Launched 1.10.1954, = STICKLEBACK 12.1954. Sold 15.7.1958 Swedish Navy = SPIGGER. Ret., museum ship 1977 Duxford.

X.52 Launched 30.12.1954. = SHRIMP 12.1954. BU 1965 Rosyth DY.

X.53 Launched 1.3.1955. = SPRAT 12.1954. BU 1966 Faslane.

X.54 Launched 5.5.1955. = MINNOW 12.1954. BU 1966 Faslane.

'XE' class 'midget' submarines 30 tons, explosive charges, all built 1944–45. XE.1–6 Vickers Armstrong, Barrow; XE.7–8 Broadbent, Huddersfield; XE.9–10 Marshall, Gainsborough; XE.11–12 Markham, Chesterfield. XE.1–6 BU 1945 Australia; XE.7 BU 1952; XE.8–9 sunk 1954 as bottom targets (XE.8 raised 5.1973 for preservation); XE.10 cancelled 6.1945; XE.11 lost 6.3.1945 collision, raised, BU 5.1945; XE.12 BU 12.1953 Metal Industries.

XENOPHON Armed ship 22, 334bm, 100·5 × 28·5ft. Purch. 1798. = INVESTIGATOR (survey vessel) 1801. BU 11.1810.

Y

YARMOUTH 50-gun ship, 608bm. Edgar, Yarmouth, 1653. BU 1680.

YARMOUTH 3rd Rate 70, 1,058bm, 151 × 40ft. Barrett, Harwich, 7.1.1695. Rebuilt 1709 as 1,110bm. Hulked 11.1740. Sold 11.9.1769.

YARMOUTH 3rd Rate 64, 1,359bm, 160 × 44ft. Deptford DY 28.12.1748. 60 guns 4.1781; receiving ship 12.1783. BU 4.1811 Plymouth.

YARMOUTH Store lighter, 106bm, 61 × 20ft. Yarmouth 1798. Rebuilt Yarmouth 1810. Coastguard 4.1828. Sold 8.1835.

YARMOUTH 2nd class cruiser, 5,250 tons, 430 × 48·5ft, 8—6in. London & Glasgow Co. 12.4.1911. Sold 2.7.1929 Alloa S. Bkg Co., Rosyth.

YARMOUTH Frigate, 'Rothesay' class, 2,380 tons, 370 (oa) × 41ft, 2—4·5in, 1—40mm, Limbo (later helo). John Brown 23.3.1959. Expended 21.6.1987 target.

YARNTON Coastal minesweeper, 'Ton' class. Pickersgill 26.3.1956. Sold Pounds 1986.

YARRA Destroyer (RAN), 700 tons, 246 (oa) × 24ft, 1—4in, 3—12pdr, 3—TT. Denny 8.4.1910. Dismantled 10.1929 Cockatoo DY; hulk sunk 22.8.1932 target.

YARRA Sloop (RAN), 1,060 tons. 250 × 36ft, 3—4in. Cockatoo DY 28.3.1935. Sunk 4.3.1942 by Japanese Squadron 300 miles south of Java.

YARRA Frigate (RAN), 2,100 tons, 370 (oa) × 41ft, 2—4·5in, 4—GWS, Limbo. Williamstown DY 30.9.1958. PO 22.11.1985; towed Pakistan 5.1992 for BU.

YARRA Minehunter (RAN), 'Huon' class, 720 tons, 172·2 (oa) × 32·5ft, 1—30mm. ADI, Newcastle, NSW, 19.1.2002.

YAXHAM Inshore minesweeper, 'Ham' class. White 21.1.1958. = WOODLARK (survey vessel) 1964. Target 1986.

YEALMPTON Minesweeper, Later 'Hunt' class. Simons, cancelled 1919.

YELLOWKNIFE MCDV (RCN), 'Kingston' class, 962 tons, 181·4 (oa) × 37·1ft, 1—40mm. Halifax SY 5.6.1997.

YEOMAN Destroyer, Modified 'W' class. Yarrow, cancelled 3.1919.

YEOMAN *See also WORCESTER 1919.*

YEOVIL Minesweeper, Later 'Hunt' class. Napier & Miller 27.8.1918. Sold 4.10.1928 Ward, Pembroke Dock.

YORK 4th Rate 60, 987bm, 146 × 39ft. Plymouth DY 4.1706. Sunk 4.2.1751 breakwater Sheerness.

YORK 4th Rate 60, 1,203bm, 150 × 43ft. Plymouth DY 10.11.1753. BU comp. 6.1772.

YORK (ex-*Betsy*) Brig-sloop 12, 65 × 22ft. Purch. 29.3.1777 North America. Captured 7.1779 by French squadron at Grenada. *Also in French hands 10.7–23.8.1778.*

YORK Storeship 14, 664bm, 14—6pdr. Purch. 3.1779. Sold 1781 East Indies.

YORK (ex-*Royal Admiral*) 3rd Rate 64, 1,433bm, 174 × 43ft, 26—24pdr, 26—18pdr, 12—12pdr. Barnard, Deptford, 24.3.1796; East Indiaman, purch. on stocks. Foundered 1.1804 North Sea.

YORK 3rd Rate 74, 1,743bm, 175 × 47·5ft. Brent, Rotherhithe, 7.7.1807. Convict ship 11.1819. BU 3.1854 Portsmouth.

YORK ABS. Req. 1915–19.

YORK Cruiser, 8,250 tons, 575 (oa) × 57ft, 6—8in, 4—4in. Palmer 17.7.1928. Struck by Italian explosive motor boat 21.3.1941; beached Suda Bay, further damaged by air attack, abandoned 22.5.1941; hulk arr. 2.1952 Bari for BU.

YORK Destroyer, Type 42 Batch 3. Swan Hunter 21.6.1982.

YORK *See also MARSTON MOOR 1654.*

YORK CASTLE *See EMPIRE COMFORT 1944.*

YOUNG HEBE Schooner, 45bm. Purch. 1843 China. Sold 7.1.1847 in Hong Kong.

YOUNG HOBLIN Flyboat, 172bm. Captured 1665. Sold 1666.

YOUNG KING Hoy, 102bm. Captured 1665. Sold 1666.

YOUNG LADY Firevessel, 63bm, 63 × 15ft. Purch. 1694. Sold 2.1695 or 1696.

YOUNG LION 10-gun vessel, 44bm. Captured 1665. Sunk 1673 foundation Sheerness.

YOUNG LION *See also LION 1665.*

YOUNG PRINCE (ex-JONGE PRINS) 4th Rate

38, 375bm. Dutch, captured 1665. Expended 1666 fireship.

YOUNG SHISH Smack, 24bm. Deptford 1673. Listed until 1688.

YOUNG SPRAGGE 6th Rate 10, 79bm. Purch. 1673. Fireship 1677. Sunk 1693 foundation Portsmouth. *This vessel may be SPRAGGE 1673 (q.v.).*

YPRES Destroyer, 2,610 tons. Fairfield, ordered 1944, = DISDAIN 3.1945, = DELIGHT 6.1946, launched 21.12.1950. *See DELIGHT 1946.*

YUKON Escort (RCN), 2,380 tons, 366 (oa) × 42ft, 4–3in, 6–TT, Limbo. Burrard 27.7.1961. Left Vancouver 25.4.1999 for use as dive site; sunk 15.7.2000 off San Diego.

Z

Z.4 (RICHARD BEITZEN) Destroyer, 2,232 tons, 374 × 37ft, 5—5in, 4—37mm, 8—TT. German, seized Oslofjord 5.1945. Arr. Inverkeithing 1.11.1948 for BU.

Z.5 Tender, 264 tons, 193 × 20ft, 2—3in. Dutch torpedo boat, cd RN 1940. = BLADE 5.1943. Arr. 10.1945 Troon for BU.

Z.6 Torpedo boat, 264 tons, 193 × 20ft, 2—3in, 4—TT. Dutch, taken into RN 1940, not cd. Arr. 2.1943 McLellan, Bo'ness, for BU.

Z.7 Torpedo boat, 264 tons, 193 × 20ft, 2—3in, 4—TT. Hulked 10.1943. BU 1946 Rees, Llanelly.

Z.8 Torpedo boat, 264 tons, 193 × 20ft, 2—3in, 4—TT. Cd RN 1940, used as tender. Hulked 1942. Arr. 22.8.1944 Cashmore, Newport, for BU.

Z.10 (HANS LODY) Destroyer, 2,270 tons, 374 × 37ft, 5—5in, 4—37mm, 8—TT. German, seized Flensburg 5.1945. Arr. 17.1.1949 Young, Sunderland, for BU.

Z.30 Destroyer, 2,603 tons, 393 × 39ft. 4—5in, 8—TT. German, seized Oslofjord 5.1945 Arr. 9.1948 Troon for BU.

Z.38 Destroyer, 2,603 tons, 400 × 39ft, 4—5in, 8—TT, German, seized Flensburg 5.1945; = NONSUCH 11.1946. BU 5.1950 West of Scotland S. Bkg. Co., Troon.

ZAMBESI Destroyer, 1,710 tons, 362·7 (oa) × 35·7ft, 4—4·5in, 5—40mm, 8—TT. Cammell Laird 21.11.1943. Arr. 12.2.1959 Ward, Briton Ferry, for BU.

ZANZIBAR (ex-PROWSE) Frigate, 'Colony' class. Walsh Kaiser 21.11.1943 on Lend-Lease (renamed 1943). Ret. USN 31.5.1946.

ZEALAND (ex-WAPEN VAN ZEELAND) 4th Rate 42, 402bm. Dutch, captured 1665. Sold 1667.

ZEALAND Flyboat 8, 420bm. Dutch, captured 1667. Sold 1668.

ZEALAND 3rd Rate 64. Dutch, seized 19.1.1796 Plymouth. Harbour service 5.1803. = JUSTITIA per AO dated 19.8.1812. Sold. 2.11.1830 for BU.

ZEALANDIA *See NEW ZEALAND 1904.*

ZEALOUS 3rd Rate 74, 1,607bm, 168·5 × 47ft. Barnard, Deptford, 25.6.1785. BU 12.1816.

ZEALOUS Ironclad, 3,176bm, 6,096 tons, 20—7in.

Pembroke Dock 7.3.1864. Sold 9.1886 Castle, Charlton.

ZEALOUS Destroyer, Modified 'W' class. Yarrow, cancelled 3.1919.

ZEALOUS Destroyer, 1,710 tons, 362·7 (oa) × 35·7ft, 4—4·5in, 5—40mm, 8—TT. Cammell Laird 28.2.1944. Tx Israeli Navy 15.7.1955 = ELATH; sunk 21.10.1967 Egyptian 'Styx' missile off Sinai.

ZEBRA Sloop 14, 306bm, 97 × 27ft. Barnard, Ipswich, 8.4.1777. Wrecked 10.1778 off northern Scotland.

ZEBRA Sloop 18, 314bm 98 × 27·5ft. Cleveley, Gravesend, 31 8.1780. Bomb vessel 1800. Sold 13.8.1812.

ZEBRA Brig-sloop 18, 'Cruizer' class, 385bm. Bombay DY 18.11.1815. Wrecked 2.12.1840 The Levant.

ZEBRA Wood screw sloop, 951bm, 185 × 33ft, 5—40pdr, 12—32pdr. Deptford DY 13.11.1860. Sold 28.8.1873 Far East.

ZEBRA Destroyer, 340 tons, 200 × 20ft, 1—12pdr, 5—6pdr, 2—TT, Thames Iron Works, Blackwall, 3.12.1895. Sold 30.7.1914.

ZEBRA Destroyer, Modified 'W' class. Yarrow, cancelled 3.1919.

ZEBRA (ex-WAKEFUL) Destroyer, 1,710 tons, 362·7 (oa) × 35·7ft, 4—4·5in, 5—40mm, 8—TT. Denny 8.3.1944 (renamed 1.1943). Arr. 12.2.1959 Cashmore, Newport, for BU.

ZEBRA *See also JUMNA 1848, WAKEFUL 1943.*

ZEEBRUGGE *See LST.3532 1945.*

ZENITH (ex-WESSEX) Destroyer, 1,710 tons, 362·7 (oa) × 35·7ft, 4—4·5in, 5—40mm, 8—TT. Denny 6.6.1944 (renamed 1.1943). Sold 5.1955 Egyptian Navy, HO 8.1956 = EL FATEH; extant 2003; for preservation?

ZENITH *See also WESSEX 1943.*

ZENOBIA Schooner 10, 112bm, 68 × 20ft. Bermuda 1806. Wrecked 10.1806 coast of Florida.

ZENOBIA Brig-sloop 18, 'Cruizer' class, 385bm. Brindley, Lynn, 7.10.1807. Sold 8.1835 for BU.

ZENOBIA (ex-*Kilkenny*) Wood paddle sloop (Indian), 684bm. Waterford 1839, purch. on stocks. Hulked 1850.